BLAW 1090

23rd Edition

David P. Twomey | Marianne M. Jennings | Stephanie M. Greene

D1451572

CENGAGE
Learning·

Australia • Brazil • Japan • Korea • Mexico • Singapore • Spain • United Kingdom • United States

BLAW 1090, 23rd Edition

Anderson's Business Law and the Legal Environment, Comprehensive Volume, 23rd Edition
David P. Twomey | Marianne M. Jennings | Stephanie M. Greene

© 2017 Cengage Learning. All rights reserved.

ALL RIGHTS RESERVED. No part of this work covered by the copyright herein may be reproduced or distributed in any form or by any means, except as permitted by U.S. copyright law, without the prior written permission of the copyright owner.

For product information and technology assistance, contact us at
Cengage Learning Customer & Sales Support, 1-800-354-9706
For permission to use material from this text or product,
submit all requests online at **cengage.com/permissions**
Further permissions questions can be emailed to
permissionrequest@cengage.com

This book contains select works from existing Cengage Learning resources and was produced by Cengage Learning Custom Solutions for collegiate use. As such, those adopting and/or contributing to this work are responsible for editorial content accuracy, continuity and completeness.

Compilation © 2016 Cengage Learning

ISBN: 978-1-337-03138-7

Cengage Learning
20 Channel Center Street
Boston, MA 02210
USA

Cengage Learning is a leading provider of customized learning solutions with office locations around the globe, including Singapore, the United Kingdom, Australia, Mexico, Brazil, and Japan. Locate your local office at: **www.international.cengage.com/region**.

Cengage Learning products are represented in Canada by Nelson Education, Ltd.

For your lifelong learning solutions, visit **www.cengage.com/custom**.

Visit our corporate website at **www.cengage.com**.

Brief Contents

Negotiable Instruments

C H A P T E R   27

Kinds of Instruments, Parties, and Negotiability

Learning Outcomes ⟨⟨⟨

After studying this chapter, you should be able to

LO.1 Explain the importance and function of negotiable instruments

LO.2 Name the parties to negotiable instruments

LO.3 Describe the concept of negotiability and distinguish it from assignability

LO.4 List the requirements for a negotiable instrument

27-1 Types of Negotiable Instruments and Parties

commercial paper–
written, transferable, signed promise or order to pay a specified sum of money; a negotiable instrument.

For convenience and as a way to facilitate transactions, businesses began to accept certain kinds of paper called **commercial paper** or negotiable instruments as substitutes for money or as a means of offering credit.[1] Negotiable commercial paper is special paper created for the special purpose of facilitating transfer of funds and payment. In addition, the use of this special paper for special purposes can create additional rights in a special party status known as a *holder in due course.* Although the details on holders in due course are covered in Chapters 28 and 29, it is important to understand that one of the purposes of the use of special paper is to allow parties to achieve the special status of holder in due course and its protections and rights. Taking each component of negotiable instruments in step-by-step sequences, from their creation to the rights associated with each, and to their transfer, helps in understanding how commercial paper is used to create rights for special persons.

Article 3 of the Uniform Commercial Code (UCC) defines the types of negotiable instruments and the parties for each.[2] Article 3 of the UCC was last amended in 2002 with those reforms adopted in some states and under consideration in others.[3] Those changes are explained in each of the relevant sections.

27-1a Definition

negotiable instrument–
drafts, promissory notes, checks, and certificates of deposit that, in proper form, give special rights as "negotiable commercial paper."

Section 3-104(a)(1) and (2) of the UCC defines a **negotiable instrument** as "an unconditional promise or order to pay a fixed amount of money, ... if it (1) is payable to bearer or order...; (2) is payable on demand or at a definite time; and (3) does not state any other undertaking or instruction ... to do any act in addition to the payment of money...."[4] A *negotiable instrument* is a record of a signed promise or order to pay a specified sum of money.[5] The former requirement that the instrument be in writing to be valid has been changed to incorporate requirements of UETA (Uniform Electronic Transactions Act) and E-Sign (Electronic Signatures in Global and National Commerce Act of 2000). Many lenders now use electronic promissory notes.[6] In addition, we now have electronic checks, or those check withdrawals from your account that you authorize over the phone or via the Internet.

Instruments are negotiable when they contain certain elements required by the UCC. These elements are listed and explained in the section titled "Requirements of Negotiability" of this chapter. However, even those instruments that do not meet the requirements for negotiability may still be referred to by their UCC names or classifications.

CPA ### 27-1b Kinds of Instruments

There are two categories of negotiable instruments: (1) promises to pay, which include promissory notes and certificates of deposit,[7] and (2) orders to pay, including drafts and checks.

---

[1] *Carlucci v. Han*, 886 F. Supp. 2d 497 (E.D. Va. 2012).
[2] The law covering negotiable instruments has been evolving and changing. The earlier version was called UCC-Commercial Paper, and the 1990 version is called UCC-Negotiable Instruments.
[3] As of January 2015, 50 states, the District of Columbia, and the Virgin Islands had adopted the 2002 changes to Article 3.
[4] U.C.C. §3-104(a)(1) and (2).
[5] See U.C.C. §3-104.
[6] Electronic Signatures in Global and National Commerce Act, 15 U.S.C. §7001 (Supp. 2014).
[7] U.C.C. §3-104(j).

FIGURE 27-1	Promissory Note

MARCH 31, 2015

Six months after date debtor undersigned hereby promises to pay to the order of Galactic Games, Inc., three thousand six hundred dollars with interest at the rate of 5.9%. This note is secured by the Video Arcade game purchased with its funds.

In the event of default, all sums due hereunder may be collected. Debtor agrees to pay all costs of collection including, but not limited to, attorney fees, costs of repossession, and costs of litigation.

/s/ JOHN R. HALDEHAND

VIDEO ARCADE, INC.

promissory note–
unconditional promise in writing made by one person to another, signed by the maker engaging to pay on demand, or at a definite time, a sum certain in money to order or to bearer. (Parties— maker, payee)

certificate of deposit (CD)–promise-to-pay instrument issued by a bank.

draft, or bill of exchange–an unconditional order in writing by one person upon another, signed by the person giving it, and ordering the person to whom it is directed to pay upon demand or at a definite time a sum certain in money to order or to bearer.

check–order by a depositor on a bank to pay a sum of money to a payee; a bill of exchange drawn on a bank and payable on demand.

cashier's check–draft drawn by a bank on itself.

Promissory Notes

A **promissory note** is a written promise made and signed by the maker to pay a *sum certain* in money to the holder of the instrument.[8] (See Figure 27-1)

Certificates of Deposit

A **certificate of deposit (CD)** is a promise to pay issued by a bank.[9] Through a CD, a bank acknowledges the customer's deposit of a specific sum of money and promises to pay the customer that amount plus interest when the certificate is surrendered.

Drafts

A **draft, or bill of exchange,** is an order by one party to pay a sum of money to a second party. (See Figure 27-2.) The party who gives the order is called the *drawer*, and the party on whom the order to pay is drawn is the *drawee*.[10] The party to whom payment is to be made is the *payee*. The drawer may also be named as the payee, as when a seller draws a draft naming a buyer as the drawee. The draft is then used as a means to obtain payment for goods delivered to that buyer. A drawee is not bound to pay a draft simply because the drawer has placed his name on it. However, the drawee may agree to pay the draft by accepting it, which then attaches the drawee's liability for payment.

Checks

Under U.C.C. §3-104(f), *check* means "a draft, other than a documentary draft, payable on demand and drawn on a bank."[11] A **check** is an order by a depositor (the drawer) on a bank or credit union (the drawee) to pay a sum of money to the order of another party (the payee).[12]

In addition to the ordinary checks just described, there are also cashier's checks, teller's checks, traveler's checks, and bank money orders. A **cashier's check** is a draft drawn by a bank on itself. U.C.C. §3-104(g) defines a cashier's check as "a draft with respect to which the drawer and drawee are the same bank or branches of the same bank."[13]

[8] *Heritage Bank v. Bruha*, 812 N.W.2d 260 (Neb. 2012).
[9] U.C.C. §3-104(j).
[10] U.C.C. §3-103(a)(2)–(3).
[11] U.C.C. §3-104(f).
[12] *Id.*
[13] U.C.C. §3-104(g).

FIGURE 27-2	Draft

```
TO:  Topa Fabrics, Inc.                                 March 17,   20 13
     1700 W. Lincoln
     Marina Del Rey, CA

     Thirty days from date                    PAY TO THE ORDER OF
     Malden Mills, Inc.

     THE SUM OF        sixteen thousand and no/100 ——————————— DOLLARS

     ACCEPTED BY:                                     Aaron Johnson
                                                      Malden Mills, Inc.

     DATE
```

---

teller's check–draft drawn by a bank on another bank in which it has an account.

traveler's check–check that is payable on demand provided it is countersigned by the person whose specimen signature appears on the check.

money order–draft issued by a bank or a nonbank.

party–person involved in a legal transaction; may be a natural person, an artificial person (e.g., a corporation), or an unincorporated enterprise (e.g., a governmental agency).

maker–party who writes or creates a promissory note.

drawer–person who writes out and creates a draft or bill of exchange, including a check.

drawee–person to whom the draft is addressed and who is ordered to pay the amount of money specified in the draft.

A **teller's check** is a draft drawn by a bank on another bank in which it has an account.[14] A **traveler's check** is a check that is payable on demand, provided it is countersigned by the person whose signature was placed on the check at the time the check was purchased.[15] Money orders are issued by both banks and nonbanks. A **money order** drawn by a bank is also a check.[16]

27-1c Parties to Instruments

CPA

A note has two original parties: the *maker* and the *payee*.[17] A draft or a check has three original parties: the *drawer*, the *drawee*, and the *payee*. The names given to the parties to these instruments are important because the liability of the parties varies depending on the parties' roles. The rights and liabilities of the various parties to negotiable instruments are covered in Chapters 28 and 29.

A **party** to an instrument may be a natural person, an artificial person such as a corporation, or an unincorporated enterprise such as a government agency.

Maker

The **maker** is the party who writes or creates a promissory note, thereby promising to pay the amount specified in the note.

Drawer

The **drawer** is the party who writes or creates a draft or check.

Drawee

The **drawee** is the party to whom the draft is addressed and who is ordered to pay the amount of money specified in the draft. The bank is the drawee on a check, and the credit union is the drawee on a share draft. A drawee on a draft has no responsibility under the draft until it has accepted that instrument.

---

[14] U.C.C. §3-104(h).
[15] U.C.C. §3-104(i).
[16] *Com. v. Pantalion*, 957 A.2d 1267 (Pa. Super. 2008). Some items are held to be checks for purposes other than Article 3 negotiability. For example, in In re *Armstrong* 291 F.2d 517 (8th Cir. 2002), the court held that gambling markers were checks for purposes of the state's "bad check" law.
[17] U.C.C. §3-103(a)(5).

Payee

payee–party to whom payment is to be made.

The **payee** is the person named in the instrument to receive payment. **For Example,** on a check with the words "Pay to the order of John Jones," the named person, John Jones, is the payee.

Acceptor

acceptor–drawee who has accepted the liability of paying the amount of money specified in a draft.

When the drawee of a draft has indicated by writing or record a willingness to pay the amount specified in the draft, the drawee has accepted liability and is called the **acceptor.**[18]

Secondary Obligor (Accommodation Party)

accommodation party–person who signs an instrument to lend credit to another party to the paper.

When a party who is not originally named in an instrument allows her name to be added to it for the benefit of another party in order to add strength to the collectability of the instrument, that party becomes a secondary obligor (formerly called an **accommodation party**) and assumes a liability role.[19] Revised Article 3 now refers to drawer, indorsers, and accommodation parties as "secondary obligors."[20]

27-2 Negotiability

negotiability–quality of an instrument that affords special rights and standing.

An instrument is a form of contract that, if negotiable, affords certain rights and protections for the parties. **Negotiability** is the characteristic that distinguishes commercial paper and instruments from ordinary contracts or what makes such paper and instruments[21] special paper. That an instrument is negotiable means that certain rights and protections may be available to the parties to the instrument under Article 3. A **nonnegotiable instrument's** terms are enforceable, but the instrument is treated simply as a contract governed by contract law.[22]

CPA

27-2a Definition of Negotiability

nonnegotiable instrument–contract, note, or draft that does not meet negotiability requirements of Article 3.

If an instrument is negotiable, it is governed by Article 3 of the UCC, and it may be transferred by negotiation. This form of transfer permits the transferee to acquire rights greater than those afforded assignees of contracts under contract law. The quality of negotiability in instruments creates opportunities for transfers and financings that streamline payments in commerce. Transfers can be made with assurance of payment without the need for investigation of the underlying contract. The process of negotiation is covered in Chapter 28. For more information on the rights of assignees of contracts, refer to Chapter 17.

---

[18] U.C.C. §3-103(a)(1).

[19] U.C.C. §3-419; In re *Rust*, 510 B.R. 562 (E.D. Ky. 2014).

[20] Revised Article 3, §3-103(12), has the following definition of a secondary obligor on an instrument "an indorser, a drawer, an accommodation party, or any other party to the instrument that has a right of recourse against another party to the instrument...." This definition was changed to be consistent with the Restatement of Surety.

[21] U.C.C. §3-104.

[22] Loan-and-supply contract is not a negotiable instrument. *Quality Oil, Inc. v. Kelley Partners, Inc.*, 657 F.2d 609 (7th Cir. 2011). A note payable when "lessee is granted possession of the premises" is not a negotiable instrument, but it is an enforceable contract. *Schiffer v. United Grocers, Inc.*, 989 P.2d 10 (Or. 1999). A deed of trust may or may not be a negotiable instrument. *Arnold v. Palmer*, 686 S.E.2d 725 (W. Va. 2009); In re *Smith*, 509 B.R. 260 (N.D. Cal. 2014).

E-COMMERCE & CYBERLAW

The Check Is in the Internet

The Check Clearing for the 21st Century Act ("Check 21") allows banks to use electronic images of checks as full and complete records of transactions, the same status formerly used only for paper checks that had been canceled. You can also pay your monthly credit card bills by preauthorizing your credit card company to withdraw the amount you specify from your account. With the bank's routing number and your account number, the company can obtain payment on the due date or any date you authorize. PayPal allows you to do the same with your bank account when you purchase items on the Internet. Paperless payment is on the increase.

CPA   27-2b **Requirements of Negotiability**

To be negotiable, an instrument (1) must be evidenced by a record and (2) must be signed (authenticated under Revised Article 3) by the maker or the drawer, (3) must contain an unconditional promise or order to pay, (4) must pay a sum certain, (5) must be payable in money, (6) must be payable on demand or at a definite time, and (7) must be payable to order or bearer, using what are known as words of negotiability.[23]

A Record (Writing)

A negotiable instrument must be evidenced by a record. The requirement of a *record*, under Revised Article 3, is satisfied by handwriting, typing, printing, electronic record, and any other method of making a record. A negotiable instrument may be partly printed and partly typewritten. No particular form is required for an instrument to satisfy the record requirement, although customers of banks may agree to use the banks' forms as part of their contractual agreement with their banks. Telephonic checks are a complete record for purposes of Article 3 rights and obligations.

Authenticated (Signed) by the Maker or Drawer

The instrument must be authenticated (signed under old Article 3) by the maker or the drawer. When a signature is used as authentication, it usually appears at the lower right-hand corner of the face of the instrument, but there is no requirement for where the signature must be placed on the instrument.[24]

The authentication may consist of the full name or of any symbol placed with the intent to authenticate the instrument. Other means of authentication that are valid as signatures include initials, figures, and marks. Electronic security devices can be used as a means of authentication for electronic records. A person signing a trade name or an assumed name is liable just as if the signer's own name had been used.

Agent. An authentication may be made by the drawer or the maker or by his or her authorized agent. **For Example,** Eileen Smith, the treasurer of Mills Company, could sign a note for her company as an agent. No particular form of authorization for an agent to authenticate an instrument is required. An authenticating agent should disclose on the instrument (1) the identity of the principal and (2) the fact that the authentication

---

[23] U.C.C. §3-104.

[24] According to Revised U.C.C. §3-103, *authenticate* means (a) to sign or (b) to execute or otherwise adopt a symbol, or encrypt or similarly process a record in whole or in part, with the present intent of the authenticating person to identify the person and adopt or accept a record.

was done in a representative capacity. When this information appears on the face of the instrument, an authorized agent is not liable on it.

The representative capacity of an officer of an organization can be shown by the authentication of the officer along with the title of the office and the organization's name.[25] **For Example,** a signature of "James Shelton, Treasurer, NorWest Utilities, Inc.," or "NorWest Utilities, Inc., by James Shelton, Treasurer," on a note is enough to show Shelton's representative capacity. NorWest Utilities, not Shelton, would be liable on the note.

Absence of Representative Capacity or Identification of Principal. If an instrument fails to show the **representative capacity** of the person who is authenticating or fails to identify the person, then the individual who authenticates the instrument is personally liable on the instrument to anyone who acquires superior rights, such as the rights of a holder in due course (see Chapter 29). Because the instrument is a final agreement, the parol evidence rule applies, and the party who authenticated is not permitted to introduce extrinsic evidence that might clarify his or her representative capacity. The party who authenticated, in order to avoid personal liability, must indicate on the face of the instrument his or her role in the principal, such as president or vice president. (For more information about the parol evidence rule, see Chapter 16.)

> **representative capacity**–action taken by one on behalf of another, as the act of a personal representative on behalf of a decedent's estate, or action taken both on one's behalf and on behalf of others, as a shareholder bringing a representative action.

However, an agent is not personally liable on a check that is drawn on the bank account of the principal and authenticated by him or her, even though the agent failed to disclose his or her representative capacity on the check. **For Example,** a check that is already imprinted with the employer's name is not the check of the employee, regardless of whether the employee only authenticates with his or her name or also adds a title such as "Payroll Clerk" or "Treasurer" near the signature.

CASE SUMMARY

A Crushing Defeat on a Note That Had the Wrong Parties

FACTS: Green Valley Growers, Inc. (GVG) was a plant nursery owned by O. Wayne Massey and others. From 2001 until the GVG's bankruptcy, KC Crushed provided GVG raw materials and construction services, including the creation of ditches and irrigation ponds, building of rock roads, beds and loading docks, as well as the work on some of the greenhouses located on the property operated by GVG. GVG took out a loan and paid $396,527.10 of the proceeds to KC Crushed. On February 27, 2007, Massey and Hurley Ray Smith (owner of KC Crushed) executed a Promissory Note that stated: "I, Wayne Massey promise to repay Ray Smith for a Promissory Note in the amount of $400,000.00 with Interest."

Smith and Massey (defendants) contend that the Note "incorrectly listed Smith as the lender and Wayne Massey as the borrower." Smith stated that the Note was in fact between KC Crushed and GVG, not himself and Massey, "I did not draft or prepare the Promissory Note. I did not

review the Promissory Note. When the Promissory Note was presented to me, I did not read it and simply signed the note as written ... I was signing on behalf of KC Crushed Concrete, not myself individually. Wayne Massey and I agreed that [GVG] would repay KC Crushed Concrete with periodic $5,000 loan repayments, as initial interest only payments." From April 2007 until December 2008, GVG paid Smith—not KC Crushed—$80,000 toward the Note, in $5,000 monthly installments.

Smith and KC Crushed moved for summary judgment that they are not liable to Randy Williams—the bankruptcy trustee for the GVG bankruptcy.

DECISION: The Note plainly stated that Massey was the borrower and Smith was the lender. But GVG wrote the $5,000 monthly checks to Smith, not to KC Crushed. Smith's argument that he did not read the Note before he signed is

---

[25] U.C.C. §3-402. In re *Bedrock Marketing, LLC,* 404 B.R. 939 (D. Utah 2009); *Free Green Can, LLC v. Green Recycling Enterprises,* LLC, Not Reported in F. Supp. 2d, 2011 WL 5130359 (N.D. Ill.), and *Arntz v. Valdez,* 2011 WL 3433018, 163 Wash. App. 1003 (Wash. App. 2011).

A Crushing Defeat on a Note That Had the Wrong Parties continued

unavailing. Parties are presumed to know the contents of a document and have an obligation to protect themselves by reading documents prior to signing.

The parties' subjective beliefs cannot contradict the intent of the parties expressed within the four corners of the document. The rights and obligations of the parties "are determined solely from the written loan agreement, and any prior oral agreements between the parties are

superseded by and merged into the loan agreement." The Note stated that the $400,000 debt ran from Massey to Smith, not from GVG to KC Crushed. The payments were not relevant because the document was clear. The payments could have been made for another purpose such as a capital contribution. [*Williams v. Houston Plants & Garden World, Inc.*, 508 B.R. 19 (S.D. Tex. 2014)]

THINKING THINGS THROUGH

When Your John Hancock Is Enough

Work through the following examples of signatures on negotiable instruments and capacity, and determine whether there would be personal liability on the part of the company executives signing the instruments.

1. Donald Schaffer owned and operated Grafton Janitorial Service, Inc. On October 6, 1998, Mr. Schaffer obtained a $25,000 line of credit for his company from First Merit Bank by executing a promissory note, which he signed both as "Donald J. Schaffer, President" and "Donald J. Schaffer, Cosigner." The note contains no guarantee provision, and Mr. Schaffer did not sign the note in the capacity as a guarantor. [*Schaffer v. First Merit Bank, N.A.*, 927 N.E.2d 15 (Ohio App. 2009)]

2. A corporate guaranty was signed as follows:

THE PRODUCERS GROUP OF FLA., INC. a Florida corporation, by the following officers solely on behalf of the corporation:

/s/ Eddie Beverly, as its President

CORPORATE PRESIDENT Eddie Beverly

/s/ Stephen Edman, as its Secretary

CORPORATE SECRETARY Steve Edman

/s/ John Bauder, as its Treasurer

CORPORATE TREASURER John Bauder

Are the officers personally liable on the guaranty?

[*Tampa Bay Economic Development Corp. v. Edman*, 598 So. 2d 172 (Fla. App. 1992)]

Promise or Order to Pay

A promissory note must contain a promise to pay money. A mere acknowledgment of a debt, such as a record stating "I.O.U.," is not a promise. A draft or check must contain an order or command to pay money.

Unconditional Promise or Order

For an instrument to be negotiable, the promise or order to pay must be unconditional.[26] **For Example,** when an instrument makes the duty to pay dependent on the completion of the construction of a building, the promise is conditional and the instrument is nonnegotiable. The instrument is enforceable as a contract, but it is not a negotiable instrument given all the rights and protections afforded under Article 3.

An order for the payment of money out of a particular fund is negotiable. The instrument can refer to a particular account or merely indicate a source of reimbursement for the drawee, such as "Charge my expense account." Nor is an instrument conditional

[26] U.C.C. §3-109(c). *Stancik v. Hersch*, 2012 WL 1567213 (Ohio App. 2012). A mortgage is not a negotiable instrument because it is not a promise to pay; it is a lien. *Gardner v. Quicken Loans*, 567 Fed. Appx. 362 (6th Cir. 2014).

when payment is to be made only from an identified fund if the issuer is a government or governmental unit or agency, or when payment is to be made from the assets of a partnership, an unincorporated association, a trust, or an estate.[27] However, the fund noted must in fact exist because payment from a fund to be created by a future event would be conditional. **For Example,** making an instrument "payable from the account I'll establish when the sale of my house occurs" is conditional because the fund's creation is tied to an event whose time of occurrence is unknown.

The standards for negotiability do not require that the issuer of the instrument be personally obligated pay it.[28] An instrument's negotiability is not destroyed by a reference to a related document. Section 3-106(b) provides, "A promise or order is not made conditional (i) by a reference to another writing for a statement of rights with respect to collateral, prepayment, or acceleration."[29] **For Example,** if a note includes the following phrase, "This note is secured by a mortgage on the property located at Hilding Lane," the note is still negotiable.[30]

Payment in Money

money—medium of exchange.

A negotiable instrument must be payable in money. **Money** is defined to include any medium of exchange adopted or authorized by the United States, a foreign government, or an intergovernmental organization. The parties to an instrument are free to decide which currency will be used for payment even though their transaction may occur in a different country.[31] **For Example,** two parties in the United States are free to agree that their note will be paid in pesos.

If the order or promise is not for money, the instrument is not negotiable. **For Example,** an instrument that requires the holder to take stock or goods in place of money is nonnegotiable. The instrument is enforceable as a contract, but it cannot qualify as a negotiable instrument for purposes of Article 3 rights.

Sum Certain

sum certain—amount due under an instrument that can be computed from its face with only reference to interest rates.

Negotiable instruments must include a statement of a **sum certain,** or an exact amount of money.[32] Without a definite statement as to how much is to be paid under the terms of the instrument, there is no way to determine how much the instrument is worth.

There are some minor variations from sum certain requirement. **For Example,** an instrument is not nonnegotiable because its interest rate provisions include changes in the rate at maturity or because it provides for certain costs and attorney fees to be recovered by the holder in the event of enforcement action or litigation.[33]

In most states, the sum payable under an instrument is certain even though it calls for the payment of a floating or variable interest rate. An instrument is negotiable even though it provides for an interest rate of 1 percent above the prime rate of a named bank. It is immaterial that the exact amount of interest that will be paid cannot be determined at the time the paper is issued because the rate may later change.[34]

[27] A check issued by a debtor in bankruptcy for payment of court-ordered obligations is not conditional because of the involvement of the court or ongoing conditions on the debtor's payments. *Ward v. Stanford*, 443 S.W.3d 334 (Tex. App. 2014).
[28] U.C.C. §3-110(c)(1)–(2) (1990); *Ocwen Loan Servicing, LLC v. Branaman*, 554 F. Supp. 2d 645 (N.D. Miss. 2008).
[29] U.C.C. §3-106(b).
[30] Reference to a bill of lading does not affect negotiability. *Regent Corp., U.S.A. v. Azmat Bangladesh, Ltd.*, 686 N.Y.S.2d 24 (1999). However, a reference to a standby agreement does affect negotiability. In re *Sabertooth, LLC*, 443 B.R. 671 (E.D. Pa. 2011).
[31] U.C.C. §3-107. *Means v. Clardy*, 735 S.W.2d 6 (Mo. App. 1987) (payment in cabinets makes a note nonnegotiable).
[32] *Heritage Bank v. Bruha*, 812 N.W.2d 260 (Neb. 2012).
[33] U.C.C. §3-106. In re *MCB Financial Group, Inc.*, 461 B.R. 914 (N.D. Ga. 2011).
[34] However, when too many documents are necessary to determine the interest rate and the interest rate floats, negotiability is affected. *Farouki v. Petra International Banking Corp.*, 63 F. Supp. 3d 84 (D.D.C. 2014).

CPA   **Time of Payment**

A negotiable instrument must be payable on demand or at a definite time.[35] If an instrument is payable "when convenient," it is nonnegotiable because the day of payment may never arrive. An instrument payable only upon the happening of a particular event that may or may not happen is not negotiable. **For Example,** a provision in a note to pay the sum certain when a person marries is not payable at a definite time because that particular event may never occur. It is immaterial whether the contingency in fact has happened because from an examination of the instrument alone, it still appears to be subject to a condition that might not occur.

Demand. An instrument is *payable on demand* when it expressly states that it is payable "on demand," at sight, or on presentation. U.C.C. §3-108(a) provides "A promise or order is 'payable on demand' if (i) it states that it is payable on demand or at sight, or otherwise indicates that it is payable at the will of the holder, or (ii) it does not state any time of payment."[36] Presentation occurs when a holder demands payment. Commercial paper is deemed to be payable on demand when no time for payment is stated in the instrument.[37]

definite time—time of payment computable from the face of the instrument.

Definite Time. The time of payment is a **definite time** if an exact time or times are specified or if the instrument is payable at a fixed time after sight or acceptance or at a time that is readily ascertainable.[38] The time of payment is definite even though the instrument provides for prepayment, for acceleration, or for extensions at the option of a party or automatically on the occurrence of a specified contingency.

CASE SUMMARY

Whenever... Paying When You Can Does Not a Negotiable Instrument Make

FACTS: Gary Vaughn signed a document stating that Fred and Martha Smith were loaning him $9,900. As to when the loan was to be repaid, the document stated, "when you can." Approximately 18 months later, the Smiths sued Vaughn for the entire amount, claiming default on the note as well as unjust enrichment. The Smiths moved for summary judgment. They contended that Vaughn was immediately liable for the entire amount but that they were willing to work out a repayment schedule. Vaughn also moved for summary judgment, arguing that he did not have to repay the Smiths because he did not have the ability to do so. The trial court denied the Smiths' motion and granted Vaughn's. The Smiths appealed.

DECISION: The court held the following: a promissory note that calls for a borrower to repay "when you can" was not payable on demand and was not a negotiable instrument. However, an issue of fact remained as to when a debt payable "when you can" became payable. There were other issues of fact, such as whether there was unjust enrichment and whether it was reasonable for the borrower to repay the debt. The language implied that there was an open-ended agreement. The parties might have a contract, but the Smiths could not demand payment as if the instrument were a demand negotiable instrument. Reversed for further factual determinations. [*Smith v. Vaughn,* **882 N.E.2d 941 (Ohio App. 2007)**]

CPA   **Missing Date.** An instrument that is not dated is deemed dated on the day it is issued to the payee. Any holder may add the correct date to the instrument.

---

[35] U.C.C. §3-108.
[36] U.C.C. §3-108(a).
[37] U.C.C. §3-112; *Universal Premium Acceptance Corp. v. York Bank's Trust Co.,* 69 F.3d 695 (3d Cir. 1995); *State v. McWilliams,* 178 P.3d 121 (Mont. 2008).
[38] *Gallwitz v. Novel,* 2011 WL 303253 (Ohio App. 2011).

Effect of Date on a Demand Instrument. The date on a demand instrument controls the time of payment, and the paper is not due before its date. Consequently, a check that is postdated ceases to be demand paper and is not properly payable before the date on the check. A bank making earlier payment does not incur any liability for doing so unless the drawer has given the bank a postdated check notice.

Words of Negotiability: Payable to Order or Bearer

payable to order–term stating that a negotiable instrument is payable to the order of any person described in it or to a person or order.

bearer–person in physical possession of commercial paper payable to bearer, a document of title directing delivery to bearer, or an investment security in bearer form.

An instrument that is not a check must be **payable to order** or **bearer.**[39] This requirement is met by such phrases as "Pay to the order of John Jones," "Pay to John Jones or order," "Pay to bearer," and "Pay to John Jones or bearer." The use of the phrase "to the order of John Jones" or "to John Jones or order" shows that the person executing the instrument had no intention of restricting payment of the instrument to John Jones. These phrases indicate that there is no objection to paying anyone to whom John Jones orders the paper to be paid. Similarly, if the person executing the instrument originally wrote that it will be paid "to bearer" or "to John Jones or bearer," there is no restriction on the payment of the paper to the original payee. However, if the instrument is not a check and it is payable on its face "to John Jones," the instrument is not negotiable.[40] Whether an instrument is bearer or order paper is important because the two instruments are transferred in different ways and because the liability of the transferors can be different.

CASE SUMMARY

The Goal Was a Hockey Team AND a Negotiable Instrument

FACTS: William Kidd served as managing director of Limeco Corporation. In 2001, negotiations began between Kidd/Limeco (defendants) and R.W. Whitaker and Monty Fletcher (plaintiffs) in connection with what later became a failed effort to purchase a hockey team in Tupelo. Whitaker and Fletcher loaned Limeco $750,000. Whitaker and Fletcher claim that Kidd concealed the fact that Limeco had no assets. Whitaker also loaned Kidd an additional $100,000, with the understanding that Kidd and Limeco would be responsible for paying back the loan Whitaker had taken out from the Peoples Bank & Trust Company in Tupelo in order to make the loan to Kidd.

On July 1, 2002, the parties entered into what they referred to as promissory notes (referred to as the "Fletcher note" and the "Whitaker note") to memorialize the terms of the loan agreements they had made in early 2002. Both Fletcher and Whitaker were granted a continuing lien on Limeco's monies, securities, and/or other property for the entire amount of the promissory notes (each in the amount of $375,000).

On December 11, 2003, Whitaker and Fletcher filed separate complaints against Limeco and Kidd for recovery of the more than $850,000 that had never been repaid. The trial court found that, because the suit was brought after the contracts' statute of limitations had expired, it had to be dismissed. Whitaker and Fletcher argued that the notes were negotiable instruments and their fraud claim was valid because of the six-year statute of limitations that applied with regard to negotiable instruments.

DECISION: The court held that words of negotiability are an absolute requirement for a negotiable instrument. Without those words, the note is simply a contract, and a suit on a contract required that it be filed within three years. Because Whitaker and Fletcher were over the three years, their suit had to be dismissed. If they had had the words of negotiability, then the suit could have proceeded because it was brought well within the time limits. [*Whitaker v. Limeco Corp.*, 32 So. 3d 429 (Miss. 2010)]

---

[39] Guaranteed student loans have too many restrictions on transfers to be negotiable instruments. *U.S. v. Carter*, 506 Fed. Appx. 853 (11th Cir. 2013).
[40] U.C.C. §3-108.

ETHICS & THE LAW

Medicaid Eligibility and Article 3 Negotiability

Kenneth Wilson was hospitalized from January 7, 2007, until his death on February 22, 2007. During the hospitalization, Kenneth's wife, Doris, sold her 100 percent stock ownership in the Brothers Delivery Service (her husband's company) to her son. The agreement provided that Kenneth, Jr., would pay $62,531 in 60 installments of $1,041.82, starting March 1, 2007. Kenneth, Jr., did not sign the promissory note for these terms. Doris never signed the purchase agreement. Doris then applied for Medicaid benefits in order to cover the costs of her husband's hospitalization. Eligibility for Medicaid requires a determination that there are insufficient personal assets to pay the bill. The Division of Social Services concluded that Doris was the owner of a promissory note, a liquid asset, that could be sold to pay the medical bills. Coverage was denied due to

excessive resources. Doris argues that there is no negotiable note because the requirements for negotiability are not met. The appellate court agreed because the underlying contract had not been signed by Doris and because there was not, as yet, a promissory note. The purchase agreement did not have words of negotiability and there was no definite time for payment because the note did not yet exist.

Discuss whether Doris attained Medicaid eligibility through a legal loophole. Does she actually have assets that could be used to pay at least part of the debt? Should legal definitions allow us to escape an obligation to pay?

[*Estate of Wilson v. Division of Social Services*, 685 S.E.2d 135 (N.C. App. 2009)]

---

order paper–instrument payable to the order of a party.

bearer paper–instrument with no payee, payable to cash or payable to bearer.

Order Paper. An instrument is payable to order, or **order paper,** when by its terms it is payable to the order of any person described in it ("Pay to the order of K. Read") or to a person or order ("Pay to K. Read or order").

Bearer Paper. An instrument is payable to bearer, or **bearer paper,** when it is payable (1) to bearer or the order of bearer, (2) to a specified person or bearer, or (3) to "cash," "the order of cash," or any other designation that does not purport to identify a person or when (4) the last or only indorsement is a blank indorsement (an indorsement that does not name the person to whom the instrument is negotiated). An instrument that does not identify any payee is payable to bearer.[41]

Whether an instrument is bearer or order paper is important for determining how the instrument is transferred (see Chapter 28) and what the liability of the parties under the instrument is. Review Figure 27-3 for more background.

CASE SUMMARY

I May Be a Thief, But under Article 3 Bearer Paper Rules, I Am Not a Forger

FACTS: Joshua Herrera found a purse in a dumpster near San Pedro and Kathryn Streets in Albuquerque. Herrera took the purse with him to a friend's house. Either Herrera or his friend called the owner of the purse and the owner retrieved the purse at some point. After the purse was returned to the owner, Herrera returned to the dumpster where he found a check and some other items. The check Herrera found was written out to "Cash" and he thought this meant that he "could get money for [the] check."

When he presented the check to the teller at a credit union to cash it, the teller instructed him to put his name on the payee line next to "Cash." Herrera added "to Joshua Herrera" next to the word "Cash" on the payee line of the check and indorsed the check.

Herrera had pleaded guilty to one count of forgery but moved to have the indictment dismissed on the grounds that adding his name to a bearer instrument was not forgery. He appealed the denial of the motion to dismiss the indictment.

[41] U.C.C. §3-104(d).

I May Be a Thief, But under Article 3 Bearer Paper Rules, I Am Not a Forger continued

DECISION: The court held that the instrument that Herrera originally found was bearer paper. By adding his named "to Joshua Herrera" to the "Pay to" line after "Cash" did not change the character of the instrument from bearer to order paper. At best, the addition of the words created an ambiguity and under the code interpretations should continue to be treated as bearer paper. Since he did not alter the nature of the instrument or convert it to a different instrument, he could not be charged with forgery. [*New Mexico v. Herrera*, 18 P.3d 326 (N.M. App. 2000); *cert. den.* 20 P.3d 810 (N.M. 2001)]

FIGURE 27-3 | **Bearer versus Order Paper**

"Pay to the order of ABC Corp."	ORDER
"Pay to the order of Bearer."	BEARER
"Pay to the order of ABC Corp. or Bearer"	BEARER
"Pay to the order of ABC Corp., Bearer"	ORDER
"Pay to the order of John Jones" (note)	ORDER
"Pay to the order of John Jones" (check)	ORDER
"Pay to John Jones" (note)	NONNEGOTIABLE
"Pay to John Jones" (check)	NEGOTIABLE/ORDER
"Pay to the order of John Jones or Bearer"	BEARER
"Pay to cash"	BEARER
"Pay to the order of cash"	BEARER

---

postdating–inserting or placing on an instrument a later date than the actual date on which it was executed.

collateral–property pledged by a borrower as security for a debt.

27-2c **Factors Not Affecting Negotiability**

Omitting a date of execution or antedating or **postdating** an instrument has no effect on its negotiability.

Provisions relating to **collateral,** such as specifying the collateral as security for the debt or a promise to maintain, protect, or give additional collateral, do not affect negotiability. **For Example,** the phrase "This note is secured by a first mortgage" does not affect negotiability.

27-2d **Ambiguous Language**

ambiguous–having more than one reasonable interpretation.

The following rules are applied when **ambiguous** language exists in words or descriptions:

1. Words control figures where conflict exists.
2. Handwriting supersedes conflicting typewritten and printed terms.
3. Typewritten terms supersede preprinted terms.
4. If there is a failure to provide for the payment of interest or if there is a provision for the payment of interest but no rate is mentioned, the judgment rate at the place of payment applies from the date of the instrument.[42]

27-2e **Statute of Limitations**

Article 3 of the UCC establishes a three-year statute of limitations for most actions involving negotiable instruments. This limitation also applies to actions for the conversion of such instruments and for breach of warranty. There is a six-year statute of limitations for suits on certificates of deposit and accepted drafts.

[42] In re *Blasco*, 352 B.R. 888 (N.D. Ala. 2006).

Make the Connection

Summary

An instrument or piece of commercial paper is a transferable, signed promise or order to pay a specified sum of money that is evidenced by a record. An instrument is negotiable when it contains the terms required by the UCC.

Negotiable instruments have two categories: (1) promises to pay and (2) orders to pay. Checks and drafts are orders to pay. Notes and certificates of deposits are promises to pay. In addition to ordinary checks, there are cashier's checks and teller's checks. A bank money order is a check even though it bears the words *money order*.

The original parties to a note are the maker and the payee. The original parties to a draft are the drawer, the drawee, and the payee. The term *party* may refer to a natural person or to an artificial person, such as a corporation. Indorsers and accommodation parties are considered secondary obligors.

The requirements of negotiability are that the instrument (1) be evidenced by a record, (2) be signed (authenticated) by the maker or the drawer, and (3) contain a promise or order (4) of an unconditional character (5) to pay in money (6) a sum certain (7) on demand or at a definite time (8) to order or bearer.

A check may be negotiable without being payable to order or bearer.

If an instrument meets the requirements of negotiability, the parties have the rights and protections of Article 3. If it does not meet the requirements of negotiability, the rights of the parties are governed under contract law.

Learning Outcomes

After studying this chapter, you should be able to clearly explain:

27-1   Types of Negotiable Instruments and Parties

LO.1   Explain the importance and function of negotiable instruments
See the discussion of negotiability that begins on page 521.
See the *New Mexico v. Herrera* case, pages 528–529.

LO.2   Name the parties to negotiable instruments
See the list of parties to instruments in the section titled "Parties to Instruments," pages 520–521.

27-2   Negotiability

LO.3   Describe the concept of negotiability and distinguish it from assignability
See *Whitaker v. Limeco Corp.* for what can happen if an instrument is not negotiable, page 527.

LO.4   List the requirements for a negotiable instrument
See the list of negotiability requirements, page 522.
See the *Williams v. Houston Plants & Garden World, Inc.* case to understand who is liable on negotiable instruments, pages 523–524.
See the *Smith v. Vaughn* case, page 526.

Key Terms

acceptor	definite time	order paper
accommodation party	draft, or bill of exchange	party
ambiguous	drawee	payable to order
bearer	drawer	payee
bearer paper	maker	postdating
cashier's check	money	promissory note
certificate of deposit (CD)	money order	representative capacity
check	negotiability	sum certain
collateral	negotiable instrument	teller's check
commercial paper	nonnegotiable instrument	traveler's check

Questions and Case Problems

1. Harold H. Heidingsfelder signed a credit agreement as vice president of J. O. H. Construction Co. for a line of credit with Pelican Plumbing Co. The credit agreement contained the following language:

> *In consideration of an open account privilege, I hereby understand and agree to the above terms.*
>
> *Should it become necessary to place this account for collection I shall personally obligate myself and my corporation, if any, to pay the entire amount due including service charges (as outlined above terms) thirty-three and one-third (33⅓%) attorney's fees, and all costs of collection, including court costs.*
> *Signed [Harold H. Heidingsfelder]*
> *Company J. O. H. Construction Co., Inc.*

When J. O. H. Construction failed to make payment, Pelican, claiming it was a holder of a negotiable instrument, sued Heidingsfelder to hold him personally liable for his failure to indicate a representative capacity on the credit agreement. He claims that a credit application is not a negotiable instrument and that he could not be held personally liable. Is he right? [*Pelican Plumbing Supply, Inc. v. J. O. H. Construction Co., Inc.*, 653 So. 2d 699 (La.)]

2. Abby Novel signed a note with the following on it: "Glen Gallwitz 1-8-2002 loaned me $5,000 at 6% interest a total of $10,000.00." The note did not contain a payment schedule or a time for repayment.

    Abby used the $10,000 as start-up money for her business and says that she orally agreed to repay the loan out of the proceeds from her first 1,000-product sales. Abby did not make any payments. Glen passed away and his son, as executor of his estate, demanded that Abby repay the $10,000 plus 6% interest for a total of $14,958 (the amount due as of April 2010). The trial court granted judgment for the estate. Abby has appealed, alleging that she repaid the note through the care she gave for Glen. The estate maintains that the instrument was a negotiable promissory note and that it is entitled to collect the amount due in cash. Who is correct and why? [*Gallwitz v. Novel*, 2011 WL 303253 (Ohio App.)]

3. Charter Bank of Gainesville had in its possession a note containing the following provision: "This note with interest is secured by a mortgage on real estate, of even date herewith, made by the maker hereof in favor of said payee…. The terms of said mortgage are by this reference made a part hereof." When the bank sued on the note, it said that it was a holder of a negotiable instrument. Is this instrument negotiable? [*Holly Hill Acres, Ltd. v. Charter Bank of Gainesville*, 314 So. 2d 209 (Fla. App.)]

4. On October 14, 1980, United American Bank of Knoxville made a $1,700,000 loan to Frederic B. Ingram. William F. Earthman, the president of the bank and a beneficiary of the loan, had arranged for the loan and prepared the loan documents. Mr. Ingram and Mr. Earthman were old friends, and Mr. Ingram had loaned Mr. Earthman money in the past. Mr. Ingram was in jail at the time of this loan and was unable to complete the documents for the loan. Mr. Earthman says that Mr. Ingram authorized him to do the loan so long as it did not cost him anything to do it.

    Also on October 14, 1980, Mr. Earthman prepared and executed a personal $1,700,000 note to Mr. Ingram, using a standard Commerce Union Bank note form. Mr. Earthman wrote "Frederic B. Ingram" in the space for identifying the lending bank and also filled in another blank stating that the note would be due "Eighteen Months after Date." With regard to the interest, Mr. Earthman checked a box signifying that the interest would be "At the Bank's 'Prime Rate' plus % per year."

    Mr. Earthman then sold both of the notes, which ended up in the hands of third parties (holders in due course) who demanded payment. Mr. Ingram raised the defense that he had not authorized Mr. Earthman to handle the transactions. The third parties said that the notes were negotiable instruments and that they were entitled to payment without listening to Mr. Ingram's defenses. Mr. Earthman said that his note to Mr. Ingram as well as the bank note from Mr. Ingram were not negotiable and that they could both raise defenses to the third parties seeking payment.

    Who is correct? What do you think of Mr. Earthman's banking processes and procedures? What ethical issues do you see in these loan transactions? [*Ingram v. Earthman*, 993 S.W.2d 611 (Tenn.)]

5. The state of Alaska was a tenant in a large office building owned by Univentures, a partnership. The state made a lease payment of $28,143.47 to Univentures with state treasury warrant No. 21045102. Charles LeViege, the managing partner of

Univentures, assigned the warrant to Lee Garcia. A dispute then arose among the Univentures partners, and the company notified the state that it should no longer pay LeViege the rent. The state placed a stop payment order on the warrant. Garcia claimed that he was a holder of a negotiable instrument and that the state owed him the money. The state claimed that a warrant did not qualify as a negotiable instrument. The warrant was in writing, was signed by the governor of the state, provided a definite sum of $28,143.47, and stated that "it will be deemed paid unless redeemed within two years after the date of issue." The warrant stated that it was "payable to the order of Univentures." Does the warrant meet the requirements for a negotiable instrument? [*National Bank v. Univentures*, 824 P.2d 1377 (Alaska)]

6. NationWide Check Corp. sold money orders through local agents. A customer would purchase a money order by paying an agent the amount of the desired money order plus a fee. The customer would then sign the money order as the remitter or sender and would fill in the name of the person who was to receive the money following the printed words "Payable to." In a lawsuit between NationWide and Banks, a payee on some of these orders, the question was raised as to whether these money orders were checks and could be negotiable even though not payable to order or to bearer. Are the money orders negotiable instruments? [*NationWide Check Corp. v. Banks*, 260 A.2d 367 (D.C.)]

7. George S. Avery signed a letter regarding the unpaid balance on a $20,000 promissory note owed to Jim Whitworth in the form of a letter addressed to Whitworth stating: "This is your note for $45,000.00, secured individually and by our Company for your security, due February 7, 1984." The letter was signed: "Your friend, George S. Avery." It was typed on stationery with the name of Avery's employer, V & L Manufacturing Co., Inc., printed at the bottom and the words "George Avery, President" printed at the top. Avery says he is not personally liable on the note. The court granted summary judgment for Whitworth and Avery appealed. Who is liable? [*Avery v. Whitworth*, 414 S.E.2d 725 (Ga. App.)]

8. Northwest Harvest Products, Inc., fell behind on its trade account with Major Products Company, Inc., and Major requested a note for the debt. Northwest sent a $79,000 corporate note. The balance on the note was incorrect, and Northwest sent a second corporate note for $79,361.89. After further discussion between the parties, Major sent a $78,445.24 note. The Chief Executive Officer of Northwest at that time signed the note "Donald H. Eoll CEO," attached a Post-It brand fax transmittal memo indicating that the note came from Donald Eoll at Northwest, and sent the note via facsimile. The note went unpaid, and Major sued both Eoll and Northwest for the debt. Is the CEO personally liable on the note? What are the parol evidence factors in this case? [*Major Products Co., Inc. v. Northwest Harvest Products, Inc.*, 979 P.2d 905 (Wash. App. 1999)]

9. Atlas Capital, LLC's sole member and manager was Weston Wade Sleater. Mr. Sleater signed two promissory notes totaling $4,000,000 as the maker of the notes. The signature blocks of the notes read, "Weston Wade Sleater & Atlas Marketing Group, L.C.," but the signature was only that of Mr. Sleater. Mr. Sleater is referred to as the maker of the note. Mr. Sleater failed to pay the notes and a bankruptcy trustee brought suit to collect the remaining amount due. Mr. Sleater maintains that the notes are not his but those of Atlas Capital. Is he correct? Is Mr. Sleater liable on the notes? Discuss the ambiguity issues as well as the way the notes were signed. [*In re Bedrock Marketing, LLC*, 404 B.R. 929 (D. Utah)]

10. Lloyd and Mario Spaulding entered into a contract to purchase property from Richard and Robert Krajcir. The two Spaulding brothers signed a promissory note to the Krajcir brothers with the following language: "The amount of $10,000 [is] to be paid sellers at the time of the initial closing [delivery of the deed]; plus, the principal amount payable to sellers at the time of the final indorsement of the subject H.U.D. loan." In litigation over the note, the Spauldings said it was not a negotiable instrument. The lower court found it to be a negotiable promissory note and the Spaulding partners appealed. Is the note negotiable? [*Krajcir v. Egid*, 712 N.E.2d 917 (Ill. App.)]

11. Is the following instrument negotiable?

> *I, Richard Bell, hereby promise to pay to the order of Lorry Motors Ten Thousand Dollars ($10,000) upon the receipt of the final distribution from the estate of my deceased aunt, Rita Dorn. This negotiable instrument is given by me as the down payment on my purchase of a 1986 Buick to be delivered in three weeks.*
>
> *Richard Bell (signature).*

12. Smith has in his possession the following instrument:

    September 1, 2003
    I, Selma Ray, hereby promise to pay Helen
    Savit One Thousand Dollars ($1,000) one
    year after date. This instrument was given for
    the purchase of Two Hundred (200) shares of
    Redding Mining Corporation, Interest 6%.
    Selma Ray (signature).

    What is this instrument? Is it negotiable?

13. Master Homecraft Co. received a promissory note
    with a stated face value from Sally and Tom Zim-
    merman. The note was payment for remodeling their
    home and contained unused blanks for installment
    payments but contained no maturity date. When
    Master Homecraft sued the Zimmermans on the
    note, the couple argued that they should not be lia-
    ble on the note because it is impossible to determine
    from its face the amount due or the date of maturity.
    Decide. [*Master Homecraft Co. v. Zimmerman*, 22
    A.2d 440 (Pa.)]

14. A note from Mark Johnson with HealthCo Interna-
    tional as payee for $28,979.15 included the follow-
    ing language:

    [p]ayable in _____, Successive Monthly
    Installments of $ Each, and in 11 Successive
    Monthly Installments of $2,414.92 Each
    thereafter, and in a final payment of
    $2,415.03 thereafter. The first installment
    being payable on the _____ day of
    _____ 20 _____, and the remaining
    installments on the same date of each month
    thereafter until paid.

    Johnson signed the note. Is it negotiable? [*Barclays
    Bank, P.L.C. v. Johnson*, 499 S.E.2d 769 (N. C. App.)]

15. The text of a handwritten note stated simply that "'I
    Robert Harrison owe Peter Jacob $25,000 ...,' /s/
    Robert Harrison." Peter Jacob sought to use the
    handwritten note as a negotiable promissory note.
    Can he? [*Jacob v. Harrison*, 49 U.C.C. Rep. Serv. 2d
    554 (Del. Super.)]

CPA Questions

1. A company has in its possession the following
   instrument:

$500.00	**Dayton, Ohio** **October 2, 1987**

   **Sixty days after the date I promise to pay
   to the order of**

   Cash

   Five Hundred **Dollars**

   at   Miami, Florida

   **Value received with interest at the rate
   of nine percent. This instrument is secured
   by a conditional sales contract.**

   No. 11 **Due** Dec. 1, 1987   Craig Burk
   Craig Burk

   This instrument is:

   a. Not negotiable until December 1, 1987.

   b. A negotiable bearer note.

   c. A negotiable time draft.

   d. A nonnegotiable note because it states that it is
   secured by a conditional sales contract.

2. The instrument shown here is a:

   **To: Middlesex National Bank
   Nassau, N.Y.**

   September 15, 1994

   **Pay to the
   order of**   Robert Silver $4,000.00

   Four Thousand and xx/100   **Dollars**

   on   October 1, 1994

   Lynn Dexter
   Lynn Dexter

   a. Draft.

   b. Postdated check.

   c. Trade acceptance.

   d. Promissory note.

3. Under the commercial paper article of the UCC, for an instrument to be negotiable, it must:

   a. Be payable to order or to bearer.

   b. Be signed to the payee.

   c. Contain references to all agreements between the parties.

   d. Contain necessary conditions of payment.

4. An instrument reads as follows:

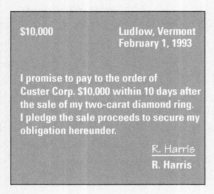

$10,000   Ludlow, Vermont
                 February 1, 1993

I promise to pay to the order of
Custer Corp. $10,000 within 10 days after
the sale of my two-carat diamond ring.
I pledge the sale proceeds to secure my
obligation hereunder.

                          R. Harris
                          R. Harris

   Which of the following statements correctly describes this instrument?

   a. The instrument is nonnegotiable because it is not payable at a definite time.

   b. The instrument is nonnegotiable because it is secured by the proceeds of the sale of the ring.

   c. The instrument is a negotiable promissory note.

   d. The instrument is a negotiable sight draft payable on demand.

5. Which of the following instruments is subject to the provisions of the Negotiable Instruments Article of the UCC?

   a. A bill of lading

   b. A warehouse receipt

   c. A certificate of deposit

   d. An investment security

6. Under the Negotiable Instruments Article of the UCC, which of the following statements is correct regarding a check?

   a. A check is a promise to pay money.

   b. A check is an order to pay money.

   c. A check does not need to be payable on demand.

   d. A check does not need to be drawn on a bank.

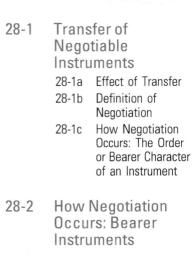

C H A P T E R   28

Transfers of Negotiable Instruments and Warranties of Parties

Learning Outcomes >>>

After studying this chapter, you should be able to

LO.1 Explain the difference between negotiation of order paper and negotiation of bearer paper

LO.2 List the types of indorsements and describe their uses

LO.3 Determine the legal effect of forged and unauthorized indorsements

LO.4 Be familiar with the forged payee impostor exceptions

LO.5 List the indorser's warranties and describe their significance

CPA   ## 28-1 Transfer of Negotiable Instruments

Much of the commercial importance of negotiable instruments lies in the ease with which they can be transferred. Negotiable instruments are transferred by a process known as *negotiation.*

28-1a Effect of Transfer

When a contract is assigned, the transferee has the rights of the transferor. The transferee is entitled to enforce the contract but, as assignee, has no greater rights than the assignor. The assignee is in the same position as the original party to the contract and is subject to any defense that could be raised in a suit on an assigned contract.

When a negotiable instrument is transferred by negotiation, the transferee becomes the *holder of the paper.* A holder who meets certain additional requirements may also be a **holder in due course.** The status of holder in due course gives immunity from certain defenses that might have been asserted against the transferor (see Chapter 29 for a discussion of the rights and role of a holder in due course).

holder in due course—a holder who has given value, taken in good faith without notice of dishonor, defenses, or that instrument is overdue, and who is afforded special rights or status.

28-1b Definition of Negotiation

Under U.C.C. §3-201(a), **negotiation** means "a transfer of possession ... of an instrument by a person other than the issuer to a person who thereby becomes a holder."[1] Negotiation, then, is simply the transfer of a negotiable instrument in such a way that the transferee becomes a holder.[2] A **holder** is different from a possessor or an assignee of the paper. A holder is a transferee in possession of an instrument that runs to her. An instrument runs to a party if it is payable to her order, is indorsed to her, or is bearer paper.

negotiation—the transfer of commercial paper by indorsement and delivery by the person to whom it is then payable in the case of order paper and by physical transfer in the case of bearer paper.

holder—someone in possession of an instrument that runs to that person (i.e., is made payable to that person, is indorsed to that person, or is bearer paper).

28-1c How Negotiation Occurs: The Order or Bearer Character of an Instrument

The order or bearer character of the paper determines how it may be negotiated. The order or bearer character of an instrument is determined according to the words of negotiability used (see Chapter 27 for a complete discussion of order and bearer words of negotiation and more examples of bearer versus order instruments). The types of instruments that qualify as bearer paper include those payable to bearer as well as those payable to the order of "Cash" or payable in blank. The character of an instrument is determined as of the time negotiation takes place even though its character originally or at the time of prior transfers may have been different.

CPA   ## 28-2 How Negotiation Occurs: Bearer Instruments

U.C.C. §3-201(b) provides, "If an instrument is payable to bearer, it may be negotiated by transfer of possession alone."[3] If an instrument qualifies for bearer status, then it is negotiated by **delivery** to another.[4] Delivery can be accomplished by actual transfer of

delivery—constructive or actual possession.

---

[1] U.C.C. §3-201(a).

[2] U.C.C. §3-201; *Bank of New York Mellon v. Deane*, 970 N.Y.S.2d 427 (N.Y. 2013); In re *Miller*, 666 F.3d 1255 (10th Cir. 2012).

[3] U.C.C. §3-201(b). In re *Hussain*, 508 B.R. 417 (9th Cir. 2014).

[4] If no payee is named, the instrument is bearer paper and is negotiated by delivery. *DCM Ltd. Partnership v. Wang*, 555 F. Supp. 2d 808 (E.D. Mich. 2008); *Waldron v. Delffs*, 988 S.W.2d 182 (Tenn. App. 1999).

possession wherein the transferee has possession of the instrument, or constructive transfer, whereby the transferee has exclusive access. **For Example,** when mortgage lenders finance a home mortgage, they often transfer the underlying promissory note on the mortgage several times through financial streams. Many of the underlying problems in the financial market's collapse in 2008 were the large bundles of the promissory notes tied to home mortgages that were in amounts above the value of the mortgaged properties. Who held the bearer promissory notes became a critical issue in foreclosures. Bearer paper is negotiated to a person taking possession of it without regard to whether such possession is lawful. Because delivery of a bearer instrument is effective negotiation, it is possible for a thief or an embezzling officer to transfer title to a bearer instrument. Such a person's presence in the chain of transfer does not affect the rights of those who have taken the bearer instrument in good faith.[5]

CASE SUMMARY

The Blank Indorsement Draws a Blank on Wrongful Foreclosure

FACTS: On September 22, 2006, Richard and Sabrina Emmons signed an adjustable rate promissory note and deed of trust with Chevy Chase Bank (now known as Capital One) for a property located in Vancleave, Mississippi. The note indicates that "[t]he Lender or anyone who takes this Note by Transfer and who is entitled to receive payments under this Note is called the 'Note Holder.'" According to the terms of the deed of trust, "MERS (Mortgage Electronic Recording System) is the beneficiary under this Security Instrument." Based on the assignment of deed of trust, executed on April 9, 2010, MERS then assigned the Emmons' deed of trust to U.S. Bank as trustee.

The deed of trust listed MERS and MERS' successors and assigns as beneficiary and nominee. On April 9, 2010, MERS assigned the deed of trust to U.S. Bank. The Emmons defaulted on their payments. The deed of trust provides for a power of sale in the event of the borrowers'

default—a right which U.S. Bank then exercised through a nonjudicial foreclosure (power of sale). The Emmons then filed suit alleging, among other things, wrongful foreclosure because they claimed U.S. Bank was not a holder of the promissory note.

DECISION: The court held that the Emmons' promissory note was a negotiable instrument that had been indorsed in blank and was therefore bearer paper. It could be further negotiated to a holder via the simple action of delivery. So the holder of the note (in this case, Capital One) would have the right to conduct a foreclosure sale should the parties fall into default on their payments. There was no wrongful foreclosure as long as the party foreclosing was a holder of the note and there had been a default. Capital One was a holder and the Emmons had defaulted. [*Emmons v. Capital One*, **2012 WL 773288 (S.D. Miss. 2012)**]

Even though a bearer instrument may be negotiated by a mere transfer of possession, the one to whom the instrument is delivered may require the bearer to indorse the instrument. This situation most commonly arises when a check payable to "Cash" is presented to a bank for payment. The reason a transferee of bearer paper would want an indorsement is to obtain the protection of an indorser's warranties from the bearer.[6] The bank wants an indorsement on a check made payable to "Cash" so that it can turn to the party cashing the check in the event payment issues arise.

---

[5] U.C.C. §§3-202 and 3-204; *Knight Pub. Co., Inc. v. Chase Manhattan Bank, N.A.*, 479 S.E.2d 478 (N.C. App. 1997); review denied 487 S.E.2d 548 (N.C. 1997); In re *Federal-Nogul Global, Inc.*, 319 B.R. 363 (D. Del. 2005).

[6] The Uniform Electronic Transactions Act (UETA), promulgated by the National Conference of Commissioners on Uniform State Laws in July 1999 and enacted in 46 states, provides that the transfer of a note by electronic record affords the transferee the same rights as a tangible written note.

ETHICS & THE LAW

Having Your Mortgage Set Aside

In cases such as the *Emmons v. Capital One* case, the borrowers bring suit seeking to have their mortgage obligations set aside on the basis of technicalities in the paperwork or the separation of the paperwork. Generally, these borrowers owe far more on their mortgages than their homes are worth.

In some cases, the mortgages have been deemed invalid or the courts have held there was no authority for foreclosure because of the problems with note transfers and the right of foreclosure. Evaluate the ethics of the borrowers in seeking to have their mortgages set aside.

CPA 28-3 **How Negotiation Occurs: Order Instruments**

indorsement–signature of the payee on an instrument.

U.C.C. §3-201(b) provides, "if an instrument is payable to an identified person, negotiation requires transfer of possession of the instrument and its indorsement by the holder."[7] A negotiable instrument that is payable to the order of a specific party is *order paper*, which can be negotiated only through indorsement and transfer of possession of the paper. **Indorsement** and transfer of possession can be made by the payee or indorsee or by an authorized agent of that person.[8]

CASE SUMMARY

The Tax Man Cometh, but He Can't Provide Your Indorsement

FACTS: Thorton Ring was behind on his property taxes for his property in Freeport, Maine. When he received a check payable to his order from Advest, Inc., in the amount of $11,347.09, he wrote the following on the back of the check: "Payable to Town of Freeport Property Taxes 2 Main St."; he sent it along with a letter to the town offices. The letter included the following: "I have paid $11,347.09 of real estate taxes and request the appropriate action to redeem the corresponding property." Ring did nothing further and his property was then liened by the tax clerk. Ring objected because he had paid the taxes. The town argued that the check was not indorsed and Ring thus had not paid the taxes in time to avoid the lien. The lower court found for the town and Ring appealed.

DECISION: There was no indorsement. Ring's name must be signed for there to be negotiation of the instrument to the town. The check had only the first part of the necessary indorsement for order paper; Ring had to indorse the instrument for further negotiation. Indorsements vary according to the method of signing and the words used along with the signature. The nature of an indorsement also affects the future of the instrument in terms of its requirements for further negotiation. [*Town of Freeport v. Ring*, 727 A.2d 901 (Me. 1999)]

blank indorsement–an indorsement that does not name the person to whom the paper, document of title, or investment security is negotiated.

28-3a Blank Indorsement

When the indorser merely signs a negotiable instrument, the indorsement is called a **blank indorsement** (Figure 28-1). A blank indorsement does not indicate the person to whom the instrument is to be paid, that is, the transferee. A blank indorsement turns an

[7] U.C.C. §3-201(b). Although the modern spelling is "endorsement," the UCC has retained the British spelling of "indorsement."
[8] UCC §3-204. The UCC spellings are "indorse" and "indorser," the spellings used in this text. However, courts (including in some cases in this text) use the modern "endorse" and "endorser." *Jenkins v. Wachovia Bank*, 711 S. E.2d 80 (Ga. App. 2011).

FIGURE 28-1   Blank Indorsement

order instrument into a bearer instrument. A person who possesses an instrument on which the last indorsement is blank is the holder.[9] **For Example,** if a check is payable to the order of Jill Barnes and Ms. Barnes indorses the check on the back "Jill Barnes," then the check that was originally an order instrument is now a bearer instrument. The check can now be transferred as bearer paper, which requires only delivery of possession. Once Jill Barnes's signature appears as a blank indorsement on the back, the check becomes transferrable simply by delivery of possession to another party.

28-3b Special Indorsement

special indorsement—an indorsement that specifies the person to whom the instrument is indorsed.

indorsee—party to whom special indorsement is made.

A **special indorsement** consists of the signature of the indorser and words specifying the person to whom the indorser makes the instrument payable, that is, the **indorsee** (Figure 28-2).[10] **For Example,** if Jill Barnes wrote on the back of the check payable to her "Pay to Jack Barnes, /s/ Jill Barnes," the check could be negotiated further only through the signature and possession of Jack Barnes. A special indorsement in this case continues an order instrument as an order instrument. If, after receiving the check, Jack Barnes simply signed it on the back, the check would become bearer paper and could be transferred through possession only.

Although words of negotiability are required on the front of negotiable instruments, it is not necessary that indorsements contain the word *order* or *bearer*. Consequently, the

E-COMMERCE & CYBERLAW

New Flexibility for Cyberspace Commercial Paper

The Check Clearing for the 21st Century Act (sometimes called "Check 21") allows banks to use images of checks as a substitute for paper checks. The substitute check is the legal equivalent of the paper check that has, for so long, dominated U.S. commerce. Under Check 21, the bank is also able to send you electronic copies of your canceled checks. Even if you still opt for paper summaries of your account activity each month, the bank need not return physical checks and can send small reproductions of your checks grouped together on the statement. Recently, you have been able to secure faster credits to your accounts for deposited checks because ATMs scan the checks in, checks that are recognized immediately as deposits. All the new regulations on check substitutes are known as Regulation CC and can be found at Regulation CC, 12 C.F.R. §229.2(zz)(2).

---

[9] In re *Smith*, 509 B.R. 260 (N.D. Cal. 2014).
[10] U.C.C. §3-205; *Chicago Title Ins. Co. v. Allfirst Bank*, 905 A.2d 366, 60 U.C.C. Rep. Serv. 2d 864 (Md. 2006).

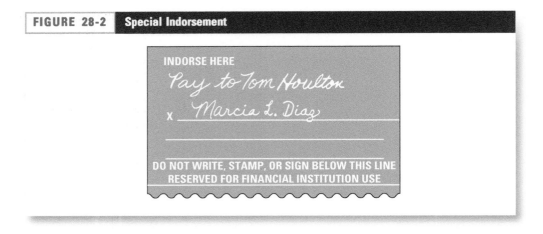

FIGURE 28-2 | **Special Indorsement**

INDORSE HERE

Pay to Tom Houlton

x ___*Marcia L. Diaz*___

DO NOT WRITE, STAMP, OR SIGN BELOW THIS LINE
RESERVED FOR FINANCIAL INSTITUTION USE

paper indorsed as shown in Figure 28-2 continues to be negotiable and may be negotiated further.[11]

An indorsement of "Pay to account [number]" is a special indorsement. In contrast, the inclusion of a notation indicating the debt to be paid is not a special indorsement.

28-3c Qualified Indorsement

qualified indorsement– an indorsement that includes words such as "without recourse" that disclaims certain liability of the indorser to a maker or a drawee.

A **qualified indorsement** is one that qualifies the effect of a blank or a special indorsement by disclaiming certain liability of the indorser to a maker or a drawee. This disclaimer is given by using the phrase "Without recourse" as part of the indorsement (Figure 28-3). Any other words that indicate an intent to limit the indorser's secondary liability in the event the maker or the drawee does not pay on the instrument can also be used.[12]

FIGURE 28-3 | **Qualified Indorsement**

INDORSE HERE

Without recourse
Diana Morris

x _____

DO NOT WRITE, STAMP, OR SIGN BELOW THIS
LINE RESERVED FOR FINANCIAL INSTITUTION USE

---

[11] Only a check may use the phrase "Pay to" on its face and remain negotiable. All other instruments require words of negotiability on their face. Indorsements, on all instruments, need only "Pay to." U.C.C. §3-110.

[12] *Antaeus Enterprises, Inc. v. SD-Barn Real Estate, LLC,* 480 F. Supp. 2d 734 (S.D.N.Y. 2007).

The qualification of an indorsement does not affect the passage of title or the negotiable character of the instrument. It merely disclaims certain of the indorser's secondary liabilities for payment of the instrument in the event the original parties do not pay as the instrument provides.

This qualified form of indorsement is most commonly used when the indorser is a person who has no personal interest in the transaction. **For Example,** an agent or an attorney who is merely indorsing a check of a third person to a client might make a qualified indorsement because he is not actually a party to the transaction.

28-3d Restrictive Indorsement

restrictive indorsement– an indorsement that restricts further transfer, such as in trust for or to the use of some other person, is conditional, or for collection or deposit.

A **restrictive indorsement** specifies the purpose of the indorsement or the use to be made of the instrument (Figure 28-4).[13] An indorsement is restrictive when it includes words showing that the instrument is to be deposited (such as "For deposit only"), when it is negotiated for collection or to an agent or a trustee, or when the negotiation is conditional.[14]

A restrictive indorsement does not prevent transfer or negotiation of the instrument once the initial restriction is honored. The indorsement "For deposit only" requires only that the first party who receives the instrument after the restriction is placed on it comply with that restriction. The indorsement "For deposit only" makes an instrument a bearer instrument for any bank. If the indorser's account number is added to a "For deposit only" indorsement, then the only party who can take the instrument after this restrictive indorsement is a bank with that account number. A restrictive indorsement reduces the risk of theft or unauthorized transfer by eliminating the bearer quality of a blank indorsement.

28-3e Correction of Name by Indorsement

Sometimes the name of the payee or the indorsee of an instrument is spelled improperly. **For Example,** H. A. Price may receive a paycheck that is payable to the order of "H. O. Price." If this error in Price's name was a clerical one and the check is indeed intended for

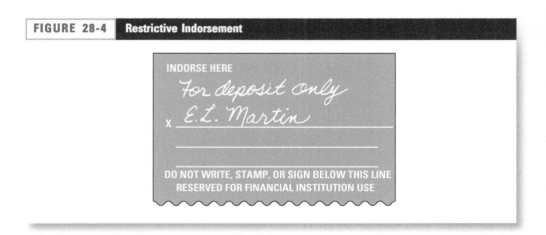

FIGURE 28-4 | **Restrictive Indorsement**

INDORSE HERE
For deposit only
X *E.L. Martin*

DO NOT WRITE, STAMP, OR SIGN BELOW THIS LINE
RESERVED FOR FINANCIAL INSTITUTION USE

---

[13] U.C.C. §3-206.
[14] *Travelers Cas. and Sur. Co. of America v. Bank of America*, 2009 WL 5176769 (Sup. Ct. N.Y.).

H. A. Price, the employee may ask the employer to write a new check payable to the proper name. However, under Article 3, a much simpler solution allows the payee or indorsee whose name is misspelled to indorse the wrong name, the correct name, or both. The person giving or paying value or taking it for collection for the instrument may require both forms of the signature.[15]

This correction of name by indorsement may be used only when it was intended that the instrument should be payable to the person making the corrective indorsement. If there were in fact two employees, one named H. A. Price and the other H. O. Price, it would be forgery for one to take the check intended for the other and, by indorsing it, obtain the benefit of the proceeds of the check.[16]

A fictitious, assumed, or trade name is treated the same as a wrong name. The same procedure for correction of a misspelled name with indorsement of both names applies to these forms of payee identification as well.[17]

28-3f Bank Indorsement

To simplify the transfer and collection of negotiable instruments from one bank to another, "any agreed method which identifies the transferor bank is sufficient for the item's further transfer to another bank."[18] A bank could simply indorse with its Federal Reserve System number instead of using its name.

Likewise, when a customer has deposited an instrument with a bank but has failed to indorse it, the bank may make an indorsement for the customer unless the instrument expressly requires the payee's personal indorsement. Furthermore, the mere stamping or marking on the item of any notation showing that it was deposited by the customer or credited to the customer's account is effective as an indorsement by the customer.

28-3g Multiple Payees and Indorsements

Ordinarily, one person is named as the payee in the instrument, but two or more payees may be named. In that case, the instrument may specify that it is payable to any one or more of them or that it is payable to all jointly. **For Example,** if the instrument is made payable "to the order of Ferns and Piercy," then Ferns and Piercy are joint payees. The indorsements of both Ferns and Piercy are required to negotiate the instrument.

alternative payees— those persons to whom a negotiable instrument is made payable, any one of whom may indorse and take delivery of it.

If the instrument is payable to **alternative payees** or if it has been negotiated to alternative indorsees, such as "Stahl or Glass" or "Stahl/Glass," it may be indorsed and delivered by either of them.

Under old Article 3, if the instrument was not clear on the relationship or types of multiple payees or indorsees, they were to be considered joint, and the signatures of all parties were required.[19] Under Revised Article 3, when a court is faced with two or more payees who are separated by a comma or other symbol, for example, "Pay to the order of Jeff Bridges—Susan Sarandon," the court must first determine whether the symbols or separating marks are sufficiently clear to make the instrument payable jointly. If the court concludes that the instrument is ambiguous, then the preference is for alternative payees, which means that either Jeff or Susan could negotiate the instrument with

[15] U.C.C. §3-204(d).
[16] *Hyatt Corp. v. Palm Beach Nat. Bank*, 840 So. 2d 300 (Fla. App. 2003).
[17] *DCM Ltd. Partnership v. Wang*, 555 F. Supp. 2d (E.D. Mich. 2008).
[18] U.C.C. §4-103.
[19] In re *Ames Dept. Stores, Inc.*, 322 B.R. 238 (S.D.N.Y. 2003).

one signature; they would not have to have the other's indorsement for negotiation. Under Revised Article 3, if the instrument is ambiguous, the payees or indorsees are considered payees in the alternative.

CASE SUMMARY

Checking Indorsements at Check City

FACTS: L & T Enterprises issued checks to one of L & T's subcontractors and one of that subcontractor's suppliers. Check City cashed the checks but did so with the indorsement of only the subcontractor, not the supplier. The subcontractor had a long, positive history with Check City. Although the reverse side of the checks contained what at cursory glance might appear to be two signatures, even minimal attention to those signatures shows they are the subcontractor's business name and the signature of a presumably authorized employee, albeit in an order that is the opposite of what is customary. Both entries are in the same handwriting, and a prudent person cashing the checks could not possibly have mistaken the two entries for proper indorsements by both the subcontractor and the subcontractor's supplier.

Check City filed suit against L & T for negligence. The trial court held that L & T owed Check City a duty and that L & T breached that duty by failing to exercise ordinary care and substantially contributing to an alteration of an instrument or forged signature. L & T appealed.

DECISION: There is a difference between the liability for a forged indorsement and a missing indorsement. Here, Check City failed to obtain the necessary signatures for the two payees. The result is that Check City has liability for the losses. Check City cannot hold L & T liable for opening the door to forgery when it failed to ensure that the signatures were there and genuine, a duty it holds as the first party to receive the check. The judgment in favor of Check City on its complaint is reversed. The parties will bear their own costs on appeal. [*Check City, Inc. v. L & T Enterprises*, 237 P.3d 910 (Utah App. 2010)]

28-3h Agent or Officer Indorsement

An instrument may be made payable to the order of an officeholder. **For Example,** a check may read "Pay to the order of Receiver of Taxes." Such a check may be received and negotiated by the person who at the time is the receiver of taxes. This general identification of a payee is a matter of convenience, and the drawer of the check is not required to find out the actual name of the receiver of taxes at that time.

If an instrument is drawn in favor of an officer of a named corporation, the instrument is payable to the corporation, the officer, or any successor to such officer. Any of these parties in possession of the instrument is the holder and may negotiate the instrument.[20]

28-3i Missing Indorsement

When the parties intend to negotiate an order instrument but for some reason the holder fails to indorse it, there is no negotiation. The transfer without indorsement has only the effect of a contract assignment.[21] If the transferee gave value for the instrument (see Chapter 29 for more information on what constitutes giving value), the transferee has the right to require that the transferor indorse the instrument unqualifiedly and thereby negotiate the instrument.

---

[20] U.C.C. §3-110(cc)(2)(li).
[21] U.C.C. §3-204(d). *Cyprus Federal Credit Union v. Cumis Ins. Soc., Inc.*, 2013 WL 7174130 (10th Cir. 2013).

THINKING THINGS THROUGH

The Minor with an Embezzling Conservator

Steven Powell died in a tragic accident at work, entitling his minor son, Cody, to approximately $252,000 in life insurance proceeds. Karen Unrue, Steven's sister, approached Elizabeth Powell, Steven's widow, and offered to manage the insurance proceeds for Cody.

The probate court appointed Karen Unrue and Travis Powell (Steven's brother) as co-conservators. The probate court also waived the bond requirement and ordered "that the funds of the minor child, [Cody], be deposited in a restricted account and that no funds be withdrawn or transferred from such account without written [o]rder of [the probate court]." The certificate of appointment and fiduciary letter included the following restriction: "No withdrawals without court order."

On Cody's behalf, Unrue received seven checks totaling $252,447.51. Three of the checks were made payable to her and Travis jointly and included the designation "Co-conservators For [Cody], A Minor" or "Co-Cn For Minor, [Cody]." The other four checks were made payable to Unrue and included the designation "As Conservator Of [Cody], A Minor." Unrue endorsed the checks without including her title as co-conservator. Unbeknownst to Travis, Unrue forged his name on the three checks made payable to her and Travis as co-conservators and took all the checks to the Pawleys Island Bank of America (BOA). Unrue had Lee Ann Yourko, a personal banker, open a certificate of deposit (CD) account titled "Karen M. Unrue Guardian [Cody]." Yourko collected the checks and took them to a teller, who processed the

checks and deposited the proceeds into the CD account. Neither Yourko nor the teller questioned the conservator designation in the payee line of the checks.

A few days later, Unrue returned to the Pawleys Island BOA with a single check for $253.67 made payable to her "As Conservator For Cody A Minor." Unrue requested Meredith Lawrence, the branch manager, to open a Uniform Gift to Minors Act (UGMA) account titled, "Karen M. Unrue—cust [Cody]—UMGA [sic]." Lawrence did not question the conservator title on the payee line of the check. Lawrence also failed to notice that Unrue endorsed the check without including her title.

Approximately a month later, after the CD matured, Unrue withdrew 100 percent of the funds, $253,991.50, from the CD account. Unrue took the funds to the Pawleys Island BOA and deposited them in the UGMA savings account. Over the next several months, Unrue made seven online transfers totaling $258,500 from the UGMA savings account to her personal checking account.

Mrs. Powell brought suit against BOA for its negligence in managing the accounts and failing to notice the indorsement requirements and restrictions imposed on the conservator.

Would Bank of America be liable? Be sure to discuss what you know about indorsement requirements and restrictive indorsements in formulating your answer.

[*Cody P. v. Bank of America, N.A.*, 720 S.E.2d 473 (S.C. App. 2011)]

CPA

28-4 Problems in Negotiation of Instruments

The issues of signatures and requirements for negotiation can become quite complex when issues such as forgery, employee misconduct, and embezzlement arise.

28-4a Forged and Unauthorized Indorsements

forged or **unauthorized indorsement**—instrument indorsed by an agent for a principal without authorization or authority.

A **forged** or **unauthorized indorsement** is not a valid indorsement.[22] Accordingly, anyone who has possession of a forged instrument is not a holder because the indorsement of the person whose signature was forged was necessary for effective negotiation of the instrument to the possessor. However, proof of forgery requires clear proof, and a split from a pattern of payments is helpful.

If payment of an instrument is made to one claiming under or through a forged indorsement, the payor ordinarily remains liable to the person who is the rightful owner of the paper. However, if the rightful owner has been negligent and contributed to the forgery or unauthorized signature problem, there are exceptions to these general rules on

[22] U.C.C. §3-403(2); Steven B. Dow, "Imposter Rule and the Problem of Agency under the Revised Uniform Commercial Code: New Risks for Bank Customers?" 16 *Comm. L.J.* 199 (2001).

liability for forged indorsements (see Chapter 29 for more information on the rights and liabilities of the parties).

CASE SUMMARY

The Great Rite-Aid Heist

FACTS: B.D.G.S., Inc., a New York corporation with headquarters in Washington, owns a warehouse in Utica, New York. In 1991, B.D.G.S. entered into an oral agreement with two local men, Anthony Balio and his employee, Peter Duniec, to manage the warehouse. Their responsibilities included finding tenants and collecting rent, which was then to be forwarded to B.D.G.S. and deposited into its bank account in Washington. Balio and Duniec formed the Beechgrove Warehouse Corporation and maintained a business account in that name at Savings Bank of Utica (SBU).

Between 1996 and 2000, B.D.G.S. believed that one of its tenants, Rite-Aid, had been falling behind and failing to make its rent payments. B.D.G.S. later discovered that Rite-Aid had been making the payments, but 16 checks had been indorsed to Beechgrove Warehouse and deposited into Beechgrove's SBU account. The checks had been made payable to DBGS (an apparent typographical error). There was a handwritten indorsement on the back of each check stating:

DBGS, Inc.
Pay to the order of

Beechgrove Warehouse
For Deposit [followed by Beechgrove's SBU account number]

A refund check from Niagara Mohawk for $427,781.82 had similarly been indorsed and deposited in the SBU account. B.D.G.S. filed suit against SBU, Balio, Duniec, and Beechgrove Warehouse. B.D.G.S. also brought a claim against SBU. The jury found that SBU had not followed reasonable commercial standards by accepting the checks for deposit. The appellate court affirmed and SBU appealed.

DECISION: The court affirmed noting that SBU was dealing with a payee forgery and it was SBU's responsibility to verify that the party with the checks was actually the payee and was authorized to deposit the checks. Because SBU was the one that had contact with Balio and Duniec it had a chance to prevent the embezzlement but its practices were not detailed enough to catch payee forgeries. [*B.D.G.S., Inc. v. Balio,* **861 N.E.2d 813 (N.Y. 2006)]**

28-4b Quasi Forgeries: The Impostor Rule

impostor rule—an exception to the rules on liability for forgery that covers situations such as the embezzling payroll clerk.

The **impostor rule** provides three exceptions to the rule that a forged indorsement is not effective to validly negotiate an instrument. If one of the three impostor exceptions applies, the instrument is still effectively negotiated, even though there may have been a forgery of an indorsement.

When the Impostor Rule Applies

The impostor rule applies in cases where an indorser is impersonating a payee and in two cases where the indorser is a dummy payee.[23]

Impersonating Payee. The impersonation of a payee in the impostor rule exception includes impersonation of the agent of the person who is named as payee. **For Example,** if Jones pretends to be the agent of Brown Corporation and thereby obtains a check payable to the order of the corporation, the impostor exception applies.

Dummy Payee. Another impostor scenario arises when the preparer of the instrument intends that the named payee will never benefit from the instrument. Such a "dummy" payee may be an actual or a fictitious person. This situation arises when the owner of a checking account wishes to conceal the true purpose of taking money from the account at

[23] *State Sec. Check Cashing, Inc. v. American General Financial Services (DE),* 972 A.2d 882 (Md. 2009).

the bank. The account owner makes out a check purportedly in payment of a debt that in fact does not exist.[24]

Dummy Payee Supplied by Employee. The third impostor situation arises when an agent or employee of the maker or the drawer has supplied the name to be used for the payee, intending that the payee should not have any interest in the paper.[25] This last situation occurs when an employee fraudulently causes an employer to sign a check made to a customer or another person, whether existing or not. The employee does not intend to send it to that person but rather intends to forge the latter's indorsement, cash the check, and keep the money. This exception to the impostor rule imposes responsibility on employers to have adequate internal controls to prevent employees from taking advantage of an accounting system with loopholes so that others are not required to bear the cost of the employer's lack of appropriate precautions.

Effect of Impostor Rule

When the impostor rule is applicable, any person may indorse the name of the payee. This indorsement is treated as a genuine indorsement by the payee and cannot be attacked on the ground that it is a forgery. This recognition of the fictitious payee's signature as valid applies even though the dummy payee of the paper is a fictitious person.[26]

Limitations on Impostor Rule

The impostor rule does not apply when there is a valid check to an actual creditor for a correct amount owed by the drawer and someone later forges the payee's name. The impostor rule does not apply in this situation even if the forger is an employee of the drawer.

Even when the unauthorized indorsement of the payee's name is effective by virtue of the impostor rule, a person forging the payee's name is subject to civil and criminal liability for making such an indorsement.

For the impostor rule to apply, the holders or the takers of the instrument must show that they took the instrument (1) in good faith and (2) for payment or collection.

CASE SUMMARY

Sorry, Charlie Walks Away with the $6.3 Million

FACTS: Won Charlie Yi solicited money from investors in the Korean–American community (plaintiffs) by representing that he would invest their money in brokerage accounts at Carlin Equities Corporation, a nationally recognized broker-dealer based in New York. Yi, however, did not invest the money he received from plaintiffs at all. Instead, Yi registered the name "Carlin Co." as a fictitious name under which he did business. He opened a bank account at Wells Fargo in the name of "Won Charlie Yi dba Carlin Co." Between January and September of 2003, Yi received eight checks, totaling $6.3 million, payable to "Carlin Co.," "Carlin Corp.," or "Carlin Corporation." Yi deposited the checks into his Wells Fargo account and absconded with plaintiffs' money. He was later apprehended by federal authorities and convicted of a variety of criminal fraud charges.

The defrauded investors filed suit against Wells Fargo to recover their losses for the bank's lack of ordinary care in

[24] *Schultz v. Bank of America*, 990 A.2d 1078 (Md. 2010).
[25] *Advocate Health and Hospitals Corp. v. Bank One*, 810 N.E.2d 962 (Ill. App. 2004).
[26] *Bank of Nichols Hills v. Bank of Oklahoma*, 196 P.3d 984 (Okla. App. 2008). *Advance Dental Care, Inc. v. SunTrust Bank*, 816 F. Supp. 2d 268 (D. Md. 2011); *State Sec. Check Cashing, Inc. v. American General Financial Services*, 972 A.2d 882 (Md. 2009).

Sorry, Charlie Walks Away with the $6.3 Million continued

being certain that the checks deposited were deposited with the intended payee. A jury found in favor of Wells Fargo and the investors appealed.

DECISION: The court affirmed the lower court's decision because the checks were made out to an intended payee. Although there were differing names on the check and the indorsements were not always precise, the parties intended the checks to go to Charlie's company and Charlie's account. Charlie was a fraudster and they lost their

money, but Wells Fargo is not liable for losses when customers write legitimate checks to those whom they later realize cannot be trusted. Losses are absorbed by banks when they fail to act in a commercially reasonable manner in honoring checks. In this situation, there were no signals that there was anything wrong with the checks because, indeed, the checks were written by the account holders. [*Unlimited Adjusting Group Inc. v. Wells Fargo Bank*, **94 Cal. Rptr. 3d. 672 (2009)**]

Negligence of Drawee not Required

The impostor rule applies without regard to whether the drawee bank acted with reasonable care.

28-4c Effect of Incapacity or Misconduct on Negotiation

A negotiation is effective even though (1) it was made by a minor or any other person lacking capacity; (2) it was an act beyond the powers of a corporation; (3) it was obtained by fraud, duress, or a mistake of any kind; or (4) the negotiation was part of an illegal transaction or was made in breach of duty. The rights of the parties in these types of negotiations depends on who holds the instrument (see Chapter 29).

28-4d Lost Instruments

The liability on lost instruments depends on who is demanding payment from whom and on whether the instrument was order or bearer paper when it was lost.

Order Instruments

If the lost instrument is order paper, the finder does not become the holder because the instrument has not been indorsed and delivered by the person to whom it was then payable. The former holder who lost it is still the rightful owner of the instrument.

Bearer Instruments

If the lost instrument is in bearer form when it is lost, the finder, as the possessor of a bearer instrument, is the holder and is entitled to enforce payment.

CPA 28-5 Warranties in Negotiation

When a negotiable instrument is transferred by negotiation, the transferors give certain implied warranties.

28-5a Warranties of Unqualified Indorser

When the transferor receives consideration for the indorsement and makes an unqualified indorsement, the warranties stated in this section are given by the transferor by implication.

No distinction is made between an unqualified blank indorsement and an unqualified special indorsement.

Scope of Warranties

The warranties of the unqualified indorser are found in Section 3-416 of the UCC and provide that the warrantor is a person entitled to enforce the instrument; that all signatures on the instrument are authentic and authorized; that the instrument has not been altered; that the instrument is not subject to a defense or claim; that the drawer of the draft has authorized the issuance of the item in the amount for which the item is drawn; and that the warrantor has no knowledge of any insolvency proceeding with respect to the maker or acceptor.[27]

Those who present an instrument for payment (see Chapter 29), or the last party in line before the payor, make three warranties: that the warrantor is entitled to enforce the draft or authorized to obtain payment or acceptance of the draft; that the draft has not been altered; and that the warrantor has no knowledge that the signature of the drawer of the draft is unauthorized.[28]

If a forged indorsement has appeared during the transfer of the instrument, and there is a refusal to pay because of that problem, the last party who is a holder may turn to her transferor to recover on the basis of these implied warranties. These warranties give those who have transferred and held the instrument recourse against those parties who were involved in the transfer of the instrument, although they were not parties to the original instrument.

What Is Not Warranted

The implied warranties stated here do not guarantee that payment of the instrument will be made. Similarly, the holder's indorsement of a check does not give any warranty that the account of the drawer in the drawee bank contains funds sufficient to cover the check. However, implied warranties do, for example, promise that the signatures on the instrument are not forged. Likewise, they promise that no one has altered the amount on the instrument. The warranties are not warranties of payment or solvency. They are simply warranties about the nature of the instrument. A holder may not be paid the amount due on the instrument, but if the lack of payment results from a forgery, the holder has rights against those who transferred the instrument with a forged signature.

Beneficiary of Implied Warranties

The implied warranties of the unqualified indorser pass to the transferee and any subsequent transferees. There is no requirement that subsequent transferees take the instrument in good faith to be entitled to the warranties. Likewise, the transferee need not be a holder to enjoy warranty protections.

Disclaimer of Warranties

Warranties may be disclaimed when the instrument is not a check. A disclaimer of warranties is ordinarily made by adding "Without warranties" to the indorsement.

Notice of Breach of Warranty

To enforce an implied warranty of an indorser, the party claiming under the warranty must give the indorser notice of the breach. This notice must be given within 30 days

---

[27] U.C.C. §3-416 (1990).
[28] U.C.C. §3-417. These warranties are for consumer accounts.

after the claimant learns or has reason to know of the breach and the identity of the indorser. If proper notice is not given, the warranty claim is reduced by the amount of the loss that could have been avoided had timely notice been given.

28-5b Warranties of Other Parties

Warranties are also made by the indorser who indorses "Without recourse" and by one who transfers by delivery only.

Qualified Indorser

The warranty liability of a qualified indorser is the same as that of an unqualified indorser.[29] A qualified indorsement means that the indorser does not assume liability for the payment of the instrument as written. (See §3-416(4).) However, a qualified indorsement does not eliminate the implied warranties an indorser makes as a transferor of an instrument. The implied warranty that is waived by a qualified indorsement is the fourth warranty on defenses. A qualified indorser still makes the other warranties on signatures and alteration but waives the warranty on defenses.

Transfer by Delivery

When the negotiable instrument is negotiated by delivery without indorsement, the warranty liability of the transferor runs only to the immediate transferee. In all other respects, the warranty liability is the same as in the case of the unqualified indorser. **For Example,** Thomas, a minor, gives Craig his note payable to bearer. Craig transfers the note for value and by delivery only to Walsh, who negotiates it to Hall. Payment is then refused by Thomas, who chooses to disaffirm his contract. Hall cannot hold Craig liable. Craig, having negotiated the instrument by delivery only, is liable on his implied warranties only to his immediate transferee, Walsh. Likewise, because Craig did not indorse the note, he is not secondarily liable for payment of the note.

Make the Connection

Summary

Negotiation is the transferring of a negotiable instrument in such a way as to make the transferee the holder. When a negotiable instrument is transferred by negotiation, the transferee becomes the holder of the instrument. If such a holder becomes a holder in due course, the holder will be immune to certain defenses.

An *order instrument* is negotiated by an indorsement and delivery by the person to whom it is then payable. A bearer instrument is negotiated by delivery alone. The order or bearer character of an instrument is determined by the face of the instrument as long as the instrument is

not indorsed. If the instrument has been indorsed, the character is determined by the last indorsement.

A number of different kinds of indorsements can be made on negotiable instruments. When an indorser merely authenticates the instrument, the indorsement is called a *blank indorsement.* If the last indorsement is a blank indorsement, the instrument is bearer paper, which may be negotiated by change of possession alone. A special indorsement consists of the authentication by the indorser and words specifying the person to whom the indorser makes the instrument payable. If the last

[29] U.C.C. §3-416(a).

indorsement is a special indorsement, the instrument is order paper and may be negotiated only by an indorsement and delivery. A qualified indorsement eliminates the liability of the indorser to answer for dishonor of the paper by the maker or the drawee. A restrictive indorsement specifies the purpose of the instrument or its use.

A forged or unauthorized indorsement is no indorsement, and the possessor of the instrument cannot be a holder. The impostor rule makes three exceptions to this rule: dummy payee; employee fraud; and impersonating a payee.

A negotiation is effective even though (1) it is made by a minor, (2) it is an act beyond the powers of a corporation, (3) it is obtained by fraud, or (4) the negotiation is part of an illegal transaction. However, the transferor may be able to set aside the negotiation under general legal principles apart from the UCC. The negotiation cannot be set aside if the instrument is held by a person paying it in good faith and without knowledge of the facts on which the rescission claim is based.

The warranties of the unqualified indorser are as follows: (1) the warrantor is a person entitled to enforce the instrument; (2) all signatures on the instrument are authentic and authorized; (3) the instrument has not been altered; (4) the instrument is not subject to a defense or claim in recoupment of any party that can be asserted against the warrantor; with respect to any item drawn on a consumer account, which does not bear a handwritten signature purporting to be the signature of the drawer, that the purported drawer of the draft has authorized the issuance of the item in the amount for which the item is drawn; and (5) the warrantor has no knowledge of any insolvency proceeding commenced with respect to the maker or acceptor or, in the case of an unaccepted draft, the drawer.

Learning Outcomes

After studying this chapter, you should be able to clearly explain:

28-1   Transfer of Negotiable Instruments
28-2   How Negotiation Occurs: Bearer Instruments
28-3   How Negotiation Occurs: Order Instruments

LO.1   Explain the difference between negotiation of order paper and negotiation of bearer paper
See the *Emmons v. Capital One* case, page 537.
See the Ethics & the Law issue "Having Your Mortgage Set Aside" to see that the note is separate from the mortgage, page 538.

LO.2   List the types of indorsements and describe their uses
See the *Town of Freeport v. Ring* case, page 538.
See *Check City, Inc. v. L & T Enterprises* for joint payee issues, page 543.

28-4   Problems in Negotiation of Instruments

LO.3   Determine the legal effect of forged and unauthorized indorsements
See the Thinking Things Through feature on minors affected by conservators misusing funds placed in trust with them, page 544.

LO.4   Be familiar with the forged payee impostor exceptions
See the *B.D.G.S., Inc. v. Balio* case, page 545.
See the *Unlimited Adjusting Group, Inc. v. Wells Fargo Bank* case, pages 546–547.

28-5   Warranties in Negotiation

LO.5   List the indorser's warranties and describe their significance
See the discussion of warranties, pages 547–549.

Key Terms

alternative payees
blank indorsement
delivery
forged or unauthorized
  indorsement

holder
holder in due course
impostor rule
indorsee
indorsement

negotiation
qualified indorsement
restrictive indorsement
special indorsement

Questions and Case Problems

1. Corey Brandon Bumgarner, who was separated from his wife, Crystal, had an accident caused by Donald Wood that resulted in $2,164.46 in damages to Corey's vehicle. Wood's insurance carrier mailed a draft in the amount of $2,164.46 drawn on Fleet Bank of Hartford, Connecticut, payable to Corey, to his box at P.O. Box 153, Hillsboro, North Carolina. The draft was negotiated at Community Bank and Trust, and the name, "Crystal Bumgarner," was handwritten on the back of the draft. Corey's name was written below Crystal Bumgarner's name. Crystal Bumgarner's driver's license number was handwritten on the front of the draft.

   Corey Bumgarner filed suit to have the insurer pay him the $2,164.46. The insurer indicated that it had sent order paper, that it had been delivered, and that there was, therefore, no claim against it or Wood. The trial court found that there had been no delivery and that Bumgarner was entitled to another check. Wood and his insurer appealed. Who is correct about delivery and why? [*Bumgarner v. Wood*, 563 S.E.2d 309, 47 U.C.C. Rep. Serv. 2d 1099 (N.C. App.)]

2. How could a check made out to "Joseph Klimas and his Attorney Fritzshall & Gleason & Blue Cross Blue Shield Company and Carpenters Welfare Fund" be negotiated further? What would be required? [*Chicago District Council of Carpenters Welfare Fund v. Gleason & Fritzshall*, 693 N.E.2d 412 (Ill. App.)]

3. An insurer issued a settlement check on a claim brought by an injured minor that was payable to "Trudy Avants attorney for minor child Joseph Walton, mother Dolores Carpenter 11762 S. Harrells Ferry Road #E Baton Rouge LA 70816." The lawyer indorsed the check. Two unknown individuals forged indorsements for the other two names and obtained payment of the check. The insurer sued the payor bank claiming that the instruments were not properly payable because of the forged indorsements. The court is unclear whether the indorsement required is one for an either/or payee or joint payee. What advice can you offer the court as it faces this issue? [*Coregis Insurance Co. v. Fleet National Bank*, 793 A.2d 254 (Conn. App.)]

4. ABCO (Abbott Development Company) made a note payable to Western State Bank of Midland. The FDIC took over Western State's operations after it failed. ABCO had defaulted on the note, after which the FDIC permitted ABCO Homes to refinance the note, making its refinancing note payable to the FDIC. The FDIC indorsed its note to SMS Financial and inadvertently sent it to SMS as part of a large batch of documents. When litigation resulted on the note, SMS claimed it was the holder. Others challenged its status, saying that SMS never had the instrument delivered to it. The lower court held SMS was not a holder and SMS appealed. Is SMS a holder? Why or why not? [*SMS Financial, L.L.C. v. ABCO Homes, Inc.*, 167 F.3d 235 (5th Cir.)]

5. Jerry O. Peavy, Jr., who did not have a bank account of his own, received a draft from CNL Insurance America in the amount of $5,323.60. The draft was drawn on CNL's account at Bank South, N.A., and was "payable to the order of Jerry Peavy and Trust Company Bank." Jerry O. Peavy, Sr., allowed his son Peavy, Jr., to deposit the draft in his account at Bank South, NA. Bank South accepted the draft and deposited it on December 29, 1992, with only the signature of Jerry Peavy, Jr. Both Mr. and Mrs. Peavy, Sr., then wrote checks on the amount of the draft using the full amount to benefit their son.

   On March 30, 1993, Bank South realized that it had improperly deposited the draft because it was lacking an indorsement from Trust Company Bank and reversed the transaction by debiting Mr. and Mrs. Peavy's account for the full amount of the draft. A bank officer then called Mr. and Mrs. Peavy, told them what had happened with the draft, and "threatened to send them to jail if they did not immediately deposit the sum of $5,323.60." The Peavys deposited that amount from the sale of some stock they owned and then filed suit against Bank South for its conversion of their son's draft and funds. Do the Peavys have a case? [*Peavy v. Bank South*, 474 S.E. 2d 690 (Ga. App.)]

6. Getty Petroleum distributes gasoline through dealer-owned stations. Customers who buy gas at a Getty station can pay by cash or credit card. When a customer uses a credit card, Getty processes the transactions, receives payment from the credit card company, and then issues computer-generated checks payable to dealers to reimburse them for their

credit card sales. Many checks, however, are not intended for negotiation and are never delivered to the payees. Instead, Getty uses these checks for bookkeeping purposes, voiding them and then crediting the check amount toward the dealer's future purchases of gasoline from Getty.

Lorna Lewis, a supervisor in Getty's credit processing department, stole over 130 checks, forged the indorsements of the payees by hand or rubber stamp, and then submitted the checks to American Express and other credit card companies to pay her own debts. The credit card companies then forwarded the checks through ordinary banking channels to Chemical Bank, where Getty had its checking account. Chemical Bank honored the checks Lewis had forged.

Getty, on discovering the larceny of Lewis, sought recovery of the amounts from the credit card companies. Getty sought payment on 31 of the checks from American Express (which had been paid by Chemical Bank). At trial, a judge held American Express liable to Getty for $58,841.60. The appeals court found that American Express was grossly negligent in taking and cashing the checks and also held it liable. American Express appealed. Who wins and why? [*Getty Petroleum Corp. v. American Exp. Travel Related Services Co., Inc.*, 683 N.E.2d 311 (N.Y.)]

7. Snug Harbor Realty Co. had a checking account in First National Bank. When construction work was obtained by Snug Harbor, its superintendent, Magee, would examine the bills submitted for labor and materials. He would instruct the bookkeeper which bills were approved, and the bookkeeper then prepared the checks in accordance with his instructions. After the checks were signed by the proper official of Snug Harbor, Magee picked them up for delivery. Instead of delivering certain checks, he forged the signatures of the respective payees as indorsers and cashed the checks. The drawee bank then debited the Snug Harbor account with the amount of the checks. Snug Harbor claimed that this was improper and sued the bank for the amount of the checks. The bank claimed that it was protected by the impostor rule. Will the bank be successful? Explain. [*Snug Harbor Realty Co. v. First National Bank*, 253 A.2d 581 (N.J. Super.)]

8. Benton, as agent for Savidge, received an insurance settlement check from Metropolitan Life Insurance Co. He indorsed it "For deposit" and deposited it in Bryn Mawr Trust Co. in Savidge's account. What were the nature and effect of this indorsement? [*Savidge v. Metropolitan Life Ins. Co.*, 110 A.2d 730 (Pa.)]

9. Allstate Insurance Company issued a check payable to "Chuk N. Tang & Rosa C. Tang HWJT" with "Bank of America" on the second line and the following explanation on the front of the check: "Settlement of our rental dwelling loss caused by fire on 11/21/93." The Tangs indorsed the check and forged the indorsement of Bank of America. When Bank of America objected, the Tangs claimed that only they needed to sign the instrument for further negotiations. The check was intended as a joint payment for Bank of America as the mortgagee on the Tangs' rental property because the insurance policy required that the mortgagee be paid first before any proceeds went to the property owners. Bank of America sued Allstate. Is Bank of America entitled to recover for the lack of its indorsement? Was its indorsement necessary for further negotiation? [*Bank of America Nat'l Trust & Savings Ass'n v. Allstate Insurance Co.*, 29 F. Supp. 2d 1129 (C.D. Cal.)]

10. When claims filed with an insurance company were approved for payment, they were given to the claims clerk, who would prepare checks to pay those claims and then give the checks to the treasurer to sign. The claims clerk of the insurance company made a number of checks payable to persons who did not have any claims and gave them to the treasurer with the checks for valid claims, and the treasurer signed all of the checks. The claims clerk then removed the false checks, indorsed them with the names of their respective payees, and cashed them at the bank where the insurance company had its account. The bank debited the account of the insurance company with the amount of these checks. The insurance company claimed that the bank could not do this because the indorsements on the checks were forgeries. Was the insurance company correct? [*General Accident Fire & Life Assur. Corp. v. Citizens Fidelity Bank & Trust Co.*, 519 S.W. 2d 817 (Ky.)]

11. Eutsler forged his brother Richard's indorsement on certified checks and cashed them at First National Bank. When Richard sought to recover the funds from the bank, the bank stated that it would press criminal charges against Eutsler. Richard asked the

bank to delay prosecution to give him time to collect directly from his brother. His brother promised to repay him the money but vanished some six months later without having paid any money. Richard sued the bank. What result? [*Eutsler v. First Nat'l Bank, Pawhuska*, 639 P.2d 1245 (Okla.)]

12. Michael Sykes, the president of Sykes Corp., hired Richard Amelung to handle the company's book-keeping and deal with all of its vendors.

    Amelung entered into an agreement with Eastern Metal Supply to help reduce Sykes's debt to Eastern. Whenever Sykes received a check, Amelung would sign it over to Eastern and allow it to keep 30 percent of the check amount. On 28 checks that totaled $200,000, Amelung indorsed the back as follows: "Sykes & Associates or Sykes Corporation, Richard Amelung." Amelung then turned the checks over to Eastern, and Eastern deposited them into its account at Barnett Bank. Eastern would then write one of its checks to Sykes Corp. for the 70 percent remaining from the checks. When Michael Sykes learned of the arrangement, he demanded the return of the 30 percent from Barnett Bank, claiming that it had paid over an unauthorized signature and that the indorsement was restricted and had been violated by the deposit into Eastern's account. What type of indorsement did Amelung make? Did he have the authority to do so? Should Sykes be reimbursed by Barnett? [*Sykes Corp. v. Eastern Metal Supply, Inc.*, 659 So. 2d 475 (Fla. App.)]

13. In January 1998, Allied Capital Partners, L.P., and American Factors Corporation were in the business of factoring accounts receivable for third-party clients. Allied assigned its factoring contract with Complete Design, Inc., to American but retained an interest in the factoring of Complete Design's invoices. On January 25, 1998, in payment of invoices issued by Complete Design, Clark Wilson Homes, Inc., issued a check for $6,823.15. The check was payable to:

Complete Design Allied Capital Partners, L.P. 2340 E. Trinity Mills Ste. 300 Carrollton, Texas 75006

On February 10, 1998, Clark Wilson issued another check for $26,329.32 made payable to:

Complete Design Allied Capital Partners, L.P. 2340 E. Trinity Mills Ste. 300 Carrollton, Texas 75006

Complete Design deposited both checks in its account at Bank One. However, Allied and American received none of the proceeds of the checks.

Complete Design subsequently declared bankruptcy, and Allied and American made demand on Bank One for damages resulting from Bank One's conversion of the two checks. Bank One denied all liability for conversion of the checks. Allied and American subsequently sued Bank One, asserting conversion. Bank One filed a motion for summary judgment asserting that, because it was ambiguous to whom the checks at issue were payable, they were payable upon a single indorsement. The trial court granted Bank One's motion. Allied and American appealed. Who is correct here? Were both signatures necessary for a proper indorsement, or will one do? [*Allied Capital Partners, L.P. v. Bank One, Texas, N.A.*, 68 S.W.3d 51 (Tex. App.)]

14. Would a bank be liable to a customer who indorsed a check "For deposit only into account #071698570" if that check were deposited into the wrong account? What if the customer's indorsement was "For deposit only"? Would any account qualify? Would any bank qualify? [*Qatar v. First American Bank of Virginia*, 885 F. Supp. 849 (E.D. Va.)]

15. What would happen if an employee directed funds to his or her account electronically? Would the UCC rules on fictitious payees apply? [*Koss Corp. v. American Exp. Co.*, 309 P.3d 898 (Ariz. App.)]

CPA Questions

1. Hand executed and delivered to Rex a $1,000 negotiable note payable to Rex or bearer. Rex then negotiated it to Ford and indorsed it on the back by merely signing his name. Which of the following is a correct statement?

a. Rex's indorsement was a special indorsement.

b. Rex's indorsement was necessary to Ford's qualification as a holder.

c. The instrument initially being bearer paper cannot be converted to order paper.

d. The instrument is bearer paper, and Ford can convert it to order paper by writing "pay to the order of Ford" above Rex's signature.

2. Jane Lane, a sole proprietor, has in her possession several checks that she received from her customers. Lane is concerned about the safety of the checks since she believes that many of them are bearer paper that may be cashed without endorsement. The checks in Lane's possession will be considered order paper rather than bearer paper if they were made payable (in the drawer's handwriting) to the order of:

a. Cash.

b. Ted Tint, and indorsed by Ted Tint in blank.

c. Bearer, and indorsed by Ken Kent, making them payable to Jane Lane.

d. Bearer, and indorsed by Sam Sole in blank.

3. West Corp. received a check that was originally made payable to the order of one of its customers, Ted Burns. The following indorsement was written on the back of the check:

   Ted Burns, without recourse, for collection only

   Which of the following describes the indorsement?

	Special	Restrictive
a.	Yes	Yes
b.	No	No
c.	No	Yes
d.	Yes	No

4. An instrument reads as follows:

   $250.00 Chicago, Illinois   April 1, 1992

   Thirty days after date I promise to pay to the order of __Cash__

   Two hundred and fifty _____ Dollars at

   New York City _____

   Value received with interest at the rate of six percent per annum. This agreement arises out of a separate agreement.

   No. 20 Due May 1, 1992   Robert Smith

   Answer "Yes" or "No" for the following questions about the previous item.

   a. The instrument is a draft.

   b. The instrument is order paper.

   c. This is a negotiable instrument.

   d. Robert Smith is the maker.

   e. The instrument may be negotiated without indorsement.

5. Ashley needs to endorse a check that had been endorsed by two other individuals prior to Ashley's receipt of the check. Ashley does not want to have surety liability, so Ashley endorses the check "without recourse." Under the Negotiable Instruments Article of the UCC, which of the following types of endorsement did Ashley make?

   a. Blank

   b. Special

   c. Qualified

   d. Restrictive

Liability of the Parties under Negotiable Instruments

Learning Outcomes

After studying this chapter, you should be able to

LO.1 Distinguish between an ordinary holder and a holder in due course

LO.2 List the requirements for becoming a holder in due course

LO.3 Explain the rights of a holder through a holder in due course

LO.4 List and explain the limited defenses not available against a holder in due course

LO.5 List and explain the universal defenses available against all holders

LO.6 Describe how the rights of a holder in due course have been limited by the Federal Trade Commission

CPA   29-1 Parties to Negotiable Instruments: Rights and Liabilities

Chapters 27 and 28 introduced the requirements for negotiable instruments and the methods for transfer of those instruments. However, the requirements of negotiability and transfer are simply preliminary steps for the discovery of the real benefit of using negotiable instruments in commerce, which is to streamline payment in commercial transactions. The rights and defenses of the parties to negotiable instruments are determined by the types of parties involved.

29-1a Types of Parties

assignee–third party to whom contract benefits are transferred.

holder–someone in possession of an instrument that runs to that person (i.e., is made payable to that person, is indorsed to that person, or is bearer paper).

holder in due course–a holder who has given value, taken in good faith without notice of dishonor, defenses, or that instrument is overdue, and who is afforded special rights or status.

Parties with rights in a negotiable instrument can be **assignees** or **holders.** A holder may be an ordinary holder or a **holder in due course.** As noted in Chapter 27, a holder in due course is a special party to an instrument with special rights beyond those of the ordinary holder.

29-1b Ordinary Holders and Assignees

A holder is a party in possession of an instrument that runs to him. An instrument "runs" to a party if it is payable to his order, is bearer paper, or is indorsed to him (see Chapter 28). Any holder has all of the rights given through and under the negotiable instrument. The holder may demand payment or bring suit for collection on the instrument. A holder can give a discharge or release from liability on the instrument. A holder who seeks payment of the instrument is required only to produce the instrument and show that the signature of the maker, drawer, or indorser is genuine. If the party obligated to pay under the instrument has no valid defense (such as forgery, which was discussed in Chapter 28), the holder is entitled to payment of the instrument.

The holder can recover from any of the parties who are liable on the instrument, regardless of the order of the signatures on the instrument. A holder could recover from the first indorser on an instrument or from the last party to indorse the instrument.

The rights of a holder are no different from the rights of a contract assignee (see Chapter 17). The assignee of a contract is in the same position and has the same rights as an ordinary holder. **For Example,** if a farmer who signed a note to pay for his tractor has a warranty problem with the tractor, he has a defense to payment on the note. Anyone who is assigned that note as an assignee or holder is also subject to the farmer's defense. (See Figure 29-1 and also the provisions on consumer credit protection under the discussion of the Federal Trade Commission rule in Chapter 32 and later in this chapter.)

CPA   29-1c The Holder-in-Due-Course Protections

The law gives certain holders of negotiable instruments special rights by protecting them from certain defenses. This protection makes negotiable instruments more attractive and allows greater ease of transfer. Unlike ordinary holders or assignees, holders in due course take free of contract assignment defenses that are good against ordinary holders or assignees. Figure 29-1 shows the different rights of holders, assignees, and holders in due course.

| FIGURE 29-1 | Assignee, Holder, and Holder-in-Due-Course Rights |

Suppose that Farmer Fred signs an installment contract to purchase a tractor from John Deere for $153,000. John Deere assigns the contract to Finance Co.

Suppose that Farmer Fred signs a negotiable promissory note for $153,000 and John Deere then transfers it to Finance Co., a holder in due course.

Suppose that Farmer Fred has a roofing company replace the roof on his home, and he signs a negotiable promissory note for $5,000. Roofing Co. transfers the note to Finance Co.

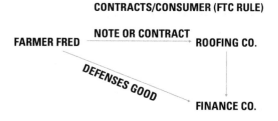

Holder in Due Course (HDC)

To obtain the preferred status of a holder in due course,[1] a person must first be a holder. However, the preferred status of HDC requires additional standards. Those holders who do not meet the standards for an HDC have all the rights of a holder. However, HDCs enjoy additional protections beyond those basic holder rights. Under U.C.C. §3-302(a), there are four requirements for becoming an HDC.[2]

---

[1] U.C.C. §3-302. Adam J. Levitin, "Finding Nemo: Rediscovering the Virtues of Negotiability in the Wake of Enron," 2007 *Columbia L. Rev.* 83 (2007).

[2] U.C.C. §3-302(a). *New Randolph Halsted Currency Exchange, Inc. v. Regent Title Ins. Agency, LLC*, 939 N.E.2d 1024 (Ill. App. 2010).

CPA

value—consideration or antecedent debt or security given in exchange for the transfer of a negotiable instrument or creation of a security interest.

Value. Value is similar to consideration (see Chapter 14). **For Example,** a person who receives a negotiable note as a gift does not give value because gifts are not supported by consideration or value.[3]

A transferee takes an instrument for value when (1) the holder has promised to do something in exchange (such as update a Web site); (2) the transferee takes the instrument as security for a loan (such as when a debtor transfers a promissory note payable to him to the transferee); or (3) the transferee receives the instrument as payment for a debt already due.[4] As with consideration, the courts do not consider whether the value is enough; they determine only whether some value has been given.[5]

Under Article 3, the original payee of a note is not an HDC unless that note is transferred to others and then back to the payee.[6]

A bank does not give value for a deposited check when it credits the depositor's account with the amount of the deposit. The bank gives value to the extent that the depositor is permitted to withdraw funds against that deposit.[7] **For Example,** if Janice deposits a $300 check into her account, which already has $400 in it, Janice's bank does not give value until Janice has written checks or withdrawn funds beyond the existing $400. The code follows FIFO (first in, first out) for drawing on funds. A bank that lets the customer draw on the funds deposited gives value.[8]

CPA

good faith—absence of knowledge of any defects in or problems; "pure heart and an empty head."

close-connection doctrine—circumstantial evidence, such as an ongoing or a close relationship, that can serve as notice of a problem with an instrument.

Good Faith. The element of **good faith** for becoming an HDC requires that a holder of a negotiable instrument act honestly in acquiring the instrument. In addition, the taker must follow reasonable standards of fair dealing.[9] Karl Llewellyn, one of the key drafters of the UCC, said that to comply with reasonable standards and good faith, the party must act with a "pure heart and an empty head."

Bad faith sometimes exists just because the transferee takes the instrument under such odd circumstances. **For Example,** if a transferee buys a note made payable to an estate from an accountant in a bar at midnight, suspicion prevents HDC status.

The **close-connection doctrine** applies in circumstances that indicate a problem with the instrument. Under this doctrine, the holder has taken so many instruments from its transferor or is so closely connected with the transferor that any knowledge the transferor has is deemed transferred to the holder, preventing holder-in-due-course status. Examples include consumer transactions where the holder in due course is a company that regularly does business with a company that has continual problems with consumer complaints.

---

[3] However, if the donor of the negotiable instrument were a holder in due course, it might be possible under a special Article 3 protection for the heir to also be a holder in due course despite the gift acquisition. U.C.C. §3-302(c) (iii). This protection for gift transfers by holders in due course is called the *shelter provision* (and is covered later in this chapter).

[4] U.C.C. §3-303.

[5] U.C.C. §3-303; *Ocwen Loan Servicing, LLC v. Branaman*, 554 F. Supp. 2d 645 (N.D. Miss. 2008); *Agriliance, LLC v. Farmpro Services, Inc.*, 328 F. Supp. 2d 958 (S.D. Iowa 2003).

[6] U.C.C. §3-302(c).

[7] U.C.C. §4-211.

[8] Allowing a deposit of a check with provisional credit does not make a bank a holder in due course, but on a cashier's check, when the bank becomes both the drawer and the drawee, the bank is obligated to pay on the instrument. *Flatiron Linen, Inc. v. First American State Bank*, 23 P.3d 1209 (Colo. 2011). If the bank does not impose provisional credit and makes the funds available immediately for the customer, it gives value and qualifies as a holder in due course. But see *Travelers Cas. and Sur. Co. of America v. Wells Fargo Bank N.A.*, 374 F.3d 521 (7th Cir. 2004).

[9] U.C.C. §3-103(a)(4); issue of whether a party is a holder in due course is always an issue of fact. *Pasack Community Bank, Inc. v. Universal Funding, LLP*, 16 A.3d 1097 (N.J. App. 2011).

CASE SUMMARY

Embezzling $29,000 and Having an HDC Cash Your Check

FACTS: Regent served as a settlement agent for closing real estate transactions. Regent cut checks to distribute funds to all the parties to such transactions. On December 23, 2005, New Randolph cashed a check from Regent, which was made out to Charae Pearson, for $1,945.99. Four days later, New Randolph cashed another check for Pearson, again from Regent, this time for $2,500. On January 11, 2006, Pearson brought Regent's check number 22221 for $29,588.31 to New Randolph. Unlike the prior checks, which spelled Pearson's name correctly, this check showed the payee as "CHAREA PAERSON." The check indicated that Pearson received it as a "LOAN PAYOFF." Pearson presented the check to Patrice Keys, manager of New Randolph. Pearson showed Keys her state identification card, which had been issued on December 30, 2005. Pearson told Keys that Regent issued the check to her to pay her a commission she earned from the sale of property.

PLS Check Cashers, which owned New Randolph, did not authorize Keys to cash checks in excess of $5,000 without approval from her supervisor. Keys contacted Sandra Arizaga of PLS. Arizaga authorized Keys to cash the check. Arizaga, who worked as director of operations for PLS, testified that she approved about three checks each week for amounts exceeding the amount of Regent's check number 22221. She spoke with Keys about the check, and then she looked up the phone number for Regent at Regent's Web site. Arizaga spoke with a woman who confirmed that Regent issued the check to Pearson in the amount shown. Arizaga then contacted American Chartered Bank, which confirmed that the check came from a valid account with sufficient funds to cover the check, and that Regent had not stopped payment on the check.

Regent introduced PLS's manual into evidence. The manual emphasizes that PLS earns its fees by cashing checks, so the employee should "[s]pend * * * time proving that the check can be cashed and not looking for excuses not to cash it." The manual identifies several signs that a check might not be valid, including several of the factors present in this case. According to the manual, the employee should "verify that the check is good" by "phoning the maker."

Police arrested Pearson, charging her with check fraud. Two days later, police arrested Tatiana Auson, an employee of Regent, on the same charge. Auson had checks intended for parties to real estate transactions canceled and then issued new checks to different payees for the amounts of the original checks. Pearson admitted that Auson gave her the three checks that New Randolph cashed for Pearson. Pearson kept about $5,000 of the proceeds from the checks, and she gave the remainder to Auson. All three checks appeared to bear the signature of Karen Hendricks, who had authority to sign checks on behalf of Regent.

Regent told its bank to stop payment on the check. New Randolph sued Regent for payment of the check, claiming that its status as a holder in due course entitled it to payment, despite the evidence that Auson and Pearson conspired to defraud Regent.

New Randolph appealed.

DECISION: Notice that disqualifies a party from being an HDC is something more than a suspicion. The verification call made in this situation showed the good faith of New Randolph. It checked to be sure that the check was good and was entitled to payment regardless of the embezzlement and breaches of fiduciary duties of their respective employees in working through the transactions. [*New Randolph Halsted Currency Exchange, Inc. v. Regent Title Insurance Co.*, 939 N.E.2d 1024 (Ill. App. 2011)]

Ignorance of the Instrument's Being Overdue or Dishonored. An instrument can be negotiated even though it has been dishonored, it is overdue,[10] or it is demand paper, such as a check, that has been outstanding for more than a reasonable time.[11] These instruments can still be transferred and the transferee is still a holder. However, the fact that the instrument is circulating at a late date or after it has been dishonored is suspicious and results in notice from the circumstances that there may be some adverse claim or defense. A person who acquires title to the instrument under such circumstances can be a holder but cannot be a holder in due course. **For Example,** buying a discounted note after its due date is notice that something may be wrong with the instrument.

[10] *Erkins v. Alaska Trustee, LLC*, 265 P.3d 292 (Alaska 2011); *Cadle Co. v. DeVincent*, 781 N.E.2d 817 (Mass. App. 2003); *Interim Capital LLC v. Herr Law Group, Ltd.*, 2011 WL 7047062 (D. Nev. 2011).
[11] *Max Duncan Family Investments, Ltd. v. NTFN Inc.*, 267 S.W.3d 447 (Tex. 2008).

Ignorance of Defenses and Adverse Claims. Prior parties on an instrument may have defenses that entitle them to withhold payment from a holder of an instrument. **For Example,** the drawer of a check, upon demand for payment by the payee, could assert as a defense to payment that the merchandise the payee delivered under the terms of their underlying contract was defective. A person who acquires an instrument with notice or knowledge that there is a defense that a party may have or that there are claims of ownership of the instrument from different parties cannot be an HDC. In general, transferees who are aware of facts that would make a reasonable person ask questions are deemed to know what they would have learned if they had asked questions.[12] Such knowledge and the failure to ask questions will cost them their special status of holder in due course; they remain simply holders.

Knowledge acquired by a holder after the instrument was acquired does not prevent the holder from being a holder in due course. The fact that a holder, after acquiring the instrument, learns of a defense does not work retroactively to destroy the holder's character as an HDC.

CASE SUMMARY

Cashing a Postdated Check from an Embezzler: HDC?

FACTS: A check dated August 10, 2007, was made payable to one of Liccardi's employees, Charles Stallone, Jr. Liccardi withheld the check from Stallone because he suspected him of embezzlement. However, the check still disappeared from the company offices, and when the disappearance was discovered, Liccardi immediately placed a stop payment on the check. JCNB Check Cashing, Inc. (JCNB), cashed the check for Stallone before the issue date (the check was postdated) and JCNB then deposited the check in its own bank account on August 9, 2007. However, the issuing bank refused to honor the check. On February 11, 2009, Robert Triffin acquired the dishonored payroll check from JCNB and sued Liccardi and Stallone for the amount of the check plus interest. Triffin's business is buying dishonored checks and attempting to collect on them.

The trial court dismissed Triffin's complaint on the grounds that he was not a holder in due course. Triffin appealed.

DECISION: The Court held that Triffin was not a holder in due course because he had taken a check that was already dishonored. In addition, Triffin could not be a holder in due course through JCNB being a holder in due course, because JCNB did not follow reasonable commercial standards when it cashed the postdated check. New Jersey's statute that regulates check cashing services requires those services to at least examine the face of the instrument before cashing it. JCNB, thus, was not a holder in due course and Triffin could not step into its shoes as an HDC. [***Triffin v. Liccardi Ford, Inc.,*** **10 A.3d 227 (N.J. Super. 2011)**]

ETHICS & THE LAW

The Corner Check Cashing Company and Good Faith

Some public policy experts have argued that no check cashing company, defined as one that takes a portion of the amount of the check as a fee for cashing checks for individuals who cannot get them cashed at banks and credit unions, should ever be allowed holder-in-due-course status.

Do you agree with this argument? Are check cashing companies ethical in their behavior? Do you believe that the state laws on check cashing firms are a means of mandating ethical conduct?

---

[12] *Specialized Loan Servicing, LLC v. January,* 119 So. 3d 582 (La. 2013); *Jelmoli Holding, Inc. v. Raymond James Financial Services, Inc.,* 470 F.3d 14 (1st Cir. 2006).

Holder Through a Holder in Due Course

holder through a holder in due course–holder of an instrument who attains holder-in-due-course status because a holder in due course has held it previous to him or her.

Those persons who become holders of the instrument after an HDC has held it are given the same protection as the HDC, provided they are not parties to any fraud or illegality that affects the instrument. This status of **holder through a holder in due course** is given in these circumstances even if the transferee from a holder in due course does not satisfy the requirements for holder-in-due-course status. This elevated or protected status is called Article 3's "shelter rule," and it allows a person who is not an HDC to hide under the "umbrella" with a holder in due course and be sheltered from claims and defenses as if actually being an HDC. **For Example,** a person who acquires an instrument as an inheritance from an estate does not give value and is missing one of the requirements for being a holder in due course. However, if the estate was an HDC, that status does transfer to the heir. Furthermore, suppose that Avery is a holder in due course of a $5,000 promissory note due May 31, 2015. Avery gives the note to his nephew Aaron for Aaron's birthday on June 1, 2015. Aaron did not give value because the note was a gift, and he has taken the note as a holder after it has already become due. Nonetheless, because Avery was a holder in due course, Aaron assumes that status under Article 3's shelter provision.

29-2 Defenses to Payment of a Negotiable Instrument

One of the key reasons for attaining HDC status is to be able to obtain payment on the negotiable instrument free of any underlying problems between the original parties to the instrument. An HDC takes an instrument free from certain types of defenses to payment. Whether a defense may be raised against an HDC claiming under a negotiable instrument depends on the nature of the defense.

CPA ### 29-2a Classification of Defenses

The importance of being a holder in due course or a holder through an HDC is that such holders are not subject to certain defenses called *limited defenses*. Another class of defenses, *universal defenses*, may be asserted against any party, whether an assignee, an ordinary holder, an HDC, or a holder through an HDC.[13]

29-2b Defenses against Assignee or Ordinary Holder

Assignees of negotiable instruments are subject to every defense raised. Similarly, a holder who does not become an HDC is subject to every payment defense just as though the instrument were not negotiable.

29-2c Limited Defenses Not Available against a Holder in Due Course

HDCs are not subject to any of the following defenses.

---

[13] Under the pre-Code law and under the 1952 Code, the universal defense was called a *real defense*, and the limited defense was called a *personal defense.* These terms have now been abandoned, but some licensing and CPA examinations may continue to use these pre-Code terms.

CPA   ## Ordinary Contract Defenses

In general terms, the defenses that could be raised in a breach of contract claim cannot be raised against an HDC. The defenses of lack, failure, or illegality of consideration with respect to the instrument's underlying transaction cannot be asserted against the holder in due course. Misrepresentation about the goods underlying the contract is also not a defense. **For Example,** a businessperson cannot refuse to pay a holder in due course on the note used to pay for her copy machine just because her copy machine does not have the speed she was promised.

Incapacity of Maker or Drawer

Ordinarily, the maker's or drawer's lack of capacity (except minors) may not be raised as a defense to payment to a holder in due course. Such incapacity is a defense, however, if the incapacity is at a legal level that makes the instrument a nullity. **For Example,** a promissory note made by an insane person for whom a court has appointed a guardian is void. In the case of a claim on the note by an HDC, the incapacity of the maker would be a defense.

CPA   ## Fraud in the Inducement

fraud in the inducement—fraud that occurs when a person is persuaded or induced to execute an instrument because of fraudulent statements.

If a person is persuaded or induced to execute the instrument because of fraudulent statements, such **fraud in the inducement** cannot be raised against a party with holder-in-due-course status. **For Example,** suppose Mills is persuaded to purchase an automobile because of Pagan's statements that the car was a demonstrator for the dealership and in good mechanical condition with a certification from the dealership's head mechanic. Mills, a car dealer, gives Pagan a note, which is negotiated until it reaches Han, who is a holder in due course. Mills meanwhile learns that the car has been in an accident and has a cracked engine block, that the head mechanic was paid to sign the certification, and that Pagan's statements were fraudulent. When Han demands payment of the note, Mills cannot refuse to pay on the ground of Pagan's fraud. Mills must pay the note because Han, as an HDC, does not take the note subject to any fraud or misrepresentation in the underlying transaction. Mills is left with the remedy of recovering from Pagan for misrepresentation or fraud.

Miscellaneous Defenses[14]

The limited defenses listed in the preceding three subsections are those most commonly raised against demands by holders in due course for payment. The following are additional limited defenses that may be asserted: (1) prior payment or cancellation of the instrument, (2) nondelivery, (3) conditional or special-purpose delivery, (4) breach of warranty, (5) duress consisting of threats, (6) unauthorized completion, and (7) theft of a bearer instrument. These defenses, however, have a very limited effect in defending against an HDC's demand for payment.

CASE SUMMARY

Fake Rolex; Good Check

FACTS: On September 23, 2011, Houston Gold Exchange issued a $3,500 check as payor to Shelly McKee as payee to buy a purported Rolex watch from her. The check was postdated September 26, 2011. McKee properly endorsed the check and presented it to RR Maloan, which cashed the check for her on September 24, 2011. On September 24, 2011,

[14] U.C.C. §3-305.

Fake Rolex; Good Check continued

Houston Gold Exchange issued a stop payment order on the check based on information that the watch was counterfeit. RR Maloan presented the check to Houston Gold Exchange's bank for payment. Houston Gold Exchange's bank refused to honor the check based on the stop payment order.

RR Maloan sued Houston Gold Exchange to collect on the check. RR Maloan maintained that it was a holder in due course entitled to collect on the check. Houston Gold Exchange was not present on the trial date, and the small claims court signed a default judgment in RR Maloan's favor. On appeal, the trial court found for Houston Gold Exchange, and RR Maloan appealed.

DECISION: A holder in due course takes the instrument free from all claims and all defenses of any party to the instrument with whom he has not dealt unless a defense that bars recovery by a holder in due course applies. RR Maloan took the check "for value" as required. "Good faith" is defined as "honesty in fact and the observance of reasonable

commercial standards of fair dealing." The record here conclusively establishes RR Maloan's good faith as that concept is defined for these purposes in the statute. No evidence was presented that the owner or any employee of RR Maloan had knowledge at the time the check was accepted that the watch was not authentic.

Because the fact of postdating did not impose a duty on RR Maloan to investigate the surrounding circumstances, Houston Gold Exchange cannot establish that RR Maloan failed to observe "reasonable commercial standards of fair dealing" by failing to investigate based on the postdating of the check.

UCC case law is very clear that fraud by the payee is not a defense against a holder in due course. McKee's asserted fraud in selling an allegedly fake Rolex to Houston Gold Exchange does not bar RR Maloan from collecting on the check as a holder in due course.

Reversed and remanded.

[*RR Maloan Investments, Inc. v. New HGE, Inc.*, 428 S.W.3d 355 (Tex. App. 2014)]

29-2d Universal Defenses Available against All Holders

Certain defenses are regarded as so basic that the social interest in preserving them outweighs the social interest of giving negotiable instruments the freely transferable qualities of money. Accordingly, such defenses are given universal effect and may be raised against all holders, whether ordinary holders, HDCs, or holders through a holder in due course. These defenses are called **universal defenses.**[15]

universal defenses— defenses that are regarded as so basic that the social interest in preserving them outweighs the social interest of giving negotiable instruments the freely transferable qualities of money; accordingly, such defenses are given universal effect and may be raised against all holders.

CPA

Fraud as to the Nature or Essential Terms of the Instrument

The fact that a person signs an instrument because the person is fraudulently deceived as to its nature or essential terms is a defense available against all holders.[16] When one person induces another to sign a note by falsely representing that, for example, it is a contract for repairs or that it is a character reference, the note is invalid, and the defense of the misrepresentation of the character of the instrument can be used against a holder in due course. **For Example,** suppose that two homeowners are asked to sign a statement for a salesperson that he was in their home and did a demonstration of a new solar water heater. Just as the homeowners are about to sign the verification statement, the salesman distracts them and then switches the verification for a purchase contract and promissory note for a $5,000 solar water heating system that the owners declined to purchase. The owners would have a defense of fraud in factum against a holder in due course of this note. The difference between fraud in the inducement—a personal defense—and fraud in factum—a universal defense—is that fraud in factum involves deception as to the documents themselves, not as to the underlying goods, services, or property.

[15] *City Rentals, Inc. v. Kessler*, 946 N.E.2d 785 (Ohio App. 2010).
[16] U.C.C. §3-305(a)(1)(iii).

C P A   Forgery or Lack of Authority

The defense that a signature was forged or signed without authority can be raised by a drawer or maker against any HDC. The fact that the negligence of the drawer helped the wrongdoer does not prevent the drawee from raising the defense of forgery. (See Chapters 28 and 30 for more discussion of the impact of forgery on liability.)

Duress Depriving Control

A party may execute or indorse a negotiable instrument in response to a force of such a nature that, under general principles of law, duress makes the transaction void rather than merely voidable. Duress of this type and level may be raised as a defense against any holder. Economic duress, in the form of a reluctance to enter into a financially demanding instrument, is not a universal defense.[17] Duress that is attempted murder is a universal defense.

Incapacity

The fact that the defendant is a minor who under general principles of contract law may avoid the obligation is a matter that may be raised against any kind of holder. Other kinds of incapacity may be raised as a defense if the effect of the incapacity is to make the instrument void, as when there has been a formal declaration of insanity.[18]

Illegality

If an instrument is void by law when executed in connection with certain conduct, such as a note for gambling or one that involves usury, such defenses may be raised against an HDC.

C P A   Alteration

alteration–unauthorized change or completion of a negotiable instrument designed to modify the obligation of a party to the instrument.

An **alteration** is an unauthorized change or completion of a negotiable instrument designed to modify the obligation of a party to the instrument.[19] **For Example,** changing the amount of an instrument from $150 to $450 is an alteration.[20]

Person Making Alteration. An alteration is a change made by a party to the instrument. Recovery on the instrument is still possible under the terms of the instrument as it originally existed, if proof of the original terms is possible.

Effect of Alteration. If the alteration to the instrument was made fraudulently, the person whose obligations under the instrument are affected by that alteration is discharged from liability on the instrument. The instrument, however, can be enforced according to its original terms or its terms as completed. This right of enforcement is given to holders in due course who had no notice of such alteration.[21] While a holder in due course would come within the protected class on alteration, such status is not required for this recovery provision in the event of alteration. **For Example,** Ryan signed a negotiable demand note for $100 made payable to Long. A subsequent holder changed the amount from $100 to

---

[17] *JPMorgan Chase Bank, N.A. v. Asia Pulp & Paper Cp., Ltd.,* 707 F.3d 853 (7th Cir. 2013).

[18] U.C.C. §3-305(a)(1)(ii). *Erkins v. Alaska Trustee LLC,* 265 P.3d 292 (Alaska 2011).

[19] U.C.C. §3-407(a); *Stahl v. St. Elizabeth Medical Center,* 948 S.W.2d 419 (Ky. App. 1997). *Farmers Deposit Bank v. Bank One,* 2005 WL 3453979 (E.D. Ky. 2005). A material alteration made based on the parties' negotiations (a 13 percent versus an 18 percent interest rate) is not fraudulent. *Darnall v. Petersen,* 592 N.W.2d 505 (Neb. App. 1999); *Knoefler v. Wojtalewicz,* 2003 WL 21496933 (Neb. App. 2003) (difference between bank interest rate and judgment interest rate is not material).

[20] However, if an instrument, such as a note, has been altered and the maker continues to pay without objection to the alteration, the alteration does not discharge the maker's liability. *Richard v. Wells Fargo Bank, N.A.,* 2013 WL 5726009 (Mo. App. 2013).

[21] U.C.C. §3-407(b), (c).

FIGURE 29-2	Defenses to Payment of Negotiable Instrument

UNIVERSAL (Available against assignees, holders, and holders in due course) (Real)	LIMITED (Available against assignees and holders but not against holders in due course) (Personal)	MIXED (Circumstances vary the availability of these defenses)
Fraud as to the nature of the instrument (fraud in factum) Forgery Unauthorized signature Incapacity (declaration) Illegality Alteration Consumer credit contracts with FTC notice	Fraud in the inducement Misrepresentation Lack of consideration Breach of warranty Cancellation Failure of delivery Unauthorized completion All ordinary contract defenses	Duress Incapacity

$700. A later holder in due course presented the note to Ryan for payment. Ryan would still be liable for the original amount of $100.

A summary of the universal and limited defenses is presented in Figure 29-2.

29-2e Denial of Holder-in-Due-Course Protection

In certain situations, the taker of a negotiable instrument is denied the status and protections of an HDC.

Participating Transferee

When the transferee is working with the lender or seller to obtain a negotiable instrument from the buyer/borrower, the transferee's holder-in-due-course status comes into question. This close-connection doctrine (discussed earlier in this chapter as an issue in the good-faith requirement for becoming a holder in due course) prevents a transferee with intimate knowledge of the transferor's business practices from becoming an HDC.[22]

The Federal Trade Commission Rule

In 1976, the Federal Trade Commission (FTC) adopted a rule that limits the rights of a holder in due course in a consumer credit transaction. The rule protects consumers who

[22] In re *Neals*, 459 B.R. 612 (D.S.C. 2011). *AIG Global Securities Lending Corp. v. Banc of America Securities LLC*, 2006 WL 1206333 (S.D.N.Y. 2006).

purchase goods or services for personal, family, or household use on credit.[23] When the note the buyer gave the seller as payment for the consumer goods is transferred to even a holder in due course, the consumer buyer may raise any defense that could have been raised against the seller. The FTC regulation requires that the following notice be included in boldface type at least 10 points in size in consumer credit contracts covered under the rule:

Notice
Any holder of this consumer credit contract is subject to all claims and defenses which the debtor could assert against the seller of goods or services obtained with the proceeds hereof. Recovery hereunder by the debtor shall not exceed amounts paid by the debtor hereunder.

When a notice preserving consumer defenses is included in a negotiable instrument, no subsequent person can be a holder in due course of the instrument.[24]

29-3 Liability Issues: How Payment Rights Arise and Defenses Are Used

In this chapter and in Chapters 27 and 28, issues surrounding the types of instruments, transfers, holders, and holders in due course have been covered. However, there are procedures under Article 3 for bringing together all of the parties, instruments, and defenses so that ultimate liability and, hopefully, payment can be determined and achieved.

CPA

29-3a The Roles of Parties and Liability

Every instrument has primary and secondary parties. The **primary party** is the party to whom the holder or holder in due course must turn first to obtain payment. The primary party on a note or certificate of deposit is the **maker.** The primary party on a draft is the **drawee,** assuming that the drawee has accepted the draft. Although a check must first be presented to the drawee bank for payment, the bank is not primarily liable on the instrument because the bank has the right to refuse to pay the check (see following and Chapter 30). The drawee bank on a check is the party to whom a holder or holder in due course turns first for payment despite the lack of primary-party status on the part of that drawee bank. The maker of a note is the party to whom holders and holders in due course must turn first for payment.

The **secondary parties** (or *secondary obligors,* as they are now called under Article 3) to an instrument are those to whom holders turn when the primary party, for whatever reason, fails to pay the instrument. Secondary parties on notes are **indorsers,** and secondary parties on checks and drafts are **drawers** and indorsers.

CPA

29-3b Attaching Liability of the Primary Parties: Presentment

Presentment occurs when the holder or HDC of an instrument orally, in writing, or by electronic communication to the primary party requests that the instrument be paid

---

primary party–party to whom the holder or holder in due course must turn first to obtain payment.

maker–party who writes or creates a promissory note.

drawee–person to whom the draft is addressed and who is ordered to pay the amount of money specified in the draft.

secondary parties–called secondary obligors under Revised Article 3; parties to an instrument to whom holders turn when the primary party, for whatever reason, fails to pay the instrument.

indorser–secondary party (or obligor) on a note.

drawer–person who writes out and creates a draft or bill of exchange, including a check.

presentment–formal request for payment on an instrument.

---

[23] The regulation does not cover purchases of real estate, securities, or consumer goods or services for which the purchase price is more than $25,000. *Fifth Third Bank v. Jones,* 168 P.3d 1 (Colo. App. 2007).

[24] U.C.C. §3-106(d). The rule changes the status of the parties as holders in due course. It does not change contract rights. *Pennsylvania Dept. of Banking v. NCAS of Delaware, LLC,* 931 A.2d 771 (Pa. 2007).

E-COMMERCE & CYBERLAW

Electronic Presentment: One Fell Swoop, All Rights, All Payments, New Laws

Because we now use debit cards, some of the UCC Article 3 provisions on checks are used far less, and the rights of the merchants and the buyers are covered under various federal and state laws on electronic funds transfers (covered in Chapter 30). Issues continue to evolve, such as the protections on debit cards and credit cards and increasing cyber security at banks and stores to prevent hackers from obtaining information, including card and pin numbers.

THINKING THINGS THROUGH

The Corner Check Cashing Company and Thieves—Who Wins?

Now is an ideal time to bring together all of the concepts you have learned in Chapters 26, 27, and 28. Analyzing this problem will help you integrate your knowledge about negotiable instruments. Sid's Salmon has purchased salmon from Fred's Fisheries. Sid wrote a check for $22,000 to Fred's. A thief broke into Fred's offices and took the cash on hand as well as the unindorsed check from Sid's. The thief took the check to the Corner Check Cashing Company (CCCC) and received $22,000 less the cashing fee of $2,000. Fred notified Sid, who then notified First Commerce Bank, the drawee of the check, of the theft. CCCC has presented the check for payment, and First Commerce refuses to pay. CCCC says it is a holder in due course.

Are you able to help First Commerce Bank develop its response to CCCC? Suppose that Fred had already indorsed the check when the thief stole it. Would CCCC be a holder in due course?

according to its terms. The primary party has the right to require that the presentment be made in a "commercially reasonable manner," which would include reasonable times for presentment, such as during business hours. The primary party can also require identification, authorization, and even a signature of receipt of the funds due under the instrument. In addition, the primary party can demand a valid indorsement on the instrument prior to making payment. Upon presentment, the primary party is required to pay according to the terms of the instrument unless there are defenses such as forgery, any of the other universal defenses for HDCs, or any defenses for holders.

If the primary party refuses to pay the instrument according to its terms, there has been a *dishonor*, and the holder is then left to turn to the secondary parties.

dishonor–status when the primary party refuses to pay the instrument according to its terms.

CPA   29-3c Dishonor and Notice of Dishonor

notice of dishonor– notice that an instrument has been dishonored; such notice can be oral, written, or electronic but is subject to time limitations.

limited defenses– defenses available to secondary parties if the presenting party is a holder in due course.

Dishonor occurs when the primary party refuses to pay the instrument according to its terms. The primary party is required to give **notice of dishonor.** The notice that the instrument has been dishonored can be oral, written, or electronic. That notice is subject to time limitations. **For Example,** a bank must give notice of dishonor by midnight of the next banking day. Nonbank primary parties must give notice of dishonor within 30 days following their receipt of notice of dishonor. Returning the dishonored check is sufficient notice of dishonor. (See Chapter 30 for more discussion of liability issues on dishonor of checks.) Upon dishonor, the holder must then turn to the secondary parties for payment.

The obligation of the secondary parties in these situations is to pay according to the terms of the instrument. These secondary parties will have **limited defenses** if the presenting party is a holder in due course. **For Example,** suppose that a check drawn on

First Interstate Bank is written by Ben Paltrow to Julia Sutherland as payment for Julia's Bentley auto that Ben purchased. Julia deposits Ben's check into her account at Ameri-Bank, and AmeriBank sends the check to First Interstate to present it for payment. First Interstate finds that Ben's account has insufficient funds and dishonors the check. Ameri-Bank must notify First Interstate by midnight of the next banking day that the check has been dishonored, and then First Interstate must notify Julia by midnight of the next banking day that Ben's check was dishonored. Julia then has 30 days to notify Ben and turn to him as a drawer, or secondary party, for payment on the check.

Make the Connection

Summary

A holder of a negotiable instrument can be either an ordinary holder or an HDC. The ordinary holder has the same rights that an assignee would have. Holders in due course and holders through an HDC are protected from certain defenses. To be an HDC, a person must first be a holder—that is, the person must have acquired the instrument by proper negotiation. The holder must then also take for value, in good faith, without notice that the paper is overdue or dishonored, and without notice of defenses and adverse claims. Those persons who become holders of the instrument after an HDC are given the same protection as the HDC through the shelter provision, provided they are not parties to any fraud or illegality affecting the instrument.

The importance of being an HDC is that those holders are not being subject to certain defenses when demand for payment is made. These defenses are limited defenses and include ordinary contract defenses, incapacity unless it makes the instrument void, fraud in the inducement, prior payment or cancellation, nondelivery of an instrument, conditional delivery, duress consisting of threats, unauthorized completion, and theft of a bearer instrument. Universal defenses may be asserted against any assignee, an ordinary holder, or HDC. Universal defenses include fraud as to the nature or essential terms of the paper, forgery or lack of authority, duress depriving control, incapacity, illegality that makes the instrument void, and alteration. Alteration is only a partial defense; an HDC may enforce the instrument according to its original terms.

The Federal Trade Commission rule on consumer credit contracts limits the immunity of an HDC from defenses of consumer buyers against their sellers. Immunity is limited in consumer credit transactions if the notice specified by the FTC regulation is included in the sales contract. When a notice preserving consumer defenses is stated in a negotiable instrument, no subsequent person can be an HDC.

Holders and HDCs are required to present instruments for payment to primary parties. Primary parties are makers and drawees. If the primary party refuses to pay, or dishonors, the instrument, it must give notice of dishonor in a timely fashion. The holder can then turn to secondary parties, drawers, and indorsers (secondary obligors) for payment.

Learning Outcomes

After studying this chapter, you should be able to clearly explain:

29-1 Parties to Negotiable Instruments: Rights and Liabilities

LO.1 Distinguish between an ordinary holder and a holder in due course

See the sections titled "Ordinary Holders and Assignees" and "The Holder-in-Due-Course Protections" for examples of distinction, pages 556–561.

LO.2 List the requirements for becoming a holder in due course

See the *Triffin v. Liccardi Ford, Inc.* case, page 560.

29-2 Defenses to Payment of a Negotiable Instrument

LO.3 Explain the rights of a holder through a holder in due course

See the *New Randolph Halsted Currency Exchange, Inc. v. Regent Title Insurance Co.* case, page 559.

LO.4 List and explain the limited defenses not available against a holder in due course

See the list of defenses in Figure 29-2, page 565.
See the *RR Maloan Investments, Inc. v. New HGE, Inc.* case, pages 562–563.

LO.5 List and explain the universal defenses available against all holders

See the Thinking Things Through discussion of the Corner Check Cashing Company, page 567.
See the ethical issue on check cashing companies, page 560.

29-3 Liability Issues: How Payment Rights Arise and Defenses Are Used

LO.6 Describe how the rights of a holder in due course have been limited by the Federal Trade Commission

See the language of the rule, page 566.

Key Terms

alteration
assignees
close-connection doctrine
dishonor
drawee
drawers
fraud in the inducement
good faith
holders
holder in due course
holder through a holder in due course
indorsers
limited defenses
maker
notice of dishonor
presentment
primary party
secondary parties
universal defenses
value

Questions and Case Problems

1. Randy Bocian had a bank account with First of America-Bank (FAB). On October 8, Bocian received a check for $28,800 from Eric Christenson as payment for constructing a pole barn on Christenson's property. Bocian deposited the check at FAB on October 9 and was permitted to draw on the funds through October 12. Bocian wrote checks totaling $12,334.21, which FAB cleared. On October 12, Christenson stopped payment on the check as the result of a contract dispute over the pole barn. Bocian's account was then overdrawn once the check was denied clearance by Christenson's bank. FAB brought suit against both Bocian and Christenson to collect its loss. Christenson counterclaimed against Bocian for his contract breach claims on the pole barn construction. FAB maintained that it had given value and was a holder in due course and that, as such, it was not required to be subject to the pole barn issues or the stop payment order. Is FAB right? [*First of America-Bank Northeast Illinois v. Bocian*, 614 N.E.2d 890 (Ill. App.)]

2. Cronin, an employee of Epicycle, cashed his final paycheck at Money Mart Check Cashing Center. Epicycle had issued a stop payment order on the check. Money Mart deposited the check through normal banking channels. The check was returned to Money Mart marked "Payment Stopped." Money Mart brought an action against Epicycle, claiming that, as a holder in due course, it was entitled to recover against Epicycle. Epicycle argued that Money Mart could not be a holder in due course because it failed to verify the check as good prior to cashing it. Is Money Mart a holder in due course? [*Money Mart Check Cashing Center, Inc. v. Epicycle Corp.*, 667 P.2d 1372 (Colo.)]

3. Halleck executed a promissory note payable to the order of Leopold. Halleck did not pay the note when due, and Leopold brought suit on the note, producing it in court. Halleck admitted that he had signed the note but claimed plaintiff Leopold was required to prove that the note had been issued for consideration and that the plaintiff was in fact the holder. Are these elements of proof required as part of the case? [*Leopold v. Halleck*, 436 N.E.2d 29 (Ill. App.)]

4. Calhoun/Johnson Company d/b/a Williams Lumber Company (Williams) sold building materials to Donald Miller d/b/a Millercraft Construction Company (Millercraft) on credit. Miller had signed a personal guaranty for the materials. Miller requested lien waivers from Williams for four of his projects

and asked for them from Fabian Boudreau, Williams's credit manager. Fabian refused to grant the waivers because Miller was $28,000 delinquent on his account. Miller agreed to bring his account current with the exception of $11,000 for which he signed a no-interest promissory note. Miller obtained the lien waivers and then defaulted on the note. Williams brought suit for payment, and Williams said there was lack of consideration and that the note was not valid. He said he must give value to be able to recover on the note. Was he correct? [*Miller v. Calhoun/Johnson Co.*, 497 S.E.2d 397 (Ga. App.)]

5. Jane bought a string of pearls from Grantham Jewelers. Jane wrote a check for $1,760 to pay for the pearls. When Jane had the pearls appraised for insurance purposes, she learned from the appraiser that the pearls were fake. Jane stopped payment on the check. However, Grantham had transferred the check to Jim Holub, who had then transferred the check back to Grantham. Is Grantham an HDC?

6. Can check cashing companies be holders in due course? What arguments can you make for and against their holder-in-due-course status? [*Dal-Tile Corp. v. Cash N' Go*, 487 S.E.2d 529 (Ga. App.)]

7. Jones, wishing to retire from a business enterprise that he had been conducting for a number of years, sold all of the assets of the business to Jackson Corp. Included in the assets were a number of promissory notes payable to the order of Jones that he had taken from his customers. Upon the maturity of one of the notes, the maker refused to pay because there was a failure of consideration. Jackson Corp. sued the maker of the note. Who should succeed? Explain.

8. Elliot, an officer of Impact Marketing, drew six postdated checks on Impact's account. The checks were payable to Bell for legal services to be subsequently performed for Impact. Financial Associates purchased them from Bell and collected on four of the checks. Payment was stopped on the last two when Bell's services were terminated. Financial argued that it was a holder in due course and had the right to collect on the checks. Impact claimed that because the checks were postdated and issued for an executory promise, Financial could not be a holder in due course. Who was correct? Why? [*Financial Associates v. Impact Marketing*, 394 N.Y.S.2d 814]

9. *D* drew a check to the order of *P*. *P* took the check postdated. *P* knew that *D* was having financial difficulties and that the particular checking account on which this check was drawn had been frequently overdrawn. Do these circumstances prevent *P* from being a holder in due course? [*Citizens Bank, Booneville v. National Bank of Commerce*, 334 F.2d 257 (10th Cir.); *Franklin National Bank v. Sidney Gotowner*, 4 U.C.C. Rep. Serv. 953 (N.Y. Supp.)]

10. Daniel, Joel, and Claire Guerrette are the adult children of Elden Guerrette, who died on September 24, 1995. Before his death, Elden purchased a life insurance policy from Sun Life Assurance Company of Canada through a Sun Life agent, Steven Hall, and named his children as his beneficiaries. Upon his death, Sun Life issued three checks, each in the amount of $40,759.35, to each of Elden's children. The checks were drawn on Sun Life's account at Chase Manhattan Bank in Syracuse, New York. The checks were given to Hall for delivery to the Guerrettes. Hall and an associate, Paul Richard, then fraudulently induced the Guerrettes to indorse the checks in blank and to transfer them to Hall and Richard, purportedly to be invested in HER, Inc., a corporation formed by Hall and Richard. Hall took the checks from the Guerrettes and turned them over to Richard, who deposited them in his account at the Credit Union on October 26, 1995. The Credit Union immediately made the funds available to Richard.

The Guerrettes quickly regretted having negotiated their checks to Hall and Richard, and they contacted Sun Life the next day to request that Sun Life stop payment on the checks. Sun Life immediately ordered Chase Manhattan to stop payment on the checks. When the checks were ultimately presented to Chase Manhattan for payment, Chase refused to pay the checks, and they were returned to the Credit Union. The Credit Union received notice that the checks had been dishonored on November 3, 1995, the sixth business day following their deposit. By the time the Credit Union received notice, however, Richard had withdrawn from his account all of the funds represented by the three checks. The Credit Union was able to recover almost $80,000 from Richard, but there remained an unpaid balance of $42,366.56.

The Credit Union filed suit against Sun Life, and all of the parties became engulfed in litigation. The Credit Union indicated it was a holder in due course and was entitled to payment on the instrument. Sun Life alleged fraud. Is the Credit Union a holder in due course? Can the parties allege the fraud defense against it? [*Maine Family Federal Credit*

Union v. Sun Life Assur. Co. of Canada, 727 A.2d 335 (Maine)]

11. G.C. Vincent was an employee of Porter County Development Corporation (PCDC). Vincent had three personal credit cards through Citibank. Vincent diverted checks to the PCDC, deposited them into his personal checking account, and issued checks drawn upon that personal account to pay part of the outstanding balance of his three Citibank-held credit card accounts. Citibank was unaware that Vincent used misappropriated funds to pay his credit card balance. PCDC filed suit to have Citibank return the embezzled funds. Citibank moved for summary judgment on the grounds that it was an HDC. The trial court granted summary judgment and PCDC appealed. Who should prevail on appeal and why? [*Porter County Development Corp. v. Citibank (South Dakota)*, N.A., 855 N.E.2d 306 (Ind. App.)]

12. Sanders gave Clary a check but left the amount incomplete. The check was given as advance payment on the purchase of 100 LT speakers. The amount was left blank because Clary had the right to substitute other LT speakers if they became available and the substitution would change the price. It was agreed that in no event would the purchase price exceed $5,000. Desperate for cash, Clary wrongfully substituted much more expensive LT speakers, thereby increasing the price to $5,700. Clary then negotiated the check to Lawrence, one of his suppliers. Clary filled in the $5,700 in Lawrence's presence, showing him the shipping order and the invoice applicable to the sale to Sanders. Lawrence accepted the check in payment of $5,000 worth of overdue debts and $700 in cash. Can Lawrence recover the full amount? Why or why not?

13. GRAS is a Michigan corporation engaged in the business of buying and selling cars. Between 1997 and 2000, Katrina Stewart was employed as a manager by GRAS. During that period, Stewart wrote checks, without authority, on GRAS's corporate account payable to MBNA and sent them to MBNA for payment of her husband's MBNA credit card account. MBNA accepted the checks and credited the proceeds to Stewart's husband's credit card debt. MBNA accepted and processed the GRAS checks in its normal manner through electronic processing. When MBNA receives a check for a credit card payment, the envelope containing the check and the payment slip is opened by machine and the check and the payment slip are electronically processed and credited to the cardholder's account balance. MBNA does not normally review checks for credit card payments. After crediting a payment check to the cardholder's account, MBNA transfers it to the bank on which it is written for collection. Pursuant to its standard practice, MBNA did not review the checks it received from Stewart. GRAS did not have a customer relationship with MBNA during the relevant time period.

GRAS sought a refund of the amounts Stewart embezzled via the MBNA application of the checks to Stewart's husband's credit card account. MBNA said it was a holder in due course. Was MBNA a holder in due course? Was MBNA subject to GRAS's defense of unauthorized instruments? [*Grand Rapids Auto Sales, Inc. v. MBNA America Bank*, 227 F. Supp. 2d 721 (W.D. Mich.)]

14. William Potts was employed by Jemoli Holdings, Inc., to liquidate assets of defunct companies. Potts had the authority to sign checks for Jemoli. Potts had a personal investment account with Raymond James Financial Services. When the stock market had its 2000 crash due to the dot-com bubble, Potts had difficulty meeting his margin calls. He began giving checks from Jemoli to Raymond James to cover the margin calls. When a representative questioned Mr. Potts about the Jemoli checks, he assured the representative that Jemoli was him, and that it was his firm. Over four months, Potts wrote checks totaling $1.5 million to Raymond James to cover loans and to make more investments. When Jemoli's principals discovered the embezzlement they brought suit to recover the funds from Raymond James. Raymond James says it was an HDC of the checks and not subject to Jemoli's claims for breach of fiduciary duty by its agent, Potts. Who is correct about the HDC status of Raymond James and why? [*Jemoli Holding, Inc. v. Raymond James Financial, Inc.*, 470 F.3d 14 (1st Cir.)]

15. Omni Trading issued two checks totaling $75,000 to Country Grain Elevators for grain it had purchased. Country Grain indorsed the checks over to the law firm of Carter & Grimsley as a retainer. Country Grain then collapsed as a business, and Omni stopped payment on the checks because all of its grain had not been delivered. Carter & Grimsley claimed it was a holder in due course and entitled to payment. However, the Department of Agriculture claimed its interest in the checks for liens and maintained that Carter & Grimsley was not a holder in due course because it had not given value.

The trial court granted summary judgment for the Department of Agriculture because the checks were indorsed as a retainer for future legal work and Carter & Grimsley had not given value. Is Carter & Grimsley a holder in due course? [*Carter & Grimsley v. Omni Trading, Inc.,* 716 N.E.2d 320 (Ill. App.)]

CPA Questions

1. Under the Commercial Paper Article of the UCC, which of the following requirements must be met for a person to be a holder in due course of a promissory note?

   a. The note must be payable to bearer.

   b. The note must be negotiable.

   c. All prior holders must have been holders in due course.

   d. The holder must be the payee of the note.

2. A maker of a note will have a real defense against a holder in due course as a result of any of the following conditions except:

   a. Discharge in bankruptcy.

   b. Forgery.

   c. Fraud in the execution.

   d. Lack of consideration.

3. Under the commercial paper article of the UCC, in a nonconsumer transaction, which of the following are real (universal) defenses available against a holder in due course?

	Material Alteration	Discharge in Bankruptcy	Breach of contract
a.	No	Yes	Yes
b.	Yes	Yes	No
c.	No	No	Yes
d.	Yes	No	No

4. A holder in due course will take free of which of the following defenses?

   a. Infancy, to the extent that it is a defense to a simple contract.

   b. Discharge of the maker in bankruptcy.

   c. A wrongful filling-in of the amount payable that was omitted from the instrument.

   d. Duress of a nature that renders the obligation of the party a nullity.

5. Mask stole one of Bloom's checks. The check was already signed by Bloom and made payable to Duval. The check was drawn on United Trust Company. Mask forged Duval's signature on the back of the check at the Corner Check Cashing Company, which in turn deposited it with its bank, Town National Bank of Toka. Town National proceeded to collect on the check from United. None of the parties mentioned were negligent. Who will bear the loss, assuming the amount cannot be recovered from Mask?

   a. Bloom

   b. Duval

   c. United Trust Company

   d. Corner Check Cashing Company

6. Robb stole one of Markum's blank checks, made it payable to himself, and forged Markum's signature to it. The check was drawn on the Unity Trust Company. Robb cashed the check at the Friendly Check Cashing Company, which in turn deposited it with its bank, Farmer's National. Farmer's National proceeded to collect on the check from Unity Trust. The theft and forgery were quickly discovered by Markum, who promptly notified Unity. None of the parties mentioned were negligent. Who will bear the loss, assuming the amount cannot be recovered from Robb?

   a. Markum

   b. Unity Trust Company

   c. Friendly Check Cashing Company

   d. Farmer's National

7. For a person to be holder in due course of a promissory note:

   a. The note must be payable in U.S. currency to the holder.

   b. The holder must be the payee of the note.

   c. The note must be negotiable.

   d. All prior holders must have been holders in due course.

Checks and Funds Transfers

Learning Outcomes <<<

After studying this chapter, you should be able to

LO.1 List and explain the duties of the drawee bank

LO.2 Explain the methods for, and legal effect of stopping payment

LO.3 Describe the liability of a bank for improper payment and collection

LO.4 Discuss the legal effect of forgeries and material alterations

LO.5 Specify the time limitations for reporting forgeries and alterations

LO.6 Describe the electronic transfer of funds and laws governing it

`CPA`   ## 30-1 **Checks**

check–order by a depositor on a bank to pay a sum of money to a payee; a bill of exchange drawn on a bank and payable on demand.

As discussed in Chapter 27, a **check** is, under Uniform Commercial Code (UCC) §3-104(f), "(i) a draft … payable on demand and drawn on a bank or (ii) a cashier's check or teller's check. An instrument may be a check even though it is described on its face by another term, such as 'money order.'"[1] The distinguishing characteristics of checks[2] and drafts are summarized in Figure 30-1. Under Article 4, the change in consumer payment patterns away from formal, signed checks is reflected with the addition of "remotely-created consumer item," which are items directing payment that are drawn on a consumer account but do not carry a handwritten signature of the drawer.[3] Consumer account is defined as a bank account used for household, family, or personal purposes.[4] These types of payments include PayPal authorizations to pay from consumer checking accounts and automatic bill payments that consumers direct via online banking.

30-1a **Nature of a Check**

Sufficient Funds on Deposit

As a practical matter, a check is drawn on the assumption that the bank has on deposit in the drawer's account an amount sufficient to pay the check. In the case of other drafts, there is no assumption that the drawee has any of the drawer's money with which to pay the instrument. In international transactions, sellers may require buyers not only to accept a draft agreeing to pay but also to back up that draft with a line of credit from the buyer's bank. That line of credit is the backup should the funds for the draft not be forthcoming from the buyer.

If a draft is dishonored, the drawer is civilly liable. If a check is drawn with intent to defraud the person to whom it is delivered, the drawer is also subject to criminal

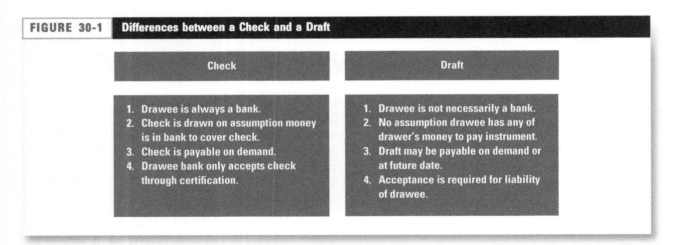

FIGURE 30-1	Differences between a Check and a Draft

Check	Draft
1. Drawee is always a bank. 2. Check is drawn on assumption money is in bank to cover check. 3. Check is payable on demand. 4. Drawee bank only accepts check through certification.	1. Drawee is not necessarily a bank. 2. No assumption drawee has any of drawer's money to pay instrument. 3. Draft may be payable on demand or at future date. 4. Acceptance is required for liability of drawee.

[1] U.C.C. §3-104(f).
[2] Checks are governed by both Article 3 of the UCC and Article 4 governing bank deposits and collections. The 2001 and 2002 versions of Article 4 are covered in this chapter, along with notations of the changes since the 1990 version. The new versions of Article 4 incorporate most provisions of the American Bankers Association Bank Collection Code. The purpose of the code was to introduce clarity into the processing of millions of electronic and paper transactions that banks must handle and to recognize the reality of electronic payments.
[3] U.C.C. §3-104(16).
[4] U.C.C. §3-104(2).

bad check laws–laws making it a criminal offense to issue a bad check with intent to defraud.

CPA

demand draft–draft that is payable upon presentment.

postdate–to insert or place on an instrument a later date than the actual date on which it was executed.

time draft–bill of exchange payable at a stated time after sight or at a definite time.

prosecution in most states. The laws under which such drawers are prosecuted are known as **bad check laws.** Most states provide that if the check is not made good within a stated period, such as 10 days, there is a presumption that the drawer originally issued the check with the intent to defraud.

Demand Paper

A draft may be payable either on demand or at a future date. A check is a form of **demand draft.** The standard form of check does not specify when it is payable, and it is therefore automatically payable on demand.

One exception arises when a check is **postdated**—that is, when the check shows a date later than the actual date of execution. Postdating a check means that the check is not payable until the date arrives, and it changes the check from a demand draft to a **time draft.**[5] However, banks are not obligated to hold a postdated check until the time used on the check unless the drawer has filed the appropriate paperwork with the bank for such a delay. Because of electronic processing, banks are not required to examine each instrument and honor postdated instrument requests unless the hold is placed into the bank's processing system by the customer (a stop payment order).

Form of the Check

A check can be in any form of writing.[6] However, bank customers may agree, as part of the contract with their bank, to use certain forms for check writing. A remotely created consumer item need only be evidenced by a *record*, not by a written document. Under Revised U.C.C. §3-104(a)(14), a *record* is defined as "information that is inscribed on a tangible medium or which is stored in an electronic or other medium and is retrievable in perceivable form."[7]

Delivery Not Assignment

The delivery of a check is not an assignment of the money on deposit, so it does not automatically transfer the rights of the depositor against the bank to the holder of the check. A check written by a drawer on his drawee bank does not result in a duty on the part of the drawee bank to the holder to pay the holder the amount of the check. An ordinary check drawn on a customer's account is direction from a customer to the bank for payment, but it does not impose absolute primary liability on the bank at the time the check is written.[8]

money order–draft issued by a bank or a nonbank.

cashier's check–draft drawn by a bank on itself.

teller's check–draft drawn by a bank on another bank in which it has an account.

Banks assume more responsibility for some types of checks than for the ordinary customer's check. **For Example,** a bank **money order** payable to John Jones is a check and has the bank as both the drawer and the drawee.[9] U.C.C. §3-104(g) defines a cashier's check as "a draft with respect to which the drawer and drawee are the same bank or branches of the same bank."[10] In other words, a **cashier's check** is a check or draft drawn by a bank again on itself. If a cashier's check is drawn on another bank in which the drawer bank has an account, it is a **teller's check.** Although the drawer and drawee may be the same on a money order or a cashier's check, the instrument does not lose its three-party character or its status as a check.

---

[5] A bank is required to comply with a postdate on a check only if it is notified of the postdate in the same way the customer issues a stop payment order.

[6] Although not required for negotiation or presentment, a printed bank check, when the customer is using a written form, is preferable because it generally carries magnetic ink figures that facilitate sorting and posting.

[7] *Smith v. Farmers Union Mut. Ins. Co.* 260 P.3d 163 (Mont. 2011).

[8] *Sapp v. Flagstar Bank, FSB*, 12 N.E.3d 913 (Ind. App. 2014).

[9] U.C.C. §3-104(f). *Lawyer's Mut. Liability Ins. Co. of North America v. Mako*, 756 S.E.2d 809 (N.C. App. 2014).

[10] U.C.C. §3-104(g). *Golden v. Citibank, N.A.*, 23 N.Y.3d 934 (N.Y. 2014).

substitute check—
electronic image of a
paper check that a bank
can create and that has
the same legal effect as
the original instrument.

Under federal laws that Article 4 recognizes, there is another form of payments known as a **substitute check,** which is an electronic image or paper printout of an electronic image of a check. A substitute check has the same legal effect as a paper check. The bank that converts the paper check into electronic form, called the *reconverting bank*, has certain duties imposed by federal regulations to be certain that the electronic version or substitute check has all of the necessary legal information such as visible indorsements, magnetic bank code strip, payee, and signature of drawer.

30-1b Certified Checks

The drawee bank may *certify* or accept a check drawn on it. Under U.C.C. §3-409(d), a certified check is "a check accepted by the bank on which it is drawn."[11] While a bank is under no obligation to certify a check, if it does so, the certification has the effect of the bank accepting primary liability on the instrument. Check certification requires that the actual certification be written on the check and authenticated by the signature of an authorized representative of the bank.[12] Upon certification, the bank must set aside, in a special account maintained by the bank, the amount of the certified check taken from the drawer's account. The certification is a promise by the bank that when the check is presented for payment, the bank will make payment according to the terms of the check. Payment is made regardless of the status of the drawer's account at that time.

A holder or drawer may request that a check be certified by a bank. When certification is at the request of the holder, all prior indorsers and the drawer are released from liability. When certification is at the request of the drawer, the indorsers and drawer, as secondary parties, are not released. Unless otherwise agreed, the delivery of a certified check, a cashier's check, or a teller's check discharges the debt for which the check is given, up to the amount of that check.[13]

CASE SUMMARY

A Cashier's Check Is Only as Good as Its Signature

FACTS: On March 26, 2012, Dale M. Smith (defendant/counter-plaintiff) presented a cashier's check for $294,500.99 for deposit in his account with State Bank (plaintiff). The check appeared to be a cashier's check drawn on Chase bank. State Bank accepted the check for deposit. The following day, March 27, 2012, Smith requested that plaintiff wire approximately $275,000 from his account to an account in Japan. Before performing this transfer, State Bank contacted a local Chase branch and spoke to a representative. A Chase representative "confirmed

the check number, the account number, verified the amount in the check and represented there were no stop-payment orders placed on the item." State Bank then processed Smith's wire transfer request.

On March 28, 2012, Chase returned the check to State Bank with the notation "refer to maker." State Bank then presented the check to Chase for payment a second time, and Chase again returned the check to State Bank. Elizabeth Roush, a Vice President and Reconciliation Manager for Chase, explained that the cashier's check was "different

[11] U.C.C. §3-409(d).
[12] Many courts treat cashier's checks and certified checks as the same because of their uniform commercial acceptability. See *Jones v. Wells Fargo Bank, N.A.*, 666 F.3d 955 (5th Cir. 2012). However, the rights of the parties are different because certification discharges all other parties to the instrument. A cashier's check does not result in the discharge of other parties on the instrument.
[13] U.C.C. §3-104(h) defines a traveler's check as "a draft drawn by a bank (i) on another bank, or (ii) payable at or through a bank."

A Cashier's Check Is Only as Good as Its Signature continued

from the form of official cashier's checks issued by Chase." The check number had an incorrect number of digits, did not include "a printed audit number to indicate its validity [,]" did not have the proper signature, and was missing a security symbol. At her deposition, Roush explained that only one authorized signature exists for all cashier's checks drawn on the account number printed on the cashier's check. This signature is electronically printed on all checks issued by Chase retail branches. Roush was immediately able to identify that the check was not issued by Chase because the signature was not an authorized signature for that account. Roush did not know who signed the check.

On May 16, 2012, State Bank filed suit against Smith and Chase. State Bank alleged that Chase wrongfully dishonored the check. The trial court granted summary judgment for Chase and State Bank appealed.

DECISION: The lack of a valid signature on a negotiable instrument is a real defense. The court held for Chase because the cashier's check did not have an authorized signature. An instrument is not valid unless it has a proper signature and no one is required to pay an instrument unless there is a valid signature. State Bank could not be an HDC of an instrument without a proper signature. And even if State Bank thought it was an HDC, the lack of an authorized signature is a real defense against an HDC seeking payment. Therefore, Chase was permitted to refuse payment because of a missing, authorized signature. [*State Bank v. Smith*, 85 U.C.C. Rep. Serv. 2d 260, 2014 WL 6088513 (Mich. App. 2014)]

E-COMMERCE & CYBERLAW

The Nigerian "I Need Your Help" E-Mails

They are quite common, those e-mails that come into our accounts asking for help in transferring funds in exchange for a percentage of those funds. They only ask that they be able to use our bank accounts in the United States so that they are able to collect the money owed to them, with your 12 to 15 percent service fee for use of your account deducted.

These are scams, accomplished by simple means. The scammers do indeed have their alleged creditors furnish large checks initially to be deposited in your account. Those checks do seem to clear. They then have you write checks in the amount deposited (less your percentage fee) to them. However, subsequent problems develop with those initially deposited checks and your bank wants you to now cover the overdraft created by the scammers cashing your check.

You end up owing the money to your bank. You have no claim based on forgery because it was your check. In short, the Nigerians win. There is no remedy under Article 3 or 4 for you, but there have been remedies under negligence by the banks in processing the transfers. Fraud is the easiest theory of recovery, but finding the scammers is a tall order. The federal government works tirelessly to alert people to the scams because it is nearly impossible for them to locate the scammers. Beware of e-mails coming your way from folks from Nigeria, Malaysia, and, well, any other country who wishes to use your bank account for processing their payments.

[*Anderson v. Branch Banking and Trust Co.*, 56 F. Supp. 3d 1345 (S.D. Fla. 2014)]

CPA   30-1c **Presentment for Obtaining Payment on a Check**

A holder of a check must take required steps to obtain payment. As discussed in Chapter 29, there are primary and secondary parties for every negotiable instrument. Primary parties are makers and drawees. Under Article 3, secondary parties are referred to as *secondary obligors* and are defined to include "an indorser, a drawer, an accommodation party, or any other party to the instrument that has a right of recourse against another party to the instrument."[14]

---

[14] U.C.C. §3-104(12).

presentment–formal request for payment on an instrument.

The process for a holder to be paid on an instrument involves mandatory steps with time limitations. The holder must first seek payment from the drawee through **present-ment.** No secondary obligor is liable on an instrument until presentment has been made. Presentment is required for checks, and presentment is made first to the drawee bank.[15]

Presentment Requirements

Presentment occurs when the holder of a check or other consumer transaction authorization demands payment.[16] Under Revised Article 3, the party presents either the check or a record for payment. If the presentment is done in person, the party to whom presentment is made can require that the presenter exhibit identification. The holder who is presenting the instrument must present the check or record for payment in a commercially reasonable manner; banks can treat the transaction as having occurred the following day when presentment is made after *the close of the business day*.[17] In the case of electronic banking, banks are permitted to impose times after which posting will occur the next day. If a check is presented to the drawee bank for payment and paid, the drawer has no liability because payment has been made. (For more details on presentment, generally, of instruments, see Chapter 29.)

C P A   Time for Presentment of a Check for Payment[18]

Under the UCC, presentment must be made within a reasonable time after the drawers and indorsers have signed the check. What constitutes a reasonable time is determined by the nature of the instrument, by commercial usage, and by the facts of the particular case.

Failure to make timely presentment discharges all secondary obligors (prior indorsers) of the instrument. It also discharges the drawer to the extent that the drawer has lost, through the bank's failure, money that was on deposit at the bank to make the payment due under the check.[19]

The UCC establishes two presumptions as to what is a reasonable time for presentment of checks. If the check is not certified and is both drawn and payable within the United States, it is presumed that 90 days after the date of the check or the date of its issuance, whichever is later, is the reasonable period in which to make presentment for payment in order to attach secondary liability to the drawer.[20] With respect to attachment of the liability of an indorser, 30 days after indorsement is the presumed reasonable time.[21]

If a check is dated with the date of issue, it may be presented immediately for payment. If it is postdated, ordinarily it may not be presented until that date arrives. However, as noted earlier, the bank need not honor the date on the postdated instrument.[22] If the holder delays in making presentment, the delay discharges the drawer if the bank itself fails during such delay. If the holder of the check does not present it for payment or

---

[15] It is important to note that the bank is unique as a drawee because its contract as a primary party is limited by its right to dishonor a check and its right to give only provisional credit.

[16] In addition to the UCC restrictions on times for presentment, banks must comply with federally imposed time constraints. Under the Expedited Funds Availability Act, 12 U.S.C. §4001 *et seq.*, banks are required to lift provisional credits on customer accounts.

[17] U.C.C. §4-107(1). *Rogers v. Bank of America, N.A.*, 73 U.C.C. Rep. Serv. 2d 47 (S.D. Ill. 2010).

[18] U.C.C. §3-501. In re *Agriprocessors*, 490 B.R. 852 (N.D. Iowa 2013).

[19] U.C.C. §3-605.

[20] Under the previous versions of Articles 3 and 4, the time was six months.

[21] U.C.C. §3-304. *Eco-Built, Inc. v. The Nat. Bank of Indianapolis*, 683 F. Supp. 2d 892 (S.D. Ind. 2010).

[22] U.C.C. §4-208(c).

collection within 90 days after an indorsement was made, the secondary obligors (indorsers) are discharged from liability to the extent that the drawer has lost, through the bank's failure, money that was on deposit at the bank to meet the payment under the check.

Under Articles 3 and 4, agreeing to honor an instrument beyond this time limit changes the obligation of the primary obligor and, as a result, changes the obligation of the secondary obligors. Such changes in the terms and conditions of payment serve to discharge the secondary obligors, a change that brings UCC Articles 3 and 4 in line with the principles of surety law (see Chapter 32).

A bank may continue to honor checks presented for payment after the 90-day period, but it does so with understanding of the discharge of liability for the primary and secondary obligors. A bank honoring a check that is overdue subjects the bank to questions about whether it exercised good faith and reasonable care in honoring it.[23]

30-1d Dishonor of a Check

If the bank refuses to make payment, the drawer is then subject to the same secondary liability as the drawer of an ordinary draft.[24] To be able to attach that secondary liability, the holder of the instrument must notify the drawer of the dishonor by the drawee. The notice of dishonor may be oral, written, or electronic.

CPA   Time for Notice of Dishonor

Banks in the chain of collection for a check must give notice of dishonor by midnight of the next banking day.[25] Others, including the payee or holder of the check, must give notice of dishonor within 30 days after learning that the instrument has been dishonored. If proper notice of dishonor is not given to the drawer of the check, the drawer will be discharged from liability to the same extent as the drawer of an ordinary draft.[26]

CPA   Overdraft

overdraft–negative balance in a drawer's account.

If the bank pays the check but the funds in the account are not sufficient to cover the amount, the excess of the payment over the amount on deposit is an **overdraft.** This overdraft is treated as a loan from the bank to the customer, and the customer must repay that amount to the bank.

If the bank account from which the check is drawn is one held by two or more persons, the joint account holder who does not sign the check that creates an overdraft is not liable for the amount of the overdraft if she received no benefit from the proceeds of that check.[27] Additional issues on overdrafts and dishonor of checks are covered in the next section, "The Customer-Bank Relationship."

[23] Article 3 changed the "negligence" of the bank to the "failure to exercise ordinary are" in §3-406. A bank need not pay a check that is presented to it after 90 days (the presumptive ordinary care period) from the date of issue (except for certified checks), but it can honor such a check and charge the customer's account if it does so in good faith.
[24] U.C.C. §3-414. PayPal is not considered a bank for purposes of Articles 3 and 4. *Zepeda v. PayPal Inc.*, 777 F. Supp. 2d 1215 (N.D. Cal. 2011).
[25] The former time frame for nonbanks was midnight of the third business day. *Troy Bank and Trust Co. v. Citizens Bank*, 166 So. 3d 57 (Ala. 2014).
[26] U.C.C. §4-213. Under Federal Reserve regulations, notice of dishonor may be given by telephone. *Security Bank and Trust Co. v. Federal Nat'l Bank*, 554 P.2d 119 (Okla. Ct. App. 1976). But it must be an official notice of dishonor and not notice that there is a problem with the check prior to it being presented for payment. *City Check Cashing, Inc. v. Manufacturers Hanover Trust Co.*, 764 A.2d 411, 43 U.C.C. Rep. Serv. 2d 768 (N.J. 2001).
[27] U.C.C. §§4-214 and 4-401(b). *Sapp v. Flagstar Bank, FSB*, 12 N.E.3d 913 (Ind. App. 2014).

ETHICS & THE LAW

Getting Hit for SOOO Many Overdraft Fees

On August 28, 2008, Cortney Hassler had a balance of $112.35 in his checking account. He made a $39.58 payment in the morning and a $140.00 debit in the afternoon. Sovereign Bank did not post the transactions in the order that they occurred but, rather, rearranged the debits so that Cortney had to pay two $33 overdraft fees on his account. A provision in his checking account agreement indicated that Sovereign had the right to pay the withdrawals in any order. Cortney filed a class-action suit against the bank for unfair trade practices and unjust enrichment.

Evaluate the legal rights of the bank to post the transactions as it did. Evaluate the ethical issues in the changes in posting order so as to maximize the overdraft fees.

[*Lunsford v. Woodforest Nat. Bank*, 299 F.R.D. 695 (N.D. Ga. 2013)]

30-1e The Customer-Bank Relationship

The relationship between banks and customers is governed by Articles 3 and 4 of the UCC as well as by several federal statutes. These laws impose duties and liabilities on both banks and customers.

Privacy

The bank owes its customer the duty of maintaining the privacy of the information that the bank acquires in connection with its relationship with the customer. Law enforcement officers and administrative agencies cannot require the disclosure of information relating to a customer's account without first obtaining the customer's consent or a search warrant or without following the statutory procedures designed to protect customers from unreasonable invasions of privacy.[28] The **USA Patriot Act** does impose certain reporting requirements on banks, financial institutions, and businesses with regard to deposits of cash and large cash payments. These reporting requirements were imposed to be able to track money laundering efforts as well as possible funding of terrorist activities.[29] For example, checks that involve amounts of more than $10,000 generally trigger the bank reporting systems under the USA Patriot Act.

> **USA Patriot Act**–federal law that, among other things, imposes reporting requirements on banks.

With the advent of the Internet and other electronic exchanges of information, it has become much easier for businesses, including banks, to exchange information about customers. All businesses are subject to federal constraints on the use of customer information. (See Chapter 32 for more information.)

Payment

A bank is under a general contractual duty to its customers to pay on demand all checks to the extent of the funds in a depositor's account.

CPA

> **stale check**–a check whose date is longer than six months ago.

Stale Checks. A bank is under no obligation to a customer to pay a check (other than one that is certified) that is presented for payment more than six months after its date. This type of check is commonly called a **stale check.**[30] However, if a bank acts in good faith, it can charge a customer's account for a check that is older than six months. Establishing that "good faith" is an uphill battle, so most banks will not cash a stale check unless and until it has verified such with its customer. Regardless of the date of the check, banks are always under an obligation to use good faith and commercial reasonableness in processing all checks.

[28] Right to Financial Privacy Act of 1978, 12 U.S.C. §3401 *et seq.*
[29] 12 U.S.C. §5311 *et seq.* 2001.
[30] U.C.C. §§3-304 and 4-404; *Commerce Bank, N.A. v. Rickett*, 748 A.2d 111 (N.J. Super. 2000).

Do not confuse the six-month stale check rule with the 90-days overdue instrument rule. The 90-day rule in Section 3-304 is the timing provision for an HDC to take a check in good faith and without notice that it is overdue. Ninety days is not the measurement for bank processing of a customer's check and six months is not the time limit for taking as an HDC. There are two separate time frames here for two different issues.

Payment after Depositor's Death. From the time of death, the bank can continue paying items until it actually knows of the customer's death.[31] The bank has the right, even with notice of the death, to continue to pay items for 10 days unless, for example, an heir or a government agency halts the payments.[32]

CPA

30-1f Stopping Payment of a Check

stop payment order— order by a depositor to the bank to refuse to make payment of a check when presented for payment.

A drawer may stop payment of a check by notifying the drawee bank in the required manner.[33] **Stop payment orders** are often used when a check is lost or mislaid. The drawer can always write a duplicate check but wants assurance that the original lost or misplaced check will not then also be presented for payment. The drawer can stop payment on the first check to prevent double-dipping. A drawer can also use a stop payment order on a check if the payee has not kept his end of the contract or has failed to provide assurances (see Chapter 25). However, the drawer must keep in mind that if a holder in due course has the check, the holder in due course can demand payment because she would not be subject to the personal defenses of breach of contract or nonperformance of contract. (See Chapter 29 and the rights of holders in due course.)

Stop payment orders are invalid for some forms of checks even when properly executed. Neither the drawer nor a bank customer can stop payment of a **certified check.** A bank customer cannot stop payment of a cashier's check.

CPA

Form of Stop Payment Order

certified check—check for which the bank has set aside in a special account sufficient funds to pay it; payment is made when check is presented regardless of amount in drawer's account at that time; discharges all parties except certifying bank when holder requests certification.

The stop payment order may be either oral or by record (written or evidence of electronic order). If oral, however, the order is binding on the bank for only 14 calendar days unless confirmed in writing within that time. A record of the stop payment order or confirmation is effective for six months. A stop payment order can be renewed for an additional six months if the customer provides the bank a written extension.

Liability to Holder for Stopping Payment

The act of stopping payment may in some cases make the drawer liable to the holder of the check. If the drawer has no proper ground for stopping payment, the drawer is liable to the holder of the check. In any case, the drawer is liable for stopping payment with respect to any holder in due course or any other party having the rights of a holder in due course unless payment was stopped for a reason that may be asserted as a defense against a holder in due course (see Chapter 29). The fact that payment of a check has been stopped does not affect its negotiable character.[34]

30-1g Wrongful Dishonor of a Check

wrongfully dishonored— error by a bank in refusing to pay a check.

A check is **wrongfully dishonored** by the drawee bank if the bank refuses to pay the amount of the check although (1) it is properly payable and (2) the account on which it is drawn is sufficient to pay the item. Dishonor for lack of funds can be a breach of contract if the customer has an agreement with the bank that it will pay overdraft items.

[31] U.C.C. §4-405(2).
[32] U.C.C. §4-405(b); *Hieber v. Uptown Nat'l Bank of Chicago,* 557 N.E.2d 408 (Ill. App. 1990).
[33] U.C.C. §4-403.
[34] *Aliaga Medical Center, S.C. v. Harris Bank N.A.,* 21 N.E.3d 1203 (Ill. App. 2014).

CPA ### Bank's Liability to Drawer of Check

If the bank improperly refuses to make payment, it is liable to the drawer for damages sustained by the drawer as a consequence of such dishonor.

Bank's Liability to Holder

If a check has not been certified, the holder has no claim against the bank for the dishonor of the check regardless of the fact that the bank was wrong in its dishonor. The bank that certifies a check is liable to the holder when it dishonors the check.

Holder's Notice of Dishonor of Check

When a check is dishonored by nonpayment, the holder must follow the procedure for notice to the secondary parties. Notice of dishonor need not be given to the drawer who has stopped payment on a check or to drawers and indorsers who are aware that there are insufficient funds on deposit to cover the check. In those circumstances, no party has reason to expect that the check will be paid by the bank.

30-1h Agency Status of Collecting Bank

agent–person or firm who is authorized by the principal or by operation of law to make contracts with third persons on behalf of the principal.

When a customer deposits negotiable instruments in a bank, the bank is regarded as being merely an **agent,** even though the customer may be given the right to make immediate withdrawals against the deposited item. Because of the bank's **agency** status, the customer remains the owner of the item and is subject to the risks of ownership involved in its collection.

agency–the relationship that exists between a person identified as a principal and another by virtue of which the latter may make contracts with third persons on behalf of the principal. (Parties–principal, agent, third person)

When a bank cashes a check deposited by its customer or cashes a check drawn by its customer based on an amount from a deposited check, it is a holder of the check deposited by its customer. The bank may still collect from the parties on the check even though the bank is an agent for collection and has the right to charge back the amount of the deposited check if it cannot be collected.

30-1i Bank's Duty of Care

A bank is required to exercise ordinary care in the handling of items. The liability of a bank is determined by the law of the state where the bank, branch, or separate office involved is located.

CPA ### Modification of Bank Duties

The parties in the bank collection process may modify their rights and duties by agreement. However, a bank cannot disclaim liability for lack of good faith or failure to exercise ordinary care, nor can it limit the measure of damages for such lack of care.

When a bank handles checks by automated processes, the bank must use the ordinary standard of care of the industry and that standard of ordinary care does not require the bank to make a physical examination of each item.

Encoding Warranty and Electronic Presentment

encoding warranty– warranty made by any party who encodes electronic information on an instrument; a warranty of accuracy.

In addition to transfer and presentment warranties, an **encoding warranty** is also given by those who transfer instruments. Under this warranty, anyone placing information on an item or transmitting the information electronically warrants that the information is correct. When there is an agreement for electronic presentment, the presenter warrants that the transfer is made properly for transmissions.[35]

---

[35] U.C.C. §§4-207 to 4-209.

Counterfeit Checks

One of the problems that banks now experience is the use of counterfeit checks. Because of automated processing, these checks can sail through bank systems and seemingly are cleared. Customers, in reliance on the check clearing, use those funds only to be told later that the check was a counterfeit and the funds credited to their account are then debited. The liability for the losses resulting from counterfeit checks will depend on whether the bank acted reasonably in its processing systems in clearing checks (particularly those for large amounts) and whether it complied with the time requirements for notifying customers of a dishonor of a deposited counterfeit check.

CASE SUMMARY

The Lawyers Who Got Taken by Their Counterfeit Clients

FACTS: Greenberg, Trager & Herbst, LLP (GTH), is a law firm specializing in construction litigation law. In September 2007, a partner at GTH received an e-mail from a representative of Northlink Industrial Limited, a Hong Kong company. Northlink was looking for legal representation to assist it in the collection of debts owed by its North American customers. Through a series of e-mails GTH agreed to represent Northlink and requested a $10,000 retainer. GTH then received a Citibank check for $197,750 from a Northlink customer and was told that it could take its retainer from those funds. On Friday, September 21, 2007, GTH deposited the check into its account at HSBC.

The next business day, Monday, September 24, HSBC processed the check through the Federal Reserve Bank of Philadelphia (FRBP) and, because of the federal funds availability law, provisionally credited GTH's account for $197,750. FRBP presented an image replacement document (IRD) of the check to Citibank that same day.

Because the routing number was not recognized by Citi's processing system, the automated sorting system directed the IRD to the reject pocket.

HSBC received the IRD with the notation "sent wrong" the next day, September 25, 2007. Because the check was marked "sent wrong," HSBC assumed that there was a problem with the routing number that required sending the check to a different Federal Reserve bank. On September 26, 2007, HSBC sent the check to the Federal Reserve Bank, San Francisco (FRBS). HSBC never informed GTH of the "administrative return" of the check.

On September 27, 2007, a GTH partner called HSBC to determine whether the check had "cleared" and if the funds were available for disbursement. GTH was informed that the funds were available. Later that day, GTH wired $187,750 from its account to Hong Kong as Northlink instructed.

On October 2, 2007, HSBC received Citibank's notice that the check was being dishonored as "RTM [return to maker] Suspect Counterfeit." HSBC contacted GTH to inform them that the check had been dishonored. HSBC then revoked its provisional settlement and charged back GTH's account.

GTH filed suit against HSBC and Citibank for failure to inform GTH that the check had been returned and dishonored on September 25 and for informing GTH over the phone that the funds had "cleared" and were available for disbursement. HSBC and Citibank moved for summary judgment.

The trial court found that HSBC had no duty under the UCC to inform GTH that the check had been returned "sent wrong" on September 25, but rather that the dishonor actually took place when HSBC discovered that the check was "Suspect Counterfeit," and dismissed the complaint.

DECISION: The bank did not owe duty to GTH to have effective procedures in place to detect counterfeit checks. The bank is only required to present the check for payment to the drawee bank, and the drawee bank and its customer are charged with the duty of monitoring properly payable items. The bank's alleged oral statement that the check had "cleared" and the funds were available for transfer was not a misrepresentation because banking rules do not allow reliance on oral representations. A check is not cleared until it actually goes through the banking system. The bank exercised ordinary care in handling the check and did not breach any duty to GTH and its alleged oral representations could not be a basis for GTH's reliance. [*Greenberg, Trager & Herbst, LLP v. HSBC Bank USA*, 934 N.Y.S.2d 43 75 U.C.C. Rep. Serv. 2d 775 (Sup. Ct. 2011)]

CPA   ## 30-2 **Liability of a Bank**

Banks can make mistakes in the payment and collection of items presented to them by their customers. **For Example,** a check may slip through and be cashed over a customer's properly executed stop payment order. The bank would be liable for this improper payment and may also be liable for improperly collecting, paying, or refusing to pay a check.

30-2a **Premature Payment of a Postdated Check**

A check may be postdated, but the bank is not liable for making payments on the check before the date stated unless the drawer has given the bank prior notice. Such a notice is similar to a stop payment order; it must provide sufficient information so that the bank is moved to action by the trigger that comes from the orderly processing of the check as it flows through its electronic processing system.[36]

30-2b **Payment over a Stop Payment Order**

A bank must be given a reasonable time in which to put a stop payment order into effect. However, if the bank makes payment of a check after it has been properly notified to stop payment, and there has been sufficient time for the order to be put into the system, the bank is liable to the drawer (customer) for the loss the drawer sustains in the absence of a valid limitation of the bank's liability.[37] The bank must have complete information on a stop payment order, such as the payee, check number, and amount, to be held responsible for the failure to stop payment.

CASE SUMMARY

When Writing "Stop" Is Not Enough to Halt a Check

FACTS: Aliaga Medical Center first opened a business checking account with Harris Bank in December 2003. Upon opening the account, Aliaga acknowledged that it received the "Harris Bank Handbook for Personal and Business Deposit Accounts." The first page of the handbook included the statement that the customer "agree[s] to the terms of this Agreement when [Aliaga] sign[s] [Harris Bank's] account opening form or signature card, make[s] deposits or withdrawals, or leave[s] funds on deposit."

The handbook also required that if Aliaga wanted to stop payment on a check it had written, the following requirements would apply:

> If you do not want us to pay a check you have written, you can order us to stop payment. Your stop payment order must include your account number, the number and date of the check, the name of the payee, and the amount. We must receive your stop payment order before our stop payment cut-off time, which is 10 a.m. Central Time (C.T.) on the next Business Day after the check is presented to us for payment. We will accept a stop payment order from any account owner regardless of who signed the check. Your stop payment order will be effective for six months. If you want the stop payment order to continue after six months, you must renew it.

Under the agreement, Harris Bank specifically "reserve[d] [its] right to pay * * * a stale check."

The agreement contained a number of other relevant notification provisions, including notice provisions that required customers to notify the Bank of any issues or problems with its account within 60 days of receiving a statement and that suit must be filed within one year of receiving the statement.

---

[36] Note that a "postdated check" is not a check but a time draft. U.C.C. §§4401 to 4-402.
[37] U.C.C. §4-403(c); *Lombino v. Bank of America, N.A.,* 797 F. Supp. 2d 1078 (D. Nev. 2011).

When Writing "Stop" Is Not Enough to Halt a Check continued

On July 10, 2010, Dr. Federico Aliaga, the plaintiff's president, issued a check in the amount of $50,000 (the check), payable to his wife, whom he was divorcing. The face of the check included the statement "void after 90 days" immediately above the signature line. Harris Bank honored the check on December 30, 2010. Aliaga never placed a stop payment order on the check, and, in fact, never communicated with Harris about the check anytime between July 10, 2010, and December 30, 2010.

In January 2011, Harris Bank sent and made available to Aliaga its December 2010 checking account statement, which showed that Harris Bank had honored the check on December 30, 2010. Aliaga, however, did not notify Harris Bank of the improper check payment within the 60-day notification period delineated in the parties' agreement. Additionally, Aliaga did not initiate this lawsuit within one year of the date Harris Bank sent or made available the December 2010 statement. Instead, Aliaga waited until October or November 2012, nearly two years after the December 2010 statement was made available, before disputing the check with Harris.

Harris moved to dismiss the complaint. The trial court granted the motion, and Aliaga appealed.

DECISION: Harris had the right to pay the check despite the "void after 90 days" language because Aliaga failed to properly stop payment of the check. Under the parties' agreement, if Aliaga did not want Harris Bank to pay a check it had written, then Aliaga had to comply with certain requirements.

Aliaga claims that under a UCC provision (810 ILCS 5/4–403(a) (West 2012)), it was only required to stop payment "in a time and manner that gives the bank a reasonable opportunity to comply" and that its notation on the check "certainly achieves this." However, Aliaga's contention is without merit for several reasons. First, the UCC permits that "[t]he effect of [its] provisions * * * may be varied by agreement."

Furthermore, even if Aliaga is correct that the stop payment provision of the agreement was neither exclusive nor meant to override the UCC, the "void" notation was ineffective because it did not comply with section 4–403(a) of the UCC by providing notice "at a time and in a manner that affords the bank a reasonable opportunity to act on it."

Aliaga also failed to comply with its obligation to timely notify Harris Bank of the alleged unauthorized payment of the check within 60 days after Harris Bank made Aliaga's December 2010 statement available to it.

Aliaga admitted that it did not comply with these terms of the agreement by providing timely notice to Harris Bank within 60 days of the date that it sent, or otherwise made available to Aliaga, the December 2010 statement. Aliaga further conceded that it did not contact Harris Bank about the payment within 60 days of receiving the December 2010 statement. As a result, Aliaga's claim is untimely.

Finally, Aliaga failed to timely commence this lawsuit within one year from the date that Harris Bank sent or made available the December 2010 statement.

Affirmed. [*Aliaga Medical Center, S.C. v. Harris Bank N.A.,* **21 N.E.3d 1203 (Ill. App. 2014)**]

CPA 30-2c **Payment on a Forged Signature of Drawer**

A forgery of the signature of the drawer occurs when the name of the drawer has been signed by another person without authority to do so with the intent to defraud by making it appear that the drawer signed the check. The bank is liable to the drawer if it pays a check on which the drawer's signature has been forged because a forgery ordinarily has no effect as a signature. The risk of loss caused by the forged signature of the drawer is placed on the bank without regard to whether the bank could have detected the forgery.[38] The reasoning behind the bank's liability for a forged drawer's signature is that the bank is presumed to know its own customers' signatures even if it does not regularly review checks for authenticity of the signature.

A bank's customer whose signature has been forged may be barred from holding the bank liable if the customer's negligence substantially contributed to the making of the forgery. This preclusion rule prevents or precludes the customer from making a forgery

[38] *Du v. Bank of America, N.A.* Not Reported in N.E.2d, 30 Mass. L. Rptr. 337, 2012 WL 5362292 (Mass. Super. 2012). Some states allow for an action for conversion of funds by the customer. *300 Broadway Healthcare Center, LLC v. Wachovia Bank, N.A.,* 39 A.3d 248 (N.J. App. 2012), but see *DMDB Adults, Inc. v. Bank of America Corp.,* 951 N.Y.S.2d 492 (N.Y.A.D. 2012).

claim against the bank. However, to enjoy the protection of the preclusion rule, the bank, if negligent in its failure to detect the forgery or alteration, must have cashed the check in good faith or have taken it for value or collection.[39]

Article 4 of the UCC extends forgery protections and rights to alterations and unauthorized signings. When an officer with authority limited to signing $5,000 checks signs a check for $7,500, the signature is unauthorized. If the principal for the drawer account is an organization and has a requirement that two or more designated persons sign negotiable instruments on its behalf, signatures by fewer than the specified number are also classified as unauthorized signatures.

CPA   30-2d **Payment on a Forged or Missing Indorsement**

A drawee bank that honors a customer's check bearing a forged indorsement must recredit the customer's account upon the drawer's discovery of the forgery and notification to the bank. A drawee bank is liable for the loss when it pays a check that lacks an essential indorsement.[40] In such a case, the instrument is not properly payable. Without proper indorsements for an order instrument and special indorsements, the person presenting the check for payment is not the holder of the instrument and is not entitled to demand or receive payment. However, the bank can then turn to the indorsers and transferors of the instrument for breach of warranty liability in that all signatures were not genuine or authorized and they did not have title. All transferors can turn to their previous transferor until liability ultimately rests with the party who first accepted the forged indorsement. This party had face-to-face contact and could have verified signatures.[41]

When a customer deposits a check but does not indorse it, the customer's bank may make an indorsement on behalf of the depositor unless the check expressly requires the customer's indorsement. A bank cannot add the missing indorsement of a person who is not its customer when an item payable is deposited in a customer's bank account.

30-2e **Alteration of a Check**

If the face of a check has been altered so that the amount to be paid has been increased, the bank is liable to the drawer for the amount of the increase when it makes payment of the greater amount.

The drawer may be barred from claiming that there was an alteration if there was negligence in writing the check or reporting its alteration. A drawer is barred from claiming alteration if the check was written negligently, the negligence substantially contributed to the making of the material alteration, and the bank honored the check in good faith and observed reasonable commercial standards in doing so. **For Example,** the drawer is barred from claiming alteration when the check was written with blank spaces that readily permitted a change of "four" to "four hundred" and the drawee bank paid out the latter sum because the alteration was not obvious. A careful drawer will write figures and words close together and run a line through or cross out any blank spaces.

30-2f **Unauthorized Collection of a Check**

A collecting bank, or a bank simply collecting an item for a customer, is protected from liability when it follows its customer's instructions. It is not required to inquire or verify

---

[39] U.C.C. §4-406(e); *Citizens Bank of Pennsylvania v. Reimbursement Technologies, Inc.*, 2014 WL 2738220 (E.D. Pa. 2014); *Rodgeres v. Bank of America, N.A.*, 73 U.C.C. Rep. Serv. 2d 47 (S.D. Ill. 2011).

[40] *Simi Management Corp. v. Bank of America, N.A.*, 930 F. Supp. 2d 1082 (N.D. Cal. 2013); *VIP Mortg. Corp. v. Bank of America, N.A.*, 769 F. Supp. 2d 20 (D. Mass. 2011).

[41] *Smith v. Farmers Union Mut. Ins. Co.*, 260 P.3d 163 (Mont. 2011).

that the customer had the authority to give such instructions. In contrast, instructions do not protect a payor bank. It has an absolute duty to make proper payment. If it does not do so, it is liable unless it is protected by estoppel or by the preclusion rule. The person giving wrongful instructions is liable for the loss caused by those instructions.

CASE SUMMARY

The Devil Shops at Neiman Marcus Using Her Boss's Checks

FACTS: Carol Young was employed as Brian P. Burns's secretary at a salary that never exceeded $75,000. Between 1995 and 2000, Young opened several credit card accounts with Neiman Marcus. In the three-year period prior to 2006, Young spent approximately $1 million at Neiman Marcus, and "the balance on [one] credit card, as of January 10, 2006, was in excess of $242,000." Young was offered entrée into Neiman Marcus's exclusive INCIRCLE® rewards program—a loyalty incentive program. Young had a personal shopper who knew of her annual salary of less than $75,000. However, the personal shopper repeatedly contacted and encouraged Young to make excessive purchases with her various Neiman Marcus cards.

Young would personally deliver on a regular basis fraudulent and forged checks drawn on Burns's Union Bank of California checking account to pay down her various [Neiman Marcus] credit card bills at the Customer Service Center in Neiman's San Francisco store. Young used three different methods for presenting Burns's checks: (a) stealing checks and forging Burns's signature; (b) stealing checks with no signature whatsoever; and (c) stealing checks with Burns's signature—checks that Burns presumed were for payments toward his own Neiman Marcus credit card account, but which were diverted to Young's credit card accounts.

Because Young managed all of Burns's accounts, the reconciliations she made had fake ledger entries for payment to third parties to cover her payments to Neiman Marcus. Burns did not detect Young's activities for three years because he did not see the bank statements, only Young did. A serendipitous examination of the ledger and canceled checks resulted in the discovery. Burns recovered what he could from his bank, an amount limited by UCC Article 4. Burns filed suit against Neiman Marcus, seeking to recover the funds paid on the checks and claiming that Neiman Marcus was subject to the defenses of forgery and unauthorized payments. The trial court granted Neiman Marcus's motion for demurrer and Burns appealed.

DECISION: The court affirmed the lower court's dismissal because it was unwilling to impose a broad duty on third parties to verify that every third-party check it receives is legitimate. Such a requirement would significantly slow down the flow and use of negotiable instruments and defeat both the purposes of Articles 3 and 4 as well as the well-defined rules for responsibility and liability when there are drawer and drawee forgeries. [*Burns v. Neiman Marcus Group, Inc.*, 173 Cal. App. 4th 479 (Cal. App. 1st Dist. 2009)]

30-2g Time Limitations

The liability of the bank to its depositor is subject to certain time limitations.

CPA   ### Forgery and Alteration Reporting Time

A customer must examine with reasonable care and promptness a bank statement and relevant checks that are paid in good faith and sent to the customer by the bank and must try to discover any unauthorized signature or alteration on the checks. The customer must notify the bank promptly after discovering either a forgery or an alteration. If the bank exercises ordinary care in paying a forged or an altered check and suffers a loss because the customer fails to discover and notify the bank of the forgery or alteration, the customer cannot assert the unauthorized signature or alteration against the bank.[42]

---

[42] *Crawford Supply Group, Inc. v. Bank of America, N.A.*, 2011 WL 1131292 (N.D. Ill. 2011).

Under the Check Truncation Act (CTA—which is part of the Check 21 statute covered in Chapter 27), banks now have the right to substitute electronic images of checks for customer billing statements. The CTA is largely implemented through Federal Reserve Board regulations found at 12 CFR §229.2. Banks do not need to provide the original check to their customers and can simply send copies of electronic images so long as the image provides enough clarity for the customer to see payee, encoding, indorsements, and so on.

With the use of substituted checks and online banking, consumers now have additional rights and time limits with substituted checks. Under the Check 21 statute, consumers have a new right to an expedited recredit to their account if a substitute check was charged improperly to their account. They have the right to see the original check if they can explain why it is necessary and that they are suffering a loss as a result of the improper charge of a substitute check to their account. Consumers have 40 calendar days from whichever of the following is later: (1) the delivery of their monthly bank statements or (2) that date on which the substitute check was made available to them for examination and/or review. If a consumer has been traveling or has been ill, the rules permit the extension of the deadline to challenge a substitute check. Consumers can even call their bank and challenge a payment, but they will not then get the benefit of all the rights and protections under Check 21 and its regulations if they choose to proceed without a written demand on a substitute check.[43] Once the demand is made, the bank must either recredit the consumer's account within one business day or explain why it believes the substitute check was charged properly to the consumer's account. The oral demand does not start this clock running for the consumer's protection. There are also fines and overdraft protections provided while the substitute check issue is in the dispute/investigation stage.

Some cases of forgery are the result of a customer's lack of care, such as when an employee is given too much authority and internal controls are lacking with the result that the employee is able to forge checks on a regular basis not easily detected by the bank. Referred to as the *fictitious payee and impostor exceptions*, this issue was covered in Chapter 28.

Customers are precluded from asserting unauthorized signatures or alterations if they do not report them within one year from the time the bank statement is received.[44] A forged indorsement must be reported within three years.

Unauthorized Signature or Alteration by Same Wrongdoer

If there is a series of improperly paid items and the same wrongdoer is involved, the customer is protected only as to those items that were paid by the bank before it received notification from the customer and during that reasonable amount of time that the customer has to examine items or statements and to notify the bank. If the customer failed to exercise reasonable promptness and failed to notify the bank but the customer can show that the bank failed to exercise ordinary care in paying the items, the loss will be allocated between the customer and the bank.[45]

Statute of Limitations

An action to enforce a liability imposed by Article 4 must be commenced within three years after the cause of action accrued.

---

[43] 12 C.F.R. 229.54(b)(1)(iii).
[44] U.C.C. §4-406.
[45] U.C.C. §4-406 (2012); *HH Computer Systems, Inc. v. Pacific City Bank*, 179 Cal. Rptr. 689 (Cal. App. 2014).

THINKING THINGS THROUGH

The Business Law Professor with the Lost Cashier's Check

Marianne Jennings obtained a cashier's check in order to pay off her car loan in the amount of $37,000. Professor Jennings mailed the cashier's check via Express Mail, requiring signature. An employee at the lender (an automaker financial arm) received the check and felt that because it did not have the signature of "Marianne Jennings" on it that it was invalid. The employee sent the check back to Professor Jennings via regular U.S. mail.

Professor Jennings, having received proof of receipt on the check, did not make her next car payment. She then received a notice of an overdue payment, a penalty for late payment, and that her late payment had been reported to the credit bureau.

Professor Jennings contacted the lender and was told that the check had been returned, and the late penalty would stand. Professor Jennings then went to the bank to discuss options. The bank indicated that it could issue a stop payment order if Professor Jennings would pay for a bond in the amount of $37,000, which would run about $1,200. The bank indicated that it could not issue a stop payment and that the cashier's check had been properly issued.

Discuss for Professor Jennings her rights in this situation, including any possible solutions to the situation. The cashier's check was never found. Also, be sure to discuss liability issues regarding the late payment, penalties, and effect on her credit rating.

30-3 Consumer Funds Transfers

Consumers are using electronic methods of payment at an increasing rate. From the swipe of the card at the grocery store checkout to the retrieval of funds from the local automated teller machine, *electronic funds transfers* represent a way of life for many consumers. A federal statute protects consumers making electronic funds transfers.

30-3a Electronic Funds Transfer Act

Electronic Funds Transfer Act (EFTA)— federal law that provides consumers with rights and protections in electronic funds transfers.

Congress passed the **Electronic Funds Transfer Act (EFTA)** to protect consumers making electronic transfers of funds.[46] **Electronic funds transfer (EFT)** means any transfer of funds (other than a transaction originated by check, draft, or similar paper instrument) that is initiated through an electronic terminal, a telephone, a computer, or a magnetic tape that authorizes a financial institution to debit or credit an account. The service available from an automated teller machine is a common form of EFT.[47]

electronic funds transfer (EFT)—any transfer of funds (other than a transaction originated by a check, draft, or similar paper instrument) that is initiated through an electronic terminal, a telephone, a computer, or a magnetic tape so as to authorize a financial institution to debit or credit an account.

30-3b Types of Electronic Funds Transfer Systems

Currently, five common types of EFT systems are in use. In some of these systems, the consumer has a card to access a machine. The consumer usually has a private code that prevents others who wrongfully obtain the card from using it.

Automated Teller Machine

The *automated teller machine (ATM)* performs many of the tasks once performed exclusively by bank employees. Once a user activates an ATM, he can deposit and withdraw funds from his account, transfer funds between accounts, make payments on loan accounts, and obtain cash advances from bank credit cards.

---

[46] 15 U.S.C. §1693 *et seq.*
[47] The majority of the states have adopted the 1990 version of Article 4A.

Pay-by-Phone System

This system facilitates paying telephone, mortgage, utility, and other bills without writing checks. The consumer calls the bank and directs the transfer of funds to a designated third party.

Direct Deposit and Withdrawal

Employees may authorize their employers to deposit wages directly to their accounts. A consumer who has just purchased an automobile on credit may elect to have monthly payments withdrawn from a bank account to be paid directly to the seller.

Point-of-Sale Terminal

The *point-of-sale terminal* allows a business with such a terminal to transfer funds from a consumer's account to the store's account. The consumer must be furnished in advance with the terms and conditions of all EFT services and must be given periodic statements covering account activity. Any automatic EFT from an individual's account must be authorized in writing in advance.

Financial institutions are liable to consumers for all damages proximately caused by the failure to make an EFT in accordance with the terms and conditions of an account. Exceptions include insufficient funds, funds subject to legal process, exceeding an established credit limit, or insufficient cash is available in an ATM.

Internet Banking

Internet banking is the customer use of computer access to bank systems to pay bills, balance accounts, transfer funds, and even obtain loans. Increasing in popularity, this form of banking still suffers from concerns about privacy and security. However, the revisions to Articles 3 and 4 recognize electronic records as valid proof of payment.

CPA   30-3c Consumer Liability

A consumer who notifies the issuer of an EFT card within two days after learning of a loss or theft of the card can be held to a maximum liability of $50 for unauthorized use of the card. If you report the loss before the card is used, you have no liability. Failure to notify within this time (after 2 days but before 60 days) will increase the consumer's liability for losses to a maximum of $500. After 60 days, you have unlimited liability. However, by the end of 60 days, you will have been through at least two monthly statements and will have had every opportunity to provide notification. Consumers have the responsibility to examine periodic statements provided by their financial institution.

CPA   30-4 Funds Transfers

The funds transfers made by businesses are governed by the UCC and Federal Reserve regulations.

30-4a What Law Governs?

In states that have adopted Article 4A of the Uniform Commercial Code, that article governs funds transfers. In addition, whenever a Federal Reserve Bank is involved, the provisions of Article 4A apply by virtue of Federal Reserve regulations.

30-4b **Characteristics of Funds Transfers**

The transfers regulated by Article 4A are characteristically made between highly sophisticated parties dealing with large sums of money. Speed of transfer is often an essential ingredient. An individual transfer may involve many millions of dollars, and the national total of such transfers on a business day can amount to trillions of dollars.

30-4c **Pattern of Funds Transfers**

In the simplest form of funds transfer, both the debtor and the creditor have separate accounts in the same bank.[48] In this situation, the debtor can instruct the bank to pay the creditor a specified sum of money by subtracting that amount from the debtor's account and adding it to the creditor's account. As a practical matter, the debtor merely instructs the bank to make the transfer.

A more complex situation is involved if each party has an account in a different bank. In that case, the funds transfer could involve only these two banks and no clearinghouse. The buyer can instruct the buyer's bank to direct the seller's bank to make payment to the seller. There is direct communication between the two banks. In a more complex situation, the buyer's bank may relay the payment order to another bank, called an **intermediary bank,** and that bank, in turn, transmits the payment order to the seller's bank. Such transactions become even more complex when two or more intermediary banks or a clearinghouse is involved.

intermediary bank–bank between the originator and the beneficiary bank in the transfer of funds.

30-4d **Scope of UCC Article 4A**

Article 4A applies to all funds transfers except as expressly excluded because of their nature or because of the parties involved.

EFTA and Consumer Transactions

Article 4A does not apply to consumer transaction payments to which the EFTA applies. If any part of the funds transfer is subject to the EFTA, the entire transfer is expressly excluded from the scope of UCC Article 4A.[49]

Credit and Debit Transfers

When the person making payment, such as the buyer, requests that payment be made to the beneficiary's bank, the transaction is called a **credit transfer.** If the beneficiary entitled to money goes to the bank according to a prior agreement and requests payment, the transaction is called a **debit transfer.** The latter transfer type is not regulated by Article 4A. Article 4A applies only to transfers begun by the person authorizing payment to another.

credit transfer– transaction in which a person making payment, such as a buyer, requests payment be made to the beneficiary's bank.

debit transfer– transaction in which a beneficiary entitled to money requests payment from a bank according to a prior agreement.

30-4e **Definitions**

Article 4A employs terms that are peculiar to that article or are used in a very different context from the contexts in which they appear elsewhere.

---

[48] The text refers to *debtor* and *creditor* in the interest of simplicity and because that situation is the most common in the business world. However, a gift may be made by a funds transfer. Likewise, a person having separate accounts in two different banks may transfer funds from one bank to another.

[49] U.C.C. §4A-108. This exclusion applies when any part of the transaction is subject to Regulation E adopted under the authority of that statute.

Funds Transfer

funds transfer–communication of instructions or requests to pay a specific sum of money to the credit of a specified account or person without an actual physical passing of money.

A **funds transfer** is more accurately described as a communication of instructions or a request to pay a specific sum of money to, or to the credit of, a specified account or person. There is no actual physical transfer or passing of money.

Originator

originator–party who originates the funds transfer.

The person starting the funds transfer is called the **originator** of the funds transfer.[50]

Beneficiary

beneficiary–person to whom the proceeds of a life insurance policy are payable, a person for whose benefit property is held in trust, or a person given property by a will; the ultimate recipient of the benefit of a funds transfer.

The **beneficiary** is the ultimate recipient of the benefit of the funds transfer. Whether the recipient is the beneficiary personally, an account owned by the beneficiary, or a third person to whom the beneficiary owes money is determined by the payment order.

Beneficiary's Bank

beneficiary's bank–the final bank, which carries out the payment order, in the chain of a transfer of funds.

The **beneficiary's bank** is the final bank in the chain of transfer that carries out the transfer by making payment or application as directed by the payment order.

Payment Order

payment order–direction given by an originator to his or her bank or by any bank to a subsequent bank to make a specified funds transfer.

The **payment order** is the direction the originator gives to the originator's bank or by any bank to a subsequent bank to make the specified funds transfer. Although called a *payment order*, it is in fact a request. No bank is required or obligated to accept a payment order unless it is so bound by a contract or a clearinghouse rule that operates independently of Article 4A.

30-4f Manner of Transmitting Payment Order

Article 4A makes no provisions for the manner of transmitting a payment order. As a practical matter, most funds transfers under Article 4A are controlled by computers, and payment orders are electronically transmitted. Article 4A, however, applies to any funds transfer payment order even if made orally, such as by telephone, or in writing. Also, the agreement of the parties or the clearinghouse and funds transfer system rules may impose some restrictions on the methods for communicating orders.

30-4g Regulation by Agreement and Funds Transfer System Rules

Article 4A, with minor limitations, permits the parties to make agreements that modify or change the provisions of Article 4A that would otherwise govern. Likewise, the rules of a clearinghouse or a funds transfer system through which the banks operate may change the provisions of the Code.

Choice of Law

When the parties enter into an agreement for a funds transfer, they may designate the law that is to apply in interpreting the agreement.

---

[50] U.C.C. §4A-201.

Clearinghouse Rules

The banks involved in a particular funds transfer may be members of the same clearinghouse. In such a case, they will be bound by the lawful rules and regulations of the house.

The rights of the parties involved in a funds transfer may be determined by the rules of FedWire, a clearinghouse system operated by the Federal Reserve System, or by CHIPS, which is a similar system operated by the New York clearinghouse.

30-4h Reimbursement of the Bank

After the beneficiary's bank accepts the payment order, it and every bank ahead of it in the funds transfer chain is entitled to reimbursement of the amount paid to or for the beneficiary. This reimbursement is due from the preceding bank. By going back along the funds transfer chain, the originator's bank, and ultimately the originator, makes payment of this reimbursement amount.

30-4i Error in Funds Transfer

There may be an error in a payment order. The effect of an error depends on its nature.

Type of Error

The error in a payment order may consist of a wrong identification or a wrong amount.

Wrong Beneficiary or Account Number. The payment order received by the beneficiary's bank may contain an error in the designation of the beneficiary or in the account number. This error may result in payment being made to or for the wrong person or account.

Excessive Amount. The payment order may call for the payment of an amount that is larger than it should be. For example, the order may wrongly add an additional zero to the specified amount.

Duplicating Amount. The payment order may be issued after a similar payment order has already been transferred, so that the second order duplicates the first. This duplication would result in doubling the proper amount paid by the beneficiary's bank.

Underpayment. The payment order may call for the payment of a smaller sum than was ordered. For example, the order may drop off one of the zeros from the amount ordered by the originator.

Effect of Error

When the error falls under one of the first three classes just discussed, the bank committing the error bears the loss because it caused the item to be wrongfully paid. In contrast, when the error is merely underpayment, the bank making the mistake can cure the fault by making a supplementary order for the amount of the underpayment. If verification by the agreed-upon security procedure would disclose an error in the payment order, a bank is liable for any loss caused by the error if it failed to verify the payment order by such a procedure. In contrast, if the security procedure followed did not reveal any error, there is no liability for accepting the payment order.

When an error of any kind is made, there may be liability under a collateral agreement of the parties, a clearinghouse or funds transfer system rule, or general principles of contract law. However, these rights may be lost in certain cases by failure to notify the involved bank that the mistake has been made.

30-4j Liability for Loss

Unless otherwise regulated by agreement or clearinghouse rule, banks have little or no liability in the funds transfer chain if they have followed the agreed-upon security procedure.

Unauthorized Order

If a bank executes or accepts an unauthorized payment order, it is liable to any prior party in the transfer chain for the loss caused. If a bank acts on the basis of an unauthorized order that nevertheless is verified by the security procedure, the bank is not liable for the loss that is caused.

Failure to Act

A bank that fails to carry out a payment order is usually liable, at the most, for interest loss and expenses. There is no liability for the loss sustained by the originator or for consequential damages suffered because payment was not made to satisfy the originator's obligation to the beneficiary.

Make the Connection

Summary

A *check* is a particular kind of draft; it is drawn on a bank and is payable on demand. A delivery of a check is not an assignment of money on deposit with the bank on which it is drawn. A check does not automatically transfer the rights of the depositor against the bank to the holder of the check, and there is no duty on the part of the drawee bank to the holder to pay the holder the amount of the check.

A check may be an *ordinary check*, a *cashier's check*, or a *teller's check*. The name on the paper is not controlling. Unless otherwise agreed, the delivery of a certified check, a cashier's check, or a teller's check discharges the debt for which it is given, up to the amount of the check.

Certification of a check by the bank is the acceptance of the check—the bank becomes the primary party. Certification may be at the request of the drawee or the holder. Certification by the holder releases all prior indorsers and the drawer from liability.

Notice of nonpayment of a check must be given to the drawer of a check. If no notice is given, the drawer is discharged from liability to the same extent as the drawer of an ordinary draft.

A depositor may stop payment on a check. However, the depositor is liable to a holder in due course unless the stop payment order was for a reason that may be raised against a holder in due course. The stop payment order may be made orally (binding for 14 calendar days) or with a record (effective for six months).

The depository bank is the agent of the depositor for the purpose of collecting a deposited item. The bank may become liable when it pays a check contrary to a stop payment order or when there has been a forgery or an alteration. The bank is not liable, however, if the drawer's negligence has substantially contributed to the forgery. A bank that pays on a forged instrument must recredit the drawer's account. A depositor is subject to certain time limitations to enforce liability of the bank. Banks are subject to reporting requirements under the USA Patriot Act.

A customer and a bank may agree that the bank should retain canceled checks and simply provide the customer with a list of paid items. The customer must examine canceled checks (or their electronic images) or paid items to see whether any were improperly paid.

An *electronic funds transfer (EFT)* is a transfer of funds (other than a transaction originated by check, draft, or other commercial paper) that is initiated through an electronic terminal, a telephone, a computer, or a magnetic tape to authorize a financial institution to debit or credit an account. The Electronic Funds Transfer Act requires that a financial institution furnish consumers with specific information containing all the terms and conditions of all EFT services. Under certain conditions, the financial institution will bear the loss for unauthorized transfers. Under other circumstances, the consumer will bear the loss.

Funds transfers regulated by UCC Article 4A are those made between highly sophisticated parties that deal with large sums of money. If any part of the funds transfer is subject to the EFTA, such as consumer transactions, the entire transfer is expressly excluded from the scope of Article 4A. A funds transfer is simply a request or an instruction to pay a specific sum of money to, or to the credit of, a specified person.

Learning Outcomes

After studying this chapter, you should be able to clearly explain:

30-1 Checks

LO.1 List and explain the duties of the drawee bank
See the discussion of duties and Ethics & the Law on overdrafts, pages 579, 582–583.

LO.2 Explain the methods for, and legal effect of stopping payment
See Thinking Things Through, "The Business Law Professor with the Lost Cashier's Check," page 589.
See the Ethics & the Law on overdraft fees, page 580.

30-2 Liability of a Bank

LO.3 Describe the liability of a bank for improper payment and collection
See the *State Bank v. Smith* case for a discussion of liability related to cashier's checks, pages 576–577.
See the E-Commerce & Cyberlaw feature on the Nigerian e-mails, page 577.

See the Ethics & the Law feature for a discussion of overdraft fees issues, page 580.
See the *Aliaga Medical Center S.C. v. Harris Bank N.A.* case for a discussion on 90-day limits on cashing checks, pages 584–585.

LO.4 Discuss the legal effect of forgeries and material alterations
See the *Greenberg, Trager & Herbst v. HSBC Bank USA* case, page 583.

LO.5 Specify the time limitations for reporting forgeries and alterations
See the *Burns v. Neiman Marcus* case, page 587.

30-3 Consumer Funds Transfers

See the EFTA discussion, page 589.

30-4 Funds Transfers

LO.6 Describe the electronic transfer of funds and laws governing it
See the discussion of Article 4A, page 591.

Key Terms

agency
agent
bad check laws
beneficiary
beneficiary's bank
cashier's check
certified check
check
credit transfer
debit transfer

demand draft
electronic funds transfer (EFT)
Electronic Funds Transfer Act
    (EFTA)
encoding warranty
funds transfer
intermediary bank
money order
originator
overdraft

payment order
postdated
presentment
stale check
stop payment orders
substitute check
teller's check
time draft
USA Patriot Act
wrongfully dishonored

Questions and Case Problems

1. William Elias was the former owner of Direct Lending, a subprime mortgage company purchased by EA Management. Sometime after the sale, Elias went to Chase Bank and had three cashier's checks drawn to third parties and payable out of Direct Lending accounts in the amount of $191,251.31.

When the new owners of Direct Lending checked their account balances online, they discovered the withdrawal for the three cashier's checks. The treasurer went to the bank and stopped payment on all three cashier's checks. Elias brought suit against the bank for wrongful dishonor and consequential damages to his businesses as a result of the dishonor. Can Elias recover? Be sure to explain which Article 4 provisions apply and why. [*EA Management v. JP Morgan Chase, N.A.*, 655 F.3d 573 (6th Cir.)]

2. Helen was a very forgetful person, so she had placed her bank code (PIN number) on the back of her debit card. A thief stole Helen's card and was able to take $100 from an ATM on the day of the theft. That same day, Helen realized that the card was gone and phoned her bank. The following morning, the thief withdrew another $100. For how much, if anything, is Helen responsible? Why?

3. Adam Paul Strege (APS) opened a checking account at U.S. Bank. Just below his signature card for the account, he wrote, "Call if I bounce a check." APS bounced several checks, and each time U.S. Bank covered those checks but it did not notify APS of the bounced check status. The result was that APS continued to write checks and U.S. Bank had to request funds from him to cover the overdrafts in his account. APS refused to pay the amount due because he argued that U.S. Bank had breached its agreement with him to report all bounced checks. Discuss whether U.S. Bank had the obligation to notify APS of the bounced checks. [*APS v. U.S. Bank*, 2009 WL 4723311 (D. Minn.)]

4. Arthur Odgers died, and his widow, Elizabeth Odgers (Elizabeth Salsman by remarriage), retained Breslow as the attorney for her husband's estate. She received a check payable to her drawn on First National City Bank. Breslow told her to deposit it in her husband's estate. She signed an indorsement "Pay to the order of Estate of Arthur J. Odgers." Breslow deposited this check in his trustee account in National Community Bank, which collected the amount of the check from the drawee, First City National Bank. Thereafter, Elizabeth, as administratrix of the estate of Arthur J. Odgers, sued National Community Bank for collecting this check and crediting Breslow's trustee account with the proceeds. Was National Community Bank liable? Explain. [*Salsman v. National Community Bank*, 246 A.2d 162 (N.J. Super.)]

5. Shipper was ill for 14 months. His wife did not take care of his affairs carefully, nor did she examine his bank statements as they arrived each month. One of Shipper's acquaintances had forged his name to a check in favor of himself for $10,000. The drawee bank paid the check and charged Shipper's account. Shipper's wife did not notify the bank for 13 months after she received the statement and the forged check. Can she compel the bank to reverse the charge? Why or why not?

6. Ann Weldon maintained an account at Trust Company Bank. James Weldon, her son and a garment broker, purchased textile goods from Sportswear Services for resale to another corporation known as Thicket Textiles. Sportswear demanded certified funds from James Weldon before it would ship the goods. When James Weldon requested a certified check from Trust Company, Trust Company officer Sweat informed James that if it issued a certified check, payment could not be stopped even if the merchandise delivered was not as promised under the terms of the contract.

Ann Weldon then obtained a $16,319.29 cashier's check drawn on her account and payable to Sportswear. James had deposited his funds into her account to cover the check. The check was delivered to Sportswear, and the goods were shipped the next day, but they were defective.

Ann Weldon went to Trust Company Bank to issue a stop payment order, and the bank, believing that the check had not yet been delivered to Sportswear, did so for $25. James Weldon then notified Sportswear of the stop payment order. After Trust Company dishonored the cashier's check, Sportswear's bank was in contact with the bank and informed it that the check had already been delivered to Sportswear. Trust Company honored the check and credited Ann Weldon's account with the $25 stop payment fee. Ann filed suit because Trust Company did not stop payment. Should payment have been stopped? Why or why not? [*Weldon v. Trust Co. Bank of Columbus*, 499 S.E.2d 393 (Ga. App.)]

7. Gloria maintains a checking account at First Bank. On the third day of January, the bank sent her a statement of her account for December accompanied by the checks that the bank had paid. One of the checks had her forged signature, which Gloria discovered on the 25th of the month when she prepared a bank reconciliation. On discovering this, Gloria

immediately notified the bank. On January 21, the bank had paid another check forged by the same party who had forged the December item. Who must bear the loss on the forged January check?

8. Dean bought a car from Cannon. As payment, Dean gave him a check drawn on South Dorchester Bank of Eastern Shore Trust Co. Cannon cashed the check at the Cambridge Bank of Eastern Shore Trust Co. The drawee bank refused payment when the check was presented on the ground that Dean had stopped payment because of certain misrepresentations made by Cannon. Will Eastern Shore Trust Co. succeed in an action against Dean for payment? [*Dean v. Eastern Shore Trust Co.*, 150 A. 797 (Md.)]

9. John G. Vowell and his wife, now deceased, had a checking account and a savings/money-market account with Mercantile Bank of Arkansas. In June 1997, Dr. Vowell and his wife allowed their daughter, Suzan Vowell, now also deceased, and her boyfriend to move in with them at their home. At that time, they knew that Suzan and her boyfriend had been involved with drugs, alcohol, writing bad checks, and stealing. They also knew that Suzan had stolen checks from them in the past and forged either Dr. Vowell's or his wife's signatures. They took precautions by hiding Mrs. Vowell's purse, which contained their checkbook, under the kitchen sink.

Beginning in June 1997, Suzan forged Mrs. Vowell's signature on 42 checks, drawn on both accounts, and committed nine unauthorized ATM withdrawals in the aggregate amount of $12,028.75. Suzan found her mother's purse hidden under the kitchen sink and stole the checkbooks and ATM card from the purse. She apparently had access to the personal identification number (PIN) for the accounts because the number was identical to the home security system code.

The Vowells received the following statements from the bank for the checking and savings accounts:

Date of Transaction	Amount	Statement date covering
July 9, 1997	$230.00	June 6–July 7, 1997
August 8, 1997	$1,235.25	July 8–August 6, 1997
August 23, 1997	$5,140.00	July 23–Aug 21, 1997
September 9, 1997	$1,423.50	Aug 7–Sept 7, 1997
September 26, 1997	$4,000.00	Aug 22–Sept 22, 1997

On September 15, 1997, Dr. Vowell had Mercantile freeze their accounts and begin investigating the alleged forgeries and other unauthorized transactions pursuant to its policy. Suzan was arrested subsequently when she tried to use the ATM card again.

The bank refused to credit the Vowells' account because it maintained that their negligence in handling their daughter caused the losses. The court found that the bank was liable for only $6,014.38, one-half of the entire sum of Suzan Vowell's unauthorized bank transactions and forgeries. The bank appealed. Can the Vowells recover? How much and why? [*Mercantile Bank of Arkansas v. Vowell*, 117 S.W.3d 603 (Ark. App.)]

10. Bogash drew a check on National Safety Bank and Trust Co. payable to the order of Fiss Corp. At the request of Fiss Corp., the bank certified the check. The bank later refused to make payment on the check because of a dispute between Bogash and the corporation over the amount due the corporation. Fiss sued the bank on the check. Can Fiss recover? [*Fiss Corp. v. National Safety Bank and Trust Co.*, 77 So. 2d 293 (N.Y. City Ct.)]

11. Rovell wrote a check to Pretty Eyes Detective Agency for $10,000 too much ($38,250). A staff member for Rovell gave a stop payment order and then issued a new check ($27,284.50). But the staff member was unsure of the check number. Pretty Eyes cashed both checks, Rovell's account was overdrawn, and he sued the bank. Is the check valid? Who gets the funds? Is it possible for Rovell to recover from the bank? [*Rovell v. American National Bank*, 232 B.R. 381, 38 U.C.C. 2d 896 (N.D. Ill. 1998)]

12. Norris, who was ill in the hospital, was visited by his sister during his last days. Norris was very fond of his sister and wrote a check to her that she deposited in her bank account. Before the check cleared, Norris died. Could the sister collect on the check even though the bank knew of the depositor's death? Explain. [In re *Estate of Norris*, 532 P.2d 981 (Colo.)]

13. Scott D. Leibling gave his bank, Mellon Bank, an oral stop payment order. Nineteen months later, the check emerged and Mellon Bank honored it. Leibling has filed suit against Mellon Bank for acting

unreasonably under the circumstances. Is Mellon Bank liable to Leibling for paying the 19-month-old check when there was an oral stop payment order? Discuss your reasons for your answer. [*Leibling, P.C. v. Mellon, PSFS (NJ) N.A.*, 710 A.2d 1067, 35 U.C.C. 2d 590 (N.J. Super.)]

14. Hixson paid Galyen Petroleum Co. money he owed by issuing three checks to Galyen. The bank refused to cash the three checks because of insufficient funds in the Hixson account to pay all three. Galyen sued the bank. What was the result? Why? [*Galyen Petroleum Co. v. Hixson*, 331 N.W.2d 1 (Neb)]

CPA Questions

1. A check has the following endorsements on the back:
   (1) Paul Frank **"without recourse"**
   (2) George Hopkins **"payment guaranteed"**
   (3) Ann Quarry **"collection guaranteed"**
   (4) Rachell Ott

   Which of the following conditions occurring subsequent to the endorsements would discharge all of the endorsers?
   a. Lack of notice of dishonor.
   b. Late presentment.
   c. Insolvency of the maker.
   d. Certification of the check.

2. Blare bought a house and provided the required funds in the form of a certified check from a bank. Which of the following statements correctly describes the legal liability of Blare and the bank?
   a. The bank has accepted; therefore, Blare is without liability.
   b. The bank has not accepted; therefore, Blare has primary liability.
   c. The bank has accepted, but Blare has secondary liability.
   d. The bank has not accepted, but Blare has secondary liability.

3. In general, which of the following statements is correct concerning the priority among checks drawn on a particular account and presented to the drawee bank on a particular day?
   a. The checks may be charged to the account in any order convenient to the bank.
   b. The checks may be charged to the account in any order provided no charge creates an overdraft.
   c. The checks must be charged to the account in the order in which the checks were dated.
   d. The checks must be charged to the account in the order of lowest amount to highest amount to minimize the number of dishonored checks.

Debtor-Creditor Relationships

C H A P T E R   31

Nature of the Debtor-Creditor Relationship

Learning Outcomes <<<

After studying this chapter, you
should be able to

LO.1   Distinguish a contract of
           suretyship from a
           contract of guaranty

LO.2   Define the parties to a
           contract of suretyship
           and a contract of
           guaranty

LO.3   List and explain the
           rights of sureties to
           protect themselves from
           loss

LO.4   Explain the defenses
           available to sureties

LO.5   Explain the nature of a
           letter of credit and the
           liabilities of the various
           parties to a letter of
           credit

31-1 Creation of the Credit Relationship

suretyship–pledge or guaranty to pay the debt or be liable for the default of another.

obligor–promisor.

surety–obligor of a suretyship; primarily liable for the debt or obligation of the principal debtor.

guaranty–agreement or promise to answer for a debt; an undertaking to pay the debt of another if the creditor first sues the debtor.

guarantor–one who undertakes ⬛ C P A the obligation of guaranty.

principal–person or firm who employs an agent; the person who, with respect to a surety, is primarily liable to the third person or creditor; property held in trust.

principal debtor–original borrower or debtor.

⬛ C P A

debtor–buyer on credit (i.e., a borrower).

obligee–promisee who can claim the benefit of the obligation.

creditor–person (seller or lender) who is owed money; also may be a secured party.

guaranty of collection–form of guaranty in which creditor cannot proceed against guarantor until after proceeding against debtor.

This section of the book deals with all aspects of debt: the creation of the debtor-creditor relationship, the statutory requirements for disclosure in those credit contracts, the means by which creditors can secure repayment of debt, and, finally, what happens when debtors are unable to repay their debts.

A debtor-creditor relationship consists of a contract that provides for the creditor to advance funds to the debtor and requires the debtor to repay that principal amount with specified interest over an agreed-upon time. The credit contract, so long as it complies with all the requirements for formation and validity covered in Chapters 11 through 17, is enforceable just like any other contract. However, credit contracts often have additional statutory obligations and relationships that provide assurances on rights and collection for both the debtor and the creditor. Chapter 32 covers the rights of both debtors and creditors in consumer credit relationships. Chapter 33 covers the additional protection that creditors enjoy when debtors offer security interests in collateral. This chapter covers the additional relationships for securing repayment of debt known as *suretyships* and *lines of credit*.

31-2 Suretyship and Guaranty

A debtor can make a separate contract with a third party that requires the third party to pay the debtor's creditor if the debtor does not pay or defaults in the performance of an obligation. This relationship, in which a third party agrees to be responsible for the debt or other obligation, is used most commonly to ensure that a debt will be paid or that a contractor will perform the work called for by a contract. **For Example,** a third-party arrangement occurs when a corporate officer agrees to be personally liable if his corporation does not repay funds received through a corporate note. Contractors are generally required to obtain a surety bond in which a third party agrees to pay damages or complete performance of the construction project in the event the contractor fails to perform in a timely manner or according to the contract terms.

31-2a Definitions

One type of agreement to answer for the debt or default of another is called a **suretyship.** The **obligor** or third party who makes good on a debtor's obligation is called a **surety.** The other kind of agreement is called a **guaranty,** and the obligor is called a **guarantor.** In both cases, the person who owes the money or is under the original obligation to pay or perform is called the **principal, principal debtor,** or **debtor.**[1] The person to whom the debt or obligation is owed is the **obligee** or **creditor.**

As discussed in Chapters 27 and 30, the revisions to Articles 3 and 4 put accommodation parties (now secondary obligors) in the same legal status as those in a surety/guarantor relationship. The revisions place secondary obligors in the position of a surety.

Suretyship and guaranty undertakings have the common feature of a promise to answer for the debt or default of another. The terms are often used interchangeably. However, certain forms of guaranty are qualified by one distinction. A surety is liable from the moment the principal is in default. The creditor or obligee can demand performance or payment from the surety without first proceeding against the principal debtor. A **guaranty of collection** is one in which the creditor generally cannot proceed directly

---

[1] Unless otherwise stated, *surety* as used in the text includes guarantor as well as surety. Often, the term *guarantee* is used for guaranty. In law, guarantee is actually one who benefits from the guaranty.

absolute guaranty—agreement that creates the same obligation for the guarantor as a suretyship does for the surety; a guaranty of **CPA** payment creates an absolute guaranty.

guaranty of payment—absolute promise to pay when a debtor defaults.

indemnity contract—agreement by one person, for consideration, to pay another person a sum of money in the event that the other person sustains a specified loss.

against the guarantor and must first attempt to collect from the principal debtor.[2] An exception is an **absolute guaranty,** which creates the same obligation as a suretyship. A **guaranty of payment** creates an absolute guaranty and requires the guarantor to pay upon default by the principal debtor.

31-2b Indemnity Contract Distinguished

Both suretyship and guaranty differ from an **indemnity contract.** An indemnity contract is an undertaking by one person, for a consideration, to pay another person a sum of money in the event that the other person sustains a specified loss. **For Example,** a fire insurance policy is an indemnity contract. The insurance you obtain when you use a rental car is also an example of an indemnity contract.

31-2c Creation of the Relationship

Suretyship, guaranty, and indemnity relationships are based on contract. The principles relating to capacity, formation, validity, and interpretation of contracts are applicable. Generally, the ordinary rules of offer and acceptance apply. Notice of acceptance usually must be given by the obligee to the guarantor.

In most states, the statute of frauds requires that contracts of suretyship and guaranty be evidenced by a record to be enforceable. No record is required when the promise is made primarily for the promisor's benefit.

When the suretyship or guaranty is created at the same time as the original transaction, the consideration for the original promise that is covered by the guaranty is also consideration for the promise of the guarantor. When the suretyship or guaranty contract is entered into after and separate from the original transaction, there must be new consideration for the promise of the guarantor.

CASE SUMMARY

Widowed Husband Has Rights of Subrogation Against His Ex-Wife's Ex-Husband for Her Divorce Attorney's Fees

FACTS: Ellen Marshall, an attorney, represented Laureen Moran, the late wife of William M. Burke, M.D. (plaintiff) in their divorce proceedings. Marshall and Burke were involved in litigation after Burke refused to pay her fee for the divorce case, which the trial court had awarded and for which Burke had guaranteed payment.

In early 1999 Burke arranged a meeting with Marshall and Moran to discuss Marshall's representation of Moran in a post-divorce action initiated by Moran's former husband, John Izmirlian. Earlier, Marshall had told Burke that Izmirlian was dishonest, concealing his income from both the Internal Revenue Service and Moran. In that meeting, which lasted two hours, they talked almost exclusively about

Moran's legal situation. Burke once again mentioned that Izmirlian was attempting to hide his finances and that he wanted to ensure Izmirlian paid his support obligations. Moran said she was unable to pay for Marshall's services and Marshall herself knew that Moran had no steady means of supporting herself, that Izmirlian had no money, and that Moran had previously discharged a fee obligation of approximately $15,000 in bankruptcy proceedings. Consequently, Marshall raised the issue of payment, asserting that litigation would be expensive and that she could not proceed without payment. According to Marshall, Burke assured her that he was "willing to throw some money at this, so that that little prick pays to support his kid" (a daughter who had

[2] On the CPA exam, the term "guarantor of collection" is used to distinguish it from a surety and the differing obligations between these two categories of backups for debtors.

lived with Burke and Moran). With that assurance, Marshall and Moran signed a retainer agreement and Marshall commenced work on the case, including arranging a meeting between the parties, which turned out to be unproductive.

Moran became very ill and Marshall cautioned Izmirlian (defendant) and Moran against proceeding; however, Burke urged Marshall to continue and again promised to pay, which Marshall confirmed in a letter. Although Marshall never received payment during her representation of Moran, she did not demand payment during Moran's illness because she relied on Burke's promise and by then had only represented Moran for a short period. Both Moran and Burke, on the other hand, deny that Burke agreed to pay plaintiff's legal fees and costs on behalf of Moran. Burke admits paying a forensic accountant who aided Moran in tracking down Izmirlian's assets.

At the conclusion of the suit between Marshall and Izmirlian, Izmirlian was ordered to "pay a counsel fee of $32,177.29 to Ellen Marshall, Esq. in accordance with the order filed February 22, 2000." Izmirlian did not pay.

Burke filed a suit alleging that Izmirlian's breach of court orders caused him harm, including compelling his payment of Marshall's fees. The court entered a default judgment against Izmirlian but later vacated it.

Izmirlian then moved for summary judgment in Burke's case against him. The trial court granted summary judgment because Burke was not entitled to proceed because he had paid Marshall as a volunteer.

Burke appealed.

DECISION: Burke was a surety and that entitles him to step into his wife's shoes for purposes of collection of those fees. Burke had agreed to pay his wife's attorney's fees. If he pays them, his wife would be entitled to collect those fees from someone else (her ex-husband). Burke then steps into the shoes of his wife and is entitled to exercise the right to collect payment from the debtor Izmirlian. Here, Marshall needed to be paid, an obligation that belonged to Burke's wife, Moran. If Moran did not pay, and Burke does, then he is entitled to collect from the debtor. Burke had the right to enforce the judgment his wife won against the debtor on payment of child support. The agreement Burke had with Marshall made him a surety for Moran's payment. He can then collect from Moran's debtors, and Izmirlian was one of those debtors.

Reversed and remanded.

[*Burke v. Izmirlian*, Not Reported in A.3d, 2011 WL 1661022 (N.J. Super. A.D. 2011)]

CPA

31-2d Rights of Sureties

exoneration–agreement or provision in an agreement that one party shall not be held liable for loss; the right of the surety to demand that those primarily liable pay the claim for which the surety is secondarily liable.

subrogation–right of a party secondarily liable to stand in the place of the creditor after making payment to the creditor and to enforce the creditor's right against the party primarily liable in order to obtain indemnity from such primary party.

Sureties have a number of rights to protect them from loss, to obtain their discharge because of the conduct of others that would be harmful to them, or to recover money that they were required to pay because of the debtor's breach.

Exoneration

A surety can be exonerated from liability, a means of discharging or relieving liability, if the creditor could have taken steps to stop or limit the surety's exposure for the debt. **For Example,** suppose that the surety learns that a debtor is about to leave the state, an act that makes it more difficult to collect debts. The surety may call on the creditor to take action against the debtor to provide a literal and figurative roadblock to the debtor's planned departure. If the creditor could proceed against the debtor who is about to leave and thereby protect the repayment and fails to do so, the surety is released or **exonerated** from liability to the extent that the surety has been harmed by such failure.

Subrogation

When a surety pays a claim that it is obligated to pay, it automatically acquires the claim and the rights of the creditor. This stepping into the shoes or position of another is known as **subrogation.**[3] That is, once the creditor is paid in full, the surety stands in

[3] *SFI Ltd. Partnership 8 v. Carroll*, 851 N.W.2d 82 (Neb. 2014).

the same position as the creditor and may collect from the debtor or enforce any rights the creditor had against the debtor to recover the amount it has paid. The effect is the same as if the creditor, on being paid, made an express assignment of all rights to the surety. Likewise, the surety acquires any rights the debtor has against the creditor. **For Example,** if the creditor has not complied with statutory requirements, the surety can enforce those rights against the creditor just as the original debtor could.

> **indemnity**–right of a person secondarily liable to require that a person primarily liable pay for loss sustained when the secondary party discharges the obligation that the primary party should have discharged; an undertaking to pay another a sum of money to indemnify when loss is incurred.

Indemnity

A surety that has made payment of a claim for which it was liable as surety is entitled to **indemnity** from the principal debtor; that is, it is entitled to demand from the principal reimbursement of the amount that it has paid.

Contribution

> **contribution**–right of a co-obligor who has paid more than a proportionate share to demand that other obligors pay their *pro rata* share.

> **co-sureties**–sureties for the same debt.

If there are two or more sureties (known as co-sureties), each is liable to the creditor or claimant for the full amount of the debt until the claim or debt has been paid in full. Between themselves, however, each co-surety is liable only for a proportionate share of the debt. Accordingly, if a surety has paid more than its share of the debt, it is entitled to demand **contribution** from its **co-sureties.** In the absence of a contrary agreement, co-sureties must share the debt repayment on a *pro rata* basis. **For Example,** Aaron and Bobette are co-sureties of $40,000 and $60,000, respectively, for Christi's $60,000 loan. If Christi defaults, Aaron owes $24,000 and Bobette owes $36,000.

CPA

31-2e Defenses of Sureties

The surety's defenses include those that may be raised by a party to any contract and special defenses that are peculiar to the suretyship relationship.

Ordinary Contract Defenses

> **fraud**–intentional making a false statement of fact, with knowledge or reckless indifference that it is false with resulting reliance by another.

> **concealment**–failure to volunteer information not requested.

Because the relationship of suretyship is based on a contract, the surety may raise any defense that a party to an ordinary contract may raise. For example, a surety may raise the defense of lack of capacity of parties, absence of consideration, fraud, or mistake.

Fraud and **concealment** are common defenses. Fraud on the part of the principal that is unknown to the creditor and in which the creditor has not taken part does not ordinarily release the surety.

Because the risk of the principal debtor's default is thrown on the surety, it is unfair for a creditor to conceal from the surety facts that are material to the surety's risk. Under

THINKING THINGS THROUGH

Pro Rata Shares for Co-Sureties

AFC Corporation borrowed $90,000 from First Bank and demanded three sureties for the loan. Anna Flynn agreed to be a surety for $45,000 for AFC's debt. Frank Conlan agreed to be a surety for $60,000, and Charles Aspen agreed to be a surety for $75,000. When AFC owed $64,000, it defaulted on the loan and demanded payment from the co-sureties. However, Frank Conlan was in bankruptcy.

How much would Anna and Charles have to pay to First Bank?

common law, the creditor was not required to volunteer information to the surety and was not required to disclose that the principal was insolvent. A modern view that is receiving increased support is that the creditor should be required to inform the surety of matters material to the risk when the creditor has reason to believe that the surety does not possess such information.

CPA ## Suretyship Defenses

Perhaps the most important thing for a surety to understand is the type of defense that does not result in a discharge of her obligation in the suretyship. The insolvency or bankruptcy of the principal debtor does not discharge the surety. The financial risk of the principal debtor is the reason that a surety was obtained from the outset. The lack of enforcement of the debt by the creditor is not a defense to the surety's obligation or a discharge. The creditor's failure to give the surety notice of default is not a defense. The creditor's right, without a specific guaranty of collection, is simply to turn to the surety for payment.[4]

> **pledge**—bailment given as security for the payment of a debt or the performance of an obligation owed to the pledgee. (Parties—pledgor, pledgee)

In some cases, the creditor may have also taken a **pledge** of collateral for the debt in addition to the commitment of a surety. It is the creditor's choice as to whether to proceed against the collateral or the surety. If, however, the creditor proceeds first against the surety, the surety then has the right of exoneration and can step into the shoes of the creditor and repossess that collateral.

Changes in the terms of the loan agreement do not discharge a compensated surety. A surety who is acting gratuitously, however, would be discharged in the event of such changes. Changes in the loan terms that would discharge a gratuitous surety's obligation include extension of the loan terms and acceptance of late payments.[5]

A surety is discharged when the principal debtor performs his obligations under the original debt contract. If a creditor refuses to accept payment from a debtor, a surety is discharged.

A surety is also discharged, to the extent of the value of the collateral, if a creditor releases back to the debtor any collateral in the creditor's possession. **For Example,** suppose that Bank One has in its possession $10,000 in gold coins as collateral for a loan to Janice in the amount of $25,000. Albert has agreed to serve as a surety for the loan to Janice in the amount of $25,000. If a Bank One manager returns the $10,000 in coins to Janice, then Albert is discharged on his suretyship obligation to the extent of that $10,000. Following the release of the collateral, the most that Albert could be held liable for in the event of Janice's default is $15,000.

A surety is also discharged from her obligation if the creditor substitutes a different debtor. A surety and a guarantor make a promise that is personal to a specific debtor and do not agree to assume the risk of an assignment or a delegation of that responsibility to another debtor. A surety also enjoys the discharge rights afforded all parties to contracts, such as the statute of limitations. If the creditor does not enforce the suretyship agreement within the time limits provided for such contract enforcement in the surety's jurisdiction, the obligation is forever discharged.[6]

Figures 31-1 and 31-2 provide summaries of the defenses and release issues surrounding suretyship and guaranty relationships.

---

[4] *Rossa v. D.L. Falk Const., Inc.,* 266 P.3d 1022 (Cal. 2012).
[5] In re *Chemtura Corp.,* 448 B.R. 635 (S.D.N.Y. 2011).
[6] *Travelers Cas. and Sur. Co. of America v. Caridi,* 73 A.3d 863 (Conn. App. 2013).

CASE SUMMARY

The Bank Tries to Take the Sure Thing Away From the Surety

FACTS: Five Corners Rialto, LLC, obtained a construction loan from Vineyard Bank to develop a 70-unit townhome project (Project), with guaranties from Thomas DelPonti and David Wood, the principals of Five Corners (Guarantors). Five Corners contracted with Advent, Inc., a general contractor, to build the project in two phases. Everything went according to schedule for the first 18 months. However, when Phase I of the Project was nearly complete, the Bank stopped funding approved payment applications, preventing completion and sale of the Phase I units, which, in turn, caused Five Corners to default on the loan.

The Bank reached an agreement with Five Corners, requiring Advent to finish Phase I so the units could be sold at auction and promising to pay the subcontractors if they discounted their bills and released any liens. Advent paid the subcontractors out of its own pocket in order to keep the project lien-free so the auction could proceed. However, the Bank foreclosed against Five Corners. The Bank (through its assignee California Bank and Trust), sued Five Corners and the Guarantors under various theories for the deficiency following a Trustee's Sale of the Deed of Trust, while Advent sued the developer and the Bank for restitution for the amounts it paid out of pocket.

The cases were consolidated and tried. The court awarded judgment in favor of Advent. The court found that the Bank breached the loan contract, exonerating the Guarantors. The court awarded attorneys' fees to Advent and the Guarantors.

The Bank appealed.

DECISION: The court held that the Guarantors had done everything expected of them and performed according to the new agreement to the extent the Bank permitted. The court did not agree with the Bank's argument that the Guarantors waived all of their defenses.

A guarantor cannot be held liable where a contract is unlawful or contravenes public policy. The rule against enforcement of illegal transactions is founded on considerations of public policy.

A guarantor's waiver of defenses is limited to legal and statutory defenses expressly set out in the agreement. A waiver of statutory defenses does not waive all defenses, especially *equitable defenses*, such as unclean hands, where to enforce the guaranty would allow a lender to profit by its own fraudulent conduct. In all suretyship and guaranty relations, the creditor owes the surety a duty of continuous good faith and fair dealing. This duty was not waived by the Guarantors in the agreement.

The judgment was affirmed in full. Advent and the Guarantors were awarded costs on appeal. [*California Bank & Trust v. DelPonti*, 232 Cal. App. 4th 162 (Cal. App. 2014)]

FIGURE 31-1	No Release of Surety

1. Fraud by debtor

2. Misrepresentation by debtor

3. Changes in loan terms (e.g., Extension of payment)—compensated surety only

4. Release of principal debtor

5. Bankruptcy of principal debtor

6. Insolvency of principal debtor

7. Death of principal debtor

8. Incapacity of principal debtor

9. Lack of enforcement by creditor

10. Creditor's failure to give notice of default

11. Failure of creditor to resort to collateral

FIGURE 31-2	Release of Surety

1. Proper performance by debtor
2. Release, surrender, or destruction of collateral (to extent of value of collateral)
3. Substitution of debtor
4. Fraud/misrepresentation by creditor
5. Refusal by creditor to accept payment from debtor
6. Change in loan terms—uncompensated surety only
7. Statute of frauds
8. Statute of limitations

31-3 Letters of Credit

letter of credit–
commercial device used
to guarantee payment to
a seller, primarily in an
international business
transaction.

issuer–party who issues
a document such as a
letter of credit or a
document of title such as
a warehouse receipt or
bill of lading.

standby letter–letter of
credit for a contractor
ensuring he will
complete the project as
contracted.

A **letter of credit** is a three-party arrangement with a payor, a beneficiary, and a party on whom the letter of credit is drawn, or **issuer.** A letter of credit is an agreement that the issuer of the letter will pay drafts drawn by the beneficiary of the letter. Letters of credit are a form of advance arrangement for financing. Sellers of goods, for example, know in advance how much money may be obtained from the issuer of the letter. A letter of credit may also be used by a creditor as a security device because the creditor knows that the drafts that the creditor draws will be accepted or paid by the issuer of the letter.[7]

The use of letters of credit arose in international trade. While international trade continues to be the primary area of use, there is a growing use of letters in domestic sales and in transactions in which the letter of credit takes the place of a surety bond. A letter of credit has been used to ensure that a borrower would repay a loan, that a tenant would pay the rent due under a lease, and that a contractor would properly perform a construction contract. This kind of letter of credit is known as a **standby letter.**

There are few formal requirements for creating a letter of credit. Although banks often use a standardized form for convenience, they may draw up individualized letters of credit for particular situations (Figure 31-3).

In international letters of credit, there are several sources of recognized standards that businesses use for the creation and execution of letters of credit. Along with the UCC, there is the Uniform Customs and Practice for Documentary Credits (or UCP), something that reflects ordinary international banking operational practices on letters of credit. The UCP is revised, generally, about every 10 years by the International Chamber of Commerce (ICC, see Chapter 7).

31-3a Definition

A letter of credit is an engagement by its issuer that it will pay or accept drafts when the conditions specified in the letter are satisfied. The issuer is usually a bank.

Three contracts are involved in letter-of-credit transactions: (1) the contract between the issuer and the customer of the issuer, (2) the letter of credit itself, and (3) the

[7] *Rafool v. Evans*, 497 B.R. 312 (C.D. Ill. 2013), discussing the character and purpose of letters of credit. See also *City of Maple Grove v. Marketline Const. Capital, LLC*, 802 N.W.2d 809 (Minn. App. 2011) for discussion of fact that a document is not a letter of credit if it requires verification of an outside event, as opposed to submission of documents.

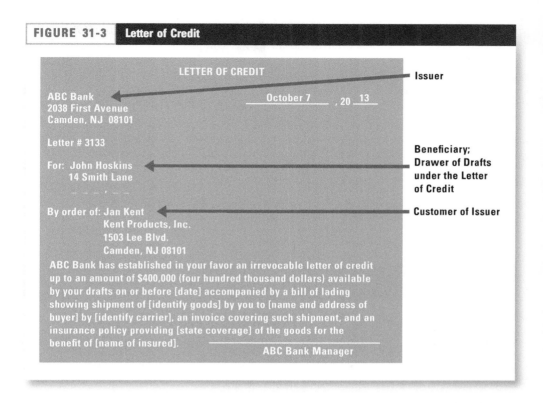

FIGURE 31-3 | **Letter of Credit**

underlying agreement, often a contract of sale, between the beneficiary and the customer of the issuer of the letter of credit (Figure 31-4).

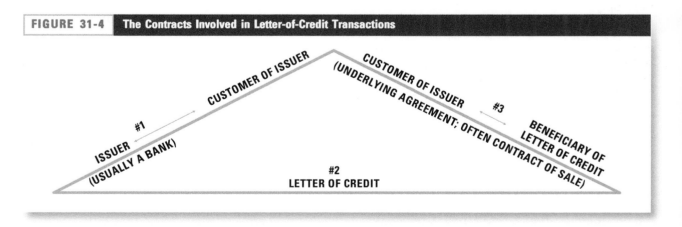

FIGURE 31-4 | **The Contracts Involved in Letter-of-Credit Transactions**

The letter of credit is completely independent from the other two contracts. Consideration is not required to establish or modify a letter of credit.

The issuer of the letter of credit is, in effect, the obligor on a third-party-beneficiary contract made for the benefit of the beneficiary of the letter. The key to the commercial success of letters of credit is their independence. **For Example,** a bank obligated to issue payment under a letter of credit "when the goods are delivered" must honor that obligation even if the buyer has complaints about the goods. It is the terms of the letter of credit that control the payment, not the relationship, contract, or problems of the beneficiary or issuer of the letter of credit.

The key to the commercial vitality and function of a letter of credit is that the issuing bank's promise is independent of the underlying contracts and the bank should not resort to them in interpreting a letter of credit. Sometimes called *the strict compliance rule*, banks must honor the letter of credit terms using strict interpretation. The respective parties are protected by a careful description of the documents that will trigger payment. The claim of a beneficiary of a letter of credit is not subject to defenses normally applicable to third-party contracts. Known as the *independence rule*, banks cannot, except in limited circumstances, delve into the underlying contract issues; the focus of the bank is only on the terms of the letter of credit.

CASE SUMMARY

The Letter of Credit and the Shoddy Mall

FACTS: In 2007, Wood Center Properties (WCP) entered into a Purchase and Sale Agreement to buy five shopping centers from Robert B. Greene and Louisville Mall Associates, LP, and several other mall property groups (collectively, the "Mall Appellants"). While performing its due diligence, WCP discovered environmental contamination at the Crestwood Shopping Center, one of the shopping centers it intended to purchase. A prior shopping center tenant, Crestwood Coin Laundry (Tenant), spilled hazardous chemicals used in its dry cleaning business. As a result of the contamination, WCP chose not to purchase Crestwood Shopping Center, and the parties amended the Purchase and Sale Agreement to reflect WCP's decision.

Shortly thereafter, Greene offered to provide WCP with an irrevocable Letter of Credit, issued by M & T Bank, in the amount of $200,000.00. The Letter of Credit's purpose was to insulate WCP from liability and fund the environmental cleanup if the Tenant failed to do so. With that inducement, Crestwood Shopping Center was put back in the contract as one of the properties being purchased by WCP. Paragraph two of the amended contract provided:

> At closing, Robert M. Greene, individually, shall deliver an irrevocable letter of credit for the benefit of Wood Center Properties, LLC in the amount of Two Hundred Thousand Dollars ($200,000.00) drawn on M & T Bank. This letter of credit shall extend for one (1) year from the date of Closing, and shall automatically renew for one (1) additional year unless Notice of non-renewal is given to [WCP] at

least 60 days prior to the expiration date on the face of the Greene Letter of Credit.

On June 13, 2007, M & T Bank issued the Letter of Credit for the benefit of WCP. The Letter of Credit contained an original expiration date of June 12, 2008, that provided:

> It is a condition of this credit that it shall be deemed automatically extended without amendment for one (1) year from the expiration date hereof, or any future expiration date, unless sixty (60) days prior to any expiration date M & T Bank notifies [WCP] in writing that M & T Bank elects not to consider this credit renewed for any such additional period.

On April 7, 2008, M & T Bank automatically renewed the Letter of Credit for a second year and provided WCP and Greene with a letter of renewal, notifying them that the Letter of Credit's new expiration date was June 12, 2009. On March 6, 2009, M & T Bank sent a second renewal letter to WCP and Greene, again giving notice that it was automatically extending the Letter of Credit for a third year and its new expiration date was June 12, 2010.

After receiving M & T Bank's March 6, 2009, letter, Greene told M & T Bank his view that the Letter of Credit was only valid for two years and should expire on June 12, 2009. Greene requested that M & T not renew the credit. Despite Greene's request, M & T did not send a nonrenewal notification to WCP. WCP sought payment under the Letter of Credit and submitted the documents to M & T that were necessary for payment.

The Letter of Credit and the Shoddy Mall continued

WCP filed a declaratory judgment action seeking the court's ruling that WCP was entitled to draw on the Letter of Credit. The court entered summary declaratory judgment in WCP's favor. Greene appealed.

DECISION: A letter of credit must be interpreted on its face, independent of other contracts and the underlying transaction. The underlying contract between the customer and the beneficiary should not be considered in interpreting the letter of credit, and should not be used to supplement or amplify the terms of the letter of credit or to add obligations thereto.

The Letter of Credit itself expressly provides that its terms shall not be amplified or interpreted by reference to any outside document.

The issuer is neither expected nor entitled to look beyond the pieces of paper to determine whether the statements they contain are true, or to determine whether under its agreement with the applicant, the beneficiary has the right to make demand under the letter of credit.

M & T Bank was only required to examine the documents presented by WCP to determine if they complied with the terms and conditions of the Letter of Credit; M & T Bank was not required to look beyond the documents to determine whether WCP's statement that it complied with [the contract] was, in fact, accurate. The court properly awarded WCP summary judgment. [*Louisville Mall Associates, LP v. Wood Center Properties, LLC,* 361 S.W.3d 323 (Ky. App. 2012)]

31-3b Parties

The parties to a letter of credit are (1) the issuer; (2) the customer who makes the arrangements with the issuer; and (3) the beneficiary, who will be the drawer of the drafts that will be drawn under the letter of credit. There may also be (4) an **advising bank**[8] if the local issuer of the letter of credit requests its **correspondent bank,** where the beneficiary is located, to notify or advise the beneficiary that the letter has been issued. **For Example,** a U.S. merchant may want to buy goods from a Spanish merchant. There may have been prior dealings between the parties so that the seller is willing to take the buyer's commercial paper as payment or to take trade acceptances drawn on the buyer. If the foreign seller is not willing to do this, the U.S. buyer, as customer, may go to a bank, the issuer, and obtain a letter of credit naming the Spanish seller as beneficiary. The U.S. bank's correspondent or advising bank in Spain will notify the Spanish seller that this has been done. The Spanish seller will then draw drafts on the U.S. buyer. Under the letter of credit, the issuer is required to accept or pay these drafts.

advising bank–bank that tells beneficiary that letter of credit has been issued.

correspondent bank–will honor the letter of credit from the domestic bank of the buyer.

31-3c Duration

A letter of credit continues for any length of time it specifies. Generally, a maximum money amount is stated in the letter, so that the letter is exhausted or used up when the issuer has accepted or paid drafts aggregating that maximum. A letter of credit may be used in installments as the beneficiary chooses. The issuer or the customer cannot revoke or modify a letter of credit without the consent of the beneficiary unless that right is expressly reserved in the letter.

31-3d Form

A letter of credit must be in writing and signed by the issuer. If the credit is issued by a bank and requires a documentary draft or a documentary demand for payment[9] or if the

---

[8] See U.C.C. §5-107; *Speedway Motorsports Intern. Ltd. v. Bronwen Energy Trading, Ltd.,* 706 S.E.2d 262 (N.C. 2011).
[9] A *documentary draft* or a *documentary demand for payment* is one for which honor is conditioned on the presentation of one or more documents. A document could be a document of title, security, invoice, certificate, notice of default, or other similar paper. U.C.C. §5-103(1)(b).

credit is issued by a nonbank and requires that the draft or demand for payment be accompanied by a document of title, the instrument is presumed to be a letter of credit (rather than a contract of guaranty). Otherwise, the instrument must conspicuously state that it is a letter of credit.

31-3e Duty of Issuer

The issuer is obligated to honor drafts drawn under the letter of credit if the conditions specified in the letter have been satisfied. The issuer takes the risk that the papers submitted are the ones required by the letter. If they are not, the issuer cannot obtain reimbursement for payment made in reliance on such documents. The issuer has no duty to verify that the papers are properly supported by facts or that the underlying transaction has been performed. It is immaterial that the goods sold by the seller in fact do not conform to the contract so long as the seller tenders the documents specified by the letter of credit. If the issuer dishonors a draft without justification, it is liable to its customer for breach of contract.[10]

ETHICS & THE LAW

When the Creditors Rule the Debtor

Very often the creditors of a business can exercise a great deal of authority over the operation of the business when it has missed a payment on its debt or has experienced some business or market setbacks. Without owning any stock in a corporation, creditors will, in more than 50 percent of all cases in which they express concern about repayment, succeed in having both boards and officers replaced in part or in toto. **For Example,** Worlds of Wonder, Inc., a creative and innovative toy manufacturer that was responsible for the first talking toy, Teddy Ruxpin, was required by demands from its secured and unsecured creditors to obtain the resignation of its founder and CEO, Donald Kingsborough. Kingsborough was paid $212,500 at his departure for "emotional distress."* For example, in 2009, the federal government, as a lender, required that the CEO of General Motors resign as a condition to receiving additional funds from the government to cover debt payments. In addition, the federal government negotiated the positions of union workers, investors, and hedge funds in the Chrysler Corporation restructuring as a condition of its receipt of federal funds.

Studies show** that creditors also have input on the following corporate actions:

Type of Decision	Percentage of Creditors with Vote
Declaration of dividends	48
Increased security	73
Restructuring of debt	55
Cap on borrowing	50
Cap on capital expenses	25
Restrictions on investment	23

Is it fair to have creditors control corporate governance? What are the risks for shareholders when creditors control the management of a company?

*"Toymaker Has Financing Pact," *New York Times*, April 2, 1988, C1 (Reuters item).
See Tim Reason, "Keeping Skin in the Game," *CFO Magazine*, February 1, 2005, **http://www.cfo.com, for a discussion of why creditors are involved and what they can do to help manage a debtor.

---

[10] *CRM Collateral II, Inc. v. TriCounty Metropolitan Transp. Dist of Oregon*, 669 F.3d 963 (9th Cir. 2012). In some cases, letters of credit are so poorly drafted that payment must be made despite evolving concerns by the parties. *Nissho Iwai Europe PLC v. Korea First Bank*, 782 N.E.2d 55 (N.Y. 2002).

31-3f Reimbursement of Issuer

When the issuer of a letter of credit makes proper payment of drafts drawn under the letter of credit, it may obtain reimbursement from its customer for such payment. Examples of improper payment include payment made after the letter has expired or a payment that is in excess of the amount authorized by the letter. No reimbursement is possible if the payment is made without the proper presentation of required documents or if the payment is made in violation of a court injunction against payment.

Make the Connection

Summary

Suretyship and guaranty undertakings have the common feature of a promise to answer for the debt or default of another. The terms are used interchangeably, but a guarantor of collection is ordinarily only secondarily liable, which means that the guarantor does not pay until the creditor has exhausted all avenues of recovery. If the guarantor has made an absolute guaranty, then its status is the same as that of a surety, which means that both are liable for the debt in the event the debtor defaults, regardless of what avenues of collection, if any, the creditor has pursued.

Surety and guaranty relationships are based on contract. Sureties have a number of rights to protect them. They are exoneration, subrogation, indemnity, and contribution. In addition to those rights, sureties also have certain defenses. They include ordinary contract defenses as well as some defenses peculiar to the suretyship relationship, such as release of collateral, change in loan terms, substitution of debtor, and fraud by the creditor.

A letter of credit is an agreement that the issuer of the letter will pay drafts drawn on the issuer by the beneficiary of the letter. The issuer of the letter of credit is usually a bank. There are three contracts involved in letter-of-credit transactions: (1) the contract between the issuer and the customer of the issuer, (2) the letter of credit itself, and (3) the underlying agreement between the beneficiary and the customer of the issuer of the letter of credit.

The parties to a letter of credit are the issuer, the customer who makes the arrangement with the issuer, and the beneficiary who will be the drawer of the drafts to be drawn under the letter of credit. The letter of credit continues for any time it specifies. The letter of credit must be in writing and signed by the issuer. Consideration is not required to establish or modify a letter of credit. If the conditions in the letter of credit have been complied with, the issuer is obligated to honor drafts drawn under the letter of credit.

Learning Outcomes

After studying this chapter, you should be able to clearly explain:

31-1   Creation of the Credit Relationship

31-2   Suretyship and Guaranty

LO.1   Distinguish a contract of suretyship from a contract of guaranty
> See the definitions and discussion of the terms related to surety and guaranty, pages 602–603.

LO.2   Define the parties to a contract of suretyship and a contract of guaranty
> See the example on corporate officers and their relationship with company debt, page 602.
> See the *Burke v. Izmirlian* case, pages 603–604.

LO.3   List and explain the rights of sureties to protect themselves from loss
> See the discussion of contribution, page 605.
> See the Thinking Things Through Feature, *Pro Rata Shares for Co-Sureties*, on page 605.

LO.4   Explain the defenses available to sureties
> See the *California Bank & Trust v. DelPonti* case, page 607.

31-3   Letters of Credit

LO.5   Explain the nature of a letter of credit and the liabilities of the various parties to a letter of credit
> See the *Louisville Mall Associates, LP v. Wood Center Properties, LLC,* case, pages 610–611.

Key Terms

absolute guaranty	fraud	obligee
advising bank	guarantor	obligor
concealment	guaranty	pledge
contribution	guaranty of collection	principal
correspondent bank	guaranty of payment	principal debtor
co-sureties	indemnity	standby letter
creditor	indemnity contract	subrogation
debtor	issuer	surety
exoneration	letter of credit	suretyship

Questions and Case Problems

1. First Interstate Bank issued a letter of credit in favor of Comdata Network. Comdata is engaged in money transfer services. It provides money to truckers on the road by way of cash advances through form checks written by truckers. When Comdata enters into a business relationship with a trucking company, it requires a letter of credit. This requirement is to secure advances made on behalf of the trucking company. One of the trucking companies defrauded the bank that issued the letter of credit. Comdata demanded that the bank make payment to it under the letter of credit for cash advances that the trucking company had not repaid. The bank, alleging fraud by the trucking company, refused. Comdata filed suit. Can Comdata force payment? [*Comdata Network, Inc. v. First Interstate Bank of Fort Dodge*, 497 N.W.2d 807 (Iowa App.)]

2. LaBarge Pipe & Steel Company agreed to sell PVF $143,613.40 of 30-inch pipe provided that PVF obtain a letter of credit for $144,000, with the letter of credit entitling LaBarge to payment if PVF did not pay for the pipe within 30 days of invoice. PVF obtained the letter of credit from First Bank but received only a facsimile copy of it. The letter of credit required LaBarge to submit the original of the letter of credit for a demand of payment.

    PVF did not pay within 30 days and LaBarge submitted a facsimile copy of the letter of credit and requested payment. First Bank denied the request for payment and LaBarge filed suit against First Bank for failure to pay. LaBarge argued that it was not disputed that PVF had not paid on the contract and First Bank was required to pay on the letter of credit. How would you explain First Bank's rights to LaBarge? [*LaBarge Pipe & Steel Co. v. First Bank*, 550 F.3d 442 (5th Cir.)]

3. On August 1, 1987, Dori Leeds signed a "guarantee of credit" with Sun Control Systems, which guaranteed "the prompt payment, when due, of every claim of [Sun Control Systems] against [Dori Leeds dba 'Blind Ambitions']." At the time she signed the guarantee of credit, Blind Ambitions was in the business of installing window treatments and installed only Faber brand blinds, which were purchased from Sun Control Systems. In 1991, Sun Control Systems sold and assigned all of its assets to Faber. Shortly thereafter, Dori assigned her interest in Blind Ambitions to David and Judith Leeds, who continued to do business as Blind Ambitions. In 1994 and 1995, Blind Ambitions made credit purchases from Faber and did not pay under the terms of those contracts. Faber brought suit against Dori Leeds as the guarantor of credit for Blind Ambitions. Dori refused to pay on the grounds that she was acting as a personal guarantor for her business, not for Blind Ambitions. Is she correct? [*Faber Industries, Ltd. v. Dori Leeds Witek*, 483 S.E.2d 443 (N.C. App.)]

4. Fern Schimke's husband, Norbert, was obligated on two promissory notes in favor of Union National Bank. Some time prior to his death, Union National Bank prepared a guaranty contract that was given to Norbert for his wife to sign. She signed the guaranty at the request of her husband without any discussion with him about the provisions of the document she was signing. On Norbert's death, the bank brought suit against Fern on the basis of the guaranty. Fern argued that because there was no consideration for the guaranty, she could not be liable. Is Fern correct? Must there be consideration for a guarantor to be responsible for payment? [*Union Nat'l Bank v. Fern Schimke*, 210 N.W.2d 176 (N.D.)]

5. In May 1989, Alma Equities Corp., owned by its sole shareholder and president, Lewis Futterman, purchased a hotel and restaurant in Vail, Colorado, from Alien for $3,900,000. Alma paid $600,000 in cash to Alien, and Alien provided a purchase money loan to Alma for the remaining amount of the sale price, with the loan secured by a deed of trust on the hotel and restaurant. The hotel and restaurant did not do well, and Futterman negotiated a friendly foreclosure on the property in 1991, whereby Alma would continue to operate the hotel and restaurant on a lease basis, with Futterman providing a personal guaranty for the lease. Alma failed to make the lease payments for the months of November and December 1991 and, following an unlawful detainer action filed by Alien for possession of the hotel and restaurant, was forced into bankruptcy. Alien turned to Futterman for satisfaction on the lease payments. Futterman said he should not have been forced to pay because Alien's unlawful detainer forced Alma into bankruptcy. Was Futterman correct? Did he have a defense? [*Alien, Inc. v. Futterman*, 924 P.2d 1063 (Colo.)]

6. Crown Corporation has borrowed $16,000,000 from Third Bank. Third Bank required four sureties for the loan. The sureties are as follows:

Andover	$4,000,0000
Busch	$8,000,0000
Chapman	$2,000,0000
Davidson	$2,000,0000

Crown has defaulted on the loan after paying back $4,000,000. How much will each surety be required to pay? What if Busch was bankrupt? How much would Andover, Chapman, and Davidson have to pay?

7. Tri County Truck & Diesel borrowed $165,000 from Security State Bank and pledged its inventory as security for the loan. In addition, Fred and Randelle Burk agreed to act as sureties for the loan. Tri County defaulted on the loan and Security Bank repossessed the collateral. The inventory was damaged while Security Bank held it, and as a result, the sale of the inventory brought only $5,257.50 at a public auction. The Burks raised the defense of the damages as a setoff to their surety amount for the remainder of the loan. Security Bank said the Burks could not raise the damages as a defense because the Burks were sureties and had guaranteed the full amount of the loan. The trial court granted summary judgment for Security Bank, and the Burks appealed. What should the court do? [*Security State Bank v. Burk*, 995 P.2d 1272 (Wash App.)]

8. UPS Capital Business Credit agreed to loan Ashford International, Inc, an American company based in Atlanta, Georgia, for the sale of computers to the Ministry of Education in Jordan. Ashford was required to obtain a letter of credit from United California Discount Corporation (UCDC) for the loan. Ashford filed for bankruptcy and UPS submitted documentation for payment on the letter of credit. UCDC responded to the payment demand with a list of requirements for compliance with the letter of credit demands. UPS satisfied all the demands and UCDC then refused to pay because UPS did not submit original documents as required by the letter of credit. UPS maintains that UCDC waived that requirement by not listing it in its demands. Who is correct and why? [*Export-Import Bank of the U.S. v. United Cal. Discount Corp.*, 738 F. Supp. 2d 1047 (C.D. Cal.)]

9. Ribaldgo Argo Consultores entered into a contract with R. M. Wade & Co. for the purchase of irrigation equipment. Ribaldgo obtained a letter of credit from Banco General, a bank with its principal place of business in Quito, Ecuador. The letter of credit required that Wade submit certain documents to obtain payment. The documents were submitted through Citibank as correspondent bank for Banco General. However, the documents were incomplete, and Citibank demanded additional information as required under the letter of credit. By the time Wade got the documents to Citibank, more than 15 days had expired, and the letter of credit required that Wade submit all documentation within 15 days of shipping the goods to obtain payment. Citibank refused to authorize the payment. Wade filed suit. Must Citibank pay? Why or why not? [*Banco General Runinahui, S.A. v. Citibank International*, 97 F.3d 480 (11th Cir.)]

10. Hugill agreed to deliver shingles to W. I. Carpenter Lumber Co. and furnished a surety bond to secure the faithful performance of the contract on his part. After a breach of the contract by Hugill, the lumber company brought an action to recover its loss from the surety, Fidelity & Deposit Co. of Maryland. The surety denied liability on the grounds that there was concealment of (a) the price to be paid for the shingles and (b) the fact that a material advance had been made to the contractor equal to the amount of

the profit that he would make by performing the contract. Decide. [*W. I. Carpenter Lumber Co. v. Hugill*, 270 P.94 (Wash.)]

11. Donaldson sold plumbing supplies. The St. Paul-Mercury Indemnity Co., as surety for him, executed and delivered a bond to the state of California for the payment of all sales taxes. Donaldson failed to pay, and the surety paid the taxes that he owed and then sued him for the taxes. What was the result? [*St. Paul-Mercury Indemnity Co. v. Donaldson*, 83 S.E.2d 159 (S.C.)]

12. Paul owed Charles a $1,000 debt due September 1. On August 15, George, for consideration, orally promised Charles to pay the debt if Paul did not. On September 1, Paul did not pay, so Charles demanded $1,000 from George. Is George liable? Why or why not?

13. First National Bank hired Longdon as a secretary and obtained a surety bond from Belton covering the bank against losses up to $100,000 resulting from Longdon's improper conduct in the performance of his duties. Both Longdon and the bank signed the application for the bond. After one year of service, Longdon was promoted to teller, and the original bond remained in effect. Shortly after Longdon's promotion, examination showed that Longdon had taken advantage of his new position and stolen $50,000. He was arrested and charged with embezzlement. Longdon had only $5,000 in assets at the time of his arrest. (a) If the bank demands a payment of $50,000 from Belton, what defense, if any, might Belton raise to deny any obligation to the bank? (b) If Belton fully reimburses the bank for its loss, under what theory or theories, if any, may Belton attempt to recover from Longdon?

14. Jack Smith was required by his bank to obtain two sureties for his line of credit of $100,000. Ellen Weiss has agreed to act as a surety for $50,000, and Allen Fox has agreed to act as a surety for $75,000. Smith has used the full $100,000 in the line of credit and is now in bankruptcy. What is the maximum liability of Weiss and Fox if the bank chooses to collect from them for Smith's default? How should the $100,000 be allocated between Weiss and Fox?

15. Industrial Mechanical had a contract with Free Flow Cooling, Ltd., a British company. Free Flow owed Industrial $171,974.44 for work Industrial had performed on a construction project in Texas. Free Flow did not pay Industrial, and Industrial filed suit against Siemens Energy & Automation as a guarantor or surety on the debt. Industrial alleges that Siemens is a surety based on a fax it received from Siemens on January 27, 1994. The fax is handwritten and states: "We have received preliminary notices and we like [sic] to point out that the contract we have signed does not allow for such action to recourse [sic] with the customer. Please advise all subcontractors and suppliers that the only recourse that they will have is against Siemens." The fax was signed "kind regards" by Arnold Schultz, Siemens's senior project manager for the Texas construction project. Nowhere in the fax did Siemens guarantee the debt of any specified entity or state that Siemens was agreeing to indemnify anyone or pay the obligations on behalf of anyone else. The fax failed to identify the principal debtor whom Siemens purportedly agreed to indemnify and failed to state that Siemens agreed to answer for that entity's debt. Can Industrial collect the amount of Free Flow's debt from Siemens? Why or why not? [*Industrial Mechanical, Inc. v. Siemens Energy & Automation, Inc.*, 495 S.E.2d 103 (Ga. App.)]

CPA Questions

1. Marbury Surety, Inc., agreed to act as a guarantor of collection of Madison's trade accounts for one year beginning on April 30, 1980, and was compensated for same. Madison's trade debtors are in default in payment of $3,853 as of May 1, 1981. As a result:

   a. Marbury is liable to Madison without any action on Madison's part to collect the amounts due.

   b. Madison can enforce the guaranty even if it is not in writing because Marbury is a del credere agent.

   c. The relationship between the parties must be filed in the appropriate county office because it is a continuing security transaction.

   d. Marbury is liable for those debts for which a judgment is obtained and returned unsatisfied.

2. Queen paid Pax and Co. to become the surety on a loan that Queen obtained from Squire. The loan is due, and Pax wishes to compel Queen to pay Squire. Pax has not made any payments to Squire in its capacity as Queen's surety. Pax will be most successful if it exercises its right to:

   a. Reimbursement (indemnification).

   b. Contribution.

   c. Exoneration.

   d. Subrogation.

3. Which of the following defenses by a surety will be effective to avoid liability?

   a. Lack of consideration to support the surety undertaking.

   b. Insolvency in the bankruptcy sense of the debtor.

   c. Incompetency of the debtor to make the contract in question.

   d. Fraudulent statements by the principal debtor that induced the surety to assume the obligation and that were unknown to the creditor.

4. For each of the numbered words or phrases, select the one best phrase from the list a through j. Each response may be used only once.

   (1) Indemnity contract

   (2) Suretyship contract

   (3) Surety

   (4) Third-party beneficiary

   (5) Co-surety

   (6) Statute of frauds

   (7) Right of contribution

   (8) Reimbursement

   (9) Subrogation

   (10) Exoneration

   a. Relationship whereby one person agrees to answer for the debt or default of another.

   b. Requires certain contracts to be in writing to be enforceable.

   c. Jointly and severally liable to creditor.

   d. Promises to pay debt on default of principal debtor.

   e. One party promises to reimburse debtor for payment of debt or loss if it arises.

   f. Receives intended benefits of a contract.

   g. Right of surety to require the debtor to pay before surety pays.

   h. Upon payment of more than his/her proportionate share, each co-surety may compel other co-sureties to pay their shares.

   i. Upon payment of debt, surety may recover payment from debtor.

   j. Upon payment, surety obtains same rights against debtor that creditor had.

5. When a principal debtor defaults and a surety pays the creditor the entire obligation, which of the following remedies gives the surety the best method of collecting from the debtor?

   a. Exoneration

   b. Contribution

   c. Subrogation

   d. Attachment

6. Which of the following bonds are an obligation of a surety?

   a. Convertible bonds

   b. Debenture bonds

   c. Municipal bonds

   d. Official bonds

Consumer Protection

32-1 General Principles

The consumer protection movement, which began in the 1960s, continues to expand with rights for consumers in everything from ads to credit collection. Consumer protection began with the goal of protecting persons of limited means and limited knowledge. One writer described consumer protection statutes as laws that protect "the little guy."[1] Over the past 20 years, however, that protection has expanded considerably in both who is protected and the types of activities that are regulated or provide consumers with statutory remedies.

32-1a Expansion of Consumer Protection

Some statutes are worded so that consumer protections apply only to natural persons. Some statutes are interpreted to apply only to consumer transactions, not to commercial transactions. However, many consumer protection statutes, once limited to individuals, now include partnerships, corporations, banks, or government entities that use goods or services as consumers. The statutes thus go beyond providing protection only for the unsophisticated and uneducated.[2] **For Example,** in defining **consumer,** courts have held that a collector paying nearly $100,000 for jade art objects, a glass manufacturer purchasing 3 million gallons of diesel oil fuel, and the city of Boston purchasing insurance are all consumers for purposes of statutory protections. Some states, such as Arizona, Arkansas, Delaware, Illinois, Iowa, Missouri, and New Jersey, even have two separate statutes, one for the protection of individual consumers and another for the protection of businesses. In addition, the protected consumer may be a firm of attorneys.[3]

> **consumer**–any buyer afforded special protections by statute or regulation.

Today, all 50 states and the District of Columbia have some version of what are called "Little FTC Acts" (the Federal Trade Commission Act [which created the FTC] discussed later in the chapter is the federal consumer protection statute that prohibits unfair or deceptive practices) or "unfair or deceptive acts or practices" ("UDAP") statutes. Although there are 51 versions of consumer protection statutes, they have several common threads. First, consumer protection statutes provide faster remedies for consumers. Statutory remedies under consumer protection statutes often mean that consumers need not establish that a tort has been committed or establish actual damage levels because the statute provides for both the elements for recovery and perhaps even a formula for recovery of damages. Second, the harms addressed by consumer statutes tend to affect the public generally and involve more than just one contract or even one seller. **For Example,** one area of consumer protection provides consumers control over both the release and content of their credit report information. The use of credit information, the granting of credit, and the use of credit to make purchases all have a profound impact on buyers, sellers, and national, state, and local economies. These protections provide a statutory formula for consumer damages when credit information is misused or is incorrect.

32-1b Who Is a Consumer?

A consumer claiming a violation of the consumer protection statute has the burden of proving that the statutory definition of consumer has been satisfied. The business accused

---

[1] Olha N. M. Rybakoff, "An Overview of Consumer Protection and Fair Trade Regulation in Delaware," 8 *Delaware L. Rev.* 63 (2005). This article provides a good history and summary of consumer protection laws.

[2] *Prime Ins. Co. v. Imperial Fire and Cas. Ins. Co.,* 151 So. 3d 670 (La. App. 2014). *Garden Catering-Hamilton Avenue, LLC v. Wally's Chicken Coop, LLC,* 30 F. Supp. 3d 117 (D. Conn. 2014).

[3] Statutes that broaden the protected group to protect buyers of goods and services are often called *deceptive trade practices statutes* instead of being referred to by the earlier term, *consumer protection statutes.* But see *Lifespan of Minnesota, Inc. v. Minneapolis Public Schools Independent School Dist. No. 1,* 841 N.W.2d 656 (Minn. App. 2014).

of unfair or deceptive trade practices then has the burden of showing that the statute does *not* apply as well as establishing exceptions and exemptions. **For Example,** some consumer protection statutes do not apply when a buyer is purchasing goods for resale.

32-1c Who Is Liable under Consumer Protection Statutes?

Those who are liable for violations of consumer protection situations are persons or enterprises that regularly enter into the type of transaction in which the injured consumer was involved. **For Example,** the merchant seller, the finance company, the bank, the leasing company, the home contractor, and any others who regularly enter into transactions with consumers are subject to the statutes. Some consumer protection statutes apply only to specific types of merchants and service providers such as auto repair and sale statutes, funeral home disclosure statutes and regulations, and swimming pool contractors.

32-1d When Is There Liability under Consumer Protection Statutes?

Consumer protection laws typically list the types of conduct that are prohibited as well as failures to act properly that are harmful to consumers. For example, the failure to disclose all of the charges related to a consumer loan or a credit purchase made by a consumer would be an omission that carries rights for the consumers and penalties for the business. *Deceptive advertising* is an act that is prohibited by consumer protection statutes that provide remedies for consumers who were deceived or misled by the ads. Deceptive advertising that is listed and described in detail in the consumer protection statutes is often easier for consumers to prove than a common law case of fraud. Consumer protection statutes do not require proof of intent. An ad might not have seemed deceptive to the merchant selling computers when he reviewed the ad copy for the newspaper. However, a consumer without the merchant's sophistication could be misled. **For Example,** suppose that a consumer sees the ad for a 19-inch flat-screen computer monitor for $158 after rebate that reads, "Compare this price with any 19-inch flat-screen monitor, and you will see we cannot be matched." The average consumer might not understand that speakers are not included with such monitors. The computer store, on the other hand, might have assumed that everyone understands that flat-screen monitors with speakers are in a different price category. Adding "no speakers" or "speakers not included" would have allowed the consumer the information needed to shop and compare.

Consumers enjoy a great deal of protection when there are omissions of material information or they are given misleading information, but consumer protection does not protect consumers from their own negligence. Consumers who sign contracts without reading or understanding what is in them are still bound. Moreover, when the contract signed by the consumer clearly states one thing, the consumer cannot introduce evidence about statements the merchant made if the contract terms are clear. Consumers must exercise reasonable care and cannot blindly trust consumer protection law to rescue them from their own blunders.

One of the areas where there have been many new consumer protections is in the area of subprime lending. In the subprime lending market, which includes "do-or-die" loans such as car title loans and home title loans as well as payday loans, there are now extensive disclosure requirements on interest rates, payments, and the effects of default. In addition, these laws have imposed stringent requirements on lenders who seek to foreclose on properties that secure those loans.

CASE SUMMARY

A Loan Modification that Finds you Owing More

FACTS: Robert and Sheryl Laughlin (Plaintiffs), who were having difficulty making their mortgage payments, applied for a HAMP modification with Bank of America, NA (BANA). HAMP is the federal Home Affordable Modification Program, a program that was one of several assistance programs created in an effort to stem the foreclosure crisis. HAMP is intended to lower a qualifying mortgagor's monthly payments to 31 percent of the [borrowers'] verified monthly gross income in order to make payments more affordable. After months of delay and inconsistent responses, BANA informed the Laughlins that they qualified for the HAMP program and would be placed in a trial period plan. BANA told the Laughlins that if they accepted a trial period plan under HAMP, they would be ineligible to short sell their house. The Laughlins opted out of the proposed HAMP modification plan in order to remain eligible for a short sale.*

A BANA representative then advised the Laughlins to accept a HAMP modification instead of attempting a short sale, but they were not allowed to have the previously offered HAMP Trial Plan reinstated. On April 11, 2012, the Laughlins resubmitted the necessary financial documentation required in order to be considered for a modification. On June 21, 2012, the Laughlins received a Notice of Intent to Foreclose. On that same day, the Laughlins received a phone call from a BANA representative, informing them that they were denied a loan modification and would need to make at least one monthly loan payment in order to qualify for any mortgage assistance programs. On June 25, 2012, the Laughlins made this payment.

On August 15, 2012, the Laughlins received a Federal Housing Agency ("FHA") Trial Period Plan Agreement ("TPP"). On the same day, Robert Laughlin spoke with a BANA representative about his concern regarding the calculation of the amount due under the loan. Robert Laughlin believed that a portion of the principal balance was being "doublecounted" because BANA was adding unpaid principal on top of the balance due on the loan. A BANA representative informed them that this was how the calculation was done. The Laughlins then [accepted the TPP].

Under the terms of the TPP, the Laughlins were obligated to make three monthly payments on or before September 15, 2013; October 15, 2013; and November 15, 2013. The Laughlins made the payments, and on November 30, 2012, were told that their loan modification request was under review and that they would receive a final loan modification within 30–45 days. They were advised to continue making the monthly trial payments in the meantime.

On January 2, 2013, BANA acknowledged the Laughlins' compliance with the FHA Trial Plan Agreement and advised in writing to continue making trial payments until a final loan modification was processed. They received their permanent loan modification offer on April 10, 2013.

The terms of the permanent loan modification offer had a modified principal balance of $680,042.78. Before the modification, their loan balance was $617,735.87. The proposed modified loan also extended the term of the loan for 30 years, providing that the loan would now mature on November 1, 2042. Finally, the proposed permanent loan modification included a balloon payment of $25,013.27, which BANA said reflected the "missed" payments from the period between the end of the TPP and before the permanent loan modification offer.

The Laughlins filed suit against BANA for breach of the duty of good faith and violation of the New Jersey consumer fraud statute (NJCFA). BANA made a motion to dismiss the case and the Laughlins opposed the motion.

DECISION: The court held that allegations of "unconscionable commercial practice, deception, fraud, false pretense, false promise, misrepresentation, or the knowing concealment, suppression, or omission of any material fact" during the loan modification process constitute unlawful conduct in violation of the NJCFA. The loan modification process, from negotiation to the signing of a permanent modification, effectively operates as a subsequent performance on the original mortgage. It would be disingenuous to hold that a loan servicer would be free from the ramifications of violating consumer rights if it engaged in unlawful conduct while participating in a loan modification.

The Court found that Plaintiffs' allegations that BANA breached its implied duty, based upon the contractual relationship between Plaintiffs and BANA, to diligently evaluate Plaintiffs for a permanent loan were actionable under the consumer protection statutes of New Jersey.

BANA's Motion to Dismiss was denied.

[*Laughlin v. Bank of America, N.A.,* 2014 WL 2602260 (D.N.J. 2014)]

*A "short sale" in real estate occurs when the outstanding loans against a property are greater than what the property is worth and the lender agrees to accept less than it is owed to permit a sale of the property that secures its note.

32-1e What Remedies Do Consumers Have?

Although consumers have the theoretical right to bring suit for defenses to contracts or enforcement when the other party does not perform, the right to prove fraud, misrepresentation, duress, or breach is often of little practical value to consumers because both the costs of litigation and the burden of proof are high. The amount that the consumer has lost may be too small to be worth pursuing when compared with the cost of litigation. Consumer protection legislation provides special remedies for consumers so that pursuing their rights in court is cost beneficial. Class-action suits provide groups of consumers options for pursuing remedies that they might not be able to pursue (due to the cost) if they were acting alone. **For Example,** the *Laughlin v. Bank of America, N.A.,* case has resulted in several class actions around the country by homeowners who were forced into similar situations as the Laughlins and they are seeking relief. Under most consumer protection statutes class actions give homeowners a chance to recover their damages as well as the costs and attorneys' fees for pursuing recovery. Under some federal statutes debtors who bring class-action suits may be able to recover a statutorily provided percentage of the net worth of the company that has violated their rights.

In addition, consumer statutes often provide initial or alternative means for consumers to enforce their rights. Consumer statutes provide procedural steps for consumers to use to try to resolve their problems with the businesses involved and to document what has happened in their contract or relationship. **For Example,** some statutes require consumers to give the business involved written notice of the consumer's complaint. Having this notice then provides the business an opportunity to examine the consumer's complaint or concerns and possibly work out a solution.

In addition to procedural remedies other than litigation, consumer protection statutes provide other ways for consumers to seek their remedies, sometimes with the help of others who are more experienced in resolving consumer protection statutory violations.

Government Agency Action

At both the federal and state levels, administrative agencies that are responsible for the enforcement of laws and regulations also have the power to take steps to obtain relief for consumers. **For Example,** the Federal Trade Commission (FTC) can file a complaint against a company for false advertising. In settling the complaint with the company that had the false ads, the FTC could require the company to refund to the consumers affected by the ads the price of the product featured in the ad.[4] The federal Consumer Financial Protection Bureau (CFPB) (see p. 630) has the same authority to bring such complaints.

Action by Attorney General

A number of states allow their state attorneys general to bring actions on behalf of consumers who are victims of fraud or other unfair conduct. In these actions, the attorney general can request that consumers' contracts be canceled and that they be given restitution of whatever they paid. These suits by attorneys general are not criminal actions; they are civil suits in which the standard of proof is a preponderance of the evidence, not proof beyond a reasonable doubt. **For Example,** the litigation brought by state attorneys general for alleged deception by tobacco companies on the health harms of using tobacco resulted in settlements by those companies. The funds were used to compensate the states for health care costs for individuals with tobacco-related illnesses for whom the state was caring. The funds were also used to pay for educational programs and ads that caution young people not to smoke and warn them about the health hazards of using tobacco.

---

[4] *F.T.C. v. Affiliate Strategies, Inc.,* 849 F. Supp. 2d 1085 (D. Kan. 2011).

Many states also permit their attorneys general to bring actions for an injunction against violations of the consumer protection statute. These statutes commonly give the attorney general the authority to obtain a voluntary cease-and-desist consent decree (see Chapter 6) for improper practices before seeking an injunction from a court. The attorney general, like the agency, can impose a penalty for a violation.

Action by Consumer

Consumer protection statutes can also provide that a consumer who has been harmed by a violation of the statutes may recover by his own suit against the business that acted improperly.[5] The consumer may either seek to recover a penalty provided for in the consumer protection statute or bring an action on behalf of consumers as a class. Consumer protection statutes are often designed to rely on private litigation as an aid to enforcement of the statutory provisions. The Consumer Product Safety Act of 1972 authorizes "any interested person" to bring a civil action to enforce a consumer product safety rule and certain orders of the Consumer Product Safety Commission.[6]

Replacement or Refund

Some state consumer protection statutes require that the consumer be made whole by the replacement of the good, the refund of the purchase price, or the repair of the item within a reasonable time.[7]

Invalidation of Consumer's Contract

Other consumer protection statutes provide that when the contract made by a consumer violates the statute, the consumer's contract is void. In such a case, the seller cannot recover from the consumer buyer for any unpaid balance. Likewise, the seller cannot repossess the goods for nonpayment. The consumer keeps the goods without making any further payment.[8]

compensatory damages—sum of money that will compensate an injured plaintiff for actual loss.

punitive damages—damages, in excess of those required to compensate the plaintiff for the wrong done, that are imposed to punish the defendant because of the particularly wanton or willful character of wrongdoing; also called exemplary damages.

32-1f What Are the Civil and Criminal Penalties under Consumer Protection Statutes?

Only certain government agencies and attorneys general can seek criminal and civil penalties against those who violate consumer protection statutes. The agency or attorney general may use those penalties to provide compensation to consumers who have been victims of the violations. When consumers successfully bring individual or class-action suits against those who violate their rights as consumers, they recover damages. Some consumer protection statutes authorize the recovery of **compensatory damages** to compensate the consumer for the loss.[9] These types of statutes are designed to put the customer in as good a position as he would have been in had there not been a deception, breach, or violation of other requirements under the consumer protection statute. Other statutes authorize the recovery of **punitive damages,** which are additional damages beyond compensatory damages and may be a percentage of the company's net worth. Under antitrust statutes that prohibit anticompetitive behavior, consumers can collect treble punitive damages for a violation. Consumers cannot claim both treble damages authorized by a

[5] *Devlin v. Wells Fargo Bank, N.A.,* 2014 WL 1155415 (W.D.N.C. 2014).
[6] 15 U.S.C. §2051 *et seq.*
[7] Note that apart from these statutes, the buyer may have protection under a warranty to repair or replace. Likewise, a revocation of acceptance under the UCC would give the right to a refund of the purchase price.
[8] *State ex rel. King v. B & B Investment Group, Inc.,* 329 P.3d 658 (N.M. 2014).
[9] *Chow v. Chak Yam Chau,* 555 Fed. Appx. 842 (11th Cir. 2014).

statute and also punitive damages under the common law. Such double recovery would be duplicative remedies for the same wrong.

32-2 Areas of Consumer Protection

The following sections discuss important areas of consumer protection. Figure 32-1 provides an overview of these areas.

32-2a Advertising

Statutes commonly prohibit fraudulent advertising. Most advertising regulations are entrusted to an administrative agency, such as the FTC, which is authorized to issue orders to stop false or misleading advertising. Statutes prohibiting false advertising are liberally interpreted.

A store is liable for false advertising when it advertises a reduced price sale of a particular item that is out of stock when the sale begins. It is no defense that the presale demand was greater than usual.

Deception

Under consumer protection statutes, *deception* rather than *fraud* is the significant element.[10] A breach of these statutes occurs even without proof that the wrongdoer intended to defraud or deceive anyone.

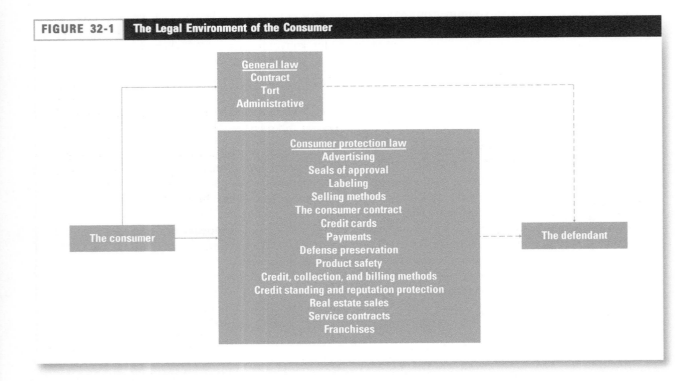

FIGURE 32-1   The Legal Environment of the Consumer

General law
Contract
Tort
Administrative

Consumer protection law
Advertising
Seals of approval
Labeling
Selling methods
The consumer contract
Credit cards
Payments
Defense preservation
Product safety
Credit, collection, and billing methods
Credit standing and reputation protection
Real estate sales
Service contracts
Franchises

The consumer

The defendant

[10] *Michael v. Mosquera-Lacy*, 200 P.3d 695 (Wash. 2009); *Williams v. Lifestyle Lift Holdings, Inc.*, 302 P.3d 523 (Wash. App. 2013).

The deception statutes and regulations represent a shift in the law and public policy. These regulations are not laws based on fault; rather, they are based on the question of whether a buyer is likely to be misled by the ad. The good faith of an advertiser or the absence of intent to deceive is immaterial. False advertising regulation protects *consumers* regardless of the advertiser's motives.

The FTC requires advertisers to maintain records of the data used as support for statements made in ads that deal with the safety, performance, efficacy, quality, or comparative price of an advertised product. The FTC can require the advertiser to produce these data and backup material. If it is in the interest of the consumer, the FTC can make this information public except to the extent that it contains trade secrets or privileged material.

Corrective Advertising

When an enterprise has made false and deceptive statements in advertising, the FTC may require new advertising to correct the former statements so that consumers are aware of the truth. This corrective advertising required by the FTC is also called *retractive advertising*. The FTC can also halt ads that it finds to be deceptive.

CASE SUMMARY

Stringing Buyers Along on Floss

FACTS: In June 2004, Pfizer Inc. ("Pfizer") launched a consumer advertising campaign for its mouthwash, Listerine Antiseptic Mouthrinse. Print ads and hang tags on the bottles in the stores featured an image of a Listerine bottle balanced on a scale against a white container of dental floss.

The campaign also featured a television commercial called the "Big Bang." The commercial announced that "Listerine's as effective as floss at fighting plaque and gingivitis. Clinical studies prove it." There had been two studies on floss vs. mouthwash, but the studies concluded that flossing was still necessary in addition to mouthwash. The studies were suggesting that mouthwash with no flossing is better than nothing at all but still concluded that there was no substitute that brought the same results as flossing.

McNeil-PPC, Inc. ("PPC") (and a division of Johnson & Johnson), the market leader in sales of string dental floss and other interdental cleaning products, brought suit alleging that Pfizer had engaged in false advertising in its conclusions about the studies and the use of floss and asked for an injunction halting the ads.

DECISION: The court held that the ads were deceptive because the studies Pfizer was using also concluded that there was no substitute for floss. The studies recommended that flossing continue. The court concluded that the ads misled consumers and granted an injunction halting them. Ads must not misrepresent the results of scientific studies and mislead consumers into doing something that could prove harmful to their dental health. [*McNeil-PPC, Inc. v. Pfizer Inc.*, 351 F. Supp. 2d 226 (S.D.N.Y. 2005)]

32-2b Labeling

Closely related to the regulation of advertising is the regulation of labeling and marking products. Various federal statutes are designed to give consumers accurate information about a product, whereas others require warnings about dangers of use or misuse. Consumer protection regulations prohibit labeling or marking products with such terms as *jumbo, giant*, and *full,* which tend to exaggerate and mislead. **For Example,** the health foods store Eating Well sold a number of foods with the label "Fat Free." This label was false, and Eating Well knew that the foods were ordinary foods not free of fat. Eating Well violated consumer protection statutes that prohibit false labeling. Sales made on

THINKING THINGS THROUGH

The Difference in Concussions and Football Helmet Ad Claims

Riddell, Inc., and Schutt Sports, Inc., both manufacture football helmets. Together, the two companies make up 90 percent of the football helmet market. Riddell's market share is slightly higher than Schutt's.

In 2002, the University of Pittsburgh conducted a study to compare concussion and recovery rates for football players. Riddell provided a grant to underwrite the study that would include salary support for two leading authors of the study, Micky Collins and Mark R. Lovell. A third author, Mark Ide, is a Riddell employee.

The study, conducted from 2002 through 2004, focused on a subset of high school players in the Pennsylvania Interscholastic Athletic Association. For "ethical reasons," the high school students studied were allowed to choose whether to use a Riddell Revolution helmet or one of the traditional helmets. The Revolution helmets supplied in 2002 to study participants were new, but the same helmets were reused in the following years. The traditional helmets were drawn from the schools' inventories and were not necessarily new. Traditional and Revolution helmets that were not new were refurbished and recertified each year by a member of the National Athletic Equipment Reconditioners Association using standards established by the National Operating Committee on Standards for Athletic Equipment.

In 2002, the authors found that athletes wearing the Revolution helmet and athletes wearing the traditional helmets during the 2002 season had nearly identical concussion rates. The data gathered in 2003 showed that the difference in the rate of concussion between the groups of athletes wearing the Revolution helmet and the athletes wearing the traditional helmets was not statistically significant, although the difference "approached" statistical significance.

In 2004, an internal study stated that the total number of participants over the three years was 2,207, with 1,173 fitted with the Revolution helmet and 1,034 equipped with traditional helmets. The internal report showed that 5.29 percent of the athletes wearing the Revolution helmet had diagnoses of cerebral concussions, while 7.16 percent of the athletes wearing traditional helmets sustained concussions.

The final three-year study considered only 2,141 of those participants, with 1,173 fitted with the Revolution and 968 fitted with traditional helmets. Using these numbers, the concussion rates were 5.3 percent and 7.6 percent, respectively, which the authors of the study described as a "statistically significant difference." According to two authors, the results "demonstrated a trend toward a lowered incidence of concussion" but the "limited size sample precludes a more conclusive statement of findings at this time."

When the study was submitted to the journal *Neurosurgery,* the reviewers found "substantial conflicts of interest" as well as flaws in design, the unknown age of the helmets, randomness, and statistical significance. The study was published with comments on its methodological flaws.

Ridell used the study in its ads, stating, "Research has shown that players wearing the Riddell Revolution football helmet are 31% less likely to suffer a concussion than players wearing traditional football helmets." Some ads added that the study showed a reduced risk of concussion "up to 41%" and others added that the 41 percent rate was only for players who had not previously suffered a concussion. Most of the advertisements also included a reference to the *Neurosurgery* article. Riddell also sent out an ad to coaches that referenced the study and developed a PowerPoint presentation with the study included to be used by sales representatives.

The sales pitches and ads were successful and Riddell was able to convert high school and college players to wearing the Riddell Revolution helmet.

Schutt Sports filed suit for false advertising, product disparagement, and deceptive trade practices. Ridell moved for summary judgment and Schutt sought an injunction to stop Ridell from using the study in its ads. Based on the *McNeil-PPC, Inc. v. Pfizer Inc.* case, what do you think the court should do?

Make a list of the ethical issues you see in the Riddell and Schutt case.

[*Riddell, Inc. v. Schutt Sports, Inc.,* 724 F. Supp. 2d 963 (W.D.Wis. 2010)]

the basis of the false labels meant that Eating Well had misled consumers about the fat content of its products.

32-2c Selling Methods

In addition to regulating ads, consumer protection statutes regulate the methods used to sell goods and services.

SPORTS & ENTERTAINMENT LAW

The NFL and Concussion Protocol

The NFL has been the target of criticism and litigation because of problems developing in retired football players that are allegedly related to the number of concussions they experienced during their careers with the NFL, including dementia, depression, and Alzheimer's. The NFL Head, Neck, and Spine Committee has developed a list of steps and procedures that teams should use when there is an injury as well as a policy on return to play. The steps are available in pamphlet guidelines as well as reproduced on wall posters to be posted in team locker rooms so that players are aware of their rights when they sustain an injury.

One part of the protocol is that there be a third-party physician available to conduct the assessment. A third-party physician is one who is not affiliated with the team, an independent doctor who evaluates the scope of the injury, recommends necessary tests, and provides information for the return-to-play decision.

In 2013, the NFL settled a lawsuit brought by former players who said that their mental ailments were caused by blows to the head that they experienced as players. The NFL has always denied the connection, but Commissioner Roger Goodell instructed the NFL's lawyers to "do the right thing for the game and the men who played it." The NFL settled the suit for $765 million. There were 4,000 former players who were plaintiffs in the class-action suit, and the suit provided a cap of $4 million damage award per player. The protocols were developed as a result of the litigation.

Home-Solicited Sales

A sale of goods or services for $25 or more made to a buyer at home may be set aside within three business days. This consumer right of rescission may be exercised merely because the buyer does not want to go through with the contract. There is no requirement that the buyer prove any seller misconduct or defect in the goods or services.[11]

When the buyer has made an oral agreement to purchase and the seller then comes to the buyer's home to work out the details, the transaction is not a home-solicited sale and cannot be rescinded under the federal regulation.[12] A sale was also not home-solicited when the seller phoned the consumer at his or her home for permission to mail the consumer a promotional brochure, and thereafter the consumer went to the seller's place of business where the contract was made.[13]

Telemarketing Fraud

High-pressure selling by telephone has attracted sham businesses and resulted in consumer contracts that are often unconscionable. The Telephone Consumer Protection Act (TCPA) gave the FTC authority to promulgate rules that restrict telemarketing.[14] The TCPA outlaws automated marketing calls without the prior express consent of the called party and prohibits calls to emergency telephone lines or patient rooms in hospitals, health care facilities, or elderly homes. The FTC has added rules that prohibit unsolicited transmissions to fax machines as well as telemarketing calls before 8 A.M. or after 9 P.M. States have additional regulations on telemarketing, including systems that require telemarketers to register with the state.

The TCPA also resulted in a National Do Not Call Registry.[15] Consumers can register to opt out of any telemarketing, except for political and charitable calls.

[11] Federal Trade Commission Regulation, 16 CFR §429:1.
[12] *Burson v. Capps*, 102 A.3d 353 (Md. 2014).
[13] In re *Deitch*, 522 B.R. 99 (E.D. Pa. 2014).
[14] 47 U.S.C. §227.
[15] 16 C.F.R. §310.8.

E-COMMERCE & CYBERLAW

Blocking WiFi to Charge More

It all started with a guest at the Marriott's Gaylord Opryland Hotel and Convention Center in Nashville, Tennessee. The guest found that he could not use any Wi-Fi hotspots in the Marriott convention space at the hotel. He filed a complaint with the Federal Communications Commission (FCC), alleging that the hotel was "jamming mobile hotspots so that you can't use them." Under a federal law that was passed at the time radio transmissions were in the infancy, it is a crime to "willfully or maliciously interfere with radio communications of any licensed station." 47 U.S.C. §333 (2014).

The investigation bureau of the FCC found that Marriott had used features of a Wi-Fi monitoring system at the Gaylord Opryland to contain and/or de-authenticate guest-created Wi-Fi hotspot access points in the conference facilities. In some cases, Marriott employees were sending de-authentication packets to the targeted access points, which would dissociate consumers' devices from their own Wi-Fi hotspot access points and disrupt their current Wi-Fi transmissions and prevent future transmissions.

The FCC also found that the purpose of the jamming was revenue. Marriott charges conference exhibitors and other attending meetings at their convention facilities at the hotel between $250 and $1,000 per device to use the Gaylord Wi-Fi services. Convention participants were left with the choice of paying twice for access (through hot-spot services or through Marriott) or having no access at all.

The FCC brought a complaint against Marriott for violating federal law. Marriott entered into a consent decree, one that contains an admission that employees were scrambling access for convention participants. Marriott agreed to pay a $600,000 fine.

Also as part of the consent decree, Marriott agreed to submit a report and compliance plan to the FCC. The hotel chain must conduct an audit of all the facilities it owns or manages to stop any similar activity and then develop a plan to prevent such activity in the future.

Businesses need to be careful about interfering with Wi-Fi, even on their own properties. Interference is an unfair and deceptive practice in addition to a violation of the federal law on radio transmissions.

32-2d The Consumer Contract

Consumer contracts are regulated in different ways.

Form of Contract

Consumer protection laws commonly regulate the form of the contract, requiring that certain items be specifically listed, that payments under the contract be itemized, and that finance charges be clear (see Chapter 33). Generally, consumer protections require that certain portions of the contract be printed in a certain font size and that a copy of the contract be furnished the consumer.

Contracts Printed on Two Sides

To be sure that consumers see all contract disclosures required by law, contracts that have their terms printed on both the front and the back of the contract must carry the warning "NOTICE: see other side for important information." Consumers must sign the back side of each sheet.

Particular Sales and Leases

The Motor Vehicle Information and Cost Savings Act requires dealers to make certain disclosures to buyers. In addition, the act prohibits selling an automobile without informing the buyer that the odometer has been reset below the true mileage. **For Example,** if a seller knows that the real mileage on a car is 120,073 miles but rolls the odometer back to 20,073 miles, the seller has committed odometer fraud, a violation that allows the buyer to recover three times the actual loss or $1,500, whichever amount is higher.[16] This federal odometer law imposes a higher standard on auto dealers. An auto dealer who may not actually know of a roll-back cannot claim lack of knowledge that the odometer was false when that conclusion was reasonably apparent from the condition of the car.[17]

The federal government regulates particular types of leases of goods. For example, under the Consumer Leasing Act of 1976, leases of autos and other durable goods require specific contract details and disclosures such as the number of lease payments as well as the amount due at the end of the lease for the consumer to purchase the leased goods.[18]

Contract Terms

Consumer protection legislation does not ordinarily affect the right of the parties to make a contract on whatever terms they choose. It is customary, however, to prohibit the use of certain clauses that are harsh for the consumer or that have too great a potential for exploitive abuse by a creditor, such as waiving a warranty limitations disclosure. The Warranty Disclosure Act requires sellers to specify whether the provided warranty protection is full or limited, a standard defined in the act itself.

Limitations on Credit: Subprime and Predatory Lending

subprime lending market—a credit market that makes loans to high-risk consumers (those who have bankruptcies, no credit history, or a poor credit history), often loaning money to pay off other debts the consumer has due.

With the economic crisis of 2008, there have been significant additional rights for consumers in credit contracts (see discussion later in the section titled "Credit Disclosures"). Part of the reforms focused on the **subprime lending market.** This credit market makes loans to consumers who have bankruptcies, no credit history, low-to-moderate incomes, or a poor credit history. Because of the higher risk of these types of loans, these credit contracts involve lower loan amounts; higher origination costs, brokers' fees, credit insurance fees; higher interest rates; significant collateral pledges; large prepayment penalties (meaning that the consumer debtor is locked into the high interest rate); and faster repayment requirements. Subprime loans have had notoriously difficult-to-read contracts.

predatory lending—a practice on the part of the subprime lending market whereby lenders take advantage of less sophisticated consumers or those who are desperate for funds by using the lenders' superior bargaining positions to obtain credit terms that go well beyond compensating them for their risk.

Part of the subprime lending market includes lenders who take advantage of less sophisticated consumers or even consumers who are just desperate for funds. These lenders use their superior bargaining positions to obtain credit terms that go well beyond compensating them for their risk. For example, title loans (loans made in exchange for title to a car or house if the borrower defaults) have been widely used in subprime markets. These types of loans, sometimes called **predatory lending,** are highly regulated by both the states and the federal government. The new wave of consumer protection on subprime loans includes limitations on interest rates, 10-day rescission periods, additional contract disclosures requirements, and the requirement of credit counseling before consumers may sign for certain types of subprime loans.

Unconscionability

The UCC has a longstanding form of consumer protection through its prohibition on "unconscionability" in contracts. The types of provisions that make contracts unconscionable include clauses that award excessive damages or the application of credit payments across purchases over time so that the consumer is never able to pay off any goods.

Some specific state statutes are aimed at activities deemed unconscionable—for example, price gouging on consumer goods or services for which the demand is abnormally greater than the supply. **For Example,** New York's statute provides: "During any abnormal disruption of the market for consumer goods and services vital and necessary for the

---

[16] 15 U.S.C. §1901 *et seq.*, as amended; recodified as 49 U.S.C. §§32701–32711.
[17] *Ukegbu v. Daniels*, 438 S.W.3d 284 (Ark. App. 2014).
[18] 15 U.S.C. §1667.

health, safety, and welfare of consumers, resulting from stress of weather, convulsion of nature, failure or shortage of electric power or other source of energy … no merchant shall sell or offer to sell any such consumer goods or services for an amount which represents an unconscionably excessive price." Such a statute protects, for example, purchasers of electric generators for home use during a hurricane-caused blackout. During floods and other natural disasters, these statutes limit what sellers can charge for water and other staples.

32-2e Credit Disclosures

While general consumer statutes prohibit deception in ads and sales practices, specific federal laws require the disclosure of all interest charges, points, and fees for all types of loans and credit contracts. These laws require disclosure of an annual percentage rate (APR) so that the consumer can see just how much the transaction costs per year and can compare alternatives.[19] The Truth in Lending Act (TILA) provides the requirements for disclosures in credit contracts and consumer rights when full disclosure is not made. When a consumer sale or contract provides for payment in more than four installments, it is subject to the TILA. The application of the TILA is required even when there is no service or finance charge for the installment payments. There are additional obligations of disclosure under the Fair Credit and Charge Card Disclosure Act,[20] the Home Equity Loan Consumer Protection Act,[21] and the Credit Card Accountability, Responsibility and Disclosure (CARD) Act of 2009.[22] The CARD Act applies to all credit cards. All of these statutes and regulations, discussed in the following sections, require advance disclosures and timing mandates.

The Federal Reserve Board was originally delegated the responsibility for enforcing TILA and has promulgated regulations to carry out the details of disclosure, but the **Consumer Financial Protection Bureau** (CFPB), created under the **Dodd-Frank Wall Street Reform and Consumer Protection Act** (DFCPA), also known as the Wall Street Reform and Consumer Financial Protection Act or the Consumer Financial Protection Act (CFPA), holds that enforcement role. Housed within the Federal Reserve, the CFPB now serves the combined roles that the Federal Reserve as well as the FTC and other federal agencies played in dealing with consumer credit laws, regulations, and issues.

32-2f Credit Cards

Credit cards and credit arrangements are so readily available that consumers tell of receiving credit cards when they apply in the name of their Labrador retrievers. Because of the extensive availability of credit cards and the ease with which they are issued, there are extensive federal regulations of credit card use and the rights of consumers with credit cards.[23]

Unsolicited Credit Cards

Federal regulations prohibit the unsolicited distribution of credit cards to persons who have not applied for them. The practice of simply sending credit cards through the mail to consumers is now illegal. The problems with rising identity theft have made this

Consumer Financial Protection Bureau–consumer protection bureau located within the Federal Reserve that now has jurisdiction over all consumer credit issues and statutes.

Dodd-Frank Wall Street Reform and Consumer Protection Act–federal legislation passed following the financial markets collapse that includes consumer protections as well as market and mortgage lending reforms.

[19] Consumer Credit Protection Act (CCPA), 15 U.S.C. §§1605, 1606, & 1636; Regulation Z adopted by the Federal Reserve, 12 C.F.R. §226.5.
[20] 15 U.S.C. §1601 *et seq.*
[21] *Id.*
[22] PL 111-24, 2009 HR 627, 15 U.S.C. §1601, amending sections 1602, 1637, 1640, 1665, 1666b, 1666e, 1666j, 1666i-2.
[23] Heidi Mandanis Schooner, "Consuming Debt: Structuring the Federal Response to Abuses in Consumer Credit," 18 *Loyola Consumer L. Rev.* 43 (2005).

protection especially important to consumers because identity thieves were able to intercept the mail and seize the unsolicited credit cards.

Credit Cards for Those under the Age of 21

The CARD Act substantially restricts the solicitation of credit card accounts from those under the age of 21. Credit card companies must have a written application in hand from those under 21 and those applications must carry the signature of a parent, guardian, or someone over the age of 21 who has the means to repay debt. The line of credit on a co-signed card for someone under the age of 21 cannot be increased without the co-signer's permission. Colleges and universities are now restricted in their partnering with credit card companies, arrangements that allowed the colleges and universities and their alumni associations to receive funds from the credit card companies in exchange for access to their students and alumni. The CARD Act limits locations for college student credit card solicitations, requires colleges and universities to disclose their financial relationships with such credit card companies, and also requires colleges and universities to provide debt counseling for their students.

Surcharge Prohibited

Under some statutes, a seller cannot add any charge to the purchase price because the buyer uses a credit card instead of paying with cash or a check.[24]

Unauthorized Use

A cardholder is not liable for more than $50 for the unauthorized use of a credit card. To even recover the $50 amount, the credit card issuer must show that (1) the credit card was an accepted card,[25] (2) the issuer gave the holder adequate notice of possible liability in such a case, (3) the issuer furnished the holder with notification means in the event of loss or theft of the credit card, (4) the issuer provided a method by which the user of the card could be identified as the person authorized to use it,[26] and (5) unauthorized use of the card had occurred or might occur as a result of loss, theft, or some other event.

The burden of proof is on the card issuer to show that the use of the card was authorized or that the holder is liable for its unauthorized use.[27]

Unauthorized Purpose Distinguished

Unauthorized use of a credit card occurs only when it is used without the permission or approval of the cardholder. The holder may authorize use by another, but only for a limited purpose, such as purchasing office supplies or a new fax machine. If the person uses the card for any item other than the purpose specified, the use remains authorized because merchants cannot know these private restrictions.[28] The same rule is applied when an employer has cards issued to employees for making employment-related purchases but that employees use for personal purposes.

[24] The Truth in Lending Act, 15 U.S.C. §1666f, permits a merchant to offer a discount to cash-paying customers but not to customers using a credit card.
[25] A credit card is accepted when the cardholder has requested and received or has signed, used, or authorized another to use the card for the purpose of obtaining money, property, labor, or services on credit.
[26] Regulation Z of the Board of Governors of the Federal Reserve, 12 C.F.R. §226.13(d), as amended, provides that the identification may be by signature, photograph, or fingerprint on the credit card or by electronic or mechanical confirmation.
[27] The Fair and Accurate Credit Transactions Act (FACTA), 15 U.S.C. §1681, requires merchants to use only the last few digits of a credit card on their receipts (a truncated number) so as to reduce the likelihood of a thief finding the receipt and using the full credit card number. *Redman v. RadioShack Corp.*, 768 F.3d 622 (7th Cir. 2014).
[28] *Hayes v. Shelby County Trustee*, 971 F. Supp. 2d 717 (W.D. Tenn. 2013).

Late Payment Fee

The contract between a credit card issuer and a holder may require the holder to pay a late payment fee. The CARD Act changed substantially the law on late payments because of so much abuse by credit card companies with regard to late fees. Under CARD, all credit card companies must have bills in consumers' hands not less than 21 days before the bill is due. In addition, the CARD Act requires conspicuous disclosures about the amount of late fees as well as the impact of a late payment on the consumer's rate of interest.

Credit Card Balance Transfers

Consumers often receive competing offers from credit card companies to transfer their balances from existing cards to what seem to be lower-interest-rate credit cards. The CARD Act imposes maximum fees allowed with these transfers and time requirements for how quickly credit card companies can change the advertised terms of the transfer. The consumer must know all terms of transferring balances, such as the upfront disclosure of transfer fees as well as potential changes in the APR once the transfer has occurred. The CARD Act also places limits on how often companies can change a credit card holder's interest rate.

32-2g Gift Cards

Gift cards have become increasingly popular. During the Christmas shopping season, many retailers' gift card revenues equal their actual sales of merchandise. However, many retailers had built in hidden expiration dates and inactivity fees. Under the CARD Act, a gift card cannot have an expiration date any earlier than five years from the time it is issued and there must be a conspicuous disclosure notice about that expiration date. Inactivity fees on gift cards and cards that decline in value are now regulated under CARD. There are now controls on those declining value fees, such as when they can be charged and what must be disclosed up front.

32-2h Payments

Under the CARD Act, consumer credit card payments are tightly regulated. The due date must specify that the time is 5:00 P.M. on that date. There had been creditor abuses that resulted when they made 9:00 A.M. the cut-off time for payments, thus depriving the debtors of the possibility that their mailed bills could get in for posting by the due date. When consumers make payments in excess of the minimum payment due on their credit card bills, the creditor must apply that extra amount to that portion of the account that carries the highest interest rate.

When and how consumers can exceed their credit limits are subject to disclosure requirements, interest rate change notices, and limitations for how long increased interest rates can apply to, for example, exceeding your credit balance. These rules all affect the amount of the minimum payment and how long the additional interest and fees can apply when a consumer has been tardy on payments or delinquent on the credit card account.

32-2i Preservation of Consumer Defenses

Consumer protection laws generally prohibit a consumer from waiving or giving up any defense provided by law. In an ordinary contract situation, when goods or services purchased or leased by a consumer are not proper or are defective, the consumer is not required to pay for the goods or services or is required to pay only a reduced amount. With the modern expansion of credit transactions, sellers and lessors have used several techniques for getting paid without regard to whether the consumer had any complaint against them. To prevent this, the FTC has adopted a regulation requiring that in every sale or lease of goods or services to a consumer, there must be a contract that gives the consumer the right to assert defenses. This notice can be found in the discussion of negotiable instruments and the rights of the parties in Chapter 28. A good deal of consumer credit issues will no longer be handled by the FTC but rather by the CFPB (see the discussion under "Credit Disclosures").

32-2j Product Safety

A variety of statutes and rules of law protects the health and well-being of consumers. Most states have laws governing the manufacture of various products and establishing product safety standards. The federal Consumer Product Safety Act provides for research and setting uniform standards for products to reduce health hazards and establishes civil and criminal penalties for the distribution of unsafe products. The Consumer Product Safety Commission (CPSC) has the authority to require recalls and obtain permanent bans on the sale of products.[29] **For Example,** the CPSC banned the sale of Bucky Balls, the magnetic building blocks toys, because it established that the product could not be made safe by labeling, warnings, or age limits. Children who swallowed the powerful magnetic pieces ended up requiring surgery due to collapsed organs drawn together by the strong magnets. (See Chapters 9 and 23.)

32-2k Credit, Collection, and Billing Methods

Various laws and regulations protect consumers from discriminatory and improper credit and collection practices.

CPA   ### Equal Credit Opportunity Act: Credit Discrimination

Under the Equal Credit Opportunity Act (ECOA), it is unlawful to discriminate against an applicant for credit on the basis of race, color, religion, national origin, gender, marital status, or age; because all or part of the applicant's income is obtained from a public assistance program; or because the applicant has in good faith exercised any right under the Consumer Credit Protection Act (CCPA). When a credit application is refused, the applicant must be furnished a written explanation. **For Example,** when Robert applied for a loan at Tradesman Bank, he was told on the phone that the loan would not be made to him because of his criminal record. Tradesman must furnish Robert with the specifics regarding that denial. Using Robert's race to decline the loan would be an ECOA violation. However, denial based on a criminal record is permitted.[30]

Fair Credit Billing Act: Correction of Errors

When a consumer believes that a credit card issuer has made a billing error, the consumer should send the creditor a written statement and explanation of the error. The creditor or card issuer must investigate and make a prompt written reply to the consumer.[31] Many credit card companies now permit consumers to file these disputes online.

---

[29] 15 U.S.C. §§2051–2081.
[30] *Semler v. General Elec. Capital Corp.*, 127 Cal. Rptr. 3d 794 (Cal. App. 2011).
[31] Fair Credit Billing Act, 15 U.S.C. §1601.

Improper Collection Methods

Unreasonable methods of debt collection are often expressly prohibited by statute or are held by courts to constitute an unreasonable invasion of privacy.[32] A creditor is liable for unreasonably attempting to collect a bill that in fact has been paid. This liability can arise under general principles of tort law as well as under special consumer protection legislation.

Fault of Agent or Employee. When improper collection methods are used, it is no defense to the creditor that the improper acts were performed by an agent, an employee, or any other person acting on behalf of the creditor. Under general principles of agency law, a creditor hiring an individual or an agency to collect a debt is liable to the debtor for damages for unlawful conduct by the collector.

CPA   **Fair Debt Collection Practices Act (FDCPA).** The federal FDCPA prohibits improper practices in the collection by third parties of debts incurred primarily for personal, family, or household purposes. For purposes of the FDCPA, collectors are defined to include attorneys who are collecting for clients as well as those who are collecting from consumers for bad checks but it does not cover original creditors who are collecting from their original debtors.[33]

Collection Letters. Under the FDCPA, collectors must comply with restrictions on correspondence with debtors. The collector must not misrepresent its status in the letterhead, for example, by stating that the collector is a law firm or lawyer.[34] A letter from a collection agency to a consumer that gives the impression a lawsuit is about to be brought against the consumer when in fact it will not be brought is also a violation of the FDCPA.[35]

A debt collection letter sent to the debtor's place of employment that reveals the nature of the correspondence is a violation of FDCPA. For example, if the words "final demand for payment" can be read through the envelope sent to the place of employment, then the collector has violated the debtor's privacy. Postcards that revealed the purpose of the collector's contact or identity would also be FDCPA violations.

What Is Not a Defense. When a collection agency violates the FDCPA, it is liable to the debtor for damages. It is no defense that the debtor owed the money that the agency was seeking to collect. When a creditor uses improper collection methods, it is no defense that the improper acts were performed by an agent, an employee, or any other person acting on behalf of the creditor.

CPA   ## 32-2l Protection of Credit Standing and Reputation

When a person purchases on credit or applies for a loan, a job, or an insurance policy, those who will extend these benefits often wish to know more about the applicant. Credit reporting agencies gather such information on borrowers, buyers, and applicants and sell the information to interested persons.

The Fair Credit Reporting Act (FCRA)[36] protects consumers from various abuses that may arise as this information is recorded and revealed. This statute governs credit reporting agencies, sometimes called *credit bureaus*.

---

[32] Fair Debt Collection Practices Act, 15 U.S.C. §1692 *et seq.*; Federal Trade Commission Regulation, 16 C.F.R. §237.
[33] *Buchanan v. Northland Group, Inc.*, 776 F.3d 393 (6th Cir. 2015) (Mich. 2015).
[34] *Plummer v. Atlantic Credit & Finance, Inc.*, 66 F. Supp. 3d 484 (S.D.N.Y. 2014).
[35] *Szczurek v. Professional Management, Inc.*, 59 F. Supp. 3d 721 (E.D. Pa. 2014).
[36] 15 U.S.C. §1681 *et seq.*

ETHICS & THE LAW

Getting Into Debt and Getting Debt Relief—from the Same Company

Howard Dvorkin is the founder and former president of Consolidated Credit Counseling Services, Inc. The company works with consumers to provide credit counseling and negotiate with lenders to help those consumers pay their debts. Mr. Dworkin has also set up companies that provide services to payday lenders. Payday lenders offer high-interest loans to consumers that are designed to be paid back once the consumers get their paychecks. Mr. Dvorkin has denied any involvement in the payday firms and said that he expects the firms to "ethically operate." However, all the companies use the same mailbox or space in the office complex where Consolidated Credit Counseling Services is located.

Some of the companies that indicate an ownership interest by Mr. Dvorkin charge interest rates between 235 percent and 782 percent on 14-day loans. When asked about this conflict Mr. Dvorkin said, "There could be some people that could

say, 'Wow, that's weird.' But I don't really have any involvement whatsoever in those businesses."*

There has been a great deal of focus on the payday loan industry Congress and a number of state legislatures. There is proposed legislation that would affect everything from disclosure requirements to limitations on interest rates for payday loans. The stories on conflicts of interest such as this one continue to appear in the media and have led to proposals that would require more disclosure about the other roles that lenders and credit counselors play, including the companies that they own or operate that are also consumer lenders.

Explain what conflicts could arise when credit counselors own lending companies and debt relief companies.

*Jason Zweig and Rachel Louise Ensign, "Credit Counselor Has Ties to Payday Lenders," *Wall Street Journal*, January 13, 2015, p. A1.

---

consumer credit–credit for personal, family, and household use.

The FCRA applies only to **consumer credit,** which is defined as credit for "personal, family, and household" use; it does not apply to business or commercial transactions.

Privacy

Credit reporting agencies are not permitted to disclose information to persons not having a legitimate use for it. It is a federal crime to obtain or to furnish a credit report for an improper purpose. On request, a credit reporting agency must tell a consumer the names and addresses of persons to whom it has made a credit report during the previous six months. It must also tell, when requested, which employers were given such a report during the previous two years.

A store may not publicly display a list of named customers from whom it will not accept checks; such action is an invasion of the privacy of those persons.

Protection from False Information

hearsay evidence–statements made out of court that are offered in court as proof of the information contained in the statements and that, subject to many exceptions, are not admissible in evidence.

Much of the information obtained by credit bureaus is based on statements made by persons, such as neighbors, when interviewed by the bureau's investigator. Sometimes the statements are incorrect. Quite often they are **hearsay evidence** and would not be admissible in a legal proceeding. Nevertheless, such statements may go on credit records without further verification and be furnished to a client of the agency, who will tend to regard them as accurate and true.

A person has a limited right to request that a credit bureau disclose the nature and substance of the information it possesses. The right to know, however, does not extend to medical information. The bureau is also not required to identify the persons giving information to its investigators, nor is it required to give the applicant a copy of, or to permit the applicant to see, any file.

CASE SUMMARY

A Crime Online in the Credit Report

FACTS: On September 11, 2012, Tony Smith (plaintiff) applied for a job as a truck driver with Dart Transit Company through Dart's student driver training program. Dart ordered a criminal background check on Smith from E-Backgroundchecks.com (BGC). Dart ordered a U.S. One-SEARCH, which is an automated computer search of BGC's nationwide criminal database programmed to return results instantaneously. U.S. OneSEARCH reports are prepared by matching identifying information provided by the end-users to identifiers contained within the public criminal records in BGC's database, and BGC's practice is to report criminal records that match a consumer's full name and date of birth.

Dart supplied the name "Tony Willie Smith," his date of birth, the state within which he works, and his Social Security number, though the Social Security number was not required. BGC's system identified six criminal records matching plaintiff's first and last name and date of birth, and which did not contain any middle name.

BGC returned these records to Dart in a two-step process as well. First, BGC provided Dart with a summary screen showing basic information about each of the matching records. BGC's system then required Dart to indicate, based on its review of the summary records, whether any records did not match Smith. Dart did not indicate that any of the records supplied by BGC were not a match to Smith and it therefore continued on to the second step of the process, which entailed BGC providing Dart with a detailed view of the criminal records that carried over from another screen. Dart was then able to review each record individually and was required to indicate whether each record would negatively affect plaintiff's employment. Following this step, BGC then completed and electronically returned the criminal background report to Dart at 4:51 P.M. on September 12, 2012.

Because the report contained public criminal record information, BGC's system automatically generated a letter to Smith, advising him that BGC had reported public record information to Dart and enclosing a copy of the report, a summary of plaintiff's rights under the FCRA, and a dispute form. The letter was dated September 12, 2012, and was mailed to Smith, which he admits he received at his home sometime after BGC transmitted the report to Dart.

Smith contacted BGC on September 17, 2012, and disputed the contents of the report he had received from Dart. Two days later, on September 19, BGC issued a corrected report removing all of the previously reported criminal records provided on the September 12 report and showing that Smith had no matching criminal records. That same day, BGC e-mailed a notice to Dart, advising Dart that it had updated Smith's criminal background report. On September 20, 2012, Dart approved plaintiff to begin the training program, which he began on September 25.

Smith filed suit against BGC, alleging that BGC inaccurately reported his criminal history on his consumer report and that in September 2012, he applied for and was denied employment with Dart due to the inaccurate information, which included convictions for possession of a controlled substance by an unregistered person, carrying firearms without a license, and criminal conspiracy. Smith alleged that BGC "continues to publish and disseminate such inaccurate information to other third parties" in violation of the FCRA.

DECISION: BGC furnished to Dart an indisputably inaccurate report that did not match plaintiff's full name and Social Security number that Dart had provided to BGC. Since BGC had in its possession information that could have been used to demonstrate the inaccuracy of the report it furnished to Dart, there is a material dispute of fact as to whether BGC's initial search procedures were in fact reasonable in this instance because while requiring a credit reporting agency to go beyond the face of court records to determine whether those records correctly report the outcome of the underlying action may be too much to ask, requiring a CRA to correctly determine which public records belong to which individual consumers is not.

BGC returned records that only matched plaintiff's first and last name, a very common name at that, and despite having Smith's complete name and Social Security number, BGC took no steps prior to issuing its initial report to confirm whether the "Tony Smith" criminal records it provided to Dart were associated with the full name and Social Security number of plaintiff.

BGC did not have a process to confirm whether its records are in fact a match to the individual. BGC even admitted that the automated computer program had no way of differentiating between individuals with the same name and date of birth, and that after it compiled its initial matching records, it then placed the burden on employers to indicate whether any records did not match the individual.

BGC's motion for summary judgment was denied. [*Smith v. E-Backgroundchecks.com, Inc.,* **81 F. Supp. 3d 1342 (N.D. Ga. 2015)**]

When a person claims that report information is erroneous, the credit bureau must take steps within a reasonable time to determine the accuracy of the disputed item.

Adverse information obtained by investigation cannot be given to a client after three months unless it is verified to determine that it is still valid. Most legal proceedings cannot be reported by a bureau after 7 years, although a bankruptcy proceeding can be reported for 10 years.

Credit Repair Organizations

These organizations, some nonprofit and others for-profit, advertise their ability to help consumers work their way out of debt and eliminate negative credit information. Congress began regulating these groups with the Credit Repair Organization Act of 1996. Both the bankruptcy reforms (see Chapter 34) and state laws have established standards and procedures to ensure that consumers are not absorbing higher costs for services that they could do for themselves. There were additional reforms under the Consumer Financial Protection Act, including requirements for disclosures.

32-2m Other Consumer Protections

Various laws aimed at protecting purchasers of real estate, buyers of services, and prospective franchisees have been adopted in the states and at the federal level.

Real Estate Development Sales: Interstate Land Sales Full Disclosure Act

development statement— statement that sets forth significant details of a real estate or property development as required by the federal Land Sales Act.

Anyone promoting the sale of a real estate development that is divided into 50 or more parcels of less than 5 acres each must file a **development statement** with the secretary of Housing and Urban Development (HUD). This statement must set forth significant details of the development as required by the federal Interstate Land Sales Full Disclosure Act (ILSFDA).[37]

property report— condensed version of a property development statement filed with the secretary of HUD and given to a prospective customer at least 48 hours before signing a contract to buy or lease property.

Anyone buying or renting one of the parcels in the subdivision must be given a **property report,** which is a condensed version of the development statement filed with the secretary of HUD. This report must be given to the prospective customer at least 48 hours before the signing of the contract to buy or lease.

State statutes complement the ILSFDA and frequently require that particular enterprises selling property disclose certain information to prospective buyers. Some state statutes provide protection for sales of real property interests such as time-sharing condominiums that are not covered under the ILSFDA.[38]

Service Contracts

The UCCC treats a consumer service contract the same as a consumer sale of goods if (1) payment is made in installments or a credit charge is made and (2) the amount financed does not exceed $25,000. The UCCC defines *services* broadly as embracing transportation, hotel and restaurant accommodations, education, entertainment, recreation, physical culture (such as athletic clubs or bodybuilding schools), hospital accommodations, funerals, and cemetery accommodations.

In some states, it is unlawful for a repair shop to make unauthorized repairs to an automobile and then refuse to return the automobile to the customer until the customer has paid for the repairs. In some states, a consumer protection statute imposes multiple

[37] 15 U.S.C. §1701 *et seq.*
[38] *Beaver v. Tarsadia Hotels,* 29 F. Supp. 3d 1294 (S.D. Cal. 2014).

damages on a repair shop that delays unreasonably in performing a contract to repair property of the consumer.[39]

Franchises

franchisee–person to whom franchise is granted.

franchisor–party granting the franchise.

franchise–(1) a privilege or authorization, generally exclusive, to engage in a particular activity within a particular geographic area, such as a government franchise to operate a taxi company within a specified city, or a private franchise as the grant by a manufacturer of a right to sell products within a particular territory or for a particular number of years; (2) the right to vote.

To protect prospective **franchisees** from deception by **franchisors** that seek to sell interests, an FTC regulation requires that the franchisor give a prospective franchisee a disclosure statement 10 days before the franchisee signs a contract or pays any money for a **franchise.** The disclosure statement provides detailed information relating to the franchisor's finances, experience, size of operation, and involvement in litigation. The FTC enforces these disclosure requirements and can impose fines.

Automobile Lemon Laws

All states have adopted special laws for the protection of consumers buying automobiles that develop numerous defects or defects that cannot be corrected. These statutes protect only persons buying automobiles for personal, family, or household use. They generally classify an automobile as a *lemon* if it cannot be put in proper or warranted condition within a specified period of time or after a specified number of repair attempts. In general, they give the buyer greater protection than is given to other buyers by the UCC or other consumer protection statutes (see Chapter 24). In some states, the seller of a car that turns out to be a lemon is required to give the buyer a brand-new replacement car. In some states, certain agencies may also bring an action to collect civil penalties from the seller of a lemon car.

Lemon laws in most states are designed to increase the prelitigation bargaining power of consumers and reduce the greater power of manufacturers to resist complaints or suits by consumers.[40] **For Example,** Abdul, who owned a paint store, purchased two automobiles from Prime Motors, one for delivering paint to his customers and the second for his wife to use for shopping and taking their children to school. Both cars were defective and in need of constant repair. Abdul claimed that he was entitled to remedies provided by the local automobile lemon law. He was wrong with respect to the store's delivery car because lemon laws do not cover cars purchased for commercial use, but the other car was protected by the lemon law because it was clearly a family car.

Make the Connection

Summary

Modern methods of marketing, packaging, and financing have reduced the ordinary consumer to a subordinate position. To protect the consumer from the hardship, fraud, and oppression that could result from being in such an inferior position, consumer protection laws, at both the state and federal levels, afford rights to consumers and impose requirements on those who deal with consumers.

When a consumer protection statute is violated, an action may sometimes be brought by the consumer against the wrongdoer. More commonly, an action is brought by an administrative agency or by the state attorney general.

Consumer protection laws are directed at false and misleading advertising; misleading or false use of labels; the methods of selling, with specific requirements on the

[39] *Raysoni v. Payless Auto Deals, LLC,* 766 S.E.2d 24 (Ga. 2014).
[40] *James Michael Leasing Co. LLC v. PACCAR, Inc.,* 772 F.3d 815 (7th Cir. 2014).

disclosure of terms and the permitting of consumer cancellation of home-solicited sales; and types of credit arrangements. The consumer is protected in a contract agreement by regulation of its form, prohibition of unconscionable terms, and limitation of the credit that can be extended to a consumer. Credit card protections include prohibition of the unauthorized distribution of credit cards and limited liability of the cardholder for the unauthorized use of a credit card. Included in consumer protection laws are the application of payments; the preservation of consumer defenses as against a transferee of the consumer's contract; product safety; the protection of credit standing and reputation; and (to some extent) real estate development sales, franchises, and service contracts. Lemon laws provide special protection to buyers of automobiles for personal, household, or family use.

Learning Outcomes

After studying this chapter, you should be able to clearly explain:

32-1   General Principles

LO.1   Explain what consumer protection laws do and the types of consumer protections

See the list of headings in this chapter to determine areas of consumer protection, page 618.

See the *Laughlin v. Bank of America* case on consumer protections in mortgage modifications, page 621.

See the *McNeil-PPC, Inc. v. Pfizer Inc.* case on page 625.

See the Thinking Things Through that deals with ads between competing football helmet manufacturers and the concussions, and a study that Ridell used in its ads that Schutt Sports says is misleading, page 626.

See the Sports & Entertainment Law feature related to the football helmet case and concussions, page 627.

32-2   Areas of Consumer Protection

LO.2   List the rights and protections consumer debtors have when a collector contacts them

See the discussion of the Fair Debt Collection Practices Act, page 634.

See the Ethics & the Law feature, "Getting Into Debt and Getting Debt Relief—from the Same Company," page 635.

See the E-Commerce & Cyberlaw feature on Marriott blocking WiFi in its hotels so that convention participants and exhibitors had to pay for WiFi, page 628.

LO.3   Give a summary of the rights of consumers with regard to credit reports

See the *Smith v. E-Backgroundchecks.com* case, page 636.

LO.4   Describe the types of protections available for consumers who have credit cards

See the discussion of the CARD Act, pages 630–632.

Key Terms

compensatory damages
consumer
consumer credit
Consumer Financial Protection
    Bureau
development statement

Dodd-Frank Wall Street Reform and
    Consumer Protection Act
franchise
franchisees
franchisors
hearsay evidence

predatory lending
property report
punitive damages
subprime lending market

Questions and Case Problems

1. The San Antonio Retail Merchants Association (SARMA) was a credit reporting agency. It was asked by one of its members to furnish information on William Douglas Thompson III. It supplied information from a file that contained data on William III and on William Daniel Thompson Jr. The agency had incorporated information related to William Jr. into the file relating to William III so that all information appeared to relate to William III. This was a negligent mistake because each William had a different Social Security number, which should have raised a suspicion that there was a mistake. In addition, SARMA should have used a number of checkpoints to ensure that incoming information would be put into the proper file. William Jr. had bad credit standing. Because of its mistake, SARMA gave a bad

report on William III, who was denied credit by several enterprises. The federal Fair Credit Reporting Act makes a credit reporting agency liable to any consumer about whom it furnishes a consumer report without following reasonable procedures to ensure maximum possible accuracy of information. William III sued SARMA for its negligence in confusing him with William Jr. Is SARMA liable? [*Thompson v. San Antonio Retail Merchants Ass'n*, 682 F.2d 509 (5th Cir.)]

2. Colgate-Palmolive Co. ran a television commercial to show that its shaving cream, Rapid Shave, could soften even the toughness of sandpaper. The commercial showed what was described as the sandpaper test. Actually, what was used was a sheet of Plexiglas on which sand had been sprinkled. The FTC claimed that this was a deceptive practice. The advertiser contended that actual sandpaper would merely look like ordinary colored paper and that Plexiglas had been used to give the viewer an accurate visual representation of the test. Could the FTC prohibit the use of this commercial? [*Federal Trade Commission v. Colgate-Palmolive Co.*, 380 U.S. 374]

3. Sharolyn Charles wrote a check for $17.93 to a Poncho's Restaurant on July 4, 1996, as payment for a meal she had there. The check was returned for insufficient funds. Poncho's forwarded the check to Check Rite for collection.

On July 19, Check Rite sent a letter to Charles, stating that "[t]his is an attempt to collect a debt" and requesting total payment of $42.93—the amount of the check plus a service charge of $25. On August 7, Check Rite sent a second letter, requesting payment of $42.93 and advising Charles that failure to pay the total amount due might result in additional liability for damages and attorneys' fees, estimated at $242.93.

Check Rite subsequently referred the matter to the law firm of Lundgren & Associates for collection. On September 8, Lundgren sent a letter to Charles offering to settle within 10 days for a total amount of $127.93—the amount of the check plus a settlement amount of $110. Lundgren further advised that it had made no decision to file suit, that it could later decide to do so, and that Charles's potential liability was $317.93. Charles immediately sent to Lundgren a money order in the amount of $17.93. On September 13, Lundgren sent a second letter, repeating the settlement offer made in the September 8 letter. Lundgren then returned

Charles's payment on September 14, declining to accept it as payment in full and repeating the settlement offer. On September 19, Lundgren sent a fourth letter to Charles, repeating the settlement offer.

On October 15, 1996, Charles filed suit in federal district court alleging violations of the Fair Debt Collections Practices Act (FDCPA). Lundgren & Associates moved to dismiss the case on grounds that an attempt to collect on a check is not a "debt" governed by FDCPA. The district court dismissed the case; Charles appealed. Should Charles win? Is she protected under the FDCPA? [*Charles v. Lundgren & Associates, P.C.*, 119 F.3d 739 (9th Cir.)]

4. Thomas was sent a credit card through the mail by a company that had taken his name and address from the telephone book. Because he never requested the card, Thomas left the card lying on his desk. A thief stole the card and used it to purchase merchandise in several stores in Thomas's name. The issuer of the credit card claimed that Thomas was liable for the total amount of the purchases made by the thief. Thomas claimed that he was not liable for any amount. The court decided that Thomas was liable for $50. Who is correct? Why?

5. On May 16, 2003, Sari Smith filed a class-action lawsuit in Cook County, Illinois, against J.M. Smucker Co. on behalf of "[a]ll purchasers in the United States of America of spreadable fruit products labeled 'Simply 100% Fruit' manufactured, produced, and sold by J.M. Smucker Co. excluding its directors, officers and employees" for consumer fraud, deceptive business practices, unjust enrichment, and breach of warranty, alleging that Smucker's Simply 100% Fruit products do not contain 100 percent fruit. The premium jam's label indicates that, for example, its Strawberry jam also contains "fruit syrup, lemon juice concentrate, fruit pectin, red grape juice concentrate and natural flavors." Is the label a form of deceptive advertising?

If you were a Smucker's executive, what would you argue in the case on deceptive ads? [*J.M. Smucker Co. v. Rudge*, 877 So. 2d 820 (Fla. App.)]

6. International Yogurt Co. (IYC) developed a unique mix for making frozen yogurt and related products. Morris and his wife purchased a franchise from the company but were not told that a franchise was not a requirement for obtaining the mix—that the company would sell its yogurt mix to anyone. The Morrises' franchise business was a failure, and they

sold it at a loss after three years. They then sued the company for fraud and for violation of the state Franchise Investment Protection Act and the state Consumer Protection Act for failing to inform them that the mix could be obtained without a franchise. IYC claimed that no liability could be imposed for failing to make the disclosure. Was it correct? [*Morris v. International Yogurt Co.*, 729 P.2d 33 (Wash.)]

7. In December 2008, Corey and Jamie Baker purchased a TV from Best Buy as well as a four-year service contract for the TV. In November 2010, Best Buy determined that the problems the Bakers were having with the TV could not be fixed, so Best Buy replaced the TV with a comparable model. Best Buy told the Bakers that if they wanted the full protection on the replacement TV, they would need to buy a new four-year policy. The Bakers and others filed suit against Best Buy for consumer fraud and false statements in advertisements because the Bakers felt that the ads depicted the service agreement as being one of full protection for four years. Under the terms of the service contract purchased by the appellants, coverage under the plan was effective from the date the product was purchased and would expire four years from the effective date. But the next paragraph of the service contract adds that "[o]ur obligations under this Plan will be fulfilled in their entirety if we replace your product." The contract further stated "Limits of Liability," defining a limit of the lesser of repair or replacements and finally stating that "[i]n the event ... we replace the product, we shall have satisfied all obligations under the Plan." What should the court decide? Was there deception, or is the contract clear enough for buyers? Discuss the factors the court will consider in deciding whether there has been consumer fraud. [*Baker v. Best Buy Stores, LP*, 812 N.W.2d 177 (Minn. App.)]

8. The town of Newport obtained a corporate MasterCard that was given to the town clerk for purchasing fuel for the town hall. The town clerk used the card for personal restaurant, hotel, and gift shop debts. The town refused to pay the card charges on the grounds that they were unauthorized. Was the town correct? [*MasterCard v. Town of Newport*, 396 N.W.2d 345 (Wis. App.)]

9. Stevens purchased a pair of softball shoes manufactured by Hyde Athletic Industries. Because of a defect in the shoes, she fell and broke an ankle. She sued Hyde under the state consumer protection act, which provided that "any person who is injured in ... business or property ... could sue for damages sustained." Hyde claimed that the act did not cover personal injuries. Stevens claimed that she was injured in her "property" because of the money that she had to spend for medical treatment and subsequent care. Decide. [*Stevens v. Hyde Athletic Industries, Inc.*, 773 P.2d 87 (Wash. App.)]

10. A consumer made a purchase on a credit card. The card issuer refused to accept the charge, and an attorney then sued the consumer for the amount due. In the complaint filed in the lawsuit, the attorney wrongly stated that interest was owed at 18 percent per annum. This statement was later corrected by an amendment of the complaint to 5 percent. The case against the consumer was ultimately settled, but the consumer then sued the attorney for penalties under the Fair Debt Collection Practices Act, claiming that the overstatement of the interest due in the original complaint was a violation of that act. The attorney defended on the ground that the act did not apply. Did it? [*Green v. Hocking*, 9 F.3d 18 (6th Cir.)]

11. Classify each of the following activities as proper or prohibited under the various consumer statutes you have studied.

    a. Calling a hospital room to talk to a debtor who is a patient there.

    b. Calling a hospital room to sell surgical stockings.

    c. Rolling back the odometer on one's car before selling it privately.

    d. No TILA disclosures on an instant tax refund program in which the lender takes 40 percent of the tax refund as a fee for advancing the money when the taxpayer files the tax return.

12. Alpha University has an arrangement with Axis Credit Card Company to collect 1 percent on all credit card charges made by students who obtain their cards through booths on the Alpha campus. Do any consumer protection statutes apply to this relationship?

13. List three areas in consumer credit cards affected by the CARD Act.

C H A P T E R   33

Secured Transactions in Personal Property

CPA # 33-1 Creation of Secured Transactions

Creditors can have some additional assurance of payment if the debtor pledges property as security for the loan. If the debtor does not pay, the creditor can then turn to the property and sell it or keep it as a means of satisfying the obligation.

A *secured transaction* is one means by which personal property is used to provide a backup plan or security for the creditor in the event the borrower does not pay. Secured transactions are governed by Article 9 of the Uniform Commercial Code (UCC). Article 9 has been revised several times, and its latest version (2001) has been adopted in some form by all states and the District of Columbia.[1]

33-1a Definitions

secured transaction–credit sale of goods or a secured loan that provides special protection for the creditor.

A **secured transaction** in personal property is created by giving the creditor a security interest in that property. A **security interest** is like a lien in personal property; it is a property right that enables the creditor to take possession of the property if the debtor does not pay the amount owed. **For Example,** if you borrow money from a bank to buy a car, the bank takes a security interest in the car. If you do not repay the loan, the bank can repossess the car and sell it to recover the money the bank has loaned you. If you purchase a side-by-side refrigerator from Kelvin's Appliances on credit, Kelvin's takes a security interest in the refrigerator. If you do not repay Kelvin's, Kelvin's can repossess the refrigerator and sell it to cover the amount you still owe.

security interest–property right that enables the creditor to take possession of the property if the debtor does not pay the amount owed.

The property that is subject to the security interest is called **collateral.** In the preceding examples, the car was the bank's collateral for the loan, and the refrigerator was Kelvin's collateral.

collateral–property pledged by a borrower as security for a debt.

Parties

The person to whom the money is owed, whether a seller or a lender, is called the **creditor** or **secured party.** The buyer on credit or the borrower is called the **debtor.**

creditor–person (seller or lender) who is owed money; also may be a secured party.

Nature of Creditor's Interest

The creditor does not own the collateral, but the security interest is a property right. That property right can ripen into possession and the right to transfer title by sale.

secured party–person owed the money, whether as a seller or a lender, in a secured transaction in personal property.

A creditor who has possession of the collateral as a means of security has a duty of care imposed under the UCC. Under the UCC, the creditor in possession must exercise reasonable care to preserve the property. The creditor is liable for any damage that results from falling short of that standard.

debtor–buyer on credit (i.e., a borrower).

Nature of Debtor's Interest

A debtor who is a borrower ordinarily owns the collateral.[2] As such, the debtor has all rights of any property owner to recover damages for the loss or improper seizure of, or damage to, the collateral.[3]

---

[1] Not all states, however, have adopted verbatim versions. For example, the application of Article 9 to governmental units varies significantly among the states. See "UCC Article 9: Personal Property Secured Transactions," 60 *Bus. Lawyer* 1725 (2005).

[2] *Heartland Bank and Trust v. The Leiter Group*, 18 N.E.3d 558 (Ill.App.2014); *Farmers-Merchants Bank & Trust Co. v. Southern Structures, LLC*, 134 So. 3d 142 (La. App. 2014).

[3] Article 9 does cover consignment arrangements. The consignor continues to own the goods, and the consignee is treated as a secured creditor with a purchase money security interest in the consigned goods.

33-1b **Creation of a Security Interest**

The attachment, or the creation of a valid security interest, occurs when the following three conditions are satisfied: There is (1) a security agreement, (2) value has been given, and (3) the debtor has rights in the collateral. These three conditions can occur in any order. A security interest will attach when the last of these conditions has been met. When the security interest attaches, it is then enforceable against the debtor and the collateral.

Agreement

C P A

security agreement—
agreement of the creditor
and the debtor that the
creditor will have a
security interest.

The **security agreement** is the contract between creditor and debtor for the security interest. This required agreement must identify the parties, contain a reasonable description of the collateral, indicate the parties' intent that the creditor has a security interest in it, describe the debt or the performance that is secured thereby, and be authenticated by the debtor.[4] Electronic authentication by debtors is acceptable under Article 9.[5] Authentication can come from the debtor's actions that indicate an understanding of a credit and secured debt agreement.[6] A security interest description is valid if it "reasonably identifies what is described."[7] Examples of reasonable identification include a specific listing, category,[8] quantity, and serial numbers. "Supergeneric descriptions"[9] such as "all the debtor's personal property" are insufficient,[10] but "livestock" is a sufficient description.[11] The requirement for description of consumer goods as collateral is more stringent than for other types of collateral.[12]

If the creditor has possession of the collateral, the security agreement may be oral regardless of the amount involved.[13] **For Example,** if you pledge your stereo system to a friend as security for the loan and the friend will keep it at his home until you have repaid him, your friend has possession of the collateral, and your oral security agreement is valid and enforceable by your friend. If the creditor does not have possession of the collateral, as in the case of credit sales and most secured loans, the security agreement must be evidenced by a record that meets all requirements.

Field warehousing, covered in Chapter 21, is another form of possession of goods that permits an oral security agreement. Credit unions and banks can possess an account

---

[4] "No magic words are necessary … to create a security interest." In re *Okke,* 513 B.R. 896 (W.D. Mich. 2014).

[5] However, the debtor must be aware that a security agreement is being signed. An electronic signature on a credit card transaction does not indicate that the debtor was aware he was agreeing to a security interest by Best Buy if the terms were not reviewed or made conspicuous in the sales receipt. In re *Cunningham,* 489 B.R. 602 (D. Kan. 2013).

[6] Article 9, §9-102(a)(69) defines "record," the new substitute for "signed agreement" of old Article 9, as "information that is inscribed on a tangible medium and is retrievable in perceivable form." Authentication need not be a signature. In re *Eyerman,* 517 B.R. 800 Bankr. (S.D. Ohio. 2014). One court held that a letter between the debtor and creditor qualified as a security agreement because it contained all of the necessary elements of description, signature, etc. In re *Loop 76, LLC,* 578 Fed. Appx. 644 (9th Cir. 2014). Not all states follow the "collage doctrine" that allows the grouping together of documents to establish a security agreement. In re *Thrun,* 495 B.R. 861 (W.D. Wis. 2013).

[7] U.C.C. §9-110.

[8] Commercial tort claims and consumer transactions cannot be sufficiently described by type of collateral. The security agreement must give more specifics. §9-108(e)(1) and (2).

[9] U.C.C. §9-108(c).

[10] The comments to §9-108 indicate that serial numbers are not necessarily required, but an outsider must be able to tell from the description what property is or is not included under the security agreement. Official Comment, §9-108, 2. "Debtor's new trucks" is insufficient. In re *LDB Media, LLC,* 497 B.R. 332 (M.D. Fla. 2013).

[11] *Baldwin v. Castro County Feeders I, Ltd.,* 678 N.W.2d 796 (S.D. 2004). All "IP assets" is also sufficient. In re *ProvideRx of Grapevine, LLC,* 507 B.R. 132 (N.D. Tex. 2014).

[12] In re *Gracy,* 522 B.R. 686 (D. Kan. 2015). "Goods purchased on [debtor's] account is insufficient." In re *Cunningham,* 489 B.R. 602 (D. Kan. 2013).

[13] U.C.C. §9-207; In re *Rowe,* 369 B.R. 73 (Mass. 2007). If there is no record the security interest itself is destroyed when the collateral is surrendered.

pledged as security if the funds cannot be used by the account holder without permission and clearance from a bank officer.

Value

value–consideration or antecedent debt or security given in exchange for the transfer of a negotiable instrument or creation of a security interest.

The creditor gives **value** either by lending money to the debtor or by delivering goods on credit. The value may be part of a contemporaneous exchange or given previously as a loan. **For Example,** a debtor who already owes a creditor $5,000 could later pledge a water scooter as collateral for that loan and give the debtor a security interest in the scooter. In fact, creditors who become nervous about repayment often request collateral later during the course of performance of a previously unsecured loan.

Rights in the Collateral

The debtor must have rights in the collateral for a security interest to attach. For example, when goods are sent "FOB place of shipment" to a debtor, the debtor has title at the time those goods are delivered to the carrier by the seller. See Chapter 23 for more information.[14] The buyer has rights in the collateral that allow for the collateral to be subject to the creditor's security interest.[14]

CPA 33-1c Purchase Money Security Interest

purchase money security interest (PMSI)–the security interest in the goods a seller sells on credit that become the collateral for the creditor/seller.

When a seller sells on credit and is given a security interest in the goods sold, that interest is called a **purchase money security interest (PMSI).** If the buyer borrows money from a third person so that the purchase can be made for cash, a security interest given in those goods to that lender is also called a purchase money security interest.[15] Certain special priority rights (discussed later in this chapter) are given in some circumstances to creditors who hold a PMSI.

CASE SUMMARY

The Best Buys on Credit

FACTS: Charles and Charity Cunningham (the Debtors) filed a joint Chapter 7 bankruptcy. The Debtors had purchased two iPods, a camera, a computer, and other items in 12 separate consumer transactions of consumer goods from Best Buy, N.A., a national retailer of consumer electronics and related products and services. Some of Debtors' purchases were made on credit provided by Capital One.

The Debtors signed a credit application, which states, "you grant the Bank a purchase money security interest in the goods purchased on your Account." Furthermore, the application states in that same section that the cardholder, the Debtors, agree to the terms and conditions of the Cardholder Agreement.

The Application has this language buried in a 16-line paragraph in a small font. A magnifying glass is necessary to find and read the language. The language appears in the ninth and tenth lines of the paragraph. The Debtors agreed, in this fine print, to the terms and conditions of the Cardholder Agreement. The Application indicates that the Cardholder Agreement would be sent to the Debtors after the Application and initial purchase of consumer products on January 16, 2010. The Cardholder Agreement is not signed. Buried in 41 numbered paragraphs in small print in the Cardholder Agreement is language that refers to Debtors granting to Capital One "a purchase money security interest in the goods purchased with your Card."

[14] U.C.C. §9-112.
[15] U.C.C. §9-107. In re *Marriage of Christodolou*, 2012 WL 4814606 (Tex. App. 2012).

The Best Buys on Credit continued

The cardholder agreement states in paragraph 17 entitled "Security," "you grant us a purchase money security interest in the goods purchased with your Card."

The 12 Best Buy receipts for the purchases all were signed by one of the Debtors, except for one transaction. The receipts contain basic information, such as the location of the Best Buy store, a brief description of items purchased and the price of these items, and the date and time of the sale. The receipts also state "Payment Type: BBY CARD/HSBC." The following language appears below the place of signature:

KEEP YOUR RECEIPT!

I HAVE READ AND AGREE TO ALL RETURN AND REFUND POLICIES PRINTED ON THE BACK OF THIS

RECEIPT AND POSTED IN THE STORE. I HAVE RECEIVED GOODS AND/OR SERVICES IN THE AMOUNT

SHOWN ABOVE. BESTBUY.COM RETURN AND EXCHANGE INFORMATION AND PRICE MATCH POLICY

MAY VARY SLIGHTLY FROM IN-STORE POLICY. PLEASE LOG ONTO WWW.BESTBUY.COM

FOR COMPLETE DETAILS.

The court did not have copies of the reverse side of the receipts, which were not provided. Regardless, it appears that the reverse side of the receipts only contains language pertinent to the return and refund policies of Best Buy. There is no reference on the receipts to security interests, purchase money or otherwise, retained by anyone. The receipts also do not contain a reference to the Application or the Cardholder Agreement. The Debtors requested a determination by the Court that Capital One does not hold a security interest, purchase money or otherwise, in the goods they purchased at Best Buy.

DECISION: A security agreement or financing statement must contain a description of the collateral that reasonably identifies the collateral. The use of categories or types of collateral defined under the UCC (i.e., inventory) is still permitted. However, in consumer transactions and a limited number of other situations, a description by type or class of collateral is ineffective as to after-acquired property. Article 9 permits "supergeneric" descriptions in the financing statement such as "all assets" or "all personal property" but not in the security agreement.

The Debtors argued that any security interest that Capital One may have never attached to the Consumer Goods because an insufficient description is fatal to the attachment of a security interest in consumer goods. Capital One argued that the description is sufficient if one combines the language contained in the application, the receipts, and the Cardholder Agreement. The issue before the Court was whether the description is sufficient to allow attachment and enforceability. The Capital One receipts do not contain a reference to a purchase money security interest or any other security interest. Capital One may not rely upon the description of the Debtors' goods purchased on the receipts because the receipts are not a component of a security agreement between the parties.

The security agreement is not enforceable in a consumer transaction because, excluding the receipts, the collateral is only described by type or class. Therefore, Capital One does not hold a security interest in the Debtors' goods. **[In re *Cunningham*, 489 B.R. 602, 80 U.C.C. Rep. Serv. 2d 576 (D. Kan. 2013)]**

CPA   33-1d **The Nature and Classification of Collateral**

The nature of the collateral in a credit transaction, as well as its classification under Article 9, affect the procedural obligations and rights of creditors. Article 9 contains an extensive list of the types of collateral, including the traditional types such as consumer goods, equipment, inventory, general intangibles, farm products, and fixtures,[16] but also accounts, accounts receivable, accounts receivable held because of credit card transactions or license fees, energy contracts, insurance policy proceeds, amounts due for services rendered, amounts earned from chartering a vessel, winnings in the state lottery, and health

---

[16] U.C.C. §9-102.

care insurance receivables. The general category of "account"[17] does not include commercial tort claims, deposit accounts, investment property, or letters of credit but does include insurance claims, lottery winnings, and property proceeds.[18]

Consumer Goods

consumer goods–goods used or bought primarily for personal, family, or household use.

Collateral that is classified as a **consumer good** results in different rights and obligations under Article 9, regardless of the type of property it is. Collateral is considered a consumer good if it is "used or bought for use primarily for personal, family, or household purposes."[19] The use of the good, and not its properties, controls its classification. **For Example,** a computer purchased by an architect for her office is not a consumer good. That same computer purchased by the same architect for use by her children at their home is a consumer good. A refrigerator purchased for the kitchen near an office conference center is not a consumer good. That same model refrigerator purchased for a home is a consumer good. The use of the goods controls the label that is applied to the collateral.

CPA

After-Acquired Collateral and Ongoing Credit

after-acquired goods– goods acquired after a security interest has attached.

floating lien–claim in a changing or shifting stock of goods of the buyer.

A creditor's rights can be expanded to include coverage of all future loans and funds advances as well as future acquisitions of collateral. If the security agreement so provides, the security interest attaches to **after-acquired goods** and applies to all loans to the debtor.[20] **For Example,** a security interest can cover the current inventory of the debtor and any future replenishments if a clause in the security agreement adds "after-acquired property" to the description of the inventory. Referred to in lay terms as a **floating lien,** the creditor's security interest covers the inventory regardless of its form or time of arrival in relation to attachment of the security interest.

After-acquired clauses in consumer credit contracts are restricted. An after-acquired property clause in a consumer security agreement can cover only goods acquired by the debtor within 10 days after the creditor gave value to the debtor.

Proceeds

The UCC defines proceeds as "whatever is received upon the sale, exchange, collection, or other disposition of collateral."[21] Collateral may change its form and character during the course of the security agreement. **For Example,** a debtor who has pledged its inventory of cars as collateral will be selling those cars. However, the buyers will sign credit contracts for the purchase of those cars. Article 9 considers the credit contracts and the right to payment under those contracts as proceeds. If the collateral has been insured and is damaged or destroyed, the debtor will receive money, another form of proceeds, from the insurance company. Proceeds are automatically subject to the creditor's security interest unless the security agreement provides to the contrary. The proceeds may be in any form, such as cash, checks, promissory notes, or other property.

[17] Deposit accounts are not considered "general intangibles" under Article 9 because of specific provisions on accounts. U.C.C. §§9-102(a)(29), 9-104, 9-109(d)(13), 9-312(b)(1), and §9-314. *ImagePoint, Inc. v. JPMorgan Chase Bank, Nat. Ass'n,* 27 F. Supp. 3d 494 (S.D.N.Y. 2014).
[18] U.C.C. §§9-102(2)(a)(5), 9-102(72), & 9-109(a)(2). A membership in a golf club can be pledged as security for a loan used to purchase the membership. *Bonem v. Golf Club of Georgia,* 591 S.E.2d 462, 52 U.C.C. Rep. Serv. 2d (West) 280 (Ga. Ct. App. 2003).
[19] U.C.C. §9-109(1).
[20] U.C.C. §9-204.
[21] U.C.C. §9-306(1).

Electronic Chattel Paper

"Electronic chattel paper" is a record of a right to funds, payment, or property that is stored in an electronic medium. **For Example,** it is possible to pledge the funds you have available in your Internet shopping account as an Article 9 security interest?[22]

CASE SUMMARY

Numismatic Nuance: Coins Are Not Money under Article 9

FACTS: On April 18, 2006, James W. Lull entered into a consignment agreement with Bowers and Merena for auction of his Standing Liberty quarter-dollar collection. On April 21, 2006, Bowers and Merena also agreed to loan to Lull $700,000, with the loan to be repaid from the auction proceeds.

The collection sold at auction for $1,119,750. After repayment of its loan to Lull and expenses of sale, Bowers held net proceeds of $455,046.11. However, Gardiner, Kapaa 382, and Yamaguchi went to Bowers and Merena and tried to claim the auction proceeds.

Gardiner's claim resulted from a March 1, 2005, loan to Lull for $3.8 million. Lull was unable to repay the loan when it became due on February 28, 2006, so in July 2006 Gardiner agreed not to take legal action to enforce the note after Lull executed a security agreement on July 19, 2006, which granted Gardiner a security interest in "all personal property and other assets" of Lull and specifically listed all commonly known categories of personal property, including goods, accounts, money, chattel paper, general intangibles, instruments, and the proceeds thereof.

Gardiner recorded a financing statement in the Bureau of Conveyances of the State of Hawaii on July 20, 2006. The financing statement described Gardiner's collateral as "All assets and all personal property of the Debtor (including, without limitations, fixtures), whether now owned or hereafter acquired or arising, and wherever located, and all proceeds and products thereof."

Kapaa 382 made short-term loans to Lull on September 20, 2005, for $933,000; on December 5, 2005, for $471,566.82; on December 15, 2005, for $165,000; and on December 19, 2005, for $400,000. On July 26, 2006, Lull executed a "Partial Settlement Agreement" in which he agreed, among other things, to "convey and transfer to [Kapaa 382] title to the Coin Collection currently consigned to Bowers and Merena Auctions, LLC for auction scheduled to occur in August 2006, by Bill of Sale[.]"

Kapaa 382 filed a financing statement with the California Secretary of State on August 22, 2006, but the financing statement listed Kapaa 382 as both the debtor and the secured party and did not mention Lull.

On July 11, 2006, Lull executed an assignment of the proceeds of the coin auction to Yamaguchi for an unpaid promissory note, dated May 16, 2006, in the amount of $700,000. The assignment was not recorded.

On December 8, 2006, Lull filed a voluntary Chapter 7 petition. Claims in the bankruptcy case exceeded $55 million, including unsecured claims of nearly $42 million. The parties involved with the coins all claimed priority.

DECISION: The coins were not money for purposes of Article 9 and could be subject to a security interest. Because the coins were collector's items they were a unique form of personal property and not used as a medium of exchange. The parties could create a security interest in the coins and be entitled to Article 9 perfection rights. **[In re _Lull_, 386 B.R. 261, 65 U.C.C. Rep. Serv. 2d 194 (D. Haw. 2008)]**

CPA   33-2 **Perfection of Secured Transactions**

The attachment of a security interest gives the creditor the important rights of enforcement of the debt through repossession of the collateral (see the section titled "Creditor's Possession and Disposition of Collateral" for more discussion of enforcement and repossession). _Attachment_ allows the secured party to resort to the collateral to collect the debt

---

[22] U.C.C. §9-105.

when the debtor defaults. However, more than one creditor may hold an attached security interest in the same collateral. A creditor who obtains a **perfected security interest** enjoys priority over unperfected interests and may in some cases enjoy priority over other perfected interests. A security interest is valid against the debtor even though it is not perfected. However, perfection provides creditors with rights superior to those of other creditors with unperfected interests. Attachment provides creditors with rights; perfection gives them priority, and a creditor can obtain perfection in collateral in several ways.

perfected security interest—security interest with priority because of filing, possession, automatic, or temporary priority status.

CPA

33-2a Perfection by Creditor's Possession

If the creditor has possession of the collateral, the security interest in the possessed goods is perfected.[23] It remains perfected until that possession is surrendered. **For Example,** when a creditor has taken a security interest in 50 gold coins and has those gold coins in his vault, his possession of the coins is perfection.

A more complex example of possession as a means of perfection is found in the commercial tool of **field warehousing.** (See Chapter 21) In this arrangement, a creditor actually has an agent on site at a buyer's place of business, and the creditor's agent controls the buyer's access to, use of, and transfer of the collateral. **For Example,** an aircraft manufacturer may have an agent on site at an aircraft dealership. That agent decides when the planes can be released to buyers and who will receive the buyers' payments or notes.[24]

field warehousing—stored goods under the exclusive control of a warehouse but kept on the owner's premises rather than in a warehouse.

CPA

33-2b Perfection for Consumer Goods

A purchase money security interest in consumer goods is perfected from the moment it attaches.[25] Known as **automatic perfection,** no other action is required for perfection as against other creditors. Because so many consumer purchases are made on credit, the UCC simplifies perfection so that creditors who are merchant sellers are not overly burdened with paperwork. However, as discussed later in this chapter in the section on priorities, the automatic perfection of a PMSI in consumer goods has some limitations. It may be destroyed by the debtor consumer's resale of the goods to a consumer who does not know of the security interest.

automatic perfection—perfection given by statute without specific filing or possession requirements on the part of the creditor.

33-2c Perfection for Health Care Insurance Receivables

Article 9 has a form of collateral known as *health care insurance receivables.* The nature of this collateral requires a unique method of perfection. When a consumer gives a creditor a security interest in health insurance proceeds that are forthcoming, the creditor need not make any filing or take any further steps to have a perfected security interest in those proceeds. The perfection is automatic.[26]

33-2d Automatic Perfection

A creditor attains automatic perfection in certain circumstances under Article 9. **For Example,** a creditor has an automatic PMSI in software that is sold with a computer that is subject to a creditor's PMSI. If you buy an IBM ThinkPad® from Best Buy on credit and get Microsoft Office software as part of your package deal, Best Buy has an automatically perfected security interest not only in the consumer goods (your new

---

[23] U.C.C. §9-305; In re *Clean Burn Fuels, LLC,* 492 B.R. 445 (N.C. 2013).
[24] U.C.C. §9-312.
[25] U.C.C. §§9-301, & 9-304; In re *Saxe,* 491 B.R. 244 (W.D. Wis. 2013).
[26] Article 9, §9-309(5).

computer) but also in the software sold with it.[27] The perfection for consumer purchase money security interests that occurs when the security interest attaches is also a form of automatic perfection.

CPA

temporary perfection– perfection given for a limited period of time to creditors.

33-2e Temporary Perfection

Some creditors are given **temporary perfection** for the collateral.[28] **For Example,** a creditor is generally given four months to refile its financing statement in a state to which a debtor has relocated. During that four-month period, the interest of the creditor is temporarily perfected in the new state despite no filing of a financing statement in that state's public records. Most creditors' agreements provide that the failure of the debtor to notify the creditor of a move constitutes a default under the credit agreement. Creditors need to know of the move so that they can refile in the debtor's new state.[29] Creditors enjoy a 20-day temporary perfection in negotiable instruments taken as collateral. Following the expiration of the 20-day period, measured from the time their security interest attaches, creditors must perfect in another way, such as by filing a financing statement or by possession.

CPA

33-2f Perfection by Control

Control is a form of possession under Article 9.[30] Control is achieved when a bank or creditor is able to require the debtor account holder to clear all transactions in that account with the bank or creditor. The debtor cannot use the funds that have been pledged as collateral without permission from the party holding the control. **For Example,** a credit union member could secure a loan with the credit union by giving the credit union a security interest in her savings account. The credit union then has control of the account and is perfected by the ability to dictate what the credit union member can do with those funds.

33-2g Perfection for Motor Vehicles

In most states, a non-Code statute provides that a security interest in a noninventory motor vehicle must be noted on the vehicle title registration. When so noted, the interest is perfected.[31] States that do not have a separate motor vehicle perfection system require financing statements, as described in the next section.

CPA

financing statement– brief statement (record) that gives sufficient information to alert third persons that a particular creditor may have a security interest in the collateral described.

33-2h Perfection by Filing a Financing Statement

The **financing statement** (known as a UCC-1) is an authenticated record statement that gives sufficient information to alert third persons that a particular creditor may have a security interest in the collateral described. With technological capabilities, the paper-signed documents are no longer a requirement. The creditor must be able to show that the documents filed were "authorized" and an "authenticated record."[32] In other words,

---

[27] Article 9, §§9-102 & 9-103.

[28] U.C.C. §9-312.

[29] U.C.C. §9-316(a).

[30] U.C.C. §9-104.

[31] U.C.C. §9-303. In re *Gracy,* 522 B.R. 686 (D. Kan. 2015).

[32] The sample financing form included with U.C.C. §9-521 does not even have a place for the debtor's signature. While a signed security agreement and signed financing statement are valid for both the security agreement and financing statement, such formalities are no longer necessary. A jail detainee's filing of a financing statement against a judge was declared invalid because the judge failed to consent. Indeed, the judge was not aware of the detainee's activities or that he owed the detainee money. *Nichols v. Branton,* 995 N.Y.S.2d 450 (N.Y. Supp. 2014).

the debtor's signature is not required for the financing statement to be valid. Article 9 gives three ways for the debtor to authorize a financing statement:

1. By authenticating a security agreement.[33]
2. By becoming bound under a security agreement, the debtor agrees to allow financing statements to be filed on the collateral in the security agreement.
3. By acquiring collateral subject to a security agreement.

An unauthorized financing statement filed without meeting one of these requirements does not provide the creditor perfected creditor status.[34]

The Content of the Financing Statement

A financing statement must provide "the name of the debtor ... the name of the secured party or representative of the secured party ... [and an indication of] the collateral covered by the financing statement."[35] The form provided with Article 9 includes much more information. Under §9-516, additional requirements are imposed for initial financing statements that include "a mailing address for the debtor [and] ... whether the debtor is an individual or organization."[36] Furthermore, §9-511 requires that the secured party of record provide an address so that there is an address for mailing notices required under other sections.

Because the filings for Article 9 perfection are electronic, the precise identification of the debtor has become critical. With electronic filings, those who will be doing searches on debtors will not find matches when the name of the debtor has not been properly entered on the financing statement. With computer technology, additional precision in debtors' names is necessary or searches are thwarted. The consequences for misspelling a debtor's name are greater in an electronic system and the risk is high. The failure to properly identify the debtor will be a loss of priority by perfection because the electronic search in the state did not uncover prior interests. Courts continue their balancing of rights, notice, and technology in dealing with proper filing and priorities that result.[37]

CASE SUMMARY

The Misplaced "9" under Article 9

FACTS: On September 8, 2005, Wells Fargo (Defendants) and the Christopher Hanson Insurance Agency entered into a promissory note and a security agreement for one million dollars. As security for the loan, Hanson assigned his interests in two separate annuity contracts, both issued by Fidelity & Guaranty Life Insurance Company ("Fidelity &

Guaranty"). The two annuity contracts were valued at one million dollars, and they were identified as "L9E00015" and "L9E00016," respectively.

That same day, Wells Fargo filed a financing statement with the Secretary of State of Missouri. The financing statement identified the "Debtor" as

---

[33] U.C.C. §9-509 permits the debtor and creditor to agree otherwise. For example, a debtor can place a requirement in the security agreement that the creditor obtain his or her signature before filing a financing statement.
[34] U.C.C. §9-510.
[35] U.C.C. §9-502(a).
[36] U.C.C. §9-516(b)(5).
[37] U.C.C. §9-506(a). In re *PTM Technologies, Inc.,* 452 B.R. 165 (M.D.N.C. 2011); In re *Webb,* 520 B.R. 748 (E.D. Ark. 2014).

The Misplaced "9" under Article 9 continued

"Christopher J. Hanson," and it describes the collateral as follows:

> All of Debtor's right, title, and interest in and to, assets and rights of Debtor, wherever located and whether now owned or hereafter acquired or arising and all proceeds and products in that certain Annuity Contract No.: LE900015 issued by Lincoln Benefit Life in the name of Debtor....

The financing statement identified the contract number as "LE900015" instead of "L9E00015," and it identified the issuer as "Lincoln Benefit Life" instead of Fidelity & Guaranty. On September 16, 2005, Wells Fargo filed an additional financing statement that correctly identified the contract number but once again mistakenly referred to the issuer of this contract as "Lincoln Benefit Life" instead of Fidelity & Guaranty.

On February 9, 2006, Hanson obtained a loan from ProGrowth Bank, Inc. As security for the loan, Hanson assigned his interests in the Fidelity & Guaranty annuity contracts to ProGrowth. On February 14, 2006, ProGrowth filed two financing statements with the Secretary of State of Missouri that identified Hanson and the Agency as the debtor and accurately described the collateral as: "Fidelity and Guaranty Life Insurance Annuity Contracts Number L9E00015 and Number L9E00016[.]"

ProGrowth filed suit seeking a declaration that Wells Fargo and Global One were not perfected secured creditors and that it had priority to the annuity funds. The district court granted summary judgment in favor of ProGrowth Bank, Inc. Wells Fargo appealed.

DECISION: The court held that Wells Fargo had enough in the financing statements to put a subsequent creditor on notice that there were interests in the debtor's property. Further, despite the transposition of the numbers of the annuities and the misidentification of the issuer, Wells had provided enough information to warrant simple clarification. Wells Fargo was a secured, perfected creditor in first position. [*ProGrowth Bank, Inc. v. Wells Fargo Bank, N.A.,* **558 F.3d 809 (8th Cir. 2008)**]*

*For a case that found a financing statement insufficient in description, see In re *Harvey Goldman & Co.,* 455 B.R. 621 (E.D. Mich. 2011).

The requirements for description of the collateral in the financing statements are now more general.[38] A security agreement can be filed as a financing statement if it contains all of the aforementioned required information.

Because the financing statement is intended as notice to third parties, it must be filed in a public place.[39] The formerly complex issues of filing location were simplified as a means of encouraging electronic systems that will be statewide, accessible across state lines, and organized simply by name in any index. The general rule is central filing for financing statements for all types of collateral. Filings for fixtures and other property-related interests have also been simplified with deferral to state laws on the proper filing location.[40]

CPA Defective Filing

When the filing of the financing statement is defective either because the statement is so erroneous or incomplete that it is seriously misleading or the filing is made in a wrong county or office, the filing fails to perfect the security interest.[41] The idea of perfection by filing is to give public notice of a creditor's interest. To the extent that the notice

---

[38] However, the sample financing form included with U.C.C. §9-521 includes boxes for all of the same information required under the previous versions Article 9.
[39] U.C.C. §9-401; *Official Committee of Unsecured Creditors of Motors Liquidation Co. v. JPMorgan Chase Bank, N.A.,* 103 A.3d 1010 (Del. 2014).
[40] U.C.C. §9-501.
[41] In re *Sterling,* 519 B.R. 586 (W.D.N.Y. 2014).

cannot be located or does not give sufficient information, the creditor then cannot rely on it to obtain the superior position of perfection.

33-2i Loss of Perfection

The perfection of the security interest can be lost if the creditor does not comply with the Article 9 requirements for continuing perfection.[42]

Possession of Collateral

When perfection is obtained because the creditor takes possession of the collateral, that perfection is lost if the creditor voluntarily surrenders the collateral to the debtor without any restrictions.

Consumer Goods

The perfection obtained by the automatic status of a PMSI is lost in some cases by removal of the goods to another state. The security interest may also be destroyed by resale of the goods to a consumer. To protect against these types of losses of protection, the creditor needs to file a financing statement. In the case of a PMSI, the perfection is good against other creditors but is not superior when it comes to buyers of the goods.

E-COMMERCE & CYBERLAW

Engines Are from Mars; Priorities Are from Financing Statements

In 2001, the International Association of Corporate Administrators promulgated Model Administrative Rules (MARS), a set of rules for the standards for search engines for court system, land, tax, and lien records. State and local governments will have different technology and standards that range from a liberal search engine to a strict search engine. A *liberal search engine* is similar to Google, which kicks back a corrected term and says, "Did you mean?" when you type in a name or word that is misspelled. A *strict search engine,* such as the simple one in Microsoft Word, will not find a word or phrase in a document unless you have spelled the search item exactly the way it appears in the document.

The MARS standards migrate toward the strict search engine. However, states have adopted different standards, and the result is that the electronic searches for debtors in various states can be very different. If there is a strict search engine in a state and the person doing the search types in "Ann Smythe," the correct spelling of the debtor's name, the financing statement against "Smythe" that was filed as "Ann Smith" will not be a match and the electronic system will kick out a "NO MATCH FOUND." Likewise, a creditor who files

under the name "House, Roger" when the debtor's actual name is "Roger House" has not perfected.* The same would be true of a financing statement filed under "Terry J. Kinderknecht" when the debtor's actual legal name is "Terrance Joseph Kinderknecht."**

Article 9 has standard rules for search logic that tend toward the "strict" end of the spectrum. The majority of states have now adopted some version of MARS, although many states have modified the rules in some respect (which has resulted in a great deal of inconsistency; furthermore, some states have not adopted any rule on search logic at all). Creditors should be cautious in their searches.

*__Pankratz Implement Company v. Citizens National Bank,__ 102 P.3d 1165 (Kan. App. 2004).

**These examples would result in a "NO MATCH FOUND" and emphasize the importance of using both the debtor's legal name and correct spelling. Furthermore, the courts in all three cases did not honor the financing statement as resulting in perfection because the names were misleading. The person doing the search is permitted to assume that the debtor has no other secured creditors. *CNH Capital America LLC v. Progreso Materials Ltd.*, Not Reported in F. Supp. 2d, 2012 WL 5305697 (S.D. Tex. 2012). See In re *EDM Corp.*, 431 B.R. 459 (Neb. 2010).

---

[42] In re *C.W. Min. Co.*, 488 B.R. 715 (D. Utah. 2013).

Lapse of Time

The perfection obtained by filing a financing statement lasts five years. The perfection may be continued for successive five-year periods by filing a continuation statement within six months before the end of each five-year period.[43] Article 9 permits a "manufactured home" exception allowing financing statements on mobile homes to be effective for 30 years.

Removal from State

In most cases, the perfection of a security interest lapses when the collateral is taken by the debtor to another state unless, as noted earlier, the creditor makes a filing in that second state within the four-month period of temporary perfection.

Motor Vehicles

If the security interest is governed by a non-Code statute creating perfection by title certificate notation, the interest, if so noted, remains perfected without regard to lapse of time or removal to another state. The perfection is lost only if a state issues a new title without the security interest notation.

CPA   33-3   Rights of Parties before Default

The rights of parties to a secured transaction are different in the time preceding the debtor's default from those in the time following the default.

33-3a   Statement of Account

To keep the record straight, the debtor may send the creditor a written statement of the amount the debtor thinks is due and an itemization of the collateral together with a request that the creditor approve the statement as submitted or correct and return the statement. Within two weeks after receiving the debtor's statement, the creditor must send the debtor a written approval or correction. If the secured creditor has assigned the secured claim, the creditor's reply must state the name and address of the assignee.[44]

33-3b   Termination Statements

termination statement—document (record), which may be requested by a paid-up debtor, stating that a security interest is no longer claimed under the specified financing statement.

A debtor who has paid his debt in full may make a written demand on the secured creditor, or the latter's assignee if the security interest has been assigned, to send the debtor a **termination statement,**[45] which states that a security interest is no longer claimed under the specified financing statement. The debtor may present this statement to the filing officer, who marks the record terminated and returns the various papers that were filed to the secured party. The termination statement clears the debtor's record so subsequent buyers or lenders will not be subject to the now-satisfied security interest. The creditor has 20 days from receipt of a demand for a termination statement from a debtor to file a termination statement (one month for consumer goods).[46]

---

[43] U.C.C. §9-516. Failure to file with the secretary of state was fatal for a priority of secured creditor when a central filing was required, despite the filing at the county level. In re *Borden*, 361 B.R. 489 (Neb. 2007).
[44] U.C.C. §9-515.
[45] U.C.C. §9-513; In re *Hickory Printing Group, Inc.*, 479 B.R. 388 (W.D.N.C. 2012).
[46] U.C.C. §9-513(b) and (c).

33-3c **Correction Statements**

Because Article 9 permits creditors and others to simply file "authorized" financing statements, debtors are given protection for abusive filings of Article 9 interests. Under Article 9, debtors are permitted to protest filed financing statements with a filing of their own correction statements. While the security interest is not abolished by such a filing, its content does provide public notice of an underlying dispute. A debtor can also file a correction statement when a creditor fails to provide a termination statement.[47]

33-4 **Priorities**

Two or more parties may have conflicting interests in the same collateral. This section discusses the rights of creditors and buyers with respect to each other and to collateral that carries a secured interest or perfected secured interest.

CPA   ### 33-4a **Unsecured Party versus Unsecured Party**

pro rata–proportionately, or divided according to a rate or standard.

When creditors are unsecured, they have equal priority. In the event of insolvency or bankruptcy of the debtor, all the unsecured creditors stand at the end of the line in terms of repayment of their debts (see Chapter 34 for more details on bankruptcy priorities). If the assets of the debtor are insufficient to satisfy all unsecured debtors, the unsecured debtors simply receive a *pro rata* share of their debts.

CPA   ### 33-4b **Secured Party versus Unsecured Party**

A secured creditor has a right superior to that of an unsecured creditor because the secured creditor can take back the collateral from the debtor's assets, while an unsecured creditor simply waits for the leftovers once all secured creditors have taken back their collateral. If the collateral is insufficient to satisfy the secured creditor's debt, the secured debtor can still stand in line with the unsecured creditors and collect any additional amount not satisfied by the collateral or a pro rata share. **For Example,** suppose that Linens Galore has a security interest in Linens R Us's inventory. Linens Galore has the right to repossess the inventory and sell it to satisfy the debt Linens R Us owes. Suppose that Linens R Us owes Linens Galore $22,000, and the sale of the inventory brings $15,000. Linens Galore still has a claim as an unsecured creditor for the remaining $7,000 due.

CPA   ### 33-4c **Secured Party versus Secured Party**

first-in-time provision–creditor whose interest attached first has priority in the collateral when two creditors have a secured interest.

If two creditors have a security interest in the same collateral, their priority is determined according to the **first-in-time provision;** that is, the creditor whose interest attached first has priority in the collateral. The secured party whose interest was last to attach must then proceed against the debtor as an unsecured creditor because the collateral was given to the creditor whose interest attached first. **For Example,** if Bob pledged his antique sign collection to Bill on January 15, 2015, with a signed security agreement in exchange for a $5,000 loan, and then pledged the same collection to Jane on February 20, 2015, with a signed security agreement, Bill has priority because his security agreement attached first.

---

[47] U.C.C. §9-518.

CPA   **33-4d Perfected Secured Party versus Secured Party**

The perfected secured creditor takes priority over the unperfected secured creditor and is entitled to take the collateral. The unperfected secured party is then left to seek remedies as an unsecured creditor because the collateral has been given to the perfected creditor. **For Example,** with respect to Bob's sign collection, if Jane filed a financing statement on February 21, 2015, she would have priority over Bill because her perfected interest would be superior to Bill's unperfected interest even though Bill's interest attached before Jane's.

CASE SUMMARY

The Bank Doesn't Win: When Secured Parties Take Priority over Overdrafts

FACTS: General Motors Acceptance Corporation (GMAC) financed the inventory of Donohue Ferrill Motor Company, Inc., which gave GMAC a security interest in its vehicle inventory and all the proceeds of that inventory. The security agreement and financing statements were executed, and GMAC properly filed the financing statements.

Shortly before Donohue Ferrill's business failed, it sold six trucks and then deposited the proceeds of $124,610.80 from the sale of those trucks into its account at Lincoln National Bank. Lincoln took the deposited funds and applied them to account overdrafts that Donohue Ferrill had. For 38 of the 62 business days of September, October, and November 1991, Donohue Ferrill's account was overdrawn. Lincoln National honored 133 overdrafts during

these three months and charged Donohue Ferrill a total of $1,995 in fees. The total amount of the overdrawn balances for those 38 days was $1,943,306.25.

GMAC objected, saying that it had priority in those funds. The trial court and court of appeals found for the bank and GMAC appealed.

DECISION: GMAC's security interest takes priority over the bank's right of setoff. The bank's interest is a statutory one, but an unsecured interest, and GMAC had a duly recorded security interest, which the bank knew of or should have known of at the time it took its offset rights. [*General Motors Acceptance Corp. v. Lincoln Nat'l Bank*, 18 S.W.3d 337 (Ky. 2000)]

---

first-to-perfect basis– rule of priorities that holds that first in time in perfecting a security interest, mortgage, judgment, lien, or other property attachment right should have priority.

The perfected secured party's interest as against other types of creditors, such as lienors, mortgagees, and judgment creditors, is also determined on a **first-to-perfect basis.** If the secured party perfects before a judgment lien or mortgage is recorded,[48] the perfected secured creditor has priority.[49] The perfected party takes priority over the secured party even when the perfected secured party is aware of the security interest prior to perfection.[50]

CPA   **33-4e Perfected Secured Party versus Perfected Secured Party**

The general rule for priority among two perfected secured creditors in the same collateral is also a first-in-time rule: The creditor who perfected first is given priority. **For Example,** again with respect to Bob's sign collection, if Bill filed a financing statement on February

---

[48] U.C.C. §9-313; *Arvest Bank v. SpiritBank, N.A.*, 191 P.3d 1228 (Ok. App. 2008), and *Fifth Third Bank v. Peoples Nat. Bank*, 929 N.E.2d 210 (Ind. App. 2010).
[49] *Banner Bank v. First Community Bank*, 854 F. Supp. 2d 846 (D. Mont. 2012).
[50] *Farm Credit of Northwest Florida, ACA v. Easom Peanut Co.*, 718 S.E.2d 590 (Ga. App. 2011).

22, 2015, Jane would still have priority because she perfected her interest first. If, however, Bill filed a financing statement on January 31, 2015, he would have priority over Jane. There are, however, three exceptions to this rule of first-in-time, first-in-right for perfected secured creditors.

CPA   ## The Purchase Money Security Interest in Inventory[51]

If the collateral is inventory, the purchase money secured creditor must do two things to prevail even over prior perfected secured creditors. The creditor must (1) perfect before the debtor receives possession of the goods that will be inventory and (2) give notice to any other secured party who has previously filed a financing statement with respect to that inventory.[52] The other secured parties must receive this notice before the debtor receives possession of the goods covered by the purchase money security interest. Compliance with these notice requirements gives the last creditor to extend credit for the inventory the priority position, which is a rule of law based on the practical notion that a debtor must be able to replenish its inventory to stay in business and keep creditors paid in a timely fashion. With this priority for subsequently perfected creditors, debtors have the opportunity to replenish inventory. **For Example,** suppose that First Bank has financed the inventory for Roberta's Exotic Pets, taken a security interest in the inventory, and filed a financing statement covering Roberta's inventory. Two months later, Animal Producers sells reptiles on credit to Roberta, taking a security interest in Roberta's inventory. To take priority over First Bank, Animal Producers would have to file the financing statement on the inventory before Roberta receives the reptiles and notify First Bank at the same time. The commercial rationale for this priority exception is to permit businesses to replenish their inventories by giving new suppliers a higher priority.

Purchase Money Security Interest—Noninventory Collateral

If the collateral is *noninventory collateral*, such as equipment, the purchase money secured creditor prevails over all others as to the same collateral if that creditor files a financing statement within 20 days after the debtor takes possession of the collateral. **For Example,** First Bank loans money to debtor Kwik Copy and properly files a financing statement covering all of Kwik Copy's present and subsequently acquired copying equipment. Second Bank then loans money to Kwik Copy for the purchase of a new copier. Second Bank's interest in the copier will be superior to First Bank's interest if Second Bank perfects its interest by filing either before the debtor receives the copier or within 20 days thereafter.

Status of Repair or Storage Lien

What happens when the debtor does not pay for the repair or storage of the collateral? In most states, a person repairing or storing goods has a lien or right to keep possession of the goods until paid for such services. The repairer or storer also has the right to sell the goods to obtain payment if the customer fails to pay and if proper notice is given.[53] Article 9 makes a statutory lien for repairs or storage superior to a perfected security interest in the same collateral.

---

[51] U.C.C. §9-103 expands the definition of a PMSI in inventory. Consignments are treated as PMSIs in inventory.
[52] U.C.C. §9-324.
[53] U.C.C. §9-333; In re *James,* 463 B.R. 719 (M.D. Pa. 2011).

CASE SUMMARY

Stephen Tolbert and His Inconsistent Tales: A BFP of a Corvette?

FACTS: In 2003, Automotive Finance Corporation ("AFC") executed a contract to provide "floorplan financing" to R American Auto, Inc., a used car dealership, for the purchase of inventory. As collateral for the financing, AFC took a security interest in all of R American's present and future inventory. AFC filed a UCC Financing Statement to record the security interest on December 16, 2003.

On August 24, 2006, R American purchased a white 2006 Corvette for its inventory. AFC took possession of the Corvette's certificate of title. On January 31, 2007, Kip Rowley, the owner of R American, gave AFC a business check for $43,220 as payment in full for the Corvette, and AFC provided Rowley with the certificate of title to the Corvette. The check was dishonored because R American's bank account had been closed. An agent of AFC went to R American's car lot to secure possession of the Corvette and discovered that it was not on the lot. AFC filed a lien on the missing vehicle.

On March 4, 2008, Steven Tolbert filed a petition seeking a release of AFC's lien on the Corvette because he claimed to be a *bona fide* purchaser" of the Corvette from Ultimate Motor Cars, LLC, on January 21, 2007. AFC filed an answer to the petition and a counterclaim against Tolbert for conversion, seeking damages for the value of the Corvette.

Tolbert testified that he paid $52,000 to Kip Rowley on November 2, 2006, and immediately took possession of the Corvette. He gave Rowley a check made out to "R American" for $50,900 and also paid $1,100 in cash. Tolbert did not receive a bill of sale and the certificate of title to the Corvette until nearly three months later on January 21, 2007. The bill of sale, issued by "Ultimate Motor Cars, Inc.," indicated that the sale was completed on January 21, 2007, and that the purchase price was $52,099. The certificate of title indicated that R American acquired the Corvette on August 24, 2006, and then transferred the Corvette to Ultimate Motor Cars on October 20, 2006. Tolbert's name was listed both as the seller of the Corvette as agent for R American and as the buyer of the Corvette as

agent for Ultimate Motor Cars. Tolbert testified that he inadvertently signed in the wrong spot as seller on the Corvette's certificate of title. Nevertheless, Tolbert was not concerned with these discrepancies because he believed Rowley did business as both R American and Ultimate Motor Cars. Tolbert said he was unaware of AFC's security interest until February 2007, when he attempted to have the Corvette titled in his name and learned about the lien.

Jason Yount, branch manager for AFC, testified that on September 7, 2006, R American paid AFC for the Corvette, and that AFC gave R American the certificate of title to the Corvette. On December 12, 2006, R American gave the certificate of title back to AFC, AFC advanced R American credit for the Corvette, and R American "refloored" the Corvette. Before reclaiming the title, on December 12, 2006, an agent of AFC physically inspected the Corvette on R American's lot, verified the Corvette's VIN, and ensured that the Corvette's certificate of title indicated that R American owned the Corvette. Yount explained that AFC would not have advanced credit to R American and accepted the Corvette's certificate of title on December 12, 2006, if at that time the certificate of title indicated that R American had transferred the Corvette to Ultimate Motor Cars on October 20, 2006.

The court issued a judgment awarding AFC $53,904.41. Tolbert appealed the judgment.

DECISION: The court affirmed the judgment for AFC because Tolbert was not a *bona fide* purchaser (BFP). There was nothing normal about his transaction. He received no documents and when he did finally receive the documents, the documents raised questions because they had different names on them and he seemed to be confused about who was selling and who was buying. Tolbert's story about the transactions differed from the paperwork trail on the financing and when the car was actually available for sale. [*Tolbert v. Automotive Finance Corp.*, 341 S.W.3d 195 (Mo. App. 2011)]

Figure 33-1 provides a summary of the priorities of various parties with respect to secured and unsecured creditor interests.

33-4f Secured Party versus Buyer of Collateral from Debtor

The debtor may sell the collateral to a third person. How does this sale affect the secured creditor?

FIGURE 33-1	Priority of Secured Interest under Article 9

CONFLICT	PRIORITY
Secured party versus secured party	First to attach
Unsecured party versus secured party	Secured party
Perfected secured party versus secured party	Perfected secured party
Perfected secured party versus perfected secured party	Party who is first to perfect
Perfected secured party versus lienor	Party who filed (financing statement or lien) first [§ 9-307(2)] (rev. § 9-317)
EXCEPTIONS	
PMSI in fixtures versus perfected secured party	PMSI creditor if perfected before annexation or within 20 days after annexation (PMSI will have priority even over prior perfected secured party) (§ 9-313, § 9-314) (rev. § 9-317)
PMSI in equipment versus perfected secured party	PMSI is perfected within 20 days after delivery [§ 9-301(2), § 9-312(4)] (rev. § 9-317)
PMSI in inventory versus perfected secured party	PMSI is perfected before delivery and if perfected secured party given notice before delivery [§ 9-312(3)] (rev. § 9-317)
PMSI in consumer goods versus buyer	Buyer unless perfection is by filing before purchase [§ 9-302(1)(d)] (rev. § 9-317)
Perfected secured party versus buyer	Buyer in ordinary course wins even with knowledge [§ 9-306(1)(d)] (rev. § 9-320)

CPA Sales in the Ordinary Course of Business

A buyer who buys goods from the debtor in the ordinary course of business is not subject to any creditor's security interest regardless of whether the interest was perfected or unperfected and regardless of whether the buyer had actual knowledge of the security interest. The reason for this protection of buyers in the ordinary course of business is that subjecting buyers to a creditor's reclaim of goods would cause great delay and hesitation in commercial and consumer sales transactions.[54]

[54] U.C.C. §9-320 covers the rights of buyers of goods.

CPA Sales Not in the Ordinary Course of Business: The Unperfected Security Interest

A sale not in the ordinary course of business is one in which the seller is not usually a seller of such merchandise. **For Example,** if a buyer purchases a computer desk from an office supply store, the sale is in the ordinary course of business. If that same buyer purchases that same computer desk from a law firm that is going out of business, that buyer is not purchasing in the ordinary course of business. If a buyer is purchasing collateral and such purchase is not in the ordinary course of business but the security interest is unperfected, such a security interest has no effect against a buyer who gives value and buys in good faith, that is, not knowing of the security interest. A buyer who does not satisfy these conditions is subject to the security interest.

CPA Sales Not in the Ordinary Course of Business: The Perfected Security Interest

If the security interest was perfected, the buyer of the collateral is ordinarily subject to the security interest unless the creditor consented to the sale.[55]

CPA Sales Not in the Ordinary Course of Business: The Consumer Debtor's Resale of Consumer Goods

When the collateral constitutes consumer goods in the hands of the debtor, a resale of the goods to another consumer destroys the automatically perfected PMSI of the consumer debtor's creditor. Assuming that the buyer who purchases from the consumer debtor has no knowledge of a security interest, she will take the collateral free and clear from the creditor's security interest even though there was perfection by that creditor. Thus, the perfection without filing option afforded consumer PMSI creditors has a flaw in its coverage when it comes to a consumer debtor selling his refrigerator to a neighbor. Without a

FIGURE 33-2 | **Priorities in Transfer of Collateral by Sale**

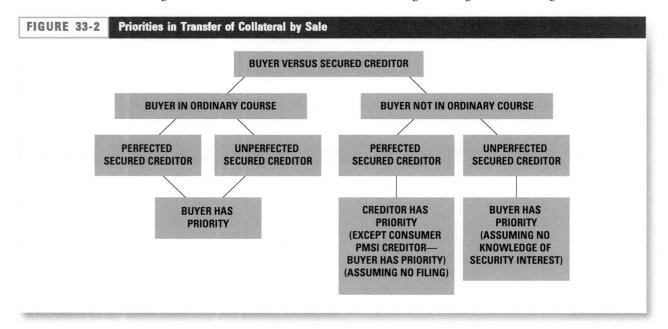

[55] U.C.C. §1-201(9) adds that a purchase from a pawnbroker will not be considered a sale in the ordinary course of business.

filed financing statement, the neighbor buyer takes the refrigerator free and clear of the creditor's security interest in it. However, consumer creditors can avoid the loss of this perfected interest by perfecting through filing. With filing, consumer PMSI creditors enjoy continuation of their interests even when the neighbor has paid the consumer debtor for the refrigerator. Figure 33-2 offers a summary of the rights of buyers of collateral with respect to the creditors who hold security interests in that collateral.

CASE SUMMARY

The Craigslist Seller with the Fake Title

FACTS: In May 2006, Jacob J. Magish agreed to purchase a certain 2001 Harley-Davidson Motorcycle from Christine and Larry Logsdon for $14,635. Magish took out a loan at a Fifth Third Bank branch in Indianapolis with a security interest in the Motorcycle favor of Fifth Third in order to borrow $15,000 for the purchase. Magish presented to Fifth Third the Logsdons' original certificate of title. As part of the transaction, Magish executed, among other documents, an Application for Certificate of Title and a Power of Attorney. Fifth Third's Closing Representative, John Wargel, copied the Logsdon Original Title and then gave the Logsdon Original Title back to Magish. Wargel instructed Magish to apply for a new title at the Indiana Bureau of Motor Vehicles ("BMV"). Wargel kept the May 31 application and the Magish file in the loan file.

Shortly after the transaction, Magish, using deception, approached the Logsdons and requested that they sign paperwork to obtain a duplicate title. The Logsdons, who had no knowledge that Magish had financed the purchase of the Motorcycle through Fifth Third, unwittingly signed an application to obtain a duplicate title and gave the application to Magish.

Magish obtained a duplicate title from the BMV in the name of the Logsdons. The Logsdons signed the Logsdon Duplicate Title as Sellers. The Logsdon Duplicate Title inactivated the Logsdon Original Title in the BMV records.

Magish, using the Logsdon Duplicate Title, submitted an application to the BMV for a new title in his name. Magish intentionally omitted Fifth Third from the June 20 application and did not list a lienholder. Magish concurrently tendered the Logsdon Duplicate Title to the BMV and failed to notate Fifth Third as lienholder. On June 28, 2006, the BMV issued a new title in Magish's name. There was no lien notated on the First Magish Title.

On October 16, 2006, Fifth Third submitted an application for an amended title to the BMV ... Fifth Third did not have the Logsdon Original Title nor the First Magish Title in its possession and so did not tender to the BMV either with the Fifth Third application.

On October 18, 2006, the BMV issued a new title listing Magish as owner and Fifth Third as lienholder. The Second Magish Title inactivated the First Magish Title in the BMV records. The whereabouts of the Second Magish Title are unknown and Fifth Third has no record of receiving it.

In 2009, the Dawsons responded to a Magish posting on Craigslist for the sale of the Motorcycle. On June 18, 2009, Magish sold and delivered the Motorcycle to the Dawsons for $13,050.00. Magish, who was terminally ill and died in August 2009, had defaulted on the loan in 2008. Magish gave the Dawsons the certificate of title that showed it was free of any lienholders. After the sale, the Dawsons submitted an application for a new title to the Motorcycle to the BMV. The BMV advised the Dawsons that, according to the BMV records, the title the Dawsons had was not the most current title. For privacy reasons the BMV would not tell the Dawsons exactly what the issue was but said it was either there was a duplicate title or a lienholder on the title. After discussions with Magish and his wife, the Dawsons determined that Fifth Third was a lienholder. The BMV refused to issue a new title to the Motorcycle to the Dawsons.

The Dawsons filed suit against Fifth Third, arguing that Fifth Third's lien against the Motorcycle should be unenforceable because, under a theory of equitable estoppel, Fifth Third should bear the loss of Magish's fraud on the Dawsons because Fifth Third's acts and omissions made the loss possible. Fifth Third filed a counterclaim, seeking replevin of the Motorcycle.

The trial court denied the Dawsons' summary judgment motion, granted Fifth Third's summary judgment motion, awarded permanent possession of the Motorcycle to Fifth Third, and ordered that the Dawsons maintain possession of the Motorcycle pending their appeal.

DECISION: There was a perfected secured creditor (Fifth Third Bank) who had a right to replevin (take back) of the Motorcycle. The bank's lienholder status was on the title and it was the only title of public record. A buyer not in the

The Craigslist Seller with the Fake Title continued

ordinary course should check for perfected secured interests prior to buying, and the Dawsons did not check the title. The Dawsons took title subject to Fifth Third Bank's security interest. The Dawsons tried to make an equitable argument that Fifth Third Bank could have prevented the problem if it

had been more careful with the title. However, the court held that they were the parties best able to check the title and because they did not check for perfected secured interests, the equities were on Fifth Third Bank's side. [*Dawson v. Fifth Third Bank*, 965 N.E.2d 730 (Ind. App. 2012)]

33-5 Rights of Parties after Default

self-help repossession— creditor's right to repossess the collateral without judicial proceedings.

When a debtor defaults on an obligation in a secured transaction, the secured creditor has the option to sue the debtor to enforce the debt or of proceeding against the collateral.

CPA

33-5a Creditor's Possession and Disposition of Collateral

breach of the peace— violation of the law in the repossession of the collateral.

Upon the debtor's default, the secured party is entitled to take the collateral from the debtor.[56] **Self-help repossession** is allowed if this can be done without causing a **breach of the peace**.[57] If a breach of the peace might occur, the seller must use court action to obtain the collateral. Breaking and entering a debtor's property is a breach of the peace.

CASE SUMMARY

I Was in My Driveway in My Underwear When They Repossessed My Car!

FACTS: Koontz entered into an agreement with Chrysler to purchase a 1988 Sundance in exchange for 60 monthly payments of $185.92. When Koontz defaulted on the contract in early 1991, Chrysler notified him that it would repossess the vehicle if he did not make up the missed payments. Koontz notified Chrysler that he would make every effort to catch up on the payments, that he did not want the vehicle to be repossessed, and that Chrysler was not to enter his private property to repossess the car. Chrysler repossessed the car, however, according to the self-help repossession statute of the UCC.

When Koontz heard the repossession in progress, he rushed outside in his underwear and hollered, "Don't take it," to the repossessor. The repossessor did not respond and proceeded to take the vehicle. Chrysler sold the car and filed a complaint against Koontz seeking a deficiency judgment

for the balance due on the loan. Koontz alleged that the repossession was a breach of the peace. From a judgment in favor of Chrysler, Koontz appealed.

DECISION: There was no breach of the peace under Article 9 standards. Koontz only yelled, "Don't take it"; there was no verbal or physical response, no threat made at the repossessor, nor was there a breach of the peace. To find otherwise would be to invite the ridiculous situation whereby a debtor could avoid a deficiency judgment by merely stepping out of his house and yelling once at those sent to repossess the collateral. Such a narrow definition of the conduct necessary to breach the peace would render the self-help repossession statute useless. [*Chrysler Credit v. Koontz*, 661 N.E.2d 1171 (Ill. App. Ct. 1996)]

---

[56] U.C.C. §9-607.
[57] The courts are divided on what is and is not a breach of the peace. *Thompson-Young v. Wells Fargo Dealer Services, Inc.*, Not Reported in N.E.3d, 2014 WL 3726900 (Ill. App. 2014). But see *Smith v. AFS Acceptance, LLC*, Not Reported in F. Supp. 2d, 2012 WL 1969415 (N.D. Ill. 2012).

The secured creditor may sell, lease,[58] or otherwise dispose of the collateral to pay the defaulted debt.[59] The sale may be private or public, at any time and place, and on any terms provided that the sale is done in a manner that is commercially reasonable. The creditor's sale eliminates all of the debtor's interest in the collateral.

33-5b Creditor's Retention of Collateral

Instead of selling the collateral, the creditor may wish to keep it and cancel the debt owed.[60]

Notice of Intention

To retain the collateral in satisfaction of the debt, the creditor must send the debtor written notice of this intent.[61]

CPA Compulsory Disposition of Collateral

In two situations, the creditor must dispose of the collateral. A creditor must sell the collateral if the debtor makes a written objection to retention within 21 days after the retention notice was sent. The creditor must also dispose of the collateral if it consists of consumer goods and the debtor has paid 60 percent or more of the cash price or of the loan secured by the security interest. The sale must be held within 90 days of the repossession. However, the debtor, after default, surrenders the right to require the resale.[62]

A creditor who fails to dispose of the collateral when required to do so is liable to the debtor for conversion of the collateral or for the penalty imposed by the Code for violation of Article 9.[63]

33-5c Debtor's Right of Redemption

The debtor may redeem the collateral at any time prior to the time the secured party has disposed of the collateral or entered into a binding contract for resale. To redeem, the debtor must tender the entire obligation that is owed plus any legal costs and expenses incurred by the secured party.[64]

33-5d Disposition of Collateral

Upon the debtor's default, the creditor may sell the collateral at a public or private sale or may lease it to a third party. The creditor must give any required notice and act in a commercially reasonable manner. Revised Article 9 imposes specific notice requirements and provides a form that, if used by the creditor, is deemed adequate notice of sale. There are different notice forms for consumer and other transactions, but the basic information required is the day, time, location for the sale, and a contact number for questions the debtor and other secured parties might have. The notice must be sent to the debtor and any other creditors with an interest in the property.[65]

---

[58] *Golden v. Prosser*, 2014 WL 4626489 (D. Minn. 2014).
[59] U.C.C. §9-611 requires the secured party to notify all other secured parties and lienholders who have filed or recorded interests in the collateral of its intent to sell the collateral. *Whitecap (U.S.) Fund I, LP v. Siemens First Capital Commercial Finance LLC,* 121 A.D.3d 584, 995 N.Y.S.2d 40 (N.Y.A.D. 2014).
[60] U.C.C. §§9-620, 9-621, and 9-624.
[61] U.C.C. §§9-620 through 9-622. If there has been no notice, repossession is a breach of the peace. *Molinski v. Chase Auto Finance Corp.*, 837 N.W.2d 166 (Wis. App. 2013).
[62] U.C.C. §9-620. *Spellman v. Independent Bankers' Bank of Florida*, 39 *Fla. L. Weekly* D1687 (Fla. App. 2014).
[63] U.C.C. §§9-625 through 9-627.
[64] U.C.C. §9-623.
[65] U.C.C. §§9-613 and 9-614. *Wilder v. Toyota Financial Services Americas Corp.*, 764 F. Supp. 2d 249 (D. Mass. 2011).

THINKING THINGS THROUGH

Repossessing and Replacing Tires

Les Schwab sold Mr. Reed four tires for $509.82 on credit. Between January 2008 and May 2008, Mr. Reed failed to make any payments. After notifying Mr. Reed of his default, Jacob Schreiber, a Les Schwab manager, went to Mr. Reed's residence. Mr. Reed's vehicle was parked in the driveway while Mr. Reed was at work. Mr. Schreiber, after consultation with two other members of the management team, removed the tires and wheels from the vehicle. They removed the tires from the wheels at the store and then returned the wheels to Mr. Reed's vehicle the next day. The purpose of removing the tires at the store was to prevent damage to the wheels by using the store's machine for the removal process.

Mr. Reed filed suit against Les Schwab for breach of the peace because his wheels were taken and they were owned by him. Only the tires were subject to repossession. Mr. Reed claimed damages from having his car immobilized and not being able to go to work because of the conversion of his property by Les Schwab employees.

Is Mr. Reed correct? Was this a breach of the peace? Explain your answer.

[*Reed v. Les Schwab Tire Centers, Inc.,* **160 Wash. App. 1020 (Wash. App. 2011)**]

ETHICS & THE LAW

Women, Children, and the Repo Guys

Repossessions of autos financed on credit are at an all-time high. Lenders explain that the growth period of the past decade inspired many to overextend themselves with credit purchases, and now the repossessions are taking place.

According to the "repo industry," about 15 percent of debtors surrender their cars voluntarily. Confrontations occur about 10 percent of the time during repossession. Many debtors change the color of their cars, change the tires and rims, or cover the vehicle identification number to foil repossession companies' efforts. One auto dealer, trying to repossess a woman's car, had two male employees scale the fence of the Murfeesboro, Tennessee, Domestic Violence Program Shelter. The shelter's security cameras spotted the men and after police were notified, they were ordered off the premises. The woman who owned the car left the shelter to make the necessary payments to bring her obligations current.

The shelter director said that if the men had come through the proper administrative channels at the shelter, the shelter would have cooperated with them. The shelter director called the men's scaling of the fence at a shelter for women and children "irresponsible."

Do you think it is ethical for the debtors to do these things? Should debtors surrender their cars voluntarily?

In two incidents in 2006, cars that were repossessed had children sleeping in them. The cars were hooked to the tow vehicle and the children were transported to the tow yards. An industry spokesman said that "repo guys" have to get in and hook the cars up as quickly as possible; they do not have time to check the inside of the vehicle.

Source: Rich Beattie, "Boom Times for Repo Guys," *New York Times,* April 18, 2003, D1, D8.

CPA 33-5e **Postdisposition Accounting**

When the creditor disposes of the collateral, the proceeds are applied in the following order. Proceeds are first used to pay the expenses of disposing of the collateral. Next, proceeds are applied to the debt owed the secured creditor making the disposition. Remaining proceeds are applied to any debts owed other creditors holding security interests in the same collateral that are subordinate to the interest of the disposing creditor.[66]

[66] U.C.C. §9-615.

Distribution of Surplus

If there is any money remaining, the surplus is paid to the debtor.[67]

Liability for Deficit

If the proceeds of the disposition are not sufficient to pay the costs and the debt of the disposing creditor, the debtor is liable for the deficiency. However, the disposition of the collateral must have been conducted in the manner required by the UCC. This means that proper notice must have been given, if required, and that the disposition must have been made in a commercially reasonable manner. Factors that determine commercial reasonableness include notice, the difference between the sale price and the value of the goods, and public versus private sale according to industry practice.[68]

Make the Connection

Summary

A security interest is an interest in personal property or fixtures that secures payment or performance of an obligation. The property that is subject to the interest is called the *collateral*, and the party holding the interest is called the *secured party*. *Attachment* is the creation of a security interest. To secure protection against third parties' claims to the collateral, the secured party must perfect the security interest. *Tangible collateral* is divided into classes: consumer goods, equipment, inventory, general intangibles, farm products, and fixtures. Under Revised Article 9, intangibles have been expanded to include bank accounts, checks, notes, and health care insurance receivables.

Perfection of a security interest is not required for its validity, but it does provide the creditor certain superior rights and priorities over other types of creditors and creditors with an interest in the same collateral. Perfection can be obtained through possession, filing, automatically (as in the case of a PMSI in consumer goods), by control for accounts under Revised Article 9, or temporarily when statutory protections are provided for creditors for limited periods of time.

Priority among creditors is determined according to their status. Unperfected, unsecured creditors simply wait to see whether there will be sufficient assets remaining after priority creditors are paid. Secured creditors have the right to take the collateral on a priority basis. As between secured creditors, the first creditor's interest to attach takes priority in the event the creditors hold security interests in the same collateral. A perfected secured creditor takes priority over an unperfected secured creditor. Perfected secured creditors with interests in the same collateral take priority generally on a first-to-perfect basis. Exceptions include PMSI inventory creditors who file a financing statement before delivery and notify all existing creditors, and equipment creditors who perfect within 20 days of attachment of their interests.

A buyer in the ordinary course of business always takes priority, even over perfected secured creditors who have knowledge of the creditor's interest. A buyer not in the ordinary course of business loses out to a perfected secured creditor but extinguishes the rights of a secured creditor unless the buyer had knowledge of the security interest. A buyer from a consumer debtor takes free and clear of the debtor's creditor's perfected security interest unless the creditor has filed a financing statement and perfected beyond just the automatic PMSI consumer goods perfection.

Upon default, a secured party may repossess the collateral from the buyer if this can be done without a breach of the peace. If a breach of the peace could occur, the secured party must use court action to regain the collateral. If the buyer has paid 60 percent or more of the cash price of the consumer goods, the seller must resell them within 90 days after repossession unless the buyer, after default, has waived this right in writing. Notice to the debtor of the sale of the collateral is usually required. A debtor may redeem the collateral prior to the time the secured party disposes of it or contracts to resell it.

---

[67] U.C.C. §9-616.
[68] *Mercado v. HFC Collection Center, Inc.*, Not Reported in F. Supp. 2d, 2013 WL 645988 (M.D. Fla. 2013).

Learning Outcomes

After studying this chapter, you should be able to clearly explain:

33-1   Creation of Secured Transactions

L0.1 Explain the requirements for creating a valid security interest

See the In re *Cunningham* case, pages 645–646.
See the *ProGrowth Bank, Inc. v. Wells Fargo Bank, N.A.*, case, pages 651–652.
See the *Dawson v. Fifth Third Bank* case, pages 661–662.

L0.2 List the major types of collateral

See the In re *Lull* case, page 648.

33-2   Perfection of Secured Transactions

L0.3 Define perfection and explain its significance in secured transactions

See E-Commerce & Cyberlaw, "Engines Are from Mars; Priorities Are from Financing Statements," page 653.

33-3   Rights of Parties before Default
33-4   Priorities

L0.4 Discuss the priorities of parties with conflicting interests in collateral when default occurs

See the *General Motors Acceptance Corp. v. Lincoln* case, page 656.
See the *Tolbert v. Automotive Finance Corp.* case for priorities of buyers and secured parties, page 658.

33-5   Rights of Parties after Default

L0.5 State the rights of the parties on the debtor's default

See the *Chrysler Credit v. Koontz* case, page 662.
See the Thinking Things Through feature on repossession of tires, page 664.
See Ethics & the Law, "Women, Children, and the Repo Guys," page 664.

Key Terms

after-acquired goods
automatic perfection
breach of the peace
collateral
consumer good
creditor
debtor
field warehousing

financing statement
first-in-time provision
first-to-perfect basis
floating lien
perfected security interest
pro rata
purchase money security interest
    (PMSI)

secured party
secured transaction
security agreement
security interest
self-help repossession
temporary perfection
termination statement
value

Questions and Case Problems

1. On October 22, 2001, Benjamin Ritchie executed a promissory note and mortgage in consideration for a $47,000 loan from WaMu. The mortgage covered both real estate located at 1790 Mount Mariah Road, Carlisle, Kentucky, and a manufactured home to be situated on the real property. The mortgage was properly filed in the Nicholas County Clerk's Office on October 31, 2001.

    Ritchie used the proceeds of the loan to purchase a manufactured home, which was subsequently rendered a total loss as a result of heavy fire damage. As the named loss payee on the insurance policy for the home, WaMu received and released the insurance proceeds to the Debtor to purchase a replacement manufactured home. WaMu failed, however, to record its lien on the certificate of title to the replacement manufactured home.

    On January 20, 2006, WaMu initiated a foreclosure action on the property. Ritchie raised the defense that WaMu no longer had a valid lien on the manufactured home. Is Ritchie correct? Explain your answer. [In re *Ritchie*, 416 B.R. 638 (6th Cir.)]

2. In 1983, Carpet Contracts owned a commercial lot and building, which it operated as a retail carpet outlet. In April of 1983, Carpet Contracts entered into a credit sales agreement with Young Electric Sign Corp. (Yesco) for the purchase of a large electronic sign for the store. The cost of the sign was $113,000, with a down payment of $25,000 and 60 monthly payments of $2,100 each.

In August 1985, Carpet Contracts agreed to sell the property to Interstate. As part of the sale, Carpet Contracts gave Interstate an itemized list showing that $64,522 of the proceeds from the sale would be used to pay for the "Electronic Sign." The property was transferred to Interstate, and the Carpet Contracts store continued to operate there, but now it paid rent to Interstate. In June 1986, Carpet Contracts asked Yesco to renegotiate the terms of the sign contract. Yesco reduced Carpet Contracts' monthly payments and filed a financing statement on the sign at the Utah Division of Corporations and Commercial Code. In December 1986, Interstate agreed to sell the property and the sign to the Webbs, who conducted a title search on the property, which revealed no interest with respect to the electronic sign. Interstate conveyed the property to the Webbs. Carpet Contracts continued its operation but was struggling financially and had not made its payments to Yesco for some time. By 1989, Yesco declared the sign contract in default and contacted the Webbs, demanding the balance due of $26,100. The Webbs then filed suit, claiming Yesco had no priority as a creditor because its financing statement was not filed in the real property records where the Webbs had done their title search before purchasing the land. Was the financing statement filed properly for perfection? [*Webb v. Interstate Land Corp.,* 920 P.2d 1187 (Utah)]

3. McLeod purchased several items from Sears, Roebuck & Co. on credit. The description of the items, in which Sears took a purchase money security interest, was as follows: "MITER SAW; LXITV-RACDC [a television, videocassette recorder, and compact disc spinner]; 25 UPRIGHT, 28 UPRIGHT [two pieces of luggage]; BRA-CELET, DIA STUDS, RING; 14K EARR, P, EARRINGS, P [diamond bracelet, ring, and earrings]; and 9-INCH E-Z-LIFT [an outdoor umbrella]." In a dispute over creditors' priorities in McLeod's bankruptcy, one creditor argued that the description of the goods was insufficient to give Sears a security interest. Does the description meet Article 9 standards? [*McLeod v. Sears, Roebuck & Co.,* 41 U.C.C. 2d (Bankr. E.D. Mich.)]

4. When Johnson Hardware Shop borrowed $20,000 from First Bank, it used its inventory as collateral for the loan. First Bank perfected its security interest by filing a financing statement. The inventory was subsequently damaged by fire. Flanders Insurance paid

Johnson Hardware $5,000 for the loss, but First Bank claimed the proceeds of the insurance. Was First Bank correct? Why or why not?

5. Consider the following cases and determine whether the financing statements as filed would be valid under Article 9. Be sure to consider the standard of "seriously misleading" under Revised Article 9.

   a. In re *Thriftway Auto Supply, Inc.,* 159 B.R. 948, 22 U.C.C. Rep. Serv. 2d 605 (W.D. Okla.). The creditor used the debtor's corporate trade name, "Thriftway Auto Stores," not its legal name, "Thriftway Auto Supply, Inc."

   b. In re *Mines Tire Co., Inc.,* 194 B.R. 23, 29 U.C.C. 2d 617 (Bankr. W.D.N.Y). The creditor used the name "Mines Company Inc." instead of "Mines Tire Company, Inc."

   c. *Mountain Farm Credit Service, ACA v. Purina Mills, Inc.,* 459 S.E.2d 75 (N.C. App.). The creditor filed the financing statement under "Warren Killian and Robert Hetherington dba Grey Daw Farms" in a situation in which the two individuals were partners running Grey Daw Farms as a partnership.

   d. *B.T. Lazarus & Co. v. Christofides,* 662 N.E.2d 41 (Ohio App.). The creditor filed a financing statement in the debtor's old name when, prior to filing, the debtor had changed its name from B.T.L., Inc., to Alma Manufacturing, Inc.

   e. In re *SpecialCare, Inc.,* 209 B.R. 13, 34 U.C.C. 2d 857 (N.D. Ga). The creditor failed to refile an amended financing statement to reflect debtor's name change from "Davidson Therapeutic Services, Inc." to "SpecialCare, Inc."

   f. *Industrial Machinery & Equipment Co. Inc. v. Lapeer County Bank & Trust Co.,* 540 N.W.2d 781 (Mich. App.). The creditor filed the financing statement under the company's trade name, KMI, Inc., instead of its legal name, Koehler Machine, Inc.

   g. *First Nat'l Bank of Lacon v. Strong,* 663 N.E.2d 432 (Ill. App.). Creditor filed the financing statement using the trade name "Strong Oil Co." instead of the legal name "E. Strong Oil Company."

6. First Union Bank of Florida loaned money to Dale and Lynn Rix for their purchase of Ann's Hallmark, a Florida corporation. First Union took a security

interest in the store's equipment, fixtures, and inventory and filed the financing statement under the names of Dale and Lynn Rix. Subsequently, the Rixes incorporated their newly acquired business as Michelle's Hallmark Cards & Gifts, Inc. When Michelle's went into bankruptcy, First Union claimed it had priority as a secured creditor because it had filed its financing statement first. Other creditors said First Union had priority against the Rixes but not against the corporation. Who was correct? What was the correct name for filing the financing statement? [In re *Michelle's Hallmark Cards & Gifts, Inc.*, 36 U.C.C. 2d 225 (Bankr. M.D. Fla.)]

7. Rawlings purchased a typewriter from Kroll Typewriter Co. for $600. At the time of the purchase, he made an initial payment of $75 and agreed to pay the balance in monthly installments. A security agreement that complied with the UCC was prepared, but no financing statement was ever filed for the transaction. Rawlings, at a time when he still owed a balance on the typewriter and without the consent of Kroll, sold the typewriter to a neighbor. The neighbor, who had no knowledge of the security interest, used the typewriter in her home. Could Kroll repossess the typewriter from the neighbor?

8. Kim purchased on credit a $1,000 freezer from Silas Household Appliance Store. After she had paid approximately $700, Kim missed the next monthly installment payment. Silas repossessed the freezer and billed Kim for the balance of the purchase price, $300. Kim claimed that the freezer, now in the possession of Silas, was worth much more than the balance due and requested that Silas sell the freezer to wipe out the balance of the debt and to leave something for her. Silas claimed that because Kim had broken her contract to pay the purchase price, she had no right to say what should be done with the freezer. Was Silas correct? Explain.

9. Benson purchased a new Ford Thunderbird automobile. She traded in her old car and used the Magnavox Employees Credit Union to finance the balance. The credit union took a security interest in the Ford. Subsequently, the Ford was involved in a number of accidents and was taken to a dealer for repairs. Benson was unable to pay for the work done. The dealer claimed a lien on the car for services and materials furnished. The Magnavox Employees Credit Union claimed priority. Which claim had priority? [*Magnavox Employees Credit Union v. Benson*, 331 N.E.2d 46 (Ind. App.)]

10. Lockovich borrowed money from a bank to purchase a motorboat. The bank took a security interest in it but never filed a financing statement. A subsequent default on the loan occurred, and the debtor was declared bankrupt. The bank claimed priority in the boat, alleging that no financing statement had to be filed. Do you agree? Why? [In re *Lockovich*, 124 B.R. 660 (W.D. Pa.)]

11. In 1987, the Muirs bought a motor home. In 1988, the Muirs created and Bank of the West acquired and perfected a security interest in the motor home. In 1992, the Muirs entered into an agreement with Gateleys Fairway Motors by which Gateleys would sell the motor home by consignment. Gateleys sold the motor home to Howard and Ann Schultz. The Schultzes did not know of the consignment arrangement or of the security interest of the bank. Gateleys failed to give the sales money to the Muirs and then filed for bankruptcy.

    The Schultzes brought suit seeking a declaration that they owned the motor home free of the bank's security interest. The trial court granted the Schultzes summary judgment. Who has title to the motor home and why? [*Schultz v. Bank of the West, C.B.C.*, 934 P.2d 421 (Or.)]

12. On April 18, 2000, Philip Purkett parked his car, on which he owed $213 in payments, in his garage and locked the garage. Later that night, TWAS, Inc., a vehicle repossession company, broke into the garage and repossessed the car without notice to Purkett. To get the car back, Purkett paid a $140 storage fee and signed a document stating that he would not hold TWAS liable for any damages. Did TWAS and Key Bank violate Article 9 requirements on repossession? [*Purkett v. Key Bank USA, Inc.*, 2001 WL 503050, 45 U.C.C. Rep. Serv. 2d 1201 (N.D. Ill.)]

13. *A* borrowed money from *B* and orally agreed that *B* had a security interest in equipment that was standing in *A*'s yard. Nothing was in writing, and no filing of any kind was made. Nine days later, *B* took possession of the equipment. What kind of interest did *B* have in the equipment after taking possession of it? [*Transport Equipment Co. v. Guaranty State Bank*, 518 F.2d 373 (10th Cir.)]

14. Cook sold Martin a new tractor truck for approximately $13,000, with a down payment of approximately $3,000 and the balance to be paid in 30 monthly installments. The sales agreement provided that "on default in any payment, Cook [could] take immediate possession of the property ... without

notice or demand. For this purpose vendor may enter upon any premises on which the property may be." Martin failed to pay the installments when due, and Cook notified him that the truck would be repossessed. Martin left the tractor truck attached to a loaded trailer and locked on the premises of a company in Memphis. Martin intended to drive to the West Coast with the trailer. When Cook located the tractor truck, no one was around. To disconnect the trailer from the truck (because he had no right to the trailer), Cook removed the wire screen over a ventilator hole by unscrewing it from the outside with his penknife. He next reached through the ventilator hole with a stick and unlocked the door of the tractor truck. He then disconnected the trailer and had the truck towed away. Martin sued Cook for unlawfully repossessing the truck by committing a breach of the peace. Decide. [*Martin v. Cook*, 114 So. 2d 669 (Miss.)]

15. Kimbrell's Furniture Co. sold a new television set and tape player to Charlie O'Neil and his wife. Each purchase was on credit, and in each instance, a security agreement was executed. Later on the same day of purchase, O'Neil carried the items to Bonded Loan, a pawnbroker, and pledged the television and tape deck as security for a loan. Bonded Loan held possession of the television set and tape player as security for its loan and contended that its lien had priority over the unrecorded security interest of Kimbrell. Who had priority? [*Kimbrell's Furniture Co. v. Sig Friedman, d/b/a Bonded Loan*, 198 S.E.2d 803 (S.C.)]

CPA Questions

1. On March 1, Green went to Easy Car Sales to buy a car. Green spoke to a salesperson and agreed to buy a car that Easy had in its showroom. On March 5, Green made a $500 down payment and signed a security agreement to secure the payment of the balance of the purchase price. On March 10, Green picked up the car. On March 15, Easy filed the security agreement. On what date did Easy's security interest attach?

    a. March 1

    b. March 5

    c. March 10

    d. March 15

2. Carr Corp. sells VCRs and videotapes to the public. Carr sold and delivered a VCR to Sutter on credit. Sutter executed and delivered to Carr a promissory note for the purchase price and a security agreement covering the VCR. Sutter purchased the VCR for personal use. Carr did not file a financing statement. Is Carr's security interest perfected?

    a. No, because the VCR was a consumer good.

    b. No, because Carr failed to file a financing statement.

    c. Yes, because Carr retained ownership of the VCR.

    d. Yes, because it was perfected at the time of attachment.

3. On July 8, Ace, a refrigerator wholesaler, purchased 50 refrigerators. This comprised Ace's entire inventory and was financed under an agreement with Rome Bank that gave Rome a security interest in all refrigerators on Ace's premises, all future-acquired refrigerators, and the proceeds of sales. On July 12, Rome filed a financing statement that adequately identified the collateral. On August 15, Ace sold one refrigerator to Cray for personal use and four refrigerators to Zone Co. for its business. Which of the following statements is correct?

    a. The refrigerators sold to Zone will be subject to Rome's security interest.

    b. The refrigerators sold to Zone will not be subject to Rome's security interest.

    c. The security interest does not include the proceeds from the sale of the refrigerators to Zone.

    d. The security interest may not cover after-acquired property even if the parties agree.

4. Fogel purchased a television set for $900 from Hamilton Appliance. Hamilton took a promissory note signed by Fogel and a security interest for the $800 balance due on the set. It was Hamilton's policy not to file a financing statement until the purchaser defaulted. Fogel obtained a loan of $500 from Reliable Finance, which took and recorded a security interest in the set. A month later, Fogel

defaulted on several loans and one of his creditors, Harp, obtained a judgment against Fogel, which was properly recorded. After making several payments, Fogel defaulted on a payment due to Hamilton, who then recorded a financing statement subsequent to Reliable's filing and the entry of the Harp judgment. Subsequently, at a garage sale, Fogel sold the set for $300 to Mobray. Which of the parties has the priority claim to the set?

a. Reliable

b. Hamilton

c. Harp

d. Mobray

5. Under the Secured Transactions Article of the UCC, which of the following items can usually be excluded from a filed original financing statement?

a. The name of the debtor.

b. The address of the debtor.

c. A description of the collateral.

d. The amount of the obligation secured.

6. Under the Secured Transactions Article of the UCC, which of the following security agreements does not need to be in writing to be enforceable?

a. A security agreement collateralizing a debt of less than $500.

b. A security agreement where the collateral is highly perishable or subject to wide price fluctuations.

c. A security agreement where the collateral is in the possession of the secured party.

d. A security agreement involving a purchase money security interest.

CHAPTER 34

Bankruptcy

Learning Outcomes >>>

After studying this chapter, you should be able to

LO.1 List the requirements for the commencement of a voluntary bankruptcy case and an involuntary bankruptcy case

LO.2 Explain the procedure for the administration of a debtor's estate

LO.3 List a debtor's duties and exemptions

LO.4 Explain the significance of a discharge in bankruptcy

LO.5 Explain when a business reorganization plan or an extended-time payment plan might be used

34-1 Bankruptcy Law

What can a person or business do when overwhelmed by debts? Bankruptcy proceedings can provide temporary and sometimes permanent relief from those debts.

Bankruptcy is a statutory proceeding with detailed procedures and requirements.

34-1a The Federal Law

Bankruptcy law is based on federal statutes that have been refined over the years. In October 2005, Congress passed the Bankruptcy Abuse Prevention and Consumer Protection Act of 2005 (BAPCPA), the law that is still in effect.[1]

Jurisdiction over bankruptcy proceedings is in courts of special jurisdiction called **bankruptcy courts,** which operate under the umbrella of the federal district courts.

bankruptcy courts—court of special jurisdiction to determine bankruptcy issues.

34-1b Types of Bankruptcy Proceedings

There are three types of bankruptcy proceedings.

CPA

Liquidation or Chapter 7 Bankruptcy

Chapter 7 bankruptcy—liquidation form of bankruptcy under federal law.

A **Chapter 7 bankruptcy** is one in which all of the debtor's assets (with some exemptions) will be **liquidated** to pay debts. Those debts that remain unpaid or are paid only partially are discharged, with some exceptions. The debtor who declares Chapter 7 bankruptcy begins again with a nearly clean slate.

liquidation—process of converting property into money whether of particular items of property or of all the assets of a business or an estate.

Chapter 7 bankruptcy is available to individuals, partnerships, and corporations. However, farmers, insurance companies, savings and loans, municipalities, Small Business Administration companies, and railroads are not entitled to declare Chapter 7 bankruptcy because they are specifically governed by other statutes or specialized sections of the Bankruptcy Code.[2]

Under the BAPCPA, consumers generally cannot go directly to a Chapter 7 liquidation bankruptcy because they must demonstrate that they do not have the means to repay the debts before they can do a Chapter 7 liquidation.[3] The means test, which is discussed later, considers the disposable income that is available after the bankruptcy court has deducted allowable expenses that are listed as part of the means section of the BAPCPA, including items such as health insurance and child support.

CPA

Reorganization or Chapter 11 Bankruptcy

Chapter 11 bankruptcy—reorganization form of bankruptcy under federal law.

Chapter 11 bankruptcy is a way for a debtor to reorganize and continue a business with protection from overwhelming debts and without the requirement of liquidation. Abercrombie & Fitch, Fuddruckers, the Chicago Cubs, Chrysler, General Motors, the Sharper Image, United Airlines, and Delta are all examples of companies that have gone through Chapter 11 bankruptcies. Stockbrokers, however, are not eligible for Chapter 11 bankruptcy.

---

[1] The act is codified at 11 U.S.C. §101 *et seq.*

[2] For example, the Small Business Investment Act governs the insolvency of small business investment companies, 11 U.S.C. §109(b). Municipalities' bankruptcies are governed by Chapter 9 of the Bankruptcy Code, and farmers' bankruptcies are covered under Chapter 11. Following the 2008 market collapse, there were a series of municipal bankruptcies because of excessive debt and pension obligations.

[3] 11 U.S.C. §707(C)(2)(a). There are exceptions to the requirements of establishing no means, such as those who incurred their debts while on active military service.

ETHICS & THE LAW

Bankruptcy Records

According to **http://www.bankruptcydata.com**, the following are the largest bankruptcies in the history of the United States:

Company	Date	Amount
Lehman Brothers	09/15/2008	$640,000,000 billion
Washington Mutual (WaMu)	09/26/2008	$327,900,000 billion
WorldCom	07/21/2002	$103,900,000 billion
General Motors	06/01/2009	$91,000,000 billion
CIT	11/01/2009	$80,400,000 billion
Enron	12/02/2001	$65,500,000 billion
Conseco	12/02/2002	$61,300,000 billion
MF Global	10/31/2011	$41,000,000 billion
Chrysler	04/20/2009	$39,300,000 billion
Thornburg Mortgage	05/05/2009	$36,500,000 billion

Total bankruptcy filings in the United States from 2008 to 2014 were as follows. Note the spike following 2008 because of the economic crisis.

Year	Total	Nonbusiness	Business
2014	936,795	909,812	26,983
2013	1,071,932	1,038,720	33,212
2012	1,221,091	1,181,016	40,075
2011	1,410,653	1,362,847	47,806
2010	1,593,081	1,536,799	56,282
2009	1,473,675	1,412,838	60,837
2008	1,117,641	1,074,108	43,533

Is there an ethical component to declaring bankruptcy? For example, actor Gary Busey's agent referred to bankruptcy as a business strategy. What are the risks of using bankruptcy as a business strategy?

CPA

Chapter 13 Bankruptcy or Payment Plans or Consumer Debt Adjustment Plans

Chapter 13 bankruptcy— proceeding of consumer debt readjustment plan bankruptcy.

Chapter 13 of the federal Bankruptcy Code provides consumers an individual form of reorganization. Chapter 13 works with consumer debtors to develop a plan to repay debt. To be eligible for **Chapter 13 bankruptcy,** the individual must owe unsecured debts of less than $383,175 and secured debts of less than $1,149.525 and have regular income.[4] Chapter 13 plays an expanded role in bankruptcy because reforms require debtors with the means to pay their debts to go first into Chapter 13 bankruptcy rather than automatically declaring Chapter 7 bankruptcy.

34-2 How Bankruptcy Is Declared

Bankruptcy can be declared in different ways. The federal Bankruptcy Code spells out the requirements and process for declaration.

CPA

34-2a Declaration of Voluntary Bankruptcy

voluntary bankruptcy— proceeding in which the debtor files the petition for relief.

A **voluntary bankruptcy** is begun when the debtor files a petition with the bankruptcy court. A joint petition may be filed by a husband and wife. When a voluntary case is

---

[4] 11 U.S.C. §109(e). These amounts were automatically increased in 2013 and are in effect for three years (through April 2016).

means test—new standard under the Reform Act that requires the court to find that the debtor does not have the means to repay creditors; goes beyond the past requirement of petitions being granted on the simple assertion of the debtor saying, "I have debts."

begun, the debtor must file a schedule of current income and current expenditures unless the court excuses this filing.

A court can dismiss an individual debtor's (consumer's) petition for abuse if the debtor does not satisfy the **means test,** which measures the debtor's ability to pay by computing the debtor's disposable income. Only those debtors who fall below their state's median disposable income will be able to continue in a Chapter 7 proceeding. Individual debtors who meet the means test are required to go into Chapter 13 bankruptcy because they have not qualified for Chapter 7 bankruptcy. The formula for applying the means test is as follows:

Debtor's current monthly income less
Allowable expenses under the Bankruptcy Code = Disposable income $\times$ 60

The debtor commits bankruptcy abuse if this number is not less than the lower of the following:

- 25 percent of the debtor's unsecured claims or $7,475, whichever is greater; or
- $12,475

A finding of abuse means that the debtor's Chapter 7 voluntary petition is dismissed.[5]

Under the BAPCPA, the bankruptcy judge also has the discretion to order the debtor's lawyer to reimburse the trustee for costs and attorney's fees and to assess a civil penalty against the lawyer if the court finds that the lawyer has not acted in good faith in filing the debtor's bankruptcy petition.[6] Lawyers are required to declare themselves (in public ads as well as in any individual meetings with clients) to be "debt relief agencies" or state that they "help people file for relief under the Bankruptcy Code." Debt relief organizations must disclose that bankruptcy may be part of what is required for relief from their debts. Lawyers who advertise their credit/bankruptcy expertise are subject to the laws and regulations that apply to debt relief agencies. If the agency/lawyer advises them to do something that causes the court to declare that there has been bankruptcy abuse, the lawyer/debt relief agency is responsible as well. As part of their role as debt counselors, lawyers are prohibited from advising clients to undertake more debt in contemplation of filing bankruptcy.[7]

Debtors are required to undergo credit counseling (from an approved nonprofit credit counseling agency) within the 180 days prior to declaring a bankruptcy. In addition, the court applies the means test described earlier to determine whether the debtor qualifies for bankruptcy.[8]

There is significant disagreement among the bankruptcy courts about the meaning of "projected income." The disagreement results from the differing situations of the debtors. **For Example,** how do courts deal with debtors who are about to experience a large drop in disposable income? And do courts then consider what happens when debtors'

[5] 11 U.S.C. §707(b). Debtor using bankruptcy to stall a lawsuit who filled out the bankruptcy forms inaccurately was held to have acted in bad faith. In re *Crest By The Sea*, 522 B.R. 540 (D.N.J. 2014). Debtors who failed to disclose their income from a rental property were guilty of bad faith. In re *Fox*, 521 B.R. 520 (D. Md. 2004).
[6] 11 U.S.C. §707(b)(4).
[7] 11 U.S.C. §§526-528. *Milavetz, Gallop & Milavetz, P.A. v. U.S.*, 559 U.S. 229 (2010).
[8] 11 U.S.C. §109(h)(2). There are exceptions to the counseling requirements; for example, active military duty, disability, and emergencies. 11 U.S.C. 111(a) is the counseling provision. The counseling must be completed prior to filing for bankruptcy or the petition can be dismissed, In re *Alvarado*, 496 B.R. 200 (N.D. Cal. 2013). However, being in prison is not an excuse for not going through counseling, and the petition may be dismissed. In re *Gordon*, 467 B.R. 639 (W.D. Ky. 2012) and In re *Kerr*, 2014 WL 6747112 (N.D. Ohio 2014).

incomes are expected to go up? If the projected income test used is applied, the bankruptcy could be dismissed. Debtors and creditors take different positions depending on which way the income goes, and the courts continue to debate the definition of projected income.[9]

CASE SUMMARY

Lawyer/Debtor in the Hoosegow: Still Eligible for Chapter 13?

FACTS: Topous obtained a judgment against Clarence Kenyon Gomery, a lawyer (Debtor), and his law firm, Gomery and Associates, PLLC. That case arose from Mr. Gomery's representation of Topous in various business transactions, including the purchase of property referred to as the Old Mitchell Creek Golf Course. Topous alleged that Mr. Gomery drafted an Operating Agreement creating a limited liability company, T & G Real Estate Development, LLC, to purchase and hold the Mitchell Creek property. Although Topous paid the full purchase price to acquire the property, Mr. Gomery defrauded Topous in the transaction by surreptitiously giving himself a one-half ownership interest in T & G in the Operating Agreement he drafted. The jury awarded ownership of the Mitchell Creek property to Topous and ordered Mr. Gomery to pay Topous damages in the net amount of $11,622.22 and imposed sanctions for Frivolous Defense and for Spoliation of Evidence (see Chapter 2) against Mr. Gomery and his law firm, jointly and severally, for $314,629.27.

Unable to pay the judgment, Mr. Gomery filed a voluntary petition under Chapter 13 on April 2, 2014.

In July 2014, Mr. Gomery was arrested and charged with solicitation of murder. Detective Gomez testified about a recorded conversation between Mr. Gomery and Dale Fisher. During the course of the recorded conversation, Mr. Gomery offered Mr. Fisher $20,000 to kill Christopher K. Cooke, the attorney who represented Topous. Detective Gomez also testified that Mr. Gomery paid Mr. Fisher $1,000 during the recorded conversation, purportedly to purchase the weapon that would be used in committing the crime. Mr. Gomery is currently incarcerated and awaiting trial on these criminal charges.

Mr. Gomery seeks confirmation of his Chapter 13 Plan. The Trustee and Topous have objected to the Plan on the grounds that the Plan is not feasible, and that neither the Plan nor the petition was filed in good faith. The Trustee has also requested that Mr. Gomery's case be converted to Chapter 7 due to the Debtor's lack of good faith.

DECISION: The Debtor's schedules failed to disclose significant and valuable assets. For example, JACCK Enterprises, LLC, in which the Debtor had an interest, appeared on the Debtor's own individual tax returns for 2009 through 2013, along with the returns of JACCK itself. Those returns reflect his income from JACCK and show him as having a one-half ownership interest in the LLC. But he did not disclose JACCK.

The Debtor's Schedules did not disclose that he owned any firearms.

Chapter 13 relief is reserved for the 'honest but unfortunate debtor.'

The court found that the Debtor had not been fair in his treatment of his creditors and was not been forthright in his dealings with the Trustee, the creditors, and this Bankruptcy Court. Under the circumstances, the court found that the Debtor had not acted in good faith.

The Court held that conversion to Chapter 7, which would allow these matters to be investigated by a Chapter 7 trustee, was in the best interests of creditors in this case.

The Debtor offered no explanation, let alone evidence, of the source of the funds he proposed to use to make the $100 monthly payments required under his proposed Plan. The Debtor was incarcerated at the time of the bankruptcy proceedings and had offered no evidence of any current income. Although the Debtor's Plan proposed increasing his payments in the future, the Debtor's attorney admitted that it is unlikely that the Debtor will resume his legal practice in the future. Because the Debtor had no current income, and limited prospects for income in the future, the Court concluded that the Debtor is not eligible to be a debtor under Chapter 13. The Debtor's case was converted to a Chapter 7 proceeding. **[In re *Gomery*, 523 B.R. 773 (W.D. Mich. 2015)]**

---

[9] In re *Turner*, 425 B.R. 918 (S.D. Ga. 2010); In re *Hilton*, 395 B.R. 433 (E.D. Wis. 2008); In re *Anstett*, 383 B.R. 380 (D.S.C. 2008); In re *Colclasure*, 383 B.R. 463 (E.D. Ark. 2008); and In re *Justice*, 418 B.R. 342 (W.D. Mo. 2009).

CPA   34-2b Declaration of Involuntary Bankruptcy

Eligibility

involuntary bankruptcy–
proceeding in which a
creditor or creditors file
the petition for relief with
the bankruptcy court.

An **involuntary bankruptcy** is begun when creditors file a petition with the bankruptcy court. An involuntary case may be commenced against any individual, partnership, or corporation, except those excluded from filing voluntary petitions. Nonprofit corporations are also exempt from involuntary proceedings.[10]

CPA   Number and Claims of Petitioning Creditors

If there are 12 or more creditors, at least 3 of those creditors whose unsecured and undisputed claims total $15,325 or more must sign the involuntary petition.[11] If there are fewer than 12 creditors, excluding employees or insiders (that is, the debtor's relatives,

---

THINKING THINGS THROUGH

Means Test Justifying the End of Debt

The following excerpt is a hypothetical case an experienced bankruptcy attorney worked through to illustrate the application of the means test.

The Brokes, a married couple in their early 40s, have two children in private schools. They are residents of Memphis, Shelby County, Tennessee; their annual gross income is $86,496. Like many debtors, the Brokes lost their home following an unsuccessful Chapter 13 case three years ago. They now rent a house for $2,000 a month. They owe back federal taxes in the amount of $9,000. They have secured debt on two cars with remaining balances of $10,000 and $6,000 and unsecured, consumer debt totaling $28,000. They desire to seek relief under Chapter 7 of the Bankruptcy Code.

The Brokes' gross monthly income is $7,208. After deducting taxes and other mandatory payroll deductions of $1,509, the couple has $5,699 in monthly income. The means test requires several additional deductions from the Brokes' gross monthly income. Section 707(b)(A)(2)(ii) provides a deduction for living and housing expenses using National Standards and Local Standards and additional Internal Revenue Service (IRS) figures. Allowable living expenses for a family of four in Ura and Ima Brokes' income bracket, based on national standards, total $1,564, while housing and utility figures for Shelby County, Tennessee, allow $1,354. In addition, there are allowable expenses for transportation. Based on IRS figures, the Brokes can subtract national ownership costs of $475 for the first car and $338 for the second, as well as regional operating and public transportation costs of $242 and $336, respectively. They can also

deduct their reasonably necessary health insurance costs, here the sum of $600, and $250 a month for private school tuition. Subtracting all of these figures from the Brokes' monthly income leaves $540.

Under §707(b)(2)(A)(iii), the Brokes can subtract payments on secured debt. The amount contractually due on their two automobiles over the next 60 months is $16,000. After dividing this total by 60 and rounding to the nearest dollar, the monthly allowable deduction for secured debt is $267. Subtracting this amount from $540 leaves $273.

Next come priority claim deductions. The Brokes are not subject to any child support or alimony claims, but they do owe $9,000 in back taxes. Again, dividing this amount by 60 yields a deductible amount of $150. Subtracting this from $273 leaves $123 in disposable monthly income. This figure would be multiplied by 60, amounting to a total of $7,380 in disposable income over the five-year period. Abuse is thus statutorily presumed because the debtors' current monthly income reduced by allowable amounts is not less than either $7,000 (25 percent of their nonpriority unsecured claims of $28,000) or $6,000. The Brokes' Chapter 7 case will therefore be dismissed (or they will be allowed voluntarily to convert their Chapter 7 case to a case under Chapter 13).

Does the means test make it more difficult for debtors to declare bankruptcy?*

*Robert J. Landry III and Nancy Hisey Mardis, "Consumer Bankruptcy Reform: Debtors' Prison without Bars or 'Just Desserts' for Deadbeats?" 36 *Golden Gate U. L Rev.* 91 (2006). Reprinted with permission.

---

[10] 11 U.S.C. §303(a). In re *C.W. Min. Co.*, 431 B.R. 307 (Utah 2009). These amounts are adjusted periodically by statutory formulas.

[11] 11 U.S.C. §303.

partners, directors, and controlling persons), any creditor whose unsecured claim is at least $15,325 may sign the petition. In the case of involuntary consumer petitions, there is disagreement as to whether the debtor will still be required to complete the credit counseling requirement prior to the granting of the automatic stay.

> **bona fide**–in good faith; without any fraud or deceit.

If a creditor holds security for a claim, only the amount of the claim in excess of the value of the security is counted. The holder of a claim that is the subject of a **bona fide** dispute may not be counted as a petitioning creditor.[12] **For Example,** David, a CPA, is an unsecured creditor of Arco Company for $16,000. Arco has a total of 10 creditors, all of whom are unsecured. Arco has not paid any of the creditors for three months. The debtor has fewer than 12 creditors. Any one of the creditors may file the petition if the unsecured portion of the amount due that creditor is at least $15,325. Because David is owed $16,000 in unsecured debts, he may file the petition alone.

CPA

Grounds for Relief for Involuntary Case

The mere filing of an involuntary case petition does not result in an order of relief. The debtor may contest the bankruptcy petition. If the debtor does not contest the petition, the court will enter an order of relief if at least one of the following grounds exists: (1) The debtor is generally not paying debts as they become due or (2) within 120 days before the filing of the petition, a custodian has been appointed for the debtor's property.

CPA

34-2c **Automatic Stay**

> **automatic stay**–order to prevent creditors from taking action such as filing suits or seeking foreclosure against the debtor.

Just the filing of either a voluntary or an involuntary petition operates as an **automatic stay,** which prevents creditors from taking action, such as filing suits or foreclosure actions, against the debtor.[13] The stay freezes all creditors in their filing date positions so that no one creditor gains an advantage over other creditors. This automatic stay ends when the bankruptcy case is closed or dismissed (for example, on a finding of abuse by the debtor who has failed to survive the means-to-pay test) or when the debtor is granted a discharge. An automatic stay means that all activity by creditors with respect to collection must stop, with some exceptions incorporated for child support and other family support issues. All litigation with the debtor is halted, and any judgments in place cannot be executed.[14]

34-2d **If the Creditors Are Wrong: Rights of Debtor in an Involuntary Bankruptcy**

If an involuntary petition is dismissed other than by consent of all petitioning creditors and the debtor, the court may award costs, reasonable attorney fees, or damages to the debtor. The damages are those that were caused by taking possession of the debtor's property. The debtor may also recover damages against any creditor who filed the petition in bad faith.

Figure 34-1 provides a summary of the requirements for declaration of bankruptcy and the standards for relief.

---

[12] 11 U.S.C. §303(b)(1). *Farmers & Merchants State Bank v. Turner*, 518 B.R. 642 (N.D. Fla. 2014).
[13] 11 U.S.C. §362. In re *Taggart*, 522 B.R. 627 (D. Or. 2014). Proceeding with the foreclosure on a home after a stay is entered is a violation of the stay order. In re *Betchan*, 524 B.R. 830 (E.D. Wash. 2015).
[14] In re *Hill*, 523 B.R. 704 (D. Mont. 2014).

| FIGURE 34-1 | Declaration of Bankruptcy | | |

	Chapter 7	Chapter 11	Chapter 13
Trustee	Yes	No	Yes
Eligible persons: Individuals Partnerships Corporations	Yes (consumer restrictions) Yes Yes	Yes (individual restrictions) Yes Yes	Yes (consumer restrictions) No No
Voluntary	Yes	Yes	Yes
Involuntary	Yes, except for farmers and nonprofits**	Yes, except for farmers and nonprofits	No
Exemptions	S & L's, credit unions, SBA, railroads, municipalities	Same as Chapter 7 plus stockbrokers*	Only individuals allowed
Requirements-Voluntary	Debts; means test applies to consumers	Debts; means test applies to consumers	Income plus <$383,175 unsecured debt; <$1,149,525 secured debt
Requirements-Involuntary	<12 = 1/$15,325 ≥12 = 3/$15,325	<12 = 1/$15,325 ≥12 = 3/$15,325	N/A

*Railroads are eligible
**Chapter 9 — Municipalities; Chapter 12 — Farmers

34-3 Administration of the Bankruptcy Estate

The administration of the bankruptcy estate varies according to the type of bankruptcy declared. This section of the chapter focuses on the process for liquidation or Chapter 7 bankruptcy. Figure 34-2 provides a flowchart view of the Chapter 7 liquidation process.

34-3a The Order of Relief

order of relief–the order from the bankruptcy judge that starts the protection for the debtor; when the order of relief is entered by the court, the debtor's creditors must stop all proceedings and work through the bankruptcy court to recover debts (if possible). Court finding that creditors have met the standards for bankruptcy petitions.

The **order of relief** is granted by the bankruptcy court and is the procedural step required for the case to proceed in bankruptcy court.[15] An order of relief is entered automatically in a voluntary case and in an involuntary case when those filing the petition have established that the debtor is unable to pay his, her, or its debts as they become due. In consumer cases and Chapter 11 cases that involve an individual, the bankruptcy court must apply the means test to determine whether the individual is eligible for declaring bankruptcy or whether there has been an abuse of the bankruptcy court and system.

34-3b List of Creditors

It is the debtor's responsibility to furnish the bankruptcy court with a list of creditors. Although imposing the responsibility for disclosing debts on the debtor may not seem to be effective, the debtor has an incentive for full disclosure. Those debts not disclosed by the debtor will not be discharged in bankruptcy.

[15] 11 U.S.C. §301.

SPORTS & ENTERTAINMENT LAW

From Millions to Nada: Celebrity Bankruptcies

- Michael Vick, who was one of the highest paid NFL players, filed for bankruptcy in 2008, from prison. Mr. Vick could not afford to pay his bills as well as the fines that were imposed when he entered a guilty plea on charges related to a dog-fighting operation. The fines were not discharged, but he was relieved of his other debts related to his personal property.

- MC Hammer, the "Hammer Time" mega star of the early 1990s, declared bankruptcy in 1996 with $9.6 million in assets and $13.7 million in debts. Mr. Hammer's problem was that he had salary costs of $500,000 per month in order to maintain his entourage.

- Kim Basinger, actress, had to declare bankruptcy after settling a contract suit by Main Line Pictures for $3.8 million for backing out of a movie deal with the company.

- Willie Nelson, Country Western singer, declared bankruptcy in 1990, a necessary result of his owing $16.7 million in taxes because the IRS won its case on Nelson's tax shelters, which were fraudulent. Mr. Nelson also said that he had too many hangers-on that he was supporting. Mr. Nelson was not able to get all of his tax debt discharged because not all tax debts are fully dischargeable and there is no discharge allowed for tax debts that resulted from fraud.

- Walt Disney declared bankruptcy in Kansas City before he moved to Hollywood. Mr. Disney ran a small animation studio there and when his only customer went bankrupt, Mr. Disney tried to continue on, living in his office and eating only canned beans. He eventually gave up, declared bankruptcy, and moved to Hollywood, where he founded an empire.

- Sir Elton John is the quintessential profligate spender whose purchases landed him in bankruptcy. By the time he declared bankruptcy in 2002, Sir Elton had credit card charges of $400,000 per month. His total debt per month was $2,000,000.

- Sinbad, the comedian, failed to pay taxes on his earnings from *Jingle All the Way*. California's Department of Revenue filed a $2.5 million lien on his home and he and his wife declared bankruptcy shortly after in 2009.

- Meat Loaf, singer, declared bankruptcy following a lawsuit filed by a former partner who wrote songs with him.

- Dionne Warwick, singer, filed for bankruptcy because of $10 million in back taxes and negligent financial management.

What are the causes of bankruptcy? What advice would you give to celebrities and athletes about management of their income and bills?

34-3c Trustee in Bankruptcy

trustee in bankruptcy—impartial person elected to administer the debtor's estate.

The **trustee in bankruptcy** is elected by the creditors. The court or the U.S. trustee will appoint an interim trustee if the creditors do not elect a trustee.

The trustee automatically becomes the owner of all of the debtor's property in excess of the property to which the debtor is entitled under exemption laws. The trustee holds all of the rights formerly owned by the debtor.

CPA ## 34-3d The Bankrupt's Estate

All of the debtor's property, with certain exceptions discussed later, is included in the *bankrupt's estate.* Property inherited by the debtor within six months after the filing of the petition also passes to the trustee.

preferences—transfers of property by a debtor to one or more specific creditors to enable these creditors to obtain payment for debts owed.

In many cases, when a debtor knows that insolvency is a problem and bankruptcy is imminent, the debtor attempts to hang onto property or reputation by making transfers of assets to friends, relatives, and creditors. However, trustees have the authority to set aside or void (1) transfers by the debtor that a creditor holding a valid claim under state law could have avoided at the commencement of the bankruptcy case, (2) **preferences,** that is, transfers of property by the debtor to a creditor, the effect of which is to enable

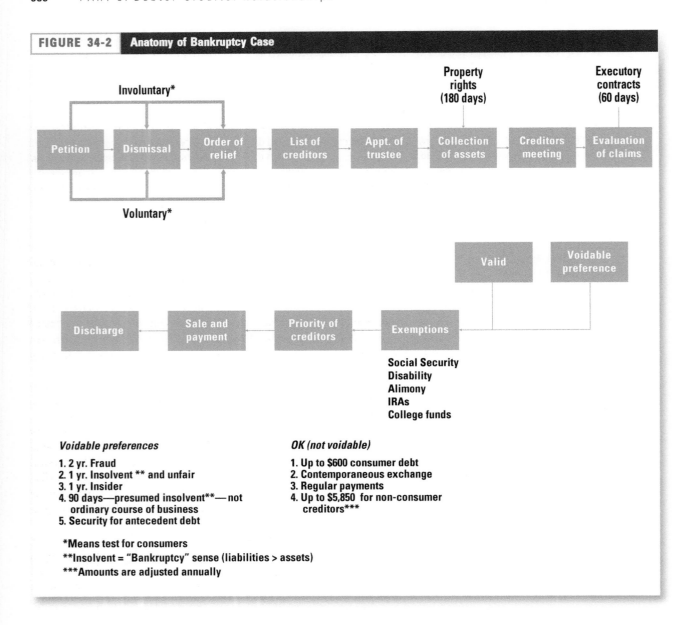

FIGURE 34-2 | **Anatomy of Bankruptcy Case**

the creditor to obtain payment of a higher percentage of the creditor's claim than the creditor would have received if the debtor's assets had been liquidated in bankruptcy, and (3) statutory liens that became effective against the debtor at the commencement of the bankruptcy.

34-3e Voidable Preferences

A debtor may not transfer property to prevent creditors from satisfying their legal claims. The trustee may void any such transfer, known as *a fraudulent transfer*, made or obligation incurred by the debtor within one year of bankruptcy when the debtor's actual intent was to hinder, delay, or defraud creditors by doing so.

The trustee may also void certain transfers of property made by a debtor merely because their effect is to make the debtor insolvent or to reduce the debtor's assets to an unreasonably low amount.[16]

CPA

insolvency—excess of debts and liabilities over assets, or inability to pay debts as they mature.

balance sheet test—comparison of assets to liabilities made to determine solvency.

preferential transfers—certain transfers of money or security interests in the time frame just prior to bankruptcy that can be set aside if voidable.

insider—full-time corporate employee or a director or their relatives.

The Insolvent Debtor

A debtor is insolvent for purposes of determining voidable transfers when the total fair value of all of the debtor's assets does not exceed the debts owed by the debtor. This test for **insolvency** under voidable transfers is commonly called the **balance sheet test** because it is merely a comparison of assets to liabilities without considering whether the debtor will be able to meet future obligations as they become due. The debtor is presumed to be insolvent in the 90 days prior to declaration of bankruptcy.

Preferential Transfers

A transfer of property by the debtor to a creditor may be set aside as **preferential transfers** and the property recovered by the debtor's trustee in bankruptcy if (1) the transfer was made to pay a debt incurred at some earlier time, (2) the transfer was made when the debtor was insolvent and within 90 days before the filing of the bankruptcy petition, and (3) the transfer resulted in the creditor receiving more than the creditor would have received in a liquidation of the debtor's estate. A debtor is presumed to be insolvent on and during the 90 days immediately preceding the date of the filing of the bankruptcy petition.[17]

Transfers made to **insiders** within the 12 months prior to the filing of the petition may be set aside.[18] **For Example,** if a building contractor transferred title to one of his model homes to the company accountant just six months before declaring bankruptcy, the transfer would be a preferential one that would be set aside. However, a transfer by an insider to a noninsider is not subject to recovery by the trustee. The sale of that same model home to a good faith buyer just three days before bankruptcy would be valid. **For Example,** the trustee in the Bernie Madoff case sought to set aside several transfers made to companies and individuals just prior to the time Mr. Madoff admitted that he had an insolvent, $50 billion Ponzi scheme. The trustee used several of the voidable preferences theories to seek a return of funds.

The trustee may not set aside certain transfers by a debtor as preferences. A transaction for present consideration, such as a cash sale, is not set aside.[19] A payment by a debtor in the ordinary course of business, such as the payment of a utility bill, will not be set aside. Under the prior bankruptcy law, a payment was not a voidable preference if it was made in the ordinary course of business and it was made according to industry terms and practices. Nonconsumer debt payments that have a value of less than $6,225 are not subject to the voidable preference standards. The expectation is that the time and effort spent by bankruptcy trustees and courts will be reduced because of the minimum amount required before a challenge can be made. In nonconsumer debts, transfers of less than $6,225 within the voidable preference period are not considered voidable preferences.

---

[16] 11 U.S.C. §548.
[17] 11 U.S.C. §547(f).
[18] 11 U.S.C. §547(b)(4)(B). In re *First Pay, Inc.*, 773 F.3d 583 (4th Cir. 2014).
[19] Payments made 50.29 days after the invoice date were not made in the ordinary course of business. In re *Quebecor World (USA), Inc.*, 518 B.R. 757 (S.D.N.Y. 2014).

CASE SUMMARY

The Honda Pilot Preference

FACTS: On July 3, 2013, Scott and Nicole Conklin (Debtors) entered into a retail installment contract with Hannigan Auto Sales, LLC, in Emmett, Idaho, to purchase a Honda Pilot. CAC agreed to finance Debtors' purchase in the amount $12,871.20. Debtors took possession of the Honda the same day.

CAC thereafter mailed a "Report of Sale and Application for Certificate of Title" to Gem County. The Application was received by Gem County on August 2, 2013, as is evidenced by a date stamp appearing on the Application. However, while the certificate of title issued for the Honda by the State of Idaho properly listed CAC as the "lienholder," it indicated that CAC's lien was "recorded" on August 6, 2013. August 2, 2013, is 30 days after July 3, 2013, the day Debtors purchased and took possession of the Honda.

Debtors filed their Chapter 7 case on September 4, 2013. On October 21, 2013, the Trustee commenced this adversary proceeding against CAC contending that because CAC's security interest in the Honda was not perfected until August 6, as evidenced by the recording date on the title, that security interest was a voidable preference.

The discrepancy between the date the Application was received by Gem County, and the lien recording date listed in the title record for the Honda occurred when the information was transmitted by Gem County to the Department to create the certificate of title. Legal Counsel for the Conklins made a request to have the date changed and, thereafter, the date in the electronic records for the Honda title certificate was changed to reflect a recording date of August 2, instead of August 6, 2013. A certified copy of a printout of the electronic record of title for the Honda, which shows August 2, 2013, as the "recorded" date for CAC's lien, was submitted in evidence.

Both parties moved for summary judgment.

DECISION: Currently under Idaho Code, there is a twenty (20) day time frame from the date of sale in which a lender can perfect a security interest. Federal bankruptcy code was amended to allow a thirty (30) day time frame to perfect a lien.

Applying the revised Idaho statute, the Court concluded Debtors and CAC had shown that the lien on the Honda was perfected under Idaho law on August 2, 2013, the 30th day after Debtors received possession of the Honda. Therefore, under §547(c)(3), Debtors' transfer of the security interest to CAC is protected from avoidance. Summary judgment for the Debtors. **[In re *Conklin*, 511 B.R. 688 (D. Idaho 2014)]**

Self-Settled Trust

Under the Reform Act, the trustee has the ability to set aside the transfer of property into a "self-settled" (a self-created personal trust) any time within the past 10 years if the trustee can establish that the trust was created with actual intent to hinder, delay, or defraud existing or future creditors.[20] This section was added to address the problem of the many assets of individuals being in personal trusts for which those individuals serve as trustees.

34-3f Proof of Claim

claim–creditor's right to payment.

proof of claim–written statement, signed by the creditor or an authorized representative, setting forth any claim made against the debtor and the basis for it.

Bankruptcy law regulates the manner in which creditors present their claims and the way in which the debtor's assets are distributed in payment of these claims.

After the debtor has filed a list of creditors, the court then sends a notice of the bankruptcy proceedings to listed creditors. The creditors who wish to participate in the distribution of the proceeds of the liquidation of the debtor's estate must file a proof of claim. A **claim** is a right to payment, whether liquidated (certain and not disputed), unliquidated, contingent, unmatured, disputed, legal, or equitable. A **proof of claim** is a written statement, signed by the creditor or an authorized representative, setting forth any claim

[20] 11 U.S.C. §548(e).

made against the debtor and the basis for it. It must ordinarily be filed within 90 days after the first meeting of creditors.[21] A creditor must file within that time even though the trustee in bankruptcy in fact knows of the existence of the creditor's claim.

CPA 34-3g **Priority of Claims**

Creditors who hold security for payment, such as a lien or a mortgage on the debtor's property, are less affected by the debtor's bankruptcy. Secured creditors may enforce their security interest to obtain payment of their claims up to the value of their security, the collateral in which they hold an interest. **For Example,** suppose that First Bank holds a mortgage on a company's office building. The mortgage amount is $750,000. The building is sold for $700,000. First Bank is entitled to the $700,000 from the sale. For the remaining portion of the debt, First Bank drops down in priority to wait with the other unsecured creditors for its remaining $50,000. Unsecured creditors with unsecured debts have a statutory order of priority following the secured creditors' rights in their collateral as outlined in the list that appears next.[22] Once the bottom of the priority list is reached, any remaining unsecured creditors share on *a pro rata* basis any remaining assets of the debtor. Any balance remaining after all creditors have been paid goes to the debtor. However, in 98 to 99 percent of all bankruptcies, no unsecured creditors receive any payments, so it is highly unlikely that the debtor would ever receive anything from the bankruptcy litigation of the debtor's property and funds.

The list that follows is the statutory one for priorities of the unsecured creditors following the payment to any secured creditors from the debtors' pledged property:

1. Allowed claims for debts to a spouse, former spouse, or child of the debtor and for alimony to, maintenance for, or support of such spouse or child (that were obligations at the time of the filing of the bankruptcy petition).[23]

2. Costs and expenses of administration of the bankruptcy case, including fees to trustees, attorneys, and accountants, and the reasonable expenses of creditors in recovering property transferred or concealed by the debtor.

3. Claims arising in the ordinary course of a debtor's business or financial affairs after the commencement of the case but before the order of relief (involuntary).

4. Claims for wages, salaries, or commissions, including vacation, severance, or sick leave pay earned within 180 days before the filing of the petition or the date of cessation of the debtor's business, whichever occurred first, limited, however, to $12,475 for each person.

5. Claims arising for contributions to employee benefit plans, based on services rendered within 180 days before the filing of the petition or when the debtor ceased doing business, whichever occurred first; the maximum amount is $12,475. Payments of key-employee retention plans are not permitted unless the plans are "essential" to keeping the key employee at the company that is in bankruptcy. Proving that they are essential requires the key employee actually to have a "bona fide" offer of employment from another company. In addition, there are limits on how much can be paid under key-employee retention plans.

6. Farm producers (up to $6,150) and fishers against debtors who operate grain storage facilities or fish storage or processing facilities, up to $6,150 per claim.

---

[21] 11 U.S.C. §302(c).
[22] 11 U.S.C. §507(1)–(6). Secured creditors' priority is determined by the priority rules related to Article 9, liens, and mortgages. In re *Restivo Auto Body, Inc.*, 772 F.3d 168 (4th Cir. 2014).
[23] In re *Coon*, 522 B.R. 357 (M.D. Ala. 2014).

7. Claims by consumer creditors, not to exceed $2,775 for each claimant, arising from the purchase of consumer goods or services when such property or services were not delivered or provided.

8. Certain taxes and penalties due government, such as income and property taxes (there are time limits, for example, three years is the general time limit, with exceptions for fraud).

9. All other unsecured creditors.

10. Tort claims for death or personal injury resulting from operation of a vehicle or vessel while intoxicated from alcohol, drug, and other substances.

11. Remainder (if any) to debtor.

Each claim must be paid in full before any lower claim is paid anything. If a class of claims cannot be paid in full, the claims in that case are paid on *a pro rata* basis. **For Example,** suppose that following the payment of all secured creditors, $10,000 is left to be distributed. The accountants who performed work on the bankruptcy are owed $15,000, and the lawyers who worked on it are owed $10,000. Because there is not enough to pay two parties in the same priority ranking, the $10,000 is split proportionately. The accountants will receive 15/25, or 3/5, of the $10,000, or $6,000, and the lawyers will receive 10/25, or 2/5, of the $10,000, or $4,000.

34-4 Debtor's Duties and Exemptions

Bankruptcy law imposes certain duties on the debtor and provides for specific exemptions of some of the debtor's estate from the claims of creditors.

34-4a Debtor's Duties

A debtor must file with the court a list of creditors, a schedule of assets and liabilities, and a statement of her financial affairs. The debtor must also appear for examination under oath at the first meeting of creditors.

CPA 34-4b Debtor's Exemptions

A debtor is permitted to claim certain property of the estate in the trustee's possession and keep it free from claims of creditors. Exemptions are provided under federal law, but state laws also provide for exemptions. Examples of exempt property from the federal code include wedding rings, property used to earn a living, one VCR, and one car. New York exemptions include "all stoves in the home, one sewing machine, the family Bible, a pew in a public house of worship, enough food for sixty days, a wedding ring, and a watch not exceeding thirty-five dollars in value."[24] California exempts tools of the trade and the family cemetery plot.[25]

The principal exemptions provided by the Bankruptcy Code are the debtor's interest in real or personal property used as a residence.[26] The homestead exemption is now greatly limited and, in effect, preempts state law on this debtor exemption. Debtors are required to have lived in the home for two years prior to bankruptcy, and the amount

---

[24] N.Y. C.P.L.R. §5205 (2014).
[25] Cal. Civ. Proc. Code §704.010-704.210 (2014).
[26] A married couple gets a single homestead exemption.

of the homestead exemption would be limited to $155,675.[27] To be able to use a higher state homestead exemption, the debtor must have lived in the home for 1,215 days (40 months).[28] Labeled as the most flagrant abuse of the existing bankruptcy system, debtors have used the homestead exemption to shift their assets into expensive homes to shield everything from bankruptcy. Known as the "mansion loophole," the changes in the Reform Act related to the homestead exemption were among the most debated and the most dramatic.[29] **For Example,** prior to the reforms actor Burt Reynolds declared bankruptcy in Florida and was relieved of millions in debt, but he was able to keep his $2.5 million Valhalla estate there. Corporate raider Paul Bilzerian, who was convicted of securities fraud, also declared bankruptcy in Florida but kept his mansion, the largest home in Hillsborough County, Florida. Former WorldCom CFO Scott Sullivan (who entered a guilty plea to fraud and other charges and is serving a five-year sentence) built a multimillion-dollar home in Florida to gain homestead protections. Wendy Gramm, who sat on Enron's board, purchased 200 acres of land in Texas and constructed a large home with her husband, former senator Phil Gramm, to take advantage of homestead exemptions then available in Texas. However, the Reform Act closed this corporate executive loophole by requiring that the $155,675 exemption apply to debtors who are convicted of securities fraud or bankruptcy fraud.[30]

Other exemptions include payments under a life insurance contract, alimony and child support payments, and awards from personal injury litigation.[31] Under the Reform Act, college savings accounts and IRAs are exempt property under the federal exemptions and can be used even by those debtors who are using state exemptions. The IRA exemption is limited to $1,245,475.[32]

CASE SUMMARY

Planning for Bankruptcy: Can You Stash Cash Away in College and Retirement Accounts?

FACTS: Leonard Bronk, a retiree living in Stevens Point, Wisconsin, incurred significant debts providing for his wife's medical care before her death in 2007, and he himself suffered a stroke in early 2009. With his medical debts mounting—they exceeded $345,000 by the time he filed for bankruptcy—Bronk sought the advice of an attorney about pre-bankruptcy exemption planning. His assets included his home, which he owned free and clear, and a certificate of deposit in the amount of $42,000. On the advice of counsel, Bronk sought to protect these nonexempt assets by converting them to exempt assets.

In May 2009, a few months before filing his Chapter 7 petition, Bronk borrowed $95,000 from Citizens Bank and mortgaged his previously unencumbered home. He used these funds to establish five college savings accounts for the benefit of his grandchildren under section 529 of the Internal Revenue Code.

Account owners control the funds in these accounts (known as "Edvest" accounts) and may designate and change account beneficiaries. Beneficiaries do not control account assets.

In addition to creating the college savings accounts using the equity in his home, Bronk converted the $42,000 certificate of deposit into an annuity with CM Life Insurance Company. The annuity contract was issued on May 4, 2009, and does not begin making payments until January 3, 2035, but it also includes a death benefit.

[27] The time requirement is at 11 U.S.C. §522(b)(3)(A), and the amount limitation is at 11 U.S.C. §522(o)(1). This amount refers to those who elect state exemptions. In the absence of state exemptions, the federal maximum is $22,975.
[28] 11 U.S.C. §522(p)(2)(B).
[29] 11 U.S.C. §522(p).
[30] 11 U.S.C. §522(q).
[31] 11 U.S.C. §522(d) (including automatic adjustments).
[32] 11 U.S.C. §522(n). There are time requirements on college savings (529) accounts in order to obtain the exemption.

Planning for Bankruptcy: Can You Stash Cash Away in College and Retirement Accounts? continued

On August 5, 2009, Bronk filed for bankruptcy under Chapter 7. The trustee objected to the college-fund and annuity transactions, arguing that Bronk had transferred his property with the intent to hinder, delay, or defraud his creditors and thus should be denied a discharge.

The judge accepted Bronk's argument about the annuity, holding that it was fully exempt as a retirement benefit as were the Edvest accounts.

Both sides appealed to the district court. The district judge agreed that Bronk was entitled to a discharge because the trustee had not proven that the asset transfers were made with intent to hinder, delay, or defraud creditors. Second, the district judge agreed with the bankruptcy judge's interpretation and upheld the decision to deny the claimed exemption for Bronk's Edvest accounts (which was reversed on remand). Finally, the judge narrowed the bankruptcy court's interpretation of "retirement benefit" and remanded the case for additional fact-finding on whether the annuity qualified under the statute.

Bronk appealed, challenging the disallowance of the exemption for his college savings accounts. The trustee filed a cross-appeal challenging the court's ruling on the annuity.

DECISION: Wisconsin's exemption statute allows debtors to exempt "[a]n interest in a college savings account" from execution by creditors. The term "interest" is not specifically defined in the statute or by regulation, but an "interest" is generally defined as "[a] legal share in something; all or part of a legal or equitable claim to or a right in property." Bronk clearly has a legal interest in each of the Edvest college savings accounts. He owned the accounts and could at any time select and change beneficiaries, transfer funds between accounts, receive distributions from the accounts, and (subject to certain limitations) remove funds from the accounts.

To qualify for full exemption, the retirement plan or contract must meet one of two additional requirements: (1) it must be employer sponsored; or (2) it must comply with the Internal Revenue Code.

The statute requires that the retirement product "provid[e] benefits" by reason of age, illness, death, etc., not that it be "purchased" by reason of age. Moreover, there is no special test for annuities.

Bronk's annuity begins paying on a fixed date—January 3, 2035—and thus does not pay benefits because of age, length of service, or the onset of an illness or disability. But the annuity also contains a death benefit. That feature brings it under the umbrella of an exemption.

To qualify for full exemption as a "retirement benefit," a retirement product must be either employer sponsored or "compl[y] with the provisions of the internal revenue code." The trustee raised this issue for the first time in the district court, and even then simply asserted—without developing an argument—that Bronk's annuity was not tax qualified. The argument was held to be waived.

The court held that the exemption statute applied to the college savings accounts. However, the court held that there were still issues about the retirement plan that required the court to make some factual findings. Because the plan was not employer-sponsored, a finding that it met the Internal Revenue Code standards was still needed. **[In re *Bronk*, 775 F.3d 871 (7th Cir. 2015)]**

34-4c Debtor's Protection against Discrimination

Federal, state, and local law may not discriminate against anyone on the basis of a discharge in bankruptcy. For example, a state cannot refuse to issue a new license to an individual if the license fees on a previous one have been discharged as a debt in the individual's declaration of bankruptcy.

34-5 Discharge in Bankruptcy

The main objectives of a bankruptcy proceeding are to collect and distribute the debtor's assets and then issue a **discharge in bankruptcy** of the debtor from obligations. The decree terminating the bankruptcy proceeding is generally a discharge that releases the debtor from most debts. Under the BAPCPA, a discharge is available only once every eight years.

discharge in bankruptcy– order of the bankruptcy court relieving the debtor from obligation to pay the unpaid balance of most claims.

34-5a Denial of Discharge

The court will refuse to grant a discharge if the debtor has (1) within one year of the filing of the petition fraudulently transferred or concealed property with intent to hinder, delay,

ETHICS & THE LAW

The Skies Are Not So Friendly to Employee Pensions

As part of its Chapter 11 bankruptcy, United Airlines was relieved of its pension liabilities. Employees and unions wonder how a company can be permitted to renege on those benefits when so many protections were built into the law under ERISA. Congressional hearings revealed that there were loopholes in the accounting processes for pension fund reporting that permitted United, and many others, to report pension numbers that made the pension funds look healthy when they really were not. The loopholes were Enron-esque in nature. Companies could spin the pension obligations off the books so that the existing levels of obligations of the plan looked small and the assets very rich.

Because of United's pension bailout, Congress changed the accounting for pension plans to avoid the problem of the rosy picture when the funds really need further funding. One interesting approach to protecting pension plans is to require companies to fund the pension plans according to the numbers they have reported to the SEC in their financials. If United had funded its plans when its SEC numbers indicated it needed to (e.g., in 1998), the plan would have been sufficiently funded. Under ERISA guidelines, it was not required to kick in funds until 2002 when it was grossly underfunded.

Were companies acting ethically on their pension accounting? Were they acting legally?*

*Marry Williams Walsh, "Pension Law Loopholes Helped United Hide Its Troubles," *New York Times,* June 7, 2005, C1.

---

or defraud creditors, (2) failed to keep proper financial records, (3) made a false oath or account,[33] (4) failed to explain satisfactorily any loss of assets, (5) refused to obey any lawful order of the court or refused to testify after having been granted immunity, (6) obtained a discharge within the last eight years,[34] (7) filed a written waiver of discharge that is approved by the court,[35] or (8) in the case of a consumer debtor, has failed to complete a personal financial management instructional course.[36] A discharge releases the debtor from the unpaid balance of most debts except for taxes, customs duties, child support obligations, and tax penalties.[37] Student loan obligations are not discharged in bankruptcy unless the loan first became due more than seven years before bankruptcy or unless not allowing a discharge would impose undue hardship on the debtor.

CASE SUMMARY

Your Living Expenses Are Fairly Minimal in Maximum Security

FACTS: Bryan Anthony Looper (Debtor) had over $300,000 in student loans that were used to finance his education at Mercer University where he obtained an A.B., an M.B.A, and another unspecified graduate degree as well as a large number of courses toward his J.D. degree. He did not make payments on these student loans.

In 1996, he was elected assessor for Putnam County, Tennessee, a position he held for two years

---

[33] The debtor must actually make a false statement. Obtaining a credit card under false pretenses is fraud. In re *Levasseur,* 737 F.3d 814 (1st Cir. 2013). However, just the use of a credit card for unnecessary purchases is not fraud, In re *Quinn,* 492 B.R. 341 (N.D. Ga. 2013).

[34] 11 U.S.C. §727(a)(8).

[35] 11 U.S.C. §523.

[36] 11 U.S.C. §727(a)(11). The financial management course requirement applies to both Chapter 7 and Chapter 13 consumer bankruptcies.

[37] Child support obligations enjoy additional protections and priorities in bankruptcy. 11 U.S.C §507(a).

Your Living Expenses Are Fairly Minimal in Maximum Security continued

and four months. He was then convicted of the first-degree murder of state senator Tommy Burks. He exhausted all of his appeals and is currently serving a life sentence without the possibility of parole. Looper has one dependent, a son born in August 1998. The circuit court for Putnam County, Tennessee, ordered Looper to pay child support of $161.00 per month plus $7,254.20 in medical expenses. Looper did not make any of the court-ordered child support payments and was in arrears by more than $23,515.00.

Looper asked to have his student loans discharged on the basis of his hardship.

DECISION: The court refused to discharge the student loans. Looper had all of his living expenses covered by the Tennessee Department of Corrections. Looper had made no effort to make any payments on any of his student loans and had also not made attempts to try and work with his lenders or apply to programs set up to help with student loans. The court also noted that Looper's circumstances were the result of his choices and conduct, not the result of unforeseen and uncontrollable events. He had three degrees and the capability of earning a living but, through poor choices, produced his own difficult circumstances. **[In re *Looper*, 2007 WL 1231700 (B. E.D. Tenn. 2007)]**

In addition, the following debts are not discharged by bankruptcy: (1) loans obtained by use of a false financial statement made with intent to deceive and on which the creditor reasonably relied, (2) debts not scheduled or listed with the court in time for allowance, (3) debts arising from fraud while the debtor was acting in a fiduciary capacity or by reason of embezzlement or larceny, (4) alimony and child support, (5) a judgment for willful and malicious injury, (6) a consumer debt to a single creditor totaling more than $650 for luxury goods or services (within 90 days of the order of relief) and cash advances exceeding $925 based on consumer open-end credit, such as a credit card (within 70 days of the order of relief),[38] (7) damages arising from drunk driving or the

FIGURE 34-3   Nondischargeable Debts in Bankruptcy

1. Taxes within three years of filing bankruptcy petition
2. Liability for obtaining money or property by false pretenses
3. Willful and malicious injuries
4. Debts incurred by driving DWI*
5. Alimony, maintenance, or child support
6. Unscheduled debts (unless actual notice)
7. Debts resulting from fraud as a fiduciary (embezzlement)
8. Government fines or penalties imposed within three years prior
9. Educational loans due within seven prior years (unless hardship)
10. Prior bankruptcy debts in which debtor waived discharge
11. Presumption on luxury goods: $650 goods; $925 cash
12. Reaffirmation agreements — Writing — Filed with court — Not rescinded prior to discharge

*Includes vessels and aircraft

[38] 11 U.S.C. §523(a)(2)(c)(i). (Amounts are adjusted each year.)

operation of vessels and aircrafts by people who are inebriated,[39] (8) loans used to pay taxes (including credit cards),[40] (9) taxes not paid as a result of a fraudulent return, although other unpaid taxes beyond the past three years can be discharged,[41] (10) pre-bankruptcy fees and assessments owed to homeowners associations, and (11) debts owed to tax-qualified retirement plans. **For Example,** one of the financial concerns facing athlete Lance Armstrong is that the litigation against him may include findings of malice with the result being that those judgments cannot be discharged in bankruptcy, thus making all those judgments a lifetime obligation. Figure 34-3 has a listing of non-dischargeable debts.

34-6 Reorganization Plans under Chapter 11

In addition to liquidation under Chapter 7, the Bankruptcy Code permits debtors to restructure the organization and finances of their businesses so that they may continue to operate. In these rehabilitation plans, the debtor keeps all of the assets (exempt and nonexempt), continues to operate the business, and makes a settlement that is acceptable to the majority of the creditors. This settlement is binding on the minority creditors.

Individuals, partnerships, and corporations in business may all be reorganized under the Bankruptcy Code. The first step is to file a plan for the debtor's reorganization. This plan may be filed by the debtor, any party in interest, or a committee of creditors. If the debtor wishes to move from a Chapter 11 proceeding (in the case of an individual debtor), the debtor must survive the means test that is now a requirement for determining eligibility for bankruptcy.

34-6a Contents of the Plan

The plan divides ownership interests and debts into those that will be affected by the adoption of the plan and those that will not be. It then specifies what will be done to those interests and claims that are affected. **For Example,** when mortgage payments are too high for the income of a corporation, a possible plan would be to reduce the mortgage payments and give the mortgage holder preferred stock to compensate for the loss sustained.

All creditors, shareholders, and other interest holders within a particular class must be treated the same way. **For Example,** the holders of first mortgage bonds must all be treated similarly. The treatment of the bondholders in the Chrysler and GM bankruptcies was a point of contention and negotiation in those reorganizations.

A plan can also provide for the assumption, rejection, or assignment of executory contracts. The trustee or debtor can, under certain circumstances, suspend performance of a contract not yet fully performed. **For Example,** collective bargaining agreements may be rejected with the approval of the bankruptcy court.[42]

34-6b Confirmation of the Plan

After the plan is prepared, the court must approve or confirm it. A plan will be confirmed if it has been submitted in good faith and if its provisions are reasonable.[43] After the plan is confirmed, the owners and creditors of the enterprise have only the rights that are specified in the plan. They cannot go back to their original contract positions.

[39] 11 U.S.C. §523(a)(9).
[40] 11 U.S.C. §523(a)(14A), (14B).
[41] 11 U.S.C. §§1129(a)(9)(c), (D), 1129(b)(2)(B), 1141(d)(6)(B).
[42] 11 U.S.C. §1113.
[43] 11 U.S.C. §1129.

C P A ## 34-7 Payment Plans under Chapter 13

The Bankruptcy Code also provides for the adoption of extended-time payment plans for individual debtors who have regular income. These debtors must owe unsecured debts of less than $383,175 and secured debts of less than $1,149,525.

An individual debtor who has a regular income may submit a plan for the installment payment of outstanding debts. If the court approves it, the debtor may then pay the debts in the installments specified by the plan even if the creditors had not originally agreed to such installment payments.

34-7a Contents of the Plan

The individual debtor plan is, in effect, a budget of the debtor's future income with respect to outstanding debts. The plan must provide for the eventual payment in full of all claims entitled to priority under the Bankruptcy Code. All creditors holding the same kind or class of claim must be treated the same way.

34-7b Confirmation of the Plan

The plan has no effect until the court approves or confirms it. A plan will be confirmed if it was submitted in good faith and is in the best interests of the creditors.[44] When the plan is confirmed, debts are payable in the manner specified in the plan.

34-7c Discharge of the Debtor

After all of the payments called for by the plan have been made, the debtor is given a discharge. The discharge releases the debtor from liability for all debts except those that would not be discharged by an ordinary bankruptcy discharge.[45] Under the bankruptcy reforms, the court cannot grant a discharge until the debtor has completed an instructional course concerning personal financial management.[46] If the debtor does not perform under the plan, the creditors can move to transfer the debtor's case to a Chapter 7 proceeding, but they would still face the means test in qualifying for this move to Chapter 7.

Make the Connection

Summary

Jurisdiction over bankruptcy cases is in U.S. district courts, which may refer all cases and related proceedings to adjunct bankruptcy courts.

Three bankruptcy proceedings are available: liquidation (Chapter 7), reorganization (Chapter 11), and extended-time payment (Chapter 13). A liquidation proceeding under Chapter 7 may be either voluntary or involuntary.

A *voluntary case* is commenced by the debtor's filing a petition with the bankruptcy court. A voluntary petition is subject to the means test to determine if the debtor meets the standard for declaring bankruptcy. An involuntary case is commenced by the creditors' filing a petition with the bankruptcy court. If there are 12 or more creditors, at least 3 whose unsecured claims total $15,325 or more

---

[44] 11 U.S.C. §1325.
[45] 11 U.S.C. §1328.
[46] 11 U.S.C. §1328(g)(1).

must sign the involuntary petition. If there are fewer than 12 creditors, any creditor whose unsecured claim is at least $15,325 may sign the petition. If the debtor contests the bankruptcy petition, it must be shown that the debtor is not paying debts as they become due.

Eligibility for Chapters 7 and 11 bankruptcy excludes railroads, municipalities, and Small Business Administration companies. Individual debtors are restricted on Chapters 7 and 11 filings by their ability to repay. If found to have the means to pay, they go into a Chapter 13 proceeding. Chapter 13 eligibility is limited to consumers with $383,175 in unsecured debt and $1,149,525 in secured debt.

An automatic stay prevents creditors from taking legal action against the debtor after a bankruptcy petition is filed. The trustee in bankruptcy is elected by the creditors and is the successor to, and acquires the rights of, the debtor. In certain cases, the trustee can avoid transfers of property to prevent creditors from satisfying their claims. Preferential transfers may be set aside. A transfer for a present consideration, such as a cash sale, is not a preference.

Bankruptcy law regulates the way creditors present their claims and how the assets of the debtor are to be distributed in payment of the claims. Some assets of the debtor are exempt from the bankruptcy estate, such as a portion of the value of the debtor's home.

Secured claims are not affected by the debtor's bankruptcy. Unsecured claims are paid in the following order of priority:

1. Support or maintenance for a spouse, former spouse, or child.
2. Costs and expenses of administration of the bankruptcy case.
3. Claims arising in the ordinary course of a debtor's business or financial affairs after the commencement of the case but before the order of relief (involuntary).
4. Claims for wages, salaries, or commissions, including vacation, severance, or sick leave pay earned within 180 days before the filing of the petition or the date of cessation of the debtor's business, limited to $12,475 for each person.
5. Claims arising for contributions (up to $6,225) to employee benefit plans based on services rendered within 180 days before the filing of the petition or when the debtor ceased doing business.
6. Farm producers (up to $6,150) and fishers against debtors who operate grain storage facilities or fish produce storage or processing facilities, up to $6,150 per claim.
7. Claims by consumer creditors, not to exceed $2,775 for each claimant.
8. Certain taxes and penalties due government units, such as income and property taxes.
9. All other unsecured creditors.
10. Remainder (if any) to debtor.

The decree terminating bankruptcy proceedings is generally a discharge that releases the debtor from most debts. Certain debts, such as income taxes, student loans, loans obtained by use of a false financial statement, alimony, and debts not listed by the debtor, are not discharged.

Under Chapter 11 bankruptcy, individuals, partnerships, and corporations in business may be reorganized so that the business can continue to operate. A plan for reorganization must be approved by the court. Under a Chapter 13 bankruptcy proceeding, individual debtors with a regular income may adopt extended-time payment plans for the payment of debts. A plan for extended-time payment must also be confirmed by the court. Federal, state, and local law may not discriminate against anyone on the basis of a discharge in bankruptcy.

Learning Outcomes

After studying this chapter, you should be able to clearly explain:

34-1 Bankruptcy Law
34-2 How Bankruptcy Is Declared

LO.1 List the requirements for the commencement of a voluntary bankruptcy case and an involuntary bankruptcy case

See the Sports & Entertainment Law discussion of celebrity bankruptcies, page 679.
See the discussion of Chapters 7, 11, and 13 and Figure 34-1, pages 672–673, 678.

See the In re *Gomery* case for a discussion of relationships between Chapter 7 and Chapter 13, page 675.

34-3 Administration of the Bankruptcy Estate

LO.2 Explain the procedure for the administration of a debtor's estate

See the list of priorities in the section titled "Priority of Claims," pages 683–684.
See In re *Conklin* on priority positions of the creditor, page 682.

34-4   Debtor's Duties and Exemptions

LO.3   List a debtor's duties and exemptions
See the discussion of the homestead exemptions, pages 684–685.
See the In re *Bronk* case for a discussion of structuring exemptions prior to bankruptcy, pages 685–686.

34-5   Discharge in Bankruptcy

LO.4   Explain the significance of a discharge in bankruptcy
See In re *Looper* for a discussion of hardship, pages 687–688.

34-6   Reorganization Plans under Chapter 11

See Ethics & the Law, "The Skies Are Not So Friendly to Employee Pensions," page 687.

34-7   Payment Plans under Chapter 13

LO.5   Explain when a business reorganization plan or an extended-time payment plan might be used
See the Ethics & the Law discussion of United Airlines, page 687.

Key Terms

automatic stay
balance sheet test
bankruptcy courts
bona fide
Chapter 7 bankruptcy
Chapter 11 bankruptcy
Chapter 13 bankruptcy

claim
discharge in bankruptcy
insiders
insolvency
involuntary bankruptcy
liquidated
means test

order of relief
preferences
preferential transfers
proof of claim
trustee in bankruptcy
voluntary bankruptcy

Questions and Case Problems

1. Hall-Mark regularly supplied electronic parts to Peter Lee. On September 11, 1992, Lee gave Hall-Mark a $100,000 check for parts it had received. Hall-Mark continued to ship parts to Lee. On September 23, 1992, Lee's check was dishonored by the bank. On September 25, 1992, Lee delivered to Hall-Mark a cashier's check for $100,000. Hall-Mark shipped nothing more to Lee after receipt of the cashier's check. On December 24, 1992, Lee filed a voluntary petition for bankruptcy. The trustee filed a complaint to have the $100,000 payment to Hall-Mark set aside as a voidable preference. Hall-Mark said it was entitled to the payment because it gave value to Lee. The trustee said that the payment was not actually made until the cashier's check was delivered on September 25, 1992, and that Hall-Mark gave no further value to Lee after that check was paid. Who was correct? [In re *Lee*, 108 F.3d 239 (9th Cir.)]

2. Orso, who had declared bankruptcy, received a structured tort settlement in a personal injury claim he had pending. The settlement would pay him an annuity each year for 30 years because the claim was the result of an auto accident that left him permanently and severely brain damaged with an IQ of about 70. His ex-wife had a pending claim for $48,000 in arrearages on Orso's $1,000 per month child support payments. His ex-wife wanted the

annuity included in the bankruptcy estate. Would this property have been included in Orso's bankruptcy estate? [In re *Orso*, 214 F.3d 637 (5th Cir.)]

3. Harold McClellan sold ice-making machinery to Bobbie Cantrell's brother for $200,000 to be paid in installment payments. McClellan took a security interest in the ice machine but did not perfect it by filing a financing statement. The brother defaulted when he owed $100,000, and McClellan brought suit. With the suit pending, the brother "sold" the ice machine to Bobbie Cantrell for $10. Bobbie then sold the machine to someone for $160,000 and refused to explain what happened to that money. McClellan added Bobbie as a defendant in his suit against her brother. Bobbie then declared bankruptcy. McClellan sought to have the various transfers set aside. The trial court refused to do so, and McClellan appealed. Should the transfers be set aside? Why or why not? [*McClellan v. Cantrell*, 217 F.3d 890 (7th Cir.)]

4. Okamoto owed money to Hornblower & Weeks-Hemphill, Noyes (a law firm and hereafter Hornblower). Hornblower filed an involuntary bankruptcy petition against Okamoto, who moved to dismiss the petition on the ground that he had more than 12 creditors and the petition could not be filed by only 1 creditor. Hornblower replied that the other creditors' claims were too small to count and,

therefore, the petition could be filed by one creditor. Decide. [In re *Okamoto*, 491 F.2d 496 (9th Cir.)]

5. Jane Leeves declared voluntary Chapter 7 bankruptcy. The trustee included the following property in her bankruptcy estate:

   • Jane's wedding ring
   • Jane's computer for her consulting business that she operated from her home
   • Jane's car payment from a client in the amount of $5,000 that was received 91 days after Jane filed bankruptcy

   After collecting all of Jane's assets, the bankruptcy trustee was trying to decide how to distribute the assets. Jane had the following creditors:

   • Mortgage company—owed $187,000 (the trustee sold Jane's house for $190,000)
   • Expenses of the bankruptcy—$3,000
   • Federal income taxes—$11,000
   • Utility bills—$1,000
   • Office supply store open account—$1,000

   The trustee had $11,500 in cash, including the $3,000 additional cash left from the sale of the house after the mortgage company was paid. How should the trustee distribute this money? What if the amount were $14,500; how should that be distributed?

6. Kentile sold goods over an extended period of time to Winham. The credit relationship began without Winham's being required to furnish a financial statement. After a time, payments were not made regularly, and Kentile requested a financial statement. Winham submitted a statement for the year just ended. Kentile requested a second statement. The second statement was false. Kentile objected to Winham's discharge in bankruptcy because of the false financial statement. Should the discharge be granted? Why or why not?

7. D. Erik Von Kiel obtained loans from the U.S. Department of Health & Human Services so that he could complete his education as an osteopathic physician. He works at the International Academy of Life (IAL) in Orem, Utah, for no salary but receives gifts from IAL that total $150,000 per year, or about $12,787 per month. He pays no taxes on these "gifts" and has received them since 2005. Dr. Von Kiel pays all but $1,000 to his ex-wife and nine children for their support. He has given up his practice, taken a vow of poverty, and works at IAL to concentrate on alternative medicine. He has signed over full authority for the management of his financial affairs to two individuals, who apparently failed to manage wisely. As a result, Dr. Von Kiel filed for bankruptcy in order to be discharged from his HHS loans. HHS says that Dr. Von Kiel should not be discharged because of bad faith. Who is correct and why? [In re *Von Kiel*, 461 B.R. 323 (E.D. Pa.)]

8. Sonia, a retailer, has the following assets: a factory worth $1 million; accounts receivable amounting to $750,000, which fall due in four to six months; and $20,000 cash in the bank. Sonia's sole liability is a $200,000 note falling due today, which she is unable to pay. Can Sonia be forced into involuntary bankruptcy under the Bankruptcy Code? [In re *35th & Morgan Development Cor*p., 510 B.R. 832 (N.D. Ill.)]

9. Samson Industries ceased doing business and is in bankruptcy proceedings. Among the creditors are five employees seeking unpaid wages. Three of the employees are owed $3,500 each, and two are owed $1,500 each. These amounts became due within 90 days preceding the filing of the petition. Where, in the priority of claims, will the employees' wage claims fall?

10. Carol Cott, doing business as Carol Cott Fashions, is worried about an involuntary bankruptcy proceeding being filed by her creditors. Her net worth, using a balance sheet approach, is $8,000 ($108,000 in assets minus $100,000 in liabilities). However, her cash flow is negative, and she has been hard pressed to meet current obligations as they mature. She is in fact some $17,000 in arrears in payments to her creditors on bills submitted during the past two months. Will the fact that Cott is solvent in the balance sheet sense result in the court's dismissing the creditors' petition if Cott objects to the petition? Explain. [*Forever Green Athletic Fields, Inc. v. Dawson*, 514 B.R. 768 (E.D. Pa.)]

11. On July 1, Roger Walsh, a sole proprietor operating a grocery, was involuntarily petitioned into bankruptcy by his creditors. At that time, and for at least 90 days prior to that time, Walsh was unable to pay current obligations. On June 16, Walsh paid the May electric bill for his business. The trustee in bankruptcy claimed that this payment was a voidable preference. Was the trustee correct? Explain.

12. Steven and Teresa Hornsby are married and have three young children. On May 25, 1993, the Hornsbys filed a voluntary Chapter 7 petition. They had by that date accumulated more than $30,000 in debt, stemming almost entirely from student loans. They wanted a discharge of their student loans on grounds of undue hardship. The Hornsbys attended

a succession of small Tennessee state colleges. Both studied business and computers, but neither graduated. Although they received several deferments and forbearances on the loans, they ultimately defaulted before making any payments. Interest had accumulated on the loans to the extent that Steven was indebted to the Tennessee Student Assistance Corporation (TSAC) for $15,058.52, and Teresa was indebted to TSAC for $18,329.15.

Steven was working for AT&T in Dallas, Texas; he made $6.53 per hour, occasionally working limited overtime hours. Teresa was employed by KinderCare Learning Center. Although she had begun work in Tennessee, she had transferred to become the director of a child care facility in Dallas. Teresa was earning $17,500 per year with medical benefits at the time of the hearing. In monthly net income, Steven earned approximately $1,083.33, and Teresa earned $1,473.33, amounting to $2,556.66 of disposable income per month. The Hornsbys' reported monthly expenses came to $2,364.90. They operated with a monthly surplus of $191.76 to $280.43, depending on whether Steven earned overtime for a particular month. Under the federal bankruptcy laws, are the Hornsbys entitled to a discharge on their student loans? Explain your answer. [In re *Hornsby*, 144 F.3d 433 (6th Cir.)]

13. TLC was an Atlanta rhythm, blues, and hip-hop band that performed at clubs in 1991. The three-woman group signed a recording contract with LaFace Records. The group's first album that LaFace produced, *Oooooohhh on the TLC Tip*, sold almost 3 million albums in 1992. The group's second album, *Crazysexycool*, also produced by LaFace, sold 5 million albums through June 1996. The two albums together had six top-of-the-chart singles.

LaFace had the right to renew TLC's contract in 1996 following renegotiation of the contract terms. In the industry, royalty rates for unknown groups, as TLC was in 1991, are generally 7 percent of the revenues for the first 500,000 albums and 8 percent for sales on platinum albums (albums that sell over 1 million copies). The royalty rate increases to 9.5

percent for all sales on an eighth album. Established artists in the industry who renegotiate often have royalty rates of 13 percent, and artists with two platinum albums can command an even higher royalty.

The three women in TLC—Tionne Watkins (T-Boz), Lisa Lopes (Left-Eye, who has since died), and Rozonda Thomas (Chili)—declared bankruptcy in July 1995. All three listed debts that exceeded their assets, which included sums owed to creditors for their cars and to Zale's and The Limited for credit purchases. Lopes was being sued by Lloyd's of London, which claimed she owed it $1.3 million it had paid on a policy held by her boyfriend on his home that was destroyed by fire. Lopes pleaded guilty to one count of arson in the destruction of the home but denied that she intended to destroy it. She was sentenced to five years probation and treatment at a halfway house.

Lopes asked that the Lloyd's claim be discharged in her bankruptcy. All three members of TLC asked that their contract with LaFace be discharged in bankruptcy because being bound to their old contract could impede their fresh financial starts.

Did the three women meet the standards for declaring bankruptcy? Evaluate whether Lopes's Lloyd's claim should be discharged. Determine whether the record contract should be discharged.

14. Place the following in order for a bankruptcy proceeding:

    a. Order of relief

    b. Collection of bankrupt's estate

    c. List of creditors

    d. Petition

    e. Evaluation of claims

    f. Voidable preferences

    g. Discharge

15. Three general unsecured creditors are owed $45,000 as follows: *A*, $15,000; *B*, $5,000; and *C*, $25,000. After all other creditors were paid, the amount left for distribution to general unsecured creditors was $9,000. How will the $9,000 be distributed?

CPA Questions

1. Which of the following statements is correct concerning the voluntary filing of a petition of bankruptcy?

   a. If the debtor has 12 or more creditors, the unsecured claims must total at least $15,325.

   b. The debtor must be solvent.

   c. If the debtor has less than 12 creditors, the unsecured claims must total at least $15,325.

   d. The petition may be filed jointly by spouses (AICPA adapted).

2. On February 28, Master, Inc., had total assets with a fair market value of $1,200,000 and total liabilities of $990,000. On January 15, Master made a monthly installment note payment to Acme Distributors Corp., a creditor holding a properly perfected security interest in equipment having a fair market value greater than the balance due on the note. On March 15, Master voluntarily filed a petition in bankruptcy under the liquidation provisions of Chapter 7 of the federal Bankruptcy Code. One year later, the equipment was sold for less than the balance due on the note to Acme.

   If a creditor challenged Master's right to file, the petition would be dismissed:

   a. If Master had less than 12 creditors at the time of filing.

   b. Unless Master can show that a reorganization under Chapter 11 of the federal Bankruptcy Code would have been unsuccessful.

   c. Unless Master can show that it is unable to pay its debts in the ordinary course of business or as they come due.

   d. If Master is an insurance company.

3. A voluntary petition filed under the liquidation provisions of Chapter 7 of the federal Bankruptcy Code:

   a. Is not available to a corporation unless it has previously filed a petition under the reorganization provisions of Chapter 11 of the federal Bankruptcy Code.

   b. Automatically stays collection actions against the debtor except by secured creditors for collateral only.

   c. Will be dismissed unless the debtor has 12 or more unsecured creditors whose claims total at least $15,325.

   d. Does not require the debtor to show that the debtor's liabilities exceed the fair market value of assets.

4. Which following conditions, if any, must a debtor meet to file a voluntary bankruptcy petition under Chapter 7 of the federal Bankruptcy Code?

	Insolvency	Three or More Creditors
a.	Yes	Yes
b.	Yes	No
c.	No	Yes
d.	No	No

5. On July 15, 1988, White, a sole proprietor, was involuntarily petitioned into bankruptcy under the liquidation provisions of the Bankruptcy Code. White's nonexempt property has been converted to $13,000 cash, which is available to satisfy the following claims:

Unsecured claim for 1986 state income tax	$10,000
Fee owed to Best & Co., CPAs, for services rendered from April 1, 1988, through June 30, 1988	$6,000
Unsecured claim by Stieb for wages earned as an employee of White during March 1988	$3,000

   There are no other claims.

   What is the maximum amount that will be distributed for the payment of the 1986 state income tax?

   a. $4,000   c. $7,000

   b. $5,000   d. $10,000

6. On May 1, 1997, two months after becoming insolvent, Quick Corp., an appliance wholesaler, filed a voluntary petition for bankruptcy under the provisions of Chapter 7 of the federal Bankruptcy Code. On October 15, 1996, Quick's board of directors had authorized and paid Erly $50,000 to repay Erly's April 1, 1996, loan to the corporation. Erly is a sibling of Quick's president. On March 15, 1996, Quick paid Kray $100,000 for inventory delivered that day. Which of the following is not relevant in determining whether the repayment of Erly's loan is a voidable preferential transfer?

   a. That Erly is an insider.

   b. That Quick's payment to Erly was made on account of an antecedent debt.

   c. Quick's solvency when the loan was made by Erly.

   d. That Quick's payment to Erly was made within one year of the filing of the bankruptcy petition.

C H A P T E R   35

Insurance

>>> **Learning Outcomes**

After studying this chapter, you should be able to

LO.1 Explain the necessity of having an insurable interest to obtain an insurance policy

LO.2 Recognize that the formation of a contract is governed by the general principles of contract law

LO.3 Explain why courts strictly construe insurance policies against insurance companies

LO.4 List and explain the five major categories of insurance

LO.5 Explain coinsurance and its purpose

LO.6 Explain incontestability clauses

By means of insurance, protection from loss and liability may be obtained.

35-1 The Insurance Contract

insurance–a plan of security against risks by charging the loss against a fund created by the payments made by policyholders.

Insurance is a contract by which one party for a stipulated consideration promises to pay another party a sum of money on the destruction of, loss of, or injury to something in which the other party has an interest or to indemnify that party for any loss or liability to which that party is subjected.

35-1a The Parties

insurer–promisor in an insurance contract.

underwriter–insurer.

insured–person to whom the promise in an insurance contract is made.

policy–paper evidencing the contract of insurance.

insurance agent–agent of an insurance company.

insurance broker–independent contractor who is not employed by any one insurance company.

The promisor in an insurance contract is called the **insurer** or **underwriter.** The person to whom the promise is made is the **insured** or the policyholder. The promise of the insurer is generally set forth in a written contract called a **policy.**

Insurance contracts are ordinarily made through an agent or broker. The **insurance agent** is an agent of the insurance company, often working exclusively for one company. For the most part, the ordinary rules of agency law govern the dealings between this agent and the applicant for insurance.[1]

An **insurance broker** is generally an independent contractor who is not employed by any one insurance company. When a broker obtains a policy for a customer, the broker is the agent of the customer for the purpose of that transaction. Under some statutes, the broker is made an agent of the insurer with respect to transmitting the applicant's payments to the insurer.

35-1b Insurable Interest

A person obtaining insurance must have an insurable interest in the subject matter insured. If not, the insurance contract cannot be enforced.

Insurable Interest in Property

A person has an insurable interest in property whenever the destruction of the property will cause a direct pecuniary loss to that person.[2]

It is immaterial whether the insured is the owner of the legal or equitable title, a lienholder, or merely a person in possession of the property.[3] **For Example,** Vin Harrington, a builder, maintained fire insurance on a building he was remodeling under a contract with its owner, Chestnut Hill Properties. The building was destroyed by fire before renovations were completed. Harrington had an insurable interest in the property to the extent of the amount owed him under the renovation contract.

To collect on property insurance, the insured must have an insurable interest at the time the loss occurs.

Insurable Interest in Life

A person who purchases life insurance can name anyone as beneficiary regardless of whether that beneficiary has an insurable interest in the life of the insured. A beneficiary who purchases a policy, however, must have an insurable interest in the life of the insured. Such an interest exists if the beneficiary can reasonably expect to receive

[1] *Tidelands Life Ins. Co. v. France*, 711 So. 2d 728 (Tex. App. 1986).
[2] *Plaisance v. Scottsdale Insurance Co.*, 2008 WL 4372888 (E.D. La. Sept. 22, 2008).
[3] See *Rydings v. Cincinnati Special Underwriters Insurance Co.*, 1 N.E.3d 40 (Ill. App. 2013) where a property insurance policy in the name of a public guardian was held to cover fire damages to certain real property included in an estate.

pecuniary gain from the continued life of the other person and, conversely, would suffer financial loss from the latter's death. Thus, a creditor has an insurable interest in the life of the debtor because he may not be paid the amount owed upon the death of the debtor.

CASE SUMMARY

She Lost Interest When He Got the House

FACTS: While Dorothy and James Morgan were still married, Dorothy purchased insurance on their home from American Security Insurance Company. The policy was issued on November 3, 1981, listing the "insured" as Dorothy L. Morgan. Shortly thereafter the Morgans entered into a separation agreement under which Dorothy deeded her interest in the house to James. The Morgans were divorced on August 26, 1982. On November 28, 1982, the house was destroyed by fire. American Security refused to pay on the policy, claiming that Dorothy had no insurable interest in the property at the time of the loss. The Morgans sued the insurer, contending that they were entitled to payment under the policy issued to Dorothy.

DECISION: Judgment for American Security. In the case of property insurance, the insurable interest must exist at the time of the loss. If the insured parts with all interest in the property prior to the loss, that individual is not covered. Dorothy had conveyed her interest in the property prior to the loss. She did not have an insurable interest at the time of the loss and therefore could not recover on the policy. James Morgan was not insured under the policy. [*Morgan v. American Security Ins. Co.*, 522 So. 2d 454 (Fla. App. 1998)]

A partner or partnership has an insurable interest in the life of each of the partners because the death of any one of them will dissolve the firm and cause some degree of loss to the partnership. A business enterprise has an insurable interest in the life of an executive or a key employee because that person's death would inflict a financial loss on the business to the extent that a replacement might not be readily available or could not be found.

In the case of life insurance, the insurable interest must exist at the time the policy is obtained. It is immaterial that the interest no longer exists when the loss is actually sustained.[4] Thus, the fact that a husband (insured) and wife (beneficiary) are divorced after the life insurance policy was procured does not affect the validity of the policy. Also, the fact that a partnership is terminated after a life insurance policy is obtained by one partner on another does not invalidate the policy.

---

[4] One who obtains insurance on his own life may legally name a beneficiary without an insurable interest or later assign the policy to one without an insurable interest. Stranger-owned life insurance policies, or "STOLI" plans, are a growing concern for insurers in the life insurance industry. Under STOLI schemes elderly individuals are able to obtain third-party financing to purchase a life insurance policy and to fund the premiums owed under that policy, with some understanding or expectation that the policy will be assigned to an individual lacking an insurable interest, following the expiration of the policy's two-year contestability period. And, these policies may be sold on the Secondary Life Insurance Market. Although an insured may generally purchase life insurance in good faith, intending to keep it for himself and later assign it to a third party, regardless of whether the third party has an insurable interest, where a person who has an interest "lends himself to one without any, as a cloak to what is, in its inception, a wager" then the contract is void as against public policy. See *Carton v. B&B Equities Group, LLC*, 827 F. Supp. 2d 1235 (D. Nev. 2011). STOLI arrangements are in violation of public policy in most states that have addressed the issue.

In *Grabner v. James*, 963 F. Supp. 2d 938 (N.D. Cal. 2013), the adult children and co-trustees of the Trabert Family Trust purchased three viatical life settlement contracts for $475,000, where the viators afflicted with AIDS sold their life insurance policy at discounts in exchange for immediate cash. When the projected demise dates (the expected payoff dates) of two of the viators did not occur, the Traberts began to suspect that the AV Reports regarding viators' life expectancies were inaccurate and that the contracts were fraudulent. Their lawsuit was dismissed by the court for waiting longer than the statutory three-year time period before filing their lawsuit.

CASE SUMMARY

Proceeds to the Surviving Partner or the Deceased Partner's Wife?

FACTS: Jewell Norred's husband, James Norred, was the business partner of Clyde Graves for 10 years. On May 7, 1979, Graves and Norred took out life insurance policies, with Graves being the beneficiary of Norred's policy and Norred being the beneficiary of Graves's policy. Premiums were paid out of partnership funds. On February 28, 1983, Graves and Norred divided the partnership assets, but they did not perform the customary steps of dissolving and winding up the partnership. Graves became the sole owner of the business and continued to pay the premiums on both insurance policies until James Norred died on December 5, 1983.

Jewell Norred sued Graves, seeking the proceeds of the insurance policy for herself, alleging that Graves had no insurable interest in the life of James Norred at the time of his death. From a judgment on behalf of the estate, Graves appealed.

DECISION: Judgment for Graves. A partner or partnership has an insurable interest in the life of one of the partners. This interest continues even if the partnership is discontinued prior to the death of one of the partners. Thus, Graves was entitled to the proceeds of the policy. [*Graves v. Norred*, 510 So.2d 816 (Ala. 1987)]

35-1c **The Contract**

The formation of a contract of insurance is governed by the general principles applicable to contracts. By statute, an insurance policy must be written. To avoid deception, many state statutes also specify the content of certain policies, in whole or in part. Some statutes specify the size and style of type to be used in printing the policies. Provisions in a policy that conflict with statutory requirements are generally void.

The Application as Part of the Contract

The application for insurance is generally attached to the policy when issued and is made part of the contract of insurance by express stipulation of the policy.

The insured is bound by all material statements in the attached application. **For Example,** insurers seek to stop the issuance of stranger-owned life insurance policies or "STOLI" plans by amending their application process to require all applicants and their brokers to fill out Policy Owner Intent Forms, requiring disclosures that, if answered honestly, will indicate a STOLI scheme and rejection of the application. And, if not answered honestly, the policy can be voided during the two-year contestability period because of the material misrepresentations.[5]

Statutory Provisions as Part of the Contract

When a statute requires that insurance contracts contain certain provisions or cover certain specified losses, a contract of insurance that does not comply with the statute will be interpreted as though it contained all the provisions required by the statute. **For Example,** Louisiana law clearly requires liability insurance coverage on all rental vehicles to protect the victims injured due to the fault of the drivers of the rental vehicles. Avis did provide liability protection for the vehicle it rented to White. However, the terms of the car rental agreement provided for termination of liability coverage in wide-ranging circumstances. White injured Terence Czop while driving intoxicated, one of the causes set forth in the rental agreement for termination of liability coverage. Because state law requires coverage on rental vehicles, the court determined that to allow termination of coverage based on a violation of the rental agreement is against public policy.[6]

[5] See *Principal Life Insurance Co. v. DeRose*, 2011 WL 4738114 (M.D. Pa. Oct. 5, 2011).
[6] *Czop v. White*, 80 So. 3d 1255 (La. App. 2011).

E-COMMERCE & CYBERLAW

Insurance Contracts & E-Sign

The Electronic Signatures in Global and National Commerce Act (E-Sign) applies broadly to the insurance business.* Thus, with consent of the consumer, contracts may be executed with electronic signatures and documents may be delivered by electronic means. E-Sign also provides protections for insurance agents against liability resulting from any deficiencies in the electronic procedures set forth in an electronic contract, provided the agent did not engage in tortious conduct and was not involved in the establishment of the electronic procedures.

Insurance providers are precluded from canceling health insurance or life insurance protection by means of electronic notices.

*15 U.S.C. §7001(i).

35-1d Antilapse and Cancellation Statutes and Provisions

If the premiums are not paid on time, the policy under ordinary contract law would lapse because of nonpayment. However, with life insurance policies, by either policy provision or statute, the insured is allowed a grace period of 30 or 31 days in which to make payment of the premium due. When there is a default in the payment of a premium by the insured, the insurer may be required by statute to (1) issue a paid-up policy in a smaller amount, (2) provide extended insurance for a period of time, or (3) pay the cash surrender value of the policy.

The contract of insurance may expressly declare that it may or may not be canceled by the insurer's unilateral act. By statute or policy provision, the insurer is commonly required to give a specific number of days' written notice of cancellation.[7]

CASE SUMMARY

Oops ... Victoria Insurance Co. didn't know that the ten-day grace period applied *after* the due date. (My goodness. The company learns something new every day.☹)

FACTS: On September 6, 2009, Robert Vietzen was injured in an automobile accident when a car driven by Dean Mandell and owned by Paulette Henry collided with his vehicle. Victoria Automobile Insurance Company ("Victoria Insurance") had issued an insurance policy for Ms. Henry's vehicle. The parties agree that Mr. Vietzen obtained a judgment against Ms. Henry in the amount of $97,000.00. Victoria Insurance refused to satisfy the judgment based on its assertion that it had cancelled Ms. Henry's policy at 12:01 a.m. on September 6, 2009, for nonpayment of the premium. Victoria Insurance had mailed a billing statement to Ms. Henry on August 24, 2009 stating that a minimum payment of $198.39 was due on September 5, 2009, with notice that if payment is not received on the due date, the policy cancels on September 6, at 12:01 a.m. Mr. Vietzen sued Victoria Insurance for failure to pay the judgment. From a decision for Victoria Insurance, Vietzen appealed.

DECISION: Judgment for Mr. Vietzen. State law includes a grace period of ten days during which an insured may cure her failure to pay a premium by its due date. An insurance company must wait until the insured has actually failed to pay her premium before mailing notice of cancellation of the policy, which can take place no fewer than ten days after the mailing of the notice. [*Vietzen v. Victoria Automobile Insurance Co.*, 9 N.E.3d 500 (Ohio App. 2014)]

[7] *Transamerican Ins. Co. v. Tab Transportation*, 906 P.2d 1341 (Cal. 1995).

35-1e Modification of Contract

As is the case with most contracts, a contract of insurance can be modified if both insurer and insured agree to the change. The insurer cannot modify the contract without the consent of the insured when the right to do so is not reserved in the insurance contract.

To make changes or corrections to the policy, it is not necessary to issue a new policy. An endorsement on the policy or the execution of a separate rider is effective for the purpose of changing the policy. When a provision of an endorsement conflicts with a provision of the policy, the endorsement controls because it is the later document.

35-1f Interpretation of Contract

A contract of insurance is interpreted by the same rules that govern the interpretation of ordinary contracts. Words are to be given their plain and ordinary meaning and interpreted in light of the nature of the coverage intended. However, an insurance policy is construed strictly against the insurer, who chooses the language of the policy, and if a reasonable construction may be given that would justify recovery, a court will do so.[8] **For Example,** Dr. Kolb consented to an elective surgical procedure on his right eye after which "something happened that caused the wound to start leaking" and resulted in loss of vision in his eye. This forced him to retire as an orthopedic surgeon. His Paul Revere Life Insurance disability income insurance policy provided income for life for a disability due to "accidental bodily injury." The policy provided benefits for a shorter duration if the disability was caused by "sickness." Dr. Kolb's vision loss was not expected and proceeded from an unidentified postsurgical cause. Applying the plain and ordinary meaning of "accidental" and "injury," the court decided that Dr. Kolb was entitled to income for life under the "injury" provision of the policy.[9]

If there is an ambiguity in the policy, the provision is interpreted against the insurer.[10] **For Example,** on August 29, 2005, the Buentes' residence in Gulfport, Mississippi, was damaged during Hurricane Katrina. Allstate tendered a check for $2,600.35 net after the deductible, under its Deluxe Homeowner's Policy. The Buentes contend that their covered losses are between $50,000 and $100,000. They brought suit against Allstate. The trial judge denied Allstate's motion to dismiss, finding that the two provisions of the policy that purport to exclude coverage for wind and rain damage were ambiguous in light of other policy provisions granting coverage for wind and rain damage and in light of the inclusion of a "hurricane deductible" as part of the policy. The court found that because the policy was ambiguous, its weather exclusion was unenforceable in the context of losses attributable to wind and rain that occur in a hurricane.[11]

35-1g Burden of Proof

When an insurance claim is disputed by the insurer, the person bringing suit has the burden of proving that there was a loss, that it occurred while the policy was in force, and that the loss was of a kind that was within the coverage or scope of the policy.[12]

A policy will contain exceptions to the coverage. This means that the policy is not applicable when an exception applies to the situation. Exceptions to coverage are generally strictly interpreted against the insurer. However, insurance policies are contracts and the

---

[8] *SWE Homes, L.P. v. Wellington Insurance Co.*, 436 S.W.3d 86 (Tex. App. 2014).
[9] *Kolb v. Paul Revere Life Insurance Co.*, 355 F.3d 1132 (8th Cir. 2004).
[10] See *Arrowood Indemnity Co. v. King*, 39 A.3d 712 (Conn. 2012); *Koziol v. Peerless Insurance Co.*, 41 A.3d 647 (R.I. 2012).
[11] *Buente v. Allstate Ins. Co.*, 422 F. Supp. 2d 690 (S.D. Miss. 2006).
[12] *Koslik v. Gulf Insurance Co.*, 673 N.W.2d 343 (Wis. App. 2003).

plain and unambiguous language of the contract will apply. **For Example,** Aroa Marketing, Inc., purchased a commercial general liability (CGL) policy from Hartford Midwest Insurance Co. The policy covered any damages that Aroa became legally obligated to pay because of "bodily injury," "property damage," or "personal and advertising injury" arising out of Aroa's business. Coverage was excluded, however, for "personal and advertising injury" arising out of "any violation of any intellectual property rights, such as copyright, patent, trademark, trade name, trade secret, service mark, or other destination of origin or authenticity." Aroa hired Tara Radcliffe to appear in and film an exercise video for its business to be used at a consumer electronics show and on a client's Internet site. Aroa used her images to sell other products, and she sued for misappropriation of her image and violation of her right of publicity. The court found that Hartford had no duty to defend or indemnify Aroa because the model's claim fell within the intellectual property exclusion.[13]

35-1h Insurer Bad Faith

As is required in the case of all contracts, an insurer must act in good faith in processing and paying claims under its policy. In some states, laws have been enacted making an insurer liable for a statutory penalty and attorney fees in case of a bad-faith failure or delay in paying a valid claim within a specified period of time.[14] A bad-faith refusal is generally considered to be any frivolous or unfounded refusal to comply with the demand of a policyholder to pay according to the policy.[15]

CASE SUMMARY

Ruining General Lafayette's* Good Name
*Check him out online.

FACTS: Don and Myna Leland owned rental property in Lake Charles, Louisiana, that was damaged by a tree falling into the building, shearing off a portion of the facade during Hurricane Rita in September 2005. By October 7, 2005, they notified their insurer, Lafayette Insurance Co., of the damages to this property. In September 2007, two years after the hurricane, the Lelands filed a lawsuit against the issuer for breach of the insurer's duty of good faith and fair dealing in adjusting losses associated with the hurricane. The jury found in favor of the Lelands, concluding that the plaintiffs sustained losses in excess of the amount paid under the defendant's policy in the amount of $144,800.00. Further, the jury concluded that the defendant: (1) failed to initiate a loss adjustment to the property within 30 days after notification of loss; (2) was arbitrary, capricious, or without probable cause in failing to pay any claim due within 60 days after receipt of satisfactory proof of loss; (3) failed to make an offer to settle the property damage within

30 days of receipt of satisfactory proof of loss; and (4) misrepresented pertinent facts or insurance policy provisions related to coverage at issue. From a judgment for the Lelands, Lafayette appealed.

DECISION: Judgment for the Lelands. The court of appeals affirmed the trial court's damages as amended as follows: $5,000 for loss of rental income, $53,000 for loss of personal income, $30,000 in interest and $45,000 each for the Lelands for mental anguish and emotional distress for a total of $178,000 in damages attributable to the insurer's breach of its duties. State law added a penalty of two times these damages, or $356,000. The insurer was also obligated to pay $144,800 in contractual damages for repairs owed under the insurance contract and $226,266 in attorneys' fees. In particular the court determined that the evidence was sufficient to support the awards for mental anguish. Mr. Leland testified extensively regarding the

---

[13] *Aroa Marketing, Inc. v. Hartford Insurance Co.,* 130 Cal. Rptr. 3d 466 (Cal. App. 2011).
[14] *Maslo v. Ameriprise Auto & Home Insurance,* 173 Cal. Rptr. 3d 854 (Cal. App. 2014).
[15] *Uberti v. Lincoln National Life Ins. Co.,* 144 F. Supp. 2d 90 (D. Conn. 2001).

Ruining General Lafayette's Good Name continued

frustrations encountered in pursuing the multiyear claim and making little progress toward a conclusion, including a record of repeated and persisted demands to the insurers regarding his property, which remained unrepaired, causing him to borrow more than $142,000 for repairs in order to avoid the city's pending action to demolish the property. Both Lelands testified to the negative impact the multiyear process had taken on their personal relationship. [***Leland v. Lafayette Insurance Co.***, **77 So.3d 1078 (La. App. 2011)**]

When it is a liability insurer's duty to defend the insured and the insurer wrongfully refuses to do so, the insurer is guilty of breach of contract and is liable for all consequential damages resulting from the breach. In some jurisdictions, an insured can recover for an excess judgment rendered against the insured when it is proven that the insurer was guilty of negligence or bad faith in failing to defend the action or settle the matter within policy limits.

If there is a reasonable basis for the insurer's belief that a claim is not covered by its policy, its refusal to pay the claim does not subject it to liability for a breach of good faith or for a statutory penalty.[16] This is so even though the court holds that the insurer is liable for the claim.

For Example, the following illustrates an insurer's bad-faith failure to pay a claim, as opposed to an insurer's reasonable basis for failure to pay. Carmela Garza's home and possessions were destroyed in a fire set by an arsonist on August 19. Carmela's husband, Raul, who was no longer living at the home, had a criminal record. An investigator for the insurer stated that while he had no specific information to implicate the Garzas in the arson, Carmela may have wanted the proceeds to finance relocation to another city. By October, however, Aetna's investigators ruled out the possibility that Garza had the motive or the opportunity to set the fire. The insurer thus no longer had a reasonable basis to refuse to pay the claim after this date. Yet it took over a year and a half and court intervention for Aetna to allow Carmela to see a copy of her policy, which had been destroyed in the fire. Two years after the fire, Aetna paid only $28,624.55 for structural damage to the fire-gutted home, which was insured for $111,000. The court held that Aetna's actions constituted a bad-faith failure to pay by the insurer.[17]

35-1i Time Limitations on Insured

The insured must comply with a number of time limitations in making a claim. For example, the insured must promptly notify the insurer of any claim that may arise, submit a proof-of-loss statement within the time set forth in the policy, and bring any court action based on the policy within a specified time period.[18]

35-1j Subrogation of Insurer

In some instances, the insured has a claim against a third person for the harm covered by the insurance policy. **For Example,** *A* sells an automobile insurance policy that provides

[16] *Shipes v. Hanover Ins. Co.*, 884 F.2d 1357 (11th Cir. 1989).
[17] See *Aetna Casualty & Surety Co. v. Garza*, 906 S.W.2d 543 (Tex. App. 1995).
[18] But see *Seeman v. Sterling Ins. Co.*, 699 N.Y.S.2d 542 (A.D. 1999), where the insured's four-month delay in notifying the insurer was excused because of his belief that only on-premises injuries were covered by his homeowners insurance policy and thus the policy would not cover an injury in which a paintball he fired at work struck his coworker in the eye.

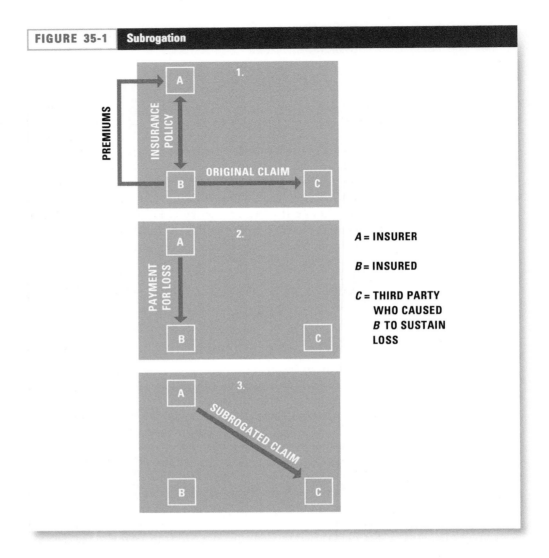

FIGURE 35-1   Subrogation

PREMIUMS

1.

A

INSURANCE POLICY

B   ORIGINAL CLAIM   C

2.

A

PAYMENT FOR LOSS

B   C

3.

A

SUBROGATED CLAIM

B   C

A = INSURER

B = INSURED

C = THIRD PARTY WHO CAUSED *B* TO SUSTAIN LOSS

subrogation–right of a party secondarily liable to stand in the place of the creditor after making payment to the creditor and to enforce the creditor's right against the party primarily liable in order to obtain indemnity from such primary party.

risk–peril or contingency against which the insured is protected by the contract of insurance.

collision coverage to *B*. *C* "rear-ends" *B*'s car at a traffic rotary in the city. *A* pays *B* the full amount of the property damage repair costs. *A* is then **subrogated** to *B*'s claim against *C*, the person who caused the harm. See Figure 35-1. When the insurer is subrogated to the insured's claim, the insurer may enforce that claim against the third person.[19]

35-2 Kinds of Insurance

Businesses today have specialized **risk** managers who identify the risks to which individual businesses are exposed, measure those risks, and purchase insurance to cover those risks (or decide to self-insure in whole or in part).

Insurance policies can be grouped into certain categories. Five major categories of insurance are considered here: (1) business liability insurance, (2) marine and inland

[19] *Stratus Services Group, Inc. v. Kash 'N Gold Ltd.,* 935 N.Y.S.2d 302 (A.D. 2011).

marine insurance, (3) fire and homeowners insurance, (4) automobile insurance, and (5) life insurance.

35-2a Business Liability Insurance

Businesses may purchase Commercial General Liability (CGL) policies. This insurance is a broad, "all-risk" form of insurance providing coverage for mostly all sums that the insured may become legally obligated to pay as damages because of "bodily injury" or "property damage" caused by an "occurrence." The insurer is obligated to defend the insured business and pay damages under CGL policies for product liability cases, actions for wrongful termination of employees, sexual harassment cases, damages caused by business advertising or employee dishonesty, and trademark infringement suits.[20] The insurer may also be obligated to pay for damages in the form of cleanup costs imposed for contamination of land, water, and air under environmental statutes.[21]

CASE SUMMARY

The Clash Between the "Auto" Insurer and the "CGL" Insurer
The Case of the Hot Defective Deep Fryer on the Moving Food Truck

FACTS: Royal Catering Company (Royal) owned a fleet of food trucks. It leased its trucks to operators who drove from site to site selling food. Royal leased one of these trucks to Esmeragdo Gomez, who, along with his wife, Irais Gomez, operated the truck. The Gomezes' food truck had two seats and two seatbelts, for a driver and a cook. The food truck was equipped with a specially designed deep fryer, grill, steam table, oven, refrigerator, and coffee maker. That equipment was built into the truck and was not designed to be used apart from the truck. On the day of the accident, Mr. Gomez was driving the food truck. A guest sat in the truck's passenger seat, and Mrs. Gomez stood in the rear of the truck. At an intersection, Mr. Gomez swerved to avoid an approaching truck. Mr. Gomez's evasive action failed to avoid a collision. Just prior to the collision, hot oil splashed on and burned Mrs. Gomez. The Gomezes and the passenger in their truck brought an action against Royal Catering for injuries sustained in connection with the accident, including a product liability claim for a defective deep fryer basket. American States Insurance Company issued automobile insurance policies to Royal. Travelers Insurance provided commercial general liability coverage (CGL) to Royal. The automobile insurer, American States, claims that the injuries should be covered under the Traveler CGL policy that,

although excluding coverage for injuries arising out of the use of automobiles, covers "mobile equipment," defined as vehicles used for a primary purpose other than transporting persons or cargo. Travelers asserts that the primary purpose of the food truck was to transport "persons and cargo" so that it is not within the "mobile equipment" exception to the Travelers' CGL auto exclusion. From a decision by the trial court that the food truck was an "auto" obligating American States to cover the claims for injury, American States appealed.

DECISION: Judgment for American States. Although the Traveler's CGL policy excluded coverage for injuries arising out of the use of automobiles, the policy contained an exception for "mobile equipment," including vehicles "maintained primarily for purposes other than transportation of persons or cargo." The primary purpose of the food truck was to serve as a mobile kitchen and not transport persons or cargo. Like a fire truck a food truck may transport persons and cargo—that is, food, but its core functional identity emerges when it operates a mobile kitchen at specified locations. [*American State Insurance Co. v. Traveler Property Casualty Co. of America*, 167 Cal. Rptr. 3d 288 (Cal. App. 2014)]

---

[20] *Charter Oak Fire Ins. Co. v. Heedon & Cos.*, 280 F.3d 730 (7th Cir. 2002).

[21] *Chemical Leaman Tank Lines, Inc. v. Aetna Casualty Co.*, 788 F. Supp. 846 (D.N.J. 1992); *United States v. Pepper's Steel, Inc.*, 823 F. Supp. 1574 (S.D. Fla. 1993). But see *Northville Industries v. National Union Fire and Ins. Co.*, 636 N.Y.S.2d 359 (A.D. 1995); *Aydin Corp. v. First State Ins. Co.*, 62 Cal. Rptr. 2d 825 (A.D. 1997).

ETHICS & THE LAW

On September 11, 2001, terrorist attacks killed 3,119 persons, devastated the U.S. airline industry, and had a severe impact on the U.S. insurance industry. In New York City, several office buildings, including One and Two World Trade Center, were destroyed, and other businesses in lower Manhattan were forced to shut down.

Business interruption insurance coverage is usually written as part of a company's commercial property insurance package. It not only covers policyholders for their lost profits and fixed charges and expenses for interruption to their business caused by physical damage or destruction to the insured's own property, but it may also cover "contingent business interruption" resulting from suspension of operations caused by damages to the property of a key supplier, distributor, or manufacturer. Such coverage, however, contains an exclusion for "war or military action." Are the September 11, 2001, terrorist attacks an "act of war" such that insurers are not responsible for business interruption claims? Can the president's words regarding war with al Qaeda be used to prove an "act of war" exclusion?

A court called upon to interpret an "act of war" exclusion will apply the plain and ordinary meaning of the policy's terms, and any ambiguity will be construed against the insurer. In *Pan American World Airways, Inc., v. Aetna Casualty & Surety Co.,** the Second Circuit Court of Appeals held that an air carrier was entitled to recover for the destruction of its plane by terrorists in Cairo, Egypt, and the damage was not excluded under the policy's "act of war" exclusion. The court reasoned in part that there was no existing "war" between recognized sovereign states.

Pressured by historic losses as a result of "9/11," insurance companies in certain areas excluded perils resulting from "terrorism" in new commercial property insurance policies. Is it fair for insurers to exclude coverage altogether for losses due to acts of terrorism? Is it best to have the community absorb the losses? Is it best to have individuals and individual businesses cover the losses? See the Terrorism Risk Insurance Program Reauthorization Act of 2014, which extends the Terrorism Insurance Act of 2002 through December 31, 2021. This law provides a federal insurance backstop in the context of the insurance marketplace where catastrophic terrorism is an uninsurable risk. The law continues the existing $100 million "trigger level" of aggregate insured losses. The Secretary of State, in concurrence with the Attorney General of the United States has authority to certify an event as an act of terrorism.

*See **Pan American World Airways, Inc. v. Aetna Casualty & Surety Co., 505 F.2d 989 (2d Cir. 1974).**

The insurer must defend when coverage is a "close issue" regarding whether the policy would provide indemnity. The duty to defend does not depend on the truth or falsity of the allegations made against the insured by a third party; rather, the factual allegations in the complaint that potentially support a covered claim are all that is needed to invoke the insurer's duty to defend.[22] It is common for the insurer to seek a declaratory judgment if it believes the policy does not call for either a defense or an indemnity. **For Example,** State Automobile Mutual Insurance Co. brought an action for declaratory judgment that it had no duty to defend and indemnify Flexdar, Inc., for the cost of cleanup of a chemical solvent discovered in the soil of Flexdar's manufacturing site, referencing its "pollution exclusion" language in its policies. The court found the language in the CGL policy in question was ambiguous and thus ruled against the insurer.[23]

Businesses may purchase policies providing liability insurance for their directors and officers. Manufacturers and sellers may purchase product liability insurance. Professional persons, such as accountants, physicians, lawyers, architects, and engineers, may obtain liability insurance protection against malpractice suits. **For Example,** the architects of the MCI Center, a sports arena in Washington, D.C., were entitled under their professional liability insurance coverage to be defended by their insurer in a lawsuit seeking only

---

[22] *Mid Continent Casualty Co. v. JHP Development Inc.*, 557 F.3d 207 (6th Cir. 2009).

[23] *State Automobile Mutual Insurance Co. v. Flexdar, Inc.*, 964 N.E.2d 845 (Ind. 2012). The court majority stated:

> After all, "[t]he insurance companies write the policies; we buy their forms or we do not buy their insurance." By more careful drafting State Auto has the ability to resolve any question of ambiguity. And in fact it has done so. In 2005 State Auto revised its policies to add an "Indiana Changes—Pollution Exclusion" endorsement. Id. At 852.

marine insurance–
policies that cover perils
relating to the
transportation of goods.

ocean marine–policies
that cover transportation
of goods in vessels in
international and coastal
trade.

inland marine–
insurance that covers
domestic shipments of
goods over land and
inland waterways.

hull insurance–
insurance that covers
physical damage on a
freight-moving vessel.

injunctive relief for the firm's alleged failure to comply with the Americans with Disabilities Act's enhanced sightline requirements.[24]

35-2b Marine Insurance

Marine insurance policies cover perils relating to the transportation of goods. **Ocean marine** insurance policies cover the transportation of goods in vessels in international and coastal trade. **Inland marine** insurance principally covers domestic shipments of goods over land and inland waterways.

Ocean Marine

Ocean marine insurance is a form of insurance that covers ships and their cargoes against "perils of the sea." Four classes of ocean marine insurance are generally available: (1) hull, (2) cargo, (3) liability, and (4) freight. **Hull insurance** covers physical damage to the vessel.[25] **Cargo insurance** protects the cargo owner against financial loss if the goods being shipped are lost or damaged at sea.[26]

CASE SUMMARY

This Coverage Is Worth a Hill of Beans

FACTS: Commodities Reserve Company (CRC) contracted to sell 1,008 tons of beans and 50 tons of seed to purchasers in Venezuela. CRC purchased the beans and seeds in Turkey and chartered space on the ship *MV West Lion.* The cargo was insured under an ocean marine policy issued by St. Paul Fire & Marine Insurance Company. The Sue and Labor Clause in CRC's ocean marine policy with St. Paul provided: "In case of any loss or misfortune, it shall be lawful and necessary to and for the Assured … to sue, labor and travel for, in and about the defense, safeguard and recovery of the said goods and merchandise … to the charges whereof, the [insurer] will contribute according to the rate and quantity of the sum hereby insured." While the ship was

sailing through Greek waters, Greek authorities seized the vessel for carrying munitions. CRC had to go to the expense of obtaining an order from a court in Crete to release the cargo. When St. Paul refused to pay the costs of the Cretan litigation to release the cargo, CRC brought suit against St. Paul.

DECISION: Judgment for CRC. The Sue and Labor Clause required CRC to sue for "recovery of the said goods and merchandise." The clause also requires the insurer to reimburse the insured for those expenses. [*Commodities Reserve Co. v. St. Paul Fire & Marine Ins. Co.*, 879 F.2d 640 (9th Cir. 1998)]

---

cargo insurance–
insurance that protects a
cargo owner against
financial loss if goods
being shipped are lost or
damaged at sea.

liability insurance–
covers the shipowner's
liability if the ship causes
damage to another ship
or its cargo.

freight insurance–
insures that shipowner
will receive payment for
transportation charges.

Cargo insurance does not cover risks prior to the loading of the insured cargo on board the vessel. An additional warehouse coverage endorsement is needed to insure merchandise held in a warehouse prior to import or export voyages.

Liability insurance covers the shipowner's liability if the ship causes damage to another ship or its cargo. **Freight insurance** ensures that the shipowner will receive payment for the transportation charges. "All-risk" policies consolidate coverage of all four classes of ocean marine insurance into one policy.[27]

---

[24] *Washington Sports and Entertainment, Inc. v. United Coastal Ins.*, 7 F. Supp. 2d 1 (D.D.C. 1998).
[25] *Lloyd's v. Labarca*, 260 F.3d 3 (1st Cir. 2001).
[26] *Kimta, A. S. v. Royal Insurance Co., Inc.*, 9 P.3d 239 (Wash. App. 2001).
[27] *Transamerican Leasing, Inc. v. Institute of London Underwriters*, 7 F. Supp. 2d 1340 (S.D. Fla. 1998).

Inland Marine

Inland marine insurance evolved from marine insurance. It protects goods in transit over land; by air; or on rivers, lakes, and coastal waters. Inland marine insurance can be used to insure property held by a bailee. Moreover, it is common for institutions financing automobile dealers' new car inventories to purchase inland marine insurance policies to insure against damage to the automobiles while in inventory.

35-2c Fire and Homeowners Insurance

fire insurance policy—a contract that indemnifies the insured for property destruction or damage caused by fire.

A **fire insurance policy** is a contract to indemnify the insured for property destruction or damage caused by fire. In almost every state, the New York standard fire insurance form is the standard policy. A **homeowners insurance policy** is a combination of the standard fire insurance policy and comprehensive personal liability insurance. It thus provides fire, theft, and certain liability protection in a single insurance contract.

homeowners insurance policy—combination of standard fire insurance and comprehensive personal liability insurance.

Fire Insurance

For fire insurance to cover fire loss, there must be an actual hostile fire that is the immediate cause of the loss. A *hostile fire* is one that becomes uncontrollable, burns with excessive heat, or escapes from the place where it is intended to be. To illustrate, when soot is ignited and causes a fire in the chimney, the fire is hostile. On the other hand, if a loss is caused by the smoke or heat of a fire that has not broken out of its ordinary container or become uncontrollable, the loss results from a friendly fire. The policy does not cover damage from a friendly fire.

By policy endorsement, however, the coverage may be extended to include loss by a friendly fire.

CASE SUMMARY

Excuse Me? The Fire Wasn't Hostile?

FACTS: Youse owned a ring that was insured with the Employers Fire Insurance Company against loss, including "all direct loss or damage by fire." Youse accidentally threw the ring into a trash burner, and it was damaged when the trash was burned. He sued the insurer.

DECISION: Judgment for insurer. A fire policy covers only loss caused by a hostile fire. The fire was not hostile because it burned in the area in which it was intended to burn. [*Youse v. Employers Fire Ins. Co.*, 238 P.2d 472 (Kan. 1951)]

coinsurance clause—clause requiring the insured to maintain insurance on property up to a stated amount and providing that to the extent that this is not done, the insured is to be deemed a coinsurer with the insurer, so that the latter is liable only for its proportionate share of the amount of insurance required to be carried.

Coinsurance. The insurer is liable for the actual amount of the loss sustained up to the maximum amount stated in the policy. An exception exists when the policy contains a coinsurance clause. A **coinsurance clause** requires the insured to maintain insurance on the covered property up to a certain amount or a certain percentage of the value (generally 80 percent). Under such a provision, if the policyholder insures the property for less than the required amount, the insurer is liable only for the proportionate share of the amount of insurance required to be carried. **For Example,** suppose that the owner of a building with a value of $400,000 insures it against loss to the extent of $240,000. The policy contains a coinsurance clause requiring that insurance of 80 percent of the value of the property be carried (in this case, $320,000). Assume that a $160,000 loss is then sustained. The insured would receive not $160,000 from the insurer but only three-fourths of that amount, which is $120,000, because the amount of the insurance carried ($240,000) is only three-fourths of the amount required ($320,000).

Some states prohibit the use of a coinsurance clause.

Assignment. Fire insurance is a personal contract, and in the absence of statute or contractual authorization, it cannot be assigned without the consent of the insurer.

Occupancy. Provisions in a policy of fire insurance relating to the use and occupancy of the property are generally strictly construed because they relate to the hazards involved.

Homeowners Insurance

In addition to providing protection against losses resulting from fire, the homeowners policy provides liability coverage for accidents or injuries that occur on the premises of the insured. Moreover, the liability provisions provide coverage for unintentional injuries to others away from home for which the insured or any member of the resident family is held responsible, such as injuries caused to others by golfing, hunting, or fishing accidents.[28] Generally, motor vehicles, including mopeds and recreational vehicles, are excluded from such personal liability coverage.

A homeowners policy also provides protection from losses caused by theft. In addition, it provides protection for all permanent residents of the household, including all family members living with the insured. Thus, a child of the insured who lives at home is protected under the homeowners policy for the value of personal property lost when the home is destroyed by fire.

35-2d Automobile Insurance

Associations of insurers, such as the National Bureau of Casualty Underwriters and the National Automobile Underwriters Association, have proposed standard forms of automobile insurance policies. These forms have been approved by the association members in virtually all states. The form used today by most insurers is the Personal Auto Policy (PAP).

Perils Covered

Part A of the policy provides liability coverage that protects the insured driver or owner from the claims of others for bodily injuries or damage to their property. Part B of the policy provides coverage for medical expenses sustained by a covered person or persons in an accident. Part C of the PAP provides coverage for damages the insured is entitled to recover from an *uninsured motorist*.[29] Part D provides coverage for loss or damage to the covered automobile. Coverage under Part D includes collision coverage and coverage of "other than collision" losses, such as fire and theft.

Covered Persons

Covered persons include the named insured or any family member (a person related by blood, marriage, or adoption or a ward or foster child who is a resident of the household). If an individual is driving with the permission of the insured, that individual is also covered. In any case, however, the language of the insurance policy is controlling. **For Example,** a court upheld State Farm Mutual's position that Robert Gaudina was not an insured under his wife's automobile policy. Gaudina had been asked to leave the household by his wife until he found a job, and his residence was not at his wife's home

[28] *American Concept Ins. Co. v. Lloyds of London,* 467 N.W.2d 480 (S.D. 1991).
[29] *Montano v. Allstate Indemnity,* 211 F.3d 1278 (10th Cir. 2002).

at the time of the accident. The policy definition was controlling, which stated: "Spouse – means your husband or wife who resides primarily with you."[30]

Use and Operation

The coverage of the PAP policy is limited to claims arising from the "use and operation" of an automobile. The term *use and operation* does not require that the automobile be in motion. Thus, the term embraces loading and unloading as well as actual travel.[31]

Notice and Cooperation

The insured is under a duty to give notice of claims, to inform, and to cooperate with the insurer. Notice and cooperation are conditions precedent to the liability of the insurer.

No-Fault Insurance

Traditional tort law (negligence law) placed the economic losses resulting from an automobile accident on the one at fault. The purpose of automobile liability insurance is to relieve the wrongdoer from the consequences of a negligent act by paying defense costs and the damages assessed. Under no-fault laws, injured persons are barred from suing the party at fault for ordinary claims. When the insured is injured while using the insured automobile, the insurer will make a payment without regard to whose fault caused the harm. However, if the automobile collision results in a permanent serious disablement or disfigurement, or death, or if the medical bills and lost wages of the plaintiff exceed a specified amount, suit may be brought against the party who was at fault.

35-2e Life Insurance

There are three basic types of life insurance: term insurance, whole life insurance, and endowment insurance.

Term insurance is written for a specified number of years and terminates at the end of that period. If the insured dies within the time period covered by the policy, the face amount is paid to the beneficiary. If the insured is still alive at the end of the time period, the contract expires, and the insurer has no further obligation. Term policies have little or no cash surrender value.

Whole life insurance (or ordinary life insurance) provides lifetime insurance protection. It also has an investment element.

Part of every premium covers the cost of insurance, and the remainder of the premium builds up a **cash surrender value** of the policy.

An **endowment insurance** policy is one that pays the face amount of the policy if the insured dies within the policy period. If the insured lives to the end of the policy period, the face amount is paid to the insured at the end of the period.

Many life insurance companies pay double the amount of the policy, called **double indemnity,** if death is caused by an accident and death occurs within 90 days afterward. A comparatively small additional premium is charged for this special protection.

In consideration of an additional premium, many life insurance companies also provide insurance against total permanent disability of the insured. **Disability** is usually defined in a life insurance policy as any "incapacity resulting from bodily injury or disease to engage in any occupation for remuneration or profit."

term insurance–policy written for a specified number of years that terminates at the end of that period.

whole life insurance–ordinary life insurance providing lifetime insurance protection.

cash surrender value–sum paid the insured upon the surrender of a policy to the insurer.

endowment insurance–insurance that pays the face amount of the policy if the insured dies within the policy period.

double indemnity–provision for payment of double the amount specified by the insurance contract if death is caused by an accident and occurs under specified circumstances.

disability–any incapacity resulting from bodily injury or disease to engage in any occupation for remuneration or profit.

[30] *Robert Gaudina v. State Farm Mutual Automobile Insurance Co.*, 8 N.E.3d 588 (Ill. App. 2014).
[31] See *American Home Insurance Co. v. First Specialty Insurance Corp.*, 894 N.E.2d 1167 (Mass. App. 2008).

Exclusions

Life insurance policies frequently provide that death is not within the protection of the policy and that a double indemnity provision is not applicable when death is caused by (1) suicide,[32] (2) narcotics, (3) the intentional act of another, (4) execution for a crime, (5) war activities, or (6) operation of aircraft.

The Beneficiary

beneficiary—person to whom the proceeds of a life insurance policy are payable, a person for whose benefit property is held in trust, or a person given property by a will; the ultimate recipient of the benefit of a funds transfer.

The recipient of life insurance policy proceeds that are payable upon the death of the insured is called the **beneficiary.** The beneficiary may be a third person or the estate of the insured, and there may be more than one beneficiary.

The beneficiary named in a policy may be barred from claiming the proceeds of the policy. It is generally provided by statute or stated by court decision that a beneficiary who has feloniously killed the insured is not entitled to receive the proceeds of the policy.

The customary policy provides that the insured reserves the right to change the beneficiary without the latter's consent. When the policy contains such a provision, the beneficiary cannot object to a change that destroys all of that beneficiary's rights under the policy and that names another person as beneficiary.

An insurance policy will ordinarily state that to change the beneficiary, the insurer must be so instructed in writing by the insured and the policy must then be endorsed by the company with the change of the beneficiary. These provisions are construed liberally. If the insured has notified the insurer but dies before the endorsement of the change by the company, the change of beneficiary is effective.[33] However, if the insured has not taken any steps to comply with the policy requirements, a change of beneficiary is not effective even though a change was intended.

Incontestability Clause

incontestability clause—provision that after the lapse of a specified time the insurer cannot dispute the policy on the ground of misrepresentation or fraud of the insured or similar wrongful conduct.

Statutes commonly require the inclusion of an **incontestability clause** in life insurance policies. Ordinarily, this clause states that after the lapse of two years, the policy cannot be contested by the insurance company.[34] The insurer is free to contest the validity of the policy at any time during the contestability period. Once the period has expired, the insurer must pay the stipulated sum upon the death of the insured and cannot claim that in obtaining the policy, the insured had been guilty of misrepresentation, fraud, or any other conduct that would entitle it to avoid the contract of insurance.[35]

Courts and legislatures have addressed the issue of "imposter fraud." In *Amex Life Assurance Co. v. Superior Court*, the California Supreme Court concluded that after the contestability period had expired, an insurer may not assert the defense that an imposter took the medical examination. Jose Morales had applied for a life insurance policy from Amex. A paramedic working for Amex met a man claiming to be Morales and took blood and urine samples, listing him as 5' 10" and weighing 172 pounds. His blood sample was HIV negative. The individual did not provide identification. Some two years later, Morales died of AIDS–related causes. Morales had listed his height as 5' 6" and his weight as 142 on his insurance application. The California Supreme Court stated that Amex, which had done nothing to protect its interest but collect premiums, could not challenge coverage based on the imposter defense.[36] Subsequent to the court's decision,

---

[32] *Mirza v. Maccabees Life and Annuity Co.,* 466 N.W.2d 340 (Mich. App. 1991).

[33] *Zeigler v. Cardona,* 830 F. Supp. 1395 (M.D. Ala. 1993).

[34] The two-year period runs from the policy's date of issue to the date the suit is filed in court. See *PHL Variable Insurance Co. v. The Sheldon Hathaway Family Insurance Trust,* 2011 WL 703839 (D. Utah Feb. 20, 2011).

[35] *Amica Life Insurance Co. v. Barbor,* 488 F. Supp. 2d 750 (N.D. Ill. 2007).

[36] *Amex Life Assurance Co. v. Superior Court,* 930 P.2d 1264 (Cal. 1997).

the California legislature amended state insurance law to provide for an "imposter defense" in that state. As set forth in the *Miller* case, Florida does not recognize an imposter defense to incontestability. The legislative purpose of such clauses is to protect beneficiaries from an insurer's refusal to honor policies by asserting pre-existing conditions, leaving beneficiaries in the untenable position of having to battle with powerful insurance companies in court.

CASE SUMMARY

The Impostor Defense: Dealing with Substitutes with Different Attributes

FACTS: The Allstate life insurance policy on which this case centers went into effect on September 20, 2000, insuring the life of John Miller. The policy stated that if the insured died while the policy was in force, Allstate would pay a death benefit to the policy beneficiaries upon receiving proof of death. As required by Fla. Stat. § 627.455, the policy further provided that it would become incontestable after remaining in force during the lifetime of the insured for a period of two years from its effective date. John Miller died on April 20, 2003—more than two years after the policy went into effect. The beneficiaries accordingly filed statements seeking to collect benefits under the policy. Rather than disburse the benefits, Allstate sought a declaratory judgment that the policy was void, alleging that the application was completed using fraudulent information and that an imposter had appeared at the medical exam in place of John Miller. The beneficiaries counterclaimed, alleging breach of contract

based on Allstate's failure to pay benefits upon proof of death in accordance with the insurance policy's terms. Allstate appealed a judgment in favor of the beneficiaries.

DECISION: Judgment for the beneficiaries. The incontestability clause works to the mutual advantage of the insured, giving the insured a guarantee against expensive litigation to defeat the policy after it has been in effect during the lifetime of the insured for a period of two years from its date of issue and giving the company a reasonable time to ascertain whether the insurance contract should remain in force. Under Florida law where the insured's death occurred after the contestability period, Allstate could not void the policy on the ground that an imposter had undergone the precoverage physical examination in the insured's place. [*Allstate Life Ins. Co. v. Miller*, 424 F.3d 1113 (11th Cir. 2005)]

Make the Connection

Summary

Insurance is a contract called a *policy*. Under an insurance policy, the insurer provides in consideration of premium payments, to pay the insured or beneficiary a sum of money if the insured sustains a specified loss or is subjected to a specified liability. These contracts are made through an insurance agent, who is an agent for the insurance company, or through an insurance broker, who is the agent of the insured when obtaining a policy for the latter.

The person purchasing an insurance contract must have an insurable interest in the insured's life or property. An insurable interest in property exists when the damage or destruction of the property will cause a direct monetary loss to the insured. In the case of property insurance, the insured must have an insurable interest at the time of loss. An insurable interest in the life of the insured exists if the purchaser would suffer a financial loss from the insured's death. This interest must exist as of the time the policy is obtained.

Ocean marine policies insure ships and their cargoes against the perils of the sea. Inland marine policies insure goods being transported by land, by air, or on inland and coastal waterways.

For fire insurance to cover a fire loss, there must be an actual hostile fire that is the immediate cause of the loss. The insurer is liable for the actual amount of the loss sustained up to the maximum amount stated in the policy. An exception exists when the policy contains a coinsurance clause requiring the insured to maintain insurance up to a certain percentage of the value of the property. To the extent this is not done, the insured is deemed a coinsurer with the insurer, and the insurer is liable for only its proportional share of the amount of insurance required to be carried. A homeowners insurance policy provides fire, theft, and liability protection in a single contract.

Automobile insurance may provide protection for collision damage to the insured's property and injury to persons. It may also cover liability to third persons for injury and property damage as well as loss by fire or theft.

A life insurance policy requires the insurer to pay a stated sum of money to a named beneficiary upon the death of the insured. It may be a term insurance policy, a whole life policy, or an endowment policy. State law commonly requires the inclusion of an incontestability clause, whereby at the conclusion of the contestability period, the insurer cannot contest the validity of the policy.

Learning Outcomes

After studying this chapter, you should be able to clearly explain:

35-1   The Insurance Contract

LO.1 Explain the necessity of having an insurable interest to obtain an insurance policy

See the Vin Harrington example of insurable interest in property, page 697.

See the discussion of a creditor's insurable interest in the life of a debtor, page 698.

LO.2 Recognize that the formation of a contract is governed by the general principles of contract law

See how insurers stop "STOLI" schemes through the application process where false answers to material questions make the insurance contract voidable by insurer, page 699.

LO.3 Explain why courts strictly construe insurance policies against insurance companies

See the discussion and examples in which the courts awarded coverage for the insured because the insurers chose the ambiguous language of the policies, page 701.

See the example in which a court determined a husband was not an insured under the contractual definition of "spouse," pages 709–710.

35-2   Kinds of Insurance

LO.4 List and explain the five major categories of insurance

See the description on business liability insurance, marine and inland insurance, fire and homeowners insurance, automobile insurance, and life insurance, pages 705–712.

See the CGL application to a food truck as "mobile" equipment, page 705.

LO.5 Explain coinsurance and its purpose

See the example of the homeowner who underinsured his property, resulting in the insurer paying a claim at a proportionate share of the amount of insurance required, pages 708–709.

LO.6 Explain incontestability clauses

See the example of the handling of imposter fraud after the incontestability period has run out, page 712.

Key Terms

beneficiary	endowment insurance	inland marine
cargo insurance	fire insurance policy	insurance
cash surrender value	freight insurance	insurance agent
coinsurance clause	homeowners insurance policy	insurance broker
disability	hull insurance	insured
double indemnity	incontestability clause	insurer

liability insurance   policy   term insurance
marine insurance   risk   underwriter
ocean marine   subrogation   whole life insurance

Questions and Case Problems

1. Mr. Keyes was injured on April 30, 2010, when he fell off Ms. Thibodeaux's roof. Mr. Keyes was cleaning and measuring the roof in preparation for painting when, unbeknownst to him, Ms. Thibodeaux sprayed a section of the metal roof with water. Mr. Keyes slipped on the wet roof and fell, seriously injuring himself. He filed the lawsuit under Ms. Thibodeaux's homeowners policy against Lighthouse Property Insurance. Mr. Keyes and Ms. Thibodeaux married in August of 2008 but physically separated four months into the marriage. Mr. Keyes and Ms. Thibodeaux have not divorced. Mr. Keyes testified that he lives in a home he owns with his grandmother and aunt. He stated that he lived in that house prior to marrying Ms. Thibodeaux and returned there after he was kicked out of her home 15 months prior to the accident. The homeowners policy precluded coverage for bodily injury to the named insured and relatives "who are residents of the insured's household." The definitions section of the policy states that the spouse of the name insured is treated as the named insured, if a resident of the same household. Lighthouse has refused coverage for Keyes under its reading of the policy. Keyes disagrees. Decide. [*Keyes v. Thibodeaux*, 85 So. 3d 1284 (La. App.)]

2. Cecil Usher owned Belize NY, Inc. (Belize), a small construction company doing business in New York City. Belize purchased a commercial general liability insurance policy from Mount Vernon Fire Insurance Co. The policy's first page, entitled "Policy Declarations," describes the insured as "Belize N.Y., Inc."; it classifies the "Form of Business" as "Corporation," the "Business Description" as "Carpentry," and indicates that Belize was afforded commercial liability insurance in the amount of $1,000,000 per occurrence and $2,000,000 in the aggregate for the period June 1, 1995, to June 1, 1996. Two classifications are listed under "Premium Computation" on the Declarations page: "Carpentry—Interior—001" and "Carpentry—001." The policy makes no further mention of these two terms. Belize performed some $60,000 of demolition work on the United House of Prayer's renovation project on 272 West 125th Street in New York City. Belize was thereafter hired to supervise subcontractors working on the job. During that period of time, a person entered the building, shot several people with a firearm, and started a fire. Seven people died and several others were injured. The estates of the victims sued Belize, Inc., for "negligence, carelessness and recklessness" regarding the fire, and Belize notified Mount Vernon of the lawsuit. Mount Vernon refused to defend or indemnify Belize because Belize was not engaging in its carpentry operations in the building at the time of the incident. It asserted that its risk is limited to carpentry operations in accordance with the classifications set forth in the policy. Belize contended that the language of the policy did not provide that the classification "Carpentry" defined covered risks, and exclusions should have been stated in the contract. Decide. [*Mount Vernon Fire Insurance Co. v. Belize NY, Inc.*, 227 F.3d 232 (2d Cir.)]

3. Gerhard Schillers was assisting his friend J.L. Loethen in removing a transmission from the bed of the Loethens' truck on the Loethens' property. While Schillers was carrying the transmission down the driveway, he fell and was seriously injured. J.L. was insured under his parents' automobile insurance policy with Shelter Mutual Insurance Company, which insured for liability, including "the loading and unloading" of the vehicle. Is Shelter Mutual liable to Schillers for the injury under its motor vehicle liability policy? Decide. [*American Family Mutual Ins. Co. v. Shelter Mutual Ins. Co.*, 747 S.W.2d 174 (Mo. App.)]

4. From the United Insurance Co., Rebecca Foster obtained a policy insuring the life of Lucille McClurkin and naming herself as beneficiary. McClurkin did not live with Foster, and Foster did not inform McClurkin of the existence of the policy. Foster paid the premiums on the policy and upon the death of McClurkin sued the United Insurance Co. for the amount of the insurance. At the trial, Foster testified vaguely that her father had told her that McClurkin was her second cousin on his side of the family. Was Foster entitled to recover on the

policy? [*Foster v. United Ins. Co.*, 158 S.E.2d 201 (S.C.)]

5. Dr. George Allard and his brother-in-law, Tom Rowland, did not get along after family land that was once used solely by Rowland was partitioned among family members after the death of Rowland's father. Rowland had a reputation in the community as a bully and a violent person. On December 17, Allard was moving cattle down a dirt road by "trolling" (leading the cattle with a bucket of feed, causing them to follow him). When he saw a forestry truck coming along the road, he led the cattle off the road onto Rowland's land to prevent frightening the cattle. When Rowland saw Allard, Rowland ran toward him screaming at him for being on his land. Allard, a small older man, retreated to his truck and obtained a 12-gauge shotgun. He pointed the gun toward the ground about an inch in front of Rowland's left foot and fired it. He stated that he fired the shot in this fashion to bring Rowland to his senses and that Rowland stepped forward into the line of fire. Allard claimed that if Rowland had not stepped forward, he would not have been hit and injured. Allard was insured by Farm Bureau homeowners and general liability policies, which did not cover liability resulting from intentional acts by the insured. Applying the policy exclusion to the facts of this case, was Farm Bureau obligated to pay the $100,000 judgment against Allard? [*Southern Farm Bureau Casualty Co. v. Allard*, 611 So. 2d 966 (Miss.)]

6. Arthur Katz testified for the U.S. government in a stock manipulation case. He also pled guilty and testified against three of his law partners in an insurance fraud case. He received a six-month sentence in a halfway house and a $5,000 fine. Katz was placed in the Federal Witness Protection Program. He and his wife changed their names to Kane and moved to Florida under the program. Both he and his wife obtained new driver's licenses and Social Security numbers. Using his new identity, "Kane" obtained two life insurance policies totaling $1.5 million. He named his wife beneficiary. A routine criminal background check on Kane found no criminal history.

From 1984 to 1987, Kane invested heavily in the stock market. On October 17, 1987, the day the stock market crashed, Kane shot and wounded his stockbroker, shot and killed the office manager, and then committed suicide. The insurers refused to pay on the policies, claiming that they never insure persons with criminal records. Mrs. Kane contended that the policies were incontestable after they had been in effect for two years. Decide. [*Bankers Security Life Ins. Society v. Kane*, 885 F.2d 820 (11th Cir.)]

7. Linda Filasky held policies issued by Preferred Risk Mutual Insurance Co. Following an injury in an automobile accident and storm damage to the roof of her home, Filasky sustained loss of income, theft of property, and water damage to her home. These three kinds of losses were covered by the policies with Preferred, but the insurer delayed unreasonably in processing her claims and raised numerous groundless objections to them. Finally, the insurer paid the claims in full. Filasky then sued the insurer for the emotional distress caused by the bad-faith delay and obstructive tactics of the insurer. The insurer defended that it had paid the claims in full and that nothing was owed Filasky. Decide. [*Filasky v. Preferred Risk Mut. Ins. Co.*, 734 P.2d 76 (Ariz.)]

8. Baurer purchased a White Freightliner tractor and agreed that his son-in-law, Britton, could use it in the trucking business. In return, Britton agreed to haul Baurer's hay and cattle, thus saving Baurer approximately $30,000 per year. Baurer insured the vehicle with Mountain West Farm Bureau Insurance Company. The policy contained an exclusionary clause that provided: "We don't insure your [truck] while it is rented or leased to others.... This does not apply to the use of your [truck] on a share expense basis." When the vehicle was destroyed, Mountain West refused to pay on the policy, contending that the arrangement between Baurer and Britton was a lease of the vehicle, which was excluded under the policy. Baurer sued, contending that it was a "share expense basis" allowed under the policy. Is the insurance policy ambiguous? What rule of contract construction applies in this case? Decide. [*Baurer v. Mountain West Farm Bureau Ins.*, 695 P.2d 1307 (Mont.)]

9. Collins obtained from South Carolina Insurance Co. a liability policy covering a Piper Colt airplane he owned. The policy provided that it did not cover loss sustained while the plane was being piloted by a person who did not have a valid pilot's certificate and a valid medical examination certificate. Collins held a valid pilot's certificate, but his medical examination certificate had expired three months before. Collins was piloting the plane when it crashed, and he was killed. The insurer denied liability because Collins did not have a valid medical certificate. It was

stipulated by both parties that the crash was in no way caused by the absence of the medical certificate. Decide. [*South Carolina Ins. Co. v. Collins*, 237 S.E.2d 358 (S.C.)]

10. Marshall Produce Co. had insured its milk- and egg-processing plant against fire. When smoke from a fire near its plant permeated the environment and was absorbed into the company's egg powder products, cans of powder delivered to the U.S. government were rejected as contaminated. Marshall Produce sued the insurance company for a total loss, but the insurer contended that there had been no fire involving the insured property and no total loss. Decide. [*Marshall Produce Co. v. St. Paul Fire & Marine Ins. Co.*, 98 N.W.2d 280 (Minn.)]

11. Amador Pena, who had three insurance policies on his life, wrote a will in which he specified that the proceeds from the insurance policies should go to his children instead of to Leticia Pena Salinas and other beneficiaries named in the policies. He died the day after writing the will. The insurance companies paid the proceeds of the policies to the named beneficiaries. The executor of Pena's estate sued Salinas and the other beneficiaries for the insurance money. Decide. [*Pena v. Salinas*, 536 S.W.2d 671 (Tex. App.)]

12. Spector owned a small automobile repair garage in rural Kansas that was valued at $80,000. He purchased fire insurance coverage against loss to the extent of $48,000. The policy contained an 80 percent coinsurance clause. A fire destroyed a portion of his parts room, causing a loss of $32,000. Spector believes he is entitled to be fully compensated for this loss, as it is less than the $48,000 of fire protection that he purchased and paid for. Is Spector correct?

13. Carman Tool & Abrasives, Inc., purchased two milling machines, FOB Taiwan, from the Dah Lih Machinery Co. Carman obtained ocean marine cargo insurance on the machines from St. Paul Fire and Marine Insurance Co. and authorized Dah Lih to arrange for the shipment of the two machines to Los Angeles, using the services of Evergreen Lines. Dah Lih booked the machinery for shipment onboard Evergreen's container ship, the *M/V Ever Giant*; arranged for the delivery of the cargo to the ship; provided all of the shipping information for the bill of lading; and was the party to whom the bill was issued. Dah Lih then delivered the bill of lading to its bank, which in turn negotiated it to Carman's bank to authorize payment to Dah Lih. After the cargo was removed from the vessel in Los Angeles but before it was delivered to Carman, the milling machines were damaged to the extent of $115,000. Is the insurer liable to Carman? Can the insurer recover from Evergreen? [*Carman Tool & Abrasives, Inc. v. Evergreen Lines*, 871 F.2d 897 (9th Cir.)]

14. Vallot was driving his farm tractor on the highway. It was struck from the rear by a truck, overturned, exploded, and burned. Vallot was killed, and a death claim was made against All American Insurance Co. The death of Vallot was covered by the company's policy if Vallot had died from "being struck or run over by" the truck. The insurance company claimed that the policy was not applicable because Vallot had not been struck; the farm tractor had been struck, and Vallot's death occurred when the overturned tractor exploded and burned. The insurance company also claimed that it was necessary that the insured be both struck and run over by another vehicle. Decide. [*Vallot v. All American Ins. Co.*, 302 So. 2d 625 (La. App.)]

15. Anderson Development Co. (ADC) manufactures organic materials at its plant in Adrian, Michigan. The Environmental Protection Agency (EPA) sent ADC a formal notification that it was considered a "potentially responsible party" (PRP) for the release of hazardous substances into the soil and groundwater. This notice was called a *PRP letter*. ADC notified its insurer Travelers of the letter, and Travelers contended that it was not prepared to defend or cover ADC in the matter. The EPA and ADC entered a consent decree wherein ADC agreed to the cleanup activities, spending more than $6 million on the cleanup. ADC brought an action against its insurer, seeking coverage under its general liability insurance policies for the cost of its defense and the cost of cleanup. Travelers responded that its policy language "defend any suit" and "damages" did not apply to this EPA action. Decide. [*Anderson Development Co. v. Travelers Indemnity Co.*, 49 F.3d 1128 (6th Cir.)]

Agency and Employment

Agency

Learning Outcomes <<<

After studying this chapter, you should be able to

LO.1 Explain the difference between an agent and an independent contractor

LO.2 Explain three methods of creating an agency relationship

LO.3 Recognize that third persons who deal with an agent are required to take notice of acts contrary to the interests of the principal

LO.4 List and explain the duties an agent owes the principal

LO.5 Explain how the Uniform Durable Power of Attorney Act changes the common law rule on incapacity of the principal

One of the most common business relationships is that of agency. By virtue of the agency device, one person can make contracts at numerous places with many different parties at the same time.

36-1 Nature of the Agency Relationship

Agency is ordinarily based on the consent of the parties and for that reason is called a *consensual relationship.* However, the law sometimes imposes an agency relationship. If consideration is present, the agency relationship is contractual.

36-1a Definitions and Distinctions

Agency is a relationship based on an express or implied agreement by which one person, the **agent,** is authorized to act under the control of and for another, the **principal,** in negotiating and making contracts with third persons.[1] The acts of the agent obligate the principal to third persons and give the principal rights against third persons. (See Figure 36-1.)

The term *agency* is frequently used with other meanings. It is sometimes used to denote the fact that one has the right to sell certain products, such as when a dealer is

agency–relationship that exists between a person identified as a principal and another by virtue of which the latter may make contracts with third persons on behalf of the principal. (Parties—principal, agent, third person)

agent–person or firm who is authorized by the principal or by operation of law to make contracts with third persons on behalf of the principal.

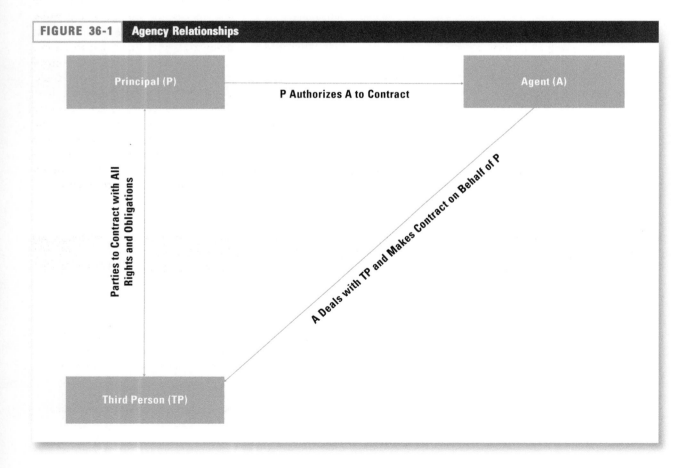

FIGURE 36-1   Agency Relationships

Principal (P)

P Authorizes A to Contract

Agent (A)

Parties to Contract with All Rights and Obligations

A Deals with TP and Makes Contract on Behalf of P

Third Person (TP)

---

[1] Restatement (Second) of Agency §1; *Union Miniere, S.A. v. Parday Corp.*, 521 N.E.2d 700 (Ind. App. 1988).

principal–person or firm who employs an agent; person who, with respect to a surety, is primarily liable to the third person or creditor; property held in trust.

said to possess an automobile agency. In other instances, the term is used to mean an exclusive right to sell certain articles within a given territory. In these cases, however, the dealer is not an agent in the sense of representing the manufacturer.

It is important to be able to distinguish agencies from other relationships because certain rights and duties in agencies are not present in other relationships.

Employees and Independent Contractors

Control and authority are characteristics that distinguish ordinary employees and independent contractors from agents.

Employees. An agent is distinguished from an ordinary employee who is not hired to represent the employer in making contracts with third persons. It is possible, however, for the same person to be both an agent and an employee. **For Example,** the driver for a spring water delivery service is an agent in making contracts between the company and its customers but is an employee with respect to the work of delivering products.

independent contractor–contractor who undertakes to perform a specified task according to the terms of a contract but over whom the other contracting party has no control except as provided for by the contract.

Independent Contractors. An **independent contractor** is bound by a contract to produce a certain result—for example, to build a house. The actual performance of the work is controlled by the contractor, not the owner. An agent or employee differs from an independent contractor in that the principal or employer has the right to control the agent or employee, but not the contractor, in the performance of the work. **For Example,** Ned and Tracy Seizer contract with Fox Building Company to build a new home on Hilton Head Island, South Carolina, according to referenced plans and specifications. Individuals hired by Fox to work on the home are subject to the authority and control of Fox, the independent contractor, not the Seizers. However, Ned and Tracy could decide to build the home themselves, hiring two individuals from nearby Beaufort, Ted Chase and Marty Bromley, to do the work the Seizers will direct each day. Because Ted and Marty would be employees of the Seizers, the Seizers would be held responsible for any wrongs committed by these employees within the scope of their employment. As a general rule, on the other hand, the Seizers are not responsible for the torts of Fox, the independent contractor, and the contractor's employees. A "right to control" test determines whether an individual is an agent, an employee, or an independent contractor.[2]

CASE SUMMARY

Why Some Businesses Use Independent Agents Rather than Employees!

FACTS: Patricia Yelverton died from injuries sustained when an automobile owned and driven by Joseph Lamm crossed the center line of a roadway and struck the automobile driven by Yelverton. Yelverton's executor brought suit against Lamm and Lamm's alleged employer, Premier Industrial Products Inc. The relationship between Lamm and Premier was governed by a written contract entitled "Independent Agent Agreement," in which Lamm, as

"Independent Agent," was given the right to sell Premier's products in a designated territory. The agreement provided that all orders were subject to acceptance by Premier and were not binding on Premier until so accepted. Lamm was paid by commission only. He was allowed to work on a self-determined schedule, retain assistants at his own expense, and sell the products of other companies not in competition with Premier. The executor claimed Lamm was an agent or

[2] *NE Ohio College of Massotherapy v. Burek*, 759 N.E.2d 869 (Ohio App. 2001).

Why Some Businesses Use Independent Agents Rather than Employees! continued

employee of Premier. Premier stated Lamm was an independent contractor.

DECISION: Judgment for Premier. Lamm had no authority to make contracts for Premier but simply took orders.

Therefore, he was not an agent. Lamm was not an employee of Premier. Premier had no right to control the way he performed his work and did not in fact do so. Lamm was an independent contractor. [*Yelverton v. Lamm*, **380 S.E.2d 621 (N.C. App. 1989)**]

A person who appears to be an independent contractor may in fact be so controlled by the other party that the contractor is regarded as an agent of, or employee of, the controlling person. **For Example,** Pierce, who was under contract to Brookville Carriers, Inc., was involved in a tractor-trailer/car collision with Rich and others. Pierce owned the tractor involved in the accident on a lease from Brookville but could use it only to haul freight for Brookville; he had no authority to carry freight on his own, and all of his operating authority belonged to Brookville. The "owner/operator" was deemed an employee rather than independent contractor for purposes of assessing the liability of the employer.[3] The separate identity of an independent contractor may be concealed so that the public believes that it is dealing with the principal. When this situation occurs, the principal is liable as though the contractor were an agent or employee.

36-1b Classification of Agents

special agent—agent authorized to transact a specific transaction or to do a specific act.

A **special agent** is authorized by the principal to handle a definite business transaction or to do a specific act. One who is authorized by another to purchase a particular house is a special agent.

general agent—agent authorized by the principal to transact all affairs in connection with a particular type of business or trade or to transact all business at a certain place.

A **general agent** is authorized by the principal to transact all affairs in connection with a particular type of business or trade or to transact all business at a certain place. To illustrate, a person who is appointed as manager by the owner of a store is a general agent.

universal agent—agent authorized by the principal to do all acts that can lawfully be delegated to a representative.

A **universal agent** is authorized by the principal to do all acts that can be delegated lawfully to a representative. This form of agency arises when a person absent because of being in the military service gives another person a blanket power of attorney to do anything that must be done during such absence.

CPA

36-1c Agency Coupled with an Interest

interest in the authority—form of agency in which an agent has been given or paid for the right to exercise authority.

An agent has an **interest in the authority** when consideration has been given or paid for the right to exercise the authority. **For Example,** when a lender, in return for making a loan of money, is given, as security, authority to collect rents due the borrower and to apply those rents to the payment of the debt, the lender becomes the borrower's agent with an interest in the authority given to collect the rents.

interest in the subject matter—form of agency in which an agent is given an interest in the property with which that agent is dealing.

An agent has an **interest in the subject matter** when, for a consideration, she is given an interest in the property with which she is dealing. Hence, when the agent is authorized to sell property of the principal and is given a lien on such property as security for a debt owed to her by the principal, she has an interest in the subject matter.

36-2 Creating the Agency

An agency may arise by appointment, conduct, ratification, or operation of law.

[3] *Rich v. Brookville Carriers, Inc.*, 256 F. Supp. 2d 26 (D. Me. 2003).

36-2a Authorization by Appointment

express authorization–authorization of an agent to perform a certain act.

The usual method of creating an agency is by **express authorization;** that is, a person is appointed to act for, or on behalf of, another.

 The authorization of the agent may be oral or in writing. **For Example,** Russell Jones, the owner of Westex, gave equipment operator Daniel Flores actual authority to sign an equipment rental agreement on behalf of Westex that acknowledged delivery of a loader to a job site.[4] However, some appointments must be made in a particular way. A majority of the states, by statute, require the appointment of an agent to be in writing when the agency is created to acquire or dispose of any interest in land. A written authorization of agency is called a **power of attorney.** An agent acting under a power of attorney is referred to as an **attorney in fact.**[5]

power of attorney–written authorization to an agent by the principal.

attorney in fact–agent authorized to act for another under a power of attorney.

36-2b Authorization by Conduct

Conduct consistent with the existence of an agency relationship may be sufficient to show authorization. The principal may have such dealing with third persons as to cause them to believe that the "agent" has authority. Thus, if the owner of a store places another person in charge, third persons may assume that the person in charge is the agent for the owner in that respect. The "agent" then appears to be authorized and is said to have *apparent authority*, and the principal is estopped from contradicting the appearance that has been created.[6]

CASE SUMMARY

The "Bulletproof Against Rust" Case. Oops! Now What?

FACTS: While constructing a hotel in Lincoln City, Oregon, the owner, Todd Taylor, became concerned about possible rusting in the exterior stucco system manufactured by ChemRex that was being installed at the hotel. The general contractor, Ramsay-Gerding, arranged a meeting with the owner, the installer, and ChemRex's territory manager for Oregon, Mike McDonald, to discuss Mr. Taylor's concerns. McDonald told those present that the SonoWall system was "bulletproof against rust," and stated that "you're getting a five-year warranty." He followed up with a letter confirming the five-year warranty on parts and labor. A year later rust discoloration appeared, and no one from ChemRex ever

fixed the problem. Taylor sued ChemRex for breach of warranty. ChemRex defended that McDonald did not have actual or apparent authority to declare such a warranty.

DECISION: Judgment for Taylor. The evidence indicated that ChemRex clothed Mike McDonald with the title of "territory manager" and gave him the actual authority to visit job sites and resolve problems. Although it denies he had actual authority, ChemRex took sufficient steps to create apparent authority to provide the five-year warranty on the stucco system. [*Taylor v. Ramsay-Gerding Construction Co.,* 196 P.3d 532 (Or. 2008)]

 The term *apparent authority* is used when there is only the appearance of authority but no actual authority, and that appearance of authority was created by the principal. The test for the existence of apparent authority is an objective test determined by the principal's outward manifestations through words or conduct that lead a third person reasonably to believe that the "agent" has authority. A principal's express restriction on authority not made known to a third person is no defense.

[4] *Jones v. Pomroy Equipment Rental, Inc.,* 438 S.W.3d 125 (Tex. App. 2014).
[5] *Lamb v. Scott,* 643 So. 2d 972 (Ala. 1994).
[6] *Intersparex Leddin KG v. AL-Haddad,* 852 S.W.2d 245 (Tenn. App. 1992).

Apparent authority extends to all acts that a person of ordinary prudence, familiar with business usages and the particular business, would be justified in believing that the agent has authority to perform. It is essential to the concept of apparent authority that the third person reasonably believe that the agent has authority. The mere placing of property in the possession of another does not give that person either actual or apparent authority to sell the property.

CPA   36-2c Agency by Ratification

An agent may attempt, on behalf of the principal, to do an act that was not authorized, or a person who is not the agent of another may attempt to act as such an agent. Very generally, notification may be express, where the principal explicitly approves the contract, or implied, where the principal does not object to the contract and accepts the contract's benefits. **For Example,** Morang-Kelly Investments, Inc., doing business as Farmer's Best Supermarket, denied that Mike Awdish was its authorized agent regarding the purchase and installation of used supermarket refrigerators at its Wyoming Street market. Nevertheless, by accepting the goods and services as well as the invoices for those goods and services for equipment still in use at the market it ratified Mr. Awdish's actions.[7]

Intention to Ratify

Initially, ratification is a question of intention. Just as in the case of authorization, when there is a question of whether the principal authorized the agent, there is a question of whether the principal intended to approve or ratify the action of the unauthorized agent.

The intention to ratify may be expressed in words, or it may be found in conduct indicating an intention to ratify. **For Example,** James Reiner signed a five-year lease of commercial space on 320 West Main Street in Avon, Connecticut, because his father, Calvin, was away on vacation, and the owner, Robert Udolf, told James that if he did not come in and sign the lease, his father would lose the opportunity to rent the space in question. James was aware that his father had an interest in the space, and while telling Robert several times that he had no authority, James did sign his name to the lease. In fact, his father took occupancy of the space and paid rent for three years and then abandoned the space. James is not liable on the remainder of the lease because the owner knew at the time of signing that James did not have authority to act. Although he did not sign the lease, Calvin ratified the lease signed by James by his conduct of moving into the space and doing business there for three years with full knowledge of all material facts relating to the transaction. The owner, therefore, had to bring suit against Calvin, not James.[8]

CPA   Conditions for Ratification

In addition to the intent to ratify, expressed in some instances with a certain formality, the following conditions must be satisfied for the intention to take effect as a ratification:

1. The agent must have purported to act on behalf of or as agent for the identified principal.

2. The principal must have been capable of authorizing the act both at the time of the act and at the time it was ratified.

3. The principal must have full knowledge of all material facts.

---

[7] *Bellevue Ventures, Inc. v. Morang-Kelly Investments, Inc.* 836 N.W.2d 898 (Mich. App. 2013).
[8] *Udolf v. Reiner,* 2000 WL 726953 (Conn. Super. May 19, 2000).

It is not always necessary, however, to show that the principal had actual knowledge. Knowledge will be imputed if a principal knows of other facts that would lead a prudent person to make inquiries or if that knowledge can be inferred from the knowledge of other facts or from a course of business. **For Example,** Stacey, without authorization but knowing that William needed money, contracted to sell one of William's paintings to Courtney for $298. Stacey told William about the contract that evening; William said nothing and helped her wrap the painting in a protective plastic wrap for delivery. A favorable newspaper article about William's art appeared the following morning and dramatically increased the value of all of his paintings. William cannot recover the painting from Courtney on the theory that he never authorized the sale because he ratified the unauthorized contract made by Stacey by his conduct in helping her wrap the painting with full knowledge of the terms of the sale. The effect is a legally binding contract between William and Courtney.

Effect of Ratification

When an unauthorized act is ratified, the effect is the same as though the act had been originally authorized. Ordinarily, this means that the principal and the third party are bound by the contract made by the agent.[9] When the principal ratifies the act of the unauthorized person, such ratification releases that person from the liability that would otherwise be imposed for having acted without authority.

CPA   ### 36-2d Proving the Agency Relationship

The burden of proving the existence of an agency relationship rests on the person who seeks to benefit by such proof. The third person who desires to bind the principal because of the act of an alleged agent has the burden of proving that the latter person was in fact the authorized agent of the principal and possessed the authority to do the act in question.[10]

36-3 Agent's Authority

When there is an agent, it is necessary to determine the scope of the agent's authority.

36-3a Scope of Agent's Authority

The scope of an agent's authority may be determined from the express words of the principal to the agent or it may be implied from the principal's words or conduct or from the customs of the trade or business.

Express Authority

If the principal tells the agent to perform a certain act, the agent has express authority to do so. Express authority can be given orally or in writing.

Incidental Authority

incidental authority— authority of an agent that is reasonably necessary to execute express authority.

An agent has implied **incidental authority** to perform any act reasonably necessary to execute the express authority given to the agent. **For Example,** if the principal authorizes the agent to purchase goods without furnishing funds to the agent to pay for them, the agent has the implied incidental authority to purchase the goods on credit.[11]

---

[9] *McCurley Chevrolet v. Rutz*, 808 P.2d 1167 (Wash. App. 1991).
[10] *Cummings, Inc. v. Nelson*, 115 P.3d 536 (Alaska 2005).
[11] *Badger v. Paulson Investment Co.*, 803 P.2d 1178 (Or. 1991).

customary authority—
authority of an agent to do
any act that, according to
the custom of the
community, usually
accompanies the
transaction for which the
agent is authorized to act.

apparent authority—
appearance of authority
created by the principal's
words or conduct.

Customary Authority

An agent has implied **customary authority** to do any act that, according to the custom of the community, usually accompanies the transaction for which the agent is authorized to act. An agent who has express authority to receive payments from third persons, for example, has the implied customary authority to issue receipts.

Apparent Authority

A person has **apparent authority** as an agent when the principal's words or conduct leads a third person to reasonably believe that the person has that authority and the third person relies on that appearance.[12]

CASE SUMMARY

CSX Gets Railroaded by Albert Arillotta

FACTS: Recovery Express and Interstate Demolition (IDEC) are two separate corporations located at the same business address in Boston. On August 22, 2003, Albert Arillotta, a "partner" at IDEC, sent an e-mail to Len Whitehead, Jr., of CSX Transportation expressing an interest in buying "rail cars as scrap." Arillotta represented himself to be "from interstate demolition and recovery express" in the e-mail. The e-mail address from which he sent his inquiry was **albert@recoveryexpress.com.** Arillotta went to the CSX rail yard, disassembled the cars, and transported them away. Thereafter CSX sent invoices for the scrap rail cars totaling $115,757.36 addressed to IDEC at its Boston office shared with Recovery Express. Whitehead believed Arillotta was authorized to act for Recovery Express, based on the e-mail's domain name, recoveryexpress.com. Recovery claims that Arillotta never worked for it. Recovery's president, Thomas Trafton, allowed the "fledgling" company to use telephone, fax, and e-mail services at its offices but never shared anything—assets, funds, books of business, or financials with IDEC—CSX sued Recovery for the invoice amount on the doctrine of "apparent authority." IDEC is now defunct. Recovery claims that Arillotta never worked for it and that it is not liable.

DECISION: Judgment for Recovery. Issuance of an e-mail address with Recovery's domain name to an individual who shared office space with Recovery did not give the individual, Albert Arillotta, apparent authority to enter contracts on Recovery's behalf. No reasonable person could conclude that Arillotta had apparent authority on the basis of an e-mail domain name by itself. Given the anonymity of the Internet, the court warned businesses to take additional action to verify a purported agent's authority to make a deal. [*CSX Transportation, Inc. v. Recovery Express, Inc.*, 415 F. Supp. 2d 6 (D. Mass. 2006)]

36-3b Effect of Proper Exercise of Authority

When an agent with authority properly makes a contract with a third person that purports to bind the principal, there is by definition a binding contract between the principal and the third person. The agent is not a party to this contract. Consequently, when the owner of goods is the principal, the owner's agent is not liable for breach of warranty with respect to the goods "sold" by the agent. The owner-principal, not the agent, was the "seller" in the sales transaction.

[12] *Alexander v. Chandler*, 179 S.W.2d 385 (Mo. App. 2005).

CPA   36-3c **Duty to Ascertain Extent of Agent's Authority**

A third person who deals with a person claiming to be an agent cannot rely on the statements made by the agent concerning the extent of authority.[13] If the agent is not authorized to perform the act or is not even the agent of the principal, the transaction between the alleged agent and the third person will have no legal effect between the principal and the third person. It is imperative that one who deals exclusively with an agent must recognize that it is his or her responsibility to ascertain the scope of that agent's authority. **For Example,** the Articles of Organization of limited liability company, Zions Gate R.V. Resort, provide that Zions Gate shall be managed by two managers, Jones and Sorpold, and the Articles require the consent and approval of both managers to constitute the act of the entity. Utah LLC law states that Articles of Organization filed with the state constitute notice of its content to third persons. Thus a 99-year RV lot lease to Oliphant signed only by manager Sorpold was invalid because Oliphant was deemed to have notice of the limitation on Sorpold's authority. Oliphant argued that it was unreasonable and unrealistic to expect individuals to acquire Articles of Organization to determine if the signatory to an agreement is authorized to act for the entity. The court responded that it is not its prerogative to question the statutory scheme enacted by the legislation.[14]

Third persons who deal with an agent whose authority is limited to a special purpose are bound at their peril to find out the extent of the agent's authority. An attorney is such an agent. Unless the client holds the attorney out as having greater authority than usual, the attorney has no authority to settle a claim without approval from the client.

Agent's Acts Adverse to Principal

The third person who deals with an agent is required to take notice of any acts that are clearly adverse to the interest of the principal. Thus, if the agent is obviously using funds of the principal for the agent's personal benefit, persons dealing with the agent should recognize that the agent may be acting without authority and that they are dealing with the agent at their peril.

The only certain way that third persons can protect themselves is to inquire of the principal whether the agent is in fact the agent of the principal and has the necessary authority. **For Example,** Ron Fahd negotiated the sale of a fire truck to the Edinburg Volunteer Fire Company on behalf of the manufacturer, Danko Company, at a price of $158,000. On Danko forms and letterhead Fahd drafted a "Proposal for Fire Apparatus" and it was signed by the president of the Fire Company and Fahd, as a dealer for Danko. Fahd gave a special $2,000 discount for prepayment of the cost of the chassis. Fahd directed that the prepayment check of $55,000 be made payable to "Ron Fahd Sales" in order to obtain the discount. The Fire Company's treasurer inquired of Fahd why the prepayment check was being made out to Fahd rather than Danko, and he accepted Fahd's answer without contacting Danko to confirm this unusual arrangement. Fahd absconded with the proceeds of the check. The Fire Company sued Danko, claiming Fahd had apparent authority to receive the prepayment. While there was some indicia of agency, the court found that the Fire Company had failed to make reasonable inquiry with Danko to verify Fahd's authority to receive the prepayment in Fahd's name, and it rejected the claim that Fahd had apparent authority to accept the prepayment check made out to Fahd as opposed to Danko.[15]

---

[13] *Breed v. Hughes Aircraft Col.,* 35 Fed. App. 864 (Fed. Cir. 2002).
[14] *Zions Gate R.V. Resort, LLC v. Oliphant,* 326 P.3d 118 (Utah App. 2014).
[15] *Edinburg Volunteer Fire Company v. Danko,* 867 N.Y.S.2d 547 (A.D. 2008).

36-3d Limitations on Agent's Authority

A person who has knowledge of a limitation on the agent's authority cannot ignore that limitation. When the third person knows that the authority of the agent depends on whether financing has been obtained, the principal is not bound by the act of the agent if the financing in fact was not obtained. If the authority of the agent is based on a writing and the third person knows that there is such a writing, the third person is charged with knowledge of limitations contained in it.

"Obvious" Limitations

In some situations, it may be obvious to third persons that they are dealing with an agent whose authority is limited. When third persons know that they are dealing with a representative of a government agency, they should recognize that such a person will ordinarily have limited authority. Third persons should recognize that a contract made with such an officer or representative may not be binding unless ratified by the principal.

The federal government places the risk on any individual making arrangements with the government to accurately ascertain that the government agent is within the bounds of his or her authority.

CASE SUMMARY

Humlen Was Had?

FACTS: The FBI approached Humlen for assistance in securing the conviction of a drug trafficker. Humlen executed an agreement with the FBI to formalize his status as an informant. The agreement he signed contained compensation figures significantly less than those he had been promised by the FBI agents with whom he was dealing. Humlen claims that five agents repeatedly assured him that he would receive the extra compensation they had discussed with him, despite the wording of the contract. It was explained that the agreement had to be "couched" in that way because it was a discoverable document in any future criminal prosecution and thus could be used to destroy his credibility. Based on the information provided by Humlen, an arrest was made, and Humlen sought the remainder of his promised monetary reward from the FBI. The FBI refused to pay him any more than the contract stipulated. When no additional payment was forthcoming, Humlen sued the U.S. government.

DECISION: Judgment for the United States. The government, unlike private parties, cannot be bound by the apparent authority of its agents. When an agent exceeds his or her authority, the government can disavow the agent's words and is not bound by an implied contract. As a general rule, FBI agents lack the requisite actual authority—either express or implied—to contractually bind the United States to remit rewards to confidential informants. Moreover, Humlen's claims directly collide with the plain language of the agreement. [*Humlen v. United States,* 49 Fed. Cl. 497 (2001)]

Secret Limitations

If the principal has clothed an agent with authority to perform certain acts but the principal gives secret instructions that limit the agent's authority, the third person is allowed to take the authority of the agent at its face value. The third person is not bound by the secret limitations of which the third person has no knowledge.

36-4 Duties and Liabilities of Principal and Agent

The creation of the principal-agent relationship gives rise to duties and liabilities.

36-4a Duties and Liabilities of Agent during Agency

While the agency relationship exists, the agent owes certain duties to the principal.

Loyalty

An agent must be loyal or faithful to the principal.[16] The agent must not obtain any secret benefit from the agency.

CASE SUMMARY

Impermissible Practices Involving Art Dealers with Russian Clients? No Way!

FACTS: On July 23, 2008, Luba Mosionzhnik, a 25 percent shareholder and vice president of the Gallery, was summoned to a meeting by Ezra Chowaiki, a 25 percent shareholder and president of the Gallery, and financial backer David Dangoor, a 50 percent shareholder. She was accused of a myriad of improprieties and fired from her employment. Section 42 of the Shareholders Agreement provided that upon termination of an employee who owned stock, he or she would be required to sell their shares to the Gallery. Mosionzhnik admitted to committing the most egregious of the alleged improper acts. She secretly opened a Swiss bank account, which she used to divert approximately $500,000 related to the Gallery's art sales, and used over $13 million of art consigned by the Gallery's clients as collateral for loans without the clients' consent. Rather than deny these allegations, at her deposition, Mosionzhnik testified that her actions were not improper and noted that "plenty of advisors take a kickback … that's not ethical but it happens because it's the art world." With respect to illegally using client art as collateral, her defense is that Chowaiki also did so and told her that such a thing was accepted practice in the industry. The Holtz accounting firm determined that Mosionzhnik shares were worth $170,000. The Gallery seeks to recover from Mosionzhnik for her improprieties. She seeks to keep the $500,000 in the Swiss bank account and believes her shares are worth $4,367,200 as valued by her experts "GMSL."

DECISION: While the Shareholder's Agreement permitted Mosionzknik to engage in private art transactions for her own benefit, the deals that led to the $500,000 secretly transferred to a Swiss bank account were all related to Gallery transactions with Russian clients. Taking a kickback on a finder's fee is legally impermissible, even if such a practice is pervasive in the art world. Consequently she must pay the $500,000 in kickbacks to the Gallery. Mosionzhnik's and Chowaiki's cross-accusations of improprieties are barred from consideration by the court by the doctrine of *in pari delicto*. The court will not intercede to resolve disputes between wrongdoers, especially with the Gallery itself benefitting from all sorts of shady practices regarding its Russian business. Mosionzhnik is nevertheless entitled to be paid the fair market valid of her shares, $170,000 as calculated by the Holtz accounting firm in accordance with the Shareholder's Agreement, because her equity is not compensation for services. [*Mosionzhnik v. Chowaiki*, 972 N.Y.S.2d 841 (A.D. 2013)]

Alternatively, the principal can approve the transaction and sue the agent for any secret profit obtained by the agent.

A contract is voidable by the principal if the agent who was employed to sell the property purchases the property, either directly or indirectly, without full disclosure to the principal.

An agent cannot act as agent for both parties to a transaction unless both know of the dual capacity and agree to it. If the agent does act in this capacity without the consent of both parties, any principal who did not know of the agent's double status can avoid the transaction.

---

[16] *Patterson Custom Homes v. Bach*, 536 F. Supp. 2d 1026 (E.D. Ill. 2008).

An agent must not accept secret gifts or commissions from third persons in connection with the agency. If the agent does so, the principal may sue the agent for those gifts or commissions. Such practices are condemned because the judgment of the agent may be influenced by the receipt of gifts or commissions.

It is a violation of an agent's duty of loyalty to make and retain secret profits or to secretly usurp the business opportunities of the principal.

CASE SUMMARY

Was Grappolini a "Bad Boy"?

FACTS: Arthur Frigo, an adjunct professor at the Kellogg Graduate School of Management, formed Lucini Italia Co. (Lucini) to import and sell premium extra virgin olive oil and other products from Italy. Lucini's officers hired Guiseppe Grappolini as their olive oil supplier. They also hired him as their consultant. Grappolini signed an exclusivity agreement and a confidentiality agreement acknowledging the confidential nature of Lucini's product development, plans, and strategies. Grappolini was "branded" as a "master cultivator" in Lucini's literature and commercials.

In 1998, Lucini and Grappolini, as his consultant, discussed adding a line of extra virgin olive oils blended with "essential oils," for example, natural extracts such as lemon and garlic. It spent more than $800,000 developing the market information, testing flavors, designing labels and packaging, creating recipes, and generating trade secrets for the new products. Vegetal-Progress s.r.l. (Vegetal) was identified as the only company in Italy that was capable of producing the superior products Lucini sought, and Grappolini was assigned responsibility to obtain an exclusive supply contract with Vegetal.

In direct contravention of his representations to Lucini, Grappolini secretly negotiated an exclusive supply contract for the Grappolini Co., not for Lucini. Moreover, Grappolini Co. began to sell flavored olive oils in the United States, which coincided with Lucini's market research and recipe development that had been disclosed to Grappolini. When Lucini officers contacted Vegetal, they acknowledged that Grappolini was a "bad boy" in procuring the contract for his own company rather than for Lucini, but they would not renege on the contract. Lucini sued Grappolini.

DECISION: Judgment for Lucini. Grappolini was Lucini's agent and owed Lucini a duty to advance Lucini's interests, not his own. When he obtained an exclusive supply agreement with Vegetal for the Grappolini Co. instead of Lucini, he was disloyal and breached his fiduciary duties. As a result, Lucini suffered lost profits and damages of $4.17 million. In addition to these damages, Grappolini was ordered to pay $1,000,000 in punitive damages to deter similar acts in the future. Additionally, a permanent injunction was issued prohibiting Grappolini from using Lucini's trade secrets. [*Lucini Italia Co. v. Grappolini*, 2003 WL 1989605 (N.D. Ill. 2003)]

An agent is, of course, prohibited from aiding the competitors of a principal or disclosing to them information relating to the business of the principal. It is also a breach of duty for the agent to knowingly deceive a principal.[17]

Obedience and Performance

An agent is under a duty to obey all lawful instructions.[18] The agent is required to perform the services specified for the period and in the way specified. An agent who does not do so is liable to the principal for any harm caused. For example, if an agent is instructed to take cash payments only but accepts a check in payment, the agent is liable for the loss caused the principal if a check is dishonored by nonpayment.

[17] *Koontz v. Rosener*, 787 P.2d 192 (Colo. App. 1990).
[18] *Stanford v. Neiderer*, 341 S.E.2d 892 (Ga. App. 1986).

Reasonable Care

It is the duty of an agent to act with the care that a reasonable person would exercise under the circumstances. **For Example,** Ethel Wilson applied for fire insurance for her house with St. Paul Reinsurance Co., Ltd., through her agent Club Services Corp. She thought she was fully covered. Unbeknown to her, however, St. Paul had refused coverage and returned her premium to Club Services, which did not refund it to Ms. Wilson or inform her that coverage had been denied. Fire destroyed her garage and St. Paul denied coverage. Litigation resulted, and St. Paul ended up expending $305,406 to settle the Wilson matter. Thereafter, St. Paul successfully sued Club Services Corp. under basic agency law principles that an agent (Club Services) is liable to its principal for all damages resulting from the agent's failure to discharge its duties.[19] In addition, if the agent possesses a special skill, as in the case of a broker or an attorney, the agent must exercise that skill.

Accounting

An agent must account to the principal for all property or money belonging to the principal that comes into the agent's possession. The agent must, within a reasonable time, give notice of collections made and render an accurate account of all receipts and expenditures. The agency agreement may state at what intervals or on what dates such accountings are to be made. An agent must keep the principal's property and money separate and distinct from that of the agent.

Information

It is the duty of an agent to keep the principal informed of all facts relating to the agency that are relevant to protecting the principal's interests.[20]

36-4b Duties and Liabilities of Agent after Termination of Agency

When the agency relationship ends, the duties of the agent continue only to the extent necessary to perform prior obligations. For example, the agent must return to the former principal any property that had been entrusted to the agent for the purpose of the agency. With the exception of such "winding-up" duties, the agency relationship is terminated, and the former agent can deal with the principal as freely as with a stranger.[21]

36-4c Duties and Liabilities of Principal to Agent

The principal must perform the contract, compensate the agent for services, make reimbursement for proper expenditures, and, under certain circumstances, must indemnify the agent for loss.

Employment According to Terms of Contract

When the contract is for a specified time, the principal is obligated to permit the agent to act as agent for the term of the contract. Exceptions are made for just cause or contract provisions that permit the principal to terminate the agency sooner. If the principal gives the agent an exclusive right to act in that capacity, the principal cannot give anyone else

---

[19] *St. Paul Reinsurance Co., Ltd. v. Club Services Corp.*, 30 Fed. Appx. 834 (10th Cir. 2002).
[20] Restatement (Second) of Agency §381; *Lumberman's Mutual Ins. Co. v. Franey Muha Alliant Ins.*, 388 F. Supp. 2d 292 (S.D.N.Y. 2005).
[21] *Corron & Black of Illinois, Inc. v. Magner*, 494 N.E.2d 785 (Ill. App. 1986).

the authority to act as agent, nor may the principal do the act to which the exclusive agent's authority relates. **For Example,** if Jill Baker gives Brett Stamos the exclusive right for six months to sell her house, she cannot give another real estate agent the right to sell it during the six-month period or undertake to sell the house herself. If the principal or another agent sells the house, the exclusive agent is entitled to full compensation just as though the act had been performed by the exclusive agent.

Compensation

The principal must pay the agent the agreed compensation.[22] If the parties have not fixed the amount of the compensation by their agreement but intended that the agent should be paid, the agent may recover the customary compensation for such services. If there is no established compensation, the agent may recover the reasonable value of the services rendered.

Repeating Transactions. In certain industries, third persons make repeated transactions with the principal. In these cases, the agent who made the original contract with the third person commonly receives a certain compensation or percentage of commissions on all subsequent renewal or additional contracts. In the insurance business, for example, the insurance agent obtaining the policyholder for the insurer receives a substantial portion of the first year's premiums and then receives a smaller percentage of the premiums paid by the policyholder in subsequent years.

Postagency Transactions. An agent is not ordinarily entitled to compensation in connection with transactions, such as sales or renewals of insurance policies, occurring after the termination of the agency even if the postagency transactions are the result of the agent's former activities. However, if the parties' employment contract calls for such compensation, it must be paid. **For Example,** real estate agent Laura McLane's contract called for her to receive $1.50 for every square foot the Atlanta Committee for the Olympic Games, Inc. (ACOG), leased at an Atlanta building; and even though she had been terminated at the time ACOG executed a lease amendment for 164,412 additional square feet, she was contractually entitled to a $246,618 commission.[23]

36-5 Termination of Agency

An agency may be terminated by the act of one or both of the parties to the agency agreement or by operation of law. When the authority of an agent is terminated, the agent loses all right to act for the principal.

36-5a Termination by Act of Parties

The duration of the agency relationship is commonly stated in the contract creating the relationship. In most cases, either party has the power to terminate the agency relationship at any time. However, the terminating party may be liable for damages to the other if the termination is in violation of the agency contract.

   When a principal terminates an agent's authority, it is not effective until the agent receives the notice. Because a known agent will have the appearance of still being an agent, notice must be given to third persons of the termination, and the agent may have the power to bind the principal and third persons until this notice is given.

---

[22] *American Chocolates, Inc. v. Mascot Pecan Co., Inc.*, 592 So. 2d 93 (Miss. 1992).
[23] *McLane v. Atlanta Market Center Management Co.*, 486 S.E.2d 30 (Ga. App. 1997).

36-5b Termination by Operation of Law

The agency relationship is a personal one, and anything that renders one of the parties incapable of performing will result in the termination of the relationship by operation of law. The death of either the principal or the agent ordinarily terminates the authority of an agent automatically even if the death is unknown to the other.[24]

An agency is also terminated by operation of law on the (1) insanity of the principal or agent, (2) bankruptcy of the principal or agent, (3) impossibility of performance, such as the destruction of the subject matter, or (4) when the country of the principal is at war with that of the agent.

CASE SUMMARY

Missing Out by Minutes

FACTS: William Moore, a fire chief for the city of San Francisco, suffered severe head injuries in a fall while fighting a fire. Moore sued the building owner, Lera, for negligence. The attorneys for the parties held a conference and reached a settlement at 5:15 P.M. Unknown to them, Moore had died at 4:50 P.M. on that day. Was the settlement agreement binding?

DECISION: No. The death of either the principal or the agent terminates the agency. Thus, the death of a client terminates the authority of his agent to act on his behalf. Because Moore died at 4:50 P.M., his attorney no longer had authority to act on his behalf, and the settlement was not enforceable. [*Moore v. Lera Development Inc.*, 274 Cal. Rptr. 658 (Cal. App. 1990)]

36-5c Disability of the Principal under the UDPAA

The Uniform Durable Power of Attorney Act (UDPAA) permits the creation of an agency by specifying that "this power of attorney shall not be affected by subsequent disability or incapacity of the principal." Alternatively, the UDPAA permits the agency to come into existence upon the disability or incapacity of the principal. For this to be effective, the principal must designate the attorney in fact in writing. The writing must contain words showing the intent of the principal that the authority conferred shall continue notwithstanding the disability or incapacity of the principal. The UDPAA, which has been adopted by most states,[25] changes the common law and the general rule that insanity of the principal terminates the agent's authority to act for the principal. Society today recognizes that it may be in the best interest of a principal and good for the business environment for a principal to designate another as an attorney in fact to act for the principal when the principal becomes incapacitated.[26] It may be prudent to grant durable powers of attorney to different persons for property matters and for health care decisions.

---

[24] *New York Life Ins. Co. v. Estate of Haelen*, 521 N.Y.S.2d 970 (N.Y. Civ. Ct. 1987).

[25] The Uniform Durable Power of Attorney Act has been adopted in some fashion in all states except Connecticut, Florida, Georgia, Illinois, Indiana, Kansas, Louisiana, and Missouri.

[26] The Uniform Probate Code and the Uniform Durable Power of Attorney Act provide for the coexistence of durable powers and guardians or conservators. These acts allow the attorney in fact to continue to manage the principal's financial affairs while the court-appointed fiduciary takes the place of the principal in overseeing the actions of the attorney in fact. See *Rice v. Flood*, 768 S.W.2d 57 (Ky. 1989).

Durable powers of attorney grant only those powers that are specified in the instrument.[27] A durable power of attorney may be terminated by revocation by a competent principal and by the death of the principal.

CASE SUMMARY

Broad Powers ... But There Is a Limit, Lucille

FACTS: On May 31, 2000, Thomas Graham made his niece Lucille Morrison his attorney in fact by executing a durable power of attorney. It was notarized and filed at the Registry of Deeds. The power of attorney granted Lucille broad powers and discretion in Graham's affairs. However, it did not contain express authority to make gifts. On October 26, 2000, Lucille conveyed 11.92 acres of property valued at between $400,000 and $700,000 to herself based on consideration of services rendered to the principal, Thomas Graham. On June 5, 2001, Lucille, as attorney in fact for Graham, conveyed Graham's house in Charlotte to her son Ladd Morrison. On June 20, 2001, she conveyed Graham's Oakview Terrace property to her brother John Hallman for $3,000 to pay for an attorney to defend Graham in a competency proceeding. Thomas Graham died on August 7, 2001, and his estate sued to set aside the deeds, alleging Lucille's breach of fiduciary duties. After a judgment for the defendants, the estate appealed.

DECISION: Judgment for the estate regarding the 11.92-acre parcel of land Lucille conveyed to herself. When an attorney in fact conveys property to herself based on consideration of services rendered to the principal, the consideration must reflect a fair and reasonable price when compared with the market value of the property. There was no testimony regarding the value of Lucille's services compared with the value of the real property. The deed must be set aside. The conveyance of Graham's home to Ladd Morrison was a gift that was not authorized by her power of attorney and must be set aside. Lucille had authority to sell the principal's property to John Hallman to obtain funds to pay an attorney to represent the principal. The estate's claim of conversion regarding this sale was denied. [*Estate of Graham v. Morrison*, **607 S.E.2d 295 (N.C. App. 2005)**]

36-5d Termination of Agency Coupled with an Interest

An agency coupled with an interest is an exception to the general rule as to the termination of an agency. Such an agency cannot be revoked by the principal before the expiration of the interest. It is not terminated by the death or insanity of either the principal or the agent.

36-5e Protection of Agent from Termination of Authority

The modern world of business has developed several methods of protecting an agent from the termination of authority for any reason.[28]

These methods include the use of an exclusive agency contract, a secured transaction, an escrow deposit, a standby letter of agreement, or a guarantee agreement.

---

[27] An attorney in fact (the holder of a power of attorney) may make decisions concerning litigation for the principal, such as deciding to settle a case, but a non-lawyer attorney in fact may not act as a lawyer to implement those decisions, nor may such an individual testify in place of an otherwise competent party in matters such as a divorce. See *Marisco v. Marisco*, 94 A.3d 947 (N.J. Super. 2013).

[28] These methods generally replace the concept of an agency coupled with an interest because of the greater protection given to the agent. Typically, the rights of the agent under these modern devices cannot be defeated by the principal, by operation of law, or by claims of other creditors.

36-5f Effect of Termination of Authority

If the principal revokes the agency, the authority to act for the principal is not terminated until the agent receives notice of revocation. As between the principal and the agent, the right of the agent to bind the principal to third persons generally ends immediately upon the termination of the agent's authority. This termination is effective without giving notice to third persons.

When the agency is terminated by the act of the principal, notice must be given to third persons. If this notice is not given, the agent may have the power to make contracts that will bind the principal and third persons. This rule is predicated on the theory that a known agent will have the appearance of still being the agent unless notice to the contrary is given to third persons.[29] **For Example,** Seltzer owns property in Boca Raton that he uses for the month of February and leases the remainder of the year. O'Neil has been Seltzer's rental agent for the past seven years, renting to individuals like Ed Tucker under a power of attorney that gives him authority to lease the property for set seasonal and off-season rates. O'Neil's right to bind Seltzer on a rental agreement ended when Seltzer faxed O'Neil a revocation of the power of attorney on March 1. A rental contract with Ed Tucker signed by O'Neil on behalf of Seltzer on March 2 will bind Seltzer, however, because O'Neil still appeared to be Seltzer's agent and Tucker had no notice to the contrary.

When the law requires giving notice in order to end the power of the agent to bind the principal, individual notice must be given or mailed to all persons who had prior dealings with the agent. In addition, notice to the general public can be given by publishing in a newspaper of general circulation in the affected geographic area a statement that the agency has been terminated.

If a notice is actually received, the power of the agent is terminated without regard to whether the method of giving notice was proper. Conversely, if proper notice is given, it is immaterial that it does not actually come to the attention of the party notified. Thus, a member of the general public cannot claim that the principal is bound on the ground that the third person did not see the newspaper notice stating that the agent's authority had been terminated.

Make the Connection

Summary

An agency relationship is created by an express or implied agreement by which one person, the agent, is authorized to make contracts with third persons on behalf of, and subject to, the control of another person, the principal. An agent differs from an independent contractor in that the principal, who controls the acts of an agent, does not have control over the details of performance of work by the independent contractor. Likewise, an independent contractor does not have authority to act on behalf of the other contracting party.

A special agent is authorized by the principal to handle a specific business transaction. A general agent is

---

[29] See *Stout Street Funding, LLC v. Johnson*, 2012 WL 1994800 (E.D. Pa. June 1, 2012). TRGC terminated its contract with Mabstract to serve as TRGC's closing agent on July 12, 2010, and obtained a court injunction barring Mabstract from engaging in any business on behalf of TRGC on July 15. Stout asserts that it had no actual notice of Mabstract's termination nor were there any red flags when it transmitted $480,000 into an escrow account held by Mabstract for a July 19 real estate transaction, which funds were misappropriated by Mabstract. It asserts that apparent authority lasts until a third party has actual notice of an agent's termination or until the third party has enough information to put that individual on inquiry.

authorized by the principal to transact all business affairs of the principal at a certain place. A universal agent is authorized to perform all acts that can be lawfully delegated to a representative.

The usual method of creating an agency is by express authorization. However, an agency relationship may be found to exist when the principal causes or permits a third person to reasonably believe that an agency relationship exists. In such a case, the "agent" appears to be authorized and is said to have apparent authority.

An unauthorized transaction by an agent for a principal may be ratified by the principal.

An agent acting with authority has the power to bind the principal. The scope of an agent's authority may be determined from the express words of the principal to the agent; this is called express authority. An agent has incidental authority to perform any act reasonably necessary to execute the authority given the agent. An agent's authority may be implied so as to enable the agent to perform any act in accordance with the general customs or usages in a business or an industry. This authority is often referred to as customary authority.

The effect of a proper exercise of authority by an agent is to bind the principal and third person to a contract. The agent, not being a party to the contract, is not liable in any respect under the contract. A third person dealing with a person claiming to be an agent has a duty to ascertain the extent of the agent's authority and a duty to take notice of any acts that are clearly adverse to the principal's interests. The third person cannot claim that apparent authority existed when that person has notice that the agent's conduct is adverse to the interests of the principal. A third person who has knowledge of limitations on an agent's authority is bound by those limitations. A third person is not bound by secret limitations.

While the agency relationship exists, the agent owes the principal the duties of (1) being loyal, (2) obeying all lawful instructions, (3) exercising reasonable care, (4) accounting for all property or money belonging to the principal, and (5) informing the principal of all facts relating to the agency that are relevant to the principal's interests. An agency relationship can be terminated by act of either the principal or the agent. However, the terminating party may be liable for damages to the other if the termination is in violation of the agency contract.

Because a known agent will have the appearance of still being an agent, notice must be given to third persons of the termination, and the agent may have the power to bind the principal and third persons until this notice is given.

An agency is terminated by operation of law upon (1) the death of the principal or agent, (2) insanity of the principal or agent, (3) bankruptcy of the principal or agent, (4) impossibility of performance, caused, for example, by the destruction of the subject matter, or (5) war. In states that have adopted the Uniform Durable Power of Attorney Act (UDPAA), an agency may be created that is not affected by subsequent disability or incapacity of the principal. In UDPAA states, the agency may also come into existence upon the "disability or incapacity of the principal." The designation of an attorney in fact under the UDPAA must be in writing.

Learning Outcomes

After studying this chapter, you should be able to clearly explain:

36-1   Nature of the Agency Relationship

LO.1 Explain the difference between an agent and an independent contractor

See the Ned and Tracy Seizer example and the "right to control" test, page 721.

36-2   Creating the Agency

LO.2 Explain three methods of creating an agency relationship

See the discussion on the usual method of creating an agency (which is by express authorization), page 723.

See the *Taylor* case where actual authority to perform some tasks created apparent authority to perform other related tasks, page 723.

See the agency by ratification example of James and Calvin Reiner, page 724.

36-3   Agent's Authority

LO.3 Recognize that third persons who deal with an agent are required to take notice of acts contrary to the interests of the principal

See the example of the Fire Company that failed to verify with the principal an agent's authority to receive a prepayment check of $55,000 made out in the agent's name, page 727.

36-4 Duties and Liabilities of Principal and Agent

L0.4 List and explain the duties an agent owes the principal

> See the discussion concerning an agent's duty of loyalty, obedience, reasonable care, accounting, and information, pages 729–731.
>
> See the *Mosionzhnik* case exposing an agent's breach of her duty of loyalty, page 729.

36-5 Termination of Agency

L0.5 Explain how the Uniform Durable Power of Attorney Act changes the common law rule on incapacity of the principal

> See the *Estate of Graham* case on the limits of a durable power of attorney, page 734.

Key Terms

agency	express authorization	interest in the subject matter
agent	general agent	power of attorney
apparent authority	incidental authority	principal
attorney in fact	independent contractor	special agent
customary authority	interest in the authority	universal agent

Questions and Case Problems

1. How does an agent differ from an independent contractor?

2. Compare authorization of an agent by (a) appointment and (b) ratification.

3. Ernest A. Kotsch executed a durable power of attorney when he was 85 years old, giving his son, Ernie, the power to manage and sell his real estate and personal property "and to do all acts necessary for maintaining and caring for [the father] during his lifetime." Thereafter, Kotsch began "keeping company" with a widow, Margaret Gradl. Ernie believed that the widow was attempting to alienate his father from him, and he observed that she was exerting a great deal of influence over his father. Acting under the durable power of attorney and without informing his father, Ernie created the "Kotsch Family Irrevocable Trust," to which he transferred $700,000, the bulk of his father's liquid assets, with the father as grantor and initial beneficiary and Ernie's three children as additional beneficiaries. Ernie named himself trustee. His father sued to avoid the trust. Ernie defended his action on the ground that he had authority to create the trust under the durable power of attorney. Decide. [*Kotsch v. Kotsch*, 608 So. 2d 879 (Fla. App.)]

4. Ken Jones, the number-one-ranked prizefighter in his weight class, signed a two-year contract with Howard Stayword. The contract obligated Stayword to represent and promote Jones in all business and professional matters, including the arrangement of fights. For these services, Jones was to pay Stayword 10 percent of gross earnings. After a year, when Stayword proved unsuccessful in arranging a title match with the champion, Jones fired Stayword. During the following year, Jones earned $4 million. Stayword sued Jones for $400,000. Jones defended himself on the basis that a principal has the absolute power at any time to terminate an agency relationship by discharging the agent, so he was not liable to Stayword. Was Jones correct?

5. Paul Strich did business as an optician in Duluth, Minnesota. Paul used only the products of the Plymouth Optical Co., a national manufacturer of optical products and supplies with numerous retail outlets and some franchise arrangements in areas other than Duluth. To increase business, Paul renovated his office and changed the sign on it to read "Plymouth Optical Co." Paul did business this way for more than three years—advertised under that name, paid bills with checks bearing the name of Plymouth Optical Co., and listed himself in the telephone and city directories by that name. Plymouth immediately became aware of what Paul was doing. However, because Paul used only Plymouth products and Plymouth did not have a franchise in Duluth, it saw no advantage at that time in prohibiting Paul from using the name and losing him as a customer. Paul contracted with the *Duluth Tribune* for advertising, making the contract in the name of Plymouth Optical Co. When the advertising bill was not paid, the *Duluth Tribune* sued Plymouth Optical Co. for payment. Plymouth's defense was that it

never authorized Paul to do business under the name, nor authorized him to make a contract with the newspaper. Decide.

6. Record owned a farm that was managed by his agent, Berry, who lived on the farm. Berry hired Wagner to bale the hay and told him to bill Record for this work. Wagner did so and was paid by Record. By the summer of the following year, the agency had been terminated by Record, but Berry remained in possession as tenant of the farm and nothing appeared changed. Late in the summer, Berry asked Wagner to bale the hay as he had done the previous year and bill Record for the work. He did so, but Record refused to pay on the ground that Berry was not then his agent. Wagner sued him. Decide. [*Record v. Wagner*, 128 A.2d 921 (N.H.)]

7. Gilbert Church owned Church Farms, Inc., in Manteno, Illinois. Church advertised its well-bred stallion Imperial Guard for breeding rights at $50,000, directing all inquiries to "Herb Bagley, Manager." Herb Bagley lived at Church Farms and was the only person available to visitors. Vern Lundberg answered the ad, and after discussions in which Bagley stated that Imperial Guard would remain in Illinois for at least a two-year period, Lundberg and Bagley executed a two-year breeding rights contract. The contract was signed by Lundberg and by Bagley as "Church Farms, Inc., H. Bagley, Mgr." When Gil Church moved Imperial Guard to Oklahoma prior to the second year of the contract, Lundberg brought suit for breach of contract. Church testified that Bagley had no authority to sign contracts for Church Farms. Decide. [*Lundberg v. Church Farms, Inc.*, 502 N.E.2d 806 (Ill.)]

8. The Holzmans signed an exclusive listing agreement with the Blum real estate brokerage firm. The contract provided that the Holzmans had an obligation to pay a commission "if they enter into a written agreement to sell the property to any person during the term of this exclusive listing agreement." The Holzmans entered into a written agreement to sell their house for $715,000 to the Noravians. On the advice of their attorney, the Holzmans included a default provision in this contract stating that in the event of default by the Holzmans, the Noravians' only remedy would be a refund of their deposit. Subsequently, the Sterns offered $850,000 for the property and the Holzmans canceled their contract with the Noravians and returned their deposit. After the exclusive listing period expired, the Holzmans executed a contract to sell their property to the

Sterns at the offered price of $850,000—with the contract calling for the Holzmans to pay half the real estate fee to Blum and half to a cooperating broker. Blum was paid this fee of $21,500. Blum brought suit against the Holzmans seeking the full commission for the Noravian contract under the exclusive listing agreement. Did Blum have a legal obligation or ethical duty to advise the Holzmans when considering the Sterns' offer that he believed they were obligated to him for the full commission under the Novarian contract? Decide. [*Holzman v. Blum*, 726 A.2d 818 (Md. App.)]

9. Tillie Flinn properly executed a durable power of attorney designating her nephew James C. Flanders and/or Martha E. Flanders, his wife, as her attorney in fact. Seven months later, Martha Flanders went to the Capitol Federal Savings and Loan Association office. She had the durable power of attorney instrument, five certificates of deposit, and a hand-printed letter identifying Martha as an attorney in fact and stating that Tillie wished to cash her five CDs that Martha had with her. At approximately 10:31 A.M., five checks were given to Martha in the aggregate amount of $135,791.34, representing the funds in the five CDs less penalties for early withdrawal. Some of the checks were drawn to the order of Martha individually and some to the order of James and Martha, as individuals. Tillie was found dead of heart disease later that day. The time of death stated on her death certificate was 11:30 A.M. The Flanderses spent the money on themselves. Bank IV, as administrator of Tillie's estate, sued Capitol Federal to recover the amount of the funds paid to the Flanderses. It contended that Capitol Federal breached its duty to investigate before issuing the checks. Capitol Federal contended that it did all that it had a duty to do. Decide. [*Bank IV v. Capitol Federal Savings and Loan Ass'n*, 828 P.2d 355 (Kan.)]

10. Lew owns a store on Canal Street in New Orleans. He paid a person named Mike and other individuals commissions for customers brought into the store. Lew testified that he had known Mike for less than a week. Boulos and Durso, partners in a wholesale jewelry business, were visiting New Orleans on a business trip when Mike brought them into the store to buy a stereo. While Durso finalized the stereo transaction with the store's manager, Boulos and Mike negotiated to buy 2 cameras, 3 videos, and 20 gold Dupont lighters. Unknown to the store's manager, Mike was given $8,250 in cash and was to deliver the merchandise later that evening to the

Marriott Hotel, where Boulos and Durso were staying. Mike gave a receipt for the cash, but it showed no sales tax or indication that the goods were to be delivered. Boulos testified that he believed Mike was the store owner. Mike never delivered the merchandise and disappeared. Boulos and Durso contended that Lew is liable for the acts of his agent, Mike. Lew denied that Mike was his agent, and the testimony showed that Mike had no actual authority to make a sale, to use a cash register, or even to go behind a sales counter. What ethical principle applies to the conduct of Boulos and Durso? Decide. [*Boulos v. Morrison*, 503 So. 2d 1 (La.)]

11. Martha Christiansen owns women's apparel stores bearing her name in New Seabury, Massachusetts; Lake Placid, New York; Palm Beach, Florida; and Palm Springs, California. At a meeting with her four store managers, she discussed styles she thought appropriate for the forthcoming season, advised them as always to use their best judgment in the goods they purchased for each of their respective stores, and cautioned "but no blue jeans." Later, Jane Farley, the manager of the Lake Placid store, purchased a line of high-quality blue denim outfits (designer jeans with jacket and vest options) from Women's Wear, Inc., for the summer season. The outfits did not sell. Martha refused to pay for them, contending that she had told all of her managers "no blue jeans" and that if it came to a lawsuit, she would fly in three managers to testify that Jane Farley had absolutely no authority to purchase denim outfits and was, in fact, expressly forbidden to do so. Women's Wear sued Martha, and the three managers testified for her. Is the fact that Martha had explicitly forbidden Farley to purchase the outfits in question sufficient to protect her from liability for the purchases made by Farley?

12. Fred Schilling, the president and administrator of Florence General Hospital, made a contract, dated August 16, 1989, on behalf of the hospital with CMK Associates to transfer the capacity to utilize 25 beds from the hospital to the Faith Nursing Home. Schilling, on behalf of the hospital, had previously made a contract with CMK Associates on May 4, 1987. Schilling had been specifically authorized by the hospital board to make the 1987 contract. The hospital refused to honor the 1989 contract because the board had not authorized it. CMK contended that Schilling had apparent authority to bind the hospital because he was president and administrator of the hospital and he had been the person who negotiated and signed a contract with CMK in 1987. Thus, according to CMK, the hospital had held out Schilling as having apparent authority to make the contract. The hospital disagreed. Decide. [*Pee Dee Nursing Home v. Florence General Hospital*, 419 S.E.2d 843 (S.C. App.)]

13. Real estate broker Donald Alley Sr. had a listing contract that gave him the exclusive right to sell Wayman Ellison's farm for at least $200,000. Ellison was told that a buyer was found. The buyer, Cora Myers, who had been paid $585,000 for her small farm because the land was needed for a commercial development, agreed to pay $380,000 for the large Ellison farm. Alley told Ellison that the sale price was $200,000. The buyer paid $380,000, however, and Alley kept the difference. When Ellison later learned of these details, he sued Alley for the $180,000. From a judgment for Ellison, Alley appealed, seeking at least his commission on the sale since he procured a ready, willing, and able buyer. Decide. [*Ellison v. Alley*, 842 S.W.2d 605 (Tenn)].

14. Francis Gagnon, an elderly gentleman, signed a power of attorney authorizing his daughter, Joan, "to sell any of my real estate and to execute any document needed to carry out the sale … and to add property to a trust of which I am grantor or beneficiary." This power was given in case Gagnon was not available to take care of matters personally because he was traveling. When Joan learned that Gagnon intended to sell his Shelburne property to Cosby for $750,000, she created an irrevocable trust naming Gagnon as beneficiary and herself as trustee. Acting then on the basis of the authority set forth in the power of attorney, she conveyed the Shelburne property to herself as trustee of the irrevocable trust, thus blocking the sale to Cosby. When Gagnon learned of this, he demanded that Joan return the Shelburne property to him, but she refused, saying she had acted within the authority set forth in the power of attorney. Did Joan violate any duty owed to Gagnon? Must she reconvey the property to Gagnon? [*Gagnon v. Coombs*, 654 N.E.2d 54 (Mass. App.)]

15. Daniels and Julian were employed by the Marriott Hotel in New Orleans and were close personal friends. One day after work, Daniels and Julian went to Werlein's music store to open a credit account. Julian, with Daniels's authorization and in her

presence, applied for credit using Daniels's name and credit history. Later, Julian went to Werlein's without Daniels and charged the purchase of a television set to Daniels's account, executing a retail installment contract by signing Daniels's name. Daniels saw the new television in Julian's home and was informed that it was charged to the Werlein's account. Daniels told Julian to continue making payments. When Werlein's credit manager first contacted Daniels to inform her that her account was delinquent, she claimed that a money order for the television was in the mail. On the second call, she asked for a "payment balance." Some four months after the purchase, she informed Werlein's that she had not authorized the purchase of the television nor ratified the purchase. Werlein's sued Daniels for the unpaid balance. Decide. [*Philip Werlein, Ltd. v. Daniels*, 536 So. 2d 722 (La. App.)]

CPA Questions

1. Generally, an agency relationship is terminated by operation of law in all of the following situations except the:

   a. Principal's death.

   b. Principal's incapacity.

   c. Agent's renunciation of the agency.

   d. Agent's failure to acquire a necessary business license.

2. Able, on behalf of Pix Corp., entered into a contract with Sky Corp., by which Sky agreed to sell computer equipment to Pix. Able disclosed to Sky that she was acting on behalf of Pix. However, Able had exceeded her actual authority by entering into the contract with Sky. If Pix wishes to ratify the contract with Sky, which of the following statements is correct?

   a. Pix must notify Sky that Pix intends to ratify the contract.

   b. Able must have acted reasonably and in Pix's best interest.

   c. Able must be a general agent of Pix.

   d. Pix must have knowledge of all material facts relating to the contract at the time it is ratified.

3. Which of the following actions requires an agent for a corporation to have a written agency agreement?

   a. Purchasing office supplies for the principal's business.

   b. Purchasing an interest in undeveloped land for the principal.

   c. Hiring an independent general contractor to renovate the principal's office building.

   d. Retaining an attorney to collect a business debt owed the principal.

4. Simmons, an agent for Jensen, has the express authority to sell Jensen's goods. Simmons also has the express authority to grant discounts of up to 5 percent of list price. Simmons sold Hemple a 10 percent discount. Hemple had not previously dealt with either Simmons or Jensen. Which of the following courses of action may Jensen properly take?

   a. Seek to void the sale to Hemple.

   b. Seek recovery of $50 from Hemple only.

   c. Seek recovery of $50 from Simmons only.

   d. Seek recovery of $50 from either Hemple or Simmons.

5. Ogden Corp. hired Thorp as a sales representative for nine months at a salary of $3,000 per month plus 4 percent of sales. Which of the following statements is correct?

   a. Thorp is obligated to act solely in Ogden's interest in matters concerning Ogden's business.

   b. The agreement between Ogden and Thorp formed an agency coupled with an interest.

   c. Ogden does not have the power to dismiss Thorp during the nine-month period without cause.

   d. The agreement between Ogden and Thorp is not enforceable unless it is in writing and signed by Thorp.

6. Frost's accountant and business manager has the authority to:

   a. Mortgage Frost's business property.

   b. Obtain bank loans for Frost.

   c. Insure Frost's property against fire loss.

   d. Sell Frost's business.

Third Persons in Agency

Learning Outcomes

After studying this chapter, you should be able to

LO.1 Explain when an agent is and is not liable to a third person as a party to a contract

LO.2 Describe how to execute a contract as an agent on behalf of a principal

LO.3 Explain the legal effect of a payment made by a third person to an authorized agent

LO.4 Explain the doctrine of *respondeat superior*

LO.5 Distinguish between the authority of a soliciting agent and that of a contracting agent

The rights and liabilities of the principal, the agent, and the third person with whom the agent deals are generally determined by contract law. In some cases, tort or criminal law may be applicable.

37-1   Liability of Agent to Third Person

The liability of the agent to the third person depends on the existence of authority and the manner of executing the contract.

37-1a   Action of Authorized Agent of Disclosed Principal

If an agent makes a contract with a third person on behalf of a disclosed principal and has proper authority to do so and if the contract is executed properly, the agent has no personal liability on the contract. Whether the principal performs the contract or not, the agent cannot be held liable by the third party. **For Example,** Lincoln Apartment Management, LP, required a vendor to sign a form before commencing work renovating Woodchase Village Apartments, which stated:

> *"Vendor understands and agrees that the legal Owner of the community is responsible for the payments of any services or materials performed or delivered, and not Lincoln, which is the property management company and Agent for the Owner of the community."*

The contractor's field manager, Jane Yang, signed the form before commencing work. After the work was performed the apartment complex was foreclosed, with the contractor still owing $59,758 for unpaid services. In a lawsuit against Lincoln by the contractor, the court determined that the owner, not the property manager, was solely liable for the debt.[1]

In speaking of an agent's action as authorized or unauthorized, it must be remembered that *authorized* includes action that, though originally *unauthorized*, was subsequently ratified by the principal. Once there is an effective ratification, the original action of the agent is no longer treated as unauthorized.

37-1b   Unauthorized Action

If a person makes a contract as agent for another but lacks authority to do so, the contract does not bind the principal. When a person purports to act as agent for a principal, an implied warranty arises that that person has authority to do so. If the agent lacks authority, there is a breach of this warranty.

If the agent's act causes loss to the third person, that third person may generally hold the agent liable for the loss.

For Example, Bruce Elieff and Todd Kurtin were equal partners and owners in a series of California real estate ventures, which included a group designated as the "Joint Entities" who were independent third-party owners. Elieff signed a settlement agreement buying out Kurtin for $48.8 million in four installments "individually and on behalf of the Elieff Separate Entities and the Joint Entities." Some $23 million of the last buyout installment was not paid by the Joint Entities. As agent for the Joint Entities, Elieff

---

[1] *Grand Master Contracting, LLC v. Lincoln Apartment Management, LP,* 724 S.E.2d 456 (Ga. App. 2012).

misstated his authority to bind the Joint Entities and he is liable to Kurtin for breach of warranty of an agent's authority.[2]

It is no defense for the agent in such a case that the agent acted in good faith or misunderstood the scope of authority. The purported agent is not liable for conduct in excess of authority when the third person knows that she is acting beyond the authority given by the principal.

An agent with a written authorization may avoid liability on the implied warranty of authority by showing the written authorization to the third person and permitting the third person to determine the scope of the agent's authority.

37-1c Disclosure of Principal

There are three degrees to which the existence and identity of the principal may be disclosed or not disclosed. An agent's liability as a party to a contract with a third person is affected by the degree of disclosure.

Disclosed Principal

disclosed principal— principal whose identity is made known by the agent as well as the fact that the agent is acting on the principal's behalf.

When the agent makes known the identity of the principal and the fact that the agent is acting on behalf of that principal, the principal is called a **disclosed principal.** The third person dealing with an agent of a disclosed principal ordinarily intends to make a contract with the principal, not the agent. Consequently, the agent is not a party to, and is not bound by, the contract that is made.[3] **For Example,** Biefeld Jewelers was the trade name of Bie-Jewel Corp., a closely held corporation of which Margie Biefeld was one of several employees. The plaintiff sought to hold her personally liable on a contract for advertising services. While Ms. Biefeld signed a contract for advertising services without reference to holding a corporate office, the plain language of the agreement established that she was acting as an agent for a disclosed principal and that the plaintiff had notice of her status.[4]

Partially Disclosed Principal

partially disclosed principal—principal whose existence is made known but whose identity is not.

When the agent makes known the existence of a principal but not the principal's identity, the principal is a **partially disclosed principal.** Because the third party does not know the identity of the principal, the third person is making the contract with the agent, and the agent is therefore a party to the contract.

Undisclosed Principal

undisclosed principal— principal on whose behalf an agent acts without disclosing to the third person the fact of agency or the identity of the principal.

When the third person is not told or does not know that the agent is acting as an agent for anyone else, the unknown principal is called an **undisclosed principal.**[5] In this case, the third person is making the contract with the agent, and the agent is a party to that contract.

---

[2] *Kurtin v. Elieff*, 155 Cal. Rptr. 3d 573 (2013).
[3] *Robinson v. Deutsche Bank Nat'l Trust Co.*, 932 F. Supp. 2d 95, 109 (D.C. Cir. 2013).
[4] *CBS Outdoor Group, Inc. v. Biefeld*, 836 N.Y.S.2d 497 (Civ. Ct. 2007).
[5] See *Castle Cheese Inc. v. MS Produce Inc.*, 2008 WL 4372856 (W.D. Pa. Sept. 19, 2008), where the court held that an agent must disclose both the identity of the principal and the fact of the agency relationship to avoid liability under a contract. One of the defendants, CVS Foods, did not establish that it had disclosed the fact it was acting as an agent, and it was held liable for breach of contract.

CASE SUMMARY

You've Got to Tell Them You're Contracting on Behalf of the Named Principal, Silly

FACTS: In 2003, Philip Steen formed Nashville Sports Leagues, LLC, for the purpose of providing a recreational sports league for a growing demographic of active adults in Middle Tennessee. Mr. Steen served as the managing member of Nashville Sports until the LLC was administratively dissolved in 2004. Three years later, in January 2007, Mr. Steen registered TN Sports, LLC, with the Tennessee Secretary of State. TN Sports performed the same functions as Nashville Sports, and Mr. Steen continued to serve as the managing member. Mr. Steen also continued to do business under the name "Nashville Sports Leagues." In correspondence, he identified himself as an executive of Nashville Sports Leagues and used an "@nashvillesports.com" e-mail address. By spring 2007, the popularity of TN Sports had grown considerably with 11,000 members on more than 175 teams. Players had their choice of six different sports with options year-round. The success of TN Sports was due at least in part to the ease of finding willing players and forming teams on the TN Sports Web site. In addition to its essential networking function, the Web site provided users with game schedules and venue information, among other details about leagues and events. In the spring of 2007, Mr. Steen moved his TN Sports Web site to ICG Link,

Inc., and it recommended that Mr. Steen build a new Web site to improve functionality. However, problems existed with the new Web site. Mr. Steen had not paid invoices from March to October, and ICG employees were instructed to "slow walk" the TN Sports Web site. The parties were unable to resolve their differences, and ICG Link filed a lawsuit against the LLC, and Mr. Steen personally, for breach of contract. The trial court found there was quasi-contract liability, less the cost to repair defects in the new Web site. It found Mr. Steen personally liable for the judgment and he appealed.

DECISION: In order for an agent to avoid personal liability on a contract, the agent must disclose the facts of the agency and the identity of the principal. Mr. Steen is the managing member of TN Sports, LLC. However, in his transactions with ICG he failed to disclose that TN Sports, LLC, was his principal, identifying himself as an executive of Nashville Sports Leagues. Thus he is personally liable for the judgment for ICG on its quasi-contract claim in the amount of $13,952, which consists of amounts owed for Web site development and hosting services, with an offset for the cost of completion of the new Web site. [*ICG Link, Inc. v. Steen*, 363 S.W.3d 533 (Tenn. App. 2011)]

37-1d Assumption of Liability

Agents may intentionally make themselves liable on contracts with third persons.[6] This situation frequently occurs when the agent is a well-established local brokerage house or other agency and when the principal is located out of town and is not known locally.

In some situations, the agent makes a contract that will be personally binding. If the principal is not disclosed, the agent is necessarily the other contracting party and is bound by the contract. Even when the principal is disclosed, the agent may be personally bound if it was the intention of the parties that the agent assume a personal obligation even though this was done to further the principal's business.[7]

CASE SUMMARY

The Thanks I Get for Being a Nice Person

FACTS: Grant Colledge was the managing member of A.T. Masterpiece Homes, a limited liability company. The trial court concluded that Colledge had assumed personal

responsibility regarding the quality of work during the construction of the Bennetts' and the Hoefferles' homes. When the construction finished, the homes were in various stages of

---

[6] *Fairchild Publications v. Rosston*, 584 N.Y.S.2d 389 (N.Y. County Sup. 1992).
[7] See *Boros v. Carter*, 537 So. 2d 1134 (Fla. App. 1989).

The Thanks I Get for Being a Nice Person continued

disrepair and structural failure. Judgment was issued against Colledge personally for $173,250 for the Bennetts and $55,250 for the Hoefferles. On appeal, Colledge contended that he should be shielded from personal liability because he was at all times acting only as an agent on behalf of a limited liability company, A.T. Masterpiece; and, he contends, any statements attributed to him where he said "I will take care of it" or "I guarantee it" were simply figures of speech and did not amount to an express assumption of personal liability.

DECISION: Judgment against Colledge. A person acting as an agent may assume personal liability on a business contract where he voluntarily undertakes a personal responsibility. For example, Colledge's statements to the Hoefferles had the effect of personally obligating himself for the structural integrity of the dormer because he made the statements with the goal of securing the Hoefferles' continuing performance on the contract. And his statements to the Bennetts led them to believe that he would personally ensure that the completed home was built properly. [*Bennett v. A.T. Masterpiece Homes at Broadsprings, LLC*, **40 A.3d 145 (Pa. Super. 2012)**]

37-1e Execution of Contract

A simple contract that would appear to be the contract of the agent can be shown by other evidence, if believed, to have been intended as a contract between the principal and the third party.

CASE SUMMARY

If You Sign as an Agent, You Don't Have to Pay

FACTS: Audrey Walton was transferred from a hospital to Mariner Health Nursing Home on January 26, 2001. Her daughter Patricia Walton signed a 30-page document, "Resident's Agent Financial Agreement." Patricia indicated in that agreement that the only method of payment would be Medicare or Medical Assistance. Medicare assistance stopped in February 2001. On January 10, 2003, Mariner Health sued both Audrey and Patricia for unpaid monthly bills amounting to $86,235. From a judgment for Mariner Health against both the patient and her daughter, Patricia appealed.

DECISION: Judgment for Patricia. As an agent, Patricia entered into the contract only for the benefit of Audrey and is personally insulated from liability by virtue of her status as an agent. *Note:* A state Nursing Home Bill of Rights did not authorize a nursing home to bring a private cause of action against a patient's agent for breach of contract unless the agent voluntarily and knowingly agreed to pay for the care with her or his own funds. [*Walton v. Mariner Health*, **894 A.2d 584 (Md. 2006)**]

To avoid any question of interpretation, an agent should execute an instrument by signing the principal's name and either *by* or *per* and the agent's name. **For Example,** if Jane R. Craig is an agent for B. G. Gray, Craig should execute instruments by signing either "B.G. Gray, by Jane R. Craig" or "B. G. Gray, per Jane R. Craig." Such a signing is in law a signing by Gray, and the agent is therefore not a party to the contract. The signing of the principal's name by an authorized agent without indicating the agent's name or identity is likewise in law the signature of the principal.

If the instrument is ambiguous as to whether the agent has signed in a representative or an individual capacity, parol evidence is admissible as between the original parties to the transaction for establishing the character in which the agent was acting.

37-1f **Torts and Crimes**

Agents are liable for harm caused to third persons by the agents' fraudulent, intentional, or negligent acts.[8] The fact that persons were acting as agents at the time or that they acted in good faith under the directions of a principal does not relieve them of liability if their conduct would impose liability on them when acting for themselves.

CASE SUMMARY

Employees Are Not Personally Liable for Roadway Accidents While at Work, Are They?

FACTS: Ralls was an employee of the Arkansas State Highway Department. While repairing a state highway, he negligently backed a state truck onto the highway, causing a collision with Mittlesteadt's car. Mittlesteadt sued Ralls, who raised the defense that, because he was acting on behalf of the state, he was not liable for his negligence.

DECISION: The fact that an employee or agent is acting on behalf of someone else does not excuse or exonerate the agent or employee from liability for torts committed by the agent or employee. Ralls was therefore liable for his negligence even though it occurred within the scope of his employment by the state. [*Ralls v. Mittlesteadt,* **596 S.W.2d 349 (Ark. 1980)**]

If an agent commits a crime, such as stealing from a third person or shooting a third person, the agent is liable for the crime without regard to the fact of acting as an agent. The agent is liable without regard to whether the agent acted in self-interest or sought to advance the interest of the principal.

37-2 Liability of Principal to Third Person

The principal is liable to the third person for the properly authorized and executed contracts of the agent and, in certain circumstances, for the agent's unauthorized contracts.

37-2a **Agent's Contracts**

The liability of a principal to a third person on a contract made by an agent depends on the extent of disclosure of the principal and the form of the contract that is executed.

CPA　**Simple Contract with Principal Disclosed**

When a disclosed principal with contractual capacity authorizes or ratifies an agent's transaction with a third person and when the agent properly executes a contract with the third person, a binding contract exists between the principal and the third person. The principal and the third person may each sue the other in the event of a breach of the contract. The agent is not a party to the contract, is not liable for its performance, and cannot sue for its breach.[9]

The liability of a disclosed principal to a third person is not discharged by the fact that the principal gives the agent money with which to pay the third person.

---

[8] *Mannish v. Lacayo*, 496 So. 2d 242 (Fla. App. 1986).
[9] *Levy v. Gold & Co., Inc.*, 529 N.Y.S.2d 133 (A.D. 1988).

ETHICS & THE LAW

Some time ago, dairy farmers owned large tracts of land in south Tempe, Arizona. The farmers used the land for grazing animals. Economic growth in this suburb of Phoenix was limited because of the state's inability at that time to attract large businesses to the area for relocation or location of new facilities.

In 1973, three farmers who owned adjoining parcels of land in the south Tempe area were approached by a local real estate agent with an offer for the purchase of their property. The amount of the offer was approximately 10 percent above the property's appraised value. The three farmers discussed the offer and concluded that with their need to retire, it was best to accept the offer and sell the land. All three signed contracts for the sale of their land.

After the contracts were entered into but before the transactions had closed, the three farmers learned that the land was being purchased by a real estate development firm

from southern California. The development firm had planned, and would be proposing to the Tempe City Council, a residential community, the Lakes. The Lakes would consist of upper-end homes in a community laced with parks, lakes, and ponds, with each house in the developed area backing up to its own dock and water recreation. The development firm had begun the project because it had learned of the plans of American Express, Rubbermaid, and Dial to locate major facilities in the Phoenix area.

The three farmers objected to the sale of their land when they learned the identity of the buyer. "If we had known who was coming in here and why, we never would have sold for such a low price." Were the farmers' contracts binding?

Is it ethical to use the strategy of an undisclosed principal? What is the role of an agent in a situation in which the third party is making a decision not as beneficial to him or her as it could or should be? Can the agent say anything?

Consequently, the liability of a buyer for the purchase price of goods is not terminated by the fact that the buyer gave the buyer's agent the purchase price to remit to the seller.

Simple Contract with Principal Partially Disclosed

A partially disclosed principal is liable for a simple contract made by an authorized agent. The third person may recover from either the agent or the principal.

Simple Contract with Principal Undisclosed

An undisclosed principal is liable for a simple contract made by an authorized agent. Although the third person initially contracted with the agent alone, the third person, on learning of the existence of the undisclosed principal, may sue that principal.[10] In most jurisdictions, third persons can sue and collect judgments from the agent or principal, or both, until the judgment is fully satisfied (joint and several liability).[11]

37-2b Payment to Agent

When the third person makes payment to an authorized agent, the payment is deemed made to the principal. Even if the agent never remits or delivers the payment to the principal, the principal must give the third person full credit for the payment so long as the third person made the payment in good faith and had no reason to know that the agent would be guilty of misconduct.[12]

[10] *McDaniel v. Hensons, Inc.*, 493 S.E.2d 529 (Ga. App. 1997).
[11] *Crown Controls, Inc. v. Smiley*, 756 P.2d 717 (Wash. 1988).
[12] This general rule of law is restated in some states by Section 2 of the Uniform Fiduciaries Act, which is expressly extended by Section 1 of the act to agents, partners, and corporate officers. Similar statutory provisions are found in a number of other states.

CASE SUMMARY

But We Already Paid!

FACTS: E.I. duPont de Nemours & Company licensed Enjay Chemical Company (now Exxon) and Johnson & Johnson to use certain chemical processes in return for which royalty payments by check were to be made to duPont. By agreement between the companies, the royalty payments to be made to duPont were to be made by check sent to a specified duPont employee, C.H.D., in its Control Division. These checks were sent during the next nine years. C.H.D. altered some of them so that he was named thereon as the payee. He then cashed them and used the money for his own purposes. Liberty Mutual Insurance Company, which insured the fidelity of duPont's employees, and duPont sued Enjay and Johnson & Johnson on the basis that they still owed the amounts embezzled by C.H.D.

DECISION: Judgment for Enjay and Johnson & Johnson. Payment to an authorized agent has the legal effect of payment to the principal regardless of whether the agent remits the payment to the principal or embezzles it. C.H.D. was the agent authorized to receive the royalty checks. Therefore, the defendants had effectively paid the royalties when they sent C.H.D. the checks. His misconduct did not revive the debts that were paid by sending him the checks. [*Liberty Mutual Ins. Co. v. Enjay Chemical Co.*, 316 A.2d 219 (Del. Super. 1974)]

Because apparent authority has the same legal effect as actual authority, a payment made to a person with apparent authority to receive the payment is deemed a payment to the apparent principal.

When a debtor makes payment to a person who is not the actual or apparent agent of the creditor, such a payment does not discharge the debt unless that person in fact pays the money to the creditor.

CASE SUMMARY

But We Already Paid!
No You Didn't

FACTS: Basic Research, LLC, ran advertisements on Rainbow Media Holdings' cable television networks from January to March 2008. Basic used an advertising agency named Icebox to place advertisements for its products. It paid Icebox up front for all of this advertising. Icebox went into bankruptcy, and it was discovered that Icebox had not paid Rainbow Networks for three months of advertising, worth $590,000. Rainbow Networks obtained a $132,000 payment from the Icebox bankruptcy estate. Rainbow now seeks payment from Basic for the remaining $406,000. Basic contends that Rainbow's only remedy was through the bankruptcy estate.

DECISION: Basic Research was a disclosed principal with whom Rainbow Networks had a credit agreement. Basic chose Icebox as its agent to place its advertisements and to make payments. Icebox didn't pay. It is Basic who is liable for the actions of its agent, and Basic is responsible for the $406,000 owed Rainbow Networks. [*Basic Research v. Rainbow Media Holdings, Inc.*, 2011 WL 2636833 (D. Utah July 6, 2011)]

37-2c Agent's Statements

A principal is bound by a statement made by an agent while transacting business within the scope of authority. This means that the principal cannot later contradict the statement of the agent and show that it is not true. Statements or declarations of an agent, in order to bind the principal, must be made at the time of performing the act to which they relate or shortly thereafter.

37-2d Agent's Knowledge

The principal is bound by knowledge or notice of any fact that is acquired by an agent while acting within the scope of actual or apparent authority. When a fact is known to the agent of the seller, the sale is deemed made by the seller with knowledge of that fact.

The rule that the agent's knowledge is imputed to the principal is extended in some cases to knowledge gained prior to the creation of the agency relationship. The notice and knowledge in any case must be based on reliable information. Thus, when the agent hears only rumors, the principal is not charged with notice.

If the subject matter is outside the scope of the agent's authority, the agent is under no duty to inform the principal of the knowledge, and the principal is not bound by it. The principal is not charged with knowledge of an agent when (1) the agent is acting adversely to the principal's interest or (2) the third party acts in collusion with the agent for the purpose of cheating the principal.

37-3 Liability of Principal for Torts and Crimes of Agent

Under certain circumstances, the principal may be liable for the torts or crimes of the agent or the employee.

CPA ### 37-3a Vicarious Liability for Torts and Crimes

Assume that an agent or an employee causes harm to a third person. Is the principal or the employer liable for this conduct? If the conduct constitutes a crime, can the principal or the employer be criminally prosecuted? The answer is that in many instances, the principal or the employer is liable civilly and may also be prosecuted criminally. That is, the principal or the employer is liable although personally free from fault and not guilty of any wrong. This concept of imposing liability for the fault of another is known as **vicarious liability.**

vicarious liability— imposing liability for the fault of another.

This situation arises both when an employer's employee or a principal's agent commits the wrong. The rules of law governing the vicarious liability of the principal and the employer are the same. In the interest of simplicity, this section is stated in terms of employees acting in the course of employment. Remember that these rules are equally applicable to agents acting within the scope of their authority. As a practical matter, some situations will arise only with agents. **For Example,** the vicarious liability of a seller for the misrepresentations made by a salesperson arises only when the seller appointed an agent to sell. In contrast, both the employee hired to drive a truck and an agent driving to visit a customer could negligently injure a third person with their vehicles. In many situations, a person employed by another is both an employee and an agent, and the tort is committed within the phase of "employee work."

respondeat superior— doctrine that the principal or employer is vicariously liable for the unauthorized torts committed by an agent or employee while acting within the scope of the agency or the course of the employment, respectively.

The rule of law imposing vicarious liability on an innocent employer for the wrong of an employee is also known as the doctrine of ***respondeat superior.*** In modern times, this doctrine can be justified on the grounds that the business should pay for the harm caused in the doing of the business, that the employer will be more careful in the selection of employees if made responsible for their actions, and that the employer may obtain liability insurance to protect against claims of third persons.

Nature of Act

The wrongful act committed by an employee may be a negligent act, an intentional act, a fraudulent act, or a violation of a government regulation. It may give rise only to civil liability of the employer, or it may also subject the employer to prosecution for crime.

Negligent Act. Historically, the act for which liability would be imposed under the doctrine of *respondeat superior* was a negligent act committed within the scope of employment.

Intentional Act. Under the common law, a master was not liable for an intentional tort committed by a servant. The modern law holds that an employer is liable for an intentional tort committed by an employee for the purpose of furthering the employer's business.[13] **For Example,** Crane Brothers, Inc., drilled a well for Stephen May. When May did not pay his bill, two Crane Brothers' employees went to May's workplace, and an altercation ensued in which May was injured. Crane Brothers, Inc., was held vicariously liable for the torts of the employees, not because the employer itself committed the wrongful acts but because it was answerable for the manner in which its agents, the two employees, conducted themselves in doing the business of the employer.[14]

Fraud. Modern decisions hold the employer liable for fraudulent acts or misrepresentations. The rule is commonly applied to a principal-agent relationship. To illustrate, when an agent makes fraudulent statements in selling stock, the principal is liable for the buyer's loss. In states that follow the common law rule of no liability for intentional torts, the principal is not liable for the agent's fraud when the principal did not authorize or know of the agent's fraud.

Government Regulation. The employer may be liable because of the employee's violation of a government regulation. These regulations are most common in the areas of business and protection of the environment. In such cases, the employer may be held liable for a penalty imposed by the government. In some cases, the breach of the regulation will impose liability on the employer in favor of a third person who is injured as a consequence of the violation.

Course of Employment

The mere fact that a tort or crime is committed by an employee does not necessarily impose vicarious liability on the employer. It must also be shown that the individual was acting within the scope of authority if an agent or in the course of employment if an employee. If an employee was not acting within the scope of employment, there is no vicarious liability.[15]

---

[13] Restatement (Second) of Agency §231.

[14] *Crane Brothers, Inc. v. May*, 556 S.E.2d 865 (Ga. App. 2001).

[15] See *Ali v. State of New York*, 981 N.Y.S.2d (App. Div. 2014) where during a phone conversation a state employee working as a security guard in the New York State Workers' Compensation Office in Brooklyn was informed of his grandmother's death. In reaction to that news, he went over to the waiting area and punched a wooden bench that was in front of the claimant, Mr. Ali, causing it to fall on Mr. Ali and injure him. Because the security guard was acting solely for personal motives unrelated to state business at the time of the incident, the state was not held vicariously liable for the security guard's actions.

CASE SUMMARY

A Hard Pill to Swallow for Walgreen: $1.4 Million in Damages

FACTS: A.E.H. was engaged in an on-and-off sexual relationship with Peterson. She filled her prescriptions, including birth control pills at a Walgreen pharmacy. Peterson began dating a Walgreen pharmacist, Audra Withers. A.E.H. became pregnant with Peterson's child. Peterson learned that he had contracted genital herpes and told Withers about the baby and that he may have exposed her to herpes. Withers became terrified, and during her shift at work she looked up A.E.H.'s prescription profile in the Walgreen computer system to see if she could find any information about her sexually transmitted disease. Peterson sent a text message to A.E.H.:

> I'm not trying to start any crap but I have a printout showing that you didn't even refill ur birth control prescription for July or august. The last time you filled ur prescription was June. I know uve lied... but the printout does not lie...

A.E.H. replied in part:

> Print out. It's illegal for u to obtain any kind of information like that regarding me...

After the child was born Peterson mailed a gift to his son. By an Internet search regarding the return address A.E.H. discovered that Peterson was married to Withers and that Withers was a Walgreen pharmacist. In a lawsuit based on negligence/malpractice the jury found that Walgreen and Withers were jointly responsible for $1.4 million in damages. Walgreen appealed.

DECISION: Judgment for A.E.H. against both Withers and Walgreen. Withers was acting within the scope of her employment with Walgreen for her actions were of the same general nature as those authorized or incidental to the actions that were authorized, using the Walgreen computer system and printer to look up customer information and patient prescription histories. Withers owed A.E.H. a duty of privacy protection by virtue of her employment as a pharmacist, and she breached this duty. Her actions are imputed to Walgreen under the doctrine of *respondeat superior*. [*Walgreen Co. v. A.E.H.*, 2014 WL 6130795 (Ind. App. 2014)]

Employee of the United States

The Federal Tort Claims Act (FTCA) declares that the United States shall be liable vicariously whenever a federal employee driving a motor vehicle in the course of employment causes harm under such circumstances that a private employer would be liable. Contrary to the general rule, the statute exempts the employee driver from liability.[16]

THINKING THINGS THROUGH

Rule No. 1: Take the Safe Course

The National Safety Council estimates that one quarter of all automobile and truck accidents involve cell phone use or texting. In fatality and injury vehicle accidents, plaintiffs' attorneys subpoena cell phone records, which often form the basis of compelling liability cases against driver-employees *and* their employers. It is a near automatic conclusion by jurors that the operator using a cell phone or texting caused the accident. Thinking Things Through, for the safety of employees and the public, as well as the extraordinary liability risks for employers, it may well be a sound business practice to ban all cell phone usage while driving on company business.

---

[16] Claims of negligent hiring are not permissible under the FTCA. See *Tonelli v. United States*, 60 F.3d 492 (8th Cir. 1995).

37-3b Negligent Hiring and Retention of Employees

In addition to a complaint against the employer based on the doctrine of *respondeat superior*, a lawsuit may often raise a second theory, that of negligent hiring or retention of an employee.[17] Unlike the *respondeat superior* theory by which the employer may be vicariously liable for the tort of an employee, the negligent hiring theory is based on the negligence of the employer in the hiring process. Under the *respondeat superior* rule, the employer is liable only for those torts committed within the scope of employment or in the furtherance of the employer's interests. The negligent hiring theory has been used to impose liability in cases when an employee commits an intentional tort, almost invariably outside the scope of employment, against a customer or the general public, and the employer knew or should have known that the employee was incompetent, violent, dangerous, or criminal.[18]

Need for Due Care in Hiring

An employer may be liable on a theory of negligent hiring when it is shown that the employer knew, or in the exercise of ordinary care should have known, that the job applicant would create an undue risk of harm to others in carrying out job responsibilities. Moreover, it must also be shown that the employer could have reasonably foreseen injury to the third party. Thus, an employer who knows of an employee's preemployment drinking problems and violent behavior may be liable to customers assaulted by that employee.

Employers might protect themselves from liability in a negligent hiring case by having each prospective employee fill out an employment application form and then checking into the applicant's work experience, background, character, and qualifications. This would be evidence of due care in hiring. Generally, the scope of a preemployment investigation should correlate to the degree of opportunity the prospective employee would have to do harm to third persons. A minimum investigation consisting of filling out an application form and conducting a personal interview would be satisfactory for hiring an outside maintenance person, but a full background inquiry would be necessary for hiring a security guard. However, such inquiry does not bar *respondeat superior* liability.

Employees with Criminal Records

The hiring of an individual with a criminal record does not by itself establish the tort of negligent hiring.[19] An employer who knows that an applicant has a criminal record has a duty to investigate to determine whether the nature of the conviction in relationship to the job to be performed creates an unacceptable risk to third persons.

Negligent Retention

Courts assign liability under negligent retention on a basis similar to that of negligent hiring. That is, the employer knew, or should have known, that the employee would create an undue risk of harm to others in carrying out job responsibilities.

A hospital is liable for negligent retention when it continues the staff privileges of a physician that it knew or should have known had sexually assaulted a female patient in the past.[20]

[17] *Medina v. Graham's Cowboys, Inc.*, 827 P.2d 859 (N.M. App. 1992).
[18] *Rockwell v. Sun Harbor Budget Suites*, 925 P.2d 1175 (Nev. 1996).
[19] *Connes v. Molalla Transportation Systems*, 831 P.2d 1316 (Colo. 1992).
[20] *Capithorne v. Framingham Union Hospital*, 520 N.E.2d 139 (Mass. 1988). A hospital may also be vicariously liable for the negligent credentialing of its physicians, as determined in *Larson v. Wasemiller*, 738 N.W.2d 300 (Minn. 2007).

CASE SUMMARY

(1) Alcohol, (2) Battery, and (3) Negligent Retention: Three Strikes and You're Out!

FACTS: Mark Livigni was manager of the National Super Markets store in Cahokia, Illinois. After drinking alcoholic beverages one evening, he stopped by the store to check the premises when he observed a 10-year-old boy's unacceptable behavior outside the store. Livigni chased the boy to a car, where he pulled another child, a 4-year-old named Farris Bryant, from the car and threw him through the air. A multicount lawsuit was brought against National and Livigni. The evidence revealed that some eight years before the incident with Farris Bryant, Livigni had thrown an empty milk crate at a subordinate employee, striking him on the arm and necessitating medical treatment, and that some two years before the incident, he threw his 13-year-old son onto a bed while disciplining him, causing the boy to sustain a broken collarbone. Livigni was promoted to store manager subsequent to the milk crate incident, and he pled guilty to aggravated battery to his child and was sentenced to two years' probation. A verdict was rendered against National for $20,000 under a *respondeat superior* theory for the battery of Farris Bryant. A verdict was also rendered against National for $15,000 for negligent retention of Livigni and for $115,000 in punitive damages for willful and wanton retention. National appealed the trial court's denial of its motions for directed verdicts on these counts.

DECISION: Judgment for Bryant. Employers that wrongfully hire or retain unfit employees expose the public to the acts of these employees, and it is not unreasonable to hold the employer accountable when the employee causes injury to another. The principle is not *respondeat superior*; rather, it is premised on the wrongful conduct of the employer itself. In addition, the employer in this case is responsible under *respondeat superior* because Livigni was prompted to act, in part, to protect store property. A dissenting opinion stated that the decision would send the wrong message to employers on the negligent retention issue and cause them to terminate any employee who has ever had an altercation on or off company premises, which is contrary to the state's public policy of rehabilitating criminal offenders. [*Bryant v. Livigni*, 619 N.E.2d 550 (Ill. App. 1993)]

37-3c Negligent Supervision and Training

A separate theory of liability in addition to the doctrine of *respondeat superior* is that of negligent supervision and training that holds the principal directly liable for its negligence in regard to training and supervision of its employees and agents. **For Example,** Monadnock Training Council, Inc., certified Robert Hebert as an "authorized Monadnock instructor" and granted him actual authority to market and promote its PR-24 police baton. In a training session run by Hebert at the Cheshire County House of Corrections in New Hampshire, Charles Herman suffered severe head trauma when training with Hebert without protective headgear in a room with unpadded cement walls. Monadnock was held directly liable for Herman's injuries based on its negligent supervision and training of Hebert.[21]

37-3d Agent's Crimes

A principal is liable for the crimes of an agent committed at the principal's direction. When not authorized, however, the principal is ordinarily not liable for an agent's crime merely because it was committed while the agent was otherwise acting within the scope of the latter's authority or employment. **For Example,** the owner of the Main Tower Cafe in Hartford, Connecticut, was not vicariously liable for injuries sustained by a patron who was shot by a bouncer while attempting to enter the bar because the bouncer's intentional and willful act was motivated by his own spleen and malevolence against the victim in

---

[21] *Herman v. Monadnock PR-24 Training Council, Inc.*, 802 A.2d 1187 (N.H. 2002).

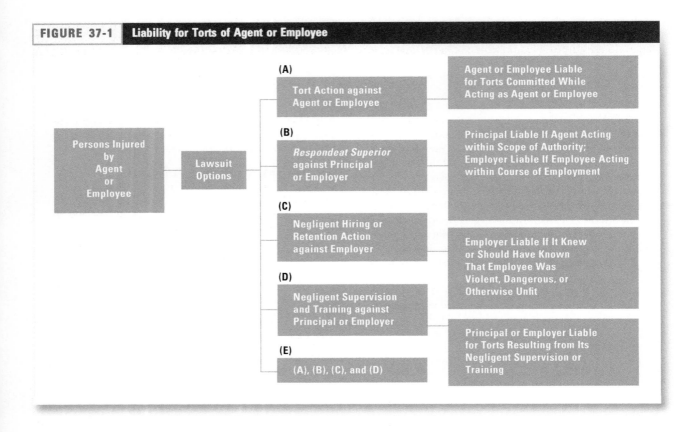

FIGURE 37-1   Liability for Torts of Agent or Employee

clear departure from his employment.[22] As an exception to the rule of nonliability just stated, courts now hold an employer criminally liable when the employee has in the course of employment violated environmental protection laws, liquor sales laws, pure food laws, or laws regulating prices or prohibiting false weights. **For Example,** an employer may be held criminally responsible for an employee's sale of liquor to a minor in violation of the liquor law even though the sale was not known to the employer and violated instructions given to the employee.

37-3e **Owner's Liability for Acts of an Independent Contractor**

If work is done by an independent contractor rather than by an employee, the owner is not liable for harm caused by the contractor to third persons or their property. Likewise, the owner is not bound by the contracts made by the independent contractor. The owner is ordinarily not liable for harm caused to third persons by the negligence of the employees of the independent contractor.[23]

[22] *Pruitt v. Main & Tower, Inc.*, 2002 WL 532467 (Conn. Super. March 14, 2002); see also *Burgess v. Lee Acceptance Corp.*, 2008 WL 5111905 (E.D. Mich. Dec. 4, 2008).
[23] *King v. Lens Creek, Ltd, Partnership*, 483 S.E.2d 265 (W. Va. 1996).

CASE SUMMARY

Plaintiffs' Attorneys Whine, "Why Do Courts Keep on Applying the 'Right to Control Test'?"

FACTS: Mark McLaurin was employed as a carpenter by Friede Goldman Offshore, Inc. Noble Drilling Inc. contracted with Friede Goldman (FG) to refit one of the offshore drilling rigs, the "Noble Clyde Boudreaux," at FG's Jackson County, Mississippi, facility. On July 30 and 31, 2002, McLaurin was assigned by Friede Goldman to construct scaffolding inside one of the pontoon extensions. A crane, operated by Friede Goldman employees, was in the process of lowering the roof structure of the pontoon for final placement. McLaurin was injured when he placed his hand in a "pinch point"—a space between two objects—while the roof was being lowered. McLaurin suffered a severely crushed left hand and arm. He received medical benefits and disability compensation from FG under the Longshore and Harbor Workers' Compensation Act. Maritime workers are also allowed to pursue separate claims against third parties responsible for their injuries, and McLaurin sued Noble Drilling for negligence. Noble Drilling sought dismissal of the case asserting that it was not responsible for the negligence of the employees of an independent contractor.

DECISION: Judgment for Noble Drilling. McLaurin testified that no one from Noble instructed him to work inside the pontoon extension or how to do his work. McLaurin's supervisor testified that Noble never told any member of his crew what to do and that he had "total control over my crew." Only FG employees were involved in the fitting work at the time of McLaurin's injury. And no Noble employee was present to observe the unsafe placement of McLaurin's hand in the pontoon extension. The mere fact that Noble could observe, inspect, and make recommendations does not establish that it had substantial control over the operation. [*McLaurin v. Noble Drilling Inc.,* **2009 WL 367401 (S.D. Miss. Feb. 10, 2009)**]

Exceptions to Owner's Immunity

There is a trend toward imposing liability on the owner when work undertaken by an independent contractor is inherently dangerous.[24] That is, the law is taking the position that if the owner wishes to engage in a particular activity, the owner must be responsible for the harm it causes. The owner cannot be insulated from such liability by the device of hiring an independent contractor to do the work.

Regardless of the nature of the activity, the owner may be liable for the torts and contracts of the independent contractor when the owner controls the conduct of the independent contractor.

In certain circumstances, such as providing security for a business, collecting bills, and repossessing collateral, there is an increased risk that torts may be committed by the individuals performing such duties. The trend of the law is to refuse to allow the use of an independent contractor for such work to insulate the employer.

Undisclosed Independent Contractor

In some situations, the owner appears to be doing the act in question because the existence of the independent contractor is not disclosed or apparent. This situation occurs most commonly when a franchisee does business under the name of the franchisor; when a concessionaire, such as a restaurant in a hotel, appears to be the hotel restaurant, although in fact it is operated by an independent concessionaire; or when the buyer of a business continues to run the business in the seller's name. In such cases of an undisclosed independent contractor, it is generally held that the apparent owner (that is, the franchisor, the grantor of the concession, or the seller) is liable for the torts and contracts of the undisclosed independent contractor.

---

[24] *Hinger v. Parker & Parsley Petroleum Co.,* 902 P.2d 1033 (N.M. App. 1995).

37-3f Enforcement of Claim by Third Person

A lawsuit may be brought by a third person against the agent or the principal if each is liable. In most states and in the federal courts, the plaintiff may sue either or both in one action when both are liable. If both are sued, the plaintiff may obtain a judgment against both, although the plaintiff is allowed to collect the full amount of the judgment only once.

37-4 Transactions with Sales Personnel

Many transactions with sales personnel do not result in a contract with the third person with whom the salesperson deals.

37-4a Soliciting and Contracting Agents

soliciting agent– salesperson.

Giving an order to a salesperson often does not give rise to a contract. A salesperson may be a **soliciting agent,** whose authority is limited to soliciting offers from third persons and transmitting them to the principal for acceptance or rejection. Such an agent does not have authority to make a contract that will bind the principal to the third person. The employer of the salesperson is not bound by a contract until the employer accepts the order, and the third person (customer) may withdraw the offer at any time prior to acceptance.

contracting agent–agent with authority to make contracts; person with whom the buyer deals.

In contrast, if the person with whom the buyer deals is a **contracting agent** with authority to make contracts, by definition a binding contract exists between the principal and the customer from the moment that the agent agrees with the customer. In other words, the contract arises when the agent accepts the customer's order.[25]

Make the Connection

- -

Summary

An agent of a disclosed principal who makes a contract with a third person within the scope of authority has no personal liability on the contract. It is the principal and the third person who may each sue the other in the event of a breach. A person purporting to act as an agent for a principal warrants by implication that there is an existing principal with legal capacity and that the principal has authorized the agent to act. The person acting as an agent is liable for any loss caused the third person for breach of these warranties. An agent of a partially disclosed or an undisclosed principal is a party to the contract with the third person. The agent may enforce the contract against the third person and is liable for its breach. To avoid problems of interpretation, an agent should execute a contract "Principal, by Agent." Agents are liable for harm caused third persons by their fraudulent, malicious, or negligent acts.

An undisclosed or a partially disclosed principal is liable to a third person on a simple contract made by an authorized agent. When a third person makes payment to an authorized agent, it is deemed paid to the principal.

A principal or an employer is vicariously liable under the doctrine of *respondeat superior* for the torts of an agent or an employee committed within the scope of authority

[25] But see the complications that developed in *Ferris v. Tennessee Log Homes, Inc.*, 2009 WL 1506724, (W.D. Ky. May 27, 2009), where Tennessee Log Homes (TLH) had a licensing agreement that explicitly granted authority to its "agent" to generate contracts for the sale of log home packages on behalf of TLH.

or the course of employment. The principal or the employer may also be liable for some crimes committed in the course of employment. An owner is not liable for torts caused by an independent contractor to third persons or their property unless the work given to the independent contractor is inherently hazardous.

A salesperson is ordinarily an agent whose authority is limited to soliciting offers (orders) from third persons and transmitting them to the principal. The principal is not bound until he or she accepts the order. The customer may withdraw an offer at any time prior to acceptance.

Learning Outcomes

After studying this chapter, you should be able to clearly explain:

37-1 Liability of Agent to Third Person

LO.1 Explain when an agent is and is not liable to a third person as a party to a contract
See the Biefeld Jewelers example in which Margie Biefeld was acting as an agent for a disclosed principal when she signed the contract and was not a party to the contract, page 743.

LO.2 Describe how to execute a contract as an agent on behalf of a principal
See the "B. G. Gray, by Jane R. Craig" example, page 745.
Learn from the mistake of Philip Steen's insufficient disclosure of his principal in the *ICG Link* case, page 744.

37-2 Liability of Principal to Third Person

LO.3 Explain the legal effect of a payment made by a third person to an authorized agent

See the discussion of a third party's payment to an authorized agent who absconds with the payment, page 747.
But see the effect of a payment by a disclosed principal to its agent who fails to pay the third party in the *Rainbow Networks* case, page 748.

37-3 Liability of Principal for Torts and Crimes of Agent

LO.4 Explain the doctrine of *respondeat superior*
See the Crane Brothers, Inc., example of employer liability for torts of the employees, page 750.
See the *Walgreen* case where the employee's negligence/malpractice was imputed to the employer under the doctrine of *respondeat superior*, page 751.

37-4 Transactions with Sales Personnel

LO.5 Distinguish between the authority of a soliciting agent and that of a contracting agent
See the discussion of the soliciting and contracting of agents, page 756.

Key Terms

contracting agent
disclosed principal
partially disclosed principal
respondeat superior
soliciting agent
undisclosed principal
vicarious liability

Questions and Case Problems

1. Richard Pawlus was an owner of Dutch City Wood Products, Inc., which did business as "Dutch City Marketing." Pawlus purchased merchandise from Rothschild Sunsystems from April 24 to June 24 using the designation "Richard Pawlus Dutch City Marketing" on orders and correspondence. In October, Rothschild was notified that Pawlus was acting on behalf of the corporation when the merchandise was purchased. Rothschild sued Pawlus for payment for the merchandise. Pawlus contended that he was an agent of the corporation and was thus not personally liable. Decide. [*Rothschild Sunsystems, Inc. v. Pawlus*, 514 N.Y.S.2d 572 (A.D.)]

2. Judith Studebaker was injured when a van owned and driven by James Ferry collided with her vehicle. On the morning of the incident, Ferry made his usual runs for the florist for whom he delivered flowers, Nettie's Flower Garden. He had made a slight detour prior to the accident to conduct personal business at a pawnshop and was returning to the flower shop at the time of the accident. Nettie's set standards for Ferry's dress and conduct, determined his territory, and set standards for his van. Studebaker brought an action against Nettie's on a *respondeat superior* theory on the belief that Ferry was Nettie's employee at the time of the accident. Nettie's defended that Ferry was an

independent contractor, not an employee. Decide. [*Studebaker v. Nettie's Flower Garden Inc.*, 842 S.W.2d 227 (Mo. App.)]

3. Lowell Shoemaker, an architect, was hired by Aff-house to work on a land development project. In September Shoemaker contacted Central Missouri Professional Services about providing engineering and surveying services for the project. Central submitted a written proposal to Shoemaker in October. About a week later, Shoemaker orally agreed that Central should proceed with the work outlined in the proposal. When the first phase of the work was completed, a bill of $5,864.00 was sent to Shoemaker. Shoemaker called Central and requested that all bills be sent directly to the owner/developer, Affhouse. When the bills were not paid, Central sued Shoemaker and Affhouse. The trial court entered a judgment against Shoemaker for $5,864 and he appealed. Shoemaker acknowledged that he did not disclose the identity of the principal to Central at the time the transaction was conducted, and explained:

> Q. *You never told Mike Bates or Central Missouri Professional Services that you were an agent for Affhouse or any other undisclosed principal?*
> A. *That's correct. I never did.*
>
> Q. *Another note I wrote down was that the subject of Affhouse came up in your conversations with Mike Bates of Central Missouri Professional Services after he sent the bill to you?*
> A. *The early part of the year, yes.*

Shoemaker contends that since he made clear to Central that he was an architect and not the developer, there was no binding oral contract between Central and him. Decide. [*Central Missouri Professional Services v. Shoemaker*, 108 S.W.3d 6 (Mo. App.)]

4. Beverly Baumann accompanied her mother to Memorial Hospital, where her mother was placed in intensive care for heart problems. A nurse asked Baumann to sign various documents, including one that authorized the hospital to release medical information and to receive the mother's insurance benefits directly. This form stated: "I understand I am financially responsible to the hospital for charges not covered by this authorization." Baumann's mother died during the course of her hospitalization. The hospital later sued Baumann to recover $19,013.42 in unpaid hospital charges based on the form she

signed, which the hospital called a "guarantee of payment." Baumann contended that she signed the document as an agent for her mother and was thus not personally liable. Decide. [*Memorial Hospital v. Baumann*, 474 N.Y.S.2d 636 (A.D.)]

5. Craig Industries was in the business of manufacturing charcoal. Craig, the corporation's president, contracted in the name of the corporation to sell the company's plants to Husky Industries. Craig did not have authority from the board of directors to make the contract, and later the board of directors voted not to accept it. Husky Industries sued Craig on the theory that he, as agent for the corporation, exceeded his authority and should be held personally liable for damages. Decide. [*Huskey Industries v. Craig*, 618 S.W.2d 458 (Mo. App. 1981)]

6. Leo Bongers died intestate. Alfred Bongers and Delores Kuhl, Leo's nephew and niece, were appointed personal representatives of his estate. Leo left more than 120 antique cars, trucks, and motorcycles. The estate hired Bauer-Moravec to sell the vehicles at auction. Auctioneer Russ Moravec suggested that the vehicles be sold at an airstrip auction in May, June, or July. The estate rejected this recommendation and insisted that the sale be conducted in January on a farm owned by the estate. On January 30, the auction took place beginning at 9:30 A.M. with temperatures below freezing and some 800 people jammed into the bid barn. One auctioneer had purchased Putnam hitch balls to be used with mylar-type ropes so that small farm tractors could tow the vehicles into and out of the bid barn. One hour into the auction, Joseph Haag was seriously injured when a hitch ball came loose from the drawbar of the tractor towing an antique Studebaker truck. Haag sued the estate, claiming that Bauer-Moravec was acting as agent for the estate and that its negligence in not properly attaching the hitch ball and in using mylar-type tow rope rather than chains should be imputed to the estate under the doctrine of *respondeat superior*. The estate defended that it was not liable for the torts of the auctioneer and its employees because the auctioneer was an independent contractor. Decide. [*Haag v. Bongers*, 589 N.W.2d 318 (Neb.)]

7. On July 11, 1984, José Padilla was working as a vacation-relief route salesperson for Frito-Lay. He testified that he made a route stop at Sal's Beverage Shop, where he was told by Mrs. Ramos that she was dissatisfied with Frito-Lay service and no longer

wanted its products in the store. He asked if there was anything he could do to change her mind. She said no and told him to pick up his merchandise. He took one company-owned merchandise rack to his van and was about to pick up another rack when Mr. Ramos said that the rack had been given to him by the regular route salesperson. Padilla said the route salesperson had no authority to give away Frito-Lay racks. A confrontation occurred over the rack, and Padilla pushed Mr. Ramos against the cash register, injuring Ramos's back. Frito-Lay has a company policy, clearly communicated to all employees, that prohibits them from getting involved in any type of physical confrontation with a customer. Frito-Lay contended that Padilla was not acting within the course and scope of his employment when the pushing incident took place and that the company was therefore not liable to Ramos. Ramos contended that Frito-Lay was responsible for the acts of its employee, Padilla. Decide. [*Frito-Lay, Inc. v. Ramos*, 770 S.W.2d 887 (Tex. App.)]

8. Jason Lasseigne, a Little League baseball player, was seriously injured at a practice session when he was struck on the head by a poorly thrown baseball from a team member, Todd Landry. The league was organized by American Legion Post 38. Claude Cassel and Billy Johnson were the volunteer coaches of the practice session. The Lasseignes brought suit on behalf of Jason against Post 38, claiming that the coaching was negligent and that Post 38 was vicariously liable for the harm caused by such negligence. Post 38 contended that it had no right to control the work of the volunteer coaches or the manner in which practices were conducted and as a result should not be held vicariously liable for the actions of the coaches. Decide. [*Lasseigne v. American Legion Post 38*, 543 So. 2d 1111 (La. App.)]

9. Moritz, a guest at Pines Hotel, was sitting in the lobby when Brown, a hotel employee, dropped a heavy vacuum cleaner on her knee. When Moritz complained, the employee insulted her and hit her with his fist, knocking her unconscious. She sued the hotel for damages. Was the hotel liable? [*Moritz v. Pines Hotel, Inc.*, 383 N.Y.S.2d 704 (A.D.)]

10. Steve Diezel, an employee of Island City Flying Service in Key West, Florida, stole a General Electric Credit Corp. (GECC) aircraft and crashed the plane while attempting to take off. GECC brought suit against Island City on the theory that it had negligently hired Diezel as an employee and was therefore legally responsible for Diezel's act of theft. Diezel had a military prison record as a result of a drug offense and had been fired by Island City twice previously but had been immediately reinstated each time. Island City claimed that the evidence was insufficient to establish that it had been negligent in employing Diezel. Decide. [*Island City Flying Service v. General Electric*, 585 So. 2d 274 (Fla.)]

11. The Bay State Harness Horse Racing and Breeding Association conducted horse races at a track where music for patrons was supplied by an independent contractor hired by the association. Some of the music played was subject to a copyright held by Famous Music Corp. The playing of that music was a violation of the copyright unless royalties were paid to Famous Music. No royalties were paid, and Famous Music sued the association, which raised the defense that the violation had been committed by an independent contractor specifically instructed not to play Famous Music's copyrighted material. Decide. [*Famous Music Corp. v. Bay State Harness Horse Racing and Breeding Association, Inc.*, 554 F.2d 1213 (1st Cir.)]

12. Steven Trujillo, told by the assistant door manager of Cowboys Bar "to show up to work tonight in case we need you as a doorman," came to the bar that evening wearing a jacket with the bar logo on it. Trujillo "attacked" Rocky Medina in the parking lot of the bar, causing him serious injury. Prior to working for Cowboys, Trujillo was involved in several fights at that bar and in its parking lot, and Cowboys knew of these matters. Medina sued Cowboys on two theories of liability: (1) *respondeat superior* and (2) negligent hiring of Trujillo. Cowboys's defense was that the *respondeat superior* theory should be dismissed because the assault was clearly not within the course of Trujillo's employment. Concerning the negligent hiring theory, Cowboys asserted that Trujillo was not on duty that night as a doorman. Decide. [*Medina v. Graham's Cowboys, Inc.*, 827 P.2d 859 (N.M. App.)]

13. Neal Rubin, while driving his car in Chicago, inadvertently blocked the path of a Yellow Cab Co. taxi driven by Robert Ball, causing the taxi to swerve and hit Rubin's car. Angered by Rubin's driving, Ball got out of his cab and hit Rubin on the head and shoulders with a metal pipe. Rubin sued Yellow Cab Co. for the damages caused by this beating, contending that the employer was vicariously liable for

the beating under the doctrine of *respondeat superior* because the beating occurred in furtherance of the employer's business, which was to obtain fares without delay. The company argued that Ball's beating of Rubin was not an act undertaken to further the employer's business. Is the employer liable under *respondeat superior?* [*Rubin v. Yellow Cab Co.*, 507 N.E.2d 114 (Ill. App.)]

14. Brazilian & Colombian Co. (B&C), a food broker, ordered 40 barrels of olives from Mawer-Gulden-Annis (MGA). MGA's shipping clerk was later told to make out the bill of lading to B&C's customer Pantry Queen; the olives were shipped directly to Pantry Queen. Eight days after delivery, the president of B&C wrote MGA to give it the name of its principal, Pantry Queen, and advised MGA to bill the principal directly. Pantry Queen was unable to pay for the olives, and MGA sued B&C for payment. B&C contended that it was well known to MGA that B&C was a food broker (agent) and the olives were shipped directly to the principal by MGA. It stated that as an agent, it was not a party to the contract and was thus not liable. Decide. [*Mawer-Gulden-Annis, Inc. v. Brazilian & Colombian Coffee Co.*, 199 N.E.2d 222 (Ill. App.)]

CPA Questions

1. Frey entered into a contract with Cara Corp. to purchase televisions on behalf of Lux, Inc. Lux authorized Frey to enter into the contract in Frey's name without disclosing that Frey was acting on behalf of Lux. If Cara repudiates the contract, which of the following statements concerning liability on the contract is *not* correct?

   a. Frey may not hold Cara liable and obtain money damages.

   b. Frey may hold Cara liable and obtain specific performance.

   c. Lux may hold Cara liable upon disclosing the agency relationship with Frey.

   d. Cara will be free from liability to Lux if Frey fraudulently stated that he was acting on his own behalf.

2. A principal will *not* be liable to a third party for a tort committed by an agent:

   a. Unless the principal instructed the agent to commit the tort.

   b. Unless the tort was committed within the scope of the agency relationship.

   c. If the agency agreement limits the principal's liability for the agent's tort.

   d. If the tort is also regarded as a criminal act.

3. Cox engaged Datz as her agent. It was mutually agreed that Datz would *not* disclose that he was acting as Cox's agent. Instead, he was to deal with prospective customers as if he were a principal acting on his own behalf. This he did and made several contracts for Cox. Assuming Cox, Datz, or the customer seeks to avoid liability on one of the contracts involved, which of the following statements is correct?

   a. Cox must ratify the Datz contracts in order to be held liable.

   b. Datz has *no* liability once he discloses that Cox was the real principal.

   c. The third party can avoid liability because he believed he was dealing with Datz as a principal.

   d. The third party may choose to hold either Datz or Cox liable.

4. Which of the following statements is (are) correct regarding the relationship between an agent and a nondisclosed principal?

   I. The principal is required to indemnify the agent for any contract entered into by the agent within the scope of the agency agreement.

   II. The agent has the same actual authority as if the principal had been disclosed.

   a. I only

   b. II only

   c. Both I and II

   d. Neither I nor II

CHAPTER 38

Regulation of Employment

Learning Outcomes <<<

After studying this chapter, you should be able to

LO.1 Explain the contractual nature of the employment relationship

LO.2 Explain how whistleblower protection under Sarbanes-Oxley is limited to conduct in violation of fraud or securities laws

LO.3 Explain how Dodd-Frank expands whistleblower protection to a wide range of financial services employees and provides incentives for whistleblowers

LO.4 Explain how the National Labor Relations Act prohibits employers from firing employees attempting to form a union and requires employers to bargain with certified unions in good faith over wages, hours, and working conditions

LO.5 Explain how ERISA protects employee pensions and benefits

LO.6 Explain the essentials of unemployment benefits, family and medical leaves, military leaves, and Social Security benefits

LO.7 Explain how OSHA is designed to ensure workers' safe and healthful working conditions

LO.8 Explain the three types of benefits provided by Workers' Compensation statutes

LO.9 Explain the sources of privacy rights and applications to telephone, e-mail, and property searches

LO.10 Explain an employer's verification obligations when hiring new employees

Employment law involves the law of contracts and the law established by lawmakers, courts, and administrative agencies.

38-1 The Employment Relationship

The relationship of an employer and an employee exists when, pursuant to an express or implied agreement of the parties, one person, the employee, undertakes to perform services or to do work under the direction and control of another, the employer, for compensation. In older cases, this relationship was called the *master-servant relationship.*

38-1a Characteristics of Relationship

An employee is hired to work under the control of the employer. An employee differs from an agent, who is to negotiate or make contracts with third persons on behalf of, and under the control of, a principal. However, a person may be both an employee and an agent for a party. An employee also differs from an independent contractor, who is to perform a contract independent of the control of the employer.[1]

38-1b Creation of Employment Relationship

The relationship of employer and employee can be created only with the consent of both parties.

Individual Employment Contracts

As in contracts generally, both parties must assent to the terms of an employment contract. Subject to statutory restrictions, the parties are free to make a contract on any terms they wish.

Collective Bargaining Contracts

Collective bargaining contracts govern the rights and obligations of employers and employees in many private and public areas of employment. Under collective bargaining, representatives of the employees bargain with a single employer or a group of employers for an agreement on wages, hours, and working conditions. The agreement worked out by the representatives of the employees, usually union officials, is generally subject to a ratification vote by the employees. Terms usually found in collective bargaining contracts are (1) identification of the work belonging exclusively to designated classes of employees, (2) wage and benefits clauses, (3) promotion and layoff clauses, which are generally tied in part to seniority, (4) a management's rights clause, and (5) a grievance procedure. A grievance procedure provides a means by which persons claiming that the contract was violated or that they were disciplined or discharged without just cause may have their cases decided by impartial labor arbitrators.

38-1c Duration and Termination of Employment Contract

In many instances, the employment contract does not state any time or duration. In such a case, it may be terminated at any time by either party. In contrast, the employment contract may state that it shall last for a specified period of time; an example would be an individual's contract to work as general manager for five years.

---

[1] *Ost v. West Suburban Travelers Limousine, Inc.,* 88 F.3d 435 (7th Cir. 1996).

Employment-at-Will Doctrine and Developing Exceptions

employment-at-will doctrine—doctrine in which the employer has historically been allowed to terminate the employment contract at any time for any reason or for no reason.

Ordinarily, a contract of employment may be terminated in the same manner as any other contract. If it is to run for a definite period of time, the employer cannot terminate the contract at an earlier date without justification. If the employment contract does not have a definite duration, it is terminable at will. Under the **employment-at-will doctrine** the employer has historically been allowed to terminate the employment contract at any time for any reason or for no reason.[2] Gradually, federal and state statutes were enacted to provide certain individual rights to workers, protecting them from workplace exploitation and discrimination by employers. And, in most states, courts have carved out narrow exceptions to the employment-at-will doctrine when the discharge violates an established public policy. **For Example,** home health care nurse Eugene Patterson continued to provide wound care to a patient after he was directed to cease the care by his employer, and he was discharged for insubordination. Patterson did so because the physician's order for the care remained in place, and he believed that state law governing the practice of nursing required him to complete the physician-directed care. The court held Patterson could sue his employer, Gentiva Health Services, for wrongful termination in violation of public policy.[3] Absent statutory protection, or a court-created contract or tort exception, the employment-at-will doctrine is still the basic default rule governing employment in the United States.

Public policy exceptions are often made to the employment-at-will doctrine when an employee is discharged in retaliation for insisting that the employer comply with the state's food and drug act or for filing a workers' compensation claim.[4] In some states, so-called whistleblower laws have been enacted to protect employees who disclose employer practices that endanger public health or safety. Also, a statutory right exists for at-will employees who are terminated in retaliation for cooperating with a federal criminal prosecution or who are terminated in violation of the public policy to provide truthful testimony.[5]

CASE SUMMARY

Pretext at the Pizzeria

FACTS: While working his nighttime cooking shift at Pizzeria Uno, Gerald Adams noticed that the restaurant's kitchen floor was saturated with a foul-smelling liquid coming from the drains. Adams left work, complaining of illness, and contacted the Department of Health about the drainage problem in the restaurant's kitchen. Upon returning to the restaurant a few days later, Adams was ordered into his manager's office. He was accused of stealing a softball shirt and taking home a work schedule. A shouting match ensued, and Adams was later arraigned on a criminal charge of disorderly conduct. The charges were eventually dropped and have since been expunged from his record. Adams contends that he was unlawfully terminated in violation of the state's whistleblower act because he notified the Board of Health regarding the unsanitary kitchen conditions. Uno contends he was fired for threatening the supervisor, which is an untenable act.

[2] *Payne v. Western & Atlantic Railroad Co.*, 82 Tenn. 507, 518–519 (1884).
[3] *Patterson v. Gentiva Health Services, Inc.*, 2011 WL 3235466 (D. S.C. July 25, 2011).
[4] *Brigham v. Dillon Companies, Inc.*, 935 P.2d 1054 (Kan. 1997).
[5] *Fitzgerald v. Salsbury Chemical, Inc.*, 613 N.W.2d 275 (Iowa 2000). In *Garcetti v. Ceballos*, 547 U.S. 410 (2006), the U.S. Supreme Court held that when public employees make statements pursuant to their official duties, the First Amendment of the Constitution does not insulate their communications from employer discipline because the employees are not speaking as citizens for First Amendment purposes. In his dissent, Justice Souter argued that a public employee should have constitutional protection when the employee acts as a whistleblower.

Pretext at the Pizzeria continued

DECISION: Judgment for Adams in the amount of $7,500. The confrontation between Adams and his employer was calculated by the employer to provoke a reaction from Adams that would serve as an excuse to fire him, a pretext for the real reason—Adam's phone call to the Board of Health. The wrongful termination and criminal charges that ensued from the verbal altercation were sufficient to establish damages for emotional distress. Adams's loss of security clearance in the National Guard, which prevented him from participating in an overseas mission in Germany, also supported the jury's finding of compensable emotional distress. [*Adams v. Uno Restaurants, Inc.*, 794 A.2d 489 (R.I. 2002)]

Other courts still follow the common law at-will rule because they believe that a court should not rewrite the contract of the parties to provide employee protection that was never intended.[6]

Employer Adjustments

Employers have revised their personnel manuals and employee handbooks and have issued directives to all employees that no assurance of continued employment exists—that the employers are not obligated to have good cause to terminate employees, just as employees are free to leave their positions with the employers. While simultaneously reserving their at-will termination powers, many employers also may design specific, apparently fair termination procedures and promulgate antiharassment and antidiscrimination policies and procedures, as seen in the *Semple v. FedEx* decision.

CASE SUMMARY

It's Not Easy to Get Around the Employment-at-Will Doctrine, Mr. Semple

FACTS: John Semple was terminated from his employment with FedEx for falsification of company documents. He appealed his termination through internal FedEx procedures without success and thereafter sued the employer in federal court, contending that his termination was in violation of the "public policy exception" to the employment-at-will doctrine in that his termination resulted from his filing internal grievances regarding harassment by his superiors and that he was protected by the employee handbook exception to the at-will doctrine. The employer disagreed.

DECISION: Judgment for FedEx. When he was hired, John Semple signed an employment contract that included the following statement:

> *I also agree that my employment and compensation can be terminated with or without cause and without notice or liability whatsoever, at any time, at the option of either the company or myself.*

The employee handbook stated in part:

> *The employment relationship between the Company and employee may be terminated at the will of either party as stated in the employment agreement signed upon application for employment. As described in that agreement, the policies and procedures set forth in this manual provide guidelines for management and employees during employment, but do not create contractual rights regarding termination otherwise.*

Semple was an employee at-will. No public policy prevented FedEx from terminating Semple's employment. Moreover, FedEx had not surrendered its statutory right to terminate at-will employees based on its employee handbook. [*Semple v. Federal Express Corp.*, 2008 WL 1793481 (D.S.D. April 17, 2008); affirmed 566 F.3d 788 (8th Cir. 2009)]

[6] See *Texas Farm Bureau Mutual Insurance Co. v. Sears*, 84 S.W.3d 604 (Tex. 2002).

Justifiable Discharge

An employer may be justified in discharging an employee because of the employee's (1) nonperformance of duties, (2) misrepresentation or fraud in obtaining the employment, (3) disobedience of proper directions, (4) disloyalty, (5) theft or other dishonesty, (6) possession or use of drugs or intoxicants, (7) misconduct, or (8) incompetence.

Employers generally have the right to lay off employees because of economic conditions, including a lack of work. Such actions are sometimes referred to as *reductions in force (RIFs)*.

Employers, however, must be very careful not to make layoffs based on age for that is a violation of the Age Discrimination in Employment Act.

In some states, a "service letter" statute requires an employer on request to furnish to a discharged employee a letter stating the reason for the discharge.

38-1d Whistleblower Protection under the Sarbanes-Oxley and Dodd-Frank Acts

The Sarbanes-Oxley Act (SOX) was enacted to restore investor confidence in financial markets following the exposure in 2001–2002 of widespread misconduct by directors and officers of publicly held companies. SOX contains reforms regarding corporate accountability, enhanced disclosure requirements, and enforcement and liability provisions. Title VIII of the Act contains protections for corporate whistleblowers.[7]

Protection Provided

SOX prohibits a publicly traded company or any agent of it from taking an adverse employment action against an employee who provides information, testifies, or "otherwise assists" in proceedings regarding (1) mail, wire, bank, or securities fraud, (2) any violation of an SEC rule or regulation, or (3) any federal law protecting shareholders against fraud.[8] The act sets forth the types of adverse employment actions that qualify for protection, specifically protecting employees from discharge, demotion, suspension, threats, harassment, failure to hire or rehire, blacklisting, or action otherwise discriminatory against employees in their terms and conditions of employment.

The act protects employees who provide information or assistance to supervisors, or a federal regulatory or law enforcement agency, or to members of Congress or a congressional committee. The act does not protect employees who provide information to the world, however. **For Example,** Nicholas Tides and Matthew Neumann were not protected under SOX when they provided a newspaper reporter information and documents about the questionable integrity of Boeing's data storage system and were fired for violating company confidentiality rules.[9]

Case law cautions that SOX whistleblower protection provisions do not provide "whistleblower protection for all employee complaints about how a public company spends its money and pays its bills."[10]

---

[7] 18 U.S.C. §1514A (2005).

[8] In *Lawson v. FMR LLC*, 134 S. Ct. 1158 (2014), the U.S. Supreme Court extended whistleblower protection under SOX to employees of private contractors and subcontractors serving public companies.

[9] *Tides v. Boeing Co.*, 644 F.3d 809 (9th Cir. 2011).

[10] *Platone v. Flyi, Inc.*, 2006 WL 3246910 (Dept. of Labor Sept. 29, 2006). See also *Welch v. Choa*, 536 F.3d 269 (4th Cir. 2008), in which CFO Welch had refused to certify an SEC quarterly report as required by SOX because of accounting irregularities and thus was fired. The court of appeals held that the conduct in question was not shown to be in violation of any fraud or securities laws listed in SOX; thus, Welch was not protected. However, in *Sylvester v. Parexel International LLC*, 2011 WL 2165854 (DOL Adm. Rev. Bd. May 25, 2011) the DOL's Administrative Review Board subsequently held that its prior ruling in *Platone v. Flyi, Inc.*—that an employee's complaint must "definitely and specifically" relate to the categories of fraud or securities violations listed in Section 806—"has evolved into an inappropriate test and is often applied too strictly."

Procedures

An individual who believes that she or he has been subject to an adverse employment action because of whistleblowing activities must file a complaint with the Department of Labor's Occupational Safety and Health Administration (OSHA) within 90 days after the asserted adverse employment action. OSHA administers 13 other federal whistleblower laws and has experienced investigators to facilitate its responsibilities under SOX.

The Dodd-Frank Expansion

The Dodd-Frank Wall Street Reform and Consumer Protection Act of 2010 (Dodd-Frank)[11] expands whistleblower protections to a wide range of financial services employees and provides expanded protections and incentives for whistleblowers.

Dodd-Frank covers almost any employee working in the financial services industry related to the extension of credit, including employees of privately held companies, and protects them from retaliation for disclosing information about fraud or unlawful conduct related to consumer financial products. It covers employees who extend credit, service loans, provide real estate settlement services, and provide financial advice, including credit counseling to consumers.[12]

Dodd-Frank requires the Securities and Exchange Commission to pay whistleblowers bounties of between 10 and 30 percent on monetary sanctions that aggregate to at least $1 million. To recover an award, a whistleblower must provide the SEC (1) voluntarily (2) with original information (3) that leads to a successful enforcement action or actions in federal court or before an agency (4) in which overall recovery totals over $1,000,000.[13]

Dodd-Frank expands on the SOX cause of action as follows:

1. Dodd-Frank expands the SOX statute of limitations from 90 to 180 days. The Dodd-Frank limitations period is six years.

2. Whistleblowers must exhaust administrative remedies under SOX at OSHA and DOL's Administrative Review Board before court review. Dodd-Frank allows an immediate lawsuit in federal district court.

3. SOX provides for actual back pay lost, as part of make whole relief, while Dodd-Frank allows recovery of double back pay as liquidated damages.

Dodd-Frank exempts whistleblower claims from predispute arbitration agreements. And it provides a burden-shifting framework for a private cause of action for employees who are retaliated against for protected activity so that once an employee has shown by a preponderance of the evidence that the protected activity was a contributing factor in an adverse employment action, the employer must show by clear and convincing evidence that it would have taken the same action in the absence of the employee's whistleblowing activities to avoid liability.

38-1e Duties of the Employee

The duties of an employee are determined primarily by the contract of employment with the employer. The law also implies certain obligations.

---

[11] The whistleblower protection provisions are codified at 15 U.S.C. §78u-6.

[12] In *Zillges v. Kenney Bank and Trust*, 24 F. Supp. 3d 795 (2014), a Dodd-Frank case was dismissed because the employee disclosure related to a violation of banking regulations, not a securities law violation.

[13] 17 C.F.R. §240.21F-1, *et seq*. To start an action a whistleblower must file a complaint with the SEC's Office of the Whistleblower, which includes a description of the misconduct, demonstrates eligibility, and declares under penalty of perjury that the information is true and accurate. Whistleblowers may submit a claim anonymously through an attorney.

Services

Employees are under the duty to perform such services as may be required by the contract of employment.

Trade Secrets

An employee may be given confidential trade secrets by the employer but must not disclose this knowledge to others. An agreement by the employee to refrain from disclosing trade secrets is binding. If the employee violates this obligation, the employer may enjoin the use of the information by the employee and by any person to whom it has been disclosed by the employee.

Former employees who are competing with their former employer may be enjoined from using information about suppliers and customers that they obtained while employees when this information is of vital importance to the employer's business. Injunctive relief is denied, however, if the information is not important or not secret.

Inventions

Employment contracts commonly provide that an employer will own any invention or discovery made by an employee, whether during work hours, after work hours, or for a period of one or two years after leaving the employment. In the absence of an express or implied agreement to the contrary, the inventions of an employee usually belong to the employee. This is true even though the employee used the time and property of the employer in the discovery. In this case, however, the employer has what is known as a **shop right** to use the invention without cost in its operations.

shop right–right of an employer to use in business without charge an invention discovered by an employee during working hours and with the employer's material and equipment.

38-1f **Rights of the Employee**

The rights of an employee are determined by the contract of employment and by the law as declared by courts, lawmakers, and administrative agencies.

Compensation

The rights of an employee with respect to compensation are governed in general by the same principles that apply to the compensation of an agent. In the absence of an agreement to the contrary, when an employee is discharged, whether for cause or not, the employer must pay wages to the expiration of the last pay period. State statutes commonly authorize employees to sue employers for wages improperly withheld and to recover penalties and attorney fees. In addition to hourly wages, payments due for vacations and certain bonuses are considered "wages" under state statutes.[14] **For Example,** Diane Beard worked for Summit Institute as a licensed practical nurse for 13 months when she walked off the job and terminated her employment. She requested her accrued vacation pay of $432, but Summit refused to pay her, claiming she had abandoned her job and thus forfeited her right to vacation pay under company policy. Accrued vacation qualifies as "wages," and she was entitled to the $432 vacation pay plus a penalty equal to 90 days' wages at the employee's rate of pay or $9,720, plus $2,400 in attorneys' fees for the trial and an additional $2,600 in attorneys' fees for the appeal. These statutes with their penalty provisions are designed as a coercive means to compel employers to promptly pay their employees.[15]

---

[14] *Knutson v. Snyder Industries, Inc.*, 436 N.W.2d 496 (Neb. 1989).
[15] *Beard v. Summit Institute of Pulmonary Medicine and Rehabilitation, Inc.*, 707 So. 2d 1233 (La. 1998); see also *Beckman v. Kansas Dep't. of Human Resources*, 43 P.3d 891 (Kan. App. 2002).

Federal Wage and Hour Law

Workers at enterprises engaged in interstate commerce are covered by the Fair Labor Standards Act (FLSA),[16] popularly known as the Wage and Hour Act. These workers cannot be paid less than a specified minimum wage.

CASE SUMMARY

What Is a "Willful" Violation?

FACTS: An action against an employer for violating the Fair Labor Standards Act must be brought within two years unless the violation was willful, in which case it may be brought within three years. McLaughlin, the Secretary of Labor, brought suit against Richland Shoe Company for failing to pay the minimum wage. Richland claimed that the suit was barred because more than two years had elapsed. McLaughlin claimed that the violation was willful, in which case the action was properly brought because three years had not expired. The parties disagreed as to what

proof was required to establish that the violation was "willful."

DECISION: To be "willful" within the statute, the violation must be intentional or made with reckless indifference to whether the statute has been satisfied. Because the case had not been tried on the basis of this standard, the case was remanded to the lower court to determine the matter in the light of the new definition of *willful*. [*McLaughlin v. Richland Shoe Co.*, 486 U.S. 128 (1998)]

The FLSA has been amended to cover domestic service workers, including housekeepers, cooks, and nannies. Executive, administrative, and professional employees and outside salespersons are exempt from both the minimum wage and overtime provisions of the law.[17] Students "working" at internships *may* be covered by the FLSA.[18]

Subminimum Wage Provisions. The FLSA allows for the employment of full-time students at institutions of higher education at wage rates below the statutory minimum. Also, individuals whose productive capacity is impaired by age, physical or mental deficiency, or injury may be employed at less than the minimum wage to prevent the curtailment of work opportunities for these individuals. In these cases, however, a special certificate is needed by the employer from the Department of Labor's (DOL) Wage and Hour Division, which has offices throughout the United States.

Wage Issues. Deductions made from wages as a result of cash or merchandise shortages and deductions for tools of the trade are not legal if they reduce wages below the

[16] P.L. 75-718, 52 Stat. 1060, 29 U.S.C. §201 *et seq.*
[17] In *Christopher v. SmithKline Beecham Corp.*, 132 S. Ct. 2156 (2012), the U.S. Supreme Court determined that pharmaceutical representatives, whose primary duty is to obtain nonbinding commitments from physicians to prescribe their drugs, are "outside salesmen" excluded from overtime pay requirements of the FLSA.
[18] A developing issue in our society is the utilization of unpaid interns—generally high school or college students—and their coverage, if any, under the FLSA and other employment laws. The FLSA does not define the terms *intern* or *trainee*. The act broadly defines the word "employee" as "to suffer or permit to work." The DOL utilizes a six-factor test for determining whether an individual is a trainee (intern) or an employee under the FLSA. In *Solis v. Laurelbrook Sanitarium and School, Inc.*, 642 F.3d 518 (6th Cir. 2011), the U.S. Court of Appeals for the Sixth Circuit determined that the DOL's test was overly rigid, and applied a "primary benefit of the relationship test" deciding that the primary benefit in that case ran to the students. In *Glatt v. Fox Searchlight Pictures, Inc.*, 2 F.R.D. 516 (S.D.N.Y. 2013) the court focused on whether the company derived an immediate advantage from the interns' work, and the court decided the case for the plaintiffs, finding that they worked as paid employees worked, and the educational benefits they received were the result of having worked as any other employee worked. Unpaid interns not considered employees are not entitled to the protections of the FLSA and Title VII of the Civil Rights Act of 1964. Practically speaking, it is up to the high schools and colleges to make sure that the internships they arrange are for the primary benefit of their students and not substitutes for regular, paid employees.

minimum wage. An employer's requirement that employees provide uniforms or tools of their own is a violation of the law to the extent that the expenses for these items reduce wages below the minimum wage.[19]

Job-related training generally is compensable under the FLSA. However, an exception exists for voluntary training not directly related to an employee's job when the employee does not perform productive work. **For Example,** Hogar, Inc., operates a nursing home and required new employees to undergo two days of unpaid training before assuming paid duties as nurses' aides, maintenance/laundry workers, and kitchen workers. Little or no instruction was offered to these "trainees," and each individual would perform the regular duties of the position for the two-day period. Hogar's practices did not fall within the training exception because the trainees performed productive work with little or no actual training during a regular shift. In a lawsuit brought by the Secretary of Labor, Hogar was ordered by the court to pay 14 hours' pay (two days' pay) for each employee so "trained," plus liquidated damages of an additional 14 hours pay.[20]

A large Pennsylvania landscape contractor whose cash wages appeared to comply with all applicable laws was found to be in violation of the FLSA because his Guatemalan and Mexican seasonal workers were required to pay employment-related costs, such as point-of-hire transportation costs, visa costs, and recruiter's fees, which reduced their real wages to below the minimum wage.[21]

Overtime Pay. Overtime must be paid at a rate of one and a half times the employee's regular rate of pay for each hour worked in excess of 40 hours in a workweek.[22]

Child Labor Provisions. The FLSA child labor provisions are designed to protect educational opportunities for minors and prohibit their employment in occupations detrimental to their health and well-being. The FLSA restricts hours of work for minors under 16 and lists hazardous occupations too dangerous for minors to perform.

38-2 Labor Relations Laws

Even if employers are not presently unionized, they are subject to certain obligations under federal labor relations law. It is important to both unionized and nonunionized employers to know their rights and obligations under the National Labor Relations Act (NLRA).[23] Employee rights and obligations are also set forth in this act. The Labor-Management Reporting and Disclosure Act regulates internal union affairs.[24]

38-2a The National Labor Relations Act

The National Labor Relations Act (NLRA), passed in 1935, was based on the federal government's power to regulate interstate commerce granted in Article 1, Section 8, of the Constitution. Congress, in enacting this law, explained that its purpose was to remove

---

[19] See Gayle Cinqugrani, "Uniform Deductions, Low Commissions Lead to DOL Penalties for FLSA Violations," *107 D.L.R. A-10* (June 6, 2012), where an investigation by the Wage and Hour Division of the DOL between November 2008 and November 2010 found that Vizza Wash LP, doing business as Wash-Tub, made illegal deductions from employees' paychecks for items such as uniforms, insurance claims, and cash register shortages, which caused the employees' pay to fall below the federal minimum wage of $7.25 per hour.

[20] *Herman v. Hogar Praderas De Amor, Inc.*, 130 F. Supp. 2d 257 (S.D.P.R. 2001).

[21] *Rivera v. Brttman Group, Ltd.*, 2008 WL 81570 (E.D. Pa. Jan. 7, 2008).

[22] DOL regulations, referred to as the *white collar exemptions* from the overtime requirements of the FLSA, took effect on August 23, 2004. Generally, executive, administrative, professional, outside sales, computer professional, and certain "highly compensated employees" are exempt from the overtime requirements if they meet the "tests" set forth in the new regulations.

[23] 29 U.S.C. §§141–169.

[24] 29 U.S.C. §§401–531.

obstructions to commerce caused by employers who denied their employees the right to join unions and refused to accept collective bargaining.[25] Congress stated that these obstructions resulted in depression of wages, poor working conditions, and diminution of purchasing power.

Section 7 of the amended NLRA is the heart of the act, stating in part that "[e]mployees shall have the right to self-organization ... to bargain collectively through representatives of their own choosing and to engage in other concerted activities for the purpose of collective bargaining or other mutual aid or protection.... and shall have the right to refrain from such activities...."

Section 8 of the NLRA contains employer and union unfair labor practices, set forth in Figure 38-1, and authorizes the National Labor Relations Board to conduct proceedings to stop such practices.

The act applies to private-sector employers with gross incomes of $500,000 or more. The Railway Labor Act applies to employees of railroad and air carriers.

38-2b National Labor Relations Board

Administration of the NLRA is entrusted to the five-member National Labor Relations Board (NLRB, or Board) and the general counsel of the Board. The general counsel is responsible for investigating and prosecuting all unfair labor practice cases. The five-member Board's major function is to decide unfair labor practice cases brought before it by the general counsel.

The Board is also responsible for conducting representation and decertification elections. This responsibility is delegated to the regional directors of the 26 regional offices located throughout the United States who (1) determine the appropriateness of each proposed bargaining unit for the purpose of collective bargaining, (2) investigate petitions for the certification or decertification of unions, and (3) conduct elections to determine the choice of the majority of those employees voting in the election. Should a majority of the employees voting select a union, the NLRB will certify that union as the exclusive representative of all employees within the unit for the purpose of bargaining with the employer to obtain a contract with respect to wages, hours, and other conditions of employment.

38-2c Election Conduct

The NLRB has promulgated preelection rules restricting electioneering activities so that the election will express the true desire of employees. The NLRA prohibits employer interference or coercion during the preelection period. The act also prohibits during this period employer statements that contain threats of reprisal or promises of benefits. **For Example,** it is a violation of Section 8(c) of the NLRA for a Southern California manufacturer to make implied threats to relocate its plant to Mexico if the employees choose union representation. Furthermore, when the company announced its intent to move to Mexico one day after the union won a representation election, the Labor Board obtained an injunction against the move.[26]

The Board prohibits all electioneering activities at polling places and has formulated a "24-hour rule," which prohibits both unions and employers from making speeches to captive audiences within 24 hours of an election. The rationale is to preserve free elections and to prevent any party from obtaining undue advantage.

[25] N.L.R.A. §1; 29 U.S.C. §141.
[26] See *Quadrtech Corp.*, N.L.R.B., No. 21–CA–33997 (settlement Dec. 11, 2000).

FIGURE 38-1   Employer and Union Unfair Labor Practices Charge

UNFAIR LABOR PRACTICES CHARGES AGAINST EMPLOYERS	SECTION OF THE NLRA*
1. Restrain or coerce employees in the exercise of their rights under Section 7; threat of reprisals or promise of benefits	8(a)(1); 8(c)
2. Dominate or interfere with the formation or administration of a labor organization or contribute financial or other support to it	8(a)(2)
3. Discriminate in regard to hire or tenure of employment or any term or condition of employment in order to encourage or discourage membership in any labor organization	8(a)(3)
4. Discharge or otherwise discriminate against employees because they have given testimony under the act	8(a)(4)
5. Refuse to bargain collectively with representatives of its employees	8(a)(5)

UNFAIR LABOR PRACTICES CHARGES AGAINST UNIONS	SECTION OF THE NLRA
1. Restrain or coerce employees in the exercise of their rights under Section 7	8(b)(1)(A)
2. Restrain or coerce an employer in the selection of its representatives	8(b)(1)(B)
3. Cause or attempt to cause an employer to discriminate against an employee	8(b)(2)
4. Refuse to bargain collectively with the employer	8(b)(3)
5. Require employees to pay excessive fees for membership	8(b)(5)
6. Engage in "featherbed practices" of seeking pay for services not performed	8(b)(6)
7. Use secondary boycotts (banned, except for publicity proviso)	8(b)(4)
8. Allow recognitional and organizational picketing by an uncertified union	8(b)(7)
9. Enter into "hot cargo" agreements, except for construction and garment industries	8(e)

* 29 U.S.C. §151.

38-2d Union Activity on Private Property

Although Section 7 of the NLRA gives employees the statutory right to self-organization, employers have the undisputed right to make rules to maintain discipline in their establishments. Generally speaking, employers may prohibit union solicitation by employees during work periods. During nonworking time, employers may prohibit activity and communications only for legitimate efficiency and safety reasons and only if the prohibitions are not manifestly intended to impede employees' exercise of their rights under the law. Nonunion employers, moreover, may not refuse to interview or retain union members because of their union membership. And even if a union pays an individual working for a nonunion employer to help organize the company, that individual is still protected under the NLRA.[27]

An employer may validly post its property against all nonemployee solicitations, including distribution of union literature, if reasonable efforts by the union through other available channels of communication would enable it to reach the employees with its message.[28]

38-2e Social Media and Section 7: Protected Activity for Union and Nonunion Workers

Section 7 of the NLRA grants all employees—union and nonunion—the right to engage in protected concerted activities pertaining to self-organization, forming, joining, or assisting a union or "for other mutual aid or protection."[29] Under Section 7, employees have a right to discuss their terms and conditions of employment with coworkers. Some employers' Internet and social media policies may be overly broad in that they may tend to chill employees' exercise of their Section 7 rights. **For Example,** the NLRB determined that a nonprofit organization, Hispanics United of Buffalo, Inc., unlawfully terminated five employees under its antiharassment policy because the employees posted comments on Facebook on a nonworkday, some of which were profane and sarcastic, in response to a complaint by a coworker, Cruz-Moore, about their job performance. The activity of the five nonunion employees was "concerted" within the protections of Section 7 of the act, because "they were taking the first step towards taking group action to defend themselves against the accusations they could reasonably believe Cruz-Moore was going to make to management." And, the fact that the employer lumped the five individuals together in terminating them, established that the employer viewed them as a group and that their activity was concerted.[30]

Though employees retain the right to talk about working conditions on social media, including discussing treatment by a supervisor in blunt language, case law will develop that not only protects Section 7 rights, but also protects employer rights to make rules to maintain discipline in the workplace and to protect the employer's reputation when a Facebook conversation on a page set to allow access to "friends of friends" involves very offensive, insulting, and disrespectful comments about supervisors or managers. The latter situation is not like a conversation between employees at a water cooler, where there is an expectation of privacy, but is more like calling the boss names on the plant floor in front

---

[27] *N.L.R.B. v. Town & Country Electric, Inc.*, 516 U.S. 85 (1995).

[28] *Lechmere, Inc. v. NLRB*, 502 U.S. 527 (1992).

[29] On June 18, 2012, the NLRB announced that it has launched a Web page describing the rights of employees to engage in concerted activity, even if they do not belong to a union. It is available at **http://www.nlrb.gov/concerted-activity.**

[30] *Hispanics United of Buffalo, Inc.*, 359 N.L.R.B. No. 37 (Dec. 14, 2012). See *Richmond District Neighborhood Center and Ian Callaghan*, 361 N.L.R.B. No. 74 (Oct. 28, 2014) where the N.L.R.B. found that the employer did not violate the NLRA when it terminated two individuals for egregious insubordinate Facebook posts.

of multiple employees and the public, as there is no expectation of privacy. This conduct does not involve protected concerted activity. Although discussion of grievances in the context of "mutual aid or protection" is protected under Section 7, an individual's personal griping is not.

38-2f Firing Employees for Union Activity

Although employers and supervisors often feel betrayed by individual employees who take leadership roles in forming organizations, the NLRA prohibits discrimination against such employees because of their union activity.

The NLRB has found evidence of discrimination against active union supporters when the employer

1. Discharges on the strength of past misdeeds that were condoned;
2. Neglects to give customary warnings prior to discharge;
3. Discharges for a rule generally unenforced;
4. Applies disproportionately severe punishment to union supporters; or
5. Effects layoffs in violation of seniority status with disproportionate impact on union supporters.

The NLRA preserves the right of the employer to maintain control over the workforce in the interest of discipline, efficiency, and pleasant and safe customer relations. Employees, on the other hand, have the right to be free from coercive discrimination resulting from union activity.

At times these two rights may collide. For example, an employee may be discharged for apparently two reasons: (1) violation of a valid company rule and (2) union activity. The employer gives the former as the reason for termination; the latter remains unstated on the employer's part, causing the filing of a Section 8(a)(3) unfair labor practice charge against the employer. These are known as *dual motive cases*. The general counsel must present on behalf of the dismissed employee a prima facie case that such protected conduct as union activity was a motivating factor in the dismissal. After this showing, the burden shifts to the employer, who must prove that the employee would have been dismissed for legitimate business reasons even absent the protected conduct.

CASE SUMMARY

The Sam Santillo Story

FACTS: Prior to his discharge, Sam Santillo was a bus driver for Transportation Management Corporation. On March 19, Santillo talked to officials of the Teamsters Union about organizing the drivers who worked with him. Over the next four days, Santillo discussed with his fellow drivers the possibility of joining the Teamsters and distributed authorization cards. On the night of March 23, George Patterson, who supervised Santillo and the other drivers, told one of the drivers that he had heard of Santillo's activities. Patterson referred to Santillo as two-faced and promised to get even with him. Later that evening, Patterson talked to Ed West, who was also a bus driver. Patterson asked, "What's with Sam and the Union?" Patterson said that he took Santillo's actions personally, recounted several favors he had done for Santillo, and added that he would remember Santillo's activities when Santillo again asked for a favor. On Monday, March 26, Santillo was discharged. Patterson told Santillo that he was being fired for leaving his keys in the bus and taking unauthorized breaks. Santillo filed charges with the Board, and the general counsel issued a complaint,

The Sam Santillo Story continued

contending that Santillo was discharged because of his union activities in distributing authorization cards to fellow employees. The evidence revealed that the practice of leaving keys in buses was commonplace among company employees and the company tolerated the practice of taking coffee breaks. The company had never taken disciplinary action against an employee for the behavior in question.

DECISION: Judgment for Santillo and the NLRB. The general counsel established a prima facie case by showing that

Santillo was involved in union-organizing activities just prior to his discharge. The employer did not meet its burden of proving that Santillo was fired for a legitimate business reason. The infractions involved were commonplace, and no discipline had ever been issued to any employee previously. The reasons given by the company were pretextual. Santillo would not have been fired had the employer not considered his effort to establish a union. [*NLRB v. Transportation Management Corp.,* 462 U.S. 393 (1983)]

38-2g Duty of Employer to Bargain Collectively

Once a union wins a representative election, the Board certifies the union as the exclusive bargaining representative of the employees. The employer then has the obligation under the NLRA to bargain with the union in good faith over wages, hours, and working conditions. These matters are *mandatory subjects of bargaining* and include seniority provisions, promotions, layoff and recall provisions, no-strike no-lockout clauses, and grievance procedures. Employers also have an obligation to bargain about the "effects" of the shutdown of a part of a business[31] and may have an obligation to bargain over the decision to relocate bargaining unit work to other plants.[32] Absent clearly expressed consent by a union, an employer violates its duty to bargain by changing a term or condition of employment without first bargaining to impasse with a union. **For Example,** Aramark Educational Services violated the NLRA when it unilaterally implemented a new, strict "Social Security no-match" policy of suspending employees with uncorrected discrepancies in their Social Security numbers prior to any discussion and impasse in bargaining with UNITE HERE Local 26.[33]

Permissive subjects of bargaining are those over which an employer's refusal to bargain is not a Section 8(a)(5) unfair labor practice. Examples are the required use of union labels, internal union affairs, and benefits for already retired workers.

38-2h Right to Work

right-to-work laws—laws restricting unions and employees from negotiating clauses in their collective bargaining agreements that make union membership compulsory.

The NLRA allows states to enact **right-to-work laws.** These laws restrict unions and employers from negotiating clauses in their collective bargaining agreements that make union membership compulsory.[34]

Advocates of such laws contend that compulsory union membership is contrary to the First Amendment right of freedom of association. Unions have attacked these laws as unfair because unions must represent all employees, and in right-to-work states where a majority of employees vote for union representation, nonunion employees receive all of the benefits of collective bargaining contracts without paying union dues.

---

[31] *First National Maintenance v. N.L.R.B.,* 452 U.S. 666 (1981).

[32] *Dubuque Packing Co. and UFCWIU, Local 150k,* 303 N.L.R.B. 66 (1991).

[33] *Aramark Educational Services, Inc.,* 335 N.L.R.B. No. 11 (Feb. 18, 2010).

[34] Right-to-work statutes declare unlawful any agreement that denies persons the right to work because of nonmembership in a union or the failure to pay dues to a union as a condition of employment. These laws have been adopted in Alabama, Arizona, Arkansas, Florida, Georgia, Idaho, Indiana Iowa, Kansas, Louisiana, Mississippi, Nebraska, Nevada, North Carolina, North Dakota, Oklahoma, South Carolina, South Dakota, Tennessee, Texas, Utah, Virginia, Wisconsin, and Wyoming.

38-2i Strike and Picketing Activity

If the parties reach an impasse in the negotiation process for a collective bargaining agreement, a union may call a strike and undertake picketing activity to enforce its bargaining demands. Strikers in such a situation are called **economic strikers.** Although the strike activity is legal, the employers may respond by hiring temporary or permanent replacement workers.

economic strikers– union strikers trying to enforce bargaining demands when an impasse has been reached in the negotiation process for a collective bargaining agreement.

Rights of Strikers

Economic strikers who unconditionally apply for reinstatement when their positions are filled by permanent replacements are not entitled to return to work at the end of the economic strike. They are, however, entitled to full reinstatement when positions become available.

CASE SUMMARY

Avoiding the Sack—The Pilots Returned before Their Positions Were Filled

FACTS: Striking pilots of Eastern Airlines made an unconditional offer to return to work on November 22, 1989. As of that date, some 227 new-hire replacement pilots were in training but had not obtained certificates from the Federal Aviation Administration permitting them to fly revenue flights. The striking pilots contended that the trainees were not permanent replacement pilots on the date they offered to go back to work because the trainees could not lawfully fly revenue flights. Eastern contended that the new-hire pilots were permanent employees and as such should not be displaced.

DECISION: The pilots' positions were not filled by permanent replacements at the time the striking pilots unconditionally applied to return to work. The new-hire replacement pilots were not qualified to fill the positions at that time. Giving preference to trainees over returning strikers would discourage employees from exercising their right to strike. [*Eastern Airlines Inc. v. Airline Pilots Association Int'l,* **970 F.2d 722 (11th Cir. 1990)]**

primary picketing–legal presentations in front of a business notifying the public of a labor dispute.

mass picketing–illegal tactic of employees massing together in great numbers to effectively shut down entrances of the employer's facility.

secondary picketing– picketing an employer with which a union has no dispute to persuade the employer to stop doing business with a party to the dispute; generally illegal under the NLRA.

Strikers responsible for misconduct while out on strike may be refused reemployment by the employer.

When employees strike to protest an employer's unfair labor practice, such as firing an employee for union-organizing activity, these unfair labor practice strikers have a right to return to their jobs immediately at the end of the strike. This right exists even if the employer has hired permanent replacements.[35]

Picketing

Placing persons outside a business at the site of a labor dispute so that they may, by signs or banners, inform the public of the existence of a labor dispute is called **primary picketing** and is legal. Should the picketing employees mass together in great numbers in front of the gates of the employer's facility to effectively shut down the entrances, such coercion is called **mass picketing;** it is illegal. **Secondary picketing** is picketing an employer with whom a union has no dispute to persuade the employer to stop doing business with a party to the dispute. Secondary picketing is generally illegal under the NLRA. An exception exists for certain product picketing at supermarkets or other

[35] *Poly America, Inc. v. N.L.R.B.,* 260 F.3d 465 (5th Cir. 2001).

multiproduct retail stores provided that it is limited to asking customers not to purchase the struck product at the neutral employer's store.[36]

38-2j Regulation of Internal Union Affairs

To ensure the honest and democratic administration of unions, Congress passed the Labor-Management Reporting and Disclosure Act (LMRDA).[37] Title IV of the LMRDA establishes democratic standards for all elections for union offices, including

1. Secret ballots in local union elections;
2. Opportunity for members to nominate candidates;
3. Advance notice of elections;
4. Observers at polling and at ballot-counting stations for all candidates;
5. Publication of results and preservation of records for one year;
6. Prohibition of any income from dues or assessments to support candidates for union office; and
7. Advance opportunity for each candidate to inspect the membership name and address lists.

38-3 Pension Plans and Federal Regulation

The Employee Retirement Income Security Act (ERISA)[38] was adopted in 1974 to protect employee pensions and benefits.

38-3a ERISA

The act sets forth fiduciary standards and requirements for administration, vesting, funding, and termination insurance.

Administration

Commonly a "benefits claims committee" is set up under the plan to make determinations about coverage issues, and courts will not disturb the finding of a benefits committee unless the determinations are "arbitrary and capricious." **For Example,** Joe Gustafson, who provided chauffeur services for senior executives at NYNEX for a number of years while classified as an independent contractor, sought benefits under ERISA because he asserted he was a common law employee of NYNEX. While the court determined he was in fact an employee entitled to overtime compensation under the Fair Labor Standards Act, the court was compelled to defer to the benefits committee's determination that Gustafson was not an employee under the NYNEX plan because he was not "on the payroll" as required by the plan guidelines. The court found that such a determination was not arbitrary or capricious.[39] Nevertheless, individuals may successfully challenge determinations of the plan administrators. **For Example,** Bell South denied ERISA-covered benefits to Suzanne Lee under both its Short Term Disability Plan and its Long Term Disability Plan. She suffered from chronic pain syndrome, and the

---

[36] *N.L.R.B. v. Fruit and Vegetable Packers, Local 760 (Tree Fruits, Inc.),* 377 U.S. 58 (1964); but see *N.L.R.B. v. Retail Clerks, Local 1001 (Safeco Title Ins. Co.),* 477 U.S. 607 (1980).
[37] 29 U.S.C. §§401–531.
[38] P.L. 93-406, 88 Stat. 829, 29 U.S.C. §§1001–1381.
[39] *Gustafson v. Bell Atlantic Corp.,* 171 F. Supp. 2d 311 (S.D.N.Y. 2001).

administrator determined that she had failed to submit "objective medical evidence" of her condition. The U.S. Court of Appeals reviewed the extensive medical record of pain care specialists supporting her diagnosis and determined that Bell South had acted arbitrarily and capriciously in denying Lee's claim of benefits.[40]

Fiduciary Standards and Reporting

Persons administering a pension fund must handle it to protect the interest of employees.[41]

The fact that an employer contributed all or part of the money to the pension fund does not entitle it to use the fund as though the employer still owned it. Persons administering pension plans must make detailed reports to the Secretary of Labor.

Vesting

Vesting is the right of an employee to pension benefits paid into a pension plan in the employee's name by the employer. Prior to ERISA, many pension plans did not vest accrued benefits until an employee had 20 to 25 years of service. Thus, an employee who was forced to terminate service after 18 years would have no pension rights or benefits. Under ERISA, employees' rights must be fully vested within five or seven years in accordance with the two vesting options available under the law.

In the past, it had been common for pension plans to contain break-in-service clauses, whereby employees who left their employment for a period longer than one year for any reason other than an on-the-job injury lost pension eligibility rights. Under the Retirement Equity Act of 1984,[42] an individual can leave the workforce for up to five consecutive years and still retain eligibility for pension benefits.

Funding

Pension funds may be broadly classified as "defined contribution plans" and "defined benefit plans."

A **defined contribution plan** is one that provides for an individual account for each plan participant and for benefits based solely on the amount contributed to the participant's account. It is also known as an *individual account plan.* These plans include 401(k) plans, employee stock option plans (ESOPs), profit-sharing plans, and stock bonus plans. Commonly, the employer establishes these plans and defines its own contributions to be matched by contributions from plan participants.

A **defined benefit plan** is an employer commitment to make specified future payments to participants upon retirement. The employer establishes a pension fund for this purpose, and the employer is contractually obligated to make those payments even if the assets set aside to finance the plan turn out to be inadequate. ERISA established an insurance plan, called the **Pension Benefit Guaranty Corporation (PBGC),** to protect employees covered under defined benefit plans should the employer go out of business.

In the case of defined benefit plans, the entire investment risk is on the employer who sponsors the plan. The employer must cover any underfunding that may result from the plan's poor performance. However, if the plan becomes overfunded, the employer may reduce or suspend its contributions.[43]

defined contribution plan–a plan providing individual accounts for each employee participant with benefits defined solely on the amounts contributed by each employee with matching contributions by the employer.

defined benefit plan–an employer established pension fund obligating the employer to make specified future payments to participants upon retirement.

Pension Benefit Guaranty Corporation (PBGC)–an insurance plan to protect employees covered by defined benefit plans in case an employer is unable to meet its payment obligations from the employer's pension fund.

---

[40] *Lee v. Bell South Telecommunications Inc.*, 318 Fed. Appx. 829 (11th Cir. 2009).
[41] *John Hancock Mutual Life Ins. Co. v. Harris Trust*, 510 U.S. 86 (1993).
[42] P.L. 98-397, 29 U.S.C. §1001.
[43] *Hughes Aircraft Co. v. Jacobson*, 523 U.S. 1093 (1998).

Defined contribution plans are the ones most frequently offered by employers today, in part because of the employers' risk of underfunding defined benefit plans. Defined contribution plans are not insured by the PBGC.

Enforcement

ERISA authorizes the Secretary of Labor and employees to bring court actions to compel the observance of statutory requirements.

38-4 Unemployment Benefits, Family Leaves, and Social Security

Generally, when employees are without work through no fault of their own, they are eligible for unemployment compensation benefits. Twelve-week maternity, paternity, or adoption leaves and family and medical leaves are available for qualifying employees. Social Security provides certain benefits, including retirement and disability benefits.

38-4a Unemployment Compensation

Unemployment compensation today is provided primarily through a federal-state system under the unemployment insurance provisions of the Social Security Act of 1935.[44] All states have laws that provide similar benefits, and the state agencies are loosely coordinated under the federal act. Agricultural employees, domestic employees, and state and local government employees are not covered by this federal-state system. Federal programs of unemployment compensation exist for federal civilian workers and former military service personnel. A separate federal unemployment program applies to railroad workers.

Eligibility

In most states, an unemployed person must be available for placement in a similar job and willing to take such employment at a comparable rate of pay. Full-time students generally have difficulty proving that they are available for work while they are still going to school.

If an employee quits a job without cause or is fired for misconduct, the employee is ordinarily disqualified from receiving unemployment compensation benefits. For example, stealing property from an employer constitutes misconduct for which benefits will be denied. Moreover, an employee's refusal to complete the aftercare portion of an alcohol treatment program has been found to be misconduct connected with work, disqualifying the employee from receiving benefits.

Funding

Employers are taxed for unemployment benefits based on each employer's "experience rating" account. Thus, employers with a stable workforce with no layoffs, who therefore do not draw on the state unemployment insurance fund, pay lower tax rates. Employers whose experience ratings are higher pay higher rates. Motivated by the desire to avoid higher unemployment taxes, employers commonly challenge the state's payment of unemployment benefits to individuals who they believe are not properly entitled to benefits. If an employee had good cause to resign her employment, she is eligible to receive benefits. **For Example,** Ms. Williams, a certified early childhood teacher, resigned her position at

---

[44] 42 U.S.C. §§301–1397e.

the Good Shepard Infant & Toddler Center because it was violating state regulations regarding child-to-staff ratios and it resisted Williams' attempt to get the matter corrected. The court found that she had good cause to resign and was eligible to receive unemployment compensation benefits.[45]

38-4b Family and Medical Leaves of Absence

The Family and Medical Leave Act of 1993 (FMLA)[46] entitles an eligible employee, whether male or female, to a total of 12 workweeks of unpaid leave during any 12-month period (1) because of the birth or adoption of the employee's son or daughter, (2) to care for the employee's spouse, son, daughter, or parent with a serious health condition, or (3) because of a serious health condition that makes the employee unable to perform the functions of his or her position. Notice should be given by the employer to an employee that the leave he or she is taking will count against FMLA entitlement in order to comply with the Secretary of Labor's regulations.[47] In the case of an employee's serious health condition or that of a covered family member, an employer may require the employee to use any accrued paid vacation, personal, medical, or sick leave toward any part of the 12-week leave provided by the act. When an employee requests leave because of the birth or adoption of a child, the employer may require the employee to use all available paid personal, vacation, and medical leave, but not sick leave, toward any FMLA leave.

To be eligible for FMLA leave, an employee must have been employed by a covered employer for at least 12 months and have worked at least 1,250 hours during the 12-month period preceding the leave. Covered employers are those that employ 50 or more employees.[48] Upon return from FMLA leave, the employee is entitled to be restored to the same or an equivalent position with equivalent pay and benefits. **For Example,** when Magda Brenlla returned to her position at LaSorsa Buick in the Bronx, New York, after quadruple bypass surgery, she was terminated by the owner, who told her that he had decided to consolidate the positions of office manager and controller, even though he had no business plan for restructuring, and soon thereafter had to hire additional help in the office. The judge upheld a jury verdict of $320,000, finding that the jury had ample evidence to conclude that the real reason for her termination was her FMLA leave.[49]

The FMLA provides specific statutory relief for violations of the provisions of the act, including pay to the employee for damages equal to lost wages and benefits or any actual monetary losses, plus interest, plus an equal amount in liquidated damages.[50]

38-4c Leaves for Military Service under USERRA

The Uniformed Services Employment and Re-Employment Rights Act (USERRA) was enacted in 1994 to encourage noncareer service in the armed services, minimize the disruption experienced in the civilian careers of reservists, and promote prompt reemployment of reservists upon return from military leave.[51] As updated in 2008, the USERRA has and will have a broad impact on U.S. employers as it provides reemployment

---

[45] *Williams v. Favored, LLC*, 443 S.W.3d 716 (Mo. App. 2014).
[46] 29 U.S.C. §§2601–2654.
[47] See *Ragsdale v. Wolverine World Wide, Inc.*, 535 U.S. 81 (2002).
[48] *Bellum v. PCE Constructors Inc.*, 407 F.3d 734 (5th Cir. 2005). Joint employers are obligated to honor FMLA-qualifying leaves. See *Grace v. USCAR*, 521 F.3d 655 (6th Cir. 2008).
[49] *Brenlla v. LaSorsa Buick*, 2002 WL 1059117 (S.D.N.Y. May 28, 2002).
[50] See *Arban v. West Publishing Co.*, 345 F.3d 390 (6th Cir. 2003), in which the U.S. Court of Appeals required the doubling of a jury verdict of $130,000 under the FMLA provision providing for liquidated damages unless the employer is able to prove that it acted "in good faith ..." and had reasonable grounds to believe it was not in violation of the FMLA. 29 U.S.C. §2617(a)(iii).
[51] 38 U.S.C. §4301.

and benefit protection rights for returning military personnel and prohibits discrimination against individuals because of their application for or performance of military service.[52]

Protections

Section 4312 of the USERRA generally requires returning reservists to be "promptly reemployed" and returned to the same or comparable positions of like seniority, status, and pay they would have had if they had not been activated. Moreover, Section 4316(c) provides that persons reemployed under the act shall not be discharged from employment within a year of their reemployment if their period of service was more than 180 days. For service of more than 30 days, the protective period is 180 days. However, the employer may terminate an individual for cause regardless of the duration of service.

Sections 4312(a)(3) and (4) provide protection for those disabled while in the service and requires employers to make reasonable efforts to accommodate each employee's disability so that each individual may return to the same or comparable positions or, if no longer qualified for the position, allow for the transfer to a position the disabled individual can perform closest to the prior position in terms of seniority, status, and pay.

Section 4323 of the act provides a full range of remedies, including back pay for loss of wages and benefits as well as liquidated damages in an amount equal to the actual damages when the employer's failure to comply with the act was willful. The act's enforcement is performed by the U.S. Justice Department's Division of Civil Rights.

CASE SUMMARY

USERRA—Because It's the Right Thing to Do!

FACTS: Michael Serricchio, an Air Force reservist, was employed as a financial advisor at Wachovia Securities and called up to active duty in the wake of September 11, 2001. Upon completion of his active duty, he sought to return to Wachovia with comparable earnings potential and opportunity for advancement. In the year prior to his activation for military duty, Mr. Serricchio was personally responsible for servicing in excess of 130 accounts, was responsible for managing in excess of $9 million dollars with his partner, and was earning $6,500 per month based on those assets. If Serricchio accepted Wachovia's reemployment offer, he would have been managing a handful of accounts, generating, according to Wachovia's own documents, a small amount in monthly commissions that had to be repaid to Wachovia to offset his monthly draw.

The employer argued that it provided the same draw and commission structure to the plaintiff and this was sufficient to fulfill its reemployment obligations under Section

4316. Serricchio contended that Wachovia's offer did not satisfy its obligation to reemploy him in a position of like pay; and the employer's failure to comply with the USERRA was willful, entitling him to double back pay as liquidated damages.

DECISION: Judgment for Serricchio. Wachovia understood that Serricchio had a right to be reinstated to his previous position as if he had never left. But even though Wachovia had a military-leave policy that expressly included that provision, the company did not offer Serricchio a position comparable to the one he held before leaving for military service. The court upheld an award of $389,453 in back pay, $389,453 in liquidated damages, $830,107 in attorneys' fees and costs, and $36,567 in interest for a total of $1.64 million. [*Serricchio v. Wachovia Securities, LLC,* 685 F.3d 169 (2d Cir. 2011)]

Defenses

In addition to an employer's right to terminate a reemployed service person for cause, employers may be excused from reemploying or continuing employment of persons under §4312(d)(1) of the act when the employer's circumstances have so changed as to make reemployment impossible, unreasonable, or an undue hardship. The burden of proof on the matter is on the employer.

38-4d Social Security

Employees and employers are required to pay Social Security taxes, which provide employees with four types of insurance protection: retirement benefits, disability benefits, life insurance benefits, and health insurance (Medicare). The federal Social Security Act established a federal program of aid for the aged, the blind, and the disabled. This is called the Supplemental Security Income (SSI) program. Payments are administered directly by the Social Security Administration, which became an independent government agency in 1995.

38-5 Employees' Health and Safety

The Occupational Safety and Health Act of 1970 (OSHA) was passed to assure every worker, so far as possible, safe and healthful working conditions and to preserve the country's human resources.[53] OSHA provides for (1) the establishment of safety and health standards and (2) effective enforcement of these standards and the other employer duties required by OSHA.

38-5a Standards

The Secretary of Labor has broad authority under OSHA to promulgate occupational safety and health standards.[54] Except in emergency situations, public hearings and publication in the *Federal Register* are required before the secretary can issue a new standard. Any person adversely affected may then challenge the validity of the standard in a U.S. Court of Appeals. The secretary's standards will be upheld if they are reasonable and supported by substantial evidence. The secretary must demonstrate a need for a new standard by showing that it is reasonably necessary to protect employees against a "significant risk" of material health impairment. The cost of compliance with new standards may run into billions of dollars. The secretary is not required to do a cost-benefit analysis for a new standard but must show that the standard is economically feasible.

38-5b Employer Duties

Employers have a "general duty" to furnish each employee a place of employment that is free from hazards that are likely to cause death or serious physical injuries.

OSHA requires employers to maintain records of occupational illness and injuries if they result in death, loss of consciousness, or one or more lost workdays or if they require medical treatment other than first aid. Such records have proven to be a valuable aid in recognizing areas of risk. They have been especially helpful in identifying the presence of occupational illnesses.

---

[53] 29 U.S.C. §651 *et seq.*
[54] *Martin v. OSHRC,* 499 U.S. 144 (1991).

38-5c **Enforcement**

The Occupational Safety and Health Administration (also identified as OSHA) is the agency within the Department of Labor that administers the act. OSHA has authority to conduct inspections and to seek enforcement action when noncompliance has occurred. Worksite inspections are conducted when employer records indicate incidents involving fatalities or serious injuries.[55] These inspections may also result from employee complaints. The act protects employees making complaints from employer retaliation. Employers have the right to require an OSHA inspector to secure a warrant before inspecting the employer's plant.

If OSHA issues a citation for a violation of workplace health or safety standards, the employer may challenge the citation before the Occupational Safety and Health Review Commission (OSHRC). Judicial review of a commission ruling is obtained before a U.S. Court of Appeals.

CASE SUMMARY

Risky Business

FACTS: On February 24, 2010, a performance was still in progress when Tilikum, a 32-year-old killer whale, seized Sea-World trainer Dawn Brancheau and pulled her off her platform into the pool causing her death. The Secretary of Labor issued citations to SeaWorld alleging two instances of "willful" violations of the general duty clause for exposing trainers to recognized hazards of drowning or injury when working with killer whales during performances. The Secretary of Labor set forth abatement procedures prohibiting trainers from working with whales unless the trainers are protected through the use of physical barriers or the use of decking systems. The Secretary proposed a penalty of $70,000. Sea-World appealed, contending that its training adequately controlled the risk. And, it asserted that trainers formally accept and control their own exposure to risks like the risks inherent in much of the sports and entertainment industries.

DECISION: Judgment for the Secretary of Labor. The general duty clause, §5(a)(1) of the Act, provides, "Each employer shall furnish to each of his employees a place of employment … free from recognized hazards … likely to cause death or serious physical harm to his employees." SeaWorld's assertion that working with killer whales is not a recognized hazard because its training controls the risk is rejected. The record of incident reports and the death of Ms. Brancheau demonstrate that a recognized hazard existed. The employer's duty to ensure a safe workplace is on the employer and not the employee. The "assumption of risk" doctrine is rejected. Moreover, the abatement procedures are feasible. [*SeaWorld of Florida, LLC v. Perez*, **748 F.3d 1202 (D.C. Cir. 2014)]**

The Occupational Safety and Health Act provides that no employer shall discharge or in any manner discriminate against employees because they filed a complaint with OSHA, testified in any OSHA proceeding, or exercised any right afforded by the act. A regulation issued by the Secretary of Labor under the act provides that if employees with no reasonable alternative refuse in good faith to expose themselves to a dangerous condition, they will be protected against subsequent discrimination. The Secretary of Labor may obtain injunctive and other appropriate relief in a U.S. district court against an employer who discriminates against employees for testifying or exercising any right under the act.

---

[55] *Chao v. Mallard Bay Drilling Co.*, 534 U.S. 235 (2002).

THINKING THINGS THROUGH

Taking Chances or Shortcuts in Violation of OSHA Standards Is Bad Management

John Carlo, Inc. (JCI), was installing a sewer line down the middle of an existing roadway in Jacksonville, Florida. The new line crossed under an existing gas line that was perpendicular to the proposed sewer line. The JCI crew worked in two stacked trench boxes, laying pipe up to the location where the pipeline crossed the trench for the sewer line. OSHA regulations require protection of employees from cave-ins; trench boxes and sloping of trench walls provide this protection. The following day, the crew removed the top trench box because both boxes would not fit under the perpendicular gas line. The crew pulled the bottom box under the perpendicular gas line and prepared the bottom of the trench to lay one joint of the sewer pipe. Project superintendent Cox had discussed this move with his foreman Jacobs. Jacobs reminded Cox that this move would leave the top portion of the trench unprotected. Cox explained that he realized the problem, but because JCI had bid the project based on 6-foot-wide trenches, they could not slope the trenches. The supervisors anticipated that just 15 minutes was needed to lay the one joint of pipe. Two crew members entered the trench to lay the pipe. The trench walls above the box (approximately 6 feet) were not sloped or otherwise protected. A large clay ball dislodged, fell into the trench, and struck one employee, who eventually died as a result.

Thinking Things Through, was it a reasonable risk for the employer to utilize the two employees in the trench for just 15 minutes to lay one joint of pipe? Of course not! The ALJ found that both supervisors "knowingly and deliberately" violated the OSHA standard because it was "more expedient to place employees in an unprotected trench ... than to take the time to adequately shore up or slope the trench to protect the employees." The $50,000 willful violation penalty was upheld by the U.S. Court of Appeals.*

In 1970, the year that OSHA became law, the American population was approximately 204,000,000; over 14,000 workers were killed in industrial accidents. In 2013, with the U.S. population at an estimated 316,500,000, some 4,405 workers were killed in work-related incidents. OSHA has drastically improved the safety and health of workers. OSHA standards are commonly devised as corrective responses to the occurrence of previous fatalities or injuries on often similarly situated work sites. Employees are empowered to refuse to expose themselves to dangerous duties under the *Whirlpool v. Marshall* U.S. Supreme Court decision.** Management and employees must always be encouraged to take the safe course!

John Carlo, Inc. v. Secretary of Labor, 2008 CCH OSHD 1 32,929.
445 U.S. 1 (1980).

38-5d State "Right-to-Know" Legislation

Laws that guarantee individual workers the "right to know" if there are hazardous substances in their workplaces have been enacted by many states in recent years. These laws commonly require an employer to make known to an employee's physician the chemical composition of certain workplace substances in connection with the employee's diagnosis and treatment by the physician. Furthermore, local fire and public health officials, as well as local neighborhood residents, are given the right to know if local employers are working with hazardous substances that could pose health or safety problems.

38-6 Compensation for Employees' Injuries

For most kinds of employment, workers' compensation statutes govern compensation for injuries. These statutes provide that an injured employee is entitled to compensation for accidents occurring in the course of employment from a risk involved in that employment.

38-6a Common Law Status of Employer

In some employment situations, common law principles apply. Workers' compensation statutes commonly do not apply to employers with fewer than a prescribed minimum number of employees or to agricultural, domestic, or casual employment. When an exempted area of employment is involved, it is necessary to consider the duties and defenses of employers apart from workers' compensation statutes.

Duties

The employer is under the common law duty to furnish an employee with a reasonably safe place in which to work, reasonably safe tools and appliances, and a sufficient number of competent fellow employees for the work involved. The employer is also under the common law duty to warn the employee of any unusual dangers particular to the employer's business.

Defenses

At common law, the employer is not liable to an injured employee if the employee is harmed by the act of a fellow employee. Similarly, an employer is not liable at common law to an employee harmed by an ordinary hazard of the work because the employee assumed such risks. If the employee is guilty of contributory negligence, regardless of the employer's negligence, the employer is not liable at common law to an injured employee.

38-6b Statutory Changes

The rising incidence of industrial accidents resulting from the increasing use of more powerful machinery and the growth of the industrial labor population led to a demand for statutory modification of common law rules relating to the liability of employers for industrial accidents.

Modification of Employer's Common Law Defenses

One type of change by statute was to modify the defenses that an employer could assert when sued by an employee for damages. For example, under the Federal Employer's Liability Act (FELA), which covers railroad workers, the injured employee must still bring an action in court and prove the negligence of the employer or other employees. However, the burden of proving the case is made lighter by limitations on employers' defenses. Under FELA, contributory negligence is a defense only in mitigation of damages; assumption of the risk is not a defense.[56]

Workers' Compensation

A more sweeping development was made by the adoption of workers' compensation statutes in every state. In addition, civil employees of the U.S. government are covered by the Federal Employees' Compensation Act. When an employee is covered by a workers' compensation statute and the injury is job connected, the employee's remedy is limited to that provided in the workers' compensation statute.[57]

Workers' compensation proceedings are brought before a special administrative agency or workers' compensation board. In contrast, a common law action for damages or an action for damages under an employer's liability statute is brought in a court of law.

---

[56] 45 U.S.C. §1 *et seq.*
[57] In *Fu v. Owens*, 622 F.3d 880 (8th Cir. 2010), Helen Fu's injuries, incurred when a coworker assaulted her at work at a Target-owned clinic in Minnesota, occurred because she was at the job, in touch with associations and conditions inseparable from it. The injuries occurred because she was on the job and thus she was subject to the exclusivity provision of the Workers' Compensation Act.

CASE SUMMARY

Locked in

FACTS: Bryant is the administrator of the estate of the deceased and the guardian of the deceased's minor child. Bryant sued Wal-Mart for damages following the death of the deceased based on the theory of false imprisonment. While working on the night restocking crew, the deceased suffered a stroke. Medical personnel arrived six minutes later but could not enter the store because management had locked all doors of the store for security reasons and no manager was present to open a door. By the time the medical crew entered the store to assist her, they were unable to revive her, and she died 15 hours later. Bryant contended that the false imprisonment occurred between the time the deceased became ill and the time the medical team was

unable to enter the store. Wal-Mart contended that Bryant's exclusive remedy is the Workers' Compensation Act.

DECISION: Judgment for Wal-Mart. It is well settled that a claim under the Workers' Compensation Act is the sole and exclusive remedy for injury or occupational disease incurred in the course of employment. In exchange for the right to recover scheduled compensation without proof of negligence on the part of the employer, employees forgo other rights and remedies they once had. Injuries to an employee's peace, happiness, and feelings are not compensable under the act. [*Bryant v. Wal-Mart Stores, Inc.*, **417 S.E.2d 688 (Ga. Ct. App. 1992)**]

For injuries arising within the course of the employee's work from a risk involved in that work, workers' compensation statutes usually provide (1) immediate medical benefits, (2) prompt periodic wage replacement, often computed as a percentage of weekly wages (ranging from 50 to 80 percent of the injured employee's wage) for a specified number of weeks, and (3) a death benefit of a limited amount.[58] In such cases, compensation is paid without regard to whether the employer or the employee was negligent. However, no compensation is generally allowed for a willful, self-inflicted injury or one sustained while intoxicated.[59]

There has been a gradual widening of the workers' compensation statutes, so compensation today is generally recoverable for both accident-inflicted injuries and occupational diseases.

38-7 Employee Privacy

Employers may want to monitor employee telephone conversations in the ordinary course of their business to evaluate employee performance and customer service; to document business transactions between employees and customers; or to meet special security, efficiency, or other needs. Employers may likewise want to monitor e-mail for what they perceive to be sound business reasons. Employers also may seek to test employees for drug use or search employee lockers for illicit drugs. Litigation may result because employees may believe that such activities violate their right to privacy.

38-7a Source of Privacy Rights

The Bill of Rights contained in the U.S. Constitution, including the Fourth Amendment, which protects against unreasonable search and seizure, provides a philosophical and legal basis for individual privacy rights for federal employees. The Fourteenth Amendment applies this privacy protection to actions taken by state and local governments that affect

[58] *Union Light & Power Co. v. DC Department of Employment Services*, 796 A.2d 665 (D.C. App. 2002).
[59] See *Beck v. Newt Brown Contractors, LLC*, 72 So. 3d 982 (La. App. 2011).

their employees. The privacy rights of individuals working in the private sector are not directly controlled by the Bill of Rights, however, because challenged employer actions are not government actions. Limited employee privacy rights in the private sector are provided by statute, case law, and collective bargaining agreements.

38-7b Monitoring Employee Telephone Conversations

The Federal Wiretapping Act[60] makes it unlawful to intercept oral and electronic communications and provides for both criminal liability and civil damages against the violator. There are two major exceptions, however. The first allows an employer to monitor a firm's telephones in the "ordinary course of business" through the use of extension telephones; a second exception applies when there is prior employee consent to the interception. If employer monitoring results in the interception of a business call, it is within the ordinary-course-of-business exception. Personal calls can be monitored, however, only to the extent necessary to determine that the call is personal, and the employer must then cease listening. **For Example,** Newell Spears taped all phone conversations at his store in trying to find out if an employee was connected to a store theft. He listened to virtually all 22 hours of intercepted and recorded telephone conversations between his employee Sibbie Deal and her boyfriend Calvin Lucas without regard to the conversations' relation to Spears's business interest. While Spears might well have legitimately monitored Deal's calls to the extent necessary to determine that the calls were personal and made or received in violation of store policy, the scope of the interception in this case was well beyond the boundaries of the ordinary-course-of-business exception and in violation of the act.[61]

Employer monitoring of employee phone calls can be accomplished without fear of violating the act if consent is established. Consent may be established by prior written notice to employees of the employer's monitoring policy. It is prudent, as well, for the employer to give customers notice of the policy through a recorded message as part of the employer's phone-answering system.

38-7c E-Mail Monitoring

Electronic mail (e-mail) is a primary means of communication in many of today's businesses, serving for some employers as an alternative to faxes, telephones, or the U.S. Postal Service. Employers may want to monitor employees' e-mail messages to evaluate the efficiency and effectiveness of their employees or for corporate security purposes, including the protection of trade secrets and other intangible property interests. When employees are disciplined or terminated for alleged wrongful activities discovered as a result of e-mail searches, however, the issue of privacy may be raised. The Electronic Communications Privacy Act of 1986 (ECPA)[62] amended the federal wiretap statute and was intended in part to apply to e-mail. However, ordinary-course-of-business and consent exceptions apply to e-mail, and it would appear that employers have broad latitude to monitor employee e-mail use. **For Example,** the e-mails that Gina Holmes sent to her personal attorney on a company-issued computer regarding litigation with the company were not protected by the attorney-client privilege because the company handbook stated that employees were prohibited from using the computer to send or receive personal e-mails. Moreover, the company warned that it would monitor its technology resources for compliance with its computer policy, and that employees "have no rights of privacy" with respect to information on the computers.[63] Very few cases involving e-mail and Web site issues

60 Title III of the Omnibus Crime Control and Safe Streets Act of 1968, 28 U.S.C. §§2510–2520.
61 *Deal v. Spears*, 580 F.2d 1153 (8th Cir. 1992); *Arias v. Mutual Central Alarm Services, Inc.*, 182 F.R.D. 407 (S.D.N.Y. 1998).
62 18 U.S.C. §§2510–2520.
63 *Holmes v. Petrovich Development Co.*, 191 Cal. App. 4th 1047 (3d Dist. 2011).

have been adjudicated so far under the ECPA. It has been held that for an employee's secure Web site to be "intercepted" in violation of the wiretap act, the electronic documents acquired must be acquired during transmission, not while in electronic storage.[64]

An employer can place itself within the consent exception of the act by issuing a policy statement to all employees that informs them of the monitoring program and its purposes and justification.

38-7d **Property Searches**

Protected by the Fourth Amendment, public-sector employees have a reasonable expectation of privacy with respect to their desks and file cabinets. However, depending on the fact-specific purpose, justification, and scope of the search, the balance of interest should favor the public employer because its interests in supervision, control, and the efficient operation of the workplace outweigh a public employee's privacy interests.[65] Search of a postal service employee's locker was held not to be a Fourth Amendment violation because well-publicized regulations informed employees that their lockers were subject to search to combat pilferage and stealing. However, the warrantless search of the desk and files of a psychiatrist employed by a state hospital was found to be a Fourth Amendment violation, exceeding the scope of a reasonable work-related search when the search examined his private possessions, including purely personal belongings, and management sought to justify the search on false grounds.[66]

In the private sector, employers may create a reasonable expectation of privacy by providing an employee a locker and allowing the employee to provide his or her own lock. A search of that locker could be an invasion of privacy.[67] If, however, the employer provides a locker and lock but retains a master key and this is known to employees, the lockers may be subject to legitimate reasonable searches by the employer. If a private-sector employer notifies all employees of its policy on lockers, desks, and office searches and the employer complies with its own policy, employees will have no actionable invasion of privacy case.

Many businesses use overt or hidden video cameras as a security method in the workplace to enhance worker safety and to prevent and/or detect theft or other criminal conduct. To avoid state constitutional or statutory claims for invasion of privacy, employers should not set up video cameras in areas where employees have a reasonable expectation of privacy.[68] Utilizing signs to notify employees and members of the public that certain areas are under video surveillance is a common business practice not likely to initiate privacy claims. Additionally, employers should disseminate their written policy on surveillance and obtain a consent form from employees acknowledging that they received this notice to preserve their consent defense.

38-7e **Drug and Alcohol Testing**

Drug and alcohol testing is an additional source of privacy concerns for employees. Public-sector employees may see drug and alcohol testing as potentially infringing on their Fourth

---

[64] *Konop v. Hawaiian Airlines, Inc.,* 302 F.3d 868 (9th Cir. 2002); *Fraser v. Nationwide Mutual Insurance Co.,* 352 F.3d 107 (3d Cir. 2003) (court held that the wiretaps act was not violated because the employer did not "intercept" the e-mail but retrieved it after it had been sent and received).

[65] *O'Connor v. Ortega,* 480 U.S. 709 (1987).

[66] *Ortega v. O'Connor,* 146 F.3d 1149 (9th Cir. 1998).

[67] *Kmart Corp. v. Trotti,* 677 S.W.2d 632 (Tex. App. 1984).

[68] See *Kline v. Security Guards, Inc.,* 386 F.3d 246 (3d Cir. 2004). Some 370 employees of Dana Corporation's Reading, Pennsylvania, facility sued the corporation and its security guard company after employees learned that a new audio and video surveillance system at the entrance of the facility allowed what was said in the area where employees "punch in" for work to be observed and heard in the guard booth. The Third Circuit Court of Appeals rejected the employer's preemption claims and remanded the matter to the state court to handle the invasion of privacy and other tort claims.

and Fifth Amendment rights, although they may be subject to this testing on the basis of reasonable suspicion. In ordinary circumstances, however, random drug testing is not permissible in the public sector except for mass transit workers and some safety-sensitive positions. The Federal Omnibus Transportation Employee Testing Act,[69] which covers certain classes of employees working in the airline, railroad, and trucking industries, makes covered employees subject to random drug and alcohol testing. Random drug and alcohol testing of employees working in safety-sensitive positions in the private sector also is permissible, as is the testing of private-sector employees on the basis of reasonable suspicion.

38-8 Employment-Related Immigration Laws

The Immigration and Naturalization Act (INA), the Immigration Reform and Control Act of 1986 (IRCA), and the Immigration Act of 1990[70] are the principal employer-related immigration laws. Administration of these laws was formerly under the Immigration and Naturalization Service and is now reorganized under the Department of Homeland Security (DHS) as the United States Bureau of Citizenship and Immigration Services (USCIS).

38-8a Employer Liability

The IRCA sets criminal and civil penalties against employers who knowingly hire aliens who have illegally entered the United States. The IRCA was designed to stop illegal immigration by eliminating job opportunities for these aliens.

38-8b Employer Verification

Upon hiring a new employee, an employer must verify that the employee is authorized to work in the United States. USCIS has designated Form I-9, Immigration Eligibility Verification Form, as the official verification form to comply with the IRCA.

The prospective employee must complete the initial portion of Form I-9, attesting under the penalty of perjury that he or she is a U.S. citizen or is authorized to work in the United States, and that the verification document(s) presented to the employer are genuine and relate to the signer. The employer must then review the documents that support the individual's right to work in the United States.

In April 2011, USCIS issued a final rule on acceptable identity documents for the I-9 employment eligibility process, divided into three sections.[71] List A documents verify identity and employment authorization and include a U.S. passport, the new U.S. passport card, and the temporary Form I-551 (permanent resident card) or a permanent resident card that includes a machine-readable immigrant visa. List B documents verify only identity; an example is a state-issued driver's license. List C documents, such as a Social Security card or official birth certificate, verify employment authorization. The employer is prohibited from requiring other documentation.[72]

E-Verify

Employers may verify new employee eligibility status through the federal government's mostly voluntary employment verification program called E-Verify. The E-Verify system is an Internet-based voluntary system that electronically compares information on I-9

[69] P.L. 102-143, 105 Stat. 952, 49 U.S.C. §1301 nt.
[70] P.L. 101-649, 8 U.S.C. §1101.
[71] See *Federal Register* (Apr. 15, 2011). USCIS stated that concerns about document fraud were among the most important reasons for this rulemaking.
[72] 8 U.S.C. §1324B (a)(b).

forms with records at the Social Security Administration and the Department of Homeland Security (DHS). In 2010, DHS instituted a U.S. passport photo matching program by comparing E-Verify data with State Department records. Employers that use E-Verify must notify applicants that they use E-Verify and cannot use the program as a prescreening tool. USCIS statistics for FY 2010 on E-Verify use showed that 98.3 percent of new hires surveyed were confirmed "work authorized" in three to five seconds.

Executive Order 12989 was amended in 2008 to require federal contractors to use E-Verify to confirm the employment eligibility of their workforce.

Under the Legal Arizona Workers Act, upheld by the Supreme Court, all an Arizona employer is required to do to avoid sanctions is to use the I-9 system and E-Verify.[73]

Many technology companies are utilizing L-1 visas as an alternative to the H-1B visas. Although the H-1B visa program requires employers to pay foreign workers the prevailing U.S. wage for a particular job, the L-1 visa has no such requirement. For example, an engineer on an L-1 visa from India may be paid the same wage rate as paid in India, rather than the much higher prevailing rate for U.S. engineers. USCIS requires each transferee, or his or her employer, to demonstrate that the transferee's responsibilities are "primarily managerial."

For Example, Brazilian corporation Granite Ebenezer established a U.S.-based affiliate, Brazil Quality Stones, Inc. (BQS), as a California corporation. Eugene dos Santos, a Brazilian citizen, served as President and CEO of both entities and owned 99 percent of the corporation's stock. Citizenship and Immigration Services determined that he was not entitled to an L-1 visa. Although BQS submitted an organizational chart with him at the top supervising five employees, only three had received pay during the quarter. The USCIS determined that BQS had not reached the level of development in which dos Santos could devote his primary attention to managerial duties as opposed to operational ones.[74]

Make the Connection

Summary

The relationship of employer and employee is created by the agreement of the parties and is subject to the principles applicable to contracts. If the employment contract sets forth a specific duration, the employer cannot terminate the contract at an earlier date unless just cause exists. If no definite time period is set forth, the individual is an at-will employee. Under the employment-at-will doctrine, an employer can terminate the contract of an at-will employee at any time for any reason or for no reason. Courts in many jurisdictions, however, have carved out exceptions to this doctrine when the discharge violates public policy or is contrary to good faith and fair dealing in the employment relationship. The Fair Labor Standards Act regulates minimum wages, overtime hours, and child labor.

Under the National Labor Relations Act, employees have the right to form a union to obtain a collective bargaining contract or to refrain from organizational activities. The National Labor Relations Board conducts elections to determine whether employees in an appropriate bargaining unit desire to be represented by a union. The NLRA prohibits employers' and unions' unfair labor practices and authorizes the NLRB to conduct proceedings to stop such practices. Economic strikes have limited reinstatement rights. Federal law sets forth democratic standards for the election of union offices.

The Employees Retirement Income Security Act (ERISA) protects employees' pensions by requiring (1) high standards of those administering the funds,

[73] *Chamber of Commerce of the United States v. Whiting*, 131 S. Ct. 624 (2011).
[74] *Brazil Quality Stones, Inc. v. Chertoff*, 531 F.3d 1063 (9th Cir. 2008).

(2) reasonable vesting of benefits, (3) adequate funding, and (4) an insurance program to guarantee payments of earned benefits.

Unemployment compensation benefits are paid to persons for a limited period of time if they are out of work through no fault of their own. Persons receiving unemployment compensation must be available for placement in a job similar in duties and comparable in rate of pay to the job they lost. Twelve-week maternity, paternity, and adoption leaves are available under the Family and Medical Leave Act. Employers and employees pay Social Security taxes to provide retirement benefits, disability benefits, life insurance benefits, and Medicare.

The Occupational Safety and Health Act provides for the (1) establishment of safety and health standards and (2) effective enforcement of these standards. Many states have enacted "right-to-know" laws, which require employers to inform their employees of any hazardous substances present in the workplace.

Workers' compensation laws provide for the prompt payment of compensation and medical benefits to persons injured in the course of employment without regard to fault. An injured employee's remedy is generally limited to the remedy provided by the workers' compensation statute. Most states also provide compensation to workers for occupational diseases.

The Bill of Rights is the source of public-sector employees' privacy rights. Private-sector employees may obtain limited privacy rights from statutes, case law, and collective bargaining agreements. Employers may monitor employee telephone calls, although once it is determined that the call is personal, the employer must stop listening or be in violation of the federal wiretap statute. The ordinary-course-of-business and consent exceptions to the Electronic Communications Privacy Act of 1986 (ECPA) give private employers a great deal of latitude to monitor employee e-mail. Notification to employees of employers' policies on searching lockers, desks, and offices reduces employees' expectations of privacy, and a search conducted in conformity with a known policy is generally not an invasion of privacy. Drug and alcohol testing is generally permissible if it is based on reasonable suspicion; random drug and alcohol testing may also be permissible in safety-sensitive positions.

Immigration laws prohibit the employment of aliens who have illegally entered the United States.

Learning Outcomes

After studying this chapter, you should be able to clearly explain:

38-1 The Employment Relationship

LO.1 Explain the contractual nature of the employment relationship

See the *FedEx* case in which the employment contract and the employee handbook both preserved the employer's at-will termination powers, page 764.
See the example of the public policy exception to the employment-at-will doctrine protecting home health care nurse Eugene Patterson, page 763.

LO.2 Explain how whistleblower protection under Sarbanes-Oxley is limited to conduct in violation of fraud or securities laws

See the example involving whistleblowers Tides and Neumann who were not protected under SOX because they disclosed information and documents to a newspaper and not a regulatory or law enforcement agency, page 765.

LO.3 Explain how Dodd-Frank expands whistleblower protection to a wide range of financial services employees and provides incentives for whistleblowers

See what a whistleblower must do to recover a bounty under Dodd-Frank, page 766.

38-2 Labor Relations Laws

LO.4 Explain how the National Labor Relations Act prohibits employers from firing employees attempting to form a union and requires employers to bargain with unions in good faith over wages, hours, and working conditions

See the *Sam Santillo* case on wrongful termination of an employee because of his union activity, pages 773–774.
See the role that the National Labor Relations Board plays in regulating employers' overly broad social media policies that are in violation of Section 7 of the NLRA, page 772.
See the discussion of mandatory and permissive subjects of bargaining, page 774.

38-3 Pension Plans and Federal Regulation

LO.5 Explain how ERISA protects employee pensions and benefits

See the Bell South example in which Ms. Lee successfully sued for disability benefits, pages 776–777.
See the discussion of defined contribution plans and defined benefit plans, page 777.

38-4   Unemployment Benefits, Family Leaves, and Social Security

`LO.6`   Explain the essentials of unemployment benefits, family and medical leaves, military leaves, and Social Security benefits

38-5   Employees' Health and Safety

`LO.7`   Explain how OSHA is designed to ensure workers' safe and healthful working conditions

See the Thinking Things Through discussion for reasons why taking chances or shortcuts in violation of OSHA standards is bad management, page 783.

See the *SeaWorld* case concerning a willful violation of the general duty clause, page 782.

38-6   Compensation for Employees' Injuries

`LO.8`   Explain the three types of benefits provided by Workers' Compensation statutes

38-7   Employee Privacy

`LO.9`   Explain the sources of privacy rights and applications to telephone, e-mail, and property searches

38-8   Employer-Related Immigration Laws

`LO.10`   Explain an employer's verification obligations when hiring new employees

Key Terms

defined benefit plan
defined contribution plan
economic strikers
employment-at-will doctrine

mass picketing
Pension Benefit Guaranty
   Corporation (PBGC)
primary picketing

right-to-work laws
secondary picketing
shop right

Questions and Case Problems

1. Robert Evjen was a full-time employee of Boise Cascade Co. At the same time, he was a full-time student at Chemata Community College. He was laid off as part of a general economy move by the employer. He applied for unemployment compensation. His claim was opposed on the ground that he was not "available for work" because he was going to school. Testimony showed that Evjen never missed work to go to classes, that he could not afford to go to school without working, and that, in case of any conflict between work and school, work came first. The employer countered that he needed to be available for all shifts of suitable work to qualify for unemployment benefits. Decide. [*Evjen v. Employment Agency*, 539 P.2d 662 (Or. App.)]

2. Michael Smyth was an operations manager at Pillsbury Co., and his employment status was that of an employee at will. Smyth received certain e-mail messages at home, and he replied to his supervisor by e-mail. His messages contained some provocative language, including the phrase "kill the backstabbing bastards" and a reference to an upcoming company party as the "Jim Jones Koolaid affair." Later, Smyth was given two weeks' notice of his termination, and he was told that his e-mail remarks were inappropriate and unprofessional. Smyth believes that he is the victim of invasion of privacy because the e-mail

messages caused his termination, and the company had promised that e-mail communications would not be intercepted and used as a basis for discipline or discharge. The company denies that it intercepted the e-mail messages and points out that Smyth himself sent the unprofessional comments to his supervisor. Is Smyth entitled to reinstatement and back pay because of the invasion of privacy? [*Smyth v. Pillsbury Co.*, 914 F. Supp. 97 (E.D. Pa.)]

3. Michael Hauck claimed that he was discharged by his employer, Sabine Pilot Service, because he refused its direction to perform the illegal act of pumping the bilges of the employer's vessel into the waterways. Hauck was an employee at will, and Sabine contends that it therefore had the right to discharge him without having to show cause. Hauck brought a wrongful discharge action against Sabine. Decide. [*Sabine Pilot Service, Inc., v. Hauck*, 687 S.W.2d 733 (Tex.)]

4. Jeanne Eenkhoorn worked as a supervisor at a business office for the New York Telephone Co. While at work, she invented a process for terminating the telephone services of delinquent subscribers. The telephone company used the process but refused to compensate her for it, claiming a shop right. Eenkhoorn then sued for damages on a quasi-contract

theory. Decide. [*Eenkhoorn v. New York Telephone Co.*, 568 N.Y.S.2d 677]

5. One Monday, a labor organization affiliated with the International Ladies Garment Workers Union, began an organizational drive among the employees of Whittal & Son. On the following Monday, six of the employees who were participating in the union drive were discharged. Immediately after the firings, the head of the company gave a speech to the remaining workers in which he made a variety of antiunion statements and threats. The union filed a complaint with the NLRB, alleging that the six employees were fired because they were engaging in organizational activity and were thus discharged in violation of the NLRA. The employer defended its position, arguing that it had a business to run and that it was barely able to survive in the global economy against cheap labor from third-world countries. It asserted that the last thing it needed was "union baloney." Was the NLRA violated?

6. David Stark submitted an application to the maintenance department of Wyman-Gordon Co. Stark was a journeyman millwright with nine years' experience at a neighboring company at the time of his application to Wyman-Gordon. Stark was vice president of the local industrial workers' union. In his preliminary interview with the company, Ms. Peevler asked if Stark was involved in union activity, and Stark detailed his involvement to her. She informed Stark that Wyman-Gordon was a nonunion shop and asked how he felt about this. Peevler's notes from the interview characterize Stark's response to this question as "seems to lean toward third-party intervention." Company officials testified that Stark's qualifications were "exactly what we were looking for," but he was not hired. Stark claimed that he was discriminated against. Wyman-Gordon denied that any discrimination had occurred. Is a job applicant (as opposed to an employee) entitled to protection from antiunion discrimination? On the facts of this case, has any discrimination taken place? [*Wyman-Gordon Co. v. N.L.R.B.*, 108 L.R.R.M. 2085 (1st Cir.)]

7. Armenda Malone and Stephen Krantz were induced to leave other employment and join ABI's CD-ROM division as national account managers in part because of a favorable commission agreement at ABI. Their employment relationship with ABI had no set duration, and as such they were employees at will. For the first two quarters of their employment, their commission reports were approved by the president of the division and paid without incident. Thereafter, a new

management team took over the division. When the mid-level manager presented third quarter commission reports based on the prior practice to the new vice president, Bruce Lowry, for approval, he was told, "You got to learn how to f—these people." Lowry then utilized severable variables—some of which the mid-level manager found "ridiculous"—to reduce the commission figures. After much discourse that carried on well into the fourth quarter, Lowry announced that a new model for determining commissions would be implemented. Commissions for both the third and fourth quarters, ending in December, were then calculated based on this model. ABI asserts that because Malone and Krantz were employees at will, the employer had the right to interpret or alter how it pays employees as it sees fit. Krantz and Malone left ABI and have sued for what they believe are the full commissions earned in the third and fourth quarters. Present a legal theory on behalf of Malone and Krantz for the payment of back commissions. Assess the strengths and weaknesses of Lowry's approach to employee relations. How would you decide this case? [*Malone v. American Business Information, Inc.*, 647 N.W.2d 569 (Neb.)]

8. Jane Richards was employed as the sole crane operator of Gale Corp. and held the part-time union position of shop steward for the plant. On May 15, Richards complained to OSHA concerning what she contended were seven existing violations of the Occupational Safety and Health Act that were brought to her attention by members of the bargaining unit. On May 21, she stated to the company's general manager at a negotiating session: "If we don't have a new contract by the time the present one expires on June 15, we will strike." On May 22, an OSHA inspector arrived at the plant, and Richards told her supervisor, "I blew the whistle." On May 23, the company rented and later purchased two large electric forklifts that were used to do the work previously performed by the crane, and the crane operator's job was abolished. Under the existing collective bargaining contract, the company had the right to lay off for lack of work. The contract also provided for arbitration, and it prohibited discipline or discharge without "just cause." On May 23, Richards was notified that she was being laid off "for lack of work" within her classification of crane operator. She was also advised that the company was not planning on using the crane in the future and that, if she were smart, she would get another job. Richards claimed that her layoff violated the

National Labor Relations Act, the Occupational Safety and Health Act, and the collective bargaining agreement. Was she correct?

9. Virgil Deemer and Thomas Cornwell, employees at a Whirlpool Corporation plant, refused to comply with a supervisor's order that they perform maintenance work on certain mesh screens located some 20 feet above the plant floor. Twelve days before a fellow employee had fallen to his death from the screens. Because they refused to do the work assigned them, they were told to punch out and go home; reprimands were placed in their files. Should employees be able to pick and choose what work they will perform? Do Deemer and Cornwell have any recourse? [*Whirlpool v. Marshall*, 445 U.S. 1]

10. In May, the nurses union at Waterbury Hospital went on strike, and the hospital was shut down. In mid-June, the hospital began hiring replacements and gradually opened many units. To induce nurses to take employment during the strike, the hospital guaranteed replacement nurses their choice of positions and shifts. If a preferred position was in a unit that was not open at that time, the hospital guaranteed that the individual would be placed in that position at the end of the strike. The strike ended in October and as the striking workers returned to work, the hospital began opening units that had been closed during the strike. It staffed many of these positions with replacement nurses. The nurses who had the positions prior to the strike and were waiting to return to work believed that they should have been called to fill these positions rather than the junior replacements who had held other positions during the strike. Decide. [*Waterbury Hospital v. NLRB*, 950 F.2d 849 (2d Cir.)]

11. Buffo was employed by the Baltimore & Ohio Railroad. Along with a number of other workers, he was removing old brakes from railroad cars and replacing them with new brakes. In the course of the work, rivet heads and scrap from the brakes accumulated on the tracks under the cars. This debris was removed only occasionally when the workers had time. Buffo, while holding an air hammer in both arms, was crawling under a car when his foot slipped on scrap on the ground, causing him to strike and injure his knee. He sued the railroad for damages under the Federal Employers Liability Act. Decide. [*Buffo v. Baltimore & Ohio Railroad Co.*, 72 A.2d 593 (Pa.)]

12. Mark Phipps was employed as a cashier at a Clark gas station. A customer drove into the station and asked him to pump leaded gasoline into her 1976 Chevrolet, an automobile equipped to receive only unleaded gasoline. The station manager told Phipps to comply with the request, but he refused, believing that his dispensing leaded gasoline into the gas tank was a violation of law. Phipps stated that he was willing to pump unleaded gas into the tank, but the manager immediately fired him. Phipps sued Clark for wrongful termination. Clark contended that it was free to terminate Phipps, an employee at will, for any reason or no reason. Decide. [*Phipps v. Clark Oil & Refining Corp.*, 396 N.W.2d 588 (Minn. App.)]

13. Reno, Nevada, police officers John Bohach and Jon Catalano communicated with each other on the Alphapage computer system, typing messages on a keyboard and sending them to each other by use of a "send" key. The computer dials a commercial paging company, which receives the message by modem, and the message is then sent to the person paged by radio broadcast. When the system was installed, the police chief warned that every Alphapage message was logged on the network, and he barred messages that were critical of department policy or discriminatory. The two police officers sought to block a department investigation into their messages and prevent disclosure of the messages' content. They claimed that the messages should be treated the same as telephone calls under federal wiretap law. The department contended that the system was essentially a form of e-mail whose messages are by definition stored in a computer, and the storage was itself not part of the communication. Was the federal wiretap law violated? [*Bohach v. City of Reno*, 932 F. Supp. 1232 (D. Nev.)]

14. Michael Kittell was employed at Vermont Weatherboard. While operating a saw at the plant, Kittell was seriously injured when a splinter flew into his eye and penetrated his head. Kittell sued Vermont Weatherboard, seeking damages under a common law theory. His complaint alleged that he suffered severe injuries solely because of the employer's wanton and willful acts and omissions. The complaint stated that he was an inexperienced worker, put to work without instructions or warning on a saw from which the employer had stripped away all safety devices. Vermont Weatherboard made a motion to dismiss the complaint on the ground that the Workers' Compensation Act provided the exclusive remedy for his injury. Decide. [*Kittell v. Vermont Weatherboard, Inc.*, 417 A.2d 926 (Vt.)]

CHAPTER 39

Equal Employment Opportunity Law

Laws of the United States reflect our society's concern that all Americans, including minorities, women, and persons with disabilities, have equal employment opportunities and that the workplace is free from discrimination and harassment. Title VII of the Civil Rights Act of 1964, as amended in 1972, 1978, and 1991, is the principal law regulating equal employment opportunities in the United States. Other federal laws require equal pay for men and women doing substantially the same work and forbid discrimination because of age or disability.

CPA ## 39-1 Title VII of the Civil Rights Act of 1964, as Amended

Title VII of the Civil Rights Act of 1964[1] seeks to eliminate employer and union practices that discriminate against employees and job applicants on the basis of race, color, religion, sex, or national origin. The law applies to the hiring process and to discipline, discharge, promotion, and benefits.

39-1a Theories of Discrimination

The Supreme Court has created, and the Civil Rights Act of 1991 has codified, two principal legal theories under which a plaintiff may prove a case of unlawful employment discrimination: disparate treatment and disparate impact.

A *disparate treatment* claim exists where an employer treats some individuals less favorably than others because of their race, color, religion, sex, or national origin. Proof of the employer's discriminatory motive is essential in a disparate treatment case.[2]

Disparate impact exists when an employer's facially neutral employment practices, such as hiring or promotion examinations, although neutrally applied and making no adverse reference to race, color, religion, sex, or national origin, have a significantly adverse or disparate impact on a protected group. In addition, the employment practice in question is not shown by the employer to be job related and consistent with business necessity. Under the disparate impact theory, it is not a defense for an employer to demonstrate that it did not intend to discriminate.

For Example, if plant manager Jones is heard telling the personnel director that the vacant welder's position should be filled by a male because "this is man's work," a qualified female applicant turned down for the job would prevail in a *disparate treatment* theory case against the employer because she was not hired because of her gender. Necessary evidence of the employer's discriminatory motive would be satisfied by testimony about the manager's "this is man's work" statement.

If the policy for hiring new pilots at Generic Airlines, Inc., required a minimum height of 5 feet 7 inches, and no adverse reference to gender was stated in this employment policy, nevertheless, the 5-feet-7-inch minimum height policy has an adverse or disparate impact on women because far fewer women than men reach this height. Such an employment policy would be set aside on a *disparate impact* theory, and a minimum height for the position would be established by the court based on evidence of job-relatedness and business necessity. A 5-feet-5-inch height requirement was set by one court for pilots.

[1] 42 U.S.C. §2000(e) *et seq.*
[2] *Woodson v. Scott Paper Co.,* 109 F.3d 913 (3d Cir. 1997).

CASE SUMMARY

Number 1 on the Charts! The Case That Created the Disparate Impact Theory

FACTS: Griggs and other black employees of the Duke Power Company's Dan River Station challenged Duke Power's requirement of a high school diploma and passing standardized general intelligence tests for transfer to more desirable "inside" jobs. The district court and Court of Appeals found no violation of Title VII because the employer did not adopt the diploma and test requirements with the purpose of intentionally discriminating against black employees. The Supreme Court granted *certiorari*.

DECISION: Judgment for Griggs. The absence of any intent on the part of the employer to discriminate was not a defense. Title VII prohibits not only overt discrimination but also practices that are fair in form but discriminatory in operation. If any employment practice, such as a diploma or testing requirement, that operates to exclude minorities at a substantially higher rate than white applicants cannot be shown to be "job-related" and consistent with "business necessity," the practice is prohibited. [*Griggs v. Duke Power Co.,* **401 U.S. 424 (1971)**]

"Disparate treatment" and "disparate impact" may both be at issue in the same case. **For Example,** as required by the city charter, the city of New Haven used objective examinations to identify those firefighters best qualified for promotion to fill vacant lieutenant and captain positions. On the basis of the examinations' results, no black candidates were eligible for immediate promotion. A rancorous public debate ensued. The city threw out the results based on the statistical racial disparity to avoid potential liability in a lawsuit based on *disparate impact* against the black candidates. White and Hispanic firefighters who passed the exams but were denied a chance for promotion by the city's refusal to certify the test results, sued the city, alleging a *disparate treatment* (intentional discrimination) case—that discarding the test results discriminated against them based on their race in violation of Title VII. The Supreme Court determined that the city rejected the test results because the higher-scoring candidates were white and that without some other justification this express race-based decision making is prohibited. The Court stated that "a strong basis in evidence" standard was necessary before the city could make an employment decision based on fear of liability under Title VII—and the Court held that the city did not meet this standard. The statistical disparity by itself was insufficient to constitute a strong basis in evidence of unlawful disparate impact. The examinations were job related and consistent with business necessity. And there was no strong basis in evidence of an equally valid, less-discriminating testing alternative. Thus, in a 5-4 decision, the U.S. Supreme Court ruled that the city had violated the civil rights of the white and Hispanic firefighters and remanded the case for further proceedings.[3]

39-1b The Equal Employment Opportunity Commission

The Equal Employment Opportunity Commission (EEOC) is a five-member body appointed by the president to establish equal employment opportunity policy under the laws it administers. The EEOC supervises the agency's conciliation and enforcement efforts.

---

[3] *Ricci v. DeStefano*, 557 U.S. 557 (2009). Contrary to the extensive presentation in the majority decision of the detailed steps taken to develop and administer the examinations, the dissent asserted that the Court had ignored substantial evidence of multiple flaws in the tests and that the Court had failed to acknowledge that better tests used in other cities have yielded less racially skewed outcomes. The decision, the dissent, and two concurrences provide an insight into the complexities of our judicial process.

The EEOC administers Title VII of the Civil Rights Act, the Equal Pay Act (EPA), the Age Discrimination in Employment Act (ADEA), Section 501 of the Rehabilitation Act (which prohibits federal-sector discrimination against persons with disabilities), and Title I (the employment provisions) of the Americans with Disabilities Act (ADA) and the ADA Amendments Act (ADAA).

Procedure

Where a state or local EEO agency with the power to act on claims of discriminatory practices exists, the charging party must file a complaint with that agency. The charging party must wait 60 days or until the termination of the state proceedings, whichever occurs first, before filing a charge with the EEOC. If no state or local agency exists, a charge may be filed directly with the EEOC so long as it is filed within 180 days of the occurrence of the discriminatory act. The commission conducts an investigation to determine whether reasonable cause exists to believe that the charge is true. If such cause is found to exist, the EEOC attempts to remedy the unlawful practice through conciliation. If the EEOC does not resolve the matter to the satisfaction of the parties, it may decide to litigate the case when systemic or unusual circumstances exist, including a "pattern or practice of discrimination." In most instances, however, the EEOC issues the charging party a *right-to-sue letter*. Thereafter, the individual claiming a violation of EEO law has 90 days to file a lawsuit in a federal district court.[4]

Pattern-or-Practice Cases. Section 707 of Title VII permits the EEOC to sue employers when it has reasonable cause to believe they are engaged in a *pattern or practice* of unlawful employment discrimination. It must establish that intentional discrimination was the defendant employer's "standard operating procedure." A first phase focuses on the employer's policy or practice, not on individual charges. Once the pattern or practice of discrimination is established, the process moves to the individual relief phase, where individual claims may be presented. The purpose of Section 707 is to provide the government with a swift and effective weapon to eliminate unlawful practices.[5]

Systemic "Class Action" Cases. The EEOC has placed renewed focus on identifying, developing, and litigating discrimination cases involving employment policies affecting large classes of individuals in every statute enforced by the agency. When an individual files a discrimination charge with the EEOC, it now may expand its investigation into that employer's related employment practices involving similarly situated individuals. Possible statutory violations discovered during the course of the investigation of the initial individual charge may lead the EEOC to bring a "systemic" case on behalf of a number of employees against the employer under Section 706 of the act.[6]

Damages

Title VII sets damages available to victims of discrimination (Figure 39-1).

---

[4] An individual who misses the filing deadline of Title VII may be able to bring a race discrimination case under the two-year time limit allowed under Section 1981 of the Civil Rights Act of 1964, codified at 42 U.S.C. §1981, and sometimes called a *Section 1981 lawsuit*. In the *Edelman v. Lynchburg College* decision, 535 U.S. 106 (2002), the U.S. Supreme Court approved an EEOC regulation that allows certain defective charges to be cured, with the cured charge relating back to the date the EEOC first received the initial charge, which was within the 300-day filing period.

[5] See *EEOC v. Mitsubishi Motor Manufacturing of America*, 102 F.3d 869 (7th Cir. 1996).

[6] Courts currently disagree on the extent of investigation and conciliation the EEOC must conduct in systemic cases. Some courts have held that the EEOC must conduct an investigation and attempt conciliation on each individual charge. See *EEOC v. CRST Van Expedited, Inc.*, 679 F.3d 657 (8th Cir. 2012). Other courts have found that the EEOC need only give the employer adequate notice that it was investigating on a class-wide basis and that it need not conciliate on behalf of each claimant. See *Serrano v. Cintas Corp.*, 699 F.3d 884 (6th Cir. 2012). The Supreme Court has recognized that the EEOC has broad discretion in conciliating claims but has not directly addressed this issue. See *Mach Mining, LLC v. EEOC*, 135 S. Ct. 1645 (2015).

| FIGURE 39-1 | **Unlawful Discrimination under Title VII of the Civil Rights Act of 1964 as Amended by the Civil Rights Act of 1991** |

DISCRIMINATORY TREATMENT IN EMPLOYMENT DECISIONS ON THE BASIS OF RACE, COLOR, RELIGION, SEX, OR NATIONAL ORIGIN

DISPARATE TREATMENT THEORY	DISPARATE IMPACT THEORY
NONNEUTRAL PRACTICE OR NONNEUTRAL APPLICATION	FACIALLY NEUTRAL PRACTICE AND NEUTRAL APPLICATION
REQUIRES PROOF OF DISCRIMINATORY INTENT	DOES NOT REQUIRE PROOF OF DISCRIMINATORY INTENT REQUIRES PROOF OF ADVERSE EFFECT ON PROTECTED GROUP AND EMPLOYER IS UNABLE TO SHOW THAT THE CHALLENGED PRACTICE IS JOB RELATED FOR THE POSITION IN QUESTION AND IS CONSISTENT WITH BUSINESS NECESSITY
EITHER PARTY HAS A RIGHT TO REQUIRE A JURY TRIAL WHEN SEEKING COMPENSATORY OR PUNITIVE DAMAGES	NO RIGHT TO A JURY TRIAL
REMEDY REINSTATEMENT, HIRING, OR PROMOTION BACK PAY LESS INTERIM EARNINGS RETROACTIVE SENIORITY ATTORNEY AND EXPERT WITNESS FEES PLUS COMPENSATORY* AND PUNITIVE DAMAGES DAMAGES CAPPED FOR CASES OF SEX AND RELIGIOUS DISCRIMINATION DEPENDING ON SIZE OF EMPLOYER:	REMEDY REINSTATEMENT, HIRING, OR PROMOTION BACK PAY LESS INTERIM EARNINGS RETROACTIVE SENIORITY ATTORNEY AND EXPERT WITNESS FEES

NUMBER OF EMPLOYEES	DAMAGES CAP
100 OR FEWER	$ 50,000
101 TO 200	100,000
201 TO 500	200,000
OVER 500	300,000
NO CAP ON DAMAGES FOR RACE CASES	

* COMPENSATORY DAMAGES INCLUDE FUTURE PECUNIARY LOSSES AND NONPECUNIARY LOSSES SUCH AS EMOTIONAL PAIN AND SUFFERING.

Section 706(k) of Title VII provides that the court in its discretion allow the prevailing party, other than the EEOC and the United States, a reasonable attorneys' fee. Thus, a court may award a prevailing individual in a Civil Rights Act lawsuit against an employer reasonable attorney fees and costs. It also may award attorneys' fees against the EEOC itself if the agency's lawsuit is without foundation. **For Example,** in *EEOC v. Peoplemark*, the federal district court awarded a temporary staffing firm, Peoplemark, the prevailing party in a lawsuit initiated by the EEOC, attorneys' fees, expert witness fees, and other expenses totaling $751,942.48, because the EEOC should have known at a certain point that there was no evidence supporting its complaint that the company maintained a policy adversely affecting a class of African Americans of denying employment to any person with a criminal record.[7]

The Arbitration Option

With the exception of transportation employees, employers can craft arbitration agreements that require employees to arbitrate any employment dispute, including statutory discrimination claims, and these mandatory arbitration clauses can be enforced in federal courts under the Federal Arbitration Act.[8] Courts do, however, require that the arbitration clauses be "fair." Moreover, a party agreeing to arbitration does not forgo substantive rights afforded by Title VII or alter federal antidiscrimination statutes. A fair arbitration clause requires adequate discovery, mandates that the arbitrator have authority to apply the same types of relief available from a court, and should not preclude an employee from vindicating statutory rights because of arbitration costs.[9]

A union may negotiate a provision in a collective bargaining agreement requiring all employment-related discrimination claims to be resolved in arbitration.[10]

39-1c Definition of "Supervisor"

Under Title VII an employer's liability for workplace harassment of employees may depend on the status of the harasser. If the harassing individual is the victim's coworker the employer is liable only if the employer was negligent in controlling working conditions. If the harasser is a "supervisor" who takes an adverse tangible employment action against the victim, the employer is strictly liable. The *Vance v. Ball State University* decision defines the word "supervisor" under Title VII of the Civil Rights Act of 1964.

CASE SUMMARY

It's About Abusing the Power Given by the Employer

FACTS: Maetta Vance sued her employer Ball State University (BSU) alleging that a fellow employee Saundra Davis created a racially hostile work environment in violation of Title VII. The trial court dismissed the case because Davis was not a "supervisor," and the matter progressed to the U.S. Supreme Court for resolution.

DECISION: Judgment for Ball State University. An employee is a "supervisor" for purposes of vicarious liability under Title VII only if the individual is empowered by the employer to take tangible employment actions against the victim, such as hiring, firing, failing to promote, reassignment with significantly different responsibilities, or a decision causing a significant change in benefits. Davis had no such authority. Moreover, there was no showing by Ms. Vance that BSU permitted harassment by a co-worker to occur. [*Vance v. Ball State University,* 133 S. Ct. 2434 (2013)]

[7] *EEOC v. Peoplemark*, 2010 WL 748250 (W.D. Mich. Feb. 26, 2010).
[8] *Circuit City Stores, Inc. v. Adams*, 532 U.S. 105 (2001).
[9] See *Circuit City II*, 279 F.3d 889 (9th Cir. 2002).
[10] For some 35 years it was widely understood that an individual may prospectively waive his or her own statutory right to a judicial forum and be compelled to resolve a statutory discrimination claim in arbitration, but a union may not prospectively waive that right for the individual in a collective bargaining agreement. See *Alexander v. Gardner-Denver Co.*, 485 U.S. 36 (1974) and *Gilmer v. Interstate/Johnson Lane Corp.*, 500 U.S. 20 (1991). In *14 Penn Plaza, LLC v. Pyett*, 556 U.S. 247 (2009), the U.S. Supreme Court, in a 5-4 decision, held that a provision in a collective bargaining agreement (CBA) negotiated under the National Labor Relations Act between a union and employer group that requires union members to arbitrate Age Discrimination in Employment Act (ADEA) claims is enforceable as a matter of federal law. Thus, the petitioner union members were precluded from bringing their ADEA case in federal court and the matter had to be resolved under the arbitration provisions of the CBA.

39-2 Protected Classes and Exceptions

To successfully pursue a Title VII lawsuit, an individual must belong to a protected class and meet the appropriate burden of proof. Exceptions exist for certain employment practices.

39-2a Race and Color

The legislative history of Title VII of the Civil Rights Act demonstrates that a primary purpose of the act is to provide fair employment opportunities for black Americans. The protections of the act are applied to blacks based on race or color.

The word *race* as used in the act applies to all members of the four major racial groupings: white, black, Native American, and Asian-Pacific. Native Americans can file charges and receive the protection of the act on the basis of national origin, race, or, in some instances, color. Individuals of Asian-Pacific origin may file discrimination charges based on race, color, or, in some instances, national origin. Whites are also protected against discrimination because of race and color.

For Example, two white professors at a predominately black university were successful in discrimination suits against the university when it was held that the university had discriminated against them on the basis of race and color in tenure decisions.[11]

39-2b Religion

Title VII requires employers to accommodate their employees' or prospective employees' religious practices. Most cases involving allegations of religious discrimination revolve around the determination of whether an employer has made reasonable efforts to accommodate religious beliefs.

If an employee's religious beliefs prohibit working on Saturday, an employer's obligation under Title VII is to try to find a volunteer to cover for the employee on Saturdays. The employer would not have an obligation to violate a seniority provision of a collective bargaining agreement or call in a substitute worker if such accommodation would require more than a *de minimis* or very small cost.

Garments Worn for Religious Reasons

Ordinarily employers have little reason to be informed or concerned about the religious practices of individual employees. However, because many Muslim women wear special clothing as part of their religious observances, which may conflict with an employer's safety or grooming standards, employers should develop appropriate and justifiable policies for their business and provide training for supervisors on how to properly handle requests for religious accommodations. **For Example,** a federal district court ruled in favor of a Muslim employee who was terminated for refusal to remove her head scarf when dealing with customers, where the employer did not strictly enforce its "company uniform policy" until after the terrorist attacks on September 11, 2001. The court did not accept the employer's argument that allowing an exception for the employee would lead to the need for many other exceptions, making its company uniform policy meaningless.[12]

---

[11] *Turgeon v. Howard University*, 571 F. Supp. 679 (D.D.C. 1983).

[12] *EEOC v. Alamo Rent-A-Car*, 432 F. Supp. 2d 1006 (D. Ariz. 2006). In a recent decision, the United States Supreme Court considered whether Abercrombie & Fitch violated Title VII when it did not hire a teenage Muslim woman who wore a headscarf because the company had a dress policy that did not allow employees to wear caps. The Court held that a job applicant does not have to show that the employer had "actual knowledge" that she was wearing the headscarf for religious reasons. She had to show only that the need for an accommodation was a motivating factor in the employer's decision not to hire her. *EEOC v. Abercrombie & Fitch Stores, Inc.*, 135 S. Ct. 2028 (2015).

Safety risks may provide a justifiable basis for a dress code. **For Example,** a court ruled that Kelly Services did not discriminate against a Muslim woman when it decided not to refer her to a client company, Nahan Printing, because she wears a khimar. She had been informed by a Kelly staffing supervisor that "you would have to take your scarf off—you cannot cover your hair," and the applicant replied that she could not remove her khimar because her religion required her to wear it. The EEOC asserted that the employer could have reasonably accommodated her by allowing her to tie her khimar back like people with long hair are allowed to do. However, the Nahan Printing executive explained that hair is permanent; a khimar is different from hair because of the risk that the khimar—like a hat—could fall off into the machinery; and the safety risk would be the worker reaching in and trying to grab it, pulling an individual into a piece of equipment or damaging equipment, or other individuals who are trying to help could potentially be hurt as well.[13]

Body Art Work Rules and Religious Beliefs

Employees have challenged employer bans on body art as religious discrimination, asserting that the employers have not made reasonable efforts to accommodate religious beliefs. EEOC's 1980 Guidelines broadly define religion "to include moral or ethical beliefs as to what is right and wrong which are sincerely held with the strength of traditional religious views."[14] The Guidelines do not limit religion to theistic practices or to beliefs professed by organized religions. **For Example,** Kimberly Cloutier was a member of the Church of Body Modification. Costco's grooming policy prohibited any "visible facial or tongue jewelry" in order to present a professional image to its customers. Ms. Cloutier wore an eyebrow ring as a religious practice. Ms. Cloutier rejected Costco's offer to return her to work if she wore a bandage or plastic retainer over the jewelry because it would violate her religious beliefs. The U.S. Court of Appeals determined that her refusal to accept an accommodation short of an exemption was an undue hardship for the employer because an exemption would negatively impact the company's policy of professionalism.[15]

Some courts, however, look for actual proof of harm to the employer in assessing whether undue hardship exists for an employer. **For Example,** the EEOC brought an action against Red Robin Gourmet Burgers, Inc., for failure to provide an exemption from its grooming policy for an employee's religious tattoos surrounding his wrists. The federal district court looked for actual proof of the restaurant's assertion that the tattoos contravened the company's "family-oriented image," such as customer complaints or other evidence, as opposed to the mere assertion. The court concluded that the employer failed to provide sufficient evidence of undue hardship in accommodating an exemption for the employee.[16]

Title VII permits religious societies to grant hiring preferences in favor of members of their religion. It also provides an exemption for educational institutions to hire employees of a particular religion if the institution is owned, controlled, or managed by a particular religious society. The exemption is a broad one and is not restricted to the religious activities of the institution.

---

[13] *EEOC v. Kelly Services, Inc.*, 598 F.3d 1022 (8th Cir. 2010).

[14] 29 C.F.R. §1605.1 (1980). The EEOC's definition of religion was derived from early Selective Service cases that moved beyond institutional religions and theistic belief structures in handling exemptions to the draft and military service. See *Welsh v. U.S.*, 398 U.S. 333, 343–44 (1970), which allows for expansion of belief systems to include nonreligious ethical or moral codes.

[15] *Cloutier v. Costco*, 390 F.3d 126 (1st Cir. 2004).

[16] *EEOC v. Red Robin Gourmet Burger, Inc.*, 2005 WL 2090677 (W.D. Wash. Aug. 29, 2005).

39-2c Sex

Employers who discriminate against female or male employees because of their sex are held to be in violation of Title VII. The EEOC and the courts have determined that the word *sex* as used in Title VII means a person's gender, not the person's sexual orientation. State and local legislation, however, may provide specific protection against discrimination based on sexual orientation.

Height, Weight, and Physical Ability Requirements

Under the *Griggs v. Duke Power* precedent, an employer must be able to show that criteria used to make an employment decision that has a disparate impact on women, such as minimum height and weight requirements, are, in fact, job related. All candidates for a position requiring physical strength must be given an opportunity to demonstrate their capability to perform the work. Women cannot be precluded from consideration just because they have not traditionally performed such work.

Pregnancy-Related Benefits

Title VII was amended by the Pregnancy Discrimination Act (PDA) in 1978. The amendment prevents employers from treating pregnancy, childbirth, and related medical conditions in a manner different from the manner in which other medical conditions are treated. Thus, women unable to work as a result of pregnancy, childbirth, or related medical conditions must be provided the same benefits as all other workers. These include temporary and long-term disability insurance, sick leave, and other forms of employee benefit programs. An employer who does not provide disability benefits or paid sick leave to other employees is not required to provide them for pregnant workers.[17]

The PDA also protects women from termination or other employment actions because of pregnancy. **For Example,** a catering manager who informed her employer that she would be taking a 12-week leave after childbirth during the busiest time of the year and was subsequently fired by her employer for "customer complaints," was able to bring suit against the employer under the PDA, where the employer's reason was a "pretext."[18] The PDA also protects women from discrimination after giving birth to a child for up to four months thereafter. **For Example,** Katherine Albin was allowed to pursue her claim against Thomas Pink clothing store that she was denied promotion to manager based on her "recent pregnancy," with the alleged discriminatory act occurring three and a half months from the date of birth of her first child.[19]

39-2d Sexual Harassment

Tangible employment action and hostile work environment are two classifications of sexual harassment.

---

[17] In *AT&T Corporation v. Hulteen*, 556 U.S. 701 (2009), the U.S. Supreme Court addressed a current effect of a pre-PDA personnel policy. Prior to the PDA of 1978, AT&T employees on "disability" leave received full-service credit toward retirement benefits for the entire period of absence. Pregnancy at that time was considered a "personal" leave of absence and women on this leave received a maximum service credit of 30 days. Upon retirement, Noreen Hulteen received seven months less service credit for the pre-PDA leave for a pregnancy than she would have had for the same leave time for a disability, and it resulted in a smaller pension benefit. The Court decided against Ms. Hulteen, determining that there was no intent to apply the PDA retroactively, and that AT&T's pre-PDA leave policy was not discriminatory when adopted.

[18] *Newman v. Deer Path Inn*, 1999 WL 1129105 (N.D. Ill. Nov. 7, 1999).

[19] *Albin v. LVMH Moet Louis Vuitton, Inc.* 2014 WL 3585492 (S.D.N.Y. July 8, 2014).

Tangible Employment Action

Sexual harassment classified as *tangible employment action* involves situations in which a supervisor performs an "official act" of the enterprise, such as discharge, demotion, or undesirable reassignment against a subordinate employee because of the employee's refusal to submit to the supervisor's demand for sexual favors. The employer is always vicariously liable for this harassment by a supervisor under the so-called aided-in-the-agency-relation standard. That is, the supervisor is aided in accomplishing the wrongful objective by the existence of the agency relationship. The employer empowered the supervisor as a distinct class of agent to make economic decisions affecting other employees under the supervisor's control. The employer can raise no affirmative defense based on the presence of an employer's antiharassment policy in such a case.

Hostile Work Environment

A second type of sexual harassment classified as *hostile work environment* occurs when a supervisor's conduct does not affect an employee's economic benefits but causes anxiety and "poisons" the work environment for the employee. Such conduct may include unwelcome sexual flirtation, propositions, or other abuses of a sexual nature, including the use of degrading words or the display of sexually explicit pictures.[20] This type of sexual harassment applies to all cases involving supervisors in which the enterprise takes no official act, including constructive discharge cases. The plaintiff must prove severe and pervasive conduct on the supervisor's part to meet the plaintiff's burden of proof.[21] The employer may raise an affirmative defense to liability for damages by proving that (1) it exercised reasonable care to prevent and promptly correct any sexually harassing behavior at its workplace and (2) the plaintiff employee unreasonably failed to take advantage of corrective opportunities provided by the employer. The existence of an employer's sexual harassment policy and notification procedures (Figure 39-2) will aid the employer in proving the affirmative defense in hostile working environment cases.

Rationale

The "primary objective of Title VII, like that of any statute meant to influence primary conduct, is not to provide redress but to avoid harm."[22] When there is no "official act" of the employer, the employer may raise an affirmative defense. This approach fosters the preventative aspect of Title VII, encouraging employers to exercise reasonable care to prevent and correct sexual harassment while providing damages only when the conduct is clearly attributed to an official action of the enterprise or when the employer has not exercised reasonable care to prevent and correct misconduct. **For Example,** Kim Ellerth alleged that she was subject to constant sexual harassment by her supervisor, Ted Slowik, at Burlington Industries. Slowik made comments about her breasts, told her to "loosen up," and warned, "You know, Kim, I could make your life very hard or very easy at Burlington." When Kim was being considered for promotion, Slowik expressed reservations that she was not "loose enough" and then reached over and rubbed her knee. She received the promotion, however. After other such incidents, she quit and filed charges

[20] According to EEOC Guidelines §1604.11(f), unwelcome sexual advances, requests for sexual favors, and other verbal or physical conduct of a sexual nature constitute sexual harassment when (1) submission to or rejection of such conduct has the purpose or effect of unreasonably interfering with an individual's work performance or creating an intimidating, hostile, or offensive working environment.

[21] *Oncale v. Sundowner Offshore Services, Inc.*, 523 U.S. 75 (1998). The Supreme Court stated in *Oncale* that it did not intend to turn Title VII into a civility code, and the Court set forth the standard for judging whether the conduct in question amounted to sexual harassment requiring that the conduct be judged from the perspective of a reasonable person in the plaintiff's position, considering all circumstances. The Court warned that "common sense" and "context" must apply in determining whether the conduct was hostile or abusive.

[22] *Faragher v. City of Boca Raton*, 524 U.S. 775, 805 (1998) (citing *Albemale Paper Co. v. Moody*, 422 U.S. 405, 418 (1975)).

FIGURE 39-2	Employer Procedure—Sexual Harassment

A. DEVELOP AND IMPLEMENT AN EQUAL EMPLOYMENT POLICY THAT SPECIFICALLY PROHIBITS SEXUAL HARASSMENT AND IMPOSES DISCIPLINE UP TO AND INCLUDING DISCHARGE. SET FORTH SPECIFIC EXAMPLES OF CONDUCT THAT WILL NOT BE TOLERATED SUCH AS:

- UNWELCOME SEXUAL ADVANCES, WHETHER OR NOT THEY INVOLVE PHYSICAL TOUCHING

- SEXUAL EPITHETS AND JOKES; WRITTEN OR ORAL REFERENCES TO SEXUAL CONDUCT; GOSSIP REGARDING ONE'S SEX LIFE; COMMENTS ON AN INDIVIDUAL'S BODY; AND COMMENTS ABOUT AN INDIVIDUAL'S SEXUAL ACTIVITY, DEFICIENCIES, OR PROWESS

- DISPLAY OF SEXUALLY SUGGESTIVE OBJECTS, PICTURES, AND CARTOONS

- UNWELCOME LEERING, WHISTLING, BRUSHING AGAINST THE BODY, SEXUAL GESTURES, AND SUGGESTIVE OR INSULTING COMMENTS

- INQUIRIES INTO ONE'S SEXUAL EXPERIENCES

- DISCUSSION OF ONE'S SEXUAL ACTIVITIES

B. ESTABLISH ONGOING EDUCATIONAL PROGRAMS, INCLUDING ROLE-PLAYING AND FILMS TO DEMONSTRATE UNACCEPTABLE BEHAVIOR.

C. DESIGNATE A RESPONSIBLE SENIOR OFFICIAL TO WHOM COMPLAINTS OF SEXUAL HARASSMENT CAN BE MADE. AVOID ANY PROCEDURE THAT REQUIRES AN EMPLOYEE TO FIRST COMPLAIN TO THE EMPLOYEE'S SUPERVISOR, BECAUSE THAT INDIVIDUAL MAY BE THE OFFENDING PERSON. MAKE CERTAIN COMPLAINANTS KNOW THAT THERE WILL BE NO RETALIATION FOR FILING A COMPLAINT.

D. INVESTIGATE ALL COMPLAINTS PROMPTLY AND THOROUGHLY.

E. KEEP COMPLAINTS AND INVESTIGATIONS AS CONFIDENTIAL AS POSSIBLE AND LIMIT ALL INFORMATION TO ONLY THOSE WHO NEED TO KNOW.

F. IF A COMPLAINT HAS MERIT, IMPOSE APPROPRIATE AND CONSISTENT DISCIPLINE.

alleging that she was constructively discharged because of the unendurable working conditions resulting from the hostile work environment created by Slowik. She did not use Burlington's sexual harassment internal complaint procedures. Because she was not a victim of a tangible employment action involving an official act of the enterprise, because she received the promotion sought, the employer will be able to raise an affirmative defense. She will be able to prove severe and pervasive conduct on the part of a supervisor under a hostile work environment theory. However, the employer may defeat liability by proving both that it exercised reasonable care to prevent and correct sexual harassing behavior through its internal company complaint policies and that Kim unreasonably failed to take advantage of the company procedures.[23]

[23] *Burlington Industries, Inc. v. Ellerth*, 524 U.S. 742 (1998); see also *Faragher v. City of Boca Raton*, 524 U.S. 775 (1998). In *Pennsylvania v. Suders*, 542 U.S. 129 (2004), the U.S. Supreme Court reviewed a decision of the Third Circuit Court of Appeals that held that a "constructive discharge," if proved, constituted a "tangible employment action" that renders the employer liable for damages and precludes an affirmative defense. The Supreme Court disagreed with the Third Circuit's reading of its *Ellerth/Faragher* decisions and made it very clear that "an official act of the enterprise" is necessary for the plaintiff to defeat the employer's right to raise an affirmative defense.

Nonsupervisors

An employer is liable for the sexual harassment caused its employees by coworkers or customers only when it knew or should have known of the misconduct and failed to take prompt remedial action.

39-2e Protection against Retaliation

Section 704(a) sets forth Title VII's antiretaliation provision in the following terms:

> *It shall be an unlawful practice for an employer to discriminate against any of his employees or applicants for employment ... because he has opposed any practice made an unlawful employment practice by this subchapter* [the opposition clause], *or because he has made a charge, testified, assisted, or participated in any manner in an investigation, proceeding, or hearing under this subchapter* [the participation clause].

Some U.S. courts of appeals had held that the retaliation provisions set forth in Section 704(a) of Title VII apply only to retaliation that takes the form of "ultimate employment actions" such as demotions, suspensions, and terminations and do not apply to ministerial matters such as reprimands and poor evaluations. The EEOC believed that the statute prohibits any adverse treatment that is based on a retaliatory motive and is reasonably likely to deter the charging party or others from engaging in protected activity. In *Burlington Northern v. White* (*Burlington*) the Supreme Court held that a plaintiff may pursue a retaliation claim under Title VII if the "employer's challenged action would have been material to a reasonable employee" and likely would have "dissuaded a reasonable worker from making or supporting a charge of discrimination."[24] By focusing on the materiality of the challenged action and the perspective of a reasonable person, this standard was designed to screen out trivial conduct while capturing those acts that are likely to dissuade employees from complaining or assisting in complaints about discrimination.

CASE SUMMARY

New Traction for the Antiretaliation Provisions Thanks to Track Laborer White

FACTS: BNSF Railway hired Shelia White as a track laborer at its Tennessee Yard. She was the only woman in the track department. When hired, she was given the job of operating forklifts as opposed to doing ordinary track labor tasks. Three months after being hired, she complained to the roadmaster that her foreman treated her differently than male employees and had twice made inappropriate remarks. The foreman was suspended without pay for 10 days and ordered to attend training on sexual harassment. Also at that time, the roadmaster reassigned the forklift duties to the former operator who was "senior" to White and assigned White to track labor duties. Six months into her employment, White refused to ride in a truck as directed by a different foreman, and she was suspended for insubordination. Thirty-seven days later, she was reinstated with full back pay, and the discipline was removed from her record. She filed a complaint with the EEOC, claiming that the reassignment to track laborer duties was unlawful gender discrimination and retaliation for her complaint about her treatment by the foreman. The 37-day suspension led to a second retaliation charge. A jury rejected her gender discrimination claim and awarded her compensatory damages for her retaliation claims. BNSF appealed, contending that Ms. White had been hired as a track laborer and it was not retaliatory to

[24] *Burlington Northern Santa Fe Railway Co. v. White*, 548 U.S. 133 (2006).

New Traction for the Antiretaliation Provisions Thanks to Track Laborer White continued

assign her to do the work she was hired to do. It also asserted that the 37-day suspension had been corrected and she had been made whole for her loss.

DECISION: Judgment for White. The Supreme Court held that the jury could reasonably conclude that the reassignment from forklift operator to track laborer duties would have been materially adverse to a reasonable employee, thus constituting retaliatory discrimination. Moreover, the Court held that an indefinite suspension without pay for a month, even if the employee later received back pay, could well act as a deterrent to filing a discrimination complaint. [*Burlington Northern Santa Fe Railway Co. v. White*, **548 U.S. 53 (2006)**]

Subsequent to the *Burlington* decision, the Supreme Court has settled the broad legal issues regarding retaliation claims under federal antidiscrimination laws, including protection of an employee who speaks out about discrimination not of her own initiative, but in answering questions during an internal investigation into rumors of sexual harassment by her supervisor[25] and also providing a "zone of interest" standard for determining whether third parties' retaliation claims are protected under Title VII.[26]

The EEOC takes the position that claims can be filed for retaliation not only under Title VII but also under the Americans with Disabilities Act, the Age Discrimination in Employment Act, and the Equal Pay Act.

39-2f National Origin

Title VII protects members of all nationalities from discrimination. The judicial principles that have emerged from cases involving race, color, and gender employment discrimination are generally applicable to cases involving allegations of discrimination related to national origin. Thus, physical standards, such as minimum height requirements, that tend to exclude persons of a particular national origin because of the physical stature of the group have been found unlawful when these standards cannot be justified by business necessity.

Adverse employment action based on an individual's lack of English language skills violates Title VII when the language requirement bears no demonstrable relationship to the successful performance of the job to which it is applied. **For Example,** Flight Services & Systems Inc. (FSS) purchased the assets of FAI, and assumed FAI's contract with Southwest Airlines to provide wheel chair attendants for Southwest in Denver. FSS took over in October 2009 and by June 2010 "only a few" Ethiopians were still employed by FSS, despite the fact that nearly 200 had held positions there when FSS took over. FSS contended that Southwest requires that FSS employees "possess the ability to communicate effectively in English." On this issue the court determined that passing the written tests required a level of English proficiency beyond what was necessary to do their jobs, thus supporting the plaintiffs' claims of national origin discrimination.[27]

39-2g Title VII Exceptions

Section 703 of Title VII defines which employment activities are unlawful. This same section, however, also exempts several key practices from the scope of Title VII enforcement. The most important are the bona fide occupational qualification exception, the testing and educational requirement exception, and the seniority system exception.

[25] *Crawford v. Metropolitan Government of Nashville*, 555 U.S. 271 (2009).
[26] *Thompson v. North American Stainless, LP*, 131 S. Ct. 863 (2011).
[27] *Tuffa v. Flight Services & Systems Inc.*, 2015 WL 273730 (D. Colo. 2015).

THINKING THINGS THROUGH

Retaliation – The Number One Risk for Employers

Since the Supreme Court's adoption of a broader definition of retaliation than was used in some judicial circuits prior to the *Burlington* decision, the number of retaliation charges filed with the EEOC has risen dramatically. Management-side employment lawyers see "retaliation as the number one risk for employers today." The litigation costs involved in a single retaliation case are substantial.

The source of unlawful retaliation can emanate from a CEO and other top executives down through middle managers or first-level managers, and it can also originate from organizational tolerance of coworker retaliation. Retaliation occurs in all types and sizes of organizations in all employment sectors of society.

Need for a Comprehensive Program. Employers must develop and implement effective antiretaliation and educational policies and procedures for their top executives, middle managers, and first-level supervisors. Additionally, each organization's highest human resource (HR) officer must have authority to independently investigate and report directly to the CEO and have authority as well to report to an appropriate board of directors' committee regarding the business justification for proposed or actual employer actions with potential retaliation liability.*

Educational Discussion of Human Nature and the Costs of Retaliation. Employers must recognize that the educational effort is going to be challenging in some cases because of the "human nature" of the controversy. For instance, an employee has gone to a supervisor's supervisor, the HR department, or the EEOC, and has charged his or her supervisor with discrimination based on race, color, religion, sex, national origin, age, or disability. If the complaint is valid, the supervisor should be appropriately disciplined. It may well be that the complaint is perceived by management or coworkers as lacking merit. How can the accused supervisor or coworkers treat the complainant as though nothing has happened? Is it not human nature for the supervisor to want to take materially adverse action against that individual? Would not the ideal solution for the supervisor be to "come up with" a business basis for terminating the complainant?

The adverse economic consequences of such an action to the employer could be severe. For example, in the Supreme Court's *Crawford v. Metropolitan Government of Nashville*** case, on remand to the district court, the employer contended that it fired Crawford for irregularities in the school system's payroll office for which Crawford was responsible. Crawford testified that she had never previously been disciplined during her 30 years of service with Metro, and local officials did not begin to investigate her job performance until after she disclosed the alleged sexual harassment by the school district's employee relations coordinator. The jury found that the reasons for firing Crawford were pretextual and awarded Crawford $420,000 in compensatory damages, $408,762 in back pay, and $727,496 in front pay, for a total monetary award of approximately $1.56 million.

Thinking Things Through, all employees at all levels should be instructed that because of the adverse impact on the complainant-victim, the potential adverse economic consequence to the employer, and the distraction and disruption to the workforce caused by ongoing litigation, violations of the employer's no-discrimination and no-retaliation policy will been enforced with major discipline—up to and including discharge!

*Some employees with poor records believe that if they have filed complaints with the EEOC, they are immune from all discipline. However, these "protected" employees are not immune from discipline or discharge. The *Burkhart v. American Railcar Industries Inc.* decision, 603 F.3d 472 (8th Cir. 2010), can be used in an educational program for executives, managers, and staff to demonstrate that employees who have engaged in protected activities under Title VII are not immune from discipline or discharge for major performance issues.

**555 U.S. 271 (2009).

Bona Fide Occupational Qualification Exception

It is not an unlawful employment practice for an employer to hire employees on the basis of religion, sex, or national origin in those certain instances where religion, sex, or national origin is a bona fide occupational qualification (BFOQ) reasonably necessary to the normal operation of a particular enterprise. **For Example,** a valid BFOQ is a men's clothing store's policy of hiring only males to do measurements for suit alterations. An airline's policy of hiring only female flight attendants is not a valid BFOQ because such a policy is not reasonably necessary to safely operate an airline.

CASE SUMMARY

It's a Woman's Choice

FACTS: Johnson Controls, Inc. (JCI), manufactures batteries. A primary ingredient in the battery-manufacturing process is lead. Occupational exposure to lead entails health risks, including the risk of harm to any fetus carried by a female employee. After eight of its employees became pregnant while maintaining blood lead levels exceeding those set by the Centers for Disease Control as dangerous for a worker planning to have a family, respondent JCI announced a policy barring all women, except those whose infertility was medically documented, from jobs involving lead exposure exceeding the OSHA standard. The United Auto Workers (UAW) brought a class action in the district court, claiming that the policy constituted sex discrimination violative of Title VII of the Civil Rights Act of 1964, as amended. The court granted summary judgment for JCI based on its BFOQ defense, and the Court of Appeals affirmed. The Supreme Court granted *certiorari*.

DECISION: Judgment for the UAW. JCI's fetal protection policy discriminated against women because the policy applied only to women and did not deal with the harmful effect of lead exposure on the male reproductive system. JCI's concerns about the welfare of the next generation do not suffice to establish a BFOQ of female sterility. Title VII, as amended, mandates that decisions about the welfare of future children be left to the parents who conceive, bear, support, and raise them rather than to the employers who hire those parents or to the courts. Moreover, an employer's tort liability for potential fetal injuries does not require a different result. If, under general tort principles, Title VII bans sex-specific fetal-protection policies, the employer fully informs the woman of the risk, and the employer has not acted negligently, the basis for holding an employer liable seems remote at best. [*UAW v. Johnson Controls*, 499 U.S. 187 (1991)]

Testing and Educational Requirements

Section 703(h) of the act authorizes the use of "any professionally developed ability test [that is not] designed, intended, or used to discriminate." Employment testing and educational requirements must be "job related"; that is, the employers must prove that the tests and educational requirements bear a relationship to job performance.

Courts will accept prior court-approved validation studies developed for a different employer in a different state or region so long as it is demonstrated that the job for which the test was initially validated is essentially the same job function for which the test is currently being used. **For Example,** a court-approved firefighters' test that has been validated in a study in California will be accepted as valid when later used in Virginia. Such application is called *validity generalization.*

The Civil Rights Act of 1991 makes it an unlawful employment practice for an employer to adjust scores or use different cutoff scores or otherwise alter the results of employment tests to favor any race, color, religion, sex, or national origin. This provision addresses the so-called race-norming issue, whereby the results of hiring and promotion tests are adjusted to ensure that a minimum number of minorities are included in application pools.

Seniority System

Section 703(h) provides that differences in employment terms based on a bona fide seniority system are sanctioned so long as the differences do not stem from an intention to discriminate. The term *seniority system* is generally understood to mean a set of rules that ensures that workers with longer years of continuous service for an employer will have a priority claim to a job over others with fewer years of service. Because such rules provide workers with considerable job security, organized labor has continually and successfully fought to secure seniority provisions in collective bargaining agreements.

39-2h Affirmative Action and Reverse Discrimination

Employers have an interest in affirmative action because it is fundamentally fair to have a diverse and representative workforce. Moreover, affirmative action is an effective means of avoiding litigation costs associated with discrimination cases while at the same time preserving management prerogatives and preserving rights to government contracts. Employers, under **affirmative action plans (AAPs),** may undertake special recruiting and other efforts to hire and train minorities and women and help them advance within the company. However, the plan may also provide job preferences for minorities and women. Such aspects of affirmative action plans have resulted in numerous lawsuits contending that Title VII of the Civil Rights Act of 1964, the Fourteenth Amendment, or collective bargaining contracts have been violated. The Supreme Court has not been able to settle the many difficult issues before it with a clear and consistent majority. The Court has decided cases narrowly, with individual justices often feeling compelled to speak in concurring or dissenting opinions.

affirmative action plan (AAP)—plan to have a diverse and representative workforce.

Affirmative Action Programs

In its 1995 *Adarand Constructors, Inc. v. Peña*[28] decision, the Supreme Court placed significant limits on the federal government's authority to implement programs favoring businesses owned by racial minorities over white-owned businesses. The decision reinstated a reverse discrimination challenge to a federal program designed to provide highway construction contracts to "disadvantaged" subcontractors in which race-based presumptions were used to identify such individuals. The Court found the program to be violative of the equal protection component of the Fifth Amendment's due process clause and announced a strict scrutiny standard for evaluating the racial classifications used in the federal government's Disadvantaged Business Enterprise (DBE) program. This standard can be satisfied only by narrowly tailored measures that further compelling governmental interests. The Court stated that programs based on disadvantage rather than race are subject only to the most relaxed judicial scrutiny. Six additional years of litigation ensued before the case involving Adarand Constructors, Inc., was finally concluded on procedural and jurisdictional grounds. *Adarand I*, as it is now called, is now the landmark Supreme Court decision setting forth the legal principles for evaluating affirmative action programs involving race and remedies.

Following the Court's *Adarand I* decision, the EEOC issued a statement on affirmative action, stating, in part:

> *Affirmative action is lawful only when it is designed to respond to a demonstrated and serious imbalance in the workforce, is flexible, is time limited, applies only to qualified workers, and respects the rights of nonminorities and men.*[29]

Reverse Discrimination

When an employer's AAP is not shown to be justified or "unnecessarily trammels" the interests of nonminority employees, it is often called *reverse discrimination*. **For Example,** a city's decision to rescore police promotional tests to achieve specific racial and gender percentages unnecessarily trammeled the interests of nonminority police officers.[30]

---

[28] 515 U.S. 200 (1995).

[29] *The Steelworkers v. Weber*, 443 U.S. 193 (1979), and *Johnson v. Santa Clara Transportation Agency*, 480 U.S. 617 (1987), are very important U.S. Supreme Court decisions in the developing law on permissible affirmative action plans.

[30] *San Francisco Police Officers Ass'n v. San Francisco*, 812 F.2d 1125 (9th Cir. 1987). See also *Barella v. Village of Freeport*, 16 F. Supp. 3d 144 (E.D.N.Y. 2014).

Executive Order

Presidential Executive Order 11246 regulates contractors and subcontractors doing business with the federal government. This order forbids discrimination against minorities and women and in certain situations requires affirmative action to be taken to offer better employment opportunities to minorities and women. The Secretary of Labor has established the Office of Federal Contract Compliance Programs (OFCCP) to administer the order.

39-3 Other Equal Employment Opportunity (EEO) Laws

Major federal laws require equal pay for men and women doing equal work and forbid discrimination against older people and those with disabilities.

39-3a Equal Pay

The Equal Pay Act prohibits employers from paying employees of one gender a lower wage rate than the rate paid employees of the other gender for equal work, or substantially equal work, in the same establishment for jobs that require substantially equal skill, effort, and responsibility and that are performed under similar working conditions.[31]

CASE SUMMARY

I Do the Same Job as Two Male Colleagues. Doesn't the Equal Pay Act Require That I Get Equal Pay?

FACTS: Jeannette Renstrom was the head grocery buyer at wholesale food distributor Nash Finch Co. at its St. Cloud, Minnesota, distribution center. She sued her employer under the Equal Pay Act because Nash Finch paid her less than two male employees who performed equal work—Bill Crosier, the head grocery buyer for the Omaha distribution center, and Dale Ebensteiner, the head grocery buyer for the Fargo and Minot distribution centers. Nash Finch seeks summary judgment.

DECISION: The term *establishment* refers to a distinct physical place of business rather than an entire business or enterprise, which may include several places of business. Each of Nash Finch's distribution centers is a separate "establishment." Because Renstrom did not work at the same establishment as the two comparators that she has identified (Crosier and Ebensteiner), her claim under the EPA must be dismissed.

Additionally, in order for the equal pay standard to apply, Ms. Renstrom needed to show that the Head Grocery Buyer jobs required equal skill, equal effort, and equal responsibility. There is little question that the job involved equal skill and responsibility. In light of the undisputed evidence that both Crosier and Ebensteiner had essentially "double work"—Crossier, because he handled 18 military facilities, and Ebensteiner, because he handled two distribution centers—Renstrom cannot meet her burden to show that the jobs required equal effort. Judgment for Nash Finch. [*Renstrom v. Nash Finch Co.,* **787 F. Supp. 2d 961 (D. Minn. 2011)**]

The Equal Pay Act does not prohibit all variations in wage rates paid men and women but only those variations based solely on gender. The act sets forth four exceptions. Variances in wages are allowed where there is (1) a seniority system, (2) a merit

[31] 29 U.S.C. §206 (d)(1).

system, (3) a system that measures earnings by quantity or quality of production, or (4) a differential based on any factor other than gender.

39-3b Age Discrimination

The Age Discrimination in Employment Act (ADEA) forbids discrimination by employers, unions, and employment agencies against persons over 40 years of age.[32] Section 4(a) of the ADEA sets forth the employment practices that are unlawful under the act, including the failure to hire because of age and the discharge of employees because of age. Section 7(b) of the ADEA allows for doubling the damages in cases of willful violations of the act. Consequently, an employer who willfully violates the ADEA is liable not only for back wages and benefits but also for an additional amount as liquidated damages.[33]

CASE SUMMARY

Miffed at Being RIF-ed

FACTS: Calvin Rhodes began his employment with Dresser Industries in 1955 as an oil industry salesman. In the throes of a severe economic downturn, Rhodes took a job selling oil field equipment at another Dresser company that became Guiberson Oil Tools. After seven months, he was discharged and told that the reason was a reduction in force (RIF) but that he would be eligible for rehiring. At that time, he was 56 years old. Within two months, Guiberson hired a 42-year-old salesperson to do the same job. Rhodes sued Guiberson for violating the ADEA. At the trial, Lee Snyder, the supervisor who terminated Rhodes, testified in part that Jack Givens, Snyder's boss who instructed Snyder to fire Rhodes, once said that he could hire two young salesmen for what some of the older salesmen were costing.

DECISION: Judgment for Rhodes. The official reason given Rhodes, that he was being terminated under a RIF, was false. Every other reason given by the employer was countered with evidence that Rhodes was an excellent salesman. Based on all of the evidence, including the statement about hiring two young salesmen for what some of the older salesmen were costing, a reasonable jury could find that Guiberson Oil discriminated against Rhodes on the basis of age. [*Rhodes v. Guiberson Oil Tools,* 75 F.3d 989 (5th Cir. 1996)]

The Older Workers Benefit Protection Act (OWBPA) of 1990[34] amends the ADEA by prohibiting age discrimination in employee benefits and establishing minimum standards for determining the validity of waivers of age claims. The OWBPA amends the ADEA by adopting an "equal benefit or equal cost" standard, providing that older workers must be given benefits at least equal to those provided for younger workers unless the employer can prove that the cost of providing an equal benefit would be more for an older worker than for a younger one.

Employers commonly require that employees electing to take early retirement packages waive all claims against their employers, including their rights or claims under the ADEA. The OWBPA requires that employees be given a specific period of time to evaluate a proposed package.

---

[32] 29 U.S.C. §623.

[33] In *Reeves v. Sanderson Plumbing Products Co., Inc.*, 530 U.S. 133 (2000), the Supreme Court reinstated a $98,490 judgment for Roger Reeves, which included $35,000 in back pay, $35,000 in liquidated damages, and $28,490.80 in front pay, and held that the plaintiff's evidence establishing a prima facie case and showing that the employer's stated reason for the termination was false was sufficient to prove that age was the motivation for the discharge. See also *Williams v. Asbury Automotive Group, Inc.*, 998 F. Supp. 2d 769 (E.D. Ark. 2014).

[34] 29 U.S.C. §623. This law reverses the Supreme Court's 1989 ruling in *Public Employees Retirement System of Ohio v. Betts*, 492 U.S. 158 (1989), which had the effect of exempting employee benefit programs from the ADEA.

Enforcement of the ADEA is the responsibility of the EEOC. Procedures and time limitations for filing and processing ADEA charges are the same as those under Title VII.[35] However, Title VII is materially different from the ADEA with respect to burdens of persuasion, and Supreme Court decisions construing Title VII do not control the construction of the ADEA. Rather, in all cases of disparate treatment, including mixed-motive cases, the plaintiff has to prove, by a preponderance of the evidence, that age was the "but for" cause of the challenged adverse employment action.[36]

39-3c Discrimination against Persons with Disabilities

The right of persons with disabilities to enjoy equal employment opportunities was established on the federal level with the enactment of the Rehabilitation Act of 1973.[37]

Although not specifically designed as an employment discrimination measure but as a comprehensive plan to meet many of the needs of persons with disabilities, the act contains three sections that provide guarantees against discrimination in employment. Section 501 is applicable to the federal government itself, Section 503 applies to federal contractors, and Section 504 applies to the recipients of federal funds.

Title I of the Americans with Disabilities Act of 1990 extends employment protection for disabled persons beyond the federal level to state and local governmental agencies and to all private employers with 15 or more employees. The ADA refers to the term *qualified individuals with disabilities* rather than the term *handicapped persons*, which is used in the Rehabilitation Act. In drafting the ADA, Congress relied heavily on the language of the Rehabilitation Act and its regulations. It was anticipated that the body of case law developed under the Rehabilitation Act would provide guidance in the interpretation and application of the ADA. However, protections for individuals were eroded by U.S. Supreme Court decisions in 1999 and 2002. Under these precedents, numerous claims of ADA plaintiffs were extinguished at the threshold stage of proving the plaintiff had a disability. With the cooperation and agreement of both the employer and disability communities, the ADA Amendments Act of 2008 (ADAAA) became law (effective January 1, 2009), effectively overturning the Supreme Court decisions and restoring the original congressional intent of providing broad coverage to protect individuals who face discrimination on the basis of disability.[38] Under Title I of the ADA, an employer may make preemployment inquiries into the ability of a job applicant to perform job-related functions. Under "user-friendly" EEOC guidelines on preemployment inquiries under the ADA, an employer may ask applicants whether they will need reasonable accommodations for the hiring process. If the answer is yes, the employer may ask for reasonable documentation of the disability. In general, the employer may not ask questions about whether an applicant will need reasonable accommodations to do the job. However, the employer

[35] In *Smith v. City of Jackson, Mississippi*, 544 U.S. 228 (2005), the U.S. Supreme Court determined that disparate impact claims of age discrimination are permitted under the ADEA. The Court relied on its Title VII *Griggs v. Duke Power Co.* precedent, which interpreted text identical to that in the ADEA, with the substitution of the word "age" for the words "race, color, religion, sex or national origin," the narrowing of the coverage of the ADEA, which permits employers to take actions that would otherwise be prohibited based on "reasonable factors other than age" (called the *RFOA provision*), and the EEOC regulations permitting disparate impact claims. The dissenting justices asserted that in the nearly four decades since the law's enactment, the Court had never read it to impose liability on an employer without proof of discriminatory intent. The *Smith v. City of Jackson* court decided the disparate impact case before it against the petitioning police officers, finding that the City's larger pay raises to younger employees were based on an RFOA that responded to the City's legitimate goal of retaining its new police officers.

[36] *Gross v. FBL Financial Services, Inc.*, 557 U.S. 167 (2009). See also *Scheick v. Tecumseh Public Schools*, 766 F.3d 523 (6th Cir. 2014).

[37] 42 U.S.C. §§701–794.

[38] 42 U.S.C. §§12101-12117; P.L. 110-325, S3406 (Sept. 25, 2008).

may make preemployment inquiries regarding the job applicant's ability to perform job-related functions.

After making a job offer (contingent upon the applicant's passing a medical examination), the employer may rescind the offer if the position in question poses a direct threat to the worker's health or safety. **For Example,** Mario Echazabal was initially offered a job at Chevron's El Segundo, California, oil refinery but the offer was rescinded when the company doctors determined that exposure to chemicals on the job would further damage his already-reduced liver functions (due to hepatitis C) and might potentially kill him. An affirmative defense then exists for employers—not only in cases where hiring an individual poses a direct threat to the health or safety of other employees in the workplace, but also when there is a direct threat to the employee in question. However, the employer must make an individualized medical risk assessment of the employee's condition.[39]

Proving a Case

The Americans with Disabilities Act, as amended in 2008, prohibits employers from discriminating "against a qualified individual on the basis of a disability." A qualified individual with a disability is one "who, with or without reasonable accommodation, can perform the essential functions of the employment position." To establish a viable claim under the act, a plaintiff must prove that (1) he or she has a disability; (2) he or she is qualified for the position; and (3) an employer has discriminated against him or her because of a disability.

The ADAAA defines the term *disability* in a three-pronged definition as follows:

1. DISABILITY: The term "disability" means, with respect to an individual—

A. a physical or mental impairment that substantially limits one or more major life activities of such individual;
B. a record of such an impairment; or
C. being regarded as having such an impairment.

The ADAAA sets forth in unmistakable language that the definition of disability "shall be construed in favor of broad coverage of individuals under this Act" and mandates that the term "substantially limits" be construed accordingly. Moreover, the determination of whether an impairment substantially limits a major life activity must be made without regard to the ameliorative effects of mitigating measures (with the exception that ameliorative effects of ordinary eyeglasses or contact lenses are considered in determinations of whether an impairment substantially limits a major life activity).

The ADAAA includes an expansive compilation of major life activities to confirm the congressional purpose of providing a broad scope of protection to individuals under the ADA.[40] In addition to establishing that the plaintiff has a disability, a plaintiff must also show that he or she is qualified for the position. **For Example,** the Department of Transportation regulations disqualify any commercial motor vehicle driver with a "current clinical diagnosis of alcoholism" for service as an over-the-road trucker. Sakari Jarvela's ADA claim against Crete Carrier Corp. failed because, disqualified by DOT as a driver, he no

---

[39] *Chevron v. Echazabal,* 536 U.S. 73 (2002).
[40] Section 3(2) of the act provides:
MAJOR LIFE ACTIVITIES—

A. IN GENERAL.—For purposes of paragraph (1), major life activities include, but are not limited to, caring for oneself; performing manual tasks; seeing, hearing, eating, sleeping, walking, standing, lifting, bending, speaking, breathing, learning, reading, concentrating, thinking, communicating, and working.
B. MAJOR BODILY FUNCTIONS.—For purposes of paragraph (1), a major life activity also includes the operation of major bodily functions, included but not limited to, functions of the immune system; normal cell growth; digestive; bowel, bladder, neurological, brain, respiratory, circulatory, endocrine, and reproductive functions.

longer could perform the essential functions of his driver's job with or without reasonable accommodations.[41]

Reasonable Accommodations under the ADA

Section 101(9) of the ADA defines an employer's obligation to make "reasonable accommodations" for individuals with disabilities to include (1) making existing facilities accessible to and usable by individuals with disabilities and (2) restructuring jobs, providing modified work schedules, and acquiring or modifying equipment or devices.[42] An employer is not obligated under the ADA to make accommodations that would be an "undue hardship" on the employer.

Seniority systems provide for a fair and uniform method of treating employees whereby employees with more years of service have a priority over employees with less years of service when it comes to layoffs, job selection, and other benefits such as days off and vacation periods. Seniority rules apply not only under collective bargaining agreements but also to many nonunion job classifications and to nonunion settings. An employer's showing that a requested accommodation conflicts with seniority rules is ordinarily sufficient to show that the requested "accommodation" is not "reasonable." **For Example,** Robert Barnett, a cargo handler for U.S. Airways, Inc., sought a less physically demanding job in the mailroom due to a back injury. Because a senior employee bid the job, U.S. Airways refused Barnett's request to accommodate his disability by allowing him to work the mailroom position. Barnett filed suit under the ADA, and the case progressed to the U.S. Supreme Court, which determined that ordinarily such a requested accommodation is not "reasonable." On remand to the trial court, Barnett was given the opportunity to show that the company allowed exceptions to the seniority rules and he fit within such exceptions.[43]

Failure to Take Action

With courts applying a less-demanding standard for coverage under the amended ADA, employers are finding requests to provide "reasonable accommodations" more common. Employers are liable for failure to take appropriate action regarding requests for reasonable accommodations. **For Example,** Jane Gagliardo had been diagnosed with multiple sclerosis that began affecting her work. The most severe symptom was fatigue, which affected her ability to think, focus, and remember. All of her symptoms were subject to being exacerbated by stress. She sought a "reasonable accommodation" under the ADA of having one major client removed from her job responsibilities. The employer took no action on this request. Moreover, while she continued to seek accommodation to no avail, the employer began disciplining her for poor job performance and ultimately fired her. She was awarded $2.3 million in compensation and punitive damages.[44]

Where a disability is obvious and known to the employer, an employee is obligated to engage in an "interactive process" regarding accommodation of a disability, even when

---

[41] *Jarvela v. Crete Carrier Corp.*, 776 F.3d 822 (11th Cir. 2015).

[42] A reasonable accommodation may also include "reassignment to a vacant position." In *Duvall v. Georgia-Pacific Consumer Products LP.*, 607 F.3d 1255 (10th Cir. 2010), the Tenth Circuit Court of Appeals was called upon to decide when a position is "vacant" for the purpose of the ADA. It determined that when a disabled employee seeks the reasonable accommodation of reassignment to a vacant position, positions within the company are "vacant" for the purpose of the ADA when they would be available to similarly suited nondisabled employees to apply for and obtain. Duvall, the employee in question, did not meet his burden of showing that the jobs he sought were available within GP, as they were occupied by a contractor service, and no GP employee had been given a contractor-filled position during the time in question.

[43] *U.S. Airways v. Barnett*, 535 U.S. 391 (2002).

[44] *Gagliardo v. Connaught Laboratories, Inc.*, 311 F.3d 565 (3d Cir. 2008). See also *Tobin v. Liberty Mutual Insurance Co.*, 553 F.3d 121 (1st Cir. 2009).

a formal request for accommodation is not made. **For Example,** 19-year-old Patrick Brady, who has cerebral palsy, was hired to work as a Wal-Mart pharmacy aide. After "a few days" on the job with no training, he was transferred to the job of collecting shopping carts and garbage in the parking lot. His supervisor, Ms. Chin, regarded Brady as "too slow" and stated that "she knew there was something wrong with him." While Brady did not request reasonable accommodations because his disability was obvious and known to the employer, Wal-Mart was found to be in violation of the ADA, and a judgment of $900,000—including $300,000 in punitive damages—was upheld by the U.S. Court of Appeals.[45] Mental disabilities frequently are not obvious to employers, and it is up to the employee to disclose nonobvious disabilities and any related limitations and a need for accommodations to his or her employer. **For Example,** Ms. Walz acknowledged that she failed to inform her employer of her bipolar disorder and obtain an accommodation. The court therefore determined that her employer had no duty to accommodate her, and her discharge for erratic and disruptive behavior, aggressiveness with a coworker, and disrespect to her supervisor was upheld.[46]

Exclusions from Coverage of the Act

The act excludes from its coverage employees or applicants who are "currently engaging in the illegal use of drugs." The exclusion does not include an individual who has been successfully rehabilitated from such use or is participating in or has completed supervised drug rehabilitation and is no longer engaging in the illegal use of drugs.

Title V of the act states that behaviors such as transvestitism, transsexualism, pedophilia, exhibitionism, compulsive gambling, kleptomania, pyromania, and psychoactive substance use disorders resulting from current illegal use of drugs are not in and of themselves considered disabilities.

39-3d GINA

The Genetic Information Nondiscrimination Act (GINA) is also administered by the EEOC.[47] GINA was enacted in 2008 to prevent discrimination on the basis of genetic information in health insurance and employment. Employees requiring fitness-for-duty or post-job-offer medical examinations have to make certain that "company doctors" do not ask for DNA tests or family medical histories. It is advisable that all medical forms and questionnaires include prominently printed language that notifies individuals: "Do not give us genetic information or family medical history."

39-4 Extraterritorial Employment

The Civil Rights Act of 1991 amended both Title VII and the ADA to protect U.S. citizens employed in foreign countries by American-owned or American-controlled companies against discrimination based on race, color, religion, national origin, sex, or disability.[48] The 1991 act contains an exemption if compliance with Title VII or the ADA would cause a company to violate the law of the foreign country in which it is located.

---

[45] *Brady v. Wal-Mart Stores, Inc.,* 531 F.3d 127 (2d Cir. 2008).

[46] *Walz v. Ameriprise Financial, Inc.,* 779 F.3d 842 (8th Cir. 2015). See also the discussion of recognizing that interacting with others as a major life activity does not mean that any cantankerous person will be deemed substantially limited in a major life activity, as discussed in *Weaving v. City of Hillsboro,* 763 F.3d 1106 (9th Cir. 2014).

[47] Pub. L. 110-233, 122 Stat. 881 (May 21, 2008).

[48] Section 109 of the Civil Rights Act of 1991, P.L. 102-166, 105 Stat. 1071.

Make the Connection

Summary

Title VII of the Civil Rights Act of 1964, as amended, forbids discrimination on the basis of race, color, religion, sex, or national origin. The EEOC administers the act. Intentional discrimination is unlawful when there is disparate treatment of individuals because of their race, color, religion, gender, or national origin. Also, employment practices that make no reference to race, color, religion, sex, or national origin, but that nevertheless have an adverse or disparate impact on the protected group, are unlawful. In disparate impact cases, the fact that an employer did not intend to discriminate is no defense. The employer must show that there is a job-related business necessity for the disparate impact practice in question. Employers have several defenses they may raise in a Title VII case to explain differences in employment conditions: (1) bona fide occupational qualifications reasonably necessary to the normal operation of the business, (2) job-related professionally developed ability tests, and (3)

bona fide seniority systems. If a state EEO agency or the EEOC is not able to resolve the case, the EEOC issues a right-to-sue letter that enables the person claiming a Title VII violation to sue in a federal district court. An affirmative action plan is legal under Title VII provided there is a voluntary "plan" justified as a remedial measure and provided it does not unnecessarily trammel the interests of whites.

Under the Equal Pay Act (EPA), employers must not pay employees of one gender a lower wage rate than the rate paid to employees of the other gender for substantially equal work. Workers over 40 years old are protected from discrimination by the Age Discrimination in Employment Act (ADEA). Employment discrimination against persons with disabilities is prohibited by the Americans with Disabilities Act (ADA). Under the ADA, employers must make reasonable accommodations without undue hardship on them to enable individuals with disabilities to work.

Learning Outcomes

After studying this chapter, you should be able to clearly explain:

39-1 Title VII of the Civil Rights Act of 1964, as Amended

LO.1 Explain the difference between the *disparate treatment* theory of employment discrimination and the *disparate impact* theory of employment discrimination
    See the discussion of the New Haven Firefighters case in which the city relied on a disparate impact theory and the firefighters asserted disparate treatment, page 796.

39-2 Protected Classes and Exceptions

LO.2 List and explain the categories of individuals protected against unlawful employment discrimination under Title VII
    See the discussion and examples of protections under Title VII applied to the categories of race and color, religion, sex, and national origin, pages 800–802, 806.

LO.3 Recognize, and know the remedies for, sexual harassment in the workplace
    See the Ellerth example and the employer's affirmative defense, pages 803–804.
    See Figure 39-2 for a presentation of an employer sexual harassment policy, page 804.

LO.4 Explain the antiretaliation provision of Title VII
    See the *White* case, which sets forth the elements of retaliatory discrimination and the remedy provided, pages 805–806.
    See why retaliation is the number one employment liability risk for employers and the antiretaliation actions proposed for employers, page 807.

39-3 Other Equal Employment Opportunity (EEO) Laws

LO.5 List and explain the laws protecting equal pay for women and men for equal work as well as the laws forbidding discrimination on the basis of age and against individuals with disabilities
    See the *Renstrom* case with the narrow meaning of the word "establishment," making her EPA case without merit, page 810.
    See the *Rhodes* case with facts and a remedy applicable to age discrimination, page 811.
    See the Patrick Brady example of the attention-getting judgment in a case where the employer failed to recognize its obligation to make a reasonable accommodation, page 815.

39-4   Extraterritorial Employment

LO.6 Explain how both Title VII of the Civil Rights Act and the ADA protect from discrimination U.S. citizens working in foreign countries for American-owned and American-controlled businesses

See the discussion of the exemption for employers where compliance would cause a company to violate the law of the country in which it is located, page 815.

Key Term

affirmative action plans (AAPs)

Questions and Case Problems

1. List the major federal statutes dealing with the regulation of equal rights in employment.

2. The EEOC notified North American Stainless (NAS) in February 2003 that Miriam Regalado had filed a charge of sex discrimination against the company. Three weeks later NAS fired her coworker Eric Thompson, a person to whom Ms. Regalado was engaged. Thompson had worked for NAS for seven years as a metallurgical engineer. Thompson filed his own charge with the EEOC and a subsequent lawsuit under Title VII of the Civil Rights Act, claiming that NAS fired him to retaliate against Regalado for filing her charge with the EEOC.

   The employer contended that because Thompson did not "engag[e] in any statutorily protected activity, either on his own behalf or on behalf of Miriam Regalado," he is not included in the class of persons for whom Congress created a retaliation cause of action. Thompson argued that the Supreme Court adopted a broad standard in its *Burlington* decision because Title VII's antiretaliation provision is worded broadly, and that there is no textual basis for making an exception to it for third-party reprisals. Decide. [*Thompson v. North American Stainless Steel, LP*, 131 S. Ct. 863]

3. Dial Corp. implemented a "work tolerance test," which all new employees were required to pass to obtain employment in its Armour Star brand sausage-making department. Of the applicants who passed the test, 97 percent were male and 38 percent were female. The EEOC "demonstrated" that the facially neutral work tolerance test "caused" a disparate impact on women. The defending employer did not deny that the employment practice in question caused the disparate impact. Rather, the employer responded that the test was "job related" and "necessary" to reduce job-related injuries at the plant and submitted evidence that the number of job injuries had been reduced after implementation of the testing program. The evidence showed that the company had initiated numerous other safety initiatives that had an impact on reducing injuries at the plant. After they failed the test, 52 women were denied jobs. Decide this case. [*EEOC v. Dial Corp.*, 2005 WL 2839977 (S.D. Iowa)]

4. Continental Photo, Inc., is a portrait photography company. Alex Riley, an African American man, applied for a position as a photographer with Continental. Riley submitted an application and was interviewed. In response to a question on a written application, Riley indicated that he had been convicted for forgery (a felony) six years before the interview, had received a suspended sentence, and was placed on five-year probation. He also stated that he would discuss the matter with his interviewer if necessary. The subject of the forgery conviction was subsequently not mentioned by Continental's personnel director in his interview with Riley. Riley's application for employment was eventually rejected. Riley inquired about the reason for his rejection. The personnel director, Geuther, explained to him that the prior felony conviction on his application was a reason for his rejection. Riley contended that the refusal to hire him because of his conviction record was actually discrimination against him because of his race in violation of Title VII. Riley felt that his successful completion of a five-year probation without incident and his steady work over the years qualified him for the job. Continental maintained that because its photographers handle approximately $10,000 in cash per year, its policy of not hiring applicants whose honesty was questionable was justified. Continental's policy excluded all applicants with felony convictions. Decide. Would the result have been different if Riley had been a convicted murderer?

[*Continental Photo, Inc.*, 26 Fair Empl. Prac. Cas. (B.N.A.) 1799 (E.E.O.C.)]

5. Beth Faragher worked part-time and summers as an ocean lifeguard for the Marine Safety Section of the city of Boca Raton, Florida. Bill Terry and David Silverman were her supervisors over the five-year period of her employment. During this period, Terry repeatedly touched the bodies of female employees without invitation and would put his arm around Faragher, with his hand on her buttocks. He made crudely demeaning references to women generally. Silverman once told Faragher, "Date me or clean the toilets for a year." She was not so assigned, however. The city adopted a sexual harassment policy addressed to all employees. The policy was not disseminated to the Marine Safety Section at the beach, however. Faragher resigned and later brought action against the city, claiming a violation of Title VII and seeking nominal damages, costs, and attorneys' fees. The city defended that Terry and Silverman were not acting within the scope of their employment when they engaged in harassing conduct and that the city should not be held liable for their actions. Are part-time employees covered by Title VII? Was Silverman's threat, "Date me or clean toilets for a year," a basis for *quid pro quo* vicarious liability against the city? Decide this case. [*Faragher v. City of Boca Raton*, 524 U.S. 775]

6. Mohen is a member of the Sikh religion whose practice forbids cutting or shaving facial hair and requires wearing a turban that covers the head. In accordance with the dictates of his religion, Mohen wore a long beard. He applied for a position as breakfast cook at the Island Manor Restaurant. He was told that the restaurant's policy was to forbid cooks to wear facial hair for sanitary and good grooming reasons and that he would have to shave his beard or be denied a position. Mohen contended that the restaurant had an obligation to make a reasonable accommodation to his religious beliefs and let him keep his beard. Is he correct?

7. Sylvia Hayes worked as a staff technician in the radiology department of Shelby Memorial Hospital. On October 1, Hayes was told by her physician that she was pregnant. When Hayes informed the doctor of her occupation as an X-ray technician, the doctor advised Hayes that she could continue working until the end of April so long as she followed standard safety precautions. On October 8, Hayes told Gail Nell, the director of radiology at Shelby, that she had discovered she was two months pregnant. On October 14, Hayes was discharged by the hospital. The hospital's reason for terminating Hayes was its concern for the safety of her fetus given the X-ray exposure that occurs during employment as an X-ray technician. Hayes brought an action under Title VII, claiming that her discharge was unlawfully based on her condition of pregnancy. She cited scientific evidence and the practice of other hospitals where pregnant women were allowed to remain in their jobs as X-ray technicians. The hospital claimed that Hayes's discharge was based on business necessity. Moreover, the hospital claimed that the potential for future liability existed if an employee's fetus was damaged by radiation encountered at the workplace. Decide. [*Hayes v. Shelby Memorial Hospital*, 546 F. Supp. 259 (N.D. Ala.)]

8. Overton suffered from depression and was made sleepy at work by medication taken for this condition. Also, because of his medical condition, Overton needed a work area away from public access and substantial supervision to complete his tasks. His employer terminated him because of his routinely sleeping on the job, his inability to maintain contact with the public, and his need for supervision. Overton argued that he is a person with a disability under the ADA and the Rehabilitation Act, fully qualified to perform the essential functions of the job, and that the employer had an obligation to make reasonable accommodations, such as allowing some catnaps as needed and providing some extra supervision. Decide. [*Overton v. Reilly*, 977 F.2d 1190 (7th Cir.)]

9. A teenage female high school student named Salazar was employed part-time at Church's Fried Chicken Restaurant. Salazar was hired and supervised by Simon Garza, the assistant manager of the restaurant. Garza had complete supervisory powers when the restaurant's manager, Garza's roommate, was absent. Salazar claimed that while she worked at the restaurant, Garza would refer to her and all other females by a Spanish term that she found objectionable. According to Salazar, Garza once made an offensive comment about her body and repeatedly asked her about her personal life. On another occasion, Garza allegedly physically removed eye shadow from Salazar's face because he claimed it was unattractive. Salazar also claimed that one night she was restrained in a back room of the restaurant while Garza and another employee fondled her. Later that night,

when Salazar told a customer what had happened, she was fired. Salazar brought suit under Title VII against Garza and Church's Fried Chicken, alleging sexual harassment. Church's, the corporate defendant, maintained that it should not be held liable under Title VII for Garza's harassment. Church's based its argument on the existence of a published fair treatment policy. Decide. [*Salazar v. Church's Fried Chicken, Inc.*, 44 Fair Empl. Prac. Cas. (B.N.A.) 472 (S.D. Tex.)]

10. Manuel Fragante applied for a clerk's job with the city and county of Honolulu. Although he placed high enough on a civil service eligibility list to be chosen for the position, he was not selected because of a perceived deficiency in oral communication skills caused by his "heavy Filipino accent." The clerks are constantly dealing with the public and the ability to speak clearly is one of the most important skills required for the position according to the city. Fragante brought suit, alleging that the defendants had discriminated against him on the basis of his national origin in violation of Title VII of the Civil Rights Act. Decide. [*Fragante v. City and County of Honolulu*, 888 F.2d 591 (9th Cir.)]

11. John Chadbourne was hired by Raytheon on February 4, 1980. His job performance reviews were uniformly high. In December 1983, Chadbourne was hospitalized and diagnosed with AIDS. In January 1984, his physician informed Raytheon that Chadbourne was able to return to work. On January 20, 1984, Chadbourne took a return-to-work physical examination required by Raytheon. The company's doctor wrote the County Communicable Disease Control director, Dr. Juels, seeking a determination of the appropriateness of Chadbourne's returning to work. Dr. Juels informed the company that "contact of employees to an AIDS patient appears to pose no risk from all evidence accumulated to date." Dr. Juels also visited the plant and advised the company doctor that there would be no medical risk to other employees at the plant if Chadbourne returned to work. Raytheon refused to reinstate Chadbourne to his position until July 19, 1984. Its basis for denying reinstatement was that coworkers might be at risk of contracting AIDS. Was Raytheon entitled to bar Chadbourne from work during the six-month period of January through July? [*Raytheon v. Fair Employment and Housing Commission*, 261 Cal. Rptr. 197 (Ct. App.)]

12. Connie Cunico, a white woman, was employed by the Pueblo, Colorado, School District as a social worker. She and other social workers were laid off in seniority order because of the district's poor financial situation. However, the school board thereafter decided to retain Wayne Hunter, a black social worker with less seniority than Cunico because he was the only black on the administrative staff. No racial imbalance existed in the relevant workforce with black persons constituting 2 percent. Cunico, who was rehired over two years later, claimed that she was the victim of reverse discrimination. She stated that she lost $110,361 in back wages plus $76,000 in attorneys' fees and costs. The school district replied that it was correct in protecting with special consideration the only black administrator in the district under the general principles it set forth in its AAP. Did the employer show that its affirmative action in retaining Hunter was justified as a remedial measure? Decide. [*Cunico v. Pueblo School District No. 6*, 917 F.2d 431 (10th Cir.)]

13. Della Janich was employed as a matron at the Yellowstone County Jail in Montana. The duties of the position of matron resemble those of a parallel male position of jailer. Both employees have the responsibility of booking prisoners, showering and dressing them, and placing them in the appropriate section of the jail depending on the offender's sex. Because 95 percent of the prisoners at the jail were men and 5 percent were women, the matron was assigned more bookkeeping duties than the jailer. At all times during Janich's employment at the jail, her male counterparts received $125 more per month as jailers. Janich brought an action under the Equal Pay Act, alleging discrimination against her in her wages because of her sex. The county sheriff denied the charge. Decide. [*Janich v. Sheriff*, 29 Fair Empl. Prac. Cas. (B.N.A.) 1195 (D. Mont.)]

14. Following a decline in cigarette sales, L & M, Inc., hired J. Gfeller as vice president of sales and charged him to turn around the sales decline. After receiving an analysis of the ages of sales personnel and first-line management, Gfeller and his assistant, T. McMorrow, instituted an intensive program of personnel changes that led to the termination of many older managers and sales representatives. A top manager who sought to justify keeping an older manager was informed that he was "not getting the message." Gfeller and McMorrow emphasized that they wanted young and aggressive people and that the

older people were not able to conform or adapt to new procedures. R. E. Moran, who had been rated a first-rate division manager, was terminated and replaced by a 27-year-old employee. Gfeller and McMorrow made statements about employees with many years' experience: "It was not 20 years' experience, but rather 1 year's experience 20 times." The EEOC brought suit on behalf of the terminated managers and sales representatives. The company vigorously denied any discriminatory attitude with regard to age. Decide. [*EEOC v. Liggett and Meyers, Inc.*, 29 F.E.P. 1611 (E.D.N.C.)]

15. Mazir Coleman had driven a school bus for the Casey County, Kentucky, Board of Education for four years. After that time, Coleman's left leg had to be amputated. Coleman was fitted with an artificial leg and underwent extensive rehabilitation to relearn driving skills. When his driving skills had been sufficiently relearned over the course of four years, Coleman applied to the county board of education for a job as a school bus driver. The board refused to accept Coleman's application, saying that it had no alternative but to deny Coleman a bus-driving job because of a Kentucky administrative regulation. That regulation stated in part: "No person shall drive a school bus who does not possess both of these natural bodily parts: feet, legs, hands, arms, eyes, and ears. The driver shall have normal use of the above named body parts." Coleman brought an action under the Rehabilitation act, claiming discrimination based on his physical handicap. The county board of education denied this charge, claiming that the reason they rejected Coleman was because of the requirement of the state regulation. Could Coleman have maintained an action for employment discrimination in light of the state regulation on natural body parts? Decide. [*Coleman v. Casey County Board of Education*, 510 F. Supp. 301 (N.D. Ky.)]

16. Marcia Saxton worked for Jerry Richardson, a supervisor at AT&T's International Division. Richardson made advances to Saxton on two occasions over a three-week period. Each time Saxton told him she did not appreciate his advances. No further advances were made, but thereafter Saxton felt that Richardson treated her condescendingly and had stopped speaking to her on a social basis at work. Four months later, Saxton filed a formal internal complaint, asserting sexual harassment, and went on "paid leave." AT&T found inconclusive evidence of sexual harassment but determined that the two employees should be separated. Saxton declined a transfer to another department, so AT&T transferred Richardson instead. Saxton still refused to return to work. Thereafter, AT&T terminated Saxton for refusal to return to work. Saxton contended that she had been a victim of hostile working environment sexual harassment. AT&T argued that while the supervisor's conduct was inappropriate and unprofessional, it fell short of the type of action necessary for sexual harassment under federal law (the *Harris* case). Decide. [*Saxton v. AT&T Co.*, 10 F.3d 526 (7th Cir.)]

Business Organizations

Types of Business Organizations

Learning Outcomes ‹‹‹

After studying this chapter, you should be able to

LO.1 Explain the advantages and disadvantages of the three principal forms of business organizations

LO.2 Recognize that the rules of law governing the rights and liabilities of joint ventures are substantially the same as those that govern partnerships

LO.3 Evaluate whether a business arrangement is a franchise protected under state or federal law

LO.4 Explain how the rights of the parties to a franchise agreement are determined by their contract

LO.5 Explain why freedom from vicarious liability is a reason for franchisors to use the franchise format

LO.6 Recognize the implications of the misclassifications of employees as franchisee-independent contractors

What form of legal organization should you have for your business? The answer will be found in your needs for money, personnel, control, tax and estate planning, and protection from liability.

40-1 Principal Forms of Business Organizations

The law of business organizations may be better understood if the advantages and disadvantages of proprietorships, partnerships, and corporations are first considered.

40-1a Individual Proprietorships

sole or individual proprietorship–form of business ownership in which one individual owns the business.

A **sole or individual proprietorship** is a form of business ownership in which one individual owns the business. The owner may be the sole worker of the business or employ as many others as needed to run the concern. Individual proprietorships are commonly used in retail stores, service businesses, and agriculture.

Advantages

The proprietor or owner is not required to expend resources on organizational fees. The proprietor, as the sole owner, controls all decisions and receives all profits. The net earnings of the business are not subject to corporate income taxes but are taxed only as personal income.

Disadvantages

The proprietor is subject to unlimited personal liability for the debts of the business and cannot limit this risk. The investment capital in the business is limited by the resources of the sole proprietor. Because all contracts of the business are made by the owner or in the owner's name by agents of the owner, the authority to make contracts terminates on the death of the owner, and the business is subject to disintegration.

40-1b Partnerships, LLPs, and LLCs

partnership–pooling of capital resources and the business or professional talents of two or more individuals (partners) with the goal of making a profit.

limited liability partnership (LLP)– partnership in which at least one partner has a liability limited to the loss of the capital contribution made to the partnership.

limited liability company (LLC)–a partnership for federal tax treatment and the limited liability feature of the corporate form of business organization.

A **partnership** involves the pooling of capital resources and the business or professional talents of two or more individuals whose goal is to make a profit. Law firms, medical associations, and architectural and engineering firms may operate under the partnership form. Today, however, these firms are likely to convert to a **limited liability partnership (LLP).** A wide range of small manufacturing, retail, and service businesses operate as partnerships. These businesses may operate under the form of organization called **limited liability company (LLC),** which allows tax treatment as a partnership with limited liability for the owners.

Advantages

The partnership form of business organization allows individuals to pool resources and then initiate and conduct their business without the requirement of a formal organizational structure.

Disadvantages

Major disadvantages of a partnership are the unlimited personal liability of each partner and the uncertain duration of the business because the partnership is dissolved by the death of one partner. Unlimited personal liability is remedied by the LLC form of business organization. Professional partnerships that convert to an LLP shield innocent partners from personal liability beyond their investment in the firm.

40-1c Corporations

corporation–artificial being created by government grant, which, for many purposes, is treated as a natural person.

Business **corporations** exist to make a profit and are created by government grant. State statutes regulating the creation of corporations require a corporate structure consisting of shareholders, directors, and officers. The shareholders, as the owners of the business, elect a board of directors, which is responsible for managing the business. The directors employ officers, who serve as the agents of the business and run day-to-day operations. Corporations range in size from incorporated one-owner enterprises to large multinational concerns.

Advantages

The major advantage to the shareholder, or investor, is that the shareholder's risk of loss from the business is limited to the amount of capital she invested in the business or paid for shares. This factor, coupled with the free transferability of corporate shares, makes the corporate form of business organization attractive to investors.

By purchasing shares, a large number of investors may contribute the capital assets needed to finance large business enterprises. As the capital needs of a business expand, the corporate form becomes more attractive.

A corporation is a separate legal entity capable of owning property, contracting, suing, and being sued in its own name. It has perpetual life. In other words, a corporation is not affected by the death of any of its shareholders or the transfer of their shares. In contrast to the case of a partnership or proprietorship, the death of an owner has no legal effect on the corporate entity.

Disadvantages

A corporation is required to pay corporate income taxes. Shareholders are required to pay personal income taxes on the amount received from a distribution of profits from the corporation. This is a form of double taxation.

Incorporation involves the expenditure of funds for organizational expenses. Documents necessary for the formation of a corporation, which are required by state law, must be prepared, and certain filing fees must be paid. State corporation laws may also require filing an annual report and other reports.

40-2 Specialized Forms of Organizations

CPA

40-2a Joint Ventures

joint venture–relationship in which two or more persons or firms combine their labor or property for a single undertaking and share profits and losses equally unless otherwise agreed.

A **joint venture,** or joint adventure, is a relationship in which two or more persons or entities combine their labor or property for a single business undertaking and share profits and losses equally or as otherwise agreed.[1] **For Example,** when a passenger died as a result of injuries sustained in a bus accident and she had purchased her bus ticket from an online ticket vendor, the plaintiff sought to recover damages for the decedent's wrongful death from both the bus company and the online ticket vendor, alleging that they were engaged in a joint venture. The court found that the elements of a joint venture were

[1] See *Abeles Inc. v. Creekstone Farms Premium Beef, LLC,* 2009 WL 2495802 (E.D.N.Y. March 30, 2009), for an in-depth discussion of the law of joint ventures. The court referenced a precedent, stating: "A joint venture has been described as a nebulous concept whose boundaries are not precisely drawn. Defining a joint venture is easier than identifying it, for each case depends upon its own facts."

satisfied: the parties manifested an intent to associate as joint venturers; they mutually contributed to the business; they each had some control over the enterprise; and they had a mechanism for sharing profits and losses.[2]

A joint venture is similar in many respects to a partnership. It differs primarily in that the joint venture typically involves the pursuit of a single limited purpose rather than an ongoing enterprise, although its accomplishment may require several years.[3] A partnership is generally a continuing business or activity but may be expressly created for a single transaction. Because the distinction is so insubstantial, most courts hold that joint ventures are subject to the same principles of law as partnerships.

CASE SUMMARY

Unilateral Action: Years of Litigation

FACTS: Prior to 1992, Drs. Kurwa and Kislinger maintained their own ophthalmologist practices in the San Gabriel Valley. They subsequently agreed to pursue a new business model at that time by creating a joint venture where, under what is called a "capitation agreement." HMOs would pay the joint venture a monthly fee based on the number of members of the HMO in exchange for their ophthalmologist services. They signed a handwritten "Agreement between Bud and Mark" in which they outlined the structure within which they would solicit business and share profits. They agreed to incorporate as a professional medical corporation to operate their joint venture business. Thus, Trans Valley Eye Associates, Inc., was formed. The joint venture had capitation agreements with three HMOs serving some 200,000 patients in the year before its demise and earned revenues of $2 million. Beginning September 26, 2003, Dr. Kurwa was suspended from the practice of medicine for 60 days and placed on five years' probation by the California Medical Board. The doctors also discovered at that time that their corporation did not contain a specific statement in its Articles of Incorporation that it was a professional medical corporation, thus making it an ordinary for-profit corporation. Dr. Kislinger unilaterally terminated the joint venture and appropriated for himself, without any compensation to Dr. Kurwa, the very successful 11-year venture. Dr. Kislinger contended that Dr. Kurwa had no standing to bring an action against him on behalf of Trans Valley. From adverse decisions in the trial court, Dr. Kurwa appealed.

DECISION: Courts in other states have recognized that joint ventures may choose to operate their venture in the corporate form without divesting themselves of the rights and obligations of joint venturers. The factual allegations in the complaint state a cause of action against Dr. Kislinger for breach of his fiduciary duty as a director of Trans Valley for misappropriating assets of the corporation. While Dr. Kurwa may have been precluded from owning shares in a professional corporation during his suspension, that does not mean Dr. Kislinger is not required to account to Dr. Kurwa for his interest in the joint enterprise or allow Dr. Kurwa to sell his shares in Trans Valley to an eligible licensed person. [*Kurwa v. Kislinger*, 138 Cal. Rptr. 3d 610 (Cal. App. 2012)]

Duration of Joint Venture

A joint venture continues for the time specified in the agreement of the parties. In the absence of a fixed-duration provision, a joint venture is ordinarily terminable at the will of any participant. When the joint venture clearly relates to a particular transaction, such as the construction of a specified bridge, the joint venture ordinarily lasts until the particular transaction or project is completed or becomes impossible to complete.

[2] *Clarke v. Sky Express, Inc. et al.*, 118 A.D.3d 935 (N.Y. App. Div. 2014).
[3] *Ride, Inc. v. APS Technology, Inc.*, 11 F. Supp. 3d 169 (D. Conn. 2014).

Liability to Third Persons

The conclusion that persons are joint venturers is important when a suit is brought by or against a third person for personal injuries or property damage. If there is a joint venture, the fault or negligence of one venturer will be imputed to the other venturers.[4]

40-2b   Unincorporated Associations

unincorporated association– combination of two or more persons for the furtherance of a common nonprofit purpose.

An **unincorporated association** is a combination of two or more persons for the furtherance of a common purpose.[5] No particular form of organization is required. Any conduct or agreement indicating an attempt to associate or work together for a common purpose is sufficient.

The authority of an unincorporated association over its members is governed by ordinary contract law. Except when otherwise provided by statute, an unincorporated association does not have any legal existence apart from its members. Thus, an unincorporated association cannot sue or be sued in its own name.

Generally, the members of an unincorporated association are not liable for the debts or liabilities of the association by the mere fact that they are members. It must usually be shown that they authorized or ratified the act in question. If either authorization or ratification by a particular member can be shown, that member has unlimited liability for the act.

CASE SUMMARY

Batters with Two Strikes Should Never Trust the Umpire, and Their Parents Should Have Little Faith That the Association Will Pay the Bills

FACTS: Golden Spike Little League was an unincorporated association of persons who joined together to promote a Little League baseball team in Ogden, Utah. They sent one of their members to arrange for credit at Smith & Edwards, a local sporting goods store. After getting credit, various members went to the store and picked up and signed for different items of baseball equipment and uniforms, at a total cost of $3,900. When Smith, the owner, requested payment, the members arranged a fundraising activity that produced only $149. Smith sued the Golden Spike Little League as an entity and the members who had picked up and signed for the equipment individually. The individual defendants denied that they had any personal liability, contending that only the Golden Spike Little League could be held responsible.

DECISION: Judgment for Smith against the individual members. The association could not be held liable because it did not have any legal existence. The persons who purchased the goods from the seller were personally liable as buyers even though they had purported to act on behalf of the unincorporated association. [*Smith & Edwards v. Golden Spike Little League*, 577 P.2d 132 (Utah 1978)]

40-2c   Cooperatives

cooperative–group of two or more persons or enterprises that acts through a common agent with respect to a common objective, such as buying or selling.

A **cooperative** consists of a group of two or more independent persons or enterprises that cooperate for a common objective or function. Thus, farmers may pool their farm products and sell them. Consumers may likewise pool their orders and purchase goods in bulk.

[4] *Kim v. Chamberlain*, 504 So. 2d 1213 (Ala. App. 1987).
[5] The National Conference of Commissioners on Uniform State Laws has adopted a Uniform Unincorporated Nonprofit Association Act. An unincorporated nonprofit association (UNA) is a default organization. Thus, if the organization is not a charitable trust or a nonprofit corporation or any other type of statutory trust it may be considered a UNA. Such organizations are governed by a variety of common law principles and statutes. The Revised Uniform Unincorporated Nonprofit Association Act provides useful information to small informal associations that may fail to consider legal and organizational issues. The text of the act is available at **http://apps.americanbar.org/intlaw/leadership/policy/ RUUNAA_Final_08.pdf**.

Incorporated Cooperatives

Statutes commonly provide for the special incorporation of cooperative enterprises. Such statutes often provide that any excess of payments over the cost of operation shall be refunded to each participant member in direct proportion to the volume of business that the member has done with the cooperative. This system contrasts with the payment of a dividend by an ordinary business corporation in which the payment of dividends is proportional to the number of shares held by the shareholder and is unrelated to the extent of the shareholder's business activities with the enterprise.

Antitrust Law Exemption

When members of a sellers' cooperative agree to sell all products at a common price, the agreement to fix prices is basically an agreement in restraint of trade and a violation of antitrust laws. The Capper-Volstead Act of 1922 expressly exempts normal selling activities of farmers' and dairy farmers' cooperatives from the operation of the federal Sherman Antitrust Act so long as the cooperatives do not conspire with outsiders to fix prices. In recent years, the Capper-Volstead exemption has been challenged in cases involving agricultural products such as mushrooms, milk, eggs, potatoes, and cattle. Some argue that the antitrust exemption should no longer apply because farms have become larger and are vertically integrated. Others maintain that farmers need this antitrust immunity because they rely on cooperatives for market access.[6]

40-3 The Franchise Business Format

franchise—privilege or authorization, generally exclusive, to engage in a particular activity within a particular geographic area, such as a government franchise to operate a taxi company within a specified city, or a private franchise as the grant by a manufacturer of a right to sell products within a particular territory or for a particular number of years.

Franchising is a *method* of doing business, not a *form* of business organization. A franchisor or franchisee could be a sole proprietor, a partnership, a limited liability company, or a corporation. The franchise agreement is a contract that sets forth the rights and obligations of the parties. Contract law governs questions that arise under the franchise agreement. Franchises are also subject to Section 5 of the Federal Trade Commission Act and state laws prohibiting deceptive, manipulative, or unfair business practices.[7] Both the FTC and state laws impose disclosure requirements on franchises. A variety of other laws may also impact franchises, such as securities, intellectual property, antitrust violations, sales, agency, employment, and tort law.

As defined by the Federal Trade Commission (FTC) a commercial business arrangement is a **franchise** if it satisfies three definitional elements: the franchisor must (1) promise to provide a trademark or other commercial symbol; (2) promise to exercise significant control or provide significant assistance in the operation of the business; and (3) require a minimum payment of at least $540 during the first six months of operations.[8]

---

[6] See Randon W. Wilson, "The Evolution of Farmers, Their Cooperatives and the Capper-Volstead Act," ABA Antitrust Section, *Agriculture and Food Committee e-Bulletin*, 4(1) (Spring 2013), **http://www.americanbar.org/content/dam/aba/publications/antitrust_law/at800006_newsletter_2013spring.authcheckdam.pdf**.

[7] 15 U.S.C. §45.

[8] Some business opportunities that do not meet the definition of a franchise (because they do not require a minimum payment or do not involve use of a trademark) may be subject to the FTC's "Business Opportunity Rule." Such opportunities may include work-at-home opportunities, such as stuffing envelopes or assembling crafts or running vending machines. The disclosure requirements for these business opportunities involve a one-page document. The disclosure requirement seeks to balance protection of consumers from deceptive practices against unnecessary and burdensome compliance costs on both sellers and buyers of business opportunities. 16 C.F.R. Part 437. Business opportunities may also be subject to state laws.

40-3a Definition and Types of Franchises

franchisor–party granting the franchise.

franchisee–person to whom franchise is granted.

The **franchisor** is the party granting the franchise, and the **franchisee** is the person to whom the franchise is granted. There are three principal types of franchises. The first is a *manufacturing* or *processing franchise*, in which the franchisor grants the franchisee authority to manufacture and sell products under the trademark(s) of the franchisor. The franchisor may supply an essential ingredient in a processing franchise, such as the syrup for an independent regional Coca-Cola bottling company. The second type of franchise is a *service franchise*, in which the franchisee renders a service to customers under the terms of a franchise agreement. The drain-cleaning service provided by Roto-Rooter is an example of a service franchise. The third type is a *distribution franchise*, in which the franchisor's products are sold to a franchisee, who then resells to customers in a geographical area. Exxon Mobil Oil Company's products are often sold to retail customers through independent distribution franchises.

A franchise benefits both the franchisor and the franchisee. The franchisor derives revenue from fees for its trademarks and other franchise fees while avoiding the risk and cost of running its own stores. The franchisee has an opportunity to run a store independently with "the expertise, goodwill and reputation of the franchisor."[9] The franchisor, however, assumes some risk to reputation by giving day-to-day control to the franchisee. The franchisee incurs some risk because it usually has less bargaining power than the franchisor. Recognizing the inequality in bargaining power, state laws often protect franchisees from the more powerful franchisor by providing specific requirements about how and when a franchise may be terminated. Consequently, a common issue in litigation is whether the business arrangement meets the definition of a franchise under the applicable state law.[10]

franchise agreement–sets forth rights of franchisee to use trademarks, etc., of franchisor.

40-3b The Franchise Agreement

The relationship between the franchisor and the franchisee is ordinarily an arm's-length relationship between two independent contractors. The respective rights of the parties are determined by the contract existing between them, called the **franchise agreement.**[11] The agreement sets forth the rights of the franchisee to use the **trademarks, trade name, trade dress,** and **trade secrets** of the franchisor. **For Example,** Burger King Corporation licenses franchisees to use the trademarks Burger King, Whopper, Croissanwich, and Whopper Jr.[12] The franchise agreement commonly requires the franchisor to provide training for the franchisee's employees, including processing or repair training. Thus, a new Chili's Bar and Grill franchise can expect to have its employees taught how to prepare and serve the food on its menu. In a distribution franchise, an Acura dealer can expect the franchisor to train its mechanics to repair the automobiles it sells. The franchise agreement also deals with terms for payment of various fees by the franchisee and sets forth compliance requirements for quality control set by the franchisor.

trademark–mark that identifies a product.

trade name–name under which a business is carried on and, if fictitious, must be registered.

trade dress–product's total image including its overall packaging look.

trade secret–formula, device, or compilation of information that is used in one's business and is of such a nature that it provides an advantage over competitors who do not have the information.

The duration of a franchise is a critical element of the franchise agreement. The franchise may last for as long as the parties agree. The laws in some states may require advance written notice of cancellation.[13] Franchise contracts generally specify the causes for which the franchisor may terminate the franchise, such as the franchisee's death, bankruptcy, failure to make payments, or failure to meet sales quotas.[14] Failure to comply with the franchise agreement may be grounds for termination. **For Example,** Burger King

[9] *Patterson v. Domino's Pizza, LLC,* 333 P.3d 723 (S. Ct. Cal. 2014).
[10] *Missouri Beverage Co., Inc. v. Shelton Brothers, Inc.,* 669 F.3d 873 (8th Cir. 2012).
[11] See *American Standard Inc. v. Meehan,* 517 F. Supp. 2d 976 (N.D. Ohio 2007).
[12] *Burger King Corp. v. Hinton, Inc.,* 203 F. Supp. 2d 1357 (S.D. Fla. 2002).
[13] See, for example, Mo. Rev. Stat. §407.405.
[14] *Smith's Sports Cycles, Inc. v. American Suzuki,* 82 So. 3d 682 (Ala. 2011).

Corp. required that a new item, value meals, "be sold in all U.S. restaurants ... and failure to comply will be considered a default under the applicable franchise agreement." The Sadiks, who owned four Burger King franchises in New York City, did not comply with the value meal requirement. The court concluded that termination of the franchises was appropriate because Burger King clearly "had the power and authority under the Franchise Agreements to impose the Value Menu on its franchisees."[15]

Franchise agreements frequently contain an arbitration provision under which a neutral party is to make a final and binding determination whether there has been a breach of the contract sufficient to justify cancellation of the franchise.[16] The arbitration provision may provide that the franchisor can appoint a trustee to run the business of the franchisee while arbitration proceedings are pending.

40-3c Special Protections under Federal and State Laws

Federal and state legislation may protect franchisees in certain industries. Holders of automobile dealership franchises are protected from bad-faith termination of their dealerships by the federal Automobile Dealers' Day in Court Act (ADDCA)[17] as well as by state law. Such legislation recognizes the disparity in bargaining power between dealers and manufacturers and the fact that dealers are dependent on the manufacturer for the supply of cars. **For Example,** electric car manufacturer Tesla Motors sells its cars directly to consumers. This practice has been strongly opposed by automobile dealers. Some states had legislation in place that prohibited auto manufacturers from selling direct to consumers. Other states have proposed legislation to prohibit such sales. While Tesla does not currently pose a threat to dealership franchises, dealers fear that larger manufacturers could seek to undercut their business by following a direct sales model.[18]

State laws may also prevent franchisors from unreasonably withholding consent for sale of the franchise. Some states have laws that specifically protect motor vehicle franchises from unreasonable termination or limitations on resale. **For Example,** a California court held that Yamaha unreasonably withheld its consent for the sale of a motorcycle franchise even though the franchisee had closed the dealership. Yamaha argued that "termination of the Franchise Agreement left Powerhouse with nothing to sell and Yamaha with nothing to approve." But the court held that the law protected the franchisee's attempt to receive fair and reasonable compensation for the value of the franchised business.[19]

CASE SUMMARY

"Reputation Poisoning" is a Material and Incurable Breach

FACTS: Giuffre contracted with Hyundai Motor America to be an authorized Hyundai dealer. After a court found that Giuffre had engaged in fraudulent, illegal, and deceptive practices, including false advertising and strong-arm sales methods, Hyundai terminated the dealership. Giuffre argued that the termination was unlawful.

---

[15] *Burger King Corp. v. E-Z Corporations*, 572 F.3d 1306 (11th Cir. 2009).

[16] *Central New Jersey Freightliner, Inc., v. Freightliner Corp.,* 987 F. Supp. 289 (D.N.J. 1998).

[17] 15 U.S.C. §§1221-1225.

[18] See Evan Puschak, *Tesla vs. the Auto Dealers of America* (Oct. 3, 2013), **http://www.msnbc.com/the-last-word/tesla-vs-the-auto-dealers-america**.

[19] *Powerhouse Motorsports Group, Inc. v. Yamaha Motor Corp., U.S.A.*, 221 Cal. App. 4th 867 (March 12, 2014).

"Reputation Poisoning" is a Material and Incurable Breach continued

DECISION: Judgment for the franchisor. A franchisor must have due cause to terminate a franchise agreement. Due cause exists if there has been a material breach of the agreement and if the breach is not cured within a reasonable time.

In this case, the illegal practices of the franchisee created a material and incurable breach. [*Giuffre Hyundai, LTD. v. Hyundai Motor America,* 756 F.3d 204 (2d Cir. 2014)]

The Petroleum Marketing Practices Act (PMPA) is a federal law that limits a franchisor's ability to terminate or refuse to renew a service station franchise.[20] The United States Supreme Court considered the reach of the PMPA in a case involving Shell Oil and several of its franchisees. The franchisees maintained that Shell discontinued a program of rent subsidies and then, as leases expired, Shell calculated higher annual rent payments. The franchisees signed lease renewals under protest but claimed that Shell's pricing practices constituted constructive termination of their franchise in violation of the PMPA. The Supreme Court held that the PMPA recognizes claims for constructive termination and constructive nonrenewal but that the franchisee must actually sever its relationship with the franchisor to benefit from the statute's protection. According to the Court, the PMPA regulates only "the circumstances in which franchisors may terminate a franchise or decline to renew a franchise relationship." It would contravene the purpose of the act, the Court stated, to allow a franchisee to obtain PMPA relief when a franchisor's conduct did not force the franchisee to end its franchise. The Court also stated that the PMPA does not prevent franchisors from responding to market demands by proposing new and different terms at the expiration of a franchise agreement. The Court noted that state law might protect the dealers where the PMPA does not reach.[21]

40-3d Disclosure

The offer and sale of a franchise requires compliance with both federal and state laws.

Federal Law

Franchise Rule—FTC rule requiring detailed disclosures and prohibiting certain practices.

Franchisors must comply with the FTC's amended **Franchise Rule,** which requires a franchisor to provide each prospective franchisee with a detailed franchise disclosure document (FDD) at least 14 calendar days before the prospective franchisee signs a binding agreement or makes any payment to the franchisor. This requirement ensures that prospective franchisees have sufficient time in which to review the disclosures. The FDD requires some 23 items of disclosure, including: (1) the business experience of the franchisor and its brokers, (2) any current and past litigation against the franchisor, (3) any previous bankruptcy, (4) the material terms of the franchise agreement, (5) initial and recurring payments, (6) restrictions on territories, (7) grounds for termination of the franchise, and (8) actual, average, or projected sales, profits, or earnings.[22] The FTC does not review the FDD but it may bring suit against the franchisor for false or misleading statements in the FDD.

---

[20] 15 U.S.C. §§2801 *et seq.*

[21] *Mac's Shell Service, Inc. v. Shell Oil Products Co., LLC,* 599 U.S. 175 (2010).

[22] See the Federal Trade Commission, *Franchise Rule Compliance Guide,* 16 C.F.R. Part 436, for details on the other disclosure items required by the FDD.

State Laws

Some 35 states require only that franchisors properly prepare FDDs. The remaining 15 states have additional requirements, including registration with a state agency. State laws may provide additional protection to franchisees, allowing them to sue for damages resulting from improper disclosure.[23]

40-3e Vicarious Liability Claims against Franchisors

In theory, a franchisor is not liable to a third person dealing with or affected by the franchise holder. This freedom from liability is one of the main reasons franchisors use franchises. If the negligence of the franchisee causes harm to a third person, the franchisor is generally not liable because the franchisee is an independent contractor. However, franchisors continue to be subject to lawsuits based on the wrongful conduct of their franchisees under the theory of either actual agency or apparent agency.[24] Plaintiffs may claim that the franchisor was the employer of persons working for the franchisee, that the franchisee was the agent of the franchisor, and, consequently, that the franchisor could be held vicariously liable for the wrongs of the franchisee's employees. Whether the franchisor stands in an employment or agency relationship with the franchisee and its employees for purposes of vicarious liability depends on the amount of control the franchisor exerts over the franchisee.[25]

CASE SUMMARY

Why Franchisors Use Franchises!

FACTS: William Roberts operated a McDonald's restaurant in Newcastle, Washington, under a franchise agreement with McDonald's Corporation. A thriving drug scene existed among employees and assistant managers at the restaurant. In May 2000, the restaurant hired 15-year-old D.L.S., and within weeks, she was part of the drug scene there. Thereafter, she left home to live with an assistant manager and use drugs. Her father, Clifford Street, and D.L.S. sued McDonald's Corp. and Roberts for introducing D.L.S. to drugs and sex. The trial court dismissed the claims against McDonald's Corp. D.L.S. and her father appealed. Mr. Street testified that "no person in their right mind would believe that McDonald's did not control what happened at the individual restaurants."

DECISION: The franchise agreement clearly provided that Roberts was not an agent of McDonald's Corporation and that McDonald's had no control over the daily operations of the restaurant. Thus, McDonald's has no liability as Roberts' actual principal. The court next considered an apparent authority theory to determine whether McDonald's created apparent authority that it operated the Newcastle restaurant and would ensure a safe working environment for young workers there. Beyond the general impression created by advertising that McDonald's restaurants offer a wholesome environment, no representations or acts of McDonald's existed to create an apparent employment relationship between McDonald's and D.L.S. D.L.S. and her parents must pursue their claims against the franchisee. [*D.L.S. v. Maybin*, 121 P.3d 1210 (Wash. App. 2005)]

[23] See *Legacy Academy, et al. v. Mamilove, LLC, et al.*, 761 S.E.2d 880 (Ga. App. 2014).
[24] *Ketterling v. Burger King Corporation*, 272 P.3d 527 (Idaho 2012).
[25] *Patterson v. Domino's Pizza, LLC*, 333 P.3d 723 (S. Ct. Cal. 2014).

To maintain uniform systems for processing or distributing goods or rendering services, franchisors often place significant controls on their franchisees' businesses. These controls are set forth in franchise agreements and operating manuals. In a lawsuit brought against a franchisor for the wrongful conduct of its franchisee, the franchise agreement and operations manuals may be used as evidence of the franchisor's right to control the franchisee and the existence of an agency relationship rather than an independent contractor relationship.[26]

To avoid negating its franchisees' independent contractor status and being liable for the wrongful conduct of a franchisee, the franchisor should make certain that the franchise agreement minimizes the number and kind of provisions that authorize the

THINKING THINGS THROUGH

Don't Finagle the Bagel!

Ken Miyamoto was president and a shareholder of Bixby's Food Systems, Inc. (Bixby's), a franchisor of bagel restaurants. The business is incorporated and provides limited liability to Miyamoto and its other corporate investors. Bixby's hired a lawyer familiar with franchise disclosure laws in Illinois and drafted a franchise offering circular (FOC) in accordance with state laws. Jan and Phillip McKay attended a meeting of existing and prospective franchisees where Miyamoto spoke and said that prospective franchisees had signed and paid for 340 development agreements; a similar statement also appeared in a Bixby's newsletter. The McKays soon thereafter executed a franchise agreement. Based on Miyamoto's view that a lease of larger retail space than recommended in Bixby's circular would bring in larger revenues, the McKays executed the larger-than-recommended lease and spent $400,000 making their restaurant operational, which was a much higher investment than projected in the FOC. When the restaurant opened, sales did not come close to the figures estimated in the FOC. After eight months of operations, Bixby's terminated the McKays' franchise for their inability to pay Bixby's franchise royalty fees. Bixby's sued the McKays for continuing to use its trademark, and the McKays counterclaimed against Bixby's, Inc., and Miyamoto as an individual for violation of the state Franchise Disclosure Act and the state Deceptive Business Practices Act.

Bixby's FOC was not shown to contain material misstatements of fact. However, the McKays listed a number of statements made by Miyamoto that were untrue concerning future events regarding costs, profitability, and financial success, like his encouraging them to rent larger-than-recommended

retail space to bring in larger revenues, which did not materialize. The court held that such statements about future events, costs, and profitability are not actionable misrepresentations under the state Franchise Disclosure Act. Corporate executives selling franchises have latitude to take the facts set forth in franchise offering circulars and project a bright future in most respects. That is, they have a legal right to put their "spin" on the facts, just as society does in governmental and personal affairs. Of course, buyers must beware and view assertions about future events, costs, and profitability with critical analysis and informed skepticism.

With his business incorporated and his circulars drafted by competent counsel, was Miyamoto immune from personal liability in this case? The answer is no. When Miyamoto told the group of prospective franchisees that some 340 development agreements had been signed and paid for and later repeated this statement in a newsletter, he was not Thinking Things Through. Through the discovery process that preceded a trial, the McKays' attorney "discovered" that Bixby's had just 15 agreements executed and paid for at the time of Miyamoto's assertion that 340 agreements were executed and paid for. Such a material misstatement of fact was a violation of the state franchising and deceptive practices laws.

The economic resources expended by Bixby's, Inc., to provide limited liability could not shield its shareholder-president from the consequences of his enormous lie. Along with Bixby's, Inc., Miyamoto was held personally liable to the McKays under the state statutes.*

*Bixby's Food Systems, Inc. v. McKay, 193 F. Supp. 2d 1053 (N.D. Ill. 2002).

[26] *J. M. v. Shell Oil Co.,* 922 S.W.2d 759 (Mo. 1996).

franchisor to control the "means" of operating the business. For example, the franchisor should not exercise control over employment-related matters.[27]

Franchisors may also insulate themselves from liability by requiring individual franchisees to take steps to publicly maintain their own individual business identities.

For Example, a gas station may post a sign stating that it is "dealer owned and operated," or a real estate franchise may list on its business sign the franchise name and the name of the local owner, such as Century 21, L & K Realty Co. All invoices, purchase orders, paychecks, and notices to employees should contain notice of the independent ownership and operation of the business. Finally, franchisors should require their franchisees to maintain appropriate comprehensive general liability insurance, workers' compensation insurance, and other appropriate insurance.

40-3f Franchises and Employee Misclassifications

The franchise agreement typically states that it does not create an employment relationship. Whether someone is a franchisee-independent contractor or an employee is determined by the actual relationship between the individual and the business, and not by a label or a franchise agreement. **For Example,** Coverall North American Inc. is one of the largest global commercial cleaning franchisors in North America, with over 9,000 franchise owners and 50,000 customers. Each individual who purchases a janitorial cleaning franchise must enter a standard unit agreement with Coverall. The agreement gives Coverall the exclusive rights to perform all billing and collection services provided by franchisees and to deduct fees before remitting payments. State law deals with whether an individual who is performing services is an independent contractor or an employee. Under one prong of the Massachusetts law, the burden is placed on Coverall to establish that the individual "is performing services that are part of an independent, separate, and distinct business from that of the employer." Coverall trains its franchisees and provides them with uniforms and identification badges; it contracted with all customers, with limited exceptions, until May 2009; and Coverall is the party billing all customers for cleaning services performed and receives a percentage of the revenues earned on every cleaning service. Accordingly, Coverall sells cleaning services, the same services provided by the "franchisees." Because the franchisees did not perform services outside the usual course of Coverall's business, Coverall failed to establish that franchisees were independent contractors.[28]

---

[27] Consider the degree of control exercised by McDonald's Corp. over its franchises. Only designated food and beverages may be served, and franchisees are required to use prescribed buildings and equipment. The franchisor dictates the level of quality, service, and cleanliness. All franchisees' employees must wear the uniforms designated by the franchisor with McDonald's logos. McDonald's dictates management, advertising, and personnel policies and requires that managers be trained at its "Hamburger University." The Illinois Court of Appeals held that the question of whether a franchise was an apparent agent of McDonald's was an issue of material fact that should go to a jury in a lawsuit involving a customer's slip and fall on ice in the franchised restaurant's bathroom. The court stated that the employees responsible for maintaining the bathroom wore "McDonald's uniforms" and were required to follow McDonald's standards of "quality, service, and cleanliness." *O'Banner v. McDonald's Corp.*, 653 N.E.2d 1267 (Ill. App. 1995). On further appeal to the Supreme Court of Illinois, the Court of Appeals was reversed because in order to recover on an apparent agency theory, the customer had to show that he actually relied on the apparent agency in going to the restaurant where he was injured. The customer failed to do so, thus losing the right to hold McDonald's Corp. liable for his injuries. *O'Banner v. McDonald's Corp.*, 670 N.E.2d 632 (Ill. 1996). See *Husain v. McDonald's Corp.*, 140 Cal. Rptr. 3d 370, 377 (Cal. App. 2012), where the form license agreement between McDonald's and the franchisor explains the essence of the "McDonald's system" is to ensure comprehensive control by McDonald's over every material aspect of the restaurant's operations so the uniformity of the McDonald's customer experience could be assured in every one of its locations.

[28] *Awauh v. Coverall North America, Inc.* 707 F. Supp. 2d 80 (D. Mass. 2010).

Cases raising similar issues were filed in Massachusetts and California in the summer of 2014 against the popular ride-sharing service, Uber. Some Uber drivers claim that the company has misclassified its drivers as independent contractors to avoid paying them the benefits it would have to pay employees.[29] The cases focus on whether or not the company controls the worker enough to qualify him or her as an employee.

The U.S. Labor Secretary stated that classifying workers as independent contractors rather than as employees has saved some employers as much as 20 to 30 percent on their labor costs. This practice gives employers an advantage in gaining business. Because their employment costs are lower, they are able to underbid employers who abide by the law and accurately report the status of their workers. Misclassification of employees as independent contractors depresses wages and reduces government revenues.

Make the Connection

Summary

The three principal forms of business organizations are sole proprietorships, partnerships, and corporations. A *sole proprietorship* is a form of business organization in which one person owns the business, controls all decisions, receives all profits, and has unlimited liability for all obligations and liabilities. A *partnership* involves the pooling of capital resources and talents of two or more persons whose goal is to make a profit; the partners are subject to unlimited personal liability. However, newly created forms of business organizations—the *limited liability company* and the *limited liability partnership*—allow for tax treatment as a partnership with certain limited liability for the owners.

A business *corporation* exists to make a profit. It is created by government grant. Its shareholders elect a board of directors whose members are responsible for managing the business. A shareholder's liability is limited to the capital the shareholder invested in the business or paid for shares. Corporate existence continues without regard to the death of shareholders or the transfer of stock by them.

The selection of the form of organization is determined by the nature of the business, tax considerations, the financial risk involved, the importance of limited liability, and the extent of management control desired.

A *joint venture* exists when two or more persons combine their labor or property for a single business undertaking and share profits and losses as agreed.

An *unincorporated association* is a combination of two or more persons for the pursuit of a common purpose.

A *cooperative* consists of two or more persons or enterprises, such as farmers, who cooperate to achieve a common objective such as the distribution of farm products.

In a franchise, the owner of a trademark, trade name, or copyright licenses others to use the mark or copyright to sell goods or services. To protect against fraud, the FTC requires that franchisors provide prospective franchisees with a disclosure statement 14 days prior to any transaction. The Automobile Dealers' Day in Court Act and the Petroleum Marketing Practices Act are federal laws that provide covered franchisees with protection from bad-faith terminations. State laws also protect franchisees in a wide range of businesses. A franchisor is not liable to third persons dealing with its franchisees. Liability of the franchisor may, however, be imposed on the ground of the apparent authority of the franchisee or the latter's control by the franchisor. Liability of the franchisor may also arise in cases of product liability.

---

[29] See Michael B. Farrell, "New Lawsuit Claims Uber Exploits Its Drivers," *Boston Globe* (June 26, 2014).

Learning Outcomes

After studying this chapter, you should be able to clearly explain:

40-1 Principal Forms of Business Organizations

LO.1 Explain the advantages and disadvantages of the three principal forms of business organizations

See the discussion on proprietorships, partnerships (LLPs and LLCs), and corporations, pages 824–825.

40-2 Specialized Forms of Organizations

LO.2 Recognize that the rules of law governing the rights and liabilities of joint ventures are substantially the same as those that govern partnerships

See the *Kurwa* case and the joint venture remedy while operating in the corporate form, page 826.

40-3 The Franchise Business Format

LO.3 Evaluate whether a business arrangement is a franchise protected under state or federal law

Consider the implications of Tesla's business model, page 830.

See the *Yamaha* example, page 830.

LO.4 Explain how the rights of the parties to a franchise agreement are determined by their contract

See the *Burger King* example involving cancellation of franchises, pages 829–830.

See the *Hyundai* case involving termination of a franchise for unethical behavior, pages 830–831.

LO.5 Explain why freedom from vicarious liability is a reason for franchisors to use the franchise format

See the *McDonald's* case in which only the franchisee was liable for the torts to the minor emanating from the McDonald's restaurant, page 832.

LO.6 Recognize the implications of the misclassifications of employees as franchisee-independent contractors

See the *Coverall* and *Uber* misclassification scheme, pages 834–835.

Key Terms

cooperative

corporations

franchise

franchise agreement

Franchise Rule

franchisee

franchisor

joint venture

limited liability company (LLC)

limited liability partnership (LLP)

partnership

sole or individual proprietorship

trade dress

trade name

trade secrets

trademarks

unincorporated association

Questions and Case Problems

1. In July 2008 Miller Brewing Co. and Coors Brewing Co. formed a joint venture to better compete with the dominant beer manufacturer, Anheuser Busch. The venture was named "MillerCoors LLC." Under the joint venture agreement, Miller Brewing Co. and Coors Brewing Company have a 50 percent voting interest in the entity, and each appoints half of the directors. Moreover, the CEOs of Miller and Coors resolve disputes, and all revenues are distributed directly to Miller and Coors, with cash returned to meet the operating needs of the joint venture. Ohio law requires just cause for the termination of beer distributors but allows a "successor manufacturer" to terminate existing distributorships without proving just cause so long as the predecessor does not exercise control over the successor. In accordance with the "successor manufacturer" exception, MillerCoors LLC notified Ohio wholesale beer distributors that it was terminating their distributorships. The distributorships sought injunctive relief. MillerCoors LLC moved for summary judgment. Decide. [*Beverage Distributors, Inc. v. Miller Brewing Co.*, 690 F.3d 788 (6th Cir.)]

2. Jerome, Sheila, Gary, and Ella agreed to purchase a tract of land and make it available for use as a free playground for neighborhood children. They called the enterprise Meadowbrook Playground. Jerome and Gary improperly hung one of the playground swings, and a child was injured. Suit was brought against Meadowbrook Playground. Can damages be recovered?

3. Morris Friedman was president of Tiny Doubles International, Inc. He sold business opportunities for Tiny Doubles Studios, which made small photographic statues of people for customers. Friedman was the primary negotiator with prospective buyers of these studio business opportunities. He advised buyers up front that the opportunities were not franchises, and, accordingly, he did not provide all of the information set forth in the disclosure rule on franchising, although he did provide full answers to all questions asked. Many businesses closed, however, because of lack of success. The FTC claims that Friedman violated its disclosure rule. Friedman disagrees. Decide. [*FTC v. Tiny Doubles Int'l, Inc.*, 1996 Bus. Franchise Guide (C.C.H.) ¶ 10,831]

4. Wolf, King, and others sold business "opportunities" in vending machines by taking out ads in newspapers throughout the country. When individuals responded, telemarketers called "fronters" would tell them of false earnings estimates, and those who could afford $16,000 to $25,000 for vending machines were turned over to "closers" who promised wonderful results. References were provided who were "shills"—they did not own vending machines but were paid to tell "stories" that were monitored by Wolf, King, and other supervisors. None of the individuals was given franchise disclosure documents. King induced one investor to mortgage her house so that she could pay $70,000 for a number of vending machines. In three years Wolf, King, and others took in some $31.3 million. The FTC alleged that the defendants violated the FTC franchise disclosure rule.

    Is there a franchise disclosure rule violation if Wolf and King were merely selling vending machines? What if Wolf and King promised exclusive territories for the machines? Why would a franchise disclosure rule be necessary in this case? Decide. [*FTC v. Wolf,* Bus. Franchise Guide ¶ 27,655 (C.C.H. D. Fla.)]

5. Katherine Apostoleres owned the rights to Dunkin' Donuts franchises in Brandon and Temple Terrace, Florida. The franchisor offered all its franchisees the right to renew their existing franchise agreements if they agreed to abide by advertising decisions favored by two-thirds of the local franchise owners in a given television market. Apostoleres refused the offer because she did not want to be bound by the two-thirds clause. Soon thereafter, Dunkin' Donuts audited her two stores. Using a "yield and usage"

analysis, it concluded that gross sales were being underreported. Based on these audits and a subsequent audit, Dunkin' Donuts gave notice of immediate termination of Apostoleres's franchises, contending that the franchise agreement had been violated. Apostoleres stated that an implied obligation of good faith exists by operation of law in every contract and that the audits were in retaliation for her refusal to accept the renewal agreement. The yield and usage test used in the audit was not specified in the franchise agreement as a measure to be used to enforce the franchisor's rights, and certain accounting experts testified as to the unreliability of this test. Was Dunkin' Donuts liable for breach of its implied obligation of good faith in this case? [*Dunkin' Donuts of America v. Minerva, Inc.*, 956 F.2d 1566 (11th Cir.)]

6. A woman claimed that she was sexually harassed by a male coworker at the franchisee's pizza store. She sued not only the harasser and the franchisee but also the franchisor, Domino's, claiming that the franchisor was the employer of those working for the franchisee and that the franchisee was the agent of the franchisor. The court recognized that the franchisor exerted control through "comprehensive and meticulous standards for marketing its trademarked brand and operating its franchises in a uniform way." Was Domino's vicariously liable for the conduct of the franchisee's employee? [*Patterson v. Domino's Pizza*, 333 P.3d 723 (S. Ct. Cal.)]

7. For a five-year period, Laurie Henry worked for James Doull, the owner of four Taco Bell franchises. During that time, she had an affair with Doull. He was the father of her two illegitimate children. Enraged over a domestic matter, Doull physically assaulted her at the Taco Bell Restaurant and then fired her and ordered her off the premises. Later, on Doull's recommendation, she was hired by a "company store" in an adjoining state. Henry brought suit against Doull, his corporate entity Taco Tia, Inc., and the Taco Bell Corporation (TBC). She did not characterize her suit as a case of sexual harassment. Rather, she contended that TBC was responsible for Doull's actions because he was TBC's agent. She sought damages for the loss of romantic and material satisfactions a person might expect from a traditional courtship and wedding. TBC denied that Doull was its employee or agent. The evidence showed that Henry knew that Doull's stores differed from TBC "company" stores. Henry insisted, having worked for

four years for Doull at stores adorned with Taco-Bell signs, that Taco Bell was responsible for Doull's actions. Decide. [*Henry v. Taco Tia, Inc.*, 606 So. 2d 1376 (La. App.)]

8. The Armory Committee was composed of officers from various National Guard units. It organized a New Year's Eve dance at a charge of $2 per person to defray costs. Perry, along with others, was a member of the Armory Committee. Libby was a paying guest at the dance who was injured by slipping on frozen ruts in the immediate approaches to the steps leading to the armory building where the dance was held. He sued Perry, Turner, and the other committee members. The evidence showed that every member of the committee had taken some part in planning or running the dance with the exception of Turner. Was the Armory Committee an unincorporated association or a joint venture? Decide. [*Libby v. Perry*, 311 A.2d 527 (Me.)]

9. The Kawasaki Shop of Aurora, Illinois (dealer), advised Kawasaki Motors Corp. (manufacturer) that it intended to move its Kawasaki franchise from New York Street to Hill Avenue, which was in the same market area. The Hill Avenue location was also the site of a Honda franchise. The manufacturer's sales manager advised the dealer that he did not want the dealer to move in with Honda at the Hill Avenue site. In February, the dealer moved to the Hill Avenue location. Effective May 1, the manufacturer terminated the dealer's franchise. The dealer brought suit against the manufacturer under the state's Motor Vehicle Franchise Act, which made it unlawful to terminate franchises for site control (requiring that the dealer's site be used exclusively as a Kawasaki dealership). The manufacturer argued that it had a right to have its products sold by a dealer who was not affiliated with a competitor. Decide. [*Kawasaki Shop v. Kawasaki Motors Corp.*, 544 N.E.2d 457 (Ill. App.)]

10. Goodward, a newly hired newspaper reporter for the *Cape Cod News*, learned that the local cranberry growers had made an agreement under which they pooled their cranberry crops each year and sold them at what they determined to be a fair price. Goodward believes that such an agreement is in restraint of trade and a violation of the antitrust laws. Is he correct?

11. Food Caterers of East Hartford, Connecticut, obtained a franchise from Chicken Delight to use that name at its store. Food Caterers agreed to the product standards and controls specified by the franchisor. The franchise contract required the franchisee to maintain a free delivery service to deliver hot, freshly prepared food to customers. The franchisee used a delivery truck that bore no sign or name. Its employee, Carfiro, was driving the truck in making a food delivery when he negligently struck and killed McLaughlin. The victim's estate sued Chicken Delight on the theory that Carfiro was its agent because he was doing work that Chicken Delight required and that benefited Chicken Delight. Was Carfiro the agent of Chicken Delight? [*McLaughlin's Estate v. Chicken Delight, Inc.*, 321 A.2d 456 (Conn.)]

12. The Girl Scouts of the United States (GSUSA) is led by the National Council. Local councils are governed by their own independent board of directors and employ their own officers and professional staff and are responsible for their own financial health. For a nominal fee, GSUSA issues a charter to the local council, which grants to that council "the right to develop, manage, and maintain Girl Scouting throughout the areas of its jurisdiction, including the right to use GSUSA's names and protected marks." Each local council has exclusive territory demarcated in its charter. The councils are not subsidiaries of GSUSA, rather the national organization relates to the councils as franchisor to franchisee. It authorizes the local councils to sell cookies and other merchandise under the "Girl Scout" trademark, which it owns. Manitou Council, a local council, makes most of its money from the sale of Girl Scout cookies and generates other income from charitable donations, fees from Girl Scout camps it owns, and investments. The GSUSA, in an effort to attract more members from minority groups and to increase revenue, sought to dissolve Manitou's territory as part of a realignment of council boundaries. Manitou sued to enjoin GSUSA from taking away its territory, which would not put it out of business, but would preclude it from representing itself as a Girl Scouts organization or otherwise using Girl Scout trademarks. Manitou Council claimed that GSUSA violated the Wisconsin Fair Dealership Law (WFDL) because it did not show good cause for termination as the law required. GSUSA defended by stating that Manitou is not a "dealer" (franchise) protected by the statute. The WFDL defines a dealership agreement as one in which the grantee is authorized to use the grantor's trademark and creates "a community of interest" between the parties "in the business of offering,

selling or distributing goods or services." Do you think that Manitou Council has the characteristics of a franchise? Should it be protected by the WFDL? Does it matter that the GSUSA and the local councils are nonprofit enterprises? [*Girl Scouts of Manitou v. GSUSA*, 549 F.3d 1079 (7th Cir.)]

13. Brenner was in the scrap iron business. Almost daily, Plitt lent Brenner money with which to purchase scrap iron. The agreement of the parties was that when the scrap was sold, Plitt would be repaid and would receive an additional sum as compensation for making the loans. The loans were to be repaid in any case without regard to whether Brenner made a profit. A dispute arose over the nature of the relationship between the two men. Plitt claimed that it was a joint venture. Decide. [*Brenner v. Plitt*, 34 A.2d 853 (Md.)]

14. Donald Salisbury, William Roberts, and others purchased property from Laurel Chapman, a partner of Chapman Realty, a franchisee of Realty World. The purchasers made payments directly to Laurel Chapman at the Realty World office, and Chapman was to make payments on the property's mortgage. However, Chapman did not make the payments and absconded with the funds. Salisbury and Roberts sued the franchisor, Realty World, claiming that Realty World was liable for the wrongful acts of the apparent agent, Chapman. Realty World and Chapman Realty were parties to a franchise agreement stating that the parties were franchisor and franchisee. The agreement contained a clause that required Chapman to prominently display a certificate in the office setting forth her status as an independent franchisee. Chapman displayed such a sign, but the plaintiffs did not recall seeing it. Chapman Realty hires, supervises, and sets the compensation for all of its employees. The plaintiffs pointed out that Chapman Realty used the service mark Realty World on its signs, both outside and inside its offices. They pointed out that a Realty World manual sets forth the general standards by which franchisees must run their businesses and that this represents clear control over the franchise. They contended that, all things considered, Realty World held out Chapman Realty as having authority to bind Realty World. Realty World disagreed, stating that both were independent businesses. Decide. [*Salisbury v. Chapman and Realty World, Inc.*, 65 N.E.2d 127 (Ill. App.)]

15. H.C. Blackwell Co. held a franchise from Kenworth Truck Co. to sell its trucks. After 12 years, the franchise was nearing expiration. Kenworth notified Blackwell that the franchise would not be renewed unless Blackwell sold more trucks and improved its building and bookkeeping systems within the next 90 days. Blackwell spent $90,000 attempting to meet the demands of Kenworth but could not do so because a year was required to make the specified changes. Kenworth refused to renew the franchise. Blackwell sued Kenworth for damages under the federal Automobile Dealers' Day in Court Act. Blackwell claimed that Kenworth had refused to renew in bad faith. Decide. [*Blackwell v. Kenworth Truck Co.*, 620 F.2d 104 (5th Cir.)]

CPA Question

1. A joint venture is a(an):
   a. Association limited to no more than two persons in business for profit.
   b. Enterprise of numerous co-owners in a nonprofit undertaking.
   c. Corporate enterprise for a single undertaking of limited duration.
   d. Association of persons engaged as co-owners in a single undertaking for profit.

Partnerships

Partnerships may be created without the formality of even a written partnership agreement when two or more individuals simply operate a business for a profit as co-owners. **For Example,** in July 2008, Paula Balzer was recruited to work for Blue Flame, a firm specializing in the business of marketing and live promotions. As of October 1, 2008, she states she was made a partner. Two firm e-mails reference her as a partner; she was paid a monthly $15,000 draw; and the firm's 2008 and 2009 tax returns listed her as a partner of Blue Flame. In October 2010, the partners had a falling-out with Paula. She disengaged from the firm on November 12, 2010, upon completion of two events she was committed to staging. The partners never executed a written partnership agreement with Paula and as a result did not believe she had partnership rights. When the firm failed to pay her certain money and expenses, the court reverted to basic partnership law that a written contract of partnership is not necessary to the formation of a partnership and concluded that a partnership existed on the basis of the facts before the court.[1] Partnership relations are governed by the partnership agreement. Only when the partnership agreement does not resolve an issue does partnership law apply. In many instances, individuals do not obtain legal advice in choosing the partnership form of business organization. Properly informed individuals today will probably not choose the partnership form of organization because partners are open to unlimited personal liability; they may choose a limited liability company to insulate the members from personal liability.

41-1 Nature and Creation

Partnerships are created by agreement. States have partnership laws that apply when there is no written agreement or to fill gaps in the partnership agreement. All states except Louisiana have adopted either the Uniform Partnership Act (UPA) or the Revised Uniform Partnership Act (RUPA), which is more detailed than the UPA.[2] Certain features of the RUPA that differ from those of the UPA are identified in the text. At common law, a partnership was considered to be an aggregate of the individual partners. Under the UPA and the RUPA, the partnership may be viewed as an entity separate from the partners for certain purposes. The RUPA enhances the entity theory of partnerships.[3] Under the aggregate theory, a partnership is characterized by the collection of its individual members. Consequently, if a partner dies or withdraws, the partnership ceases to exist. Under the entity theory, the partnership continues to exist as distinct from its partners, even if a partner dies or withdraws.[4] Even under the entity theory, however, each partner remains personally liable for the obligations of the partnership.[5] The 1994 or 1997 versions of the Revised Uniform Partnership Act apply in 38 states.[6] Limited partnerships (LPs) and limited liability partnerships (LLPs) differ significantly from general partnerships and are discussed in the next chapter.

41-1a Definition

A **partnership** (also called a **general partnership**) is a relationship created by the voluntary "association of two or more persons to carry on as co-owners a business for profit."[7] The persons so associated are called **partners** or **general partners.** A partner is the agent

---

partnership–pooling of capital resources and the business or professional talents of two or more individuals (partners) with the goal of making a profit.

general partnership– partnership in which the partners conduct as co-owners a business for profit, and each partner has a right to take part in the management of the business and has unlimited liability.

partner–one of two or more persons who jointly own and carry on a business for profit.

general partners– partners who publicly and actively engage in the transaction of firm business.

---

[1] *Balzer v. Millward*, 2011 WL 1547211 (D. Conn. April 21, 2011).
[2] The Louisiana Civil Code has many provisions similar to those in the UPA and RUPA.
[3] See *Mission West v. Republic*, 873 A.2d 372 (Md. App. 2005).
[4] See *Robertson v. Jacobs Cattle Co.*, 830 N.W.2d 191 (Neb. 2013).
[5] The UPA or the RUPA is in effect in all states except Louisiana.
[6] The RUPA was approved in 1992 and amended in 1993, 1994, and 1997. States that have adopted the RUPA provide for a transition period after passage during which only newly created partnerships come under the new law, with all partnerships in the state eventually being governed by the RUPA (see R.U.P.A. §1206(a)).
[7] U.P.A. §6(1).

of the partnership and of each partner with respect to partnership matters. A partner is not an employee of the partnership even when doing work that would ordinarily be done by an employee.

CASE SUMMARY

A Partner Is Not an Employee

FACTS: Ford and Mitcham were partners engaged in construction. Ford was killed at work. His widow made a claim for workers' compensation against the partnership. Mitcham opposed the claim on the ground that Ford was a partner, not an employee.

DECISION: Workers' compensation denied. While a working partner does work, a partner is not an employee. The essential element of an employment relationship is the right of the employer to control the employee. Although a partner is required to act in a proper manner, a partner is not subject to the control of the partnership in the same sense as an employee and therefore is not an "employee" of the partnership for the purpose of workers' compensation. [*Ford v. Mitcham*, 298 So. 2d 34 (Ala. App. 1974)]

41-1b Characteristics of a Partnership

A partnership has distinguishing characteristics:

1. A partnership is a voluntary, consensual relationship.
2. A partnership involves partners' contributions of capital, services, or a combination of these.
3. The partners are associated as co-owners to transact the business of the firm for profit.

unincorporated association— combination of two or more persons for the furtherance of a common nonprofit purpose.

If profit is not the object, the group will commonly be an **unincorporated association.**

Under the UPA, the partnership is not an entity separate from its partners and cannot bring suit in its own name, unless a special statute or procedural rule specifically allows. In RUPA states, however, partnerships are recognized as entities and suit may be brought against the partnership. In either case, plaintiffs must name the individual partners to have access to their individual assets.

41-1c Rights of Partners

The rights of partners are determined by the partnership agreement. If written, this agreement is interpreted by the same rules that govern the interpretation of any other written document. Any matter not covered by the partnership agreement may be covered by a provision of the UPA or RUPA, depending on which version the state has adopted.

41-1d Partnership Agreement

Partnership agreements are typically written to cover numerous, complex issues. However, there is no requirement that they be in writing unless compliance with a statute of frauds is required. **For Example,** the world's highest-paid performers in the early 1990s, the New Kids on the Block, who grossed $74.1 million in one year, were a group started by promoter Maurice Starr. He obtained $60,000 from James Martorano, who was connected with organized crime, and $50,000 from businessman Jeffrey Furst to finance the initial recording and promotion of the group. Martorano and Furst testified that, ultimately, all three agreed with a handshake that 50 percent of the profits from the group would be shared between Martorano as a silent partner and Furst, who would also provide limousine service and security. They testified that Starr would keep half of the profits. Starr denied that a partnership existed because he believed that such an alleged business arrangement would have had to be reduced to writing with great detail. However, based on the evidence, which included damaging testimony that Starr tried to buy some witnesses' silence, a jury decided that a binding oral partnership agreement existed.[8]

To reduce or avoid disputes and litigation, partnership agreements should be in writing. Courts will enforce partnership agreements, under the standards of the law of contracts, according to the terms of the agreement.[9] **For Example,** dentist Steven Schwartz was terminated from a three-dentist practice "without cause" by vote of his two other partners. The partnership agreement allowed for termination of a partner as long as either party gave the other 90 days' notice. The appeals court held that the written terms of the agreement were determinative. The parties were sophisticated and highly educated professionals and the provision was not in violation of public policy.[10]

The formal document that is prepared to evidence the contract of the parties is termed a **partnership agreement, articles of partnership,** or **articles of copartnership.** The partnership agreement governs the partnership during its existence and may contain provisions relating to dissolution. (See Figure 41-1.)

partnership agreement—
document prepared to evidence the contract of the parties. (Parties—partners or general partners)

articles of partnership—
see *partnership agreement.*

articles of copartnership—see *partnership agreement.*

FIGURE 41-1	Partnership Agreement

PARTNERSHIP AGREEMENT
THIS IS A PARTNERSHIP AGREEMENT EXECUTED AT CINCINNATI, OHIO, THIS 9TH DAY OF SEPTEMBER, 1998, BY AND AMONG LOUIS K. HALL, SHARON B. YOUNG, AND C. LYNN MUELLER, INDIVIDUALS RESIDING IN CINCINNATI, OHIO, HEREINAFTER SOMETIMES REFERRED TO INDIVIDUALLY AS "PARTNER" AND COLLECTIVELY AS "PARTNERS."

RECITALS
THE PARTNERS TO THIS AGREEMENT DESIRE TO ACQUIRE A CERTAIN PARCEL OF REAL ESTATE AND TO DEVELOP SUCH REAL ESTATE FOR LEASE OR SALE, ALL FOR INVESTMENT PURPOSES. THIS AGREEMENT IS BEING EXECUTED TO DELINEATE THE BASIS OF THEIR RELATIONSHIP.

PROVISIONS
1. NAME; AND PRINCIPAL OFFICES. THE NAME OF THE PARTNERSHIP SHALL BE: HALL, YOUNG AND MUELLER, ASSOCIATES. ITS PRINCIPAL PLACE OF BUSINESS SHALL BE AT: 201 RIVER ROAD, CINCINNATI, OHIO 45238.
2. PURPOSE. THE PURPOSE OF THE PARTNERSHIP SHALL BE TO PURCHASE AND OWN FOR INVESTMENT PURPOSES, A CERTAIN PARCEL OF REAL ESTATE LOCATED AT 602 SIXTH STREET, CINCINNATI, OHIO, AND TO ENGAGE IN ANY OTHER TYPE OF INVESTMENT ACTIVITIES THAT THE PARTNERSHIP MAY FROM TIME TO TIME HEREINAFTER UNANIMOUSLY AGREE UPON.
3. CAPITAL CONTRIBUTIONS. THE CAPITAL OF THE PARTNERSHIP SHALL BE THE AGGREGATE AMOUNT OF CASH AND PROPERTY CONTRIBUTED BY THE PARTNERS. A CAPITAL ACCOUNT SHALL BE MAINTAINED FOR EACH PARTNER.
  A. CAPITAL CONTRIBUTIONS. ANY ADDITIONAL CAPITAL WHICH MAY BE REQUIRED BY THE PARTNERSHIP SHALL BE CONTRIBUTED TO THE PARTNERSHIP BY THE PARTNERS IN THE SAME RATIO AS THAT PARTNER'S ORIGINAL CONTRIBUTION TO CAPITAL AS TO THE TOTAL OF ALL ORIGINAL CAPITAL CONTRIBUTIONS TO THE PARTNERSHIP UNLESS OTHERWISE AGREED BY THE PARTNERS.

---

[8] Judy Rakowsky, "New Kids' Profits on the Block," *Boston Globe*, November 18, 1995.
[9] *Krajacich v. Great Falls Clinic*, 276 P.3d 922 (Mont. 2012).
[10] *Schwartz v. Family Dental Group*, P.C., 943 A.2d 1122 (Conn. App. 2008).

CPA　41-1e **Determining the Existence of a Partnership**

If the parties agree to operate a business for profit as co-owners, a partnership is created even though the parties may not have labeled their new relationship as such.[11] The law is concerned with the substance of the relationship rather than the name. Conversely, a partnership does not arise if the parties do not agree to the elements of a partnership even though they call it one.[12]

CASE SUMMARY

The Case of the Absolutely Dumbfounded Investor (Partner)

FACTS: David Byker, an accountant, and Tom Mannes, a real estate professional, agreed to engage in an ongoing business enterprise to raise investment funds for separate real estate–related ventures and to share equally in the profits, losses, and expenses. Over the years, the parties pursued various individual limited partnerships, sharing equally in commissions, financing fees, and termination costs. Byker and Mannes then created a subsequent entity, Pier 1000, Ltd., to own and manage a marina. This venture was not successful, and they took profits from a prior entity and borrowed money to continue operations. The unsuccessful marina was later returned to its previous owners in exchange for assumption of Byker's and Mannes's direct obligations to that business. The nine-year business relationship between them ceased. Later, Byker approached Mannes and requested that he share in the payments resulting from losses that were incurred from their various entities. Mannes was, in his words, "absolutely dumbfounded" by the request, and he refused payment. Byker sued, contending that a general partnership was underlying all their business affairs. Mannes asserted that he merely invested in separate business ventures with Byker and that there were no other understandings between them.

DECISION: Judgment for David Byker. Partnership law does not require that individuals be aware of their status as "partners" to have a legal partnership. The intent to create a partnership is not required if the acts and the conduct of the parties otherwise evidence that the parties carried on as co-owners of a business for profit. No writing is needed to form a partnership. No name or tax ID number is necessary to attain legal status as a partnership, nor is it required that the parties must aggregate all entities under a general partnership tax return. Mannes filed his tax returns based on his share of the income and expense from the individual legal entities that existed with the legal status of each entity controlling his tax obligations. However, additional evidence indicated that a partnership existed, including the general agreement in principle from the beginning that they would share profits and losses together in their real estate investment business. While they should have created a legal entity to address the situation that precipitated the lawsuit, because they did not, partnership law applies. [*Byker v. Mannes*, 641 N.W.2d 210 (Mich. 2002)]

A partnership is shown to exist when it is established that the parties have agreed to the formation of a business organization that has the characteristics of a partnership. The burden of proving the existence of a partnership is on the person who claims that one exists.[13]

When the nature of the relationship is not clear, the following rules aid in determining whether the parties have created a partnership.

CPA　**Control**

The presence or absence of control of a business enterprise is significant in determining whether there is a partnership and whether a particular person is a partner.

---

[11] *Swecker v. Swecker*, 360 S.W.3d 422 (Tenn. App. 2011).
[12] See *Cleland v. Thirion*, 704 N.Y.S.2d 316 (A.D. 2000).
[13] *MacArthur v. Stein*, 934 P.2d 214 (Mont. 1997).

CPA   Sharing Profits and Losses

The fact that the parties share profits and losses is strong evidence of a partnership.[14]

CPA   Sharing Profits

An agreement that does not provide for sharing losses but does provide for sharing profits is evidence that the parties are partners. If the partners share profits, it is assumed that they will also share losses. Sharing profits is prima facie evidence of a partnership. However, a partnership is not to be inferred when profits are received in payment (1) of a debt, (2) of wages, (3) of an annuity to a deceased partner's surviving spouse or representative, (4) of interest, or (5) for the goodwill of the business.[15] **For Example,** the fact that one doctor receives one-half of the net income does not establish that doctor as a partner of another doctor when the former was guaranteed a minimum annual amount. Also, federal income tax and Social Security contributions were deducted from the payments to the doctor, thus indicating that the relationship was that of employer and employee. If there is no evidence of the reason for receiving the profits, a partnership of the parties involved exists.

CPA   Gross Returns

The sharing of gross returns is itself very slight, if any, evidence of a partnership.

CPA   Contribution of Skill or Labor

The fact that all persons have not contributed capital to an enterprise does not establish that the enterprise is not a partnership. A partnership may be formed even though some of its members furnish only skill or labor.

CPA   Fixed Payment

When a person who performs continuing services for another receives a fixed payment that does not depend on the existence of profit and is not affected by losses, that person is not a partner.

CPA   41-1f Partners as to Third Persons

In some instances, persons who are in fact not partners may be held liable to third persons as though they were partners. This liability arises when they conduct themselves in such a manner that others are reasonably led to believe that they are partners and to act in reliance on that belief to their injury.[16] A person who is held liable as a partner under such circumstances is termed a *nominal partner, a partner by estoppel,* or an *ostensible partner.*

Partnership liability may arise by estoppel when a person who in fact is not a partner represents herself as a partner or consents to another representing her as a partner. The person is liable to any such person to whom such representation is made. To prevail on a partnership by estoppel claim, the plaintiff must have reasonably relied on the representation of partnership or joint venture status. **For Example,** purchasers of condominiums at Las Vegas Cay Club sued those who represented that they were in a partnership with the developer. The purchasers claimed that they relied on marketing materials that indicated Cay Clubs was in a partnership with certain entities and that they bought the condominiums relying on the expertise and resources of these purported partners to develop the luxury resort. When the developers abandoned the project, the purchasers were left

---

[14] *Botsee Gates v. Houston,* 897 N.E.2d 532 (Ind. App. 2008).
[15] U.P.A. §7(4).
[16] U.P.A. §16(1); *Andrews v. Elwell,* 367 F. Supp. 2d 35 (D. Mass. 2005).

with "worthless property." The court concluded that under Nevada law partnership by estoppel applied because the purchasers reasonably relied on the representation that Cay Clubs was in a partnership with established developers.[17] Under the RUPA, an apparent partnership or partnership by estoppel is called a *purported* partnership, and a third person who relies on the partnership's representations that the purported partner had authority to bind the partnership can hold it liable as if the purported partner were an actual partner with authority.[18] Under the RUPA, a partnership can limit potential liability with a publicly recorded statement of partnership authority or limitation on partner authority.[19]

CPA ## 41-1g Partnership Property

In general, partnership property consists of all property contributed by the partners or acquired for the firm or with its funds.

There is usually no limitation on the type and amount of property that a partnership may acquire. The firm may own real as well as personal property unless it is prohibited from doing so by statute or by the partnership agreement.

The parties may agree that real estate owned by one of the partners should become partnership property. When this intent exists, the particular property constitutes partnership property even if it is still in the name of the original owner.

Article 2 of the RUPA recognizes that partnerships are "entities" that can acquire and own property in the partnership's name. If a partner desires to retain an interest in property contributed to the partnership in RUPA states, the partner must condition the transfer of the property to the partnership to reflect this interest or set forth the condition in the partnership agreement. Otherwise, the property becomes partnership property under the entity theory, and the contributing partner has no right to get it back, even in liquidation.[20]

41-1h Tenancy in Partnership

tenancy in partnership—ownership relationship that exists between partners under the Uniform Partnership Act.

Under the UPA, partners hold title to firm property by **tenancy in partnership.**[21] The characteristics of such a tenancy are as follows:

1. Each partner has an equal right to use firm property for partnership purposes in the absence of a contrary agreement.

2. A partner possesses no divisible interest in any specific item of partnership property that can be voluntarily sold, assigned, or mortgaged by a partner.

charging order—order by a court, after a business partner's personal assets are exhausted, requiring that the partner's share of the profits be paid to a creditor until the debt is discharged.

3. A creditor of a partner cannot proceed against any specific items of partnership property. The creditor can proceed only against the partner's interest in the partnership. This is done by applying to a court for a **charging order.** By this procedure, the share of any profits that would be paid to the debtor-partner is paid to a receiver on behalf of the creditor, or the court may direct the sale of the interest of the debtor-partner in the partnership.

4. Upon the death of a partner, the partnership property vests in the surviving partners for partnership purposes and is not subject to the rights of the surviving spouse of the deceased partner.

[17] In re *Cay Clubs*, 130 Nev. Adv. 14 (2014).
[18] R.U.P.A. §308.
[19] R.U.P.A. §303.
[20] R.U.P.A. §204.
[21] U.P.A. §25(1); *Krause v. Vollmar*, 614 N.E.2d 1136 (Ohio App. 1992).

CPA   ## 41-1i Assignment of a Partner's Interest

Although a partner cannot transfer specific items of partnership property in the absence of authority to so act on behalf of the partnership, a partner's interest in the partnership may be voluntarily assigned by the partner. The assignee does not become a partner without the consent of the other partners. Without this consent, the assignee is entitled to receive only the assignor's share of the profits during the continuance of the partnership and the assignor's interest upon the dissolution of the firm. The assignee has no right to participate in the management of the partnership or to inspect the books of the partnership.

41-2 Authority of Partners

The scope of a partner's authority is determined by the partnership agreement and by the nature of the partnership. **For Example,** in a family farming partnership, the agreement specified that whenever there were more than two managing partners, the approval of a majority of the managing partners was required to act on behalf of the partnership. One of the managing partners entered into a series of grain contracts on behalf of the partnership, which led to substantial losses. The court found that he had no right to bind the partnership to the contracts without a majority vote of the managing partners. The consequences for the unauthorized partner were grave. Because he did not have authority and did not act in good faith, he was held personally liable for the partnership's losses.[22]

41-2a Authority of Majority of Partners

When there are more than two partners in a firm, the decision of the majority prevails in matters involving how the ordinary functions of the business will be conducted. Thus, if a majority of the partners of a firm decide to increase the firm's advertising and enter into a contract for that purpose, the transaction is valid and binds the firm and all of the partners.

Majority action is not binding if it contravenes the partnership agreement. For such matters, unanimous action is required.[23] Thus, the majority of the members cannot change the nature of the business against the protests of the minority.

When there is an even number of partners, an even division on a matter that requires majority approval is always a possibility. In such a case, the partnership is deadlocked. When the partners are evenly divided on any question, one partner has no authority to act.

If the division is over a basic issue and the partners persist in the deadlock so that it is impossible to continue the business, any one of the partners may petition the court to order the dissolution of the firm.

41-2b Express Authority of Individual Partners

express authority— authority of an agent to perform a certain act.

An individual partner may have **express authority** to perform certain acts either because the partnership agreement provides for such authority or because a sufficient number of partners have agreed to it.

A partner's authority to act for the firm is similar to that of an agent to act for a principal. Thus, in addition to express authority, a partner has the authority to do those acts that are customary for a member of a partnership conducting the particular business of that partnership.[24] As in the case of an agent, the acts of a partner in excess of authority do not ordinarily bind the partnership.

[22] *Elting v. Elting,* 849 N.W.2d 444 (Neb. 2014).
[23] U.P.A. §18(h).
[24] *Ball v. Carlson,* 641 P.2d 303 (Colo. App. 1981).

41-2c Customary Authority of Individual Partners

A partner, by virtue of being a comanager of the business, customarily has certain powers necessary and proper for carrying out that business. The scope of such powers varies with the nature of the partnership and with the business customs and usages of the area in which the partnership operates.

A partner may make any contract necessary to transact the firm's business.

CASE SUMMARY

"Jerry Should Have Run It by Me," Silvio Seethed

FACTS: Silvio Giannetti and his daughter and son-in-law, Anne Marie and Jerry Pruzinsky, are partners in a general partnership known as Giannetti Investment Company (GIC), which owns and operates Brougham Manor Apartments. Jerry entered into an access agreement with Omnicom, a provider of cable television services, giving Omnicom the right to enter Brougham Manor for purposes of installing, maintaining, and promoting cable service. Some time later, when he learned of the contract, Silvio denied Omnicom access to the property. Omnicom was unable to repair a signal leakage problem and was forced to discontinue cable service. Omnicom sued GIC for breach of contract. GIC contended that Jerry did not sign the agreement in the partnership name and thereby failed to bind GIC.

DECISION: Judgment for Omnicom. A contract executed in the name of a partner is binding on the partnership. Jerry executed the contract in the usual course of GIC's business, for it is a typical activity for an apartment complex to contract for cable television. [*Omnicom v. Giannetti Investment Co.*, 561 N.W.2d 138 (Mich. App. 1997)]

A partner can sell the firm's goods in the regular course of business, make purchases within the scope of the business, and borrow money for firm purposes. When borrowing money, a partner may execute commercial paper in the firm's name or give security such as a mortgage.[25] A partner may purchase insurance, hire employees, and adjust claims for or against the firm. Notice given to a partner is effective notice to the partnership.[26]

41-2d Limitations on Authority

The partners may agree to limit the powers of each partner. When a partner, contrary to such an agreement, executes a contract on behalf of the firm with a third person, the firm is bound if the third person was unaware of the limitation and the partner violating the agreement is liable to the other partners for any loss caused by the breach of the limitation.[27] Under the UPA, if the third person knew of the limitation, the firm would not be bound.[28] Under the RUPA, the term *knew* is confined to actual knowledge,[29] which is cognitive awareness. Under the RUPA, a partnership may file a statement of partnership authority setting forth any restrictions on a general partner's authority.[30] **For Example,** Bernard Roeger was a general partner of RNR, with three limited partners. Restrictions were clearly set forth in the partnership agreement limiting Roeger's borrowing authority to no more than $650,000 for the construction of a building on partnership property. Roeger on behalf of RNR entered a construction loan agreement with People's Bank

[25] *U.S. Leather v. H&W Partnership*, 60 F.3d 222 (5th Cir. 1995).
[26] *Cham, Hill, Inc., v. Block & Veatch*, 557 N.W.2d 829 (Wis. App. 1996).
[27] *Blankenship v. Smalley*, 324 P.3d 573 (Or. App. 2014).
[28] U.P.A. §9(4).
[29] R.U.P.A. §102(a).
[30] R.U.P.A. §303.

| FIGURE 41-2 | Limitations on Authority of Individual Partner to Bind Partnership |

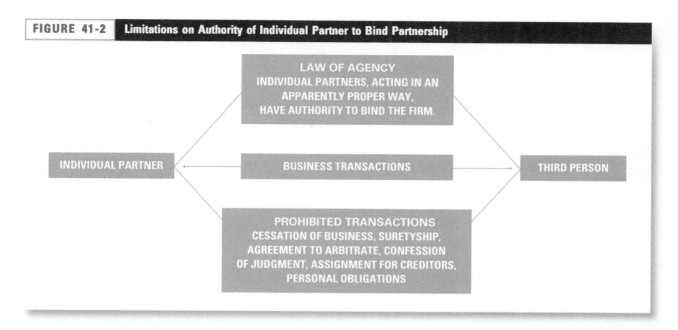

with a note and mortgage in the amount of $990,000, and over an 18-month period, the bank disbursed an aggregate sum of $952,699. The bank did not request a written consent from any of the other partners or review the partnership agreement. When the loan was not paid, the bank foreclosed on the property. RNR defended on behalf of the partnership that the bank negligently failed to investigate and discover the limitation on Roeger's authority to borrow. The case was decided for the bank because it had no actual knowledge or notice of the restriction on the general partner's authority. The court also pointed out that the partnership could have protected itself by filing a statement of partnership authority setting forth the restrictions on the general partner under RUPA section 303.[31]

A third person must not assume that a partner has all of the authority that the partner purports to have. If there is anything that would put a reasonable person on notice that the partner's powers are limited, the third person is bound by that limitation.

The third person must be on the alert for the following prohibited transactions because they warn that the partner with whom the third person deals has either restricted authority or no authority at all. (See Figure 41-2.)

41-2e Prohibited Transactions

A partner cannot enter into certain transactions on behalf of the partnership unless expressly authorized to do so. A third person entering into such a transaction does so at the risk that the partner has not been authorized. The following are prohibited transactions.

Cessation of Business

A partner cannot bind the firm by a contract that would make it impossible for the firm to conduct its usual business.[32]

---

[31] *RNR Investments, Ltd. v. People's First Community Bank,* 812 So. 2d 561 (Fla. App. 2002).
[32] *Wales v. Roll,* 769 P.2d 899 (Wyo. 1989).

CASE SUMMARY

Family Feud

FACTS: The Patel family, consisting of parents and a son, was a partnership that owned and operated a motel. The parents made a contract to sell the motel, but thereafter the son refused to sell. He claimed that the contract of sale was not binding.

DECISION: Judgment for the son. The motel was not an asset held by the partnership for sale. It was an asset that was essential for the running of the partnership/business. Accordingly, neither one partner nor a majority had implied authority to sell the motel. To the contrary, the unanimous consent of all partners was required for the sale of the motel because such a sale would make it impossible to continue the partnership business. [*Patel v. Patel,* 260 Cal. Rptr. 255 (Cal. App. 1989)]

Suretyship

A partner has no implied authority to bind the firm by contracts of surety, guarantee, or indemnity for purposes other than firm business.[33]

Arbitration

A partner cannot submit controversies of the firm to arbitration "unless authorized by the other partners or unless they have abandoned the business."[34]

Confession of Judgment

All partners should have an opportunity to defend in court. Consequently, a partner cannot confess judgment against the firm on one of its obligations. Exceptions exist when the other partners consent or when they have abandoned the business.

Assignment for Creditors

A partner cannot make a general assignment of firm property for the benefit of creditors unless authorized by the other partners or unless they have abandoned the business.

Personal Obligations

A partner cannot discharge personal obligations or claims of the firm by interchanging them in any way.

41-3 Duties, Rights, and Liabilities of Partners

The rights and duties of partners are based on their dual capacity of agent and co-owner.

41-3a Duties of Partners

In many respects, the duties of a partner are the same as those of an agent.

Loyalty and Good Faith

Each partner must act in good faith toward the partnership. One partner must not take advantage of the other(s) by the slightest misrepresentation or concealment.[35] Famous

---

[33] *First Interstate Bank of Oregon v. Bergendahl,* 723 P.2d 1005 (Or. App. 1986).
[34] U.P.A. §9(3)(e).
[35] *Brosseau v. Ranzau,* 81 S.W.3d 381 (Tex. App. 2002).

language from a decision authored by Justice Cardozo describes the duty of partners and joint venturers to each other, as follows: "Not honesty alone, but the punctilio of an honor the most sensitive, is then the standard of behavior."[36] Each partner also owes a duty of loyalty to the firm. This duty requires a partner's devotion to the firm's business and bars making any secret profit at the expense of the firm.[37]

Moreover, the duty of loyalty bars the use of the firm's property for personal benefit or the exploitation of a business opportunity of the partnership for personal gain. A partner cannot promote a competing business. A partner who does so is liable for damages sustained by the partnership.

Each partner also owes a fiduciary duty of good faith to all other partners. This duty extends to any transaction connected with the formation, conduct, or liquidation of the partnership.

A breach of fiduciary duty requires the complete forfeiture of all compensation during the period of the breach. **For Example,** general partners Michael Morton and Scott DeGraff breached their fiduciary duty to their partners when they did not disclose the parts of a deal they were keeping for themselves relating to a proposed relocation of the partnership's Las Vegas nightclub, Drink. Morton and DeGraff had been paid $833,190 in management fees during the period of time they were found to be in breach of their fiduciary duty to the partnership. The court ordered them to return these funds to the partnership.[38]

Obedience

Each partner is obligated to perform all duties and to obey all restrictions imposed by the partnership agreement or by the vote of the required number of partners.[39] **For Example,** when the partnership agreement required that each partner in an insurance sales firm give his "entire time" to the business and "not engage in any other business that would work to the disadvantage of the partnership," Richard Levatino's engaging in an insurance-related business outside the firm was a breach of the partnership agreement and was a proper basis for the assessment of punitive damages.[40]

Other Duties

The RUPA states that a partner must refrain from engaging in grossly negligent or intentional misconduct in transacting firm business.[41] Partners are accountable as a fiduciary and must hold as trustee for the firm any profits derived by a partner without the consent of the other partners.[42]

CPA   41-3b Rights of Partners as Owners

Each partner, in the absence of a contrary agreement, has the following rights. These rights stem from the fact that the partner is a co-owner of the partnership business.

CPA   Management

Each partner has a right to take an equal part in transacting the business of the firm. It is immaterial that one partner contributed more than another or that one contributed only services.

[36] *Meinhard v. Salmon,* 164 N.E. 545, 546 (N.Y. 1928).
[37] Under R.U.P.A. 404(e), partners may pursue their own interests without automatically violating their fiduciary duties to the firm.
[38] *Caparos v. Morton,* 845 N.E.2d 773 (Ill. App. 2006).
[39] *Cobin v. Rice,* 823 F. Supp. 1419 (D. Ind. 1993).
[40] *Gates, Duncan, and VanCamp v. Levatino,* 962 S.W.2d 21 (Tenn. App. 1997).
[41] R.U.P.A. §404(c).
[42] U.P.A. §21; R.U.P.A. §404(b)(1).

Incidental to the right to manage the partnership, each partner has the right to possession of the partnership property for the purposes of the partnership.

CPA   Inspection of Books

All partners are equally entitled to inspect the books of the firm. "The partnership books shall be kept, subject to any agreement between the partners, at the principal place of business of the partnership, and every partner shall at all times have access to and may inspect and copy any of them."[43]

CPA   Share of Profits

Each partner is entitled to a share of the profits. The partners may provide, if they so wish, that profits shall be shared in unequal proportions. In the absence of such a provision in the partnership agreement, each partner is entitled to an equal share of the profits without regard to the amount of capital contributed or services performed for the partnership.

CPA   Compensation

In the absence of a contrary agreement, a partner is not entitled to compensation for services performed for the partnership. There is no right to compensation even if the services are unusual or more extensive than the services rendered by other partners. Consequently, when one partner becomes seriously ill and the other partners transact all of the firm's business, they are not entitled to compensation for those services. The sickness of a partner is considered a risk assumed in the relationship. No agreement can be inferred that the active partners are to be compensated even though the services rendered by them are such that they would ordinarily be rendered in the expectation of receiving compensation. As an exception, "a surviving partner is entitled to reasonable compensation for services performed in winding up the partnership affairs."[44]

Partners may agree that one of the partners will work full time as manager of the business and receive for such services a salary in addition to the managing partner's share of the profits.

Repayment of Loans

A partner is entitled to the return of any money advanced to or for the firm. Such amounts must be separate and distinct from original or additional contributions to the capital of the firm.

CPA   Payment of Interest

In the absence of an agreement to the contrary, contributions to capital do not draw interest. The theory is that the profits constitute sufficient compensation. Advances by a partner in the form of loans are treated as if they were made by a stranger and bear interest from the date the advance is made. When the partnership business continues after dissolution, a retiring partner is entitled to interest on the value of her interest in the partnership.[45]

CPA   Contribution and Indemnity

A partner who pays more than a proportionate share of the debts of the firm has a right to contribution from the other partners. Under this principle, if an employee of a

---

[43] U.P.A. §19. See *Smith v. Brown & Jones*, 633 N.Y.S.2d 436 (Sup. Ct. 1995).
[44] U.P.A. §18(f).
[45] *Lewis v. Edwards*, 554 S.E.2d 17 (N.C. App. 2001).

partnership negligently injures a third person while acting within the scope of employment and if the injured party collects damages from one partner, the latter may enforce contribution from the other partners to divide the loss proportionately among them.

The partnership must indemnify every partner for payments made and personal liabilities reasonably incurred in the ordinary and proper conduct of its business or for the preservation of its business or property. A partner has no right, however, to indemnity or reimbursement if the partner has (1) acted in bad faith, (2) negligently caused the necessity for payment, or (3) previously agreed to assume the expense alone.[46]

CPA ### Distribution of Capital

After the payment of all creditors and the repayment of loans made to the firm by partners, every partner is entitled to receive a share of the firm property upon dissolution. Unless otherwise stated in the partnership agreement, all partners are entitled to the return of their capital contributions.

After such distribution is made, each partner is the sole owner of the fractional part distributed to that partner rather than a co-owner of all the property as during the existence of the partnership.

CPA ## 41-3c Liability of Partners and Partnership

The liability of a partnership and of the partners for the acts of individual partners and of employees is governed by the same principles that apply to the liability of an employer or a principal for the acts of an employee or agent. A partner may be vicariously liable for the acts of his partners, even if those acts are fraudulent. **For Example,** Joseph Palilla had a common law partnership in a used auto sales business with Lowell Andrews. Andrews bought used cars, purportedly to resell them, but never delivered the money to the sellers. Even though Palilla was unaware of his partner's fraud, the court held that the embezzlement was imputed to the innocent partner.[47]

joint liability–apportions partners' responsibility for partnership debt equally.

CPA ### Nature and Extent of Partner's Liability

joint and several liability–disproportionate satisfaction of partnership debt rendering each partner liable for the entire debt with the right to contribution from other partners.

Partners are **jointly liable** on all firm contracts. They are **jointly and severally liable** for all torts committed by an employee or one of the partners in the scope of the partnership business.[48] When partners are liable for the wrongful injury caused a third person, the latter may sue all or any of the members of the firm.

Partners who have satisfied a claim against the partnership have the right to contribution from the other partners, whereby the liability is apportioned among all partners. Unlike the UPA, partners under the RUPA are jointly and severally liable for both tort and contract obligations of the firm.[49] However, the RUPA alters the traditional applications of "joint and several" liability by requiring that the creditors and tort victims satisfy their claims against the partnership before pursuing the personal assets of a partner.

---

[46] *Gramacy Equities Corp. v. DuMont*, 531 N.E.2d 629 (N.Y.A.D.1988).
[47] In re *Palilla*, 439 B.R. 248 (D. Colo. 2013).
[48] See *Wayne Smith Construction v. Wolman, Durberstein*, 604 N.E.2d 157 (Ohio 1992), where the Ohio Supreme Court described joint liability and joint and several liability as follows: Joint liability apportions responsibility for a contractual debt equally, in the absence of a partnership agreement to the contrary, among the partners and thereby limits the creditor's execution on one individual partner's personal property to a *pro rata* share of the debt. Joint and several liability, on the other hand, allows for disproportionate satisfaction of the partnership obligation by rendering each general partner responsible for the entire amount of the partnership debt.
[49] R.U.P.A. §307(d).

CASE SUMMARY

"Joint Liability" and "Joint and Several Liability": A Big Difference

FACTS: PNC Bank sued two of the eight general partners of Washington Square Enterprises, Farinacci and Gruttadauria, for the unpaid balance of their partnership's business line of credit. The trial court entered judgment in the amount of $4,190.33 plus interest against each of the two partners. The trial court determined that the eight general partners were jointly liable, not jointly and severally liable, for the debt to PNC. In addition, it issued a separate judgment against Farinacci and Gruttadauria in the amount of one-eighth each of the entire debt of $33,522. PNC appealed, contending that the trial court should have found the partners jointly and severally liable or that the trial court should have apportioned the debt according to the percentages of each partner's ownership interest in the partnership, rather than dividing the debt equally among the eight partners.

DECISION: The trial court properly decided the case, holding the two partners jointly liable. In 2007 Ohio adopted the Revised Uniform Partnership Act (RUPA) effective January 1, 2010, which provides that all partners are liable jointly and severally for all obligations of the partnership unless otherwise agreed by the claimant or provided by law. However, the new law states that the RUPA language does not apply to partnerships formed prior to January 1, 2009. The Washington Square Partnership was formed in 1978. "Joint liability" apportions responsibility for a contractual debt equally among all general partners in the absence of a partnership agreement to the contrary. PNC Bank's contention that the judgment be apportioned according to the percentage of the partners' ownership interests is without legal precedent. [*PNC Bank N.A. v. Farinacci*, 964 N.E.2d 1124 (Ohio App. 2011)]

CPA ## Liability of New Partners

A person admitted as a partner into an existing partnership has *limited liability* for all obligations of the partnership arising before such admission. The preadmission claim may be satisfied only out of partnership property and does not extend to the individual property of the newly admitted partner.[50] **For Example,** Citizens Bank was unsuccessful in its attempt to satisfy part of a $1.2 million deficiency judgment against the Parkham-Woodman Medical partnership from the individual property of Dr. Hunley, who had joined the practice after the underlying obligation leading to the deficiency judgment was assumed.[51]

Effect of Dissolution on Partner's Liability

A partner remains liable after dissolution of the partnership unless expressly released by the creditors or unless all claims against the partnership have been satisfied. The dissolution of the partnership does not of itself discharge the existing liability of any partner. The individual property of a deceased partner may be reached to satisfy obligations of the partnership that were incurred while the deceased partner was alive. However, the individual creditors of the deceased partner have priority over the partnership creditors with respect to such property.[52]

41-3d Enforcement and Satisfaction of Creditors' Claims

A firm may be sued in the name of all individual partners doing business as the partnership, such as "*Plaintiff v. A, B, C, doing business as the Ajax Warehouse.*" The partners

[50] U.P.A. §17; see also U.P.A. §41(1), (7).
[51] *Citizens Bank v. Parkman Woodman Medical Associates*, 874 F. Supp. 705 (D. Mass. 1995).
[52] U.P.A. §36.

named are bound by the judgment against the firm if they have been properly served in the suit.

If a debt is contractual in origin, common law requires that the partnership's assets be resorted to and exhausted before partnership creditors can reach a partner's individual assets.[53]

Personal creditors of a partner must first pursue the assets of that partner for satisfaction of their claims. After a partner's personal assets are exhausted, the creditor may enforce the unpaid portion of a judgment by obtaining a charging order against the partner's interest in the partnership. Under such an order, a court requires that the partner's share of the profits be paid to the creditor until the debt is discharged.

41-4 Dissolution and Termination

The end of a partnership's existence is marked by dissolution and termination.

CPA ## 41-4a Effect of Dissolution

Dissolution is the "change in the relationship of the partners caused by any partner ceasing to be associated in the carrying on as distinguished from the winding-up of the business."[54] Dissolution does not necessarily mean that the business has ended. If the partnership agreement provides that the business is to be continued by the remaining partner(s), it will continue without a winding up, and the former partner's interest will be bought out according to the partnership agreement. Also, when breach of the partnership agreement causes dissolution, innocent partners may continue the business, provided they pay the breaching partner the value of his or her interest.[55]

If no legal basis exists to continue the business, dissolution ends the right of the partnership to exist as a going concern, but it does not end the existence of the partnership.[56] Dissolution is followed by a winding-up period at the conclusion of which the partnership's legal existence terminates.

Dissolution reduces the authority of the partners. From the moment of dissolution, the partners lose authority to act for the firm "except so far as may be necessary to wind up partnership affairs or to complete transactions begun but not then finished."[57] The vested rights of the partners are not extinguished by dissolving the firm, and the existing liabilities remain.

41-4b Dissolution by Act of the Parties

A partnership may be dissolved by action of the parties. However, certain acts of the parties do not cause a dissolution.

Agreement

A partnership may be dissolved in accordance with the terms of the original agreement of the parties. This may be by the expiration of the period for which the relationship was to continue or by the performance of the object for which the partnership was organized.[58] The relationship may also be dissolved by subsequent agreement. The partners may agree to dissolve the firm before the lapse of the time specified in the articles of partnership or before the attainment of the object for which the firm was created.

---

[53] *McCune & McCune v. Mountain Bell Tel. Co.,* 758 P.2d 914 (Utah 1988).
[54] U.P.A. §29.
[55] U.P.A. §38 (2)(b).
[56] *Sheppard v. Griffin,* 776 S.W.2d 119 (Tenn. App. 1989).
[57] U.P.A. §33.
[58] U.P.A. §31(1)(a).

Expulsion

A partnership is dissolved by the expulsion of any partner from the business, whether or not authorized by the partnership agreement.[59]

Alienation of Interest

Neither a voluntary sale of a partner's interest nor an involuntary sale for the benefit of creditors works a dissolution of the partnership.

Withdrawal

A partner has the power to withdraw from the partnership at any time. However, if the withdrawal violates the partnership agreement, the withdrawing partner becomes liable to the copartners for damages for breach of contract.[60] When the relationship is for no definite purpose or time, a partner may withdraw without liability at any time.

CASE SUMMARY

The Business School Graduate Who Should Have Taken Business Law

FACTS: Geoffrey Buehler and Antonio Gelman formed a partnership by oral agreement after they graduated from business school. They aimed to raise $600,000 to search for and acquire a business with growth potential. They planned to sell the business at a profit. When they disagreed over ownership interest in the partnership, Buehler withdrew from the partnership. Gelman sued for breach of contract, claiming that Buehler could not unilaterally terminate his obligations under the agreement.

DECISION: Judgment for Buehler. New York's version of the Uniform Partnership Act states that a partnership may be dissolved by "the express will of any partner when no definite or particular undertaking is specified" in the partnership agreement. The critical issue is whether the partnership agreement set forth a "definite term" or identified a particular objective to be achieved. The temporal framework for the partnership plan was flexible. The length of time for soliciting investors, identifying the business, and purchasing and operating the enterprise before the sale could not be determined with reasonable certainty. The plan was also too "amorphous" to meet the statutory "particular undertaking" standard. Consequently, the breach of contract claim must be dismissed. [*Gelman v. Buehler*, 986 N.E.2d 914 (N.Y. App. 2013)]

41-4c Dissolution by Operation of Law

A partnership is dissolved by **operation of law** in the following instances.

operation of law— attaching of certain consequences to certain facts because of legal principles that operate automatically, as contrasted with consequences that arise because of the voluntary action of a party designed to create those consequences.

Death

A partnership is dissolved immediately upon the death of any partner. Thus, when the executor of a deceased partner carries on the business with the remaining partner, there is legally a new firm.

Bankruptcy

Bankruptcy of the firm or of one of the partners causes the dissolution of the firm; insolvency alone does not.

[59] *Susman v. Cypress Venture*, 543 N.E.2d 184 (Ill. App. 1989).
[60] *BPR Group v. Bendetson*, 906 N.E.2d 956 (Mass. 2009).

Illegality

A partnership is dissolved by an event that makes it unlawful for the business of the partnership to be carried on or for the members to carry it on in partnership. For example, when a statute specifies that it is unlawful for judges to engage in the practice of law, a law firm is dissolved when one of its members becomes a judge.

41-4d Dissolution by Decree of Court

A court may decree the dissolution of a partnership for proper cause. A court will not order the dissolution for trifling causes or temporary grievances that do not involve a permanent harm or injury to the partnership.

The filing of a complaint seeking a judicial dissolution does not in itself cause a dissolution of the partnership; it is the decree of the court that has that effect.

A partner may obtain a decree of dissolution for any of the following reasons.

Insanity

A partner has been judicially declared insane or of unsound mind.

Incapacity

One of the partners has become incapable of performing the terms of the partnership agreement.

Misconduct

One of the partners has been guilty of conduct that substantially prejudices the continuance of the business. The habitual drunkenness of a partner is a sufficient cause for judicial dissolution.

Impracticability

One of the partners persistently or willfully acts in such a way that it is not reasonably practicable to carry on the partnership business. Dissolution will be granted when dissensions are so serious and persistent that continuance is impracticable or when all confidence and cooperation between the partners have been destroyed. If management of the partnership is deadlocked, a court may exercise its discretion to dissolve the partnership.[61]

CASE SUMMARY

Strategy = Squeeze Out Dyas
Ethics (Trust, Fairness, Loyalty, Doing No Harm) = None
Law = Dissociation, Dissolution

FACTS: Edward Dyas and Joseph Della Ratta were equal owners of two hotels in Ocean City, Maryland. The "old" hotel was completed in 1988 and the "new" hotel was completed in 2006, with both properties owned under their Spa Motel General Partnership (Spa). They were also developers and equal owners of the Maresol Condominium project in Ocean City, which was completed in 2004 and held under Dyas's and Della Ratta's Bay View Limited Liability Company (Bay View). Della Ratta owned the construction company that built these projects, "DRI," and he also owned

[61] *Maree et al. v. ROMAR Joint Venture*, 763 S.E.2d 899 (Ga. App. 2014).

"CMC," the company that managed the two hotels. Dyas believed that Della Ratta was attempting to squeeze him out from ownership of Spa and Bay View. Under Dyas's analysis, Della Ratta's strategy in the general partnership, Spa, was to call for a very substantial capital contribution to pay claims asserted by CMC for alleged advances made by it to pay for operational expenses and to pay claims to DRI for the new hotel's construction costs. Dyas contended that those calls were unauthorized because the underlying claims could not be substantiated and the partnership agreement required that the developers first seek a commercial loan.

With respect to Bay View, Dyas's theory of Della Ratta's squeeze-out strategy involved two ploys. First, that Della Ratta sought personally to purchase the loan from Severn Bank and obtain from it an assignment of the security instrument, on which Della Ratta then would foreclose, so that he could buy in at the foreclosure sale. Severn Bank, however, would not assign the loan to Della Ratta. Dyas further alleged that, as an alternate squeeze-out strategy, Della Ratta wrongfully refused to sell condominium units

in Maresol. The resulting illiquidity would deprive Bay View of the cash needed to repay Severn Bank, so that Della Ratta could buy Maresol at a foreclosure sale conducted by Severn Bank. After a 10-day trial, the circuit court concluded that Dyas had proven these allegations. The ultimate findings of the trial court were that it was "no longer reasonably practicable to carry on the business" of Spa or of Bay View and that Dyas "had proved to the court's satisfaction facts sufficient for the court to grant a dissolution" of the entities. The court further ordered dissociation of Della Ratta as a partner in Spa. The court supervised the winding up of the general partnership. Della Ratta appealed.

DECISION: Judgment for Dyas. A review of Della Ratta's activities while a partner in Spa demonstrates satisfactory grounds for the dissociation and dissolution determinations of the trial court since his conduct was such that it was "not reasonably practicable to carry on the business in partnership with him." [*Della Ratta v. Dyas*, 961 A.2d 629 (Md. App. 2008)]

Lack of Success

The partnership cannot continue in business except at a loss.

Equitable Circumstances

A decree of dissolution will be granted under any other circumstances that equitably call for a dissolution. Such a situation exists when one partner was induced by fraud to enter into the partnership.

CPA 41-4e Dissociation under the RUPA

Under the RUPA and its "entity" concept, a partner can leave the firm and not disrupt the partnership's legal existence. The RUPA uses the term *dissociation* for the departure of a partner[62] and reserves the term *dissolution* for those instances when a partner's departure results in the winding up and termination of the business.[63]

A partner has the absolute power to dissociate at will, just as a partner has the power to withdraw under the UPA, even if it is wrongful.[64] If wrongful, the partner is liable for damages for breach of contract.

A partner's dissociation from a firm ends the individual's right to participate in the management of the business.[65] It also ends the duty of loyalty owed the firm, and the individual may compete with the firm once dissociated.[66] If the partnership business continues after a partner dissociates from a firm, the partnership must buy out the dissociated

[62] R.U.P.A. §601 cmt 1.
[63] R.U.P.A. §801.
[64] R.U.P.A. §601(1), 602(a).
[65] In a two-person partnership, when one partner withdraws, the partnership is dissolved by operation of law because there cannot be a one-person partnership. The buyout rule of RUPA §701(b) does not apply, and the dissolution procedures take over. See *Corrales v. Corrales*, 129 Cal. Rptr. 3d 428 (Cal. App. 2011).
[66] R.U.P.A. §404(2).

partner's interest based on his share of the higher of the liquidation value of the firm or the value of the firm's business as a going concern on the date of dissociation, with interest.[67]

The RUPA created "notices" to deal with lingering authority of a dissociated partner based on apparent authority. To avoid liability, notice of lack of authority or liability should be given to customers and creditors regarding the dissociation of a partner. A filing with the Secretary of State limits liability and authority to 90 days after filing.[68] If no notice is given or filed, the partnership may be bound by the acts of a dissociated partner for up to two years after dissociation based on apparent authority.[69]

CPA   41-4f **Notice of Dissolution**

Under some circumstances, one partner may continue to possess the power to make a contract that binds the partnership even though the partnership has been dissolved.

Notice to Partners

When the firm is dissolved by the act of a partner, notice must be given to the other partners unless that partner's act clearly shows an intent to withdraw from or to dissolve the firm. If the withdrawing partner acts without notice to the other partners, that partner is bound by contracts created for the firm.

When the dissolution is caused by the act, death, or bankruptcy of a partner, each partner is liable to the copartners for a share of any liability created by any other partner acting for the partnership without knowledge or notice of the act, death, or bankruptcy of the partner who caused the dissolution.

CPA   ### Notice to Third Persons

When dissolution is caused by the act of a partner or of the partners, notice must be given to third parties. A notice should expressly state that the partnership has been dissolved. Circumstances from which a termination may be inferred are generally not sufficient notice.

Thus, the fact that the partnership checks added the abbreviation *Inc.* after the partnership name was not sufficient notice that the partnership did not exist and that the business had been incorporated.

Actual notice of dissolution must be given to persons who have dealt with the firm.

CASE SUMMARY

Notice Necessary!

FACTS: Paul Babich ran a business under the name of House of Paul. The business became a partnership between Babich, Dyson, and Schnepp but continued under the same name. The partners arranged for printing advertising material with Philipp Lithographing Company, making contracts on three separate occasions for such printing. During the course of these dealings, the House of Paul became a corporation. When the printing bills were not paid in full, Philipp sued the partners as individuals. They claimed they were not liable because the corporation had made the contracts.

---

[67] R.U.P.A. §701(b). In *Rapport v. Gelfand*, 129 Cal. Rptr. 3d 670, 680 (Cal. App. 2011), the court interpreted the term *liquidation value* as used in R.U.P.A. §701(b) to mean the sale price of the separate assets based on their market value as determined by a willing and knowledgeable buyer and a willing and knowledgeable seller, neither of whom is under any compulsion to buy or sell. Thus, for purposes of section 701, subdivision (b), "liquidation value" does not incorporate the common definition of "liquidation," which generally implies some urgency for immediate cash.
[68] R.U.P.A. §704.
[69] R.U.P.A. §702.

DECISION: Whether or not the House of Paul was a corporation with respect to a particular contract was not important because no notice had been given of its change from a partnership to a corporation. Having originally done business with the defendant as a partnership, Philipp could hold the individual persons liable as partners until notice to the contrary was given to Philipp. [*Philipp Lithographing Co. v. Babich,* 135 N.W.2d 343 (Wis. 1965)]

For persons who have had no dealings with the firm, a publication of the fact of dissolution is sufficient. Such notice may be by newspaper publication, by posting a placard in a public place, or by any similar method. Failure to give proper notice continues the power of each partner to bind the others with respect to third persons on contracts within the scope of the business.

When dissolution has been caused by operation of law, notice to third persons is not required. As between the partners, however, the UPA requires knowledge or notice of dissolution by death and bankruptcy.

41-4g Winding Up Partnership Affairs

Most established partnerships deal with the question of how to proceed with the business upon the death of a partner in the written partnership agreement. The agreement may set forth a method for establishing the value of the deceased partner's interest as of the date of death or allow for the remaining partners to purchase the deceased partner's interest. The agreement may also allow for the continuation of the business as usual while the valuation process is completed. However, in the absence of an agreement, either express or implied, permitting the surviving partners to continue the business, the partners must wind up the business and account for the share of the deceased partner.[70]

When dissolution is obtained by court decree, the court may appoint a receiver to conduct the winding up of the partnership business. This may be done in the usual manner, or the receiver may sell the business as a going concern to those partners who wish to continue its operation.

With a few exceptions, all partners have the right to participate in the winding up of the business.[71]

CPA   41-4h Distribution of Assets

Creditors of the firm have first claim on the assets of the partnership.[72] Difficulty arises when there is a contest between the creditors of the firm and the creditors of the individual partners. The general rule is that firm creditors have first claim on assets of the firm. The individual creditors share in the remaining assets, if any.

After the firm's liabilities to nonpartners have been paid, the assets of the partnership are distributed as follows: (1) each partner is entitled to a refund of advances made to or for the firm, (2) contributions to the capital of the firm are then returned, and (3) the remaining assets, if any, are divided equally as profits among the partners unless there is some other agreement. A partner who contributes only services to the partnership is not considered to have made a capital contribution, absent an agreement to the contrary.

---

[70] *Chaney v. Burdett,* 560 S.E.2d 21 (Ga. 2002); *King v. Stoddard,* 104 Cal. Rptr. 903 (Cal. App. 1972).
[71] U.P.A. §37. In *Urbain v. Beierling,* 835 N.W.2d 455 (Mich. App. 2013), the court found that a partner who was excluded from the winding up should have been given the right to participate, but she could not show that she was damaged.
[72] *Holmes v. Holmes,* 849 P.2d 1140 (Or. App. 1993).

CASE SUMMARY

Are Time and Labor Capital Contributions? Fred Ott Says They Ought to Be

FACTS: Fred Ott and Charles Corley were partners doing business as "Lakewood Associates, a general partnership." Corley provided the capital to purchase the land to be sold by the partnership, called Lakewood Estates. Corley brought suit for the dissolution of the partnership, and Ott contended that his contributions of time and labor in improving Lakewood Estates should be credited to him as capital contributions in the distribution of assets.

DECISION: Judgment for Corley. There was no evidence of any agreement between the partners that Ott's services should be credited as capital contributions. Therefore, the value of the services could not be credited as capital contributions in the distribution of assets. [*Corley v. Ott,* **485 S.E.2d 97 (S.C. 1997)]**

If the partnership has sustained a loss, the partners assume it equally in the absence of a contrary agreement. Distribution of partnership assets must be made on the basis of actual value when it is clear that the book values are merely nominal or arbitrary amounts.

A provision in a partnership agreement that upon the death of a partner the interest of the partner shall pass to that partner's surviving spouse is valid. Such a provision takes effect against the contention that it is not valid because it does not satisfy the requirements applicable to wills.

41-4i Continuation of Partnership Business

As a practical matter, the business of the partnership is commonly continued after dissolution and winding up. In all cases, however, there is a technical dissolution, winding up, and termination of the life of the original partnership.

If the business continues, either with the surviving partners or with additional partners, it is a new partnership. Again, as a practical matter, the liquidation of the old partnership may in effect be merely a matter of bookkeeping entries, with all partners contributing again or relending to the new business any payment to which they would be entitled from the liquidation of the original partnership.

Make the Connection

Summary

A *partnership* is a relationship created by the voluntary association of two or more persons to carry on as co-owners a business for profit.

A partnership agreement governs the partnership during its existence and may also contain provisions relating to dissolution. The partnership agreement will generally be in writing, and this may be required by the statute of frauds. The existence of a partnership may be found from the existence of shared control in the running of the business and the fact that the parties share profits and losses. The sharing of gross returns, as opposed to profits, is slight evidence of a partnership.

Partners hold title to firm property by tenancy in partnership. A creditor of a partner cannot proceed against any specific item of partnership property but must obtain a charging order to seize the debtor-partner's share of the profits. An assignee of a partner's interest does not become a partner without the consent of the other partners and is entitled only to a share of the profits and the assignor's interest upon dissolution.

When there are more than two partners in a firm, the decisions of the majority prevail on ordinary matters relating to the firm's business unless the partnership agreement provides otherwise. A partner's authority to act for the firm is similar to that of an agent to act for a principal. A partner may not bind the firm by a contract that makes it impossible for the firm to conduct its business.

A partner's duties are the same as those of an agent. If there is no contrary agreement, each partner has the right to take an equal part in the management of the business, to inspect the books, to share in the profits, and after payment of all of the firm's debts and the return of capital, to share in the firm's property or surplus upon dissolution.

Partners have unlimited personal liability for partnership liabilities. Partners are jointly liable on all firm contracts. They are jointly and severally liable for all torts committed by one of the partners or by a firm employee within the scope of the partnership's business. A partner remains liable after dissolution unless expressly released by creditors. An incoming partner is not liable for the existing debts of the partnership unless the new partner expressly assumes those debts.

Dissolution ends the right of the partnership to exist as a going concern. Dissolution is followed by a winding-up period and the distribution of assets. A partnership may be dissolved by the parties themselves in accordance with the terms of the partnership agreement, by the expulsion of a partner, by the withdrawal of a partner, or by the bankruptcy of the firm or one of the partners. A court may order dissolution of a partnership upon the petition of a partner because of the insanity, incapacity, or major misconduct of a partner. Dissolution may be decreed because of lack of success, impracticability, or other circumstances that equitably call for dissolution. Notice of dissolution, except dissolution by operation of law, must be given. Actual notice must be given to those who have dealt with the firm as a partnership.

All partners generally have a right to participate in the winding up of the business. After the firm's liabilities to nonpartners have been paid, the assets are distributed among the partners as follows: (1) refund of advances, (2) return of contributions to capital, and (3) division of remaining assets in accordance with the partnership agreement or, if no agreement is stated, division of net assets equally among the partners.

Learning Outcomes

After studying this chapter, you should be able to clearly explain:

41-1   Nature and Creation

LO.1 Explain how partnerships are created by agreement, and understand that only when the partnership agreement does not resolve an issue does partnership law apply

See the example of the dentist who was terminated from the three-person dental partnership without cause by majority vote, where the partnership agreement allowed for such a termination, page 843.

LO.2 Understand that no writing is needed to form a partnership, nor a tax ID number, nor a partnership name. All that is needed is clear evidence that the partners carried on as co-owners of a business for profit

See the *Byker* case where one individual who carried on a business for a profit was dumbfounded to find out that he was, by law, a partner, page 844.

41-2   Authority of Partners

LO.3 Distinguish between express authority and customary authority of a partner to act for a partnership

See the discussion on the role of individual partners to act as expressly directed by a majority of partners (express authority) and to act on their own to make ordinary contracts necessary to transact the firm's business (customary authority), pages 847–848.

41-3   Duties, Rights, and Liabilities of Partners

LO.4 List the duties of partners to one another

See the discussion and examples of partners' duties of loyalty, good faith, and obedience, pages 850–851.

LO.5 Explain the nature and extent of a partner's liability on firm contracts and torts

41-4   Dissolution and Termination

LO.6 Describe how a partnership may be dissolved by the acts of partners, by operation of law, and by order of the court

See the *Della Ratta* case involving partnership dissolution by decree of court because of impracticability, pages 857–858.

See the *Gelman* case discussing unilateral termination of an oral partnership agreement, page 856.

Key Terms

articles of copartnership
articles of partnership
charging order
express authority
general partners

general partnership
jointly and severally liable
jointly liable
operation of law
partners

partnership
partnership agreement
tenancy in partnership
unincorporated association

Questions and Case Problems

1. Ray, Linda, and Nancy form a partnership. Ray and Linda contribute property and cash. Nancy contributes only services. Linda dies, and the partnership is liquidated. After all debts are paid, the surplus is not sufficient to pay back Linda's estate and Ray for the property and cash originally contributed by Linda and Ray. Nancy claims that the balance should be divided equally among Ray, Linda's estate, and Nancy. Is she correct?

2. Baxter, Bigelow, Owens, and Dailey were partners in a New York City advertising agency. Owens, who was in poor health and wanted to retire, advised the partners that she had assigned her full and complete interest in the partnership to her son, Bartholomew, a highly qualified person with 10 years of experience in the advertising business. Baxter, Bigelow, and Dailey refused to allow Bartholomew to attend management meetings and refused his request to inspect the books. Bartholomew pointed out that his mother had invested as much in the firm as any other partner. He believed, as assignee of his mother's full and complete partnership interest, that he is entitled to (a) inspect the books as he sees fit and (b) participate fully in the management of the firm. Was Bartholomew correct?

3. Amy Gargulo and Paula Frisken operated as a partnership Kiddies Korner, an infants' and children's clothing store. They operated the business very successfully for three years, with both Paula and Amy doing the buying and Paula keeping the books and paying the bills. Amy and Paula decided to expand the business when an adjoining store became vacant. At the same time, they incorporated the business. Children's Apparel, Inc., was a major supplier to the business before the expansion. After the expansion, business did not increase as anticipated, and when a nationally known manufacturer of children's apparel opened a factory outlet nearby, the business could no longer pay its bills. Children's Apparel, which had supplied most of the store's stock after expansion, sued Amy and Paula as partners for bills due for

expansion stock. Children's Apparel did not know that Amy and Paula had incorporated. Amy and Paula contended that the business was incorporated and that they therefore were not liable for business debts occurring after incorporation. Were Amy and Paula correct?

4. Calvin Johnson and Rudi Basecke did business as the Stockton Cheese Co., a partnership, which owned a building and equipment. The partners agreed to dissolve the partnership but never got around to completing the winding-up process. Calvin continued to use the building and to pay insurance on it but removed Rudi's name as an insured on the policy. When the building was later destroyed by fire, Calvin claimed the proceeds of the fire insurance policy because he and his wife were the named insureds on the policy and they had paid the premiums. Rudi claimed that although the partnership was dissolved before the fire, the winding up of the partnership was not completed at the time of the fire. He therefore claimed that he was entitled to half of the net proceeds of the policy. Decide. [*State Casualty v. Johnson*, 766 S.W.2d 113 (Mo. App.)]

5. Samuel Shaw purchased a ticket through Delta Airlines to fly a "Delta Connection" flight on SkyWest Airlines to Elko, Nevada. He was seriously injured when the SkyWest plane crashed near Elko. SkyWest's relationship with Delta was a contractual business referral arrangement, whereby Delta benefits through its charges for issuing tickets to connecting passengers to and from smaller communities, and SkyWest benefits from revenue generated by passengers sent to it by Delta. Both firms make a profit from this arrangement. SkyWest and Delta are often mentioned together by Delta in national print advertisements. Shaw believed that regardless of how the airlines characterize themselves, these airlines are in fact partners because they share profits from their combined efforts. Delta contended that it had no control over SkyWest's airplane operations and that sharing profits as compensation for services does not

create a partnership. Decide. [*Shaw v. Delta Airlines, Inc.*, 798 F. Supp. 1453 (D. Nev.)]

6. After graduating from Vanderbilt University with a degree in economics, James Pettes worked for Video Magic, a video rental business. In 1987, Dr. Gordon Yukon, a pediatrician, wanted to invest in a two-store video business called Rent-a-Flick. One store was located on Quince Road and the other in Germantown. Pettes testified that Yukon paid $42,000 for the business and that he and Yukon agreed they would be partners. Pettes would manage the two stores and earn the same amount he earned at Video Magic. Pettes testified that he worked 70 to 80 hours a week and that his "sweat equity" was a capital contribution to the partnership. He also testified that Yukon frequently referred to him as a partner. According to Pettes, in 1992, the parties agreed to divide the business, with the Germantown store going to Yukon and the Quince Road store to Pettes. In December 1992, Pettes made a written demand for an accounting. On January 5, 1993, Dr. Yukon "fired" Pettes. Sutherland, an employee, testified that when she questioned Yukon about firing a partner, Yukon did not deny that there was a partnership but stated that Pettes could not prove there was a partnership because there was no written agreement. Pettes sued for breach of an oral partnership agreement and an accounting. Decide. [*Pettes v. Yukon*, 912 S.W.2d (Tenn. App.)]

7. Two brothers, Eugene and Marlowe Mehl, formed a partnership to operate the family farm. One year, Eugene Mehl withdrew $7,200 from the partnership account and bought the Dagmar Bar. The warranty deed and the liquor license to the bar were obtained in the names of Eugene Mehl and his wife, Bonnie. In a subsequent lawsuit, Marlowe claimed that the bar was a partnership asset. Decide. [*Mehl v. Mehl*, 786 P.2d 1173 (Mont.)]

8. Summers and Dooley formed a partnership to collect trash. Summers became unable to work and he hired a third man to do his work and paid him out of his personal funds. Summers suggested to Dooley that the third man be paid from the partnership funds, but Dooley refused to do so. Summers sued Dooley for reimbursement of the money he spent to pay the third man. Decide.

9. Thomas Bartomeli decided to leave his employment to join his brother Raymond full-time in a small construction company. The brothers each contributed individual assets to the company and worked together to acquire equipment with both signing notes jointly to acquire certain equipment. Thomas considered himself a partner in the company; Raymond often referred to Thomas as his partner. It was the practice of the company to garage the equipment at Thomas's house. In 1983, the company was incorporated, but Thomas never held any shares in the company. On several occasions, Thomas's careless operation of equipment resulted in loss or damage to the company. Raymond became dissatisfied with Thomas's work performance, and on January 17, 1991, Thomas was removed as secretary of the corporation.

On April 19, 1991, Thomas went to the company office and demanded a blank check from the secretary. Raymond found out about this demand and fired him. On April 20, 1991, Thomas demanded from Raymond either 50 percent of the company or certain equipment owned by the company. On April 22, 1991, Thomas was removed as vice president of the company. Raymond attempted to reach an agreement with Thomas on a division of company assets at that point but was not successful. Thereafter, Thomas sued his brother, alleging that Raymond had breached the brothers' contract of partnership. Because the company was a corporation, is it legally inconsistent for Thomas to contend that there was a contract for partnership in the company? How would you decide this case? [*Bartomeli v. Bartomeli*, 783 A.2d 1050 (Ct. App.)]

10. Friedman, the "O" Street Carpet Shop, Inc., and Langness formed a partnership known as NFL Associates. "O" Street Carpet's net contribution to capital was $5,004; Langness contributed $14,000 in cash; and Friedman contributed his legal services, on which no value was placed by the articles of partnership. The articles stated that Friedman was entitled to 10 percent of the profits and that Langness was to receive payments of $116.66 per month. The partnership's accountant treated the payments to Langness as a return of her capital. Years later, the partnership sold the rental property owned by the partnership, and the partnership was wound up. Friedman claimed that he was entitled to 10 percent of the partnership capital upon dissolution. Langness claimed that Friedman was not entitled to a capital distribution and that the monthly payments to her should not have been treated as a return of capital. Decide. [*Langness v. "O" Street Carpet, Inc.*, 353 N.W.2d 709 (Neb.)]

11. Ross, Marcos, and Albert are partners. Ross and Marcos each contributed $60,000 to the partnership; Albert contributed $30,000. At the end of the fiscal year, distributable profits total $150,000. Ross claims $60,000 as his share of the profits. Is he entitled to this sum?

12. Leland McElmurry was one of three partners of MHS Enterprises, a Michigan partnership. Commonwealth Capital Investment Corp. sued the partnership and obtained a judgment of $1,137,285 against it, but the partnership could not pay the judgment. Commonwealth then sued McElmurry for the entire debt on the theory that, as a partner of MHS, he was liable for its debts. What, if any, is McElmurry's liability? [*Commonwealth Capital Investment Corp. v. McElmurry*, 302 N.W.2d 222 (Mich. App.)]

13. Thomas Smith and Jackie Lea were partners in the logging business. In January 1981, they joined Gordon Redd and went into business running a sawmill, calling the business Industrial Hardwood Products (IHP). Smith and Lea used their logging equipment at the mill site. Smith hauled 400 loads of gravel, worth some $26,000, from his father's land for the mill yard in the process of getting the mill operational. Smith and Lea received $300 a week compensation for their work, which was reported on federal W-2 forms. They worked up to 65 hours per week and were not paid overtime. All three discussed business decisions. Smith and Lea had the authority to write checks and to hire and fire employees. Lea left the business in 1983 and was paid $20,000 by Redd. The testimony indicated that the three individuals agreed in January 1981 that as soon as the bank was paid off and Redd was paid his investment, Lea and Smith would be given an interest in the mill. No written agreement existed. Redd invested $410,452 in the business and withdrew $500,475 from it. As of December 31, 1986, IHP had sufficient retained earnings to retire the bank debt. In April 1987, Smith petitioned the Chancery Court for dissolution of the "partnership" and an accounting. Redd denied that any partnership agreement was formed and asserted that Smith was an employee because he was paid wages. He offered to pay Smith $50,000 for the gravel and use of his equipment. Decide. [*Smith v. Redd*, 593 So. 2d 989 (Miss.)]

14. Mason and Phyllis Ledbetter operated a business in Northbrook, Illinois, as a partnership called Ledbetters' Nurseries that specialized in the sale of garden lilies. The grounds of the nurseries were planted with numerous species of garden lilies, and hundreds of people toured the Ledbetters' gardens every day. After a tour, Sheila Clark offered to buy the facilities at a "top-notch price." Mason felt he could not refuse the high offer, and he signed a contract to sell all the facilities, including all flowers and the business name. When Phyllis refused to go along with the contract, Clark sued the Ledbetters' Nurseries partnership, seeking to obtain specific performance of the sales contract. Decide.

15. St. John Transportation Co., a corporation, made a contract with the partnership of Bilyeu and Herstel, contractors, by which the latter was to construct a ferryboat. Herstel, a member of the firm of contractors, executed a contract in the firm name with Benbow for certain materials and labor in connection with the construction of the ferryboat. In an action brought by Benbow to enforce a lien against the ferryboat, the *James Johns*, it was contended that all members of the firm were bound by the contract made by Herstel. Do you agree? [*Benbow v. The Ferryboat James Johns*, 108 P. 634 (Or.)]

CPA Questions

1. Acorn and Bean were general partners in a farm machinery business. Acorn contracted, on behalf of the partnership, to purchase 10 tractors from Cobb Corp. Unknown to Cobb, Acorn was not authorized by the partnership to make such contracts. Bean refused to allow the partnership to accept delivery of the tractors, and Cobb sought to enforce the contract. Cobb will:

   a. Lose, because Acorn's action was beyond the scope of Acorn's implied authority.

   b. Prevail, because Acorn had implied authority to bind the partnership.

   c. Prevail, because Acorn had apparent authority to bind the partnership.

   d. Lose, because Acorn's express authority was restricted, in writing, by the partnership agreement.

2. Upon dissolution of a general partnership, distributions will be made on account of:
   I. Partners' capital accounts.
   II. Amounts owed partners with respect to profits.
   III. Amounts owed partners for loans to the partnership in the following order:

   a. III, I, II

   b. I, II, III

   c. II, III, I

   d. III, II, I

3. Which of the following statements is correct with respect to a limited partnership?

   a. A limited partner may *not* be an unsecured creditor of the limited partnership.

   b. A general partner may *not* also be a limited partner at the same time.

   c. A general partner may be a secured creditor of the limited partnership.

   d. A limited partnership can be formed with limited liability for all partners.

4. When a partner in a general partnership lacks actual or apparent authority to contract on behalf of the partnership, and the party contracted with is aware of this fact, the partnership will be bound by the contract if the other partners:

	Ratify the Contract	*Amend the Partnership Agreement*
a.	Yes	Yes
b.	Yes	No
c.	No	Yes
d.	No	No

LPs, LLCs, and LLPs

Learning Outcomes <<<

After studying this chapter, you should be able to

LO.1 Explain the history of making limited liability available to general partnerships

LO.2 Explain the extent of a founding general partner's liability for the debts of the firm, and how unlimited liability can be avoided by utilization of a corporate general partner

LO.3 Explain the nature and extent of a limited partner's liability for the debts of the firm

LO.4 Explain the advantages of a limited liability company

LO.5 Understand that an LLC is not liable for the conduct of its promoters prior to organization

LO.6 Understand that unless modified in an operating agreement, managers of LLCs owe member-investors the traditional duties of loyalty and care

LO.7 Explain how a limited liability partnership "shields" innocent partners from liability to third parties

42-1 The Arrival of Partnership Limited Liability

Individuals owning businesses or professional firms are concerned about exposing their personal wealth to liability beyond that invested in their businesses or firms. As discussed previously, limited liability is not a feature of general partnership law. The concept of making limited liability available to general partnerships was considered by the RUPA Drafting Committee when it began its work to revise the Uniform Partnership Act in 1987, but the concept was rejected. A limited partnership form of business organization had existed since 1916 under the Uniform Limited Partnership Act with limited partners (investors) having limited liability, but the firm's general partners were exposed to personal liability for firm debts under this act. The concept of full limited liability for partnerships began to take hold in 1986 when businesses forming limited partnerships under the Revised Uniform Limited Partnership Act utilized corporate general partners, with the general partners avoiding personal liability by the simple expedient of incorporating.

An IRS ruling classifying a Wyoming limited liability company (LLC) as a partnership for tax purposes led to the rapid spread of LLC statutes to every state within six years of the IRS ruling.[1] As part of the limited liability trend established by the swift enactment of LLC laws throughout the country, most states have also enacted limited liability partnership (LLP) acts. Like LLCs, they provide businesses and those offering professional services the benefit of single taxation as a partnership as well as limited liability.

42-2 Limited Partnership

A limited partnership is a special kind of partnership.

42-2a Formation of Limited Partnerships

The Uniform Limited Partnership Act (ULPA) was approved by the National Conference of Commissioners on Uniform State Law in 1916. It was revised in 1976 as the Revised Uniform Limited Partnership Act (RULPA) and was amended in 1985. All states except Louisiana have adopted a version of the RULPA.

Members of a Limited Partnership

limited partnership—partnership that can be formed by "one or more general partners and one or more limited partners."

limited partner—partner who neither takes part in the management of the partnership nor appears to the public to be a general partner.

general partner—partnership in which the partners conduct as co-owners a business for profit, and each partner has a right to take part in the management of the business and has unlimited liability; general partners publicly and actively engage in the transaction of firm business.

In a **limited partnership** certain members contribute capital but have limited liability for firm debts. The most these members can lose is their investment. These members are known as **limited partners.** The partners who manage the business are called **general partners.** General partners are personally liable for the firm's debts.[2] A limited partnership can be formed by "one or more general partners and one or more limited partners."[3]

Certificate of Limited Partnership

Unlike a general partnership, a limited partnership can be created only by executing a certificate of limited partnership.

Under the 1985 amendments to the RULPA, the certificate requires the following information: (1) the limited partnership's name, (2) the address of the partnership's registered office and the name and business address of its agent for service of process, (3) the name and business address of each general partner, (4) the partnership's mailing address, and (5) the latest date on which the limited partnership is to dissolve. The names of the limited partners (the investors) are not required in order to preserve the confidentiality of the investors'

---

[1] Rev. Rul. 88-76, 1988—2 C.B. 360.
[2] *Brooke v. Mt. Hood Meadows, Ltd.,* 725 P.2d 925 (Or. App. 1986).
[3] R.U.L.P.A. §101(7).

names from competitors. New investors may be admitted as limited partners without the significant administrative burden involved in amending the certificate, as was required under the ULPA. The RULPA provides that the certificate should be filed with the Office of the Secretary of State, as opposed to the local filing required under the ULPA.

If a limited partnership certificate is not filed, all participants have the status and liability of general partners in a general partnership. However, technical defects in the certificate do not prevent formation of a limited partnership if there has been substantial, good-faith compliance with the filing requirements.[4]

CPA Limited Partnership Agreement

The RULPA embodies the policy of freedom of contract and maximum flexibility regarding the limited partnership agreement.[5] Most limited partnership agreements are drafted almost exclusively by their founding general partners. Courts resolve ambiguities against the drafting general partners and in favor of the reasonable expectations of the limited partners. **For Example,** when the general partners of the Nantucket Island Associates Limited Partnership unilaterally amended the limited partnership agreement to add a new class of preferred limited partnership units with superior rights to existing unit holders, the court construed the ambiguous language in the agreement against the general partners. The general partners were found to be in breach of the agreement by adding the new class of units.[6]

42-2b Characteristics of Limited Partnerships

A limited partnership has the following characteristics.

CPA Capital Contributions

Under the ULPA, a limited partner contributed either cash or property but not services. Under the RULPA, however, a limited partner may contribute services.

CPA Firm Name

With certain exceptions, a limited partner's name cannot appear in the firm name. Under the RULPA, the words *limited partnership* must appear without abbreviation in the firm name.

CPA Management and Control of the Firm

The general partners manage the business and are personally liable for firm debts. However, general partners may avoid personal liability by incorporating. Limited partners (the investors) have the right to a share of the profits and a return of capital upon dissolution; they also have limited liability. The limitation of liability is lost, however, if they participate in the control of the business.

The RULPA lists a number of "safe harbor" activities in which limited partners may engage without losing their protection from liability. These activities include:

1. Being a contractor for, or an agent or employee of, the limited partnership or of a general partner;
2. Consulting with and advising a general partner regarding the partnership business;
3. Acting as a surety for the limited partnership; and
4. Voting on partnership matters, such as dissolving and winding up the limited partnership or removing a general partner.

[4] R.U.L.P.A. §201(b); *Fabry Partnership v. Christensan*, 794 P.2d 719 (Nev. 1990).
[5] See *Gotham Partners, L.P. v. Hallowood Realty Partners, LP*, 817 A.2d 160 (Del. 2002).
[6] In re *Nantucket Island Associates Limited Partnership Unit Holders Litigation*, 810 A.2d 351 (Del. Ch. 2002).

Right to Sue

A limited partner may bring a derivative action on behalf of the limited partnership to enforce a claim that the limited partnership possesses against others but that the partnership refuses to enforce.[7] This derivative suit is filed in the name of the limited partner, and the partnership is named as a defendant, with the limited partnership deriving the benefits of the action.

Limited partners may sue their partnership's general partner to protect the limited partners' interest. General partners today are commonly corporations with their own boards of directors and management teams, with the limited partnership format providing investment and tax incentives for investor–limited partners and the general partners reserving to themselves broad authority to act in the general partners' sole discretion and often in the general partners' own best interest. **For Example,** Donald Weedon and others formed a limited partnership under Delaware law to raise capital for the securities broker–dealer business. The partnership agreement, as allowed by Delaware law, gave the corporate general partners and its directors the right to restrict their fiduciary duties in managing the partnership and gave the general partner broad power to act, even in conflicted situations, subject only to very loose constraints of a subjective bad-faith standard. Nonemployee limited partners referred to by the court as the "outside investors" brought suit against the corporate general partners and members of the general partner's board of directors and top management for squeezing out all nonemployee limited partners and paying less than the fair value for their units in violation of fiduciary duties and the partnership agreement. The trial court decided in favor of the plaintiffs, stating in part:

> … *Even given the wide discretion the partnership agreement gives to the defendants to issue new units without fear of liability, the defendants managed to step out of bounds in one important respect. By deciding to permit the general partner's outside directors to acquire new units at a favorable price and by denying the same opportunity to Outside Investors, the defendants breached their contractual duties. This decision, I find, was not undertaken in good faith but instead as quid pro quo for the outside directors' willing assent to the issuance of a large number of new units to management and employees.…*

The plaintiffs received a make-whole remedy from the court with monetary damages tied to fair market values.[8]

Dissolution

The dissolution and winding up of limited partnerships is governed by the same principles applicable to general partnerships.

42-3 Limited Liability Companies

Limited liability company (LLC) acts were rapidly adopted by state legislatures throughout the country following a favorable tax ruling on this form of organization by the Internal Revenue Service.[9] This corporate-sounding entity is considered in this chapter because it is a form of limited partnership.

---

[7] *Garber v. Stevens*, 941 N.Y.S.2d 127 (A.D. 2012).
[8] *Gelfman v. Weeden Investors, L.P.*, 859 A.2d 89 (Del. Ch. 2004).
[9] IRS Rev. Rul. 88-76. LLCs have been adopted by every state and the District of Columbia. A Uniform Limited Liability Company Act was approved by the National Conference of Commissioners on Uniform State Law.

CPA   42-3a **Characteristics of LLCs**

The IRS has determined that an LLC may qualify for partnership federal tax treatment. Unlike a corporation, an LLC pays no federal taxes on its income as an entity. Instead, the income (or losses, deductions, and credits) flows through to the LLC's owners (called *members*) based on their proportionate interest in the company. The members report the income on their personal tax returns. The LLC combines this tax advantage with the limited liability feature of the corporate form of business organization. The owners and managers are not personally liable for the debts and obligations of the entity, provided that these individuals fulfill their common law duty to disclose that they are acting as agents for the limited liability company.

CPA   **Formation**

As set forth previously, general partnerships may be created without the formality of a written partnership agreement when two individuals operate a business for profit as co-owners. LLCs, however, require a formal filing of articles of organization with the Secretary of State in a manner similar to a filing of articles of incorporation by a corporation or a certificate of limited partnership for a limited partnership.

The articles for an LLC must contain the name, purpose, duration, registered agent, and principal office of the LLC. An LLC must use the words *limited liability company* or *LLC* in the company's name. The LLC is a legal entity with authority to conduct business in its own name.[10] LLC acts are characterized as "flexible statutes" because they generally permit owners to engage in the private ordering of relationships, with broad freedom of contract to govern these relationships as set forth in their operating agreements.[11]

Liability of Promoters

Before the LLC is formally organized, promoters prepare for the conduct of business. Promoters may enter into contracts or seek investors for the new entity. An LLC is generally not liable for the preformation contracts of its promoters.

CASE SUMMARY

All Bottled Up!

FACTS: Clifford Hansen was an entrepreneur who sought to purchase a water bottling company in South Carolina. He approached Robert Fields for help locating investors and securing financing. Fields and Hansen worked together for some time. But Fields began to work on behalf of his own company, Fields Company LLC, as well as other LLCs. He found investors to purchase the water bottling company on behalf of these entities and cut Hansen out of the deal.

Hansen sued Fields Company LLC for breach of fiduciary duty, breach of contract, and several torts. A jury found for Hansen with damages over one million dollars. Fields Company LLC appealed.

DECISION: Judgment for Fields Company, LLC. The LLC is not liable for its promoter's preincorporation contracts unless the contract was ratified expressly or implicitly by

---

[10] An individual has a right to appear before a court and represent himself or herself. However, a member of an LLC who as such is not personally liable for the LLC's actions cannot appear before a court on behalf of the LLC entity. The LLC may appear in court only through counsel. Thus, a nonattorney member of an LLC was not allowed to represent the LLC in a court case. *Collier v. Cobalt, LLC*, 2002 WL 726640 (E.D. La. April 22, 2002). See also *Gobe Media Group, LLC v. Cisneros*, 959 A.2d 892 (N.J. Super. 2008).

[11] *Elf Atochem N. America, Inc. v. Jaffari*, 727 A.2d 286 (Del. Super. Ct. 1999).

All Bottled Up! continued

accepting its benefits. There was no evidence that Fields LLC ratified any contract with Hansen or that it accepted any benefits of Fields' or his related entities' contracts with Hansen. The general rule regarding a corporation's liability for torts is that a promoter is not liable for torts that its promoters committed before it came into existence. An LLC is not liable for torts committed by its promoter prior to organization because (1) there is no agency relationship between a promoter and a non-existent LLC; (2) the injured party may seek recourse from the promoter directly; and (3) the potential for such liability would stifle investment. **[*Hansen v. Fields Company, LLC,* 763 S.E.2d 31 (S.C. 2014)]**

CPA Capital Contributions

An ownership interest in an LLC may be issued for cash, property, or services.

If there is no operating agreement, statutory provisions govern the relationship between the members and the operation of the company.[12] If there is an operating agreement, the members must comply with its terms, including provisions on capital contributions. **For Example,** William Eichengrun claimed that his capital contribution to the LLC was in services, not cash, because he was the LLC's managing member. However, in proceedings to dissolve the LLC and distribute its assets, Eichengrun was not allowed to participate in the distribution because the operating agreement required that "initial capital contributions" of members be in cash or the fair market value of property.[13]

CPA Management

Management of an LLC is vested in its members. An *operating agreement*, equivalent to the bylaws of a corporation or a partnership agreement, sets forth the specific management authority of members and managers.

The operating agreement need not be in writing. All amendments must be unanimous unless otherwise agreed to by the members. Oral amendments may modify written terms unless otherwise set forth in the operating agreement. To promote certainty in management, it is recommended that the operating agreement be in writing and that it be changed only by written amendments adopted by a specified percentage or number of members.

The management structure created in the operating agreement may provide for the company to be member managed. However, members commonly delegate authority to run the entity to managers who may or may not be required to be members of the LLC. A member is not entitled to compensation for services performed for an LLC unless it is stipulated in the operating agreement. (Members receive profits and losses according to the terms of the operating agreement.)

In a member-managed company, each member has equal rights in management, with decisions made by a majority vote of the members.[14] In a manager-managed company, nonmanager members have no rights in management except for extraordinary matters, such as amending the operating agreement or consenting to merge with another entity.

Managers have the same fiduciary duties to the entity as corporate officers have to a corporation. LLC acts are characterized as "flexible statutes" allowing broad freedom of contract to govern relationships, as spelled out in detail in operating agreements. The parties are free to waive or modify the duties of loyalty and care owed by managers to

---

[12] *Germano v. Beaujean,* 997 N.E.2d 1238 (Ohio App. 2013).
[13] *KSI Rockville, LLC v. Eichengrun,* 760 N.Y.S.2d 520 (A. D. 2003).
[14] *IIC Holdings, LLC v. HR Software Acquisition Group, Inc.,* 750 N.Y.S.2d 425 (Sup. Ct. 2002).

members in the operating agreement. Unless modified by the operating agreement, however, state LLC acts may apply fiduciary duties to managers who would qualify as fiduciaries under traditional equitable principles.

CASE SUMMARY

Golf Course Owner Out of Bounds

FACTS: Minority members in a Delaware limited liability company, Peconic Bay, LLC, brought a breach of fiduciary duty action against the LLC's manager and its majority interest holder regarding the sale of the LLC at an auction, in which the LLC was purchased by the manager. The "manager" was Gatz Properties, LLC, which was managed and partially owned by William Gatz. Peconic Bay, LLC, held a long-term lease on valuable property in New York that allowed the LLC to operate a first-rate Robert Trent Jones, Jr., designed golf course, called Long Island National Golf Course. The golf management company, American Golf, held a sublease on the property after it opened in 1999, never made a profit, and let the course fall into disrepair. Gatz knew in 2004 that American Golf would exercise its early termination option in 2010, yet he did nothing to plan for its exit. Rather, Gatz made a series of decisions that placed Peconic Bay in an economically vulnerable position. Then Gatz decided to put Peconic Bay on the auction block without engaging an experienced broker to market it to golf course managers or owners. Gatz, on behalf of Gatz Properties, was the only bidder to show up. Knowing this fact before formulating his bid, Gatz purchased Peconic Bay for a nominal value over the debt and merged Peconic Bay into Gatz Properties.

DECISION: Judgment for the minority members. The LLC agreement made it clear that the manager could enter into a self-dealing transaction, such as its purchase of the LLC, only if it proved that the terms were fair. The LLC agreement essentially incorporated a core element of the traditional fiduciary duty of loyalty. The manager's defense that his voting power gave him a license to exploit the minority shareholders fundamentally misunderstands Delaware law. The manager was free not to vote his membership interest for a sale. But he was not free to create a situation of distress by failing to cause the LLC to explore its market alternatives and then buying the LLC for a nominal price. The purpose of the duty of loyalty is in large measure to prevent the exploitation by a fiduciary of his self-interest to the disadvantage of the minority. The fair price requirement of that duty, which is incorporated in the LLC agreement here, makes sure that if the conflicted fiduciary engages in self-dealing, he pays a price that is as much as an arms-length purchaser would pay. [*Auriga Capital Corp. v. Gatz Properties, LLC,* **40 A.3d 839 (Del. Ch. 2012)**]

In some states, members of manager-managed LLCs owe no fiduciary duty to the LLC unless a member exercises some or all of the authority of a manager pursuant to the operating agreement.[15]

CPA Distributions

Profits and losses are shared according to the terms of the operating agreement.

Liquidating distributions must first be applied to return all contributions not previously returned, and the remainder is distributed per capita to members unless members alter these rules in the operating agreement.

---

[15] In *Remora Investments, LLC v. Orr*, 673 S.E.2d 845 (Va. 2009), the Virginia Supreme Court held that nothing in the statutory provisions relating to LLCs provides for fiduciary duties between members of an LLC or between a member and a manager of an LLC. The statutory standard of conduct for a manager of an LLC is to discharge duties in accordance with his or her good-faith business judgment of the best interests of the company, rather than by imposing fiduciary duties on members. In contrast, the Uniform Limited Liability Act of 2006, which has been adopted in Idaho, Iowa, Nebraska, Utah, and Wyoming, states that members of an LLC owe each other the fiduciary duties of loyalty and care. See *Bush v. Sage Health Care, LLC*, 203 P.3d 694 (Idaho 2009). See also *Melcher v. Apollo Medical Fund Management*, 208 N.Y.S.2d 207 (A.D. 2006), referencing Delaware Code, Title 6 §18-110(c).

Any distribution made when the company is insolvent is unlawful. Each member or manager who votes to make an unlawful distribution is in violation of his or her fiduciary duty to the firm and is personally liable for the amount of distribution improperly paid.[16] However, the individual may compel contribution from all other responsible members and managers.

LLC Property

The LLC is an independent entity separate and distinct from the members. The LLC owns and holds property in its own name.[17]

Assignment

An interest in an LLC is personal property and is generally assignable. However, LLC members cannot transfer the right to participate in management without the consent of the other members of the LLC.

CASE SUMMARY

"I'm in Charge," said the Admiral's Daughter.
"No, You're Not," said the Admiral's New Wife.

FACTS: Admiral Dewey Monroe and his wife Lou Ann Monroe formed an LLC in 2003, with Dewey holding an 80% membership interest and Lou Ann a 20% membership interest, respectively. The LLC provided that Lou Ann would be the managing member. Dewey died in 2004 and bequeathed his entire estate to his daughter, Janet Ott. Janet called a meeting of the company, seeking to remove Lou Ann and elect herself as the company's new managing member, asserting that she had inherited her father's full LLC membership upon his death under his will. The LLC asserted that Janet had inherited only Dewey's right to share profits

and losses and to receive distributions but did not inherit a right to the management and control of the company.

DECISION: Judgment for the LLC and Lou Ann. Dewey Monroe was dissociated from the company upon his death by operation of law, terminating all his rights as a member to participate in the management and control of the company. Only the right to share profits and losses and to receive distributions survived to be inherited by Janet under his will. [*Ott v. Monroe*, 719 S.E.2d 309 (Va. 2011)]

A creditor's right against a member's interest in an LLC is limited to a *charging order*. The creditor with such an order has only the rights of an assignee of an interest in an LLC.

Dissolution

Most LLC statutes provide that an LLC will dissolve by the consent of the members or upon the death, retirement, resignation, expulsion, or bankruptcy of a member. Statutes also provide, however, that the business of the LLC may be continued with the consent of all of the remaining members. With a change in IRS regulations away from its four-factor corporate characteristics test, discussed in the following section, some states have begun to amend LLC laws to give limited liability companies the option of perpetual existence.

Situations in which it is not reasonably practicable to carry on the business in conformity with the operating agreement may arise. The LLC statute commonly permits a court

---

[16] *Florence Cement Co. v. Vitttaino*, 807 N.W.2d 461 (Mich. App. 2011).
[17] *Northeast Realty, LLC v. Misty Bayou, LLC*, 920 So. 2d 938 (La. App. 2006).

FIGURE 42-1	**Comparison of General Partnership, Limited Partnership, Limited Liability Company, and Limited Liability Partnership**			
	General Partnership	**Limited Partnership**	**Limited Liability Company (LLC)**	**Limited Liability Partnership (LLP)**
Creation	No formality required.	Filing a certificate of limited partnership with appropriate state office.	Filing articles of organization with Secretary of State.	Registration of LLP filed with state government.
Liability	Unlimited liability of each partner for firm debts.	General partners: unlimited liability for firm debts. Limited partners: no liability beyond loss of investment.	All members are liable for LLC debts to the extent of their capital contributions and equity in firm. No personal liability beyond this.	No liability for partners beyond their contributions and equity in firm, except unlimited personal liability for their own wrongful acts and those of persons whom they supervise.
Management	All partners according to their partnership agreement or the UPA or RUPA.	General partners according to their partnership agreement or the UPA or RUPA. Limited partners excluded.	By members of firm, who may delegate authority to managers.	All partners according to partnership agreement or the UPA.
Dissolution	As set forth in the partnership agreement or the UPA or RUPA.	As set forth in the partnership agreement or the ULPA or RULPA.	As set forth in LLC statute or articles of organization.	As set forth in partnership agreement or the UPA or RUPA.

to decree dissolution of the LLC when such a situation occurs.[18] **For Example,** Haley and Talcott each had a 50 percent interest in a real estate LLC. They had a falling out. The operating agreement contained an exit mechanism to buy out Haley's share, but the

[18] *Venture Sales, LLC v. Perkins*, 86 So. 3d 910 (Miss. 2012).

mechanism could not relieve Haley of his obligation as a personal guarantor for the LLC's mortgage. Because the LLC was deadlocked and the exit mechanism was not an adequate remedy, the court ordered the dissolution of the LLC and the sale of its property.[19]

Upon the winding up of an LLC, the assets are distributed according to the operating agreement. Should the agreement fail to provide for this event, the assets will be distributed according to the state's LLC statute.

Tax Classification

The IRS applied a four-factor corporate characteristics test to determine whether an LLC would be taxed as a partnership or a corporation. If the LLC had more than two of the characteristics, it would not qualify for taxation as a partnership. The factors were continuity of life, centralized management, limited liability, and free transferability of interest. The four-factor test became obsolete when the IRS implemented its so-called check-the-box entity classification election procedure available to unincorporated associations that are not publicly traded.[20] Now, if an LLC wants to be classified as a partnership, all it needs to do is make that election by checking the box on the appropriate IRS form.

Disregarding the LLC Entity

Some LLC statutes provide that courts may disregard the LLC entirely and hold the owners personally liable beyond their investments to the same extent as done in corporate law when exceptional circumstances demand.[21] Courts will disregard the corporate entity and hold individuals liable to prevent injustice, but doing so is the exception rather than the rule.[22]

CASE SUMMARY

Piercing the LLC Veil

FACTS: Kaycee Land and Livestock entered into a contract with Flahive Oil and Gas, LLC, allowing it to use the surface of its real property. Kaycee alleged that Flahive Oil and Gas caused environmental contamination of its real property. Because the LLC had no assets at the time of suit, Kaycee sought to pierce the limited liability company veil and disregard the LLC entity of Flahive Oil and Gas and hold Roger Flahive, the managing member of the LLC who directed all operations on the property, individually liable for the contamination. The question presented to the court was, "In the absence of fraud, is the remedy of piercing the veil available against a company formed under the Wyoming Limited Liability Company Act?"

DECISION: The equitable remedy of piercing the corporate veil is available under the Wyoming Limited Liability Company Act. When corporations fail to follow the statutorily mandated formalities, commingle funds, or ignore restrictions in their articles of incorporation regarding separate treatment of the corporate property, the courts deem it appropriate to disregard the separate identity and do not permit shareholders to be sheltered from liability to third parties for damages caused by the corporation's acts. No public policy exists to treat LLCs differently than corporations regarding veil piercing. [*Kaycee Land and Livestock v. Flahive*, 46 P.3d 323 (Wyo. 2002)]

---

[19] *Haley v. Talcott*, 864 A.2d 86 (Del. Ch. 2004).
[20] Treas. Reg. 301.7701 *et seq.*
[21] *Net Jets Aviation, Inc. v. LHC Communications, LLC*, 537 F.3d 168 (2d Cir. 2008); but see *Serio v. Baystate Properties, LLC*, 39 A.3d 131 (Md. App. 2012).
[22] See *Hibbs v. Berger*, 430 S.W.3d 296 (2014).

42-3b LLCs and Other Entities

LLCs are distinguishable from Subchapter S corporations and limited partnerships.

LLC Distinguished from a Subchapter S Corporation

Under a Subchapter S corporation (so named from Subchapter S of the Internal Revenue Code), shareholders of a close corporation may be treated as partners for tax purposes and retain the benefit of limited liability under the corporate form. An S corporation is limited to 100 shareholders who must be U.S. citizens or resident aliens.[23] Although partnerships and corporations may generally not be shareholders, employee stock ownership plans (ESOPs) and nonprofit entities may be. In contrast, an LLC has no limit on the number of owners, and there is no restriction on the types of entities or persons who may own an LLC. Thus, partnerships, corporations, and foreign investors may be owners of an LLC. Because substantial taxes on appreciated assets are payable on the liquidation of an S corporation, it is generally not feasible to convert an existing S corporation to an LLC.

CPA ### LLC Distinguished from a Limited Partnership

Limited partners in a limited partnership have the advantage of limited liability. However, every limited partnership must have a general partner who manages the business, and this partner can be subject to unlimited liability. This structural feature is a major disadvantage of the limited partnership form that does not exist in a limited liability company (LLC). Also, individual limited partners may lose their limited liability if they participate in the control of the business. Under an LLC, the members may actively participate in the control of the business and still receive limited liability protection. As stated previously in this chapter, a general partner may avoid unlimited liability on a sizeable limited partnership project by incorporating.

Usage

The LLC will in many instances replace general and limited partnerships as well as close corporations and S corporations. The LLC will not replace the publicly traded corporation, however, because publicly traded companies and LLCs must be classified as corporations for tax purposes.[24]

42-4 Limited Liability Partnerships

As part of the limited liability trend established by the swift enactment of LLC laws throughout the country, most states have enacted limited liability partnership (LLP) acts. Like LLCs, they provide businesses and those offering professional services the benefit of single taxation as a partnership as well as limited liability.[25]

---

[23] See IRS, S Corporations, **http://www.irs.gov/Businesses/Small-Businesses-&-Self-Employed/S-Corporations.**

[24] See IRS Notice 88-75, 1988, 1988-2 CB 386. The traditional corporation retains many advantages, such as the low corporate income tax on corporate profits, which allows accumulation of capital for expansion or the distribution of all corporate earnings as compensation as well as providing fringe benefits for employee-owners with pretax dollars (IRC §§79, 119, 162).

[25] The 1994 Revised Uniform Partnership Act (RUPA) was amended in 1996 to include two new articles: Article 10, dealing with limited liability partnerships, and Article 11, dealing with foreign limited liability partnerships. Articles 1 through 11 constitute the Uniform Limited Liability Partnership Act.

CPA   42-4a Extent of Limited Liability

In a general partnership, partners are jointly liable for partnership debts and jointly and severally liable for partnership torts. LLP statutes were initially drafted to shield innocent partners from vicarious negligence or malpractice liability of their partners. Some states now provide "full shields" for innocent partners that eliminate the vicarious personal liability of these partners for the obligations of the partnership and free them from any obligation to contribute personal assets beyond their investments in the partnership. However, the "liability shield" of a registered limited liability partnership applies only to a partner's liability to third parties and does not shield against breaches of the partnership's or partners' obligations to each other. In every state, however, LLP partners remain fully liable for their own negligence and continue to have unlimited liability for the wrongful acts of those whom they directly supervise and control.

CASE SUMMARY

A Limited Shield

FACTS: Phillip Kuslansky sued his former law partners for breach of contract for failure to pay him the value of his interest in the registered limited liability partnership upon his withdrawal from the partnership. His former partners moved to dismiss the complaint, contending that they were shielded from liability with respect to the plaintiff partner who had withdrawn from the partnership. From a judgment for the defendant former partners, Kuslansky appealed.

DECISION: Judgment for Kuslansky. The state LLP law does not shield general partners in registered limited liability partnerships from personal liability for breaches of the partnership's or partners' obligations to each other. [*Kuslansky v. Kuslansy, Robbins, Stechel and Cunningham, LLP,* 858 N.Y.S.2d 213 (A.D. 2008)]

Professional LLPs continue to be subject to professional regulations, and the appropriate regulating boards set the amount and type of malpractice insurance that firms must carry to operate as an LLP.

To illustrate the effects of a change from a general partnership to an LLP, consider the case of surgeons Jones, Smith, and Gray, who were partners. Jones inadvertently removed Miller's healthy kidney rather than his diseased kidney, and a jury returned a verdict of $2 million. Under general partnership law, Smith and Gray, although innocent partners, are jointly and severally liable along with Jones, and their personal assets can be reached to pay the judgment if necessary. Under an LLP, only partnership assets and the personal assets of Jones are available to pay the judgment. Smith's and Gray's personal assets cannot be reached.

CPA   42-4b Registration and Usage

LLP statutes are designed to permit the conversion of existing general partnerships into limited liability partnerships. The statutes require registration with the Secretary of State, and the name of the partnership must contain the term *limited liability partnership* or *LLP*.

Traditional partnership agreements, like those used by many accounting and law firms and other professional partnerships, can be converted into limited liability partnership agreements without major redrafting or renegotiating of the underlying agreements. Consequently, many professional firms organize under this form of partnership.

ETHICS & THE LAW

The S & L Crisis

When the Office of the Special Counsel concluded its work in both civil and criminal litigation against officers, directors, and consultants involved with failed savings and loan institutions in the late 1980s, it released a report on its work. On the civil side, the Office of the Special Counsel had obtained settlements from defendants in civil suits of $2.9 billion in restitution. Accounting firms, along with lawyers and consultants, comprised 71 percent of the defendants.

Because most accounting firms were organized as partnerships, the result was that many partners were required to dig into their personal assets to meet the restitution requirements imposed by the federal government. Since the creation

of LLPs, all of the largest accounting firms in the United States have restructured, with most choosing the LLP for conducting business. All forms of restructuring will ensure limited personal liability for their principals.

Was the restructuring undertaken to avoid liability? Does limited liability insulate those who make decisions from liability for those decisions? Financiers attempt to determine what stake the officers in a corporation have in the corporation. Stock ownership and exposure to losses through the value of those shares are seen as a positive influence. Do liability limitations reduce the stake a principal has? Is it good to have decision makers separated from the costs of those decisions?

Make the Connection

Summary

A limited partnership consists of one or more limited partners who contribute cash, property, or services without liability for losses beyond their investment, and one or more general partners, who manage the business and have unlimited personal liability. A limited partner's protection from unlimited liability may be lost if the partner participates in the control of the business. "Safe harbor" activities for limited partners are set forth in the RULPA. General partners may avoid personal liability by incorporating. A certificate of limited partnership must be filed when the partnership is formed for the law to apply. Otherwise, general partnership law applies.

A limited liability company is a hybrid form of business organization that combines the tax advantages of a partnership with the limited liability feature of the corporation. It must be formed in accordance with state law in

order to have effect, and the designation LLC must appear with the company's name. Management of an LLC is vested in its members, and members can delegate authority to run the entity to managers, the terms of which are set forth in the company's operating agreement. Members receive profits and losses according to the operating agreement. A member's interest in an LLC is assignable, but consent of the other members is needed for the assignee to participate in the firm's management.

A limited liability partnership allows existing partnerships to convert to this form without major renegotiation of the underlying partnership agreement. Innocent partners in a limited liability partnership are not personally liable for the torts of other partners beyond their investment in the firm.

Learning Outcomes

After studying this chapter, you should be able to clearly explain:

42-1 The Arrival of Partnership Limited Liability

LO.1 Explain the history of making limited liability available to general partnerships

See the presentation of the developing law of partnership limited liability, page 868.

42-2 Limited Partnership

LO.2 Explain the extent of a founding general partner's liability for the debts of the firm, and how unlimited liability can be avoided by utilization of a corporate general partner

See the discussion of general partners' avoidance of personal liability through incorporation, page 868.

LO.3 Explain the nature and extent of a limited partner's liability for the debts of the firm

42-3   Limited Liability Companies

LO.4 Explain the advantages of a limited liability company See the discussion of the advantages of an LLC, including the tax advantages of treatment as a partnership with the limited liability feature of a corporation, page 871.

LO.5 Understand that an LLC is not liable for the conduct of its promoters prior to organization

See the *Hansen* case, pages 871–872.

LO.6 Understand that unless modified in an operating agreement, managers of LLCs owe member-investors the traditional duties of loyalty and care

See the *Auriga Capital* case, where the manager's conduct breached his fiduciary duties to minority members, page 873.

42-4   Limited Liability Partnerships

LO.7 Explain how a limited liability partnership "shields" innocent partners from liability to third parties

See the example involving Dr. Jones's removal of the wrong kidney, with innocent partners Smith's and Gray's personal assets being shielded from liability from a large judgment beyond partnership and Dr. Jones' assets, page 878.

Key Terms

general partners	limited partners	limited partnership

Questions and Case Problems

1. What is the principal advantage of an LLP over an LLC?

2. Alan Waung, a Hong Kong businessperson, purchased a golf course in Saginaw, Michigan, as an investment. As an avid golfer, Alan anticipates spending several weeks during the year at his "Northern Pines" course. He has been informed that a Subchapter S corporation would allow him and his family-member shareholders to be treated as partners for U.S. tax purposes while retaining the limited liability of the corporate form. Advise Mr. Waung on this matter. What form of business organization would you recommend?

3. Kate Haley, an experienced builder, formed a limited partnership in August 2011, along with two limited partners, Drs. Growbioski and Gailen, who each provided $100,000 to the partnership for initial capital for the construction of a medical office building near Stowe, Vermont. With the bustle of getting building and environmental permits and placating abutters to the property, as well as lining up suppliers and subcontractors and getting the job started, Kate simply did not find an opportunity to take the long drive to file the certificate of limited partnership with the Secretary of State's office in Montpelier. A confluence of bad weather, an accident causing serious personal injury, financing disappointments, labor difficulties, design problems, and some personal problems resulted in the project being stopped before completion with some $550,000 in overdue bills. Dr. Growbioski has been approached by several suppliers and craftsmen seeking payment for supplies and work performed. As a limited partner, he believes that he is not liable for firm debts beyond his investment, which was $100,000. Explain to Dr. Growbioski his obligations at this point.

4. Gilroy, Sims & Associates, Ltd., was a limited partnership engaged in real estate development. The original general partners were Richard Gilroy and William Sims. Thomas Green and John Murphy, Jr., were listed as limited partners, along with certain other individuals, on the certificate of limited partnership. Green and Murphy took an active role in the day-to-day operations of the real estate developed by the limited partnership. Financing was obtained to construct the venture's building in St. Louis in 1968, with a mortgage that was payable to American National Insurance Company over 27 years. In 1976, Green and Murphy became general partners of Gilroy, Sims. They executed a Restated Agreement and agreed to "unlimited liability for the debts of the partnership." In the fall of 1990, the partnership stopped making mortgage payments. After foreclosure by American National, a deficiency of $1,437,840 was outstanding. Green and Murphy

believed they were absolved from any personal liability beyond the assets of the firm because they were limited partners when the debt was incurred in 1968. Decide. [*American National Ins. Co. v. Gilroy, Sims & Associates, Ltd.*, 874 F. Supp. 971 (E.D. Mo.)]

5. Sabastian Hafner joined a start-up business with a business plan focused on making breads without common food allergens, such as wheat, yeast, dairy, and gluten, to be marketed in a major metropolitan area. The five founders of the business, including Sabastian, selected the limited liability company (LLC) as their form of business organization. The Articles of Organization for the limited liability company were duly filed with the Secretary of State. The Operating Agreement simply provided that founding member Jillian Lopez would be the sole manager of the firm, and it set a salary for her at $40,000 per year. She hired employees to perform production, delivery, and sales work. Sabastian and the other three members spent nights and early mornings "pitching in" at the bakery. After two months of diligent work, Sabastian, a second-year MBA student, sought back pay for the 40 hours each week he spent at the bakery during the previous eight weeks. He pointed out to the other members of the LLC that state law authorizes employees to sue for their wages. What are Sabastian's rights regarding pay for the service he performed for the LLC?

6. Hurwitz and Padden practiced law as equal partners for a short period of time before converting to an LLC. Some three years later, Padden informed Hurwitz that he intended to leave the firm. When they could not agree on how to divide $200,000 in fees relating to work acquired before the dissolution of the LLC, Hurwitz filed suit seeking an equal division of the fees under partnership principles. Padden contended that partnership principles should not apply to the dissolution of an LLC even though the state's LLC law incorporated the definition and use of the term *dissolution* from the UPA. Decide. [*Hurwitz v. Padden*, 581 N.W.2d 359 (Minn. App.)]

7. Don Mason and Beth Daley were managers and members of Pacific Beach Developers, LLC (PBD), a start-up real estate development company focusing on rehabilitating older properties for increased rental values and possible resale. Daley made a contract with San Diego Architects Associates (SDAA) to provide plans for the rehabilitation of a 60-unit building on Ingraham Street for $97,000, signing the contract "Beth Daley, manager P.B.D. LLC." Financing for the Ingraham Street property fell through, and PBD's option on the property expired. Although Daley notified SDAA that the "Ingraham Street deal was off," SDAA had nearly completed its work, and SDAA brought suit for the contract price against both the LLC and Beth Daley. At the point the lawsuit was initiated, PBD had no working capital remaining, and Don and Beth had "moved on," having taken jobs as mutual fund salespersons. Advise Beth of her legal obligations to SDAA.

8. John and Amelia have general commitments from a number of individuals to invest in their Sproondrift Cove Club golf course and distinctive residential community in Duval County. John wants to form a limited partnership. He realizes that every limited partnership must have a general partner who manages the business and is subject to unlimited liability for all debts and liabilities of the limited partnership. But he says that is no problem because the general partner can be a corporation and can limit its liability exposure by simply creating a "shell" corporation. John stated to Amelia, "As officers of the corporate general partner, you and I can operate the business without the limited partners interfering ... we run the show!" Amelia responded, "John, what you propose seems so very complicated, risky, and expensive. A number of our investors are relatives who may want to be listened to, and some of our investors are professionals who could give us some valuable advice. Maybe a limited liability company would be a better entity for us." Compare the advantages and disadvantages of an LLC with a limited partnership and recommend the most appropriate form of business organization for this venture.

9. Hacienda Farms, Ltd., was organized as a limited partnership with Ricardo de Escamilla as the general partner and James L. Russell and H. W. Andrews as limited partners. The partnership raised vegetables and truck crops that were marketed principally through a produce concern controlled by Andrews. All three individuals decided which crops were to be planted. The general partner had no power to withdraw money from the partnership's two bank accounts without the signature of one of the limited partners. After operating for some seven and one-half months under these procedures, the limited partners demanded that the general partner resign as farm manager, which he did. Six weeks later, the partnership went into bankruptcy. Laurance Holzman, as trustee in bankruptcy, brought an action against Russell and Andrews, claiming that they had become liable to the creditors of the partnership as general partners because they had taken part in the control of the partnership business. How would

you decide the case under the ULPA? Would the outcome be different under the RULPA? [*Holzman v. de Escamilla*, 195 P.2d 833 (Cal. App.)]

10. Jerome Micco was a major shareholder and corporate officer of Micco and Co., Inc., which was a limited partner in Harbor Creek, Ltd., a limited partnership formed to build a condominium complex. Hommel, an electrical contractor, was the successful bidder on certain electrical work for the project. For several months, Hommel worked under the direction of the construction supervisor and was paid by the limited partnership for his work. Because of financial difficulties, the supervisor was released. Thereafter, Jerome Micco played a major role in the building of the project, directing the work to be performed. Hommel submitted payment invoices directly to Micco. When Hommel was not paid, he sued Micco, contending that Micco was a limited partner who ran the operation personally and was personally responsible for the debt. Micco argued that he was an employee or agent of a corporation (Micco and Co., Inc.) and thus could not be held liable for the debt. The evidence reveals that Micco had no occasion to tell Hommel that he was acting as a corporate officer. Is it ethical for a corporate officer and shareholder to seek to avoid individual liability in this case? How would you decide the case? [*Hommel v. Micco*, 602 N.E.2d 1259 (Ohio App.)]

11. Ralph and Maureen K. Hagan (collectively Hagan) owned the Stuart Court Apartments in Richmond, Virginia. On April 30, 1994, Hagan executed an agreement with Adams Property Associates, Inc. (Adams), giving Adams the exclusive right to sell the property for $1,600,000. The agreement provided that if the property was "sold or exchanged" within one year, with or without Adams's assistance, Hagan would pay Adams a fee of 6 percent of the "gross sales amount." Seven days before the year expired, Hagan, Roy T. Tepper, and Lynn Parsons formed a limited liability company, Hagan, Parsons, & Tepper, LLC (HPT). By deed dated April 23, 1995, Hagan transferred the property to HPT. Adams

contends it is entitled to a commission from Hagan pursuant to the April 1994 agreement. Hagan contends the transaction was just a contribution of capital to a new company, not a sale. Decide. [*Hagan v. Adams Property Associates, Inc.*, 482 S.E.2d 805 (Va. 1997)]

12. Peter Kertesz formed an LLC and operated it in South Florida under the business name "Mourning Flowers." The LLC specialized in the sale of flowers to funeral homes. Although Kertesz was initially the only member and manager, he ultimately granted ownership interests totaling 55 percent of the LLC to six individuals. In mid-2007, the members had a falling out that culminated in the majority removing Kertesz as managing member. Kertesz alleged that shortly after this, the LLC's distributors and clients "threatened to terminate their relationship with the LLC if Kertesz was not brought back into the operations of the LLC." These actions, Kertesz claimed, caused the LLC to suffer irreparable harm. Kertesz sought the judicial dissolution of the LLC on the basis of these circumstances and an alleged deadlock in management of the LLC. He sought the appointment of a receiver to protect the assets and goodwill of the LLC. What relief, if any, is Kertesz entitled to? [*Kertesz v. The Spa Floral, LLC*, 994 So. 2d 473 (Fla. App.)]

13. Thomas Banner assigned his voting rights and his right to receive distributions in the Hut at Avon, LLC, to Elizabeth Condo as part of a divorce settlement. When the other members of the Hut Group, Thomas Connors and George Roberts, learned of the unapproved assignment, they contacted Banner and expressed the view that the assignment violated the anti-assignment clause of the operating agreement, which required the primary consent of all the members. After some negotiations, Banner agreed to sell his entire rights to Connors and Roberts for $125,000. Condo sued these members in court for the destruction of the value of the assignment. The LLC defended that the assignment was in violation of the operating agreement and thus was void. Decide. [*Condo v. Connors*, 266 P.3d 1110 (Colo. 2011)]

CPA Question

1. Which of the following statements is correct with respect to a limited partnership?

    a. A limited partner may *not* be an unsecured creditor of the limited partnership.

    b. A general partner may *not* also be a limited partner at the same time.

    c. A general partner may be a secured creditor of the limited partnership.

    d. A limited partnership can be formed with limited liability for all partners.

Corporation Formation

Learning Outcomes

After studying this chapter, you should be able to

LO.1 Recognize that a corporation is a separate legal entity, distinct and apart from its stockholders and that individual shareholders are not liable for claims against the corporation

LO.2 Explain the wide range of power given to corporations under modern corporate codes

LO.3 Understand that the promoter is personally liable for preincorporation contracts

LO.4 Understand that after a corporate charter has been dissolved the owners and officers may be personally responsible for contracts made in the corporate name if they knew or should have known of the dissolution

LO.5 Explain a stockholder's option when he or she objects to a proposed consolidation or merger of the corporation

LO.6 Recognize that liabilities of predecessor corporations can be imposed on successor corporations when the transaction is a de facto merger or a continuation of the predecessor

The corporation is one of the most important forms of business organization.

43-1 Nature and Classes

A *corporation* is an artificial person that is created by government action.

43-1a The Corporation as a Person

corporation–artificial being created by government grant, which for many purposes is treated as a natural person.

certificate of incorporation–written approval from the state or national government for a corporation to be formed.

A **corporation** is an artificial person created by government action and granted certain powers. It exists in the eyes of the law as a person, separate and distinct from the persons who own the corporation.

The concept that the corporation is a distinct legal person means that the corporation's property is owned not by the persons who own shares in the corporation but by the corporation itself. Debts of the corporation are debts of this artificial person, not of the persons running the corporation or owning shares of stock in it.[1] The corporation can sue and be sued in its own name, but shareholders cannot be sued or held liable for corporate actions or obligations.[2] The cardinal rule is that a corporation has a legal existence separate and apart from its officers and shareholders.[3] Consequently, even a sole shareholder is not ordinarily liable for corporate acts.[4]

CASE SUMMARY

Personal Liability versus Corporate Liability

FACTS: Thomas Sauers asked a family friend, Robert Crozier, to lend him money to expand his auto glass business. Crozier loaned $180,000 pursuant to an oral agreement. The loan was to purchase an existing auto glass company and to be a down payment on two buildings for corporate purposes. Crozier gave Sauers four checks made out to T & M Corp. The buildings were never purchased but Sauers testified that the funds were used to cover operating expenses of T & M Corp. Crozier sued for repayment of the loan amount, maintaining that Thomas Sauers was personally liable for the repayment of the loan.

DECISION: Judgment for Sauers. The parties understood that the funds were for corporate purposes, were advanced to the corporation, were deposited in the corporation's account, and were used for corporate purposes. There was no evidence that Sauers agreed to be personally responsible for repaying the loan. The complaint against Sauers must be dismissed. [*Crozier v. Sauers*, **109 A.D.3d 507 (N.Y. App. Div. 2013)**]

articles of incorporation–See *certificate of incorporation.*

charter–grant of authority from a government to exist as a corporation. Generally replaced today by a certificate of incorporation approving the articles of incorporation.

A corporation is formed by obtaining approval of a **certificate of incorporation, articles of incorporation,** or a **charter** from the state or national government.[5]

[1] *American Truck Lines, Inc. v. Albino*, 424 S.E.2d 367 (Ga. App. 1992).

[2] Also, a corporation does not have standing to pursue a claim on behalf of its sole shareholder. See *Accurate Printers, Inc. v. Stark*, 671 S.E.2d 228 (Ga. App. 2008).

[3] *Hayes v. Collins*, 538 S.E.2d 785 (Ga. App. 2000).

[4] If a court finds that a corporation is merely the alter ego of an individual shareholder, the court may "pierce the corporate veil" and hold the individual personally liable. Piercing the corporate veil is addressed in Chapter 44, Shareholders Rights in Corporations.

[5] *Charter, certificate of incorporation,* and *articles of incorporation* are all terms used to refer to the documents that serve as evidence of a government's grant of corporate existence and powers. Most state incorporation statutes now provide for a certificate of incorporation issued by the Secretary of State, but a Revised Model Business Corporation Act (RMBCA) has done away with the certificate of incorporation. Under the RMBCA, corporate existence begins when articles of incorporation are filed with the Secretary of State. An endorsed copy of the articles together with a fee, receipt, or acknowledgment replaces the certificate of incorporation. See RMBCA §§1.25 and 2.03.

43-1b Classifications of Corporations

Corporations may be classified in terms of their relationship to the public, the source of their authority, and the nature of their activities.

Public, Private, and Quasi-Public Corporations

A **public corporation** is one established for governmental purposes and for the administration of public affairs. A city is a public or municipal corporation acting under authority granted to it by the state.

A **private corporation** is one organized for charitable and benevolent purposes or for purposes of finance, industry, and commerce. Private corporations are often called *public* in business circles when their stock is sold to the public.

A **quasi-public corporation,** sometimes known as a public service corporation or a public utility, is a private corporation furnishing services on which the public is particularly dependent, such as a gas or electric company.

Public Authorities

The public increasingly demands that government perform services. Some of these are performed directly by government. Others are performed by separate corporations or **authorities** created by government. **For Example,** a city parking facility may be organized as a separate municipal parking authority, or a public housing project may be operated as an independent housing authority.

Domestic and Foreign Corporations

A corporation is called a **domestic corporation** with respect to the state under whose law it has been incorporated. Any other corporation going into that state is called a **foreign corporation.** Thus, a corporation holding a Texas charter is a domestic corporation in Texas but a foreign corporation in all other states.[6]

Special Service Corporations

Corporations formed for transportation, banking, insurance, and savings and loan operations and similar specialized functions are subject to separate codes or statutes with regard to their organization. In addition, federal and state laws and administrative agencies regulate in detail the way these businesses are conducted.

Close Corporations

A corporation whose shares are held by a single shareholder or a small group of shareholders is known as a **close corporation.** Its shares are not traded publicly. Many such corporations are small firms that are incorporated to obtain either the advantage of limited liability or a tax benefit, or both.

Many states have statutes that have liberalized corporation law as it applies to close corporations. **For Example,** a brother and sister inherited their parents' stock in a domestic close corporation, Hall's Mortuary, Inc., a prominent and successful funeral home in

public corporation—corporation that has been established for governmental purposes and for the administration of public affairs.

private corporation—corporation organized for charitable and benevolent purposes or for purposes of finance, industry, and commerce.

quasi-public corporation—private corporation furnishing services on which the public is particularly dependent, for example, a gas and electric company.

authorities—corporations formed by government that perform public service.

domestic corporation—corporation that has been incorporated by the state in question as opposed to incorporation by another state.

foreign corporation—corporation incorporated under the laws of another state.

close corporation—corporation whose shares are held by a single shareholder or a small group of shareholders.

[6] Failure of a foreign corporation to obtain a certificate of authority to do business within the state, under that state's door-closing statute, may mean that the foreign corporation cannot enforce a contract entered into in the state. For Example, TradeWinds Environmental Restoration, Inc., a New York–based company, entered into a contract with Alabama contractor BBC to do structural-drying services at a number of coastal condominiums after Hurricane Ivan in 2004. TradeWinds performed the work under the contract valued at $400,000. When TradeWinds sued for the money owed under the contract, the court determined that the "labor" performed is not an article of commerce nor is the agreement to supply it an act of commerce. The court determined that TradeWinds' business was intrastate, rather than interstate, and without a certificate of authority to perform the work, TradeWinds could not enforce the contract. *TradeWinds Environmental Restoration, Inc. v. Brown Brothers Construction, LLC*, 999 So. 2d 875 (Ala. 2008).

Louisiana. Nancy was the secretary-treasurer, a director, and the shareholder of 50 percent of the corporation's stock. Hall was president, a director, and the shareholder of the other 50 percent of the corporation's stock. The siblings had a falling out that involved Nancy demanding more participation in the management of the business. Hall maintained that he and Nancy were deadlocked in the management of corporate affairs and petitioned the court for involuntary dissolution and the appointment of a liquidator. The court applied a statute, nearly identical to the Delaware statute, "designed to obviate a deadlocked vote of two equal shareholders" of a close corporation and ordered the dissolution of the corporation.[7]

CPA Subchapter S Corporations

Subchapter S is a subdivision of the Internal Revenue Code. If corporate shareholders meet the requirements of this subdivision, they may elect Subchapter S status, which allows the shareholders to be treated as partners for tax purposes and retain the benefit of limited liability under the corporate form. A Subchapter S corporation is limited to 100 shareholders.[8]

Professional Corporations

A corporation may be organized for the purpose of conducting a profession, such as law, medicine, accounting, architecture, or engineering. Each officer, director, and shareholder of a professional corporation must be licensed to practice the profession. Professional incorporation does not shield a practitioner from personal liability relating to the professional services rendered. State laws vary, with some states recognizing professional corporations, or P.C.s, and other states recognizing a Professional Limited Liability Company (PLLC). In addition to approval from the Secretary of State, professional corporations may need approval from the state professional licensing body.

Nonprofit Corporations

eleemosynary corporation–corporation organized for a charitable or benevolent purpose.

A *nonprofit corporation* (or an **eleemosynary corporation**), is one that is organized for charitable or benevolent purposes. Nonprofit corporations include hospitals, nursing homes, and universities.[9] Special procedures for incorporation are prescribed, and provision is made for a detailed examination of and hearing regarding the purpose, function, and methods of raising money for the enterprise. State laws vary and may require a nonprofit corporation to include a brief statement of its purpose.[10]

Benefit Corporations

benefit corporation–for-profit corporation that sets a goal to create a public benefit while still providing economic returns to its investors.

Benefit, or **B-corporations** are for-profit corporations that set a goal to create a public benefit while still providing economic returns to their investors. **For Example,** Patagonia, registered under California's benefit corporation statute, uses the benefit corporation to emphasize its commitment to the environment. State laws typically recognize that directors will take benefits to society or the environment into account when making corporate decisions and require benefit corporations to adopt independent, third-party standards to measure their success or failure. At least 26 states have benefit corporation statutes and several have legislation pending. The state of Washington recognizes a social purpose corporation, or SPC.

---

[7] *Judson v. Davis*, 916 So. 2d 1106 (La. App. 2005).
[8] See IRS, S Corporations, **http://www.irs.gov/Businesses/Small-Businesses-&-Self-Employed/S-Corporations.**
[9] The Committee on Corporate Laws of the American Bar Association has prepared a Model Nonprofit Corporation Act. A revised Model Nonprofit Corporation Act was approved in 1986.
[10] See *Peters Creek United Presbyterian Church v. Washington Presbytery of Penn.*, 90 A.3d 95 (2014).

43-1c Corporations and Governments

The power of governments to create and regulate corporations may involve several issues.

Power to Create

By definition a corporation is created by government. Thus, the right to be a corporation must be obtained from the proper governmental agency. The federal government may create corporations whenever appropriate to carry out the powers granted to it.

Generally, a state by virtue of its **police power** may create any kind of corporation for any purpose. Most states have a **general corporation code,** which lists certain requirements, and anyone who satisfies the requirements and files the necessary papers with the government may automatically form a corporation. In 1950, the American Bar Association (ABA) published a Model Business Corporation Act (MBCA) to assist legislative bodies in the modernization of state corporation laws. An updated version was published in 1969. Statutory language similar to that contained in the 1969 version of the MBCA has been adopted in whole or in part by 35 states. A complete revision of the model act was approved in 1984 (RMBCA).[11] Jurisdictions following the model act have made numerous modifications to reflect differing views about balancing the interests of public corporations, shareholders, and management. Caution must therefore be exercised in making generalizations about model act jurisdictions. There is no *uniform* corporation act.

Power to Regulate

Subject to constitutional limitations, corporations may be regulated by statutes.

Protection of the Corporation as a Person. The Constitution of the United States prohibits the national government and state governments from depriving any person of life, liberty, or property without due process of law. Many state constitutions contain a similar limitation on their respective state governments. A corporation is regarded as a "person" within the meaning of such provisions.

The federal Constitution prohibits a state from denying to any person within its jurisdiction the equal protection of the laws. No such express limitation is placed on the federal government, although the due process clause binding the federal government is liberally interpreted so that it prohibits substantial inequality of treatment.

Recall the *Citizens United* case in Chapter 4 in which the Supreme Court held that the government may not suppress political speech on the basis of the speaker's corporate identity.[12]

Protection of the Corporation as a Citizen. For certain purposes, such as determining the right to bring a lawsuit in a federal court, a corporation is a citizen of any state in which it has been incorporated and of the state where it has its principal place of business.

43-2 Corporate Powers

Except for limitations in the federal Constitution or the state's own constitution, a state legislature may give corporations any lawful powers. The RMBCA contains a general provision on corporate powers granting a corporation "the same powers as an individual to do all things necessary or convenient to carry out its business and affairs."[13]

police power—power to govern; the power to adopt laws for the protection of the public health, welfare, safety, and morals.

general corporation code—state's code listing certain requirements for creation of a corporation.

---

[11] The Revised Model Business Corporation Act (1984) was approved by the Committee on Corporate Laws Section of Business Law of the American Bar Association. Model act citations are to the 1984 Revised Model Business Corporation Act (RMBCA) unless designated otherwise.

[12] *Citizens United v. Federal Election Com'n,* 558 U.S. 310 (2010).

[13] RMBCA §3.02. State statutes generally contain similar broad catchall grants of powers.

43-2a **Particular Powers**

Modern corporation codes give corporations a wide range of powers.

Perpetual Life

One of the distinctive features of a corporation is its perpetual or continuous life—the power to continue as an entity forever or for a stated period of time regardless of changes in stock ownership or the death of any shareholders.

Corporate Name

A corporation must have a name to identify it. As a general rule, it may select any name for this purpose. Most states require that the corporate name contain some word indicating the corporate character[14] and that the name not be the same as, or deceptively similar to, the name of any other corporation. Some statutes prohibit the use of a name that is likely to mislead the public.

Corporate Seal

A corporation may have a distinctive seal. However, a corporation need not use a seal in the transaction of business unless it is required by statute or a natural person in transacting that business would be required to use a seal.

Bylaws

C P A

bylaws–rules and regulations enacted by a corporation to govern the affairs of the corporation and its shareholders, directors, and officers.

Bylaws are the rules and regulations enacted by a corporation to govern the affairs of the corporation and its shareholders, directors, and officers.

Bylaws are adopted by shareholders, although in some states they may be adopted by the directors of the corporation. Approval by the state or an amendment of the corporate charter is not required to make the bylaws effective.

The bylaws are subordinate to the general law of the state, the statute under which the corporation is formed, and the charter of the corporation.[15] Bylaws that conflict with such superior authority or that are in themselves unreasonable are invalid. Bylaws that are valid are binding on all shareholders regardless of whether they know of the existence of those bylaws or were among the majority that consented to their adoption. Bylaws are not binding on third persons, however, unless they have notice or knowledge of them.

Stock

A corporation may issue certificates representing corporate stock. Under the RMBCA, authorized, but unissued, shares may be issued at the price set by the board of directors. Under UCC Article 8 (1978 and 1994 versions), securities may be "uncertificated," or not represented by an instrument.

Making Contracts

Corporation codes give corporations the power to make contracts.

Borrowing Money

Corporations have the implied power to borrow money in carrying out their authorized business purposes.

---

[14] RMBCA §4.01(a) declares that the corporate name must contain the word *corporation, company, incorporated,* or *limited* or an abbreviation of one of these words.
[15] *Roach v. Bynum,* 403 So. 2d 187 (Ala. 1981).

Executing Negotiable Instruments

Corporations have the power to issue or indorse negotiable instruments and to accept drafts.

Issuing Bonds

A corporation may exercise its power to borrow money by issuing bonds.

Transferring Property

The corporate property may be leased, assigned for the benefit of creditors, or sold. In many states, however, a solvent corporation may not transfer all of its property without the consent of all or a substantial majority of its shareholders.

A corporation, having power to incur debts, may mortgage or pledge its property as security for those debts. This rule does not apply to public service companies, such as street transit systems and gas and electric companies.

Acquiring Property

A corporation has the power to acquire and hold such property as is reasonably necessary for carrying out its express powers.

Buying Back Stock

Generally, a corporation may purchase its own stock if it is solvent at the time and the purchase does not impair capital. Stock that is reacquired by the corporation that issued it is commonly called **treasury stock.**

treasury stock– corporate stock that the corporation has reacquired.

Although treasury stock retains the character of outstanding stock, it has an inactive status while it is held by the corporation.[16] Thus, the treasury shares cannot be voted nor can dividends be declared on them.

Doing Business in Another State

A corporation has the power to engage in business in other states. However, such power does not exempt the corporation from satisfying valid restrictions imposed by the foreign state in which it seeks to do business.

Participating in an Enterprise

Corporations may generally participate in an enterprise to the same extent as individuals. They may enter into joint ventures and partnerships. A corporation may also be a limited partner. The RMBCA authorizes a corporation "to be a promoter, partner, member, associate, or manager of any partnership, joint venture, trust, or other entity."[17]

Paying Employee Benefits

The RMBCA empowers a corporation "to pay pensions and establish pension plans, pension trusts, profit-sharing plans, share bonus plans, share option plans, and benefit or incentive plans for any or all of its current or former directors, officers, employees, and agents."[18]

---

[16] When a corporation reacquires its own shares, it has the choice of retiring them and thus restoring them to the status of authorized, but unissued, shares or of treating them as still issued and available for transfer. The latter are described as treasury shares.

[17] RMBCA §3.02(9).

[18] RMBCA §3.02(12).

Charitable Contributions

The RMBCA authorizes a corporation, without any limitation, "to make donations for the public welfare or for charitable, scientific, or educational purposes."[19] In some states, a limitation is imposed on the amount that can be donated for charitable purposes.

43-2b *Ultra Vires* Acts

ultra vires—act or contract that the corporation does not have authority to do or make.

When a corporation acts in excess of or beyond the scope of its powers, the corporation's act is described as ***ultra vires.*** Such an action is improper in the same way that it is improper for an agent to act beyond the scope of the authority given by the principal. It is also improper with respect to shareholders and creditors of the corporation because corporate funds have been diverted to unauthorized uses.

The modern corporation statute will state that every corporation formed under it will have certain powers unless the articles of incorporation expressly exclude some of the listed powers, and then the statute will list every possible power that is needed to run a business. In some states, the legislature makes a blanket grant of all power that a natural person running the business would possess.[20] The net result is that the modern corporation possesses such a broad scope of powers that it is difficult to find an action that is *ultra vires*. If a mining corporation should begin to manufacture television sets, that might be an *ultra vires* transaction but such an extreme departure rarely happens.

Because nonprofit corporations have a more restricted range of powers than business corporations, actions not authorized by the charters of nonprofit corporations are more likely to be found *ultra vires*.[21]

43-3 Creation and Termination of the Corporation

All states have general laws governing the creation of corporations.

CPA

43-3a Promoters

promoters—persons who plan the formation of the corporation and sell or promote the idea to others.

Corporations come into existence as the result of the activities of one or more persons known as **promoters** who bring together persons interested in the enterprise, aid in obtaining subscriptions to stock, and set in motion the machinery that leads to the formation of the corporation itself.

A corporation is not liable on a contract made by its promoter for its benefit unless the corporation takes some affirmative action to adopt the contract, such as express words of adoption or acceptance of the contract's benefits.[22] A corporation may also become bound by such contracts through assignment or novation.

The promoter is personally liable for all contracts made on behalf of the corporation before its existence unless the promoter is exempted by the terms of the agreement or by the circumstances surrounding it.[23]

---

[19] RMBCA §3.02(13).

[20] Note the broad powers granted under RMBCA §3.02; see also *MIC v. Battle Mountain Corp.*, 70 P.3d 1176 (Colo. 2003), where Colorado's *ultra vires* statute prohibits claims that a corporation is acting beyond the scope of its powers.

[21] *Lovering v. Seabrook Island Property Owners Ass'n*, 344 S.E.2d 862 (S.C. App. 1986). But see *St. Louis v. Institute of Med. Ed. & Res.*, 786 S.W.2d 885 (Mo. App. 1990).

[22] The *Hansen v. Fields Company, LLC* case, summarized in Chapter 42, addresses the distinction between an LLC's liability and that of the promoter.

[23] See *GS Petroleum, Inc. v. R and S Fuel, Inc.*, 2009 WL 1554680 (Del. Super. June 4, 2009), where the court found that the promoters were not liable on the preincorporation contract for the sale of a Shell gas station. The court reasoned that the terms of the contract did not intend promoter liability, and the business was incorporated by the buyer before taking possession of the business.

A promoter is liable for all torts committed in connection with the promoter's activities. The corporation is not ordinarily liable for the torts of the promoter, but it may become liable by its conduct after incorporation. If a promoter induces making a contract by fraud, the corporation is liable for the fraud if it assumes or ratifies the contract with knowledge or notice of such fraud.

A promoter stands in a fiduciary relation to the corporation and to stock subscribers and cannot make secret profits at their expense. Accordingly, if a promoter makes a secret profit on a sale of land to the corporation, the promoter must surrender the profit to the corporation.

The corporation is not liable in most states for the expenses and services of the promoter unless it subsequently promises to pay for them or the corporation's charter or a statute imposes such liability on it.

43-3b Incorporation

incorporator—one or more natural persons or corporations who sign and file appropriate incorporation forms with a designated government official.

One or more natural persons or corporations may act as **incorporators** of a corporation by signing and filing appropriate forms with a designated government official.[24] These papers are filed in duplicate, and a filing fee must be paid. The designated official (usually the Secretary of State), after being satisfied that the forms conform to statutory requirements, stamps "Filed" and the date on each copy. The official then retains one copy and returns the other copy, along with a filing fee receipt, to the corporation.[25]

Statutes may require incorporators to give some form of public notice, such as by advertising in a newspaper, of their intention to form a corporation, stating its name, address, and general purpose.

43-3c Application for Incorporation

In most states, the process of forming a corporation is begun by filing an application for a certificate of incorporation. This application contains or is accompanied by articles of incorporation. The instrument is filed with the Secretary of State and sets forth certain information about the new corporation. The articles of incorporation must contain (1) the name of the corporation, (2) the number of shares of stock the corporation is authorized to issue, (3) the street address of the corporation's initial registered office and the name of its initial registered agent, and (4) the name and address of each incorporator.[26] The articles of incorporation may also state the purpose or purposes for which the corporation is organized. If there is no "purpose clause," the corporation automatically has the purpose of engaging in any lawful business.[27] Also, if no reference is made to the duration of the corporation in the articles of incorporation, it will automatically have perpetual duration.[28]

43-3d The Certificate of Incorporation

Most state incorporation statutes now provide for a certificate of incorporation to be issued by the Secretary of State after articles of incorporation that conform to state requirements have been filed. The Revised Model Business Corporation Act (RMBCA) has eliminated the certificate of incorporation in an effort to reduce the volume of paperwork handled by the Secretary of State.

[24] RMBCA §2.01.
[25] RMBCA §1.25.
[26] RMBCA §2.02.
[27] RMBCA §3.01.
[28] RMBCA §3.02.

Under the RMBCA, corporate existence begins when the articles are filed with the Secretary of State.[29] In some states, corporate existence begins when the proper government official issues a certificate of incorporation. In other states, it does not begin until an organizational meeting is held by the new corporation.

43-3e Proper and Defective Incorporation

corporation de jure—corporation with a legal right to exist by virtue of law.

If the procedure for incorporation has been followed, the corporation has a legal right to exist. It is then called a **corporation de jure,** meaning that it is a corporation by virtue of law.

The law usually overlooks defects that are not material and holds that the corporation is a corporation de jure.

The RMBCA abolishes objections to irregularities and defects in incorporating. It provides that the

secretary of state's filing of the articles of incorporation is conclusive proof that the incorporators satisfied all conditions precedent to incorporation....[30]

De Facto Corporation

The defect in the incorporation may be so substantial that it cannot be ignored, and the corporation will not be accepted as a corporation de jure, yet compliance may be sufficient for recognizing that there is a corporation. When this occurs, the association is called a **de facto** corporation.

de facto—existing in fact as distinguished from as of right, as in the case of an officer or a corporation purporting to act as such without being elected to the office or having been properly incorporated.

Although conflict exists among authorities, the traditional elements of a de facto corporation are that (1) a valid law exists under which the corporation could have been properly incorporated, (2) an attempt to organize the corporation has been made in good faith, (3) a genuine attempt to organize in compliance with statutory requirements has been made, and (4) corporate powers have been used.

Corporation by Estoppel

The defect in incorporation may be so great that by law the association cannot be accepted as a de facto corporation. In such a case, there is no corporation. If the individuals involved proceed to run the business in spite of such irregularity, they may be held personally liable as partners for the business's debts.[31] This rule is sometimes not applied when a person has dealt with the business as though it were a corporation.[32] In such instances, the party is estopped from denying that the "corporation" had legal existence. In effect, there is **corporation by estoppel** with respect to that party.

corporation by estoppel—corporation that comes about when parties estop themselves from denying that the corporation exists.

Several jurisdictions that follow the 1969 MBCA have expressly retained the doctrines of corporation by estoppel and de facto corporations.[33] Other courts interpreting the language of the 1969 MBCA, however, have held that the doctrines of de facto corporation and corporation by estoppel no longer exist.

The language of the 1984 version allows some jurisdictions sufficient room for the de facto and estoppel doctrines to operate through Section 2.04 of the MBCA.

With respect to preincorporation debts, the 1984 act imposes liability only on persons who act as, or on behalf of, a corporation while knowing that no corporation

---

[29] RMBCA §2.03(a).
[30] RMBCA §2.03(b).
[31] In a minority of states, a court will not hold individuals liable as partners but will hold liable the person who committed the act on behalf of the business on the theory that that person was an agent who acted without authority and is therefore liable for breach of the implied warranties of the existence of a principal possessing capacity and of proper authorization.
[32] *Am. South Bank v. Holland*, 669 So. 2d 151 (Ala. Civ. App. 1994).
[33] See Ga. Bus. Corp Code §22-5103; Minn. Bus. Corp Act §301:08. See also *H. Rich Corp. v. Feinberg*, 518 So. 2d 377 (Fla. App. 1987).

exists.[34] Courts may allow a corporation to sue to enforce a preincorporation agreement if the corporation had a "personal stake" in the agreement.[35]

43-3f Insolvency, Bankruptcy, and Reorganization

When a corporation has financial troubles so serious that it is insolvent, the best thing may be to go through bankruptcy or reorganization proceedings. The law with respect to bankruptcy and reorganizations is discussed in Chapter 34.

43-3g Forfeiture of Charter

In states that have adopted the RMBCA, the Secretary of State may commence proceedings to administratively dissolve a corporation if (1) the corporation does not pay franchise taxes within 60 days after they are due, (2) the corporation does not file its annual report within 60 days after it is due, or (3) the corporation is without a registered agent or registered office for 60 days or more.[36] After a corporate charter has been dissolved, the owners and officers of the dissolved corporation are not shielded from personal liability by using the corporate name when making contracts if they knew or should have known of the dissolution. **For Example,** on October 2, 2004, Dinky, Inc., was involuntarily dissolved for failure to file an annual report and pay an annual franchise tax. Elaine Kostopulos, the president and sole shareholder of Dinky, Inc., had incorporated her business in 1989 and regularly purchased products manufactured by Benetton USA, Inc., since that time. During the five years after Dinky was dissolved, she continued to operate as a corporation, ordering and making payments to Benetton through June 7, 2009. Between June and November 2009, Benetton sought payment of over $200,000 owed by Dinky. Ms. Kostopulos claims she was unaware of the dissolution until late 2009, when payment problems arose. Dinky applied for reinstatement at that time. With corporate status reinstated, Ms. Kostopulos contended that she was not personally liable for the debts incurred by the dissolved corporation during the time of its dissolution. The court determined that Ms. Kostopulos could not escape personal liability by reinstating her corporation, holding that "she should have known" about the dissolution of Dinky, over such a long period of time.[37]

After a corporation is dissolved, a contract made by an officer of the dissolved corporation cannot be enforced against the other party to the contract. **For Example,** a lucrative contract with Florio Entertainment, Inc., was signed "Louis Lofredo, LL Associates as company president" using a letterhead "LL Associates, Inc." In fact, the corporation "LL Associates, Inc." had been dissolved years before the contract was negotiated and signed, and Lofredo had made no effort to reinstate the corporation. LL Associates, Inc., had no legal existence and thus could not be a party to the contract and could not enforce the contract.[38]

A corporation whose powers are suspended for nonpayment of taxes cannot sue or defend a lawsuit while its taxes remain unpaid.[39] Upon payment of taxes, however, corporate powers are revived. Thus, if a corporation filed a timely appeal while its powers were suspended, it could proceed with the appeal after paying its taxes.[40]

---

[34] RMBCA §2.04.

[35] *De La Garza v. Clean Oil Innovations, Inc.*, 2013 WL 1222109 (S.D. Tex. March 20, 2013).

[36] RMBCA §14.20.

[37] *Benetton U.S.A. Corp. v. Dinky, Inc.*, 2011 WL 5024549 (N.D. Ill. Oct. 19, 2011). But see section 2.04 of the 1984 RMBCA, which provides that all persons purporting to act for or on behalf of a corporation "knowing that there was no incorporation" under the act are jointly and severally liable for all liabilities while so acting. There would be no liability for an individual who did not and should not have known of the dissolution.

[38] *Animazing Entertainment, Inc. v. Louis Lofredo Associates, Inc.*, 88 F. Supp. 2d 265 (S.D.N.Y. 2000).

[39] *Kaufman, Inc. v. Performance Plastering, Inc.*, 39 Cal. Rptr. 3d 33 (Cal. App. 2006).

[40] See *Bourhis v. Lord*, 295 P.3d 895 (Cal. 2013).

43-3h Judicial Dissolution

Judicial dissolution of a corporation may be decreed when its management is deadlocked and the deadlock cannot be broken by the shareholders.[41] In some states, a "custodian" may be appointed for a corporation when the shareholders are unable to break a deadlock in the board of directors and irreparable harm is threatened to, or sustained by, the corporation because of the deadlock.

43-3i Voluntary Dissolution

State laws describe the requirements for voluntary dissolution of a corporation. For example, publication in a paper of general circulation may be required. Compliance with such statutes is important to protect the company from subsequent claims. A state law may state that a claim against the corporation will be barred unless the claim is brought within two years of publication of the notice of dissolution.[42]

consolidation (of corporations)– combining of two or more corporations in which the corporate existence of each one ceases and a new corporation is created.

43-4 Consolidations, Mergers, and Conglomerates

Two or more corporations may be combined to form a new structure or enterprise.

CPA

43-4a Definitions

Enterprises may be combined by a consolidation or merger of corporations or by the formation of a conglomerate.

CPA

Consolidation

In a **consolidation** of two or more corporations, the separate existence of the two corporations ceases, and a new corporation with the property and assets of the old corporations comes into being (Figure 43-1).

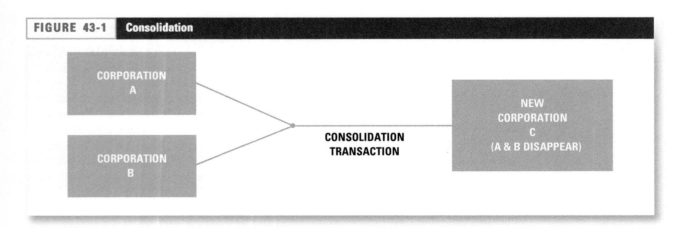

FIGURE 43-1   Consolidation

---

[41] After a shareholder has requested dissolution of a corporation, a state statute may offer an option to the corporation or other existing shareholders to purchase shares owned by the petitioning shareholder(s) for "fair value" in lieu of dissolution. See *Dawkins v. Hickman Family Corp.*, 2010 WL 4683472 (N.D. Miss. Nov. 10, 2010).

[42] *Lewis Oil, Inc. v. Bourbon Mini-Mart, Inc.*, 16 N.E.3d (Ind. App. 2014). Lewis Oil gave reasonable notice of voluntary dissolution in a paper of general circulation. The notice stated that claims against the corporation had to be filed within two years after publication of the notice. A suit by a liquor store claiming that Lewis Oil contributed to environmental contamination on the property was dismissed because it was time-barred by the notice of dissolution.

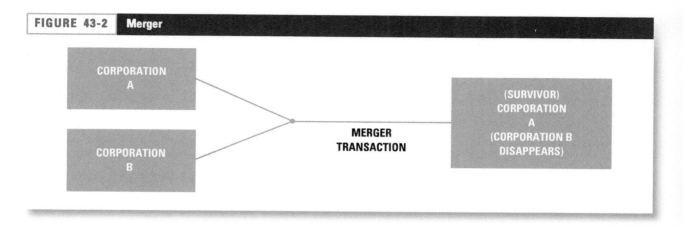

FIGURE 43-2   Merger

When a consolidation occurs, the new corporation ordinarily succeeds to the rights, powers, and immunities of its component parts. However, limitations may be imposed by constitution, statute, or certificate of incorporation.

CPA   Merger

merger (of corporations)— combining of corporations by which one absorbs the other and continues to exist, preserving its original charter and identity while the other corporation ceases to exist.

When two corporations **merge,** one absorbs the other. One corporation retains its original charter and identity and continues to exist; the other disappears, and its corporate existence terminates (Figure 43-2).

A stockholder who objects to a proposed consolidation or merger or who fails to convert existing shares into stock of the new or continuing corporation may apply to a court to appraise the value of the stock that she holds.[43] Should either party act arbitrarily, vexatiously, or not in good faith in the appraisal process, the courts have the right to assess court costs and attorney fees. The new or continuing corporation is then required to pay the "fair value" of the stock to the stockholder.[44]

CASE SUMMARY

The Sound of Music: $63.44 per Share

FACTS: The Trapp Family Lodge, Inc. (TFL), was incorporated in 1962 as a holding company for certain assets of the Von Trapp family, including the Trapp Family Lodge, a resort hotel complex located in Stowe, Vermont, and other assets, including certain royalty rights related to the family's story as portrayed in a Broadway musical and a movie. A majority of TFL shareholders approved a merger with a new corporation in 1994, and the merger took place on January 28, 1995. The dissenting shareholders, holding 76,529 of the corporation's 198,000 outstanding shares,

were paid $33.84 per share as fair value by the TFL board of directors. The dissenting shareholders brought suit seeking a higher price as fair value. After the trial court set the fair value of $63.44, TFL appealed.

DECISION: Judgment for the dissenting shareholders. Dissenters' rights statutes were enacted in response to the common law rule that required unanimous consent from shareholders to make fundamental changes in a corporation. Under this rule minority shareholders could block corporate

---

[43] *Delaware Open MRI Radiology v. Kessler*, 898 A.2d 290 (Del. Ch. 2006).
[44] See *Spenlinhauer v. Spencer Press Inc.*, 959 N.E.2d 436 (Mass. App. 2011), where a minority shareholder dissented to a proposed merger, and after executing a cash-out merger, the court determined the "fair value" of the minority shares as the pro rata percentage of the net selling price.

The Sound of Music: $63.44 per Share continued

change by refusing to cooperate in hope of establishing a nuisance value for their shares. In response, legislatures enacted statutes authorizing corporate changes by majority vote. To protect the interests of minority shareholders, statutes generally permit a dissenting minority to demand that the corporation buy back shares at fair value. The basic concept of fair value is that the stockholder is entitled to be paid for his or her "proportionate interest in a going concern." The trial court properly rejected the fact-specific appraisal made on behalf of the majority shareholders because it

lacked thoroughness and credibility, unjustifiably reducing the value of the lodge operations and overstating income taxes to reduce after-tax cash flows. The court accepted the appraisal made on behalf of the minority shareholders that utilized the average of a net asset value method of evaluation and a discounted cash flow method of evaluation, and yielded a value of $63.44 per share. **[In re *75,629 Shares of Common Stock of Trapp Family Lodge, Inc.*, 725 A.2d 927 (Vt. 1999)]**

Conglomerate

conglomerate—relationship of a parent corporation to subsidiary corporations engaged in diversified fields of activity unrelated to the field of activity of the parent corporation.

Conglomerate describes the relationship of a parent corporation to subsidiary corporations engaged in diversified fields of activity unrelated to the parent corporation's field of activity. **For Example,** a wire-manufacturing corporation that owns all the stock of a newspaper corporation and of a drug-manufacturing corporation would be described as a conglomerate. In contrast, if the wire-manufacturing company owned a mill that produced the metal used in making the wire and a mine that produced the ore that was used by the mill, the relationship would probably be described as an *integrated industry* rather than as a conglomerate. This term is merely a matter of usage rather than of legal definition. Likewise, when the parent company is not engaged in production or the rendering of services, it is customary to call it a *holding company*.

Without regard to whether the enterprise is a holding company or whether the group of corporations constitutes a conglomerate or an integrated industry, each part is a distinct corporation to which ordinary corporation law applies. In some instances, additional principles apply because of the nature of the relationships existing among the several corporations involved.

43-4b Legality

Consolidations, mergers, and asset acquisitions between enterprises are prohibited by federal antitrust legislation when the effect is to lessen competition in interstate commerce. A business corporation may not merge with a charitable corporation because this combination would divert the assets of the respective corporations to purposes not intended by their shareholders.

43-4c Liability of Successor Corporations

When corporations are combined in any way, the question of who is liable for the debts and obligations of the predecessor corporation arises.

Mergers and Consolidations

Generally, the enterprise engaging in or continuing the business after a merger or consolidation succeeds to all of the rights and property of the predecessor, or disappearing, corporation.[45]

[45] *Corporate Express Office Products, Inc. v. Phillips*, 847 So. 2d 406 (Fla. 2003).

CASE SUMMARY

A Marshmallow of a Case for the Plaintiff Marsh USA

FACTS: The Orleans Parish School Board ("School Board") in New Orleans, Louisiana, hired Johnson & Higgins, Inc. (J&H), in 1996, creating an ongoing insurance consulting agreement between them. The terms of the agreement provided that the School Board would pay J&H, Inc., for its consulting services and would later be reimbursed by the insurance carrier eventually selected by the School Board. Pursuant to their agreement, over the next few years, J&H's Mrs. Ippolito prepared several Requests for Proposals ("RFP") on behalf of the School Board. The School Board paid its fees for this consulting work without complaint. During this time, Johnson & Higgins merged with Marsh McLennan, a company that thereafter merged into Marsh USA, Inc. In 2001, Mrs. Ippolito prepared, at the request of the School Board, two more requests for proposals. Per the terms of the RFPs, Marsh was to receive $70,000 as its consulting fee under NO. 7656 and a $5,000 consulting fee

under NO. 7657. Mrs. Ippolito and her staff spent several months working on the project for the School Board. The School Board never paid Marsh for the services and Marsh USA, Inc., sued the School Board for breach of contract, seeking payment of $75,000. The School Board asserted that Marsh USA was not a proper party to the lawsuit and that no contract had existed with it. From a judgment for Marsh USA, Inc., the School Board appealed.

DECISION: Judgment for Marsh USA, Inc. When two corporations merge or consolidate, the new successor corporation acquires all of the assets and rights of the former corporation. The minutes of a School Board meeting reflect the School Board's awareness of the merger in this case as well as its continuing contract with the firm. [*Marsh Advantage America v. Orleans Parish School Board*, 995 So. 2d 53 (La. App. 2008)]

The enterprise continuing the business is also subject to all of the debts and liabilities of the predecessor corporation.[46]

Liabilities of predecessor corporations can be imposed on a successor corporation when the transaction is a de facto merger[47] or the successor is a mere continuation of the predecessor. **For Example,** Steven Stepp manufactured pleasure boats through Thoroughbred Power Boats, Inc., until August 1996 at which time Thoroughbred Power Boats, Inc., ceased manufacturing and selling boats. In August 1996, Velocity Power Boats, Inc., began manufacturing and selling pleasure boats at the same location. Stephen Stepp and his wife were the only officers and board members of both corporations. Finding that Velocity was merely a "new hat" for Thoroughbred Power Boats, Inc., with the same or similar management and ownership, Velocity Power Boats, Inc., was held liable as a successor corporation for damages for a May 6, 1995, boating accident caused by a defective Thoroughbred Power Boats, Inc., manufactured boat.[48]

Asset Sales

In contrast with a merger or consolidation, a corporation may merely purchase the assets of another business. In that case, the purchaser does not become liable for the obligations of the predecessor business. **For Example,** Hull Corporation sold one of its operating divisions to SP Industries, Inc. (SPI), for $6 million under an asset purchase agreement (APA) that stated that the buyer SPI assumed no liability for preclosing claims against Hull. In fact as Hull and SPI were negotiating the APA, Hull was having difficulties regarding engineering and installation work the division had performed in China for Berg Chilling Systems, Inc. Berg Chilling sued SPI under the doctrine of successor liability for the payment of a

[46] *Beck v. Roper Whitney, Inc.*, 190 F. Supp. 2d 524 (W.D.N.Y. 2001).
[47] *Ulanet v. D'Artagnan, Inc.*, 170 F. Supp. 2d 356 (E.D.N.Y. 2001); see *Callahan & Sons, Inc. v. Dykeman Electric Co. Inc.*, 266 F. Supp. 2d 208 (D. Mass 2003).
[48] *Paten v. Thoroughbred Power Boats, Inc.*, 294 F.3d 640 (5th Cir. 2002).

$1,650,000 arbitration award because of the defective work done by Hull in China. The court held that SPI did not assume Hull's contractual liability to Berg under any exception to the traditional corporate rule of successor nonliability.[49]

Corporations may seek to avoid liability for the obligations of a predecessor corporation by attempting to disguise a consolidation or merger as being merely a sale of assets. Courts will not recognize such a transaction and will impose a successor's liability on the successor corporation.[50] In addition, even when the old corporate entity is not formally dissolved, a finding of a de facto merger resulting in successor liability may occur.

CASE SUMMARY

Corporate Shell Games Not Allowed

FACTS: Since 1976, McGhan/Cal. Inc., a manufacturer of prostheses used in breast augmentation surgery, and later McGhan/Del., received numerous complaints about its implants. It also received inquiries from the Food and Drug Administration. In April 1977, Mary Marks had surgery; two McGhan implants were used. Because of defects in the McGhan implants, Marks underwent three additional operations, eventually having the McGhan products replaced with implants manufactured by another company. In June 1977, McGhan/Cal. was acquired by a Delaware subsidiary of 3M, called McGhan/Del. Inc. McGhan/Del. removed the implants from the market in April 1979. On January 1, 1981, 3M's wholly owned subsidiary, McGhan/Del. Inc., was reorganized as a division of 3M and dissolved. In January 1982, following her fourth surgery, Marks brought a product liability suit against 3M. 3M contended that it was not liable for the actions of the predecessor corporation.

DECISION: The transaction between the 3M subsidiary McGhan/Del. Inc. and McGhan/Cal. Inc. amounted to a de facto merger of the seller and the purchaser. McGhan/Cal. changed its name, distributed 3M stock to its shareholders, and dissolved, and all key employees signed employment contracts to work for the purchaser. No cash was paid for the business. The transaction was not an assets sale. The second reorganization amounted to a continuation of the de facto merger. Public policy requires that 3M, having accepted the benefits of a going concern, should also assume the costs that all other going concerns must bear. It should not be allowed to avoid liability to an injured person by merely shuffling paper and manipulating corporate entities. [*Marks v. Minnesota Mining and Manufacturing Co.,* 232 Cal. Rptr. 594 (Cal. App. 1986)]

Make the Connection

Summary

A *corporation* is an artificial person created by government action. It exists as a separate and distinct entity possessing certain powers. In most states, the corporation comes into existence when the Secretary of State issues a certificate of incorporation. The most common forms of corporations are private business corporations whose stock is sold to the public (publicly held) and close corporations, which are business firms whose shares are not traded publicly.

Corporations may be formed for purposes other than conducting a business. For example, there are nonprofit corporations, municipal corporations, and public authorities for governmental purposes.

An *ultra vires* act occurs when a corporation acts beyond the scope of the powers given it. Because states now grant broad powers to corporations, it is unlikely that a modern corporation would act beyond the scope of its powers.

[49] *Berg Chilling Systems Inc. v. Hull Corp.,* 435 F.3d 455 (3d Cir. 2006).
[50] *State v. Westwood Squibb Pharmaceutical Co., Inc.,* 981 F. Supp. 760 (W.D.N.Y. 1997).

A *promoter* is a person who brings together the persons interested in the enterprise and sets in motion all that must be done to form a corporation. A corporation is not liable on contracts made by its promoter for the corporation unless it adopts the contracts. The promoter is personally liable for contracts made for the corporation before its existence. A promoter stands in a fiduciary relation to the corporation and stockholders.

The procedures for incorporation are set forth in the statutes of each state. In most states, the corporation comes into existence on issuance of the certificate of incorporation. When all requirements have been satisfied, the corporation is a corporation de jure. When there has not been full compliance with all requirements for incorporation, a de facto corporation may be found to exist. Or when sufficient compliance for a de facto corporation does not exist, in some jurisdictions a third person may be estopped from denying the legal existence of the "corporation" with which it did business (corporation by estoppel).

A corporation has the power to continue as an entity forever or for a stated period of time regardless of changes in the ownership of the stock or the death of a shareholder. It may make contracts, issue stocks and bonds, borrow money, execute commercial paper, transfer and acquire property, acquire its own stock if it is solvent and the purchase does not impair capital, and make charitable contributions. Subject to limitations, a corporation has the power to do business in other states. A corporation may also participate in a business enterprise to the same extent as an individual; that is, it may be a partner in a partnership, or it may enter a joint venture or other enterprise. Special service corporations, such as banks, insurance companies, and railroads, are subject to separate statutes governing their organization and powers.

Two or more corporations may be combined to form a new enterprise. This combination may be a consolidation, with a new corporation coming into existence, or a merger, in which one corporation absorbs the other.

Learning Outcomes

After studying this chapter, you should be able to clearly explain:

43-1   Nature and Classes

LO.1 Recognize that a corporation is a separate legal entity, distinct and apart from its stockholders and that individual shareholders are not liable for claims against the corporation

43-2   Corporate Powers

LO.2 Explain the wide range of power given to corporations under modern corporate codes

See the RMBCA general provision granting corporations "the same powers as an individual to do all things necessary or convenient to carry out its business and affairs," page 887.

43-3   Creation and Termination of the Corporation

LO.3 Understand that the promoter is personally liable for preincorporation contracts

LO.4 Understand that after a corporate charter has been dissolved the owners and officers may be personally responsible for contracts made in the corporate name if they knew or should have known of the dissolution

See the example where Ms. Kostopulos was personally liable for debts incurred during the time of dissolution because she should have known about the dissolution, page 893.

43-4   Consolidations, Mergers, and Conglomerates

LO.5 Explain a stockholder's option when he or she objects to a proposed consolidation or merger of the corporation

See the *Trapp Family Lodge* case, page 895.

LO.6 Recognize that liabilities of predecessor corporations can be imposed on successor corporations when the transaction is a de facto merger or a continuation of the predecessor

See the example of Velocity Power Boats, Inc., which became essentially a "new hat" for Thoroughbred Power Boats, Inc., with liability as a corporate successor for a defective Thoroughbred boat, page 897.

Key Terms

articles of incorporation	charter	corporation by estoppel
authorities	close corporation	corporation de jure
benefit corporation	conglomerate	de facto
bylaws	consolidation	domestic corporation
certificate of incorporation	corporation	eleemosynary corporation

foreign corporation
general corporation code
incorporators
merge

police power
private corporation
promoters
public corporation

quasi-public corporation
treasury stock
ultra vires

Questions and Case Problems

1. Edwin Edwards and Karen Davis owned EEE, Inc., which owned three convenience stores, all of which sold gasoline. Reid Ellis delivered to the three convenience stores $26,675.02 worth of gasoline for which he was not paid. Ellis proved that Edwards and Davis owned the business, ran it, and in fact personally ordered the gasoline. He claimed that they were personally liable for the debt owed him by EEE, Inc. Decide. [*Ellis v. Edwards*, 348 S.E.2d 764 (Ga. App.)]

2. Clinton Investors Company, as landlord, entered into a three-year lease with the Clifton Park Learning Center as tenant. The lease was executed by Bernie Watkins who represented himself as the treasurer of the Learning Center. On May 31, 1984, the day before the lease term began, Watkins signed a rider to the lease. He again signed as treasurer of the tenant, identifying the tenant as "the Clifton Park Learning Center, Inc." Watkins had not consulted an attorney regarding the formation of the corporation. He mistook the reservation of the business name with the Secretary of State for the filing of a certificate of incorporation. On February 11, 1985, a certificate of incorporation was filed. By March 1986, the Learning Center had become delinquent in rental payments and other fees in the amount of $18,103. Clinton sued Watkins and the Learning Center for the amounts due. Watkins claimed that only the corporation was liable. Decide. [*Clinton Investors Co. v. Watkins*, 536 N.Y.S. 2d 270 (A.D. 1989)]

3. Compare and contrast consolidations, mergers, and conglomerates.

4. On January 27, 1982, Joe Walker purchased a wheel-loader machine from Thompson & Green Machinery Co. (T&G). Walker signed a promissory note for $37,886.30 on behalf of "Music City Sawmill, Inc., by Joe Walker, President." When Sawmill was unable to make payments on the loader, the machine was returned to T&G. T&G brought suit against Sawmill and subsequently discovered that Sawmill had not been incorporated on January 27, 1982, when the machine was purchased but had been incorporated the next day. T&G then sued Walker individually. The lawsuit was Walker's first notice that Sawmill was not incorporated on the date of the sale. Walker's defense was that T&G dealt with Sawmill as a corporation and did not intend to bind him personally on the note and therefore was estopped to deny Sawmill's corporate existence. Decide based on the 1969 MBCA. What would be the result if the RMBCA applied? [*Thompson & Green Machinery Co. v. Music City Lumber Co., Inc., Music City Sawmill Co., Inc.*, 683 S.W.2d 340 (Tenn. App.)]

5. North Pole, Inc., approved a plan to merge with its subsidiary, Santa's Workshop, Inc. The merger plan provided that certain of Workshop's shareholders would receive $3.50 per share. The highest independent appraisal of the stock was $4.04 per share. Hirschfeld, Inc., a shareholder, claimed that the fair value was $16.80 per share. Workshop offered to make its corporate books and records available to Hirschfeld to assess the validity of the $16.80 demand. This offer was declined. Hirschfeld did not attempt to base the $16.80 demand on any recognizable method of stock valuation. Hirschfeld contended that it had a right to get the asking price. Refer to RMBCA §§13.02, 13.28, and 13.31. Could Hirschfeld have blocked the merger until Workshop paid the $16.80? Decide. [*Santa's Workshop v. Hirschfeld, Inc.*, 851 P.2d 265 (Colo. App.)]

6. Richard Ramlall was hired by CloseCall (MD) Inc. to negotiate a billing dispute with Verizon involving some $2 million in asserted overcharges. CloseCall (MD) agreed to a contingent fee "bonus" for its negotiators of 10 percent of the refund. The negotiations were successful. However, before he could collect his fee CloseCall (MD) merged with MVCC Acquisition Corp., a wholly owned subsidiary of MobilePro Corp., which was created for the express purpose of merging with CloseCall (MD). MVCC survived and CloseCall (MD) dissolved. MVCC then changed its name to CloseCall (DE). The merger agreement between CloseCall and MVCC referenced the 10 percent bonus due on the Verizon billing dispute. The surviving Delaware corporation created by the merger of CloseCall (MD) into MVCC is CloseCall (DE). Ramlall sued CloseCall (DE) for the bonus as the successor corporation of

CloseCall (MD). CloseCall (DE) contends that after the merger CloseCall (DE) did not owe any money to Ramlall. Is CloseCall (DE) a successor corporation? Is it liable to Ramlall for the "bonus fee"? [*Ramlall v. Mobile Pro Corp.*, 30 A.2d 1003 (Md. App.)]

7. The Community Youth Center (CYC) Corporation failed to pay its annual registration fee in 2000 and was automatically dissolved by the state corporation commission. CYC continued to operate and held itself out as a corporation well into 2005 when it obtained a loan from the First Community Bank to finance a swimming pool at its facility. The loan was secured by the CYC property. After the corporation defaulted on its loan payments, the bank foreclosed and subsequently purchased the property at a foreclosure sale. CYC contended that the president, vice president, and treasurer of CYC had no standing to make the 2005 loan transaction because CYC's corporate status had been terminated. The bank contended that under the doctrine of corporation by estoppel, CYC continued to exist in 2005, and, consequently, the officer-directors had authority to borrow money and grant a deed of trust, thereby giving the bank a valid lien on the property. Decide. [*First Community Bank, N.A. v. Community Youth Center*, 2010 WL 8696179 (Ca. Cir. Ct.)]

8. Emmick was a director and shareholder of Colonial Manors, Inc. (CM). He organized another corporation named Oahe Enterprises, Inc. To obtain shares of the Oahe stock, Emmick transferred CM shares arbitrarily valued by him at $19 per share to Oahe. The CM shares had a book value of $.47 per share, but Emmick believed that the stock would increase to a value of $19. The directors of Oahe approved Emmick's payment with the valuation of $19 per share. Golden sued Emmick on the ground that he had fraudulently deceived Oahe Corp. about the value of the CM shares and thus had made a secret profit when he received the Oahe shares that had a much greater value than the CM shares he gave in exchange. Emmick contended that his firm opinion was that the future potential value of CM shares would surely reach $19 per share. Decide. [*Golden v. Oahe Enterprises, Inc.*, 295 N.W.2d 160 (S.D.)]

9. Madison Associates purchased control of the majority of shares of 79 Realty Corp. from the Kimmelmans and the Zauders, who then resigned as directors. The Alpert group, which owned the remaining 26 percent of 79 Realty refused to sell their shares. Partners of Madison Associates replaced the Kimmelmans and Zauders as directors of 79 Realty Corp., and as controlling directors, they approved a plan to merge 79 Realty Corp. with the Williams Street Corp., which was owned by Madison Associates. A shareholders' meeting was called, and the merger was approved by two-thirds of the shareholders. The Alpert group's shares were then forcibly canceled, with the price paid for these shares determined at their fair market value. The Alpert group brought suit contending that the merger was unlawful because the sole purpose was to benefit the Madison Associates. Decide. [*Alpert v. 28 Williams Street Corp.*, 473 N.E.2d 19 (N.Y.)]

10. The Seabrook Island Property Owners Association, Inc., is a nonprofit corporation organized under state law to maintain streets and open spaces owned by property owners of Seabrook Island. Seabrook Island Co. is the developer of Seabrook Island and has majority control of the board of directors of the association. The association's bylaws empower the board of directors to levy an annual maintenance charge. Neither the association's charter nor its bylaws authorize the board to assess any other charges. When the board levied, in addition to the annual maintenance charge, an emergency budget assessment on all members to rebuild certain bridges and to revitalize the beach, the Loverings and other property owners challenged in court the association's power to impose the assessment. Decide. [*Lovering v. Seabrook Island Property Owners Ass'n*, 344 S.E.2d 862 (S.C. App.)]

11. Adams and two other persons were promoters for a new corporation, Aldrehn Theaters Co. The promoters retained Kridelbaugh to perform legal services in connection with the incorporation of the new business and promised to pay him $1,500. Aldrehn was incorporated through Kridelbaugh's services, and the promoters became its only directors. Kridelbaugh attended a meeting of the board of directors at which he was told that he should obtain a permit for the corporation to sell stock because the directors wished to pay him for his previous services. The promoters failed to pay Kridelbaugh, and he sued the corporation. Was the corporation liable? [*Kridelbaugh v. Aldrehn Theaters Co.*, 191 N.W. 803 (Iowa)]

12. On August 19, 1980, Joan Ioviero injured her hand when she slipped and fell while leaving the dining room at the Hotel Excelsior in Venice, Italy. This hotel was owned by an Italian corporation, Cigahotels, S.p.A. (The designation *S.p.A.* stands for *Societa per Azionean*, the Italian term for *corporation*.)

In 1973, a firm called Ciga Hotels, Inc., was incorporated in New York. Its certificate of incorporation was amended in 1979, changing the name of the firm to Landia International Services, Inc. This New York corporation was employed by the Italian corporation Cigahotels, S.p.A., to provide sales and promotional services in the United States and Canada. Ioviero sought to hold the New York corporation liable for her hand injury at the Venice hotel. She pointed to the similarity of the first corporate name used by the New York firm to the name Cigahotels, S.p.A., and the fact that the New York firm represented the interests of the Italian firm in the United States as clear evidence that the two firms were the same single legal entity. She asked that the court disregard the separate corporate entities. The New York corporation moved that the case be dismissed because it was duly incorporated in New York and did not own the Excelsior Hotel in which Ioviero was injured. Decide. [*Ioviero v. CigaHotel, Inc., aka Landia I.S., Inc.*, 475 N.Y.S.2d 880 (A.D.)]

13. William Sullivan was ousted from the presidency of the New England Patriots Football Club, Inc. Later, he borrowed $5,348,000 to buy 100 percent control of the voting shares of the corporation. A condition of the loan was that he reorganize the Patriots so that the income from the corporation could be devoted to repayment of the personal loan and the team's assets could be used as collateral. Sullivan, therefore, arranged for a cash freeze-out merger of the holders of the 120,000 shares of nonvoting stock. David Coggins, who owned 10 shares of nonvoting stock and took special pride in the fact that he was an owner of the team, refused the $15-a-share buyout and challenged the merger in court. He contended that the merger was not for a legitimate corporate purpose but to enable Sullivan to satisfy his personal loan. Sullivan contended that legitimate business purposes were given in the merger proxy statement, such as the National Football League's policy of discouraging public ownership of teams. Coggins responded that before the merger, Sullivan had 100 percent control of the voting stock and thus control of the franchise and that no legal basis existed to eliminate public ownership. Decide. [*Coggins v. New England Patriots Football Club*, 492 N.E.2d 1112 (Mass.)]

CPA Questions

1. Which of the following statements is correct concerning the similarities between a limited partnership and a corporation?

   a. Each is created under a statute and must file a copy of its certificate with the proper state authorities.

   b. All corporate stockholders and all partners in a limited partnership have limited liability.

   c. Both are recognized for federal income tax purposes as taxable entities.

   d. Both are allowed statutorily to have perpetual existence.

2. Rice is a promoter of a corporation to be known as Dex Corp. On January 1, 1985, Rice signed a nine-month contract with Roe, a CPA, which provided that Roe would perform certain accounting services for Dex. Rice did not disclose to Roe that Dex had not been formed. Prior to the incorporation of Dex on February 1, 1985, Roe rendered accounting services pursuant to the contract. After rendering accounting services for an additional period of six months pursuant to the contract, Roe was discharged without cause by the board of directors of Dex. In the absence of any agreements to the contrary, who will be liable to Roe for breach of contract?

   a. Both Rice and Dex

   b. Rice only

   c. Dex only

   d. Neither Rice nor Dex

3. In general, which of the following must be contained in articles of incorporation?

   a. The names of the states in which the corporation will be doing business

   b. The name of the state in which the corporation will maintain its principal place of business

   c. The names of the initial officers and their terms of office

   d. The classes of stock authorized for issuance

Shareholder Rights in Corporations

Learning Outcomes >>>

After studying this chapter, you should be able to

LO.1 Explain how to calculate the book value of a share of stock

LO.2 Distinguish between stocks and bonds

LO.3 Distinguish between subscriptions for and transfers of stock

LO.4 Explain the rights of shareholders

LO.5 Explain the nature of a shareholder derivative lawsuit

LO.6 Explain the exceptions to the limited liability of shareholders

The two most common instruments used to provide funds for a corporation are stocks and bonds.

44-1   Corporate Stocks and Bonds

Ownership of a corporation is represented by stock. A *bond* is a corporate debt.

44-1a   Nature of Stock

An interest in a corporation is based on ownership of one or more shares of stock of the corporation. Each share represents a fractional interest in the total property of the corporation. The shareholder does not own or have an interest in any specific property of the corporation; the corporation is the owner of all of its property. The terms *share, stock*, and *share of stock* mean the same thing.

outstanding—name for shares of a company that have been issued to stockholders.

capital stock—declared money value of the outstanding stock of the corporation.

par value—specified monetary amount assigned by an issuing corporation for each share of its stock.

Capital and Capital Stock

Capital refers to the net assets of the corporation. Shares that have been issued to holders are said to be **outstanding. Capital stock** refers to the value received by the corporation for its outstanding stock.

Valuation of Stock

Corporate stock may have a specified **par value.** This means that the person subscribing to the stock and acquiring it from the corporation must pay that amount.

Shares may be issued with no par value. In that case, no amount is stated in the certificate, and the amount that the subscriber pays the corporation is determined by the board of directors. The Revised Model Business Corporation Act (RMBCA) eliminates the concept of par value, so stock issued by corporations in states following the RMBCA is always no par.

book value—value found by dividing the value of the corporate assets by the number of shares outstanding.

The value found by dividing the value of the net corporate assets by the number of shares outstanding is the **book value** of the shares. **For Example,** Roger Eggett entered a Shareholder Agreement in 1995 with Todd Cusick and Curtis Chisholm, forming the Wasatch Energy Corporation. The terms of the Shareholder Agreement provided that should a shareholder separate from the corporation, the remaining shareholders would have the option to purchase that shareholder's corporate stock. The remaining shareholders, as per the Shareholder Agreement, would either purchase the stock for book value, if the separating shareholder voluntarily left the corporation, or for par value, if the shareholder was terminated for cause. The Shareholder Agreement defined *book value* as the shareholder's net equity in the corporation, which would be determined by Wasatch's certified year-end financial statements. The Shareholder Agreement defined *par value* as the original price the shareholder paid for the stock. Egget tendered his resignation two years later and offered to sell his stock according to the Shareholder Agreement "for the audited book value of the corporation as of June 30, 1997 divided by the number of shares he owned." Wasatch Corp. responded by firing Egget, wrongly asserting the firing was for cause, and tendered him a check for the par value of his stock, $1,217, Eggett's original investment. Eggett sued and was awarded the book value of his shares, $135,671, plus $60,000 in attorney fees.[1] The **market value** of a share of stock is the price at which that stock can be voluntarily bought or sold in the open market.

market value—price at which a share of stock can be voluntarily bought or sold in the open market.

---

[1] *Eggett v. Wasatch Energy Corp.*, 29 P.3d 668 (Utah App. 2001).

There can be a substantial difference between book value and market value. If an agreement refers to book value or market value a court may construe the term strictly even if the result in interpretation yields vastly different amounts. **For Example,** a family partnership agreement provided for a buyout based on book value. The book value of the partnership was calculated at $177,808. The fair market value, however, was in excess of $30 million. The court found that the agreement was unambiguous and enforced it even though doing so resulted in a windfall to the purchaser.[2]

44-1b Certificates of Stock and Uncertificated Shares

certificate of stock–document evidencing a shareholder's ownership of stock issued by a corporation.

A corporation ordinarily issues a **certificate of stock** or *share certificate* as evidence of the shareholder's ownership of stock. The issuance of such certificates is not essential either to the existence of a corporation or to the ownership of its stock. Many companies have stopped issuing paper stock certificates and use electronic registration to create a more secure and efficient system.[3]

In states that have adopted the 1978 and 1994 amendments to Article 8 of the UCC, uncertificated shares may be issued. Uncertificated shares are not represented by instruments. Their ownership and transfer are registered on the books maintained by, or on behalf of, the issuer corporation.[4] The registered stockholder is considered the stockholder of record. Registered owners may have either physical certificates or uncertificated ownership.

44-1c Kinds of Stock

The stock of a corporation may be divided into two or more classes.

Classification by Preferences

CPA

common stock–stock that has no right or priority over any other stock of the corporation as to dividends or distribution of assets upon dissolution.

CPA

preferred stock–stock that has a priority or preference as to payment of dividends or upon liquidation, or both.

CPA

Common stock is ordinary stock that has no preferences. Each share usually entitles the holder to have one vote, to receive a share of the profits in the form of dividends when declared, and to participate in the distribution of capital upon dissolution of the corporation. **Preferred stock** has a priority over common stock. The priority may be with respect to either dividends or the distribution of capital upon dissolution of the corporation, or both. Preferred stock is ordinarily nonvoting.

Cumulative Preferred Stock. The right to receive dividends depends on the declaration of dividends by the board of directors for a particular period of time. If there is no fund from which the dividends may be declared or if the directors do not declare them from an available fund, the shareholder has no right to dividends. The fact that a shareholder has not received dividends for the current year does not in itself give the right to accumulate or carry over into the next year a claim for those dividends. However, in the absence of a statement that the right to dividends is noncumulative, courts frequently hold that preferred stock has the right to accumulate dividends for each year in which there was a surplus available for dividend payment but dividends were not declared.

Participating Preferred Stock. Sometimes the preferred stock is given the right of participation. If it is, then after the common shares receive dividends or a capital distribution is made equal to that first received by the preferred stock, both kinds participate or share equally in the balance.

---

[2] See *Estate of Cohen v. Booth Computer*, 22 A.3d 991 (N.J. App. Div. 2011).
[3] Some stock certificates are collectors' items. Walt Disney Co. stopped issuing paper stock certificates in 2013. It was one of the last large companies to stop issuing paper stock certificates.
[4] U.C.C. §8-102(1)(b). The 1978 and 1994 amendments to Article 8 of the UCC have been adopted in all of the states except Alabama.

Duration of Shares

Ordinarily, shares continue to exist for the life of the corporation. However, any kind of share, whether common or preferred, may be made terminable at an earlier date.

Fractional Shares

A corporation may issue fractional shares or scrip or certificates representing fractional shares. These can be sold or combined for the acquisition of whole shares.

44-1d Characteristics of Bonds

A **bond** is an instrument promising to repay a loan of money to a corporation. Typically, the loan is for a relatively long period of time, generally five years or longer. A bond obligates the corporation to pay the bondholder the amount of the loan, called the *principal*, at a stated time, called the **maturity date,** and to pay a fixed amount of *interest* at regular intervals, commonly every six months. The relationship between the bondholder and the issuing corporation is that of creditor and debtor. Companies and government entities may use bonds to finance a wide variety of projects. Unlike dividends, which are discretionary, bond interest must be paid. A bond may be secured by a mortgage or lien on corporate property. A **debenture** is an unsecured bond of the corporation with no specific corporate assets pledged as security for payment.

Bonds are negotiable securities.[5] Bonds held by owners whose names and addresses are registered on the books of the corporation are called **registered bonds.**

44-1e Terms and Control

The contractual terms of a particular bond issue are set forth in an agreement called a **bond indenture** or **deed.** An **indenture trustee,** usually a commercial banking institution, represents the interests of the bondholders in making sure that the corporation meets the terms and covenants of the bond issue.[6] For example, the terms of the bond indenture may require a **sinking fund,** by which the borrowing corporation is required to set aside a fixed amount of money each year toward the ultimate payment of the bonds.

Bondholders do not vote for directors or have the right to vote on matters on which shareholders vote. However, when the debt is risky, it is highly likely that significant restraints on the corporation's freedom of action will be imposed by the terms of the indenture.

44-2 Acquisition of Shares

Shares may be acquired from the corporation or from an existing shareholder.

44-2a Nature of Acquisition

Shares of stock may be acquired (1) from the corporation by subscription, either before or after the corporation is organized, or (2) by transfer of existing shares from a shareholder or from the corporation. The transfer may be voluntary, as by a sale, gift, or bequest by will, or involuntary, as by an execution sale to pay the judgment of a creditor. The transfer may also take place by operation of law—as when the stock of a shareholder passes to the shareholder's trustee in bankruptcy.

[5] U.C.C. §8-105.
[6] *Lorenc v. CSX Corp.,* CCH Sec. L. Rep. 95298 (W.D. Pa. 1990).

---

bond–a debt investment; a loan to a corporation or government entity usually for a defined period of time at a fixed interest rate.

maturity date–date that a corporation is required to repay a loan to a bondholder.

debenture–unsecured bond of a corporation, with no specific corporate assets pledged as security for payment.

registered bonds–bonds held by owners whose names and addresses are registered on the books of the corporation to ensure proper payment.

bond indenture–agreement setting forth the contractual terms of a particular bond issue.

deed–instrument by which the grantor (owner of land) conveys or transfers the title to a grantee.

indenture trustee–usually a commercial banking institution, to represent the interests of the bondholders and ensure that the terms and covenants of the bond issue are met by the corporation.

sinking fund–fixed amount of money set aside each year by the borrowing corporation toward the ultimate payment of bonds.

44-2b Statute of Frauds

Under the 1978 version of Article 8, a contract for the sale of corporate shares must be evidenced by a writing, or it cannot be enforced.[7] The 1994 version of Article 8 renders the statute of frauds inapplicable to contracts for the sale or purchase of securities.[8] The commentary notes explain that the 1978 statute's potential for filtering out fraudulent claims is outweighed by the obstacles the statute presents to the development of modern commercial practices in the securities business.

No writing is required for a contract by which a broker agrees with a customer to buy or sell securities for the customer. That is an agency agreement, not a sale made between the customer and the broker.

44-2c Subscription

stock subscription—contract or agreement to buy a specific number and kind of shares when they are issued by the corporation.

A **stock subscription** is a contract or an agreement to buy a specific number and kind of shares when the corporation issues them. As in the case of any other contract, the agreement to subscribe to shares of a corporation may be avoided for fraud.

Subscription before Incorporation

In many states, a preincorporation subscription of shares is an offer to the corporation. According to this view, it is necessary for the corporation to accept the subscription offer either expressly or by conduct. A few states hold that subscriptions automatically become binding contracts when the organization of the corporation has been completed. In some states, the preincorporation subscription is irrevocable for a stated period. The RMBCA provides that "a subscription for shares entered into before incorporation is irrevocable for six months unless the subscription agreement provides a longer or shorter period or all the subscribers agree to revocation."[9]

Subscription after Incorporation

acceptance—unqualified assent to the act or proposal of another; as the acceptance of a draft (bill of exchange), of an offer to make a contract, of goods delivered by the seller, or of a gift or deed.

Subscriptions may be made after incorporation. In that event, the transaction is like any other contract with the corporation. The offer of the subscription may come from the subscriber or from the corporation. In either case, there must be an **acceptance.** Upon acceptance, the subscriber immediately becomes a shareholder with all the rights, privileges, and liabilities of a shareholder even though she has not paid any of the purchase price. Moreover, the subscriber is a shareholder even though no share certificate has been issued. In contrast with a contract for immediate subscription to shares, the contract may be one for the future issue of shares. In that case, the contracting party has only a contract and is not a shareholder as of the formation of the contract.

44-2d Transfer of Shares

In the absence of a valid restriction, a shareholder may transfer shares to anyone.

Restrictions on Transfer

Restrictions on the transfer of stock are valid if they are not unreasonable. It is lawful to require that the corporation or other stockholders be given the first right to purchase stock before a shareholder may sell stock to an outsider.

Such restrictions are widely used, particularly in close corporations, so current shareholders can control the ownership and management of the corporation and prevent outsiders from "invading the business;" also, restrictions serve to maintain parity among shareholders.

---

[7] U.C.C. §8-319(a); *Goldfinger v. Brown*, 564 N.Y.S.2d 461 (A.D. 1991).
[8] U.C.C. §8-113.
[9] RMBCA §6.20(a).

CASE SUMMARY

Restrictions on Transfer of Stock Are Legal, Morris

FACTS: In 1974 Billy Fought, Brady Morris, Clayton Strong, and John Peyton organized Vicksburg Mold and Die, Inc., for the purpose of designing and manufacturing plastic and metal products. Each individual was issued 25 shares of stock. The shareholders entered into a stock redemption agreement requiring a stockholder wishing to sell his stock to offer proportionate shares to each stockholder. Morris was elected president and Fought vice president, and all four individuals worked at the plant. Strong retired in 1979 and sold his shares in accordance with the stock redemption plan. In 1983, Peyton decided to sell his shares and agreed to sell them all to Morris, thus giving Morris control of the corporation. Fought sued Morris for breach of his fiduciary duty to Fought and for the value of Fought's pro rata share of Peyton's stock.

DECISION: Judgment for Fought. Section 2 of the stock redemption agreement was designed to maintain a balance of power in the four-person close corporation. Before stock could be sold to others, it had to be offered to each shareholder on a pro rata basis. Each individual had an opportunity to maintain the initial balance of power. By purchasing all of Peyton's stock, Morris bought control of the corporation. In doing so, he violated the stock redemption agreement and thus breached his fiduciary duty as a director, officer, and shareholder. [*Fought v. Morris*, 543 So. 2d 167 (Miss. 1989)]

A provision giving a corporation the right to purchase a shareholder's shares on the death of the shareholder is valid.[10]

A restriction on the right of a certificate's purchaser to transfer his stock is not valid unless the restriction is conspicuously noted on the certificate or the transferee had actual knowledge of the restriction. A restriction on the transfer of stock is strictly interpreted.[11]

When no restrictions exist, the issuer has a duty to register the transfer. **For Example,** Richard Jones purchased 1,000 certificated shares of International Generic Corporation (IGC) from Madison Tucker on March 30, 2016, at fair market value. Tucker properly indorsed the certificates to Jones on that date, and her signatures were duly notarized. On September 15, 2016, Jones presented the securities to IGC to register the transfer of shares and to collect dividends for the second quarter (April 1 through June 30) and the third quarter (July 1 through September 30). IGC refused to register the shares in Jones's name, believing him to be a person of questionable integrity that it did not want as an "owner" of IGC. Under either the 1978 or 1994 version of Article 8 of the UCC, it was improper for IGC to fail to register the stock that had been transferred to a bona fide purchaser, Jones. No restrictions existed on the certificate, and IGC had a duty to register the transfer and was liable for its failure to do so. Jones was entitled to the dividends from the date of presentation of the stock for transfer. Prior to that date, the issuer, IGC, was entitled to treat the registered owner, Madison Tucker, as exclusively entitled to exercise the rights of ownership, including the right to dividends. Thus, IGC was not liable to Jones for the second-quarter dividends. However, dividends declared after the date of presentment, which included the third-quarter dividend declared in October 2016 with a record date in October, must be paid to Jones by IGC.

[10] See *Puritas Metal Products v. Cook*, 972 N.E2d 615 (Ohio 2012), where a trial court incorrectly determined that the decedent's death resulted in a "transfer" under the corporation's code of regulation. In fact, the decedent's shares were in a marital trust, and upon his death the shares were retained by the trustee of the trust, his wife, to administer and vote as she saw fit.

[11] *Capano v. Wilmington Country Club, Inc.*, 2001 WL 1359254 (Del. Ch. Nov. 1, 2001).

Interest Transferred

The transfer of shares may be absolute; that is, it may divest all ownership and make the transferee the full owner. The transfer may be of only a partial interest in the stock, or the transfer may be for security, such as when stock is pledged to secure the repayment of a loan.

44-2e Mechanics of Transfer

When stock is represented by a certificate, the ownership of shares is transferred by the delivery of the certificate of stock, indorsed by its owner in blank or to a specified person. Ownership may also be transferred by the delivery of the certificate accompanied by a separate assignment or power of attorney executed by the owner.[12]

A delivery from the owner of the shares directly to the transferee is not required. It can be made to an intermediary. When there is no delivery of the share certificate to anyone, however, there is no transfer of ownership of the shares.

A physical transfer of the certificate without a necessary indorsement is effective as between the parties. Thus, a gift of shares is binding even though no indorsement has been made. An indorsement is required to make the transferee a bona fide purchaser.

44-2f Effect of Transfer

The transfer of existing shares of stock may raise questions between the parties to the transfer as well as between the parties and the corporation.

Validity of Transfer

Because a transfer of shares is a transfer of ownership, the transfer must satisfy the requirements governing any other transfer of property or agreement to transfer property.[13] As between the parties, a transfer may be set aside for any ground that would warrant similar relief under property law. If the transfer has been obtained by duress, the transferor may obtain a rescission of the transfer.

Negotiability

Under common law, the transferee of shares of stock had no greater right than the transferor because the certificate and the shares represented by the certificate were nonnegotiable. By statute, the common law rule has been changed by imparting negotiability to certificated stock. Just as various defenses cannot be asserted against the holder in due course of a commercial paper, statutory law provides that similar defenses cannot be raised against the person acquiring the certificate in good faith and for value. Against such a person, the defense cannot be raised that the transferor did not own the shares or did not have authority to deliver the certificate or that the transfer was made in violation of a restriction on transfer not known to the person and not noted conspicuously on the certificate.

Statements sent by the issuer identifying the ownership of uncertificated securities are neither certificated securities nor negotiable instruments. Although certificated securities have the quality of negotiability, they are not commercial paper within Article 3 of the UCC.

Secured Transaction

Corporate stock is frequently delivered to a creditor as security for a debt owed by the shareholder. Thus, a debtor borrowing money from a bank may deliver shares of stock

---

[12] U.C.C. §8-309. See *Kesling v. Kesling*, 967 N.E.2d 66, 68 (Ind. App. 2012), where the corporate bylaws set forth the two methods of transferring stock in the corporation.
[13] *Gallant v. Kanterman*, 294 A.D.2d 59 (N.Y. App. Div. 1998).

to the bank as collateral security for the repayment of the loan. A broker's customer purchasing stock on margin may leave the stock in the possession of the broker as security for the payment of any balance due. The delivery of the security to the creditor is a pledge. This gives rise to a perfected security interest without any filing by the creditor. In itself, the pledge does not make the pledgee of the corporate stock the owner of the stock.

Effect of Transfer on Corporation

The corporation is entitled to treat as the owner of shares the person whose name is on the corporation's books as the owner. Therefore, until there is a transfer on its books, the corporation may still treat a transferor of shares as the owner. The corporation may properly refuse to recognize a transferee when the corporation is given notice or has knowledge that the transfer is void or in breach of trust. In such a case, the corporation properly refuses to register a transfer until the rights of the parties have been determined. The corporation may also refuse to register the transfer of shares when the outstanding certificate is not surrendered to it or there is a lack of satisfactory proof that the certificate has been lost, destroyed, or stolen.

44-2g Lost, Destroyed, and Stolen Share Certificates

The owner of a lost, destroyed, or stolen share certificate is entitled to a replacement if the owner files a sufficient indemnity bond and requests the new certificate within a reasonable time before the issuer has notice that the original certificate has been acquired by a bona fide purchaser. A *share* is the actual property of the shareholder, while the *certificate* is merely the authentic evidence of the stockholder's ownership of shares.[14] If, after the new security is issued, a bona fide purchaser appears with the original certificate, the corporation must register a transfer of the security to that person and accept that person as the owner of the shares.

CPA   ## 44-3 Rights of Shareholders

The rights of shareholders stem from their status as owners.

CPA   ## 44-3a Ownership Rights

Shareholder control over the corporation is indirect. Periodically (ordinarily once a year), the shareholders elect directors and by this means control the corporation. At other times, however, the shareholders have no right or power to control corporate activity so long as it is conducted within lawful channels.

CPA   ### Certificates of Stock

A shareholder has the right to have a properly executed certificate as evidence of ownership of shares. An exception is made when the corporation is authorized to issue uncertificated securities.

CPA   ### Transfer of Shares

Unless limited by a valid restriction, a shareholder has the right to transfer her shares. The shareholder may sell the shares at any price or transfer them as a gift. The fact that the seller sells at a price higher than the market price is not unlawful even if the seller is a director or an officer.

---

[14] *Rosso v. Rosso*, 701 N.W.2d 355 (Neb. 2005).

CASE SUMMARY

It's the Real Thing, Controlling Shares in Coke-Anderson, and You Have to Pay a Premium

FACTS: Paul Warlick, Jr., was the president and chief executive officer and a stockholder of Coca-Cola Bottling Company of Anderson, S.C. (Coke-Anderson). He controlled a majority of the shares of stock of the company. Warlick agreed to sell this controlling interest in Coke-Anderson to Coke-Asheville for a price greater than the market value of the shares. Wayne Shoaf, a minority shareholder, brought suit against Warlick, contending that Warlick had violated his fiduciary duty to the corporation by receiving an unlawful premium for the sale of the majority interest in Coke-Anderson.

DECISION: Judgment for Warlick. Paying or receiving a premium for the controlling shares of stock in a corporation is not unlawful. A majority shareholder who is also a director and an officer is generally under no duty to minority shareholders to refrain from receiving a premium on the sale of the controlling stock. [*Shoaf v. Warlick,* **380 S.E.2d 865 (S.C. App. 1989)**]

CPA   ## 44-3b Right to Vote

The right to vote means the right to vote at shareholders' meetings for the election of directors and on other special matters that shareholders must vote on. **For Example,** a proposal to change the capital structure of the corporation or a proposal to sell all or substantially all assets of the corporation must be approved by the shareholders.

CPA   ## Who May Vote

Ordinarily, only shareholders of record—those common shareholders in whose name the stock appears on the books of the corporation—are entitled to vote. The board of directors may fix a date for closing the corporate books for this purpose.

CPA   ## Number of Votes

Unless there is a provision to the contrary, for each share owned, each shareholder is entitled to one vote on each matter to be voted. This procedure is called *straight voting,* and it is the normal method for shareholder voting on corporate matters. However, in the case of voting to elect directors only, **cumulative voting** is mandatory in nearly half of the states. This requirement is imposed by either state constitution or state statute. Cumulative voting is permitted by law in other states when provided for in the articles of incorporation or bylaws.

cumulative voting– system of voting for directors in which each shareholder has as many votes as the number of voting shares owned multiplied by the number of directors to be elected, and such votes can be distributed for the various candidates as desired.

Cumulative voting is a form of voting that is designed to give proportional representation on the board of directors to minority shareholders. Under a cumulative voting plan, each shareholder has as many votes as the number of shares owned multiplied by the number of directors to be elected. A shareholder may cast all of these votes for one candidate or may divide the votes between two or more candidates. This system enables minority shareholders to cast all of their votes for a candidate who will represent their interests on the board of directors.

Under straight voting, minority shareholders would always be outvoted. **For Example,** assume that minority shareholder Tyler Feldberg owned 400 shares of stock and majority shareholder C. J. Jones controlled the remaining 600 shares. Also assume that five directors are to be elected to the board. If straight voting were used for the election of directors, C. J., with 600 shares, would always outvote Tyler's 400 shares.

However, under cumulative voting, Tyler would be allowed 2,000 votes (400 shares times five directors), and C. J. would be allowed 3,000 votes (600 shares times five directors). The five candidates with the highest number of votes will be elected. If Tyler casts 1,000 votes for each of two directors and C. J. casts 1,000 votes for each of three directors, Tyler, who owns 40 percent of the stock, is able to elect two-fifths of the board to represent his interests.

Voting by Proxy

voting by proxy–authorizing someone else to vote the shares owned by the shareholder.

A shareholder has the right to authorize another to vote the shares owned by the shareholder. This procedure is known as **voting by proxy.** In the absence of restrictions to the contrary, any person, even someone who is not a shareholder, may act as a proxy. The authorization from the shareholder may be made by any writing.[15] The authorization is also commonly called a **proxy.**

proxy–written authorization by a shareholder to another person to vote the stock owned by the shareholder; the person who is the holder of such a written authorization.

Voting Agreements and Trusts

Shareholders, as a general rule, are allowed to enter into an agreement by which they concentrate their voting strength for the purpose of electing directors or voting on any other matter.

A **voting trust** is created when by agreement a group of shareholders or all of the shareholders transfer their shares in trust to one or more persons as trustees. The trustees are authorized to vote the stock during the life of the trust agreement.[16] In general, such agreements are upheld if their object is lawful. In some jurisdictions, such trusts cannot run beyond a stated number of years. There are some signs of a relaxation as to time. Several states have abandoned all time limitations, several have extended the time limitation, and many provide for an extension or renewal of the agreement.

voting trust–transfer by two or more persons of their shares of stock of a corporation to a trustee who is to vote the shares and act for such shareholders.

CPA

44-3c Preemptive Offer of Shares

If the capital stock of a corporation is increased, shareholders ordinarily have the **preemptive right** to subscribe to the same percentage of the new shares that their old shares represented of the former total of capital stock. This right is given to enable shareholders to maintain their relative interests in the corporation.

preemptive right–shareholder's right upon the increase of a corporation's capital stock to be allowed to subscribe to such a percentage of the new shares as the shareholder's old shares bore to the former total capital stock.

The existence of a preemptive right may make it impossible to conclude a transaction in which the corporation is to transfer a block of stock as consideration. Moreover, practical difficulties arise as to how stock should be allocated among shareholders of different classes.

The RMBCA provides that shareholders do not have preemptive rights unless the articles of incorporation provide for them.

CPA

44-3d Inspection of Books

A shareholder has the right to inspect the books of the shareholder's corporation. In some states, there are no limitations on this right. In most states, the inspection must be made in good faith, for proper motives, and at a reasonable time and place.[17] **For Example,** shareholders have a proper purpose to inspect the books and records of a corporation to determine whether the directors and officers engaged in self-dealing to the detriment of the corporation.[18] Some courts have even allowed shareholders to demand the production of documents that fall under the attorney-client privilege.[19] In many states, a shareholder

---

[15] RMBCA §7.07.
[16] *Bettner Trust v. Bettner*, 495 N.E.2d 194 (Ind. App. 1986).
[17] RMBCA §16.02(c); *Leary v. Foley*, 884 So. 2d 655 (La. App. 2004).
[18] *Sunlitz Holding Co. v. Trading Block Holdings, Inc.*, 17 N.E.3d 715 (Ill. App. 2014).
[19] *Wal-Mart Stores, Inc. v. Indiana Electrical Workers Pension Trust Fund IBEW*, 2014 WL 3638848 (Del. July 23, 2014).

must own a certain percentage of the outstanding stock of a corporation (commonly 5 percent) or must own at least one share of stock for a minimum amount of time (commonly six months) to have the right to inspect the books. A shareholder is not relegated to accepting opinions and numbers offered by a company's auditor and may employ an expert accountant of his own to review and analyze the books and records of the corporation.[20] If a corporation unreasonably refuses inspection, a court may require the corporation to pay the shareholder's litigation costs, including reasonable attorneys' fees.[21]

A shareholder is entitled to inspect the records to determine the financial condition of the corporation, the quality of its management, and any matters relating to rights or interests in the corporate business, such as the value of stock.[22]

CASE SUMMARY

When Shareholders Investigate Bribery and a Corporate Cover-Up, Even Privileged Documents Must Be Produced

FACTS: In April 2012, the *New York Times* ran a story about bribery at WalMex, a Mexican subsidiary of Wal-Mart. The article described a scheme of illegal bribery payments made to Mexican officials at the direction of WalMex CEO, Eduardo Castro-Wright, between 2002 and 2005. The article stated that WalMex received benefits such as zoning changes and rapid and favorable processing of permits and licenses for new stores in exchange for bribes. The *NYT* article stated that Wal-Mart executives were aware of the conduct no later than September 2005. A stockholder of Wal-Mart, the Electrical Workers Pension Trust Fund IBEW (IBEW), demanded to inspect the books and records of the corporation with the purpose of investigating the bribery allegations and breaches of fiduciary duty by Wal-Mart or WalMex executives in connection with the bribery allegations. Wal-Mart produced approximately 3,000 documents, including documents regarding its compliance with the Foreign Corrupt Practices Act and minutes and materials referencing the WalMex Allegations. Wal-Mart declined to provide documents that it believed were not necessary and essential to the stated purposes or that were protected by the attorney-client privilege and work-product doctrine.

The Court of Chancery held that Wal-Mart had to produce these additional documents because they were "necessary and essential" to achieve a "proper purpose," as required by Section 220 of the Delaware Code. According to Section 220, documents are "necessary and essential" if they address

the "crux of the shareholder's purpose" and if that information "is unavailable from another source."

DECISION: Judgment for the shareholder, IBEW. There is a fiduciary exception to the attorney-client privilege. Ordinarily, a corporation may assert the privilege even when stockholders request privileged information. But when the corporation is in suit against its stockholders and is potentially acting against shareholder interests, the stockholders may show cause why the privilege should not be invoked. Section 220 of the Delaware Code requires that shareholders demonstrate that the corporate documents they request are "necessary and essential" for a legitimate shareholder purpose. The record showed that IBEW's purpose in seeking the information was to investigate the handling of the WalMex Investigation, whether a cover-up took place, and what details were shared with the Wal-Mart Board. Once a stockholder has satisfied the "necessary and essential" requirements, it must then show that there is good cause for access to the privileged documents. Good cause existed in this case because the stockholders had a "colorable claim" based on Wal-Mart's public statements about alleged illegalities in Mexico. The fact that the information would be difficult to obtain from another source also supported a good cause finding. [*Wal-Mart Stores, Inc. v. Indiana Electrical Workers Pension Trust Fund IBEW,* 2014 WL 3638848 (Del. July 23, 2014)]

A shareholder is entitled to inspect the books to obtain information needed for a lawsuit against the corporation or its directors or officers, to organize the other shareholders

---

[20] *Missouri v. III Investments, Inc.,* 80 S.W.3d 855 (Mo. App. 2002).
[21] *Clark v. Anjacko, Inc.,* 333 P.2d 779 (Ariz. App. 2014).
[22] *Ihrig v. Frontier Equity Exchange,* 128 P.3d 993 (Kan. App. 2006).

into an "opposition" party to remove the board of directors at the next election, or to buy the shares of other shareholders.[23]

Inspection has frequently been refused when it was sought merely from idle curiosity or for "speculative purposes." Inspection has sometimes been denied on the ground that it was sought merely to obtain a mailing list of persons who would be solicited to buy products of another enterprise. Inspection has also been refused when the object of the shareholder was to advance political or social beliefs without regard to the welfare of the corporation. Cases that deny the right of inspection do so when it would be harmful to the corporation[24] or is sought only for the purpose of annoying, harassing, or causing vexation or of aiding competitors of the corporation.

Form of Books

There are generally no requirements regarding the form of corporate books and records. The RMBCA recognizes that corporate books and records may be stored in modern data storage systems. "A corporation shall maintain its records in written form or in any other form capable of conversion into written form within a reasonable time."[25]

Financial Statements

The RMBCA requires a corporation to furnish annual financial statements. These statements include a balance sheet at the end of the fiscal year, an income statement for that year, and a statement of changes in shareholders' equity for that year.[26] A number of state statutes contain similar provisions and set forth a statutory penalty for any officer responsible for providing the financial statements who fails to perform such duties after written request.

CPA   ## 44-3e Dividends

A shareholder has the right to receive a proportion of dividends as they are declared, subject to the relative rights of other shareholders to preferences, accumulation of dividends, and participation. There is no absolute right that dividends be declared, but dividends, when declared, must be paid in the manner indicated.

CPA   ### Funds Available for Declaration of Dividends

Statutes commonly provide that no dividends may be declared unless there is an "earned surplus" for their payment. Earned surplus, also known as *retained earnings*, consists of the accumulated profits earned by the corporation since its formation less prior dividend distributions. Dividend payments are prohibited if the corporation is insolvent or would be rendered insolvent by the payment of the dividend.

wasting assets corporation–corporation designed to exhaust or use up the assets of the corporation, such as by extracting oil, coal, iron, and other ores.

As an exception to these rules, a wasting assets corporation may pay dividends out of current net profits without regard to the preservation of the corporate assets. **Wasting assets corporations** are those designed to exhaust or use up the assets of the corporation (for example, by extracting oil, coal, iron, and other ores) as compared with manufacturing

---

[23] See *Kelley Manufacturing Co. v. Martin*, 674 S.E.2d 92 (Ga. App. 2009), where the court determined that two shareholders showed a proper purpose for seeking inspection of books: to enforce the company's bylaws; to ensure proper corporate governance and to determine if corporate waste, mismanagement, and other breaches of fiduciary duty were occurring; to inspect corporate records to protect the shareholders substantial ownership interest; and to inspect records related to the shareholders' removal as trustees, directors, officers, and employees of the corporation.

[24] *Retail Property Investors, Inc., v. Skeens*, 471 S.E.2d 181 (Va. 1996).

[25] RMBCA §16.01(d).

[26] RMBCA §16.20. See *Troccoli v. Lab Contract Industries, Inc.*, 687 N.Y.S.2d 400 (A.D. 1999).

plants whose object is to preserve the plant as well as to continue to manufacture. A wasting assets corporation may also be formed for the purpose of buying and liquidating a stock of merchandise from a company that has received a discharge in bankruptcy court.

In some states, statutes provide that dividends may be declared from earned surplus or from current net profits without regard to the existence of a deficit from former years.

C P A ### Discretion of Directors

Assuming that a fund is available for the declaration of dividends, it is then a matter primarily within the discretion of the board of directors whether a dividend shall be declared. The fact that there is an earned surplus that could be used for dividends does not mean that they must be declared. This rule is not affected by the nature of the shares. Thus, the fact that the shareholders hold cumulative preferred shares does not give them any right to demand a declaration of dividends or to interfere with an honest exercise of discretion by the directors.

Maintaining an adequate cash and working capital position is an important practical consideration in determining whether to declare a cash dividend. In general, courts refuse to substitute their judgment for the judgment of the directors of the corporation and interfere with their decision on dividend declaration only when it is shown that their conduct is harmful to the welfare of the corporation or its shareholders.[27]

Form of Dividends

Customarily, a dividend is paid in money. However, it may be paid in property, such as a product manufactured by the corporation; in shares of other corporations held by the corporation; or in shares of the corporation itself.

Effect of Transfer of Shares

When a corporation declares a cash or property dividend, the usual practice is for the board of directors to declare a dividend as of a certain date—the *declaration date*—payable to shareholders of record on a stated future date—the *record date*—with a *payment date* following the record date, usually by some 30 days. The person who is the owner of the shares on the record date is entitled to the dividend even if the shares are transferred prior to the payment date.

If the dividend consists of shares in the corporation declaring the dividend, ownership of the dividend is determined by the date of distribution. Whoever is the owner of the shares when the stock dividend is distributed is entitled to the stock dividend. The reason for this variation from the cash dividend rule is that the declaration of a stock dividend has the effect of diluting the existing corporate assets among a larger number of shares. The value of the holding represented by each share is diminished as a result. Unless the person who owns the stock on the distribution date receives a proportionate share of the stock dividend, the net effect will be to lessen that person's holding.

44-3f Capital Distribution

Upon dissolution of the corporation, shareholders are entitled to receive any balance of the corporate assets that remains after the payment of all creditors. Certain classes of stock may have a preference or priority in this distribution.

---

[27] *Gabelli & Co. v. Liggett Group, Inc.*, 479 A.2d 276 (Del. Super. 1984).

CPA   ## 44-3g Shareholders' Actions

When the corporation has the right to sue its directors, officers, or third persons for damages caused by them to the corporation or for breach of contract, one or more shareholders may bring such action if the corporation refuses to do so. This is a **derivative (secondary) action** in that the shareholder enforces only the cause of action of the corporation and any money recovery is paid into the corporate treasury.

derivative (secondary) action–secondary action for damages or breach of contract brought by one or more corporate shareholders against directors, officers, or third persons.

In a derivative action, when a corporation has failed to enforce a right, a shareholder bringing such a suit must show that a demand was made on the directors to enforce the right in question. The shareholder must show (1) that the directors refused to enforce the right[28] or (2) that a demand that the directors enforce the right is excused because the directors are deemed incapable of making an impartial decision regarding the pursuit of the litigation. Additionally, where a special litigation committee (SLC) is formed by the board of directors with full authority to decide what position to take with regard to a derivative lawsuit, demand on the entire board may be excused on a case-by-case basis.

CASE SUMMARY

"Curb Your Enthusiasm," Defendants Greenberg and Smith Argue

FACTS: Plaintiff stockholders sued derivatively CEO Maurice Greenberg, CFO Howard Smith, and other former officers who had served on American Insurance Group's (AIG's) board of directors. The plaintiffs took this action on behalf of the corporation for damages the former officers had caused AIG by having the corporation engage in illegal acts. In one example, the plaintiffs asserted that AIG had created a fictional reinsurance business transaction with General Reinsurance Corp. to inflate loss reserves, thus making AIG appear to be a healthier company than it actually was and inflating AIG's stock price. AIG's board of directors formed a special litigation committee (SLC) to look into the stockholder plaintiffs' allegations, giving full authority to the SLC to address the litigation. The SLC investigated all matters and decided to join this action as a direct plaintiff on behalf of the corporation, asserting breach of fiduciary duty and indemnification claims against former CEO Greenberg and former CFO Smith. The defendants, Greenberg and Smith, contended that the stockholder plaintiffs had to make a demand on the full board. Moreover, they asserted that under procedural law, boards of directors should not be lightly bypassed by derivative plaintiffs.

DECISION: Judgment for the stockholder plaintiffs. Corporation law seeks to ensure that boards are not lightly bypassed by derivative plaintiffs and not allowed to usurp the board's right to manage the affairs of the corporation. AIG's board's primacy in decision making has been fully honored. The SLC chose to have AIG sue Greenberg and Smith itself, to seek dismissal of certain defendants, and to otherwise take no position on the plaintiffs' claims. The board gave the SLC full authority to make this decision, and through the SLC the board asserted control over the lawsuit. Demand on the full board is thus excused and the plaintiffs are free to proceed against the defendants. [*AIG, Inc. v. Greenberg,* 965 A.2d 763 (Del. Ch. 2009)]

A special litigation committee is vested with enormous power to pursue a corporate claim or seek dismissal of a derivative suit. But courts will defer to the business judgment and conclusions of the SLC only if the directors involved possess a disinterested independence and do not have relationships that prevent an unprejudicial exercise of judgment.[29]

[28] *Marx. v. Akers,* 666 N.E.2d 1034 (N.Y. 1996). But see *Potter v. Hughes,* 546 F.3d 1051 (9th Cir. 2008).
[29] In re *Comverse Technology, Inc.,* 766 N.Y.S.2d 10 (A.D. 2008).

CASE SUMMARY

It's Not Good Retailing to Publicly Tout "Low Cost Manufacturing – High Retail Pricing" on Wall Street: Wall Street Abuts Main Street

FACTS: Shareholders of Abercrombie & Fitch Co. filed a derivative suit on behalf of the company against several officers and directors alleging that the defendants caused Abercrombie to make misleading public statements between June 2 and August 18, 2005, which caused stock prices to rise and then fall once the falsity of the statements were revealed. According to the complaint, Abercrombie adopted a business model of selling products with a low manufacturing cost at high retail prices, resulting in a high per-unit margin. The company sought to create such a desired brand that it could "train" its customers to not expect a sale or markdowns and instead just pay the high price. This approach manifested itself most particularly in Abercrombie's denim products. Abercrombie issued reports indicating that its denim sales were strong and that its high gross margin business strategy was working. The shareholders allege that these statements were misleading because company insiders knew that Abercrombie was amassing a large surplus of inventory such that there would have to be dramatic markdowns to clear out the inventory, causing a negative correction in the company's stock price. The stock price eventually did fall, which kicked off a spate of lawsuits and regulatory investigations. During this time, when the insiders are alleged to have known that the price would soon fall, five of the defendants—Singer, Jeffries, Bachmann, Kessler, and Griffin—sold a large number of their personally owned shares of Abercrombie stock. The corporation formed an SLC, consisting of board members Allan Tuttle and Lauren Brisky. During the investigation Mr. Tuttle recused himself from considering claims against Mr. Singer, Abercrombie's president, COO, and CFO, due to a prior relationship at the Gucci company. The SLC recommended that the corporation seek dismissal of the suit, and the district court granted a motion to dismiss. The shareholders appealed.

DECISION: The court of appeals reversed the district court, having serious doubts about Mr. Tuttle's independence because he recused himself from considering the claims against the person at the very center of the alleged improper activity. When Tuttle recused himself from considering the claims against Singer, he essentially launched a signal flare that he was not independent. Mr. Singer, as the COO, appears to have been heavily involved in the strategy of touting the success of the business model to the market. He was also alleged to have engaged in insider trading. Without a demonstration that its SLC was independent, the corporation's motion to dismiss based on the SLC's recommendation could not be granted. [*Booth Family Trust v. Jeffries,* 640 F.3d 134 (6th Cir. 2011)]

Mere allegations that a director and other directors move in the same social circles or are characterized as close friends is not enough to negate a director's independence for presuit demand excusal purposes.

Lawsuits may be brought by minority shareholders against majority shareholders who are oppressive toward minority shareholders. Oppressive conduct may include payment of grossly excessive salaries and fringe benefits to the majority stockholders who are also officers of the corporation. Shareholders may bring a derivative action to obtain a dissolution of the corporation by judicial decree.[30]

44-4 Liability of Shareholders

A shareholder is ordinarily protected from the liabilities of the corporation. Some exceptions exist, however.

[30] *Miller v. Up In Smoke, Inc.,* 738 F. Supp. 2d 878 (N.D. Ind. 2010). But see *Whithorn v. Whithorn Farms, Inc.,* 195 P.3d 836 (Mont. 2008).

44-4a **Limited Liability**

The liability of a shareholder is generally limited. This means that the shareholder is not personally liable for the debts and liabilities of the corporation. The capital contributed by shareholders may be exhausted by the claims of creditors, but there is no personal liability for any unpaid balance.

44-4b **Ignoring the Corporate Entity**

Ordinarily a corporation is regarded and treated as a separate legal entity, and the law does not look behind a corporation to see who owns or controls it.

The fact that two corporations have identical shareholders does not justify a court's regarding the two corporations as one. Similarly, the fact that there is a close working relationship between two corporations does not in itself constitute any basis for ignoring their separate corporate entities when they in fact are separately run enterprises.

"Piercing the Corporate Veil"

A court may disregard the corporate entity, or figuratively "pierce the corporate veil," when exceptional circumstances warrant. The decision whether to disregard the corporate entity is made on a case-by-case basis, weighing all factors before the court. Factors that may lead to piercing the corporate veil and imposing liability on its owners (the shareholders) are (1) the failure to maintain adequate corporate records and the commingling of corporate and other funds,[31] (2) grossly inadequate capitalization,[32] (3) the diversion by shareholders of corporate funds or assets,[33] (4) the formation of the corporation to evade an existing obligation, (5) the formation of the corporation to perpetrate a fraud or conceal illegality, and (6) a determination that injustice and inequitable consequences would result if the corporate entity were recognized.[34]

CASE SUMMARY

Sometimes "Parents" Have to Pay the Rent in Business, Too

FACTS: Inter-Tel is an Arizona corporation that designs, manufacturers, and sells telecommunication services primarily to businesses. Inter-Tel Technology Inc. (Technologies) operates Inter-Tel's retail division. On July 2, 1998, Technologies purchased Integrated Telecom Services Corp. (ITS), with Inter-Tel, the Arizona parent, paying for the stock. ITS was Inter-Tel's first retail branch in Kentucky, selling Inter-Tel's products from an office building in Louisville it leased from Linn Station Properties. After ITS was acquired by Technologies, ITS no longer possessed any financial independence. ITS could not maintain a bank account, hold any funds, or pay any bills. All of ITS's regional offices were transformed from independent dealers of communications equipment into direct sales "branches" of Inter-Tel. ITS employees became employees of Inter-Tel and were paid by Inter-Tel from its headquarters in Arizona. When a customer purchased a telecommunications system from ITS the payment went directly into a "lock box" or

---

[31] *East Market v. Tycorp Pizza IV, Inc.*, 625 S.E.2d 191, 198 (N.C. App. 2006).

[32] In *Trevino v. MERSCORP, Inc.*, 583 F. Supp. 2d 521 (D. Del. 2008), the court determined that a shortage of capital is not per se a reason to pierce the corporate veil; rather, a more relevant inquiry would be "Was the entity established to defraud its creditors?" An example of grossly inadequate capitalization is found in *Klokke Corp. v. Classic Exposition, Inc.*, 912 P.2d 929 (Or. App. 1996), in which Classic's two shareholders invested $1,000 of capital to start a business and immediately took out a $200,000 loan. The business remained undercapitalized until part of it was sold. However, the two shareholders effectively withdrew all of the proceeds of the sale in October 1991, and the business was again without sufficient capital, leaving it unable to meet its financial obligations. The court held that the shareholders were personally liable up to the amount withdrawn in October 1991 after the partial sale of the business.

[33] See *Trustees of the National Elevator Industry Pension Fund v. Lutyk*, 332 F.3d 188 (3d Cir. 2003).

[34] *Barton v. Moore*, 558 N.W.2d 746 (Minn. 1997).

Sometimes "Parents" Have to Pay the Rent in Business, Too continued

depository account controlled by Inter-Tel. Once the funds were placed in this account, they belonged to Inter-Tel. Inter-Tel paid all the vendors who provided ITS with goods and services. Inter-Tel paid ITS's rent for the Linn Station Road property from the time Technologies acquired ITS until ITS abandoned the premises in 2002. Linn Properties sued ITS for unpaid rent and failure to maintain the property, and a default judgment was entered against ITS for $332,900. ITS was a defunct corporation without any assets, so Linn Properties sought to pierce the corporate veil to collect the debt from Technologies and Inter-Tel.

DECISION: Judgment for Linn Properties. Limited liability for corporate entities is described by some scholars as springing from both democratic and economic principles in the early days of the United States. The "imposition of limited liability was perceived as a means of encouraging the small-scale entrepreneur, and of keeping entry into business markets competitive and democratic," assuring that the corporate world was not dominated by industrialists who had the immense personal wealth to withstand any business risk. The economic rationale was that the public would benefit from investment by shareholders who would be willing to take risks in industry, manufacturing, and general commercial development if personal liability could be avoided should their ventures not succeed. By the twentieth century, deliberate misuse of the corporate form by shareholders who were either individuals or other corporations had led courts to authorize piercing the corporate veil. The equitable doctrine of veil piercing cannot be thwarted by having two entities, rather than one, dominate the subsidiary and dividing the conduct between the two so that each can point the finger to some extent at the other. Inter-Tel and Technologies together exercised complete control and dominion over ITS, causing it to lose any semblance of separate corporate existence. Technologies and Inter-Tel transferred all of ITS's income and assets to themselves, thus deriving all of the benefits from the business while leaving behind a shell entity from which a legitimate creditor could recover nothing. Under these circumstances there was the requisite domination and injustice to justify piercing ITS's corporate veil to hold both Technologies and Inter-Tel responsible for the default judgment previously obtained by Linn Station against ITS. [*Inter-Tel Technologies Inc. v. Linn Station Properties, LLC,* 360 S.W.3d 152 (Ky. 2012)]

"Alter Ego" Theory

Some courts express their reasons for disregarding the corporate entity by stating that the corporation is the "*alter ego*" of the wrongdoer. A corporation is a separate and distinct person from the person or persons who own the corporation. However, when a corporation is so dominated and controlled by a shareholder(s), officer(s), or director(s) that the separate personalities of the individual and the corporation no longer exist and there is a wrongful use of that control, the courts will disregard the corporate entity so as not to sanction a fraud or injustice.[35]

For Example, V&M Industries, Inc., owned land on which some 40,000-plus used tires caught fire. It took nearly a week to extinguish the fire and it caused severe air pollution in the St. Louis area. Vernon Leirer originally owned 99 percent of V&M corporate stock; all corporate officers other than Leirer were nonfunctioning; the corporation was inadequately capitalized; no stock certificates were issued; and corporate records were generally not kept. At a time just before the fire, when Leirer was no longer a shareholder or officer, he exercised total direction and control over the corporation and "ran the show." The court held that to adhere to the fiction of separate corporate existence would sanction fraud. It concluded that V&M, Inc., was the *alter ego* for Leirer, and Leirer was personally responsible for civil penalties under the Environmental Protection Act.[36]

Limited liability is important to our economy because it encourages investors to make investments in high-risk ventures. It should be disregarded only in exceptional circumstances. When fraud or deceit is absent, other circumstances for piercing the corporate veil must be so strong as to clearly indicate that the corporation is the alter ego of the controlling person.

---

[35] *Dishon v. Ponthie,* 918 So. 2d 1132 (La. App. 2005).
[36] *Illinois v. V&M Industries,* 700 N.E.2d 746 (Ill. App. 1998).

Obtaining Advantages of Corporate Existence

Courts will not go behind the corporate identity merely because the corporation has been formed to obtain tax savings or to obtain limited liability for its shareholders. Similarly, the corporate entity will not be ignored merely because the corporation does not have sufficient assets to pay the claims against it.

One-person, family, and other closely held corporations are permissible and entitled to all of the advantages of corporate existence. The fact that the principal shareholder runs or oversees the day-to-day operations does not justify ignoring the corporate entity.

44-4c Other Exceptions to Limited Liability

Liability may be imposed on a shareholder as though there were no corporation when the court ignores the corporate entity either because of the particular circumstances of the case or because the corporation is so defectively organized that it is deemed not to exist.

Wage Claims

Statutes sometimes provide that the shareholders shall have unlimited liability for the wage claims of corporate employees. This exception has been abandoned in some states in recent years or has been confined to corporate officers who are active in corporate decision making.[37]

Unpaid Subscriptions

Most states prohibit the issuance of par value shares for less than par or except for "money, labor done, or property actually received." Whenever shares issued by a corporation are not fully paid for, the original subscriber receiving the shares, or any transferee who does not give value or who knows that the shares were not fully paid for, is liable for the unpaid balance if the corporation is insolvent and the money is required to pay its creditors.[38]

CASE SUMMARY

You've Got to Pay for Your Stock, Silly

FACTS: On July 19, 1984, Keith and Joan Bryan incorporated Bryan's Inc. The corporation was authorized to issue 100 shares of stock with a par value of $1,000 per share. The corporation issued 50 shares to Keith and 50 shares to Joan, although it did not receive any payment in labor, services, money, or property for the stock. On August 30, 1984, Bryan's Inc. bought Hanewald's dry goods store, giving Hanewald a promissory note for part of the purchase price. The business was not successful, and after four months, Keith and Joan Bryan decided to close the store. They disbursed all of the corporation's funds in payment of all bills except for the debt owed Hanewald. No corporate funds were available to pay this debt. Hanewald sued the Bryans individually for the amount owed. The Bryans contended that they were not personally liable for the corporation's debts.

DECISION: Judgment for Hanewald. Organizing a corporation to avoid personal liability is legitimate and a primary advantage to doing business in the corporate form. But proper capitalization is the principal prerequisite for this limited liability. Keith and Joan Bryan's failure to pay for their stock makes them liable to Hanewald, the corporate creditor, to the extent that the stock was not paid for. Because the debt to Hanewald, $36,000, was less than the par value of their stock, $100,000, the Bryans are personally liable for the entire corporate debt owed to Hanewald. [*Hanewald v. Bryan's, Inc.*, 429 N.W.2d 414 (N.D. 1988)]

[37] *Cusimano v. Metro Auto, Inc.*, 860 P.2d 532 (Colo. App. 1993).
[38] *Frasier v. Trans-Western Land Corp.*, 316 N.W.2d 612 (Neb. 1982). But see *Brunfield v. Horn*, 547 So. 2d 415 (Ala. 1989).

If the corporation has issued the shares as fully paid for, has given them as a bonus, or has agreed to release the subscriber for the unpaid balance, the corporation cannot recover that balance. The fact that the corporation is thus barred does not prevent creditors of the corporation from bringing an action to compel payment of the balance. The same rules are applied when stock is issued as fully paid for in return for property or services that were overvalued so that the stock is not actually paid for in full. A conflict of authority exists, however, as to whether the shareholder is liable from the mere fact that the property or service given for the shares was in fact overvalued by the directors or whether it must also be shown that the directors acted in bad faith in making the erroneous valuation. The trend of modern statutes is, in the absence of proof of fraud, to prohibit disputing the valuation placed by the corporation on services or property.

Unauthorized Dividends

If dividends are improperly paid out of capital, shareholders are generally liable to creditors to the extent of such depletion of capital. In some states, the liability of a shareholder depends on whether the corporation was insolvent at the time and whether debts were existing at the time.

44-4d The Professional Corporation

The extent to which incorporation limits the liability of shareholders of a professional corporation depends on the interpretation of the statute under which the corporation was formed.

Act of Shareholder in Creating Liability

The statutes that authorize the formation of professional corporations usually require that share ownership be limited to duly licensed professionals. If a shareholder in a professional corporation, such as a corporation of physicians, negligently drives the professional corporation's automobile in going to attend a patient or is personally obligated on a contract made for the corporation or is guilty of malpractice, the physician-shareholder is liable without limit for the liability that has been created. This is the same rule of law that applies in the case of the ordinary business corporation.

Professional corporation statutes generally repeat the rule governing malpractice liability by stating that the liability of a shareholder for malpractice is not affected by the fact of incorporation.

Malpractice Liability of an Associate

The liability of a shareholder in a professional corporation for the malpractice of an associate varies from state to state depending on the language of the professional corporation statute in effect and on the court decisions under the statute.[39]

If the statute provides for limited liability, as in a business corporation, then where doctors *A, B,* and *C* are a professional corporation, *A* and *B* will not be liable for the malpractice of *C* beyond the extent of corporate assets. If the statute provides for vicarious personal liability, as in a partnership, and doctors *A, B,* and *C* are a professional corporation, each will have unlimited liability for any malpractice liability incurred by the others. Often the statutory reference to malpractice liability is not very clear, and the courts are called on to resolve the question of the liability of a professional shareholder for the malpractice of an associate.

---

[39] ABA Model Professional Corporation Act Amendments (1984) §34 offers three alternative positions regarding the liability of shareholders: (1) limited liability, as in a business corporation, (2) vicarious personal liability, as in a partnership, and (3) personal liability limited in amount and conditioned on financial responsibility in the form of insurance or a surety bond.

Make the Connection

Summary

The ownership of a corporation is evidenced by a holder's shares of stock that have been issued by the corporation. Common stock is ordinary stock that has no preferences but entitles the holder to (1) participate in the control of the corporation by exercising one vote per share of record, (2) share in the profits in the form of dividends, and (3) participate, upon dissolution, in the distribution of net assets after the satisfaction of all creditors (including bondholders). Other classes of stock exist, such as preferred stock, that have priority over common stock with regard to distribution of dividends and/or assets upon liquidation. Shares may be acquired by subscription of an original issue or by transfer of existing shares.

Bonds are debt securities, and a bondholder is a creditor rather than an owner of the corporation. Bondholders' interests are represented by an indenture trustee who is responsible for ensuring that the corporation complies with the terms of the bond indenture.

Shareholders control the corporation, but this control is indirect. Through their voting rights, they elect directors, and by this means, they can control the corporation.

Preemptive rights, if they exist, allow shareholders to maintain their voting percentages when the corporation issues additional shares of stock. Shareholders have the right to inspect the books of the corporation unless it would be harmful to the corporation. Shareholders also have the right to receive dividends when declared at the discretion of the directors. Shareholders may bring a derivative action on behalf of the corporation for damages to the corporation. Shareholders are ordinarily protected from liability for the acts of the corporation.

Ordinarily, each corporation is treated as a separate person, and the law does not look beyond the corporate identity merely because the corporation was formed to obtain tax savings or limited liability. The fact that two corporations have the same shareholders does not justify disregarding the separate corporate entities. However, when a corporation is formed to perpetrate a fraud, a court ignores the corporate form, or "pierces the corporate veil." The corporate form is also ignored to prevent injustice or because of the functional reality that the two corporations in question are one.

Learning Outcomes

After studying this chapter, you should be able to clearly explain:

44-1   Corporate Stocks and Bonds

LO.1 Explain how to calculate the book value of a share of stock
See the example in which Roger Eggett was awarded the book value of his stock, page 904.

LO.2 Distinguish between stocks and bonds
See the discussion of stocks as an ownership interest in a corporation and bonds as a corporate debt, page 904.

44-2   Acquisition of Shares

LO.3 Distinguish between subscriptions for and transfers of stock
See the discussion of stock subscriptions for new issues of stock, page 907.
See the discussion of transfers of shares and the impact of restrictions, pages 907–908.

44-3   Rights of Shareholders

LO.4 Explain the rights of shareholders

See the discussion of shareholder ownership rights, including the right to vote, inspect books and records, and receive dividends when declared, pages 911–915.

LO.5 Explain the nature of a shareholder derivative lawsuit
See the *AIG* case, where stockholder plaintiffs were excused from making a demand on the full board, page 916.
See the Abercrombie & Fitch Co. litigation where the court did not defer to the special litigation committee (SLC) because one of the two members was not "independent," page 917.

44-4   Liability of Shareholders

LO.6 Explain the exceptions to the limited liability of shareholders
See the *Inter-Tel* case where "grandparent" and "parent" corporations transferred all income and assets to themselves, and as a result the corporate entities were disregarded to accomplish justice, pages 918–919.

Key Terms

acceptance	deed	preferred stock
bond	derivative (secondary)	proxy
bond indenture	action	registered bonds
book value	indenture trustee	sinking fund
capital stock	market value	stock subscription
certificate of stock	maturity date	voting by proxy
common stock	outstanding	voting trust
cumulative voting	par value	wasting assets
debenture	preemptive right	corporations

Questions and Case Problems

1. Monica Beam, a shareholder of Martha Stewart Living Omnimedia, Inc. (MSO), filed a derivative action against Martha Stewart and the other MSO board of directors, alleging that Stewart breached her duties to MSO by illegally selling ImClone stock and mishandling media attention, thereby jeopardizing the financial future of MSO. Ms. Beam asserted that it would be a futile act to make a demand on the corporation because a majority of the outside directors were not independent of Stewart. Ms. Beam pleaded the particularized facts that director Darla Moore attended a wedding reception hosted by Stewart's personal lawyer for his daughter and was a longtime friend of Stewart; and that director Naomi Seligman made a phone call to publisher John Wiley, Inc., to express concern over a planned book critical of Stewart. Should Ms. Beam be excused from making a demand on the board of directors to pursue the derivative action because the outside directors were not independent of Stewart? [*Beam v. Stewart*, 845 A.2d 1040 (Del)]

2. Six members of the Weston family, who owned 6.8 percent of the stock of Weston Paper and Manufacturing Company, brought suit against three corporate directors and CFIS, a firm hired by the company to make the annual evaluation of the company's stock for allocating stock options to its employees. The Westons stated that their claims against the defendants were personal claims, alleging that they were injured by CFIS and the three directors who kept the price of the stock low to obtain more shares of stock through the stock option plan. From an adverse ruling on their right to maintain a direct action against the directors, the Westons appealed. How would you decide this case? [*Weston v. Weston Paper and Manufacturing Co.*, 74 Ohio 377]

3. Tomlinson and Hubbard were two of five shareholders in Multimedia Software Distributors, a corporation. The corporation was formed in 1992 and filed for bankruptcy in 1994. In 1996, Tomlinson filed a claim in his own name, alleging that Hubbard had breached his fiduciary duties to Tomlinson by diverting proceeds owned by Multimedia to another business owned by Hubbard. Hubbard contends that Tomlinson is an improper plaintiff. Decide. [*Hubbard v. Tomlinson*, 747 N.E.2d 69 (Ind. App.)]

4. Equivest, a partnership, owned 10,000 shares of Altec International, Inc. Equivest pledged these shares to secure loans by Lloyds Bank. Sometime after pledging the stock, Equivest transferred beneficial ownership of 350 shares of Altec stock to Thorn Hoffman and 350 shares to John Erikson. Thereafter, in 1988, Altec elected to be treated as a Subchapter S corporation, which necessitated that shareholders return their old stock certificates in exchange for new stock certificates. Neither Erikson nor Hoffman had certificates to return because their stock had been pledged by Equivest to Lloyds Bank. Altec had knowledge that Erikson and Hoffman were the beneficial owners of 700 shares of Altec stock. However, Altec distributed cash dividends to Equivest, the registered owner of the 10,000 shares during the period from 1988 until March 14, 1990. Equivest defaulted on its loan to Lloyds Bank and Lloyds sold all of the pledged stock, including Hoffman's and Erikson's 700 shares, at public auction. Hoffman and Erikson contend that Altec should have made all cash distributions to them as shareholders, not Equivest. Altec contends that it complied with the UCC by making distributions to the owner of record. Do you think the distribution should have gone to Hoffman and Erikson or to

Equivest? [*Hoffman v. Altec Int'l Inc.*, 546 N.W.2d 162 (Wis. App.)]

5. The stock of West End Development Co. was subject to a transfer restriction. This restriction required that any shareholder selling shares first offer every other shareholder the right to purchase a proportion of the shares being sold. The proportions were to be the same as the percentages of the outstanding shares that the other shareholders already owned. This restriction was stated in the articles of incorporation but was not stated on the stock certificate of the corporation. The Taylors owned stock in the company and sold their stock to Vroom, an officer of the corporation, without first offering any stock to the other shareholders, as required by the restriction. The other shareholders brought an action against Vroom to recover from him the percentages of the shares they would have been entitled to if the Taylors had followed the transfer restriction. Decide. [*Irwin v. West End Development Co.*, 481 F.2d 34 (10th Cir.)]

6. Siebrecht organized Siebrecht Realty Co., a corporation, and then transferred his building to the corporation in exchange for its stock. The corporation rented different parts of the building to different tenants. Elenkrieg, an employee of one of the tenants, fell and was injured because of the defective condition of a stairway. She sued Siebrecht individually on the ground that the corporation had been formed by him for the purpose of securing limited liability. Decide. [*Elenkrieg v. Siebrecht*, 144 N.E. 519 (N.Y.)]

7. U.S. Die Casting, Inc., is a closely held Ohio corporation that owns 5 percent of Security First Corporation, a Delaware corporation. David Slyman is the president of U.S. Die and its sole shareholder. The defendant, Security First, entered into a merger agreement with Mid Am, Inc., a large regional bank holding company. After the announcement of the merger, Security First's stock increased significantly. The merger agreement required Security First to pay a termination fee of $2 million plus third-party expenses not to exceed $250,000 contingent on the occurrence of certain events within one year after termination should Security First pull out of the merger. The merger did not go through, and the market price for Security First dropped significantly. According to Security First, it did not go through with the merger because it realized that Mid Am's "management philosophy and direction were fundamentally different from its own." Security First paid Mid Am $275,000 in expenses and agreed to pay an

additional $2 million if a certain event occurred within one and one-half years after termination. U.S. Die submitted a written demand to Security First pursuant to Section 220 of the Delaware Code to inspect all of its books and records related to the Mid Am merger and its termination. Security First refused to comply. The Court of Chancery granted U.S. Die's demand and Security First appealed. Should U.S. Die be allowed to inspect Security First's books? [*Security First Corp. v. U.S. Die Casting, Inc.*, 687 A.2d 563 (Del.)]

8. Ken and Charlotte Maschmeier were the majority shareholders of Southside Press; each owned 1,300 shares. Marty and Larry Maschmeier, who each owned 1,200 shares of the corporation, had a falling out with Ken and Charlotte and were terminated as employees of the business. Ken and Charlotte started a new corporation, which employed most of the employees of the old corporation and which took most of its former customers. Gross receipts of Southside Press went from $613,258 down to $18,172 two years later. The $18,172 figure was from the lease of equipment. Ken and Charlotte continued to draw from Southside annual salaries of $20,000, which were in excess of the gross receipts of the business. Marty and Larry brought suit against Ken and Charlotte, alleging "oppressive" conduct. Ken and Charlotte stated that they had paid Marty and Larry excellent salaries when they were employed by the corporation. Ken and Charlotte contended that they had a right to start a new corporation as they saw fit. Decide. [*Maschmeier v. Southside Press, Inc.*, 435 N.W.2d 377 (Iowa App.)]

9. Gladys Boles and 28 other owners of property at Hidden Valley Lakes Development sued the corporate developer, National Development Co. Inc. (NDC); NDC's parent, Sunstates Corporation; and the individual behind both corporations, Clyde Engle, for breach of contract and fraud. The centerpiece of this development, Crystal Lake, a 30-acre recreational lake, failed to hold water; and it was determined that it could never do so. Instead of having a 30-acre lake as the centerpiece, the plaintiffs had a 30-acre hole in the ground. While the controversy over NDC's breach of contract was pending, Engle made a "proposal" to the CEO of NDC to transfer $2.4 million in receivables to Sunstates in exchange for an unsecured promissory note. Evidence showed that all of Sunstates' assets thereafter were transferred to Engle, making the note NDC

held from Sunstates worthless. Sunstates purchased approximately $1.9 million of oriental art, antique jewelry, rare books, and other collectibles, which were maintained in Engle's home in Illinois. Likewise, Sunstates purchased a Rolls Royce from Libco, a corporation in which Engle was the majority shareholder. This automobile also appeared to be in Engle's possession or control. Engles regrets that the lake did not work out, a risk that the developer and the homeowners have to live with, and points out that NDC is a separate legal entity with limited liability for its shareholders. Engle asserts that he is not personally liable for damages in this case. Decide. [*Boles v. National Development Co., Inc.*, 175 N.W.3d 226 (Tenn. App.)]

10. Ed Klein was the sole shareholder, director, and chief executive officer of The Gun Exchange, Inc., a retail firearms dealership. The inventory of The Gun Exchange had been pledged as security for a $622,500 debt owed to InterFirst Bank. It also owed $231,484.60 to Sporting Goods, Inc.; this debt was unsecured. On May 20, InterFirst Bank notified Klein of its intention to foreclose on the inventory and sell it at public auction. InterFirst Bank further advised Klein that, pursuant to his personal guarantee, he would be responsible for any deficiency following the sale. Klein immediately incorporated The Gun Store, Inc., for the purpose of purchasing the assets of The Gun Exchange at the foreclosure sale. Before the foreclosure sale, Klein obtained a $650,000 line of credit from CharterBank on behalf of The Gun Store. At the sale, Klein purchased the assets of The Gun Exchange for $650,000 even though the highest prior bid was $175,000. (Had the $175,000 bid been accepted, Klein would have been personally liable for the deficiency to InterFirst Bank.)

After the foreclosure sale, no funds existed to pay the unsecured creditors of The Gun Exchange. Following the sale, The Gun Store began operating as a retail firearms dealer with the inventory purchased from the foreclosure sale. It operated in the same location and with the same personnel as The Gun Exchange. Sporting Goods, Inc., sued Klein individually for the $231,484.60. Klein contended that the corporate form under which he did business insulated him as a shareholder from liability for corporate obligations. Decide. Is it ethical to seek limited liability under the corporate form, as Klein did in this case? [*Klein v. Sporting Goods, Inc.*, 772 S.W.2d 173 (Tex. Civ. App.)]

11. Ibanez owned shares of stock in Farmers Underwriters. He left the stock certificate lying on top of his desk in his office. Many persons continually passed through the office, and one day Ibanez realized that someone had taken the certificate from the top of his desk. Ibanez applied to Farmers Underwriters for a duplicate stock certificate. The corporation refused to issue a duplicate on the ground that it was Ibanez's own fault that the original certificate had been stolen. Ibanez claimed that he was entitled to a new certificate even though he had been at fault. Was he correct? [*Ibanez v. Farmers Underwriters Ass'n*, 534 P.2d 1336 (Cal.)]

12. On March 3, 2002, pursuant to a public offering, First All State Trucking Corp. (FAST) issued securities to investors in denominations of $1,000. The interest rate was 7 percent per year payable semiannually, and the maturity date was March 3, 2010. The rights and obligations of the issuer, FAST, and the holders of the securities were set forth in an indenture agreement. Because the securities were not secured by a mortgage or lien on corporate property, Alec believes that they are shares of preferred stock. Is Alec correct? Fully explain the type of security involved, and discuss the extent of the holders' voting rights.

13. Linhart owned shares of stock in First National Bank. She borrowed money from the bank and pledged the stock as security. She later decided to transfer 70 head of cattle and the shares of stock to her son, but she could not deliver the share certificate to him because it was held by the bank. She therefore executed a bill of sale reciting the transfer of the cattle and the stock to the son. She gave him the bill of sale, and he had the bill recorded. After her death, the son brought an action to determine the ownership of the stock. Was the son the owner of the shares?

14. Birt was a hospital patient. The doctor who treated him was a shareholder of a professional corporation organized under the Indiana Medical Professional Corporation Act. Birt claimed that the doctor who treated him was guilty of malpractice, and he sued the doctor. He also sued the professional corporation and all of its officers, directors, and shareholders. These other defendants asserted that they were not liable because the corporate entity shielded them. The plaintiff claimed that the corporation was not a shield because in fact all of the persons were rendering medical services and should be held liable as

in a partnership. The statute did not expressly regulate the matter of limited liability beyond declaring that it did not change the law between a person supplying medical services and the patient. Decide. [*Birt v. St. Mary Mercy Hospital,* 370 N.E.2d 379 (Ind. App.)]

15. Ronald Naquin, an employee of Air Engineered Systems & Services, Inc., owned one-third of its outstanding shares. After six years, he was fired and an offer was made to buy out his interest in Air Engineered at a price that Naquin thought inadequate. He then formed a competing business and made a written request to examine the corporate records of Air Engineered. This request was denied. Naquin filed suit to require Air Engineered to allow him to examine the books. Air Engineered raised the defense that he was a competitor seeking to gain unfair competitive advantage. Decide. [*Naquin v. Air Engineered Systems & Services, Inc.,* 463 So. 2d 992 (La. App.)]

CPA Questions

1. A stockholder's right to inspect books and records of a corporation will be properly denied if the stockholder:

   a. Wants to use corporate stockholder records for a personal business.

   b. Employs an agent to inspect the books and records.

   c. Intends to commence a stockholder's derivative suit.

   d. Is investigating management misconduct.

2. The limited liability of a stockholder in a closely held corporation may be challenged successfully if the stockholder:

   a. Undercapitalized the corporation when it was formed.

   b. Formed the corporation solely to have limited personal liability.

   c. Sold property to the corporation.

   d. Was a corporate officer, a director, or an employee.

3. Price owns 2,000 shares of Universal Corp.'s $10 cumulative preferred stock. During its first year of operations, cash dividends of $5 per share were declared on the preferred stock but were never paid. In the second year, dividends on the preferred stock were neither declared nor paid. If Universal is dissolved, which of the following statements is correct?

   a. Universal will be liable to Price as an unsecured creditor for $10,000.

   b. Universal will be liable to Price as a secured creditor for $20,000.

   c. Price will have priority over the claims of Universal's bond owners.

   d. Price will have priority over the claims of Universal's unsecured judgment creditors.

4. Under the Revised Model Business Corporation Act, a dissenting stockholder's appraisal right generally applies to which of the following corporate actions?

	Consolidations	Shares from mergers
a.	Yes	Yes
b.	Yes	No
c.	No	Yes
d.	No	No

Securities Regulation

Learning Outcomes ‹‹‹

After studying this chapter, you should be able to

LO.1 Explain the meaning of state "blue sky laws"

LO.2 Define "security"

LO.3 Compare and distinguish between the Securities Act of 1933 and the Securities Exchange Act of 1934

LO.4 Explain the changes that the JOBS Act has had on registration exemptions

LO.5 Explain how the 1934 act's policy of fostering reliance on market integrity is served by Rule 10b-5 private investor lawsuits when investors are injured by material misstatements by the issuer

LO.6 Explain the factors that subject an individual to liability for insider trading

LO.7 Explain how the primary and secondary markets are regulated by the SEC as well as private enforcement organizations

45-1 State Regulation

To protect the public from the sale of fraudulent securities, many states have adopted statutes regulating the intrastate sale of securities.

CPA

blue sky laws–state statutes designed to protect the public from the sale of worthless stocks and bonds.

State laws regulating securities are called **blue sky laws.** The term *blue sky* is derived from the purpose of such laws, which is to prevent the sale of speculative schemes that have no more value than the blue sky. The state statutes vary in detail. They commonly contain (1) an antifraud provision prohibiting fraudulent practices and imposing criminal penalties for violations, (2) broker-dealer licensing provisions regulating the persons engaged in the securities business, and (3) provisions for the registration of securities, including disclosure requirements, with a designated government official.

A Uniform Securities Act, covering the foregoing three categories of regulations, exists to provide guidance to states in updating their securities laws. This act also contains alternative regulations that can be adopted by states with different regulatory philosophies.

Congress reallocated responsibility between state and federal security regulators in the National Securities Markets Improvement Act (NSMIA)[1] recognizing that the dual system of state and federal regulation of securities resulted in duplicative regulation and expenses. The NSMIA allows the states to investigate and bring enforcement actions for fraud or deceit or for unlawful conduct by a broker or dealer in connection with securities transactions.[2]

45-2 History of Federal Regulation and Market Trends

The federal system for regulation of securities sales and the secondary market began following the stock market crash of 1929 and the resulting Great Depression. The Securities Act of 1933 and the Securities Exchange Act of 1934, both covered in detail in this chapter, were the beginning of the extensive federal regulatory structure for capital markets. In response to market events that revealed loopholes and gaps in regulation, Congress has continued to refine securities regulation.

In the mid-1980s there was substantial abuse of penny stocks in "pump and dump" schemes as well as "churning" of accounts. Abuse of penny stocks resulted in significant investor losses and fraudulent offerings. Penny stocks are those that are not listed on the exchanges and that trade over the counter below $5. The Securities Enforcement Remedies and Penny Stock Reform Act of 1990[3] required more regulation and increased disclosure to reduce penny stock fraud. The act imposed more stringent regulations on broker-dealers who recommend penny stocks to clients. **For Example,** the SEC charged Oppenheimer & Co. with failure to respond to red flags about the unregistered sales of billions of shares of penny stocks. Oppenheimer admitted to wrongdoing and paid fines of $10 million to the SEC and $10 million to the Treasury Department's Financial Crimes Enforcement Network.[4]

The Market Reform Act of 1990[5] was enacted to provide the SEC with powers to deal with market volatility. The act was passed in response to the savings and loan crisis

---

[1] P.L. 104-290, 110 Stat 3416, 15 U.S.C. §78a nt.
[2] The 1996 act amends §18(c) of the 1933 Securities Act to accomplish this result.
[3] P.L. 101-429, 104 Stat. 931, 15 U.S.C. §77g.
[4] Press Release, SEC, "SEC Charges Oppenheimer with Securities Law Violations Related to Improper Penny Stock Sales" (Jan. 27, 2015), **http://www.sec.gov/news/pressrelease/2015-14.html.**
[5] P.L. 101-432, 104 Stat. 963, 15 U.S.C. §78a.

in the 1980s and 1990s.[6] Under the law, the SEC has the power to suspend all trading when markets are excessively volatile. Also, the SEC may require "large traders" to identify themselves and provide information concerning their trading.

The Private Securities Litigation Reform Act (PSLRA) of 1995[7] was passed in response to increasing abuses in private securities litigation, including lawyers filing suits on behalf of plaintiff shareholders who were unaware that they were involved in those suits. The intent of the act is to reduce the number of lawsuits brought against issuers of securities and accounting firms.

Congress passed sweeping legislation in response to widespread accounting fraud that began with Enron's collapse in 2001 (Sarbanes-Oxley Act). The financial crisis in 2008 led to the Dodd-Frank Wall Street Reform and Consumer Protection Act (Dodd-Frank), which seeks to prevent another financial crisis and to restore investor confidence in the market. Because of the widespread economic impact of the 2008 crisis, Congress passed the Jumpstart Our Business Startups (JOBS) Act in 2012 to encourage investment in companies, especially smaller companies, by providing easier access to capital markets. The role of the SEC is to protect investors even as it oversees efficient operation of the markets through monitoring compliance with the law and enforcing its rules and regulations. Its role and regulations expand as market events and activities change.

45-2a The Securities Act of 1933

primary offerings–the original distribution of securities by the issuing corporations.

The 1933 act deals with the original distribution of securities by the issuing corporations, or **primary offerings.** The 1933 act is a disclosure statute designed to secure essential facts for the investor who is buying shares from the company. The 1934 act focuses on the secondary distribution of securities in the national securities exchanges and in the over-the-counter markets. That is, the 1933 act regulates the sale of securities by a corporation to the first owner, a primary offering. An offer or sale of securities to the public in interstate commerce requires that a registration statement be filed with the SEC unless an exemption applies. The exemptions are discussed later in this chapter.

Applicability and Definition of Security

securities–stocks and bonds issued by a corporation. Under some investor protection laws, the term includes any interest in an enterprise that provides unearned income to its owner.

For the securities acts to apply, the transaction must involve a "security" within the meaning of the acts.[8] Congress adopted a definition of **security** sufficiently broad to encompass virtually any instrument that might be sold as an investment.

The 1933 act applies to the sale of securities, including (1) stocks, (2) corporate bonds, and (3) any conceivable type of corporate interest or instrument that has the characteristics of an investment security, including convertible securities and variable annuities.

The definition of *security* includes not only investment instruments such as stocks and bonds but also "investment contracts." The definition of an *investment contract*, developed by the Supreme Court, is sufficiently broad to allow the securities acts to apply to a wide range of investment transactions or schemes, including the sale of bottled

---

[6] A savings and loan or "thrift" is a financial institution that accepts savings deposits and makes payments for individuals such as mortgages or car payments. During the S&L crisis 747 out of the 3,234 saving and loan associations in the United States failed. Many S&Ls became insolvent when they could not attract sufficient capital. Some CEOs invented creative accounting strategies to make the S&Ls look profitable while they were actually losing money.

[7] P.L. 104-67, 109 Stat. 737, 15 U.S.C. §78a nt.

[8] The Supreme Court has consistently held that the definition of a security set forth in §3(a)(10) of the 1934 act is identical to the definition set forth in §2(1) of the 1933 act. The definition of security under these acts is not to be confused with the narrower definition in Article 8 of the Uniform Commercial Code. See *SEC v. Infinity Group Co.,* 993 F. Supp. 321 (E.D. Pa. 1998).

whiskey, cattle-breeding programs, and a limited liability partnership to operate local telephone companies.[9] Under the Supreme Court's definition, an investment contract exists if the following elements are present: (1) an investment of money, (2) a common enterprise, and (3) an expectation of future profits from the efforts of others. **For Example,** the sale of citrus groves to investors, coupled with the execution of service contracts to plant, harvest, and sell the fruit and the distribution of the profits of the venture to the investors, is an investment contract. An instrument denominated as a "note" may, in fact, be a "security" subject to regulation under the 1934 act.[10]

registration statement—document disclosing specific financial information regarding the security, the issuer, and the underwriter.

CASE SUMMARY

10,000 Investors Wish They Had Missed This Opportunity

FACTS: "Opportunity doesn't always knock … sometimes it rings" (ETS Payphones promotional brochure). And sometimes it hangs up. So it did for the 10,000 people who invested a total of $300 million in the payphone sale-and-leaseback arrangements touted by ETS under that slogan. Charles Edwards was the chairman, chief executive officer, and sole shareholder of ETS Payphones, Inc. Acting partly through a subsidiary, ETS sold payphones to the public via independent distributors. The payphones were offered packaged with a site lease, a five-year leaseback and management agreement, and a buyback agreement. The purchase price for the payphone packages was approximately $7,000. Under the leaseback and management agreement, purchasers received $82 per month, a 14 percent annual return. Purchasers were not involved in the day-to-day operation of the payphones they owned. ETS selected the site for the phones, installed the equipment, arranged for connection and long distance service, collected coin revenues, and maintained and repaired the phones. Under the buyback agreement, ETS promised to refund the full purchase price of the package at the end of the lease or within 180 days of the purchaser's request. The payphones did not generate enough revenue for ETS to make the payments required by the leaseback agreements, so the company depended on funds from

new investors to meet its obligations. In September 2000, ETS filed for bankruptcy protection. The SEC brought this civil enforcement action alleging that Edwards and ETS had violated the registration requirements and antifraud provisions of the 1933 act. The district court concluded that the arrangement was an "investment contract" subject to the securities laws. The Court of Appeals for the Eleventh Circuit reversed the lower court because the scheme offered a contractual entitlement to a fixed, rather than a variable, return.

DECISION: Judgment for the SEC. Congress's purpose in enacting the securities laws was to regulate investments in whatever form they are made and by whatever name they are called. To that end, it enacted a broad definition of "security" sufficient to encompass virtually any instrument that might be sold as an investment. The U.S. Supreme Court applied the *Hovey* test for an investment contract finding (1) an investment of money, (2) a common enterprise, and (3) an expectation of future "profits" from the efforts of others, including fixed returns based on contracts. The Court determined that the ETS investment scheme can be an "investment contract" and thus a "security" under the securities laws. It reversed and remanded the case to the Court of Appeals. [*SEC v. Edwards*, 540 U.S. 389 (2004)]

prospectus—information provided to each potential purchaser of securities setting forth the key information contained in the registration statement.

45-2b The Filing Requirements: Registration Statements

A **registration statement** is a document disclosing specific financial information regarding the security, the issuer, and the underwriter. The seller must also provide a prospectus to each potential purchaser of the securities. The **prospectus** sets forth the key information contained in the registration statement. The object is to provide the interested investor detailed information about the security and the enterprise. The SEC does not approve or disapprove the securities as being good or bad investments but only reviews the form

[9] *SEC v. Shiner*, 268 F. Supp. 2d 1333 (S.D. Fla. 2003).
[10] *SEC v. Wallenbrock*, 313 F.3d 532 (9th Cir. 2002).

registration requirements—provisions of the Securities Act of 1933 requiring advance disclosure to the public of a new securities issue through filing a statement with the SEC and sending a prospectus to each potential purchaser.

and content of the registration statement and the prospectus to ensure full disclosure. The requirements of advance disclosure to the public through the filing of the registration statement with the SEC and the sending of a prospectus to each potential purchaser are commonly referred to as the **registration requirements** of the 1933 act.

The JOBS Act and Dodd-Frank have made it easier for smaller reporting companies and emerging growth companies to comply with registration and disclosure rules for primary offerings. If a company qualifies as a smaller reporting company (based on equity amount or less than $50 million in annual revenue) or an emerging growth company (EGC) (total annual gross revenues of less than $1 billion during its most recent fiscal year), then the registration requirements are easier and less costly for their primary offerings. One of the helpful provisions for an ECG or smaller reporting companies is that the initial SEC filing may be made on a confidential basis. The confidential filing is a way for these companies to determine if they can meet regulatory standards without the public disclosure that the SEC has rejected their offering. They can then withdraw the offering until such time as they can meet the regulatory requirements without the taint of having been denied registration.

The Registration Process

Section 5 of the 1933 act provides for the division of the registration process into three time periods: (1) the prefiling period, (2) the waiting period or quiet period, from the date of filing with the SEC to the date the registration statement becomes effective (a minimum of 20 days but commonly extended for additional 20-day periods after each amendment by the issuer in compliance with SEC requirements for additional information), and (3) the posteffective period. The time divisions allow the public an opportunity to study the information disclosed in the registration process before a sale can be made. Permissible, required, and prohibited activities during these time periods are set forth in Figure 45-1.

CPA ## Regulation A Offerings

Regulation A provides a simplified registration process for small issues of securities by small businesses. Regulation A originally allowed registration exemptions for offerings of securities up to $5 million in a 12-month period. The Jumpstart Our Business Startups (JOBS) Act, signed into law in 2012, expanded Regulation A to allow emerging enterprises to raise public capital efficiently and to allow more choices to investors through a simpler SEC registration process. The new regulation, sometimes referred to as Regulation A+, increases the amount of capital a business can raise in a Regulation A offering from $5 million to $50 million.[11] One of the primary benefits of the new regulation is that it allows companies to register only with the SEC and exempts them from registering with state financial regulators.[12] If Regulation A companies meet certain standards, they can avoid onerous reporting and disclosure requirements. The new regulation allows investment by both accredited and nonaccredited investors, with some limits on the amount a nonaccredited investor may invest.[13] One of the significant advantages of Regulation A is that it allows companies to "test the waters" through general solicitation and advertising before filing an offering statement. In other words, issuers can solicit interest in a potential offering before incurring substantial expenses either before or after filing the offering statement. Once the offering statement has been filed, the issuer must provide a

[11] Before the amount was increased and the state regulation requirement was changed, Regulation A offerings were rarely used.
[12] The revised Regulation A creates two tiers: a Tier 1 offering allows up to $20 million in 12 months; a Tier 2 offering allows up to $50 million in 12 months. The requirements and benefits of the tiers differ. Tier 1 offerings still require state registration, while Tier 2 offerings require registration only with the SEC.
[13] Tier 2 offerings limit a nonaccredited investor to 10 percent of the greater of annual income or net worth.

FIGURE 45-1   Registration Periods

	PROHIBITED OR REQUIRED ACTIVITIES	PERMITTED ACTIVITIES
PREFILING PERIOD	ISSUER MUST NOT SELL OR OFFER FOR SALE A SECURITY BEFORE REGISTRATION STATEMENT IS FILED.	ISSUER MAY PLAN WITH UNDERWRITERS THE DISTRIBUTION OF THE SECURITY.
WAITING PERIOD	NO FINAL SALE OF A SECURITY PERMITTED DURING THIS PERIOD.	PRELIMINARY PROSPECTUS* CONTAINING INFORMATION FROM THE REGISTRATION STATEMENT BEING REVIEWED BY THE SEC MAY BE DISTRIBUTED TO INVESTORS, WHO MAY MAKE OFFERS. ADVERTISEMENTS MAY BE PLACED IN FINANCIAL PUBLICATIONS, IDENTIFYING PARTICULARS OF THE SECURITY, FROM WHOM A PROSPECTUS CAN BE OBTAINED, AND BY WHOM ORDERS WILL BE EXECUTED.**
POSTEFFECTIVE PERIOD	MUST PROVIDE A COPY OF FINAL PROSPECTUS WITH EVERY WRITTEN OFFER, CONFIRMATION OF SALE, OR DELIVERY OF SECURITY. MUST UPDATE PROSPECTUS WHENEVER IMPORTANT NEW DEVELOPMENTS OCCUR OR AFTER NINE MONTHS.	SALES OF THE SECURITY MAY BE COMPLETED.

*The preliminary prospectus is commonly called the *red herring* prospectus because of the red ink caption required by the SEC, informing the public that a registration statement has been filed but is not yet effective and that no final sale can be made until after the effective date. A red herring prospectus does not include key details such as price and the number of shares offered.

**These advertisements are sometimes called *tombstone ads* because they are commonly framed by a black ink border.

preliminary offering circular or provide information to potential investors on where the most current preliminary offering circular can be obtained, such as a Web site.

Financial statements for a Regulation A offering are less extensive than those required for a public offering but issuers must file balance sheets and financial statements for the two previous fiscal years. Only companies that are organized in and have their principal place of business in the United States or Canada are eligible for Regulation A exemptions. Issuers considered "bad actors" by the SEC are not eligible.[14]

CPA Regulation D Exemptions

Certain private and limited offerings of securities are exempt from the registration requirements under Regulation D, which includes three different types of exemptions.

CPA **Rule 506 Exemption.** Regulation D is a rule that provides general permission to offer and sell to a potentially indefinite number of individuals who meet the definition of

[14] "Bad actors" would be those who have had difficulties with the SEC, such as investigations, sanctions, fines, or any types of criminal convictions.

accredited investor.[15] Regulation D is commonly referred to as the *private placement exemption*. Under the Rule 506 exemption, specific information must be provided to all buyers if any buyers are nonaccredited investors; the number of nonaccredited investors is limited to no more than 35 investors. Under Rule 506(b) a company may not use general solicitation or advertising to market the securities. Under the JOBS Act, the SEC made changes to Rule 506 that allow general solicitation if all purchasers of the securities are accredited investors and the issuer takes reasonable steps to verify that the purchasers are accredited investors. The new rule on general solicitation was a response to the need for companies to communicate more efficiently with potential investors in a market where both capital and information flow swiftly.

CPA **Rule 505 Exemption.** Rule 505 of Regulation D exempts from registration offerings of less than $5 million to no more than 35 nonaccredited purchasers over a 12-month period. No limit exists on the number of accredited investors who may participate. No general solicitation or general advertising is permitted under Rule 505. If any prospective investors are nonaccredited, the issuer must furnish all investors specific information on the issuer, its business, and the securities offered for sale.

CPA **Rule 504 Exemption.** Under Rule 504 of Regulation D, an issuer can offer and sell securities up to $1 million within a 12-month period without registration and without most of the restrictions contained in Rules 505 and 506.

CPA **Restrictions.** Securities acquired under Rules 506, 505, and 504 exemptions from registration are considered restricted securities. Their resale may require registration. Rules requiring registration of these Regulation D securities prior to resale ensure that investors purchase these securities as an investment rather than for public distribution. When there is no attempt to make public distributions, investors ordinarily fit within one of several exemptions to registration upon resale. Generally, all restrictions expire after two years. Companies do not have to register their offering of securities with the SEC if they are relying on Rule 504, 505, or 506 under Regulation D. Companies relying on these exemptions must, however, file a "Form D," which provides the names and addresses of the company's promoters, executive officers, and directors and some details about the offering.[16]

Intrastate Offerings Exemption

An intrastate offering exemption may be used to finance local business operations through local investment. SEC Rule 147 provides stringent standards for the exemption. The company must be organized in the state where it is offering securities and it must meet the so-called Triple 80 requirement.[17] All of the offerees and purchasers must be residents of the same state where the offering is made. The exemption may be lost if a sale is made to even one out-of-state person. The exemption does not limit the number of persons who may purchase the securities and there is no limit on the size of the offering.[18]

[15] The term *accredited investor* is defined to include virtually every type of institution that participates in the private placement market, such as banks, stock brokerage firms, insurance companies, mutual fund companies, and retirement plans with assets in excess of $5 million. A director, an executive officer, or a general partner of the company selling the securities is an accredited investor. An individual is considered an accredited investor if he or she has a net worth of at least $1 million, not including the value of his or her primary residence or if his or her income exceeds $200,000 in each of the two most recent calendar years or joint income with a spouse exceeds $300,000 for those years and there is a reasonable expectation of the same income level in the current year.

[16] A company's Form D can be accessed from the SEC's EDGAR database.

[17] 17 C.F.R. §230.147 (2015). Rule 147 offerings must meet the so-called Triple 80 requirements: 80 percent of the offeror's assets must be in one state, 80 percent of its revenue must be earned within that state, and 80 percent of the proceeds from the offering must be used within that state.

[18] Several states have enacted or proposed state crowdfunding legislation, relying on the intrastate exemption. The SEC has stated that general advertising or solicitation through the Internet does not make such local crowdfunding efforts ineligible for the exemption if there are sufficient disclaimers to ensure that offers are made only to state residents.

Crowdfunding Exemption

Crowdfunding has become a popular way to raise money by attracting relatively small individual contributions form a large number of people. The JOBS Act requires the SEC to create a crowdfunding exemption that would allow companies to raise $1 million in any 12-month period. Under the proposed rule, companies must use an intermediary that is registered with the SEC. The proposed rule also limits individual investors in the amount they can invest in crowdfunding in any 12-month period.[19]

CPA   Enforcement of the 1933 Act

Issuers, sellers, and "aiders and abettors" may be subject to civil and criminal liability under the 1933 act.

CPA   **Issuer's Civil Liability for False or Misleading Statements.** The Securities Act of 1933 imposes civil liability under section 11 for making materially false or misleading statements in a registration statement and for omitting any required material fact. An issuing company has virtually no defense if there has been a false statement and a loss.

CPA   **Civil Liability of Sellers of Securities.** Section 12 of the 1933 act applies to those who "offer or sell" securities and employ any device or scheme to defraud or obtain money by means of untrue statements of material facts. This section makes such persons or firms liable to purchasers for damages sustained.

CPA   **Criminal Liability.** Section 24 of the 1933 act imposes criminal penalties on anyone who willfully makes untrue statements of material facts or omits required material facts from a registration statement. Section 17 of the act makes it unlawful for any person to employ any device, scheme, or artifice to defraud in the offer or sale of securities.

CPA   45-2c The Securities Exchange Act of 1934

The 1934 Securities Exchange Act regulates the sale of securities from one owner to another, the secondary markets. Other federal laws supplement the 1934 act by regulating other market participants.[20] These laws cover holding companies in utility businesses, trustees for debt securities, mutual funds, and investment advisors.

CPA   Registration and Reporting Requirements

Exchanges, brokers, and dealers who deal in securities traded in interstate commerce or on any national security exchange must register with the SEC unless exempted by it.

---

[19] The proposed rules state that investors whose annual income or net worth is less than $100,000 may invest up to the greater of $2,000 or 5 percent of annual income or net worth. Investors whose annual income or net worth is more than $100,000 may invest up to 10 percent of annual income or net worth up to a maximum amount of $100,000. Net worth does not include the value of an investor's primary residence.

[20] The Public Utility Holding Company Act of 1935 (15 U.S.C. §79 *et seq.*) provides comprehensive regulation of holding companies and their subsidiaries in interstate gas and electric utilities businesses. The Trust Indenture Act of 1939 (15 U.S.C. §§77aaa to 77bbb) was enacted to protect the interests of the holders of bonds and other debt securities offered to the public in interstate commerce by requiring the appointment of independent institutional trustees. The Investment Company Act of 1940 (15 U.S.C. §§80a-1 to 80a-52) provides for the registration and comprehensive regulation of mutual funds and all other investment companies. The Investment Advisers Act of 1940 (15 U.S.C. §§80b-1 to 80b-21) requires registration with the Securities and Exchange Commission of all persons engaged in the business of providing investment advice in interstate commerce. In 1970, the Securities Investors Protection Act was enacted to protect investors from the business failures of brokers and dealers.

Companies whose securities are listed on a national securities exchange and unlisted companies with assets in excess of $10 million and a class of equity securities, such as common stock that is held of record by either (1) 2,000 or more persons or (2) 500 or more persons who are not accredited investors, are subject to the reporting requirements of the act. The JOBS Act requires the SEC to adopt rules permitting crowdfunding. Under such rules, companies will be able to exclude holders of securities issued under the crowdfunding exemption.

CPA   **Principal Reports.** Publicly traded companies must disclose information to the SEC on an ongoing basis. Domestic issuers must submit annual reports on Form 10-K. Form 10-K provides an overview of the company's business and financial condition and must include audited financial statements. It is similar, but distinct, from the annual report to shareholders. Publicly traded companies must also file quarterly reports on Form 10-Q. Companies must report material changes or events, such as acquisitions, bankruptcy, or the resignation of directors, on Form 8-K.

CPA   **Certifications and Disclosure Controls.** The Sarbanes-Oxley Act of 2002 requires written certification of the 10-K and 10-Q reports by each company's CEO and CFO. Section 302(a) of the act requires CEOs and CFOs to certify that:

(1) the signing officer has reviewed the report;

(2) based on the officer's knowledge, the report does not contain any untrue statement of a material fact or omit to state a material fact necessary in order to make the statements made, in light of the circumstances under which such statements were made, not misleading;

(3) based on such officer's knowledge, the financial statements, and other financial information included in the report, fairly present in all material respects the financial condition and results of operations of the issuer as of, and for, the periods presented in the report;

(4) the signing officers—

(A) are responsible for establishing and maintaining internal controls....

A "knowing" misrepresentation in connection with the certification process is punishable by fine up to $1 million and imprisonment of up to 10 years. A "willful" misrepresentation in connection with the certification process is punishable by fine up to $5 million and imprisonment of up to 20 years.[21]

Section 304 of Sarbanes Oxley contains a clawback provision. If an issuer is required to prepare an accounting restatement due to fraudulent activity or noncompliance with financial reporting requirements, the CEO and CFO must reimburse the issuer for any bonus or incentive-based compensation received during the 12-month period following the issuance of the restated financial statements.[22] **For Example,** Carl Jasper, the CFO of semiconductor manufacturer Maxim Integrated Products, issued backdated stock options without properly expensing them. During the years 2000 to 2005, Jasper regularly backdated stock options so that options were granted at the lowest possible price to employees. He concealed millions of dollars in expenses from investors and significantly overstated the company's income. Because Jasper had certified false financial statements in 10-Ks and 10-Qs, Section 304 required that he reimburse Maxim $1.8 million in bonuses and profits from the sale of Maxim stock during the relevant period.[23]

---

[21] 18 U.S.C. §1350(c).

[22] The Dodd-Frank Act also requires the SEC to implement a rule that requires national securities exchanges to prohibit the listing of any security of a company that fails to adopt a clawback policy.

[23] *SEC v. Jasper*, 678 F.2d 1116 (9th Cir. 2012). He also paid a civil fine of $360,000 and was barred from serving as an officer or director of a publicly traded company for two years.

Before Sarbanes-Oxley was implemented, many public companies published pro forma (provided in advance) financial results in press releases before filing their official quarterly reports with the SEC. This approach allowed these companies to cast their "financials" in a favorable light. The SEC financial statements are prepared under a set of accounting conventions called *generally accepted accounting principles*, or GAAP. Pro forma financial results are not prepared using GAAP, and they may not provide a true and accurate picture of a company's financial status. Section 401 of the Sarbanes-Oxley Act instructed the SEC to issue rules requiring the presentation of pro forma financial statements in a manner that does not contain material misstatements or omit material facts and can be reconciled with financial results using GAAP. SEC Regulation G imposes a broad range of limitations on the use of pro forma results. If a company issues a press release saying that its pro forma earnings will be $5 million for the quarter when its official GAAP earnings will be just $4 million, the company will have to disclose both figures and explain what expenses were excluded from the pro forma figures and why.

CPA Antifraud Provision

Section 10(b) of the 1934 act makes it unlawful for any person to use any manipulative or deceptive device in contravention of SEC rules. Under the authority of section 10(b) of the 1934 act, the SEC has promulgated *Rule 10b-5*. This rule is the principal antifraud rule relating to the secondary distribution of securities. The rule states:

> *It shall be unlawful for any person, directly or indirectly, by use of any means or instrumentality of interstate commerce, or of the mails or of any facility of any national securities exchange,*
>
> *(a) To employ any device, scheme, or artifice to defraud,*
> *(b) To make any untrue statement of a material fact or to omit to state a material fact necessary in order to make the statements made, in the light of the circumstances under which they were made, not misleading, or*
> *(c) To engage in any act, practice, or course of business that operates or would operate as a fraud or deceit upon any person, in connection with the purchase or sale of any security.[24]*

CPA Private Actions. Rule 10b-5 applies to all securities, whether registered or not, as long as use is made of the mail, interstate commerce, or a national stock exchange. Subject to the safe harbor provisions of the Private Securities Litigation Reform Act as discussed in the following section, under Rule 10b-5, a civil action for damages may be brought by any private investor who purchased or sold a security and was injured because of false, misleading, or undisclosed information.[25]

CPA Liability for "Material Misstatements or Omissions of Fact." Rule 10b-5 prohibits the making of any untrue statement of a "material" fact or the omission of a material fact necessary to render statements made not misleading. The SEC considers information "material" if there is a substantial likelihood that it would have been viewed by a reasonable investor as having significantly altered the total mix of information made available and if a reasonable investor would have considered the fact important in making an investment decision. In every Rule 10b-5 case, the plaintiff must show "reliance" on the misrepresentation and resulting injury.

---

[24] 17 C.F.R. §240.10b-5.
[25] *Miller v. Thane International, Inc.*, 519 F.3d 879 (9th Cir. 2008).

In *Basic, Inc. v. Levinson*, the Supreme Court dealt with the question of what should be the standard of "materiality" in merger cases as well as the standard for determining whether or not the plaintiffs relied on the misrepresentation.

CASE SUMMARY

Why Silence Is Golden

FACTS: In December 1978, Combustion Engineering, Inc., and Basic, Inc., agreed to merge. During the preceding two years, representatives of the two companies had meetings regarding the possibility of a merger. During this time, Basic made three public statements denying that any merger negotiations were taking place or that it knew of any corporate developments that would account for the heavy trading activity in its stock. Certain former shareholders who sold this stock between Basic's first public denial of merger activity and the public announcement of the merger brought a section 10(b) and Rule 10b-5 action against Basic and some of its directors. The former shareholders contended that Basic had made material misrepresentations in its public statements denying merger activity. Basic raised the defense that the alleged misrepresentations were not material and that there was no showing of reliance by the shareholders on Basic's statements.

DECISION: The standard for materiality applicable to preliminary merger discussions is to be decided on a case-by-case basis depending on the probability that the transaction will be consummated and on its significance to the issuer. There is a presumption of reliance by the shareholders on the misstatements of the corporations. This presumption is supported by the policy of the 1934 act, which is to foster reliance on market integrity. However, the presumption may be rebutted by showing that the market price was not affected by the misrepresentation. The case is remanded for further proceedings consistent with this opinion. [***Basic, Inc. v. Levinson***, 485 U.S. 224 (1988)]

In the pharmaceutical industry "materiality" of adverse event reports is a "fact-specific" inquiry. It requires consideration of the source and content and context of the reports, as set forth in the *Matrixx Initiatives* case.

CASE SUMMARY

Rule No. 1 For Corporate Finance Executives: Be Very Careful About What You Say

FACTS: Matrixx develops, manufactures, and markets over-the-counter pharmaceutical products. Its core product, Zicam Cold Remedy, with its active ingredient, zinc gluconate, accounted for approximately 70 percent of Matrixx's sales. Individuals who purchased Matrixx securities between October 22, 2003, and February 6, 2004, filed a securities fraud class action against Matrixx under Section 10(b) of the 1934 Act. In October 2003 Matrixx made a statement to the market that Zicam was "poised for growth in the upcoming cold and cough season." It expressed its expectations that revenues would "be up in excess of 50%." In January 2004 it raised its revenue guidance, predicting an 80 percent increase.

On January 30, 2004, Dow Jones Newswires reported that the Food and Drug Administration (FDA) was "looking into complaints that an over-the-counter common-cold medicine manufactured by a unit of Matrixx Initiatives, Inc., may be causing some users to lose their sense of smell" in light of at least three product liability lawsuits. Matrixx's stock fell from $13.55 to $11.97 per share after the report. In response, on February 2, Matrixx issued a press release that stated in part:

> Matrixx believes statements alleging that intranasal Zicam products caused anosmia (loss of smell) are completely unfounded and misleading. In no clinical trial of intranasal zinc gluconate gel products has there been a single report of lost or diminished olfactory function (sense of smell). Rather, the safety and efficacy of zinc gluconate for the treatment of symptoms related to the common cold have been well established ...

The day after Matrixx issued this press release, its stock price bounced back to $13.40 per share. On February 6,

Rule No. 1 For Corporate Finance Executives: Be Very Careful About What You Say continued

2004, *Good Morning America*, a nationally broadcast morning news program, reported that Dr. Jafek had discovered more than a dozen patients suffering from anosmia after using Zicam. It also noted that four lawsuits had been filed against Matrixx. The price of Matrixx stock plummeted to $9.94 per share that same day. Zicam again issued a press release largely repeating its February 2 statement.

Prior to these public statements, between October 2003 and February 2004, medical experts had revealed to Matrixx a plausible causal relationship between Zicam Cold Remedy and anosmia. For example, Dr. Linschoten sent abstracts of studies to Matrixx that had confirmed "zinc's toxicity." In September 2003 Matrixx learned of a planned national medical conference presentation by Dr. Jafek of the University of Colorado finding that 10 patients suffered loss of smell after Zicam use. The investors claim that the information the company had about the causal relationship between Zicam and anosmia were material facts necessary in order to make the statements made by Matrixx to the market not misleading. Matrixx defended that the investors had not alleged a statistically significant correlation between the use of Zicam and anosmia so as to make failure to publicly disclose complaints and the University of Colorado study a material omission.

DECISION: The "materiality" requirement of a Section 10(b) claim by investors that Matrixx made statements that were misleading as to material facts was satisfied in this case. There is a substantial likelihood that the disclosure of the omitted facts asserted in this case would have been viewed by a reasonable investor as having significantly altered the "total mix" of information made available by the company. Section 10(b) and Rule 10b-5 do not create an affirmative duty to disclose any and all material information (silence, absent a duty to disclose, is not misleading under Rule 10b-5). However, disclosure is required in order to make the statements made by Matrixx to the market not misleading. Matrixx told the market that revenues were going to rise 50 then 80 percent, yet it had information that its leading revenue product caused loss of the sense of smell. Matrixx also stated that reports its product caused anosmia were "completely unfounded and misleading," yet it had contrary information that a reasonable investor would deem material. The FDA and medical professionals do not limit the evidence considered for assessing causation to statistically significant data nor should investors be so limited. [*Matrixx Initiatives, Inc. v. Siracusano*, 131 S. Ct. 1309 (2011)]

Reliance and the Fraud-on-the Market Theory. The United States Supreme Court has stated that to prevail in a securities fraud case under section 10(b) and Rule 10b-5, a plaintiff must prove: "(1) a material misrepresentation or omission by the defendant; (2) scienter; (3) a connection between the misrepresentation or omission and the purchase or sale of a security; (4) reliance upon the misrepresentation or omission; (5) economic loss; and (6) loss causation."[26] The Court has long recognized the difficulty of proving reliance on a material misstatement or omission. In *Basic v. Levinson*, the Supreme Court held that requiring direct proof of reliance "would place an unnecessarily unrealistic evidentiary burden on the Rule 10b-5 plaintiff who has traded on an impersonal market."[27] The **fraud-on-the-market** theory creates a presumption that securities fraud plaintiffs relied on the misrepresentation. The theory assumes that the market price of shares reflect publicly available information, including material misrepresentations. Several companies have challenged the fraud-on-the-market theory, arguing that *Basic v. Levinson* should be overruled because the premise on which it is founded—market efficiency—is no longer tenable. The Supreme Court, however, has refused to "jettison" *Basic's* fraud-on-the-market theory.[28]

fraud-on-the-market–a theory that in an open and developed securities market, the price of a stock is determined by the information on the company available to the public, and misleading statements will defraud purchasers of stock even if they do not directly rely on these statements.

[26] In *Amgen, Inc. v. Connecticut Retirement Plans and Trust Funds*, 133 S. Ct. 1184 (2013), the Court held that plaintiffs who employ the fraud-on-the-market theory of reliance do not need to establish materiality of alleged misstatements or omissions of fact at the class certification stage.

[27] *Basic v. Levinson*, 485 U.S. 224, 245 (1988).

[28] See *Halliburton Co. v. Erica P. John Fund, Inc.*, 134 S. Ct. 2398 (2014). In this case, Halliburton claimed that each securities fraud plaintiff should have to prove that he actually relied on the defendant's misrepresentation in deciding to buy or sell a company's stock. The Court disagreed, emphasizing that the fraud-on-the-market theory allows a defendant to rebut the presumption of reliance on market information. Moreover, the Court stated that even though the efficient market theory has been criticized, Halliburton did not identify a "fundamental shift in economic theory" to justify overruling *Basic*. In dissent, three justices stated that *Basic's* fraud-on-the-market theory should be abandoned based on "logic" and "economic realities."

CPA **Litigation Reform Act**

The Private Securities Litigation Reform Act (PSLRA, or the Litigation Reform Act) of 1995 was passed because of (1) congressional concern over an excess of frivolous private securities lawsuits, (2) the financial burdens placed on accountants and other professional advisors by such litigation, and (3) concern that the investors in a class-action lawsuit have their interests fairly represented. Important features of the act are as follows.

CPA **Safe Harbor Rules.** Issuers of securities frequently believed that lawsuits against them under Rule 10b-5 occurred simply because the corporation made a projection that failed to materialize. The Litigation Reform Act provides shelter for issuers from private liability for forward-looking statements that were not known to be false when made and that were accompanied by meaningful cautionary statements informing investors of contingencies that could cause results to differ from projected results.

To preserve the protections of the PSLRA, quarterly and annual reports to the SEC (Forms 10-Q and 10-K) and quarterly and annual reports to stockholders, as well as corporate press releases on financial matters, now commonly utilize the expression *forward-looking statements* regarding corporate statements that estimate or project the short-term and long-term outlook for a business. Moreover, these reports typically include a section entitled "Cautionary Statements" or "Risk Factors," and contain a statement such as:

> *Forward-looking statements as contained in this report involve a number of risks, including but not limited to product demand, pricing, market acceptance, supply problems, intellectual property rights and litigation, and risks in product and technology development.*

Corporations do not have to caution against every conceivable factor that may cause results to differ from the issuer's forward-looking statements. **For Example,** Ivax Corporation, a drug company, issued a press release including optimistic assumptions about future events. Attached to the release was an italicized warning that stated in specific detail the kinds of misfortunes that could befall Ivax and could cause results to differ from its forward-looking statements. This cautionary statement did not mention that a large goodwill writedown could occur; and when a writedown did occur, Ivax stock declined sharply. Harris, Wolpin, and others brought a Rule 10b-5 fraud suit against Ivax based on the omission of a warning about the writedown risk. The court held that the cautionary statements were sufficient to warn an investor of risks similar to that actually realized and the statements satisfied Ivax's burden to warn under the statute. Ivax was not required to list all risk factors, and the failure to mention one risk that in fact occurred did not "blow Ivax out of the safe harbor."[29]

CPA **Litigation Reform.** The Litigation Reform Act places a heightened pleading requirement on plaintiffs attempting to plead fraud in securities cases and requires not only that the plaintiffs specify each statement alleged to have been false or misleading and the reason for the belief but also that the plaintiffs plead "scienter"—the mental state embracing intent to deceive, manipulate, or defraud.[30] In the *Matrixx Initiatives* case, the Supreme Court held that the investors adequately pleaded scienter, where the allegations gave rise to the compelling inference that Matrixx elected not to disclose the reports of adverse events not because it believed they were meaningless, but because it understood their likely effect on the market.[31]

---

[29] *Harris v. Ivax Corp.*, 182 F.3d 799 (11th Cir. 1999).
[30] See In re *Lucent Technologies Inc., Securities Litigation*, 307 F. Supp. 2d 633 (D. N.J. 2004).
[31] *Matrixx Initiatives, Inc. v. Siracusano*, 131 S. Ct. 1309, 1324 (2011); see also *Frank v. Dana Corp.*, 646 F.3d 954 (6th Cir. 2011).

The Litigation Reform Act also provides for *proportionate liability*, as opposed to joint and several liability, for defendants who are found not to have knowingly committed a violation of the security laws. In addition, securities fraud is eliminated as a predicate for private RICO actions absent a prior criminal conviction.[32] Under the act, frivolous private securities lawsuits require payment of the defendant's reasonable attorney fees.

CPA **Class-Action Reforms.** Reforms were necessary to protect against "lawyer-driven lawsuits" in which a class-action counsel would direct a "professional" plaintiff to buy a security to have standing to bring a class-action lawsuit. Thereafter, the class-action counsel would race to the courthouse to file before any other plaintiff and thus be able to claim enhanced standing to represent the class. The Litigation Reform Act provides that the status of lead plaintiff must be offered to the person with the largest financial interest in the case.

Aiders and Abettors. For many years the courts and the SEC held aiders and abettors, such as banks, accountants, trustees, and attorneys, liable in private actions under section 10(b) of the Securities Exchange Act of 1934 and Rule 10b-5. The broad language of the act and the rule arguably allowed private parties to sue aiders and abettors for fraud or deceit in connection with the sale of securities. In a 1994 decision, the Supreme Court limited the liability of such aiders and abettors. In *Central Bank of Denver v. First Interstate Bank of Denver*, the Court made a distinction between primary violators who directly misstate or omit material facts that investors rely on and secondary violators or aiders and abettors.[33] Aiders and abettors are liable in private actions, the Court held, only if investors can show reliance on their material misstatements or omissions. Thus, a plaintiff who sues an attorney, an accountant, or a bank for securities fraud must sue that party as a primary violator and show reliance on that party's material misstatements or omissions.

In 2008, the Court again limited the liability of third parties in securities fraud cases. In *Stoneridge Investment Partners, LLC v. Scientific Atlanta, Inc.*, investors maintained that Scientific Atlanta and Motorola helped giant cable TV firm Charter Communications inflate its financial statements to bolster its stock price.[34] The companies allegedly helped Charter to generate $17 million in phony revenues. Investors maintained that the two companies should be treated as primary violators because they were involved in a scheme to defraud investors, even though they did not issue any public statements. The Court found that the investors had no knowledge of the companies' deceptive acts and could not show reliance "except in an indirect chain that was too remote for liability." The Court stated that the companies were subject to criminal laws preventing such fraudulent scheming and to SEC enforcement actions, but that liability did not extend to private investors.

In 2011, the Court considered whether a mutual fund investment advisor was liable to investors under section 10(b) and Rule 10b-5 for false statements included in the mutual fund prospectuses. The Court held that investment advisors cannot be sued under federal securities law for false statements made by the fund they advised.[35] The Court held that Janus Capital Group, the investment advisor, did not "make" the false statements, rather the mutual fund itself made the statements. The Court held that only a party "with ultimate authority over the statement including its content and whether and how to communicate it" is the one that "makes" the statement within the meaning of Rule 10b-5.

---

[32] The RICO Act is discussed in Chapter 7.
[33] 511 U.S. 164 (1994).
[34] 552 U.S. 148 (2008).
[35] *Janus Capital Group, Inc. v. First Derivative Traders*, 131 S. Ct. 2296 (2011).

CPA   ## 45-2d Trading on Insider Information

Illegal insider trading occurs when a person who owes a fiduciary duty to a company buys or sells a security while in possession of material nonpublic information. Enforcing insider trading laws is a high priority for the SEC. In recent years, the SEC has pursued insider trading cases against financial professionals, hedge fund managers, corporate insiders, and attorneys.

insider information– privileged information on company business known only to employees.

Section 10(b) and Rule 10b-5 form a basis for imposing sanctions for trading on **insider information.** Those accused of insider trading may face both criminal and civil actions. The Insider Trading and Securities Fraud Enforcement Act of 1988, which amended the 1934 act, gave the SEC authority to bring an action against an individual purchasing or selling a security while in possession of material inside information. Persons who "aid or abet" in the violation may also be held liable under the act.

Individuals convicted of criminal insider trading may be sentenced up to 20 years in prison per violation and can face fines of up to $5 million or twice the gain from the offense. In a civil action by the SEC, an individual may have to disgorge any profits from the offense and may have to pay fines not to exceed the greater of $1 million or three times the amount of the profit gained or loss avoided. Individuals can be barred from serving as an officer or a director of a public company, or from acting as a securities broker or an investment advisor. Attorneys and accountants may be barred from serving before the SEC. **For Example,** Mathew Martoma, formerly a portfolio manager for SAC Capital Advisors, was sentenced to nine years in prison for his role in carrying out one of the biggest insider trading schemes ever. He was convicted of using inside information about a clinical trial for an experimental Alzheimer's drug to make illegal trades in the shares of two drug companies. The information allowed SAC to generate $275 million in profits. Martoma was also ordered to forfeit a $9.38 million bonus as well as his Florida home. He was the eighth employee of SAC to be convicted or plead guilty to insider trading charges. SAC, a highly successful hedge fund, pleaded guilty to insider trading. SAC paid record fines of $1.2 billion to the federal government and $600 million to the SEC. Steven A. Cohen, the founder and owner of the hedge fund, was not charged with any criminal wrongdoing. He closed the hedge fund and reorganized it as a family office that manages his own money.[36]

Under the 1988 insider trading act, "controlling persons," including employers whose lax supervision may allow employees to commit insider trading violations, are subject to civil penalties.[37] The SEC must prove "knowing" or "reckless" behavior by the controlling person. The 1988 law establishes bounty programs that allow the SEC to reward informants giving information on insider trading activity. The reward is up to 10 percent of any penalty imposed.

Broker-dealers and investment advisors are also required to establish and maintain procedures to prevent the misuse of material nonpublic information.[38] **For Example,** in 2014, the SEC charged Wells Fargo Advisors LLC with failing to maintain adequate controls to prevent one of its employees from trading on a customer's nonpublic information. After learning confidentially from his client that Burger King was being acquired by a New York-based private equity firm, a Wells Fargo broker traded on that information.

[36] See Michael Bobelian, "What Does Martoma's Conviction Mean for SAC Capital's Steven Cohen," FORBES (Feb. 7, 2014), **http://www.forbes.com/sites/michaelbobelian/2014/02/07/what-does-martomas-conviction-mean-for-sac-capitals-steven-cohen/.** The SEC filed an administrative complaint against Steven A. Cohen maintaining that he failed to supervise his senior employees in a reasonable manner.
[37] P.L. 100-704, 102 Stat. 4677, 15 U.S.C. §78u-1(a)(2).
[38] Section 15(g) of the 1934 Exchange Act and Section 204A of the Investment Advisers Act of 1940 require broker-dealers and investment advisors to establish, maintain, and enforce policies and procedures to prevent the misuse of material nonpublic information.

Wells Fargo agreed to pay a $5 million penalty to settle the SEC's charges. The case was the first in which the SEC charged a broker-dealer with failure to protect a customer's material nonpublic information.[39]

Classical Theory of Insider Trading

The classical theory of insider trading states that a corporate insider, such as an officer or a director, violates section 10(b) and Rule 10b-5 by using material nonpublic information about the corporation to trade in the corporation's securities. Underlying insider liability is the concept that there is a special relationship of trust and confidence between the shareholders of a corporation and those insiders who have obtained confidential information by virtue of their position. An **insider** may be a director or corporate employee. A **temporary insider** is someone retained by the corporation for professional services, such as an attorney, accountant, or investment banker. Insiders and temporary insiders are liable for inside trading when they fail to disclose material nonpublic information before trading on it and thus make a secret profit. A **tippee** is an individual who receives information from an insider or a temporary insider. A tippee is subject to the insider's fiduciary duty to shareholders when the insider has breached the fiduciary duty to shareholders by improperly disclosing the information to the tippee and when the tippee knows or should know that there has been a breach.[40] Such a breach occurs when an insider benefits personally from her disclosure. When the insider does not breach a fiduciary duty, a tippee does not violate the securities laws. The Supreme Court has made it clear that an insider must breach a fiduciary duty in disclosing material nonpublic information and that the breach must involve a personal benefit.[41] Some courts have held that a tippee must know that the insider received a personal benefit by disclosing the material nonpublic information. What constitutes a "personal benefit" is a question that is likely to be hotly contested in litigation.[42]

insider—full-time corporate employee or a director.

temporary insider—someone retained by a corporation for professional services on an as-needed basis, such as an attorney, accountant, or investment banker.

tippee—individual who receives information about a corporation from an insider or temporary insider.

CASE SUMMARY

No Secrets from Secrist!

FACTS: On March 6, 1973, Dirks, an investment analyst, received information from Secrist, a former officer of Equity Funding of America, alleging that the assets of Equity Funding were vastly overstated as the result of fraudulent corporate practices. On investigation by Dirks, certain corporation employees corroborated the charges of fraud. Neither Dirks nor his firm owned or traded any Equity Funding stock, but throughout his investigation, he openly discussed the information he had obtained with a number of clients and investors. The information from Dirks induced them to sell Equity Funding stock in excess of $16 million. On March 27, the New York Stock Exchange halted trading of Equity Funding stock, and a subsequent investigation revealed the vast fraud that had taken place. The SEC, investigating Dirks's role in

---

[39] Press Release, SEC, "Wells Fargo Advisors Admits Failing to Maintain Controls and Producing Altered document, Agrees to Pay $5 Million Penalty" (Sept. 22, 2014), **http://www.sec.gov/News/PressRelease/Detail/PressRelease/1370543012047.**

[40] *United States v. Chestman*, 974 F.2d 564 (2d Cir. 1991).

[41] *Dirks v. SEC*, 468 U.S. 646 (1983).

[42] In *United States v. Newman*, the Court of Appeals for the Second Circuit held that there was insufficient evidence that two hedge fund portfolio managers had knowledge of a breach of fiduciary duty and personal benefit by the sources of the inside information. The court found that evidence that the insiders were friends with the tippees or received "career advice" from the tippees was not enough to show they received a personal benefit. 773 F.3d 438 (2d Cir. 2014). The Justice Department sought a rehearing *en banc* of the Second Circuit's interpretation of "personal benefit."

No Secrets from Secrist! continued

the exposure of the fraud, claimed that Dirks had aided and abetted violations of the Securities Act of 1933, the Securities Exchange Act of 1934, and SEC Rule 10b-5 by repeating the allegations of fraud to members of the investment community who later sold their Equity Funding stock.

DECISION: Judgment for Dirks. Secrist, the insider, did not violate any fiduciary duty to shareholders when he disclosed

information about the fraudulent practices to the tippee, Dirks. Secrist received no monetary or personal benefit for the information but was motivated by the desire to expose the fraud. Because the insider did not breach his fiduciary duty when he gave nonpublic information to Dirks, Dirks breached no duty when he passed the information on to investors. [*Dirks v. SEC,* 463 U.S. 646 (1983)]

Misappropriation Theory of Insider Trading

Individuals who misappropriate or steal valuable nonpublic information in breach of a fiduciary duty to their employer and trade in securities on that information are guilty of insider trading as "misappropriators." **For Example,** an employee working for a financial printing firm was found guilty of insider trading under section 10(b) and Rule 10b-5.[43] While proofreading a financial document being prepared for a client firm, he figured out the identity of tender offer targets. Soon after that, he traded on this valuable nonpublic information to his advantage.

It is no defense to a section 10(b) and Rule 10b-5 criminal charge of participating in a "scheme to defraud" that the victim of the fraud (an employer) had no economic interest in the securities traded. The convictions of a stockbroker and a columnist for the *Wall Street Journal* were upheld under section 10(b) of the 1934 act. The columnist violated his fiduciary duty to his employer by revealing prepublication information about his column to the stockbroker. The stockbroker then used the information to trade in the securities identified in the column.[44]

Where an individual misappropriates confidential information for security trading purposes in breach of a fiduciary duty owed to the source of the information rather than to the shareholders who sold securities to the individual, that individual may be convicted of security fraud in violation of section 10(b) and Rule 10b-5.

CASE SUMMARY

The Case of the Dastardly Misappropriator

FACTS: James O'Hagan was a partner in the law firm of Dorsey & Whitney in Minneapolis, Minnesota. In July 1988, Grand Metropolitan PLC, a company based in London, England, retained Dorsey & Whitney as local counsel to represent Grand Met regarding a potential tender offer for the common stock of the Pillsbury Company

headquartered in Minneapolis. O'Hagan did no work on the Grand Met representation. Dorsey & Whitney withdrew from representing Grand Met on September 9, 1988. Less than a month later, on October 4, 1988, Grand Met publicly announced its tender offer for Pillsbury stock. Previously, on August 18, 1988, while Dorsey & Whitney was

[43] *SEC v. Materia,* 745 F.2d 197 (2d Cir. 1984).
[44] *Carpenter v. United States,* 484 U.S. 19 (1987).

The Case of the Dastardly Misappropriator continued

still representing Grand Met, O'Hagan began purchasing call options for Pillsbury stock. Each option gave him the right to purchase 100 shares of Pillsbury stock by a specified date in September 1988. Later in August and September, O'Hagan purchased additional Pillsbury call options. By the end of September, he owned 2,500 unexpired Pillsbury options, apparently more than any other individual investor. O'Hagan also purchased, in September 1988, some 5,000 shares of Pillsbury common stock at a price just under $39 per share. When Grand Met announced its tender offer in October, the price of Pillsbury stock rose to nearly $60 per share. O'Hagan then sold his Pillsbury call options and common stock, making a profit of more than $4.3 million. O'Hagan was charged and convicted of securities fraud in violation of section 10(b) and Rule 10b-5. On appeal, he claimed that he was not a "misappropriator," for he had no fiduciary duty to the Pillsbury shareholders from whom he purchased calls and stock; in fact, he had not even worked on the transaction at the law firm.

DECISION: Judgment against O'Hagan. "Misappropriation" requires that there be "deceptive" conduct "in connection with" a securities transaction. A fiduciary who pretends loyalty to the principal while secretly converting the principal's information for personal gain dupes or defrauds the principal. O'Hagan's failure to disclose his personal trading to his law firm and its client, Grand Met, was a breach of his fiduciary duty and was "deceptive" conduct "in connection with" a securities transaction. The misappropriation theory is designed to protect the integrity of the securities market against "outsiders" like O'Hagan who have access to confidential information that will affect a company's stock price when revealed but have no fiduciary or other duty to the company's shareholders. [*United States v. O'Hagan*, 521 U.S. 642 (1997)]

Regulation FD

The SEC adopted Regulation FD (Fair Disclosure) in 2000 to end the practice of selective disclosure by issuers of securities to security analysts and selected institutional investors of important nonpublic information, such as advance warnings of negative or positive earnings results, before disclosing the information to the general public. Many companies disclosed material information in meetings and during conference calls. Shareholders and the general public were at a disadvantage regarding such information. Those privy to the early release of the information were able to make a profit or avoid a loss at the expense of the uninformed general public. Regulation FD changed the way companies disclose information. As companies increasingly use social media for corporate disclosure, the SEC considered whether information provided through social media complied with Regulation FD. **For Example,** in July 2012, Netflix CEO, Reed Hastings, posted on his personal Facebook page: "Congrats to Ted Sarandos, and his amazing content licensing team. Netflix monthly viewing exceeded 1 billion hours for the first time ever in June. When House of Cards and Arrested Development debut, we'll blow these records away. Keep going Ted, we need even more!" This information arguably did not comply with Regulation FD because it was a disclosure of material information. The SEC questioned whether the posting was "private," even though Mr. Hastings had more than 200,000 Facebook followers. The SEC did not pursue the case but offered additional guidance regarding disclosures through social media. Companies that make disclosures over social media channels should give advance warning that information will be disclosed through its Web site, or through social media such as Facebook or Twitter. Companies may also use technology that provides investors with alerts that new information has been posted.

Remedy for Investors

Investors who lack the inside information possessed by the insider and sell their stock during the relevant time period may recover damages from any insider who made use of undisclosed information. Recovery is by a civil action based on Rule 10b-5.

45-2e Disclosure of Ownership and Short-Swing Profits

Corporate directors and officers owning equity securities in their corporation and any shareholder owning more than 10 percent of any class of the corporation's equity securities are statutorily defined as insiders and must file with the SEC a disclosure statement regarding such ownership and all related transactions. This disclosure is required under section 16(a) of the 1934 act. Under section 403(a) of the Sarbanes-Oxley Act, these individuals must electronically report transactions in company stock to the SEC by the second business day after the transaction. Moreover, the transaction must be posted on the SEC's and the company's Web sites within one day after the filing date.

Section 16 is designed to prevent the unfair use of information available to these corporate insiders. This section prevents insiders from participating in short-term trading in their corporation's securities.

short-swing profit–profit realized by a corporate insider from selling securities less than six months after purchase.

If such a person sells at a profit any of these securities less than six months after their purchase, the profit is called a **short-swing profit.** Under section 16(b), the corporation may sue a director, an officer, or a major stockholder for a short-swing profit.[45] The corporation may recover that profit even if the corporate insider had no fraudulent intent in acquiring and selling the securities. The corporation must bring the lawsuit within two years after the date the profit was realized.[46]

45-2f Tender Offers

A corporation or group of investors may seek to acquire control of another corporation by making a general offer to all shareholders of the target corporation to purchase their shares for cash at a specified price. This type of offer is called a **cash tender offer.** The offer to purchase is usually contingent on the tender of a fixed number of shares sufficient to ensure takeover. The bid price is ordinarily higher than the prevailing market price. Should more shares be tendered than the offeror is willing to purchase, the tender offeror must purchase shares from each shareholder on a pro rata basis.

cash tender offer–general offer to all shareholders of a target corporation to purchase their shares for cash at a specified price.

The Williams Act amended the 1934 act[47] to ensure that public shareholders have adequate information about the cash tender offer. Under section 14(d) of the Williams Act, a person making a tender offer must file appropriate SEC forms. These forms provide information about the background and identity of the person filing, the source of funds used to make stock purchases, the amount of stock beneficially owned, the purpose of the purchases, any plan the purchaser proposes to follow if it gains control over the target corporation, and any contracts or understandings that it has with other persons concerning the target corporation.[48]

Section 14(e) of the Williams Act is the antifraud section. It prohibits fraudulent, deceptive, or manipulative practices. SEC Rule 14e-1 requires any tender offer to remain open for a minimum of 20 business days from the date it is first published or given to security holders.[49] Federal and state legislation, as well as administrative regulation, is aimed at requiring disclosure of information and allowance of a reasonable length of

---

[45] *Levy v. Southbrook International Investments, Ltd.*, 263 F.3d 10 (2d Cir. 2001); *Donaghue v. Natural Microsystems Corp.*, 198 F. Supp. 2d 487 (S.D.N.Y. 2002).

[46] *Credit Suisse Securities (USA) LLC v. Simmonds*, 132 S. Ct. 1414 (2012).

[47] P.L. 90-439, 82 Stat. 454, 15 U.S.C. §78m(d), (e).

[48] Section 14(d) requires a filing by any person making a tender offer that, if successful, would result in the acquisition of 5 percent of any class of an equity security required to be registered under the 1934 Act. Section 13(d) of the act requires disclosure to the issuer, the SEC, and the appropriate stock exchange when a person acquires 5 percent of a class of equity security through stock purchases on exchanges or through private purchases. The person may have acquired the stock for investment purposes, not for control, but must still file disclosure forms under §13(d). See *SEC v. Bilzerian*, 814 F. Supp. 116 (D. D.C. 1993). Section 14(d) applies only to shares to be acquired by tender offer.

[49] For certain types of securities, under certain conditions, the SEC may allow shorter periods for tender offers.

time for consideration of the facts. These requirements are designed to make agreement to takeovers the result of voluntary action based on full knowledge of material facts.

As far as the courts are concerned, takeovers must be regarded with a neutral eye. If there is misrepresentation or other misconduct, the law will interfere. Otherwise, freedom of contract requires that courts not interfere with the judgment of the contracting parties.

CPA 45-2g SEC Enforcement under the 1934 Act

Dodd-Frank Enforcement Powers

The Dodd-Frank Act of 2010[50] contains numerous reforms and initiatives to help restore market trust and reform Wall Street to protect the economy, American consumers, investors, and businesses. To prevent another financial crisis the act created the Financial Stability Oversight Council to oversee the various government agencies responsible for regulating financial institutions. Many sections of the act require various studies to be undertaken and mandate or permit rulemaking by the Commodity Futures Trading Commission and the SEC.

Dodd-Frank further increased the SEC's power. In addition to issuing cease-and-desist orders, the SEC can seek disgorgement and civil penalties. Furthermore, the SEC can bring administrative proceedings against any person, not just regulated persons, for violations of the federal securities laws. With its new power, the SEC has substantially increased the number of administrative proceedings it brings against unregulated persons in a variety of actions including fraud and insider trading. Members of the securities industry have questioned the fairness of the SEC's new power.[51]

Enforcement and Whistleblowers

Section 922 of Dodd-Frank authorized the SEC to create a whistleblower program to encourage individuals to provide the SEC with information that would lead to the discovery and prosecution of violations of the federal securities laws. The program, implemented in 2012, allows a monetary award to whistleblowers who provide original information that leads to successful enforcement actions resulting in monetary sanctions over $1 million. It also protects the identity of the informant and prohibits retaliation by employers. In 2014, the SEC announced its largest whistleblower award since the program began. A single individual received $30 million, an amount that the SEC noted could have been higher had the whistleblower not delayed unreasonably in reporting the violation. According to the SEC, whistleblowers provide information about fraudulent activity that would otherwise be difficult to detect. The SEC has interpreted the Dodd-Frank whistleblower reward provisions to include whistleblowers from outside the United States. At least one court, however, has held that the act does not apply extraterritorially.[52]

[50] P.L. 111-203, 124 Stat. 1376, 15 U.S.C. §8305 (2012).
[51] The fairness of the SEC's power is questioned because the SEC brings the charges, an Administrative Law Judge within the agency hears the case, and the SEC commissioners make the final decision as to the fate of those charged. Between October 2010 and May 2015, the SEC won 90 percent of its cases against defendants before its own judges. See Jean Eaglesham, "In-House Judges Help SEC Rack Up Wins," *Wall Street Journal*, May 6, 2015, p. A1.
[52] *Liu Meng-Lin v. Siemens AG*, 763 F.3d 175 (2d Cir. 2014). The whistleblower discovered that Siemens employees were indirectly making improper payments to officials in North Korea and China in connection with the sale of medical equipment in those countries. He reported the conduct to his superiors through internal company procedures. After he was fired, he reported the payments to the SEC, suggesting that Siemens had violated the Foreign Corrupt Practices Act. The plaintiff was a citizen and resident of Taiwan, employed as a compliance officer for the health care division of Siemens China Ltd. The court held that Dodd-Frank whistleblower protection does not extend to foreign workers employed abroad by foreign corporations because "a statute is presumed in the absence of clear congressional intent to the contrary, to apply only domestically...."

Enforcement and Third–Party Market Participants

The financial crisis of 2008 triggered numerous lawsuits by institutional investors against Wall Street securities firms, claiming that securities firms misrepresented risks when advising clients about complex investments. In response, the Dodd-Frank Act directed the SEC to study the need for establishing a new, uniform federal fiduciary standard of care for broker-dealers and investment advisors. The SEC is in the comment stage of developing this uniform standard, and the standard as proposed would impose a fiduciary duty on both broker-dealers and investment advisors.

Currently, investment advisors and broker-dealers are regulated by different laws.[53] Investment advisors owe a fiduciary duty to their clients. Broker-dealers generally do not owe a fiduciary duty to their clients under federal law. An investment advisor has a duty of good faith and full and fair disclosure; a duty to recommend only securities suitable for the investor; and a duty of loyalty to serve the best interests of his client.[54] Broker-dealers are exempt from the Investment Advisers Act if the advice to clients is "solely incidental" to the conduct of business as a broker or dealer and the broker-dealer receives no "special compensation" for providing the advice.[55] Nevertheless, FINRA rules require that a broker-dealer recommend only investments that are suitable for the customer and anti-fraud provisions of the securities laws protect investors as well. Those who favor the rule maintain that the rules will strengthen investor protection against conflicted investment advice. Opponents in the financial industry say that it would significantly raise regulatory and liability costs for brokers and force them to drop middle-income clients with modest investable assets.[56]

Regulation of Attorneys and Accountants by the SEC

Accountants play a vital role in financial reporting under the federal securities laws administered by the SEC. Sections 1, 12, 17, and 24 of the 1933 act and section 10(b) of the 1934 act are the sections under which accountants may be subject to liability.

An accountant who prepares any statement, opinion, or other legal paper filed with the SEC with the preparer's consent is deemed to be practicing before the SEC. Because it relies so heavily on accountants, the SEC has promulgated Rule 2(e), which regulates and provides the basis for discipline of accountants, attorneys, and consultants who practice before the SEC.[57] Under Rule 2(e), the SEC may suspend or disbar from practice before it those who are unqualified or unethical or who have violated federal securities laws or SEC rules.[58] SEC Rules also state that "[a]ny ... person who has been convicted of a felony or a misdemeanor involving moral turpitude shall be forthwith suspended from appearing or practicing before the Commission."[59]

---

[53] Investment advisors are regulated by the Investment Advisers Act of 1940 and are subject to the antifraud provisions of the Securities Act of 1933 and the Securities Exchange Act of 1934. Broker-dealers are regulated under both the Securities Act and the Exchange Act as well as by FINRA rules and state regulations.

[54] Investment Advisers Act of 1940, §206.

[55] Investment Advisers Act of 1940 §202(a)(11)(C).

[56] In 2015, the Department of Labor proposed a revision to its regulation that redefines what it means to be a fiduciary under the Employee Retirement Income Security Act (ERISA) and the Internal Revenue Code.

[57] 17 C.F.R. §201.2e.

[58] Rule 2(e) provides: "Suspension and disbarment. (1) The Commission may deny, temporarily or permanently, the privilege of appearing or practicing before it in any way to any person who is found by the Commission after notice of an opportunity for hearing in the matter (i) not to possess the requisite qualifications to represent others, or (ii) to be lacking in character or integrity or to have engaged in unethical or improper professional conduct, or (iii) to have willfully violated, or willfully aided and abetted, the violation of any provision of the federal securities laws (15 U.S.C. §§77a to 80B-20), or the rules and regulations thereunder." 17 C.F.R. §201.2e.

[59] 15 U.S.C. §78d-3, 17 C.F.R. §201.102(e)(2).

Section 307 of the Sarbanes-Oxley Act gave authority to the SEC to establish minimum standards of professional conduct for attorneys practicing before the SEC in the representation of publicly held companies. The act and SEC rules require that attorneys report evidence of material violations of securities laws, up the chain of command, to the companies' general counsel, CEO, audit committees, or the full board of directors. Lawyers can make a quiet withdrawal; that is, they do not have to go to the SEC, but they are under a professional obligation to not represent a client in an ongoing fraud on the market.

The ABA Model Rules of Professional Conduct, which serve as a basis for most states' ethics rules for lawyers, were revised to free lawyers from their duty of confidentiality to those clients who use the lawyers' advice to commit a crime or fraud.[60] The ABA also revised its Model Rules to allow a lawyer who knows that an officer or employee of a corporation will likely harm the company to refer the matter to higher-up officials of the organization.[61]

Regulation of Corporate Officers and Auditors

Provisions of the Dodd-Frank Act impacting executives and executive compensation give the SEC additional enforcement tools in the activities of officers and directors in preparing financial statements. These tools include clawback provisions that allow for the recoupment of executive compensation and bonuses based on financial performance when that performance turns out to be falsified.

Additional provisions of the Dodd-Frank Act impacting auditors' roles in developing financial information for release to the markets are covered in Chapter 47. In addition, the Litigation Reform Act amends the 1934 act by requiring auditors who discover illegal acts to notify management and the board of directors and, in some cases, to notify the SEC if the issuer does not.[62] Auditors are relieved from liability for any such disclosure to the SEC.

45-3 Industry Self-Regulation

The Financial Industry Regulatory Authority (FINRA) is the largest independent, not-for-profit regulator for all securities firms doing business in the United States. The National Association of Securities Dealers (NASD) and the New York Stock Exchange merged their member regulation functions into this one self-regulatory organization. FINRA is authorized by Congress to protect investors by ensuring that the securities industry is fair and honest. The agency writes and enforces rules for securities firms and brokers; monitors compliance with its rules; fosters market transparency; and educates investors. FINRA administers the largest dispute resolution forum for investors and registered firms.[63] Most agreements between investors and stockbrokers include mandatory arbitration agreements. It provides a BrokerCheck system, which allows investors to check out the professional and disciplinary backgrounds of firms and brokers online.[64] FINRA also refers fraud and insider trading cases to the SEC for investigation.

[60] Model Rule 1.6, "Confidentiality of Information."
[61] Model Rule 1.13, "Organization as Client."
[62] P.L. 104-671, 109 Stat. 763, 15 U.S.C. §78j-I nt.
[63] FINRA oversees some 629,640 registered securities representatives. In 2014, FINRA brought 1,397 disciplinary actions against registered brokers and firms; it imposed fines totaling $134 million and ordered restitution to harmed investors of $32.3 million. See **http://www.finra.org/ABOUTFINRA.**
[64] **http://www.finra.org/brokercheck.**

ETHICS & THE LAW

Problem: Conflicts of Interest—Remedy: Commonsense Rules

An investigation into Merrill Lynch by the New York Attorney General's Office revealed that while certain Merrill analysts were publicly recommending certain technology companies that were investment banking clients of the firm, internal e-mails indicated that these analysts believed the same companies were "crap" and "junk." One wrote to a colleague questioning his "positive" recommendation of a company whose numbers seemed weak to her, and his response to her was, he had written "pos," in place of [expletive deleted].

The public and retail clients believed that the firm's analysts were independent of the investment banking function of the firm and that the recommendations were made solely with retail clients' interests in mind. The New York Attorney General's Office concluded, however, that analysts and investment bankers were closely involved in each other's

work and were not independent; that the analyst department's compensation was tied to the results of the investment banking department's results; and that analysts were negotiating with investment banking clients for ratings.

The SEC has eliminated these problems with the following rules: (1) Investment banking divisions may not supervise firms' analysts, (2) compensation for analysts may not be linked to specific investment banking transactions, (3) analysts must disclose whether they own shares in a company they recommend and certify that their recommendations are their true opinions, (4) analysts appearing in public forums before the media must disclose whether they have an interest in the company being discussed, and (5) firms must make comprehensive disclosures about their rating systems and the firms they represent as investment banking clients.

45-3a Arbitration of Securities Disputes

Both NASD and securities firms with seats on the New York Stock Exchange have adopted codes of arbitration that allow customers and members to submit disputes to arbitration. The arbitration rights are contractual and are set forth in writing when opening an account with the securities firms. Investors who have agreed to arbitrate their securities disputes can be compelled to arbitrate, rather than sue, in courts. NASD and NYSE arbitrations are now administered by FINRA. Courts are very reluctant to vacate an arbitration award.

Make the Connection

Summary

State blue sky laws, which apply only to intrastate transactions, protect the public from the sale of fraudulent securities. The term *security* is defined sufficiently broadly to encompass not only stocks and bonds but also any conceivable type of corporate interest that has investment characteristics.

Two principal laws provide the basic framework for federal regulation of the sale of securities in interstate commerce. The Securities Act of 1933 deals with the issue or original distribution of securities by issuing corporations. The 1933 act requires registration of primary offering

securities unless they are exempt. There are a number of exemptions that have been expanded under the JOBS Act that allow smaller offerings and offerings to accredited investors to offer securities for sale without the costs of full registration. These offerings require disclosures and may have limits on distribution and resale but allow companies to raise capital more easily. Criminal and civil penalties exist for fraudulent statements made in the registration process.

The Securities Exchange Act of 1934 regulates the secondary distribution or sale of securities on exchanges.

These acts are administered by the Securities and Exchange Commission. The 1934 act provides reporting requirements for companies whose securities are listed on a national exchange and unlisted companies that have assets in excess of $10 million and 2,000 or more holders of record or 500 or more unaccredited shareholders. The JOBS Act has made it easier for smaller reporting companies and emerging growth companies to comply with registration and disclosure requirements.

Rule 10b-5 is the principal antifraud rule under the 1934 act. Trading on "inside information" is unlawful and may subject those involved to a civil penalty of three times the profit made on the improperly disclosed information.

Under 10b-5, there can be liability on the part of individuals and companies for withholding or misrepresenting material information about the company and its financial performance. Cash tender offers are regulated by the SEC under authority of the Williams Act.

The SEC and private regulatory organizations have a wide variety of tools that are used for enforcement including fines and penalties as well as sanctions that can prohibit practice before the SEC or employment by individuals in publicly traded companies or the securities industry. The securities industry provides arbitration procedures to resolve disputes between customers and firms.

Learning Outcomes

After studying this chapter, you should be able to clearly explain:

45-1   State Regulation

LO.1 Explain the meaning of state "blue sky laws"
See the discussion of the common-content features of state securities laws such as antifraud provisions, licensing provisions, and regulation of securities, page 928.

45-2   History of Federal Regulation and Market Trends

LO.2 Define "security"
See the *Edwards* case as an example of the broad definition of *security* sufficient to encompass virtually any instrument that might be sold as an investment, page 930.

LO.3 Compare and distinguish between the Securities Act of 1933 and the Securities Exchange Act of 1934
See the discussion regarding the regulation of the original issue of securities, pages 929–934.
See the discussion regarding the secondary distribution of securities designed to prevent fraudulent and manipulative practices on the securities exchanges, page 934.

LO.4 Explain the changes that the JOBS Act has had on registration exemptions
See the discussion on Regulation D, Rule 506, referring to private placement offerings and the change that the JOBS Act made regarding general solicitation of accredited investors, pages 932–933.
See the discussion on the SEC's proposed crowdfunding exemption, page 934.

LO.5 Explain how the 1934 act's policy of fostering reliance on market integrity is served by Rule 10b-5 private investor lawsuits when investors are injured by material misstatements by the issuer
See the *Basic Inc.* case on the fraud-on-the-market theory and "materiality" in merger cases, page 937.
See the *Matrixx* case on "materiality" in the pharmaceutical industry, pages 937–938.

LO.6 Explain the factors that subject an individual to liability for insider trading
See the *Dirks* case that illustrates the rule that when the insider does not breach a fiduciary duty, a tippee does not violate securities laws, pages 942–943.
See the *O'Hagan* case regarding outsiders who have access to confidential information that will affect a company's stock price, pages 943–944.

LO.7 Explain how the primary and secondary markets are regulated by the SEC as well as private enforcement organizations
See the discussion regarding false and misleading statements in the registration process of the 1933 act, page 934.
See the SEC's enforcement powers under Dodd-Frank including its powers to bring administrative proceedings against defendants, to reward whistleblowers, to regulate attorneys and accountants, and to regulate officers and accountants in the preparation of financial statements, pages 946–948.

45-3   Industry Self-Regulation
See the section on industry self-regulation and FINRA's role, page 948.

Key Terms

blue sky laws

cash tender offer

fraud-on-the-market

insider

insider information

primary offering

prospectus

registration requirements

registration statement

security

short-swing profit

temporary insider

tippee

Questions and Case Problems

1. Lawrence D. Polizzotto, a former vice president at First Solar Inc., spoke in one-on-one phone calls with some analysts and investors. He stated that the company was unlikely to receive a much-anticipated loan guarantee from the U.S. Department of Energy. The next morning, this information was disclosed in a press release. The stock price dropped 6 percent. Has Polizzotto violated any SEC rules or regulations? [*In the Matter of Lawrence D. Polizzotto*, Adm. Proc. File No. 3-15458 (September 6, 2013)]

2. Corporation A was involved in merger discussions with Corporation B. During this time, Corporation A made public statements denying that any merger negotiations were taking place or that it knew of any corporate developments that would account for heavy trading activity in its stock. A class of former shareholders who sold Corporation A stock after the public denial of merger activity and the announcement of the merger some six weeks later sued Corporation A, contending that it made material misrepresentations of fact in denying the merger activity. Corporation A stock increased 25 percent upon the merger announcement. Corporation A stated that at the time of its denial of merger activity it was just involved in preliminary negotiations and its actions were not material until negotiations reached an agreement in principle. Moreover, it asserted that the shareholders made no showing that they relied on the denial statement. Decide.

3. *Business Week* magazine is sent to a national distributor of magazines, Curtis Circulations Co., which sells the magazines to various wholesalers, including Hudson News. *Business Week* publishes a column entitled "Inside Wall Street," and the evidence shows that stocks discussed favorably in the column tend to increase in value after release to the public. *Business Week* has a strict confidentiality policy prior to release of the magazine to the public applicable to all employees involved in production and distribution. This policy also applies to Hudson News. Gregory

Savage, an employee of Hudson News, and the "top person" in the delivery room area, arranged to have the "Inside Wall Street" column faxed to his neighbor, a stockbroker named Larry Strath, prior to the close of the market on Thursday and prior to release to the public that evening. Strath traded on the information and passed it on to Joseph Falcone, who likewise traded on the basis of this information. While Falcone paid Strath $200 for a copy of the column each week, he contends that the information he received was too remote from the *Business Week* confidentiality policy to be actionable by the SEC. What theory do you believe the SEC pursued against Falcone? What are the elements of the theory? How would you decide this case? [*United States v. Falcone*, 257 F.3d 226 (2d Cir.)]

4. Minnesota Prostate Research Labs, Inc. (MPRL), made an initial public offering of its shares in August 1998. It stated in its prospectus that research on laboratory animals indicated that the lab may have discovered a cure for prostate cancer in humans. MPRL pointed out as well that results in animal testing did not necessarily mean that the same positive result would occur in humans. MPRL shares initially traded at $10 per share in 1999 and rose to $18 in August 2001, when the MPRL prostate cancer drug was finally approved for sale to the public. Tuttle reviewed the initial prospectus and analysts' reports on the drug and purchased 10,000 shares at $18 per share on August 18, 2001. In September 2002, an independent study of the four leading prostate medicines indicated that MPRL's product was as effective as sugar pills in curing prostate cancer and other prostate symptoms. The price of MPRL shares plummeted to $6 per share. Tuttle is contemplating a Rule 10b-5 securities fraud class-action lawsuit against MPRL. Advise him of his chances of success in this lawsuit and any expenses that he would be exposed to other than the cost of his attorney.

5. The following transactions in Heritage Cosmetics Co., Inc., stock took place: On January 21, Jones,

the corporation's vice president of marketing, purchased 1,000 shares of stock at $25 per share. On January 24, Sylvan, a local banker and director of Heritage, purchased 500 shares of stock at $26 per share. On January 30, McCarthy, a secretary at Heritage, purchased 300 shares of stock at $26.50. On February 12, Winfried, a rich investor from New England, purchased 25,000 shares at an average price of $26 per share. At that time, Heritage had a total of 200,000 shares of stock outstanding. On June 14, Winfried sold his entire holding in Heritage at an average price of $35 per share. In a local newspaper interview, Winfried was quoted regarding his reasons for selling the stock: "I have not had the pleasure of meeting any person from Heritage, but I have the highest regard for the Heritage Company, ... I sold my stock simply because the market has gone too high and in my view is due for a correction." After independently reading Winfried's prediction on the stock market, Jones, Sylvan, and McCarthy sold their shares on June 15 for $33 per share. On June 20, Heritage Co. demanded that Jones, Sylvan, McCarthy, and Winfried pay the corporation the profits made on the sale of the stock. Was the corporation correct in making such a demand on each of these people?

6. Dorozhko hacked into the corporate network of Thomson Financial on October 17, 2007, at 2:15 P.M. and gained access to IMS Health's soon-to-be-released negative earnings announcement due out at 5:00 P.M. He purchased $41,670 worth of put options. IMS shares were trading at $29.56 at the close on October 17. On October 18, 2007, IMS Health's stock price plunged at the opening of trading to $21.20 per share on the negative news issued at 5:00 P.M. on October 17. Within six minutes, Dorozhko sold the put options for a net profit of $286,456. Did Dorozhko's "hacking and trading" violate either the traditional or misappropriation theories of "insider trading"?

7. Mary Dale worked in the law office of Emory Stone, an attorney practicing securities law. While proofreading Mary's keying of a document relating to the merger of two computer software companies, Emory joked to her, "If I weren't so ethical, I could make a few bucks on this info. Nomac Software stock prices are going to take off when this news hits 'The Street.'" That evening, Mary told her friend Rick Needleworth, a stockbroker, what her boss had said. Needleworth bought 500 shares of Nomac Software stock the next day and sold it three days later when the news of the merger was made public. He made a profit of $3,500. Did Dale, Stone, or Needleworth violate any securities law(s) or ethical principles with respect to the profit made by Needleworth?

8. International Advertising, Inc. (IA), would like to raise $10 million in new capital to open new offices in Eastern Europe. It believes it could raise the capital by selling shares of stock to its directors and executive officers as well as to its bank and a large insurance company whose home office is located near IA's headquarters. Opposition to the financing plan exists because of the trouble, time, and cost involved with registering with the SEC. Advise IA how best to proceed with the registration of the new issue of stock.

9. Dubois sold Hocking a condominium that included an option to participate in a rental pool arrangement. Hocking elected to participate in the arrangement. Under it, the rental pool's agent rented condominiums, pooled the income, and after deducting a management fee, distributed the income to the owners on a pro rata basis. Hocking brought a Rule 10b-5 fraud action against Dubois. Dubois contended that the sale of the condominium was not a security under the securities acts so Hocking could not bring a securities suit against her. Was Dubois correct? [*Hocking v. Dubois*, 839 F.2d 290 (9th Cir.)]

10. William Rubin, president of Tri-State Mining Co., sought a loan from Bankers Trust Co. To secure the loan, he pledged worthless stock in six companies and represented that the stock was worth $1.7 million. He also arranged for fictitious quotations to appear in an investment reporting service used by the bank to value the pledged securities. The bank loaned Rubin $475,000 and took the securities as pledged collateral. In a criminal action against Rubin under section 17(a) of the 1933 act, Rubin's defense was that the pledging of securities did not constitute an offer or sale of securities under the act. Was Rubin correct? [*Rubin v. United States*, 449 U.S. 424]

11. J. C. Cowdin, a director of Curtis-Wright Co., phoned Robert Gintel, a partner of Cady, Roberts & Co., a stock brokerage house, and advised him that Curtis-Wright's quarterly dividend had been cut. Gintel immediately entered orders selling Curtis-Wright shares for his customers' accounts. The stock was selling at over $40 a share when the orders were executed but fell to $30 soon after the dividend cut was announced to the public. The SEC contended that the firm, Cady, Roberts & Co., and Gintel

violated section 10(b) of the 1934 act, Rule 10b-5, and section 17(a) of the 1933 act. Gintel and Cady, Roberts & Co. disagreed. Decide. [In re *Cady, Roberts & Co.*, 40 SEC 907]

12. In a January 2000 prospectus for its initial public offering of shares, Apex Oil Discovery Co. (AODC) estimated a sizable volume of oil production based on the studies of two geologists and a test well at one of its Oklahoma properties. A cautionary statement advised that the projections were only estimates based on the opinion of the two experts and a test well, and that actual production could vary significantly. Lutz bought 10,000 shares of Apex in May 2000 for $20 per share. By October 2000, 12 of its 15 drilling operations under way that year turned out to be dry holes. On October 18, 2000, AODC stock fell to $6 per share. Lutz brought a private securities civil action under SEC Rule 10b-5 against AODC, alleging that the AODC oil production estimates that induced him to buy the stock were fraudulent as evidenced by the 80 percent failure rate of its drilling operations. What defense, if any, does AODC have in this case? Decide.

13. Douglas Hansen, Leo Borrell, and Bobby Lawrence were three psychiatrists who recognized the need for an inpatient treatment facility for adolescents and children in their community. They became limited partners in building a for-profit psychiatric facility. Each had a 6.25 percent interest in the partnership. Healthcare International, Inc., the general partner with a 75 percent interest, had expertise in hospital construction, management, and operation. Hansen, Borrell, and Lawrence asserted that the managerial control of the partnership was undertaken and operated by the general partner to the exclusion of the limited partners. The doctors claimed that their interest was a security—"an investment contract"— that gave them status to file a securities suit against the general partner under the 1934 act. The general partner disagreed. Decide. [*L & B Hospital Ventures, Inc. v. Health-care International, Inc.*, 894 F.2d 150 (5th Cir.)]

14. Texas International Speedway, Inc. (TIS), filed a registration statement and prospectus with the Securities and Exchange Commission offering a total of $4,398,900 in securities to the public. The proceeds of the sale were to be used to finance the construction of an automobile speedway. The entire issue was sold on the offering date. TIS did not meet with success, and the corporation filed a petition for bankruptcy. Huddleston and Bradley instituted a class-action suit in U.S. district court on behalf of themselves and other purchasers of TIS securities. Their complaint alleged violations of section 10(b) of the 1934 act. The plaintiffs sued most of the participants in the offering, including the accounting firm of Herman & MacLean. Herman & MacLean had issued an opinion concerning certain financial statements and a pro forma balance sheet that were contained in the registration statement and prospectus. The plaintiffs claimed that the defendants had engaged in a fraudulent scheme to misrepresent or conceal material facts regarding the financial condition of TIS, including the costs incurred in building the speedway. Herman & MacLean contended that the case should be dismissed because section 11 of the 1933 act provides an express remedy for a misrepresentation in a registration statement, so an action under section 10(b) of the 1934 act is precluded. Decide. [*Herman & MacLean v. Huddleston*, 459 U.S. 375]

15. Melvin J. Ford, president of International Loan Network, Inc. (ILN), promoted ILN's financial enrichment programs to ILN members and prospective members with evangelical fervor at revival-style "President's Night" gatherings. His basic philosophy was this:

> The movement of money creates wealth. What we believe is that if you organize people and get money moving, it can actually create wealth.

One ILN program was the Maximum Consideration Program, which, somewhat like a chain letter, provided $5,000 awards to members who sold $3,000 worth of new memberships called PRAs and made a deposit on the purchases of nonresidential real estate. According to Ford, an individual purchasing $16,000 worth of PRAs could receive an award of up to $80,000 because "all of a sudden the velocity of money increases to such a point, the ability to create wealth expands to such a degree, that we could come back and give somebody an award for up to $80,000." The SEC contended that ILN was selling unregistered investment contracts in violation of the 1933 act. ILN disagreed, contending that the program never guaranteed a return and was thus not an investment contract. Decide. Could ILN have provided full disclosure to investors concerning the program in a prospectus if required by the 1933 act? [*SEC v. ILN, Inc.*, 968 F.2d 1304 (D.C. Cir.)]

Management of Corporations

Learning Outcomes ⟨⟨⟨

After studying this chapter, you should be able to

LO.1 Explain how shareholders, as owners of the corporation, exercise limited control over management by voting at shareholders' meetings to elect directors

LO.2 Explain the qualifications and powers of directors

LO.3 Explain the liability of directors and the meaning of the business judgment rule (BJR)

LO.4 Explain the obligation of officers—who have access to corporate information and agency powers—to not violate their fiduciary duties to the corporation

LO.5 Explain the rationale for the "say-on-pay" provision of the Dodd-Frank Act

LO.6 Explain how directors, officers, and the corporation itself may be criminally liable for regulatory offenses

47-1 Shareholders

A corporation is managed, directly or indirectly, by its shareholders, board of directors, and officers.[1] As owners, the shareholders have the right to control the corporation.

47-1a Extent of Management Control by Shareholders

As a practical matter, control of the shareholders is generally limited to voting at shareholders' meetings to elect directors. In this sense, shareholders indirectly determine the management policies of the business. At shareholders' meetings, shareholders may also vote to amend bylaws, approve shareholder resolutions, or vote on so-called extraordinary corporate matters. *Extraordinary matters* include the sale of corporate assets outside the regular course of the corporation's business or the merger or dissolution of the corporation.

47-1b Meetings of Shareholders

To have legal effect, action by the shareholders must ordinarily be taken at a regular or special meeting.

Regular Meetings

The time and place of regular or stated meetings are usually prescribed by the articles of incorporation or the bylaws. Notice to shareholders of such meetings is ordinarily not required, but it is usually given as a matter of good business practice. Some statutes require that notice of all meetings be given.

Special Meetings

Generally, notice must be given specifying the subject matter of special meetings. Unless otherwise prescribed, special meetings are called by the directors. It is sometimes provided that a special meeting may be called by a certain percentage of shareholders.[2] Notice of the day, hour, and place of a special meeting must be given to all shareholders. The notice must include a statement of the nature of the business to be transacted, and no other business may be transacted at this meeting.

Quorum

quorum—minimum number of persons, shares represented, or directors who must be present at a meeting in order to lawfully transact business.

A valid meeting requires the presence of a quorum of the voting shareholders. A **quorum** is the minimum number of persons (shareholders or persons authorized to vote a stated proportion of the voting stock) required to transact business. If a quorum is present, a majority of those present may act on any matter unless there is an express requirement of a higher affirmative vote.

When a meeting opens with a quorum, the quorum is generally not broken if shareholders leave the meeting and those remaining are not sufficient to constitute a quorum.

[1] State corporate codes as well as federal laws such as the Securities Act of 1933 and the Securities Exchange Act of 1934, as amended by the Sarbanes Oxley Act of 2002 and the Dodd-Frank Act of 2010, impact the management of corporations. Articles of incorporation and corporate bylaws also impact corporate management. Chapter 43, Corporation Formation, and Chapter 45, Securities Regulation, provide background on these issues.
[2] N.Y. Bus. Corp. Law §603.

47-1c **Action without Meeting**

A number of statutes provide for corporate action by shareholders without holding a meeting. The Revised Model Business Corporation Act (RMBCA) provides that "action required or permitted by this Act to be taken at a shareholders' meeting may be taken without a meeting if the action is taken by all shareholders entitled to vote on the action."[3] The action must be evidenced by a written consent describing the action taken, signed by all shareholders entitled to vote on the action, and delivered to the corporation for inclusion in the minutes.

47-2 Directors

A state's corporate law or the articles of incorporation delegate powers to the board of directors. The board has oversight responsibility for a company's business affairs, including (1) approving strategic plans, (2) reviewing operating and financial results, (3) approving SEC filings, (4) approving the hiring of executives, (5) evaluating management's performance and approving executive compensation packages, (6) appointing and meeting with auditors, and (7) evaluating and acting on extraordinary matters, such as the merger, acquisition, or sale of the business.

Most states now permit the number of directors to be fixed by the bylaws. Many specify that the board of directors shall consist of not less than three directors; a few authorize one or more.[4] Professional corporation legislation often authorizes or is interpreted as authorizing a one- or two-person board of directors.

47-2a **Qualifications**

Eligibility for membership on a board of directors is determined by statute, articles of incorporation, or bylaws.[5] In the absence of a contrary provision, any person (including a nonresident, a minor, or a person who is not a shareholder) is eligible for membership. Bylaws may require that a director own stock in the corporation although this requirement is not ordinarily imposed.

CPA   ### 47-2b **Powers of Directors**

The board of directors has authority to manage the corporation. Courts will not interfere with the board's discretion in the absence of (1) illegal conduct or (2) fraud harming the rights of creditors, shareholders, or the corporation.

The board of directors may enter into any contract or transaction necessary to carry out the business for which the corporation was formed. The board may appoint officers and other agents to act for the company, or it may appoint several of its own members as an executive committee to act for the board between board meetings. (See Figure 47-1.) Broad delegation of authority, however, may involve the risk of being treated as an unlawful abdication of the board's management power.

---

[3] RMBCA §7.04(a).
[4] Del. Code §141(b). See also RMBCA §8.03.
[5] In family-owned businesses, shareholder agreements are often utilized to impose restrictions on the voting of shares and eligibility standards for membership on the board of directors to maintain continuity of management, ownership, and control of a corporation. See *Miniat v. EMI*, 315 F.3d 712 (7th Cir. 2002).

CASE SUMMARY

The Case of Medoff, the Marathon Man

FACTS: The Boston Athletic Association (BAA) is a non-profit corporation created to sponsor the annual Boston Marathon. The BAA authorized its president, William Cloney, to negotiate contracts for it. Cloney executed a contract with attorney Marshall Medoff, giving Medoff exclusive power to promote the marathon. The BAA transferred to Medoff all rights to use the marathon name and logos. The contract's financial terms were extremely favorable to Medoff, who could renew the contract from year to year. When the BAA's board members learned of the contract, they declared that it was beyond the authorization vested in Cloney. The board brought an action to have the contract set aside. Medoff contended that Cloney had authority to make the contract and that therefore the contract bound the corporation.

DECISION: Judgment for the BAA. It is the obligation of the board to direct the corporation. Consistent with this obligation, a board may delegate general managerial functions to corporate officers, but certain powers cannot be delegated. The contract made with Medoff surrendered virtually complete control of the marathon to Medoff. The board in this case improperly delegated to Cloney the authority to make such a contract, which prevented accomplishment of the BAA's corporate purpose, that of sponsoring the marathon. Authority to make such a contract was beyond the power of the board to delegate. [*Boston Athletic Association v. International Marathon, Inc.*, **467 N.E.2d 58 (Mass. 1984)**]

FIGURE 47-1   Powers of Directors

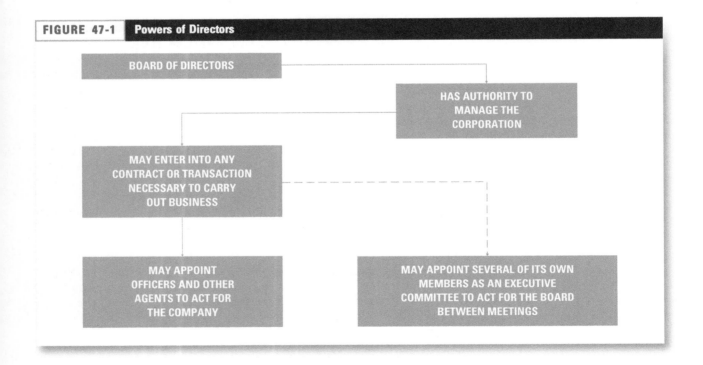

BOARD OF DIRECTORS

HAS AUTHORITY TO MANAGE THE CORPORATION

MAY ENTER INTO ANY CONTRACT OR TRANSACTION NECESSARY TO CARRY OUT BUSINESS

MAY APPOINT OFFICERS AND OTHER AGENTS TO ACT FOR THE COMPANY

MAY APPOINT SEVERAL OF ITS OWN MEMBERS AS AN EXECUTIVE COMMITTEE TO ACT FOR THE BOARD BETWEEN MEETINGS

CPA   47-2c ## Conflict of Interest

A director is disqualified from taking part in corporate action involving a matter in which the director has an undisclosed conflicting interest. The corporation generally may avoid any transaction because of a director's undisclosed conflict of interest.

A number of states provide by statute that a director's conflict of interest does not impair the transaction or contract entered into or authorized by the board of directors if the disqualified director disclosed the interest and if the contract or transaction is fair and reasonable with respect to the corporation. Thus, a director may lend money to a corporation if the board of directors is informed of the transaction and the terms approximate the market rate for businesses with similar credit ratings. Some states simply require notice of the conflicting interests and abstaining from all participation in the transaction. **For Example,** Delos Yancey, Jr., and Delos Yancey III were directors of State Mutual Insurance Co. Subsequently, they formed North American Services, Inc., and served as directors of both companies. State Mutual decided to sell one of its companies, Atlas Life Insurance, Inc. North American expressed an interest in purchasing Atlas, and thereafter the Yanceys recused themselves from State Mutual's decision-making process in selling the company. State Mutual sold Atlas to North American at a $5.2 million loss. Some two years later, North American resold Atlas for a $22.6 million gain, and a shareholder derivative suit was brought against the Yanceys. The court decided the case in favor of the Yanceys, holding that they complied with the state's "safe harbor" law by giving notice of their conflicting interest to State Mutual and thereafter abstaining from all participation in the corporate transaction.[6]

To prevent conflicts of interest and covert compensation schemes, section 402(a) of the federal Sarbanes-Oxley Act[7] prohibits all loans either directly or indirectly to directors and executive officers by their corporations. The act makes an exception for companies in the consumer credit business, which may make loans to directors and officers on terms no more favorable than those offered to the general public.

Prior to Sarbanes-Oxley, it was a common practice for publicly traded companies to provide low-interest loans to company officers. **For Example,** Bernard Ebbers, while CEO of WorldCom, Inc., used company stock as collateral for bank loans to buy additional shares of WorldCom stock. When WorldCom's share prices weakened in late 2000 and Ebbers needed to put up additional collateral to cover his loans, WorldCom's board of directors agreed to lend him more than $400 million at just over 2 percent interest with no fixed due date. The company rate was far below the personal loan rate at banks near company headquarters of between 9.75 percent and 16.67 percent and well below margin loan rates at 5 percent. Another scandal involved business conglomerate Tyco International Ltd. Tyco maintained a "key employee loan fund" that was used like a revolving line of credit by Tyco executives Dennis Kozlowski and Martin Swartz to fund their lavish lifestyles. Sarbanes-Oxley responded to these abuses with language that is broad and far-reaching, prohibiting all direct personal loans by public companies, such as relocation loans, tax loans, and loans to purchase securities.

47-2d Meetings of Directors

Action by directors is ordinarily taken at a meeting of the board of directors. Bylaws sometimes require the meeting to be held at a particular place. Generally, a director is not allowed to vote by proxy. Most states permit action to be taken by the board of directors without holding an actual meeting. A meeting may be required, however, if the action requires a writing signed by all directors.

47-2e Liability of Directors

In dealing with the corporation, the directors act in a fiduciary capacity. It is into their care that the stockholders have entrusted the control of the corporate property and the management of the business.

[6] *Fisher v. State Mutual Insurance Co.,* 290 F.3d 1256 (11th Cir. 2002).
[7] P.L. 107-204, 116 Stat. 745.

CPA   **The Business Judgment Rule**

Courts recognize that the decisions of corporate directors often involve weighing and balancing legal, ethical, commercial, promotional, public relations, and other factors. Accordingly, courts will not sit in judgment or second guess the wisdom of decisions made by directors. If the directors have acted in good faith on the basis of adequate information, courts will not enjoin the course of action taken by the directors.[8] Moreover, if directors' decisions cause loss to the corporation, the directors will not be held personally liable for it. This principle is called the **business judgment rule (BJR).** It is one of the most important protections against personal liability for officers and directors.

business judgment rule (BJR)–rule that allows management immunity from liability for corporate acts where there is a reasonable indication that the acts were made in good faith with due care.

CPA   **The Traditional Rule.** Courts apply the business judgment rule as a presumption that in making a business decision, the directors acted (1) on an informed basis, (2) in good faith, and (3) in the honest belief that the action taken was in the best interest of the corporation. The party challenging the directors' actions has the burden of proving that the director did not act on an informed basis or in good faith or in the best interest of the corporation.[9] (See the *Disney* case.)

CASE SUMMARY

Problem: "A Mismatch of Cultures and Styles"
Solution: $140 Million Severance Payment
Shareholders: Not Happy!

FACTS: In 1995, Michael Ovitz was a founder of Creative Artists Agency (CAA), an agency with 1,400 of Hollywood's top actors, directors, writers, and musicians. Ovitz was considered one of the most powerful figures in Hollywood at that time. Because of the untimely death of Disney's prior president in a helicopter crash, Walt Disney Co. CEO Michael Eisner focused on hiring Ovitz as president. The chairman of Disney's compensation committee, Irwin Russell, in consultation with Eisner, negotiated the Ovitz employment agreement (OEA). As part of the OEA, if Disney fired Ovitz for any reason other than gross negligence or malfeasance, Ovitz would be entitled to a nonfault termination (NFT) package consisting of his remaining salary for the five-year period, bonuses, and the immediate vesting of stock options. Russell met with a compensation expert for advice on the contract and had telephone conversations with two compensation committee members, Sidney Poitier and Ignatio Lozano. CEO Eisner telephoned each member of the board of directors to inform them of his plan to hire Ovitz. On September 26, 1995, the Compensation Committee had a one-hour meeting to discuss several topics, including the OEA. Thereafter, the full board of directors met and elected Ovitz president of Disney. After he joined Disney, it soon became apparent that a "mismatch of cultures and styles" ensued and that Ovitz was not succeeding as president. The trial provided the following example:

> *In January 1996, a corporate retreat was held at Walt Disney World in Orlando, Florida. At that retreat, Ovitz failed to integrate himself in the group of executives by declining to participate in group activities, insisting on a limousine, when the other executives, including Eisner, were taking a bus, and making inappropriate demands of the park employees. In short, Ovitz "was a little elitist for the egalitarian Walt Disney World cast members [employees]," and a poor fit with his fellow executives.*

When it became clear that Ovitz was not working out, Eisner considered his options. Sanford Litvak, Disney's general counsel, advised Eisner and other directors that Ovitz had not been shown to have been grossly negligent or malfeasant

---

[8] In discharging their duties, directors are not individually liable if, acting in good faith, they rely upon "the opinion of counsel for the corporation" or "written reports setting forth financial data concerning the corporation and prepared by an independent public accountant or certified public accountant or firm of such accountants"—which opinions or statements turn out to be flawed. *Casey v. Brennan*, 344 N.J. Super. 83 (2002).

[9] *Huang Group v. LTI*, 760 N.E.2d 14 (Ohio App. 2002).

Problem: "A Mismatch of Cultures and Styles" continued

in his year at Disney, and no cause existed to avoid the NFT payments. Eisner decided it was necessary to terminate Ovitz on a nonfault basis and notified the board members. The board members supported this decision under the nonfault termination agreement. Ovitz was ultimately paid $140 million in severance pay. Stockholders brought a derivative suit, asserting that Eisner and the board of directors had breached their fiduciary duties in connection with Ovitz's hiring and termination. Years of litigation cumulated in a 37-day trial that ended on January 19, 2005.

DECISION: Judgment for the defendants. Eisner's actions should not serve as a model for directors and CEOs. By virtue of his imperial nature as CEO, he handicapped the board's decision-making abilities, stacking the board with his friends who, although not necessarily beholden to him in a legal sense, were more willing to support him unconditionally than truly independent directors. He failed to keep the board informed as he should have and failed to better involve the board in the process of hiring Ovitz, usurping the role for himself. Nevertheless, Eisner did not violate the law. Despite the legitimate criticisms leveled at Eisner, especially at having enthroned himself as the omnipotent and infallible monarch of his personal Magic Kingdom, Eisner's actions were taken in good faith and did not breach his fiduciary duty of care because he was not grossly negligent, nor was any other director in violation of a fiduciary duty. The redress for failures that arise from faithful management (not in violation of fiduciary duties) must come from the markets, not the courts. Corporate decisions are made, risks are taken, the results become apparent, capital flows accordingly, and shareholder value increases or decreases. [**In re** *Walt Disney Co. Derivative Litigation,* **907 A.2d 693 (Del. Ch. 2005)**]

CPA   **Application in Corporate Control Transactions.** When a corporation receives a takeover bid, the target board of directors may tend to take actions that favor the board's interests over the interests of shareholders. Courts have recognized the potential for director self-interest in this situation. (See the *Van Gorkom* case.)

CASE SUMMARY

Directors—Independent Evaluators, Not Pawns

FACTS: Jerome Van Gorkom was chairman and chief executive officer of Trans Union Inc. On September 13, Van Gorkom arranged a meeting with Jay Pritzker, a well-known takeover specialist and a social acquaintance, to determine his interest in acquiring Trans Union. On Thursday, September 18, Pritzker made an offer of $55 per share (a price suggested by Van Gorkom). Pritzker wanted a decision to be made by the board no later than Sunday, September 21. On Friday, Van Gorkom called a special meeting of the board of directors for noon the following day; no agenda was announced. At the directors' meeting, Van Gorkom made a 20-minute oral analysis of the merger transaction. He showed that the company was having difficulty generating sufficient income to offset its increasingly large investment tax credits. Van Gorkom discussed his meeting with Pritzker and the reasons for the meeting. Copies of the proposed merger agreement were delivered too late to be studied before or during the meeting. No consultants or investment advisors were called on to support the merger price of $55 per share. The merger was approved at the end of the two-hour meeting. Certain shareholders brought a class-action suit against the directors, contending that the board's decision was not the product of informed business judgment. The directors responded that their good-faith decision was shielded by the business judgment rule.

DECISION: Judgment for the shareholders. Directors cannot claim the protection of the business judgment rule if they have been grossly negligent in exercising their judgment. The directors approved the merger based on a 20-minute oral analysis by the president, Van Gorkom, at a hastily called board meeting with no prior notice of its purpose. No investment consultants or other experts were employed to assess the intrinsic value of the company, nor were the merger documents containing the terms of the merger available for study by the directors. Deciding to sell the company without any information and deliberation was gross negligence. The directors therefore could not claim the protection of the business judgment rule when they voted to "sell" the company for $55 per share. The directors are personally liable for damages. [*Smith v. Van Gorkom,* **488 A.2d 858 (Del. 1985)**]

Protection of Directors. In the wake of court decisions holding directors personally liable for damages for gross negligence and in the wake of the resulting general reluctance of individuals to serve as directors, states have passed statutes to protect directors. The aim of the various state laws is essentially the same: to reduce the risk of personal liability for directors who act in good faith when their decisions are challenged. The laws permit a corporation, by a stockholder-approved amendment to its charter or certificate of incorporation, to protect its directors from monetary liability for duty-of-care violations (gross negligence) provided they have not acted in bad faith, breached their duty of loyalty, or gained an improper personal benefit.[10] The laws provide for indemnification and advancement of expenses. **For Example,** the certificate of incorporation of Jennifer Convertibles, Inc., a Delaware corporation, includes an exculpatory clause that protects directors from liability for breach of fiduciary duty except in cases of breach of duty of loyalty, bad faith, knowing violation of the law, or improper personal benefit. Delaware's General Corporate Law, section 102(b)(7), states that a corporation may include an exculpation clause in its certificate of incorporation.[11] Statutes intended to protect directors from liability have raised questions about whether the business judgment rule applies to officers. Although most courts recognize that the business judgment rule applies to both directors and officers,[12] several courts have held that the rule applies only to independent directors, not to officers if the state statute refers only to directors.[13]

Actions against Directors

Actions against directors should be brought by the corporation. If the corporation fails to act, as is the case when the directors alleged to be liable control the corporation, shareholders may bring the action in a representative capacity for the corporation.[14] **For Example,** Risa Weinberger, a shareholder, became concerned that the president and majority shareholder of American Composting Inc., James Willits, was using corporate funds for his own personal benefit. Corporate bank statements showed payments to his ex-wife of $283,068.48, payments to the law firm that represented him in his divorce of $145,789, and a "loans to shareholders" balance that increased from $21,075 in 2004 to $444,642 by September 2011. The court determined that Ms. Weinberger could pursue the shareholder derivative suit on behalf of American Composting Inc. because Willets controlled the board of directors and a demand on the board would be futile.[15]

Removal of Director

Ordinarily, directors are removed by vote of the shareholders. In some states, the board of directors may remove a director and elect a successor on the ground that the removed director (1) did not accept office, (2) failed to satisfy the qualifications for office, (3) was continually absent from the state without a leave of absence granted by the board, generally for a period of six months or more, (4) was discharged in bankruptcy, (5) was

---

[10] See Del. Code §102(b)(7); N.Y. Bus. Corp. Law §§721–723; Ohio Gen. Corp. Law §1701.59; Ind. Bus. Corp. Law, ch. 35, §1(e); Mo. Gen. Bus. Corp. Law 351.355 §§2, 7.

[11] In *KDW Restructuring & Liquidation Services LLC v. Greenfield*, 2012 WL 2125986 (S.D.N.Y. June 12, 2012), the court found that there were sufficient facts in the complaint against Harley Greenfield, Jennifer's CEO, to support claims for breach of duty of loyalty and breach of the duty to act in good faith regarding a 2009 transaction causing a net loss of $11 million at the end of the 2009 fiscal year.

[12] See, for example, *FDIC v. Loudermilk, et al.*, 761 S.E.2d 332 (Ga. 2014).

[13] Several decisions by federal district courts in California ruled that the business judgment rule applies only to independent directors, under California law. These cases involved suits by the Federal Deposit Insurance Corporation against officers at failed banks. The FDIC sued the officers for negligence in generating and acquiring risky residential loans. See, for example, *FDIC v. Perry*, 2012 WL 589569 (C.D. Cal. 2012); *FDIC v. Faigin*, 2013 WL 3389490 (C.D. Cal. 2013).

[14] In re *Abbott Laboratories Derivative Shareholder Litigation*, 325 F.3d 795 (7th Cir. 2003).

[15] *Weinberger v. American Composting, Inc.*, 2012 WL 1190970 (E.D. Ark. Apr. 9, 2012).

convicted of a felony, (6) was unable to perform the duties of director because of any illness or disability, generally for a period of six months or more, or (7) had been judicially declared of unsound mind.[16]

The RMBCA provides for removal of directors "with or without cause" by a majority vote of the shareholders unless the articles of incorporation provide that directors may be removed only for cause.[17] **For Example,** former Conseco, Inc., director Dennis Murray, Sr., was unsuccessful in his action against the board of directors in challenging his removal from the board. The court held that the directors had unlimited authority to remove a fellow director without regard for the reasons why the other directors wished to remove him.[18] Directors may always be voted out of office at a regular meeting of shareholders held for the election of directors.

47-3   Officers, Agents, and Employees

Corporations generally have a president, at least one vice president, a secretary, a treasurer, and, frequently, a chief executive officer (CEO). The duties of these officers are generally set forth in the corporation's bylaws. The duty of the secretary to keep minutes of the proceedings of shareholders and directors is commonly included. Corporation codes generally expressly permit the same person to be both secretary and treasurer. In large corporations, there is often a recording secretary and a corresponding secretary.

Sometimes the officers are elected by the shareholders, but usually they are appointed by the board of directors. The RMBCA follows the general pattern of providing for the appointment of officers by the board of directors.[19] Ordinarily, no particular formality is required to make such appointments. Unless prohibited, a director may hold an executive office.

Officers ordinarily hire the employees and agents of the corporation.

47-3a Powers of Officers

The officers of a corporation are its agents. Consequently, their powers are controlled by the laws of agency.[20] As in the case of any other agency, a third person has the burden of proving that a particular officer had the authority he or she purported to have.

The fact that the officer or employee acting on behalf of the corporation is a major shareholder does not give either any greater agency powers. Moreover, the person dealing with the officer or employee is charged with knowledge of any limitation on authority contained in the recorded corporate charter or articles of incorporation.

When the nature of the transaction is unusual, that unusual nature should alert a third person to the necessity of specific authorization from the corporation.

President

It is sometimes held that, in the absence of some limitation on authority, the president of a corporation has by virtue of that office the authority to act as agent on behalf of the corporation within the scope of the business in which the corporation is empowered to engage. It has also been held, however, that the president has such broad powers only when the president is the general manager of the corporation. In instances in which a corporation has a president and a chief executive officer, the CEO has authority to exercise personal

---

[16] See California Corp Code §807, recognizing grounds (1), (2), (5), and (7).
[17] RMBCA §8.08(a).
[18] *Murray v. Conseco, Inc.*, 766 N.E.2d 38 (Ind. App. 2002).
[19] RMBCA §8.40(a).
[20] *Credit Corp. v. Nuova Pasta Co.*, 815 F. Supp. 268 (N.D. Ill. 1993).

judgment and discretion in the administrative and executive functions of the corporation as endowed by its bylaws and the resolutions of the board of directors. When a corporation has both a CEO and a president, the CEO is ordinarily the officer entrusted with the broader decisional powers, whereas the president is the executing officer. The president does not have authority by virtue of his office to make a contract that would require action by the board of directors or shareholders due to its unusual character.[21]

The president cannot make a contract to fix long-term or unusual contracts of employment, release a claim of the corporation, promise that the corporation will later repurchase shares issued to a subscriber, or mortgage a corporate property.[22]

It is ordinarily held that the president of a business corporation is not authorized to execute commercial paper in the name of the corporation. However, the president may do so when authorized by the board of directors to borrow money for the corporation.

Other Officers and Employees

The authority of corporate employees and other officers, such as the secretary or treasurer, is generally limited to the duties of their office. However, the authority may be extended by the conduct of the corporation in accordance with the general principles governing apparent authority based on the conduct of the principal. An unauthorized act may, of course, be ratified. The authority of the general manager of the corporation is determined by principles of ordinary agency law.

47-3b Liability Relating to Fiduciary Duties

The relationship of officers to the corporation, like that of directors, is a fiduciary one. Officers, because of their access to corporate information developed in the pursuit of their daily duties on behalf of the corporation, have an obligation to inform the directors of material information relating to the business. Officers have an obligation not to make any secret financial gain at the expense of the corporation. Because of their level of knowledge of the business, officer-directors have a high fiduciary duty to the corporation.

Corporate Opportunities

If an officer diverts a corporate opportunity, the corporation may recover from the officer the profits of which the corporation has been deprived.

CASE SUMMARY

Ruling Wisely and Decently?

FACTS: Demoulas Super Markets, Inc. (DSM), was owned by brothers George and Telemachus Demoulas, each owning an equal number of shares of stock. From 1964 through May 1971, the company grew from 5 stores to a chain of 14 supermarkets, including 2 stores in New Hampshire. George died suddenly on June 27, 1971, and, at his death, Telemachus assumed control of DSM under the terms of a voting trust. In 1990, George's son Arthur, age 22 and a shareholder of DSM, brought a shareholder derivative action on behalf of DSM, contending that since George's death, Telemachus had diverted business opportunities away from DSM into other businesses that were solely owned by Telemachus's branch of the family. The evidence showed that in the 1970s two new corporations were formed that operated

---

[21] *French v. Chosin Few, Inc.*, 173 F. Supp. 2d 451 (W.D.N.C. 2001).
[22] *Schmidt v. Farm Credit Services*, 977 F.2d 511 (10th Cir. 1992).

Ruling Wisely and Decently? continued

supermarkets in New Hampshire; DSM supplied the financing and management, but ownership was held in the name of Telemachus's sister and daughter. By 1986, these stores grew into a single supermarket chain operating under the Market Basket name and entirely owned by members of Telemachus's branch of the family. The trial court judge determined that Telemachus had diverted these corporate opportunities from DSM, and the court ordered the transfer of the assets and liabilities of the new corporations back to DSM. In her decision, the judge cited lines from *Ulysses*, by Alfred Lord Tennyson, in which Ulysses speaks lovingly of his son, Telemachus, expressing the belief that he would rule wisely and decently after his death. Telemachus denied that any acts were improper or gave rise to liability and charged that the judge was not impartial, as evidenced by her quotation from Tennyson's poem.

DECISION: Judgment against Telemachus. Judicial bias was not present, and the literary reference was simply the judge's stylistic way of stating the theme of her decision against Telemachus, based on the facts she had found. Telemachus had a fiduciary duty to DSM. A fiduciary violates his duty of loyalty by advancing the pecuniary interests of a child or a sibling in a manner that would constitute a breach if he had acted for himself. The record is clear that the New Hampshire companies were set up under Telemachus's direction and were independent in name only, with DSM managing and financing them. The return to DSM of the assets and liabilities of the diverted business was the proper remedy. **[*Demoulas v. Demoulas Super Markets, Inc.*, 677 N.E.2d 159 (Mass. 1997); see also 787 N.E.2d 1059 (Mass. 2003)]**

An opportunity that would be advantageous to the corporation must first be offered to the corporation before an officer or a director, who owes a fiduciary duty to the corporation, can take advantage of the opportunity. Full disclosure is required. Only if the opportunity is rejected by a majority of disinterested directors may the officer then take advantage of the opportunity. **For Example,** Nancy Harris was president of the Northeast Harbor Golf Club, Inc. In her capacity as club president, she learned of an opportunity to purchase the Gilpin property, which adjoined the golf club. Her private purchase of the property constituted the taking of a corporate opportunity and resulted in her liability to the club. Harris believed that her purchase, in a separate transaction, of the Smallidge land, which was adjacent to three of the golf club's holes and could be developed, was not usurpation of a corporate opportunity because she learned of the availability independently of the club. However, this also was a corporate opportunity because it was so closely related to the club's business. She was obligated to disclose the opportunity to the corporation and let it decide whether to pursue it.[23]

Officers may avail themselves of all opportunities lying outside the field of their duties as officers when business opportunities come to them in an individual capacity.[24]

Secret Profits

Officers are liable to the corporation for secret profits made in connection with, or at the expense of, the business of the corporation.

Duty of Loyalty

A corporate officer, while still employed by his or her firm, may be in breach of the officer's fiduciary duty of loyalty by recruiting key management employees to join a competing company. However, an officer may legally make arrangements before leaving the firm to compete in the future. The line separating mere preparation from active competition may be difficult to discern and, if misjudged, may lead to significant liability for the officer and a competitor aider and abettor, as is evidenced by the *Security Title v. Pope* case.

[23] *Northeast Harbor Golf Club v. Harris*, 725 A.2d 1018 (Me. 1999); see *Anderson v. Bellino*, 658 N.W.2d 645 (Neb. 2003).
[24] *Hill v. Southeastern Floor Covering Co.*, 596 So. 2d 874 (Miss. 1992).

CASE SUMMARY

Walkin' with Linda Pope

FACTS: Linda Pope ran one of the largest and most successful title insurance branches in the title insurance industry for Security Title Insurance. First American Title Insurance sought to regain its top position in title insurance sales through its Talon division by recruiting key people from other companies who had relationships with key customers and other key employees. Talon recruited Pope. While still employed by Security Title, Pope secretly solicited key management employees to join Talon–First American and planned to bring all 40 employees with her. Over drinks and dinner, she arranged for a Talon official to help with the recruiting by telling Security Title employees about Talon's beneficial compensation, signing bonuses, medical benefits, and superior computer system. When Security Title discovered Pope's plan to leave Security Title, it fired her and "walked her out." Thirty-five employees walked out with her. Security Title asserted that Pope's actions, aided

and abetted by Talon, resulted in $12,194,335 in lost profits. Security Title sued Pope for breach of fiduciary duty of loyalty and sued Talon–First American as an aider and abettor. Pope defended that she was merely making arrangements to compete in the future.

DECISION: Judgment for Security Title. Pope breached her fiduciary duty by improperly recruiting Security Title employees for Talon while she was still employed by Security Title. First American's argument that Pope had merely discussed her plans with the other employees and was only preparing to compete with Security Title flies in the face of a wealth of evidence presented to the jury. She secretly solicited key management employees to join a competitor and enticed employees to leave by telling them of bonuses and benefits. [*Security Title Agency, Inc. v. Pope*, 200 P.3d 977 (Ariz. App. 2008)]

47-3c Agents and Employees

The authority, rights, and liabilities of an agent or employee of a corporation are governed by the same rules as those applicable when the principal or employer is a natural person. The authority of corporate employees is also governed by general agency principles. **For Example,** R. Bryan Smith, president of Allstate Building Systems applied for a credit account with 84 Lumber Company. The first sentence of the application stated: "BY SIGNING BELOW I HEREBY CERTIFY THAT I AM THE OWNER, GENERAL PARTNER OR PRESIDENT OF THE ABOVE BUSINESS,..." The instructions on the first page of the contract state, "If the Applicant is a corporation, then President must sign the application." The language is a certification that the individual signing the contract has the authority to sign the contract in a representative capacity for the company. Immediately following this clause is the language, "I DO UNCONDITIONALLY ... PERSONALLY GUARANTEE THIS CREDIT ACCOUNT AND PAYMENTS OF ANY AND ALL AMOUNTS DUE BY THE ABOVE BUSINESS." Mr. Smith signed both in a representative capacity and personally guaranteed the contract. He agreed to be personally responsible for the $27,611 owed on the account and the court enforced the agreement as written.[25]

The fact that a person is acting on behalf of a corporation does not serve as a shield from the liability that would be imposed for acts done on behalf of a natural person.

[25] *84 Lumber Co. v. Smith*, 356 S.W.3d 380 (Tenn. 2011); but see *Stamina Products, Inc. v. Zinctec USA Inc.*, 90 A.D.3d 1021 (A.D.2d 2011), where Anthyony Yau signed a contract on behalf of Zinctec, solely as a corporate officer, and did not bind himself individually under the agreement.

47-3d **Executive Compensation under Dodd-Frank**

The economic downturn in 2008 prompted many companies to take a hard look at executive compensation. There was widespread perception that executive pay practices contributed to the financial crisis. According to this view, some executives took excessive risks to realize short-term gains at the expense of long-term shareholder value and financial stability. As some CEOs pursued risky strategies or investments, boards were often complacent and failed to rein in the senior executives. Furthermore, boards approved executive compensation plans that rewarded excessive risk-taking.

Several sections of the Dodd-Frank Act require greater accountability by the board of directors to shareholders about executive compensation. The law took effect on July 21, 2010, with directions for the SEC to promulgate rules addressing issues such as executive pay, pay for performance, the independence of compensation committees, and claw-back provisions for erroneous payments to executives based on inaccurate financial statements. The following sections explain these provisions and the progress on SEC Rules.

Section 951. Say on Pay (Rule effective 2011)

This section requires that shareholders have a nonbinding vote to approve or disapprove executive compensation. Shareholders must first hold a "say-on-frequency" vote to determine how frequently shareholders will vote—every year, second year, or third year. The say-on-pay rule responds to the complaint that directors are not sufficiently accountable to shareholders when awarding executive pay packages. Boards are frequently influenced by management, especially the CEO, and may make decisions about pay that ignore their obligations to maximize shareholder value. The advisory shareholder vote is designed to increase the accountability of the board of directors to the shareholders and to encourage the board to consider shareholder interests when designing executive pay. Section 951 also requires a nonbinding vote on golden parachute payments. It is triggered whenever shareholders are asked to approve an acquisition, a merger, a consolidation, a sale, or other disposition of all or substantially all the assets of the company.

Section 952. Compensation Committee (Rule effective 2012)

This rule requires that most companies listed on the national exchanges have independent compensation committees. Compensation consultants, legal counsel, or other advisors to the compensation committee must also be independent.

Section 953. Pay for Performance: Executive Compensation Disclosures (Rule proposed)

The federal securities laws require clear disclosure about CEO compensation to enhance transparency for investors in publicly held companies. Information about executive pay is located in several sources including the company's annual proxy statement, the company's annual report on form 10-K, and registration statements to register securities for sale to the public. Annual proxy statements containing information on executive pay can be accessed easily on the SEC's Web site. The "pay for performance" section of the rule requires disclosure of "the relationship between executive compensation actually paid and the financial performance of the issuer, taking into account any change in the value of the shares of stock and dividends of the issuer and any distributions."

The SEC approved a rule that requires most public companies to state the ratio of the CEO's pay to that of the average employee. This rule will take effect in 2017. This rule and the pay for performance rule are controversial because some companies maintain that they unduly burden reporting companies without substantial benefit to shareholders.[26]

Section 954. Recovery of Erroneously Awarded Compensation (Rule proposed)

This rule would require exchanges to prohibit the listing of securities of issuers that have not developed and implemented compensation claw-back policies. A claw-back policy requires current or former executive officers to repay to the issuer any "incentive-based compensation including stock options awarded as compensation received during the three year period preceding the date on which the issuer is required to prepare an accounting restatement, based on the erroneous data, in excess of what would have been paid to the executive officer under the accounting restatement." The idea is that executives should not benefit from pay that is supposed to be related to performance when it is later discovered that it was related to fraudulent actions. Clawback provisions could curb the problem of high pay for poor performance.

47-4   Liability

Limited liability is a major reason for incorporating. Management, however, is not free from all civil and criminal liability simply because the corporate form is used.

47-4a   Liability of Management to Third Persons

Officers and managers of a corporation are not personally liable to third parties for the economic consequences of their advice so long as they acted in good faith to advance the interests of the corporation, even if they cause the corporation to refuse to deal with or break its contract with these third persons.

Ordinarily, the management of a corporation (its directors, officers, and executive employees) is not liable to third persons for the effect of its management or advice. The liability of a director or an officer for misconduct may usually be enforced only by the corporation or by shareholders bringing a derivative action on behalf of the corporation. Ordinarily, directors or officers are not liable to a third person for loss caused by the negligent performance of their duties as directors or officers even if, because of such negligence, the corporation is in turn liable to the third person to whom the corporation owed the duty to use care or was under a contract obligation to render a particular service.

However, in those rare cases when a director or an officer has in some way participated in or directed the tortious act, personal liability will attach. **For Example,** a corporate officer and director may be held personally liable for the tort of fraud in the inducement regarding a false promise to grant an insurance agency an exclusive territory selling viatical settlements, by which life insurance policies of terminally ill people are purchased at a discount in exchange for an immediate cash settlement.[27]

---

[26] There is some evidence that the financial crisis and the regulations that followed have made an impact on Wall Street. The gap between what bank CEOs take home in comparison to other bank employees has narrowed since the financial crisis. In 2014, CEOs made on average 124 times what the average worker at a bank makes, down from 273 in 2006. In 2006, the five CEOS at J.P. Morgan Chase, Goldman Sachs, Morgan Stanley, Bank of America, and Citigroup took home $173.6 million all together. In 2014, that number was down to $92.5 million. Peter Rudegeair, "Pay Gap Between Wall Street CEOs and Employees Narrows," *Wall Street Journal* (Apr. 6, 2015), available at **http://www .wsj.com/articles/a-pay-gap-narrows-on-wall-street-1428267898.**

[27] *First Financial USA, Inc. v. Steinger*, 760 So. 2d 996 (Fla. App. 2000).

ETHICS & THE LAW

Executive Compensation

Is it worth it to pay large sums of money to rock star CEOs? One study shows that the highest paid CEOs are the worst performers. According to the study, the 5 percent of CEOs who were the highest paid were running companies that performed 15 percent worse than their peers. Overconfidence is one reason that top CEOs don't have high-performing companies. The research also found that the longer CEOs stayed with a company, the more poorly the company performed. This correlation may be attributed to the fact that CEOs appoint allies to their boards who are likely to go along with the CEO's decisions—even the bad decisions.*

Consider the case of Larry Ellison, CEO of Oracle. In 2012, Ellison was paid $96.2 million; in 2013, $78.4 million. He stepped down as CEO in September 2014. Mr. Ellison received a token salary of $1 but received large stock grants. Using Dodd-Frank's say-on-pay provision, a union-affiliated group, Change to Win, urged Oracle shareholders to vote against the pay package for Mr. Ellison in 2012 and 2013. The organization noted that "Mr. Ellison's pay far outstrips that of the highest paid executives at the companies Oracle has identified as peers" (including Google and Microsoft). Oracle shareholders voted overwhelmingly against Ellison's pay package.

Despite some high-profile votes against executive compensation packages, most are not challenged.

The Wall Street Journal's annual compensation survey looked at 2013 compensation for CEOs at 300 publicly traded companies in the United States. The survey noted that CEO pay rose by a median of 5.5 percent while companies' median profit rose 8 percent. Compensation for ordinary employees in the private-sector rose an average of 1.8 percent.

Top Ten Earners in 2013

Compensation packages vary in the amount of cash, stock option grants, restricted stock grants, and performance awards.**

Oracle	Larry Ellison	$76.9
CBS	Leslie Moonves	$65.4
Liberty Global	Michael Fries	$45.5
Freeport-McMoRan	Richard Adkerson	$38.9
Viacom	Philippe Dauman	$36.8
Walt Disney	Robert Iger	$33.4
Time Warner	Jeffrey Bewkes	$32.4
Aetna	Mark Bertollini	$31.2
Estee Lauder	Fabrizio Freda	$30.9
General Electric	Jeffrey Immelt	$28.2

Do you think that say-on-pay legislation will impact CEO compensation? Will it increase directors' willingness to listen to shareholders? Will directors be likely to respond to advisory votes in order to preserve their seats on the board? Or, is say-on-pay legislation an intrusion on free enterprise?

*See Michael J. Cooper, Huseyin Gulin, and P. Raghavendra Rau, *Performance for Pay? The Relation Between CEO Incentive Compensation and Future Stock Price Performance* (October 1, 2014). Available at SSRN: **http://ssrn.com/abstract=1572085** or **http://dx.doi.org/10.2139/ssrn.1572085**.
Theo Francis and Joann S. Lublin, *CEO Pay Rises Moderately; a Few Reap Huge Rewards*, WSJ (May 27, 2014), **http://www.wsj.com/articles/ceo-pay-rises-moderately-a-few-reap-huge-rewards-1401235102.

47-4b Criminal Liability

Officers and directors, as well as the corporation itself, may be criminally accountable for business regulatory offenses.

Active Participation

Officers and directors, as in the case of agents, are personally responsible for any crimes committed by them even when they act on behalf of the corporation.[28] At the local level, they may be criminally responsible for violation of ordinances relating to sanitation, safety, and hours of closing.

At the state level, they may be criminally liable for conducting a business without obtaining necessary licenses or after the corporate certificate of incorporation has been forfeited.

[28] *Joy Management Co. v. City of Detroit*, 455 N.W.2d 55 (Mich. App. 1990).

At the federal level, officers and directors may be criminally liable for tax and securities law violations as well as egregious environmental protection law and worker safety law violations. International transactions may lead to potential criminal exposure. Under the Foreign Corrupt Practices Act, it is a crime for a U.S. firm to make payments or gifts to a foreign officer to obtain business. Not only is the U.S. corporation subject to a fine but also the officers and individuals involved are subject to fine and imprisonment.

Responsible Corporate Officer Doctrine

Officers and directors may be criminally liable under a number of federal and state statutes for failure to prevent the commission of a crime if they are found to be the "responsible corporate officers." These statutes include the Food, Drug and Cosmetic Act, the Federal Hazardous Substances Act, the Occupational Safety and Health Act, the Federal Water Pollution Act, and, at the state level, the California Corporate Criminal Liability Act.

For Example, Gary Lundgren was a shareholder and officer of KIE, Inc., which owned and operated a sewage treatment plant on Ketron Island. He knew of the facility's discharge of pollutants into Puget Sound without a permit. As the "responsible corporate officer," he was held personally liable for a $250,000 penalty because he controlled the

THINKING THINGS THROUGH

Responsible Corporate Officers—The Park Doctrine Revisited

Food safety violations may give rise to civil and criminal prosecution for companies as well as for corporate executives. In 2013, the United States Department of Justice brought criminal charges against five former officials and employees of Peanut Corporation of America (PCA), including the president and owner of the company, Stewart Parnell.

The charges stem from a salmonella outbreak that was traced to the PCA roasting plant in Georgia. An investigation by the FDA revealed that the processing plant was not properly cleaned. The roof leaked and there was poor ventilation and inadequate pest control. According to the FDA, at least nine people died and more than 700 became ill due to tainted peanut products. More than 100 people who were sickened settled their civil suit against PCA for $12 million. PCA went bankrupt and is no longer in business.

Parnell and his brother, who also worked for the company, were convicted on 97 felony counts, including fraud, conspiracy, and obstruction of justice. Other employees reached plea agreements with the government.

The criminal case involved a six-year conspiracy in which employees failed to notify customers that laboratory tests showed salmonella was present in the product. Employees also falsified certificates of analysis, which summarized lab results.

The government has rarely used criminal provisions to charge individual food industry executives and employees. In *United States v. Park*, 421 U.S. 658 (1975), the United States

Supreme Court decided a case that led to what is now known as the Park Doctrine, a doctrine that allows corporate executives to be prosecuted criminally, even for unintentional violations of food and drug laws by their companies.

The charges against Parnell were likely pursued because the deception was particularly callous about consumer safety. An e-mail notified PCA's president that salmonella testing was not yet available on a shipment—to which the president replied "s**t, just ship it. I cannot afford to loose (sic) another customer."

On September 19, 2014, a federal jury convicted Parnell on charges of mail and wire fraud and the introduction of misbranded food into interstate commerce with the intent to defraud or mislead. Parnell was also convicted of obstruction of justice. Parnell, who could face more than 30 years in prison, is seeking to overturn the jury's conviction.*

The case is one of the first felony convictions of a food processor under the Federal Food, Drug and Cosmetic Act. The case demonstrates the government's interest in food safety cases and its willingness to use the Park Doctrine against executives.**

*Michelle Gillette and Mina Nasseri, *Guilty Convictions in Salmonella Trial May Signify Landmark in Criminal Food-Safety Prosecutions*, Consumer Product Matters (Sept. 22, 2014), **http://www.martindale.com/products-liability-law/article_Mintz-Levin-Cohn-Ferris-Glovsky-Popeo-PC_2178980.htm**.
Press Release, "United States Department of Justice, All Defendants Convicted in Trial of Former Peanut Company Officials," *United States v. Stewart Parnell et al.*, **http://www.justice.gov/civil/current-and-recent cases.

facility with knowledge of the violations.[29] The California Corporate Criminal Liability Act requires managers in control of corporate operations who have knowledge of "serious concealed dangers" to employees or customers to notify the appropriate regulatory authority or be subject to criminal liability.[30]

Liability of the Corporation Itself

A corporation itself may be convicted of a criminal offense if its agent committed the offense acting within the scope of the agent's authority. **For Example,** Steenberg Homes, Inc., was convicted of negligent criminal homicide in the deaths of two cyclists who were killed when the company's trailer truck, loaded with timber, disengaged from the tractor. If safety chains had been properly attached, the accident would not have happened. The corporation's failure to establish and enforce safety procedures was a cause of the deaths of the cyclists.[31]

Punishment of Corporations

Under the Organizational Federal Sentencing Guidelines, organizations, including corporations, trusts, pension funds, unions, and nonprofit organizations, are subject to greatly increased fines for criminal convictions. However, corporations and other covered organizations that implement an effective compliance program designed to prevent and detect corporate crimes and voluntarily disclose such crimes to the government will be subject to much lower fines under the guidelines.[32]

47-4c Indemnification of Officers, Directors, Employees, and Agents

While performing what they believe to be their duty, officers, directors, employees, and agents of corporations may commit acts for which they are later sued or criminally prosecuted. The RMBCA broadly authorizes the corporation to indemnify these persons if they acted in good faith and in a manner reasonably believed to be in, or not opposed to, the interests of the corporation and had no reason to believe that their conduct was unlawful.[33] In some states, statutes require the corporation to indemnify directors and officers for reasonable expenses incurred by them in defending unwarranted suits brought against them by shareholders.

47-4d Liability for Corporate Debts

Because the corporation is a separate legal person, debts that it owes are ordinarily the obligations of the corporation only. Consequently, neither directors nor officers are individually liable for corporate debts, even though it may have been their acts that gave rise to the debts.

In some states, liability for corporate debts is imposed on the corporation's officers and directors when the corporation improperly engages in business.

47-4e Protection of Shareholders

Shareholders may obtain protection from misconduct by management and by the majority of the shareholders. Shareholders may protect themselves by voting at annual elections

[29] *State Department of Ecology v. Lundgren*, 971 P.2d 948 (Wash. App. 1999).
[30] Cal. Penal Code §387 (West 2006).
[31] *State v. Steenberg Homes, Inc.*, 859 N.W.2d 668 (Wis. App. 1998).
[32] U.S. Sentencing Commission Guidelines Manual §§8C2.5(f), 8C2.6 (2014).
[33] Subchapter 8E, added in 1980 and revised in 1994.

for new directors and for new officers. Shareholders may take remedial action at a special meeting called for that purpose. Objecting shareholders may bring a legal action when the management misconduct complained of constitutes a legal wrong.[34]

47-4f Civil Liability of the Corporation

A corporation is liable to third persons for the acts of its officers, employees, and agents to the same extent that a natural person is liable for the acts of agents and employees. The ordinary rules of agency law determine the extent to which the corporation is liable to a third person for a contract made or a tort committed by management personnel, employees, and agents.

Make the Connection

Summary

Ordinarily, stockholder action is taken at a regular or special meeting of the stockholders. The presence of a quorum of the voting shareholders is required.

Management of a corporation is under the control of a board of directors elected by the shareholders. Courts will not interfere with the board's judgment in the absence of unusual conduct such as fraud. A director is disqualified from taking part in corporate action when the director has a conflict of interest. Action by directors is usually taken at a properly called meeting of the board. Directors act in a fiduciary capacity in dealing with the corporation. Directors who act in good faith and have exercised reasonable care are not liable for losses resulting from their management decisions under the business judgment rule. Ordinarily, directors are removed by shareholders.

Officers of a corporation, including a CEO, president, vice president, secretary, and treasurer, are usually selected and removed by the board of directors. Officers are agents of the corporation, and their powers are governed by the law of agency. Their relations with the corporation are fiduciary in nature, and they are liable for any secret profits and for diverting corporate opportunities to their own advantage.

Directors and officers, as in the case of agents generally, are personally responsible for any torts or crimes they commit even if they act on behalf of the corporation. The corporation itself may be prosecuted for crimes and is subject to fines if convicted. The ordinary rules of agency law determine the extent to which a corporation is liable for a contract made or tort committed by a director, an officer, a corporate agent, or an employee.

Learning Outcomes

After studying this chapter, you should be able to clearly explain:

47-1 Shareholders

LO.1 Explain how shareholders, as owners of the corporation, exercise limited control over management by voting at shareholders' meetings to elect directors
See the discussion of shareholder voting and meetings, page 978.

47-2 Directors

LO.2 Explain the qualifications and powers of directors
See the discussion regarding the broad authority of directors to manage the corporation, page 979.

LO.3 Explain the liability of directors and the meaning of the business judgment rule (BJR)
See the *Walt Disney* case in which an unsuccessful action taken by directors was protected by the BJR, pages 982–983.

[34] *Christner v. Anderson, Nietzke & Co.*, 444 N.W.2d 779 (Mich. 1989).

See the *Van Gorkom* case in which directors were not protected by the BJR because they were grossly negligent in their judgment, page 983.

47-3   Officers, Agents, and Employees

LO.4   Explain the obligation of officers—who have access to corporate information and agency powers—to not violate their fiduciary duties to the corporation

See the *Demoulas Super Markets* case regarding diverting corporate opportunities, pages 986–987.

See the *Security Title v. Pope* case regarding a manager's duty of loyalty, page 988.

LO.5   Explain the rationale for the "say-on-pay" provision of the Dodd-Frank Act

See the examples of executive compensation practices leading to the financial crisis of 2008–2009, page 989.

See Ethics & the Law on Executive Pay, page 991.

47-4   Liability

LO.6   Explain how directors, officers, and the corporation itself may be criminally liable for regulatory offenses

See the Gary Lundgren example in which, as a "responsible corporate officer," Gary was held personally liable for environmental law violations, pages 992–993.

See the Thinking Things Through segment about criminal conviction of an executive under the "responsible corporate officer" doctrine, page 992.

Key Terms

business judgment rule (BJR)   quorum

Questions and Case Problems

1. Shareholders of Bear Stearns sued the directors of the corporation for damages for violation of the directors' fiduciary duties in effecting a stock-for-stock merger with J.P. Morgan Chase for an implied value of $10 per share while the company's stock had previously reached a 15-month high of $160. On March 10, 2008, information began leaking into the market that Bear Stearns had a liquidity problem. On March 13, 2008, the company was forced to seek emergency financing from the Federal Reserve and J.P. Morgan Chase. By the weekend of March 14–16, the company could no longer operate without major financing. In an effort to preserve some shareholder value while averting the uncertainty of bankruptcy (where stockholders would likely receive nothing), and represented by teams of legal and financial experts and relying on their financial advisor Lazard Freres & Co.'s opinion that the "exchange ratio is fair, from a financial point of view, to the shareholders," the board of directors approved the initial merger agreement. The shareholder plaintiffs contended that the ultimate $10 share price paid was inadequate and they presented their experts who vigorously dissected the board's decisions. What defense, if any, would you raise on behalf of the Bear Stearns board of directors? [In re *Bear Stearns Litigation*, 870 N.Y.S.2d 709]

2. In 1996, Congress offered national banks the opportunity to become Subchapter S entities.

Amboy Bancorporation was a small, highly profitable New Jersey Bank that was overcapitalized. Amboy's president and CEO utilized Bank Advisory Group, Inc. (BAG), to calculate the fair value of individual shares of Amboy stock. The board of directors approved a merger cash buyout program designed to reduce the shareholder base to below the 75 qualified shareholders necessary to obtain Subchapter S status. BAG incorrectly applied a minority and marketability discount to its evaluation of the fair value of the stock, bringing it down from $110 per share to $70.13 per share. Casey and other shareholders who cashed out under the plan at $73 per share sued the board of directors individually for damages for approving such a flawed plan. Are directors personally liable when they act in reliance on a report by an outside expert whose advice is flawed? If a public accounting firm or an attorney gave the flawed advice, would the directors be personally liable? [*Casey v. Brennan*, 344 N.J. Super. 83]

3. The majority shareholder and president of Dunaway Drug Stores, Inc., William B. Dunaway, was structuring and executing the sale of virtually all of the corporation's assets to Eckerd Drug Co. While doing this, he negotiated a side noncompete agreement with Eckerd, giving Dunaway $300,000 plus a company car in exchange for a covenant not to compete for three years. He simultaneously amended

two corporate leases with Eckerd, thereby decreasing the value of the corporation's leasehold estates. The board of directors approved the asset sale. Minority shareholders brought a derivative action against William Dunaway, claiming breach of his fiduciary duty in negotiating the undisclosed noncompete agreement, which did not require him to perform any service for buyer Eckerd Drug. Did William Dunaway make sufficient disclosure about all of the negotiations of the asset sale to Eckerd Drug? Did William Dunaway violate any fiduciary duty to the corporation? Decide. [*Dunaway v. Parker*, 453 S.E.2d 43 (Ga. App.)]

4. Larry Phillips was hired for a two-year period as executive secretary of the Montana Education Association (MEA). Six months later, he was fired. He then sued MEA for breach of contract and sued the directors and some of the other employees of MEA on the theory that they had caused MEA to break the contract with him and were therefore guilty of the tort of maliciously interfering with his contract with MEA. The evidence showed that the individual defendants, without malice, had induced the corporation to break the contract with Phillips but that this had been done to further the welfare of the corporation. Was MEA liable for breach of contract? Were the individual defendants shielded from personal liability? [*Phillips v. Montana Education Ass'n*, 610 P.2d 154 (Mont.)]

5. Christy Pontiac, a corporation, was indicted for theft by swindle and forgery involving a GM cash rebate program. Hesli, a middle-management employee of Christy Pontiac, had forged the cash rebate applications for two cars so that the rebate money was paid to Christy Pontiac instead of its customers. When confronted by a customer who should have received a rebate, the president of the dealership attempted to negotiate a settlement. The president did not contact GM headquarters until after an investigation was begun by the state attorney general. Christy Pontiac argued that it could not be held responsible for a crime involving specific intent because only natural persons, as opposed to corporations, can form such intent. Decide. [*State v. Christy Pontiac-GMC, Inc.*, 354 N.W.2d 17 (Minn.)]

6. Larry G. Snodgrass and Mark Swinnea owned equal interests in two business entities, ERI Consulting Engineers, Inc. (ERI), and Malmeba Company, Ltd., which they operated together for approximately 10 years. ERI manages asbestos abatement projects for contractors. It leased office space from Malmeba, their partnership that owned the building. Snodgrass and ERI purchased Swinnea's interest in ERI in 2001. ERI paid Swinnea $497,500 to redeem Swinnea's ERI stock, and Snodgrass transferred his half-interest in Malmeba to Swinnea. ERI agreed to employ Swinnea for six years, and Swinnea agreed not to compete with ERI. At the same time, ERI agreed to continue leasing from Malmeba for six years. Unknown to Snodgrass, the wives of Swinnea and Chris Power, an ERI employee, had created a new company called Air Quality Associates a month before Swinnea and Snodgrass executed the buyout agreement. Air Quality Associates was created to perform mold abatement but later engaged in asbestos abatement as a contractor even though neither wife had experience in the asbestos abatement field. Swinnea did not disclose the existence of Air Quality Associates to Snodgrass during the ERI buyout negotiations. Over a 33-month period Snodgrass suffered a total loss of profits of $178,000 for business lost to Swinnea. Was Swinnea free to outmaneuver Snodgrass in their buyout agreement as part of the competitive spirit of America? Do owners have a fiduciary duty to each other in negotiating a buyout agreement with a noncompete clause? Are Swinnea's action's so contrary to our public sense of justice and propriety to merit exemplary damages? [*ERI Consulting Engineers, Inc. v. Swinnea*, 318 S.W.3d 867 (Tex.); *Swinnea v. ERI Consulting Engineers*, 364 S.W.3d 421 (Tex. App.)]

7. Discuss the power of a corporation's president to employ a sales manager and to agree that the manager should be paid a stated amount per year plus a percentage of any increase in the dollar volume of sales that might take place.

8. Richard Grassgreen was executive vice president and then president and chief operating officer of Kinder-Care, Inc., the largest proprietary provider of child care in the country. The company was restructured in 1989 and changed its name to the Enstar Group, Inc. Between 1985 and 1990, while Grassgreen served as the corporation's investment manager, he invested millions of dollars of company money in junk bond deals with Michael Milken, and he secretly retained some $355,000 in commitment fees. When the corporation discovered this, Grassgreen repaid the corporation. It sued him to recover any compensation paid him over the five-year period during which the secret payments were made, some

$5,197,663. Grassgreen defended that his conduct caused little, if any, damage to the corporation because the corporation did not lose any money on any of the investments for which he received personal fees. Decide. [*Enstar Group, Inc. v. Grassgreen*, 812 F. Supp. 1562 (M.D. Ala.)]

9. Danny Hill, the general manager of Southeastern Floor Covering Co., Inc. (SE), had full authority to run the business. His responsibilities included preparing and submitting bid proposals to general contractors for floor coverings and ceilings on construction projects. Hill prepared and submitted a bid for a job for Chata Construction Co. for asbestos encapsulation, ceramic tile, ceilings, carpets, and vinyl tile flooring. However, because SE was not licensed by the EPA, the asbestos work was withdrawn. In the past, SE had used Larry Barnes's company, which was EPA licensed, to do asbestos work under a subcontract agreement. Hill did not pursue a subcontract with Barnes for the Chata job. Rather, Hill and Barnes worked up a bid together and submitted it to Chata for the asbestos work. The bid was accepted, and Hill made $90,000 from the Chata job. Two years later, SE found out about Hill's role in the asbestos work done for Chata, and the corporation sued him for the lost profits. Hill argued that SE was not licensed by the EPA to do asbestos work and thus could not claim a lost corporate opportunity when it was not qualified to do the work. Decide. Are any ethical principles applicable to this case? [*Hill v. Southeastern Floor Covering Co.*, 596 So. 2d 874 (Miss.)]

10. A director of a corporation cannot lend money to the corporation because that would create the danger of a conflict of interest between the director's status as a director and as a creditor. Appraise this statement.

11. Hamway and other minority shareholders brought an action against majority shareholders of Libbie Rehabilitation Center, Inc., including Frank Giannotti, CEO-director; Alex Grossman, president-director; Henry Miller, vice president-director; Ernest Dervishian, secretary and corporate attorney; and Lewis Cowardin, treasurer-director. The minority shareholders contended that the corporation paid excessive salaries to these director-officers and was wasting corporate assets. Prior to coming to Libbie, Giannotti had been a carpet and tile retailer, Grossman a pharmacist, Miller a real estate developer, Dervishian a lawyer, and Cowardin a jeweler. The evidence showed that the extent of their work

for the corporation was very limited. For example, Cowardin, Libbie's finance officer, who was paid $78,121, demonstrated no knowledge of the Medicare and Medicaid programs, the principal source of Libbie's income. Although he claimed to have spent 20 to 25 hours a week on corporate duties, he reported on the tax return for his jewelry business that he spent 75 percent of his working time in that business. One expert witness for the plaintiff testified that the five men were performing the management functions of one individual. The director-officers contended that the business was making a profit and that all salaries were approved by a board of directors that had extensive business experience. Were the directors within their rights to elect themselves officers and set pay for themselves as they saw fit? Did they violate any legal or ethical duty to their shareholders?

12. Anthony Yee was the president of Waipahu Auto Exchange, a corporation. As part of his corporate duties, he arranged financing for the company. Federal Services Finance Corp. drew 12 checks payable to the order of Waipahu Auto Exchange. These were then indorsed by its president, "Waipahu Auto Exchange, Limited, by Anthony Yee, President," and were cashed at two different banks. Bishop National Bank of Hawaii, on which the checks were drawn, charged its depositor, Federal Services, with the amount of the checks. Federal Services then sued Bishop National Bank to restore to its account the amount of the 12 checks on the ground that Bishop National Bank had improperly made payment on the checks because Anthony Yee had no authority to cash them. Did Yee have authority to indorse and cash the checks? [*Federal Services Finance Corp. v. Bishop Natl Bank of Hawaii*, 190 F.2d 442 (9th Cir.)]

13. Klinicki and Lundgren incorporated Berlinair, Inc., a closely held Oregon corporation. Lundgren was president and responsible for developing business. Klinicki served as vice president and director responsible for operations and maintenance. Klinicki owned one-third of the stock, and Lundgren controlled the rest. They both met with BFR, a consortium of Berlin travel agents, about contracting to operate some charter flights. After the initial meeting, all contracts with BFR were made by Lundgren, who learned that there was a good chance that the BFR contract would be available. He incorporated Air Berlin Charter Co. (ABC) and was its sole owner. He presented BFR with a contract proposal, and it

awarded the contract to ABC. Although Lundgren was using Berlinair's working time and facilities, he managed to keep the negotiations a secret from Klinicki. When Klinicki discovered Lundgren's actions, he sued him for usurping a corporate opportunity for Berlinair. Lundgren contended that it was not a usurpation of corporate opportunity because Berlinair did not have the financial ability to undertake the contract with BFR. Decide. Are any ethical principles applicable to this case? Consider the applicability of Chief Justice Cardozo's statement in *Meinhard v. Salmon*, 164 N.E. 545 (N.Y. 1928), concerning the level of conduct for fiduciaries: "A trustee is held to something stricter than the morals of the marketplace. Not honesty alone, but the punctilio of an honor the most sensitive is then the standard of behavior...." [*Klinicki v. Lundgren*, 695 P.2d 906 (Or.)]

14. Rudolph Redmont, the president of Abbott Thinlite Corp., left Abbott to run Circle Corp. in competition with his former employer. It was claimed that he diverted contracts from his former employer to his new one, having gained the advantage of specific information about the deals in progress while employed by Abbott. Abbott sued Redmont and Circle Corp. to recover lost profits. Redmont contended that all of the contracts in question were made after he left Abbott, at which time his fiduciary duty to Abbott had ceased. Decide. [*Abbott Thinlite Corp. v. Redmont*, 475 F.2d 85 (2d Cir.)]

15. William Gurtler was president and a board member of Unichem Corp., which produced and sold chemical laundry products. While president of Unichem, he encouraged his plant manager to leave to join a rival business, which Gurtler was going to join in the near future. Moreover, Gurtler sold Unichem products to his son, G. B. Gurtler, at a figure substantially below their normal price and on credit even though G. B. had no credit history. Gurtler made the sales with full knowledge that G. B. was going to start a rival business. Also at that time, Gurtler was aware that his wife was soliciting Unichem employees to join the new Gurtler Chemical Co., and he helped her design Gurtler's label so that it would look like Unichem's. Gurtler guaranteed a $100,000 bank loan for the new Gurtler Chemical Co. with funds to be disbursed after he left Unichem. One month later, he became president of Gurtler Chemical Co. Unichem sued Gurtler for breach of fiduciary duty and for the loss of profits that resulted. Gurtler contended that his sales to G. B. guaranteed needed revenue to Unichem and constituted a sound business decision that should be applauded and that was protected under the business judgment rule. Decide. Are any ethical principles applicable to this case? [*Unichem Corp. v. Gurtler*, 498 N.E.2d 724 (Ill. App.)]

CPA Questions

1. Davis, a director of Active Corp., is entitled to:
   a. Serve on the board of a competing business.
   b. Take sole advantage of a business opportunity that would benefit Active.
   c. Rely on information provided by a corporate officer.
   d. Unilaterally grant a corporate loan to one of Active's shareholders.

2. Absent a specific provision in its articles of incorporation, a corporation's board of directors has the power to do all of the following *except:*
   a. Repeal the bylaws.
   b. Declare dividends.
   c. Fix compensation of directors.
   d. Amend the articles of incorporation.

3. Which of the following statements is correct regarding fiduciary duty?
   a. A director's fiduciary duty to the corporation may be discharged by merely disclosing his or her self-interest.
   b. A director owes a fiduciary duty to the shareholders but *not* to the corporation.
   c. A promoter of a corporation to be formed owes no fiduciary duty to anyone, unless the contract engaging the promoter so provides.
   d. A majority shareholder as such may owe a fiduciary duty to fellow shareholders.

P A R T 8

Real Property and Estates

Real Property

Learning Outcomes

After studying this chapter, you should be able to

LO.1 List the types of real property interests, the rights of the parties and their liabilities

LO.2 Distinguish between liens, licenses, and easements

LO.3 Discuss the nature and form of real property ownership

LO.4 Explain the liability of landowners for injury to others on their property

LO.5 Discuss the forms of co-ownership and parties' rights

LO.6 Describe how deeds convey title to land

LO.7 Describe the characteristics and effect of a mortgages

48-1 Nature of Real Property

real property–land and all rights in land.

Real property has special characteristics of permanence and uniqueness. These characteristics have strongly influenced the rules that society has developed to resolve disputes concerning real property.

48-1a Land

land–earth, including all things embedded in or attached thereto, whether naturally or by the act of humans.

Land means more than the surface of the earth. It is composed of the soil and all things of a permanent nature affixed to the ground, such as shrubs, grass, trees, and other growing, natural products. The word also includes the waters on the ground and minerals that are embedded beneath the surface.

easement–permanent right that one has in the land of another, as the right to cross another's land or an easement of way.

Technically, land extends downward to the earth's center and upward indefinitely. The general view is that the owner of the land owns the space above that land subject to the right of flying aircraft that do not interfere with the use of the land and are not dangerous to persons or property on the land.

CPA

48-1b Easements

dominant tenement–land that is benefited by an easement.

An **easement** is the right to use another's property, such as the right to cross another's land. Rights in another person's land also include profits, or the right to remove minerals. The easement belongs to the land that is benefited. The benefited land is called the **dominant tenement**, and the land that is subject to the easement is called the **servient tenement.**[1]

servient tenement–land that is subject to an easement.

Creation of Easement

Because an easement is an interest in land, an oral promise to create an easement is not binding because of the statute of frauds. An oral grant of an easement would be a license (see the section titled "Licenses"). An easement created by agreement is transferred by deed. However, an easement may also be created by implication. An **easement by implication** arises when one conveys a portion the land that has been used as a dominant estate in relation to the part retained. **For Example,** if water pipes or drain pipes run from the part of the land conveyed through the part retained, there is an implied right to continue using the pipes. For an easement to be implied, the use, as in this case with the pipes, must be apparent, continuous, and reasonably necessary.

easement by implication–easement not specifically created by deed that arises from the circumstances of the parties and the land location and access.

An easement by implication arises when one subdivides land and sells a portion to which no entry can be made except over the land retained or over the land of a stranger. The grantee's right to use the land retained by the grantor for the purpose of going to and from the land conveyed is known as a **way of necessity.**

way of necessity–grantee's right to use land retained by the grantor for going to and from the conveyed land.

An easement may be created by **prescription.** Under prescription, a person acquires an easement by adverse use, or use contrary to the landowner's use, for a statutory period. No easement is acquired by prescription if the use of the land is with the permission of the owner.

prescription–acquisition of a right to use the land of another, as an easement, by making hostile, visible, and notorious use of the land, continuing for the period specified by the local law.

Termination of Easement

Once an easement has been granted, it cannot be destroyed by the act of the grantor. A "revocation" attempted without the easement owner's consent has no effect.

An easement may be lost by nonuse when surrounding circumstances show an intent to abandon the easement.[2] **For Example,** when a surface transit system had an easement to maintain trolley tracks but abandoned the easement when the tracks were removed and

---

[1] *Gaw v. Seldon*, 85 So. 3d 312 (Miss. App. 2012).
[2] *Howard v. U.S.*, 964 N.E.2d 779 (Ind. 2012).

all surface transportation was discontinued, the easement was lost through abandonment. Likewise, when the owner of the easement planted a flower bed on the land across the end of the path of the easement, the intent to abandon the easement was evident.

CASE SUMMARY

Freddie and Peggy's Speed Bumps on the Easement Get Bumped

FACTS: Adrian and Charline Wingate (Appellees) own and occupy a home adjoining Gloria Dianne and Freddie L. Wingate's (Appellants) property. On February 1, 1999, Appellant Freddie L. Wingate and his (now deceased) wife, Peggy Ann Wingate (now Peggy Dianne), granted an easement over and across their property, providing ingress and egress to Adrian and Charline, which was recorded. Around October 21, 2009, Freddie and Peggy placed speed bumps across a paved portion of the easement, which is used by Adrian and Charline to gain access to their residence. Freddie and Peggy also placed concrete barriers on either side of the speed bumps to prevent vehicles from going around the speed bumps. The speed bumps have proven dangerous to drivers and their passengers and have damaged vehicles passing over them. Adrian and Charline demanded summary judgment as well as a permanent injunction restraining Freddie and Peggy from keeping the speed bumps across the easement. The court granted summary judgment and ordered the removal of the speed bumps. Peggy and Freddie appealed.

DECISION: The court held that there were issues of fact about the burden that the speed bumps caused the dominant easement holders. The issues that require examination are whether there are underlying reasons for the control of ingress and egress, whether the easement language offers guidance on what the servient interest holder can do, and if there are other means for accomplishing whatever safety goals the servient interest holder may have. Dominant interest holders do not have a right of absolute prohibition of ingress and egress restrictions unless such is spelled out in the easement grant itself. The decision was reversed and the lower court was required to hold a trial on all of these issues. [*Dianne v. Wingate*, 84 So. 3d 427 (Fla. App. 2012)]

THINKING THINGS THROUGH

The Dryer Vent That Dumped on the Doc

Danetta Garfink owns a condominium unit at The Cloisters at Charles Condominiums. Garfink purchased her unit (one of the model units) in 1991 during the development and construction phase of the project. The original construction included installed household appliances in each unit, a clothes dryer among them. As originally installed, the clothes dryer was connected and vented into the furnace room, rather than to the outside of the building, contrary to the terms of the construction contract, and in violation of prevailing building codes and regulations.

In 2000, the clothes dryer malfunctioned and Garfink purchased a replacement from Sears, Roebuck & Co. After viewing the existing vent system, however, Sears refused to install the replacement because a "fire hazzard [sic] was identified."

Garfink took it upon herself to have the venting system rerouted. The new system was routed from the dryer through the wall of the laundry room into the adjoining garage, then through the garage and then the exterior wall. Garfink's immediate neighbor, Dr. Oscar Kantt, found that the new vent was within 17 feet of the front door of his residence, and Dr. Kantt complained about the discharge. Garfink says she has an easement for the dryer vent. Analyze whether she does have an easement. Be sure to think through the types of easements.

[*Garfink v. Cloisters at Charles, Inc.*, 897 A.2d 206 (Md. 2006)]

CPA   ## 48-1c Profits

profit–right to take a part of the soil or produce of another's land, such as timber or water.

Profits are rights to take part of the soil, subsurface materials, or resources or produce from land that belongs to another. **For Example,** profits could include the right to remove coal from the land of another and the right to use the water from another's land.

CPA 48-1d Licenses

license–personal privilege to do some act or series of acts upon the land of another, as the placing of a sign thereon, not amounting to an easement or a right of possession.

A **license** is a personal, revocable privilege to perform an act or series of acts on the land of another. Unlike an easement, a license is not an interest in land. **For Example,** the person allowed to come into the house to use the telephone has a license. The advertising company that has permission to paint a sign on the side of a building also has a license. A ticket to see a movie is a license.

A license may be terminated at the will of the licensor. It continues only as long as the licensor is the owner of the land.

SPORTS & ENTERTAINMENT LAW

The New England Patriots and Their Season License Holders

In its litigation against StubHub, Inc., over StubHub's listing of its tickets for resale, the New England Patriots alleged that StubHub was engaged in intentional interference with advantageous relations through StubHub's knowing solicitation of ticket holders to violate the terms on which their tickets for access to Patriots home football games are granted (i.e., the license restrictions on transfer of the tickets). Massachusetts' Supreme Court had already held that tickets to entertainment events are revocable licenses, which a venue owner may revoke at any time and for any reason. The Patriots argued that StubHub, by offering season ticket holders' tickets for sale online, was interfering with its license rights. StubHub argued that a ticket was not a license but more like a bearer instrument that could be transferred easily. Not surprisingly, the Patriots continued their winning streak in court. The result is, because 95 percent of the tickets held to a Patriots game are season tickets, there is no open secondary market for ticket sales to Patriots games. Fans have only the license holder options afforded for selling their tickets.

[Yarde Metals, Inc. v. New England Patriots, LP., 834 N.E.2d 450 (2005); New England Patriots, LP. and NPS LLC, Herman v. Admit One Ticket Agency, 912 N.E.2d 450 (Mass. 2009)]

CPA 48-1e Liens

lien–claim or right, against through judgment or levy.

tax lien–lien on property for nonpayment of taxes.

judgment lien–lien obtained through the courts.

mechanic's lien–claim by laborers or materials suppliers for property improvements.

Real property may be subject to **liens** that arise by the voluntary act of the owner of the land. **For Example,** the lien of a mortgage is created when the owner borrows money and uses the land as security for repayment of the debt.

Liens may also arise involuntarily, as in the case of **tax liens, judgment liens,** and **mechanic's liens.** In the case of taxes and judgments, the liens provide a means for enforcing the obligations of the owner of the land to pay the taxes or the judgment. Mechanic's liens give persons furnishing labor and materials in the improvement of real estate the right to proceed against the real estate for the collection of the amounts due them.

48-1f Fixtures

Under the laws relating to fixtures, personal property becomes real property.

CPA Definition

fixture–personal property attached to or adapted to real estate.

A **fixture** is personal property that is attached to the earth or placed in a building in such a way or under such circumstances that it is considered part of the real property.

A person may buy a refrigerator, an air conditioner, a furnace, or some other item that is used in a building and then have the item installed. The question of whether such an item is a fixture, and therefore part of a building, can arise in a variety of situations: (1) The real estate tax assessor assesses the building and adds in the value of the item on the theory that it is part of the building, (2) the buyer of the item owns and then sells the building, and the new owner of the building claims that the item stays with the building, (3) the buyer places a mortgage on the building, and the mortgagee claims that the item is bound by the mortgage, (4) the buyer is a tenant in the building in which the item is installed, and the landlord claims that the item must stay in the building when the tenant leaves, and (5) the buyer does not pay in full for the item, and the seller of the item has a security interest that the seller wishes to enforce against the buyer or against the landlord of the building in which the buyer installs the item. The seller of the item may also assert a claim against the mortgagee of the building or against the buyer of the building. The determination of the rights of these parties depends on the common law of fixtures, as occasionally modified by statute.

Tests of a Fixture

In the absence of an agreement between the parties, the courts apply three tests to determine whether personal property has become a fixture.

Annexation. Generally, personal property becomes a fixture if it is so attached to the realty that it cannot be removed without materially damaging the real property or destroying the personal property itself. If the property is so affixed as to lose its specific identity, such as bricks in a wall, it becomes part of the realty. When cabinets are attached to kitchen walls so as to be immovable, they are fixtures.

Adaptation. Personal property especially adapted or suited to the use made of the building may constitute a fixture such as the pipes for a church organ.

Intent. One controlling test is the intention of the person affixing the property. Intent is considered as of the time the property was affixed.[3] In the absence of direct proof of such intent, courts resort to the nature of the property, the method of its attachment, and all the surrounding circumstances to determine intent.

The fact that machinery installed in a plant would be very difficult and expensive to move or is so delicate that the moving would cause damage is significant in reaching the conclusion that the owner installed the equipment as a permanent addition and intended to make the equipment fixtures. **For Example,** when the floors in a large apartment house are made of concrete and covered with a thin sheet of plywood to which wall-to-wall carpeting is stapled, the carpeting constitutes a fixture that cannot be removed from the building. Removal would probably destroy the carpeting because it was cut to size. In addition, the carpeting is necessary to make the building livable as an apartment.

CPA   Movable Machinery and Equipment

Machinery and equipment that are movable are ordinarily held not to be fixtures even though, in order to move them, it is necessary to unbolt them from the floor or to disconnect electrical wires or water pipes. **For Example,** refrigerators, freezers, and gas and electric ranges are not fixtures. They do not lose their character as personal property when they are readily removable after disconnecting pipes or unplugging wires. A portable window air conditioner that rests on a rack that is affixed to the windowsill by screws and is connected directly to the building only by an electric cord plug is not a fixture.

The mere fact that an item may be unplugged, however, does not establish that it is not a fixture. **For Example,** a computer and its related hardware constitute fixtures when there is such a mass of wires and cables under the floor that the installation gives the impression of permanence.

---

[3] In re *Treadwell*, 520 B.R. 788 (W.D. Mo. 2014).

CPA Trade Fixtures

Equipment that a tenant attaches to a rented building and uses in a trade or business is ordinarily removable by the tenant when the tenant permanently leaves the premises. Such equipment is commonly called a *trade fixture.*[4]

CASE SUMMARY

The Lake Home "Stripped" of Fixtures

FACTS: Denny Ryerson (Debtor) filed his Chapter 11 bankruptcy case on August 30, 2013, and Anaconda (mortgage creditor) asked for relief from the stay to sell the property securing the mortgage notes. The property securing the notes is located on the shore of Lake Coeur d'Alene. A residence and related structures sit on two contiguous lakefront lots, and there are two additional lots adjacent thereto. The two primary lots total 2.18 acres. The residence, a luxury custom home, is about 11,000 square feet in size. There is a separate 1,500 square foot caretaker residence and a separate 900 square foot garage with a dwelling unit over it. The court valued the lots and residences, excluding moveable personal property (i.e., extensive furniture and art), at $9,000,000.

Anaconda commenced foreclosure on the deeds of trust. There was a $7,000,000 bid that Anaconda obtained for the residence property. At a separate foreclosure sale on April 15, Anaconda obtained a $145,000 bid for the adjacent lots.

Ryerson was entitled to remove personal property such as furniture and art, but he also removed fixtures and Anaconda sought remedies for the loss of the improperly removed fixtures. Anaconda requested that the court order the Debtor, who had "stripped" over $550,000 worth of "fixtures" from the property, be required to return them.

The Debtor maintained that the items are not fixtures and sought to sell the non-fixture personal property and devote the proceeds to payment of creditors under the Chapter 11 plan.

DECISION: The court decided for the debtor with respect to some of the property and the creditor in others.

1. under Idaho law, recessed "can" lighting, in-cabinet lighting, wall sconces, installed indirect lighting, and outdoor "carriage lights" were fixtures, but suspended or hanging lighting, including large chandeliers, were not;
2. the French-made gas and electric range, though a wedding present from debtor to his wife, was "installed" in a manner that spoke objectively to the intent that it be a permanent accession, and so was a fixture;
3. the other appliances were not fixtures;
4. the house's sound system was a fixture because of its integration into the walls;
5. the house's standby generators were not fixtures because they could be removed from their concrete bases;
6. the two large bronze statues on the property were not fixtures because they could be moved from their bases without damage; and
7. the dock built for use in conjunction with the property was not a fixture because it could be detached and moved.

The decisions were based on degree of attachment, damage upon removal, relationship of the item to the property, and whether its use could be transferred elsewhere. **[In re Ryerson, 519 B.R. 275 (D. Idaho 2014)]**

fee simple estate–highest level of land ownership; full interest of unlimited duration.

life estate–an estate for the duration of a life.

CPA 48-2 Nature and Form of Real Property Ownership

A person's interest in real property may be defined in terms of the period of time for which the person will remain the owner as (1) a **fee simple estate** or (2) a **life estate.** These estates are termed *freehold estates*, which are interests of uncertain duration. At the time of creation of a freehold estate, a termination date is not known. When a person

[4] *Steel Farms, Inc. v. Croft & Reed, Inc.*, 297 P.3d 222 (Idaho 2012); *Taco Bell of America, Inc. v. Com. Transp. Com'r*, 710 S.E.2d 478 (Va. 2011).

leasehold estate—interest of a tenant in rented land.

owns property for a specified period of time, this interest is not regarded as a freehold estate; it is a **leasehold estate,** subject to special rules of law.

estate in fee—largest estate possible in which the owner has absolute and entire interest in the land.

48-2a Fee Simple Estate

An **estate in fee,** a fee simple, or a fee simple absolute lasts forever. The owner of such a land interest held in fee simple has the absolute and entire interest in the land. The important characteristics of this estate are that (1) it is alienable, or transferable, during life, (2) it is alienable by will, (3) it passes to heirs of the owner if it is not specifically devised (transferred by will), (4) it is subject to rights of the owner's surviving spouse, and (5) it can be attached or used to satisfy debts of the owner before or after death.

fee simple defeasibles—fee simple interest that can be lost if restrictions on its use are violated.

There are other forms of the fee simple estate generally used for control of land use. **Fee simple defeasibles** are interests that give the grantee all the rights of a fee simple holder provided that the grantee complies with certain restrictions. **For Example,** the grant "To Ralph Watkins so long as he uses the property for school purposes" is an example of a fee simple defeasible. Watkins will have all the rights of a fee simple holder provided that he uses the property for school purposes. If Watkins ever stops using the property for school purposes, the property reverts back to the grantor.

48-2b Life Estate

A *life estate* (or life tenancy), as its name indicates, lasts only during the life of a person (ordinarily its owner). Upon the death of the person by whose life the estate was measured, the owner of the life estate has no interest remaining to pass to heirs or by will. **For Example,** a grant of a life estate would be "To my husband, Nathan Jones, for life, and then to my children." Jones would hold title to the property only for the time he is alive. When Jones dies, he cannot give the property away by will. If Jones conveys the property while he is alive, the grantee for the property holds title to the land only until Jones's death.

48-2c Future Interests

In several of the examples given to illustrate fee simple and life estates, interests were created in more than one person. **For Example,** in the preceding life estate example, the children of the grantor are given an interest in the land at the same time that Jones is. However, the interests of the children will not take effect until Jones dies. The children have a future interest in the land. Their interest is referred to as a **remainder interest** because they have the remaining interest in the land once the life estate ends.

remainder interest—land interest that follows a life estate.

possibility of reverter—nature of the interest held by the grantor after conveying land outright but subject to a condition or provision that may cause the grantee's interest to become forfeited and the interest to revert to the grantor or heirs.

In the Watkins fee simple defeasible example, the grantor has a future interest if Watkins violates the restriction. The grantor's interest is called a **possibility of reverter.** It is a future interest because it cannot exist unless Watkins violates the use restriction placed on his present interest.

48-3 Liability to Third Persons for Condition of Real Property

A person entering the land of another may be injured by the condition of the land. Who is liable for such harm?

CPA

48-3a Common Law Rule

Under the common law, liability to a person who enters the land of another is controlled by the status of the injured person—that is, whether the person injured was a **trespasser,** a **licensee,** or an **invitee.** A different duty is owed by the owner (or occupier, as when a tenant is leasing property) of land to persons in each of these three categories.

Trespassers

For a trespasser, the landowner ordinarily owes the duty of refraining from causing intentional harm only once the presence of the trespasser is known. The landowner is not under any duty to warn of dangers or to make the premises safe to protect the trespasser from harm. The most significant exception to this rule arises in the case of small children. Even when children are trespassers, they are generally afforded greater protection through the **attractive nuisance doctrine. For Example,** the owner of a tract of land was held liable for the death of a seven-year-old child who drowned in a creek on that land. Snow had covered the ice on the creek, and children running across the land did not know of the creek's location or the danger of the ice. The landowner had a duty to fence the creek, put up warnings, or control the children's access.[5]

Licensees

Licensees are on the premises with the permission of the landowner, who owes the duty of warning of nonobvious dangers that are known to the owner. A host must warn a guest of such dangers. **For Example,** when a sliding glass door is "invisible" if the patio lights are on and the house lights are off, the owner must warn guests of the presence of the glass. The owner is liable if he has not warned guests of the danger and a guest is injured in shattering the glass. An owner, however, owes no duty to a licensee to take any steps to learn of the presence of dangers that are unknown to the owner.

Invitees

Invitees are persons who enter another's land by invitation. The entry is connected with the owner's business or with an activity the occupier conducts on the land. Business customers, for example, are invitees.

Owners have a duty to take reasonable steps to discover any danger and a duty to warn the invitee or to correct the danger. **For Example,** a store must make a reasonable inspection of the premises to determine that there is nothing on the floor that would be dangerous, such as a slippery substance that might cause a patron to fall. The store must correct the condition, appropriately rope off the danger area, or give suitable warning. If the owner of the premises fails to take the degree of care required and an invitee is harmed as a result, then the owner is liable for such harm.

In most states, the courts have expanded the concept of invitees beyond the category of customers, or those whose presence will economically benefit the occupier. Invitees now usually include members of the public who are invited onto the premises and who cannot be reasonably expected to make an inspection of the premises before using them and would not be able to make necessary repairs to dangerous conditions. Some courts have also made inroads into the prior law by treating a recurring licensee, such as a letter carrier, as an invitee. For more information on landowner liability, refer to Chapter 9 on torts.

trespasser–person who is on the land of another without permission or authorization.

licensee–someone on another's premises with the permission of the occupier, whose duty is to warn the licensee of nonobvious dangers.

invitee–person who enters another's land by invitation.

attractive nuisance doctrine–a rule imposing liability upon a landowner for injuries sustained by small children playing on the land when the landowner permits a condition to exist or maintains equipment that a reasonable person should realize would attract small children who could not realize the danger. The rule does not apply if an unreasonable burden would be imposed upon the landowner in taking steps to protect the children.

---

[5] *Peguero v. Tau Kappa Epsilon Local Chapter*, 106 A.3d 565 (N.J. Super. A.D. 2015).

CASE SUMMARY

A Loose Clothes Line, a Saved Cow, and a Broken Back

FACTS: On March 10, 2006, Rodney Wrinkle (appellant/plaintiff) and his friend Raymond Lee observed four or five cows wandering loose in front of property belonging to Gene and Charlene Norman (defendants), and some of the cattle were straying toward the highway that ran between Wrinkle's and the Normans' property. Wrinkle was riding his lawn tractor, and he signaled to approaching cars to slow down. Initially riding on his lawn tractor and then going on foot, Wrinkle proceeded to herd the cattle into the Normans' yard. The Normans' gate was open, and Wrinkle herded the cows through the gate toward a pen.

A clothesline wire was attached to a pole in the Normans' yard. As Wrinkle herded the cattle across the Normans' yard toward the cow pen, one calf strayed into the clothesline wire, caught the line around its neck, and began to choke. Wrinkle grabbed the back of the clothesline and walked around to the other side, flipping the line several times in order to remove the line from the calf's neck. The calf took off running toward the gate of the pen, apparently catching the clothesline somehow, so that the clothesline caught Wrinkle from behind. Wrinkle's feet went out from under him, and he landed on his back on a concrete pad.

Wrinkle immediately experienced severe pain. Lee helped him get home, and Wrinkle eventually went to the hospital, where he was diagnosed with a broken back. He was hospitalized for 30 days. Afterward, he approached the Normans in person about the injury and later wrote a letter in which he asked that they submit to their insurance carrier a claim for $44,115.72, which was the outstanding balance on his hospital bill. The Normans refused to arrange for payment of the medical expenses.

Wrinkle then filed an action grounded in negligence alleging that the Normans had created a dangerous condition on their property that presented an unreasonable risk of harm by leaving their gate open and by leaving a clothesline wire running across the ground.

The Normans filed a motion for summary judgment. The court granted the Normans' motion for summary judgment, holding that Wrinkle was a trespasser on the Normans' property and they had breached no duty toward him. The Court of Appeals affirmed. Wrinkle appealed.

DECISION: Although the rescuer was somewhere between a licensee and invitee, the question is what to do about Samaritans who enter the property of another to help that property owner.

The duty of reasonable care is essentially the same as the duty under the theory that the Normans were negligent in the manner of storing their clothesline. Because Wrinkle asserts that the injury occurred on the Normans' property and in the course of attempting to protect the Normans' calf, it is that theory of negligence that governs the duty of care.

The court held that the Normans could be held liable under a theory of negligence and that there was a question of fact that required the case to go to a jury to make the determination of whether the Normans had exercised reasonable care in hanging their clothes.

DISSENT: A duty to remove any object from one's property that could in any fashion somehow be a factor in an injury to another person entering one's property simply increases the possibility of liability and litigation to an absurd level. [*Wrinkle v. Norman*, 301 P.3d 312 (Kan. 2013)]

48-4 Co-Ownership of Real Property

Real property may be owned by one or several persons, and the method of co-ownership determines the extent of the owners' rights.

48-4a Multiple Ownership

Several persons may have *concurrent interests* (or interests that exist at the same time) in the same real property. The forms of multiple ownership for real property are the same as those for personal property. Real property can be held by tenants in common, by joint tenants with right of survivorship, by tenants by the entirety, or under community property rights. When co-owners sell property, they hold the proceeds of sale by the same kind of tenancy as that in which they held the original property.

48-4b **Condominiums**

condominium—
combination of co-
ownership and individual
ownership.

A **condominium** is a combination of co-ownership and individual ownership. **For Example,** persons owning an office building or an apartment house by condominium are co-owners of the land and of the halls, lobby, elevators, stairways, exits, surrounding land, incinerator, laundry rooms, and other areas used in common. Each apartment or office in the building, however, is individually owned and is transferred in the same way as other forms of real property.

Control and Expense

In some states, owners of the various units in the condominium have equal voice in its management and share an equal part of its expenses. In others, control and liability for expenses are shared by a unit owner in the same ratio that the value of the unit bears to the value of the entire condominium project. In all states, unit owners have equal rights to use the common areas. An owners' association is created by the condominium owners to operate the common areas of the condominium property and resolve any disputes among owners.

The owner of each condominium unit makes the repairs required by the owner's deed or contract of ownership. The owner is prohibited from making any major change that would impair or damage the safety or value of an adjoining unit.

Collection of Expenses from Unit Owner

When a unit owner fails to pay the owner's share of taxes, operating expenses, and repairs, the owners' association generally has the right to a lien against that owner's unit for the amount due.

Tort Liability

Most condominium projects fail to make provision for the liability of unit owners for a tort occurring in the common areas. A few states expressly provide that when a third person is injured in a common area, a suit may be brought only against the condominium association. Any judgment recovered is a charge against the association to be paid off as a common expense. When the condominium association is incorporated, the same result should be obtained by applying ordinary principles of corporation law. Under principles of corporation law, liability for torts occurring on the premises of the corporation would not be the liability of individual shareholders.

cooperative—group of
two or more persons or
enterprises that acts
through a common agent
with respect to a
common objective, such
as buying or selling.

deed—an instrument by
which the grantor (owner
of land) conveys or
transfers the title to a
grantee.

grantor—owner who
transfers or conveys an
interest in land to a new
owner.

grantee—new owner of a
land conveyance.

CPA

transferee—buyer or
vendee.

Cooperatives Distinguished

Ownership in a condominium is different from ownership in a **cooperative.** An apartment cooperative is typically a corporation that owns an apartment complex. The "ownership" interests of the apartment occupants are as stockholders of the corporation.

48-5 **Transfer of Real Property by Deed**

Although many of the technical limitations of the feudal system and earlier common law on transfer of land have disappeared, much of the law relating to the modern deed originated in those days.

48-5a **Definitions**

A **deed** is an instrument or writing by which an owner or **grantor** transfers or conveys an interest in land to a new owner. The new owner is called a **grantee** or **transferee.** Real property may be either sold or given as a gift. A deed, however, is necessary to transfer title to land, even if it is a gift.

In contrast to the situation with a contract, no consideration is required to make a deed effective. Although consideration is not required to make a deed valid or to transfer title by deed, the absence of consideration may show that the owner makes the transfer to defraud creditors. The creditors may then be able to set aside the fraudulent transfer.

C P A

quitclaim deed–deed by which the grantor purports to give up only whatever right or title the grantor may have in the property without specifying or warranting transfer of any particular interest.

48-5b Classification of Deeds

Deeds may be classified according to the interest conveyed as **quitclaim deeds** or **warranty deeds.** A quitclaim deed merely transfers whatever interest, if any, the grantor may have in the property without specifying that interest in any way. A warranty deed transfers a specified interest and warrants or guarantees that such interest is transferred. Figure 48-1 is a sample warranty deed.

C P A

48-5c Execution of Deeds

warranty deed–deed by which the grantor conveys a specific estate or interest to the grantee and makes one or more of the covenants of title.

Ordinarily, the grantor must sign, by signature or mark, a deed. A deed must be executed and delivered by a person having capacity. A deed may be set aside by the grantor for fraud by the grantee if third persons have not acquired rights in the land in good faith.

C P A

48-5d Delivery and Acceptance of Deeds

A deed has no effect and title does not pass until the deed has been delivered. Delivery is a matter of intent as shown by words and conduct; no particular form of ceremony is required. The essential intent in delivering a deed is not merely that the grantor intends to hand over physical control and possession of the paper on which the deed is written but also that the grantor intends thereby to transfer the ownership of the property described in the deed. That intent can be shown by handing it to the grantee or placing the deed, addressed to the grantee, in the mail or by giving it to a third person with directions to give it to the grantee.

acceptance–unqualified assent to the act or proposal of another, such as the acceptance of a draft (bill of exchange), of an offer to make a contract, of goods delivered by the seller, or of a gift or deed.

An effective delivery of a deed may be made symbolically, or constructively, such as by delivering to the grantee the key to a locked box and informing the grantee that the deed to the property is in the box. **For Example,** the delivery of a safe deposit box key has been held to constitute delivery of a deed that was in the box.

Generally, there must be an **acceptance** by the grantee. In all cases, an acceptance is presumed unless the grantee disclaims the transfer.

C P A

48-5e Recording of Deeds

recorder–public official in charge of deeds.

The owner of land may record the deed in the office of a public official, sometimes called a **recorder** or *commissioner of deeds.* The recording is not required to make the deed effective to pass title, but it is done so that the public will know that the grantee is the present owner and thereby prevent the former owner from making any future transfer or transaction relating to the property.

race statute–statute under which the first party to record the deed holds the title.

notice statute–statute under which the last good-faith or bona fide purchaser holds the title.

When no document is recorded, states have statutes for determining who obtains title and who will be left to take action against the party that has conveyed the property to more than one person. **For Example,** suppose that Grant conveys a tract of land to Dee. Dee does not record her deed. Grant then conveys the same tract of land to Joe, who also does not record his deed, but Joe is unaware of Dee's acquisition. Then Grant conveys the same property to Larry who knows about Dee and Joe but records his deed. Who will hold title, and who will be left to pursue Grant for remedies? Under **race statutes,** the first party to record the deed holds title, so Larry holds title. Under **notice statutes,** the last good-faith or bona fide purchaser (BFP), someone who does not know

FIGURE 48-1	Form of Warranty Deed

THIS DEED, made the twentieth day of November, two thousand and . . . between James K. Damron, residing at 132 Spring Street in the Borough of Manhattan, City and State of New York, party of the first part, and Terrence S. Bloemker, residing at 14 Steinway Street in the Borough of Queens, City and State of New York, party of the second part,

WITNESSETH, that the party of the first part, in consideration of the sum of one dollar ($1), lawful money of the United States, and other good and valuable consideration paid by the party of the second part, does hereby grant and release unto the party of the second part, his heirs and assigns forever,

ALL that certain lot, piece, and parcel of land situated in the Borough of Manhattan, City and County of New York, and State of New York, and bounded and described as follows:

Beginning at a point on the northerly side of Spring Street, distant two hundred (200) feet westerly from the corner formed by the intersection of the northerly side of Spring Street with the westerly side of 6th Avenue, running thence northerly parallel with 6th Avenue one hundred (100) feet, thence westerly and parallel with said Spring Street one hundred (100) feet; thence southerly, again parallel with said 6th Avenue one hundred (100) feet to the northerly side of Spring Street, and thence easterly along the said northerly side of Spring Street one hundred (100) feet to the point or place of beginning.

Together with the appurtenances and all the estate and rights of the party of the first part in and to said premises.

TO HAVE AND TO HOLD the premises herein granted unto the party of the second part, his heirs and assigns forever.

AND the party of the first part covenants as follows:

First. That the party of the first part is seised of the said premises in fee simple, and has good right to convey the same;

Second. That the party of the second part shall quietly enjoy the said premises;

Third. That the said premises are free from encumbrances except as expressly stated;

Fourth. That the party of the first part will execute or procure any further necessary assurance of the title to said premises;

IN WITNESS WHEREOF, the party of the first part has hereunto set his hand and seal the day and year first above written.

JAMES K. DAMRON

(L.S.)

In presence of:

DIANA L. REILMAN } S.S.:*

State of New York

County of New York

On the twentieth day of November in the year two thousand and . . . , before me personally came James K. Damron, to me known and known to me to be the individual described in, and who executed, the foregoing instrument, and he acknowledged that he executed the same.

DIANA L. REILMAN

Notary Public, New York County

*Acknowledgment before a notary public is not essential to the effectiveness of a deed, but it is typically required to qualify the deed for recording.

notice-race statute—statute under which the first bona fide purchaser to record the deed holds the title.

about the previous conveyances, takes title. Under notice, Joe holds title because he is the last BFP. Larry knows about the prior transactions and that fact controls title, not the recording of his deed under notice statutes. Under **notice-race** or **race-notice statutes,** the first BFP to record the deed holds title. So, if Dee records first, she holds title. If Joe records first, he will. Larry has recorded but does not meet the second requirement of race-notice, which is that one must be the first BFP to record to take title in a race-notice statute. Suppose that Larry is a BFP, but Joe is not because he is aware of the conveyance to Dee. Under race, Larry holds title. Under notice, Larry holds title. Under race-notice, Larry wins again. If Dee records her deed, all of these issues are moot because recording the deed is complete notice for all subsequent purchasers.

The fact that a deed is recorded provides notice to the world about who holds title. The recording of a deed, however, is only such notice if the deed was properly executed. Likewise, the grantee of land cannot claim any protection by virtue of the recording of a deed when (1) a claim is made by one whose title is superior to that of the owner of record, (2) the grantee had notice or knowledge of the adverse claim when title was acquired, (3) a person acting under a hostile claim was then in possession of the land, (4) the grantee received the land as a gift, or (5) the transfer to the grantee was fraudulent.

CASE SUMMARY

The Double-Deeded Property to the Incurious Neighbors

FACTS: In January 1986, Norman and Mildred Dahl conveyed the disputed property (a 1.667 acre tract located in McKenzie County) to Harry and Linda Chornuk by warranty deed, but the deed was not recorded until June 24, 2010. On June 17, 2005, after Norman Dahl's death, Mildred Dahl conveyed the same property by warranty deed to the Nelsons as part of the conveyance of approximately 44.5 acres. The deed was recorded on July 5, 2005.

In 2010, the Chornuks sued the Nelsons to quiet title to the property. The district court quieted title in favor of the Chornuks. The court found that the Chornuks' actions were sufficient to put a prudent person on notice that someone else had an interest in the property and that the Nelsons

were required to conduct further inquiry before purchasing the property from Mildred Dahl. The court found the Nelsons had constructive notice of the Chornuks' interest and were not good-faith purchasers.

The Nelsons appealed.

DECISION: The Chornuks held title to the property because they were the first good-faith purchasers to record. The Nelsons recorded first, but they were not good-faith purchasers because they had seen the Chornuks on the property and never asked questions about their presence or reasons for improving and caring for the property. Judgment affirmed. [*Chornuk v. Nelson,* 857 N.W.2d 587 (N.D. 2014)]

48-5f Additional Protection of Buyers

In addition to the protection given to buyers and third persons by the recorded title to property, a buyer is generally protected by procuring title insurance or an abstract of title. An **abstract of title** is a summarized report of the title to the property as shown by the records, together with a report of all judgments, mortgages, and similar recorded claims against the property.

48-5g Grantor's Warranties

The warranties of the grantor relate to the title transferred by the grantor and to the fitness of the property for use.

CPA   ### Warranties of Title

In the common law deed, the grantor may expressly warrant or make certain *covenants* as to the title conveyed. The statutes authorizing a short form of deed provide that, unless otherwise stated in the deed, the grantor is presumed to have made certain **warranties of title.**

covenants (or warranties) of title–grantor's covenants of a deed that guarantee such matters as the right to make the conveyance, to ownership of the property, to freedom of the property from encumbrances, or that the grantee will not be disturbed in the quiet enjoyment of the land.

covenant of seisin–guarantee that the grantor of an interest in land owns the estate conveyed to a new owner.

covenant of right to convey–guarantee that the grantor of an interest in land, if not the owner, has the right or authority to make the conveyance to a new owner.

covenant against encumbrances–guarantee that conveyed land is not subject to any right or interest of a third person.

covenant of quiet enjoyment–covenant by the grantor of an interest in land to not disturb the grantee's possession of the land.

limited covenant–any covenant that does not provide the complete protection of a full covenant.

covenant of further assurances–promise that the grantor of an interest in land will execute any additional documents required to perfect the title of the grantee.

CPA

The more important of the **covenants (or warranties) of title** that the grantor may make are (1) **covenant of seisin,** or guarantee that the grantor owns the estate conveyed, (2) **covenant of right to convey,** or guarantee that the grantor, if not the owner as in the case of an agent, has the right or authority to make the conveyance, (3) **covenant against encumbrances,** or guarantee that the land is not subject to any right or interest of a third person, such as a lien or an easement, (4) **covenant of quiet enjoyment,** or guarantee by the grantor that the grantee's possession of the land will not be disturbed either by the grantor, in the case of a **limited covenant,** or by the grantor or any person claiming title under the grantor, in the case of a general covenant, and (5) **covenant of further assurances,** or guarantee that the grantor will execute any additional documents that may be required to perfect the title of the grantee.

Fitness for Use

Courts in most states hold that when a builder or real estate developer sells a new house to a home buyer, the buyer gets an implied warranty that the house and foundation are fit for occupancy or use. This warranty arises regardless of whether the house was purchased before, during, or after completion of construction.[6] This first buyer is not responsible for the builder warranty when the house is resold. However, there is authority that the second buyer may recover from the original contractor for breach of the implied warranty even though there is no privity of contract.[7]

48-5h Grantee's Covenants

In a deed, the grantee may agree to do or to refrain from doing certain acts. Such an agreement becomes a binding contract between the grantor and the grantee. The grantor may recover from the grantee for its breach. The right to enforce the covenant also runs with the land owned by the grantor to whom the promise was made. **For Example,** a promise not to use a tract of land for a parking lot between two adjoining landowners would be passed (conveyed) to any buyers who subsequently acquire these tracts. For more information on covenants, see Chapter 49, Environmental Law and Land Use Controls.

48-6 Other Methods of Transferring Real Property

Title to real property can also be acquired by eminent domain and by adverse possession.

48-6a Eminent Domain

Under **eminent domain,** property is taken from its private owner for a public purpose. The title is then taken by a government or public authority. There are constitutionally protected rights of property owners under eminent domain. Known as the "takings clause," this portion of the Fifth Amendment to the U.S. Constitution requires compensation when private property is taken for public use. Two important issues arise under the takings clause: whether there is a taking of property and whether the property is taken for a public use. With respect to whether a taking has occurred, it is not necessary that the owner be physically deprived of the property but that normal use of the property has been

[6] *Richards v. Powercraft Homes, Inc.*, 678 P.2d 427 (Ariz. 1984); *Hernandez v. Chisesi Investments, L.L.C.*, 164 So. 3d 912 (La. App. 2014).
[7] Many states have passed statutes that govern the extent of the implied warranty of habitability. Although the statutes vary, the types of defects covered include defects in construction, design, and appearance. See *Corry v. Jahn*, 972 N.E.2d 907 (Ind. App. 2012).

eminent domain—power of government and certain kinds of corporations to take private property against the objection of the owner, provided the taking is for a public purpose and just compensation is made for it.

impaired or lost. Whether there is a public use for the taking is a question that continues to be challenged in court because the definition of public purpose is so broad. **For Example,** property can be taken to build a freeway as well as for the preservation of a historic site. In the eminent domain cases after 2000, much of the litigation centered on whether revitalizations of areas with urban blight were permissible takings. Eminent domain has activated a concerned public as state and local governments take more and more houses and land for purposes of economic development.

CASE SUMMARY

Little Pink Houses, for You, but Not for Me...Anymore

FACTS: In 1978, the city of New London, Connecticut, undertook a redevelopment plan for purposes of creating a redeveloped area in and around the existing park at Fort Trumball. The plan had the goals of achieving all the related ambience a state park should have, including the absence of pink cottages and other architecturally eclectic homes. Part of the redevelopment plan was the city's deal with Pfizer Corporation for the location of its research facility in the area. The preface to the city's development plan stated that it would *"create jobs increase tax and other revenues, encourage public access to and use of the city's waterfront, and eventually 'build momentum' for the revitalization of the rest of the city, including its downtown area."*

Susette Kelo, and other property owners whose homes would be razed and whose land would be taken to allow for the park, Pfizer's facility, and other redevelopment (15 total owners including Kelo), asked to be permitted to stay in the area. The city refused their request.

Kelo and the other homeowners filed suit challenging New London's legal authority to take their homes. The trial court issued an injunction preventing New London from taking certain of the properties but allowing others to be taken. Those property owners who were held subject to eminent domain appealed.

The appellate court found for New London on all claims; the landowners appealed.

DECISION: In a 5-4 decision delivered by Justice Stevens, joined by Justices Kennedy, Souter, Ginsberg, and Breyer,

the U.S. Supreme Court upheld the decision of the Connecticut Supreme Court. New London's taking of the homes of Kelo and others qualifies as a "public use." Local governments cannot take private land simply to give to a particular private party, but when the takings are part of a carefully considered economic development plan, then the takings are constitutional. Public purpose is a broad category for purposes of determining when takings are constitutional. Economic development is a legitimate and constitutionally protected public purpose. Local governments' determinations that areas are economically distressed are enough to justify a program of economic development and local authorities are entitled to make that determination. The courts will not second-guess local authorities.

AFTERMATH: Ms. Kelo's home and 15 others were razed. Pfizer merged with Wyeth in 2009 and closed all company operations in New London. The Fort Trumball area has no houses, no research park, no businesses, and is now undeveloped land. However, following Hurricane Irene, officials from the city of New London announced that the citizens of their fair city could dump their branches and fallen trees at the site where Ms. Kelo's home once sat. A new mayor of New London announced a plan in 2015 to turn the area into a park to serve as a memorial to those who lost their homes to eminent domain. Forty-five states changed their eminent domain statutes to prevent takings such as those in *Kelo.* [*Kelo v. City of New London*, 545 U.S. 469 (2005)]

adverse possession—hostile possession of real estate, which when actual, visible, notorious, exclusive, and continued for the required time, will vest the title to the land in the person in such adverse possession.

48-6b Adverse Possession

Title to land may be acquired by possessing it adversely for a statutorily prescribed period of time. A possessor who complies with the requirements for **adverse possession** can gain title. Those who adversely possess property gain title to property even though they had no right to use the property at the beginning of their use or possession.

To acquire title by adverse possession, the possession must be (1) actual, (2) visible and notorious, (3) exclusive, (4) hostile, and (5) continuous for a required period of time.

THINKING THINGS THROUGH

Putting the Brakes on Eminent Domain

Bailey's Brake Service, a bit of an eyesore at a main intersection near a failing downtown area of Mesa, Arizona, was a family-founded, owned, and operated business that had been open in its existing location since 1970. Lenhart's True Value Hardware store was also a longstanding Mesa business with a location south and east of Bailey's and a desire for a better location. The Lenharts had purchased the property abutting Bailey's but felt that the street facing Bailey's property was necessary for its location.

The city did a taking by eminent domain and then "reissued" the property to Lenhart's for its store. The Baileys challenged the city's taking in the Superior Court as unconstitutional, but the court held that the taking was constitutional as part of the city's plan for redevelopment and revitalization of the area. The Baileys appealed the trial court decision. Should the Baileys get their property back? Was this a proper eminent domain taking?

[*Bailey v. Myers*, 76 P.3d 898 (Az. Ct. App. 2003)]

State statutes control the required time period, but the typical range is 10 to 20 years. Use or possession of land under a mistaken belief that one is the owner still qualifies for the "hostile" possession required under the fourth element listed.[8]

mortgage—interest in land given by the owner to a creditor as security for the payment of the creditor for a debt, the nature of the interest depending upon the law of the state where the land is located. (Parties— mortgagor, mortgagee)

`CPA`

48-7 Mortgages

An agreement that creates an interest in real property as security for an obligation until that obligation is repaid is a **mortgage.**

The property owner, whose interest in the property is given as security, is the *mortgagor.*

The person who receives the security is the *mortgagee.*

48-7a Characteristics of a Mortgage

A mortgage has three characteristics: (1) the termination of the mortgagee's interest on the performance of the obligation secured by the mortgage, (2) the right of the mortgagee to enforce the mortgage by foreclosure on the mortgagor's failure to perform, and (3) the mortgagor's right to redeem or regain the property.

48-7b Property Subject to Mortgage

In general, any form of property that may be sold or conveyed may be mortgaged. It is immaterial whether the right is a present right, a future interest, or merely a right in the land of another. It is not necessary that the mortgagor have complete or absolute ownership in the property. Mortgagors may mortgage any type of land interest they own.

`CPA` ### 48-7c Form of Mortgage

Because a mortgage of real property transfers an interest in the property, it must be in writing under the statute of frauds. As a general rule, no particular form of language is required if the language used expresses the intent of the parties to create a mortgage. Many state statutes provide a standardized form for mortgage language that may be used.

---

[8] The state with the shortest period for adverse possession is Texas, whose adverse possession period can be as short as three years. The state with the longest adverse possession period is Wyoming, with 40 years.

48-7d Creative Forms of Financing

In many situations in which a buyer seeks to purchase property, the conventional methods for obtaining a mortgage are not available because of affordability or qualifications required for a loan. Many creative forms of financing have been developed to help buyers purchase property. **For Example,** residential land buyers, particularly during the real estate boom in 2005–2006, could obtain an **adjustable rate mortgage (ARM),** in which the lower interest rates applied at the beginning of the mortgage help the buyer qualify for the loan. The ARM changes interest rates along with the market, going up and down, unless the ARM has a fixed minimum rate. Other buyers may have the seller finance their purchase through the use of a land or an installment contract. Some new forms of financing, such as the **reverse mortgage,** permit those who have paid off their mortgages on their property to get the value out of their property by having a mortgage company take a mortgage out on the property and pay them money over time. Many senior citizens are able to obtain the additional monthly income they may need by this form of financing, which permits them to draw on their equity in their land. Because of the collapse of the subprime mortgage market in 2007–2008, these creative forms of financing are now under extensive state and federal regulation. In addition, state and federal reforms (under Dodd-Frank) require additional disclosures about the full cost of financing a real property purchase through a mortgage, especially in the types of mortgages in which payments and interest rates fluctuate. (See Chapter 31 for more information.)

adjustable rate mortgage (ARM)– mortgage with variable financing charges over the life of the loan.

reverse mortgage– mortgage in which the owners get their equity out of their home over a period of time and return the house to the lender upon their deaths.

48-7e Recording or Filing of Mortgage

An unrecorded mortgage is still valid and binding between and among the parties. A mortgage cannot be set aside on the ground that it has not been recorded. However, recording the mortgage does protect the mortgagee in terms of priority as against other creditors. The recording statutes, including the problems with MERS, also apply to mortgages.

E-COMMERCE & CYBERLAW

MERS and Problems

Mortgage Electronic Registration Systems, Inc. (MERS), was the system used by most lenders for purposes of recording their mortgages for loans on residential property and, thereby, attaining their secured interest and priority. About one-half of the residential mortgages in the United States were recorded in MERS. The effect was that MERS was listed as the mortgagee on the public records. Debtors wanted to know, "Who is MERS?" The result has been litigation around the country, brought by homeowners facing foreclosure. These suits have alleged that MERS had not perfected its security interest in the mortgaged property because the note was split (and sold off in bundles that were then the foundation of collateralized debt obligations on Wall Street) from the deed of trust or mortgage. And MERS was not their mortgagee. Further, the debtors were unable to fight foreclosure because it became difficult to determine who actually was the mortgagee for purposes of determining default, rights, and redemption. The debtors have argued that their notes were unenforceable without an accompanying mortgage and mortgagee. With the note unenforceable, the debtors argued that they could not be in default because no money was due and owing. The argument has not fared well in deed-of-trust lending, but the litigation continues around the country. Known as the "lost chain of title" cases, the result has been investigations by state attorneys general of how loan and mortgage documents were transferred (including allegations of robo-signing by transferees for transferors). As one writer noted, MERS has had a destructive effect on 400 years of recorded property rights in the United States because the chain of title has been lost in so many cases.

[*Rostami v. BAC Home Loans Servicing, L.P.*, 2013 WL 100946 (D. Nev. 2013)]

Source: David E. Woolley, "MERS: The Unreported Effects of Lost Chain of Title on Real Property Owners," 8 *Hastings Bus. L J.*, 365 (2012).

48-7f Responsibilities of the Parties

The mortgagor and mortgagee have the following duties and liabilities when a mortgage is placed on real property.

CPA Taxes, Assessments, and Insurance

The duty to pay taxes and assessments rests with the mortgagor. In the absence of an agreement, neither party is under a duty to insure the mortgaged property. Both parties, however, may insure their respective interests. It is common practice for the mortgagor to obtain a single policy of insurance on the property payable to the mortgagee and the mortgagor generally according to the standard mortgagee clause that pays the outstanding loan balance first.

Impairment of Security

The mortgagor is liable to the mortgagee for any damage to the property caused by the mortgagor that impairs the security of the mortgage by materially reducing the value of the property. Both the mortgagor and the mortgagee have a right of action against a third person who wrongfully injures the property.

48-7g Transfer of Interest

Questions arise as to transfers by the mortgagor and the mortgagee of their respective interests and of the liability of a transferee of the mortgagor.

CPA Transfer by Mortgagor

The mortgagor may ordinarily transfer the property without the consent of the mortgagee. Such a transfer passes only the interest of the mortgagor and does not divest or impair a properly recorded mortgage.

The transfer of the property by the mortgagor does not affect the liability of the mortgagor to the mortgagee. Unless the mortgagee has agreed to substitute the mortgagor's grantee for the mortgagor, the mortgagor remains liable for the mortgage debt as though no transfer had been made.[9]

CPA Liability of the Parties in a Transfer by a Mortgagor

assumption–mortgage transfers in which the transferee and mortgagor are liable and the property is subject to foreclosure by the mortgagee if payments are not made.

There are two ways to transfer mortgaged property, and each way has different results in terms of personal liability for the transferee. In the assumption of a mortgage, the transferee agrees to assume liability. In an **assumption,** the mortgagor remains liable, the transferee is liable, and the property is subject to foreclosure by the mortgagee in the event the payments are not made. **For Example,** if Bob sold his house with a $175,000 mortgage for $200,000 to Jane, Jane could pay Bob $25,000 cash and then agree to assume Bob's mortgage. Jane may get the benefit of a lower interest rate by assuming Bob's mortgage. Both Bob and Jane are personally liable, and the mortgagee may foreclose on the property if the payments are not made.

The second method of transfer is called a "subject to" transfer. In this type of transfer, the property is subject to foreclosure, but the transferee does not agree to assume the mortgage personally. The mortgagor remains liable in this type of transfer, too.

Transfer by Mortgagee

In most states, a mortgage may be transferred or assigned by the mortgagee.

---

[9] *Regan v. Jeff D.*, 339 P.3d 1162 (Idaho 2014).

48-7h Rights of Mortgagee after Default

foreclosure–procedure for enforcing a mortgage resulting in the public sale of the mortgaged property and, less commonly, in merely barring the right of the mortgagor to redeem the property from the mortgage.

Upon the mortgagor's default, the mortgagee in some states is entitled to obtain possession of the property and collect the rents or to have a receiver appointed for that purpose. In all states, the mortgagee may enforce the mortgage by **foreclosure,** a judicial procedure resulting in sale of the mortgaged property. Generally, upon any default under the terms of the mortgage agreement, the mortgagee has the right to accelerate the debt or declare that the entire mortgage debt is due. The mortgagee generally has this right even though the default related only to paying an installment or to doing some act, such as maintaining insurance on the property or producing receipts for taxes.

A sale resulting from the foreclosure of the mortgage ends the mortgage lien (subject to rights of redemption), and the property passes free of the mortgage to the buyer at the sale. However, the extinction of the mortgage by foreclosure does not destroy the debt that was secured by the mortgage. The mortgagor remains liable for any unpaid balance or deficiency. In many states, the mortgagor is generally given credit for the fair value of the property if it was purchased by the mortgagee.[10]

48-7i Rights of Mortgagor after Default

stay (or delay) of foreclosure–delay of foreclosure obtained by the mortgagor to prevent undue hardship.

After default, the mortgagor may seek to stop or stay foreclosure or to redeem the mortgaged land.

Stay of Foreclosure

In certain cases authorized by statute, a **stay (or delay) of foreclosure** may be obtained by the mortgagor to prevent undue hardship.

redemption–buying back of one's property, which has been sold because of a default, upon paying the amount that had been originally due together with interest and costs.

Redemption

The right of **redemption** is the right of the mortgagor to pay off the mortgage lien and all foreclosure expenses and, by so doing, acquire title to the property. State laws vary, but the right of redemption generally runs from the time of default through to six months after the foreclosure sale.

Make the Connection

Summary

Real property includes land, buildings, fixtures, and rights in the land of another. Some land interests include the right to use the land, such as easements. Easements can be granted or arise by implication or prescription.

The interest held by a person in real property may be defined in terms of the period of time for which the person will remain the owner. The interest may be a fee simple estate, which lasts forever, or a life estate, which lasts for the life of a person. These estates are known as *freehold estates*. If the ownership interest exists for a specified number of days, months, or years, the interest is a leasehold estate.

Personal property may be attached to, or associated with, real property in such a way that it becomes real property. In such a case, it is called a *fixture*. To determine whether property has in fact become a fixture, the courts

[10] *BMO Harris Bank, N.A. v. Wildwood Creek Ranch, LLC,* 340 P.3d 1071 (Ariz. 2015).

look to the method of attachment, to how the property is adapted to the realty, and to the intent of the person originally owning the personal property.

Under common law, the liability of a landowner for injury to third persons on the premises depends on the status of the third persons as trespassers, licensees, or invitees. Many jurisdictions, however, are ignoring these common law distinctions in favor of an ordinary negligence standard or are giving licensees the same protection as invitees.

Real property may be the subject of multiple ownership. The forms of multiple ownership are the same as those for personal property. In addition, there are special forms of co-ownership for real property, such as condominiums and cooperatives.

A *deed* is an instrument by which a grantor transfers an interest in land to a grantee. A deed can be a quitclaim deed or a warranty deed. To be effective, a deed must be signed or sealed by the grantor and delivered to the grantee. Recording the deed is not required to make the deed effective to pass title, but recording provides notice to the public that the grantee is the present owner. The warranties of the grantor relate to the title transferred by the grantor and to the fitness of the property for use. In the absence of any express warranty in the deed, no warranty of fitness arises under the common law in the sale or the conveyance of real estate. Most states today hold that when a builder or real estate developer sells a new home to a buyer, an implied warranty of habitability arises. Title to real estate may also be acquired by eminent domain and adverse possession.

An agreement that creates an interest in real property as security for an obligation and that ends upon the performance of the obligation is a mortgage. A mortgage must be in writing under the statute of frauds. If the mortgage is unrecorded, it is valid between the parties. The mortgage should be recorded to put good-faith purchasers on notice of the mortgage. A purchaser of the mortgaged property does not become liable for the mortgage debt unless the purchaser assumes the mortgage. The mortgagor still remains liable unless the mortgagee agrees to a substitution of parties. If the mortgagor defaults, the mortgagee may enforce the mortgage by foreclosure. Such foreclosure may be delayed because of undue hardship.

Learning Outcomes

After studying this chapter, you should be able to clearly explain:

48-1   Nature of Real Property

LO.1 List the types of real property interests, the rights of the parties and their liabilities
See *Kelo v. City of New London*, page 1015.

LO.2 Distinguish between liens, licenses, and easements
See *Dianne v. Wingate* for a discussion of easement holder rights, page 1003.
See the Sports & Entertainment Law discussion of the New England Patriots, page 1004.

48-2   Nature and Form of Real Property Ownership

LO.3 Discuss the nature and form of real property ownership
See In re *Ryerson* that covers stripping a home of property and the court's analysis as to what is a fixture and what is personal property, page 1006.

48-3   Liability to Third Persons for Condition of Real Property

LO.4 Explain the liability of landowners for injury to others on their property
See the slip-and-fall example in the section titled "Invitees," page 1008.

See the *Wrinkle v. Norman* case for coverage of the duty of landowners to Samaritans who come onto their property to help, page 1009.

48-4   Co-Ownership of Real Property

LO.5 Discuss the forms of co-ownership and parties' rights
See the example of the rights of condominium owners, page 1010.

48-5   Transfer of Real Property by Deed

LO.6 Describe how deeds convey title to land
See the *Chornuk v. Nelson* case for a discussion of multiple deed transfers and the rights of the parties, page 1013.

48-6   Other Methods of Transferring Real Property

Explain eminent domain and adverse possession.
See the *Kelo* case, page 1015.

48-7   Mortgages

LO.7 Describe the characteristics and effect of a mortgages
See the *For Example* discussion of Bob and Jane in the section titled "Liability of the Parties in a Transfer by a Mortgagor," page 1018.

Key Terms

abstract of title	fee simple defeasibles	prescription
acceptance	fee simple estate	profits
adjustable rate mortgage (ARM)	fixture	quitclaim deeds
adverse possession	foreclosure	race statutes
assumption	grantee	race-notice statute
attractive nuisance doctrine	grantor	real property
condominium	invitee	recorder
cooperative	judgment liens	redemption
covenant against encumbrances	land	remainder interest
covenant of further assurances	leasehold estate	reverse mortgage
covenant of quiet enjoyment	license	servient tenement
covenant of right to convey	licensee	stay (or delay) of foreclosure
covenant of seisin	liens	tax liens
covenants (or warranties) of title	life estate	transferee
deed	limited covenant	trespasser
dominant tenement	mechanic's liens	warranties of title
easement	mortgage	warranty deeds
easement by implication	notice statutes	way of necessity
eminent domain	notice-race statute	
estate in fee	possibility of reverter	

Questions and Case Problems

1. In 1972, Donald and Joyce Carnahan purchased a 1-acre lot located on a 22-acre lake. The purchase included a portion of the lake bed. The Carnahans used the lake for recreational activity in both winter and summer, and their activities included motorboats, jet skis, and wave runners. In 1991, the Moriah Property Owners Association, Inc., acquired title to the majority of the lots along the lake and imposed restrictive covenants on the use of the lake, including one that prohibited all motors on the lake except for those powered by 12-volt batteries. The Carnahans filed suit to establish a prescriptive easement in their right to use the lake for all their activities. Do you think the Carnahans acquired an easement by prescription? [*Carnahan v. Moriah Property Owners Association, Inc.*, 716 N.E.2d 437 (Ind.)]

2. Bunn and his wife claimed that they had an easement to enter and use the swimming pool on neighboring land. A contract between the former owners of the Bunns' property and the adjacent apartment complex contained a provision that the use of the apartment complex's swimming pool would be available to the purchaser and his family. No reference to the pool was made in the contract between the former owners and the Bunns, nor was there any reference to it in the deed conveying the property to the Bunns. Decide. [*Bunn v. Offutt*, 222 S.E.2d 522 (Va.)]

3. Harald Dude's real estate dealings began breaking bad in 2003. After securing a $1.9 million loan from Washington Mutual on a house he owned in Aspen, Mr. Dude quickly sought to borrow another $500,000 from Wells Fargo. The Washington Mutual mortgage was not yet recorded because of a defect in the property description. To satisfy Wells Fargo, Mr. Dude had to complete a form for the bank's title insurance company, Stewart Title. On that form, he was asked to disclose existing liens and loans on the property, at least those that hadn't already turned up in Stewart Title's title search. Knowing that the company had failed to discover the existence of the Washington Mutual loan and worried that disclosing it now might scotch any chance he had of winning a second loan from Wells Fargo, Mr. Dude decided to conceal its existence. The plan worked: Stewart Title and Wells Fargo proceeded with the second loan just as Mr. Dude had hoped. Discuss who will have priority in the land if Mr. Dude defaults. Does it matter that Mr. Dude

failed to disclose the loan and lien of Washington Mutual? What can we learn from situations such as this one? [*Stewart Title Guaranty Company v. Dude*, 708 F.3d 1191 (10th Cir.)]

4. After executing the various deeds, J. M. Fernandez Jr. placed them in a closet (with other valuable papers) for safekeeping until they could be physically delivered to the various grantees, including Sylvia Sheppard, when she returned to Key West. This closet was in the home that Fernandez shared with Betty DeMerritt. They were not married but lived together the final 15 years of Fernandez's life. Shortly thereafter, Fernandez was debilitated by a stroke and became a total invalid. He never regained his health and died before Sylvia Sheppard could return to Key West to receive physical delivery of the deed personally from him. When Sylvia Sheppard did arrive in Key West, Betty DeMerritt gave her the deed. This took place two or three days after the death of Fernandez. When questioned as to why she turned the deed over to Sylvia, Betty DeMerritt stated, "I knew he wanted me to do it … because he couldn't do it." She was speaking of Fernandez's physical disability. Does Sylvia have title to the property? Was there delivery? [*Kerr v. Fernandez*, 792 So. 2d 685 (Fla.)]

5. Kenneth Corson, 10, lived with his mother, Lynda Lontz, in an apartment building owned by Bruno and Carolyn Kosinski. While playing with other children who lived in the same building, Corson was drawn to a stairwell that provided access to the building's laundry room and roof. Corson and the other children climbed to the roof and discovered an area where they could jump from the roof of their building to that of the building next door. The children engaged in roof-hopping for several days. On the last day, Corson misjudged his jump and fell the three stories to the ground below. Corson and his mother filed suit against the Kosinskis to collect damages for Corson's injuries. What theory might be used to hold the Kosinskis liable? [*Corson by Lontz v. Kosinski*, 801 F. Supp. 75 (N.D. Ill.)]

6. Determine whether the following would be fixtures or personal property.

   a. Refrigerator in a home

   b. Refrigerators in an apartment complex with furnished units

   c. Refrigerators in a restaurant kitchen

   d. Refrigeration/freezer units in a grocery store

   e. Mini-refrigerator in a student dorm

7. What is the relationship between trespass and adverse possession?

8. At approximately 3:00 A.M., on February 3, 2000, Sonya Winchell was driving two of her friends through a Fort Wayne Taco Bell drive-thru. When Winchell arrived in line, there was one car in front of her at the speaker. Winchell noticed that the occupants of the car, Remco Guy and Ariel Graham, were taking a long time placing their order and then got out of their car. At that point, Winchell yelled out her window, "Can we get moving, we are hungry!" Guy approached Winchell's car, stuck his head in the window, and "started cussing everybody out." Guy removed his head from the window, stuck it back in, and asked, "You got an f-ing problem?" Winchell responded by "drill[ing] him in the nose." Guy then pulled a gun out of his pants and shot Winchell. One of Winchell's passengers and others summoned police officers who were in a nearby parking lot. Winchell survived the shooting, and Guy was convicted of attempted murder. Winchell filed a civil action against Guy and Graham, and against Taco Bell, alleging negligence. Is Taco Bell liable for the injuries that occur on its property? [*Winchell v. Guy*, 857 N.E.2d 1024 (Ind.)]

9. Miller executed a deed to real estate, naming Zieg as grantee. He placed the deed in an envelope on which was written "To be filed at my death" and put the envelope and deed in a safe deposit box in the National Bank that had been rented in the names of Miller and Zieg. After Miller's death, Zieg removed the deed from the safe deposit box. Moseley, as executor under Miller's will, brought an action against Zieg to declare the deed void. Decide. [*Moseley v. Zieg*, 146 N.W.2d 72 (Neb.)]

10. Henry Lile owned a house. When the land on which it was situated was condemned for a highway, he moved the house to the land of his daughter, Sarah Crick. In the course of construction work, blasting damaged the house. Sarah Crick sued the contractors, Terry & Wright, who claimed that Lile should be joined in the action as a plaintiff and that Sarah could not sue by herself because it was Lile's house. Were the defendants correct? [*Terry & Wright v. Crick*, 418 S.W.2d 217 (Ky.)]

11. Bradt believed that his backyard ran all the way to a fence. Actually, a strip on Bradt's side of the fence belonged to his neighbor, Giovannone, but Bradt never intended to take land away from anyone. Bradt later brought an action against Giovannone to

determine who owned the strip on Bradt's side of the fence. Who is the owner? Why? [*Bradt v. Giovannone*, 315 N.Y.S.2d 96]

12. Robert E. Long owned land in the City of Hampton that he leased to Adams Outdoor Advertising Limited Partnership. Adams had an advertising billboard placed on the property. On October 6, 1993, Long notified Adams that he was terminating the lease. Adams accepted the termination and told Long that it would have the electrical service disconnected and would schedule demolition of the billboard for the first week in November. Long wanted to use the billboard to advertise his own business and filed suit to enjoin Adams from destroying the billboard. Long maintained that the billboard was part of the land and that it belonged to him. Adams asserted that it owned the billboard as a lessee. The trial court found for Long, and Adams appealed. Decide. [*Adams Outdoor Adv., Ltd., Part. v. Long*, 483 S.E.2d 224 (Va.)]

13. The Friersons have a two-story building in Easley, South Carolina, that shares a common wall with an adjacent two-story building owned by David and Patricia Watson. An outdoor stairway located on the Watsons' property provides access to the second floor of both buildings. A dispute arose when David Watson began to construct apartments on the second floor of his building and proposed to close off a connecting indoor hallway between the two properties at the top of the stairs located inside the building. The Friersons maintained that they had an easement to use both the outdoor stairway and the indoor hallway for access.

The Friersons' predecessors-in-interest, E. C, E. O., and D. M. Frierson, purchased the building in 1929 from the "Estate of R. F. Smith, Inc." The 1929 deed, dated January 14 and recorded on January 23, expressly conveyed "an easement in a certain four foot stairway in the back of the building, with right of ingress and egress on said stairway to the second story of said building." On January 21, 1929, two days before the deed was recorded, the parties to the sale executed a "Memorandum of Agreement" that granted an easement for the use of the hallway. The memo was not recorded. The Friersons brought suit to stop Watson's construction.

The Friersons claimed that Watson's construction violated their easement by eliminating the hallway, which denied them access to the second floor of their building.

The circuit court determined that the Friersons had established an easement for use of the hallway by grant and by prescription and granted the Friersons' motion. David Watson appealed. Who is correct on this easement issue? Explain why. [*Frierson v. Watson*, 636 S.E. 2d 872 (S.C. App.)]

14. Martin Manufacturing decided to raise additional long-term capital by mortgaging an industrial park it owned. First National Loan Co. agreed to lend Martin $1 million and to take a note and first mortgage on the land and building. The mortgage was duly recorded. Martin sold the property to Marshall, who took the property and assumed the mortgage debt. Does Marshall have any personal liability on the mortgage debt? Is Martin still liable on the mortgage debt? Explain.

15. Christine and Steve Mallock buried their son in a burial plot purchased at Southern Memorial Park, Inc. Each year the Mallocks conducted a memorial service for their son at his burial plot. On the seventh anniversary of their son's death, the Mallocks went to their son's grave at 11:00 A.M. for the annual service, which generally took 30 minutes. When they arrived, they discovered that a tent and chairs set up for funeral services on the plot next to their son's grave were actually resting on his gravesite. The Mallocks asked Southern's management if the tent and chairs could be moved until they could conduct their service. The managers refused, and the Mallocks went ahead with their ceremony, cutting it to five minutes, after they moved the chairs and tents by themselves. Southern's managers called the police and had the Mallocks evicted. Southern claimed that the Mallocks had no rights on the property except for the grave and that their deed for the plot did not award an easement for access. Did the Mallocks have the right to access to the gravesite? [*Mallock v. Southern Memorial Park, Inc.*, 561 So. 2d 330 (Fla. Ct. App.)]

16. *O* conveys property to *A* on December 1, 2015. *O* conveys the same property to *B* who does not know about *A* and who records his deed on December 2, 2015. *O* then conveys the same property to *C*. Who has title to the property?

CPA Questions

The topic of insurance has been eliminated from the content outline for the CPA exam as of October 2009. However, the exam lags behind the content change, and real property questions have continued to be released as questions on the exam.

1. Which of the following statements is correct with respect to a real estate mortgage?

    a. It must be signed only by the mortgagor (borrower).

    b. It must be recorded in order to be effective between the mortgagor and the mortgagee.

    c. It does *not* have to be recorded to be effective against third parties without notice if it is a purchase money mortgage.

    d. It is effective even if *not* delivered to the mortgagee.

2. To be enforceable against the mortgagor, a mortgage must meet all the following requirements *except*:

    a. Be delivered to the mortgagee.

    b. Be in writing and signed by the mortgagor.

    c. Be recorded by the mortgagee.

    d. Include a description of the debt and land involved.

3. Ritz owned a building in which there was a duly recorded first mortgage held by Lyn and a recorded second mortgage held by Jay. Ritz sold the building to Nunn. Nunn assumed the Jay mortgage and had no actual knowledge of the Lyn mortgage. Nunn defaulted on the payments to Jay. If both Lyn and Jay foreclosed and the proceeds of the sale were insufficient to pay both Lyn and Jay, then:

    a. Jay would be paid after Lyn was fully paid.

    b. Jay and Lyn would be paid proportionately.

    c. Nunn would be personally liable to Lyn but not to Jay.

    d. Nunn would be personally liable to Lyn and Jay.

4. Which of the following deeds will give a real property purchaser the greatest protection?

    a. Quitclaim

    b. Bargain and sale

    c. Special warranty

    d. General warranty

Environmental Law and Land Use Controls

Learning Outcomes ⟨⟨⟨

After studying this chapter, you should be able to

LO.1 List and describe the federal statutes that regulate various aspects of the environment

LO.2 Explain how environmental laws are enforced and describe the criminal penalties for violation of environmental laws

LO.3 Define *nuisance* and list the remedies available

LO.4 Explain the role and application of covenants and zoning laws

49-1   Statutory Environmental Law

As the United States changed from a rural, agricultural society to an urban, industrial one, new laws were needed to prevent the pollution of the environment.

49-1a   Air Pollution Regulation

Legislative History of Air Pollution Regulation

The first legislation that dealt with air pollution, passed in 1955, was the Air Pollution Control Act, which was simply a statutory recognition of a concern about air quality. Even the first statute regulating air pollution, the **Clean Air Act,** passed in 1963, produced no response from the states, which were charged with the responsibility of developing pollution standards and enforcement mechanisms. It was not until the 1970 amendments to the Clean Air Act that the federal law on air pollution got some teeth, for it was in those amendments that Congress established the federal agency responsible for enforcing the law, the Environmental Protection Agency (EPA). The EPA was authorized to establish national air quality standards and see that the states developed plans for the implementation of those standards.

Modern Legislation and Requirements

Under the 1970 Clean Air Act,[1] as well as the 1977 and 1990 amendments to it, states must measure sulfur dioxide, carbon monoxide, and hydrocarbons and then take appropriate steps to bring their air quality within the federal limits established for each of these. States that do not meet federal standards are called **nonattainment areas,** or *dirty areas*, and their plans for implementation are strictly reviewed by the EPA, which can halt federal highway funding in the event the implementation plan is not followed. Those states that do meet the federal standards must still have a plan to remain at that level.

For nonattainment areas, the EPA developed an **emissions offset policy,** which controls whether new factories can be built. For a new plant to obtain a permit to begin operations in a nonattainment area, the business proposing the new plant must be able to show that (1) the plant will have the greatest possible emissions controls, which means having better-than-existing emissions standards, (2) the business has all of its other plants and operations in compliance with federal emissions standards, and (3) the new plant's emissions will be offset by reductions in emissions in other facilities in the area. This last requirement is often referred to as the **bubble concept,** which requires an examination of all emissions from all sources in an area. Before any new operations with emissions can be permitted, the business seeking approval must be able to show that overall emissions in the area will not increase.

The 1990 amendments to the Clean Air Act increased the role of the bubble concept with the ability of businesses to transfer their emissions permits. Those businesses that can reduce their emissions below their allowable amounts or that can eliminate their emissions are free to transfer their permit rights to emit to someone else who can then use them without affecting total emissions in the bubble area. There is a market exchange for emissions permits because the EPA will not, under the 1990 act, issue any additional permits beyond the rights to emissions that already exist. Today, approximately 10 percent of all the emissions permit rights are owned by environmental groups.

Clean Air Act–federal legislation that establishes standards for air pollution levels and prevents further deterioration of air quality.

nonattainment areas–"dirty" areas that do not meet federal standards under the Clean Air Act.

emissions offset policy–controls whether new factories can be built in a nonattainment area.

bubble concept–method for determining total emissions in one area; all sources are considered in an area.

[1] 42 U.S.C. §1857 *et seq.*

New Developments in Air Quality: The U.S. Supreme Court and the EPA

In *Environmental Defense v. Duke Energy*, 549 U.S. 561 (2007), the U.S. Supreme Court heard a case in which the EPA had brought suit against Duke Energy for implementing modifications to its coal-fired electricity plants without first filing for approval from the agency. Duke maintained that only major modifications to power plants required EPA approval, a standard the EPA had been following for years. However, the EPA based its expanded permit requirements for even minor modifications under the Prevention of Significant Deterioration (PSD) regulations. The utilities challenged the agency's authority to act on greenhouse gases and global warming issues because there was no statutory provision that covered such an expansion. The Court held that the EPA could step up its permit requirements and still be within its statutory authority in choosing which modifications to regulate via permit. The standard has now evolved to one that goes beyond best available technology (BAT) to maximum achievable control technology (MACT), a standard that is not controlled by cost alone, but under recent rulings cost must be considered and weighed.

In *Massachusetts v. EPA*, 549 U.S. 497 (2007), the Court held that the Clean Air Act mandated EPA action on greenhouse gases and global warming. In *Michigan v. EPA*, 135 S.Ct. 2699 (2015), the court held that the EPA must consider cost in researching and promulgating rules with regard to plant emissions. The court held that cost is relevant under the statutes that give the EPA its authority. The EPA efforts against primarily coal-fired plants can continue, but the agency will have to examine the costs of, for example, reducing mercury emissions vs. the benefits obtained.

One expansion of EPA authority has been the EPA rule promulgated to address downwind pollution from coal and gas-fired power plants—that is, pollution that drifts from one state to others. The EPA now requires the upwind states to reduce emissions that result in air pollution problems downwind. Upwind states (there are 28) must control sources within their borders from emitting pollution that travels across state lines in a way that prevents downwind states' attainment of their air quality levels.[2] Known as the **Transport Rule,** this regulation is also referred to as a "good neighbor" provision, and its impact has been the shutdown of coal-fired facilities.

From 2009 forward, there has been increasing expansion of EPA authority through rules that were implemented regardless of the costs to business. **For Example,** the *Michigan v. EPA* case held that the EPA had acted unreasonably under the so-called mercury rules, where the cost of power plant compliance would have been $9.6 billion a year, but the quantifiable benefits from the reduction would be only $4 million to $6 million. The Court's 5-4 holding was one that allowed EPA expansion with the caveat that the agency employ cost/benefit analysis.

Transport Rule–the rule promulgated to address downwind pollution from coal and gas-fired power plants.

49-1b **Water Pollution Regulation**

The first meaningful regulation in water pollution began at about the same time as effective air pollution regulation. The first legislation with enforcement power was passed in 1972 as the Federal Water Pollution Control Act and then amended and renamed in 1977 as the **Clean Water Act.**[3] Under the Clean Water Act, the EPA has developed **effluent guidelines,** which are ranges for discharges organized according to industrial groups and for

Clean Water Act–federal legislation that regulates water pollution through a control system.

effluent guidelines–EPA standards for maximum ranges of discharge into water.

---

[2] *EME Homer City Generation, L.P. v. EPA*, 134 S. Ct. 1584 (2014). The Transport Rule continues to be a subject of litigation. *Westar Energy, Inc. v. E.P.A.*, 608 Fed.Appx. 1 (C.A.D.C. 2014); Emma E. Schoedel, "The Siren's Song of a Trickle-Down Bureaucracy: The Transport Rule, The Problem of Air Contamination Crossing State Lines, and the EPA Crossing Its Line," 53 *Duquesne Law Review* 629 (2015).

[3] 33 U.S.C. §1251 *et seq.* The pollution of navigable waters had been regulated by the Rivers and Harbors Act of 1899, which required a permit for discharging into navigable rivers, streams, and lakes.

National Pollutant Discharge Elimination System (NPDES)–EPA system for regulating point source emissions into water.

point sources–direct discharges into bodies of water.

best conventional treatment–a water treatment that is generally used among industries; not always the best treatment available.

best available treatment–a water treatment that is the most current and best available through research, even though it may not be the treatment used most frequently.

Safe Drinking Water Act–a federal law that establishes national standards for contaminants in drinking water.

Oil Pollution Act–federal law that assigns cleanup liability for oil spills in U.S. waters.

Resource Recovery Act–early federal solid waste disposal legislation that provided funding for states and local governments with recycling programs.

specific plants in each of these groups. The guidelines establish the maximum amounts that can be discharged, and those maximums are coupled with a permit system that requires each plant to obtain a permit from the EPA before discharging anything into any type of pool, pond, river, lake, stream, or ocean.[4] **For Example,** a plant that releases hot water from a steam generator must still have a permit just to release hot water into the stream near the plant. The EPA also has standards for the treatment of water that is used in a plant's production process before that water can be discharged.[5] **For Example,** a plant must still have a permit to discharge water even though that water is cleaner as it is discharged from the plant than it was when it was brought in to be used in production or manufacturing. However, the EPA is permitted to use cost-benefit analysis in setting the standards for the quality of the water that is released back into the river, lake, and other bodies of water. All discharges into the waterways require a **National Pollutant Discharge Elimination System (NPDES)** permit from the EPA. This type of permit is required only for direct dischargers, or **point sources,** and is not required of plants that discharge into sewer systems (although these secondary dischargers may still be required to pretreat their discharges). Obtaining a permit requires EPA and state approval as well as public hearings.

The permits also impose requirements on the permit holder. If the plant is going to release a conventional pollutant, the EPA can require the plant to pretreat the substance with the **best conventional treatment** (BCT). However, the EPA can also require the **best available treatment** (BAT) standard, which is the highest standard imposed. Until 2009, the standard for requiring BAT was solely the consideration of environmental effects and not the economic effects on the applicant. However, the U.S. Supreme Court has held that the EPA can use cost-benefit analysis to allow variances from those standards. In the *Entergy Corporation v. Riverkeeper* case, Entergy's cost of bringing cooling water intake structures to the higher level that the EPA requires for new structures would have been nine times the existing costs. The Court held that the additional benefit achieved was too small to justify the cost of bringing the cooling water facilities up to BAT standards.[6] With this decision as well as the decision in *Michigan v. EPA*, the court has held that cost is a factor in the validity of EPA rules on both air and water pollution controls.

There are other federal statutes that address water pollution issues. The **Safe Drinking Water Act** requires the EPA to establish national standards for contaminants in drinking water. The **Oil Pollution Act** is a federal law passed following the oil spill from the *Exxon Valdez* off the coast of Alaska, which resulted in damage to the waters, fish, and birds in that area. Under this law, companies are financially responsible for the cleanup of their spills that occur in U.S. waters. The act also provides for substantial penalties for failure to take action to clean up a spill, and those penalties can be as high as $25,000 per day or $3,000 per barrel if the spill is the result of negligence or willful misconduct.[7] Failure to report a spill carries penalties of up to five years in prison and/or $250,000 per individual and $500,000 for corporations. In addition, civil penalties for the failure to clean up an oil spill can cost the company up to $50,000,000 in penalties.

---

[4] Even the placement of dirt from adjoining property into a stream can be a CWA violation. *Sackett v. EPA*, 132 S. Ct. 1367 (2012).

[5] In *Coeur Alaska v. Southeast Alaska Conservation*, 557 U.S. 261 (2009), the court held that a project in an Alaskan lake under the supervision of the Army Corps of Engineers did not require an EPA permit process for the operator to obtain permission to dump fill dirt into the lake.

[6] *Entergy Corporation v. Riverkeeper, Inc.*, 556 U.S. 208 (2009).

[7] 33 U.S.C. §2701 *et seq.* The act establishes a cleanup fund for those spills in which the party to blame is unknown or is financially unable to pay the cost of cleanup. The act also requires that boats be double-hulled. The *Exxon Shipping Co. v. Baker*, 554 U.S. 471 (2008) case went through the courts several times before Exxon's initial penalty of $4.5 billion was reduced to maritime limitations of $507.5 million. *Exxon Valdez v. Exxon Mobil*, 568 F.3d 1077 (9th Cir. 2009). Following the 2010 BP Deepwater Horizon rig explosion, BP paid a criminal penalty of $4.5 billion. The civil penalty settlement, which is the settlement of all states and federal claims against BP, is $18.7 billion. Total costs, penalties, and settlements in the case resulted in BP paying out $43.7 billion.

ETHICS & THE LAW

Spreading the Manure a Little Too Thick

Mahard Egg Farm, Inc., headquartered in Texas and with operations in Oklahoma, is the country's 17th largest egg producer. Mahard's poultry operations generated significant amounts of manure—estimated to be in excess of 50,000 tons of dry manure per year. Mahard applied poultry manure to its agricultural fields, with the result being that when it rained and the soil washed into creeks and rivers, the waterways also had high levels of nutrients.

In addition, Mahard stored manure on its farms and the manure piles often resulted in what are called "inactive manure lagoons," with the resulting smells and flies as well

as seepage of the manure and the nutrients into the groundwater.

Mahard has some NPDES permits for some of its facilities, but it did not for others. In addition, Mahard did not comply with its permit requirements for grass buffers as well as control of soil flow.

Develop a list of possible environmental violations. Does it matter for purposes of EPA discharge regulations that the nutrients came from nature (i.e., the manure)? What are the risks for a business when its operations are not in compliance?

Toxic Substances Control Act (TOSCA)–first federal law to control the manufacture, use, and disposal of toxic substances.

Resource Conservation and Recovery Act (RCRA)–federal law that regulates the disposal of potentially harmful substances and encourages resource conservation and recovery.

Comprehensive Environmental Response, Compensation, and Liability Act (CERCLA)–federal law that assigns liability for cleanup of hazardous sites.

Superfund sites–areas designated by the EPA for cleanup.

Superfund Amendment and Reauthorization Act–federal law that expands scope and operation of CERCLA.

potentially responsible parties (PRPs)–those beyond actual polluters who could be responsible for cleanup costs.

49-1c Solid Waste Disposal Regulation

The disposal of solid waste (garbage) has also been regulated since the 1960s, but the initial legislation simply provided money for research by state and local governments on how to dispose of solid waste.[8] In 1970, the **Resource Recovery Act** provided federal money for cities and states with recycling programs.

After several major open-dumping problems that produced community-wide illnesses, including those in the Love Canal area near Buffalo, New York, Congress passed the **Toxic Substances Control Act (TOSCA),** which controls the manufacture, use, and disposal of toxic substances, a list of which the EPA developed. Along with TOSCA, Congress passed the **Resource Conservation and Recovery Act (RCRA),** which regulates the disposal of potentially harmful substances through a permit system and uses federal grants to encourage the restoration of damaged resources.[9] **For Example,** many strip mine locations were restored due to the RCRA.

In 1980, Congress passed the **Comprehensive Environmental Response, Compensation, and Liability Act (CERCLA),**[10] which authorizes the U.S. president to issue funds to be used for the cleanup of areas that were once disposal sites for hazardous wastes. The act set up a trust fund for cleanups, to be reimbursed by the company responsible for such hazardous wastes. The funds in the trust are available for government use but are not subject to attachment by private citizens who seek to get an area cleaned up by removing the hazardous waste. Under CERCLA, the EPA has the authority to designate **Superfund sites,** or parcels of land that are deemed to have, or potentially have, hazardous wastes that require cleanup.

The **Superfund Amendment and Reauthorization Act** authorizes the EPA to bring suit for the purpose of collecting the costs of cleanup from those who are responsible for the hazardous wastes on the site. The act and its judicial interpretations provide a very broad definition of who is responsible under CERCLA for the costs of cleanup. Four classes of parties, known as **potentially responsible parties (PRPs),** can be held liable under CERCLA. "Owners and operators" of contaminated property are liable under the statute.

---

[8] See the Solid Waste Disposal Act, 42 U.S.C. §3251 *et seq.*, and the Resource Recovery and Policy Act of 1970, 42 U.S.C. §3251 *et seq.*
[9] 42 U.S.C. §6901 *et seq.*
[10] 42 U.S.C. §9601 *et seq.*

Owners include present owners as well as past owners, whether or not they are responsible for the hazardous wastes being dumped on the property. *Operators* include those who are leasing the property, again regardless of whether they are responsible for the hazardous waste being dumped. **For Example,** many gas stations have been designated as Superfund sites because the underground tanks have leaks, causing gas to seep into the soil. Current and past owners of such a station are responsible under CERCLA as well as an owner who has converted the station into some other use.[11]

Other responsible parties under CERCLA include anyone who transported hazardous waste to a site and anyone who hired another or arranged to transport hazardous waste to the site. Lenders were, at one time, also held liable for cleanup costs in the event they took back property from a debtor. However, the Asset Conservation, Lender Liability, and Deposit Insurance Protection Act of 1996 provides an exclusion for lenders provided the lender does not actually participate in the management or operational affairs of the facility of the debtor.[12]

CASE SUMMARY

Don't Blame Me, I'm Only the Arranger

FACTS: In 1960, Brown & Bryant, Inc. (B & B), began operating an agricultural chemical distribution business. Using its own equipment, B & B applied its products to customers' farms. B & B opened its business on a 3.8 acre parcel of former farmland in Arvin, California, and in 1975, expanded operations onto an adjacent .9 acre parcel of land owned jointly by the Atchison, Topeka & Santa Fe Railway Company, and the Southern Pacific Transportation Company (Railroads). Waste water and chemical runoff from the facility was allowed to seep into the ground water below.

During its years of operation, B & B stored and distributed various hazardous chemicals (D-D) on its property sold by Shell Oil Company (Shell). When B & B purchased chemicals from Shell, Shell would arrange for delivery by common carrier, f.o.b. destination. When the product arrived, it was transferred from tanker trucks to a bulk storage tank located on B & B's primary parcel. During each of these transfers leaks and spills could—and often did—occur. Although the common carrier and B & B used buckets to catch spills from hoses and gaskets connecting the tanker trucks to its bulk storage tank, the buckets sometimes overflowed or were knocked over, causing chemical spills onto the ground during the transfer process.

In the late 1970s Shell took several steps to encourage the safe handling of its products. Shell provided distributors

with detailed safety manuals and instituted a voluntary discount program for distributors that made improvements in their bulk handling and safety facilities. Later, Shell required distributors to obtain an inspection by a qualified engineer and provide self-certification of compliance with applicable laws and regulations. B & B's Arvin facility was inspected twice and B & B had made a number of recommended improvements to its facilities. Despite these improvements, B & B remained a "[s]loppy [o]perator." The EPA soon discovered significant contamination of soil and ground water.

By 1989, B & B was insolvent and ceased all operations, and the Arvin facility was designated as a Superfund site. By 1998, the Governments had spent more than $8 million in cleanup costs.

In 1991, EPA (Governments) ordered the Railroads to conduct certain cleanup processes. The Railroads did so, incurring expenses of more than $3 million in the process. Seeking to recover at least a portion of these costs, the Railroads brought suit against B & B.

The District Court held that both the Railroads and Shell were PRPs under CERCLA—the Railroads because they were owners of a portion of the facility, and Shell because it had "arranged for" the disposal of hazardous substances through its sale and delivery of chemicals.

---

[11] Courts do require some proof of causation between a company's conduct and the resulting toxic contamination. *NCR Corp. v. George A. Whiting Paper Co.*, 768 F.3d 682 (7th Cir. 2014).

[12] "Participating" does not include monitoring or enforcing the security agreement, monitoring or inspecting the premises, providing financial advice, mandating cleanup of hazardous materials, restructuring the loan, foreclosing, or selling or leasing the property.

Don't Blame Me, I'm Only the Arranger continued

Although the court found the parties liable, it did not impose joint and several liability on Shell and the Railroads for the entire cleanup cost. The court apportioned the Railroads' liability as 9% of the Governments' total response cost. Based on estimations of chemicals spills of Shell products, the court held Shell liable for 6% of the total site response cost.

The state and local governments appealed the District Court's apportionment, and Shell cross-appealed the court's finding of liability. Applying a theory of arranger liability, the Ninth Circuit held that Shell arranged for the disposal of a hazardous substance.

The Court of Appeals held Shell and the Railroads jointly and severally liable for the Governments' cost of responding to the contamination of the Arvin facility.

The Railroads and Shell appealed.

DECISION: The primary pollution at the Arvin facility was contained in the southeastern portion of the facility most distant from the Railroads' parcel and the spills of hazardous chemicals that occurred on the Railroad parcel contributed to no more than 10% of the total site contamination, some of which did not require cleanup.

The court reversed the Court of Appeals' conclusion that the Railroads are subject to joint and several liability for all costs arising out of the contamination of the Arvin facility.

The court held that Shell should not be held liable as an arranger under CERCLA because it did not arrange for disposal and it ran responsible programs to get distributors to comply with its standards. However, there was not intent on the part of Shell to dump the chemicals by arranging for their delivery. The court also held that the Railroads' share of the site cleanup costs was reasonably apportioned at 9% and that the parties were not joint and severally liable. The judgment was reversed. [***Burlington Northern Railway/Shell Oil Co. v. U.S.,*** **556 U.S. 599 (2009)]**

CERCLA liability has been extended to those who merge or buy corporations; these parties also buy into CERCLA liability, and liability under CERCLA cannot be avoided by a transfer of ownership. The U.S. Supreme Court has ruled in *United States v. Bestfoods*, 525 U.S. 51 (1998), that a parent corporation is not automatically liable under CERCLA for a subsidiary corporation's conduct but may be responsible if the subsidiary is simply a shell. In other words, CERCLA liability of parent corporations for the actions of their subsidiaries is governed by corporate law on piercing the corporate veil (see Chapter 3 for more information).

 THINKING THINGS THROUGH

The Leaking Barrels GE Sold

For over 30 years, GE manufactured electric capacitors containing Pyranol at its plants located in New York. GE met its Pyranol needs by purchasing polychlorinated biphenyl (PCB) from Monsanto. GE then refined the PCBs it purchased until the PCBs attained the level of purity necessary for the Pyranol used in the capacitors.

Pyranol that fell short of GE purity standards was deemed "scrap Pyranol" and was stored in 55-gallon drums on site. Over time, GE accumulated a glut of scrap Pyranol and had Frederic H. Fletcher, local manufacturer, "chemical scrapper," and businessman, purchase the scrap Pyranol from GE at bargain prices for his industrial needs.

For approximately 10 years, ending in 1967, Fletcher purchased about 200,000 gallons, or 3,600 55-gallon drums, of Pyranol from GE. Fletcher was not prompt on his payments and by August 1967, Fletcher's account was delinquent. Fletcher told GE that the scrap Pyranol he received had markedly declined and he ended his relationship with GE.

In 1987, EPA found hundreds of drums containing scrap Pyranol and other chemicals at Fletcher's business. The drums were unmarked and several had leaked. The EPA filed suit against GE to recoup costs associated with the Fletcher site's cleanup as an arranger. Explain whether GE is an arranger and whether GE should be held liable for the cost of the Fletcher cleanup.

[*U.S. v. General Elec. Co.*, 670 F.3d 377 (1st Cir. 2012)]

One of the new key areas for minimizing CERCLA liability is that of the self-audit, a company's internal investigation of its operations and lands to determine whether any environmental hazards are on its properties. Many companies wanted to know, for the sake of financial planning and minimizing harm, whether they had any Superfund issues. However, they did not want their voluntary investigations and cleanups to work against them. To encourage these types of internal investigations and self-reporting, the EPA developed its Incentives for Self-Policing, Disclosure, Correction, and Prevention of Violations. Under this EPA program, companies can have their penalties reduced and not waive any rights if they follow the procedures and meet the following requirements: (1) the violations were uncovered as part of a self-audit, (2) the violations were uncovered voluntarily, (3) the violations were reported to the EPA within 10 days, (4) the discovery was made independently and disclosed independently and no one was threatening disclosure, (5) the violations are corrected within 60 days, (6) there is a written agreement that the conduct will not happen again, (7) there is no history of repeat violations, (8) no serious harm came to anyone as a result of the conduct, and (9) the company cooperates completely with the EPA. If these requirements are met, the company is eligible for reductions in fines and penalties of up to 75 percent.

CERCLA has been so effective that designated Superfund sites estimates place the number of currently undeveloped brownfields at 425,000. "**Brownfields,**" are sites defined by the EPA as "real property, the expansion, redevelopment, or reuse of which may be complicated by the presence or potential presence of a hazardous substance, pollutant, or contaminant." The Small Business Liability Relief and Brownfields Revitalization Act brings together 75 federal agencies that work through the *Federal Partnership Action Agenda* to provide funding for proposals to clean up and use these brownfields (42 U.S.C.A. §9601). The EPA has a process for becoming an "innocent landowner," someone who seeks to develop the brownfield but wants an exemption from CERCLA exposure. That designation then allows the applicant to obtain federal funding for purposes of cleaning up and developing the brownfield.

brownfields–land that is a designated Superfund cleanup site but which lies fallow because no one is willing to risk liability by buying the property, even when the hazardous waste has been removed, or property no one is willing to spend the money to remove the hazardous waste.

National Environmental Policy Act (NEPA)– federal law that mandates study of a project's impact on the environment before it can be undertaken by any federal agency.

environmental impact statement (EIS)–formal report prepared under NEPA to document findings on the impact of a federal project on the environment.

Noise Control Act– federal law that controls noise emissions from low-flying aircraft.

49-1d Environmental Quality Regulation

The federal statutes on air, water, and solid waste pollution are directed at private parties in their use of land. However, the federal government also regulates itself in terms of its operations and impact on the environment. The **National Environmental Policy Act (NEPA)** requires federal agencies to consider the impact on the environment of their proposed projects.[13] An agency must prepare a report, called an **environmental impact statement (EIS),** that documents the impact of the proposed federal project on the environment and covers consideration of practical and feasible alternatives with a lesser impact.[14] **For Example,** the federal government was required to file an EIS for the Alaska oil pipeline, the extermination of wild horses, the construction of a post office, the implementation of a change in national park airport procedures that would permit jets to land, and highway construction.

49-1e Other Environmental Regulations

In addition to the major categories of environmental laws just covered, several other important statutes regulate specific areas of the environment. The **Noise Control Act** sets standards for noise from low-flying aircraft for the protection of landowners who are

---

[13] 42 U.S.C. §4321 *et seq.*
[14] For contrasting cases of when an EIS is required, see *Kentucky Coal Ass'n, Inc. v. Tennessee Valley Authority*, 68 F. Supp. 3d 685 (W.D. Ky. 2014), and *Confederated Tribes of Grand Ronde Community of Oregon v. Jewell*, 75 F. Supp. 3d 387 (D.D.C. 2014).

in flight paths.[15] The **Endangered Species Act (ESA)** gives the secretary of the interior the responsibility of identifying and protecting endangered terrestrial species, while the secretary of commerce is responsible for endangered marine species.[16] These cabinet-level federal officers have the authority to curtail any development, noise, or other act that threatens those species on their endangered lists.[17]

CASE SUMMARY

The Loggers and the Naturalists Can't Be Friends: Oregon—Where the Spotted Owl Comes Flying in the Trees

FACTS: Two U.S. agencies halted logging in the Pacific Northwest because it endangered the habitat of the northern spotted owl and the red-cockaded woodpecker, both endangered species. Sweet Home Chapter (respondents) is a group of landowners, logging companies, and families dependent on the forest products industries in the Pacific Northwest. They brought suit seeking clarification of the authority of the secretary of the interior and the director of the Fish and Wildlife Service (petitioners) to include habitation modification as a harm covered by the Endangered Species Act (ESA).

The federal district court found for the secretary and director and held that they had the authority to protect the northern spotted owl through a halt to logging. The court of appeals reversed. Babbitt, the secretary of the interior, appealed.

DECISION: The statutory word *harm* encompasses direct as well as indirect injuries. The broad purpose of the ESA supports the secretary's decision to extend protection against

activities that cause the precise harms Congress enacted the statute to avoid—that is, to provide a means whereby the ecosystems upon which endangered species and threatened species depend may be conserved.

When it enacted the ESA, Congress delegated broad administrative and interpretive power to the secretary. The proper interpretation of a word such as *harm* involves a complex policy choice. When Congress has entrusted the secretary with broad discretion, courts should not substitute their views of wise policy. The judgment of the Court of Appeals was reversed.* [*Babbitt v. Sweet Home Chapter of Communities for a Great Oregon,* 515 U.S. 687 (1995)]

*Following this decision, Congress passed a rider to a budget-reduction bill that suspended environmental laws in many national forests in Washington and Oregon. The logging industry, paper products processors, and environmentalists have since worked together to find mutually acceptable solutions to logging and the protection of endangered species. Known as the "Sustainable Forestry Initiative," the goal is ecofriendly logging.

Endangered Species Act (ESA)–federal law that identifies and protects species that are endangered from development or other acts that threaten their existence.

49-1f State Environmental Regulation

All states have some form of environmental regulation, and their environmental agencies work closely with the EPA on enforcement and standards.[18] All states have some form of hazardous waste controls that define hazardous waste differently and carry a range of penalties for violations. **For Example,** Oregon imposes a fine of $3,500 per animal killed as a result of hazardous waste dumping. Other states mandate disclosure of the history of property use before that property can be sold, transferred, or mortgaged.

49-2 Enforcement of Environmental Laws

Federal environmental laws can be enforced through criminal sanctions, penalties, injunctions, and suits by private citizens. In addition to federal enforcement rights, certain common law remedies exist for the protection of property rights, such as the remedies for nuisance.

[15] 42 U.S.C. §4901.
[16] 16 U.S.C. §1530 *et seq.*
[17] The authority to bring suit rests with both landowners and environmentalists. *Bennett v. Spear,* 520 U.S. 154 (1997). See also *Northwest Coalition for Alternatives to Pesticides v. U.S. E.P.A.,* 920 F. Supp. 2d 1168 (W.D. Wash. 2013).
[18] *Chico Service Station, Inc. v. Sol Puerto Rico Ltd.,* 633 F.3d 20 (1st Cir. 2011).

49-2a Parties Responsible for Enforcement

The EPA is the primary federal agency responsible for the enforcement of federal environmental laws, including those on air and water pollution, solid waste disposal, toxic substance control, and noise pollution. The EPA establishes emissions standards through regulation and then enforces them with a system of permits and sanctions for violations. The EPA works closely with state environmental agencies in enforcement.

The **Council on Environmental Quality (CEQ)** was established in 1966 as a part of the executive branch to establish national policy on environmental quality and then make recommendations for legislation for the implementation of that policy. Other federal agencies with responsibility for enforcement of federal environmental laws include the Department of Commerce, the Department of the Interior, the U.S. Forest Service, and the Bureau of Land Management.

Private citizens also have the right to enforce federal environmental laws through private litigation. **For Example,** a private citizen can bring a suit to halt the construction of a dam by the federal government if the agency responsible failed to conduct an environmental impact study or if the EIS is inadequate.[19]

Council on Environmental Quality (CEQ)–federal agency that establishes national policies on environmental quality and then recommends legislation to implement these policies.

49-2b Criminal Penalties

Most of the federal environmental laws carry criminal penalties for violations. Figure 49-1 provides a summary of those penalties to which both companies and their employees are subject.

49-2c Civil Remedies

Although criminal remedies are costly to businesses, the EPA also has the authority to have the polluting activity halted through the use of **injunction.** The EPA simply brings suit against a business and shows that it is engaged in unauthorized dumping, the release of emissions in excess of a permit, or discharge without a permit. A court can then order the business to halt the activity that is resulting in the violation. In some cases, the effect of the injunction is to shut down the business. The business is then required to negotiate with the EPA to meet certain standards before the EPA will agree to have the injunction lifted.

Private citizens can also bring suit for injunctions against companies that are in violation of federal law or not in compliance with statutory procedures. **For Example,** private citizens have filed suit against developers to stop construction when there is an issue of possible violation of the Endangered Species Act.

injunction–order of a court of equity to refrain from doing (negative injunction) or to do (affirmative or mandatory injunction) a specified act.

49-2d Private Remedies: Nuisance

Conduct that unreasonably interferes with the enjoyment or use of land is a **nuisance,**[20] which may be smoke from a chemical plant that damages the paint on neighboring houses. It may be noise, dirt, or vibration from passing heavy trucks. Some conduct is clearly so great an interference that it is easy to conclude that it constitutes a nuisance, but not every interference is a nuisance. Furthermore, determining whether the interference is sufficiently great to be halted as unreasonable is frequently difficult. The fact that the activity or business is lawful and is conducted in a lawful manner does not mean that it is not a nuisance. The effect on others determines whether there is a nuisance.[21]

nuisance–conduct that harms or prejudices another in the use of land or that harms or prejudices the public.

[19] *Alliance for the Wild Rockies v. Austin*, 55 F. Supp. 3d 1294 (D. Mont. 2014).
[20] *Kitsap County v. Kitsap Rifle and Revolver Club*, 337 P.3d 328 (Wash. App. 2014).
[21] A drive-in theater that affects a neighbor is not a nuisance. *Blue Ink, Ltd. v. Two Farms, Inc.*, 96 A.3d 810 (Md. App. 2014).

FIGURE 49-1	Penalties for Violations of Federal Environmental Laws

Act	Penalties	Private suit
Clean Air Act	$25,000 per day; up to 1 year of imprisonment; 15 years and/or $1,000,000 for willful or repeat violations; $10,000 rewards	Citizen suits; authorized EPA suit for injunctive relief
Clean Water Act	$25,000 per day, up to 1 year; $50,000 and/or 3 years for violations with knowledge; $100,000 and/or 6 years for subsequent violations	Citizen suits; authorized EPA suit for injunctive relief
Resource Conservation Recovery Act (Solid Waste Disposal Act)	$250,000 and/or 15 years' of imprisonment for intentional violations; $1,000,000 for corporations, $50,000 and/or 5 years for others	Citizen and negligence suits (after EPA refuses to handle)
Hazardous Substance/ Response Trust	Fund for cleanup	EPA suit for injunctive relief and reimbursement of trust funds
Oil Pollution Act	$25,000 per day, or $1,000 per barrel; $3,000 per barrel if willful or negligent; $250,000 and/or 5 years for failure to report	Private suits

A neighbor's expansion of a pond in order to attract more water fowl that then roosted in the neighbors' property is a nuisance even though no law was broken.[22]

The courts attempt to balance the social utility of the activity with the resulting harm. The mere fact that there is harm does not establish that there is a nuisance. When community welfare outweighs the harm to land and owners, the activity is not a nuisance.[23] **For Example,** courts have held that smoke, fumes, and noise from public utilities and power plants were not nuisances, although they did create harm. The interests of the community in the activity of the public utilities outweighed the interests of those affected.

Those affected by a nuisance are entitled to damages for the loss of the use of the land or for harm that is caused by the nuisance. Sometimes, an injunction that stops the conduct is necessary. If the nuisance is permanent, the damages are the loss in value of the land. If the nuisance can be stopped, the measure of damages is the reduction in value of the property during the time of the nuisance.[24]

---

[22] *Schillaci v. Sarris*, 997 N.Y.S.2d 504 (N.Y.A.D. 2014).
[23] *Hurley v. Port Blakely Tree Farms L.P.*, 332 P.3d 469 (Wash. App. 2014).
[24] *Valley Estates, Ltd. Partnership v. Pangle*, 448 S.W.3d 235 (Ark. App. 2014).

Private and Public Nuisances

private nuisance—
nuisance that affects
only one or a few
individuals.

public nuisance—
nuisance that affects the
community or public at
large.

When a nuisance affects only one or a few persons, it is called a **private nuisance.** When it affects the community or public at large, it is called a **public nuisance.** Planting trees or erecting a fence, although otherwise lawful, constitutes a public nuisance when it creates a traffic hazard by obscuring an intersection. For example, the smell and harmful pollutants from a grain processing plant near Muscatine, Iowa, were examples of public nuisances that entitled the nearby residents to some form of relief.[25] The existence of a statutory environmental protection procedure may bar or supersede the common law of nuisance.

Remedy for Nuisance

A criminal nuisance may be terminated by abatement or closure by government authority. A civil nuisance may be stopped by an injunction, and the injured person may sue for money damages for the harm caused.

When an injunction is issued, the court must exercise great care to halt the nuisance while avoiding going too far by enjoining conduct that is otherwise lawful.[26]

CASE SUMMARY

Moooving to the Nuisance

FACTS: Spur Industries operated a cattle feedlot near Young-town and Sun City, Arizona (communities 14 to 15 miles west of Phoenix). Spur had been operating the feedlot since 1956, and the area had been agricultural since 1911.

In 1959 Del E. Webb began development of the Sun City area, a retirement community. Webb purchased the 20,000 acres of land for about $750 per acre.

In 1960 Spur began an expansion program in which its operating area grew from 5 acres to 115 acres.

At the time of the suit, Spur was feeding between 20,000 and 30,000 head of cattle, which produced 35 to 40 pounds of wet manure per head per day, or over one million pounds per day. And despite the admittedly good feedlot management and good housekeeping practices of Spur, the resulting odor and flies produced an annoying if not unhealthy situation as far as the senior citizens of southern Sun City were concerned. There is no doubt that some of the citizens of Sun City were unable to enjoy the outdoor

living which Del Webb had advertised. Del Webb was faced with sales resistance from prospective purchasers as well as strong and persistent complaints from the people who had purchased homes in that area. Nearly 1,300 lots could not be sold. Webb then filed suit alleging Spur's operation was a nuisance because of the flies and odors constantly drifting over Sun City. The trial court enjoined Spur's operations and Spur appealed.

DECISION: The court held that because Del Webb had "moved to the nuisance" that Spur could not be required to shut down its operations. Rather, Spur would have to relocate because of the court's actions of balancing the interests of the important cattle industry in Arizona with the equally important housing/retirement industry. However, Del Webb would have to compensate Spur for the costs of the move—$11 million. [*Spur Industries, Inc. v. Del E. Webb Development Co.*, 494 P.2d 700 (Az. 1972)]

The Technological Environment of the Law of Nuisance

As technology changes, new ways of manufacturing, new methods of transportation, and new ways of living develop. Groups such as NIMBYs (not in my backyard) have become active in challenging everything from cell phone towers to wind turbines. The courts and legislatures are working to find ways to accommodate advancement with the impact of the

[25] *Freeman v. Grain Processing Corp.*, 848 N.W.2d 58 (Iowa 2014).
[26] *City of South Milwaukee v. Kester*, 830 N.W.2d 710 (Wis. App. 2013) (case in which an injunction was issued to stop the public nuisance of a sex offender living in close proximity to an elementary school).

E-COMMERCE & CYBERLAW

Data Barns, Nuisance, and E-Commerce

Data barns are Internet services centers that are generally located in rural areas. They are becoming increasingly important because of our increasing reliance on cloud storage technology. For example, Microsoft bought 75 acres of bean fields in Grant County, Washington, to set up a digital warehouse. The issue of nuisance arose because Microsoft installed 40 diesel generators that operate as a backup source of power when there are transmission failures. The generators, located next to

an elementary school, produce smoke and noise. The emissions from the generators are now classified as a *toxic pollutant* under Washington state law. The courts are weighing the need for the data barns versus the effect on neighboring properties and those in close proximity. In these situations, the courts will use a balancing approach to find a way to accommodate e-commerce without affecting the quality of life of those who live near these facilities.

forces that allow that advancement on those who live near these new technology sites. Also, the parties affected are working together. For example, federal and local laws protect the placement of cell towers so that neighbors cannot impede progress. However, in Arizona, the towers are disguised with artificial foliage that gives the towers the appearance of tall palm trees. Aesthetics are protected as technology advances.

49-2e Private Remedies: Due Diligence

due diligence—process of checking the environmental history and nature of land prior to purchase.

Another method by which problems with land are remedied is through sales transactions in which the buyer demands that a situation or problem on the land be fixed before signing a contract for purchase. **Due diligence** is the process by which the buyer conducts a thorough investigation of the property and its current and former uses to determine whether any problems with respect to environmental law or nuisance exist. Due diligence is conducted through a search of public records, an inspection of the land, and, often, when problems appear in these first two steps, some soil testing. This advance determination of problems is a civil means for land cleanup because sellers will be unable to transfer their properties until they meet the buyers' standards, determined by a close examination of the property for violations.

49-3 Land Use Controls

In addition to environmental laws, other restrictions, both private and public, place controls and limits on how land can be used.

49-3a Restrictive Covenants in Private Contracts

restrictive covenants—covenants in a deed by which the grantee agrees to refrain from doing specified acts.

Real estate developers find that when there are consistent patterns in the appearance of a neighborhood's homes and buildings (for example, similarity of design instead of a hodgepodge look), the property values are enhanced. To make sure this consistency is maintained, developers place **restrictive covenants** on the land that obligate the buyers to honor limitations in their use of their property, the nature of buildings that will be maintained or constructed on the land, and so on. If a restrictive covenant is valid, it binds buyers who had actual notice or knowledge of the restrictions. The notice comes from a notation in the deed about the covenants; the covenants then are said to "run with the land." That is, all owners are subject to them and all owners in that development have the right to stop another owner from violating the covenant.

A restrictive covenant must be clearly stated to be effective. Contract rules apply in interpreting covenants. If any uncertainty exists, the covenant will be construed strictly in favor of the free use of the land. When there is no uncertainty and no reason to depart from the meaning of the words of the covenant, a court will enforce those words.

Because of property rights, courts interpret restrictive covenants narrowly to permit the greatest possible use of the land. However, courts often disagree as to what is permitted by a restrictive covenant. **For Example,** there has been a great deal of litigation over restrictive covenants that require building design such as "traditional New England fashion, with pitched roofs, clapboard siding, and double-hung windows."[27]

Restrictive covenants that violate laws or constitutional rights are not valid. For example, a restrictive covenant that discriminates against persons with disabilities is void because it violates the Fair Housing Act.[28]

A restrictive covenant that has not been enforced or observed is no longer valid. For example, if houses in a neighborhood have had their roofs replaced with materials that did not comply with the restrictive covenants but no one objects, those new materials become the standard for the neighborhood, not the covenant materials.[29]

49-3b Public Zoning

zoning—restrictions imposed by government on the use of designated land to ensure an orderly physical development of the regulated area.

By **zoning,** a governmental unit such as a city adopts an ordinance imposing restrictions on the use of the land. The object of zoning is to ensure an orderly physical development of the regulated area. In effect, zoning is the same as restrictive covenants; the difference is in the source of authority. In most cases, zoning is based on an ordinance of a local political subdivision, such as a municipality or a county. Restrictive covenants, on the other hand, are created by agreement of the parties.

The zoning power permits any regulation that is conducive to advancing public health, welfare, and safety. The object of a particular zoning regulation may be to prevent high-density population.

Some zoning ordinances may be conservation inspired. An ordinance may prohibit or regulate the extraction of natural resources from any land within the zoned area. The fact that a zoning restriction limits the owner in the use of a property does not amount to a "taking" of property for which compensation must be made.[30] If, however, the zoning law deprived the owner of use of the land in any fashion, that would be a "taking" that required compensation.

Nonconforming Use

nonconforming use—use of land that conflicts with a zoning ordinance at the time the ordinance goes into effect.

When the use of land is in conflict with a zoning ordinance at the time the ordinance goes into effect, such use is described as a **nonconforming use. For Example,** when a zoning ordinance that requires a setback of 25 feet from the boundary line is adopted, an existing building that has a 10-foot setback is a nonconforming use.

A nonconforming use has a constitutionally protected right to continue, but if the nonconforming use is discontinued, it cannot be resumed.[31] The right to a

---

[27] *Lynch v. Town of Pelham*, 104 A.3d 1047 (N.H. 2014). Generally, these design covenants are upheld, so you find McDonald's is able to secure a place in a town with restrictive covenants, but the McDonald's will look like the other business buildings in the town and not its traditional free-standing model involving red and yellow colors.

[28] *Bhogaita v. Altamonte Heights Condominium Ass'n, Inc.*, 765 F.3d 1277 (11th Cir. 2014) (issue of restriction on pets when a resident suffered from post-traumatic stress disorder).

[29] *Oakwood Meadows Homeowners Ass'n v. Urban*, 2014 WL 2935908 (Mich. App. 2014) (lax enforcement on the construction of sheds and other buildings in violation of covenants).

[30] *California-Nevada Annual Conference of the Methodist Church v. City and County of San Francisco*, 74 F. Supp. 3d 1144 (N.D. Cal. 2014).

[31] *Day v. Town of Phippsburg*, 110 A.3d 645 (Me. 2014).

SPORTS & ENTERTAINMENT LAW

The Star Wars Studio

Quietly over the years, beginning in the 1970s when the money from his films began to roll in, George "Star Wars" Lucas has been acquiring land in Marin County (6,000 acres in total) with the goal of preserving its natural beauty and stopping its development. In fact, 97 percent of the acreage cannot be developed under deed restrictions. Mr. Lucas has planted 8,000 trees on the land and restored pathways for walking and hiking.

However, Mr. Lucas always intended to build a studio complex there, a 269,000-square-foot facility that would be located on a little over 1,000 of the acres. The plan has been 27 years in the making and was canceled last week because of what Mr. Lucas called "regulatory delay" and fierce opposition from the neighborhoods around the planned site. The neighbors opposed the facility, known as the Grady Ranch project, because it would employ 463 people and bring too much noise and traffic into the area. Neighbors indicated that regardless of county approval that they would file suits that would delay the project until their concerns were fully litigated. More details on the project can be found at Victoria Baret, "Millionaire NIMBYs 1; Billionaire Filmmaker 0," **http://www.forbes.com/sites/victoriabarret/2012/04/18/how-star-wars-george-lucas-lost-out-to-a-california-subdivision/** *Forbes*, May 2, 2012, p. 18.

nonconforming use may be lost by abandonment. If a garage is a nonconforming use and its owner stops using it as a garage and uses it for storing goods, a return to the use of the property as a garage will be barred by abandonment.

At times, a real estate development or building construction is only partly completed when a zoning ordinance that would prohibit such development or building is adopted. To avoid hardship for the persons involved, it is customary to exempt partly finished projects from the zoning ordinance just as though they were existing nonconforming uses.[32]

variance—permission of a landowner to use the land in a specified manner that is inconsistent with the zoning ordinance.

Variance

The administrative agency charged with the enforcement of a zoning ordinance may grant a **variance.** This permits the owner of the land to use it in a specified manner that is inconsistent with the zoning ordinance.

CASE SUMMARY

No Tattoos in My Neighborhood

FACTS: Hold Fast Tattoo (Plaintiff) wished to open a tattoo studio on North Sheridan Road in the City of North Chicago and obtained a prospective lessor at its desired location. In accordance with North Chicago's zoning ordinance, Hold Fast Tattoo applied for a special use permit to operate a tattoo studio at that location. On June 21, 2007, the Zoning Board of Appeals of North Chicago recommended approval of the permit to its city council. The proposal was discussed at two council meetings, on July 9, 2007, and July 16, 2007, and Hold Fast Tattoo's request for a special use permit was ultimately denied. The city council informed Hold Fast that its special use permit was denied because it was "not the kind of business" the council wanted in North Chicago. Hold Fast filed suit.

DECISION: The court held that there were no First Amendment violations in prohibiting the tattoo parlor because the tattoo parlor was not speaking; its clients were the ones speaking and they were not prohibited from having tattoos. This control only related to where they could obtain tattoos. The court also held that cities are permitted to have zoning plans and regulations that restrict certain types of businesses

---

[32] See, for example, *Anderton v. City of Cedar Hill*, 447 S.W.3d 84 (Tex. App. 2014).

No Tattoos in My Neighborhood continued

as long as there is a public purpose. The city was worried about the level of traffic and congestion from the business and the court found that there was a legitimate public purpose in excluding tattoo parlors from the area. **[*Hold Fast Tattoo, LLC v. City of North Chicago*, 580 F. Supp. 2d 656 (N.D. Ill. 2008)]** *

*Other states have held that tattoos are a form of protected speech and refused to allow denial of licenses and zoning permits solely based on the tattoo reasoning. *Coleman v. City of Mesa*, 284 P.3d 853 (Ariz. 2012); *Jucha v. City of North Chicago*, 63 F. Supp. 2d 820 (N.D. Ill. 2014); *Anderson v. City of Hermosa Beach*, 621 F.3d 1051 (9th Cir. 2014). The tattoo-zoning issue has a split among the federal circuits as well as in the states and may require a U.S. Supreme Court decision.

spot zoning–allowing individual variation in zoning.

Agencies ordinarily are reluctant to permit a variance when neighboring property owners object because, to the extent that variation is permitted, the basic plan of the zoning ordinance is defeated. Likewise, the allowance of an individual variation, or **spot zoning,** may result in such inequality as to be condemned by the courts.[33] In addition, there is a consideration of practical expediency. If variances are readily granted, every property owner will request a variance and flood the agency with these requests.

When the desired use of land is in harmony with the general nature of surrounding areas, a zoning variance is usually granted. A zoning variance is not granted on the ground of hardship, however, when the landowner created the hardship by purchasing land that was subject to a zoning ordinance.

Make the Connection

Summary

Public and private regulations apply to land use. The public regulations consist of environmental laws and zoning. Environmental laws exist at both the state and the federal levels. At the federal level, regulations govern air pollution through limits on emissions and permits for discharges; water pollution with permit requirements, discharge prohibitions, and treatment standards; solid waste disposal with limitations on dumping and liability for cleanup when hazardous materials are found on property; and environmental quality through the use of advance studies on projects and their impact on the environment. Other federal regulations on the environment protect endangered species, set standards for drinking water, and impose liability for oil spills as well as safety standards for oil tankers.

Environmental laws are primarily enforced at the federal level by the Environmental Protection Agency (EPA), but other federal agencies as well as state agencies work together to enforce these laws, using criminal and civil penalties and injunctions to halt pollution. Private citizens also have the right to bring suit under federal statutes to enforce the requirements imposed.

A *nuisance* is a public or private interference with the use and enjoyment of land, and individuals can bring suit to halt nuisances. Courts perform a balancing test in deciding how to handle concerns about nuisances. They seek to balance the use and enjoyment of land with the economic interests of all involved parties.

Restrictive covenants in deeds are valid land use restrictions that pass from owner to owner and are enforceable as long as they do not violate any constitutional rights. *Zoning* is a public means of regulating land use. Zoning laws are part of an overall plan for development adopted by a governmental entity. Some landowners can obtain variances from zoning laws, and some preexisting uses are permitted to continue with the protection of a nonconforming use.

[33] *City of Ocean Springs v. Psycamore, LLC*, 124 So. 3d 658 (Miss. 2013).

Learning Outcomes

After studying this chapter, you should be able to clearly explain:

49-1 Statutory Environmental Law

LO.1 List and describe the federal statutes that regulate various aspects of the environment

See the *Massachusetts v. EPA* discussion, page 1027.

See the *Environmental Defense v. Duke Energy* discussion, page 1027.

See the discussion of the liability for CERCLA cleanup in *Burlington Northern Railway/Shell Oil Co. v. U.S.*, pages 1030–1031.

49-2 Enforcement of Environmental Laws

LO.2 Explain how environmental laws are enforced and describe the criminal penalties for violation of environmental laws

See the list of penalties in Figure 49-1, page 1035.

Study the Thinking Things Through feature "The Leaking Barrels GE Sold" and GE Pyranol, page 1031. See the *Babbitt v. Sweet Home Chapter of Communities for a Great Oregon* case, page 1033.

LO.3 Define *nuisance* and list the remedies available

See the *Spur Industries v. Del Webb* case, page 1036. See the E-Commerce & Cyberlaw feature "Data Barns, Nuisance, and E-Commerce" for a discussion of nuisance in the technology age, page 1037.

49-3 Land Use Controls

LO.4 Explain the role and application of covenants and zoning laws

See the *Hold Fast Tattoo, LLC v. City of North Chicago* case for a discussion of zoning and rights of owners, pages 1039–1040.

Key Terms

best available treatment
best conventional treatment
brownfields
bubble concept
Clean Air Act
Clean Water Act
Comprehensive Environmental Response, Compensation, and Liability Act (CERCLA)
Council on Environmental Quality (CEQ)
due diligence
effluent guidelines
emissions offset policy
Endangered Species Act (ESA)

environmental impact statement (EIS)
injunction
National Environmental Policy Act (NEPA)
National Pollutant Discharge Elimination System (NPDES)
Noise Control Act
nonattainment areas
nonconforming use
nuisance
Oil Pollution Act
point sources
potentially responsible parties (PRPs)
private nuisance

public nuisance
Resource Conservation and Recovery Act (RCRA)
Resource Recovery Act
restrictive covenants
Safe Drinking Water Act
spot zoning
Superfund Amendment and Reauthorization Act
Superfund sites
Toxic Substances Control Act (TOSCA)
Transport Rule
variance
zoning

Questions and Case Problems

1. Union Electric wishes to construct a new coal-fired plant in the northeastern corner of Arizona. Union plans to use the maximum achievement technology for the scrubbers on the plant to reduce emissions. Will Union be able to obtain a permit from the EPA to build and operate the new power plant? Discuss the issues that Union faces.

2. Federal Oil Co. was loading a tanker with fuel oil when the loading hose snapped for some unknown reason and about 1,000 gallons of oil poured into the ocean. Federal Oil was prosecuted for this water

pollution. It raised the defense that it had exercised due care, was not at fault in any way, and had not intended to pollute the water. What statutes could be used to prosecute Federal Oil? What are the potential penalties?

3. Philip Carey Co. owned a tract of land in Plymouth Township, Pennsylvania, on which it deposited a large pile of manufacturing waste containing asbestos. Carey sold the land to Celotex, and Celotex sold the land to Smith Land & Improvement Corp. The EPA notified Smith that unless it took steps to

eliminate the asbestos hazard, the EPA would do the work and pursue reimbursement. Smith cleaned up the land to the EPA's satisfaction at a cost of $218,945.44. Smith asked Celotex and Carey for reimbursement. Which firms have liability for the cleanup costs? [*Smith Land & Improvement Corp. v. Celotex*, 851 F.2d 86 (3d Cir.)]

4. The McConnells bought a home in Sherwood Estates. The land was subject to a restrictive covenant that "no building, fence, or other structure" could be built on the land without the approval of the developer of the property. The McConnells built a dog pen in their yard that consisted of a cement base with fencing surrounding the base. They claimed that approval was not required on the theory that the restrictive covenant did not apply because it showed an intent to restrict only major construction, not minor additions to the landscape. A lawsuit was brought to compel the McConnells to remove the dog pen because prior approval had not been obtained. Are restrictive covenants applied this expansively to homeowners? Must the McConnells have prior approval? [*Sherwood Estates Homes Ass'n, Inc. v. McConnell*, 714 S.W.2d 848 (Mo. App.)]

5. General Automotive operates Grand Auto Parts Stores, which receive used automotive batteries from customers as trade-ins. General's policy in disposing of these batteries had been to drive a screwdriver through each spent battery and then sell them to a battery-cracking plant operated by Morris P. Kirk & Sons, Inc., which extracted and smelted the lead. After the lead was extracted from the batteries, Kirk washed and crushed the battery casings, loaded them into a dump truck, and then dumped them. Tons of pieces of crushed batteries were dumped onto Catellus Development Corp.'s property. Under CERCLA, Catellus sought to recover from General the costs of cleaning up the hazardous battery parts from its property. General maintained that it was not liable because it sold the batteries to Kirk, and Kirk did the dumping. Was General correct? [*Catellus Development Corp. v. United States*, 34 F.3d 748 (9th Cir.)]

6. A zoning ordinance of the city of Dallas, Texas, prohibited the use of property in a residential district for gasoline filling stations. Lombardo brought an action against the city to test the validity of the ordinance. He contended that the ordinance violated the rights of the owners of property in such districts. Do you agree with this contention? [*Lombardo v. City of Dallas*, 73 S.W.2d 475 (Tex.)]

7. Taback began building a vacation home on a parcel of wooded land. It was to be a three-story house, 31 feet high. This height violated the local zoning ordinance that limited residential homes to two and one-half stories, not exceeding 35 feet. When Taback learned of this violation, he applied for a zoning variance. Because of the delay of the zoning board and because winter was approaching, Taback finished the construction of the building as a three-story house. At a later hearing before the zoning board, he showed that it would be necessary for him to rebuild the third floor to convert the house into a two and one-half story house. The zoning board recognized that Taback's violation could not be seen from neighboring properties. Was Taback entitled to a zoning variance? [*Taback v. Town of Woodstock Zoning Board of Appeals*, 521 N.Y.S.2d 838 (App. Div.)]

8. The EPA has increased its BACT standards to impose greenhouse gas emissions standards for passenger cars, light-duty trucks, and medium-duty passenger vehicles and all businesses that emit greenhouse gases. The emissions from these small businesses and vehicles are not *per se* pollutants, but, rather, greenhouse gases. Does the EPA have the authority to regulate these emissions in vehicles? What about the costs associated with additional permits? [*Utility Air Regulatory Group v. E.P.A.*, 134 S. Ct. 2427]

9. The Stallcups lived in a rural section of the state. In front of their house ran a relatively unused, unimproved public county road. Wales Trucking Co. transported concrete pipe from the plant where it was made to a lake where the pipe was used to construct a water line to bring water to a nearby city. In the course of four months, Wales made 825 trips over the road, carrying from 58,000 to 72,000 pounds of pipe per trip and making the same number of empty return trips. Because the heavy use of the road by Wales cut up the dirt and made it like ashes, the Stallcups sued Wales for damages caused by the deposit of dust on their house and for the physical annoyance and discomfort it caused. Wales defended its position on the ground that it had not been negligent and that its use of the road was not unlawful. Decide. [*Wales Trucking Co. v. Stallcup*, 465 S.E.2d 44 (Tex. App.)]

10. Some sections of the city of Manitou Springs have hills of varying degrees of slope. To protect against water drainage and erosion, the city adopted a hillside zoning ordinance that required homes on hillsides to be surrounded by more open land than in

the balance of the city. Sellon owned land on a hillside and claimed that the hillside ordinance was unconstitutional because it did not treat all homeowners equally. Was the ordinance valid? [*Sellon v. City of Manitou Springs*, 745 P.2d 229 (Colo.)]

11. Patrick Bossenberry owned a house in a planned community area. Each lot in the area was limited by a restrictive covenant to use for a single-family dwelling. The covenant defined *family* as a blood or marital relationship between most of the occupants. Bossenberry rented his building to Kay-Jan, Inc., which wanted to use the building as a care home for not more than six adult mentally retarded persons. The neighbors sought to enjoin this use as a breach of the covenant. A number of Michigan statutes had been adopted that advanced the public policy of providing care for mentally retarded persons. Could the neighbors prevent the use of the property as a care home for mentally retarded adults? [*Craig v. Bossenberry*, 351 N.W.2d 596 (Mich. App.)]

12. Kenneth and Mary Norpel purchased a house, and Kenneth attached a 35-foot flagpole to it. He did not obtain the permission of the architectural committee of the Stone Hill Community Association. This consent was required by a restrictive covenant to which the Norpel house was subject. The association objected to the flagpole from which Norpel then flew the American flag. The association brought an action to compel the removal of the pole. Norpel claimed that as a combat veteran of World War II, he had a constitutionally protected right to fly the American flag. Can he be compelled to remove the flagpole?

13. In 1997, Isbell purchased a building in San Diego with the intent to open an adult entertainment establishment there. Because this building was located within 1,000 feet of a residential area, however, a San Diego zoning ordinance precluded him from operating there. Isbell applied for a variance but was unsuccessful. He then filed suit, arguing that the city's ordinance violates the First Amendment, and that its standards for variances violate the equal protection clause. Can the city restrict the operation of this business? What must the city be able to establish? [*Isbell v. City of San Diego*, 258 F.3d 1108 (9th Cir.)]

14. Explain why a company would want to perform a self-audit to determine whether it has any environmental violations.

15. Gregory Mills lives next to Dean Kimbley. Mills kept a journal of Kimbley's activities, and even videotaped a few of the activities, including Kimbley's smoking marijuana and standing drunk in his backyard and yelling, "Hi, neighbor!" Kimbley also threw a snowball into Mills' yard and nearly hit Mills' girlfriend with it. When Mills listed his property for sale because of the issues with Kimbley, Kimbley sent a pizza delivery man to Mills' door and told him to offer $125,000 to buy Mills' home. Kimbley then hired a real estate agent and took a tour of Mills' home with that real estate agent. Kimbley also drove an All Terrain Cycle onto Mills' lawn. Is this a nuisance case? Are these the elements of nuisance? Explain why or why not. [*Mills v. Kimbley*, 909 N.E.2d 1068 (Ind. App.)]

CPA Questions

1. Which of the following remedies is available against a real property owner to enforce the provisions of federal acts regulating air and water pollution?

	Citizen Suits against the Environmental Protection Agency to Enforce Compliance	State Suits to Enforce the Laws against Violators	Citizen Suits against Violators to Enforce the Laws
a.	Yes	Yes	Yes
b.	Yes	Yes	No
c.	No	Yes	Yes
d.	Yes	No	Yes

2. Under the Comprehensive Environmental Response, Compensation, and Liability Act (CERCLA), commonly known as Superfund, which of the following parties would be liable to the Environmental Protection Agency (EPA) for the expense of cleaning up a hazardous waste disposal site?

I. The current owner or operator of the site

II. The person who transported the wastes to the site

III. The person who owned or operated the site at the time of the disposal

   a. I and II

   b. I and III

   c. II and III

   d. I, II, and III

3. The National Environment Policy Act was passed to enhance and preserve the environment. Which of the following is not true?

    a. The act applies to all federal agencies.

    b. The act requires that an environmental impact statement be provided if any proposed federal legislation may significantly affect the environment.

    c. Enforcement of the act is primarily accomplished by litigation of persons who decide to challenge federal government decisions.

    d. The act provides generous tax breaks to those companies that help accomplish national environmental policy.

4. Which of the following actions should a business take to qualify for leniency if an environmental violation has been committed?

	Conduct Environmental Audits	Report Environmental Violations to the Government
a.	Yes	Yes
b.	Yes	No
c.	No	Yes
d.	No	No

Leases

Learning Outcomes

After studying this chapter, you should be able to

LO.1   List the ways in which a lease may be terminated

LO.2   List and explain the rights and duties of the parties to a lease

LO.3   Describe a landlord's liability for a tenant's and a third person's injuries sustained on the premises

LO.4   Define *sublease* and *assignment of a lease* and distinguish between them

50-1 Creation and Termination

Leases are governed by the common law of property as modified by judicial decisions and statutes.[1]

50-1a Definition and Nature

lease—agreement between the owner of property and a tenant by which the former agrees to give possession of the property to the latter in consideration of the payment of rent. (Parties—landlord or lessor, tenant or lessee)

lessor—one who conveys real or personal property by a lease; a landlord.

landlord—one who leases real property to another.

lessee—one who has a possessory interest in real or personal property under a lease; a tenant.

tenant—one who holds or possesses real property by any kind of right or title; one who pays rent for the temporary use and occupation of another's real property under a lease.

A **lease** is the relationship in which one person is in lawful possession of real property owned by another. In common usage, *lease* also refers to the agreement that creates that relationship.

The person who owns the real property and permits the occupation of the premises is known as the **lessor,** or **landlord.** The **lessee,** or **tenant,** is the one who occupies the property. A lease establishes the relationship of landlord and tenant.

50-1b Creation of the Lease Relationship

The relationship of landlord and tenant is created by an express or implied contract. An oral lease is valid at common law, but statutes in most states require written leases for certain tenancies. Many states provide that a lease for a term exceeding one year must be in writing.

Antidiscrimination

Statutes in many states prohibit an owner who rents property for profit from discriminating against prospective tenants on the basis of race, color, religion, or national origin. Also, the federal *Fair Housing Act* prohibits such discrimination. In addition, landlords are subject to the Americans with Disabilities Act (ADA) and must make reasonable accommodations for tenants with disabilities. **For Example,** a tenant whose physician has prescribed a comfort pet must be allowed to have that pet in his or her apartment even if the complex does not allow pets.[2] However, the use of medical marijuana in leased premises is not protected under the ADA.[3]

Unconscionability

At common law, the parties to a lease had freedom to include such terms as they chose. However, that freedom has been curbed in some states that require that leases follow the pattern of UCC section 2-302 and not include terms and conditions that are unconscionable. **For Example,** a provision in a residential lease stating that the landlord cutting off heat or water will not constitute an eviction is unconscionable. Such a clause does not prevent the tenant from recovering on the grounds of unconscionability or for breach of the implied warranty of habitability when there has been no heat or water.

50-1c Classification of Tenancies

Tenancies are classified by duration as tenancies for years, from year to year, at will, and by sufferance.

---

[1] A uniform act, the Uniform Residential Landlord and Tenant Act (URLTA), has been adopted in some form, often just in sections, in 21 states. URLTA does not apply to dorm rooms, fraternities, homeless shelters, or halfway houses. *Picken v. Multnomah County,* 2012 WL 1151037 (D. Or. 2012).

[2] *Bhogaita v. Altamonte Heights Condominium Ass'n, Inc.,* 765 F.3d 1277 (11th Cir. 2014).

[3] *Forest City Residential Management, Inc. ex rel. Plymouth Square Ltd. Dividend Housing Ass'n v. Beasley,* 71 F. Supp. 3d 715 (E.D. Mich. 2014).

CPA

tenancy for years—
tenancy for a fixed period of time, even though the time is less than a year.

periodic tenancy—
tenancy that continues indefinitely for a specified rental period until terminated; often called a month-to-month tenancy.

CPA

tenancy at will—holding of land for an indefinite period that may be terminated at any time by the landlord or by the landlord and tenant acting together.

CPA

tenancy at sufferance—
lease arrangement in which the tenant occupies the property at the discretion of the landlord.

Tenancy for Years

A **tenancy for years** is one under which the tenant has a lease that runs for a definite duration. The expression "for years" is used to describe such a tenancy whether the duration of the tenancy is for only six months or as long as 10 years.

Periodic Tenancy

A **periodic tenancy** is one under which a tenant has a lease that has an indefinite duration and under which the tenant pays annual, monthly, or weekly rent. This tenancy does not terminate at the end of a year, month, or week except with proper notice. Proper notice, in most states, means giving notice for at least one period before ending the lease.[4] **For Example,** on a month-to-month tenancy, the notice must be at least one month prior to ending the lease.

In almost all states, a periodic tenancy is implied if the tenant, with the consent of the landlord, stays in possession of property after a tenancy for years. Consent exists when there is an express statement or by conduct, such as when a landlord continues to accept rent.[5]

Tenancy at Will

When a lease runs for an indefinite period, which may be terminated at any time by the landlord or the tenant, a **tenancy at will** exists. A person who possesses land for an indefinite period with the owner's permission but without any agreement as to rent is a tenant at will. Statutes in some states and decisions in others require advance notice of termination of this kind of tenancy.

Tenancy at Sufferance

When a tenant remains in possession after the termination of the lease without permission of the landlord, the landlord may treat the tenant as either a trespasser or a tenant.[6] Until the landlord elects to do one or the other, a **tenancy at sufferance** exists. **For Example,** if John's one-year lease expired on January 31, 2016, and John remained in the apartment for a week, he would be a tenant at sufferance during that week. If John's landlord accepted a rental payment at the end of the first week, John would be a *periodic* or *month-to-month tenant.* In this situation, John was a tenant for years, a tenant at sufferance, and then a periodic tenant.[7]

50-1d Termination of Lease

A lease is generally not terminated by the death, insanity, or bankruptcy of either party except in the case of a tenancy at will. Leases may be terminated in the following ways.

Termination by Notice

Unless prohibited by statute, a lease may give the landlord the power to terminate it by giving notice to the tenant. In states that follow the common law on termination by notice, it is immaterial why the landlord terminates. A provision in a lease giving the landlord the right to terminate the lease by notice is strictly construed against the landlord.

Expiration of Term in a Tenancy for Years

A tenancy for years ends upon the expiration of the term. There is no requirement that one party give the other any notice of termination. However, a lease may require express

[4] *Meek v. Mallory and Evans, Inc.,* 734 S.E.2d 109 (Ga. App. 2012). URLTA §1.303.
[5] In re *2408 W. Kennedy, LLC,* 512 B.R. 708 (M.D. Fla. 2014).
[6] *Coinmach Corp. v. Aspenwood Apartment Corp.,* 417 S.W.3d 909 (Tex. 2013).
[7] *Brittany Sobery Family Ltd. Partnership v. Coinmach Corp.,* 392 S.W.3d 46 (Mo. App. 2013).

notice in this type of lease with a specified term except when a statute prohibits the landlord from imposing such a requirement.

Notice in a Periodic Tenancy

In the absence of an agreement of the parties, notice for termination of a periodic tenancy is now usually governed by statute. It is common practice for the parties to require 30 or 60 days' notice to end a tenancy from year to year.

Destruction of Property

By either an express provision in a lease or under a statutory provision, tenants are released from their liability to pay rent if the leased premises are destroyed. Alternatively, the amount of rent may be reduced in proportion to the loss. **For Example,** a tenant may only be able to use one-half of the property, so the rent would be cut in half. Such statutes do not require the landlord to repair or restore the property to its former condition. When the lease covers rooms or an apartment in a building, a destruction of the leased premises terminates the lease.

Fraud

Because a lease is based on a contract, a lease agreement is subject to the contract defense of fraud. (See Chapter 13.)

Transfer of the Tenant

Residential leases may contain a provision for termination if there is a change in the tenant's circumstances, such as the tenant's being transferred by an employer to another city or on the tenant's being called into active military service. Such provisions are strictly construed against the tenant. Tenants should be certain to request personal circumstances provisions in their leases that are broad enough to cover these types of job events and military duty.

50-1e Notice of Termination

When notice of termination is required, no particular words are necessary to constitute a sufficient notice so long as the words used clearly indicate the intention of the party. The notice, whether given by the landlord or the tenant, must be definite. Statutes sometimes require that the notice be in writing. In the absence of such a provision, however, oral notice is generally sufficient.

50-1f Renewal of Lease

When a lease terminates for any reason, the landlord and the tenant ordinarily enter into a new agreement if they wish to extend or renew the lease. The power to renew the lease may be stated in the original lease by declaring that the lease runs indefinitely, as from year to year, subject to being terminated by either party's giving written notice of a specified number of days or months before the termination date. Renewal provisions are strictly construed against the tenant.

The lease may require the tenant to give written notice of intention to renew the lease. In such a case, there is no renewal if the tenant does not give the required notice but merely remains on the premises after the expiration of the original term.[8]

---

[8] *Faison v. RTFX, Inc.,* 6 N.E.3d 376 (Ill. App. 2014).

50-2 Rights and Duties of Parties

The rights and duties of the landlord and tenant are based on principles of real estate law and contract law. There is an increasing tendency to treat the residential lease like any other type of consumer contract and to govern the rights and duties of the parties by general principles of contract law.

50-2a Possession

possession–exclusive dominion and control of property.

The tenant has the right to acquire **possession** of the property and to remain in possession of that property until the term of the lease has expired or he or she is removed according to legal proceedings provided to landlords for removal of tenants in breach of the lease.

Right of Possession

By making a lease, the lessor or landlord agrees to give possession of the premises to the tenant at the time specified in the lease. If the landlord rents a building that is being constructed, there is an implied promise in the contract that the leased premises will be ready for occupancy on the date specified in the lease for the beginning of the lease term.

If the landlord interferes with the tenant's possession, the landlord has breached the lease agreement, and legal remedies are available to the tenant. *Interference* is generally defined to be an eviction that occurs by judicial proceedings or when the landlord prevents access by the tenant, as when the locks are changed and the tenant does not have a key. If the landlord wrongfully deprives the tenant of the use of one room when the tenant is entitled to use an entire apartment or building, there is a partial eviction. An eviction in violation of the lease or law entitles the tenant to collect damages from the landlord for interference with possession of the leased premises.

Covenant of Quiet Enjoyment

covenant of quiet enjoyment–covenant by the grantor of an interest in land to not disturb the grantee's possession of the land.

Most written leases today contain an express promise by the landlord called a **covenant of quiet enjoyment.** Such a provision protects the tenant from interference with possession by the landlord or the landlord's agent, but it does not impose liability on the landlord for the unlawful acts of third persons.[9]

Constructive Eviction

constructive eviction– act or omission of the landlord that substantially deprives the tenant of the use and enjoyment of the premises.

A **constructive eviction** occurs when some act or omission of the landlord substantially deprives the tenant of the use and enjoyment of the premises.

To establish a constructive eviction, the tenant must show that the condition of the property is such that it is impossible for the tenant to remain in possession. In addition, constructive eviction is not established unless the tenant actually leaves the premises. If the tenant continues to occupy the premises for more than a reasonable time after what is claimed to be a constructive eviction, the tenant waives or loses the right to object to the landlord's conduct. The definition of constructive eviction requires the establishment of conditions so awful that a tenant is forced to leave. The tenant's remaining behind in the leased premises contradicts one of the elements required for establishing constructive eviction.[10] **For Example,** a condition of constructive eviction would be sewage backing up

[9] *Haslam-James v. Lawrence*, 39 A.3d 1121 (Conn. 2012).
[10] Some states prohibit a landlord of residential property from willfully turning off the utilities of a tenant for the purpose of evicting the tenant. *City and County of San Francisco v. Sainez*, 77 Cal. App. 4th 1302, 92 Cal. Rptr. 2d 418 (Cal. App. 2009) (imposing civil penalty of $663,000 for shutting off utilities for 530 days). Such conduct is also a violation of URLTA §§2.104 and 4.105. *Mik v. Federal Home Loan Mortgage Corp.*, 743 F.3d 149 (6th Cir. 2014).

through the bathtub. The tenant could claim that the sewage in the apartment constituted constructive eviction, but the tenant would also need to move out of the apartment.

50-2b Use of Premises

The lease generally specifies those uses authorized for the tenant. In the absence of express or implied restrictions, a tenant is entitled to use the premises for any lawful purpose for which they are adapted or for which they are ordinarily employed or in a manner contemplated by the parties in executing the lease. A provision specifying the use to be made of the property is strictly construed against the tenant.

Change of Use

If the tenant uses the property for any purpose other than the one specified, the landlord has the option to declare the lease terminated.

Continued Use of Property

A tenant is ordinarily required to give the landlord notice of nonuse or vacancy of the premises. This notice is a practical issue; landlords need to be aware when premises are vacant because there is an increased danger of damage to the premises by vandalism or fire. Also, there is commonly a provision in the landlord's fire insurance policy making it void if a vacancy continues for a specified time.

Rules

The modern lease generally contains a blanket agreement by the tenant to abide by the provisions of rules and regulations adopted by the landlord. These rules are generally binding on the tenant whether they exist at the time the lease was made or are adopted afterward.

Prohibition of Pets

A lease restriction prohibiting pet ownership is valid, as are cleaning fees for violations of the restriction.

50-2c Rent

The tenant is under a duty to pay rent as compensation to the landlord. The amount of rent agreed to by the parties may be subject to government regulation, as when a city or county has enacted rent control laws.

Time of Payment

The time of payment of rent is ordinarily fixed by the lease. However, statutes or custom may require rent to be paid monthly or may require a substantial deposit before the lease begins.

CPA Assignment

If the lease is assigned (the tenant's entire interest is transferred to a third person), the assignee is liable to the landlord for the rent. However, the assignment does not in itself discharge the tenant from the duty to pay the rent. If the assignee of the lease does not make the lease payments, the landlord may bring an action for the rent against either the original tenant or the assignee, or both, but is entitled to payment of only what is due under the lease, not a double amount as collected from each party. A **sublessee** (a person

sublessee—person with lease rights for a period of less than the term of the original lease (also *subtenant*).

to whom part of a tenant's interest is transferred) ordinarily is not liable to the original lessor for rent unless that liability has been expressly assumed or is imposed by statute.

Rent Escalation

escalation clause—
provision for the automatic increase of the rent at periodic intervals.

When property is rented for a long term, it is common to include some provision for the automatic increase of the rent at periodic intervals. Such a provision is often tied to increases in the cost of living or in the landlord's operating costs and is called an **escalation clause.** There may, however, also be rent controls that would prohibit such rent increases.[11]

50-2d **Repairs and Condition of Premises**

In the absence of an agreement to the contrary, the tenant has no duty to make repairs. When the landlord makes repairs, reasonable care must be exercised to make them in a proper manner. The tenant is liable for any damage to the premises caused by his or her willful or negligent acts.

Inspection of Premises

Under the URLTA, the landlord has the right to enter the leased premises for emergency purposes or with notice to the tenant for repairs, evaluations, and estimates.

Housing Laws

Various laws protect tenants by requiring landlords to observe specified safety, health, and fire prevention standards. Some statutes require a landlord who leases a building for dwelling purposes to keep it in a condition fit for habitation. Leases commonly require the tenant to obey local ordinances and laws relating to the care and use of the premises.

Landlords must comply with the ADA. Compliance means that landlords cannot discriminate on the basis of disability in deciding whether to rent to a particular tenant.[12] Also, landlords are required to make reasonable modifications to accommodate tenants with disabilities, which can include everything from making sure that sidewalks on the property are smooth enough for operation of wheelchairs to permitting guide dogs to live with their sight-impaired owners.

 THINKING THINGS THROUGH

The Rotting Balcony

Cayetano Giron stepped out onto the balcony of the apartment that he and his wife Robin leased from Jane Bailey. After taking four steps onto the balcony, Cayetano's foot sank into the soft floorboards and he fell toward the railing. He tried to grab the railing, but the railing broke off in his hand and he fell from the balcony to the street below (a two-story fall) and was injured. Robin had notified Mrs. Bailey, shortly after moving into the apartment, that the wooden balcony was "a little lopped." No repair attempts were made. Cayetano brought suit to recover for his injuries. Can he recover from Mrs. Bailey? Why or why not? **[Giron v. Bailey, 985 A.2d 1003 (2009)]**

In the summer of 2015, six students were killed and seven were injured when a balcony collapsed during one of the student's 21st birthday celebration. Would the landlord be liable? What if the balcony had passed inspection less than one year ago?

[11] *Fisher v. City of Berkeley, California,* 475 U.S. 260 (1986); N.Y. Comp. Codes R. & Regs. tit. 9, §2520.1 (2014).
[12] *Short v. Manhattan Apartments, Inc.,* 915 F. Supp. 2d 375 (S.D.N.Y. 2012).

One of the developing areas of landlord-tenant law involves landlords' rights with regard to leasing to convicts and those who are registered as sex offenders. About 600,000 inmates are released from prisons each year, and their housing choices generally involve leasing.[13] The federal government requires public housing authorities to screen and evict tenants for drug-related or "safety-threatening" behavior. Public housing authorities that receive federal funds must include a lease clause that requires automatic lease termination for any drug or violent criminal activity, even if the activity does not occur on the landlord's property.

CASE SUMMARY

But I'm Innocent!!!

FACTS: Several young men, grandsons of William Lee and Barbara Hill, both of whom were residents on leases of the Oakland Housing Authority (OHA), were caught in the apartment complex parking lot smoking marijuana. The daughter of Pearlie Rucker, who resided with her and was listed on the OHA lease as a resident, was found with cocaine and a crack cocaine pipe three blocks from Rucker's apartment. On three instances within a two-month period, Herman Walker's, another OHA resident, caregiver and two others were found with cocaine in Walker's apartment.

After OHA initiated the eviction proceedings in state court against the Hills, Rucker, and Walker (respondents), they commenced actions against OHA in federal district court, challenging the Department of Housing and Urban Development's (HUD's) interpretation of the federal statute requiring eviction of tenants for criminal activity or the failure to control criminal activity in their apartments. The tenants of OHA argued that the federal statute and HUD regulations result in the eviction of "innocent" tenants and are unconstitutional.

The district court issued a preliminary injunction, enjoining OHA from terminating the leases of the tenants. A panel of the court of appeals reversed, and the full court of appeals reversed the panel and reinstated the district court's injunction. HUD appealed to the U.S. Supreme Court.

DECISION: Congress, wanting to ensure the safety of public housing, allowed the eviction for criminal activity in leased property even when the tenants were not involved. There are no constitutional issues as long as the proper processes under state law for eviction are followed. [*Department of Housing and Urban Development v. Rucker*, 535 U.S. 125 (2002)]

ETHICS & THE LAW

Screening Tenants for Criminal Records

There are several suits pending around the country against landlords who refuse to rent to tenants who have criminal records. The suits are brought by nonprofit groups that seek to help ex-cons with rehabilitation by getting them housing and jobs. However, the landlords note that once they are aware of criminal history and rent to that tenant, then they can be held liable for any crimes that individual might commit against tenants in their rental properties. San Francisco and Newark have ordinances that prohibit landlords from asking about criminal history. Many landlords have an individual review of applicants, not a blanket policy where they consider the nature of the crime, the time spent in prison, and the time since being released from prison. Discuss the ethical issues in setting policies on screening applicants with criminal records.

---

[13] Meghan L. Schneider, "From Criminal Confinement to Social Confinement: Helping Ex-Offenders Obtain Public Housing with a Certificate of Rehabilitation," 36 *New. Eng. J. on Crim. & Civil Confinement*, 335 (2010).

CPA   ## Warranty of Habitability

warranty of habitability–
implied warranty that the
leased property is fit for
dwelling by tenants.

At common law, a landlord was not bound by any obligation that the premises be fit for use unless the lease contained an express warranty to that effect. Most jurisdictions now reject this view and have created a **warranty of habitability** to protect tenants. The warranty of habitability requires, in most states, that the premises have running water, have heat in winter, and be free from structural defects and infestation. If the landlord breaches a warranty of habitability, the tenant is entitled to damages. These damages may be offset against the rent that is due, or if no rent is due, the tenant may bring an independent lawsuit to recover damages from the landlord.[14]

CASE SUMMARY

Don't Let the Bedbugs Bite

FACTS: Geoffrey Green lived in a rent-control apartment in New York City. Bedbugs in his apartment forced him and his partner, Dana Shapiro, to sleep with the lights on, and rotate between sleeping in the bedroom, the kitchen, and the living room. They did not use the bedroom between May and August in 2005 and 2006.

Mr. Green testified that from April 2005 through July 2008, he did not have a single full night's sleep during the summer months. Lack of sleep affected Mr. Green's relationship with Ms. Shapiro and his ability to get to work on time.

Mr. Green withheld rent from October 2005 through January 2007, but only for the prime bedbug months, that is, non-winter months, during this period for a total amount of $5,665.84. His landlord (Petitioner) brought a forcible detainer action to have him evicted. Mr. Green counterclaimed for his damages from the bedbugs. Mr. Green offered into evidence two zip-loc bags containing dead bedbugs.

The exterminator for the complex had come to spray the building but said he never saw any live or dead bedbugs in the Green/Shapiro apartment except the specimens that Mr. Green had shown him, in a zip lock bag.* The exterminator believed Green and Shapiro (Respondents) may have brought the bedbugs with them from their previous apartment. Theresa Lonng, a neighbor, testified that she had bedbugs in her apartment, but that she also had them in her apartment in the building next door, where she had lived until moving next to Mr. Green and Ms. Shapiro.

DECISION: The presence of bedbugs was a breach of the warranty of habitability, regardless of where the bugs came from. As the court noted, those who travel run the risk of bedbugs and landlords must be prepared to eliminate the bugs, wherever and however they land.

The court did question the credibility of tenants who would stay in a bug-infested place for three years without some more diligent form of action. However, the court awarded the tenants a rent abatement to cover September 2005 through December 2006. The first documented notification to the landlord regarding the alleged condition was in September 2005. That was the first documented phone call to the exterminator, and the tenants withheld their rent in September and October of 2005. Based on the log of bites that was kept by the tenants for January 2007 forward, the court found that the tenants had failed to establish the presence of bedbugs from January 2007 forward, and that the bites documented were in all likelihood other insect bites.

The tenants received a 12 percent abatement in rent, for the period of September 2005 through December 2006, totaling $2724.21. [*Bender v. Green,* 874 N.Y.S.2d 786 (N.Y. Civ. Ct. 2009)]

*The court used the terms "zip lock" and "zip-loc" rather than the registered term, "Ziploc."

Abatement and Escrow Payment of Rent

To protect tenants from unsound living conditions, statutes sometimes provide that a tenant is not required to pay rent as long as the premises are not fit to live in. As a compromise, some statutes require the tenant to continue to pay the rent but require that it be paid into an escrow or agency account. The money in the escrow account is paid to the landlord only upon proof that the necessary repairs have been made to the premises.

[14] *Erlach v. Sierra Asset Servicing, LLC,* 173 Cal. Rptr. 3d 159 (Cal. App. 2014).

50-2e Improvements

In the absence of a special agreement, neither the tenant nor the landlord is under a duty to make improvements, as contrasted with repairs.[15] Either party may, as a term of the original lease, agree to make improvements, in which case a failure to perform will result in liability in an action for damages for breach of contract brought by the other party. In the absence of an agreement to the contrary, improvements become part of the realty and belong to the landlord.

50-2f Taxes and Assessments

In the absence of an agreement to the contrary, the landlord, not the tenant, is usually under a duty to pay taxes and/or assessments. The lease may provide for an increase in rent if taxes on the rented property are increased.[16]

If taxes or assessments are increased because of improvements made by the tenant, the landlord is liable for such increases if the improvements remain with the property. If the improvements can be removed by the tenant, the amount of the increase must be paid by the tenant.

50-2g Tenant's Deposit

A landlord may require a tenant to make a deposit to protect the landlord from any default on the part of the tenant.[17] There may be statutory limits on the amount of the deposit. Some states provide tenants with protections on these deposits. For example, the landlord may have to hold the deposits in a trust fund or be responsible for paying interest for the period the deposit is held. The landlord may be subject to a penalty if the money is used before the lease would allow for its use.

50-2h Protection from Retaliation

The URLTA and most state laws protect tenants from retaliation by the landlord for the tenants' exercise of their lawful rights or reporting the landlord for violations of housing and sanitation codes. The types of retaliation from which reporting tenants are protected include refusing to renew a lease and evicting the tenant.

50-2i Remedies of Landlord

If a tenant fails to pay rent, the landlord may bring an ordinary lawsuit to collect the amount due and in some states may seize and hold the property of the tenant.

Landlord's Lien

In the absence of an agreement or a statute, the landlord does not have a lien on the personal property or crops of the tenant for money due for rent. The parties may create, by express or implied contract, a lien in favor of the landlord for rent and also for advances, taxes, or damages for failure to make repairs. In the absence of a statutory provision, the lien of the landlord is superior to the claims of all other persons except prior lienors and good-faith purchasers.

---

[15] The Americans with Disabilities Act requires commercial landlords and tenants to comply with legal requirements for access by the disabled. Shopping centers, medical offices, banks, and professional buildings must be in compliance. *Brooks Shopping Centers, LLC v. DCHWWC Restaurants, Inc.*, 929 N.Y.S.2d 354 (N.Y. App. 2012). *Anderson v. Little League Baseball, Inc.*, 794 F. Supp. 342 (D. Ariz. 1992).

[16] *Reach Community Development v. Stanley*, 274 P.3d 211 (Or. App. 2012).

[17] URLTA §2.101.

Suit for Rent

Whether or not the landlord has a lien for unpaid rent, the landlord may collect rent from the tenant as specified in the lease. In some states, the landlord is permitted to bring a combined action against the tenant to recover the possession of the premises and the overdue rent at the same time.

Recovery of Possession

A lease commonly provides that on the breach of any of its provisions by the tenant, such as the failure to pay rent, the lease terminates or the landlord may exercise the option to declare the lease terminated. When the lease is terminated for any reason, the landlord then has the right to evict the tenant and retake possession of the property.

A landlord cannot lock out a tenant for overdue rent. The landlord must employ legal process to regain possession even if the lease expressly gives the landlord the right to self-help.

The landlord may resort to legal process to evict the tenant to enforce the right to possession of the premises. Statutes in many states provide a summary remedy to recover possession that is much more efficient than the slow common law remedies. Often referred to as a **forcible entry and detainer,** this action restores the property to the landlord's possession unless the tenant complies with payment requirements.

forcible entry and detainer—action by the landlord to have the tenant removed for nonpayment of rent.

Landlord's Duty to Mitigate Damages

If the tenant leaves the premises before the expiration of the lease, is the landlord under any duty to rent the premises again to reduce the rent or damages for which the departing tenant will be liable? By common law and majority rule, a tenant holds a possessory estate in land, and if the tenant abandons it, there is no duty on the landlord to find a new tenant for the premises. But a growing minority view places greater emphasis on the contractual aspects of a lease. Under this view, when the tenant abandons the property, thereby defaulting on the contract, the landlord has a duty to seek to mitigate the damages caused by the tenant's breach and make a reasonable effort to rent the abandoned property.

50-3 Liability for Injury on Premises

When the tenant, a member of the tenant's family, or a third person is injured because of the condition of the premises, the question of who is liable for the damages sustained by the injured person arises.

50-3a Landlord's Liability to Tenant

At common law, in the absence of a covenant to keep the premises in repair, the landlord was not liable for the tenant's personal injuries caused by the defective condition of the premises that, by the lease, are placed under the control of the tenant. However, recent cases have imposed liability on landlords for their failure to keep leased premises in repair, even when there is no covenant of repair. Tenants must still take reasonable precautions when they are aware of a defect. Giving the landlord notice, avoiding the broken step, and even stepping carefully are required when the tenant becomes aware of a dangerous condition and the landlord has not had an opportunity to make repairs.[18]

---

[18] *Mauskopf v. 1528 Owners Corp.,* 958 N.Y.S.2d 759 (N.Y.A.D. 2013).

Crimes of Third Persons

Ordinarily, the landlord is not liable to the tenant for crimes committed on the premises by third persons, such as when a third person enters the premises and commits larceny or murder.[19] The landlord is not required to establish a security system to protect the tenant from crimes of third persons.

In contrast, when the criminal acts of third persons are reasonably foreseeable, the landlord may be held liable for the harm caused a tenant. **For Example,** when a tenant has repeatedly reported that the deadbolt on the apartment door is broken, the landlord is liable for the tenant's loss when a thief enters through the door because such criminal conduct was foreseeable. Likewise, when the landlord of a large apartment complex does not take reasonable steps to prevent repeated criminal acts, the landlord is liable to the tenant for the harm caused by the foreseeable criminal act of a third person.

CASE SUMMARY

Parking Outside the Gate and Living in a Gated Community: High Risk

FACTS: Arnel Management Company manages the Pheasant Ridge Apartments. Pheasant Ridge is a 620-unit, multibuilding apartment complex with over 1,000 residents, situated on 20.59 acres in Rowland Heights, California. Before the gated entrance to the complex are two parking lots; one is a visitor lot, and the other is the parking lot for the leasing office, located on the other side of the road. There are two security gates just past the parking lot. The gates are remote-control operated. Most of the property's parking spaces lie behind these gates by the apartments.

Yu Fang Tan and his wife, Chun Kuei Chang, and their child moved into Pheasant Ridge in July 2002 and received one assigned parking space. Tenants could pay an additional fee for a garage, but Tan chose not to rent one. Tenants with a second car could park in unassigned parking spaces located throughout the complex, or in one of the two lots—as long as the car was removed from the leasing office lot before 7:00 A.M.

At around 11:30 P.M. on December 28, 2002, Tan returned home and tried to find an unassigned open parking space because his wife had parked the family's other car in their assigned space. Unable to locate an available space, he parked in the leasing office parking lot outside the gated area. As Tan was parking his car, an unidentified man

approached him and asked for help. When Tan opened his window, the man pointed a gun and told him to get out of the car because the man wanted it. Tan responded, "Okay. Let me park my car first." But then the car rolled a little, and at that point, the assailant shot Tan in the neck. The incident rendered Tan a quadriplegic. Tan and Chang filed suit against Arnel for their negligent management of the complex as well as its policy of not providing sufficient parking inside the gated area and of charging more for such additional spaces. The trial court granted judgment on the pleadings for Arnel, and Tan and Chang appealed.

DECISION: Judgment for Tan. There had been a chain of events at the apartment complex and, particularly, in the parking lots that put the landlord on notice that there was a need for additional precautions. An expert had recommended various solutions that did not require a great deal of expense such as (1) moving the existing security gates from the back of the access road, and (2) installing "very similar" gates before the visitor and leasing office parking lots. The expert also noted that you don't get much more foreseeability in a property situation than was present in this situation. Reversed. [*Yu Fang Tan v. Arnel Management Co.,* 170 Cal. App. 4th 1087, 88 Cal. Rprt. 3d 754 (2009)]

Limitation of Liability

A number of courts, however, have restricted the landlord's power to limit liability in the case of residential, as distinguished from commercial, leasing. A provision in a residential lease excusing a landlord from liability for damage caused by water, snow, or ice is void.

[19] *Galanis v. CMA Management Co.,* ____ So. 3d ____, 2014 WL 5556196 (Miss. App. 2014). A co-tenant's application revealing credit-card fraud criminal history does not result in liability of landlord for tenant's murder.

Indemnification of Landlord

The modern lease commonly contains a provision declaring that the tenant will indemnify the landlord for any liability of the landlord to a third person that arises from the tenant's use of the rented premises.

50-3b Landlord's Liability to Third Persons

A landlord is ordinarily not liable to third persons injured because of the condition of any part of the rented premises that is in the possession of a tenant by virtue of a lease. If the landlord retains control over a portion of the premises, such as hallways or stairways, however, a landlord's liability exists for injuries to third persons caused by failure to exercise proper care in connection with that part of the premises. Most courts impose liability on the landlord for harm caused to a third person when the landlord was obligated, under a contract with the tenant, to correct the condition that caused the harm or to keep the premises in repair.

CPA

50-3c Tenant's Liability to Third Persons

A tenant in possession has control of the property and is liable when his or her failure to use due care under the circumstances causes harm to (1) licensees, such as a person allowed to use a telephone, and (2) invitees, such as customers entering a store. For both classes, the liability is the same as that of an owner in possession of property. It is likewise immaterial whether the property is used for residential or business purposes.

The liability of the tenant to third persons is not affected by the fact that the landlord may have contracted in the lease to make repairs that, if made, would have avoided the injury. The tenant can be protected, however, in the same manner that the landlord can be protected: by procuring liability insurance for indemnity against loss from claims of third persons.

SPORTS & ENTERTAINMENT LAW

The Quarter Pipe 360 Liability Issue

Timothy Lucier, two days shy of his thirteenth birthday, went with his father and several of his friends to Impact (a commercial skate park located in East Providence, Rhode Island) to skateboard to celebrate his birthday. At the skate park, Timothy's father signed the waiver that was required of all who used the park. Timothy donned a helmet, kneepads, and elbow pads, and then he and his friends used the skate park half pipes and quarter pipes. At one point, Timothy climbed on top of the quarter pipe, and as he pushed forward to go down the ramp, the front wheel of his skateboard caught inside a "nub" or "little tiny hole" in the ramp, causing the tail of his skateboard to swing around in a clockwise direction. Timothy twisted off the skateboard and fell on his right leg, causing a spiral fracture in his right leg. Timothy said that after he fell, he looked back at the ramp and saw that there was a split in the wood covering the ramp.

Timothy's parents filed suit against Impact Recreation, Ltd., the operator of the skateboard facility, and Eugene Voll, Impact's landlord. They alleged that there had been a failure by the landlord to ensure that the commercial tenant was not engaging in an activity that was inherently dangerous to the public at large.

Voll required Impact to have insurance, obtain signed waivers from all participants, and obtain his approval prior to the installation of any equipment. Do you believe the landlord is liable to the Luciers? Why or why not?

[Lucier v. Impact Recreation, LTD., 864 A.2d 635 (R.I. 2005)]

50-4 Transfer of Rights

Both the landlord and the tenant have property and contract rights with respect to the lease. Can they be transferred or assigned? A landlord who sells his property transfers the rights in the leased premises to the buyer. The tenant also has transfer rights that are covered next.

CPA

50-4a Tenant's Assignment of Lease and Sublease

assignment—transfer of a right. Generally used in connection with personal property rights, as rights under a contract, commercial paper, an insurance policy, a mortgage, or a lease. (Parties—assignor, assignee)

sublease—a transfer of the premises by the lessee to a third person, the sublessee or subtenant, for a period of less than the term of the original lease.

An **assignment** of a lease is a transfer by the tenant of the tenant's entire interest in the premises to a third person. A tenancy for years may be assigned by the tenant unless the tenant is restricted from making such an assignment by the terms of the lease or by a statute. A **sublease** is a transfer to a third person, the *sublessee*, of less than the tenant's entire interest, or full lease term.

Limitations on Rights

The lease may contain provisions denying or limiting the right to assign or sublet. Such restrictions protect the landlord from new tenants who might damage the property or be financially irresponsible.

Restrictions in the lease are construed liberally in favor of the tenant. No violation of a provision prohibiting assignment or subleasing occurs when the tenant merely permits someone else to use the premises.

Effect of Assignment or Sublease

An assignee or a sublessee has no greater rights than the original lessee.[20] An assignee becomes bound by the obligations of the lease by the act of taking possession of the premises.

Neither the act of subletting nor the landlord's agreement to it releases the original tenant from liability under the terms of the original lease. When a lease is assigned, the original tenant remains liable for the rent that becomes due thereafter.

The tenant should require the sublessee to perform all obligations under the original lease and to indemnify the tenant for any loss caused if the sublessee defaults. Such liability on the part of the sublessee requires an express covenant. The fact that the sublease is made "subject to" the terms of the original lease merely recognizes the superiority of the original lease but does not impose any duty on the sublessee to perform the tenant's obligation under the original lease. If the sublessee promises to assume the obligations of the original lease, the landlord, as a third-party beneficiary, may recover from the sublessee for breach of the provisions of the original lease.

Make the Connection

Summary

The agreement between a lessor and a lessee by which the latter holds possession of real property owned by the former is a lease. Statutes in many states prohibit discrimination by an owner who rents property. Statutes in some states require that the lease not be unconscionable.

Tenancies are classified according to duration as tenancies for years, from year to year, at will, and at sufferance.

A lease is generally not terminated by the death, insanity, or bankruptcy of either party except for a tenancy at will. Leases are usually terminated by the expiration of the

[20] *First Hudson Capital LLC v. Seaborn*, 862 N.Y.S.2d 501 (N.Y.A.D. 2008).

specified term, notice, surrender, forfeiture, or destruction of the property or because of fraud. A tenant has the right to acquire possession at the beginning of the lease and has the right to retain possession until the lease is ended. Evictions may be either actual or constructive. The tenant is under a duty to pay rent as compensation to the landlord.

An assignment of a lease by the tenant is a transfer of the tenant's entire interest in the property to a third person; a sublease is a transfer of less than an entire interest—in either space or time. A lease may prohibit both an assignment and a sublease. If the lease is assigned, the assignee is liable to the landlord for the rent. Such an assignment, however, does not discharge the tenant from the duty to pay rent. In a sublease, the sublessee is not liable to the original lessor for rent unless that liability has been assumed or is imposed by statute.

The tenant need not make repairs to the premises, absent an agreement to the contrary. A warranty of habitability was not implied at common law, but most states now reject this view and imply in residential leases a warranty that the premises are fit for habitation.

A landlord is usually liable to the tenant only for injuries caused by latent defects or by defects that are not apparent but of which the landlord had knowledge. The landlord is not liable to the tenant for crimes of third persons unless they are reasonably foreseeable.

Learning Outcomes

After studying this chapter, you should be able to clearly explain:

50-1 Creation and Termination

LO.1 List the ways in which a lease may be terminated
See the discussion of the types of tenancies, page 1047.
See the Ethics & the Law feature on screening tenants for criminal records, page 1052.
See *Department of Housing and Urban Development v. Rucker* for a discussion of federal housing policy on eviction for drug use, page 1052.

50-2 Rights and Duties of Parties

LO.2 List and explain the rights and duties of the parties to a lease
See the *Bender v. Green* case, page 1053.

See the Thinking Things Through feature about the rotting balcony, page 1051.

50-3 Liability for Injury on Premises

LO.3 Describe a landlord's liability for a tenant's and a third person's injuries sustained on the premises
See the *Yu Fang Tan v. Arnel Management Co.* case, page 1056.
See the Sports & Entertainment Law discussion of the quarter pipe, page 1057.

50-4 Transfer of Rights

LO.4 Define *sublease* and *assignment of a lease* and distinguish between them
See the discussion of transfer of rights, pages 1057–1058.

Key Terms

assignment
constructive eviction
covenant of quiet enjoyment
escalation clause
forcible entry and detainer
landlord

lease
lessee
lessor
periodic tenancy
possession
sublease

sublessee
tenancy at sufferance
tenancy at will
tenancy for years
tenant
warranty of habitability

Questions and Case Problems

1. Johnny C. Carpenter and Harvey E. Hill died of asphyxiation when a fire broke out in their Hattiesburg, Mississippi, apartment on the morning of February 20, 1983. There were no smoke detectors in the apartment at the time of the fire, as required under Hattiesburg City Ordinance 2021. The administrators of the estates of Carpenter and Hill filed suit against London, Stetelman, and Kirkwood, the owners and managers of the apartment complex. Who is liable? [*Hill v. London,*

Stetelman, and Kirkwood, Inc., 906 F.2d 204 (5th Cir.)]

2. Petra Valoma and her three roommates rented an apartment in New York City with a security deposit of $2,850, two months of rent for $5,700, and a property loss payment of $800. Less than a month after the group of four took possession of the property, they found bedbugs. The manager sent an exterminator each week for six weeks, with no effective results. The four had to move out and lost most of their furniture because it was infected with bedbugs. The four sought to recover the rent that they had paid as well as damages for their lost furniture. What can they recover? [*Valoma v. G-Way Management, LLC*, 918 N.Y.S.2d 401 (N.Y. Cir. Ct.)]

3. Rod had a five-year lease in a building owned by Darwood and had agreed to pay $800 a month rent. After two years, Rod assigned his rights under the lease to Kelly. Kelly moved in and paid the rent for a year and then, owing two months' rent, moved out without Darwood's knowledge or consent. Darwood demanded that Rod pay him the past-due rent. Must Rod do so? Why or why not?

4. Sue A. Merrill injured her right shoulder when she fell as she was ascending the front steps leading to the porch and front door of the mobile home that her daughter, Sherri Pritchard, rented from Alvina Jansma. The step became loose during the time Ms. Pritchard rented the home. Prior to the fall, Ms. Pritchard had attempted to repair the step by securing it with nails. When that failed, she informed the manager of the property that the step was loose. The manager suggested that Ms. Pritchard try using screws to secure the step. Ms. Pritchard told the manager that she did not have a screw gun. The manager had one and said she would screw the step into place. Subsequently, and without Ms. Pritchard's knowledge, the manager attempted to repair the step. Apparently, that effort was unsuccessful and Ms. Merrill fell when the step separated from the porch as she stepped on it. Ms. Merrill filed a negligence claim against Ms. Jansma to recover for her medical expenses, lost wages, and damages for emotional distress and pain and suffering. Could Ms. Merrill recover? [*Merrill v. Jansma*, 86 P.3d 270 (Wyo.)]

5. Jennifer Sanchez and her three children lived in a two-story townhome operated by CAA (the Cincinnati Community Action Agency). CAA is a nonprofit entity that provides housing for single mothers in financial need. Sanchez requested maintenance on an area behind her toilet on the second floor of the townhome. Josh Hill, a maintenance employee for CAA, came to fix the area. Hill's plan was to simply plaster over the moist area. However, Ms. Sanchez's boyfriend and the father of her children, Ruben, was present and offered his expertise as someone who earned a living doing drywall work. He loaned Hill a box cutter to cut out the moist portion of the wall and Ruben walked Hill through the repair. As Hill finished the work, Ms. Sanchez called Ruben downstairs and Hill left.

The two- and four-year-olds ended up in the bathroom near the repair area and found the box cutter. In a fight over the box cutter, the four-year-old (V.R.) sliced her finger trying to seize it from the two-year-old. V.R. had to have several surgeries for nerve and tendon damage. Ms. Sanchez, Ruben, and V.R. sued CAA alleging that it had breached its duty as a landowner and caused the injury for their failure to maintain the premises. Can they recover? [In re *V.R.,* 2014 WL 6090396 (Ohio App.)]

6. On June 21, 1997, Julio Ramos was helping his cousin move out of a second-floor apartment. He positioned himself on the outer side of the second-floor balcony railing, his feet between its spindles, to pass furniture to a friend on the ground below. While perched in this precarious position, Ramos held onto the railing with one hand and used his other hand to move the furniture. The reason for this method of removing the furniture was that many pieces were too large to be taken down the stairs. After approximately an hour of moving furniture in this manner, Ramos heard some cracking and felt the railing giving way. He released the furniture and attempted to grab onto the railing with both hands, but the spindles broke, and Ramos fell to the ground.

Ramos brought suit against the landlord to recover for his injuries. How does this case compare to the *Tan* case? Should the landlord in this case be held liable? [*Ramos v. Granajo*, 822 A.2d 936 (R.I.)]

7. A tenant leased an apartment in which so much noise emanated from surrounding apartments late at night and in the wee hours of the morning that he could not get much sleep. The tenant brought suit against the landlord, alleging that the landlord had breached the implied warranty of habitability. Is the tenant correct? Can noise be a breach of the warranty

of habitability? [*Nostrand Gardens Co-op v. Howard*, 634 N.Y.S.2d 505]

8. James Santelli was staying at a motel owned by Abu Rahmatullah for several months as he worked at a nearby construction project.

   Joseph Pryor had been previously employed at the motel as a general maintenance man. There was no criminal background check done on Pryor. Pryor had a prior conviction and was wanted at the time he was hired for probation violations. When he left his job at the motel, Pryor kept his master keycard. Pryor used the keycard to enter Santelli's room and later confessed to robbing and killing him, with a resulting sentence of 85 years. Mr. Santelli's widow brought suit against Rahmatullah for his negligence in hiring Pryor. Can Rahmatullah be held liable for Mr. Santelli's death? [*Santelli v. Rahmatullah*, 966 N.E.2d 661 (Ind. App.)]

9. During the remodeling of an apartment building, tenants had so much dust from the construction settle in their apartment that they experienced damage to their expensive sound and recording equipment. They had rented the very specialized and large apartment because it was suitable to use as a recording studio. Would the presence of the dust be grounds for constructive eviction? Would it be a breach of the warranty of habitability? [*Minjak Co. v. Rudolph*, 528 N.Y.S.2d 554]

10. Cantanese leased a building for the operation of his drugstore from Saputa. He moved his drugstore from Saputa's building to another location but continued to pay rent to Saputa. Saputa, fearing that he was losing his tenant, entered the premises without Cantanese's permission and made extensive alterations to the premises to suit two physicians who had agreed to rent the premises from Saputa. Cantanese informed Saputa that he regarded the making of the unauthorized repairs as grounds for canceling the lease. Saputa then claimed that Cantanese was liable for the difference between the rent that Cantanese had agreed to pay and the rent that the doctors would pay for the remainder of the term of the Cantanese lease. Was Cantanese liable for such rent? [*Saputa v. Cantanese*, 182 So. 2d 826 (La. App.)]

11. Sargent rented a second-floor apartment in a building owned by Ross. Anna, Sargent's four-year-old daughter, fell from an outdoor stairway and was killed. Sargent brought suit against Ross for her daughter's death. Ross contended that she did not have control over the stairway and therefore was not liable for its condition. Was this defense valid? [*Sargent v. Ross*, 308 A.2d 528 (N.H.)]

12. Charles leased a house from Donald for four years. The rent agreed on was $850 per month. After two years, Charles assigned his rights under the lease to Smith, who moved in and paid rent regularly for a year. Owing rent, Smith moved out sometime later without Donald's knowledge or consent. Donald demanded that Charles pay the rent. Is Charles liable?

13. Green rented an apartment from Stockton Realty. The three-story building had a washroom and clothesline on the roof for use by the tenants. The clothesline ran very near the skylight, and there was no guard rail between the clothesline and the skylight. Green's friend, who was 14 years old, was helping Green remove clothes from the line when she tripped on an object and fell against the skylight. The glass was too weak to support her weight, and she fell to the floor below, sustaining serious injuries. Is the landlord responsible for damages for the injury sustained? Decide. [*Reiman v. Moore*, 180 P.2d 452 (Cal.)]

14. Suzanne Andres was injured when she fell from the balcony of her second-floor apartment in the Roswell-Windsor Village Apartments. Andres was leaning against the railing on the balcony when it gave out, and she and the railing fell to the ground. Andres filed suit against Roswell-Windsor for its failure to maintain the railing. Roswell-Windsor maintains that the railing was not in a common area and was in Andres's exclusive possession and that she was responsible for its maintenance or at least letting the manager know the railing needed repairs. Should Andres recover from the landlord for her injuries? [*Andres v. Roswell-Windsor Village Apartments*, 777 F.2d 671 (11th Cir.)]

15. Williams, an elderly man who was sensitive to heat, rented an apartment in the Parker House. His apartment was fully air-conditioned, which enabled him to stand the otherwise unbearable heat of the summer. The landlord was dissatisfied with the current rent, and although the lease had a year to run, insisted that Williams agree to an increase. Williams refused. The landlord attempted to force Williams to pay the increase by turning off the electricity and thereby stopping the apartment's air conditioners. He also sent up heat on the hot days. After one week of such treatment, Williams, claiming that he had been evicted, moved out. Has there been an eviction? Explain.

CPA Questions

1. Which of the following provisions must be included to have an enforceable written residential lease?

	A Description of the Leased Premises	A Due Date for the Payment of Rent
a.	Yes	Yes
b.	Yes	No
c.	No	Yes
d.	No	No

2. Bronson is a residential tenant with a 10-year written lease. In the absence of specific provisions in the lease to the contrary, which of the following statements is correct?

   a. The premises may not be sublet for less than the full remaining term.

   b. Bronson may not assign the lease.

   c. The landlord's death will automatically terminate the lease.

   d. Bronson's purchase of the property will terminate the lease.

3. Which of the following provisions must be included in a residential lease agreement?

   a. A description of the leased premises.

   b. The due date for payment of rent.

   c. A requirement that the tenant have public liability insurance.

   d. A requirement that the landlord will perform all structural repairs to the property.

Decedents' Estates and Trusts

Learning Outcomes

After studying this chapter, you should be able to

LO.1 Define *testamentary capacity* and *testamentary intent*

LO.2 Discuss how a valid will is created

LO.3 Explain how a will may be modified or revoked

LO.4 Describe briefly the probate and contest of a will

LO.5 Describe the ordinary pattern of distribution by intestacy

LO.6 Explain the nature of a trust

Uniform Probate Code (UPC)–uniform statute on wills and administration of estates.

decedent–person whose estate is being administered.

testate–condition of leaving a will upon death.

intestate–condition of dying without a will as to any property.

testate distribution– distribution of an estate in accordance with the will of the decedent.

will–instrument executed with the formality required by law by which a person makes a disposition of his or her property to take effect upon death.

testator, testatrix–man, woman who makes a will.

legacy–gift of money made by will.

bequest–gift of personal property by will.

legatee–beneficiary who receives a gift of personal property by will.

devise–gift of real estate made by will.

devisee–beneficiary of a devise.

testamentary capacity– sufficient mental capacity to understand that a writing being executed is a will and what that entails.

51-1   Wills

What happens to your property after you die? There is a process for estate administration that is governed by state statutes and judicial decisions. There is wide variation in state law and there are only 17 states that have adopted the **Uniform Probate Code (UPC).**[1]

When a **decedent** has died with a valid will, he or she is said to have died **testate,** and the will determines who is entitled to receive the estate property after creditors have been paid. If the decedent did not make a valid will, laws for **intestate** distribution determine the distribution.

51-1a   Definitions

Testate distribution describes the distribution that is made when the decedent leaves a valid will. A **will** is ordinarily a writing that provides for a distribution of property upon death but that confers no rights prior to that time. A man who makes a will is called a **testator;** a woman, a **testatrix.**

A gift of personal property by will is a **legacy** or **bequest,** in which case the beneficiary may also be called a **legatee.** A gift of real property by will is a **devise,** and the beneficiary may be called a **devisee.**

51-1b   Parties to Will

Each state has variations on the qualifications of persons who wish to make a will. The following requirements are typical.

Testator

Generally, the right to make a will is limited to persons 18 or older. The testator must have **testamentary capacity,**[2] which means that a person must have sufficient mental capacity to understand that the writing that is being executed is a will—that is, that it disposes of the person's property after death. The testator must also have a reasonable appreciation of who the beneficiaries of his will are as well as a grasp of the identity of relatives and friends and the nature and extent of the property that will be given and to whom upon death.

Testamentary capacity is challenged by surviving relatives quite often. Eccentric behavior does not mean that the individual lacks capacity. The excessive and continued use of alcohol or multiple medications, producing mental deterioration, may be sufficient to justify the conclusion that the decedent lacked testamentary capacity. However, there can be lucid periods even among those who suffer from addictions. Expert testimony, the observations of friends and relatives, and the conduct of the decedent prior to death are all relevant factors in determining whether there was testamentary capacity.[3]

---

[1] The Uniform Probate Code has been adopted in Alaska, Arizona, Colorado, Florida, Hawaii, Idaho, Maine, Massachusetts, Michigan, Minnesota, Montana, Nebraska, New Mexico, North Dakota, South Carolina, South Dakota, and Utah. Other states have adopted portions or select provisions of the UPC. The predominant form of the UPC continues to be the 1969 version, but the 1990 and 2003 versions have been integrated into existing UPC states' statutes.
[2] In re *Estate of Rosen,* 23 N.E.3d 116 (Mass. App. 2014).
[3] *Parish v. Parish,* 704 S.E.2d 99 (Va. 2011).

CASE SUMMARY

Paranoia, Dementia, and Alzheimer's: Enough to Void a Will?

FACTS: Patricia Watson, the decedent, was raised in Missouri, but taught elementary school in California where she had three marriages and one daughter who was murdered in 1980. Ms. Watson retained close ties with her half siblings, Richard Ivie, Jimmie Ivie, Ladonna Small, and Bernard Ivie ("the Ivies").

When Watson retired from teaching in February 2002, and she married Smith. At the time of their marriage, Watson was 70 years old and Smith was 60 years old. Watson had substantial income and approximately $1 million in assets, including her home in California, real estate in Missouri, a pension from the California State Teachers' Retirement System (CALSTRS), and several bank accounts, retirement accounts, and vehicles. Smith had filed for bankruptcy in 1997 and had minimal income and assets. Watson created her original trust on May 9, 2002, about three months after marrying Smith. At the same time, Watson also created a will with a provision "pouring over" all of her estate's assets into the trust. Watson's Missouri attorney, Reginald Young, prepared the documents. All of Watson's property was conveyed into the trust. They moved to Missouri in 2004.

The Ivies were the sole beneficiaries of the trust. The trust provided "It is expressly the Grantor's intention that her husband, Arnold L. Smith, not receive any part of the Trust Estate."

Watson began showing signs that her mental health was progressively deteriorating. She saw a doctor who wrote in his report: "She thinks her husband is trying to poison her with rat poison. She denies hallucinations, but apparently gets very angry quickly on questioning.... At this time the patient seems to have paranoia."

According to her sister, Watson wanted a divorce from Smith because he had ruined her life. Watson also told one of her brothers that she thought she was losing her mind, that she was afraid of Smith, and that she thought he was trying to poison her.

Watson had a neuro-psychological evaluation at the Mayo Clinic in October 2005. Test results showed "a mild to moderate degree of cognitive impairment." The Mayo Clinic physician concluded that Watson's diagnosis was vascular dementia.

A second physician stated without qualification in November 2006 that the diagnosis was Alzheimer's dementia.

Before Watson executed the first trust amendment, she was no longer able to care for herself. She needed help with all of her daily living activities. By May 2007, at a family gathering, Watson did not recognize the children of one of her brothers and other previously known family members.

Roughly one month after leaving the hospital following a hospitalization, on July 27, 2007, Watson signed the first trust amendment decreasing the Ivies' share of her property and granting Smith a share. The amendment also added a "no-contest" clause, the purpose of which was to cause anyone challenging the trust to lose his or her share.

Watson's mental health continued to worsen. At some point after July 2007, she visited one of her neighbors and took off her own clothes in the neighbor's living room. In-home nurses' reports reflect that Watson's dementia was uncontrolled, she was paranoid and experienced forgetfulness and mood swings.

From early December 2007 to mid-January 2008, Watson retitled her checking account and money market account from the trust to her own name individually and signed documents to "pay on death" to Smith. Watson removed the Ivies from all accounts and beneficiary status.

The in-home nursing staff noted that her forgetfulness continued and that she had bouts of confusion. In late January, she asked Smith, "Am I still your wife? Are we married?" In late March, she was disoriented in her home and could not find the bathroom. In April, she wanted her lawn hand-pulled instead of mowed. In May, she was hospitalized after falling, and hospital reports repeatedly showed that she was "Confused/Disoriented/Senile/Irrational/Non–Compliant." On June 5, back at home, Watson said that she saw a baby while staring at the ceiling and that she was hearing voices.

Watson lived in a nursing home until July 2, 2008, which was the day she signed the second trust amendment. The second trust amendment further reduced the Ivies' shares in the trust estate and increased Smith's share. Because Reginald Young recognized that Watson's mental health had deteriorated and because he anticipated controversy over the changes to Watson's estate plan, he prepared a memorandum for his file stating that he believed she understood what she was doing.

Watson died April 10, 2009. After Watson's death, the Ivies filed to set aside the trust amendments, beneficiary designations, and various property transfers. The court entered judgment for the Ivies. The court found that Watson lacked testamentary capacity with regard to her estate plan. Smith appealed.

DECISION: There was substantial evidence to support a finding that Watson lacked testamentary capacity to make the

Paranoia, Dementia, and Alzheimer's: Enough to Void a Will? continued

changes to her estate plan. Although the testamentary capacity standard takes into account the ability of persons who have been diagnosed with some form of mental defect to make a valid will or trust, it remains a factual issue of whether a person had testamentary capacity at the particular time of execution. Lower courts are in the best position to

decide precisely when a person has testamentary capacity, and the bizarre and declining behaviors of the Testator indicate that she did not understand what she was doing through the changes and to whom.

Affirmed. [*Ivie v. Smith*, **439 S.W.3d 189 (Mo. 2014)**]

Beneficiary

beneficiary—person to whom the proceeds of a life insurance policy are payable, a person for whose benefit property is held in trust, or a person given property by a will; the ultimate recipient of the benefit of a funds transfer.

Generally, the capacity of the **beneficiary** is not an issue. However, when part of a decedent's estate passes to a minor, a guardian may be appointed to administer that interest for the minor. If a will directs that any share payable to a minor be held by a particular person as trustee for the minor, the minor's interest will be so held, and a guardian is not required. Statutes often provide that if the estate or interest of the minor is not large, it may be paid directly to the minor or to the parent or person by whom the minor is maintained.

51-1c Testamentary Intent

testamentary intent—designed to take effect at death, as by disposing of property or appointing a personal representative.

To execute a valid will, testators must demonstrate an intent to transfer property upon their deaths. This mental state is called **testamentary intent.**[4] This is the testator's intent that certain persons become the owners of certain property upon his or her death. However, there is still testamentary intent when the testator designates an executor only and does not make any disposition of property.

51-1d Form

Because the privilege of disposing of property by will is purely statutory, the will must be executed in the manner required by state statutes. Unless statutory requirements are met, the will is invalid, and the testator is considered to have died intestate. In such a case, the decedent's property will be distributed according to the laws of intestacy of the particular state.

Writing

Ordinarily, a will must be in writing. Some state statutes, however, permit oral wills in limited circumstances, and the use of videotaped wills is gaining some legal ground.

Signature

A written will must be signed by the testator. In case of physical incapacity, the testator may be assisted in signing the will.[5] Witnesses to the will can then verify that simple marks were indeed made by the testator while experiencing a physically debilitating condition.

Generally, a will must be signed at the bottom or end. The purpose of this requirement is to prevent unscrupulous persons from taking a will that has been validly signed and writing or typing additional provisions in the space below the signature.

[4] In re *Estate of Tyler*, 80 A.3d 797 (Pa. Super. 2013).
[5] In re *Estate of Shapiro*, 995 N.Y.S.2d 805 (N.Y. App. 2014).

E-COMMERCE & CYBERLAW

Where There's a Video, Is There a Will?

With technology, wills are no longer always just written but may be supplemented with electronic verification. The American Bar Association's Web site (**http://www.abanet.org**) offers the following thoughts on the new trend in video wills:

More and more people are preparing a video in which they read the will and explain why certain gifts were made and others not made. The video recording might also show the execution of the will. Should a disgruntled relative decide to

challenge the will, the video can provide compelling proof that the person making the will was mentally competent and observed the formalities of execution.

Keep in mind that videos do not last forever and are subject to damage. You should consult a lawyer before making such a video to find out about your state's laws on video wills. Generally, such a video would supplement the will and is not always a substitute for a validly executed will.

Attestation

attestation clause—clause that indicates a witness has observed either the execution of the will or the testator's acknowledgment of the writing as the testator's will.

self-proved wills—wills that eliminate some formalities of proof by being executed according to statutory requirements.

acknowledgment—admission or confirmation, generally of an instrument and usually made before a person authorized to administer oaths, such as a notary public.

affidavit—statement of facts under oath; executed before a notary public or anyone authorized to administer oaths.

Attestation is the act of witnessing the execution of a will. Generally, attestation consists of a witness signing the will following a clause that declares that the witness either saw the testator sign the will or that the testator told the witness that he or she did indeed sign the will. The clause that describes what the witness saw or knows is called an **attestation clause.** Statutes often require that attestation be made by the witnesses in the presence of the testator and in the presence of each other. Most states and the Uniform Probate Code (UPC) require two witnesses; a few states require three.

Self-proved wills are wills that carry a presumption that they are valid if executed according to the requirements set forth by statute. The UPC recognizes self-proved wills. A will may be simultaneously executed, attested, and made self-proving by acknowledgment by the testator and by affidavits of the witnesses.

The **acknowledgment** and **affidavits** must each be made before an officer authorized to administer oaths under state law, such as a notary. The acknowledgement and affidavits must carry an official seal, such as a notary's seal, which must be evidenced by the officer's certificate under official seal.

The self-proving provisions attached to the will are not a part of the will. Self-proving provisions allow a will to be admitted to probate without requiring the testimony of the witnesses to the will. The will itself must still meet the requirements of the law. The execution of a valid will is a condition precedent to use of the self-proving provisions.

In some states, a witness cannot be a beneficiary under the will. In those states, use of a beneficiary as a witness will not affect the will, but the witness's share is limited to whatever his or her intestate share would have been if there had been no will. Under the UPC, a will can be validly witnessed by an interested person.

Date

There is generally no requirement that a testator date a will, but a dated will does reduce confusion. When there are several wills, the most recent one will control when there are conflicting provisions between and among the wills.

51-1e Modification of Will

A will may be modified by executing a *codicil*, a separate writing that amends a will. The will, except as changed by the codicil, remains the same. The effect is that the provisions of the codicil are substituted for those provisions of the will that are inconsistent with the codicil. A codicil must be executed with all the formality of a will and is treated in all other respects the same as a will.

A will cannot be modified merely by crossing out a clause and writing in what the testator wishes. Such an **interlineation** is not operative unless it is executed with the same formality required of a will or, in some states, unless the will is republished in its interlineated form.

interlineation–writing between the lines or adding to the provisions of a document, the effect thereof depending upon the nature of the document.

revoke–testator's act of taking back his or her will and its provisions.

51-1f Revocation of Will

At any time during the testator's life, the testator may **revoke** the will made or make changes in its terms. It may be revoked by act of the testator or by operation of law. A testator must have the same degree of mental capacity to revoke a will as is required to make one.

Revocation by Act of Testator

A will or a codicil is revoked when the testator destroys, burns, or tears it or crosses out the provisions of the will or codicil with the intention to revoke them. The revocation may be in whole or in part.[6]

CASE SUMMARY

When Wife #2 Finds Wife #1's Will with a Lot of Lines Through It

FACTS: On June 15, 1982, Shirley Joyce Speers signed a "Last Will and Testament." It named her husband, Ralph Speers, as her executor. It also gave her daughter, Sherr Arlene Ross, her household furnishings and appliances, and her son, Daniel Eugene Speers, her livestock. Her husband was named the beneficiary of the rest of the estate, provided he paid the estate's expenses. If he failed to do so, his share went to their children and grandsons. The will was probably witnessed and signed, but not notarized. The witnesses did not see any lines or strikeouts in the will when they signed it. Shirley died on April 20, 1997, and the will was not probated at the time of her death.

After his wife's death, Ralph married Ann Speers. Ralph died some time before June 2005, and Ann then discovered a copy of Shirley's will with lines through it and cross-outs. She filed a petition seeking to admit the will to probate. The will she submitted contained several handwritten strikeouts and interlineations. Shirley's children objected to the admission of the will, arguing that it was invalid because the original will was destroyed. The court found for Ann and the children appealed. The Court of Appeals reversed and Ann appealed.

DECISION: The court affirmed, holding that the original will was not self-proving because of the lack of a notary seal and because its strike-outs indicated that Shirley had revoked its provisions. The result was a completely different distribution of property under state intestacy law for Shirley's estate and, as a result, for Ralph's. Whether the will was admitted determined whether Ann or the children inherited Ralph's property. A dissent in the case concluded that the will should be admitted and that the witnesses' testimony had been clouded by the cross-outs and lines in the copy of the will. [**In re Estate of Speers,** 179 P.3d 1265 (Okl. 2008)]

Revocation by Operation of Law

In certain instances, statutes provide that a change of circumstances has the effect of a revocation. **For Example,** when a person marries after executing a will, the will is revoked or is presumed revoked unless it was made in contemplation of marriage or unless it provided for the future spouse. In some states, the revocation is not total but is effective only

---

[6] In re *Estate of Irvine,* 264 P.3d 127 (Mont. 2011).

to the extent of allowing the spouse to take such share of the estate as that to which the spouse would have been entitled had there been no will.

The birth or adoption of a child after the execution of a will commonly works a revocation or partial revocation of the will as to that child. In the case of a partial revocation, the child is entitled to receive the same share as if the testator had died intestate.

The divorce of the testator does not in itself work a revocation. However, the majority of courts hold that if a property settlement is carried out on the basis of the divorce, a prior will of the testator is revoked, at least to the extent of the legacy given to the divorced spouse.

51-1g Election to Take against the Will

To protect the husband or wife of a testator, the surviving spouse may generally ignore the provisions of a will and elect to take against the will. In such a case, the surviving spouse receives the share of the estate he or she would have received had the testator died without leaving a will or receives a fractional share specified by statute.

The right to take against the will is generally barred by certain kinds of misconduct by the surviving spouse. If a spouse is guilty of desertion or nonsupport that would have justified the decedent's obtaining a divorce, the surviving spouse usually cannot elect to take against the will.

51-1h Disinheritance

disinherited—excluded from sharing in the estate of a decedent.

With some exceptions, any person may be **disinherited** or excluded from sharing in the estate of a decedent.[7] A person who would inherit if there were no will is excluded from

---

SPORTS & ENTERTAINMENT LAW

Wills, Estates, & Probate Mistakes of the Rich and Famous

Philip Seymour Hoffman's sudden death offered some insights into the importance of effective estate planning, even by those who are young. For example, from Heath Ledger's estate we learn that it is important to keep your will updated. Mr. Ledger had not updated his will following the birth of his daughter. Mr. Hoffman's will only mentioned his first child, not the two who were born following the will's execution. While courts can step in and include the other children, there is always the chance of misunderstandings, challenges, and, perhaps most importantly, how the children's inheritance and care is to be handled.

When there are partners who are not married, there are complications. Who will manage any inheritance the children receive? Is the partner to be the trustee? Also, part of estate planning could include marriage because marriage does save estate taxes. For example, Mr. Hoffman gave his $35 million estate to the mother of his three children, Marianne O'Donnell. If the two had been married, there would be no estate tax.

Because they were not married, there is a personal exemption of $5.34 million and the remainder of the estate is taxes, at about 50 percent, so $15 million of Mr. Hoffman's estate will go to the federal government.

If Mr. Hoffman had established a trust for his children and partner, his estate would have simply "poured over" into the trust and his probate would have been completely private.

James Gandolfini's untimely death resulted in a payment of $30 million in taxes of his $70 million estate. He had likewise not structured his estate to minimize taxes. His young daughter will receive the bulk of the estate when she turns 21.

Robin Williams' death has resulted in a probate battle over his personal property items between his third wife and his children. The children want to have personal items, such as Mr. Williams' suspenders from his hit television series, "Mork and Mindy." While Mr. Williams had taken care with trusts and appropriate planning for his major property interests, the little items have proven to be a source of contention in probate.

---

[7] One exception, for example, is a surviving spouse. A surviving spouse has marital property rights and cannot be disinherited completely.

receiving any part of a decedent's estate if the decedent has left a will giving everything to other persons.

51-1i Special Types of Wills

In certain situations, special types of wills are used.

Holographic Wills

A **holographic will** is an unwitnessed will that is written by the testator entirely by hand. Some states make no distinction between holographic and other wills. Other states apply the general law of wills to holographic wills, with certain variations. Some states require that a holographic will be dated. Under the UPC, a holographic will is valid, whether witnessed or not, if the signatures and the material provisions are in the handwriting of the testator.[8]

Living Wills

Living wills are documents that individuals use to decide in advance what level of life-sustaining medical treatments that want if they become unable to express their wishes and are in an irreversible, incurable condition (Figure 51-1). Living wills are legal in most states. Such personal wishes are entitled to constitutional protection as long as they are expressed clearly.

51-2 Administration of Decedents' Estates

A decedent's estate consists of the assets the decedent owned at death, and the administration of the estate requires a determination of who is entitled to receive that property. If the decedent owed debts, those debts must be paid first. After those payments, any balance must be distributed according to the terms of the will or by the intestate law if the decedent did not leave a valid will.

51-2a Definitions

The decedent has the privilege of naming the person who will administer the estate. A man named in a will to administer the estate of the decedent is an **executor**; a woman, an **executrix.** If the decedent failed to name an executor or executrix or did not leave a will, the law permits another person, usually a close relative, to be appointed to wind up the estate. This person is an **administrator** or **administratrix.** Administrators and executors are referred to generally under the UPC as **personal representatives** of the decedents because they represent the decedents or stand in their place.

51-2b Probate of Will

Probate is the act by which the proper court or official accepts a will and declares that the instrument satisfies the statutory requirements as the will of the testator. Until a will is probated, it has no legal effect.

When witnesses have signed a will, generally they must appear and state that they saw the testator sign the will (unless the will is self-proving). If those witnesses cannot be found, have died, or are outside the jurisdiction, the will may be probated nevertheless.

holographic will—unwitnessed will written by hand.

living will—document by which individuals may indicate that if they become unable to express their wishes and are in an irreversible, incurable condition, they do not want life-sustaining medical treatments.

executor, executrix—man, woman named in a will to administer the estate of the decedent.

administrator, administratrix—person (man, woman) appointed to wind up and settle the estate of a person who has died without a will.

personal representatives—administrators and executors who represent decedents under the UPC.

probate—procedure for formally establishing or proving that a given writing is the last will and testament of the person who purportedly signed it.

[8]Determination of the validity of a holographic will requires the court to examine the nature of the document submitted for probate. In re *Succession of Duskin*, 153 So. 3d 567 (La. App. 2014).

FIGURE 51-1   **Living Will**

Living Will

INSTRUCTIONS:

This is an important legal document It sets forth your directions regarding medical treatment. You have the right to refuse treatment you do not want. You may make changes in any of these directions, or add to them, to conform them to your personal wishes.

I, _John Jones_ , being of sound mind, make this statement as a directive to be followed if I become permanently unable to participate in decisions regarding my medical care. These instructions reflect my firm and settled commitment to decline medical treatment under the circumstances indicated below:

I direct my attending physician to withhold or withdraw treatment that serves only to prolong the process of my dying, if I should be in an incurable or irreversible mental or physical condition with no reasonable expectation of recovery.

These instructions apply if I am (a) in a terminal condition; (b) permanently unconscious; or (c) if I am conscious but have irreversible brain damage and will never regain the ability to make decisions and express my wishes.

I direct that treatment be limited to measures to keep me comfortable and to relieve pain, including any pain that might occur by withholding or withdrawing treatment.

While I understand that I am not legally required to be specific about future treatments, if I am in the condition(s) described above I feel especially strongly about the following forms of treatment:

I do not want cardiac resuscitation.
I do not want mechanical respiration.
I do not want tube feeding.
I do not want antibiotics.
I do want maximum pain relief.

Other directions (insert personal instructions): _NONE_

These directions express my legal right to refuse treatment, under the law of [name of state]. I intend my instructions to be carried out, unless I have rescinded them in a new writing or by clearly indicating that I have changed my mind.

Sign and date here in the presence of two adult witnesses, who should also sign.

Keep the signed original with your personal papers at home. Give copies of the signed original to your doctor, family, lawyer, and others who might be involved in your care.

Signed: _John Jones_
Witness: _Earl Hummel_
  Address: _7852 Bailey Avenue_
  Buffalo, New York
Witness: _Ramona Yaley_
  Address: _8921 Clinton Street_
  Buffalo, New York

When no witnesses are required, it is customary to require two or more persons to identify the signature of the testator at the time of probate.

After the probate witnesses have made their statements under oath, the official or court will ordinarily admit the will to probate in the absence of any circumstances indicating that the writing should not be probated. A certificate or decree that officially declares that the will is the will of the testator and has been admitted to probate is then issued.

Any qualified person who wishes to object to the probate of the will on the ground that it is not a proper will may appear before the official or court prior to the entry of the decree of probate. A person may petition after probate to have the probate of the will set aside.

51-2c Will Contest

The probate of a will may be refused or set aside on the ground that the will is not the free expression of the intention of the testator. It may be attacked on the ground of (1) a lack of mental capacity to execute a will, (2) undue influence, duress, fraud, or mistake existing at the time of the execution of the will that induced or led to its execution, or (3) forgery.[9] With the exception of mental capacity, these terms consist of the same elements they do in contract law.

If any one of these problems exists, the probate court can refuse to admit the will for probate. The decedent's estate is then distributed as if there had been no will unless an earlier will can be probated.

CASE SUMMARY

There's a Melody in the Heirs

FACTS: John C. Ramsey Sr. (Senior) executed a will in the last months of his life that left the bulk of his estate to Melody Taylor, his paramour. Senior's relationships with his son and grandsons were strained, and his will included the following clause:

I have intentionally provided significant, yet smaller amounts for my son and grandsons because they have for several years alienated my affections by being irresponsible, contentious, and constantly seeking financial support from me rather than providing for themselves.

I have made provisions for MELODY J. TAYLOR because MELODY J. TAYLOR provides me care and support.

Senior was suffering from cancer and renal failure, and his pain was extraordinary. His doctors prescribed high doses of morphine that Melody administered. Senior died from an overdose of morphine.

John Ramsey Jr. (Junior), Senior's son, challenged the validity of the will on the grounds of undue influence as well as felonious killing of a testator by a beneficiary. The trial court found there was undue influence and refused to admit the will to probate. Melody appealed.

DECISION: Judgment for Melody. There was a long history of bad blood between Junior and Senior. Further, Senior had disinherited Junior long before Melody came into the picture. The clear statement in the will that he knew he was leaving out Junior and why was indicative of clear thinking and lack of duress from Melody. Senior also had independent advice on his will and took his time in executing it. Melody's administration of the fatal drug dose was pursuant to physician's instructions, and she was still entitled to inherit under the valid will that was admitted to probate. [*Ramsey v. Taylor*, 999 P.2d 1178 (Or. App. 2000)]

51-2d When Administration Is Not Necessary

No administration is required when the decedent did not own any property at the time of death. In some states, special statutes provide for a simplified administration when the decedent leaves only a small estate. Likewise, when all property owned by the decedent

---

[9] *Shoaf v. Shoaf*, 727 S.E.2d 301 (N.C. App. 2012).

was owned with another person as joint tenants with right of survivorship, no administration is required.

51-2e Appointment of Personal Representative

Both executors and administrators must be appointed to their roles by a court or an officer designated by law. The appointment is made by granting to the personal representative **letters testamentary,** in the case of an executor, or **letters of administration,** in the case of an administrator.

51-2f Proof of Claims against the Estate

State statutes vary widely on how **claims** against a decedent's estate are presented. In very general terms, statutes provide for some form of public notice of the grant of letters testamentary or letters of administration. Creditors are then required to give notice of their claims within a period specified by either statute or a court order (for example, within six months). In most states, failure to present a claim within the specified time bars the claim.

51-2g Construction of a Will

The will of a decedent is interpreted according to the ordinary or plain meaning evidenced by its words. The court will strive to give effect to every provision of the will to avoid concluding that any part of the decedent's estate was not disposed of by the will.[10]

letters testamentary–written authorization given to an executor of an estate as evidence of appointment and authority.

letters of administration–written authorization given to an administrator of an estate as evidence of appointment and authority.

claims–right to payment.

ETHICS & THE LAW

Preparing Your Client's Will When You're the Beneficiary

John Richard Tomlan, an attorney, befriended Katherine Rice, a 90-year-old nursing home resident, shortly after she was admitted to the home in 1993. Ms. Rice, unmarried and childless, had Parkinson's disease as well as dementia. Mr. Tomlan handled several legal items for her, including the sale of her cabin and the necessary legal paperwork for its closing. In 1998, Tomlan prepared a will that left her substantial estate to a niece and nephew, with the remainder of the estate to various philanthropic organizations.

Later, Ms. Rice told Mr. Tomlan that she wanted to leave the bulk of her estate to him. He explained that he could not ethically prepare such a will. Ms. Rice never contacted another attorney to make the change in the will. After that point, Mr. Tomlan began transferring Ms. Rice's assets into accounts that were joint and survivorship accounts with him. He was then able to convince her to give him a durable power of attorney so that he had control over all of her assets, including investment accounts, property, and bank

accounts. Using that power, he had $1,000,000 in shares of stock transferred solely to him.

Mr. Tomlan maintained that everything was a gift that Ms. Rice had directed be given to him. When Ms. Rice died at the age of 99, Mr. Tomlan failed to probate her estate despite questions and demands from Ms. Rice's niece. Eventually, the estate was processed and had just over $200,000 left. However, with the property that had been gifted to Mr. Tomlan, the estate was valued at over $2.1 million. Ms. Rice's niece reported Mr. Tomlan to the state bar of Ohio and he was given an indefinite suspension of his license to practice law. Clients are dependent upon absolute trust and arms-length relationships with their lawyers. When friendship and gifting enter the picture, the power of lawyer over client is one that dissipates estates.

[*Disciplinary Counsel v. Tomlan*, 885 N.E.2d 895 (Ohio 2008)]

---

[10] In re *Estate of Nalaschi,* 90 A.3d 8 (Pa. Super. 2014).

51-2h **Testate Distribution of an Estate**

general legacies— certain sums of money bequeathed to named persons by the testator; to be paid out of the decedent's assets generally without specifying any particular fund or source from which the payment is to be made.

specific legacies— identified property bequeathed by a testator; also called *specific devises.*

abate—put a stop to a nuisance; reduce or cancel a legacy because the estate of the decedent is insufficient to make payment in full.

adeemed—canceled; as in a specifically bequeathed property being sold or given away by the testator prior to death, thus canceling the bequest.

antilapse statutes— statutes providing that the children or heirs of a deceased beneficiary may take the legacy in the place of the deceased beneficiary.

The last phase of the administration of the estate by the decedent's personal representative is the distribution of property remaining after the payment of all debts and taxes in accordance with the provisions of the will or by intestacy rules if there was no valid will.

There are various types of gifts under a will. A testator can bequeath to named persons certain sums of money called **general legacies,** or gifts in which no particular money is specified. The testator may also bequeath identified property called **specific legacies** or *specific devises.* **For Example,** a testator may give "$1,000 to *A*; $1,000 to *B*; my automobile to *C.*" The first two bequests are general; the third is specific. After such specific bequests, the testator may make a bequest of everything remaining, called a *residuary bequest,* such as "the balance of my estate to *D.*"

Abatement of Legacies

Assume in the preceding example that after all debts are paid, and only $1,500 and the automobile remain. What disposition is to be made?

Legacies **abate** or bear loss in the following order: (1) residuary, (2) general, (3) specific. The law also holds that legacies of the same class abate proportionately. **For Example,** in the hypothetical case, *C,* the specific legatee, would receive the automobile; *A* and *B,* the general legatees, would each receive $750; and *D,* the residuary legatee, would receive nothing.

Ademption of Property

When specifically bequeathed property is sold or given away by the testator prior to death, the bequest is considered **adeemed,** or canceled. The specific legatee in this instance is not entitled to receive any property or money. *Ademption* has the same consequence as though the testator had formally canceled the bequest. **For Example,** if Aunt Claire left her 2011 Honda Accord to her niece, Helen, but Aunt Claire sold the Honda Accord in 2014 and died in 2015, Helen receives nothing from Aunt Claire's estate because the bequest of the Honda is adeemed or canceled.

Antilapse Statutes

If the beneficiary named in the testator's will died before the testator and the testator did not make any alternate provision applicable in such a case, the gift ordinarily does not lapse. **Antilapse statutes** commonly provide that the gift to the deceased beneficiary

THINKING THINGS THROUGH

Close Enough for a Will?

Gloria Waterloo had difficulty with her handwriting. When Rabbi Zimmerman and his wife came to visit her at a hospice facility, she asked his wife, Sandie, to take dictation and write out her will, a resulting one-page document that listed five provisions. One of the provisions left $3,000,000 to Rabbi Zimmerman and appointed him guardian of her estate. After the provisions were dictated, Gloria went through and signed them all and then signed her name. No one witnessed the will. Gloria died less than a month later. Her heirs moved to set aside the will. Give a list of the possible theories her heirs could use to challenge the will.

[In re *Estate of Waterloo,* 250 P.3d 558 (Ariz. App. 2011)]

shall not lapse but that the children or heirs of that beneficiary may take the legacy in the place of the deceased beneficiary. An antilapse statute does not apply if the testator specified a disposition that should be made of the gift if the original legatee had died.

51-2i Intestate Distribution of an Estate

If the decedent does not effectively dispose of all property by will or does not have a will, the decedent's property is distributed to certain relatives. Because such persons acquire or succeed to the rights of the decedent and because the circumstances under which they do so is the absence of an effective will, it is said that they acquire title by **intestate succession.**

intestate succession—distribution, made as directed by statute, of a decedent's property not effectively disposed of by will.

The right of intestate succession or inheritance is not a basic right of the citizen or an inalienable right. It exists only because the state legislature so provides. It is within the power of the state legislature to modify or destroy the right to inherit property.

Although wide variations exist among the statutory provisions of the states, a common pattern of intestate distribution exists.

Spouses

The surviving spouse of the decedent, whether husband or wife, shares in the estate. Generally, the amount received is a fraction that varies with the number of children. If no children survive, the spouse is generally entitled to take the entire estate. Otherwise, the surviving spouse ordinarily receives a one-half or one-third share of the estate.

Lineals

lineals—relationship that exists when one person is a direct descendant of the other; also called *lineal descendants*.

Lineals, or lineal descendants, are blood descendants of the decedent. Lineal descendants include children and grandchildren. That portion of the estate that is not distributed to the surviving spouse is generally distributed to lineals.

Parents

If the estate has not been fully distributed by this time, the remainder is commonly distributed to the decedent's parents.

Collateral Heirs

These are persons who are not descendants of the decedent but are related through a common ancestor. Generally, brothers and sisters and their descendants share any part of the estate that has not already been distributed. Statutes vary as to how far distribution will be made to the descendants of brothers and sisters. Under some statutes, a degree of relationship is specified, such as first cousins, and no person more remotely related to the decedent is permitted to share in the estate.

right of escheat—right of the state to take the property of a decedent that has not been distributed.

If the entire estate is not distributed within the permitted degree of relationship, the property that has not been distributed is given to the state government. This right of the state to take the property is the **right of escheat.** Under some statutes, the right of escheat arises only when there is no relative of the decedent, however remotely related.

Distribution *Per Capita* and *Per Stirpes*

per capita—method of distributing estate assets on an equal-per-person basis.

The fact that different generations of distributees may be entitled to receive the estate creates a problem of determining the proportions in which distribution is to be made (Figure 51-2). When all the distributees stand in the same degree of relationship to the decedent, distribution is made *per capita,* each receiving the same share. **For Example,** if the decedent is survived by three children—*A, B,* and *C*—each of them is entitled to receive one-third of the estate.

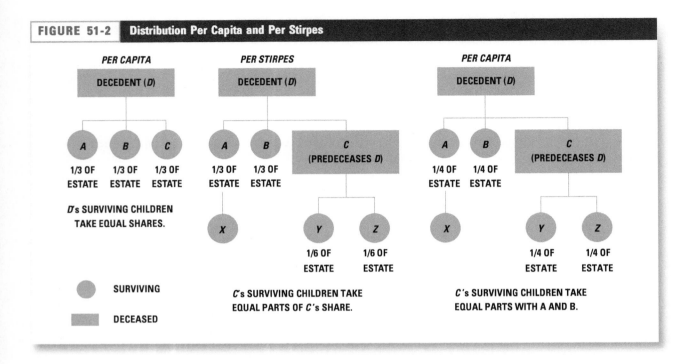

FIGURE 51-2   Distribution Per Capita and Per Stirpes

If the distributees stand in different degrees of relationship, distribution is made in as many equal parts as there are family lines, or *stirpes*, represented in the nearest generation. Parents take to the exclusion of their children or subsequent descendants, and when members of the nearest generation have died, their descendants take by way of representation. This is called **distribution *per stirpes***, or *stirpital distribution*. **For Example,** Thomas dies leaving two living children, *A* and *B*, and one child, *C*, who predeceased him but left two children (Thomas's grandchildren, *D* and *E*). *A* and *B* would each take one-third of Thomas's estate, and *D* and *E* would, under a ***per stirpes*** distribution, split a one-third interest, each receiving one-sixth of the estate.

distribution *per stirpes*— distribution of an estate made in as many equal parts as there are family lines represented in the nearest generation; also known as *stirpital distribution*.

***per stirpes*—**method for distribution of an estate that divides property equally down family lines.

Murder of Decedent

Statutes generally provide that a person who murders the decedent cannot inherit from the victim by intestacy. In the absence of such a statute, courts are divided over whether the heir may inherit.

CASE SUMMARY

When Mother and Daughter Die: The Son-in-Law's Rights

FACTS: Deanna Edwards Palladino and Brandon Palladino were high school sweethearts who married in 2007. On December 17, 2008, Brandon killed his mother-in-law, Dianne Edwards (hereinafter the decedent), by strangling her to death. The decedent's will bequeathed her entire estate to Deanna, her only child. In October 2009, Brandon was indicted for the crime of murder in the second degree for causing the death of the decedent. Deanna, who was not criminally charged in connection with the decedent's death, stood by Brandon and believed in his innocence.

When Mother and Daughter Die: The Son-in-Law's Rights continued

In February 2010, approximately 14 months after her mother's death, Deanna died intestate of an accidental drug overdose. Although the decedent's will had been admitted to probate in October 2009, none of the decedent's estate had been distributed to Deanna prior to Deanna's death. Deanna was survived by one distributee, Brandon. Brandon designated his mother, Donna DiRusso, as the administrator of Deanna's estate. According to DiRusso's petition for letters of administration, Deanna's estate consisted only of funds received as the beneficiary of the decedent's retirement plan and the expected inheritance from the decedent.

On October 12, 2010, approximately 10 months after Deanna's death, Brandon pleaded guilty to manslaughter in the first degree, in connection with the death of the decedent. During the plea proceeding, Brandon admitted to entering the decedent's home on December 17, 2008, for the purpose of taking her jewelry. While Brandon was in the decedent's bedroom taking jewelry from her jewelry box, the decedent returned home and the two got into a physical fight. Brandon placed the decedent in a choke hold and squeezed as the decedent was resisting and scratching him. Brandon admitted that he intended to cause the decedent serious physical injury but asserted that he did not intend to kill her. However, Brandon subsequently moved for leave to file a late notice of appeal from the judgment of conviction, and his motion was granted by this Court by decision and order dated April 4, 2012.

The decedent's estranged sister, Donna Larsen, submitted objections to the account arguing that Brandon forfeited his interest in any property that would pass to him from the decedent's estate through Deanna's estate, due to his conviction for causing the decedent's death.

DiRusso moved to dismiss the objections, and Larsen cross-moved for summary judgment on the objections. In a decision and order dated March 28, 2012, the Surrogate's Court denied DiRusso's motion and granted Larsen's motion in part. DiRusso appealed.

DECISION: The issue here is whether a wrongdoer should be prevented from indirectly profiting from his or her own wrongdoing. May Brandon inherit assets of the decedent's estate indirectly through Deanna's estate?

There is a clear causal link between the wrongdoing and the benefits sought. But for Brandon's killing of the decedent, the estate of Deanna would not likely include any assets from the decedent's estate. Deanna's "intervening estate" should not be used to allow Brandon to profit from his unlawful killing of the decedent.

Allowing Brandon to inherit the assets of the decedent's estate through Deanna's estate would be rewarding Brandon's criminal behavior.

Affirmed. **[In re *Edwards*, 991 N.Y.S.2d 431 (N.Y.A.D. 2014)]**

Uniform Simultaneous Death Act–law providing that when survivorship cannot be established, the property of each person shall be disposed of as though he or she had survived the other.

Death of Distributee after Decedent

The persons entitled to distribution of a decedent's estate are determined as of the date of death. If a distributee dies after that, the rights of the distributee are not lost but pass from the original decedent's estate to the deceased distributee's estate.

Simultaneous Death

The **Uniform Simultaneous Death Act**[11] provides that when survivorship cannot be established, the property of each person shall be disposed of as if he or she had survived the other.

trust–transfer of property by one person to another with the understanding or declaration that such property be held for the benefit of another; the holding of property by the owner in trust for another, upon a declaration of trust, without a transfer to another person. (Parties—settlor, trustee, beneficiary)

51-3 Trusts

A **trust** is a legal device by which property, real or personal, is held by one person for the benefit of another. Legal problems in the area of trusts invariably require a determination of the nature of the relationship created by the trust and the rights and obligations of the parties with respect to that relationship.

---

[11] The 1940 version of this act has been adopted in all states except Louisiana and Ohio. The newest version of the act (1993) has been adopted in one-third of the states.

settlor—one who settles property in trust or creates a trust.

donor—person making a gift.

trustor—donor or settlor who is the owner of property.

trustee—party who has legal title to estate and manages it.

cestui que trust—beneficiary of the trust.

trust corpus—fund or property that is transferred to the trustee also called *trust fund, trust estate,* and *trust res.*

principal—property held in trust.

income—money earned by the principal, or property in trust, and distributed by the trustee.

living trust—trust created to take effect within the lifetime of the settlor; also called *inter vivos* trust.

testamentary trust—trust that takes effect upon the settlor's death.

trust agreement—instrument creating a trust; also called *deed of trust.*

legal title—title held by the trustee in a trust situation.

equitable title—beneficial interest in a trust.

spendthrift trust—a trust that, prevents creditors of the beneficiary from reaching the principal or income held by the trustee and precludes beneficiary assignments.

51-3a Definitions

The property owner who creates the trust is the **settlor.** (The word *settlor* is taken from the old legal language of "settling the property in trust.") The settlor is sometimes called the **donor** or **trustor.** The person to whom the property is transferred in trust is the **trustee.** The person for whose benefit the trustee holds the property is the beneficiary (or *cestui que trust*).

Property held in trust is sometimes called the **trust corpus,** *trust fund, trust estate,* or *trust res.* A distinction is made between the **principal,** or the property in trust, and the **income** that is earned by the principal and distributed by the trustee.

If the trust is created to take effect within the lifetime of the settlor, it is a **living trust,** or an *inter vivos trust.* If the trust is provided for in the settlor's will and is to become effective only when the will takes effect after death, the trust is called a **testamentary trust.**

51-3b Creation of Trusts

The requirements for creating a trust are not uniform, but there are certain typical requirements.

Capacity of Beneficiary

The capacity of the beneficiary of the trust to hold property or to contract is immaterial. Many trusts are created because the beneficiary lacks legal or actual capacity to manage the property. The trustee, as the holder of legal title, must have capacity.

Formality

In creating a trust, it is common practice to execute a writing, called a **trust agreement** or *deed of trust.* No particular form of language is necessary to create a trust as long as the property, the trust purpose, and the beneficiaries are designated. If an *inter vivos* trust relates to an interest in land, the statute of frauds requires that the trust be in writing with the details of the trust included. A writing signed by the trustee and referring to a deed from the trustor can satisfy this requirement. When the trust depends on a transfer of title to land, there must be a valid transfer of the title to the trustee. If a trust is created by the will of the settlor, there must be a writing that meets the requirements of a will.

Intention

The settler must express some intention to place property in trust. It is not necessary, however, that the word *trust* or *trustee* be used. The settlor will ordinarily name a trustee, but failure to do so is not fatal to the trust because a trustee will be appointed by the court.

Identity of Beneficiary

Every trust must have a beneficiary. In a private trust, the beneficiaries must be identified by name, description, or designation of the class to which the beneficiaries belong. In a charitable trust, it is sufficient that the beneficiaries be members of the public at large or a general class of the public.

51-3c Nature of Beneficiary's Interest

When property is transferred to a trust, the trustee has **legal title** and the beneficiary has **equitable title.** The beneficiary may transfer or assign such interest in the trust. The beneficiary's creditors may reach that interest in satisfaction of their claims. However, the trustor can protect beneficiaries from creditors by creating a **spendthrift trust,** which does not allow creditors of the beneficiary to attach the beneficial interest, nor is the beneficiary permitted to assign or pledge that interest.[12]

---

[12] However, see In re *Marriage of Beevers,* 2013 WL 3872784 (Ill. App. 2013).

51-3d Powers of Trustee

A trustee can exercise only those powers that are given by law or the trust instrument or those that the court will construe as being given by implication. Modern trusts commonly give the trustee discretion to make decisions on matters that could not be foreseen by the settlor. **For Example,** the trustee may be authorized to expend principal as well as income when, in the trustee's opinion, it is necessary for the education or medical care of a beneficiary.

51-3e Duties of Trustee

The duty of a trustee is to administer the trust. The trustee who accepts the appointment must take all necessary steps to carry out the trust in a proper manner.

Performance

A trustee is under a duty to carry out the trust according to its terms and is personally liable for any loss sustained from an unjustified failure to perform such duties. A trustee cannot delegate the performance of personal duties.

Due Care

The trustee is under a duty to use reasonable skill, prudence, and diligence in the performance of trust duties. More simply stated, the trustee must use the care that would be exercised by a reasonable person under the circumstances.

Loyalty

A trustee is entitled to compensation but is not permitted to profit personally from the position of trustee.[13]

Possession and Preservation of Trust Property

The trustee has a duty to take possession of trust property and to preserve it from loss or damage. If the property includes accounts receivable or outstanding debts, the trustee is responsible for collecting them.

Production of Income

By either express or implied direction, the trustee is required to invest the money or property in enterprises or transactions that will yield an income to the estate. A trustee must invest the trust property as a reasonable and prudent investor would.

Accounting and Information

A trustee must keep accurate records so that it can be determined whether the trust has been properly administered. On request by a beneficiary, the trustee must furnish information about the trust. Periodically or at certain times, as determined by the law in each state, a trustee must file an account in court. At such time, the court examines the stewardship of the trust.

In some trusts, the trustee must balance the interests of the life beneficiary (the party entitled to the income from the trust while he or she is alive) with those of the eventual recipients of the trust *res*. **For Example,** a testator might put this provision in her will: "To my husband in trust for his life, and upon his death in fee simple to my children." How does the trustee account for rental income? What if the rental properties need

---

[13] *Whitman v. Whitman*, 2012 WL 367055 (Ohio App. 2012).

| FIGURE 51-3 | Trust Principal/Income Allocation |

PRINCIPAL	PAYABLE FROM PRINCIPAL	INCOME	PAYABLE FROM INCOME
Original trust property	Loans (principal)	Rent	Loans (interest)
Proceeds and gains from sale	Litigation expenses	Interest	Taxes
Insurance payments	Permanent improvements	Cash	Insurance premiums
New property purchased with principal	Costs of purchase	Dividends	Repairs
Stock dividends		Royalties	
Stock splits			

repairs? Do the repairs come from the income, or are they taken from principal? There are clear rules for the allocation of income and principal and the expenses of operation of the trust and the trust properties. These rules are summarized in Figure 51-3.

51-3f Remedies for Breach of Trust

A breach of trust may occur in a variety of ways. The manner in which a trust is breached affects the remedies available. These remedies include the following: (1) A money judgment against the trustee for losses, (2) an injunction, (3) criminal prosecution for misconduct, (4) recovery of trust property, (5) removal of the trustee for misconduct, and (6) recovery from any third parties who participated in a breach of trust.

51-3g Termination of Trust

A trust may be terminated (1) by its own terms—for example, the trust is an education fund that has a termination date of college graduation, (2) because of the impossibility of attaining the object of the trust—for example, the trust is for the trustor's grandchild and his only child has died before having any children, (3) via revocation by the settlor when allowed by the terms of the trust, but trusts are presumed irrevocable unless the trust document permits revocation, (4) by merger of all interests in the same person (as when there is only one trustee and one beneficiary and they are the same person), or (5) upon the request of all the beneficiaries, as approved by a court, when there is no express purpose that requires continuation of the trust.

Make the Connection

Summary

A *will* is a writing that provides for a disposition of property to take effect upon death. A man who makes a will is called a *testator*; a woman, a *testatrix*. The person to whom

property is left by will is a *beneficiary*. A *legacy* is a gift of personal property by will; a gift of real property by will is a *devise*. A testator must have testamentary capacity to make a will and must manifest some intention that the will is to be effective only upon death. The will must be signed by the testator and be witnessed.

A will may be modified by a codicil or revoked either by the act of the testator or by operation of law.

Probate is the process by which a proper court official accepts a will. Probate may be refused or set aside on grounds that the will is not the free expression of the testator.

A *holographic* will is an unwitnessed will written entirely in the handwriting of the testator. A *self-proved will* may be admitted to probate without the testimony of subscribing witnesses. A *living will* allows a person to make wishes known regarding life-sustaining medical treatment.

If there is a valid will, the last phase of administration of the estate is the distribution of property after the payment of all debts and taxes. *General legacies* are bequests of money, whereas *specific legacies* or *specific devises* are gifts of identified personal or real property. Legacies abate in the following order: residuary, general, and specific. If a beneficiary named in the will has died before the testator and no alternate provision has been made for that beneficiary, antilapse statutes provide that the gift will not lapse. In that event, the children or heirs of the beneficiary may take the legacy in the place of the deceased beneficiary.

If the decedent does not dispose of all property by will or does not have a will, the property will be distributed according to state intestacy statutes. A surviving spouse may generally elect to take the statutory allocation instead of that provided in the will.

The estate of the testator will be administered by the person appointed in the will (the *executor*) or, if there is no will, by a person appointed by the court (an *administrator*). Creditors who have claims against the estate are required to give notice of their claims to the personal representative; otherwise, the claims will be barred.

A *trust* is a legal device by which property is held by one person for the benefit of another. The settlor creates the trust, and the person for whose benefit the trustee holds the property is the beneficiary. Property held in trust is called the *trust corpus, trust fund, trust estate,* or *trust res.*

A trust is usually created by a trust agreement or deed of trust. No particular form or language is required. A trust is not created unless an active duty is placed on the trustee to manage the property in some manner. A trustee's acceptance of duties is presumed.

Legal title to trust property is given to the trustee, and the beneficiary holds equitable title. A beneficiary may transfer an interest in the trust except in the case of a spendthrift trust.

The trustee can exercise only those powers that are given by law or the trust instrument. The trustee must administer the trust and carry out the trust in a proper manner. A trustee is liable for breach of the terms of the trust agreement. A trust comes to an end when its terms so provide or when it becomes impossible to attain the object of the trust.

Learning Outcomes

After studying this chapter, you should be able to clearly explain:

51-1   Wills

LO.1 Define *testamentary capacity* and *testamentary intent*
See *Ivie v. Smith* for a case discussion of a testator who lacks capacity, pages 1065–1066.
See the Sports & Entertainment feature on the mistakes that the rich and famous make in their estate plans and wills, page 1069.

LO.2 Discuss how a valid will is created
See the discussion of the *Ramsey v. Taylor* case, page 1072.

LO.3 Explain how a will may be modified or revoked
See the In re *Estate of Speers* case, page 1068.

51-2   Administration of Decedents' Estates

LO.4 Describe briefly the probate and contest of a will
See the Ethics & the Law discussion of a lawyer's duties, page 1073.

LO.5 Describe the ordinary pattern of distribution by intestacy
See Figure 51-2, page 1076.
See the In re *Edwards* case for a discussion of a son-in-law inheriting his mother-in-law's estate after confessing to killing her, pages 1076–1077.

51-3   Trusts

LO.6 Explain the nature of a trust
See the sections titled "Creation of Trusts," "Nature of Beneficiary's Interest," and "Powers of Trustee" on trust terminology and creation, pages 1078–1079.

Key Terms

abate
acknowledgment
adeemed
administrator
administratrix
affidavits
antilapse statutes
attestation clause
beneficiary
bequest
cestui que trust
claims
decedent
devise
devisee
disinherited
distribution *per stirpes*
donor
equitable title
executor
executrix

general legacies
holographic will
income
interlineations
intestate
intestate succession
legacy
legal title
legatee
letters of administration
letters testamentary
lineal
living trust
living wills
per capita
per stirpes
personal representatives
principal
probate
revoke
right of escheat

self-proved wills
settlor
specific legacies
spendthrift trust
testamentary capacity
testamentary intent
testamentary trust
testate
testate distribution
testator
testatrix
trust
trust agreement
trust corpus
trustee
trustor
Uniform Probate Code (UPC)
Uniform Simultaneous Death Act
will

Questions and Case Problems

1. After an eleven-month struggle with esophageal cancer, Leonard R. Brener died on December 8, 2001, at age 85. He had never married. He had no children. He had a long and successful career as a stockbroker. The value of his estate approximated $8 million. Several nieces and nephews survived him. He had originally left nearly all of his estate to The Carroll Center for the Blind, the Perkins School for the Blind, and Beth Israel Deaconess Medical Center, Inc. The gifts to these nonprofit organizations during Brener's life and through his will were complicated and made through detailed living, testamentary, and pour-over trusts. During the last five weeks of his life he was hospitalized and drafted and executed the final version of his will, which made one niece and her husband the primary beneficiaries of his estate. The nonprofit organizations sought to have the will set aside for lack of testamentary capacity.

   During those five weeks of terminal illness, Brener spoke of suicide by jumping out of the window, complained of depression, and often complained to his lawyer that he did not understand all the estate planning tools that were being used in his

will. The staff at the hospital testified that Brener did not seem confused and was aware that he was dying and wanted to be sure his affairs were in order. [*Maimonides School v. Coles,* 881 N.E.2d 778 (Mass. App.)]

2. Gerald "Pat" Arrington was diagnosed with a brain tumor. At the time of the diagnosis, he was married to Brenda Arrington, but they were separated pending their divorce. Brenda and Pat had no children, but Pat had five children from a previous marriage. Patricia Daley had lived with Pat since she was born. Pat referred to her as his only "stable" child. After Patricia married David Daley, the two stayed with Pat at his ranch and helped him with the cattle and working the land.

   Pat executed a new will one year before his death and following the brain tumor diagnosis that left everything to Patricia because Pat felt that Brenda would just sell his ranch and he did not want it to be sold. After Pat died, Patricia, as executrix of the estate, had the will admitted to probate. Brenda challenged the admission of the will to probate because she said that he gave his property to someone who was not legally his child and that showed he lacked capacity. The will was witnessed by two employees of a bank and both testified that Pat seemed to be his usual self and that he had done business at the bank for 20 years. What should the court do with the will and the challenge to it and why? [In re *Estate of Arrington*, 365 S.W.3d 463 (Tex. App.)]

3. Iona wrote her will. The following year, she wrote another will that expressly revoked the earlier will. Later, while cleaning house, she came across the second will. She mistakenly thought that it was the first will and tore it up because the first will had been revoked. Iona died shortly thereafter. The beneficiaries named in the second will claimed that the second will should be probated. The beneficiaries named in the first will claimed that the second will had been revoked when it was torn up. Had the second will been revoked?

4. Logsdon, who had three children, disliked one of them without any reason. In his will, he left only a small amount to the child he disliked and gave the bulk of his estate to the remaining two. On his death, the disliked child claimed that the will was void and had been obtained by undue influence. Do you agree? [*Logsdon v. Logsdon*, 104 N.E.2d 622 (Ill.)]

5. Field executed a will. On her death, the will was found in her safe deposit box, but the part of it containing the fifth bequest had been torn from the will. This torn fragment was also found in the box. There was no evidence that anyone other than Field had ever opened the box. A proceeding was brought to determine whether the will was entitled to be probated. Had the will been revoked? Was the will still valid with a portion torn from it? [*Flora v. Hughes*, 228 S.W.2d 27 (Ky.)]

6. Miller wrote a will that was 11 pages long and enclosed it in an envelope, which she sealed. She then wrote on the envelope "My last will & testament" and signed her name below this statement. This was the only place where she signed her name on any of the papers. Was this signature sufficient to allow this writing to be admitted to probate as her will? [*Miller's Executor v. Shannon*, 299 S.W.2d 103 (Ky.)]

7. Ms. Lingenfelter's will was offered for probate and was opposed. Ms. Lingenfelter (the testatrix) was sick, highly nervous, and extremely jealous, and she committed suicide a week after executing the will. She had, however, seemed to understand the will when she discussed it with an attorney. The will disinherited her husband because she feared he was not faithful to her despite the fact that he was seriously ill when she wrote the will. He died the day after she executed the will, and she grieved his death terribly for one week before committing suicide. Did she have the capacity to make a will? Should it be admitted to probate? [In re *Lingenfelter's Estate*, 241 P.2d 990 (Cal.)]

8. Copenhaver wrote a will in ink, which was found with her other papers in her bedroom at her death. Pencil lines had been drawn through every provision of the will and the signature. There was no evidence as to the circumstances under which this had been done. Was the will revoked? Why or why not? [*Franklin v. Maclean*, 66 S.E.2d 504 (Va.)]

9. George Baxter executed a will that left the bulk of his estate to the Church of Christ in New Boston, Texas. Two members of the church served as the witnesses for the will. Is the will valid? [In re *Estate of Gordon*, 519 S.W.2d 902 (Tex.)]

10. Jeanette Wall worked for D. J. Sharron for many years. Sharron executed a will, leaving his entire estate to Jeanette. He re-executed the same will sometime thereafter with the same provisions. Sharron's children contested the will, offering evidence that Sharron was a very sick man, physically as well as mentally, and that Wall was active in Sharron's business as well as his personal life. They offered no evidence that Wall had any involvement in the procurement of the original or the re-executed will. Who is entitled to the estate? Why? [*Wall v. Hodges*, 465 So. 2d 359 (Ala. App.)]

11. In 1984, Alexander Tolin executed a will under which the residue of his estate was to be devised to his friend Adair Creaig. The will was prepared by Steven Fine, Tolin's attorney, and executed in Fine's office. Fine retained the original will and gave a blue-backed photocopy to Tolin. In 1989, Tolin executed a codicil to the will that changed the residuary beneficiary from Creaig to Broward Art Guild, Inc. Fine prepared the codicil, and retained the original, giving Tolin a blue-backed photocopy of the original executed codicil.

    Tolin died in 1990. Six months before his death, he told his neighbor Ed Weinstein, who was a retired attorney, that he made a mistake and wished to revoke the codicil and reinstate Creaig as the residuary beneficiary. Weinstein told Tolin he could do this by tearing up the original codicil. Tolin handed Weinstein a blue-backed document that

Tolin said was the original codicil. Weinstein looked at the document; it appeared to him to be the original, and gave it back to Tolin. Tolin then tore up and destroyed the document with the intent and for the purpose of revocation.

Some time after Tolin's death, Weinstein spoke with Fine and found out for the first time that Fine had the original will and codicil. Creaig filed a petition to determine if there had been a revocation of the codicil. From a judgment that Tolin's destruction of a copy of the codicil was not an effective revocation of the codicil, Creaig appealed. Who is correct about the revocation and why? [In re *Estate of Tolin*, 622 So. 2d 988 (Fla.)]

12. Valerie and Flora are the beneficiaries of a trust left to them by their mother upon her death. Their mother named Art Casanelli, a family friend, as the trustee. Flora has seen Art driving a new car and has learned that he just purchased a new and rather large home. She is concerned about the trust funds and Art's unfettered access to them. How can she determine whether Art is using trust funds? What happens if she finds that he is?

13. Can a murderer inherit property from his victim? Why or why not?

14. James Horne's will provides that his estate is to be distributed to his heirs *per capita*. Upon his death, two of his three children are surviving and his deceased child left two children (James's grandchildren). His will provides that all his property is to be distributed *per capita* to these children and grandchildren. How will the property be distributed? How would it be distributed if he had provided for a *per stirpes* distribution?

15. Justin Whitman is the adult son of Jeffrey Whitman, an attorney who has served as the trustee for a trust of which Justin is the beneficiary. The trust was established for Justin by his grandfather, Jeffrey's father. Justin asked his father/trustee for an accounting of the principal and income of the trust. Jeffrey asked for the accounting in 2007 and received nothing by 2008 and filed suit for the accounting. Is Jeffrey entitled to receive the accounting? What could a court do in order to obtain the accounting? [*Whitman v. Whitman*, 2012 WL 367055 (Ohio App.)]

How to Find the Law

In order to determine what the law on a particular question or issue is, it may be necessary to examine (1) compilations of constitutions, treaties, statutes, executive orders, proclamations, and administrative regulations; (2) reports of state and federal court decisions; (3) digests of opinions; (4) treatises on the law; and (5) loose-leaf services. These sources can be either researched traditionally or using fee and/or non-fee-based computerized legal research, accessed through the World Wide Web.

Compilations

In the consideration of a legal problem in business it is necessary to determine whether the matter is affected or controlled by a constitution, national or state; by a national treaty; by an Act of Congress, a state legislature, or a city ordinance; by a decree or proclamation of the President of the United States, a governor, or a mayor; or by a regulation of a federal, state, or local administrative agency.

Each body or person that makes laws, regulations, or ordinances usually compiles and publishes at the end of each year or session all of the matter that it has adopted. In addition to the periodical or annual volumes, it is common to compile all the treaties, statutes, regulations, or ordinances in separate volumes. To illustrate, the federal Anti-Injunction Act may be cited as the Act of March 23, 1932, 47 Stat. 70, 29 U.S.C. § 101 et seq. This means that this law was enacted on March 23, 1932, and that it can be found at page 70 in Volume 47 of the reports that contain all of the statutes adopted by the Congress.

The second part of the citation, 29 U.S.C. § 101 et seq., means that in the collection of all of the federal statutes, which is known as the United States Code, the full text of the statute can be found in the sections of the 29th title beginning with Section 101.

Court Decisions

For complicated or important legal cases or when an appeal is to be taken, a court will generally write an opinion, which explains why the court made the decision. Appellate courts as a rule write opinions. The great majority of these decisions, particularly in the case of the appellate courts, are collected and printed. In order to avoid confusion, the opinions of each court are ordinarily printed in a separate set of reports, either by official reporters or private publishers.

In the reference "*Pennoyer v. Neff*, 95 U.S. 714, 24 L.Ed. 565," the first part states the names of the parties. It does not necessarily tell who was the plaintiff and who was the defendant. When an action is begun in a lower court, the first name is that of the plaintiff and the second name that of the defendant. When the case is appealed, generally the name of the person taking the appeal appears on the records of the higher court as the first one and that of the adverse party as the second. Sometimes, therefore, the original order of the names of the parties is reversed.

The balance of the reference consists of two citations. The first citation, 95 U.S. 714, means that the opinion which the court filed in the case of *Pennoyer v. Neff* may be found on page 714 of the 95th volume of a series of books in which are printed officially the opinions of the United States Supreme Court. Sometimes the same opinion is printed in two different sets of volumes. In the example, 24 L.Ed. 565 means that in the 24th volume of another set of books, called Lawyer's Edition, of the United States Supreme Court Reports, the same opinion begins on page 565.

In opinions by a state court there may also be two citations, as in the case of *Morrow v. Corbin*, 122 Tex. 553, 62 S.W.2d 641. This means that the opinion in the lawsuit between Morrow and Corbin may be found in the 122nd volume of the reports of the highest court of Texas, beginning on page 553; and also in Volume 62 of the Southwestern Reporter, Second Series, at page 641.

The West Publishing Company publishes a set of sectional reporters covering the entire United States. They are called "sectional" because each reporter, instead of being limited to a particular court or a particular state, covers the decisions of the courts of a particular section of the country. Thus the decisions of the courts of Arkansas, Kentucky, Missouri, Tennessee, and Texas are printed by the West Publishing company as a group in a sectional reporter called the Southwestern Reporter.[1] Because of the large number of decisions involved, generally only the opinions of the state appellate courts are printed. A number of states[2] have discontinued publication of the opinions of their courts, and those opinions are now found only in the West reporters.

The reason for the "Second Series" in the Southwestern citation is that when there were 300 volumes in the original series, instead of calling the next volume 301, the publisher called it Volume 1, Second Series. Thus 62 S.W.2d Series really means the 362nd volume of the Southwestern Reporter. Six to eight volumes appear in a year for each geographic section.

In addition to these state reporters, the West Publishing Company publishes a Federal Supplement, which primarily reports the opinions of the Federal District Courts; the Federal Reporter, which primarily reports the decisions of the United States Courts of Appeals; and the Supreme Court Reporter, which reports the decisions of the United States Supreme Court. The Supreme Court decisions are also reported in a separate set called the Lawyers' Edition, published by the Lawyers Cooperative Publishing Company.

The reports published by the West Publishing Company and Lawyers Cooperative Publishing Company are unofficial reports, while those bearing the name or abbreviation of the United States or of a state, such as "95 U.S. 714" or "122 Tex. 553" are official reports. This means that in the case of the latter, the particular court, such as the United States Supreme Court, has officially authorized that its decisions be printed and that by federal statute such official printing is made. In the case of the unofficial reporters, the publisher prints the decisions of a court on its own

initiative. Such opinions are part of the public domain and not subject to any copyright or similar restriction.

Digests of Opinions

The reports of court decisions are useful only if one has the citation, that is, the name and volume number of the book and the page number of the opinion one is seeking. For this reason, digests of the decisions have been prepared. These digests organize the entire field of law under major headings, which are then arranged in alphabetical order. Under each heading, such as "Contracts," the subject is divided into the different questions that can arise with respect to that field. A master outline is thus created on the subject. This outline includes short paragraphs describing what each case holds and giving its citation.

Treatises and Restatements

Very helpful in finding a case or a statute are the treatises on the law. These may be special books, each written by an author on a particular subject, such as Williston on Contracts, Bogert on Trusts, Fletcher on Corporations, or they may be general encyclopedias, as in the case of *American Jurisprudence, American Jurisprudence, Second,* and *Corpus Juris Secundum.*

Another type of treatise is found in the restatements of the law prepared by the American Law Institute. Each restatement consists of one or more volumes devoted to a particular phase of the law, such as the Restatement of the Law of Contracts, Restatement of the Law of Agency, and Restatement of the Law of Property. In each restatement, the American Law Institute, acting through special committees of judges, lawyers, and professors of law, has set forth what the law is; and in many areas where there is no law or the present rule is regarded as unsatisfactory, the restatement specifies what the Institute deems to be the desirable rule.

Loose-Leaf Services

A number of private publishers, notably Commerce Clearing House and Prentice-Hall, publish loose-leaf books devoted to particular branches of the law. Periodically, the publisher sends to the purchaser a number of pages that set forth any decision, regulation, or statute made or adopted since the prior set of pages was prepared. Such services are unofficial.

---

[1] The sectional reporters are: Atlantic—A. (Connecticut, Delaware, District of Columbia, Maine, Maryland, New Hampshire, New Jersey, Pennsylvania, Rhode Island, Vermont); Northeastern—N.E. (Illinois, Indiana, Massachusetts, New York, Ohio); Northwestern—N.W. (Iowa, Michigan, Minnesota, Nebraska, North Dakota, South Dakota, Wisconsin); Pacific—P. (Alaska, Arizona, California, Colorado, Hawaii, Idaho, Kansas, Montana, Nevada, New Mexico, Oklahoma, Oregon, Utah, Washington, Wyoming); Southeastern—S.E. (Georgia, North Carolina, South Carolina, Virginia, West Virginia); Southwestern—S.W. (Arkansas, Kentucky, Missouri, Tennessee, Texas); and Southern—So. (Alabama, Florida, Louisiana, Mississippi). There is also a special New York State reporter known as the New York Supplement and a special California State reporter known as the California Reporter.

[2] See, for example, Alaska, Florida, Iowa, Kentucky, Louisiana, Maine, Mississippi, Missouri, North Dakota, Oklahoma, Texas, and Wyoming.

Computerized Legal Research

National and local computer services are providing constantly widening assistance for legal research. The database in such a system may be opinions, statutes, or administrative regulations stored word for word; or the later history of a particular case giving its full citation and showing whether the case has been followed by other courts; or the text of forms and documents. By means of a terminal connected to the system, the user can retrieve the legal information at a great saving of time and with the assurance that it is up-to-date.

There are two leading, fee-based systems for computer-aided research. Listed alphabetically, they are LEXIS and WESTLAW.

A specialized service of legal forms for business is provided by Shepard's BUSINESS LAW CASE MANAGEMENT SYSTEM. A monthly fee is required for usage.

Numerous free, private sites offer a lot of legal resources. The federal government offers a variety of case law, regulations, and code enactments, either pending or newly promulgated. To find the most comprehensive source of government-maintained legal information, go to **http://www.house.gov**. The United States Supreme Court has information about both its current term and past terms at **www.supremecourt.gov**. Another website that provides excellent information about current controversies that reach the United States Supreme Court is **www.scotusblog.com**.

State governments provide access to regulations and codes online. As an example, go to the State of California's site, **http://www.leginfo.ca.gov**. You can access an array of information about both state and federal government through links at **www.USA.gov**.

The Constitution of the United States

We the people of the United States of America, in order to form a more perfect union, establish justice, insure domestic tranquility, provide for the common defense, promote the general welfare, and secure the blessings of liberty to ourselves and our posterity, do ordain and establish this Constitution for the United States of America.

Article I

SECTION 1

All legislative powers herein granted shall be vested in a Congress of the United States, which shall consist of a Senate and House of Representatives.

SECTION 2

1. The House of Representatives shall be composed of members chosen every second year by the people of the several States, and the electors in each State shall have the qualifications requisite for electors of the most numerous branch of the State legislature.

2. No person shall be a representative who shall not have attained to the age of twenty-five years, and been seven years a citizen of the United States, and who shall not, when elected, be an inhabitant of that State in which he shall be chosen.

3. Representatives and direct taxes shall be apportioned among the several States which may be included within this Union, according to their respective numbers, which shall be determined by adding to the whole number of free persons, including those bound to service for a term of years, and excluding Indians not taxed, three fifths of all other persons.[1] The actual enumeration shall be made within three years after the first meeting of the Congress of the United States, and within every subsequent term of ten years, in such manner as they shall by law direct. The number of representatives shall not exceed one for every thirty thousand, but each State shall have at least one representative; and until such enumeration shall be made, the State of New Hampshire shall be entitled to choose three, Massachusetts eight, Rhode Island and Providence Plantations one, Connecticut five, New York six, New Jersey four, Pennsylvania eight, Delaware one, Maryland six, Virginia ten, North Carolina five, South Carolina five, and Georgia three.

4. When vacancies happen in the representation from any State, the executive authority thereof shall issue writs of election to fill such vacancies.

5. The House of Representatives shall choose their speaker and other officers; and shall have the sole power of impeachment.

SECTION 3

1. The Senate of the United States shall be composed of two senators from each State, chosen by the legislature thereof, for six years; and each senator shall have one vote.

2. Immediately after they shall be assembled in consequence of the first election, they shall be divided as equally as may be into three classes. The seats of the senators of the first class shall be vacated at the expiration of the second year, of the second class at the expiration of the fourth year, and of the third class at the expiration of the sixth year, so that one third may be chosen every second year; and if vacancies happen by resignation, or otherwise, during the recess of the legislature of any State, the executive thereof may make temporary appointments until the next meeting of the legislature, which shall then fill such vacancies.[2]

3. No person shall be a senator who shall not have attained to the age of thirty years, and been nine years a citizen of the United States, and who shall not, when elected, be an inhabitant of that State for which he shall be chosen.

4. The Vice President of the United States shall be President of the Senate, but shall have no vote, unless they be equally divided.

[1] See the 14th Amendment.

[2] See the 17th Amendment.

5. The Senate shall choose their other officers, and also a president pro tempore, in the absence of the Vice President, or when he shall exercise the office of the President of the United States.

6. The Senate shall have the sole power to try all impeachments. When sitting for that purpose, they shall be on oath or affirmation. When the President of the United States is tried, the chief justice shall preside: and no person shall be convicted without the concurrence of two thirds of the members present.

7. Judgment in cases of impeachment shall not extend further than to removal from office, and disqualification to hold and enjoy any office of honor, trust or profit under the United States: but the party convicted shall nevertheless be liable and subject to indictment, trial, judgment and punishment, according to law.

SECTION 4

1. The times, places, and manner of holding elections for senators and representatives, shall be prescribed in each State by the legislature thereof; but the Congress may at any time by law make or alter such regulations, except as to the places of choosing senators.

2. The Congress shall assemble at least once in every year, and such meeting shall be on the first Monday in December, unless they shall by law appoint a different day.

SECTION 5

1. Each House shall be the judge of the elections, returns and qualifications of its own members, and a majority of each shall constitute a quorum to do business; but a smaller number may adjourn from day to day, and may be authorized to compel the attendance of absent members, in such manner, and under such penalties as each House may provide.

2. Each House may determine the rules of its proceedings, punish its members for disorderly behavior, and, with the concurrence of two thirds, expel a member.

3. Each House shall keep a journal of its proceedings, and from time to time publish the same, excepting such parts as may in their judgment require secrecy; and the yeas and nays of the members of either House on any question shall, at the desire of one fifth of those present, be entered on the journal.

4. Neither House, during the session of Congress, shall, without the consent of the other, adjourn for more than three days, nor to any other place than that in which the two Houses shall be sitting.

SECTION 6

1. The senators and representatives shall receive a compensation for their services, to be ascertained by law, and paid out of the Treasury of the United States. They shall in all cases, except treason, felony, and breach of the peace, be privileged from arrest during their attendance at the session of their respective Houses, and in going to and returning from the same; and for any speech or debate in either House, they shall not be questioned in any other place.

2. No senator or representative shall, during the time for which he was elected, be appointed to any civil office under the authority of the United States, which shall have been created, or the emoluments whereof shall have been increased during such time; and no person holding any office under the United States shall be a member of either House during his continuance in office.

SECTION 7

1. All bills for raising revenue shall originate in the House of Representatives; but the Senate may propose or concur with amendments as on other bills.

2. Every bill which shall have passed the House of Representatives and the Senate, shall, before it becomes a law, be presented to the President of the United States; if he approves he shall sign it, but if not he shall return it, with his objections to that House in which it shall have originated, who shall enter the objections at large on their journal, and proceed to reconsider it. If after such reconsideration two thirds of that House shall agree to pass the bill, it shall be sent, together with the objections, to the other House, by which it shall likewise be reconsidered, and if approved by two thirds of that House, it shall become a law. But in all such cases the votes of both Houses shall be determined by yeas and nays, and the names of the persons voting for and against the bill shall be entered on the journal of each House respectively. If any bill shall not be returned by the President within ten days (Sundays excepted) after it shall have been presented to him, the same shall be a law, in like manner as if he had signed it, unless the Congress by their adjournment prevent its return, in which case it shall not be a law.

3. Every order, resolution, or vote to which the concurrence of the Senate and the House of Representatives may be necessary (except on a question of adjournment) shall be presented to the President of the United States; and before the same shall take effect, shall be approved

by him, or being disapproved by him, shall be repassed by two thirds of the Senate and House of Representatives, according to the rules and limitations prescribed in the case of a bill.

SECTION 8

The Congress shall have the power

1. To lay and collect taxes, duties, imposts, and excises, to pay the debts and provide for the common defense and general welfare of the United States; but all duties, imposts, and excises shall be uniform throughout the United States;

2. To borrow money on the credit of the United States;

3. To regulate commerce with foreign nations, and among the several States, and with the Indian tribes;

4. To establish a uniform rule of naturalization, and uniform laws on the subject of bankruptcies throughout the United States;

5. To coin money, regulate the value thereof, and of foreign coin, and fix the standard of weights and measures;

6. To provide for the punishment of counterfeiting the securities and current coin of the United States;

7. To establish post offices and post roads;

8. To promote the progress of science and useful arts, by securing for limited times to authors and inventors the exclusive rights to their respective writings and discoveries;

9. To constitute tribunals inferior to the Supreme Court;

10. To define and punish piracies and felonies committed on the high seas, and offenses against the law of nations;

11. To declare war, grant letters of marque and reprisal, and make rules concerning captures on land and water;

12. To raise and support armies, but no appropriation of money to that use shall be for a longer term than two years;

13. To provide and maintain a navy;

14. To make rules for the government and regulation of the land and naval forces;

15. To provide for calling forth the militia to execute the laws of the Union, suppress insurrections and repel invasions;

16. To provide for organizing, arming, and disciplining the militia, and for governing such part of them as may be employed in the service of the United States, reserving to the States respectively, the appointment of the officers, and the authority of training the militia according to the discipline prescribed by Congress;

17. To exercise exclusive legislation in all cases whatsoever, over such district (not exceeding ten miles square) as may, by cession of particular States, and the acceptance of Congress, become the seat of the government of the United States, and to exercise like authority over all places purchased by the consent of the legislature of the State in which the same shall be, for the erection of forts, magazines, arsenals, dockyards, and other needful buildings; and

18. To make all laws which shall be necessary and proper for carrying into execution the foregoing powers, and all other powers vested by this Constitution in the government of the United States, or in any department or officer thereof.

SECTION 9

1. The migration or importation of such persons as any of the States now existing shall think proper to admit, shall not be prohibited by the Congress prior to the year one thousand eight hundred and eight, but a tax or duty may be imposed on such importation, not exceeding ten dollars for each person.

2. The privilege of the writ of habeas corpus shall not be suspended, unless when in cases of rebellion or invasion the public safety may require it.

3. No bill of attainder or ex post facto law shall be passed.

4. No capitation, or other direct, tax shall be laid, unless in proportion to the census or enumeration hereinbefore directed to be taken.[3]

5. No tax or duty shall be laid on articles exported from any State.

6. No preference shall be given by any regulation of commerce or revenue to the ports of one State over those of another: nor shall vessels bound to, or from, one State be obliged to enter, clear, or pay duties in another.

7. No money shall be drawn from the treasury, but in consequence of appropriations made by law; and a regular statement and account of the receipts and expenditures of all public money shall be published from time to time.

[3] See the 16th Amendment.

8. No title of nobility shall be granted by the United States: and no person holding any office of profit or trust under them, shall, without the consent of the Congress, accept of any present, emolument, office, or title, of any kind whatever, from any king, prince, or foreign State.

SECTION 10

1. No State shall enter into any treaty, alliance, or confederation; grant letters of marque and reprisal; coin money; emit bills of credit; make anything but gold and silver coin a tender in payment of debts; pass any bill of attainder, ex post facto law, or law impairing the obligation of contracts, or grant any title of nobility.

2. No State shall, without the consent of the Congress, lay any imposts or duties on imports or exports, except what may be absolutely necessary for executing its inspection laws: and the net produce of all duties and imposts laid by any State on imports or exports, shall be for the use of the treasury of the United States; and all such laws shall be subject to the revision and control of the Congress.

3. No State shall, without the consent of the Congress, lay any duty of tonnage, keep troops, or ships of war in time of peace, enter into any agreement or compact with another State, or with a foreign power, or engage in war, unless actually invaded, or in such imminent danger as will not admit of delay.

Article II

SECTION 1

1. The executive power shall be vested in a President of the United States of America. He shall hold his office during the term of four years, and, together with the Vice President, chosen for the same term, be elected as follows:

2. Each State shall appoint, in such manner as the legislature thereof may direct, a number of electors, equal to the whole number of senators and representatives to which the State may be entitled in the Congress: but no senator or representative, or person holding an office of trust or profit under the United States, shall be appointed an elector.

The electors shall meet in their respective States, and vote by ballot for two persons, of whom one at least shall not be an inhabitant of the same State with themselves. And they shall make a list of all the persons voted for, and of the number of votes for each; which list they shall sign and certify, and transmit sealed to the seat of the government of the United States, directed to the president of the Senate. The president of the Senate shall, in the presence of the Senate and House of Representatives, open all the certificates, and the votes shall then be counted. The person having the greatest number of votes shall be the President, if such number be a majority of the whole number of electors appointed; and if there be more than one who have such majority, and have an equal number of votes, then the House of Representatives shall immediately choose by ballot one of them for President; and if no person have a majority, then from the five highest on the list the said House shall in like manner choose the President. But in choosing the President, the votes shall be taken by States, the representation from each State having one vote; a quorum for this purpose shall consist of a member or members from two thirds of the States, and a majority of all the States shall be necessary to a choice. In every case, after the choice of the President, the person having the greatest number of votes of the electors shall be the Vice President. But if there should remain two or more who have equal votes, the Senate shall choose from them by ballot the Vice President.[4]

3. The Congress may determine the time of choosing the electors, and the day on which they shall give their votes; which day shall be the same throughout the United States.

4. No person except a natural born citizen, or a citizen of the United States, at the time of the adoption of this Constitution, shall be eligible to the office of President; neither shall any person be eligible to that office who shall not have attained to the age of thirty-five years, and been fourteen years a resident within the United States.

5. In the case of removal of the President from office, or of his death, resignation, or inability to discharge the powers and duties of the said office, the same shall devolve on the Vice President, and the Congress may by law provide for the case of removal, death, resignation, or inability, both of the President and Vice President, declaring what officer shall then act as President, and such officer shall act accordingly, until the disability be removed, or a President shall be elected.

6. The President shall, at stated times, receive for his services a compensation, which shall neither be

[4] Superseded by the 12th Amendment.

increased nor diminished during the period for which he shall have been elected, and he shall not receive within that period any other emolument from the United States, or any of them.

7. Before he enter on the execution of his office, he shall take the following oath or affirmation:—"I do solemnly swear (or affirm) that I will faithfully execute the office of President of the United States, and will to the best of my ability, preserve, protect and defend the Constitution of the United States."

SECTION 2

1. The President shall be commander in chief of the army and navy of the United States, and of the militia of the several States, when called into the actual service of the United States; he may require the opinion, in writing, of the principal officer in each of the executive departments, upon any subject relating to the duties of their respective office, and he shall have power to grant reprieves and pardons for offenses against the United States, except in cases of impeachment.

2. He shall have power, by and with the advice and consent of the Senate, to make treaties, provided two thirds of the senators present concur; and he shall nominate, and by and with the advice and consent of the Senate, shall appoint ambassadors, other public ministers and consuls, judges of the Supreme Court, and all other officers of the United States, whose appointments are not herein otherwise provided for, and which shall be established by law: but the Congress may by law vest the appointment of such inferior officers, as they think proper, in the President alone, in the courts of law, or in the heads of departments.

3. The President shall have power to fill up all vacancies that may happen during the recess of the Senate, by granting commissions which shall expire at the end of their next session.

SECTION 3

He shall from time to time give to the Congress information of the state of the Union, and recommend to their consideration such measures as he shall judge necessary and expedient; he may, on extraordinary occasions, convene both Houses, or either of them, and in case of disagreement between them with respect to the time of adjournment, he may adjourn them to such time as he shall think proper; he shall receive ambassadors and other public ministers; he shall take care that the laws be faithfully executed, and shall commission all the officers of the United States.

SECTION 4

The President, Vice President, and all civil officers of the United States, shall be removed from office on impeachment for, and conviction of, treason, bribery, or other high crimes and misdemeanors.

Article III

SECTION 1

The judicial power of the United States shall be vested in one Supreme Court, and in such inferior courts as the Congress may from time to time ordain and establish. The judges, both of the Supreme and inferior courts, shall hold their offices during good behavior, and shall, at stated times, receive for their services, a compensation, which shall not be diminished during their continuance in office.

SECTION 2

1. The judicial power shall extend to all cases, in law and equity, arising under this Constitution, the laws of the United States, and treaties made, or which shall be made, under their authority;—to all cases affecting ambassadors, other public ministers and consuls;—to all cases of admiralty and maritime jurisdiction;—to controversies to which the United States shall be a party;—to controversies between two or more States; between a State and citizens of another State;[5]—between citizens of different States;—between citizens of the same State claiming lands under grants of different States, and between a State, or the citizens thereof, and foreign States, citizens or subjects.

2. In all cases affecting ambassadors, other public ministers and consuls, and those in which a State shall be party, the Supreme Court shall have original jurisdiction. In all the other cases before mentioned, the Supreme Court shall have appellate jurisdiction, both as to law and to fact, with such exceptions, and under such regulations as the Congress shall make.

3. The trial of all crimes, except in cases of impeachment, shall be by jury; and such trial shall be held in the State where the said crimes shall have been committed; but when not committed within any State, the trial shall be at such place or places as the Congress may by law have directed.

[5] See the 11th Amendment.

SECTION 3

1. Treason against the United States shall consist only in levying war against them, or in adhering to their enemies, giving them aid and comfort. No person shall be convicted of treason unless on the testimony of two witnesses to the same overt act, or on confession in open court.

2. The Congress shall have power to declare the punishment of treason, but no attainder of treason shall work corruption of blood, or forfeiture except during the life of the person attainted.

Article IV

SECTION 1

Full faith and credit shall be given in each State to the public acts, records, and judicial proceedings of every other State. And the Congress may by general laws prescribe the manner in which such acts, records and proceedings shall be proved, and the effect thereof.

SECTION 2

1. The citizens of each State shall be entitled to all privileges and immunities of citizens in the several States.[6]

2. A person charged in any State with treason, felony, or other crime, who shall flee from justice, and be found in another State, shall on demand of the executive authority of the State from which he fled, be delivered up to be removed to the State having jurisdiction of the crime.

3. No person held to service or labor in one State under the laws thereof, escaping into another, shall in consequence of any law or regulation therein, be discharged from such service or labor, but shall be delivered up on claim of the party to whom such service or labor may be due.[7]

SECTION 3

1. New States may be admitted by the Congress into this Union; but no new State shall be formed or erected within the jurisdiction of any other State, nor any State be formed by the junction of two or more States, or parts of States, without the consent of the legislatures of the States concerned as well as of the Congress.

2. The Congress shall have power to dispose of and make all needful rules and regulations respecting the territory or other property belonging to the United States; and nothing in this Constitution shall be so construed as to prejudice any claims of the United States, or of any particular State.

SECTION 4

The United States shall guarantee to every State in this Union a republican form of government, and shall protect each of them against invasion; and on application of the legislature, or of the executive (when the legislature cannot be convened) against domestic violence.

Article V

The Congress, whenever two thirds of both Houses shall deem it necessary, shall propose amendments to this Constitution, or, on the application of the legislature of two thirds of the several States, shall call a convention for proposing amendments, which in either case, shall be valid to all intents and purposes, as part of this Constitution when ratified by the legislatures of three fourths of the several States, or by conventions in three fourths thereof, as the one or the other mode of ratification may be proposed by the Congress; provided that no amendment which may be made prior to the year one thousand eight hundred and eight shall in any manner affect the first and fourth clauses in the ninth section of the first article; and that no State, without its consent, shall be deprived of its equal suffrage in the Senate.

Article VI

1. All debts contracted and engagements entered into, before the adoption of this Constitution, shall be as valid against the United States under this Constitution, as under the Confederation.[8]

2. This Constitution, and the laws of the United States which shall be made in pursuance thereof; and all treaties made, or which shall be made, under the authority of the United States, shall be the supreme law of the land; and the judges in every State shall be bound thereby, anything in the Constitution or laws of any State to the contrary notwithstanding.

3. The senators and representatives before mentioned, and the members of the several State legislatures, and all executive and judicial officers, both of the United States and of the several States, shall be bound by oath or affirmation to support this Constitution; but no

---

[6] See the 14th Amendment, Sec. 1.
[7] See the 13th Amendment.

[8] See the 14th Amendment, Sec. 4.

religious test shall ever be required as a qualification to any office or public trust under the United States.

Article VII

The ratification of the conventions of nine States shall be sufficient for the establishment of this Constitution between the States so ratifying the same.

Done in Convention by the unanimous consent of the States present the seventeenth day of September in the year of our Lord one thousand seven hundred and eighty-seven, and of the independence of the United States of America the twelfth. In witness whereof we have hereunto subscribed our names.

Amendments

First Ten Amendments passed by Congress Sept. 25, 1789.

Ratified by three-fourths of the States December 15, 1791.

Amendment I

Congress shall make no law respecting an establishment of religion, or prohibiting the free exercise thereof; or abridging the freedom of speech, or of the press; or the right of the people peaceably to assemble, and to petition the government for a redress of grievances.

Amendment II

A well regulated militia, being necessary to the security of a free State, the right of the people to keep and bear arms, shall not be infringed.

Amendment III

No soldier shall, in time of peace be quartered in any house, without the consent of the owner, nor in time of war, but in a manner to be prescribed by law.

Amendment IV

The right of the people to be secure in their persons, houses, papers, and effects, against unreasonable searches and seizures, shall not be violated, and no warrants shall issue, but upon probable cause, supported by oath or affirmation, and particularly describing the place to be searched, and the person or things to be seized.

Amendment V

No person shall be held to answer for a capital, or otherwise infamous crime, unless on a presentment or indictment of a grand jury, except in cases arising in the land or naval forces, or in the militia, when in actual service in time of war or public danger; nor shall any person be subject for the same offense to be twice put in jeopardy of life or limb; nor shall be compelled in any criminal case to be a witness against himself, nor be deprived of life, liberty, or property, without due process of law; nor shall private property be taken for public use without just compensation.

Amendment VI

In all criminal prosecutions, the accused shall enjoy the right to a speedy and public trial, by an impartial jury of the State and district wherein the crime shall have been committed, which district shall have been previously ascertained by law, and to be informed of the nature and cause of the accusation; to be confronted with the witnesses against him; to have compulsory process for obtaining witnesses in his favor, and to have the assistance of counsel for his defense.

Amendment VII

In suits at common law, where the value in controversy shall exceed twenty dollars, the right of trial by jury shall be preserved, and no fact tried by a jury shall be otherwise reexamined in any court of the United States, then according to the rules of the common law.

Amendment VIII

Excessive bail shall not be required, nor excessive fines imposed, nor cruel and unusual punishments inflicted.

Amendment IX

The enumeration in the Constitution of certain rights shall not be construed to deny or disparage others retained by the people.

Amendment X

The powers not delegated to the United States by the Constitution, nor prohibited by it to the States, are reserved to the States respectively, or to the people.

Amendment XI

Passed by Congress March 5, 1794. Ratified January 8, 1798.

The judicial power of the United States shall not be construed to extend to any suit in law or equity, commenced or prosecuted against one of the United States by citizens of another State, or by citizens or subjects of any foreign State.

Amendment XII

Passed by Congress December 12, 1803. Ratified September 25, 1804.

The electors shall meet in their respective States, and vote by ballot for President and Vice President, one of whom, at least, shall not be an inhabitant of the same State with themselves; they shall name in their ballots the person voted for as President, and in distinct ballots, the person voted for as Vice President, and they shall make distinct lists of all persons voted for as President and of all persons voted for as Vice President, and of the number of votes for each, which lists they shall sign and certify, and transmit sealed to the seat of the government of the United States, directed to the President of the Senate;—The President of the Senate shall, in the presence of the Senate and House of Representatives, open all the certificates and the votes shall then be counted;—The person having the greatest number of votes for President, shall be the President, if such number be a majority of the whole number of electors appointed; and if no person have such majority, then from the persons having the highest numbers not exceeding three on the list of those voted for as President, the House of Representatives shall choose immediately, by ballot, the President. But in choosing the President, the votes shall be taken by States, the representation from each State having one vote; a quorum for this purpose shall consist of a member or members from two thirds of the States, and a majority of all the States shall be necessary to a choice. And if the House of Representatives shall not choose a President whenever the right of choice shall devolve upon them, before the fourth day of March next following, then the Vice President shall act as President, as in the case of the death or other constitutional disability of the President. The person having the greatest number of votes as Vice President shall be the Vice President, if such number be a majority of the whole number of electors appointed, and if no person have a majority, then from the two highest numbers on the list, the Senate shall choose the Vice President; a quorum for the purpose shall consist of two thirds of the whole number of Senators, and a majority of the whole number shall be necessary to a choice. But no person constitutionally ineligible to the office of President shall be eligible to that of Vice President of the United States.

Amendment XIII

Passed by Congress February 1, 1865. Ratified December 18, 1865.

SECTION 1

Neither slavery nor involuntary servitude, except as punishment for crime whereof the party shall have been duly convicted, shall exist within the United States, or any place subject to their jurisdiction.

SECTION 2

Congress shall have power to enforce this article by appropriate legislation.

Amendment XIV

Passed by Congress June 16, 1866. Ratified July 23, 1868.

SECTION 1

All persons born or naturalized in the United States, and subject to the jurisdiction thereof, are citizens of the United States and of the State wherein they reside. No State shall make or enforce any law which shall abridge the privileges or immunities of citizens of the United States; nor shall any State deprive any person of life, liberty, or property, without due process of law; nor deny to any person within its jurisdiction the equal protection of the laws.

SECTION 2

Representatives shall be apportioned among the several States according to their respective numbers, counting the whole number of persons in each State, excluding Indians not taxed. But when the right to vote at any election for the choice of electors for President and Vice President of the United States, representatives in Congress, the executive and judicial officers of a State, or the members of the legislature thereof, is denied to any of the male inhabitants of such State, being twenty-one years of age, and citizens of the United States, or in any way abridged, except for participation in rebellion, or other crime, the basis of representation therein shall be reduced in the proportion which the number of such male citizens shall bear to the whole number of male citizens twenty-one years of age in such State.

SECTION 3

No person shall be a senator or representative in Congress, or elector of President and Vice President, or hold any office, civil or military, under the United States, or under any State, who having previously taken an oath, as a member of Congress, or as an officer of the United States, or as a member of any State legislature, or as an executive or judicial officer of any State, to support the Constitution of the United States, shall have engaged in insurrection or rebellion against the same, or given aid or comfort to the enemies thereof. But Congress may by a vote of two thirds of each House, remove such disability.

SECTION 4

The validity of the public debt of the United States, authorized by law, including debts incurred for payment of pensions and bounties for services in suppressing insurrection or rebellion, shall not be questioned. But neither the United States nor any State shall assume or pay any debt or obligation incurred in aid of insurrection or rebellion against the United States, or any claim for the loss or emancipation of any slave; but all such debts, obligations, and claims shall be held illegal and void.

SECTION 5

The Congress shall have power to enforce, by appropriate legislation, the provisions of this article.

Amendment XV

Passed by Congress February 27, 1869. Ratified March 30, 1870.

SECTION 1

The right of citizens of the United States to vote shall not be denied or abridged by the United States or by any State on account of race, color, or previous condition of servitude.

SECTION 2

The Congress shall have power to enforce this article by appropriate legislation.

Amendment XVI

Passed by Congress July 12, 1909. Ratified February 25, 1913.

The Congress shall have power to lay and collect taxes on incomes, from whatever source derived, without apportionment among the several States, and without regard to any census or enumeration.

Amendment XVII

Passed by Congress May 16, 1912. Ratified May 31, 1913.

The Senate of the United States shall be composed of two senators from each State, elected by the people thereof, for six years; and each senator shall have one vote. The electors in each State shall have the qualifications requisite for electors of the most numerous branch of the State legislature.

When vacancies happen in the representation of any State in the Senate, the executive authority of such State shall issue writs of election to fill such vacancies: Provided, That the legislature of any State may empower the executive thereof to make temporary appointments until the people fill the vacancies by election as the legislature may direct.

This amendment shall not be so construed as to affect the election or term of any senator chosen before it becomes valid as part of the Constitution.

Amendment XVIII

Passed by Congress December 17, 1917. Ratified January 29, 1919.

After one year from the ratification of this article, the manufacture, sale, or transportation of intoxicating liquors within, the importation thereof into, or the exportation thereof from the United States and all territory subject to the jurisdiction thereof for beverage purposes is hereby prohibited.

The Congress and the several States shall have concurrent power to enforce this article by appropriate legislation.

This article shall be inoperative unless it shall have been ratified as an amendment to the Constitution by the legislatures of the several States, as provided in the Constitution, within seven years from the date of the submission hereof to the States by Congress.

Amendment XIX

Passed by Congress June 5, 1919. Ratified August 26, 1920.

The right of citizens of the United States to vote shall not be denied or abridged by the United States or by any State on account of sex.

The Congress shall have power by appropriate legislation to enforce the provisions of this article.

Amendment XX

Passed by Congress March 3, 1932. Ratified January 23, 1933.

SECTION 1

The terms of the President and Vice President shall end at noon on the 20th day of January, and the terms of Senators and Representatives at noon on the 3d day of January, of the years in which such terms would have ended if this article had not been ratified; and the terms of their successors shall then begin.

SECTION 2

The Congress shall assemble at least once in every year, and such meeting shall begin at noon on the 3d day of January, unless they shall by law appoint a different day.

SECTION 3

If, at the time fixed for the beginning of the term of the President, the President-elect shall have died, the Vice President-elect shall become President. If a President shall not have been chosen before the time fixed for the beginning of his term, or if the President-elect shall have failed to qualify, then the Vice President-elect shall act as President until a President shall have qualified; and the Congress may by law provide for the case wherein neither a President-elect nor a Vice President-elect shall have qualified, declaring who shall then act as President, or the manner in which one who is to act shall be selected, and such person shall act accordingly until a President or Vice President shall have qualified.

SECTION 4

The Congress may by law provide for the case of the death of any of the persons from whom the House of Representatives may choose a President whenever the right of choice shall have devolved upon them, and for the case of the death of any of the persons from whom the Senate may choose a Vice President whenever the right of choice shall have devolved upon them.

SECTION 5

Sections 1 and 2 shall take effect on the 15th day of October following the ratification of this article.

SECTION 6

This article shall be inoperative unless it shall have been ratified as an amendment to the Constitution by the legislatures of three-fourths of the several States within seven years from the date of its submission.

Amendment XXI

Passed by Congress February 20, 1933. Ratified December 5, 1933.

SECTION 1

The eighteenth article of amendment to the Constitution of the United States is hereby repealed.

SECTION 2

The transportation or importation into any State, Territory, or possession of the United States for delivery or use therein of intoxicating liquors in violation of the laws thereof, is hereby prohibited.

SECTION 3

This article shall be inoperative unless it shall have been ratified as an amendment to the Constitution by conventions in the several States, as provided in the Constitution, within seven years from the date of the submission thereof to the States by the Congress.

Amendment XXII

Passed by Congress March 24, 1947. Ratified February 26, 1951.

SECTION 1

No person shall be elected to the office of the President more than twice, and no person who has held the office of President, or acted as President, for more than two years of a term to which some other person was elected President shall be elected to the office of the President more than once. But this article shall not apply to any person holding the office of President when this article was proposed by the Congress, and shall not prevent any person who may be holding the office of President, or acting as President, during the term within which this article becomes operative from holding the office of President or acting as President during the remainder of such term.

SECTION 2

This article shall be inoperative unless it shall have been ratified as an amendment to the Constitution by the legislatures of three-fourths of the several States within seven years from the date of its submission to the States by the Congress.

Amendment XXIII

Passed by Congress June 16, 1960. Ratified April 3, 1961.

SECTION 1

The District constituting the seat of Government of the United States shall appoint in such manner as the Congress may direct:

A number of electors of President and Vice President equal to the whole number of Senators and

Representatives in Congress to which the District would be entitled if it were a State, but in no event more than the least populous State; they shall be in addition to those appointed by the States, but they shall be considered, for the purposes of the election of President and Vice President, to be electors appointed by a State; and they shall meet in the District and perform such duties as provided by the twelfth article of amendment.

SECTION 2

The Congress shall have power to enforce this article by appropriate legislation.

Amendment XXIV

Passed by Congress August 27, 1962. Ratified February 4, 1964.

SECTION 1

The right of citizens of the United States to vote in any primary or other election for President or Vice President, for electors for President or Vice President, or for Senator or Representative in Congress, shall not be denied or abridged by the United States or any State by reason of failure to pay any poll tax or other tax.

SECTION 2

The Congress shall have power to enforce this article by appropriate legislation.

Amendment XXV

Passed by Congress July 6, 1965. Ratified February 23, 1967.

SECTION 1

In case of the removal of the President from office or of his death or resignation, the Vice President shall become President.

SECTION 2

Whenever there is a vacancy in the office of the Vice President, the President shall nominate a Vice President who shall take office upon confirmation by a majority vote of both Houses of Congress.

SECTION 3

Whenever the President transmits to the President pro tempore of the Senate and the Speaker of the House of Representatives his written declaration that he is unable to discharge the powers and duties of his office, and until he transmits to them a written declaration to the contrary, such powers and duties shall be discharged by the Vice President as Acting President.

SECTION 4

Whenever the Vice President and a majority of either the principal officers of the executive departments or of such other body as Congress may by law provide, transmit to the President pro tempore of the Senate and the Speaker of the House of Representatives their written declaration that the President is unable to discharge the powers and duties of his office, the Vice President shall immediately assume the powers and duties of the office as Acting President.

Thereafter, when the President transmits to the President pro tempore of the Senate and the Speaker of the House of Representatives his written declaration that no inability exists, he shall resume the powers and duties of his office unless the Vice President and a majority of either the principal officers of the executive department or of such other body as Congress may by law provide, transmit within four days to the President pro tempore of the Senate and the Speaker of the House of Representatives their written declaration that the President is unable to discharge the powers and duties of his office. Thereupon Congress shall decide the issue, assembling within forty-eight hours for that purpose if not in session. If the Congress, within twenty-one days after receipt of the latter written declaration, or, if Congress is not in session, within twenty-one days after Congress is required to assemble, determines by two-thirds vote of both Houses that the President is unable to discharge the powers and duties of his office, the Vice President shall continue to discharge the same as Acting President; otherwise, the President shall resume the powers and duties of his office.

Amendment XXVI

Passed by Congress March 23, 1971. Ratified July 5, 1971.

SECTION 1

The right of citizens of the United States, who are eighteen years of age or older, to vote shall not be denied or abridged by the United States or by any State on account of age.

Amendment XXVII

Passed by Congress September 25, 1789. Ratified May 18, 1992.

No law, varying the compensation for the services of the Senators and Representatives, shall take effect, until an election of Representatives shall have intervened.

Uniform Commercial Code (Selected Sections)

(Adopted in fifty-two jurisdictions; all fifty States, although Louisiana has adopted only Articles 1, 3, 4, 7, 8, and 9; the District of Columbia; and the Virgin Islands.)

Articles

1. General Provisions
2. Sales

    2A. Leases

3. Negotiable Instruments
4. Bank Deposits and Collections

    4A. Funds Transfers

5. Letters of Credit
6. Repealer of Article 6—Bulk Transfers and [Revised] Article 6—Bulk Sales
7. Warehouse Receipts, Bills of Lading and Other Documents of Title
8. Investment Securities
9. Secured Transactions

Article 1 General Provisions

Part 1 Short Title, Construction, Application and Subject Matter of the Act

* * * *

§1—103. SUPPLEMENTARY GENERAL PRINCIPLES OF LAW APPLICABLE

Unless displaced by the particular provisions of this Act, the principles of law and equity, including the law merchant and the law relative to capacity to contract, principal and agent, estoppel, fraud, misrepresentation, duress, coercion, mistake, bankruptcy, or other validating or invalidating cause shall supplement its provisions.

* * * *

§1—201. GENERAL DEFINITIONS

* * * *

(3) "Agreement" means the bargain of the parties in fact as found in their language or by implication from other circumstances including course of dealing or usage of trade or course of performance as provided in this Act (Sections 1—205 and 2—208). Whether an agreement has legal consequences is determined by the provisions of this Act, if applicable; otherwise by the law of contracts (Section 1—103). (Compare "Contract".)

(4) "Bank" means any person engaged in the business of banking.

(5) "Bearer" means the person in possession of an instrument, document of title, or certificated security payable to bearer or indorsed in blank.

(6) "Bill of lading" means a document evidencing the receipt of goods for shipment issued by a person engaged in the business of transporting or forwarding goods, and includes an airbill. "Airbill" means a document serving for air transportation as a bill of lading does for marine or rail transportation, and includes an air consignment note or air waybill.

* * * *

(9) "Buyer in ordinary course of business" means a person that buys goods in good faith, without knowledge that the sale violates the rights of another person in the goods, and in the ordinary course from a person, other than a pawnbroker, in the business of selling goods of that kind. A person buys goods in the ordinary course if the sale to the person comports with the usual or customary practices in the kind of business in which the seller is engaged or with the seller's own usual or customary practices. A person that sells oil, gas, or other minerals at the wellhead or minehead is a person in the business of selling goods of that kind. A buyer in ordinary course of business may buy for cash, by exchange of other property, or on secured or unsecured credit, and may acquire goods or documents of title under a pre-existing contract for sale. Only a buyer that takes

possession of the goods or has a right to recover the goods from the seller under Article 2 may be a buyer in ordinary course of business. A person that acquires goods in a transfer in bulk or as security for or in total or partial satisfaction of a money debt is not a buyer in ordinary course of business.

(10) "Conspicuous": A term or clause is conspicuous when it is so written that a reasonable person against whom it is to operate ought to have noticed it. A printed heading in capitals (as: NON-NEGOTIABLE BILL OF LADING) is conspicuous. Language in the body of a form is "conspicuous" if it is in larger or other contrasting type or color. But in a telegram any stated term is "conspicuous". Whether a term or clause is "conspicuous" or not is for decision by the court.

(11) "Contract" means the total legal obligation which results from the parties' agreement as affected by this Act and any other applicable rules of law. (Compare "Agreement".)

* * * *

(15) "Document of title" includes bill of lading, dock warrant, dock receipt, warehouse receipt or order for the delivery of goods, and also any other document which in the regular course of business or financing is treated as adequately evidencing that the person in possession of it is entitled to receive, hold and dispose of the document and the goods it covers. To be a document of title a document must purport to be issued by or addressed to a bailee and purport to cover goods in the bailee's possession which are either identified or are fungible portions of an identified mass.

* * * *

(17) "Fungible" with respect to goods or securities means goods or securities of which any unit is, by nature or usage of trade, the equivalent of any other like unit. Goods which are not fungible shall be deemed fungible for the purposes of this Act to the extent that under a particular agreement or document unlike units are treated as equivalents.

* * * *

(19) "Good faith" means honesty in fact in the conduct or transaction concerned.

(20) "Holder" with respect to a negotiable instrument, means the person in possession if the instrument is payable to bearer or, in the cases of an instrument payable to an identified person, if the identified person is in possession. "Holder" with respect to a document of title means the person in possession if the goods are deliverable to bearer or to the order of the person in possession.

* * * *

(23) A person is "insolvent" who either has ceased to pay his debts in the ordinary course of business or cannot pay his debts as they become due or is insolvent within the meaning of the federal bankruptcy law.

(24) "Money" means a medium of exchange authorized or adopted by a domestic or foreign government and includes a monetary unit of account established by an intergovernmental organization or by agreement between two or more nations.

(25) A person has "notice" of a fact when

(a) he has actual knowledge of it; or

(b) he has received a notice or notification of it; or

(c) from all the facts and circumstances known to him at the time in question he has reason to know that it exists.

* * * *

(37) "Security interest" means an interest in personal property or fixtures which secures payment or performance of an obligation. The term also includes any interest of a consignor and a buyer of accounts, chattel paper, a payment intangible, or a promissory note in a transaction that is subject to Article 9. The special property interest of a buyer of goods on identification of those goods to a contract for sale under Section 2—401 is not a "security interest", but a buyer may also acquire a "security interest" by complying with Article 9. Except as otherwise provided in Section 2—505, the right of a seller or lessor of goods under Article 2 or 2A to retain or acquire possession of the goods is not a "security interest", but a seller or lessor may also acquire a "security interest" by complying with Article 9. The retention or reservation of title by a seller of goods notwithstanding shipment or delivery to the buyer (Section 2—401) is limited in effect to a reservation of a "security interest".

Whether a transaction creates a lease or security interest is determined by the facts of each case; however, a transaction creates a security interest if the consideration the lessee is to pay the lessor for the right to possession and use of the goods is an obligation for the term of the lease not subject to termination by the lessee, and

(a) the original term of the lease is equal to or greater than the remaining economic life of the goods,

(b) the lessee is bound to renew the lease for the remaining economic life of the goods or is bound to become the owner of the goods,

(c) the lessee has an option to renew the lease for the remaining economic life of the goods for no additional consideration or nominal additional consideration upon compliance with the lease agreement, or

(d) the lessee has an option to become the owner of the goods for no additional consideration or nominal additional consideration upon compliance with the lease agreement.

A transaction does not create a security interest merely because it provides that

(a) the present value of the consideration the lessee is obligated to pay the lessor for the right to possession and use of the goods is substantially equal to or is greater than the fair market value of the goods at the time the lease is entered into,

(b) the lessee assumes risk of loss of the goods, or agrees to pay taxes, insurance, filing, recording, or registration fees, or service or maintenance costs with respect to the goods,

(c) the lessee has an option to renew the lease or to become the owner of the goods,

(d) the lessee has an option to renew the lease for a fixed rent that is equal to or greater than the reasonably predictable fair market rent for the use of the goods for the term of the renewal at the time the option is to be performed, or

(e) the lessee has an option to become the owner of the goods for a fixed price that is equal to or greater than the reasonably predictable fair market value of the goods at the time the option is to be performed.

* * * *

(39) "Signed" includes any symbol executed or adopted by a party with present intention to authenticate a writing.

(40) "Surety" includes guarantor.

* * * *

(43) "Unauthorized" signature means one made without actual, implied or apparent authority and includes a forgery.

(44) "Value". Except as otherwise provided with respect to negotiable instruments and bank collections (Sections 3—303, 4—210 and 4—211) a person gives "value" for rights if he acquires them

(a) in return for a binding commitment to extend credit or for the extension of immediately available credit whether or not drawn upon and whether or not a chargeback is provided for in the event of difficulties in collection; or

(b) as security for or in total or partial satisfaction of a pre-existing claim; or

(c) by accepting delivery pursuant to a preexisting contract for purchase; or

(d) generally, in return for any consideration sufficient to support a simple contract.

(45) "Warehouse receipt" means a receipt issued by a person engaged in the business of storing goods for hire.

(46) "Written" or "writing" includes printing, typewriting or any other intentional reduction to tangible form.

* * * *

§1—203. OBLIGATION OF GOOD FAITH

Every contract or duty within this Act imposes an obligation of good faith in its performance or enforcement.

§1—204. TIME; REASONABLE TIME; "SEASONABLY"

(1) Whenever this Act requires any action to be taken within a reasonable time, any time which is not manifestly unreasonable may be fixed by agreement.

(2) What is a reasonable time for taking any action depends on the nature, purpose and circumstances of such action.

(3) An action is taken "seasonably" when it is taken at or within the time agreed or if no time is agreed at or within a reasonable time.

§1—205. COURSE OF DEALING AND USAGE OF TRADE

(1) A course of dealing is a sequence of previous conduct between the parties to a particular transaction which is fairly to be regarded as establishing a common basis of understanding for interpreting their expressions and other conduct.

(2) A usage of trade is any practice or method of dealing having such regularity of observance in a place, vocation or trade as to justify an expectation that it will be observed with respect to the transaction in question. The existence and scope of such a usage are to be proved as facts. If it is established that such a usage is embodied in a written trade code or similar writing the interpretation of the writing is for the court.

(3) A course of dealing between parties and any usage of trade in the vocation or trade in which they are engaged or of which they are or should be aware give particular meaning to and supplement or qualify terms of an agreement.

(4) The express terms of an agreement and an applicable course of dealing or usage of trade shall be construed wherever reasonable as consistent with each other; but

when such construction is unreasonable express terms control both course of dealing and usage of trade and course of dealing controls usage trade.

(5) An applicable usage of trade in the place where any part of performance is to occur shall be used in interpreting the agreement as to that part of the performance.

(6) Evidence of a relevant usage of trade offered by one party is not admissible unless and until he has given the other party such notice as the court finds sufficient to prevent unfair surprise to the latter.

* * * *

Article 2 Sales

§2—102. SCOPE; CERTAIN SECURITY AND OTHER TRANSACTIONS EXCLUDED FROM THIS ARTICLE

Unless the context otherwise requires, this Article applies to transactions in goods; it does not apply to any transaction which although in the form of an unconditional contract to sell or present sale is intended to operate only as a security transaction nor does this Article impair or repeal any statute regulating sales to consumers, farmers or other specified classes of buyers.

§2—103. DEFINITIONS AND INDEX OF DEFINITIONS

(1) In this Article unless the context otherwise requires

    (a) "Buyer" means a person who buys or contracts to buy goods.

    (b) "Good faith" in the case of a merchant means honesty in fact and the observance of reasonable commercial standards of fair dealing in the trade.

    (c) "Receipt" of goods means taking physical possession of them.

    (d) "Seller" means a person who sells or contracts to sell goods.

§2—104. DEFINITIONS: "MERCHANT"; "BETWEEN MERCHANTS"; "FINANCING AGENCY"

(1) "Merchant" means a person who deals in goods of the kind or otherwise by his occupation holds himself out as having knowledge or skill peculiar to the practices or goods involved in the transaction or to whom such knowledge or skill may be attributed by his employment of an agent or broker or other intermediary who by his occupation holds himself out as having such knowledge or skill.

§2—105. DEFINITIONS: TRANSFERABILITY; "GOODS"; "FUTURE" GOODS; "LOT"; "COMMERCIAL UNIT"

(1) "Goods" means all things (including specially manufactured goods) which are movable at the time of identification to the contract for sale other than the money in which the price is to be paid, investment securities (Article 8) and things in action. "Goods" also includes the unborn young of animals and growing crops and other identified things attached to realty as described in the section on goods to be severed from realty (Section 2—107).

(2) Goods must be both existing and identified before any interest in them can pass. Goods which are not both existing and identified are "future" goods. A purported present sale of future goods or of any interest therein operates as a contract to sell.

(3) There may be a sale of a part interest in existing identified goods.

(4) An undivided share in an identified bulk of fungible goods is sufficiently identified to be sold although the quantity of the bulk is not determined. Any agreed proportion of such a bulk or any quantity thereof agreed upon by number, weight or other measure may to the extent of the seller's interest in the bulk be sold to the buyer who then becomes an owner in common.

(5) "Lot" means a parcel or a single article which is the subject matter of a separate sale or delivery, whether or not it is sufficient to perform the contract.

(6) "Commercial unit" means such a unit of goods as by commercial usage is a single whole for purposes of sale and division of which materially impairs its character or value on the market or in use. A commercial unit may be a single article (as a machine) or a set of articles (as a suite of furniture or an assortment of sizes) or a quantity (as a bale, gross, or carload) or any other unit treated in use or in the relevant market as a single whole.

* * * *

§2—107. GOODS TO BE SEVERED FROM REALTY: RECORDING

(1) A contract for the sale of minerals or the like (including oil and gas) or a structure or its materials to be removed from realty is a contract for the sale of goods within this Article if they are to be severed by the seller but until severance a purported present sale thereof which is not effective as a transfer of an interest in land is effective only as a contract to sell.

(2) A contract for the sale apart from the land of growing crops or other things attached to realty and capable of severance without material harm thereto but not described in subsection (1) or of timber to be cut is a contract for the sale of goods within this Article whether the subject matter is to be severed by the buyer or by the seller even though it forms part of the realty at the time of contracting, and the parties can by identification effect a present sale before severance.

(3) The provisions of this section are subject to any third party rights provided by the law relating to realty records, and the contract for sale may be executed and recorded as a document transferring an interest in land and shall then constitute notice to third parties of the buyer's rights under the contract for sale.

§2—201. FORMAL REQUIREMENTS; STATUTE OF FRAUDS

(1) Except as otherwise provided in this section a contract for the sale of goods for the price of $500 [some states have increased this amount to $5,000] or more is not enforceable by way of action or defense unless there is some writing sufficient to indicate that a contract for sale has been made between the parties and signed by the party against whom enforcement is sought or by his authorized agent or broker. A writing is not insufficient because it omits or incorrectly states a term agreed upon but the contract is not enforceable under this paragraph beyond the quantity of goods shown in such writing.

(2) Between merchants if within a reasonable time a writing in confirmation of the contract and sufficient against the sender is received and the party receiving it has reason to know its contents, it satisfies the requirements of subsection (1) against such party unless written notice of objection to its contents is given within ten days after it is received.

(3) A contract which does not satisfy the requirements of subsection (1) but which is valid in other respects is enforceable

(a) if the goods are to be specially manufactured for the buyer and are not suitable for sale to others in the ordinary course of the seller's business and the seller, before notice of repudiation is received and under circumstances which reasonably indicate that the goods are for the buyer, has made either a substantial beginning of their manufacture or commitments for their procurement; or

(b) if the party against whom enforcement is sought admits in his pleading, testimony or otherwise in court that a contract for sale was made, but the contract is not enforceable under this provision beyond the quantity of goods admitted; or

(c) with respect to goods for which payment has been made and accepted or which have been received and accepted (Sec. 2—606).

§2—202. FINAL WRITTEN EXPRESSION: PAROL OR EXTRINSIC EVIDENCE

Terms with respect to which the confirmatory memoranda of the parties agree or which are otherwise set forth in a writing intended by the parties as a final expression of their agreement with respect to such terms as are included therein may not be contradicted by evidence of any prior agreement or of a contemporaneous oral agreement but may be explained or supplemented

(a) by course of dealing or usage of trade (Section 1—205) or by course of performance (Section 2—208); and

(b) by evidence of consistent additional terms unless the court finds the writing to have been intended also as a complete and exclusive statement of the terms of the agreement.

* * * *

§2—204. FORMATION IN GENERAL

(1) A contract for sale of goods may be made in any manner sufficient to show agreement, including conduct by both parties which recognizes the existence of such a contract.

(2) An agreement sufficient to constitute a contract for sale may be found even though the moment of its making is undetermined.

(3) Even though one or more terms are left open a contract for sale does not fail for indefiniteness if the parties have intended to make a contract and there is a reasonably certain basis for giving an appropriate remedy.

§2—205. FIRM OFFERS

An offer by a merchant to buy or sell goods in a signed writing which by its terms gives assurance that it will be held open is not revocable, for lack of consideration, during the time stated or if no time is stated for a reasonable time, but in no event may such period of irrevocability exceed three months; but any such term of assurance on a form supplied by the offeree must be separately signed by the offeror.

§2—206. OFFER AND ACCEPTANCE IN FORMATION OF CONTRACT

(1) Unless other unambiguously indicated by the language or circumstances

(a) an offer to make a contract shall be construed as inviting acceptance in any manner and by any medium reasonable in the circumstances;

(b) an order or other offer to buy goods for prompt or current shipment shall be construed as inviting acceptance either by a prompt promise to ship or by the prompt or current shipment of conforming or non-conforming goods, but such a shipment of non-conforming goods does not constitute an acceptance if the seller seasonably notifies the buyer that the shipment is offered only as an accommodation to the buyer.

(2) Where the beginning of a requested performance is a reasonable mode of acceptance an offeror who is not notified of acceptance within a reasonable time may treat the offer as having lapsed before acceptance.

§2—207. ADDITIONAL TERMS IN ACCEPTANCE OR CONFIRMATION

(1) A definite and seasonable expression of acceptance or a written confirmation which is sent within a reasonable time operates as an acceptance even though it states terms additional to or different from those offered or agreed upon, unless acceptance is expressly made conditional on assent to the additional or different terms.

(2) The additional terms are to be construed as proposals for addition to the contract. Between merchants such terms become part of the contract unless:

(a) the offer expressly limits acceptance to the terms of the offer;

(b) they materially alter it; or

(c) notification of objection to them has already been given or is given within a reasonable time after notice of them is received.

(3) Conduct by both parties which recognizes the existence of a contract is sufficient to establish a contract for sale although the writings of the parties do not otherwise establish a contract. In such case the terms of the particular contract consist of those terms on which the writings of the parties agree, together with any supplementary terms incorporated under any other provisions of this Act.

§2—208. COURSE OF PERFORMANCE OR PRACTICAL CONSTRUCTION

(1) Where the contract for sale involves repeated occasions for performance by either party with knowledge of the nature of the performance and opportunity for objection to it by the other, any course of performance accepted or acquiesced in without objection shall be relevant to determine the meaning of the agreement.

(2) The express terms of the agreement and any such course of performance, as well as any course of dealing and usage of trade, shall be construed whenever reasonable as consistent with each other; but when such construction is unreasonable, express terms shall control course of performance and course of performance shall control both course of dealing and usage of trade (Section 1—205).

(3) Subject to the provisions of the next section on modification and waiver, such course of performance shall be relevant to show a waiver or modification of any term inconsistent with such course of performance.

§2—209. MODIFICATION, RESCISSION AND WAIVER

(1) An agreement modifying a contract within this Article needs no consideration to be binding.

(2) A signed agreement which excludes modification or rescission except by a signed writing cannot be otherwise modified or rescinded, but except as between merchants such a requirement on a form supplied by the merchant must be separately signed by the other party.

(3) The requirements of the statute of frauds section of this Article (Section 2—201) must be satisfied if the contract as modified is within its provisions.

(4) Although an attempt at modification or rescission does not satisfy the requirements of subsection (2) or (3) it can operate as a waiver.

(5) A party who has made a waiver affecting an executory portion of the contract may retract the waiver by reasonable notification received by the other party that strict performance will be required of any term waived, unless the retraction would be unjust in view of a material change of position in reliance on the waiver.

§2—210. DELEGATION OF PERFORMANCE; ASSIGNMENT OF RIGHTS

* * * *

(5) An assignment of "the contract" or of "all my rights under the contract" or an assignment in similar general terms is an assignment of rights and unless the language or the circumstances (as in an assignment for security) indicate the contrary, it is a delegation of performance of the duties of the assignor and its acceptance by the assignee constitutes a promise by him to perform those duties. This promise is enforceable by either the assignor or the other party to the original contract.

§2—301. GENERAL OBLIGATIONS OF PARTIES

The obligation of the seller is to transfer and deliver and that of the buyer is to accept and pay in accordance with the contract.

§2—302. UNCONSCIONABLE CONTRACT OR CLAUSE

(1) If the court as a matter of law finds the contract or any clause of the contract to have been unconscionable at the time it was made the court may refuse to enforce the contract, or it may enforce the remainder of the contract without the unconscionable clause, or it may so limit the application of any unconscionable clause as to avoid any unconscionable result.

(2) When it is claimed or appears to the court that the contract or any clause thereof may be unconscionable the parties shall be afforded a reasonable opportunity to present evidence as to its commercial setting, purpose and effect to aid the court in making the determination.

§2—303. ALLOCATIONS OR DIVISION OF RISKS

Where this Article allocates a risk or a burden as between the parties "unless otherwise agreed", the agreement may not only shift the allocation but may also divide the risk or burden.

§2—304. PRICE PAYABLE IN MONEY, GOODS, REALTY, OR OTHERWISE

(1) The price can be made payable in money or otherwise. If it is payable in whole or in part in goods each party is a seller of the goods which he is to transfer.

(2) Even though all or part of the price is payable in an interest in realty the transfer of the goods and the seller's obligations with reference to them are subject to this Article, but not the transfer of the interest in realty or the transferor's obligations in connection therewith.

§2—305. OPEN PRICE TERM

(1) The parties if they so intend can conclude a contract for sale even though the price is not settled. In such a case the price is a reasonable price at the time for delivery if

(a) nothing is said as to price; or

(b) the price is left to be agreed by the parties and they fail to agree; or

(c) the price is to be fixed in terms of some agreed market or other standard as set or recorded by a third person or agency and it is not so set or recorded.

(2) A price to be fixed by the seller or by the buyer means a price for him to fix in good faith.

(3) When a price left to be fixed otherwise than by agreement of the parties fails to be fixed through fault of one party the other may at his option treat the contract as cancelled or himself fix a reasonable price.

(4) Where, however, the parties intend not to be bound unless the price be fixed or agreed and it is not fixed or agreed there is no contract. In such a case the buyer must return any goods already received or if unable so to do must pay their reasonable value at the time of delivery and the seller must return any portion of the price paid on account.

§2—306. OUTPUT, REQUIREMENTS AND EXCLUSIVE DEALINGS

(1) A term which measures the quantity by the output of the seller or the requirements of the buyer means such actual output or requirements as may occur in good faith, except that no quantity unreasonably disproportionate to any stated estimate or in the absence of a stated estimate to any normal or otherwise comparable prior output or requirements may be tendered or demanded.

(2) A lawful agreement by either the seller or the buyer for exclusive dealing in the kind of goods concerned imposes unless otherwise agreed an obligation by the seller to use best efforts to supply the goods and by the buyer to use best efforts to promote their sale.

§2—307. DELIVERY IN SINGLE LOT OR SEVERAL LOTS

Unless otherwise agreed all goods called for by a contract for sale must be tendered in a single delivery and payment is due only on such tender but where the circumstances give either party the right to make or demand delivery in lots the price if it can be apportioned may be demanded for each lot.

§2—308. ABSENCE OF SPECIFIED PLACE FOR DELIVERY

Unless otherwise agreed

(a) the place for delivery of goods is the seller's place of business or if he has none his residence; but

(b) in a contract for sale of identified goods which to the knowledge of the parties at the time of contracting are in some other place, that place is the place for their delivery; and

(c) documents of title may be delivered through customary banking channels.

§2—309. ABSENCE OF SPECIFIC TIME PROVISIONS; NOTICE OF TERMINATION

(1) The time for shipment or delivery or any other action under a contract if not provided in this Article or agreed upon shall be a reasonable time.

§2—310. OPEN TIME FOR PAYMENT OR RUNNING OF CREDIT; AUTHORITY TO SHIP UNDER RESERVATION

Unless otherwise agreed

(a) payment is due at the time and place at which the buyer is to receive the goods even though the place of shipment is the place of delivery; and

(b) if the seller is authorized to send the goods he may ship them under reservation, and may tender the documents of title, but the buyer may inspect the goods after their arrival before payment is due unless such inspection is inconsistent with the terms of the contract (Section 2—513).

* * * *

§2—312. WARRANTY OF TITLE AND AGAINST INFRINGEMENT; BUYER'S OBLIGATION AGAINST INFRINGEMENT

(1) Subject to subsection (2) there is in a contract for sale a warranty by the seller that

(a) the title conveyed shall be good, and its transfer rightful; and

(b) the goods shall be delivered free from any security interest or other lien or encumbrance of which the buyer at the time of contracting has no knowledge.

(2) A warranty under subsection (1) will be excluded or modified only by specific language or by circumstances which give the buyer reason to know that the person selling does not claim title in himself or that he is purporting to sell only such right or title as he or a third person may have.

(3) Unless otherwise agreed a seller who is a merchant regularly dealing in goods of the kind warrants that the goods shall be delivered free of the rightful claim of any third person by way of infringement or the like but a buyer who furnishes specifications to the seller must hold the seller harmless against any such claim which arises out of compliance with the specifications.

§2—313. EXPRESS WARRANTIES BY AFFIRMATION, PROMISE, DESCRIPTION, SAMPLE

(1) Express warranties by the seller are created as follows:

(a) Any affirmation of fact or promise made by the seller to the buyer which relates to the goods and becomes part of the basis of the bargain creates an express warranty that the goods shall conform to the affirmation or promise.

(b) Any description of the goods which is made part of the basis of the bargain creates an express warranty that the goods shall conform to the description.

(c) Any sample or model which is made part of the basis of the bargain creates an express warranty that the whole of the goods shall conform to the sample or model.

(2) It is not necessary to the creation of an express warranty that the seller use formal words such as "warrant" or "guarantee" or that he have a specific intention to make a warranty, but an affirmation merely of the value of the goods or a statement purporting to be merely the seller's opinion or commendation of the goods does not create a warranty.

§2—314. IMPLIED WARRANTY: MERCHANTABILITY; USAGE OF TRADE

(1) Unless excluded or modified (Section 2—316), a warranty that the goods shall be merchantable is implied in a contract for their sale if the seller is a merchant with respect to goods of that kind. Under this section the serving for value of food or drink to be consumed either on the premises or elsewhere is a sale.

(2) Goods to be merchantable must be at least such as

(a) pass without objection in the trade under the contract description; and

(b) in the case of fungible goods, are of fair average quality within the description; and

(c) are fit for the ordinary purposes for which such goods are used; and

(d) run, within the variations permitted by the agreement, of even kind, quality and quantity within each unit and among all units involved; and

(e) are adequately contained, packaged, and labeled as the agreement may require; and

(f) conform to the promises or affirmations of fact made on the container or label if any.

(3) Unless excluded or modified (Section 2—316) other implied warranties may arise from course of dealing or usage of trade.

§2—315. IMPLIED WARRANTY: FITNESS FOR PARTICULAR PURPOSE

Where the seller at the time of contracting has reason to know any particular purpose for which the goods are required and that the buyer is relying on the seller's skill or judgment to select or furnish suitable goods, there is unless excluded or modified under the next section an implied warranty that the goods shall be fit for such purpose.

§2—316. EXCLUSION OR MODIFICATION OF WARRANTIES

(1) Words or conduct relevant to the creation of an express warranty and words or conduct tending to negate or limit warranty shall be construed wherever reasonable as consistent with each other; but subject to the provisions of this Article on parol or extrinsic evidence (Section 2—202) negation or limitation is inoperative to the extent that such construction is unreasonable.

(2) Subject to subsection (3), to exclude or modify the implied warranty of merchantability or any part of it the language must mention merchantability and in case of a writing must be conspicuous, and to exclude or modify any implied warranty of fitness the exclusion must be by a writing and conspicuous. Language to exclude all implied warranties of fitness is sufficient if it states, for example, that "There are no warranties which extend beyond the description on the face hereof."

(3) Notwithstanding subsection (2)

(a) unless the circumstances indicate otherwise, all implied warranties are excluded by expressions like "as is", "with all faults" or other language which in common understanding calls the buyer's attention to the exclusion of warranties and makes plain that there is no implied warranty; and

(b) when the buyer before entering into the contract has examined the goods or the sample or model as fully as he desired or has refused to examine the goods there is no implied warranty with regard to defects which an examination ought in the circumstances to have revealed to him; and

(c) an implied warranty can also be excluded or modified by course of dealing or course of performance or usage of trade.

(4) Remedies for breach of warranty can be limited in accordance with the provisions of this Article on liquidation or limitation of damages and on contractual modification of remedy (Sections 2—718 and 2—719).

§2—317. CUMULATION AND CONFLICT OF WARRANTIES EXPRESS OR IMPLIED

Warranties whether express or implied shall be construed as consistent with each other and as cumulative, but if such construction is unreasonable the intention of the parties shall determine which warranty is dominant. In ascertaining that intention the following rules apply:

(a) Exact or technical specifications displace an inconsistent sample or model or general language of description.

(b) A sample from an existing bulk displaces inconsistent general language of description.

(c) Express warranties displace inconsistent implied warranties other than an implied warranty of fitness for a particular purpose.

§2—318. THIRD PARTY BENEFICIARIES OF WARRANTIES EXPRESS OR IMPLIED

Note: If this Act is introduced in the Congress of the United States this section should be omitted. (States to select one alternative.)

Alternative A

A seller's warranty whether express or implied extends to any natural person who is in the family or household of his buyer or who is a guest in his home if it is reasonable to expect that such person may use, consume or be affected by the goods and who is injured in person by breach of the warranty. A seller may not exclude or limit the operation of this section.

Alternative B

A seller's warranty whether express or implied extends to any natural person who may reasonably be expected to use, consume or be affected by the goods and who is injured in person by breach of the warranty. A seller may not exclude or limit the operation of this section.

Alternative C

A seller's warranty whether express or implied extends to any person who may reasonably be expected to use, consume or be affected by the goods and who is injured by breach of the warranty. A seller may not exclude or limit the operation of this section with respect to injury to the person of an individual to whom the warranty extends.

§2—319. F.O.B. AND F.A.S. TERMS

(1) Unless otherwise agreed the term F.O.B. (which means "free on board") at a named place, even though used only in connection with the stated price, is a delivery term under which

(a) when the term is F.O.B. the place of shipment, the seller must at that place ship the goods in the manner provided in this Article (Section 2—504) and bear the expense and risk of putting them into the possession of the carrier; or

(b) when the term is F.O.B. the place of destination, the seller must at his own expense and risk transport the goods to that place and there tender delivery of them in the manner provided in this Article (Section 2—503);

(c) when under either (a) or (b) the term is also F.O.B. vessel, car or other vehicle, the seller must in addition at his own expense and risk load the goods on board. If the term is F.O.B. vessel the buyer must name the vessel and in an appropriate case the seller must comply with the provisions of this Article on the form of bill of lading (Section 2—323).

(2) Unless otherwise agreed the term F.A.S. vessel (which means "free alongside") at a named port, even though used only in connection with the stated price, is a delivery term under which the seller must

(a) at his own expense and risk deliver the goods alongside the vessel in the manner usual in that port or on a dock designated and provided by the buyer; and

(b) obtain and tender a receipt for the goods in exchange for which the carrier is under a duty to issue a bill of lading.

(3) Unless otherwise agreed in any case falling within subsection (1)(a) or (c) or subsection (2) the buyer must seasonably give any needed instructions for making delivery, including when the term is F.A.S. or F.O.B. the loading berth of the vessel and in an appropriate case its name and sailing date. The seller may treat the failure of needed instructions as a failure of cooperation under this Article (Section 2—311). He may also at his option move the goods in any reasonable manner preparatory to delivery or shipment.

(4) Under the term F.O.B. vessel or F.A.S. unless otherwise agreed the buyer must make payment against tender of the required documents and the seller may not tender nor the buyer demand delivery of the goods in substitution for the documents.

§2—320. C.I.F. AND C. & F. TERMS

(1) The term C.I.F. means that the price includes in a lump sum the cost of the goods and the insurance and freight to the named destination. The term C. & F. or C.F. means that the price so includes cost and freight to the named destination.

(2) Unless otherwise agreed and even though used only in connection with the stated price and destination, the term C.I.F. destination or its equivalent requires the seller at his own expense and risk to

(a) put the goods into the possession of a carrier at the port for shipment and obtain a negotiable bill or bills of lading covering the entire transportation to the named destination; and

(b) load the goods and obtain a receipt from the carrier (which may be contained in the bill of lading) showing that the freight has been paid or provided for; and

(c) obtain a policy or certificate of insurance, including any war risk insurance, of a kind and on terms then current at the port of shipment in the usual amount, in the currency of the contract, shown to cover the same goods covered by the bill of lading and providing for payment of loss to the order of the buyer or for the account of whom it may concern; but the seller may add to the price the amount of the premium for any such war risk insurance; and

(d) prepare an invoice of the goods and procure any other documents required to effect shipment or to comply with the contract; and

(e) forward and tender with commercial promptness all the documents in due form and with any indorsement necessary to perfect the buyer's rights.

(3) Unless otherwise agreed the term C. & F. or its equivalent has the same effect and imposes upon the seller the same obligations and risks as a C.I.F. term except the obligation as to insurance.

(4) Under the term C.I.F. or C. & F. unless otherwise agreed the buyer must make payment against tender of the required documents and the seller may not tender nor the buyer demand delivery of the goods in substitution for the documents.

* * * *

§2—322. DELIVERY "EX-SHIP"

(1) Unless otherwise agreed a term for delivery of goods "ex-ship" (which means from the carrying vessel) or in equivalent language is not restricted to a particular ship and requires delivery from a ship which has reached a place at the named port of destination where goods of the kind are usually discharged.

(2) Under such a term unless otherwise agreed

(a) the seller must discharge all liens arising out of the carriage and furnish the buyer with a direction which puts the carrier under a duty to deliver the goods; and

(b) the risk of loss does not pass to the buyer until the goods leave the ship's tackle or are otherwise properly unloaded.

* * * *

§2—324. "NO ARRIVAL, NO SALE" TERM

Under a term "no arrival, no sale" or terms of like meaning, unless otherwise agreed,

(a) the seller must properly ship conforming goods and if they arrive by any means he must tender them on arrival but he assumes no obligation that the goods will arrive unless he has caused the non-arrival; and

(b) where without fault of the seller the goods are in part lost or have so deteriorated as no longer to conform to the contract or arrive after the contract time, the buyer may proceed as if there had been casualty to identified goods (Section 2—613).

* * * *

§2—326. SALE ON APPROVAL AND SALE OR RETURN; RIGHTS OF CREDITORS

(1) Unless otherwise agreed, if delivered goods may be returned by the buyer even though they conform to the contract, the transaction is

(a) a "sale on approval" if the goods are delivered primarily for use, and

(b) a "sale or return" if the goods are delivered primarily for resale.

(2) Goods held on approval are not subject to the claims of the buyer's creditors until acceptance; goods held on sale or return are subject to such claims while in the buyer's possession.

(3) Any "or return" term of a contract for sale is to be treated as a separate contract for sale within the statute of frauds section of this Article (Section 2—201) and as contradicting the sale aspect of the contract within the provisions of this Article or on parol or extrinsic evidence (Section 2—202).

§2—327. SPECIAL INCIDENTS OF SALE ON APPROVAL AND SALE OR RETURN

(1) Under a sale on approval unless otherwise agreed

(a) although the goods are identified to the contract the risk of loss and the title do not pass to the buyer until acceptance; and

(b) use of the goods consistent with the purpose of trial is not acceptance but failure seasonably to notify the seller of election to return the goods is acceptance, and if the goods conform to the contract acceptance of any part is acceptance of the whole; and

(c) after due notification of election to return, the return is at the seller's risk and expense but a merchant buyer must follow any reasonable instructions.

(2) Under a sale or return unless otherwise agreed

(a) the option to return extends to the whole or any commercial unit of the goods while in substantially their original condition, but must be exercised seasonably; and

(b) the return is at the buyer's risk and expense.

§2—328. SALE BY AUCTION

(1) In a sale by auction if goods are put up in lots each lot is the subject of a separate sale.

(2) A sale by auction is complete when the auctioneer so announces by the fall of the hammer or in other customary manner. Where a bid is made while the hammer is falling in acceptance of a prior bid the auctioneer may in his discretion reopen the bidding or declare the goods sold under the bid on which the hammer was falling.

(3) Such a sale is with reserve unless the goods are in explicit terms put up without reserve. In an auction with reserve the auctioneer may withdraw the goods at any time until he announces completion of the sale. In an auction without reserve, after the auctioneer calls for bids on an article or lot, that article or lot cannot be withdrawn unless no bid is made within a reasonable time. In either case a bidder may retract his bid until the auctioneer's announcement of completion of the sale, but a bidder's retraction does not revive any previous bid.

(4) If the auctioneer knowingly receives a bid on the seller's behalf or the seller makes or procures such a bid, and notice has not been given that liberty for such bidding is reserved, the buyer may at his option avoid the sale or take the goods at the price of the last good faith bid prior to the completion of the sale. This subsection shall not apply to any bid at a forced sale.

§2—401. PASSING OF TITLE; RESERVATION FOR SECURITY; LIMITED APPLICATION OF THIS SECTION

Each provision of this Article with regard to the rights, obligations and remedies of the seller, the buyer, purchasers or other third parties applies irrespective of title to the goods except where the provision refers to such title. Insofar as situations are not covered by the other provisions of this Article and matters concerning title became material the following rules apply:

(1) Title to goods cannot pass under a contract for sale prior to their identification to the contract

(Section 2—501), and unless otherwise explicitly agreed the buyer acquires by their identification a special property as limited by this Act. Any retention or reservation by the seller of the title (property) in goods shipped or delivered to the buyer is limited in effect to a reservation of a security interest. Subject to these provisions and to the provisions of the Article on Secured Transactions (Article 9), title to goods passes from the seller to the buyer in any manner and on any conditions explicitly agreed on by the parties.

(2) Unless otherwise explicitly agreed title passes to the buyer at the time and place at which the seller completes his performance with reference to the physical delivery of the goods, despite any reservation of a security interest and even though a document of title is to be delivered at a different time or place; and in particular and despite any reservation of a security interest by the bill of lading

    (a) if the contract requires or authorizes the seller to send the goods to the buyer but does not require him to deliver them at destination, title passes to the buyer at the time and place of shipment; but

    (b) if the contract requires delivery at destination, title passes on tender there.

(3) Unless otherwise explicitly agreed where delivery is to be made without moving the goods,

    (a) if the seller is to deliver a document of title, title passes at the time when and the place where he delivers such documents; or

    (b) if the goods are at the time of contracting already identified and no documents are to be delivered, title passes at the time and place of contracting.

(4) A rejection or other refusal by the buyer to receive or retain the goods, whether or not justified, or a justified revocation of acceptance revests title to the goods in the seller. Such revesting occurs by operation of law and is not a "sale".

* * * *

§2—403. POWER TO TRANSFER; GOOD FAITH PURCHASE OF GOODS; "ENTRUSTING"

(1) A purchaser of goods acquires all title which his transferor had or had power to transfer except that a purchaser of a limited interest acquires rights only to the extent of the interest purchased. A person with voidable title has power to transfer a good title to a good faith purchaser for value. When goods have been delivered under a transaction of purchase the purchaser has such power even though

    (a) the transferor was deceived as to the identity of the purchaser, or

    (b) the delivery was in exchange for a check which is later dishonored, or

    (c) it was agreed that the transaction was to be a "cash sale", or

    (d) the delivery was procured through fraud punishable as larcenous under the criminal law.

(2) Any entrusting of possession of goods to a merchant who deals in goods of that kind gives him power to transfer all rights of the entruster to a buyer in ordinary course of business.

(3) "Entrusting" includes any delivery and any acquiescence in retention of possession regardless of any condition expressed between the parties to the delivery or acquiescence and regardless of whether the procurement of the entrusting or the possessor's disposition of the goods have been such as to be larcenous under the criminal law.

(4) The rights of other purchasers of goods and of lien creditors are governed by the Articles on Secured Transactions (Article 9), Bulk Transfers (Article 6) and Documents of Title (Article 7).

§2—501. INSURABLE INTEREST IN GOODS; MANNER OF IDENTIFICATION OF GOODS

(1) The buyer obtains a special property and an insurable interest in goods by identification of existing goods as goods to which the contract refers even though the goods so identified are non-conforming and he has an option to return or reject them. Such identification can be made at any time and in any manner explicitly agreed to by the parties. In the absence of explicit agreement identification occurs

    (a) when the contract is made if it is for the sale of goods already existing and identified;

    (b) if the contract is for the sale of future goods other than those described in paragraph (c), when goods are shipped, marked or otherwise designated by the seller as goods to which the contract refers;

    (c) when the crops are planted or otherwise become growing crops or the young are conceived if the contract is for the sale of unborn young to be born within twelve months after contracting or for the sale of crops to be harvested within twelve months or the next normal harvest season after contracting whichever is longer.

(2) The seller retains an insurable interest in goods so long as title to or any security interest in the goods

remains in him and where the identification is by the seller alone he may until default or insolvency or notification to the buyer that the identification is final substitute other goods for those identified.

(3) Nothing in this section impairs any insurable interest recognized under any other statute or rule of law.

§2—502. BUYER'S RIGHT TO GOODS ON SELLER'S INSOLVENCY

(1) Subject to subsections (2) and (3) and even though the goods have not been shipped a buyer who has paid a part or all of the price of goods in which he has a special property under the provisions of the immediately preceding section may on making and keeping good a tender of any unpaid portion of their price recover them from the seller if:

(a) in the case of goods bought for personal, family, or household purposes, the seller repudiates or fails to deliver as required by the contract; or

(b) in all cases, the seller becomes insolvent within ten days after receipt of the first installment on their price.

(2) The buyer's right to recover the goods under subsection (1)(a) vests upon acquisition of a special property, even if the seller had not then repudiated or failed to deliver.

(3) If the identification creating his special property has been made by the buyer he acquires the right to recover the goods only if they conform to the contract for sale.
As amended in 1999.

§2—503. MANNER OF SELLER'S TENDER OF DELIVERY

(1) Tender of delivery requires that the seller put and hold conforming goods at the buyer's disposition and give the buyer any notification reasonably necessary to enable him to take delivery. The manner, time and place for tender are determined by the agreement and this Article, and in particular

(a) tender must be at a reasonable hour, and if it is of goods they must be kept available for the period reasonably necessary to enable the buyer to take possession; but

(b) unless otherwise agreed the buyer must furnish facilities reasonably suited to the receipt of the goods.

(2) Where the case is within the next section respecting shipment tender requires that the seller comply with its provisions.

(3) Where the seller is required to deliver at a particular destination tender requires that he comply with subsection (1) and also in any appropriate case tender documents as described in subsections (4) and (5) of this section.

(4) Where goods are in the possession of a bailee and are to be delivered without being moved

(a) tender requires that the seller either tender a negotiable document of title covering such goods or procure acknowledgment by the bailee of the buyer's right to possession of the goods; but

(b) tender to the buyer of a non-negotiable document of title or of a written direction to the bailee to deliver is sufficient tender unless the buyer seasonably objects, and receipt by the bailee of notification of the buyer's rights fixes those rights as against the bailee and all third persons; but risk of loss of the goods and of any failure by the bailee to honor the non-negotiable document of title or to obey the direction remains on the seller until the buyer has had a reasonable time to present the document or direction, and a refusal by the bailee to honor the document or to obey the direction defeats the tender.

(5) Where the contract requires the seller to deliver documents

(a) he must tender all such documents in correct form, except as provided in this Article with respect to bills of lading in a set (subsection (2) of Section 2—323); and

(b) tender through customary banking channels is sufficient and dishonor of a draft accompanying the documents constitutes non-acceptance or rejection.

§2—504. SHIPMENT BY SELLER

Where the seller is required or authorized to send the goods to the buyer and the contract does not require him to deliver them at a particular destination, then unless otherwise agreed he must

(a) put the goods in the possession of such a carrier and make such a contract for their transportation as may be reasonable having regard to the nature of the goods and other circumstances of the case; and

(b) obtain and promptly deliver or tender in due form any document necessary to enable the buyer to obtain possession of the goods or otherwise required by the agreement or by usage of trade; and

(c) promptly notify the buyer of the shipment. Failure to notify the buyer under paragraph (c) or to make a proper contract under paragraph (a) is a ground for rejection only if material delay or loss ensues.

* * * *

§2—506. RIGHTS OF FINANCING AGENCY

(1) A financing agency by paying or purchasing for value a draft which relates to a shipment of goods acquires to the extent of the payment or purchase and in addition to its own rights under the draft and any document of title securing it any rights of the shipper in the goods including the right to stop delivery and the shipper's right to have the draft honored by the buyer.

(2) The right to reimbursement of a financing agency which has in good faith honored or purchased the draft under commitment to or authority from the buyer is not impaired by subsequent discovery of defects with reference to any relevant document which was apparently regular on its face.

§2—507. EFFECT OF SELLER'S TENDER; DELIVERY ON CONDITION

(1) Tender of delivery is a condition to the buyer's duty to accept the goods and, unless otherwise agreed, to his duty to pay for them. Tender entitles the seller to acceptance of the goods and to payment according to the contract.

(2) Where payment is due and demanded on the delivery to the buyer of goods or documents of title, his right as against the seller to retain or dispose of them is conditional upon his making the payment due.

§2—508. CURE BY SELLER OF IMPROPER TENDER OR DELIVERY; REPLACEMENT

(1) Where any tender or delivery by the seller is rejected because non-conforming and the time for performance has not yet expired, the seller may seasonably notify the buyer of his intention to cure and may then within the contract time make a conforming delivery.

(2) Where the buyer rejects a non-conforming tender which the seller had reasonable grounds to believe would be acceptable with or without money allowance the seller may if he seasonably notifies the buyer have a further reasonable time to substitute a conforming tender.

§2—509. RISK OF LOSS IN THE ABSENCE OF BREACH

(1) Where the contract requires or authorizes the seller to ship the goods by carrier

    (a) if it does not require him to deliver them at a particular destination, the risk of loss passes to the buyer when the goods are duly delivered to the carrier even though the shipment is under reservation (Section 2—505); but

    (b) if it does require him to deliver them at a particular destination and the goods are there duly tendered while in the possession of the carrier, the risk of loss passes to the buyer when the goods are there duly so tendered as to enable the buyer to take delivery.

(2) Where the goods are held by a bailee to be delivered without being moved, the risk of loss passes to the buyer

    (a) on his receipt of a negotiable document of title covering the goods; or

    (b) on acknowledgment by the bailee of the buyer's right to possession of the goods; or

    (c) after his receipt of a non-negotiable document of title or other written direction to deliver, as provided in subsection (4)(b) of Section 2—503.

(3) In any case not within subsection (1) or (2), the risk of loss passes to the buyer on his receipt of the goods if the seller is a merchant; otherwise the risk passes to the buyer on tender of delivery.

(4) The provisions of this section are subject to contrary agreement of the parties and to the provisions of this Article on sale on approval (Section 2—327) and on effect of breach on risk of loss (Section 2—510).

§2—510. EFFECT OF BREACH ON RISK OF LOSS

(1) Where a tender or delivery of goods so fails to conform to the contract as to give a right of rejection the risk of their loss remains on the seller until cure or acceptance.

(2) Where the buyer rightfully revokes acceptance he may to the extent of any deficiency in his effective insurance coverage treat the risk of loss as having rested on the seller from the beginning.

(3) Where the buyer as to conforming goods already identified to the contract for sale repudiates or is otherwise in breach before risk of their loss has passed to him, the seller may to the extent of any deficiency in his effective insurance coverage treat the risk of loss as resting on the buyer for a commercially reasonable time.

§2—511. TENDER OF PAYMENT BY BUYER; PAYMENT BY CHECK

(1) Unless otherwise agreed tender of payment is a condition to the seller's duty to tender and complete any delivery.

(2) Tender of payment is sufficient when made by any means or in any manner current in the ordinary course of business unless the seller demands payment in legal tender and gives any extension of time reasonably necessary to procure it.

(3) Subject to the provisions of this Act on the effect of an instrument on an obligation (Section 3—310), payment by check is conditional and is defeated as between the parties by dishonor of the check on due presentment.

As amended in 1994.

§2—512. PAYMENT BY BUYER BEFORE INSPECTION

(1) Where the contract requires payment before inspection non-conformity of the goods does not excuse the buyer from so making payment unless

(a) the non-conformity appears without inspection; or

(b) despite tender of the required documents the circumstances would justify injunction against honor under this Act (Section 5—109(b)).

(2) Payment pursuant to subsection (1) does not constitute an acceptance of goods or impair the buyer's right to inspect or any of his remedies.

§2—513. BUYER'S RIGHT TO INSPECTION OF GOODS

(1) Unless otherwise agreed and subject to subsection (3), where goods are tendered or delivered or identified to the contract for sale, the buyer has a right before payment or acceptance to inspect them at any reasonable place and time and in any reasonable manner. When the seller is required or authorized to send the goods to the buyer, the inspection may be after their arrival.

(2) Expenses of inspection must be borne by the buyer but may be recovered from the seller if the goods do not conform and are rejected.

(3) Unless otherwise agreed and subject to the provisions of this Article on C.I.F. contracts (subsection (3) of Section 2—321), the buyer is not entitled to inspect the goods before payment of the price when the contract provides

(a) for delivery "C.O.D." or on other like terms; or

(b) for payment against documents of title, except where such payment is due only after the goods are to become available for inspection.

(4) A place or method of inspection fixed by the parties is presumed to be exclusive but unless otherwise expressly agreed it does not postpone identification or shift the place for delivery or for passing the risk of loss. If compliance becomes impossible, inspection shall be as provided in this section unless the place or method fixed was clearly intended as an indispensable condition failure of which avoids the contract.

* * * *

§2—601. BUYER'S RIGHTS ON IMPROPER DELIVERY

Subject to the provisions of this Article on breach in installment contracts (Section 2—612) and unless otherwise agreed under the sections on contractual limitations of remedy (Sections 2—718 and 2—719), if the goods or the tender of delivery fail in any respect to conform to the contract, the buyer may

(a) reject the whole; or

(b) accept the whole; or

(c) accept any commercial unit or units and reject the rest.

§2—602. MANNER AND EFFECT OF RIGHTFUL REJECTION

(1) Rejection of goods must be within a reasonable time after their delivery or tender. It is ineffective unless the buyer seasonably notifies the seller.

(2) Subject to the provisions of the two following sections on rejected goods (Sections 2—603 and 2—604),

(a) after rejection any exercise of ownership by the buyer with respect to any commercial unit is wrongful as against the seller; and

(b) if the buyer has before rejection taken physical possession of goods in which he does not have a security interest under the provisions of this Article (subsection (3) of Section 2—711), he is under a duty after rejection to hold them with reasonable care at the seller's disposition for a time sufficient to permit the seller to remove them; but

(c) the buyer has no further obligations with regard to goods rightfully rejected.

(3) The seller's rights with respect to goods wrongfully rejected are governed by the provisions of this Article on Seller's remedies in general (Section 2—703).

§2—603. MERCHANT BUYER'S DUTIES AS TO RIGHTFULLY REJECTED GOODS

(1) Subject to any security interest in the buyer (subsection (3) of Section 2—711), when the seller has no agent or place of business at the market of rejection a merchant buyer is under a duty after rejection of goods in his possession or control to follow any reasonable instructions received from the seller with respect to the goods and in the absence of such instructions to make reasonable efforts to sell them for the seller's account if they are perishable or threaten to decline in value speedily. Instructions are not reasonable if on demand indemnity for expenses is not forthcoming.

(2) When the buyer sells goods under subsection (1), he is entitled to reimbursement from the seller or out of the proceeds for reasonable expenses of caring for and selling them, and if the expenses include no selling commission then to such commission as is usual in the trade or if there is none to a reasonable sum not exceeding ten per cent on the gross proceeds.

(3) In complying with this section the buyer is held only to good faith and good faith conduct hereunder is neither acceptance nor conversion nor the basis of an action for damages.

§2—604. BUYER'S OPTIONS AS TO SALVAGE OF RIGHTFULLY REJECTED GOODS

Subject to the provisions of the immediately preceding section on perishables if the seller gives no instructions within a reasonable time after notification of rejection the buyer may store the rejected goods for the seller's account or reship them to him or resell them for the seller's account with reimbursement as provided in the preceding section. Such action is not acceptance or conversion.

§2—605. WAIVER OF BUYER'S OBJECTIONS BY FAILURE TO PARTICULARIZE

(1) The buyer's failure to state in connection with rejection a particular defect which is ascertainable by reasonable inspection precludes him from relying on the unstated defect to justify rejection or to establish breach

(a) where the seller could have cured it if stated seasonably; or

(b) between merchants when the seller has after rejection made a request in writing for a full and final written statement of all defects on which the buyer proposes to rely.

(2) Payment against documents made without reservation of rights precludes recovery of the payment for defects apparent on the face of the documents.

§2—606. WHAT CONSTITUTES ACCEPTANCE OF GOODS

(1) Acceptance of goods occurs when the buyer

(a) after a reasonable opportunity to inspect the goods signifies to the seller that the goods are conforming or that he will take or retain them in spite of their non-conformity; or

(b) fails to make an effective rejection (subsection (1) of Section 2—602), but such acceptance does not occur until the buyer has had a reasonable opportunity to inspect them; or

(c) does any act inconsistent with the seller's ownership; but if such act is wrongful as against the seller it is an acceptance only if ratified by him.

(2) Acceptance of a part of any commercial unit is acceptance of that entire unit.

§2—607. EFFECT OF ACCEPTANCE; NOTICE OF BREACH; BURDEN OF ESTABLISHING BREACH AFTER ACCEPTANCE; NOTICE OF CLAIM OR LITIGATION TO PERSON ANSWERABLE OVER

(1) The buyer must pay at the contract rate for any goods accepted.

(2) Acceptance of goods by the buyer precludes rejection of the goods accepted and if made with knowledge of a non-conformity cannot be revoked because of it unless the acceptance was on the reasonable assumption that the non-conformity would be seasonably cured but acceptance does not of itself impair any other remedy provided by this Article for non-conformity.

(3) Where a tender has been accepted

(a) the buyer must within a reasonable time after he discovers or should have discovered any breach notify the seller of breach or be barred from any remedy; and

(b) if the claim is one for infringement or the like (subsection (3) of Section 2—312) and the buyer is sued as a result of such a breach he must so notify the seller within a reasonable time after he receives notice of the litigation or be barred from any remedy over for liability established by the litigation.

(4) The burden is on the buyer to establish any breach with respect to the goods accepted.

(5) Where the buyer is sued for breach of a warranty or other obligation for which his seller is answerable over

(a) he may give his seller written notice of the litigation. If the notice states that the seller may come in and defend and that if the seller does not do so he will be bound in any action against him by his buyer by any determination of fact common to the two litigations, then unless the seller after seasonable receipt of the notice does come in and defend he is so bound.

(b) if the claim is one for infringement or the like (subsection (3) of Section 2—312) the original seller may demand in writing that his buyer turn over to him control of the litigation including settlement or else be barred from any remedy over and if he also agrees to bear all expense and to satisfy any adverse judgment, then unless the buyer after seasonable receipt of the demand does turn over control the buyer is so barred.

(6) The provisions of subsections (3), (4) and (5) apply to any obligation of a buyer to hold the seller harmless against infringement or the like (subsection (3) of Section 2—312).

§2—608. REVOCATION OF ACCEPTANCE IN WHOLE OR IN PART

(1) The buyer may revoke his acceptance of a lot or commercial unit whose non-conformity substantially impairs its value to him if he has accepted it

    (a) on the reasonable assumption that its non-conformity would be cured and it has not been seasonably cured; or

    (b) without discovery of such non-conformity if his acceptance was reasonably induced either by the difficulty of discovery before acceptance or by the seller's assurances.

(2) Revocation of acceptance must occur within a reasonable time after the buyer discovers or should have discovered the ground for it and before any substantial change in condition of the goods which is not caused by their own defects. It is not effective until the buyer notifies the seller of it.

(3) A buyer who so revokes has the same rights and duties with regard to the goods involved as if he had rejected them.

§2—609. RIGHT TO ADEQUATE ASSURANCE OF PERFORMANCE

(1) A contract for sale imposes an obligation on each party that the other's expectation of receiving due performance will not be impaired. When reasonable grounds for insecurity arise with respect to the performance of either party the other may in writing demand adequate assurance of due performance and until he receives such assurance may if commercially reasonable suspend any performance for which he has not already received the agreed return.

(2) Between merchants the reasonableness of grounds for insecurity and the adequacy of any assurance offered shall be determined according to commercial standards.

(3) Acceptance of any improper delivery or payment does not prejudice the party's right to demand adequate assurance of future performance.

(4) After receipt of a justified demand failure to provide within a reasonable time not exceeding thirty days such assurance of due performance as is adequate under the

circumstances of the particular case is a repudiation of the contract.

§2—610. ANTICIPATORY REPUDIATION

When either party repudiates the contract with respect to a performance not yet due the loss of which will substantially impair the value of the contract to the other, the aggrieved party may

    (a) for a commercially reasonable time await performance by the repudiating party; or

    (b) resort to any remedy for breach (Section 2—703 or Section 2—711), even though he has notified the repudiating party that he would await the latter's performance and has urged retraction; and

    (c) in either case suspend his own performance or proceed in accordance with the provisions of this Article on the seller's right to identify goods to the contract notwithstanding breach or to salvage unfinished goods (Section 2—704).

§2—611. RETRACTION OF ANTICIPATORY REPUDIATION

(1) Until the repudiating party's next performance is due he can retract his repudiation unless the aggrieved party has since the repudiation cancelled or materially changed his position or otherwise indicated that he considers the repudiation final.

(2) Retraction may be by any method which clearly indicates to the aggrieved party that the repudiating party intends to perform, but must include any assurance justifiably demanded under the provisions of this Article (Section 2—609).

(3) Retraction reinstates the repudiating party's rights under the contract with due excuse and allowance to the aggrieved party for any delay occasioned by the repudiation.

§2—612. "INSTALLMENT CONTRACT"; BREACH

(1) An "installment contract" is one which requires or authorizes the delivery of goods in separate lots to be separately accepted, even though the contract contains a clause "each delivery is a separate contract" or its equivalent.

(2) The buyer may reject any installment which is non-conforming if the non-conformity substantially impairs the value of that installment and cannot be cured or if the non-conformity is a defect in the required documents; but if the non-conformity does not fall within subsection (3) and the seller gives adequate assurance of its cure the buyer must accept that installment.

(3) Whenever non-conformity or default with respect to one or more installments substantially impairs the value of the whole contract there is a breach of the whole. But the aggrieved party reinstates the contract if he accepts a non-conforming installment without seasonably notifying of cancellation or if he brings an action with respect only to past installments or demands performance as to future installments.

§2—613. CASUALTY TO IDENTIFIED GOODS

Where the contract requires for its performance goods identified when the contract is made, and the goods suffer casualty without fault of either party before the risk of loss passes to the buyer, or in a proper case under a "no arrival, no sale" term (Section 2—324) then

(a) if the loss is total the contract is avoided; and

(b) if the loss is partial or the goods have so deteriorated as no longer to conform to the contract the buyer may nevertheless demand inspection and at his option either treat the contract as voided or accept the goods with due allowance from the contract price for the deterioration or the deficiency in quantity but without further right against the seller.

§2—614. SUBSTITUTED PERFORMANCE

(1) Where without fault of either party the agreed berthing, loading, or unloading facilities fail or an agreed type of carrier becomes unavailable or the agreed manner of delivery otherwise becomes commercially impracticable but a commercially reasonable substitute is available, such substitute performance must be tendered and accepted.

(2) If the agreed means or manner of payment fails because of domestic or foreign governmental regulation, the seller may withhold or stop delivery unless the buyer provides a means or manner of payment which is commercially a substantial equivalent. If delivery has already been taken, payment by the means or in the manner provided by the regulation discharges the buyer's obligation unless the regulation is discriminatory, oppressive or predatory.

§2—615. EXCUSE BY FAILURE OF PRESUPPOSED CONDITIONS

Except so far as a seller may have assumed a greater obligation and subject to the preceding section on substituted performance:

(a) Delay in delivery or non-delivery in whole or in part by a seller who complies with paragraphs (b) and (c) is not a breach of his duty under a contract for sale if performance as agreed has been made impracticable by the occurrence of a contingency the nonoccurrence of which was a basic assumption on which the contract was made or by compliance in good faith with any applicable foreign or domestic governmental regulation or order whether or not it later proves to be invalid.

(b) Where the causes mentioned in paragraph (a) affect only a part of the seller's capacity to perform, he must allocate production and deliveries among his customers but may at his option include regular customers not then under contract as well as his own requirements for further manufacture. He may so allocate in any manner which is fair and reasonable.

(c) The seller must notify the buyer seasonably that there will be delay or non-delivery and, when allocation is required under paragraph (b), of the estimated quota thus made available for the buyer.

* * * *

§2—702. SELLER'S REMEDIES ON DISCOVERY OF BUYER'S INSOLVENCY

(1) Where the seller discovers the buyer to be insolvent he may refuse delivery except for cash including payment for all goods theretofore delivered under the contract, and stop delivery under this Article (Section 2—705).

(2) Where the seller discovers that the buyer has received goods on credit while insolvent he may reclaim the goods upon demand made within ten days after the receipt, but if misrepresentation of solvency has been made to the particular seller in writing within three months before delivery the ten day limitation does not apply. Except as provided in this subsection the seller may not base a right to reclaim goods on the buyer's fraudulent or innocent misrepresentation of solvency or of intent to pay.

(3) The seller's right to reclaim under subsection (2) is subject to the rights of a buyer in ordinary course or other good faith purchaser under this Article (Section 2—403). Successful reclamation of goods excludes all other remedies with respect to them.

§2—703. SELLER'S REMEDIES IN GENERAL

Where the buyer wrongfully rejects or revokes acceptance of goods or fails to make a payment due on or before delivery or repudiates with respect to a part or the whole, then with respect to any goods directly affected and, if the breach is of the whole contract

(Section 2—612), then also with respect to the whole undelivered balance, the aggrieved seller may

> (a) withhold delivery of such goods;
>
> (b) stop delivery by any bailee as hereafter provided (Section 2—705);
>
> (c) proceed under the next section respecting goods still unidentified to the contract;
>
> (d) resell and recover damages as hereafter provided (Section 2—706);
>
> (e) recover damages for non-acceptance (Section 2—708) or in a proper case the price (Section 2—709);
>
> (f) cancel.

§2—704. SELLER'S RIGHT TO IDENTIFY GOODS TO THE CONTRACT NOTWITHSTANDING BREACH OR TO SALVAGE UNFINISHED GOODS

(1) An aggrieved seller under the preceding section may

> (a) identify to the contract conforming goods not already identified if at the time he learned of the breach they are in his possession or control;
>
> (b) treat as the subject of resale goods which have demonstrably been intended for the particular contract even though those goods are unfinished.

(2) Where the goods are unfinished an aggrieved seller may in the exercise of reasonable commercial judgment for the purposes of avoiding loss and of effective realization either complete the manufacture and wholly identify the goods to the contract or cease manufacture and resell for scrap or salvage value or proceed in any other reasonable manner.

§2—705. SELLER'S STOPPAGE OF DELIVERY IN TRANSIT OR OTHERWISE

(1) The seller may stop delivery of goods in the possession of a carrier or other bailee when he discovers the buyer to be insolvent (Section 2—702) and may stop delivery of carload, truckload, planeload or larger shipments of express or freight when the buyer repudiates or fails to make a payment due before delivery or if for any other reason the seller has a right to withhold or reclaim the goods.

(2) As against such buyer the seller may stop delivery until

> (a) receipt of the goods by the buyer; or
>
> (b) acknowledgment to the buyer by any bailee of the goods except a carrier that the bailee holds the goods for the buyer; or

> (c) such acknowledgment to the buyer by a carrier by reshipment or as warehouseman; or
>
> (d) negotiation to the buyer of any negotiable document of title covering the goods.

(3) ****

> (a) To stop delivery the seller must so notify as to enable the bailee by reasonable diligence to prevent delivery of the goods.
>
> (b) After such notification the bailee must hold and deliver the goods according to the directions of the seller but the seller is liable to the bailee for any ensuing charges or damages.
>
> (c) If a negotiable document of title has been issued for goods the bailee is not obliged to obey a notification to stop until surrender of the document.
>
> (d) A carrier who has issued a non-negotiable bill of lading is not obliged to obey a notification to stop received from a person other than the consignor.

§2—706. SELLER'S RESALE INCLUDING CONTRACT FOR RESALE

(1) Under the conditions stated in Section 2—703 on seller's remedies, the seller may resell the goods concerned or the undelivered balance thereof. Where the resale is made in good faith and in a commercially reasonable manner the seller may recover the difference between the resale price and the contract price together with any incidental damages allowed under the provisions of this Article (Section 2—710), but less expenses saved in consequence of the buyer's breach.

(2) Except as otherwise provided in subsection (3) or unless otherwise agreed resale may be at public or private sale including sale by way of one or more contracts to sell or of identification to an existing contract of the seller. Sale may be as a unit or in parcels and at any time and place and on any terms but every aspect of the sale including the method, manner, time, place and terms must be commercially reasonable. The resale must be reasonably identified as referring to the broken contract, but it is not necessary that the goods be in existence or that any or all of them have been identified to the contract before the breach.

(3) Where the resale is at private sale the seller must give the buyer reasonable notification of his intention to resell.

(4) Where the resale is at public sale

> (a) only identified goods can be sold except where there is a recognized market for a public sale of futures in goods of the kind; and

(b) it must be made at a usual place or market for public sale if one is reasonably available and except in the case of goods which are perishable or threaten to decline in value speedily the seller must give the buyer reasonable notice of the time and place of the resale; and

(c) if the goods are not to be within the view of those attending the sale the notification of sale must state the place where the goods are located and provide for their reasonable inspection by prospective bidders; and

(d) the seller may buy.

(5) A purchaser who buys in good faith at a resale takes the goods free of any rights of the original buyer even though the seller fails to comply with one or more of the requirements of this section.

(6) The seller is not accountable to the buyer for any profit made on any resale. A person in the position of a seller (Section 2—707) or a buyer who has rightfully rejected or justifiably revoked acceptance must account for any excess over the amount of his security interest, as hereinafter defined (subsection (3) of Section 2—711).

* * * *

§2—708. SELLER'S DAMAGES FOR NON-ACCEPTANCE OR REPUDIATION

(1) Subject to subsection (2) and to the provisions of this Article with respect to proof of market price (Section 2—723), the measure of damages for non-acceptance or repudiation by the buyer is the difference between the market price at the time and place for tender and the unpaid contract price together with any incidental damages provided in this Article (Section 2—710), but less expenses saved in consequence of the buyer's breach.

(2) If the measure of damages provided in subsection (1) is inadequate to put the seller in as good a position as performance would have done then the measure of damages is the profit (including reasonable overhead) which the seller would have made from full performance by the buyer, together with any incidental damages provided in this Article (Section 2—710), due allowance for costs reasonably incurred and due credit for payments or proceeds of resale.

§2—709. ACTION FOR THE PRICE

(1) When the buyer fails to pay the price as it becomes due the seller may recover, together with any incidental damages under the next section, the price

(a) of goods accepted or of conforming goods lost or damaged within a commercially reasonable time after risk of their loss has passed to the buyer; and

(b) of goods identified to the contract if the seller is unable after reasonable effort to resell them at a reasonable price or the circumstances reasonably indicate that such effort will be unavailing.

(2) Where the seller sues for the price he must hold for the buyer any goods which have been identified to the contract and are still in his control except that if resale becomes possible he may resell them at any time prior to the collection of the judgment. The net proceeds of any such resale must be credited to the buyer and payment of the judgment entitles him to any goods not resold.

(3) After the buyer has wrongfully rejected or revoked acceptance of the goods or has failed to make a payment due or has repudiated (Section 2—610), a seller who is held not entitled to the price under this section shall nevertheless be awarded damages for non-acceptance under the preceding section.

§2—710. SELLER'S INCIDENTAL DAMAGES

Incidental damages to an aggrieved seller include any commercially reasonable charges, expenses or commissions incurred in stopping delivery, in the transportation, care and custody of goods after the buyer's breach, in connection with return or resale of the goods or otherwise resulting from the breach.

§2—711. BUYER'S REMEDIES IN GENERAL; BUYER'S SECURITY INTEREST IN REJECTED GOODS

(1) Where the seller fails to make delivery or repudiates or the buyer rightfully rejects or justifiably revokes acceptance then with respect to any goods involved, and with respect to the whole if the breach goes to the whole contract (Section 2—612), the buyer may cancel and whether or not he has done so may in addition to recovering so much of the price as has been paid

(a) "cover" and have damages under the next section as to all the goods affected whether or not they have been identified to the contract; or

(b) recover damages for non-delivery as provided in this Article (Section 2—713).

(2) Where the seller fails to deliver or repudiates buyer may also

(a) if the goods have been identified recover them as provided in this Article (Section 2—502); or

(b) in a proper case obtain specific performance or replevy the goods as provided in this Article (Section 2—716).

(3) On rightful rejection or justifiable revocation of acceptance a buyer has a security interest in goods in his possession or control for any payments made on their price and any expenses reasonably incurred in their inspection, receipt, transportation, care and custody and may hold such goods and resell them in like manner as an aggrieved seller (Section 2—706).

§2—712. "COVER"; BUYER'S PROCUREMENT OF SUBSTITUTE GOODS

(1) After a breach within the preceding section the buyer may "cover" by making in good faith and without unreasonable delay any reasonable purchase of or contract to purchase goods in substitution for those due from the seller.

(2) The buyer may recover from the seller as damages the difference between the cost of cover and the contract price together with any incidental or consequential damages as hereinafter defined (Section 2—715), but less expenses saved in consequence of the seller's breach.

(3) Failure of the buyer to effect cover within this section does not bar him from any other remedy.

§2—713. BUYER'S DAMAGES FOR NON-DELIVERY OR REPUDIATION

(1) Subject to the provisions of this Article with respect to proof of market price (Section 2—723), the measure of damages for non-delivery or repudiation by the seller is the difference between the market price at the time when the buyer learned of the breach and the contract price together with any incidental and consequential damages provided in this Article (Section 2—715), but less expenses saved in consequence of the seller's breach.

(2) Market price is to be determined as of the place for tender or, in cases of rejection after arrival or revocation of acceptance, as of the place of arrival.

§2—714. BUYER'S DAMAGES FOR BREACH IN REGARD TO ACCEPTED GOODS

(1) Where the buyer has accepted goods and given notification (subsection (3) of Section 2—607) he may recover as damages for any non-conformity of tender the loss resulting in the ordinary course of events from the seller's breach as determined in any manner which is reasonable.

(2) The measure of damages for breach of warranty is the difference at the time and place of acceptance between the value of the goods accepted and the value they would have had if they had been as warranted, unless special circumstances show proximate damages of a different amount.

(3) In a proper case any incidental and consequential damages under the next section may also be recovered.

§2—715. BUYER'S INCIDENTAL AND CONSEQUENTIAL DAMAGES

(1) Incidental damages resulting from the seller's breach include expenses reasonably incurred in inspection, receipt, transportation and care and custody of goods rightfully rejected, any commercially reasonable charges, expenses or commissions in connection with effecting cover and any other reasonable expense incident to the delay or other breach.

(2) Consequential damages resulting from the seller's breach include

(a) any loss resulting from general or particular requirements and needs of which the seller at the time of contracting had reason to know and which could not reasonably be prevented by cover or otherwise; and

(b) injury to person or property proximately resulting from any breach of warranty.

§2—716. BUYER'S RIGHT TO SPECIFIC PERFORMANCE OR REPLEVIN

(1) Specific performance may be decreed where the goods are unique or in other proper circumstances.

(2) The decree for specific performance may include such terms and conditions as to payment of the price, damages, or other relief as the court may deem just.

(3) The buyer has a right of replevin for goods identified to the contract if after reasonable effort he is unable to effect cover for such goods or the circumstances reasonably indicate that such effort will be unavailing or if the goods have been shipped under reservation and satisfaction of the security interest in them has been made or tendered. In the case of goods bought for personal, family, or household purposes, the buyer's right of replevin vests upon acquisition of a special property, even if the seller had not then repudiated or failed to deliver.

§2—717. DEDUCTION OF DAMAGES FROM THE PRICE

The buyer on notifying the seller of his intention to do so may deduct all or any part of the damages resulting from any breach of the contract from any part of the price still due under the same contract.

§2—718. LIQUIDATION OR LIMITATION OF DAMAGES; DEPOSITS

(1) Damages for breach by either party may be liquidated in the agreement but only at an amount which is reasonable in the light of the anticipated or actual harm caused by the breach, the difficulties of proof of loss, and the inconvenience or nonfeasibility of otherwise obtaining an adequate remedy. A term fixing unreasonably large liquidated damages is void as a penalty.

(2) Where the seller justifiably withholds delivery of goods because of the buyer's breach, the buyer is entitled to restitution of any amount by which the sum of his payments exceeds

    (a) the amount to which the seller is entitled by virtue of terms liquidating the seller's damages in accordance with subsection (1), or

    (b) in the absence of such terms, twenty per cent of the value of the total performance for which the buyer is obligated under the contract or $500, whichever is smaller.

(3) The buyer's right to restitution under subsection (2) is subject to offset to the extent that the seller establishes

    (a) a right to recover damages under the provisions of this Article other than subsection (1), and

    (b) the amount or value of any benefits received by the buyer directly or indirectly by reason of the contract.

(4) Where a seller has received payment in goods their reasonable value or the proceeds of their resale shall be treated as payments for the purposes of subsection (2); but if the seller has notice of the buyer's breach before reselling goods received in part performance, his resale is subject to the conditions laid down in this Article on resale by an aggrieved seller (Section 2—706).

§2—719. CONTRACTUAL MODIFICATION OR LIMITATION OF REMEDY

(1) Subject to the provisions of subsections (2) and (3) of this section and of the preceding section on liquidation and limitation of damages,

    (a) the agreement may provide for remedies in addition to or in substitution for those provided in this Article and may limit or alter the measure of damages recoverable under this Article, as by limiting the buyer's remedies to return of the goods and repayment of the price or to repair and replacement of non-conforming goods or parts; and

    (b) resort to a remedy as provided is optional unless the remedy is expressly agreed to be exclusive, in which case it is the sole remedy.

(2) Where circumstances cause an exclusive or limited remedy to fail of its essential purpose, remedy may be had as provided in this Act.

(3) Consequential damages may be limited or excluded unless the limitation or exclusion is unconscionable. Limitation of consequential damages for injury to the person in the case of consumer goods is prima facie unconscionable but limitation of damages where the loss is commercial is not.

§2—720. EFFECT OF "CANCELLATION" OR "RESCISSION" ON CLAIMS FOR ANTECEDENT BREACH

Unless the contrary intention clearly appears, expressions of "cancellation" or "rescission" of the contract or the like shall not be construed as a renunciation or discharge of any claim in damages for an antecedent breach.

§2—721. REMEDIES FOR FRAUD

Remedies for material misrepresentation or fraud include all remedies available under this Article for non-fraudulent breach. Neither rescission or a claim for rescission of the contract for sale nor rejection or return of the goods shall bar or be deemed inconsistent with a claim for damages or other remedy.

§2—722. WHO CAN SUE THIRD PARTIES FOR INJURY TO GOODS

Where a third party so deals with goods which have been identified to a contract for sale as to cause actionable injury to a party to that contract

    (a) a right of action against the third party is in either party to the contract for sale who has title to or a security interest or a special property or an insurable interest in the goods; and if the goods have been destroyed or converted a right of action is also in the party who either bore the risk of loss under the contract for sale or has since the injury assumed that risk as against the other;

    (b) if at the time of the injury the party plaintiff did not bear the risk of loss as against the other party to the contract for sale and there is no arrangement between them for disposition of the recovery, his suit or settlement is, subject to his own interest, as a fiduciary for the other party to the contract;

    (c) either party may with the consent of the other sue for the benefit of whom it may concern.

§2—723. PROOF OF MARKET PRICE: TIME AND PLACE

(1) If an action based on anticipatory repudiation comes to trial before the time for performance with respect to some or all of the goods, any damages based on market price (Section 2—708 or Section 2—713) shall be determined according to the price of such goods prevailing at the time when the aggrieved party learned of the repudiation.

(2) If evidence of a price prevailing at the times or places described in this Article is not readily available the price prevailing within any reasonable time before or after the time described or at any other place which in commercial judgment or under usage of trade would serve as a reasonable substitute for the one described may be used, making any proper allowance for the cost of transporting the goods to or from such other place.

(3) Evidence of a relevant price prevailing at a time or place other than the one described in this Article offered by one party is not admissible unless and until he has given the other party such notice as the court finds sufficient to prevent unfair surprise.

§2—724. ADMISSIBILITY OF MARKET QUOTATIONS

Whenever the prevailing price or value of any goods regularly bought and sold in any established commodity market is in issue, reports in official publications or trade journals or in newspapers or periodicals of general circulation published as the reports of such market shall be admissible in evidence. The circumstances of the preparation of such a report may be shown to affect its weight but not its admissibility.

§2—725. STATUTE OF LIMITATIONS IN CONTRACTS FOR SALE

(1) An action for breach of any contract for sale must be commenced within four years after the cause of action has accrued. By the original agreement the parties may reduce the period of limitation to not less than one year but may not extend it.

(2) A cause of action accrues when the breach occurs, regardless of the aggrieved party's lack of knowledge of the breach. A breach of warranty occurs when tender of delivery is made, except that where a warranty explicitly extends to future performance of the goods and discovery of the breach must await the time of such performance the cause of action accrues when the breach is or should have been discovered.

(3) Where an action commenced within the time limited by subsection (1) is so terminated as to leave available a remedy by another action for the same breach such other action may be commenced after the expiration of the time limited and within six months after the termination of the first action unless the termination resulted from voluntary discontinuance or from dismissal for failure or neglect to prosecute.

(4) This section does not alter the law on tolling of the statute of limitations nor does it apply to causes of action which have accrued before this Act becomes effective.

Article 2 Amendments (Excerpts)

Part 1 Short Title, General Construction and Subject Matter

* * * *

§2—103. DEFINITIONS AND INDEX OF DEFINITIONS

(1) In this article unless the context otherwise requires

* * * *

(b) "Conspicuous", with reference to a term, means so written, displayed, or presented that a reasonable person against which it is to operate ought to have noticed it. A term in an electronic record intended to evoke a response by an electronic agent is conspicuous if it is presented in a form that would enable a reasonably configured electronic agent to take it into account or react to it without review of the record by an individual. Whether a term is "conspicuous" or not is a decision for the court. Conspicuous terms include the following:

  (i) for a person:

   (A) a heading in capitals equal to or greater in size than the surrounding text, or in contrasting type, font, or color to the surrounding text of the same or lesser size;

   (B) language in the body of a record or display in larger type than the surrounding text, or in contrasting type, font, or color to the surrounding text of the same size, or set off from surrounding text of the same size by symbols or other marks that call attention to the language; and

  (ii) for a person or an electronic agent, a term that is so placed in a record or display that the person or electronic agent cannot proceed without taking action with respect to the particular term.

(c) "Consumer" means an individual who buys or contracts to buy goods that, at the time of contracting, are intended by the individual to be used primarily for personal, family, or household purposes.

(d) "Consumer contract" means a contract between a merchant seller and a consumer.

* * * *

(j) "Good faith" means honesty in fact and the observance of reasonable commercial standards of fair dealing.

(k) "Goods" means all things that are movable at the time of identification to a contract for sale. The term includes future goods, specially manufactured goods, the unborn young of animals, growing crops, and other identified things attached to realty as described in Section 2—107. The term does not include information, the money in which the price is to be paid, investment securities under Article 8, the subject matter of foreign exchange transactions, and choses in action.

* * * *

(m) "Record" means information that is inscribed on a tangible medium or that is stored in an electronic or other medium and is retrievable in perceivable form.

(n) "Remedial promise" means a promise by the seller to repair or replace the goods or to refund all or part of the price upon the happening of a specified event.

* * * *

(p) "Sign" means, with present intent to authenticate or adopt a record,

(i) to execute or adopt a tangible symbol; or

(ii) to attach to or logically associate with the record an electronic sound, symbol, or process.

* * * *

Part 2 Form, Formation, Terms and Readjustment of Contract; Electronic Contracting

§2—201. FORMAL REQUIREMENTS; STATUTE OF FRAUDS

(1) A contract for the sale of goods for the price of $5,000 or more is not enforceable by way of action or defense unless there is some record sufficient to indicate that a contract for sale has been made between the parties and signed by the party against whom which enforcement is sought or by the party's authorized agent or broker. A record is not insufficient because it omits or incorrectly states a term agreed upon but the contract is not enforceable under this subsection beyond the quantity of goods shown in the record.

(2) Between merchants if within a reasonable time a record in confirmation of the contract and sufficient against the sender is received and the party receiving it has reason to know its contents, it satisfies the requirements of subsection (1) against such party the recipient unless notice of objection to its contents is given in a record within 10 days after it is received.

(3) A contract which does not satisfy the requirements of subsection (1) but which is valid in other respects is enforceable

(a) if the goods are to be specially manufactured for the buyer and are not suitable for sale to others in the ordinary course of the seller's business and the seller, before notice of repudiation is received and under circumstances which reasonably indicate that the goods are for the buyer, has made either a substantial beginning of their manufacture or commitments for their procurement; or

(b) if the party against whom which enforcement is sought admits in the party's pleading, or in the party's testimony or otherwise under oath that a contract for sale was made, but the contract is not enforceable under this paragraph beyond the quantity of goods admitted; or

(c) with respect to goods for which payment has been made and accepted or which have been received and accepted (Sec. 2—606).

(4) A contract that is enforceable under this section is not rendered unenforceable merely because it is not capable of being performed within one year or any other applicable period after its making.

* * * *

§2—207. TERMS OF CONTRACT; EFFECT OF CONFIRMATION

If (i) conduct by both parties recognizes the existence of a contract although their records do not otherwise establish a contract, (ii) a contract is formed by an offer and acceptance, or (iii) a contract formed in any manner is confirmed by a record that contains terms additional to or different from those in the contract being confirmed, the terms of the contract, subject to Section 2—202, are:

(a) terms that appear in the records of both parties;

(b) terms, whether in a record or not, to which both parties agree; and

(c) terms supplied or incorporated under any provision of this Act.

* * * *

Part 3 General Obligation and Construction of Contract
* * * *

§2—312. WARRANTY OF TITLE AND AGAINST INFRINGEMENT; BUYER'S OBLIGATION AGAINST INFRINGEMENT

(1) Subject to subsection (2) there is in a contract for sale a warranty by the seller that

(a) the title conveyed shall be good, good and its transfer rightful and shall not, because of any colorable claim to or interest in the goods, unreasonably expose the buyer to litigation; and

(b) the goods shall be delivered free from any security interest or other lien or encumbrance of which the buyer at the time of contracting has no knowledge.

(2) Unless otherwise agreed a seller that is a merchant regularly dealing in goods of the kind warrants that the goods shall be delivered free of the rightful claim of any third person by way of infringement or the like but a buyer that furnishes specifications to the seller must hold the seller harmless against any such claim that arises out of compliance with the specifications.

(3) A warranty under this section may be disclaimed or modified only by specific language or by circumstances that give the buyer reason to know that the seller does not claim title, that the seller is purporting to sell only the right or title as the seller or a third person may have, or that the seller is selling subject to any claims of infringement or the like.

§2—313. EXPRESS WARRANTIES BY AFFIRMATION, PROMISE, DESCRIPTION, SAMPLE; REMEDIAL PROMISE

(1) In this section, "immediate buyer" means a buyer that enters into a contract with the seller.

* * * *

(4) Any remedial promise made by the seller to the immediate buyer creates an obligation that the promise will be performed upon the happening of the specified event.

§2—313A. OBLIGATION TO REMOTE PURCHASER CREATED BY RECORD PACKAGED WITH OR ACCOMPANYING GOODS

(1) This section applies only to new goods and goods sold or leased as new goods in a transaction of purchase in the normal chain of distribution. In this section:

(a) "Immediate buyer" means a buyer that enters into a contract with the seller.

(b) "Remote purchaser" means a person that buys or leases goods from an immediate buyer or other person in the normal chain of distribution.

(2) If a seller in a record packaged with or accompanying the goods makes an affirmation of fact or promise that relates to the goods, provides a description that relates to the goods, or makes a remedial promise, and the seller reasonably expects the record to be, and the record is, furnished to the remote purchaser, the seller has an obligation to the remote purchaser that:

(a) the goods will conform to the affirmation of fact, promise or description unless a reasonable person in the position of the remote purchaser would not believe that the affirmation of fact, promise or description created an obligation; and

(b) the seller will perform the remedial promise.

(3) It is not necessary to the creation of an obligation under this section that the seller use formal words such as "warrant" or "guarantee" or that the seller have a specific intention to undertake an obligation, but an affirmation merely of the value of the goods or a statement purporting to be merely the seller's opinion or commendation of the goods does not create an obligation.

(4) The following rules apply to the remedies for breach of an obligation created under this section:

(a) The seller may modify or limit the remedies available to the remote purchaser if the modification or limitation is furnished to the remote purchaser no later than the time of purchase or if the modification or limitation is contained in the record that contains the affirmation of fact, promise or description.

(b) Subject to a modification or limitation of remedy, a seller in breach is liable for incidental or consequential damages under Section 2—715, but the seller is not liable for lost profits.

(c) The remote purchaser may recover as damages for breach of a seller's obligation arising under subsection (2) the loss resulting in the ordinary course of events as determined in any manner that is reasonable.

(5) An obligation that is not a remedial promise is breached if the goods did not conform to the affirmation of fact, promise or description creating the obligation when the goods left the seller's control.

§2—313B. OBLIGATION TO REMOTE PURCHASER CREATED BY COMMUNICATION TO THE PUBLIC

(1) This section applies only to new goods and goods sold or leased as new goods in a transaction of purchase in the normal chain of distribution. In this section:

(a) "Immediate buyer" means a buyer that enters into a contract with the seller.

(b) "Remote purchaser" means a person that buys or leases goods from an immediate buyer or other person in the normal chain of distribution.

(2) If a seller in advertising or a similar communication to the public makes an affirmation of fact or promise that relates to the goods, provides a description that relates to the goods, or makes a remedial promise, and the remote purchaser enters into a transaction of purchase with knowledge of and with the expectation that the goods will conform to the affirmation of fact, promise, or description, or that the seller will perform the remedial promise, the seller has an obligation to the remote purchaser that:

(a) the goods will conform to the affirmation of fact, promise or description unless a reasonable person in the position of the remote purchaser would not believe that the affirmation of fact, promise or description created an obligation; and

(b) the seller will perform the remedial promise.

(3) It is not necessary to the creation of an obligation under this section that the seller use formal words such as "warrant" or "guarantee" or that the seller have a specific intention to undertake an obligation, but an affirmation merely of the value of the goods or a statement purporting to be merely the seller's opinion or commendation of the goods does not create an obligation.

(4) The following rules apply to the remedies for breach of an obligation created under this section:

(a) The seller may modify or limit the remedies available to the remote purchaser if the modification or limitation is furnished to the remote purchaser no later than the time of purchase. The modification or limitation may be furnished as part of the communication that contains the affirmation of fact, promise or description.

(b) Subject to a modification or limitation of remedy, a seller in breach is liable for incidental or consequential damages under Section 2—715, but the seller is not liable for lost profits.

(c) The remote purchaser may recover as damages for breach of a seller's obligation arising under subsection (2) the loss resulting in the ordinary course of events as determined in any manner that is reasonable.

(5) An obligation that is not a remedial promise is breached if the goods did not conform to the affirmation of

fact, promise or description creating the obligation when the goods left the seller's control.

* * * *

§2—316. EXCLUSION OR MODIFICATION OF WARRANTIES.

* * * *

(2) Subject to subsection (3), to exclude or modify the implied warranty of merchantability or any part of it in a consumer contract the language must be in a record, be conspicuous and state "The seller undertakes no responsibility for the quality of the goods except as otherwise provided in this contract," and in any other contract the language must mention merchantability and in case of a record must be conspicuous. Subject to subsection (3), to exclude or modify the implied warranty of fitness the exclusion must be in a record and be conspicuous. Language to exclude all implied warranties of fitness in a consumer contract must state "The seller assumes no responsibility that the goods will be fit for any particular purpose for which you may be buying these goods, except as otherwise provided in the contract," and in any other contract the language is sufficient if it states, for example, that "There are no warranties which extend beyond the description on the face hereof." Language that satisfies the requirements of this subsection for the exclusion and modification of a warranty in a consumer contract also satisfies the requirements for any other contract.

(3) Notwithstanding subsection (2):

(a) unless the circumstances indicate otherwise, all implied warranties are excluded by expressions like "as is", "with all faults" or other language which in common understanding calls the buyer's attention to the exclusion of warranties, makes plain that there is no implied warranty, and in a consumer contract evidenced by a record is set forth conspicuously in the record; and

(b) when the buyer before entering into the contract has examined the goods or the sample or model as fully as desired or has refused to examine the goods after a demand by the seller there is no implied warranty with regard to defects which an examination ought in the circumstances to have revealed to the buyer; and

(c) an implied warranty can also be excluded or modified by course of dealing or course of performance or usage of trade.

* * * *

§2—318. THIRD PARTY BENEFICIARIES OF WARRANTIES EXPRESS OR IMPLIED

(1) In this section:

(a) "Immediate buyer" means a buyer that enters into a contract with the seller.

(b) "Remote purchaser" means a person that buys or leases goods from an immediate buyer or other person in the normal chain of distribution.

Alternative A to subsection (2)

(2) A seller's warranty whether express or implied to an immediate buyer, a seller's remedial promise to an immediate buyer, or a seller's obligation to a remote purchaser under Section 2—313A or 2—313B extends to any natural person who is in the family or household of the immediate buyer or the remote purchaser or who is a guest in the home of either if it is reasonable to expect that the person may use, consume or be affected by the goods and who is injured in person by breach of the warranty, remedial promise or obligation. A seller may not exclude or limit the operation of this section.

Alternative B to subsection (2)

(2) A seller's warranty whether express or implied to an immediate buyer, a seller's remedial promise to an immediate buyer, or a seller's obligation to a remote purchaser under Section 2—313A or 2—313B extends to any natural person who may reasonably be expected to use, consume or be affected by the goods and who is injured in person by breach of the warranty, remedial promise or obligation. A seller may not exclude or limit the operation of this section.

Alternative C to subsection (2)

(2) A seller's warranty whether express or implied to an immediate buyer, a seller's remedial promise to an immediate buyer, or a seller's obligation to a remote purchaser under Section 2—313A or 2—313B extends to any person that may reasonably be expected to use, consume or be affected by the goods and that is injured by breach of the warranty, remedial promise or obligation. A seller may not exclude or limit the operation of this section with respect to injury to the person of an individual to whom the warranty, remedial promise or obligation extends.

* * * *

Part 5 Performance
* * * *

§2—502. BUYER'S RIGHT TO GOODS ON SELLER'S INSOLVENCY

(1) Subject to subsections (2) and (3) and even though the goods have not been shipped a buyer who that has paid a part or all of the price of goods in which the buyer has a special property under the provisions of the immediately preceding section may on making and keeping good a tender of any unpaid portion of their price recover them from the seller if:

(a) in the case of goods bought by a consumer, the seller repudiates or fails to deliver as required by the contract; or

(b) in all cases, the seller becomes insolvent within ten days after receipt of the first installment on their price.

(2) The buyer's right to recover the goods under subsection (1) vests upon acquisition of a special property, even if the seller had not then repudiated or failed to deliver.

(3) If the identification creating the special property has been made by the buyer, the buyer acquires the right to recover the goods only if they conform to the contract for sale.

* * * *

§2—508. CURE BY SELLER OF IMPROPER TENDER OR DELIVERY; REPLACEMENT

(1) Where the buyer rejects goods or a tender of delivery under Section 2—601 or 2—612 or except in a consumer contract justifiably revokes acceptance under Section 2—608(1)(b) and the agreed time for performance has not expired, a seller that has performed in good faith, upon seasonable notice to the buyer and at the seller's own expense, may cure the breach of contract by making a conforming tender of delivery within the agreed time. The seller shall compensate the buyer for all of the buyer's reasonable expenses caused by the seller's breach of contract and subsequent cure.

(2) Where the buyer rejects goods or a tender of delivery under Section 2—601 or 2—612 or except in a consumer contract justifiably revokes acceptance under Section 2—608(1)(b) and the agreed time for performance has expired, a seller that has performed in good faith, upon seasonable notice to the buyer and at the seller's own expense, may cure the breach of contract, if the cure is appropriate and timely under the

circumstances, by making a tender of conforming goods. The seller shall compensate the buyer for all of the buyer's reasonable expenses caused by the seller's breach of contract and subsequent cure.

§2—509. RISK OF LOSS IN THE ABSENCE OF BREACH

(1) Where the contract requires or authorizes the seller to ship the goods by carrier

>(a) if it does not require the seller to deliver them at a particular destination, the risk of loss passes to the buyer when the goods are delivered to the carrier even though the shipment is under reservation (Section 2—505); but

>(b) if it does require the seller to deliver them at a particular destination and the goods are there tendered while in the possession of the carrier, the risk of loss passes to the buyer when the goods are there so tendered as to enable the buyer to take delivery.

(2) Where the goods are held by a bailee to be delivered without being moved, the risk of loss passes to the buyer

>(a) on the buyer's receipt of a negotiable document of title covering the goods; or

>(b) on acknowledgment by the bailee to the buyer of the buyer's right to possession of the goods; or

>(c) after the buyer's receipt of a non-negotiable document of title or other direction to deliver in a record, as provided in subsection (4)(b) of Section 2—503.

(3) In any case not within subsection (1) or (2), the risk of loss passes to the buyer on the buyer's receipt of the goods.

* * * *

§2—513. BUYER'S RIGHT TO INSPECTION OF GOODS
* * * *

(3) Unless otherwise agreed, the buyer is not entitled to inspect the goods before payment of the price when the contract provides

>(a) for delivery on terms that under applicable course of performance, course of dealing, or usage of trade are interpreted to preclude inspection before payment; or

>(b) for payment against documents of title, except where such payment is due only after the goods are to become available for inspection.

* * * *

Part 6 Breach, Repudiation and Excuse
* * * *

§2—605. WAIVER OF BUYER'S OBJECTIONS BY FAILURE TO PARTICULARIZE

(1) The buyer's failure to state in connection with rejection a particular defect or in connection with revocation of acceptance a defect that justifies revocation precludes the buyer from relying on the unstated defect to justify rejection or revocation of acceptance if the defect is ascertainable by reasonable inspection

>(a) where the seller had a right to cure the defect and could have cured it if stated seasonably; or

>(b) between merchants when the seller has after rejection made a request in a record for a full and final statement in record form of all defects on which the buyer proposes to rely.

(2) A buyer's payment against documents tendered to the buyer made without reservation of rights precludes recovery of the payment for defects apparent on the face of the documents.

* * * *

§2—607. EFFECT OF ACCEPTANCE; NOTICE OF BREACH; BURDEN OF ESTABLISHING BREACH AFTER ACCEPTANCE; NOTICE OF CLAIM OR LITIGATION TO PERSON ANSWERABLE OVER
* * * *

(3) Where a tender has been accepted

>(a) the buyer must within a reasonable time after the buyer discovers or should have discovered any breach notify the seller; however, failure to give timely notice bars the buyer from a remedy only to the extent that the seller is prejudiced by the failure and

>(b) if the claim is one for infringement or the like (subsection (3) of Section 2—312) and the buyer is sued as a result of such a breach the buyer must so notify the seller within a reasonable time after the buyer receives notice of the litigation or be barred from any remedy over for liability established by the litigation.

* * * *

§2—608. REVOCATION OF ACCEPTANCE IN WHOLE OR IN PART
* * * *

(4) If a buyer uses the goods after a rightful rejection or justifiable revocation of acceptance, the following rules apply:

(a) Any use by the buyer that is unreasonable under the circumstances is wrongful as against the seller and is an acceptance only if ratified by the seller.

(b) Any use of the goods that is reasonable under the circumstances is not wrongful as against the seller and is not an acceptance, but in an appropriate case the buyer shall be obligated to the seller for the value of the use to the buyer.

* * * *

§2—612. "INSTALLMENT CONTRACT"; BREACH
* * * *

(2) The buyer may reject any installment which is non-conforming if the non-conformity substantially impairs the value of that installment to the buyer or if the non-conformity is a defect in the required documents; but if the non-conformity does not fall within subsection (3) and the seller gives adequate assurance of its cure the buyer must accept that installment.

(3) Whenever non-conformity or default with respect to one or more installments substantially impairs the value of the whole contract there is a breach of the whole. But the aggrieved party reinstates the contract if the party accepts a non-conforming installment without seasonably notifying of cancellation or if the party brings an action with respect only to past installments or demands performance as to future installments.

* * * *

Part 7 Remedies

§2—702. SELLER'S REMEDIES ON DISCOVERY OF BUYER'S INSOLVENCY
* * * *

(2) Where the seller discovers that the buyer has received goods on credit while insolvent the seller may reclaim the goods upon demand made within a reasonable time after the buyer's receipt of the goods. Except as provided in this subsection the seller may not base a right to reclaim goods on the buyer's fraudulent or innocent misrepresentation of solvency or of intent to pay.

* * * *

§2—705. SELLER'S STOPPAGE OF DELIVERY IN TRANSIT OR OTHERWISE

(1) The seller may stop delivery of goods in the possession of a carrier or other bailee when the seller discovers the buyer to be insolvent (Section 2—702) or when the buyer repudiates or fails to make a payment due before delivery or if for any other reason the seller has a right to withhold or reclaim the goods.

* * * *

§2—706. SELLER'S RESALE INCLUDING CONTRACT FOR RESALE

In an appropriate case involving breach by the buyer, the seller may resell the goods concerned or the undelivered balance thereof. Where the resale is made in good faith and in a commercially reasonable manner the seller may recover the difference between the contract price and the resale price together with any incidental or consequential damages allowed under the provisions of this Article (Section 2—710), but less expenses saved in consequence of the buyer's breach.

* * * *

§2—708. SELLER'S DAMAGES FOR NON-ACCEPTANCE OR REPUDIATION

(1) Subject to subsection (2) and to the provisions of this Article with respect to proof of market price (Section 2—723)

(a) the measure of damages for non-acceptance by the buyer is the difference between the contract price and the market price at the time and place for tender together with any incidental or consequential damages provided in this Article (Section 2—710), but less expenses saved in consequence of the buyer's breach; and

(b) the measure of damages for repudiation by the buyer is the difference between the contract price and the market price at the place for tender at the expiration of a commercially reasonable time after the seller learned of the repudiation, but no later than the time stated in paragraph (a), together with any incidental or consequential damages provided in this Article (Section 2—710), but less expenses saved in consequence of the buyer's breach.

(2) If the measure of damages provided in subsection (1) or in Section 2—706 is inadequate to put the seller in as good a position as performance would have done then the measure of damages is the profit (including reasonable overhead) which the seller would have made from full performance by the buyer, together with any incidental or consequential damages provided in this Article (Section 2—710).

§2—709. ACTION FOR THE PRICE

(1) When the buyer fails to pay the price as it becomes due the seller may recover, together with any incidental or consequential damages under the next section, the price

(a) of goods accepted or of conforming goods lost or damaged within a commercially reasonable time after risk of their loss has passed to the buyer; and

(b) of goods identified to the contract if the seller is unable after reasonable effort to resell them at a reasonable price or the circumstances reasonably indicate that such effort will be unavailing.

* * * *

§2—710. SELLER'S INCIDENTAL AND CONSEQUENTIAL DAMAGES

(1) Incidental damages to an aggrieved seller include any commercially reasonable charges, expenses or commissions incurred in stopping delivery, in the transportation, care and custody of goods after the buyer's breach, in connection with return or resale of the goods or otherwise resulting from the breach.

(2) Consequential damages resulting from the buyer's breach include any loss resulting from general or particular requirements and needs of which the buyer at the time of contracting had reason to know and which could not reasonably be prevented by resale or otherwise.

(3) In a consumer contract, a seller may not recover consequential damages from a consumer.

* * * *

§2—713. BUYER'S DAMAGES FOR NON-DELIVERY OR REPUDIATION

(1) Subject to the provisions of this Article with respect to proof of market price (Section 2—723), if the seller wrongfully fails to deliver or repudiates or the buyer rightfully rejects or justifiably revokes acceptance

(a) the measure of damages in the case of wrongful failure to deliver by the seller or rightful rejection or justifiable revocation of acceptance by the buyer is the difference between the market price at the time for tender under the contract and the contract price together with any incidental or consequential damages provided in this Article (Section 2—715), but less expenses saved in consequence of the seller's breach; and

(b) the measure of damages for repudiation by the seller is the difference between the market price at the expiration of a commercially reasonable time after the buyer learned of the repudiation, but no later than the time stated in paragraph (a), and the contract price together with any incidental or consequential damages provided in this Article (Section 2—715), but less expenses saved in consequence of the seller's breach.

* * * *

§2—725. STATUTE OF LIMITATIONS IN CONTRACTS FOR SALE

(1) Except as otherwise provided in this section, an action for breach of any contract for sale must be commenced within the later of four years after the right of action has accrued under subsection (2) or (3) or one year after the breach was or should have been discovered, but no longer than five years after the right of action accrued. By the original agreement the parties may reduce the period of limitation to not less than one year but may not extend it; however, in a consumer contract, the period of limitation may not be reduced.

(2) Except as otherwise provided in subsection (3), the following rules apply:

(a) Except as otherwise provided in this subsection, a right of action for breach of a contract accrues when the breach occurs, even if the aggrieved party did not have knowledge of the breach.

(b) For breach of a contract by repudiation, a right of action accrues at the earlier of when the aggrieved party elects to treat the repudiation as a breach or when a commercially reasonable time for awaiting performance has expired.

* * * *

Article 2A Leases

§2A—102. SCOPE

This Article applies to any transaction, regardless of form, that creates a lease.

§2A—103. DEFINITIONS AND INDEX OF DEFINITIONS

* * * *

(e) "Consumer lease" means a lease that a lessor regularly engaged in the business of leasing or selling makes to a lessee who is an individual and who takes under the lease primarily for a personal, family, or household purpose [, if the total payments to be made under the lease contract, excluding payments for options to renew or buy, do not exceed $___].

* * * *

(g) "Finance lease" means a lease with respect to which:

(i) the lessor does not select, manufacture or supply the goods;

(ii) the lessor acquires the goods or the right to possession and use of the goods in connection with the lease; and

(iii) one of the following occurs:

(A) the lessee receives a copy of the contract by which the lessor acquired the goods or the right to possession and use of the goods before signing the lease contract;

(B) the lessee's approval of the contract by which the lessor acquired the goods or the right to possession and use of the goods is a condition to effectiveness of the lease contract;

(C) the lessee, before signing the lease contract, receives an accurate and complete statement designating the promises and warranties, and any disclaimers of warranties, limitations or modifications of remedies, or liquidated damages, including those of a third party, such as the manufacturer of the goods, provided to the lessor by the person supplying the goods in connection with or as part of the contract by which the lessor acquired the goods or the right to possession and use of the goods; or

(D) if the lease is not a consumer lease, the lessor, before the lessee signs the lease contract, informs the lessee in writing (a) of the identity of the person supplying the goods to the lessor, unless the lessee has selected that person and directed the lessor to acquire the goods or the right to possession and use of the goods from that person, (b) that the lessee is entitled under this Article to any promises and warranties, including those of any third party, provided to the lessor by the person supplying the goods in connection with or as part of the contract by which the lessor acquired the goods or the right to possession and use of the goods, and (c) that the lessee may communicate with the person supplying the goods to the lessor and receive an accurate and complete statement of those promises and warranties, including any disclaimers and limitations of them or of remedies.

* * * *

(h) "Goods" means all things that are movable at the time of identification to the lease contract, or are fixtures (Section 2A—309), but the term does not include money, documents, instruments, accounts, chattel paper, general intangibles, or minerals or the like, including oil and gas, before extraction. The term also includes the unborn young of animals.

(i) "Installment lease contract" means a lease contract that authorizes or requires the delivery of goods in separate lots to be separately accepted, even though the lease contract contains a clause "each delivery is a separate lease" or its equivalent.

(j) "Lease" means a transfer of the right to possession and use of goods for a term in return for consideration, but a sale, including a sale on approval or a sale or return, or retention or creation of a security interest is not a lease. Unless the context clearly indicates otherwise, the term includes a sublease.

(k) "Lease agreement" means the bargain, with respect to the lease, of the lessor and the lessee in fact as found in their language or by implication from other circumstances including course of dealing or usage of trade or course of performance as provided in this Article. Unless the context clearly indicates otherwise, the term includes a sublease agreement.

(l) "Lease contract" means the total legal obligation that results from the lease agreement as affected by this Article and any other applicable rules of law. Unless the context clearly indicates otherwise, the term includes a sublease contract.

* * * *

(o) "Lessee in ordinary course of business" means a person who in good faith and without knowledge that the lease to him [or her] is in violation of the ownership rights or security interest or leasehold interest of a third party in the goods, leases in ordinary course from a person in the business of selling or leasing goods of that kind but does not include a pawnbroker. "Leasing" may be for cash or by exchange of other property or on secured or unsecured credit and includes receiving goods or documents of title under a pre-existing lease contract but does not include a transfer in bulk or as security for or in total or partial satisfaction of a money debt.

(p) "Lessor" means a person who transfers the right to possession and use of goods under a lease. Unless the context clearly indicates otherwise, the term includes a sublessor.

(q) "Lessor's residual interest" means the lessor's interest in the goods after expiration, termination, or cancellation of the lease contract.

* * * *

§2A—104. LEASES SUBJECT TO OTHER LAW

(1) A lease, although subject to this Article, is also subject to any applicable:

(a) certificate of title statute of this State: (list any certificate of title statutes covering automobiles, trailers, mobile homes, boats, farm tractors, and the like);

(b) certificate of title statute of another jurisdiction (Section 2A—105); or

(c) consumer protection statute of this State, or final consumer protection decision of a court of this State existing on the effective date of this Article.

§2A—105. TERRITORIAL APPLICATION OF ARTICLE TO GOODS COVERED BY CERTIFICATE OF TITLE

Subject to the provisions of Sections 2A—304(3) and 2A—305(3), with respect to goods covered by a certificate of title issued under a statute of this State or of another jurisdiction, compliance and the effect of compliance or noncompliance with a certificate of title statute are governed by the law (including the conflict of laws rules) of the jurisdiction issuing the certificate until the earlier of (a) surrender of the certificate, or (b) four months after the goods are removed from that jurisdiction and thereafter until a new certificate of title is issued by another jurisdiction.

* * * *

§2A—108. UNCONSCIONABILITY

(1) If the court as a matter of law finds a lease contract or any clause of a lease contract to have been unconscionable at the time it was made the court may refuse to enforce the lease contract, or it may enforce the remainder of the lease contract without the unconscionable clause, or it may so limit the application of any unconscionable clause as to avoid any unconscionable result.

(2) With respect to a consumer lease, if the court as a matter of law finds that a lease contract or any clause of a lease contract has been induced by unconscionable conduct or that unconscionable conduct has occurred in the collection of a claim arising from a lease contract, the court may grant appropriate relief.

(3) Before making a finding of unconscionability under subsection (1) or (2), the court, on its own motion or that of a party, shall afford the parties a reasonable opportunity to present evidence as to the setting, purpose, and effect of the lease contract or clause thereof, or of the conduct.

(4) In an action in which the lessee claims unconscionability with respect to a consumer lease:

(a) If the court finds unconscionability under subsection (1) or (2), the court shall award reasonable attorney's fees to the lessee.

(b) If the court does not find unconscionability and the lessee claiming unconscionability has brought or maintained an action he [or she] knew to be groundless, the court shall award reasonable attorney's fees to the party against whom the claim is made.

(c) In determining attorney's fees, the amount of the recovery on behalf of the claimant under subsections (1) and (2) is not controlling.

§2A—109. OPTION TO ACCELERATE AT WILL

(1) A term providing that one party or his [or her] successor in interest may accelerate payment or performance or require collateral or additional collateral "at will" or "when he [or she] deems himself [or herself] insecure" or in words of similar import must be construed to mean that he [or she] has power to do so only if he [or she] in good faith believes that the prospect of payment or performance is impaired.

(2) With respect to a consumer lease, the burden of establishing good faith under subsection (1) is on the party who exercised the power; otherwise the burden of establishing lack of good faith is on the party against whom the power has been exercised.

Part 2 Formation and Construction of Lease Contract

§2A—201. STATUTE OF FRAUDS

(1) A lease contract is not enforceable by way of action or defense unless:

(a) the total payments to be made under the lease contract, excluding payments for options to renew or buy, are less than $1,000; or

(b) there is a writing, signed by the party against whom enforcement is sought or by that party's authorized agent, sufficient to indicate that a lease contract has been made between the parties and to describe the goods leased and the lease term.

(2) Any description of leased goods or of the lease term is sufficient and satisfies subsection (1)(b), whether or not it is specific, if it reasonably identifies what is described.

(3) A writing is not insufficient because it omits or incorrectly states a term agreed upon, but the lease

contract is not enforceable under subsection (1)(b) beyond the lease term and the quantity of goods shown in the writing.

(4) A lease contract that does not satisfy the requirements of subsection (1), but which is valid in other respects, is enforceable:

(a) if the goods are to be specially manufactured or obtained for the lessee and are not suitable for lease or sale to others in the ordinary course of the lessor's business, and the lessor, before notice of repudiation is received and under circumstances that reasonably indicate that the goods are for the lessee, has made either a substantial beginning of their manufacture or commitments for their procurement;

(b) if the party against whom enforcement is sought admits in that party's pleading, testimony or otherwise in court that a lease contract was made, but the lease contract is not enforceable under this provision beyond the quantity of goods admitted; or

(c) with respect to goods that have been received and accepted by the lessee.

(5) The lease term under a lease contract referred to in subsection (4) is:

(a) if there is a writing signed by the party against whom enforcement is sought or by that party's authorized agent specifying the lease term, the term so specified;

(b) if the party against whom enforcement is sought admits in that party's pleading, testimony, or otherwise in court a lease term, the term so admitted; or

(c) a reasonable lease term.

§2A—202. FINAL WRITTEN EXPRESSION: PAROL OR EXTRINSIC EVIDENCE

Terms with respect to which the confirmatory memoranda of the parties agree or which are otherwise set forth in a writing intended by the parties as a final expression of their agreement with respect to such terms as are included therein may not be contradicted by evidence of any prior agreement or of a contemporaneous oral agreement but may be explained or supplemented:

(a) by course of dealing or usage of trade or by course of performance; and

(b) by evidence of consistent additional terms unless the court finds the writing to have been

intended also as a complete and exclusive statement of the terms of the agreement.

* * * *

§2A—205. FIRM OFFERS

An offer by a merchant to lease goods to or from another person in a signed writing that by its terms gives assurance it will be held open is not revocable, for lack of consideration, during the time stated or, if no time is stated, for a reasonable time, but in no event may the period of irrevocability exceed 3 months. Any such term of assurance on a form supplied by the offeree must be separately signed by the offeror.

§2A—206. OFFER AND ACCEPTANCE IN FORMATION OF LEASE CONTRACT

(1) Unless otherwise unambiguously indicated by the language or circumstances, an offer to make a lease contract must be construed as inviting acceptance in any manner and by any medium reasonable in the circumstances.

(2) If the beginning of a requested performance is a reasonable mode of acceptance, an offeror who is not notified of acceptance within a reasonable time may treat the offer as having lapsed before acceptance.

§2A—207. COURSE OF PERFORMANCE OR PRACTICAL CONSTRUCTION

(1) If a lease contract involves repeated occasions for performance by either party with knowledge of the nature of the performance and opportunity for objection to it by the other, any course of performance accepted or acquiesced in without objection is relevant to determine the meaning of the lease agreement.

(2) The express terms of a lease agreement and any course of performance, as well as any course of dealing and usage of trade, must be construed whenever reasonable as consistent with each other; but if that construction is unreasonable, express terms control course of performance, course of performance controls both course of dealing and usage of trade, and course of dealing controls usage of trade.

(3) Subject to the provisions of Section 2A—208 on modification and waiver, course of performance is relevant to show a waiver or modification of any term inconsistent with the course of performance.

§2A—208. MODIFICATION, RESCISSION AND WAIVER

(1) An agreement modifying a lease contract needs no consideration to be binding.

(2) A signed lease agreement that excludes modification or rescission except by a signed writing may not be otherwise modified or rescinded, but, except as between merchants, such a requirement on a form supplied by a merchant must be separately signed by the other party.

(3) Although an attempt at modification or rescission does not satisfy the requirements of subsection (2), it may operate as a waiver.

(4) A party who has made a waiver affecting an executory portion of a lease contract may retract the waiver by reasonable notification received by the other party that strict performance will be required of any term waived, unless the retraction would be unjust in view of a material change of position in reliance on the waiver.

* * * *

§2A—216. THIRD-PARTY BENEFICIARIES OF EXPRESS AND IMPLIED WARRANTIES

Alternative A

A warranty to or for the benefit of a lessee under this Article, whether express or implied, extends to any natural person who is in the family or household of the lessee or who is a guest in the lessee's home if it is reasonable to expect that such person may use, consume, or be affected by the goods and who is injured in person by breach of the warranty. This section does not displace principles of law and equity that extend a warranty to or for the benefit of a lessee to other persons. The operation of this section may not be excluded, modified, or limited, but an exclusion, modification, or limitation of the warranty, including any with respect to rights and remedies, effective against the lessee is also effective against any beneficiary designated under this section.

Alternative B

A warranty to or for the benefit of a lessee under this Article, whether express or implied, extends to any natural person who may reasonably be expected to use, consume, or be affected by the goods and who is injured in person by breach of the warranty. This section does not displace principles of law and equity that extend a warranty to or for the benefit of a lessee to other persons. The operation of this section may not be excluded, modified, or limited, but an exclusion, modification, or limitation of the warranty, including any with respect to rights and remedies, effective against

the lessee is also effective against the beneficiary designated under this section.

Alternative C

A warranty to or for the benefit of a lessee under this Article, whether express or implied, extends to any person who may reasonably be expected to use, consume, or be affected by the goods and who is injured by breach of the warranty. The operation of this section may not be excluded, modified, or limited with respect to injury to the person of an individual to whom the warranty extends, but an exclusion, modification, or limitation of the warranty, including any with respect to rights and remedies, effective against the lessee is also effective against the beneficiary designated under this section.

* * * *

§2A—219. RISK OF LOSS

(1) Except in the case of a finance lease, risk of loss is retained by the lessor and does not pass to the lessee. In the case of a finance lease, risk of loss passes to the lessee.

(2) Subject to the provisions of this Article on the effect of default on risk of loss (Section 2A—220), if risk of loss is to pass to the lessee and the time of passage is not stated, the following rules apply:

(a) If the lease contract requires or authorizes the goods to be shipped by carrier

(i) and it does not require delivery at a particular destination, the risk of loss passes to the lessee when the goods are duly delivered to the carrier; but

(ii) if it does require delivery at a particular destination and the goods are there duly tendered while in the possession of the carrier, the risk of loss passes to the lessee when the goods are there duly so tendered as to enable the lessee to take delivery.

(b) If the goods are held by a bailee to be delivered without being moved, the risk of loss passes to the lessee on acknowledgment by the bailee of the lessee's right to possession of the goods.

(c) In any case not within subsection (a) or (b), the risk of loss passes to the lessee on the lessee's receipt of the goods if the lessor, or, in the case of a finance lease, the supplier, is a merchant; otherwise the risk passes to the lessee on tender of delivery.

§2A—220. EFFECT OF DEFAULT ON RISK OF LOSS

(1) Where risk of loss is to pass to the lessee and the time of passage is not stated:

(a) If a tender or delivery of goods so fails to conform to the lease contract as to give a right of rejection, the risk of their loss remains with the lessor, or, in the case of a finance lease, the supplier, until cure or acceptance.

(b) If the lessee rightfully revokes acceptance, he [or she], to the extent of any deficiency in his [or her] effective insurance coverage, may treat the risk of loss as having remained with the lessor from the beginning.

(2) Whether or not risk of loss is to pass to the lessee, if the lessee as to conforming goods already identified to a lease contract repudiates or is otherwise in default under the lease contract, the lessor, or, in the case of a finance lease, the supplier, to the extent of any deficiency in his [or her] effective insurance coverage may treat the risk of loss as resting on the lessee for a commercially reasonable time.

* * * *

§2A—304. SUBSEQUENT LEASE OF GOODS BY LESSOR

(1) Subject to Section 2A—303, a subsequent lessee from a lessor of goods under an existing lease contract obtains, to the extent of the leasehold interest transferred, the leasehold interest in the goods that the lessor had or had power to transfer, and except as provided in subsection (2) and Section 2A—527(4), takes subject to the existing lease contract. A lessor with voidable title has power to transfer a good leasehold interest to a good faith subsequent lessee for value, but only to the extent set forth in the preceding sentence. If goods have been delivered under a transaction of purchase the lessor has that power even though:

(a) the lessor's transferor was deceived as to the identity of the lessor;

(b) the delivery was in exchange for a check which is later dishonored;

(c) it was agreed that the transaction was to be a "cash sale"; or

(d) the delivery was procured through fraud punishable as larcenous under the criminal law.

(2) A subsequent lessee in the ordinary course of business from a lessor who is a merchant dealing in goods of that kind to whom the goods were entrusted by the existing lessee of that lessor before the interest of the subsequent lessee became enforceable against that lessor obtains, to the extent of the leasehold interest transferred, all of that lessor's and the existing lessee's rights to the goods, and takes free of the existing lease contract.

(3) A subsequent lessee from the lessor of goods that are subject to an existing lease contract and are covered by a certificate of title issued under a statute of this State or of another jurisdiction takes no greater rights than those provided both by this section and by the certificate of title statute.

§2A—305. SALE OR SUBLEASE OF GOODS BY LESSEE

(1) Subject to the provisions of Section 2A—303, a buyer or sublessee from the lessee of goods under an existing lease contract obtains, to the extent of the interest transferred, the leasehold interest in the goods that the lessee had or had power to transfer, and except as provided in subsection (2) and Section 2A—511(4), takes subject to the existing lease contract. A lessee with a voidable leasehold interest has power to transfer a good leasehold interest to a good faith buyer for value or a good faith sublessee for value, but only to the extent set forth in the preceding sentence. When goods have been delivered under a transaction of lease the lessee has that power even though:

(a) the lessor was deceived as to the identity of the lessee;

(b) the delivery was in exchange for a check which is later dishonored; or

(c) the delivery was procured through fraud punishable as larcenous under the criminal law.

(2) A buyer in the ordinary course of business or a sublessee in the ordinary course of business from a lessee who is a merchant dealing in goods of that kind to whom the goods were entrusted by the lessor obtains, to the extent of the interest transferred, all of the lessor's and lessee's rights to the goods, and takes free of the existing lease contract.

(3) A buyer or sublessee from the lessee of goods that are subject to an existing lease contract and are covered by a certificate of title issued under a statute of this State or of another jurisdiction takes no greater rights than those provided both by this section and by the certificate of title statute.

* * * *

§2A—501. DEFAULT: PROCEDURE

(1) Whether the lessor or the lessee is in default under a lease contract is determined by the lease agreement and this Article.

(2) If the lessor or the lessee is in default under the lease contract, the party seeking enforcement has rights and remedies as provided in this Article and, except as limited by this Article, as provided in the lease agreement.

(3) If the lessor or the lessee is in default under the lease contract, the party seeking enforcement may reduce the party's claim to judgment, or otherwise enforce the lease contract by self-help or any available judicial procedure or nonjudicial procedure, including administrative proceeding, arbitration, or the like, in accordance with this Article.

(4) Except as otherwise provided in Section 1—106 (1) or this Article or the lease agreement, the rights and remedies referred to in subsections (2) and (3) are cumulative.

(5) If the lease agreement covers both real property and goods, the party seeking enforcement may proceed under this Part as to the goods, or under other applicable law as to both the real property and the goods in accordance with that party's rights and remedies in respect of the real property, in which case this Part does not apply.

§2A—502. NOTICE AFTER DEFAULT

Except as otherwise provided in this Article or the lease agreement, the lessor or lessee in default under the lease contract is not entitled to notice of default or notice of enforcement from the other party to the lease agreement.

§2A—503. MODIFICATION OR IMPAIRMENT OF RIGHTS AND REMEDIES

(1) Except as otherwise provided in this Article, the lease agreement may include rights and remedies for default in addition to or in substitution for those provided in this Article and may limit or alter the measure of damages recoverable under this Article.

(2) Resort to a remedy provided under this Article or in the lease agreement is optional unless the remedy is expressly agreed to be exclusive. If circumstances cause an exclusive or limited remedy to fail of its essential purpose, or provision for an exclusive remedy is unconscionable, remedy may be had as provided in this Article.

(3) Consequential damages may be liquidated under Section 2A—504, or may otherwise be limited, altered, or excluded unless the limitation, alteration, or exclusion is unconscionable. Limitation, alteration, or exclusion of consequential damages for injury to the person in the case of consumer goods is prima facie unconscionable but limitation, alteration, or exclusion of damages where the loss is commercial is not prima facie unconscionable.

(4) Rights and remedies on default by the lessor or the lessee with respect to any obligation or promise collateral or ancillary to the lease contract are not impaired by this Article.

As amended in 1990.

§2A—504. LIQUIDATION OF DAMAGES

(1) Damages payable by either party for default, or any other act or omission, including indemnity for loss or diminution of anticipated tax benefits or loss or damage to lessor's residual interest, may be liquidated in the lease agreement but only at an amount or by a formula that is reasonable in light of the then anticipated harm caused by the default or other act or omission.

(2) If the lease agreement provides for liquidation of damages, and such provision does not comply with subsection (1), or such provision is an exclusive or limited remedy that circumstances cause to fail of its essential purpose, remedy may be had as provided in this Article.

(3) If the lessor justifiably withholds or stops delivery of goods because of the lessee's default or insolvency (Section 2A—525 or 2A—526), the lessee is entitled to restitution of any amount by which the sum of his [or her] payments exceeds:

(a) the amount to which the lessor is entitled by virtue of terms liquidating the lessor's damages in accordance with subsection (1); or

(b) in the absence of those terms, 20 percent of the then present value of the total rent the lessee was obligated to pay for the balance of the lease term, or, in the case of a consumer lease, the lesser of such amount or $500.

(4) A lessee's right to restitution under subsection (3) is subject to offset to the extent the lessor establishes:

(a) a right to recover damages under the provisions of this Article other than subsection (1); and

(b) the amount or value of any benefits received by the lessee directly or indirectly by reason of the lease contract.

§2A—505. CANCELLATION AND TERMINATION AND EFFECT OF CANCELLATION, TERMINATION, RESCISSION, OR FRAUD ON RIGHTS AND REMEDIES

(1) On cancellation of the lease contract, all obligations that are still executory on both sides are discharged, but any right based on prior default or performance

survives, and the cancelling party also retains any remedy for default of the whole lease contract or any unperformed balance.

(2) On termination of the lease contract, all obligations that are still executory on both sides are discharged but any right based on prior default or performance survives.

(3) Unless the contrary intention clearly appears, expressions of "cancellation," "rescission," or the like of the lease contract may not be construed as a renunciation or discharge of any claim in damages for an antecedent default.

(4) Rights and remedies for material misrepresentation or fraud include all rights and remedies available under this Article for default.

(5) Neither rescission nor a claim for rescission of the lease contract nor rejection or return of the goods may bar or be deemed inconsistent with a claim for damages or other right or remedy.

§2A—506. STATUTE OF LIMITATIONS

(1) An action for default under a lease contract, including breach of warranty or indemnity, must be commenced within 4 years after the cause of action accrued. By the original lease contract the parties may reduce the period of limitation to not less than one year.

(2) A cause of action for default accrues when the act or omission on which the default or breach of warranty is based is or should have been discovered by the aggrieved party, or when the default occurs, whichever is later. A cause of action for indemnity accrues when the act or omission on which the claim for indemnity is based is or should have been discovered by the indemnified party, whichever is later.

(3) If an action commenced within the time limited by subsection (1) is so terminated as to leave available a remedy by another action for the same default or breach of warranty or indemnity, the other action may be commenced after the expiration of the time limited and within 6 months after the termination of the first action unless the termination resulted from voluntary discontinuance or from dismissal for failure or neglect to prosecute.

(4) This section does not alter the law on tolling of the statute of limitations nor does it apply to causes of action that have accrued before this Article becomes effective.

* * * *

§2A—508. LESSEE'S REMEDIES

(1) If a lessor fails to deliver the goods in conformity to the lease contract (Section 2A—509) or repudiates the lease contract (Section 2A—402), or a lessee rightfully rejects the goods (Section 2A—509) or justifiably revokes acceptance of the goods (Section 2A—517), then with respect to any goods involved, and with respect to all of the goods if under an installment lease contract the value of the whole lease contract is substantially impaired (Section 2A—510), the lessor is in default under the lease contract and the lessee may:

   (a) cancel the lease contract (Section 2A—505(1));

   (b) recover so much of the rent and security as has been paid and is just under the circumstances;

   (c) cover and recover damages as to all goods affected whether or not they have been identified to the lease contract (Sections 2A—518 and 2A—520), or recover damages for nondelivery (Sections 2A—519 and 2A—520);

   (d) exercise any other rights or pursue any other remedies provided in the lease contract.

(2) If a lessor fails to deliver the goods in conformity to the lease contract or repudiates the lease contract, the lessee may also:

   (a) if the goods have been identified, recover them (Section 2A—522); or

   (b) in a proper case, obtain specific performance or replevy the goods (Section 2A—521).

(3) If a lessor is otherwise in default under a lease contract, the lessee may exercise the rights and pursue the remedies provided in the lease contract, which may include a right to cancel the lease, and in Section 2A—519(3).

(4) If a lessor has breached a warranty, whether express or implied, the lessee may recover damages (Section 2A—519(4)).

(5) On rightful rejection or justifiable revocation of acceptance, a lessee has a security interest in goods in the lessee's possession or control for any rent and security that has been paid and any expenses reasonably incurred in their inspection, receipt, transportation, and care and custody and may hold those goods and dispose of them in good faith and in a commercially reasonable manner, subject to Section 2A—527(5).

(6) Subject to the provisions of Section 2A—407, a lessee, on notifying the lessor of the lessee's intention to do so, may deduct all or any part of the damages resulting from any default under the lease contract

from any part of the rent still due under the same lease contract.

§2A—509. LESSEE'S RIGHTS ON IMPROPER DELIVERY; RIGHTFUL REJECTION

(1) Subject to the provisions of Section 2A—510 on default in installment lease contracts, if the goods or the tender or delivery fail in any respect to conform to the lease contract, the lessee may reject or accept the goods or accept any commercial unit or units and reject the rest of the goods.

(2) Rejection of goods is ineffective unless it is within a reasonable time after tender or delivery of the goods and the lessee seasonably notifies the lessor.

* * * *

§2A—512. LESSEE'S DUTIES AS TO RIGHTFULLY REJECTED GOODS

(1) Except as otherwise provided with respect to goods that threaten to decline in value speedily (Section 2A—511) and subject to any security interest of a lessee (Section 2A—508(5)):

    (a) the lessee, after rejection of goods in the lessee's possession, shall hold them with reasonable care at the lessor's or the supplier's disposition for a reasonable time after the lessee's seasonable notification of rejection;

    (b) if the lessor or the supplier gives no instructions within a reasonable time after notification of rejection, the lessee may store the rejected goods for the lessor's or the supplier's account or ship them to the lessor or the supplier or dispose of them for the lessor's or the supplier's account with reimbursement in the manner provided in Section 2A—511; but

    (c) the lessee has no further obligations with regard to goods rightfully rejected.

(2) Action by the lessee pursuant to subsection (1) is not acceptance or conversion.

§2A—513. CURE BY LESSOR OF IMPROPER TENDER OR DELIVERY; REPLACEMENT

(1) If any tender or delivery by the lessor or the supplier is rejected because non-conforming and the time for performance has not yet expired, the lessor or the supplier may seasonably notify the lessee of the lessor's or the supplier's intention to cure and may then make a conforming delivery within the time provided in the lease contract.

(2) If the lessee rejects a non-conforming tender that the lessor or the supplier had reasonable grounds to believe would be acceptable with or without money allowance, the lessor or the supplier may have a further reasonable time to substitute a conforming tender if he [or she] seasonably notifies the lessee.

* * * *

Revised Article 3 Negotiable Instruments

Part 1 General Provisions and Definitions

§3—102. SUBJECT MATTER

(a) This Article applies to negotiable instruments. It does not apply to money, to payment orders governed by Article 4A, or to securities governed by Article 8.

(b) If there is conflict between this Article and Article 4 or 9, Articles 4 and 9 govern.

(c) Regulations of the Board of Governors of the Federal Reserve System and operating circulars of the Federal Reserve Banks supersede any inconsistent provision of this Article to the extent of the inconsistency.

§3—103. DEFINITIONS

(a) In this Article:

    (1) "Acceptor" means a drawee who has accepted a draft.

    (2) "Drawee" means a person ordered in a draft to make payment.

    (3) "Drawer" means a person who signs or is identified in a draft as a person ordering payment.

    (4) "Good faith" means honesty in fact and the observance of reasonable commercial standards of fair dealing.

    (5) "Maker" means a person who signs or is identified in a note as a person undertaking to pay.

    (6) "Order" means a written instruction to pay money signed by the person giving the instruction. The instruction may be addressed to any person, including the person giving the instruction, or to one or more persons jointly or in the alternative but not in succession. An authorization to pay is not an order unless the person authorized to pay is also instructed to pay.

    (7) "Ordinary care" in the case of a person engaged in business means observance of reasonable

commercial standards, prevailing in the area in which the person is located, with respect to the business in which the person is engaged. In the case of a bank that takes an instrument for processing for collection or payment by automated means, reasonable commercial standards do not require the bank to examine the instrument if the failure to examine does not violate the bank's prescribed procedures and the bank's procedures do not vary unreasonably from general banking usage not disapproved by this Article or Article 4.

(8) "Party" means a party to an instrument.

§3—104. NEGOTIABLE INSTRUMENT

(a) Except as provided in subsections (c) and (d), "negotiable instrument" means an unconditional promise or order to pay a fixed amount of money, with or without interest or other charges described in the promise or order, if it:

(1) is payable to bearer or to order at the time it is issued or first comes into possession of a holder;

(2) is payable on demand or at a definite time; and

(3) does not state any other undertaking or instruction by the person promising or ordering payment to do any act in addition to the payment of money, but the promise or order may contain (i) an undertaking or power to give, maintain, or protect collateral to secure payment, (ii) an authorization or power to the holder to confess judgment or realize on or dispose of collateral, or (iii) a waiver of the benefit of any law intended for the advantage or protection of an obligor.

(b) "Instrument" means a negotiable instrument.

(c) An order that meets all of the requirements of subsection (a), except paragraph (1), and otherwise falls within the definition of "check" in subsection (f) is a negotiable instrument and a check.

(d) A promise or order other than a check is not an instrument if, at the time it is issued or first comes into possession of a holder, it contains a conspicuous statement, however expressed, to the effect that the promise or order is not negotiable or is not an instrument governed by this Article.

(e) An instrument is a "note" if it is a promise and is a "draft" if it is an order. If an instrument falls within the definition of both "note" and "draft," a person entitled to enforce the instrument may treat it as either.

(f) "Check" means (i) a draft, other than a documentary draft, payable on demand and drawn on a bank or (ii) a

cashier's check or teller's check. An instrument may be a check even though it is described on its face by another term, such as "money order."

(g) "Cashier's check" means a draft with respect to which the drawer and drawee are the same bank or branches of the same bank.

(h) "Teller's check" means a draft drawn by a bank (i) on another bank, or (ii) payable at or through a bank.

(i) "Traveler's check" means an instrument that (i) is payable on demand, (ii) is drawn on or payable at or through a bank, (iii) is designated by the term "traveler's check" or by a substantially similar term, and (iv) requires, as a condition to payment, a countersignature by a person whose specimen signature appears on the instrument.

(j) "Certificate of deposit" means an instrument containing an acknowledgment by a bank that a sum of money has been received by the bank and a promise by the bank to repay the sum of money. A certificate of deposit is a note of the bank.

* * * *

§3—106. UNCONDITIONAL PROMISE OR ORDER

(a) Except as provided in this section, for the purposes of Section 3—104(a), a promise or order is unconditional unless it states (i) an express condition to payment, (ii) that the promise or order is subject to or governed by another writing, or (iii) that rights or obligations with respect to the promise or order are stated in another writing. A reference to another writing does not of itself make the promise or order conditional.

(b) A promise or order is not made conditional (i) by a reference to another writing for a statement of rights with respect to collateral, prepayment, or acceleration, or (ii) because payment is limited to resort to a particular fund or source.

(c) If a promise or order requires, as a condition to payment, a countersignature by a person whose specimen signature appears on the promise or order, the condition does not make the promise or order conditional for the purposes of Section 3—104(a). If the person whose specimen signature appears on an instrument fails to countersign the instrument, the failure to countersign is a defense to the obligation of the issuer, but the failure does not prevent a transferee of the instrument from becoming a holder of the instrument.

(d) If a promise or order at the time it is issued or first comes into possession of a holder contains a statement, required by applicable statutory or administrative law, to the effect that the rights of a holder or transferee are subject to claims or defenses that the issuer could assert against the original payee, the promise or order is not thereby made conditional for the purposes of Section 3—104(a); but if the promise or order is an instrument, there cannot be a holder in due course of the instrument.

§3—107. INSTRUMENT PAYABLE IN FOREIGN MONEY

Unless the instrument otherwise provides, an instrument that states the amount payable in foreign money may be paid in the foreign money or in an equivalent amount in dollars calculated by using the current bank-offered spot rate at the place of payment for the purchase of dollars on the day on which the instrument is paid.

§3—108. PAYABLE ON DEMAND OR AT DEFINITE TIME

(a) A promise or order is "payable on demand" if it (i) states that it is payable on demand or at sight, or otherwise indicates that it is payable at the will of the holder, or (ii) does not state any time of payment.

(b) A promise or order is "payable at a definite time" if it is payable on elapse of a definite period of time after sight or acceptance or at a fixed date or dates or at a time or times readily ascertainable at the time the promise or order is issued, subject to rights of (i) prepayment, (ii) acceleration, (iii) extension at the option of the holder, or (iv) extension to a further definite time at the option of the maker or acceptor or automatically upon or after a specified act or event.

(c) If an instrument, payable at a fixed date, is also payable upon demand made before the fixed date, the instrument is payable on demand until the fixed date and, if demand for payment is not made before that date, becomes payable at a definite time on the fixed date.

§3—109. PAYABLE TO BEARER OR TO ORDER

(a) A promise or order is payable to bearer if it:

(1) states that it is payable to bearer or to the order of bearer or otherwise indicates that the person in possession of the promise or order is entitled to payment;

(2) does not state a payee; or

(3) states that it is payable to or to the order of cash or otherwise indicates that it is not payable to an identified person.

(b) A promise or order that is not payable to bearer is payable to order if it is payable (i) to the order of an identified person or (ii) to an identified person or order. A promise or order that is payable to order is payable to the identified person.

(c) An instrument payable to bearer may become payable to an identified person if it is specially indorsed pursuant to Section 3—205(a). An instrument payable to an identified person may become payable to bearer if it is indorsed in blank pursuant to Section 3—205(b).

§3—110. IDENTIFICATION OF PERSON TO WHOM INSTRUMENT IS PAYABLE

(a) The person to whom an instrument is initially payable is determined by the intent of the person, whether or not authorized, signing as, or in the name or behalf of, the issuer of the instrument. The instrument is payable to the person intended by the signer even if that person is identified in the instrument by a name or other identification that is not that of the intended person. If more than one person signs in the name or behalf of the issuer of an instrument and all the signers do not intend the same person as payee, the instrument is payable to any person intended by one or more of the signers.

(b) If the signature of the issuer of an instrument is made by automated means, such as a check-writing machine, the payee of the instrument is determined by the intent of the person who supplied the name or identification of the payee, whether or not authorized to do so.

(c) A person to whom an instrument is payable may be identified in any way, including by name, identifying number, office, or account number.

§3—111. PLACE OF PAYMENT

Except as otherwise provided for items in Article 4, an instrument is payable at the place of payment stated in the instrument. If no place of payment is stated, an instrument is payable at the address of the drawee or maker stated in the instrument. If no address is stated, the place of payment is the place of business of the drawee or maker. If a drawee or maker has more than one place of business, the place of payment is any place of business of the drawee or maker chosen by the person entitled to enforce the instrument. If the drawee or maker has no place of business, the place of payment is the residence of the drawee or maker.

§3—112. INTEREST

(a) Unless otherwise provided in the instrument, (i) an instrument is not payable with interest, and (ii) interest on an interest-bearing instrument is payable from the date of the instrument.

(b) Interest may be stated in an instrument as a fixed or variable amount of money or it may be expressed as a fixed or variable rate or rates. The amount or rate of interest may be stated or described in the instrument in any manner and may require reference to information not contained in the instrument. If an instrument provides for interest, but the amount of interest payable cannot be ascertained from the description, interest is payable at the judgment rate in effect at the place of payment of the instrument and at the time interest first accrues.

§3—113. DATE OF INSTRUMENT

(a) An instrument may be antedated or postdated. The date stated determines the time of payment if the instrument is payable at a fixed period after date. Except as provided in Section 4—401(c), an instrument payable on demand is not payable before the date of the instrument.

(b) If an instrument is undated, its date is the date of its issue or, in the case of an unissued instrument, the date it first comes into possession of a holder.

§3—114. CONTRADICTORY TERMS OF INSTRUMENT

If an instrument contains contradictory terms, typewritten terms prevail over printed terms, handwritten terms prevail over both, and words prevail over numbers.

§3—115. INCOMPLETE INSTRUMENT

(a) "Incomplete instrument" means a signed writing, whether or not issued by the signer, the contents of which show at the time of signing that it is incomplete but that the signer intended it to be completed by the addition of words or numbers.

(b) Subject to subsection (c), if an incomplete instrument is an instrument under Section 3—104, it may be enforced according to its terms if it is not completed, or according to its terms as augmented by completion. If an incomplete instrument is not an instrument under Section 3—104, but, after completion, the requirements of Section 3—104 are met, the instrument may be enforced according to its terms as augmented by completion.

(c) If words or numbers are added to an incomplete instrument without authority of the signer, there is an alteration of the incomplete instrument under Section 3—407.

(d) The burden of establishing that words or numbers were added to an incomplete instrument without authority of the signer is on the person asserting the lack of authority.

§3—116. JOINT AND SEVERAL LIABILITY; CONTRIBUTION

(a) Except as otherwise provided in the instrument, two or more persons who have the same liability on an instrument as makers, drawers, acceptors, indorsers who indorse as joint payees, or anomalous indorsers are jointly and severally liable in the capacity in which they sign.

(b) Except as provided in Section 3—419(e) or by agreement of the affected parties, a party having joint and several liability who pays the instrument is entitled to receive from any party having the same joint and several liability contribution in accordance with applicable law.

(c) Discharge of one party having joint and several liability by a person entitled to enforce the instrument does not affect the right under subsection (b) of a party having the same joint and several liability to receive contribution from the party discharged.

* * * *

§3—118. STATUTE OF LIMITATIONS

(a) Except as provided in subsection (e), an action to enforce the obligation of a party to pay a note payable at a definite time must be commenced within six years after the due date or dates stated in the note or, if a due date is accelerated, within six years after the accelerated due date.

(b) Except as provided in subsection (d) or (e), if demand for payment is made to the maker of a note payable on demand, an action to enforce the obligation of a party to pay the note must be commenced within six years after the demand. If no demand for payment is made to the maker, an action to enforce the note is barred if neither principal nor interest on the note has been paid for a continuous period of 10 years.

(c) Except as provided in subsection (d), an action to enforce the obligation of a party to an unaccepted draft to pay the draft must be commenced within three years after dishonor of the draft or 10 years after the date of the draft, whichever period expires first.

(d) An action to enforce the obligation of the acceptor of a certified check or the issuer of a teller's check, cashier's check, or traveler's check must be commenced within three years after demand for payment is made to the acceptor or issuer, as the case may be.

(e) An action to enforce the obligation of a party to a certificate of deposit to pay the instrument must be commenced within six years after demand for payment is made to the maker, but if the instrument states a due date and the maker is not required to pay before that date, the six-year period begins when a demand for payment is in effect and the due date has passed.

(f) An action to enforce the obligation of a party to pay an accepted draft, other than a certified check, must be commenced (i) within six years after the due date or dates stated in the draft or acceptance if the obligation of the acceptor is payable at a definite time, or (ii) within six years after the date of the acceptance if the obligation of the acceptor is payable on demand.

(g) Unless governed by other law regarding claims for indemnity or contribution, an action (i) for conversion of an instrument, for money had and received, or like action based on conversion, (ii) for breach of warranty, or (iii) to enforce an obligation, duty, or right arising under this Article and not governed by this section must be commenced within three years after the [cause of action] accrues.

* * * *

Part 2 Negotiation, Transfer, and Indorsement

§3—201. NEGOTIATION

(a) "Negotiation" means a transfer of possession, whether voluntary or involuntary, of an instrument by a person other than the issuer to a person who thereby becomes its holder.

(b) Except for negotiation by a remitter, if an instrument is payable to an identified person, negotiation requires transfer of possession of the instrument and its indorsement by the holder. If an instrument is payable to bearer, it may be negotiated by transfer of possession alone.

* * * *

§3—203. TRANSFER OF INSTRUMENT; RIGHTS ACQUIRED BY TRANSFER

(a) An instrument is transferred when it is delivered by a person other than its issuer for the purpose of giving to the person receiving delivery the right to enforce the instrument.

(b) Transfer of an instrument, whether or not the transfer is a negotiation, vests in the transferee any right of the transferor to enforce the instrument, including any right as a holder in due course, but the transferee cannot acquire rights of a holder in due course by a transfer, directly or indirectly, from a holder in due course if the transferee engaged in fraud or illegality affecting the instrument.

(c) Unless otherwise agreed, if an instrument is transferred for value and the transferee does not become a holder because of lack of indorsement by the transferor, the transferee has a specifically enforceable right to the unqualified indorsement of the transferor, but negotiation of the instrument does not occur until the indorsement is made.

(d) If a transferor purports to transfer less than the entire instrument, negotiation of the instrument does not occur. The transferee obtains no rights under this Article and has only the rights of a partial assignee.

§3—204. INDORSEMENT

(a) "Indorsement" means a signature, other than that of a signer as maker, drawer, or acceptor, that alone or accompanied by other words is made on an instrument for the purpose of (i) negotiating the instrument, (ii) restricting payment of the instrument, or (iii) incurring indorser's liability on the instrument, but regardless of the intent of the signer, a signature and its accompanying words is an indorsement unless the accompanying words, terms of the instrument, place of the signature, or other circumstances unambiguously indicate that the signature was made for a purpose other than indorsement. For the purpose of determining whether a signature is made on an instrument, a paper affixed to the instrument is a part of the instrument.

(b) "Indorser" means a person who makes an indorsement.

(c) For the purpose of determining whether the transferee of an instrument is a holder, an indorsement that transfers a security interest in the instrument is effective as an unqualified indorsement of the instrument.

(d) If an instrument is payable to a holder under a name that is not the name of the holder, indorsement may be made by the holder in the name stated in the instrument or in the holder's name or both, but signature in both names may be required by a person paying or taking the instrument for value or collection.

§3—205. SPECIAL INDORSEMENT; BLANK INDORSEMENT; ANOMALOUS INDORSEMENT

(a) If an indorsement is made by the holder of an instrument, whether payable to an identified person or payable to bearer, and the indorsement identifies a person to whom it makes the instrument payable, it is a "special indorsement." When specially indorsed, an instrument becomes payable to the identified person and may be negotiated only by the indorsement of that person. The principles stated in Section 3—110 apply to special indorsements.

(b) If an indorsement is made by the holder of an instrument and it is not a special indorsement, it is a "blank indorsement." When indorsed in blank, an instrument becomes payable to bearer and may be negotiated by transfer of possession alone until specially indorsed.

(c) The holder may convert a blank indorsement that consists only of a signature into a special indorsement by writing, above the signature of the indorser, words identifying the person to whom the instrument is made payable.

(d) "Anomalous indorsement" means an indorsement made by a person who is not the holder of the instrument. An anomalous indorsement does not affect the manner in which the instrument may be negotiated.

§3—206. RESTRICTIVE INDORSEMENT

(a) An indorsement limiting payment to a particular person or otherwise prohibiting further transfer or negotiation of the instrument is not effective to prevent further transfer or negotiation of the instrument.

(b) An indorsement stating a condition to the right of the indorsee to receive payment does not affect the right of the indorsee to enforce the instrument. A person paying the instrument or taking it for value or collection may disregard the condition, and the rights and liabilities of that person are not affected by whether the condition has been fulfilled.

(c) If an instrument bears an indorsement (i) described in Section 4—201(b), or (ii) in blank or to a particular bank using the words "for deposit," "for collection," or other words indicating a purpose of having the instrument collected by a bank for the indorser or for a particular account, the following rules apply:

(1) A person, other than a bank, who purchases the instrument when so indorsed converts the instrument unless the amount paid for the instrument is received by the indorser or applied consistently with the indorsement.

(2) A depositary bank that purchases the instrument or takes it for collection when so indorsed converts the instrument unless the amount paid

by the bank with respect to the instrument is received by the indorser or applied consistently with the indorsement.

(3) A payor bank that is also the depositary bank or that takes the instrument for immediate payment over the counter from a person other than a collecting bank converts the instrument unless the proceeds of the instrument are received by the indorser or applied consistently with the indorsement.

(4) Except as otherwise provided in paragraph (3), a payor bank or intermediary bank may disregard the indorsement and is not liable if the proceeds of the instrument are not received by the indorser or applied consistently with the indorsement.

(d) Except for an indorsement covered by subsection (c), if an instrument bears an indorsement using words to the effect that payment is to be made to the indorsee as agent, trustee, or other fiduciary for the benefit of the indorser or another person, the following rules apply:

(1) Unless there is notice of breach of fiduciary duty as provided in Section 3—307, a person who purchases the instrument from the indorsee or takes the instrument from the indorsee for collection or payment may pay the proceeds of payment or the value given for the instrument to the indorsee without regard to whether the indorsee violates a fiduciary duty to the indorser.

(2) A subsequent transferee of the instrument or person who pays the instrument is neither given notice nor otherwise affected by the restriction in the indorsement unless the transferee or payor knows that the fiduciary dealt with the instrument or its proceeds in breach of fiduciary duty.

(e) The presence on an instrument of an indorsement to which this section applies does not prevent a purchaser of the instrument from becoming a holder in due course of the instrument unless the purchaser is a converter under subsection (c) or has notice or knowledge of breach of fiduciary duty as stated in subsection (d).

(f) In an action to enforce the obligation of a party to pay the instrument, the obligor has a defense if payment would violate an indorsement to which this section applies and the payment is not permitted by this section.

§3—207. REACQUISITION

Reacquisition of an instrument occurs if it is transferred to a former holder, by negotiation or otherwise. A former holder who reacquires the instrument may cancel indorsements made after the reacquirer first became a holder of the instrument. If the cancellation causes the instrument to be payable to the reacquirer or to bearer, the reacquirer may negotiate the instrument. An indorser whose indorsement is canceled is discharged, and the discharge is effective against any subsequent holder.

Part 3 Enforcement of Instruments

§3—301. PERSON ENTITLED TO ENFORCE INSTRUMENT

"Person entitled to enforce" an instrument means (i) the holder of the instrument, (ii) a nonholder in possession of the instrument who has the rights of a holder, or (iii) a person not in possession of the instrument who is entitled to enforce the instrument pursuant to Section 3—309 or 3—418(d). A person may be a person entitled to enforce the instrument even though the person is not the owner of the instrument or is in wrongful possession of the instrument.

§3—302. HOLDER IN DUE COURSE

(a) Subject to subsection (c) and Section 3—106(d), "holder in due course" means the holder of an instrument if:

(1) the instrument when issued or negotiated to the holder does not bear such apparent evidence of forgery or alteration or is not otherwise so irregular or incomplete as to call into question its authenticity; and

(2) the holder took the instrument (i) for value, (ii) in good faith, (iii) without notice that the instrument is overdue or has been dishonored or that there is an uncured default with respect to payment of another instrument issued as part of the same series, (iv) without notice that the instrument contains an unauthorized signature or has been altered, (v) without notice of any claim to the instrument described in Section 3—306, and (vi) without notice that any party has a defense or claim in recoupment described in Section 3—305(a).

(b) Notice of discharge of a party, other than discharge in an insolvency proceeding, is not notice of a defense under subsection (a), but discharge is effective against a person who became a holder in due course with notice of the discharge. Public filing or recording of a document does not of itself constitute notice of a defense, claim in recoupment, or claim to the instrument.

(c) Except to the extent a transferor or predecessor in interest has rights as a holder in due course, a person does not acquire rights of a holder in due course of an instrument taken (i) by legal process or by purchase in an execution, bankruptcy, or creditor's sale or similar proceeding, (ii) by purchase as part of a bulk transaction not in ordinary course of business of the transferor, or (iii) as the successor in interest to an estate or other organization.

(d) If, under Section 3—303(a)(1), the promise of performance that is the consideration for an instrument has been partially performed, the holder may assert rights as a holder in due course of the instrument only to the fraction of the amount payable under the instrument equal to the value of the partial performance divided by the value of the promised performance.

(e) If (i) the person entitled to enforce an instrument has only a security interest in the instrument and (ii) the person obliged to pay the instrument has a defense, claim in recoupment, or claim to the instrument that may be asserted against the person who granted the security interest, the person entitled to enforce the instrument may assert rights as a holder in due course only to an amount payable under the instrument which, at the time of enforcement of the instrument, does not exceed the amount of the unpaid obligation secured.

(f) To be effective, notice must be received at a time and in a manner that gives a reasonable opportunity to act on it.

(g) This section is subject to any law limiting status as a holder in due course in particular classes of transactions.

§3—303. VALUE AND CONSIDERATION

(a) An instrument is issued or transferred for value if:

(1) the instrument is issued or transferred for a promise of performance, to the extent the promise has been performed;

(2) the transferee acquires a security interest or other lien in the instrument other than a lien obtained by judicial proceeding;

(3) the instrument is issued or transferred as payment of, or as security for, an antecedent claim against any person, whether or not the claim is due;

(4) the instrument is issued or transferred in exchange for a negotiable instrument; or

(5) the instrument is issued or transferred in exchange for the incurring of an irrevocable obligation to a third party by the person taking the instrument.

(b) "Consideration" means any consideration sufficient to support a simple contract. The drawer or maker of an instrument has a defense if the instrument is issued without consideration. If an instrument is issued for a promise of performance, the issuer has a defense to the extent performance of the promise is due and the promise has not been performed. If an instrument is issued for value as stated in subsection (a), the instrument is also issued for consideration.

§3—304. OVERDUE INSTRUMENT

(a) An instrument payable on demand becomes overdue at the earliest of the following times:

(1) on the day after the day demand for payment is duly made;

(2) if the instrument is a check, 90 days after its date; or

(3) if the instrument is not a check, when the instrument has been outstanding for a period of time after its date which is unreasonably long under the circumstances of the particular case in light of the nature of the instrument and usage of the trade.

(b) With respect to an instrument payable at a definite time the following rules apply:

(1) If the principal is payable in installments and a due date has not been accelerated, the instrument becomes overdue upon default under the instrument for nonpayment of an installment, and the instrument remains overdue until the default is cured.

(2) If the principal is not payable in installments and the due date has not been accelerated, the instrument becomes overdue on the day after the due date.

(3) If a due date with respect to principal has been accelerated, the instrument becomes overdue on the day after the accelerated due date.

(c) Unless the due date of principal has been accelerated, an instrument does not become overdue if there is default in payment of interest but no default in payment of principal.

§3—305. DEFENSES AND CLAIMS IN RECOUPMENT

(a) Except as stated in subsection (b), the right to enforce the obligation of a party to pay an instrument is subject to the following:

(1) a defense of the obligor based on (i) infancy of the obligor to the extent it is a defense to a simple contract, (ii) duress, lack of legal capacity, or illegality of the transaction which, under other law, nullifies the obligation of the obligor, (iii) fraud that induced the obligor to sign the instrument with neither knowledge nor reasonable opportunity to learn of its character or its essential terms, or (iv) discharge of the obligor in insolvency proceedings;

(2) a defense of the obligor stated in another section of this Article or a defense of the obligor that would be available if the person entitled to enforce the instrument were enforcing a right to payment under a simple contract; and

(3) a claim in recoupment of the obligor against the original payee of the instrument if the claim arose from the transaction that gave rise to the instrument; but the claim of the obligor may be asserted against a transferee of the instrument only to reduce the amount owing on the instrument at the time the action is brought.

(b) The right of a holder in due course to enforce the obligation of a party to pay the instrument is subject to defenses of the obligor stated in subsection (a)(1), but is not subject to defenses of the obligor stated in subsection (a)(2) or claims in recoupment stated in subsection (a)(3) against a person other than the holder.

(c) Except as stated in subsection (d), in an action to enforce the obligation of a party to pay the instrument, the obligor may not assert against the person entitled to enforce the instrument a defense, claim in recoupment, or claim to the instrument (Section 3—306) of another person, but the other person's claim to the instrument may be asserted by the obligor if the other person is joined in the action and personally asserts the claim against the person entitled to enforce the instrument. An obligor is not obliged to pay the instrument if the person seeking enforcement of the instrument does not have rights of a holder in due course and the obligor proves that the instrument is a lost or stolen instrument.

(d) In an action to enforce the obligation of an accommodation party to pay an instrument, the accommodation party may assert against the person entitled to enforce the instrument any defense or claim in recoupment under subsection (a) that the accommodated party could assert against the person entitled to enforce the instrument, except the defenses of discharge in insolvency proceedings, infancy, and lack of legal capacity.

§3—306. CLAIMS TO AN INSTRUMENT

A person taking an instrument, other than a person having rights of a holder in due course, is subject to a claim of a property or possessory right in the instrument or its proceeds, including a claim to rescind a negotiation and to recover the instrument or its proceeds. A person having rights of a holder in due course takes free of the claim to the instrument.

§3—307. NOTICE OF BREACH OF FIDUCIARY DUTY

(a) In this section:

(1) "Fiduciary" means an agent, trustee, partner, corporate officer or director, or other representative owing a fiduciary duty with respect to an instrument.

(2) "Represented person" means the principal, beneficiary, partnership, corporation, or other person to whom the duty stated in paragraph (1) is owed.

(b) If (i) an instrument is taken from a fiduciary for payment or collection or for value, (ii) the taker has knowledge of the fiduciary status of the fiduciary, and (iii) the represented person makes a claim to the instrument or its proceeds on the basis that the transaction of the fiduciary is a breach of fiduciary duty, the following rules apply:

(1) Notice of breach of fiduciary duty by the fiduciary is notice of the claim of the represented person.

(2) In the case of an instrument payable to the represented person or the fiduciary as such, the taker has notice of the breach of fiduciary duty if the instrument is (i) taken in payment of or as security for a debt known by the taker to be the personal debt of the fiduciary, (ii) taken in a transaction known by the taker to be for the personal benefit of the fiduciary, or (iii) deposited to an account other than an account of the fiduciary, as such, or an account of the represented person.

(3) If an instrument is issued by the represented person or the fiduciary as such, and made payable to the fiduciary personally, the taker does not have notice of the breach of fiduciary duty unless the taker knows of the breach of fiduciary duty.

(4) If an instrument is issued by the represented person or the fiduciary as such, to the taker as payee, the taker has notice of the breach of fiduciary duty if the instrument is (i) taken in payment of or as security for a debt known by the taker to be the personal debt of the fiduciary, (ii) taken in a transaction known by the taker to be for the personal benefit of the fiduciary, or (iii) deposited to an account other than an account of the fiduciary, as such, or an account of the represented person.

§3—308. PROOF OF SIGNATURES AND STATUS AS HOLDER IN DUE COURSE

(a) In an action with respect to an instrument, the authenticity of, and authority to make, each signature on the instrument is admitted unless specifically denied in the pleadings. If the validity of a signature is denied in the pleadings, the burden of establishing validity is on the person claiming validity, but the signature is presumed to be authentic and authorized unless the action is to enforce the liability of the purported signer and the signer is dead or incompetent at the time of trial of the issue of validity of the signature. If an action to enforce the instrument is brought against a person as the undisclosed principal of a person who signed the instrument as a party to the instrument, the plaintiff has the burden of establishing that the defendant is liable on the instrument as a represented person under Section 3—402(a).

(b) If the validity of signatures is admitted or proved and there is compliance with subsection (a), a plaintiff producing the instrument is entitled to payment if the plaintiff proves entitlement to enforce the instrument under Section 3—301, unless the defendant proves a defense or claim in recoupment. If a defense or claim in recoupment is proved, the right to payment of the plaintiff is subject to the defense or claim, except to the extent the plaintiff proves that the plaintiff has rights of a holder in due course which are not subject to the defense or claim.

§3—309. ENFORCEMENT OF LOST, DESTROYED, OR STOLEN INSTRUMENT

(a) A person not in possession of an instrument is entitled to enforce the instrument if (i) the person was in possession of the instrument and entitled to enforce it when loss of possession occurred, (ii) the loss of possession was not the result of a transfer by the person or a lawful seizure, and (iii) the person cannot reasonably obtain possession of the instrument because the instrument was destroyed, its whereabouts cannot be determined, or it is in the wrongful possession of an unknown person or a person that cannot be found or is not amenable to service of process.

(b) A person seeking enforcement of an instrument under subsection (a) must prove the terms of the instrument and the person's right to enforce the instrument. If that proof is made, Section 3—308 applies to the case as if the person seeking enforcement had produced the instrument. The court may not enter judgment in favor of the person seeking enforcement unless it finds that the person required to pay the instrument is adequately protected against loss that might occur by reason of a claim by another person to enforce the instrument. Adequate protection may be provided by any reasonable means.

§3—310. EFFECT OF INSTRUMENT ON OBLIGATION FOR WHICH TAKEN

(a) Unless otherwise agreed, if a certified check, cashier's check, or teller's check is taken for an obligation, the obligation is discharged to the same extent discharge would result if an amount of money equal to the amount of the instrument were taken in payment of the obligation. Discharge of the obligation does not affect any liability that the obligor may have as an indorser of the instrument.

(b) Unless otherwise agreed and except as provided in subsection (a), if a note or an uncertified check is taken for an obligation, the obligation is suspended to the same extent the obligation would be discharged if an amount of money equal to the amount of the instrument were taken, and the following rules apply:

(1) In the case of an uncertified check, suspension of the obligation continues until dishonor of the check or until it is paid or certified. Payment or certification of the check results in discharge of the obligation to the extent of the amount of the check.

(2) In the case of a note, suspension of the obligation continues until dishonor of the note or until it is paid. Payment of the note results in discharge of the obligation to the extent of the payment.

(3) Except as provided in paragraph (4), if the check or note is dishonored and the obligee of the obligation for which the instrument was taken is the person entitled to enforce the instrument, the obligee may enforce either the instrument or the obligation. In the case of an instrument of a third person which is negotiated to the obligee by the obligor, discharge of the obligor on the instrument also discharges the obligation.

(4) If the person entitled to enforce the instrument taken for an obligation is a person other than the obligee, the obligee may not enforce the obligation to the extent the obligation is suspended. If the obligee is the person entitled to enforce the instrument but no longer has possession of it because it was lost, stolen, or destroyed, the obligation may not be enforced to the extent of the amount payable on the instrument, and to that extent the obligee's rights against the obligor are limited to enforcement of the instrument.

(c) If an instrument other than one described in subsection (a) or (b) is taken for an obligation, the effect is (i) that stated in subsection (a) if the instrument is one on which a bank is liable as maker or acceptor, or (ii) that stated in subsection (b) in any other case.

* * * *

§3—312. LOST, DESTROYED, OR STOLEN CASHIER'S CHECK, TELLER'S CHECK, OR CERTIFIED CHECK.

(1) "Check" means a cashier's check, teller's check, or certified check.

(2) "Claimant" means a person who claims the right to receive the amount of a cashier's check, teller's check, or certified check that was lost, destroyed, or stolen.

(3) "Declaration of loss" means a written statement, made under penalty of perjury, to the effect that (i) the declarer lost possession of a check, (ii) the declarer is the drawer or payee of the check, in the case of a certified check, or the remitter or payee of the check, in the case of a cashier's check or teller's check, (iii) the loss of possession was not the result of a transfer by the declarer or a lawful seizure, and (iv) the declarer cannot reasonably obtain possession of the check because the check was destroyed, its whereabouts cannot be determined, or it is in the wrongful possession of an unknown person or a person that cannot be found or is not amenable to service of process.

(4) "Obligated bank" means the issuer of a cashier's check or teller's check or the acceptor of a certified check.

* * * *

Part 4 Liability of Parties

§3—401. SIGNATURE

(a) A person is not liable on an instrument unless (i) the person signed the instrument, or (ii) the person is represented by an agent or representative who signed the instrument and the signature is binding on the represented person under Section 3—402.

(b) A signature may be made (i) manually or by means of a device or machine, and (ii) by the use of any name, including a trade or assumed name, or by a word, mark, or symbol executed or adopted by a person with present intention to authenticate a writing.

§3—402. SIGNATURE BY REPRESENTATIVE

(a) If a person acting, or purporting to act, as a representative signs an instrument by signing either the name of the represented person or the name of the signer, the represented person is bound by the signature to the same extent the represented person would be bound if the signature were on a simple contract. If the represented person is bound, the signature of the representative is the "authorized signature of the represented person" and the represented person is liable on the instrument, whether or not identified in the instrument.

(b) If a representative signs the name of the representative to an instrument and the signature is an authorized signature of the represented person, the following rules apply:

(1) If the form of the signature shows unambiguously that the signature is made on behalf of the represented person who is identified in the instrument, the representative is not liable on the instrument.

(2) Subject to subsection (c), if (i) the form of the signature does not show unambiguously that the signature is made in a representative capacity or (ii) the represented person is not identified in the instrument, the representative is liable on the instrument to a holder in due course that took the instrument without notice that the representative was not intended to be liable on the instrument. With respect to any other person, the representative is liable on the instrument unless the representative proves that the original parties did not intend the representative to be liable on the instrument.

(c) If a representative signs the name of the representative as drawer of a check without indication of the representative status and the check is payable from an account of the represented person who is identified on the check, the signer is not liable on the check if the signature is an authorized signature of the represented person.

§3—403. UNAUTHORIZED SIGNATURE

(a) Unless otherwise provided in this Article or Article 4, an unauthorized signature is ineffective except as the signature of the unauthorized signer in favor of a person who in good faith pays the instrument or takes it for value. An unauthorized signature may be ratified for all purposes of this Article.

(b) If the signature of more than one person is required to constitute the authorized signature of an organization, the signature of the organization is unauthorized if one of the required signatures is lacking.

(c) The civil or criminal liability of a person who makes an unauthorized signature is not affected by any provision of this Article which makes the unauthorized signature effective for the purposes of this Article.

§3—404. IMPOSTORS; FICTITIOUS PAYEES

(a) If an impostor, by use of the mails or otherwise, induces the issuer of an instrument to issue the instrument to the impostor, or to a person acting in concert with the impostor, by impersonating the payee of the instrument or a person authorized to act for the payee, an indorsement of the instrument by any person in the name of the payee is effective as the indorsement of the payee in favor of a person who, in good faith, pays the instrument or takes it for value or for collection.

(b) If (i) a person whose intent determines to whom an instrument is payable (Section 3—110(a) or (b)) does not intend the person identified as payee to have any interest in the instrument, or (ii) the person identified as payee of an instrument is a fictitious person, the following rules apply until the instrument is negotiated by special indorsement:

(1) Any person in possession of the instrument is its holder.

(2) An indorsement by any person in the name of the payee stated in the instrument is effective as the indorsement of the payee in favor of a person who, in good faith, pays the instrument or takes it for value or for collection.

(c) Under subsection (a) or (b), an indorsement is made in the name of a payee if (i) it is made in a name substantially similar to that of the payee or (ii) the instrument, whether or not indorsed, is deposited in a depositary bank to an account in a name substantially similar to that of the payee.

(d) With respect to an instrument to which subsection (a) or (b) applies, if a person paying the instrument or taking it for value or for collection fails to exercise ordinary care in paying or taking the instrument and that failure substantially contributes to loss resulting from payment of the instrument, the person bearing the loss may recover from the person failing to exercise ordinary care to the extent the failure to exercise ordinary care contributed to the loss.

§3—405. EMPLOYER'S RESPONSIBILITY FOR FRAUDULENT INDORSEMENT BY EMPLOYEE

(a) In this section:

(1) "Employee" includes an independent contractor and employee of an independent contractor retained by the employer.

(2) "Fraudulent indorsement" means (i) in the case of an instrument payable to the employer, a forged indorsement purporting to be that of the employer, or (ii) in the case of an instrument with respect to which the employer is the issuer, a forged indorsement purporting to be that of the person identified as payee.

(3) "Responsibility" with respect to instruments means authority (i) to sign or indorse instruments on behalf of the employer, (ii) to process instruments received by the employer for book-keeping purposes, for deposit to an account, or for other disposition, (iii) to prepare or process instruments for issue in the name of the employer, (iv) to supply information determining the names or addresses of payees of instruments to be issued in the name of the employer, (v) to control the disposition of instruments to be issued in the name of the employer, or (vi) to act otherwise with respect to instruments in a responsible capacity. "Responsibility" does not include authority that merely allows an employee to have access to instruments or blank or incomplete instrument forms that are being stored or transported or are part of incoming or outgoing mail, or similar access.

(b) For the purpose of determining the rights and liabilities of a person who, in good faith, pays an instrument or takes it for value or for collection, if an employer entrusted an employee with responsibility with respect to the instrument and the employee or a person acting in concert with the employee makes a fraudulent indorsement of the instrument, the indorsement is effective as the indorsement of the person to whom the instrument is payable if it is made in the name of that person. If the person paying the instrument or taking it for value or for collection fails to exercise ordinary care in paying or taking the instrument and that failure substantially contributes to loss resulting from the fraud, the person bearing the loss may recover from the person failing to exercise ordinary care to the extent the failure to exercise ordinary care contributed to the loss.

(c) Under subsection (b), an indorsement is made in the name of the person to whom an instrument is payable if (i) it is made in a name substantially similar to the name of that person or (ii) the instrument, whether or not indorsed, is deposited in a depositary bank to an account in a name substantially similar to the name of that person.

§3—406. NEGLIGENCE CONTRIBUTING TO FORGED SIGNATURE OR ALTERATION OF INSTRUMENT

(a) A person whose failure to exercise ordinary care substantially contributes to an alteration of an instrument or to the making of a forged signature on an instrument is precluded from asserting the alteration or the forgery against a person who, in good faith, pays the instrument or takes it for value or for collection.

(b) Under subsection (a), if the person asserting the preclusion fails to exercise ordinary care in paying or taking the instrument and that failure substantially contributes to loss, the loss is allocated between the person precluded and the person asserting the preclusion according to the extent to which the failure of each to exercise ordinary care contributed to the loss.

(c) Under subsection (a), the burden of proving failure to exercise ordinary care is on the person asserting the preclusion. Under subsection (b), the burden of proving failure to exercise ordinary care is on the person precluded.

§3—407. ALTERATION

(a) "Alteration" means (i) an unauthorized change in an instrument that purports to modify in any respect the obligation of a party, or (ii) an unauthorized addition of words or numbers or other change to an incomplete instrument relating to the obligation of a party.

(b) Except as provided in subsection (c), an alteration fraudulently made discharges a party whose obligation is affected by the alteration unless that party assents or is precluded from asserting the alteration. No other alteration discharges a party, and the instrument may be enforced according to its original terms.

(c) A payor bank or drawee paying a fraudulently altered instrument or a person taking it for value, in good faith and without notice of the alteration, may enforce rights with respect to the instrument (i) according to its original terms, or (ii) in the case of an incomplete instrument altered by unauthorized completion, according to its terms as completed.

§3—408. DRAWEE NOT LIABLE ON UNACCEPTED DRAFT

A check or other draft does not of itself operate as an assignment of funds in the hands of the drawee available for its payment, and the drawee is not liable on the instrument until the drawee accepts it.

§3—409. ACCEPTANCE OF DRAFT; CERTIFIED CHECK

(a) "Acceptance" means the drawee's signed agreement to pay a draft as presented. It must be written on the draft and may consist of the drawee's signature alone. Acceptance may be made at any time and becomes effective when notification pursuant to instructions is given or the accepted draft is delivered for the purpose of giving rights on the acceptance to any person.

(b) A draft may be accepted although it has not been signed by the drawer, is otherwise incomplete, is overdue, or has been dishonored.

(c) If a draft is payable at a fixed period after sight and the acceptor fails to date the acceptance, the holder may complete the acceptance by supplying a date in good faith.

(d) "Certified check" means a check accepted by the bank on which it is drawn. Acceptance may be made as stated in subsection (a) or by a writing on the check which indicates that the check is certified. The drawee of a check has no obligation to certify the check, and refusal to certify is not dishonor of the check.

§3—410. ACCEPTANCE VARYING DRAFT

(a) If the terms of a drawee's acceptance vary from the terms of the draft as presented, the holder may refuse the acceptance and treat the draft as dishonored. In that case, the drawee may cancel the acceptance.

(b) The terms of a draft are not varied by an acceptance to pay at a particular bank or place in the United States, unless the acceptance states that the draft is to be paid only at that bank or place.

(c) If the holder assents to an acceptance varying the terms of a draft, the obligation of each drawer and indorser that does not expressly assent to the acceptance is discharged.

§3—411. REFUSAL TO PAY CASHIER'S CHECKS, TELLER'S CHECKS, AND CERTIFIED CHECKS

(a) In this section, "obligated bank" means the acceptor of a certified check or the issuer of a cashier's check or teller's check bought from the issuer.

(b) If the obligated bank wrongfully (i) refuses to pay a cashier's check or certified check, (ii) stops payment of a teller's check, or (iii) refuses to pay a dishonored teller's check, the person asserting the right to enforce the check is entitled to compensation for expenses and loss of interest resulting from the nonpayment and may recover consequential damages if the obligated bank refuses to pay after receiving notice of particular circumstances giving rise to the damages.

(c) Expenses or consequential damages under subsection (b) are not recoverable if the refusal of the obligated bank to pay occurs because (i) the bank suspends payments, (ii) the obligated bank asserts a claim or defense of the bank that it has reasonable grounds to believe is available against the person entitled to enforce the instrument, (iii) the obligated bank has a reasonable doubt whether the person demanding payment is the person entitled to enforce the instrument, or (iv) payment is prohibited by law.

§3—412. OBLIGATION OF ISSUER OF NOTE OR CASHIER'S CHECK

The issuer of a note or cashier's check or other draft drawn on the drawer is obliged to pay the instrument (i) according to its terms at the time it was issued or, if not issued, at the time it first came into possession of a holder, or (ii) if the issuer signed an incomplete instrument, according to its terms when completed, to the extent stated in Sections 3—115 and 3—407. The obligation is owed to a person entitled to enforce the instrument or to an indorser who paid the instrument under Section 3—415.

§3—413. OBLIGATION OF ACCEPTOR

(a) The acceptor of a draft is obliged to pay the draft (i) according to its terms at the time it was accepted, even though the acceptance states that the draft is payable "as originally drawn" or equivalent terms, (ii) if the acceptance varies the terms of the draft, according to the terms of the draft as varied, or (iii) if the acceptance is of a draft that is an incomplete instrument, according to its terms when completed, to the extent stated in Sections 3—115 and 3—407. The obligation is owed to a person entitled to enforce the draft or to the drawer or an indorser who paid the draft under Section 3—414 or 3—415.

(b) If the certification of a check or other acceptance of a draft states the amount certified or accepted, the obligation of the acceptor is that amount. If (i) the certification or acceptance does not state an amount, (ii) the amount of the instrument is subsequently raised, and (iii) the instrument is then negotiated to a holder in due course, the obligation of the acceptor is the amount of the instrument at the time it was taken by the holder in due course.

§3—414. OBLIGATION OF DRAWER

(a) This section does not apply to cashier's checks or other drafts drawn on the drawer.

(b) If an unaccepted draft is dishonored, the drawer is obliged to pay the draft (i) according to its terms at the time it was issued or, if not issued, at the time it first came into possession of a holder, or (ii) if the drawer signed an incomplete instrument, according to its terms when completed, to the extent stated in Sections 3—115 and 3—407. The obligation is owed to a person entitled to enforce the draft or to an indorser who paid the draft under Section 3—415.

(c) If a draft is accepted by a bank, the drawer is discharged, regardless of when or by whom acceptance was obtained.

(d) If a draft is accepted and the acceptor is not a bank, the obligation of the drawer to pay the draft if the draft is dishonored by the acceptor is the same as the obligation of an indorser under Section 3—415(a) and (c).

(e) If a draft states that it is drawn "without recourse" or otherwise disclaims liability of the drawer to pay the draft, the drawer is not liable under subsection (b) to pay the draft if the draft is not a check. A disclaimer of the liability stated in subsection (b) is not effective if the draft is a check.

(f) If (i) a check is not presented for payment or given to a depositary bank for collection within 30 days after its date, (ii) the drawee suspends payments after expiration of the 30-day period without paying the check, and (iii) because of the suspension of payments, the drawer is deprived of funds maintained with the drawee to cover payment of the check, the drawer to the extent deprived of funds may discharge its obligation to pay the check by assigning to the person entitled to enforce the check the rights of the drawer against the drawee with respect to the funds.

§3—415. OBLIGATION OF INDORSER

(a) Subject to subsections (b), (c), and (d) and to Section 3—419(d), if an instrument is dishonored, an indorser is obliged to pay the amount due on the instrument (i) according to the terms of the instrument at the time it was indorsed, or (ii) if the indorser indorsed an incomplete instrument, according to its terms when completed, to the extent stated in Sections 3—115 and 3—407. The obligation of the indorser is owed to a person entitled to enforce the instrument or to a subsequent indorser who paid the instrument under this section.

(b) If an indorsement states that it is made "without recourse" or otherwise disclaims liability of the indorser, the indorser is not liable under subsection (a) to pay the instrument.

(c) If notice of dishonor of an instrument is required by Section 3—503 and notice of dishonor complying with that section is not given to an indorser, the liability of the indorser under subsection (a) is discharged.

(d) If a draft is accepted by a bank after an indorsement is made, the liability of the indorser under subsection (a) is discharged.

(e) If an indorser of a check is liable under subsection (a) and the check is not presented for payment, or given to a depositary bank for collection, within 30 days after the day the indorsement was made, the liability of the indorser under subsection (a) is discharged.

As amended in 1993.

§3—416. TRANSFER WARRANTIES

(a) A person who transfers an instrument for consideration warrants to the transferee and, if the transfer is by indorsement, to any subsequent transferee that:

> (1) the warrantor is a person entitled to enforce the instrument;
>
> (2) all signatures on the instrument are authentic and authorized;
>
> (3) the instrument has not been altered;
>
> (4) the instrument is not subject to a defense or claim in recoupment of any party which can be asserted against the warrantor; and
>
> (5) the warrantor has no knowledge of any insolvency proceeding commenced with respect to the maker or acceptor or, in the case of an unaccepted draft, the drawer.

(b) A person to whom the warranties under subsection (a) are made and who took the instrument in good faith may recover from the warrantor as damages for breach of warranty an amount equal to the loss suffered as a result of the breach, but not more than the amount of the instrument plus expenses and loss of interest incurred as a result of the breach.

(c) The warranties stated in subsection (a) cannot be disclaimed with respect to checks. Unless notice of a claim for breach of warranty is given to the warrantor within 30 days after the claimant has reason to know of the breach and the identity of the warrantor, the liability of the warrantor under subsection (b) is discharged to the extent of any loss caused by the delay in giving notice of the claim.

(d) A [cause of action] for breach of warranty under this section accrues when the claimant has reason to know of the breach.

§3—417. PRESENTMENT WARRANTIES

(a) If an unaccepted draft is presented to the drawee for payment or acceptance and the drawee pays or accepts the draft, (i) the person obtaining payment or acceptance, at the time of presentment, and (ii) a previous transferor of the draft, at the time of transfer, warrant to the drawee making payment or accepting the draft in good faith that:

> (1) the warrantor is, or was, at the time the warrantor transferred the draft, a person entitled to enforce the draft or authorized to obtain payment or acceptance of the draft on behalf of a person entitled to enforce the draft;
>
> (2) the draft has not been altered; and
>
> (3) the warrantor has no knowledge that the signature of the drawer of the draft is unauthorized.

(b) A drawee making payment may recover from any warrantor damages for breach of warranty equal to the amount paid by the drawee less the amount the drawee received or is entitled to receive from the drawer because of the payment. In addition, the drawee is entitled to compensation for expenses and loss of interest resulting from the breach. The right of the drawee to recover damages under this subsection is not affected by any failure of the drawee to exercise ordinary care in making payment. If the drawee accepts the draft, breach of warranty is a defense to the obligation of the acceptor. If the acceptor makes payment with respect to the draft, the acceptor is entitled to recover from any warrantor for breach of warranty the amounts stated in this subsection.

(c) If a drawee asserts a claim for breach of warranty under subsection (a) based on an unauthorized indorsement of the draft or an alteration of the draft, the warrantor may defend by proving that the indorsement is effective under Section 3—404 or 3—405 or the drawer is precluded under Section 3—406 or 4—406 from asserting against the drawee the unauthorized indorsement or alteration.

(d) If (i) a dishonored draft is presented for payment to the drawer or an indorser or (ii) any other instrument is presented for payment to a party obliged to pay the instrument, and (iii) payment is received, the following rules apply:

> (1) The person obtaining payment and a prior transferor of the instrument warrant to the person making payment in good faith that the warrantor is, or was, at the time the warrantor transferred the instrument, a person entitled to enforce the instrument or authorized to obtain payment on behalf of a person entitled to enforce the instrument.
>
> (2) The person making payment may recover from any warrantor for breach of warranty an amount equal to the amount paid plus expenses and loss of interest resulting from the breach.

(e) The warranties stated in subsections (a) and (d) cannot be disclaimed with respect to checks. Unless notice of a claim for breach of warranty is given to the warrantor within 30 days after the claimant has reason to know of the breach and the identity of the warrantor, the liability of the warrantor under subsection (b) or (d) is discharged to the extent of any loss caused by the delay in giving notice of the claim.

(f) A [cause of action] for breach of warranty under this section accrues when the claimant has reason to know of the breach.

§3—418. PAYMENT OR ACCEPTANCE BY MISTAKE

(a) Except as provided in subsection (c), if the drawee of a draft pays or accepts the draft and the drawee acted on the mistaken belief that (i) payment of the draft had not been stopped pursuant to Section 4—403 or (ii) the signature of the drawer of the draft was authorized, the drawee may recover the amount of the draft from the person to whom or for whose benefit payment was made or, in the case of acceptance, may revoke the acceptance. Rights of the drawee under this subsection are not affected by failure of the drawee to exercise ordinary care in paying or accepting the draft.

(b) Except as provided in subsection (c), if an instrument has been paid or accepted by mistake and the case is not covered by subsection (a), the person paying or accepting may, to the extent permitted by the law governing mistake and restitution, (i) recover the payment from the person to whom or for whose benefit payment was made or (ii) in the case of acceptance, may revoke the acceptance.

(c) The remedies provided by subsection (a) or (b) may not be asserted against a person who took the instrument in good faith and for value or who in good faith changed position in reliance on the payment or acceptance. This subsection does not limit remedies provided by Section 3—417 or 4—407.

(d) Notwithstanding Section 4—215, if an instrument is paid or accepted by mistake and the payor or acceptor recovers payment or revokes acceptance under subsection (a) or (b), the instrument is deemed not to have been paid or accepted and is treated as dishonored, and the person from whom payment is recovered has rights as a person entitled to enforce the dishonored instrument.

§3—419. INSTRUMENTS SIGNED FOR ACCOMMODATION

(a) If an instrument is issued for value given for the benefit of a party to the instrument ("accommodated party") and another party to the instrument ("accommodation party") signs the instrument for the purpose of incurring liability on the instrument without being a direct beneficiary of the value given for the instrument, the instrument is signed by the accommodation party "for accommodation."

(b) An accommodation party may sign the instrument as maker, drawer, acceptor, or indorser and, subject to subsection (d), is obliged to pay the instrument in the capacity in which the accommodation party signs. The obligation of an accommodation party may be enforced notwithstanding any statute of frauds and whether or not the accommodation party receives consideration for the accommodation.

* * * *

(e) An accommodation party who pays the instrument is entitled to reimbursement from the accommodated party and is entitled to enforce the instrument against the accommodated party. An accommodated party who pays the instrument has no right of recourse against, and is not entitled to contribution from, an accommodation party.

§3—420. CONVERSION OF INSTRUMENT

(a) The law applicable to conversion of personal property applies to instruments. An instrument is also converted if it is taken by transfer, other than a negotiation, from a person not entitled to enforce the instrument or a bank makes or obtains payment with respect to the instrument for a person not entitled to enforce the instrument or receive payment. An action for conversion of an instrument may not be brought by (i) the issuer or acceptor of the instrument or (ii) a payee or indorsee who did not receive delivery of the instrument either directly or through delivery to an agent or a co-payee.

(b) In an action under subsection (a), the measure of liability is presumed to be the amount payable on the instrument, but recovery may not exceed the amount of the plaintiff's interest in the instrument.

(c) A representative, other than a depositary bank, who has in good faith dealt with an instrument or its proceeds on behalf of one who was not the person entitled to enforce the instrument is not liable in conversion to that person beyond the amount of any proceeds that it has not paid out.

§3—501. PRESENTMENT

(a) "Presentment" means a demand made by or on behalf of a person entitled to enforce an instrument (i) to pay the instrument made to the drawee or a party obliged to pay the instrument or, in the case of a note or accepted draft payable at a bank, to the bank, or (ii) to accept a draft made to the drawee.

(b) The following rules are subject to Article 4, agreement of the parties, and clearing-house rules and the like:

(1) Presentment may be made at the place of payment of the instrument and must be made at the place of payment if the instrument is payable at a bank in the United States; may be made by any commercially reasonable means, including an oral, written, or electronic communication; is effective when the demand for payment or acceptance is received by the person to whom presentment is made; and is effective if made to any one of two or more makers, acceptors, drawees, or other payors.

(2) Upon demand of the person to whom presentment is made, the person making presentment must (i) exhibit the instrument, (ii) give reasonable identification and, if presentment is made on behalf of another person, reasonable evidence of authority to do so, and (...) sign a receipt on the instrument for any payment made or surrender the instrument if full payment is made.

(3) Without dishonoring the instrument, the party to whom presentment is made may (i) return the instrument for lack of a necessary indorsement, or (ii) refuse payment or acceptance for failure of the presentment to comply with the terms of the instrument, an agreement of the parties, or other applicable law or rule.

(4) The party to whom presentment is made may treat presentment as occurring on the next business day after the day of presentment if the party to whom presentment is made has established a

cut-off hour not earlier than 2 P.M. for the receipt and processing of instruments presented for payment or acceptance and presentment is made after the cut-off hour.

§3—502. DISHONOR

(a) Dishonor of a note is governed by the following rules:

(1) If the note is payable on demand, the note is dishonored if presentment is duly made to the maker and the note is not paid on the day of presentment.

(2) If the note is not payable on demand and is payable at or through a bank or the terms of the note require presentment, the note is dishonored if presentment is duly made and the note is not paid on the day it becomes payable or the day of presentment, whichever is later.

(3) If the note is not payable on demand and paragraph (2) does not apply, the note is dishonored if it is not paid on the day it becomes payable.

(b) Dishonor of an unaccepted draft other than a documentary draft is governed by the following rules:

(1) If a check is duly presented for payment to the payor bank otherwise than for immediate payment over the counter, the check is dishonored if the payor bank makes timely return of the check or sends timely notice of dishonor or nonpayment under Section 4—301 or 4—302, or becomes accountable for the amount of the check under Section 4—302.

(2) If a draft is payable on demand and paragraph (1) does not apply, the draft is dishonored if presentment for payment is duly made to the drawee and the draft is not paid on the day of presentment.

(3) If a draft is payable on a date stated in the draft, the draft is dishonored if (i) presentment for payment is duly made to the drawee and payment is not made on the day the draft becomes payable or the day of presentment, whichever is later, or (ii) presentment for acceptance is duly made before the day the draft becomes payable and the draft is not accepted on the day of presentment.

(4) If a draft is payable on elapse of a period of time after sight or acceptance, the draft is dishonored if presentment for acceptance is duly made and the draft is not accepted on the day of presentment.

(c) Dishonor of an unaccepted documentary draft occurs according to the rules stated in subsection (b)(2), (3),

and (4), except that payment or acceptance may be delayed without dishonor until no later than the close of the third business day of the drawee following the day on which payment or acceptance is required by those paragraphs.

(d) Dishonor of an accepted draft is governed by the following rules:

(1) If the draft is payable on demand, the draft is dishonored if presentment for payment is duly made to the acceptor and the draft is not paid on the day of presentment.

(2) If the draft is not payable on demand, the draft is dishonored if presentment for payment is duly made to the acceptor and payment is not made on the day it becomes payable or the day of presentment, whichever is later.

(e) In any case in which presentment is otherwise required for dishonor under this section and presentment is excused under Section 3—504, dishonor occurs without presentment if the instrument is not duly accepted or paid.

(f) If a draft is dishonored because timely acceptance of the draft was not made and the person entitled to demand acceptance consents to a late acceptance, from the time of acceptance the draft is treated as never having been dishonored.

§3—503. NOTICE OF DISHONOR

(a) The obligation of an indorser stated in Section 3—415 (a) and the obligation of a drawer stated in Section 3—414 (d) may not be enforced unless (i) the indorser or drawer is given notice of dishonor of the instrument complying with this section or (ii) notice of dishonor is excused under Section 3—504(b).

(b) Notice of dishonor may be given by any person; may be given by any commercially reasonable means, including an oral, written, or electronic communication; and is sufficient if it reasonably identifies the instrument and indicates that the instrument has been dishonored or has not been paid or accepted. Return of an instrument given to a bank for collection is sufficient notice of dishonor.

(c) Subject to Section 3—504(c), with respect to an instrument taken for collection by a collecting bank, notice of dishonor must be given (i) by the bank before midnight of the next banking day following the banking day on which the bank receives notice of dishonor of the instrument, or (ii) by any other person within 30 days following the day on which the person receives notice of dishonor. With respect to any other instrument, notice of dishonor must be given within 30 days following the day on which dishonor occurs.

* * * *

§3—601. DISCHARGE AND EFFECT OF DISCHARGE

(a) The obligation of a party to pay the instrument is discharged as stated in this Article or by an act or agreement with the party which would discharge an obligation to pay money under a simple contract.

(b) Discharge of the obligation of a party is not effective against a person acquiring rights of a holder in due course of the instrument without notice of the discharge.

§3—602. PAYMENT

(a) Subject to subsection (b), an instrument is paid to the extent payment is made (i) by or on behalf of a party obliged to pay the instrument, and (ii) to a person entitled to enforce the instrument. To the extent of the payment, the obligation of the party obliged to pay the instrument is discharged even though payment is made with knowledge of a claim to the instrument under Section 3—306 by another person.

(b) The obligation of a party to pay the instrument is not discharged under subsection (a) if:

> (1) a claim to the instrument under Section 3—306 is enforceable against the party receiving payment and (i) payment is made with knowledge by the payor that payment is prohibited by injunction or similar process of a court of competent jurisdiction, or (ii) in the case of an instrument other than a cashier's check, teller's check, or certified check, the party making payment accepted, from the person having a claim to the instrument, indemnity against loss resulting from refusal to pay the person entitled to enforce the instrument; or

> (2) the person making payment knows that the instrument is a stolen instrument and pays a person it knows is in wrongful possession of the instrument.

§3—603. TENDER OF PAYMENT

(a) If tender of payment of an obligation to pay an instrument is made to a person entitled to enforce the instrument, the effect of tender is governed by principles of law applicable to tender of payment under a simple contract.

(b) If tender of payment of an obligation to pay an instrument is made to a person entitled to enforce the instrument and the tender is refused, there is discharge, to the extent of the amount of the tender, of the obligation of an indorser or accommodation party having a right of recourse with respect to the obligation to which the tender relates.

(c) If tender of payment of an amount due on an instrument is made to a person entitled to enforce the instrument, the obligation of the obligor to pay interest after the due date on the amount tendered is discharged. If presentment is required with respect to an instrument and the obligor is able and ready to pay on the due date at every place of payment stated in the instrument, the obligor is deemed to have made tender of payment on the due date to the person entitled to enforce the instrument.

§3—604. DISCHARGE BY CANCELLATION OR RENUNCIATION

(a) A person entitled to enforce an instrument, with or without consideration, may discharge the obligation of a party to pay the instrument (i) by an intentional voluntary act, such as surrender of the instrument to the party, destruction, mutilation, or cancellation of the instrument, cancellation or striking out of the party's signature, or the addition of words to the instrument indicating discharge, or (ii) by agreeing not to sue or otherwise renouncing rights against the party by a signed writing.

(b) Cancellation or striking out of an indorsement pursuant to subsection (a) does not affect the status and rights of a party derived from the indorsement.

§3—605. DISCHARGE OF INDORSERS AND ACCOMMODATION PARTIES

(a) In this section, the term "indorser" includes a drawer having the obligation described in Section 3—414(d).

(b) Discharge, under Section 3—604, of the obligation of a party to pay an instrument does not discharge the obligation of an indorser or accommodation party having a right of recourse against the discharged party.

(c) If a person entitled to enforce an instrument agrees, with or without consideration, to an extension of the due date of the obligation of a party to pay the instrument, the extension discharges an indorser or accommodation party having a right of recourse against the party whose obligation is extended to the extent the indorser or accommodation party proves that the extension caused loss to the indorser or accommodation party with respect to the right of recourse.

(d) If a person entitled to enforce an instrument agrees, with or without consideration, to a material modification of the obligation of a party other than an extension of the due date, the modification discharges the obligation of an indorser or accommodation party having a right of recourse against the person whose obligation is modified to the extent the modification causes loss to the indorser or accommodation party with respect to the right of recourse. The loss suffered by the indorser or accommodation party as a result of the modification is equal to the amount of the right of recourse unless the person enforcing the instrument proves that no loss was caused by the modification or that the loss caused by the modification was an amount less than the amount of the right of recourse.

(e) If the obligation of a party to pay an instrument is secured by an interest in collateral and a person entitled to enforce the instrument impairs the value of the interest in collateral, the obligation of an indorser or accommodation party having a right of recourse against the obligor is discharged to the extent of the impairment. The value of an interest in collateral is impaired to the extent (i) the value of the interest is reduced to an amount less than the amount of the right of recourse of the party asserting discharge, or (ii) the reduction in value of the interest causes an increase in the amount by which the amount of the right of recourse exceeds the value of the interest. The burden of proving impairment is on the party asserting discharge.

(f) If the obligation of a party is secured by an interest in collateral not provided by an accommodation party and a person entitled to enforce the instrument impairs the value of the interest in collateral, the obligation of any party who is jointly and severally liable with respect to the secured obligation is discharged to the extent the impairment causes the party asserting discharge to pay more than that party would have been obliged to pay, taking into account rights of contribution, if impairment had not occurred. If the party asserting discharge is an accommodation party not entitled to discharge under subsection (e), the party is deemed to have a right to contribution based on joint and several liability rather than a right to reimbursement. The burden of proving impairment is on the party asserting discharge.

* * * *

(h) An accommodation party is not discharged under subsection (c), (d), or (e) unless the person entitled to enforce the instrument knows of the accommodation or has notice under Section 3—419(c) that the instrument was signed for accommodation.

(i) A party is not discharged under this section if (i) the party asserting discharge consents to the event or conduct that is the basis of the discharge, or (ii) the instrument or a separate agreement of the party provides for waiver of discharge under this section either specifically or by general language indicating that parties waive defenses based on suretyship or impairment of collateral.

* * * *

Revised Article 4 Bank Deposits and Collections

Part 1 General Provisions and Definitions

§4—103. VARIATION BY AGREEMENT; MEASURE OF DAMAGES; ACTION CONSTITUTING ORDINARY CARE

(a) The effect of the provisions of this Article may be varied by agreement, but the parties to the agreement cannot disclaim a bank's responsibility for its lack of good faith or failure to exercise ordinary care or limit the measure of damages for the lack or failure. However, the parties may determine by agreement the standards by which the bank's responsibility is to be measured if those standards are not manifestly unreasonable.

(b) Federal Reserve regulations and operating circulars, clearing-house rules, and the like have the effect of agreements under subsection (a), whether or not specifically assented to by all parties interested in items handled.

* * * *

§4—104. DEFINITIONS AND INDEX OF DEFINITIONS

(1) "Account" means any deposit or credit account with a bank, including a demand, time, savings, passbook, share draft, or like account, other than an account evidenced by a certificate of deposit;

* * * *

(3) "Banking day" means the part of a day on which a bank is open to the public for carrying on substantially all of its banking functions;

(4) "Clearing house" means an association of banks or other payors regularly clearing items;

* * * *

(7) "Draft" means a draft as defined in Section 3—104 or an item, other than an instrument, that is an order;

(8) "Drawee" means a person ordered in a draft to make payment;

* * * *

(10) "Midnight deadline" with respect to a bank is midnight on its next banking day following the banking day on which it receives the relevant item or notice or from which the time for taking action commences to run, whichever is later;

* * * *

§4—105. "BANK"; "DEPOSITARY BANK"; "PAYOR BANK"; "INTERMEDIARY BANK"; "COLLECTING BANK"; "PRESENTING BANK"

In this Article:

(1) "Bank" means a person engaged in the business of banking, including a savings bank, savings and loan association, credit union, or trust company;

(2) "Depositary bank" means the first bank to take an item even though it is also the payor bank, unless the item is presented for immediate payment over the counter;

(3) "Payor bank" means a bank that is the drawee of a draft;

(4) "Intermediary bank" means a bank to which an item is transferred in course of collection except the depositary or payor bank;

(5) "Collecting bank" means a bank handling an item for collection except the payor bank;

(6) "Presenting bank" means a bank presenting an item except a payor bank.

§4—106. PAYABLE THROUGH OR PAYABLE AT BANK: COLLECTING BANK

(a) If an item states that it is "payable through" a bank identified in the item, (i) the item designates the bank as a collecting bank and does not by itself authorize the bank to pay the item, and (ii) the item may be presented for payment only by or through the bank.

Alternative A

(b) If an item states that it is "payable at" a bank identified in the item, the item is equivalent to a draft drawn on the bank.

Alternative B

(b) If an item states that it is "payable at" a bank identified in the item, (i) the item designates the bank as a collecting bank and does not by itself authorize the bank to pay the item, and (ii) the item may be presented for payment only by or through the bank.

(c) If a draft names a nonbank drawee and it is unclear whether a bank named in the draft is a co-drawee or a collecting bank, the bank is a collecting bank.

§4—107. SEPARATE OFFICE OF BANK

A branch or separate office of a bank is a separate bank for the purpose of computing the time within which and determining the place at or to which action may be taken or notices or orders shall be given under this Article and under Article 3.

§4—108. TIME OF RECEIPT OF ITEMS

(a) For the purpose of allowing time to process items, prove balances, and make the necessary entries on its books to determine its position for the day, a bank may fix an afternoon hour of 2 P.M. or later as a cutoff hour for the handling of money and items and the making of entries on its books.

(b) An item or deposit of money received on any day after a cutoff hour so fixed or after the close of the banking day may be treated as being received at the opening of the next banking day.

§4—109. DELAYS

(a) Unless otherwise instructed, a collecting bank in a good faith effort to secure payment of a specific item drawn on a payor other than a bank, and with or without the approval of any person involved, may waive, modify, or extend time limits imposed or permitted by this [act] for a period not exceeding two additional banking days without discharge of drawers or indorsers or liability to its transferor or a prior party.

(b) Delay by a collecting bank or payor bank beyond time limits prescribed or permitted by this [act] or by instructions is excused if (i) the delay is caused by interruption of communication or computer facilities, suspension of payments by another bank, war, emergency conditions, failure of equipment, or other circumstances beyond the control of the bank, and (ii) the bank exercises such diligence as the circumstances require.

§4—110. ELECTRONIC PRESENTMENT

(a) "Agreement for electronic presentment" means an agreement, clearing-house rule, or Federal Reserve regulation or operating circular, providing that presentment of an item may be made by transmission of an image of an item or information describing the item ("presentment notice") rather than delivery of the item itself. The agreement may provide for procedures governing retention, presentment, payment, dishonor, and other matters concerning items subject to the agreement.

* * * *

§4—111. STATUTE OF LIMITATIONS

An action to enforce an obligation, duty, or right arising under this Article must be commenced within three years after the [cause of action] accrues.

§4—201. STATUS OF COLLECTING BANK AS AGENT AND PROVISIONAL STATUS OF CREDITS; APPLICABILITY OF ARTICLE; ITEM INDORSED "PAY ANY BANK"

(a) Unless a contrary intent clearly appears and before the time that a settlement given by a collecting bank for an item is or becomes final, the bank, with respect to an item, is an agent or sub-agent of the owner of the item and any settlement given for the item is provisional. This provision applies regardless of the form of indorsement or lack of indorsement and even though credit given for the item is subject to immediate withdrawal as of right or is in fact withdrawn; but the continuance of ownership of an item by its owner and any rights of the owner to proceeds of the item are subject to rights of a collecting bank, such as those resulting from outstanding advances on the item and rights of recoupment or setoff. If an item is handled by banks for purposes of presentment, payment, collection, or return, the relevant provisions of this Article apply even though action of the parties clearly establishes that a particular bank has purchased the item and is the owner of it.

(b) After an item has been indorsed with the words "pay any bank" or the like, only a bank may acquire the rights of a holder until the item has been:

(1) returned to the customer initiating collection; or

(2) specially indorsed by a bank to a person who is not a bank.

§4—202. RESPONSIBILITY FOR COLLECTION OR RETURN; WHEN ACTION TIMELY

(a) A collecting bank must exercise ordinary care in:

(1) presenting an item or sending it for presentment;

(2) sending notice of dishonor or nonpayment or returning an item other than a documentary draft to the bank's transferor after learning that the item has not been paid or accepted, as the case may be;

(3) settling for an item when the bank receives final settlement; and

(4) notifying its transferor of any loss or delay in transit within a reasonable time after discovery thereof.

(b) A collecting bank exercises ordinary care under subsection (a) by taking proper action before its midnight deadline following receipt of an item, notice, or settlement. Taking proper action within a reasonably longer time may constitute the exercise of ordinary care, but the bank has the burden of establishing timeliness.

(c) Subject to subsection (a)(1), a bank is not liable for the insolvency, neglect, misconduct, mistake, or default of another bank or person or for loss or destruction of an item in the possession of others or in transit.

* * * *

§4—205. DEPOSITARY BANK HOLDER OF UNINDORSED ITEM

If a customer delivers an item to a depositary bank for collection:

(1) the depositary bank becomes a holder of the item at the time it receives the item for collection if the customer at the time of delivery was a holder of the item, whether or not the customer indorses the item, and, if the bank satisfies the other requirements of Section 3—302, it is a holder in due course; and

(2) the depositary bank warrants to collecting banks, the payor bank or other payor, and the drawer that the amount of the item was paid to the customer or deposited to the customer's account.

* * * *

§4—207. TRANSFER WARRANTIES

(a) A customer or collecting bank that transfers an item and receives a settlement or other consideration warrants to the transferee and to any subsequent collecting bank that:

(1) the warrantor is a person entitled to enforce the item;

(2) all signatures on the item are authentic and authorized;

(3) the item has not been altered;

(4) the item is not subject to a defense or claim in recoupment (Section 3—305(a)) of any party that can be asserted against the warrantor; and

(5) the warrantor has no knowledge of any insolvency proceeding commenced with respect to the

maker or acceptor or, in the case of an unaccepted draft, the drawer.

(b) If an item is dishonored, a customer or collecting bank transferring the item and receiving settlement or other consideration is obliged to pay the amount due on the item (i) according to the terms of the item at the time it was transferred, or (ii) if the transfer was of an incomplete item, according to its terms when completed as stated in Sections 3—115 and 3—407. The obligation of a transferor is owed to the transferee and to any subsequent collecting bank that takes the item in good faith. A transferor cannot disclaim its obligation under this subsection by an indorsement stating that it is made "without recourse" or otherwise disclaiming liability.

(c) A person to whom the warranties under subsection (a) are made and who took the item in good faith may recover from the warrantor as damages for breach of warranty an amount equal to the loss suffered as a result of the breach, but not more than the amount of the item plus expenses and loss of interest incurred as a result of the breach.

(d) The warranties stated in subsection (a) cannot be disclaimed with respect to checks. Unless notice of a claim for breach of warranty is given to the warrantor within 30 days after the claimant has reason to know of the breach and the identity of the warrantor, the warrantor is discharged to the extent of any loss caused by the delay in giving notice of the claim.

(e) A cause of action for breach of warranty under this section accrues when the claimant has reason to know of the breach.

§4—208. PRESENTMENT WARRANTIES

(a) If an unaccepted draft is presented to the drawee for payment or acceptance and the drawee pays or accepts the draft, (i) the person obtaining payment or acceptance, at the time of presentment, and (ii) a previous transferor of the draft, at the time of transfer, warrant to the drawee that pays or accepts the draft in good faith that:

(1) the warrantor is, or was, at the time the warrantor transferred the draft, a person entitled to enforce the draft or authorized to obtain payment or acceptance of the draft on behalf of a person entitled to enforce the draft;

(2) the draft has not been altered; and

(3) the warrantor has no knowledge that the signature of the purported drawer of the draft is unauthorized.

(b) A drawee making payment may recover from a warrantor damages for breach of warranty equal to the amount paid by the drawee less the amount the drawee received or is entitled to receive from the drawer because of the payment. In addition, the drawee is entitled to compensation for expenses and loss of interest resulting from the breach. The right of the drawee to recover damages under this subsection is not affected by any failure of the drawee to exercise ordinary care in making payment. If the drawee accepts the draft (i) breach of warranty is a defense to the obligation of the acceptor, and (ii) if the acceptor makes payment with respect to the draft, the acceptor is entitled to recover from a warrantor for breach of warranty the amounts stated in this subsection.

(c) If a drawee asserts a claim for breach of warranty under subsection (a) based on an unauthorized indorsement of the draft or an alteration of the draft, the warrantor may defend by proving that the indorsement is effective under Section 3—404 or 3—405 or the drawer is precluded under Section 3—406 or 4—406 from asserting against the drawee the unauthorized indorsement or alteration.

(d) If (i) a dishonored draft is presented for payment to the drawer or an indorser or (ii) any other item is presented for payment to a party obliged to pay the item, and the item is paid, the person obtaining payment and a prior transferor of the item warrant to the person making payment in good faith that the warrantor is, or was, at the time the warrantor transferred the item, a person entitled to enforce the item or authorized to obtain payment on behalf of a person entitled to enforce the item. The person making payment may recover from any warrantor for breach of warranty an amount equal to the amount paid plus expenses and loss of interest resulting from the breach.

(e) The warranties stated in subsections (a) and (d) cannot be disclaimed with respect to checks. Unless notice of a claim for breach of warranty is given to the warrantor within 30 days after the claimant has reason to know of the breach and the identity of the warrantor, the warrantor is discharged to the extent of any loss caused by the delay in giving notice of the claim.

(f) A cause of action for breach of warranty under this section accrues when the claimant has reason to know of the breach.

* * * *

§4—211. WHEN BANK GIVES VALUE FOR PURPOSES OF HOLDER IN DUE COURSE

For purposes of determining its status as a holder in due course, a bank has given value to the extent it has a security interest in an item, if the bank otherwise complies with the requirements of Section 3—302 on what constitutes a holder in due course.

As amended in 1990.

§4—212. PRESENTMENT BY NOTICE OF ITEM NOT PAYABLE BY, THROUGH, OR AT BANK; LIABILITY OF DRAWER OR INDORSER

(a) Unless otherwise instructed, a collecting bank may present an item not payable by, through, or at a bank by sending to the party to accept or pay a written notice that the bank holds the item for acceptance or payment. The notice must be sent in time to be received on or before the day when presentment is due and the bank must meet any requirement of the party to accept or pay under Section 3—501 by the close of the bank's next banking day after it knows of the requirement.

(b) If presentment is made by notice and payment, acceptance, or request for compliance with a requirement under Section 3—501 is not received by the close of business on the day after maturity or, in the case of demand items, by the close of business on the third banking day after notice was sent, the presenting bank may treat the item as dishonored and charge any drawer or indorser by sending it notice of the facts.

* * * *

§4—214. RIGHT OF CHARGE-BACK OR REFUND; LIABILITY OF COLLECTING BANK: RETURN OF ITEM

(a) If a collecting bank has made provisional settlement with its customer for an item and fails by reason of dishonor, suspension of payments by a bank, or otherwise to receive settlement for the item which is or becomes final, the bank may revoke the settlement given by it, charge back the amount of any credit given for the item to its customer's account, or obtain refund from its customer, whether or not it is able to return the item, if by its midnight deadline or within a longer reasonable time after it learns the facts it returns the item or sends notification of the facts. If the return or notice is delayed beyond the bank's midnight deadline or a longer reasonable time after it learns the facts, the bank may revoke the settlement, charge back the credit, or obtain refund from its customer, but it is liable for any loss resulting from the delay. These rights to revoke, charge back, and obtain refund terminate if and when a settlement for the item received by the bank is or becomes final.

(b) A collecting bank returns an item when it is sent or delivered to the bank's customer or transferor or pursuant to its instructions.

(c) A depositary bank that is also the payor may charge back the amount of an item to its customer's account or obtain refund in accordance with the section governing return of an item received by a payor bank for credit on its books (Section 4—301).

(d) The right to charge back is not affected by:

(1) previous use of a credit given for the item; or

(2) failure by any bank to exercise ordinary care with respect to the item, but a bank so failing remains liable.

(e) A failure to charge back or claim refund does not affect other rights of the bank against the customer or any other party.

(f) If credit is given in dollars as the equivalent of the value of an item payable in foreign money, the dollar amount of any charge-back or refund must be calculated on the basis of the bank-offered spot rate for the foreign money prevailing on the day when the person entitled to the charge-back or refund learns that it will not receive payment in ordinary course.

§4—215. FINAL PAYMENT OF ITEM BY PAYOR BANK; WHEN PROVISIONAL DEBITS AND CREDITS BECOME FINAL; WHEN CERTAIN CREDITS BECOME AVAILABLE FOR WITHDRAWAL

(a) An item is finally paid by a payor bank when the bank has first done any of the following:

(1) paid the item in cash;

(2) settled for the item without having a right to revoke the settlement under statute, clearing-house rule, or agreement; or

(3) made a provisional settlement for the item and failed to revoke the settlement in the time and manner permitted by statute, clearing-house rule, or agreement.

(b) If provisional settlement for an item does not become final, the item is not finally paid.

* * * *

§4—216. INSOLVENCY AND PREFERENCE

(a) If an item is in or comes into the possession of a payor or collecting bank that suspends payment and the item has not been finally paid, the item must be returned by the receiver, trustee, or agent in charge of the closed bank to the presenting bank or the closed bank's customer.

(b) If a payor bank finally pays an item and suspends payments without making a settlement for the item with its customer or the presenting bank which settlement is or becomes final, the owner of the item has a preferred claim against the payor bank.

(c) If a payor bank gives or a collecting bank gives or receives a provisional settlement for an item and thereafter suspends payments, the suspension does not prevent or interfere with the settlement's becoming final if the finality occurs automatically upon the lapse of certain time or the happening of certain events.

(d) If a collecting bank receives from subsequent parties settlement for an item, which settlement is or becomes final and the bank suspends payments without making a settlement for the item with its customer which settlement is or becomes final, the owner of the item has a preferred claim against the collecting bank.

§4—301. DEFERRED POSTING; RECOVERY OF PAYMENT BY RETURN OF ITEMS; TIME OF DISHONOR; RETURN OF ITEMS BY PAYOR BANK

(a) If a payor bank settles for a demand item other than a documentary draft presented otherwise than for immediate payment over the counter before midnight of the banking day of receipt, the payor bank may revoke the settlement and recover the settlement if, before it has made final payment and before its midnight deadline, it

> (1) returns the item; or
>
> (2) sends written notice of dishonor or nonpayment if the item is unavailable for return.

(b) If a demand item is received by a payor bank for credit on its books, it may return the item or send notice of dishonor and may revoke any credit given or recover the amount thereof withdrawn by its customer, if it acts within the time limit and in the manner specified in subsection (a).

(c) Unless previous notice of dishonor has been sent, an item is dishonored at the time when for purposes of dishonor it is returned or notice sent in accordance with this section.

(d) An item is returned:

> (1) as to an item presented through a clearing house, when it is delivered to the presenting or last collecting bank or to the clearing house or is sent or delivered in accordance with clearing-house rules; or
>
> (2) in all other cases, when it is sent or delivered to the bank's customer or transferor or pursuant to instructions.

§4—302. PAYOR BANK'S RESPONSIBILITY FOR LATE RETURN OF ITEM

(a) If an item is presented to and received by a payor bank, the bank is accountable for the amount of:

> (1) a demand item, other than a documentary draft, whether properly payable or not, if the bank, in any case in which it is not also the depositary bank, retains the item beyond midnight of the banking day of receipt without settling for it or, whether or not it is also the depositary bank, does not pay or return the item or send notice of dishonor until after its midnight deadline; or
>
> (2) any other properly payable item unless, within the time allowed for acceptance or payment of that item, the bank either accepts or pays the item or returns it and accompanying documents.

(b) The liability of a payor bank to pay an item pursuant to subsection (a) is subject to defenses based on breach of a presentment warranty (Section 4—208) or proof that the person seeking enforcement of the liability presented or transferred the item for the purpose of defrauding the payor bank.

§4—303. WHEN ITEMS SUBJECT TO NOTICE, STOP-PAYMENT ORDER, LEGAL PROCESS, OR SETOFF; ORDER IN WHICH ITEMS MAY BE CHARGED OR CERTIFIED

(a) Any knowledge, notice, or stop-payment order received by, legal process served upon, or setoff exercised by a payor bank comes too late to terminate, suspend, or modify the bank's right or duty to pay an item or to charge its customer's account for the item if the knowledge, notice, stop-payment order, or legal process is received or served and a reasonable time for the bank to act thereon expires or the setoff is exercised after the earliest of the following:

> (1) the bank accepts or certifies the item;
>
> (2) the bank pays the item in cash;
>
> (3) the bank settles for the item without having a right to revoke the settlement under statute, clearing-house rule, or agreement;
>
> (4) the bank becomes accountable for the amount of the item under Section 4—302 dealing with the payor bank's responsibility for late return of items; or
>
> (5) with respect to checks, a cutoff hour no earlier than one hour after the opening of the next banking day after the banking day on which the bank received the check and no later than the close of that next banking day or, if no cutoff hour is fixed,

the close of the next banking day after the banking day on which the bank received the check.

(b) Subject to subsection (a), items may be accepted, paid, certified, or charged to the indicated account of its customer in any order.

§4—401. WHEN BANK MAY CHARGE CUSTOMER'S ACCOUNT

(a) A bank may charge against the account of a customer an item that is properly payable from the account even though the charge creates an overdraft. An item is properly payable if it is authorized by the customer and is in accordance with any agreement between the customer and bank.

(b) A customer is not liable for the amount of an overdraft if the customer neither signed the item nor benefited from the proceeds of the item.

(c) A bank may charge against the account of a customer a check that is otherwise properly payable from the account, even though payment was made before the date of the check, unless the customer has given notice to the bank of the postdating describing the check with reasonable certainty. The notice is effective for the period stated in Section 4—403(b) for stop-payment orders, and must be received at such time and in such manner as to afford the bank a reasonable opportunity to act on it before the bank takes any action with respect to the check described in Section 4—303. If a bank charges against the account of a customer a check before the date stated in the notice of postdating, the bank is liable for damages for the loss resulting from its act. The loss may include damages for dishonor of subsequent items under Section 4—402.

(d) A bank that in good faith makes payment to a holder may charge the indicated account of its customer according to:

(1) the original terms of the altered item; or

(2) the terms of the completed item, even though the bank knows the item has been completed unless the bank has notice that the completion was improper.

§4—402. BANK'S LIABILITY TO CUSTOMER FOR WRONGFUL DISHONOR; TIME OF DETERMINING INSUFFICIENCY OF ACCOUNT

(a) Except as otherwise provided in this Article, a payor bank wrongfully dishonors an item if it dishonors an item that is properly payable, but a bank may dishonor an item that would create an overdraft unless it has agreed to pay the overdraft.

(b) A payor bank is liable to its customer for damages proximately caused by the wrongful dishonor of an item. Liability is limited to actual damages proved and may include damages for an arrest or prosecution of the customer or other consequential damages. Whether any consequential damages are proximately caused by the wrongful dishonor is a question of fact to be determined in each case.

(c) A payor bank's determination of the customer's account balance on which a decision to dishonor for insufficiency of available funds is based may be made at any time between the time the item is received by the payor bank and the time that the payor bank returns the item or gives notice in lieu of return, and no more than one determination need be made. If, at the election of the payor bank, a subsequent balance determination is made for the purpose of reevaluating the bank's decision to dishonor the item, the account balance at that time is determinative of whether a dishonor for insufficiency of available funds is wrongful.

§4—403. CUSTOMER'S RIGHT TO STOP PAYMENT; BURDEN OF PROOF OF LOSS

(a) A customer or any person authorized to draw on the account if there is more than one person may stop payment of any item drawn on the customer's account or close the account by an order to the bank describing the item or account with reasonable certainty received at a time and in a manner that affords the bank a reasonable opportunity to act on it before any action by the bank with respect to the item described in Section 4—303. If the signature of more than one person is required to draw on an account, any of these persons may stop payment or close the account.

(b) A stop-payment order is effective for six months, but it lapses after 14 calendar days if the original order was oral and was not confirmed in writing within that period. A stop-payment order may be renewed for additional six-month periods by a writing given to the bank within a period during which the stop-payment order is effective.

(c) The burden of establishing the fact and amount of loss resulting from the payment of an item contrary to a stop-payment order or order to close an account is on the customer. The loss from payment of an item contrary to a stop-payment order may include damages for dishonor of subsequent items under Section 4—402.

§4—404. BANK NOT OBLIGED TO PAY CHECK MORE THAN SIX MONTHS OLD

A bank is under no obligation to a customer having a checking account to pay a check, other than a certified check, which is presented more than six months after its date, but it may charge its customer's account for a payment made thereafter in good faith.

§4—405. DEATH OR INCOMPETENCE OF CUSTOMER

(a) A payor or collecting bank's authority to accept, pay, or collect an item or to account for proceeds of its collection, if otherwise effective, is not rendered ineffective by incompetence of a customer of either bank existing at the time the item is issued or its collection is undertaken if the bank does not know of an adjudication of incompetence. Neither death nor incompetence of a customer revokes the authority to accept, pay, collect, or account until the bank knows of the fact of death or of an adjudication of incompetence and has reasonable opportunity to act on it.

(b) Even with knowledge, a bank may for 10 days after the date of death pay or certify checks drawn on or before the date unless ordered to stop payment by a person claiming an interest in the account.

§4—406. CUSTOMER'S DUTY TO DISCOVER AND REPORT UNAUTHORIZED SIGNATURE OR ALTERATION

(a) A bank that sends or makes available to a customer a statement of account showing payment of items for the account shall either return or make available to the customer the items paid or provide information in the statement of account sufficient to allow the customer reasonably to identify the items paid. The statement of account provides sufficient information if the item is described by item number, amount, and date of payment.

(b) If the items are not returned to the customer, the person retaining the items shall either retain the items or, if the items are destroyed, maintain the capacity to furnish legible copies of the items until the expiration of seven years after receipt of the items. A customer may request an item from the bank that paid the item, and that bank must provide in a reasonable time either the item or, if the item has been destroyed or is not otherwise obtainable, a legible copy of the item.

(c) If a bank sends or makes available a statement of account or items pursuant to subsection (a), the customer must exercise reasonable promptness in examining the statement or the items to determine whether any payment was not authorized because of an alteration of an item or because a purported signature by or on behalf of the customer was not authorized. If, based on the statement or items provided, the customer should reasonably have discovered the unauthorized payment, the customer must promptly notify the bank of the relevant facts.

(d) If the bank proves that the customer failed, with respect to an item, to comply with the duties imposed on the customer by subsection (c), the customer is precluded from asserting against the bank:

> (1) the customer's unauthorized signature or any alteration on the item, if the bank also proves that it suffered a loss by reason of the failure; and

> (2) the customer's unauthorized signature or alteration by the same wrongdoer on any other item paid in good faith by the bank if the payment was made before the bank received notice from the customer of the unauthorized signature or alteration and after the customer had been afforded a reasonable period of time, not exceeding 30 days, in which to examine the item or statement of account and notify the bank.

(e) If subsection (d) applies and the customer proves that the bank failed to exercise ordinary care in paying the item and that the failure substantially contributed to loss, the loss is allocated between the customer precluded and the bank asserting the preclusion according to the extent to which the failure of the customer to comply with subsection (c) and the failure of the bank to exercise ordinary care contributed to the loss. If the customer proves that the bank did not pay the item in good faith, the preclusion under subsection (d) does not apply.

(f) Without regard to care or lack of care of either the customer or the bank, a customer who does not within one year after the statement or items are made available to the customer (subsection (a)) discover and report the customer's unauthorized signature on or any alteration on the item is precluded from asserting against the bank the unauthorized signature or alteration. If there is a preclusion under this subsection, the payor bank may not recover for breach or warranty under Section 4—208 with respect to the unauthorized signature or alteration to which the preclusion applies.

§4—407. PAYOR BANK'S RIGHT TO SUBROGATION ON IMPROPER PAYMENT

If a payor has paid an item over the order of the drawer or maker to stop payment, or after an account has been closed, or otherwise under circumstances giving a basis for objection by the drawer or maker, to prevent unjust enrichment and only to the extent necessary to prevent loss to the bank by reason of its payment of the item, the payor bank is subrogated to the rights

(1) of any holder in due course on the item against the drawer or maker;

(2) of the payee or any other holder of the item against the drawer or maker either on the item or under the transaction out of which the item arose; and

(3) of the drawer or maker against the payee or any other holder of the item with respect to the transaction out of which the item arose.

* * * *

Article 4A Funds Transfers

Part 1 Subject Matter and Definitions

§4A—104. FUNDS TRANSFER—DEFINITIONS

(a) "Funds transfer" means the series of transactions, beginning with the originator's payment order, made for the purpose of making payment to the beneficiary of the order. The term includes any payment order issued by the originator's bank or an intermediary bank intended to carry out the originator's payment order. A funds transfer is completed by acceptance by the beneficiary's bank of a payment order for the benefit of the beneficiary of the originator's payment order.

(b) "Intermediary bank" means a receiving bank other than the originator's bank or the beneficiary's bank.

(c) "Originator" means the sender of the first payment order in a funds transfer.

(d) "Originator's bank" means (i) the receiving bank to which the payment order of the originator is issued if the originator is not a bank, or (ii) the originator if the originator is a bank.

§4A—105. OTHER DEFINITIONS

(1) "Authorized account" means a deposit account of a customer in a bank designated by the customer as a source of payment of payment orders issued by the customer to the bank. If a customer does not so designate an account, any account of the customer is an authorized account if payment of a payment order from that account is not inconsistent with a restriction on the use of that account.

(2) "Bank" means a person engaged in the business of banking and includes a savings bank, savings and loan association, credit union, and trust company. A branch or separate office of a bank is a separate bank for purposes of this Article.

(3) "Customer" means a person, including a bank, having an account with a bank or from whom a bank has agreed to receive payment orders.

(4) "Funds-transfer business day" of a receiving bank means the part of a day during which the receiving bank is open for the receipt, processing, and transmittal of payment orders and cancellations and amendments of payment orders.

(5) "Funds-transfer system" means a wire transfer network, automated clearing house, or other communication system of a clearing house or other association of banks through which a payment order by a bank may be transmitted to the bank to which the order is addressed.

(6) "Good faith" means honesty in fact and the observance of reasonable commercial standards of fair dealing.

(7) "Prove" with respect to a fact means to meet the burden of establishing the fact (Section 1—201(8)).

* * * *

§4A—106. TIME PAYMENT ORDER IS RECEIVED

(a) The time of receipt of a payment order or communication cancelling or amending a payment order is determined by the rules applicable to receipt of a notice stated in Section 1—201(27). A receiving bank may fix a cut-off time or times on a funds-transfer business day for the receipt and processing of payment orders and communications cancelling or amending payment orders. Different cut-off times may apply to payment orders, cancellations, or amendments, or to different categories of payment orders, cancellations, or amendments. A cut-off time may apply to senders generally or different cut-off times may apply to different senders or categories of payment orders. If a payment order or communication cancelling or amending a payment order is received after the close of a funds-transfer business day or after the appropriate cut-off time on a funds-transfer business day, the receiving bank may treat the payment order or communication as received at the opening of the next funds-transfer business day.

(b) If this Article refers to an execution date or payment date or states a day on which a receiving bank is required to take action, and the date or day does not fall on a funds-transfer business day, the next day that is a funds- transfer business day is treated as the date or day stated, unless the contrary is stated in this Article.

* * * *

§4A—108. EXCLUSION OF CONSUMER TRANSACTIONS GOVERNED BY FEDERAL LAW

This Article does not apply to a funds transfer any part of which is governed by the Electronic Fund Transfer Act of 1978 (Title XX, Public Law 95—630, 92 Stat. 3728, 15 U.S.C. §1693 et seq.) as amended from time to time.

* * * *

Revised Article 9 Secured Transactions

§9—102. DEFINITIONS AND INDEX OF DEFINITIONS

(1) "Accession" means goods that are physically united with other goods in such a manner that the identity of the original goods is not lost.

(2) "Account", except as used in "account for", means a right to payment of a monetary obligation, whether or not earned by performance, (i) for property that has been or is to be sold, leased, licensed, assigned, or otherwise disposed of, (ii) for services rendered or to be rendered, (iii) for a policy of insurance issued or to be issued, (iv) for a secondary obligation incurred or to be incurred, (v) for energy provided or to be provided, (vi) for the use or hire of a vessel under a charter or other contract, (vii) arising out of the use of a credit or charge card or information contained on or for use with the card, or (viii) as winnings in a lottery or other game of chance operated or sponsored by a State, governmental unit of a State, or person licensed or authorized to operate the game by a State or governmental unit of a State. The term includes health-care insurance receivables. The term does not include (i) rights to payment evidenced by chattel paper or an instrument, (ii) commercial tort claims, (iii) deposit accounts, (iv) investment property, (v) letter-of-credit rights or letters of credit, or (vi) rights to payment for money or funds advanced or sold, other than rights arising out of the use of a credit or charge card or information contained on or for use with the card.

* * * *

(5) "Agricultural lien" means an interest, other than a security interest, in farm products:

(A) which secures payment or performance of an obligation for:

(i) goods or services furnished in connection with a debtor's farming operation; or

(ii) rent on real property leased by a debtor in connection with its farming operation;

(B) which is created by statute in favor of a person that:

(i) in the ordinary course of its business furnished goods or services to a debtor in connection with a debtor's farming operation; or

(ii) leased real property to a debtor in connection with the debtor's farming operation; and

(C) whose effectiveness does not depend on the person's possession of the personal property.

(6) "As-extracted collateral" means:

(A) oil, gas, or other minerals that are subject to a security interest that:

(i) is created by a debtor having an interest in the minerals before extraction; and

(ii) attaches to the minerals as extracted; or

(B) accounts arising out of the sale at the wellhead or minehead of oil, gas, or other minerals in which the debtor had an interest before extraction.

(7) "Authenticate" means:

(A) to sign; or

(B) to execute or otherwise adopt a symbol, or encrypt or similarly process a record in whole or in part, with the present intent of the authenticating person to identify the person and adopt or accept a record.

* * * *

(11) "Chattel paper" means a record or records that evidence both a monetary obligation and a security interest in specific goods, a security interest in specific goods and software used in the goods, a security interest in specific goods and license of software used in the goods, a lease of specific goods, or a lease of specific goods and license of software used in the goods. In this paragraph, "monetary obligation" means a monetary obligation secured by the goods or owed under a lease of the goods and includes a monetary obligation with respect to software used in the goods. The term does not include (i) charters or other contracts involving the use or hire of a vessel or (ii) records that evidence a right to payment arising out of the use of a credit or charge card or information contained on or for use with the card. If a transaction is evidenced by records that include an instrument or

series of instruments, the group of records taken together constitutes chattel paper.

(12) "Collateral" means the property subject to a security interest or agricultural lien. The term includes:

(A) proceeds to which a security interest attaches;

(B) accounts, chattel paper, payment intangibles, and promissory notes that have been sold; and

(C) goods that are the subject of a consignment.

(13) "Commercial tort claim" means a claim arising in tort with respect to which:

(A) the claimant is an organization; or

(B) the claimant is an individual and the claim:

(i) arose in the course of the claimant's business or profession; and

(ii) does not include damages arising out of personal injury to or the death of an individual.

* * * *

(19) "Consignee" means a merchant to which goods are delivered in a consignment.

(20) "Consignment" means a transaction, regardless of its form, in which a person delivers goods to a merchant for the purpose of sale and:

(A) the merchant:

(i) deals in goods of that kind under a name other than the name of the person making delivery;

(ii) is not an auctioneer; and

(iii) is not generally known by its creditors to be substantially engaged in selling the goods of others;

(B) with respect to each delivery, the aggregate value of the goods is $1,000 or more at the time of delivery;

(C) the goods are not consumer goods immediately before delivery; and

(D) the transaction does not create a security interest that secures an obligation.

(21) "Consignor" means a person that delivers goods to a consignee in a consignment.

(22) "Consumer debtor" means a debtor in a consumer transaction.

(23) "Consumer goods" means goods that are used or bought for use primarily for personal, family, or household purposes.

(24) "Consumer-goods transaction" means a consumer transaction in which:

(A) an individual incurs an obligation primarily for personal, family, or household purposes; and

(B) a security interest in consumer goods secures the obligation.

(25) "Consumer obligor" means an obligor who is an individual and who incurred the obligation as part of a transaction entered into primarily for personal, family, or household purposes.

(26) "Consumer transaction" means a transaction in which (i) an individual incurs an obligation primarily for personal, family, or household purposes, (ii) a security interest secures the obligation, and (iii) the collateral is held or acquired primarily for personal, family, or household purposes. The term includes consumer-goods transactions.

(27) "Continuation statement" means an amendment of a financing statement which:

(A) identifies, by its file number, the initial financing statement to which it relates; and

(B) indicates that it is a continuation statement for, or that it is filed to continue the effectiveness of, the identified financing statement.

(28) "Debtor" means:

(A) a person having an interest, other than a security interest or other lien, in the collateral, whether or not the person is an obligor;

(B) a seller of accounts, chattel paper, payment intangibles, or promissory notes; or

(C) a consignee.

(29) "Deposit account" means a demand, time, savings, passbook, or similar account maintained with a bank. The term does not include investment property or accounts evidenced by an instrument.

(30) "Document" means a document of title or a receipt of the type described in Section 7—201(2).

(31) "Electronic chattel paper" means chattel paper evidenced by a record or records consisting of information stored in an electronic medium.

(32) "Encumbrance" means a right, other than an ownership interest, in real property. The term includes mortgages and other liens on real property.

(33) "Equipment" means goods other than inventory, farm products, or consumer goods.

(34) "Farm products" means goods, other than standing timber, with respect to which the debtor is engaged in a farming operation and which are:

(A) crops grown, growing, or to be grown, including:

   (i) crops produced on trees, vines, and bushes; and

   (ii) aquatic goods produced in aquacultural operations;

(B) livestock, born or unborn, including aquatic goods produced in aquacultural operations;

(C) supplies used or produced in a farming operation; or

(D) products of crops or livestock in their unmanufactured states.

(35) "Farming operation" means raising, cultivating, propagating, fattening, grazing, or any other farming, livestock, or aquacultural operation.

* * * *

(39) "Financing statement" means a record or records composed of an initial financing statement and any filed record relating to the initial financing statement.

(40) "Fixture filing" means the filing of a financing statement covering goods that are or are to become fixtures and satisfying Section 9—502(a) and (b). The term includes the filing of a financing statement covering goods of a transmitting utility which are or are to become fixtures.

(41) "Fixtures" means goods that have become so related to particular real property that an interest in them arises under real property law.

(42) "General intangible" means any personal property, including things in action, other than accounts, chattel paper, commercial tort claims, deposit accounts, documents, goods, instruments, investment property, letter-of-credit rights, letters of credit, money, and oil, gas, or other minerals before extraction. The term includes payment intangibles and software.

* * * *

(44) "Goods" means all things that are movable when a security interest attaches. The term includes (i) fixtures, (ii) standing timber that is to be cut and removed under a conveyance or contract for sale, (iii) the unborn young of animals, (iv) crops grown, growing, or to be grown, even if the crops are produced on trees, vines, or bushes, and (v) manufactured homes. The term also includes a computer program embedded in goods and any supporting information provided in connection with a transaction relating to the program if (i) the program is associated with the goods in such a manner that it customarily is considered part of the goods, or (ii) by becoming the owner of the goods, a person acquires a right to use the program in connection with the goods. The term does not include a computer program embedded in goods that consist solely of the medium in which the program is embedded. The term also does not include accounts, chattel paper, commercial tort claims, deposit accounts, documents, general intangibles, instruments, investment property, letter-of-credit rights, letters of credit, money, or oil, gas, or other minerals before extraction.

* * * *

(46) "Health-care-insurance receivable" means an interest in or claim under a policy of insurance which is a right to payment of a monetary obligation for health-care goods or services provided.

(47) "Instrument" means a negotiable instrument or any other writing that evidences a right to the payment of a monetary obligation, is not itself a security agreement or lease, and is of a type that in ordinary course of business is transferred by delivery with any necessary indorsement or assignment. The term does not include (i) investment property, (ii) letters of credit, or (iii) writings that evidence a right to payment arising out of the use of a credit or charge card or information contained on or for use with the card.

(48) "Inventory" means goods, other than farm products, which:

   (A) are leased by a person as lessor;

   (B) are held by a person for sale or lease or to be furnished under a contract of service;

   (C) are furnished by a person under a contract of service; or

   (D) consist of raw materials, work in process, or materials used or consumed in a business.

(49) "Investment property" means a security, whether certificated or uncertificated, security entitlement, securities account, commodity contract, or commodity account.

* * * *

(51) "Letter-of-credit right" means a right to payment or performance under a letter of credit, whether or not the beneficiary has demanded or is at the time entitled to demand payment or performance. The term does not include the right of a beneficiary to demand payment or performance under a letter of credit.

(52) "Lien creditor" means:

   (A) a creditor that has acquired a lien on the property involved by attachment, levy, or the like;

(B) an assignee for benefit of creditors from the time of assignment;

(C) a trustee in bankruptcy from the date of the filing of the petition; or

(D) a receiver in equity from the time of appointment.

* * * *

(55) "Mortgage" means a consensual interest in real property, including fixtures, which secures payment or performance of an obligation.

(56) "New debtor" means a person that becomes bound as debtor under Section 9—203(d) by a security agreement previously entered into by another person.

(57) "New value" means (i) money, (ii) money's worth in property, services, or new credit, or (iii) release by a transferee of an interest in property previously transferreed to the transferee. The term does not include an obligation substituted for another obligation.

* * * *

(61) "Payment intangible" means a general intangible under which the account debtor's principal obligation is a monetary obligation.

* * * *

(64) "Proceeds", except as used in Section 9—609 (b), means the following property:

(A) whatever is acquired upon the sale, lease, license, exchange, or other disposition of collateral;

(B) whatever is collected on, or distributed on account of, collateral;

(C) rights arising out of collateral;

(D) to the extent of the value of collateral, claims arising out of the loss, non-conformity, or interference with the use of, defects or infringement of rights in, or damage to, the collateral; or

(E) to the extent of the value of collateral and to the extent payable to the debtor or the secured party, insurance payable by reason of the loss or non-conformity of, defects or infringement of rights in, or damage to, the collateral.

* * * *

(69) "Record", except as used in "for record", "of record", "record or legal title", and "record owner", means information that is inscribed on a tangible medium or which is stored in an electronic or other medium and is retrievable in perceivable form.

* * * *

(72) "Secured party" means:

(A) a person in whose favor a security interest is created or provided for under a security agreement, whether or not any obligation to be secured is outstanding;

(B) a person that holds an agricultural lien;

(C) a consignor;

(D) a person to which accounts, chattel paper, payment intangibles, or promissory notes have been sold;

(E) a trustee, indenture trustee, agent, collateral agent, or other representative in whose favor a security interest or agricultural lien is created or provided for; or

(F) a person that holds a security interest arising under Section 2—401, 2—505, 2—711(3), 2A—508(5), 4—210, or 5—118.

(73) "Security agreement" means an agreement that creates or provides for a security interest.

* * * *

(78) "Tangible chattel paper" means chattel paper evidenced by a record or records consisting of information that is inscribed on a tangible medium.

(79) "Termination statement" means an amendment of a financing statement which:

(A) identifies, by its file number, the initial financing statement to which it relates; and

(B) indicates either that it is a termination statement or that the identified financing statement is no longer effective.

* * * *

§9—103. PURCHASE-MONEY SECURITY INTEREST; APPLICATION OF PAYMENTS; BURDEN OF ESTABLISHING

(a) In this section:

(1) "purchase-money collateral" means goods or software that secures a purchase-money obligation incurred with respect to that collateral; and

(2) "purchase-money obligation" means an obligation of an obligor incurred as all or part of the price of the collateral or for value given to enable the debtor to acquire rights in or the use of the collateral if the value is in fact so used.

(b) A security interest in goods is a purchase-money security interest:

(1) to the extent that the goods are purchase-money collateral with respect to that security interest;

(2) if the security interest is in inventory that is or was purchase-money collateral, also to the extent that the security interest secures a purchase-money obligation incurred with respect to other inventory in which the secured party holds or held a purchase-money security interest; and

(3) also to the extent that the security interest secures a purchase-money obligation incurred with respect to software in which the secured party holds or held a purchase-money security interest.

(c) A security interest in software is a purchase-money security interest to the extent that the security interest also secures a purchase-money obligation incurred with respect to goods in which the secured party holds or held a purchase-money security interest if:

(1) the debtor acquired its interest in the software in an integrated transaction in which it acquired an interest in the goods; and

(2) the debtor acquired its interest in the software for the principal purpose of using the software in the goods.

(d) The security interest of a consignor in goods that are the subject of a consignment is a purchase-money security interest in inventory.

(e) In a transaction other than a consumer-goods transaction, if the extent to which a security interest is a purchase-money security interest depends on the application of a payment to a particular obligation, the payment must be applied:

(1) in accordance with any reasonable method of application to which the parties agree;

(2) in the absence of the parties' agreement to a reasonable method, in accordance with any intention of the obligor manifested at or before the time of payment; or

(3) in the absence of an agreement to a reasonable method and a timely manifestation of the obligor's intention, in the following order:

(A) to obligations that are not secured; and

(B) if more than one obligation is secured, to obligations secured by purchase-money security interests in the order in which those obligations were incurred.

(f) In a transaction other than a consumer-goods transaction, a purchase-money security interest does not lose its status as such, even if:

(1) the purchase-money collateral also secures an obligation that is not a purchase-money obligation;

(2) collateral that is not purchase-money collateral also secures the purchase-money obligation; or

(3) the purchase-money obligation has been renewed, refinanced, consolidated, or restructured.

(g) In a transaction other than a consumer-goods transaction, a secured party claiming a purchase-money security interest has the burden of establishing the extent to which the security interest is a purchase-money security interest.

(h) The limitation of the rules in subsections (e), (f), and (g) to transactions other than consumer-goods transactions is intended to leave to the court the determination of the proper rules in consumer-goods transactions. The court may not infer from that limitation the nature of the proper rule in consumer-goods transactions and may continue to apply established approaches.

§9—104. CONTROL OF DEPOSIT ACCOUNT

(a) A secured party has control of a deposit account if:

(1) the secured party is the bank with which the deposit account is maintained;

(2) the debtor, secured party, and bank have agreed in an authenticated record that the bank will comply with instructions originated by the secured party directing disposition of the funds in the deposit account without further consent by the debtor; or

(3) the secured party becomes the bank's customer with respect to the deposit account.

(b) A secured party that has satisfied subsection (a) has control, even if the debtor retains the right to direct the disposition of funds from the deposit account.

§9—105. CONTROL OF ELECTRONIC CHATTEL PAPER

A secured party has control of electronic chattel paper if the record or records comprising the chattel paper are created, stored, and assigned in such a manner that:

(1) a single authoritative copy of the record or records exists which is unique, identifiable and, except as otherwise provided in paragraphs (4), (5), and (6), unalterable;

(2) the authoritative copy identifies the secured party as the assignee of the record or records;

(3) the authoritative copy is communicated to and maintained by the secured party or its designated custodian;

(4) copies or revisions that add or change an identified assignee of the authoritative copy can be made only with the participation of the secured party;

(5) each copy of the authoritative copy and any copy of a copy is readily identifiable as a copy that is not the authoritative copy; and

(6) any revision of the authoritative copy is readily identifiable as an authorized or unauthorized revision.

§9—106. CONTROL OF INVESTMENT PROPERTY

(a) A person has control of a certificated security, uncertificated security, or security entitlement as provided in Section 8—106.

(b) A secured party has control of a commodity contract if:

(1) the secured party is the commodity intermediary with which the commodity contract is carried; or

(2) the commodity customer, secured party, and commodity intermediary have agreed that the commodity intermediary will apply any value distributed on account of the commodity contract as directed by the secured party without further consent by the commodity customer.

(c) A secured party having control of all security entitlements or commodity contracts carried in a securities account or commodity account has control over the securities account or commodity account.

§9—107. CONTROL OF LETTER-OF-CREDIT RIGHT

A secured party has control of a letter-of-credit right to the extent of any right to payment or performance by the issuer or any nominated person if the issuer or nominated person has consented to an assignment of proceeds of the letter of credit under Section 5—114(c) or otherwise applicable law or practice.

§9—108. SUFFICIENCY OF DESCRIPTION

(a) Except as otherwise provided in subsections (c), (d), and (e), a description of personal or real property is sufficient, whether or not it is specific, if it reasonably identifies what is described.

(b) Except as otherwise provided in subsection (d), a description of collateral reasonably identifies the collateral if it identifies the collateral by:

(1) specific listing;

(2) category;

(3) except as otherwise provided in subsection (e), a type of collateral defined in [the Uniform Commercial Code];

(4) quantity;

(5) computational or allocational formula or procedure; or

(6) except as otherwise provided in subsection (c), any other method, if the identity of the collateral is objectively determinable.

(c) A description of collateral as "all the debtor's assets" or "all the debtor's personal property" or using words of similar import does not reasonably identify the collateral.

(d) Except as otherwise provided in subsection (e), a description of a security entitlement, securities account, or commodity account is sufficient if it describes:

(1) the collateral by those terms or as investment property; or

(2) the underlying financial asset or commodity contract.

(e) A description only by type of collateral defined in [the Uniform Commercial Code] is an insufficient description of:

(1) a commercial tort claim; or

(2) in a consumer transaction, consumer goods, a security entitlement, a securities account, or a commodity account.

§9-109 SCOPE

* * * *

This article does not apply to:

(1) a landlord's lien, other than an agricultural lien;

(2) a lien, other than an agricultural lien, given by statute or other rule of law for services or materials, but Section 9—333 applies with respect to priority of the lien;

(3) an assignment of a claim for wages, salary, or other compensation of an employee;

(4) a sale of accounts, chattel paper, payment intangibles, or promissory notes as part of a sale of the business out of which they arose;

(5) an assignment of accounts, chattel paper, payment intangibles, or promissory notes which is for the purpose of collection only;

(6) an assignment of a right to payment under a contract to an assignee that is also obligated to perform under the contract;

(7) an assignment of a single account, payment intangible, or promissory note to an assignee in full or partial satisfaction of a preexisting indebtedness;

(8) a transfer of an interest in or an assignment of a claim under a policy of insurance, other than an

assignment by or to a health-care provider of a health-care-insurance receivable and any subsequent assignment of the right to payment, but Sections 9—315 and 9—322 apply with respect to proceeds and priorities in proceeds;

(9) an assignment of a right represented by a judgment, other than a judgment taken on a right to payment that was collateral;

(10) a right of recoupment or set-off, but:

(A) Section 9—340 applies with respect to the effectiveness of rights of recoupment or set-off against deposit accounts; and

(B) Section 9—404 applies with respect to defenses or claims of an account debtor;

(11) the creation or transfer of an interest in or lien on real property, including a lease or rents thereunder, except to the extent that provision is made for:

(A) liens on real property in Sections 9—203 and 9—308;

(B) fixtures in Section 9—334;

(C) fixture filings in Sections 9—501, 9—502, 9—512, 9—516, and 9—519; and

(D) security agreements covering personal and real property in Section 9—604;

(12) an assignment of a claim arising in tort, other than a commercial tort claim, but Sections 9—315 and 9—322 apply with respect to proceeds and priorities in proceeds; or

(13) an assignment of a deposit account in a consumer transaction, but Sections 9—315 and 9—322 apply with respect to proceeds and priorities in proceeds.

* * * *

§9—201. GENERAL EFFECTIVENESS OF SECURITY AGREEMENT

(a) Except as otherwise provided in [the Uniform Commercial Code], a security agreement is effective according to its terms between the parties, against purchasers of the collateral, and against creditors.

(b) A transaction subject to this article is subject to any applicable rule of law which establishes a different rule for consumers and [insert reference to (i) any other statute or regulation that regulates the rates, charges, agreements, and practices for loans, credit sales, or other extensions of credit and (ii) any consumer-protection statute or regulation].

(c) In case of conflict between this article and a rule of law, statute, or regulation described in subsection (b),

the rule of law, statute, or regulation controls. Failure to comply with a statute or regulation described in subsection (b) has only the effect the statute or regulation specifies.

(d) This article does not:

(1) validate any rate, charge, agreement, or practice that violates a rule of law, statute, or regulation described in subsection (b); or

(2) extend the application of the rule of law, statute, or regulation to a transaction not otherwise subject to it.

§9—202. TITLE TO COLLATERAL IMMATERIAL

Except as otherwise provided with respect to consignments or sales of accounts, chattel paper, payment intangibles, or promissory notes, the provisions of this article with regard to rights and obligations apply whether title to collateral is in the secured party or the debtor.

§9—203. ATTACHMENT AND ENFORCEABILITY OF SECURITY INTEREST; PROCEEDS; SUPPORTING OBLIGATIONS; FORMAL REQUISITES

(a) A security interest attaches to collateral when it becomes enforceable against the debtor with respect to the collateral, unless an agreement expressly postpones the time of attachment.

(b) Except as otherwise provided in subsections (c) through (i), a security interest is enforceable against the debtor and third parties with respect to the collateral only if:

(1) value has been given;

(2) the debtor has rights in the collateral or the power to transfer rights in the collateral to a secured party; and

(3) one of the following conditions is met:

(A) the debtor has authenticated a security agreement that provides a description of the collateral and, if the security interest covers timber to be cut, a description of the land concerned;

(B) the collateral is not a certificated security and is in the possession of the secured party under Section 9—313 pursuant to the debtor's security agreement;

(C) the collateral is a certificated security in registered form and the security certificate has been delivered to the secured party under Section 8—301 pursuant to the debtor's security agreement; or

(D) the collateral is deposit accounts, electronic chattel paper, investment property, or letter-of-credit rights, and the secured party has control under Section 9—104, 9—105, 9—106, or 9—107 pursuant to the debtor's security agreement.

(c) Subsection (b) is subject to Section 4—210 on the security interest of a collecting bank, Section 5—118 on the security interest of a letter-of-credit issuer or nominated person, Section 9—110 on a security interest arising under Article 2 or 2A, and Section 9—206 on security interests in investment property.

(d) A person becomes bound as debtor by a security agreement entered into by another person if, by operation of law other than this article or by contract:

(1) the security agreement becomes effective to create a security interest in the person's property; or

(2) the person becomes generally obligated for the obligations of the other person, including the obligation secured under the security agreement, and acquires or succeeds to all or substantially all of the assets of the other person.

(e) If a new debtor becomes bound as debtor by a security agreement entered into by another person:

(1) the agreement satisfies subsection (b)(3) with respect to existing or after-acquired property of the new debtor to the extent the property is described in the agreement; and

(2) another agreement is not necessary to make a security interest in the property enforceable.

(f) The attachment of a security interest in collateral gives the secured party the rights to proceeds provided by Section 9—315 and is also attachment of a security interest in a supporting obligation for the collateral.

(g) The attachment of a security interest in a right to payment or performance secured by a security interest or other lien on personal or real property is also attachment of a security interest in the security interest, mortgage, or other lien.

(h) The attachment of a security interest in a securities account is also attachment of a security interest in the security entitlements carried in the securities account.

(i) The attachment of a security interest in a commodity account is also attachment of a security interest in the commodity contracts carried in the commodity account.

§9—204. AFTER-ACQUIRED PROPERTY; FUTURE ADVANCES

(a) Except as otherwise provided in subsection (b), a security agreement may create or provide for a security interest in after-acquired collateral.

(b) A security interest does not attach under a term constituting an after-acquired property clause to:

(1) consumer goods, other than an accession when given as additional security, unless the debtor acquires rights in them within 10 days after the secured party gives value; or

(2) a commercial tort claim.

(c) A security agreement may provide that collateral secures, or that accounts, chattel paper, payment intangibles, or promissory notes are sold in connection with, future advances or other value, whether or not the advances or value are given pursuant to commitment.

§9—205. USE OR DISPOSITION OF COLLATERAL PERMISSIBLE

(a) A security interest is not invalid or fraudulent against creditors solely because:

(1) the debtor has the right or ability to:

(A) use, commingle, or dispose of all or part of the collateral, including returned or repossessed goods;

(B) collect, compromise, enforce, or otherwise deal with collateral;

(C) accept the return of collateral or make repossessions; or

(D) use, commingle, or dispose of proceeds; or

(2) the secured party fails to require the debtor to account for proceeds or replace collateral.

(b) This section does not relax the requirements of possession if attachment, perfection, or enforcement of a security interest depends upon possession of the collateral by the secured party.

§9—206. SECURITY INTEREST ARISING IN PURCHASE OR DELIVERY OF FINANCIAL ASSET

(a) A security interest in favor of a securities intermediary attaches to a person's security entitlement if:

(1) the person buys a financial asset through the securities intermediary in a transaction in which the person is obligated to pay the purchase price to the securities intermediary at the time of the purchase; and

(2) the securities intermediary credits the financial asset to the buyer's securities account before the buyer pays the securities intermediary.

(b) The security interest described in subsection (a) secures the person's obligation to pay for the financial asset.

* * * *

§9—207. RIGHTS AND DUTIES OF SECURED PARTY HAVING POSSESSION OR CONTROL OF COLLATERAL

(a) Except as otherwise provided in subsection (d), a secured party shall use reasonable care in the custody and preservation of collateral in the secured party's possession. In the case of chattel paper or an instrument, reasonable care includes taking necessary steps to preserve rights against prior parties unless otherwise agreed.

(b) Except as otherwise provided in subsection (d), if a secured party has possession of collateral:

(1) reasonable expenses, including the cost of insurance and payment of taxes or other charges, incurred in the custody, preservation, use, or operation of the collateral are chargeable to the debtor and are secured by the collateral;

(2) the risk of accidental loss or damage is on the debtor to the extent of a deficiency in any effective insurance coverage;

(3) the secured party shall keep the collateral identifiable, but fungible collateral may be commingled; and

(4) the secured party may use or operate the collateral:

(A) for the purpose of preserving the collateral or its value;

(B) as permitted by an order of a court having competent jurisdiction; or

(C) except in the case of consumer goods, in the manner and to the extent agreed by the debtor.

(c) Except as otherwise provided in subsection (d), a secured party having possession of collateral or control of collateral under Section 9—104, 9—105, 9—106, or 9—107:

(1) may hold as additional security any proceeds, except money or funds, received from the collateral;

(2) shall apply money or funds received from the collateral to reduce the secured obligation, unless remitted to the debtor; and

(3) may create a security interest in the collateral.

(d) If the secured party is a buyer of accounts, chattel paper, payment intangibles, or promissory notes or a consignor:

(1) subsection (a) does not apply unless the secured party is entitled under an agreement:

(A) to charge back uncollected collateral; or

(B) otherwise to full or limited recourse against the debtor or a secondary obligor based on the nonpayment or other default of an account debtor or other obligor on the collateral; and

(2) subsections (b) and (c) do not apply.

§9—208. ADDITIONAL DUTIES OF SECURED PARTY HAVING CONTROL OF COLLATERAL

(a) This section applies to cases in which there is no outstanding secured obligation and the secured party is not committed to make advances, incur obligations, or otherwise give value.

(b) Within 10 days after receiving an authenticated demand by the debtor:

(1) a secured party having control of a deposit account under Section 9—104(a)(2) shall send to the bank with which the deposit account is maintained an authenticated statement that releases the bank from any further obligation to comply with instructions originated by the secured party;

(2) a secured party having control of a deposit account under Section 9—104(a)(3) shall:

(A) pay the debtor the balance on deposit in the deposit account; or

(B) transfer the balance on deposit into a deposit account in the debtor's name;

(3) a secured party, other than a buyer, having control of electronic chattel paper under Section 9—105 shall:

(A) communicate the authoritative copy of the electronic chattel paper to the debtor or its designated custodian;

(B) if the debtor designates a custodian that is the designated custodian with which the authoritative copy of the electronic chattel paper is maintained for the secured party, communicate to the custodian an authenticated record releasing the designated custodian from any further obligation to comply with instructions originated by the secured party and instructing the custodian to comply with instructions originated by the debtor; and

(C) take appropriate action to enable the debtor or its designated custodian to make copies of or revisions to the authoritative copy which add or change an identified assignee of the authoritative copy without the consent of the secured party;

(4) a secured party having control of investment property under Section 8—106(d)(2) or 9—106(b) shall send to the securities intermediary or commodity intermediary with which the security entitlement or commodity contract is maintained an authenticated record that releases the securities intermediary or commodity intermediary from any further obligation to comply with entitlement orders or directions originated by the secured party; and

(5) a secured party having control of a letter-of-credit right under Section 9—107 shall send to each person having an unfulfilled obligation to pay or deliver proceeds of the letter of credit to the secured party an authenticated release from any further obligation to pay or deliver proceeds of the letter of credit to the secured party.

§9—209. DUTIES OF SECURED PARTY IF ACCOUNT DEBTOR HAS BEEN NOTIFIED OF ASSIGNMENT

(a) Except as otherwise provided in subsection (c), this section applies if:

(1) there is no outstanding secured obligation; and

(2) the secured party is not committed to make advances, incur obligations, or otherwise give value.

(b) Within 10 days after receiving an authenticated demand by the debtor, a secured party shall send to an account debtor that has received notification of an assignment to the secured party as assignee under Section 9—406(a) an authenticated record that releases the account debtor from any further obligation to the secured party.

* * * *

§9—301. LAW GOVERNING PERFECTION AND PRIORITY OF SECURITY INTERESTS

Except as otherwise provided in Sections 9—303 through 9—306, the following rules determine the law governing perfection, the effect of perfection or nonperfection, and the priority of a security interest in collateral:

(1) Except as otherwise provided in this section, while a debtor is located in a jurisdiction, the local law of that jurisdiction governs perfection, the effect of perfection or nonperfection, and the priority of a security interest in collateral.

(2) While collateral is located in a jurisdiction, the local law of that jurisdiction governs perfection, the effect of perfection or nonperfection, and the priority of a possessory security interest in that collateral.

(3) Except as otherwise provided in paragraph (4), while negotiable documents, goods, instruments, money, or tangible chattel paper is located in a jurisdiction, the local law of that jurisdiction governs:

(A) perfection of a security interest in the goods by filing a fixture filing;

(B) perfection of a security interest in timber to be cut; and

(C) the effect of perfection or nonperfection and the priority of a nonpossessory security interest in the collateral.

(4) The local law of the jurisdiction in which the wellhead or minehead is located governs perfection, the effect of perfection or nonperfection, and the priority of a security interest in as-extracted collateral.

* * * *

§9—309. SECURITY INTEREST PERFECTED UPON ATTACHMENT

The following security interests are perfected when they attach:

(1) a purchase-money security interest in consumer goods, except as otherwise provided in Section 9—311(b) with respect to consumer goods that are subject to a statute or treaty described in Section 9—311(a);

(2) an assignment of accounts or payment intangibles which does not by itself or in conjunction with other assignments to the same assignee transfer a significant part of the assignor's outstanding accounts or payment intangibles;

(3) a sale of a payment intangible;

(4) a sale of a promissory note;

(5) a security interest created by the assignment of a health-care-insurance receivable to the provider of the health-care goods or services;

(6) a security interest arising under Section 2—401, 2—505, 2—711(3), or 2A—508(5), until the debtor obtains possession of the collateral;

(7) a security interest of a collecting bank arising under Section 4—210;

(8) a security interest of an issuer or nominated person arising under Section 5—118;

(9) a security interest arising in the delivery of a financial asset under Section 9—206(c);

(10) a security interest in investment property created by a broker or securities intermediary;

(11) a security interest in a commodity contract or a commodity account created by a commodity intermediary;

(12) an assignment for the benefit of all creditors of the transferor and subsequent transfers by the assignee thereunder; and

(13) a security interest created by an assignment of a beneficial interest in a decedent's estate; and

(14) a sale by an individual of an account that is a right to payment of winnings in a lottery or other game of chance.

§9—310. WHEN FILING REQUIRED TO PERFECT SECURITY INTEREST OR AGRICULTURAL LIEN; SECURITY INTERESTS AND AGRICULTURAL LIENS TO WHICH FILING PROVISIONS DO NOT APPLY

(a) Except as otherwise provided in subsection (b) and Section 9—312(b), a financing statement must be filed to perfect all security interests and agricultural liens.

(b) The filing of a financing statement is not necessary to perfect a security interest:

(1) that is perfected under Section 9—308(d), (e), (f), or (g);

(2) that is perfected under Section 9—309 when it attaches;

(3) in property subject to a statute, regulation, or treaty described in Section 9—311(a);

(4) in goods in possession of a bailee which is perfected under Section 9—312(d)(1) or (2);

(5) in certificated securities, documents, goods, or instruments which is perfected without filing or possession under Section 9—312(e), (f), or (g);

(6) in collateral in the secured party's possession under Section 9—313;

(7) in a certificated security which is perfected by delivery of the security certificate to the secured party under Section 9—313;

(8) in deposit accounts, electronic chattel paper, investment property, or letter-of-credit rights which is perfected by control under Section 9—314;

(9) in proceeds which is perfected under Section 9—315; or

(10) that is perfected under Section 9—316.

(c) If a secured party assigns a perfected security interest or agricultural lien, a filing under this article is not required to continue the perfected status of the security interest against creditors of and transferees from the original debtor.

§9—311. PERFECTION OF SECURITY INTERESTS IN PROPERTY SUBJECT TO CERTAIN STATUTES, REGULATIONS, AND TREATIES

(a) Except as otherwise provided in subsection (d), the filing of a financing statement is not necessary or effective to perfect a security interest in property subject to:

(1) a statute, regulation, or treaty of the United States whose requirements for a security interest's obtaining priority over the rights of a lien creditor with respect to the property preempt Section 9—310(a);

(2) [list any certificate-of-title statute covering automobiles, trailers, mobile homes, boats, farm tractors, or the like, which provides for a security interest to be indicated on the certificate as a condition or result of perfection, and any non Uniform Commercial Code central filing statute]; or

(3) a certificate-of-title statute of another jurisdiction which provides for a security interest to be indicated on the certificate as a condition or result of the security interest's obtaining priority over the rights of a lien creditor with respect to the property.

* * * *

§9—312. PERFECTION OF SECURITY INTERESTS IN CHATTEL PAPER, DEPOSIT ACCOUNTS, DOCUMENTS, GOODS COVERED BY DOCUMENTS, INSTRUMENTS, INVESTMENT PROPERTY, LETTER-OF-CREDIT RIGHTS, AND MONEY; PERFECTION BY PERMISSIVE FILING; TEMPORARY PERFECTION WITHOUT FILING OR TRANSFER OF POSSESSION

(a) A security interest in chattel paper, negotiable documents, instruments, or investment property may be perfected by filing.

(b) Except as otherwise provided in Section 9—315 (c) and (d) for proceeds:

(1) a security interest in a deposit account may be perfected only by control under Section 9—314;

(2) and except as otherwise provided in Section 9—308(d), a security interest in a letter-of-credit

right may be perfected only by control under Section 9—314; and

(3) a security interest in money may be perfected only by the secured party's taking possession under Section 9—313.

(c) While goods are in the possession of a bailee that has issued a negotiable document covering the goods:

(1) a security interest in the goods may be perfected by perfecting a security interest in the document; and

(2) a security interest perfected in the document has priority over any security interest that becomes perfected in the goods by another method during that time.

(d) While goods are in the possession of a bailee that has issued a nonnegotiable document covering the goods, a security interest in the goods may be perfected by:

(1) issuance of a document in the name of the secured party;

(2) the bailee's receipt of notification of the secured party's interest; or

(3) filing as to the goods.

(e) A security interest in certificated securities, negotiable documents, or instruments is perfected without filing or the taking of possession for a period of 20 days from the time it attaches to the extent that it arises for new value given under an authenticated security agreement.

(f) A perfected security interest in a negotiable document or goods in possession of a bailee, other than one that has issued a negotiable document for the goods, remains perfected for 20 days without filing if the secured party makes available to the debtor the goods or documents representing the goods for the purpose of:

(1) ultimate sale or exchange; or

(2) loading, unloading, storing, shipping, transshipping, manufacturing, processing, or otherwise dealing with them in a manner preliminary to their sale or exchange.

(g) A perfected security interest in a certificated security or instrument remains perfected for 20 days without filing if the secured party delivers the security certificate or instrument to the debtor for the purpose of:

(1) ultimate sale or exchange; or

(2) presentation, collection, enforcement, renewal, or registration of transfer.

(h) After the 20-day period specified in subsection (e), (f), or (g) expires, perfection depends upon compliance with this article.

§9—313. WHEN POSSESSION BY OR DELIVERY TO SECURED PARTY PERFECTS SECURITY INTEREST WITHOUT FILING

(a) Except as otherwise provided in subsection (b), a secured party may perfect a security interest in negotiable documents, goods, instruments, money, or tangible chattel paper by taking possession of the collateral. A secured party may perfect a security interest in certificated securities by taking delivery of the certificated securities under Section 8—301.

(b) With respect to goods covered by a certificate of title issued by this State, a secured party may perfect a security interest in the goods by taking possession of the goods only in the circumstances described in Section 9—316(d).

(c) With respect to collateral other than certificated securities and goods covered by a document, a secured party takes possession of collateral in the possession of a person other than the debtor, the secured party, or a lessee of the collateral from the debtor in the ordinary course of the debtor's business, when:

(1) the person in possession authenticates a record acknowledging that it holds possession of the collateral for the secured party's benefit; or

(2) the person takes possession of the collateral after having authenticated a record acknowledging that it will hold possession of collateral for the secured party's benefit.

(d) If perfection of a security interest depends upon possession of the collateral by a secured party, perfection occurs no earlier than the time the secured party takes possession and continues only while the secured party retains possession.

(e) A security interest in a certificated security in registered form is perfected by delivery when delivery of the certificated security occurs under Section 8—301 and remains perfected by delivery until the debtor obtains possession of the security certificate.

(f) A person in possession of collateral is not required to acknowledge that it holds possession for a secured party's benefit.

(g) If a person acknowledges that it holds possession for the secured party's benefit:

(1) the acknowledgment is effective under subsection (c) or Section 8—301(a), even if the

acknowledgment violates the rights of a debtor; and

(2) unless the person otherwise agrees or law other than this article otherwise provides, the person does not owe any duty to the secured party and is not required to confirm the acknowledgment to another person.

(h) A secured party having possession of collateral does not relinquish possession by delivering the collateral to a person other than the debtor or a lessee of the collateral from the debtor in the ordinary course of the debtor's business if the person was instructed before the delivery or is instructed contemporaneously with the delivery:

(1) to hold possession of the collateral for the secured party's benefit; or

(2) to redeliver the collateral to the secured party.

(i) A secured party does not relinquish possession, even if a delivery under subsection (h) violates the rights of a debtor. A person to which collateral is delivered under subsection (h) does not owe any duty to the secured party and is not required to confirm the delivery to another person unless the person otherwise agrees or law other than this article otherwise provides.

§9—314. PERFECTION BY CONTROL

(a) A security interest in investment property, deposit accounts, letter-of-credit rights, or electronic chattel paper may be perfected by control of the collateral under Section 9—104, 9—105, 9—106, or 9—107.

(b) A security interest in deposit accounts, electronic chattel paper, or letter-of-credit rights is perfected by control under Section 9—104, 9—105, or 9—107 when the secured party obtains control and remains perfected by control only while the secured party retains control.

(c) A security interest in investment property is perfected by control under Section 9—106 from the time the secured party obtains control and remains perfected by control until:

(1) the secured party does not have control; and

(2) one of the following occurs:

(A) if the collateral is a certificated security, the debtor has or acquires possession of the security certificate;

(B) if the collateral is an uncertificated security, the issuer has registered or registers the debtor as the registered owner; or

(C) if the collateral is a security entitlement, the debtor is or becomes the entitlement holder.

§9—315. SECURED PARTY'S RIGHTS ON DISPOSITION OF COLLATERAL AND IN PROCEEDS

(a) Except as otherwise provided in this article and in Section 2—403(2):

(1) a security interest or agricultural lien continues in collateral notwithstanding sale, lease, license, exchange, or other disposition thereof unless the secured party authorized the disposition free of the security interest or agricultural lien; and

(2) a security interest attaches to any identifiable proceeds of collateral.

(b) Proceeds that are commingled with other property are identifiable proceeds:

(1) if the proceeds are goods, to the extent provided by Section 9—336; and

(2) if the proceeds are not goods, to the extent that the secured party identifies the proceeds by a method of tracing, including application of equitable principles, that is permitted under law other than this article with respect to commingled property of the type involved.

(c) A security interest in proceeds is a perfected security interest if the security interest in the original collateral was perfected.

(d) A perfected security interest in proceeds becomes unperfected on the 21st day after the security interest attaches to the proceeds unless:

(1) the following conditions are satisfied:

(A) a filed financing statement covers the original collateral;

(B) the proceeds are collateral in which a security interest may be perfected by filing in the office in which the financing statement has been filed; and

(C) the proceeds are not acquired with cash proceeds;

(2) the proceeds are identifiable cash proceeds; or

(3) the security interest in the proceeds is perfected other than under subsection (c) when the security interest attaches to the proceeds or within 20 days thereafter.

(e) If a filed financing statement covers the original collateral, a security interest in proceeds which remains perfected under subsection (d)(1) becomes unperfected at the later of:

(1) when the effectiveness of the filed financing statement lapses under Section 9—515 or is terminated under Section 9—513; or

(2) the 21st day after the security interest attaches to the proceeds.

§9—316. CONTINUED PERFECTION OF SECURITY INTEREST FOLLOWING CHANGE IN GOVERNING LAW

(a) A security interest perfected pursuant to the law of the jurisdiction designated in Section 9—301(1) or 9—305(c) remains perfected until the earliest of:

(1) the time perfection would have ceased under the law of that jurisdiction;

(2) the expiration of four months after a change of the debtor's location to another jurisdiction; or

(3) the expiration of one year after a transfer of collateral to a person that thereby becomes a debtor and is located in another jurisdiction.

(b) If a security interest described in subsection (a) becomes perfected under the law of the other jurisdiction before the earliest time or event described in that subsection, it remains perfected thereafter. If the security interest does not become perfected under the law of the other jurisdiction before the earliest time or event, it becomes unperfected and is deemed never to have been perfected as against a purchaser of the collateral for value.

(c) A possessory security interest in collateral, other than goods covered by a certificate of title and as-extracted collateral consisting of goods, remains continuously perfected if:

(1) the collateral is located in one jurisdiction and subject to a security interest perfected under the law of that jurisdiction;

(2) thereafter the collateral is brought into another jurisdiction; and

(3) upon entry into the other jurisdiction, the security interest is perfected under the law of the other jurisdiction.

(d) Except as otherwise provided in subsection (e), a security interest in goods covered by a certificate of title which is perfected by any method under the law of another jurisdiction when the goods become covered by a certificate of title from this State remains perfected until the security interest would have become unperfected under the law of the other jurisdiction had the goods not become so covered.

(e) A security interest described in subsection (d) becomes unperfected as against a purchaser of the goods for value and is deemed never to have been perfected as against a purchaser of the goods for value if the applicable requirements for perfection under Section 9—311(b) or 9—313 are not satisfied before the earlier of:

(1) the time the security interest would have become unperfected under the law of the other jurisdiction had the goods not become covered by a certificate of title from this State; or

(2) the expiration of four months after the goods had become so covered.

(f) A security interest in deposit accounts, letter-of-credit rights, or investment property which is perfected under the law of the bank's jurisdiction, the issuer's jurisdiction, a nominated person's jurisdiction, the securities intermediary's jurisdiction, or the commodity intermediary's jurisdiction, as applicable, remains perfected until the earlier of:

(1) the time the security interest would have become unperfected under the law of that jurisdiction; or

(2) the expiration of four months after a change of the applicable jurisdiction to another jurisdiction.

(g) If a security interest described in subsection (f) becomes perfected under the law of the other jurisdiction before the earlier of the time or the end of the period described in that subsection, it remains perfected thereafter. If the security interest does not become perfected under the law of the other jurisdiction before the earlier of that time or the end of that period, it becomes unperfected and is deemed never to have been perfected as against a purchaser of the collateral for value.

§9—317. INTERESTS THAT TAKE PRIORITY OVER OR TAKE FREE OF SECURITY INTEREST OR AGRICULTURAL LIEN

(a) A security interest or agricultural lien is subordinate to the rights of:

(1) a person entitled to priority under Section 9—322; and

(2) except as otherwise provided in subsection (e), a person that becomes a lien creditor before the earlier of the time:

(A) the security interest or agricultural lien is perfected; or

(B) one of the conditions specified in Section 9—203(b)(3) is met and a financing statement covering the collateral is filed.

(b) Except as otherwise provided in subsection (e), a buyer, other than a secured party, of tangible chattel paper, documents, goods, instruments, or a security certificate takes free of a security interest or agricultural lien if the buyer gives value and receives delivery of the collateral without knowledge of the security interest or agricultural lien and before it is perfected.

(c) Except as otherwise provided in subsection (e), a lessee of goods takes free of a security interest or agricultural lien if the lessee gives value and receives delivery of the collateral without knowledge of the security interest or agricultural lien and before it is perfected.

(d) A licensee of a general intangible or a buyer, other than a secured party, of accounts, electronic chattel paper, general intangibles, or investment property other than a certificated security takes free of a security interest if the licensee or buyer gives value without knowledge of the security interest and before it is perfected.

(e) Except as otherwise provided in Sections 9—320 and 9—321, if a person files a financing statement with respect to a purchase-money security interest before or within 20 days after the debtor receives delivery of the collateral, the security interest takes priority over the rights of a buyer, lessee, or lien creditor which arise between the time the security interest attaches and the time of filing.

§9—318. NO INTEREST RETAINED IN RIGHT TO PAYMENT THAT IS SOLD; RIGHTS AND TITLE OF SELLER OF ACCOUNT OR CHATTEL PAPER WITH RESPECT TO CREDITORS AND PURCHASERS

(a) A debtor that has sold an account, chattel paper, payment intangible, or promissory note does not retain a legal or equitable interest in the collateral sold.

(b) For purposes of determining the rights of creditors of, and purchasers for value of an account or chattel paper from, a debtor that has sold an account or chattel paper, while the buyer's security interest is unperfected, the debtor is deemed to have rights and title to the account or chattel paper identical to those the debtor sold.

§9—319. RIGHTS AND TITLE OF CONSIGNEE WITH RESPECT TO CREDITORS AND PURCHASERS

(a) Except as otherwise provided in subsection (b), for purposes of determining the rights of creditors of, and purchasers for value of goods from, a consignee, while the goods are in the possession of the consignee, the consignee is deemed to have rights and title to the goods identical to those the consignor had or had power to transfer.

(b) For purposes of determining the rights of a creditor of a consignee, law other than this article determines the rights and title of a consignee while goods are in the consignee's possession if, under this part, a perfected security interest held by the consignor would have priority over the rights of the creditor.

§9—320. BUYER OF GOODS

(a) Except as otherwise provided in subsection (e), a buyer in ordinary course of business, other than a person buying farm products from a person engaged in farming operations, takes free of a security interest created by the buyer's seller, even if the security interest is perfected and the buyer knows of its existence.

(b) Except as otherwise provided in subsection (e), a buyer of goods from a person who used or bought the goods for use primarily for personal, family, or household purposes takes free of a security interest, even if perfected, if the buyer buys:

    (1) without knowledge of the security interest;

    (2) for value;

    (3) primarily for the buyer's personal, family, or household purposes; and

    (4) before the filing of a financing statement covering the goods.

(c) To the extent that it affects the priority of a security interest over a buyer of goods under subsection (b), the period of effectiveness of a filing made in the jurisdiction in which the seller is located is governed by Section 9—316(a) and (b).

(d) A buyer in ordinary course of business buying oil, gas, or other minerals at the wellhead or minehead or after extraction takes free of an interest arising out of an encumbrance.

(e) Subsections (a) and (b) do not affect a security interest in goods in the possession of the secured party under Section 9—313.

* * * *

§9—322. PRIORITIES AMONG CONFLICTING SECURITY INTERESTS IN AND AGRICULTURAL LIENS ON SAME COLLATERAL

(a) Except as otherwise provided in this section, priority among conflicting security interests and agricultural liens in the same collateral is determined according to the following rules:

(1) Conflicting perfected security interests and agricultural liens rank according to priority in time of filing or perfection. Priority dates from the earlier of the time a filing covering the collateral is first made or the security interest or agricultural lien is first perfected, if there is no period thereafter when there is neither filing nor perfection.

(2) A perfected security interest or agricultural lien has priority over a conflicting unperfected security interest or agricultural lien.

(3) The first security interest or agricultural lien to attach or become effective has priority if conflicting security interests and agricultural liens are unperfected.

(b) For the purposes of subsection (a)(1):

(1) the time of filing or perfection as to a security interest in collateral is also the time of filing or perfection as to a security interest in proceeds; and

(2) the time of filing or perfection as to a security interest in collateral supported by a supporting obligation is also the time of filing or perfection as to a security interest in the supporting obligation.

(c) Except as otherwise provided in subsection (f), a security interest in collateral which qualifies for priority over a conflicting security interest under Section 9—327, 9—328, 9—329, 9—330, or 9—331 also has priority over a conflicting security interest in:

(1) any supporting obligation for the collateral; and

(2) proceeds of the collateral if:

(A) the security interest in proceeds is perfected;

(B) the proceeds are cash proceeds or of the same type as the collateral; and

(C) in the case of proceeds that are proceeds of proceeds, all intervening proceeds are cash proceeds, proceeds of the same type as the collateral, or an account relating to the collateral.

(d) Subject to subsection (e) and except as otherwise provided in subsection (f), if a security interest in chattel paper, deposit accounts, negotiable documents, instruments, investment property, or letter-of-credit rights is perfected by a method other than filing, conflicting perfected security interests in proceeds of the collateral rank according to priority in time of filing.

(e) Subsection (d) applies only if the proceeds of the collateral are not cash proceeds, chattel paper, negotiable documents, instruments, investment property, or letter-of-credit rights.

(f) Subsections (a) through (e) are subject to:

(1) subsection (g) and the other provisions of this part;

(2) Section 4—210 with respect to a security interest of a collecting bank;

(3) Section 5—118 with respect to a security interest of an issuer or nominated person; and

(4) Section 9—110 with respect to a security interest arising under Article 2 or 2A.

(g) A perfected agricultural lien on collateral has priority over a conflicting security interest in or agricultural lien on the same collateral if the statute creating the agricultural lien so provides.

§9—323. FUTURE ADVANCES

(a) Except as otherwise provided in subsection (c), for purposes of determining the priority of a perfected security interest under Section 9—322(a)(1), perfection of the security interest dates from the time an advance is made to the extent that the security interest secures an advance that:

(1) is made while the security interest is perfected only:

(A) under Section 9—309 when it attaches; or

(B) temporarily under Section 9—312(e), (f), or (g); and

(2) is not made pursuant to a commitment entered into before or while the security interest is perfected by a method other than under Section 9—309 or 9—312(e), (f), or (g).

(b) Except as otherwise provided in subsection (c), a security interest is subordinate to the rights of a person that becomes a lien creditor to the extent that the security interest secures an advance made more than 45 days after the person becomes a lien creditor unless the advance is made:

(1) without knowledge of the lien; or

(2) pursuant to a commitment entered into without knowledge of the lien.

(c) Subsections (a) and (b) do not apply to a security interest held by a secured party that is a buyer of accounts, chattel paper, payment intangibles, or promissory notes or a consignor.

(d) Except as otherwise provided in subsection (e), a buyer of goods other than a buyer in ordinary course of business takes free of a security interest to the extent that it secures advances made after the earlier of:

(1) the time the secured party acquires knowledge of the buyer's purchase; or

(2) 45 days after the purchase.

(e) Subsection (d) does not apply if the advance is made pursuant to a commitment entered into without knowledge of the buyer's purchase and before the expiration of the 45-day period.

(f) Except as otherwise provided in subsection (g), a lessee of goods, other than a lessee in ordinary course of business, takes the leasehold interest free of a security interest to the extent that it secures advances made after the earlier of:

(1) the time the secured party acquires knowledge of the lease; or

(2) 45 days after the lease contract becomes enforceable.

(g) Subsection (f) does not apply if the advance is made pursuant to a commitment entered into without knowledge of the lease and before the expiration of the 45 day period.

§9—324. PRIORITY OF PURCHASE-MONEY SECURITY INTERESTS

(a) Except as otherwise provided in subsection (g), a perfected purchase-money security interest in goods other than inventory or livestock has priority over a conflicting security interest in the same goods, and, except as otherwise provided in Section 9—327, a perfected security interest in its identifiable proceeds also has priority, if the purchase-money security interest is perfected when the debtor receives possession of the collateral or within 20 days thereafter.

(b) Subject to subsection (c) and except as otherwise provided in subsection (g), a perfected purchase-money security interest in inventory has priority over a conflicting security interest in the same inventory, has priority over a conflicting security interest in chattel paper or an instrument constituting proceeds of the inventory and in proceeds of the chattel paper, if so provided in Section 9—330, and, except as otherwise provided in Section 9—327, also has priority in identifiable cash proceeds of the inventory to the extent the identifiable cash proceeds are received on or before the delivery of the inventory to a buyer, if:

(1) the purchase-money security interest is perfected when the debtor receives possession of the inventory;

(2) the purchase-money secured party sends an authenticated notification to the holder of the conflicting security interest;

(3) the holder of the conflicting security interest receives the notification within five years before the debtor receives possession of the inventory; and

(4) the notification states that the person sending the notification has or expects to acquire a purchase-money security interest in inventory of the debtor and describes the inventory.

(c) Subsections (b)(2) through (4) apply only if the holder of the conflicting security interest had filed a financing statement covering the same types of inventory:

(1) if the purchase-money security interest is perfected by filing, before the date of the filing; or

(2) if the purchase-money security interest is temporarily perfected without filing or possession under Section 9—312(f), before the beginning of the 20-day period thereunder.

(d) Subject to subsection (e) and except as otherwise provided in subsection (g), a perfected purchase-money security interest in livestock that are farm products has priority over a conflicting security interest in the same livestock, and, except as otherwise provided in Section 9—327, a perfected security interest in their identifiable proceeds and identifiable products in their unmanufactured states also has priority, if:

(1) the purchase-money security interest is perfected when the debtor receives possession of the livestock;

(2) the purchase-money secured party sends an authenticated notification to the holder of the conflicting security interest;

(3) the holder of the conflicting security interest receives the notification within six months before the debtor receives possession of the livestock; and

(4) the notification states that the person sending the notification has or expects to acquire a purchase-money security interest in livestock of the debtor and describes the livestock.

(e) Subsections (d)(2) through (4) apply only if the holder of the conflicting security interest had filed a financing statement covering the same types of livestock:

(1) if the purchase-money security interest is perfected by filing, before the date of the filing; or

(2) if the purchase-money security interest is temporarily perfected without filing or possession under Section 9—312(f), before the beginning of the 20-day period thereunder.

(f) Except as otherwise provided in subsection (g), a perfected purchase-money security interest in software has priority over a conflicting security interest in the same collateral, and, except as otherwise provided in Section 9—327, a perfected security interest in its identifiable proceeds also has priority, to the extent that the purchase-money security interest in the goods in which the software was acquired for use has priority in the goods and proceeds of the goods under this section.

(g) If more than one security interest qualifies for priority in the same collateral under subsection (a), (b), (d), or (f):

> (1) a security interest securing an obligation incurred as all or part of the price of the collateral has priority over a security interest securing an obligation incurred for value given to enable the debtor to acquire rights in or the use of collateral; and
>
> (2) in all other cases, Section 9—322(a) applies to the qualifying security interests.

§9—325. PRIORITY OF SECURITY INTERESTS IN TRANSFERRED COLLATERAL

(a) Except as otherwise provided in subsection (b), a security interest created by a debtor is subordinate to a security interest in the same collateral created by another person if:

> (1) the debtor acquired the collateral subject to the security interest created by the other person;
>
> (2) the security interest created by the other person was perfected when the debtor acquired the collateral; and
>
> (3) there is no period thereafter when the security interest is unperfected.

(b) Subsection (a) subordinates a security interest only if the security interest:

> (1) otherwise would have priority solely under Section 9—322(a) or 9—324; or
>
> (2) arose solely under Section 2—711(3) or 2A—508(5).

§9—326. PRIORITY OF SECURITY INTERESTS CREATED BY NEW DEBTOR

(a) Subject to subsection (b), a security interest created by a new debtor which is perfected by a filed financing statement that is effective solely under Section 9—508 in collateral in which a new debtor has or acquires rights is subordinate to a security interest in the same collateral which is perfected other than by a filed financing statement that is effective solely under Section 9—508.

(b) The other provisions of this part determine the priority among conflicting security interests in the same collateral perfected by filed financing statements that are effective solely under Section 9—508. However, if the security agreements to which a new debtor became bound as debtor were not entered into by the same original debtor, the conflicting security interests rank according to priority in time of the new debtor's having become bound.

* * * *

§9—330. PRIORITY OF PURCHASER OF CHATTEL PAPER OR INSTRUMENT

(a) A purchaser of chattel paper has priority over a security interest in the chattel paper which is claimed merely as proceeds of inventory subject to a security interest if:

> (1) in good faith and in the ordinary course of the purchaser's business, the purchaser gives new value and takes possession of the chattel paper or obtains control of the chattel paper under Section 9—105; and
>
> (2) the chattel paper does not indicate that it has been assigned to an identified assignee other than the purchaser.

(b) A purchaser of chattel paper has priority over a security interest in the chattel paper which is claimed other than merely as proceeds of inventory subject to a security interest if the purchaser gives new value and takes possession of the chattel paper or obtains control of the chattel paper under Section 9—105 in good faith, in the ordinary course of the purchaser's business, and without knowledge that the purchase violates the rights of the secured party.

(c) Except as otherwise provided in Section 9—327, a purchaser having priority in chattel paper under subsection (a) or (b) also has priority in proceeds of the chattel paper to the extent that:

> (1) Section 9—322 provides for priority in the proceeds; or
>
> (2) the proceeds consist of the specific goods covered by the chattel paper or cash proceeds of the specific goods, even if the purchaser's security interest in the proceeds is unperfected.

(d) Except as otherwise provided in Section 9—331 (a), a purchaser of an instrument has priority over a security interest in the instrument perfected by a method other than possession if the purchaser gives value and takes possession of the instrument in good faith and without knowledge that the purchase violates the rights of the secured party.

(e) For purposes of subsections (a) and (b), the holder of a purchase-money security interest in inventory gives new value for chattel paper constituting proceeds of the inventory.

(f) For purposes of subsections (b) and (d), if chattel paper or an instrument indicates that it has been assigned to an identified secured party other than the purchaser, a purchaser of the chattel paper or instrument has knowledge that the purchase violates the rights of the secured party.

* * * *

§9—333. PRIORITY OF CERTAIN LIENS ARISING BY OPERATION OF LAW

(a) In this section, "possessory lien" means an interest, other than a security interest or an agricultural lien:

(1) which secures payment or performance of an obligation for services or materials furnished with respect to goods by a person in the ordinary course of the person's business;

(2) which is created by statute or rule of law in favor of the person; and

(3) whose effectiveness depends on the person's possession of the goods.

(b) A possessory lien on goods has priority over a security interest in the goods unless the lien is created by a statute that expressly provides otherwise.

§9—334. PRIORITY OF SECURITY INTERESTS IN FIXTURES AND CROPS

(a) A security interest under this article may be created in goods that are fixtures or may continue in goods that become fixtures. A security interest does not exist under this article in ordinary building materials incorporated into an improvement on land.

(b) This article does not prevent creation of an encumbrance upon fixtures under real property law.

(c) In cases not governed by subsections (d) through (h), a security interest in fixtures is subordinate to a conflicting interest of an encumbrancer or owner of the related real property other than the debtor.

(d) Except as otherwise provided in subsection (h), a perfected security interest in fixtures has priority over a conflicting interest of an encumbrancer or owner of the real property if the debtor has an interest of record in or is in possession of the real property and:

(1) the security interest is a purchase-money security interest;

(2) the interest of the encumbrancer or owner arises before the goods become fixtures; and

(3) the security interest is perfected by a fixture filing before the goods become fixtures or within 20 days thereafter.

(e) A perfected security interest in fixtures has priority over a conflicting interest of an encumbrancer or owner of the real property if:

(1) the debtor has an interest of record in the real property or is in possession of the real property and the security interest:

(A) is perfected by a fixture filing before the interest of the encumbrancer or owner is of record; and

(B) has priority over any conflicting interest of a predecessor in title of the encumbrancer or owner;

(2) before the goods become fixtures, the security interest is perfected by any method permitted by this article and the fixtures are readily removable:

(A) factory or office machines;

(B) equipment that is not primarily used or leased for use in the operation of the real property; or

(C) replacements of domestic appliances that are consumer goods;

(3) the conflicting interest is a lien on the real property obtained by legal or equitable proceedings after the security interest was perfected by any method permitted by this article; or

(4) the security interest is:

(A) created in a manufactured home in a manufactured-home transaction; and

(B) perfected pursuant to a statute described in Section 9—311(a)(2).

(f) A security interest in fixtures, whether or not perfected, has priority over a conflicting interest of an encumbrancer or owner of the real property if:

(1) the encumbrancer or owner has, in an authenticated record, consented to the security interest or disclaimed an interest in the goods as fixtures; or

(2) the debtor has a right to remove the goods as against the encumbrancer or owner.

(g) The priority of the security interest under paragraph (f)(2) continues for a reasonable time if the debtor's right to remove the goods as against the encumbrancer or owner terminates.

(h) A mortgage is a construction mortgage to the extent that it secures an obligation incurred for the construction of an improvement on land, including the acquisition cost of the land, if a recorded record of the mortgage so indicates. Except as otherwise provided in subsections (e) and (f), a security interest in fixtures is subordinate to a construction mortgage if a record of the mortgage is recorded before the goods become fixtures and the goods become fixtures before the completion of the construction. A mortgage has this priority to the same extent as a construction mortgage to the extent that it is given to refinance a construction mortgage.

(i) A perfected security interest in crops growing on real property has priority over a conflicting interest of an encumbrancer or owner of the real property if the debtor has an interest of record in or is in possession of the real property.

* * * *

§9—336. COMMINGLED GOODS

(a) In this section, "commingled goods" means goods that are physically united with other goods in such a manner that their identity is lost in a product or mass.

(b) A security interest does not exist in commingled goods as such. However, a security interest may attach to a product or mass that results when goods become commingled goods.

(c) If collateral becomes commingled goods, a security interest attaches to the product or mass.

(d) If a security interest in collateral is perfected before the collateral becomes commingled goods, the security interest that attaches to the product or mass under subsection (c) is perfected.

(e) Except as otherwise provided in subsection (f), the other provisions of this part determine the priority of a security interest that attaches to the product or mass under subsection (c).

(f) If more than one security interest attaches to the product or mass under subsection (c), the following rules determine priority:

(1) A security interest that is perfected under subsection (d) has priority over a security interest that is unperfected at the time the collateral becomes commingled goods.

(2) If more than one security interest is perfected under subsection (d), the security interests rank equally in proportion to the value of the collateral at the time it became commingled goods.

* * * *

§9—501. FILING OFFICE

(a) Except as otherwise provided in subsection (b), if the local law of this State governs perfection of a security interest or agricultural lien, the office in which to file a financing statement to perfect the security interest or agricultural lien is:

(1) the office designated for the filing or recording of a record of a mortgage on the related real property, if:

(A) the collateral is as-extracted collateral or timber to be cut; or

(B) the financing statement is filed as a fixture filing and the collateral is goods that are or are to become fixtures; or

(2) the office of [ ] [or any office duly authorized by [ ]], in all other cases, including a case in which the collateral is goods that are or are to become fixtures and the financing statement is not filed as a fixture filing.

(b) The office in which to file a financing statement to perfect a security interest in collateral, including fixtures, of a transmitting utility is the office of [ ]. The financing statement also constitutes a fixture filing as to the collateral indicated in the financing statement which is or is to become fixtures.

Legislative Note: The State should designate the filing office where the brackets appear. The filing office may be that of a governmental official (e.g., the Secretary of State) or a private party that maintains the State's filing system.

§9—502. CONTENTS OF FINANCING STATEMENT; RECORD OF MORTGAGE AS FINANCING STATEMENT; TIME OF FILING FINANCING STATEMENT

(a) Subject to subsection (b), a financing statement is sufficient only if it:

(1) provides the name of the debtor;

(2) provides the name of the secured party or a representative of the secured party; and

(3) indicates the collateral covered by the financing statement.

(b) Except as otherwise provided in Section 9—501 (b), to be sufficient, a financing statement that covers as-extracted collateral or timber to be cut, or which is filed as a fixture filing and covers goods that are or are to become fixtures, must satisfy subsection (a) and also:

(1) indicate that it covers this type of collateral;

(2) indicate that it is to be filed [for record] in the real property records;

(3) provide a description of the real property to which the collateral is related [sufficient to give constructive notice of a mortgage under the law of this State if the description were contained in a record of the mortgage of the real property]; and

(4) if the debtor does not have an interest of record in the real property, provide the name of a record owner.

(c) A record of a mortgage is effective, from the date of recording, as a financing statement filed as a fixture filing or as a financing statement covering as-extracted collateral or timber to be cut only if:

(1) the record indicates the goods or accounts that it covers;

(2) the goods are or are to become fixtures related to the real property described in the record or the collateral is related to the real property described in the record and is as-extracted collateral or timber to be cut;

(3) the record satisfies the requirements for a financing statement in this section other than an indication that it is to be filed in the real property records; and

(4) the record is [duly] recorded.

(d) A financing statement may be filed before a security agreement is made or a security interest otherwise attaches.

Legislative Note: Language in brackets is optional. Where the State has any special recording system for real property other than the usual grantor-grantee index (as, for instance, a tract system or a title registration or Torrens system) local adaptations of subsection (b) and Section 9—519(d) and (e) may be necessary. See, e.g., Mass. Gen. Laws Chapter 106, Section 9—410.

§9—503. NAME OF DEBTOR AND SECURED PARTY

(a) A financing statement sufficiently provides the name of the debtor:

(1) if the debtor is a registered organization, only if the financing statement provides the name of the debtor indicated on the public record of the debtor's jurisdiction of organization which shows the debtor to have been organized;

(2) if the debtor is a decedent's estate, only if the financing statement provides the name of the decedent and indicates that the debtor is an estate;

(3) if the debtor is a trust or a trustee acting with respect to property held in trust, only if the financing statement:

(A) provides the name specified for the trust in its organic documents or, if no name is specified, provides the name of the settlor and additional information sufficient to distinguish the debtor from other trusts having one or more of the same settlors; and

(B) indicates, in the debtor's name or otherwise, that the debtor is a trust or is a trustee acting with respect to property held in trust; and

(4) in other cases:

(A) if the debtor has a name, only if it provides the individual or organizational name of the debtor; and

(B) if the debtor does not have a name, only if it provides the names of the partners, members, associates, or other persons comprising the debtor.

(b) A financing statement that provides the name of the debtor in accordance with subsection (a) is not rendered ineffective by the absence of:

(1) a trade name or other name of the debtor; or

(2) unless required under subsection (a)(4)(B), names of partners, members, associates, or other persons comprising the debtor.

(c) A financing statement that provides only the debtor's trade name does not sufficiently provide the name of the debtor.

(d) Failure to indicate the representative capacity of a secured party or representative of a secured party does not affect the sufficiency of a financing statement.

(e) A financing statement may provide the name of more than one debtor and the name of more than one secured party.

§9—504. INDICATION OF COLLATERAL

A financing statement sufficiently indicates the collateral that it covers if the financing statement provides:

(1) a description of the collateral pursuant to Section 9—108; or

(2) an indication that the financing statement covers all assets or all personal property.

As amended in 1999.

* * * *

§9—506. EFFECT OF ERRORS OR OMISSIONS

(a) A financing statement substantially satisfying the requirements of this part is effective, even if it has minor errors or omissions, unless the errors or omissions make the financing statement seriously misleading.

(b) Except as otherwise provided in subsection (c), a financing statement that fails sufficiently to provide the name of the debtor in accordance with Section 9—503(a) is seriously misleading.

(c) If a search of the records of the filing office under the debtor's correct name, using the filing office's standard search logic, if any, would disclose a financing statement that fails sufficiently to provide the name of the debtor in accordance with Section 9—503(a), the name provided does not make the financing statement seriously misleading.

(d) For purposes of Section 9—508(b), the "debtor's correct name" in subsection (c) means the correct name of the new debtor.

* * * *

§9—509. PERSONS ENTITLED TO FILE A RECORD

(a) A person may file an initial financing statement, amendment that adds collateral covered by a financing statement, or amendment that adds a debtor to a financing statement only if:

(1) the debtor authorizes the filing in an authenticated record or pursuant to subsection (b) or (c); or

(2) the person holds an agricultural lien that has become effective at the time of filing and the financing statement covers only collateral in which the person holds an agricultural lien.

(b) By authenticating or becoming bound as debtor by a security agreement, a debtor or new debtor authorizes the filing of an initial financing statement, and an amendment, covering:

(1) the collateral described in the security agreement; and

(2) property that becomes collateral under Section 9—315(a)(2), whether or not the security agreement expressly covers proceeds.

(c) By acquiring collateral in which a security interest or agricultural lien continues under Section 9—315(a)(1), a debtor authorizes the filing of an initial financing statement, and an amendment, covering the collateral and property that becomes collateral under Section 9—315(a)(2).

(d) A person may file an amendment other than an amendment that adds collateral covered by a financing statement or an amendment that adds a debtor to a financing statement only if:

(1) the secured party of record authorizes the filing; or

(2) the amendment is a termination statement for a financing statement as to which the secured party of record has failed to file or send a termination statement as required by Section 9—513(a) or (c), the debtor authorizes the filing, and the termination statement indicates that the debtor authorized it to be filed.

(e) If there is more than one secured party of record for a financing statement, each secured party of record may authorize the filing of an amendment under subsection (d).

§9—510. EFFECTIVENESS OF FILED RECORD

(a) A filed record is effective only to the extent that it was filed by a person that may file it under Section 9—509.

(b) A record authorized by one secured party of record does not affect the financing statement with respect to another secured party of record.

(c) A continuation statement that is not filed within the six-month period prescribed by Section 9—515(d) is ineffective.

* * * *

§9—513. TERMINATION STATEMENT

(a) A secured party shall cause the secured party of record for a financing statement to file a termination statement for the financing statement if the financing statement covers consumer goods and:

(1) there is no obligation secured by the collateral covered by the financing statement and no commitment to make an advance, incur an obligation, or otherwise give value; or

(2) the debtor did not authorize the filing of the initial financing statement.

(b) To comply with subsection (a), a secured party shall cause the secured party of record to file the termination statement:

(1) within one month after there is no obligation secured by the collateral covered by the financing statement and no commitment to make an advance, incur an obligation, or otherwise give value; or

(2) if earlier, within 20 days after the secured party receives an authenticated demand from a debtor.

(c) In cases not governed by subsection (a), within 20 days after a secured party receives an authenticated demand from a debtor, the secured party shall cause the secured party of record for a financing statement to send to the debtor a termination statement for the financing statement or file the termination statement in the filing office if:

(1) except in the case of a financing statement covering accounts or chattel paper that has been sold or goods that are the subject of a consignment, there is no obligation secured by the collateral covered by the financing statement and no commitment to make an advance, incur an obligation, or otherwise give value;

(2) the financing statement covers accounts or chattel paper that has been sold but as to which the account debtor or other person obligated has discharged its obligation;

(3) the financing statement covers goods that were the subject of a consignment to the debtor but are not in the debtor's possession; or

(4) the debtor did not authorize the filing of the initial financing statement.

(d) Except as otherwise provided in Section 9—510, upon the filing of a termination statement with the filing office, the financing statement to which the termination statement relates ceases to be effective. Except as otherwise provided in Section 9—510, for purposes of Sections 9—519(g), 9—522(a), and 9—523(c), the filing with the filing office of a termination statement relating to a financing statement that indicates that the debtor is a transmitting utility also causes the effectiveness of the financing statement to lapse.

* * * *

§9—515. DURATION AND EFFECTIVENESS OF FINANCING STATEMENT; EFFECT OF LAPSED FINANCING STATEMENT

(a) Except as otherwise provided in subsections (b), (e), (f), and (g), a filed financing statement is effective for a period of five years after the date of filing.

(b) Except as otherwise provided in subsections (e), (f), and (g), an initial financing statement filed in connection with a public-finance transaction or manufactured-home transaction is effective for a period of 30 years after the date of filing if it indicates that it is filed in connection with a public-finance transaction or manufactured-home transaction.

(c) The effectiveness of a filed financing statement lapses on the expiration of the period of its effectiveness unless before the lapse a continuation statement is filed pursuant to subsection (d). Upon lapse, a financing statement ceases to be effective and any security interest or agricultural lien that was perfected by the financing statement becomes unperfected, unless the security interest is perfected otherwise. If the security interest or agricultural lien becomes unperfected upon lapse, it is deemed never to have been perfected as against a purchaser of the collateral for value.

(d) A continuation statement may be filed only within six months before the expiration of the five-year period specified in subsection (a) or the 30-year period specified in subsection (b), whichever is applicable.

(e) Except as otherwise provided in Section 9—510, upon timely filing of a continuation statement, the effectiveness of the initial financing statement continues for a period of five years commencing on the day on which the financing statement would have become ineffective in the absence of the filing. Upon the expiration of the five-year period, the financing statement lapses in the same manner as provided in subsection (c), unless, before the lapse, another continuation statement is filed pursuant to subsection (d). Succeeding continuation statements may be filed in the same manner to continue the effectiveness of the initial financing statement.

(f) If a debtor is a transmitting utility and a filed financing statement so indicates, the financing statement is effective until a termination statement is filed.

(g) A record of a mortgage that is effective as a financing statement filed as a fixture filing under Section 9—502(c) remains effective as a financing statement filed as a fixture filing until the mortgage is released or satisfied of record or its effectiveness otherwise terminates as to the real property.

* * * *

§9—601. RIGHTS AFTER DEFAULT; JUDICIAL ENFORCEMENT; CONSIGNOR OR BUYER OF ACCOUNTS, CHATTEL PAPER, PAYMENT INTANGIBLES, OR PROMISSORY NOTES

(a) After default, a secured party has the rights provided in this part and, except as otherwise provided in Section 9—602, those provided by agreement of the parties.

A secured party:

(1) may reduce a claim to judgment, foreclose, or otherwise enforce the claim, security interest, or agricultural lien by any available judicial procedure; and

(2) if the collateral is documents, may proceed either as to the documents or as to the goods they cover.

(b) A secured party in possession of collateral or control of collateral under Section 9—104, 9—105, 9—106, or 9—107 has the rights and duties provided in Section 9—207.

(c) The rights under subsections (a) and (b) are cumulative and may be exercised simultaneously.

(d) Except as otherwise provided in subsection (g) and Section 9—605, after default, a debtor and an obligor have the rights provided in this part and by agreement of the parties.

(e) If a secured party has reduced its claim to judgment, the lien of any levy that may be made upon the collateral by virtue of an execution based upon the judgment relates back to the earliest of:

(1) the date of perfection of the security interest or agricultural lien in the collateral;

(2) the date of filing a financing statement covering the collateral; or

(3) any date specified in a statute under which the agricultural lien was created.

(f) A sale pursuant to an execution is a foreclosure of the security interest or agricultural lien by judicial procedure within the meaning of this section. A secured party may purchase at the sale and thereafter hold the collateral free of any other requirements of this article.

(g) Except as otherwise provided in Section 9—607 (c), this part imposes no duties upon a secured party that is a consignor or is a buyer of accounts, chattel paper, payment intangibles, or promissory notes.

* * * *

§9—604. PROCEDURE IF SECURITY AGREEMENT COVERS REAL PROPERTY OR FIXTURES

(a) If a security agreement covers both personal and real property, a secured party may proceed:

(1) under this part as to the personal property without prejudicing any rights with respect to the real property; or

(2) as to both the personal property and the real property in accordance with the rights with respect

to the real property, in which case the other provisions of this part do not apply.

(b) Subject to subsection (c), if a security agreement covers goods that are or become fixtures, a secured party may proceed:

(1) under this part; or

(2) in accordance with the rights with respect to real property, in which case the other provisions of this part do not apply.

(c) Subject to the other provisions of this part, if a secured party holding a security interest in fixtures has priority over all owners and encumbrancers of the real property, the secured party, after default, may remove the collateral from the real property.

(d) A secured party that removes collateral shall promptly reimburse any encumbrancer or owner of the real property, other than the debtor, for the cost of repair of any physical injury caused by the removal. The secured party need not reimburse the encumbrancer or owner for any diminution in value of the real property caused by the absence of the goods removed or by any necessity of replacing them. A person entitled to reimbursement may refuse permission to remove until the secured party gives adequate assurance for the performance of the obligation to reimburse.

* * * *

§9—607. COLLECTION AND ENFORCEMENT BY SECURED PARTY

(a) If so agreed, and in any event after default, a secured party:

(1) may notify an account debtor or other person obligated on collateral to make payment or otherwise render performance to or for the benefit of the secured party;

(2) may take any proceeds to which the secured party is entitled under Section 9—315;

(3) may enforce the obligations of an account debtor or other person obligated on collateral and exercise the rights of the debtor with respect to the obligation of the account debtor or other person obligated on collateral to make payment or otherwise render performance to the debtor, and with respect to any property that secures the obligations of the account debtor or other person obligated on the collateral;

(4) if it holds a security interest in a deposit account perfected by control under Section 9—104(a)(1), may apply the balance of the deposit

account to the obligation secured by the deposit account; and

(5) if it holds a security interest in a deposit account perfected by control under Section 9—104(a)(2) or (3), may instruct the bank to pay the balance of the deposit account to or for the benefit of the secured party.

(b) If necessary to enable a secured party to exercise under subsection (a)(3) the right of a debtor to enforce a mortgage nonjudicially, the secured party may record in the office in which a record of the mortgage is recorded:

(1) a copy of the security agreement that creates or provides for a security interest in the obligation secured by the mortgage; and

(2) the secured party's sworn affidavit in recordable form stating that:

(A) a default has occurred; and

(B) the secured party is entitled to enforce the mortgage nonjudicially.

(c) A secured party shall proceed in a commercially reasonable manner if the secured party:

(1) undertakes to collect from or enforce an obligation of an account debtor or other person obligated on collateral; and

(2) is entitled to charge back uncollected collateral or otherwise to full or limited recourse against the debtor or a secondary obligor.

(d) A secured party may deduct from the collections made pursuant to subsection (c) reasonable expenses of collection and enforcement, including reasonable attorney's fees and legal expenses incurred by the secured party.

(e) This section does not determine whether an account debtor, bank, or other person obligated on collateral owes a duty to a secured party.

§9—608. APPLICATION OF PROCEEDS OF COLLECTION OR ENFORCEMENT; LIABILITY FOR DEFICIENCY AND RIGHT TO SURPLUS

(a) If a security interest or agricultural lien secures payment or performance of an obligation, the following rules apply:

(1) A secured party shall apply or pay over for application the cash proceeds of collection or enforcement under Section 9—607 in the following order to:

(A) the reasonable expenses of collection and enforcement and, to the extent provided for by

agreement and not prohibited by law, reasonable attorney's fees and legal expenses incurred by the secured party;

(B) the satisfaction of obligations secured by the security interest or agricultural lien under which the collection or enforcement is made; and

(C) the satisfaction of obligations secured by any subordinate security interest in or other lien on the collateral subject to the security interest or agricultural lien under which the collection or enforcement is made if the secured party receives an authenticated demand for proceeds before distribution of the proceeds is completed.

(2) If requested by a secured party, a holder of a subordinate security interest or other lien shall furnish reasonable proof of the interest or lien within a reasonable time. Unless the holder complies, the secured party need not comply with the holder's demand under paragraph (1)(C).

(3) A secured party need not apply or pay over for application noncash proceeds of collection and enforcement under Section 9—607 unless the failure to do so would be commercially unreasonable. A secured party that applies or pays over for application noncash proceeds shall do so in a commercially reasonable manner.

(4) A secured party shall account to and pay a debtor for any surplus, and the obligor is liable for any deficiency.

(b) If the underlying transaction is a sale of accounts, chattel paper, payment intangibles, or promissory notes, the debtor is not entitled to any surplus, and the obligor is not liable for any deficiency.

§9—609. SECURED PARTY'S RIGHT TO TAKE POSSESSION AFTER DEFAULT

(a) After default, a secured party:

(1) may take possession of the collateral; and

(2) without removal, may render equipment unusable and dispose of collateral on a debtor's premises under Section 9—610.

(b) A secured party may proceed under subsection (a):

(1) pursuant to judicial process; or

(2) without judicial process, if it proceeds without breach of the peace.

(c) If so agreed, and in any event after default, a secured party may require the debtor to assemble the collateral and make it available to the secured party at a place to be designated by the secured party which is reasonably convenient to both parties.

§9—610. DISPOSITION OF COLLATERAL AFTER DEFAULT

(a) After default, a secured party may sell, lease, license, or otherwise dispose of any or all of the collateral in its present condition or following any commercially reasonable preparation or processing.

(b) Every aspect of a disposition of collateral, including the method, manner, time, place, and other terms, must be commercially reasonable. If commercially reasonable, a secured party may dispose of collateral by public or private proceedings, by one or more contracts, as a unit or in parcels, and at any time and place and on any terms.

(c) A secured party may purchase collateral:

(1) at a public disposition; or

(2) at a private disposition only if the collateral is of a kind that is customarily sold on a recognized market or the subject of widely distributed standard price quotations.

(d) A contract for sale, lease, license, or other disposition includes the warranties relating to title, possession, quiet enjoyment, and the like which by operation of law accompany a voluntary disposition of property of the kind subject to the contract.

(e) A secured party may disclaim or modify warranties under subsection (d):

(1) in a manner that would be effective to disclaim or modify the warranties in a voluntary disposition of property of the kind subject to the contract of disposition; or

(2) by communicating to the purchaser a record evidencing the contract for disposition and including an express disclaimer or modification of the warranties.

(f) A record is sufficient to disclaim warranties under subsection (e) if it indicates "There is no warranty relating to title, possession, quiet enjoyment, or the like in this disposition" or uses words of similar import.

§9—611. NOTIFICATION BEFORE DISPOSITION OF COLLATERAL

(a) In this section, "notification date" means the earlier of the date on which:

(1) a secured party sends to the debtor and any secondary obligor an authenticated notification of disposition; or

(2) the debtor and any secondary obligor waive the right to notification.

(b) Except as otherwise provided in subsection (d), a secured party that disposes of collateral under Section 9—610 shall send to the persons specified in subsection (c) a reasonable authenticated notification of disposition.

(c) To comply with subsection (b), the secured party shall send an authenticated notification of disposition to:

(1) the debtor;

(2) any secondary obligor; and

(3) if the collateral is other than consumer goods:

(A) any other person from which the secured party has received, before the notification date, an authenticated notification of a claim of an interest in the collateral;

(B) any other secured party or lienholder that, 10 days before the notification date, held a security interest in or other lien on the collateral perfected by the filing of a financing statement that:

(i) identified the collateral;

(ii) was indexed under the debtor's name as of that date; and

(iii) was filed in the office in which to file a financing statement against the debtor covering the collateral as of that date; and

(C) any other secured party that, 10 days before the notification date, held a security interest in the collateral perfected by compliance with a statute, regulation, or treaty described in Section 9—311(a).

(d) Subsection (b) does not apply if the collateral is perishable or threatens to decline speedily in value or is of a type customarily sold on a recognized market.

(e) A secured party complies with the requirement for notification prescribed by subsection (c)(3)(B) if:

(1) not later than 20 days or earlier than 30 days before the notification date, the secured party requests, in a commercially reasonable manner, information concerning financing statements indexed under the debtor's name in the office indicated in subsection (c)(3)(B); and

(2) before the notification date, the secured party:

(A) did not receive a response to the request for information; or

(B) received a response to the request for information and sent an authenticated notification of disposition to each secured party or other lienholder named in that response whose financing statement covered the collateral.

§9—612. TIMELINESS OF NOTIFICATION BEFORE DISPOSITION OF COLLATERAL

(a) Except as otherwise provided in subsection (b), whether a notification is sent within a reasonable time is a question of fact.

(b) In a transaction other than a consumer transaction, a notification of disposition sent after default and 10 days or more before the earliest time of disposition set forth in the notification is sent within a reasonable time before the disposition.

* * * *

§9—615. APPLICATION OF PROCEEDS OF DISPOSITION; LIABILITY FOR DEFICIENCY AND RIGHT TO SURPLUS

(a) A secured party shall apply or pay over for application the cash proceeds of disposition under Section 9—610 in the following order to:

(1) the reasonable expenses of retaking, holding, preparing for disposition, processing, and disposing, and, to the extent provided for by agreement and not prohibited by law, reasonable attorney's fees and legal expenses incurred by the secured party;

(2) the satisfaction of obligations secured by the security interest or agricultural lien under which the disposition is made;

(3) the satisfaction of obligations secured by any subordinate security interest in or other subordinate lien on the collateral if:

(A) the secured party receives from the holder of the subordinate security interest or other lien an authenticated demand for proceeds before distribution of the proceeds is completed; and

(B) in a case in which a consignor has an interest in the collateral, the subordinate security interest or other lien is senior to the interest of the consignor; and

(4) a secured party that is a consignor of the collateral if the secured party receives from the consignor an authenticated demand for proceeds before distribution of the proceeds is completed.

(b) If requested by a secured party, a holder of a subordinate security interest or other lien shall furnish reasonable proof of the interest or lien within a reasonable time.

Unless the holder does so, the secured party need not comply with the holder's demand under subsection (a)(3).

(c) A secured party need not apply or pay over for application noncash proceeds of disposition under Section 9—610 unless the failure to do so would be commercially unreasonable. A secured party that applies or pays over for application noncash proceeds shall do so in a commercially reasonable manner.

(d) If the security interest under which a disposition is made secures payment or performance of an obligation, after making the payments and applications required by subsection (a) and permitted by subsection (c):

(1) unless subsection (a)(4) requires the secured party to apply or pay over cash proceeds to a consignor, the secured party shall account to and pay a debtor for any surplus; and

(2) the obligor is liable for any deficiency.

(e) If the underlying transaction is a sale of accounts, chattel paper, payment intangibles, or promissory notes:

(1) the debtor is not entitled to any surplus; and

(2) the obligor is not liable for any deficiency.

(f) The surplus or deficiency following a disposition is calculated based on the amount of proceeds that would have been realized in a disposition complying with this part to a transferee other than the secured party, a person related to the secured party, or a secondary obligor if:

(1) the transferee in the disposition is the secured party, a person related to the secured party, or a secondary obligor; and

(2) the amount of proceeds of the disposition is significantly below the range of proceeds that a complying disposition to a person other than the secured party, a person related to the secured party, or a secondary obligor would have brought.

(g) A secured party that receives cash proceeds of a disposition in good faith and without knowledge that the receipt violates the rights of the holder of a security interest or other lien that is not subordinate to the security interest or agricultural lien under which the disposition is made:

(1) takes the cash proceeds free of the security interest or other lien;

(2) is not obligated to apply the proceeds of the disposition to the satisfaction of obligations secured by the security interest or other lien; and

(3) is not obligated to account to or pay the holder of the security interest or other lien for any surplus.

* * * *

§9—617. RIGHTS OF TRANSFEREE OF COLLATERAL

(a) A secured party's disposition of collateral after default:

1) transfers to a transferee for value all of the debtor's rights in the collateral;

2) discharges the security interest under which the disposition is made; and

3) discharges any subordinate security interest or other subordinate lien [other than liens created under [cite acts or statutes providing for liens, if any, that are not to be discharged]].

(b) A transferee that acts in good faith takes free of the rights and interests described in subsection (a), even if the secured party fails to comply with this article or the requirements of any judicial proceeding.

(c) If a transferee does not take free of the rights and interests described in subsection (a), the transferee takes the collateral subject to:

(1) the debtor's rights in the collateral;

(2) the security interest or agricultural lien under which the disposition is made; and

(3) any other security interest or other lien.

* * * *

§9—620. ACCEPTANCE OF COLLATERAL IN FULL OR PARTIAL SATISFACTION OF OBLIGATION; COMPULSORY DISPOSITION OF COLLATERAL

(a) Except as otherwise provided in subsection (g), a secured party may accept collateral in full or partial satisfaction of the obligation it secures only if:

(1) the debtor consents to the acceptance under subsection (c);

(2) the secured party does not receive, within the time set forth in subsection (d), a notification of objection to the proposal authenticated by:

(A) a person to which the secured party was required to send a proposal under Section 9—621; or

(B) any other person, other than the debtor, holding an interest in the collateral subordinate to the security interest that is the subject of the proposal;

(3) if the collateral is consumer goods, the collateral is not in the possession of the debtor when the debtor consents to the acceptance; and

(4) subsection (e) does not require the secured party to dispose of the collateral or the debtor waives the requirement pursuant to Section 9—624.

(b) A purported or apparent acceptance of collateral under this section is ineffective unless:

(1) the secured party consents to the acceptance in an authenticated record or sends a proposal to the debtor; and

(2) the conditions of subsection (a) are met.

(c) For purposes of this section:

(1) a debtor consents to an acceptance of collateral in partial satisfaction of the obligation it secures only if the debtor agrees to the terms of the acceptance in a record authenticated after default; and

(2) a debtor consents to an acceptance of collateral in full satisfaction of the obligation it secures only if the debtor agrees to the terms of the acceptance in a record authenticated after default or the secured party:

(A) sends to the debtor after default a proposal that is unconditional or subject only to a condition that collateral not in the possession of the secured party be preserved or maintained;

(B) in the proposal, proposes to accept collateral in full satisfaction of the obligation it secures; and

(C) does not receive a notification of objection authenticated by the debtor within 20 days after the proposal is sent.

(d) To be effective under subsection (a)(2), a notification of objection must be received by the secured party:

(1) in the case of a person to which the proposal was sent pursuant to Section 9—621, within 20 days after notification was sent to that person; and

(2) in other cases:

(A) within 20 days after the last notification was sent pursuant to Section 9—621; or

(B) if a notification was not sent, before the debtor consents to the acceptance under subsection (c).

(e) A secured party that has taken possession of collateral shall dispose of the collateral pursuant to Section 9—610 within the time specified in subsection (f) if:

(1) 60 percent of the cash price has been paid in the case of a purchase-money security interest in consumer goods; or

(2) 60 percent of the principal amount of the obligation secured has been paid in the case of a nonpurchase-money security interest in consumer goods.

(f) To comply with subsection (e), the secured party shall dispose of the collateral:

(1) within 90 days after taking possession; or

(2) within any longer period to which the debtor and all secondary obligors have agreed in an agreement to that effect entered into and authenticated after default.

(g) In a consumer transaction, a secured party may not accept collateral in partial satisfaction of the obligation it secures.

* * * *

§9—623. RIGHT TO REDEEM COLLATERAL

(a) A debtor, any secondary obligor, or any other secured party or lienholder may redeem collateral.

(b) To redeem collateral, a person shall tender:

(1) fulfillment of all obligations secured by the collateral; and

(2) the reasonable expenses and attorney's fees described in Section 9—615(a)(1).

(c) A redemption may occur at any time before a secured party:

(1) has collected collateral under Section 9—607;

(2) has disposed of collateral or entered into a contract for its disposition under Section 9—610; or

(3) has accepted collateral in full or partial satisfaction of the obligation it secures under Section 9—622.

* * * *

§9—625. REMEDIES FOR SECURED PARTY'S FAILURE TO COMPLY WITH ARTICLE

(a) If it is established that a secured party is not proceeding in accordance with this article, a court may order or restrain collection, enforcement, or disposition of collateral on appropriate terms and conditions.

(b) Subject to subsections (c), (d), and (f), a person is liable for damages in the amount of any loss caused by a failure to comply with this article. Loss caused by a failure to comply may include loss resulting from the debtor's inability to obtain, or increased costs of, alternative financing.

(c) Except as otherwise provided in Section 9—628:

(1) a person that, at the time of the failure, was a debtor, was an obligor, or held a security interest in

or other lien on the collateral may recover damages under subsection (b) for its loss; and

(2) if the collateral is consumer goods, a person that was a debtor or a secondary obligor at the time a secured party failed to comply with this part may recover for that failure in any event an amount not less than the credit service charge plus 10 percent of the principal amount of the obligation or the time-price differential plus 10 percent of the cash price.

(d) A debtor whose deficiency is eliminated under Section 9—626 may recover damages for the loss of any surplus. However, a debtor or secondary obligor whose deficiency is eliminated or reduced under Section 9—626 may not otherwise recover under subsection (b) for noncompliance with the provisions of this part relating to collection, enforcement, disposition, or acceptance.

(e) In addition to any damages recoverable under subsection (b), the debtor, consumer obligor, or person named as a debtor in a filed record, as applicable, may recover $500 in each case from a person that:

(1) fails to comply with Section 9—208;

(2) fails to comply with Section 9—209;

(3) files a record that the person is not entitled to file under Section 9—509(a);

(4) fails to cause the secured party of record to file or send a termination statement as required by Section 9—513(a) or (c);

(5) fails to comply with Section 9—616(b)(1) and whose failure is part of a pattern, or consistent with a practice, of noncompliance; or

(6) fails to comply with Section 9—616(b)(2).

(f) A debtor or consumer obligor may recover damages under subsection (b) and, in addition, $500 in each case from a person that, without reasonable cause, fails to comply with a request under Section 9—210. A recipient of a request under Section 9—210 which never claimed an interest in the collateral or obligations that are the subject of a request under that section has a reasonable excuse for failure to comply with the request within the meaning of this subsection.

(g) If a secured party fails to comply with a request regarding a list of collateral or a statement of account under Section 9—210, the secured party may claim a security interest only as shown in the list or statement included in the request as against a person that is reasonably misled by the failure.

* * * *

§9—627. DETERMINATION OF WHETHER CONDUCT WAS COMMERCIALLY REASONABLE

(a) The fact that a greater amount could have been obtained by a collection, enforcement, disposition, or acceptance at a different time or in a different method from that selected by the secured party is not of itself sufficient to preclude the secured party from establishing that the collection, enforcement, disposition, or acceptance was made in a commercially reasonable manner.

(b) A disposition of collateral is made in a commercially reasonable manner if the disposition is made:

(1) in the usual manner on any recognized market;

(2) at the price current in any recognized market at the time of the disposition; or

(3) otherwise in conformity with reasonable commercial practices among dealers in the type of property that was the subject of the disposition.

(c) A collection, enforcement, disposition, or acceptance is commercially reasonable if it has been approved:

(1) in a judicial proceeding;

(2) by a bona fide creditors' committee;

(3) by a representative of creditors; or

(4) by an assignee for the benefit of creditors.

(d) Approval under subsection (c) need not be obtained, and lack of approval does not mean that the collection, enforcement, disposition, or acceptance is not commercially reasonable.

Copyright 2002 by the American Law Institute and the National Conference of Commissioners on Uniform State Laws. Reproduced with permission.

A

abate—put a stop to a nuisance; reduce or cancel a legacy because the estate of the decedent is insufficient to make payment in full.

absolute guaranty—agreement that creates the same obligation for the guarantor as a suretyship does for the surety; a guaranty of payment creates an absolute guaranty.

absolute privilege—complete defense against the tort of defamation, as in the speeches of members of Congress on the floor and witnesses in a trial.

abstract of title—history of the transfers of title to a given piece of land, briefly stating the parties to and the effect of all deeds, wills, and judicial proceedings relating to the land.

acceptance—unqualified assent to the act or proposal of another, such as the acceptance of an offer to make a contract; the acceptance of a draft (bill of exchange); the acceptance of goods delivered by a seller, or a gift of a deed.

acceptor—drawee who has accepted the liability of paying the amount of money specified in a draft.

accommodation party—person who signs an instrument to lend credit to another party to the paper.

accord and satisfaction—agreement to substitute for an existing debt some alternative form of discharging that debt, coupled with the actual discharge of the debt by the substituted performance.

acknowledgment—admission or confirmation, generally of an instrument and usually made before a person authorized to administer oaths, such as a notary public.

acquired distinctiveness—through advertising, use and association, over time, an ordinary descriptive word or phrase has taken on a new source-identifying meaning and functions as a mark in the eyes of the public.

act-of-state doctrine—doctrine whereby every sovereign state is bound to respect the independence of every other sovereign state, and the courts of one country will not sit in judgment of another government's acts done within its own territory.

adeemed—canceled; as in a specifically bequeathed property being sold or given away by the testator prior to death, thus canceling the bequest.

adjustable rate mortgage (ARM)—mortgage with variable financing charges over the life of the loan.

administrative agency—government body charged with administering and implementing legislation.

administrative law—law governing administrative agencies.

administrative law judge—judicial figure who hears administrative agency actions.

Administrative Procedure Act—federal law that establishes the operating rules for administrative agencies.

administrative regulations—rules made by state and federal administrative agencies.

administrator, administratrix—person (man, woman) appointed to wind up and settle the estate of a person who has died without a will.

admissibility—the quality of the evidence in a case that allows it to be presented to the jury.

adverse possession—hostile possession of real estate, which when actual, visible, notorious, exclusive, and continued for the required time, will vest the title to the land in the person in such adverse possession.

advising bank—bank that tells beneficiary that letter of credit has been issued.

affidavit—statement of facts under oath; executed before a notary public or anyone authorized to administer oaths.

affirm—action taken by an appellate court that approves the decision of the court below.

affirmative action plan (AAP)—plan to have a diverse and representative workforce.

after-acquired goods—goods acquired after a security interest has attached.

agency—the relationship that exists between a person identified as a principal and another by virtue of which the latter may make contracts with third persons on behalf of the principal. (Parties–principal, agent, third person)

agent—person or firm who is authorized by the principal or by operation of law to make contracts with third persons on behalf of the principal.

airbill—document of title issued to a shipper whose goods are being sent via air.

alteration—unauthorized change or completion of a negotiable instrument designed to modify the obligation of a party to the instrument.

alternative payees—those persons to whom a negotiable instrument is made payable, any one of whom may indorse and take delivery of it.

ambiguous—having more than one reasonable interpretation.

answer—what a defendant must file to admit or deny facts asserted by the plaintiff.

anticipatory breach—promisor's repudiation of the contract prior to the time that performance is required when such repudiation is accepted by the promisee as a breach of the contract.

anticipatory repudiation—repudiation made in advance of the time for performance of the contract obligations.

antilapse statutes—statutes providing that the children or heirs of a deceased beneficiary may take the legacy in the place of the deceased beneficiary.

apparent authority—appearance of authority created by the principal's words or conduct.

appeal—taking a case to a reviewing court to determine whether the judgment of the lower court or administrative agency was correct. (Parties—appellant, appellee)

appellate jurisdiction—the power of a court to hear and decide a given class of cases on appeal from another court or administrative agency.

arbitration—the settlement of disputed questions, whether of law or fact, by one or more arbitrators by whose decision the parties agree to be bound.

Article 2—section of the Uniform Commercial Code that governs contracts for the sale of goods.

articles of copartnership—see *partnership agreement.*

articles of incorporation—see *certificate of incorporation.*

articles of partnership—see *partnership agreement.*

assignee—third party to whom contract benefits are transferred.

assignment—transfer of a right. Generally used in connection with personal property rights, as rights under a contract, commercial paper, an insurance policy, a mortgage, or a lease. (Parties—assignor, assignee)

assignor—party who assigns contract rights to a third party.

association tribunal—a court created by a trade association or group for the resolution of disputes among its members.

assumption—mortgage transfers in which the transferee and mortgagor are liable and the property is subject to foreclosure by the mortgagee if payments are not made.

attestation clause—clause that indicates a witness has observed either the execution of the will or the testator's acknowledgment of the writing as the testator's will.

attorney in fact—agent authorized to act for another under a power of attorney.

attorney-client privilege—right of individual to have discussions with his/her attorney kept private and confidential.

attractive nuisance doctrine—a rule imposing liability upon a landowner for injuries sustained by small children playing on the land when the landowner permits a condition to exist or maintains equipment that a reasonable person should realize would attract small children who could not realize the danger. The rule does not apply if an unreasonable burden would be imposed upon the

landowner in taking steps to protect the children.

authorities—corporations formed by government that perform public service.

automatic perfection—perfection given by statute without specific filing or possession requirements on the part of the creditor.

automatic stay—order to prevent creditors from taking action such as filing suits or seeking foreclosure against the debtor.

B

bad check laws—laws making it a criminal offense to issue a bad check with intent to defraud.

bailee—person who accepts possession of a property.

bailee's lien—specific, possessory lien of the bailee upon the goods for work done to them. Commonly extended by statute to any bailee's claim for compensation, eliminating the necessity of retention of possession.

bailment—relationship that exists when personal property is delivered into the possession of another under an agreement, express or implied, that the identical property will be returned or will be delivered in accordance with the agreement. (Parties—bailor, bailee)

bailment for mutual benefit—bailment in which the bailor and bailee derive a benefit from the bailment.

bailor—person who turns over the possession of a property.

balance sheet test—comparison of assets to liabilities made to determine solvency.

bankruptcy—procedure by which one unable to pay debts may surrender all assets in excess of any exemption claim to the court for administration and distribution to creditors, and the debtor is given a discharge that releases him from the unpaid balance due on most debts.

bankruptcy courts—court of special jurisdiction to determine bankruptcy issues.

battle of the forms—merchants' exchanges of invoices and purchase orders with differing boilerplate terms.

bearer—person in physical possession of commercial paper payable to bearer, a

document of title directing delivery to bearer, or an investment security in bearer form.

bearer paper—instrument with no payee, payable to cash or payable to bearer.

bedrock view—a strict constructionist interpretation of a constitution.

beneficiary—person to whom the proceeds of a life insurance policy are payable, a person for whose benefit property is held in trust, or a person given property by a will; the ultimate recipient of the benefit of a funds transfer.

benefit corporation—for-profit corporation that sets a goal to create a public benefit while still providing economic returns to its investors.

beneficiary's bank—the final bank, which carries out the payment order, in the chain of a transfer of funds.

bequest—gift of personal property by will.

best available treatment—a water treatment that is the most current and best available through research, even though it may not be the treatment used most frequently.

best conventional treatment—a water treatment that is generally used among industries; not always the best treatment available.

bicameral—a two-house form of the legislative branch of government.

bilateral contract—agreement under which one promise is given in exchange for another.

bill of lading—document issued by a carrier acknowledging the receipt of goods and the terms of the contract of transportation.

bill of sale—writing signed by the seller reciting that the personal property therein described has been sold to the buyer.

blackmail—extortion demands made by a nonpublic official.

blank indorsement—an indorsement that does not name the person to whom the paper, document of title, or investment security is negotiated.

blocking laws—laws that prohibit the disclosure, copying, inspection, or removal of documents located in the enacting country in compliance with orders from foreign authorities.

blue sky laws—state statutes designed to protect the public from the sale of worthless stocks and bonds.

bona fide—in good faith; without any fraud or deceit.

bond—a debt investment; a loan to a corporation or government entity usually for a defined period of time at a fixed interest rate.

bond indenture—agreement setting forth the contractual terms of a particular bond issue.

book value—value found by dividing the value of the corporate assets by the number of shares outstanding.

breach—failure to act or perform in the manner called for in a contract.

breach of the peace—violation of the law in the repossession of the collateral.

brownfields—land that is a designated Superfund cleanup site but which lies fallow because no one is willing to risk liability by buying the property, even when the hazardous waste has been removed, or property no one is willing to spend the money to remove the hazardous waste.

bubble concept—method for determining total emissions in one area; all sources are considered in an area.

business ethics—balancing the goal of profits with values of individuals and society.

business judgment rule (BJR)—rule that allows management immunity from liability for corporate acts where there is a reasonable indication that the acts were made in good faith with due care.

bylaws—rules and regulations enacted by a corporation to govern the affairs of the corporation and its shareholders, directors, and officers.

C

cancellation provision—crossing out of a part of an instrument or a destruction of all legal effect of the instrument, whether by act of party, upon breach by the other party, or pursuant to agreement or decree of court.

capital stock—declared money value of the outstanding stock of the corporation.

cargo insurance—insurance that protects a cargo owner against financial loss if goods being shipped are lost or damaged at sea.

carrier—individual or organization undertaking the transportation of goods.

case law—law that includes principles that are expressed for the first time in court decisions.

cash surrender value—sum paid the insured upon the surrender of a policy to the insurer.

cash tender offer—general offer to all shareholders of a target corporation to purchase their shares for cash at a specified price.

cashier's check—draft drawn by a bank on itself.

cause of action—right to damages or other judicial relief when a legally protected right of the plaintiff is violated by an unlawful act of the defendant.

cease-and-desist order—order issued by a court or administrative agency to stop a practice that it decides is improper.

certificate of deposit (CD)—promise-to-pay instrument issued by a bank.

certificate of incorporation—written approval from the state or national government for a corporation to be formed.

certificate of stock—document evidencing a shareholder's ownership of stock issued by a corporation.

certified check—check for which the bank has set aside in a special account sufficient funds to pay it; payment is made when check is presented regardless of amount in drawer's account at that time; discharges all parties except certifying bank when holder requests certification.

cestui que trust—beneficiary of the trust.

CF—cost and freight.

Chapter 7 bankruptcy—liquidation form of bankruptcy under federal law.

Chapter 11 bankruptcy—reorganization form of bankruptcy under federal law.

Chapter 13 bankruptcy—proceeding of consumer debt readjustment plan bankruptcy.

charging order—order by a court, after a business partner's personal assets are exhausted, requiring that the partner's share of the profits be paid to a creditor until the debt is discharged.

charter—grant of authority from a government to exist as a corporation. Generally replaced today by a certificate of incorporation approving the articles of incorporation.

check—order by a depositor on a bank to pay a sum of money to a payee; a bill of exchange drawn on a bank and payable on demand.

choice-of-law clause—clause in an agreement that specifies which law will govern should a dispute arise.

chose in action—intangible personal property in the nature of claims against another, such as a claim for accounts receivable or wages.

CIF—cost, insurance, and freight.

civil disobedience—the term used when natural law proponents violate positive law.

civil laws—the laws that define the rights of one person against another.

claim—creditor's right to payment.

Clayton Act—a federal law that prohibits price discrimination.

Clean Air Act—federal legislation that establishes standards for air pollution levels and prevents further deterioration of air quality.

Clean Water Act—federal legislation that regulates water pollution through a control system.

close corporation—corporation whose shares are held by a single shareholder or a small group of shareholders.

close-connection doctrine—circumstantial evidence, such as an ongoing or a close relationship, that can serve as notice of a problem with an instrument.

COD—cash on delivery.

coinsurance clause—clause requiring the insured to maintain insurance on property up to a stated amount and providing that to the extent that this is not done, the insured is to be deemed a coinsurer with the insurer, so that the latter is liable only for its proportionate share of the amount of insurance required to be carried.

collateral—property pledged by a borrower as security for a debt.

comity—principle of international and national law that the laws of all nations and states deserve the respect legitimately demanded by equal participants.

commerce clause—that section of the U.S. Constitution allocating business regulation between federal and state governments.

commercial impracticability—situation that occurs when costs of performance rise suddenly and performance of a contract will result in a substantial loss.

commercial lease—any nonconsumer lease.

commercial paper—written, transferable, signed promise or order to pay a specified sum of money; a negotiable instrument.

commercial unit—standard of the trade for shipment or packaging of a good.

commission merchant—bailee to whom goods are consigned for sale.

commission or factorage—consignee's compensation.

common carrier—carrier that holds out its facilities to serve the general public for compensation without discrimination.

common law—the body of unwritten principles originally based upon the usages and customs of the community that were recognized and enforced by the courts.

common stock—stock that has no right or priority over any other stock of the corporation as to dividends or distribution of assets upon dissolution.

community property—cotenancy held by husband and wife in property acquired during their marriage under the law of some of the states, principally in the southwestern United States.

comparative negligence—defense to negligence that allows plaintiff to recover reduced damages based on his level of fault.

compensatory damages—sum of money that will compensate an injured plaintiff for actual loss.

complaint—the initial pleading filed by the plaintiff in many actions, which in many states may be served as original process to acquire jurisdiction over the defendant.

composition of creditors—agreement among creditors that each shall accept a part payment as full payment in consideration of the other creditors doing the same.

Comprehensive Environmental Response, Compensation, and Liability Act (CERCLA)—federal law that assigns liability for cleanup of hazardous sites.

computer crimes—wrongs committed using a computer or with knowledge of computers.

concealment—failure to volunteer information not requested.

condition—stipulation or prerequisite in a contract, will, or other instrument.

condition precedent—event that if unsatisfied would mean that no rights would arise under a contract.

condition subsequent—event whose occurrence or lack thereof terminates a contract.

condominium—combination of co-ownership and individual ownership.

confidential relationship—relationship in which, because of the legal status of the parties or their respective physical or mental conditions or knowledge, one party places full confidence and trust in the other.

conflict of interest—conduct that compromises an employee's allegiance to that company.

conglomerate—relationship of a parent corporation to subsidiary corporations engaged in diversified fields of activity unrelated to the field of activity of the parent corporation.

consent decrees—informal settlements of enforcement actions brought by agencies.

consequential damages—damages the buyer experiences as a result of the seller's breach with respect to a third party; also called *special damages.*

consideration—promise or performance that the promisor demands as the price of the promise.

consignee—(1) person to whom goods are shipped; (2) dealer who sells goods for others.

consignment—bailment made for the purpose of sale by the bailee. (Parties—consignor, consignee)

consignor—(1) person who delivers goods to the carrier for shipment; (2) party with title who turns goods over to another for sale.

consolidation (of corporations)—combining of two or more corporations in which the corporate existence of each one ceases and a new corporation is created.

conspiracy—agreement between two or more persons to commit an unlawful act.

constitution—a body of principles that establishes the structure of a government and the relationship of the government to the people who are governed.

constructive bailment—bailment imposed by law as opposed to one created by contract, whereby the bailee must preserve the property and redeliver it to the owner.

constructive delivery—See "*symbolic delivery.*"

constructive eviction—act or omission of the landlord that substantially deprives the tenant of the use and enjoyment of the premises.

consumer—any buyer afforded special protections by statute or regulation.

consumer credit—credit for personal, family, and household use.

Consumer Financial Protection Bureau—consumer protection bureau located within the Federal Reserve that now has jurisdiction over all consumer credit issues and statutes.

consumer goods—goods used or bought primarily for personal, family, or household use.

consumer lease—lease of goods by a natural person for personal, family, or household use.

Consumer Product Safety Improvement Act (CPSIA)—federal law that sets standards for the types of paints used in toys, a response to the lead paint found in toys made in China; requires tracking for international production; increases penalties.

contract—a binding agreement based on the genuine assent of the parties, made for a lawful object, between competent parties, in the form required by law, and generally supported by consideration.

contract carrier—carrier that transports on the basis of individual contracts that it makes with each shipper.

contract interference—tort in which a third party interferes with others' freedom to contract.

contract of adhesion—contract offered by a dominant party to a party with inferior bargaining power on a take-it-or-leave-it basis.

contract under seal—contract executed by affixing a seal or making an impression on the paper or on some adhering substance such as wax attached to the document.

contracting agent—agent with authority to make contracts; person with whom the buyer deals.

Contracts for the International Sale of Goods (CISG)—uniform international contract code contracts for international sale of goods.

contractual capacity—ability to understand that a contract is being made and to understand its general meaning.

contribution—right of a co-obligor who has paid more than a proportionate share to demand that other obligors pay their *pro rata* share.

contributory negligence—negligence of the plaintiff that contributes to injury and at common law bars recovery from the defendant although the defendant may have been more negligent than the plaintiff.

Controlling the Assault of Non-Solicited Pornography and Marketing (CAN-SPAM) Act—allows private companies to bring suit against spammers for their unauthorized use of Internet Service Providers (ISPs).

conversion—act of taking personal property by a person not entitled to it and keeping it from its true owner or prior possessor without consent.

cooperative—group of two or more persons or enterprises that acts through a common agent with respect to a common objective, such as buying or selling.

copyright—exclusive right given by federal statute to the creator of a literary or an artistic work to use, reproduce, and display the work.

corporation—artificial being created by government grant, which for many purposes is treated as a natural person.

corporation by estoppel—corporation that comes about when parties estop themselves from denying that the corporation exists.

corporation de jure—corporation with a legal right to exist by virtue of law.

correspondent bank—will honor the letter of credit from the domestic bank of the buyer.

cost plus—method of determining the purchase price or contract price equal to the seller's or contractor's costs plus a stated percentage as the profit.

co-sureties—sureties for the same debt.

cotenancy—when two or more persons hold concurrent rights and interests in the same property.

Council on Environmental Quality (CEQ)—federal agency that establishes national policies on environmental quality and then recommends legislation to implement these policies.

counterclaim—a claim that the defendant in an action may make against the plaintiff.

counteroffer—proposal by an offeree to the offeror that changes the terms of, and thus rejects, the original offer.

course of dealing—pattern of performance between two parties to a contract.

court—a tribunal established by government to hear and decide matters properly brought to it.

covenant against encumbrances—guarantee that conveyed land is not subject to any right or interest of a third person.

covenant of further assurances—promise that the grantor of an interest in land will execute any additional documents required to perfect the title of the grantee.

covenant of quiet enjoyment—covenant by the grantor of an interest in land to not disturb the grantee's possession of the land.

covenant of right to convey—guarantee that the grantor of an interest in land, if not the owner, has the right or authority to make the conveyance to a new owner.

covenant of seisin—guarantee that the grantor of an interest in land owns the estate conveyed to a new owner.

covenants (or warranties) of title—grantor's covenants of a deed that guarantee such matters as the right to make the conveyance, to ownership of the property, to freedom of the property from encumbrances, or that the grantee will not be disturbed in the quiet enjoyment of the land.

credit transfer—transaction in which a person making payment, such as a buyer, requests payment be made to the beneficiary's bank.

creditor—person (seller or lender) who is owed money; also may be a secured party.

crime—violation of the law that is punished as an offense against the state or government.

criminal laws—the laws that define wrongs against society.

cross-examination—the examination made of a witness by the attorney for the adverse party.

cumulative voting—system of voting for directors in which each shareholder has as many votes as the number of voting shares owned multiplied by the number of directors to be elected, and such votes can be distributed for the various candidates as desired.

customary authority—authority of an agent to do any act that, according to the custom of the community, usually accompanies the transaction for which the agent is authorized to act.

cybersquatters—term for those who register and set up domain names on the Internet for resale to the famous users of the names in question.

D

de facto—existing in fact as distinguished from as of right, as in the case of an officer or a corporation purporting to act as such without being elected to the office or having been properly incorporated.

debenture—unsecured bond of a corporation, with no specific corporate assets pledged as security for payment.

debit transfer—transaction in which a beneficiary entitled to money requests payment from a bank according to a prior agreement.

debtor—buyer on credit (i.e., a borrower).

decedent—person whose estate is being administered.

deed—instrument by which the grantor (owner of land) conveys or transfers the title to a grantee.

defamation—untrue statement by one party about another to a third party.

defendant—party charged with a violation of civil or criminal law in a proceeding.

defined benefit plan—an employer established pension fund obligating the employer to make specified future payments to participants upon retirement.

defined contribution plan—a plan providing individual accounts for each employee participant with benefits defined solely on the amounts contributed by each employee with matching contributions by the employer.

definite time—time of payment computable from the face of the instrument.

delegated powers—powers expressly granted the national government by the Constitution.

delegation—transfer to another of the right and power to do an act.

delegation of duties—transfer of duties by a contracting party to another person who is to perform them.

delivery—constructive or actual possession.

demand draft—draft that is payable upon presentment.

demurrer—a pleading to dismiss the adverse party's pleading for not stating a cause of action or a defense.

deposition—the testimony of a witness taken out of court before a person authorized to administer oaths.

depositor—person, or bailor, who gives property for storage.

derivative (secondary) action—secondary action for damages or breach of contract brought by one or more corporate shareholders against directors, officers, or third persons.

development statement—statement that sets forth significant details of a real estate or property development as required by the federal Land Sales Act.

devise—gift of real estate made by will.

devisee—beneficiary of a devise.

direct damages—losses that are caused by breach of a contract.

direct examination—examination of a witness by his or her attorney.

directed verdict—a direction by the trial judge to the jury to return a verdict in favor of a specified party to the action.

disability—any incapacity resulting from bodily injury or disease to engage in any occupation for remuneration or profit.

discharge in bankruptcy—order of the bankruptcy court relieving the debtor from obligation to pay the unpaid balance of most claims.

disclosed principal—principal whose identity is made known by the agent as well as the fact that the agent is acting on the principal's behalf.

discovery—procedures for ascertaining facts prior to the time of trial in order to eliminate the element of surprise in litigation.

dishonor—status when the primary party refuses to pay the instrument according to its terms.

disinherited—excluded from sharing in the estate of a decedent.

Dispute Settlement Body (DSB)—means provided by the World Trade Organization for member nations to resolve trade disputes rather than engage in unilateral trade sanctions or a trade war.

distinctiveness—capable of serving the source-identifying function of a mark.

distribution *per stirpes*—distribution of an estate made in as many equal parts as there are family lines represented in the nearest generation; also known as *stirpital distribution.*

distributor—entity that takes title to goods and bears the financial and commercial risks for the subsequent sale of the goods.

divestiture order—a court order to dispose of interests that could lead to a monopoly.

divisible contract—agreement consisting of two or more parts, each calling for corresponding performances of each part by the parties.

document of title—document treated as evidence that a person is entitled to receive, hold, and dispose of the document and the goods it covers.

Dodd-Frank Wall Street Reform and Consumer Protection Act—federal legislation passed following the financial markets collapse that includes consumer protections as well as market and mortgage lending reforms.

domestic corporation—corporation that has been incorporated by the state in question as opposed to incorporation by another state.

dominant tenement—land that is benefited by an easement.

donee—recipient of a gift.

donor—person making a gift.

double indemnity—provision for payment of double the amount specified by the insurance contract if death is caused by an accident and occurs under specified circumstances.

draft, or bill of exchange—an unconditional order in writing by one person upon another, signed by the person giving it, and ordering the person to whom it is directed to pay upon demand or at a definite time a sum certain in money to order or to bearer.

drawee—person to whom the draft is addressed and who is ordered to pay the amount of money specified in the draft.

drawer—person who writes out and creates a draft or bill of exchange, including a check.

due diligence—process of checking the environmental history and nature of land prior to purchase.

due process—the constitutional right to be heard, question witnesses, and present evidence.

due process clause—a guarantee of protection against the loss of property or rights without the chance to be heard.

dumping—selling goods in another country at less than fair value.

duress—conduct that deprives the victim of free will and that generally gives the victim the right to set aside any transaction entered into under such circumstances.

duty—obligation of law imposed on a person to perform or refrain from performing a certain act.

E

easement—permanent right that one has in the land of another, as the right to cross another's land or an easement of way.

easement by implication—easement not specifically created by deed that arises from the circumstances of the parties and the land location and access.

economic duress—threat of financial loss.

Economic Espionage Act (EEA)—federal law that makes it a felony to copy, download, transmit, or in any way transfer proprietary files, documents, and information from a computer to an unauthorized person.

economic strikers—union strikers trying to enforce bargaining demands when an impasse has been reached in the negotiation process for a collective bargaining agreement.

effects doctrine—doctrine stating that U.S. courts will assume jurisdiction and will apply antitrust laws to conduct outside of the United States when the activity of business firms has a direct and substantial effect on U.S. commerce; the rule has been modified to require that the effect on U.S. commerce also be direct and foreseeable.

effluent guidelines—EPA standards for maximum ranges of discharge into water.

electronic funds transfer (EFT)—any transfer of funds (other than a transaction originated by a check, draft, or similar paper instrument) that is initiated through an electronic terminal, a telephone, a computer, or a magnetic tape so as to authorize a financial institution to debit or credit an account.

Electronic Funds Transfer Act (EFTA)—federal law that provides consumers with rights and protections in electronic funds transfers.

eleemosynary corporation—corporation organized for a charitable or benevolent purpose.

embezzlement—statutory offense consisting of the unlawful conversion of property entrusted to the wrongdoer.

eminent domain—power of government and certain kinds of corporations to take private property against the objection of the owner, provided the taking is for a public purpose and just compensation is made for it.

emissions offset policy—controls whether new factories can be built in a nonattainment area.

employment-at-will doctrine—doctrine in which the employer has historically been allowed to terminate the employment contract at any time for any reason or for no reason.

en banc—the term used when the full panel of judges on the appellate court hears a case.

encoding warranty—warranty made by any party who encodes electronic information on an instrument; a warranty of accuracy.

Endangered Species Act (ESA)—federal law that identifies and protects species that are endangered from development or other acts that threaten their existence.

endowment insurance—insurance that pays the face amount of the policy if the insured dies within the policy period.

entitlement theory—another name for Nozick's theory that we all have certain rights that must be honored and protected by government.

environmental impact statement (EIS)—formal report prepared under NEPA to document findings on the impact of a federal project on the environment.

equitable title—beneficial interest in a trust.

equity—the body of principles that originally developed because of the inadequacy of the rules then applied by the common law courts of England.

escalation clause—provision for the automatic increase of the rent at periodic intervals.

escheat—transfer to the state of the title to a decedent's property when the owner of the property dies intestate and is not survived by anyone capable of taking the property as heir.

estate in fee—largest estate possible in which the owner has absolute and entire interest in the land.

estoppel—principle by which a person is barred from pursuing a certain course of action or of disputing the truth of certain matters.

ethical egoism—theory of ethics that we should all act in our own self-interest; the Ayn Rand theory that separates guilt from acting in our own self-interest.

ethics—a branch of philosophy dealing with values that relate to the nature of human conduct and values associated with that conduct.

ex post facto **law**—a law making criminal an act that was lawful when done or that increases the penalty when done. Such laws are generally prohibited by constitutional provisions.

exculpatory clause—provision in a contract stating that one of the parties is not liable for damages in case of breach; also called *limitation-of-liability clause.*

executed contract—agreement that has been completely performed.

execution—the carrying out of a judgment of a court, generally directing that property owned by the defendant be sold and the proceeds first be used to pay the execution or judgment creditor.

executive branch—the branch of government (e.g., the president) formed to execute the laws.

executor, executrix—person (man, woman) named in a will to administer the estate of the decedent.

executory contract—agreement by which something remains to be done by one or both parties.

exhaustion of administrative remedies—requirement that an agency make its final decision before the parties can go to court.

existing goods—goods that physically exist and are owned by the seller at the time of a transaction.

exoneration—agreement or provision in an agreement that one party shall not be held liable for loss; the right of the surety to demand that those primarily liable pay the claim for which the surety is secondarily liable.

expert witness—one who has acquired special knowledge in a particular field as through practical experience or study, or both, whose opinion is admissible as an aid to the trier of fact.

export sale—direct sale to customers in a foreign country.

express authority—authority of an agent to perform a certain act.

express authorization—authorization of an agent to perform a certain act.

express contract—agreement of the parties manifested by their words, whether spoken or written.

express warranty—statement by the defendant relating to the goods, which statement is part of the basis of the bargain.

extortion—illegal demand by a public officer acting with apparent authority.

F

factor—bailee to whom goods are consigned for sale.

false imprisonment—intentional detention of a person without that person's consent; called the *shopkeeper's tort* when shoplifters are unlawfully detained.

FAS—free alongside the named vessel.

federal district court—a general trial court of the federal system.

Federal Register—government publication issued five days a week that lists all administrative regulations, all presidential proclamations and executive orders, and other documents and classes of documents that the president or Congress direct to be published.

Federal Register Act—federal law requiring agencies to make public disclosure of proposed rules, passed rules, and activities.

Federal Sentencing Guidelines—federal standards used by judges in determining mandatory sentence terms for those convicted of federal crimes.

federal system—the system of government in which a central government is given power to administer to national concerns while individual states retain the power to administer to local concerns.

fee simple defeasibles—fee simple interest that can be lost if restrictions on its use are violated.

fee simple estate—highest level of land ownership; full interest of unlimited duration.

felony—criminal offense that is punishable by confinement in prison for more than one year or by death, or that is expressly stated by statute to be a felony.

field warehousing—stored goods under the exclusive control of a warehouse but kept on the owner's premises rather than in a warehouse.

Fifth Amendment—constitutional protection against self-incrimination; also guarantees due process.

finance lease—three-party lease agreement in which there is a lessor, a lessee, and a financier.

financing statement—brief statement (record) that gives sufficient information to alert third persons that a particular creditor may have a security interest in the collateral described.

fire insurance policy—a contract that indemnifies the insured for property destruction or damage caused by fire.

firm offer—offer stated to be held open for a specified time, under the UCC, with respect to merchants.

first-in-time provision—creditor whose interest attached first has priority in the collateral when two creditors have a secured interest.

first-to-perfect basis—rule of priorities that holds that first in time in perfecting a security interest, mortgage, judgment, lien, or other property attachment right should have priority.

fixture—personal property attached to or adapted to real estate.

floating lien—claim in a changing or shifting stock of goods of the buyer.

FOB place of destination—shipping contract that requires the seller to deliver goods to the buyer.

FOB place of shipment—contract that requires the seller to arrange for shipment only.

forbearance—refraining from doing an act.

forcible entry and detainer—action by the landlord to have the tenant removed for nonpayment of rent.

foreclosure—procedure for enforcing a mortgage resulting in the public sale of the mortgaged property and, less commonly, in merely barring the right of the mortgagor to redeem the property from the mortgage.

foreign corporation—corporation incorporated under the laws of another state.

Foreign Corrupt Practices Act (FCPA)—federal law that makes it a felony to influence decision makers in other countries for the purpose of obtaining business, such as contracts for sales and services; also imposes financial reporting requirements on certain U.S. corporations.

Foreign Trade Antitrust Improvements Act—the act that requires that the defendant's conduct have a "direct, substantial, and reasonably foreseeable effect" on domestic commerce.

forged or unauthorized indorsement—instrument indorsed by an agent for a principal without authorization or authority.

forgery—fraudulently making or altering an instrument that apparently creates or alters a legal liability of another.

formal contracts—written contracts or agreements whose formality signifies the parties' intention to abide by the terms.

Fourth Amendment—privacy protection in the U.S. Constitution; prohibits unauthorized searches and seizures.

franchise—privilege or authorization, generally exclusive, to engage in a particular activity within a particular geographic area, such as a government franchise to operate a taxi company within a specified city, or a private franchise as the grant by a manufacturer of a right to sell products within a particular territory or for a particular number of years.

franchise agreement—sets forth rights of franchisee to use trademarks, etc., of franchisor.

Franchise Rule—FTC rule requiring detailed disclosures and prohibiting certain practices.

franchisee—person to whom franchise is granted.

franchising—granting of permission to use a trademark, trade name, or copyright under specified conditions; a form of licensing.

franchisor—party granting the franchise.

fraud—intentional making a false statement of fact, with knowledge or reckless indifference that it is false with resulting reliance by another.

fraud in the inducement—fraud that occurs when a person is persuaded or induced to execute an instrument because of fraudulent statements.

fraud-on-the-market—a theory that in an open and developed securities market, the price of a stock is determined by the information on the company available to the public, and misleading statements will defraud purchasers of stock even if they do not directly rely on these statements.

Freedom of Information Act—federal law permitting citizens to request documents and records from administrative agencies.

freight insurance—insures that shipowner will receive payment for transportation charges.

full warranty—obligation of a seller to fix or replace a defective product within a reasonable time without cost to the buyer.

funds transfer—communication of instructions or requests to pay a specific sum of money to the credit of a specified account or person without an actual physical passing of money.

fungible goods—homogeneous goods of which any unit is the equivalent of any other unit.

future goods—goods that exist physically but are not owned by the seller and goods that have not yet been produced.

G

garnishment—the name given in some states to attachment proceedings.

general agent—agent authorized by the principal to transact all affairs in connection with a particular type of business or trade or to transact all business at a certain place.

general corporation code—state's code listing certain requirements for creation of a corporation.

general jurisdiction—the power to hear and decide most controversies involving legal rights and duties.

general legacies—certain sums of money bequeathed to named persons by the testator; to be paid out of the decedent's assets generally without specifying any particular fund or source from which the payment is to be made.

general partner—partnership in which the partners conduct as co-owners a business for profit, and each partner has a right to take part in the management of the business and has unlimited liability; general partners publicly and actively engage in the transaction of firm business.

general partners—managers of a partnership who have personal liability for the partnership debts.

gift—title to an owner's personal property voluntarily transferred by a party not receiving anything in exchange.

gift causa mortis—gift, made by the donor in the belief that death was immediate and impending, that is revoked or is revocable under certain circumstances.

good faith—absence of knowledge of any defects or problems; "pure heart and an empty head."

goods—anything movable at the time it is identified as the subject of a transaction.

grantee—new owner of a land conveyance.

grantor—owner who transfers or conveys an interest in land to a new owner.

gratuitous bailment—bailment in which the bailee does not receive any compensation or advantage.

guarantor—one who undertakes the obligation of guaranty.

guaranty—agreement or promise to answer for a debt; an undertaking to pay the debt of another if the creditor first sues the debtor.

guaranty of collection—form of guaranty in which creditor cannot proceed against guarantor until after proceeding against debtor.

guaranty of payment—absolute promise to pay when a debtor defaults.

guest—transient who contracts for a room or site at a hotel.

H

hearing officer (or examiner)—another name for an administrative law judge.

hearsay evidence—statements made out of court that are offered in court as proof of the information contained in the statements and that, subject to many exceptions, are not admissible in evidence.

holder—someone in possession of an instrument that runs to that person (i.e., is made payable to that person, is indorsed to that person, or is bearer paper).

holder in due course—a holder who has given value, taken in good faith without notice of dishonor, defenses, or that instrument is overdue, and who is afforded special rights or status.

holder through a holder in due course—holder of an instrument who attains holder-in-due-course status because a holder in due course has held it previous to him or her.

holographic will—unwitnessed will written by hand.

homeowners insurance policy—combination of standard fire insurance and comprehensive personal liability insurance.

hotelkeeper—one regularly engaged in the business of offering living accommodations to all transient persons.

hull insurance—insurance that covers physical damage on a freight-moving vessel.

I

identification—point in the transaction when the buyer acquires an interest in the goods subject to the contract.

identified—term applied to particular goods selected by either the buyer or the seller as the goods called for by the sales contract.

illusory promise—promise that in fact does not impose any obligation on the promisor.

impeach—using prior inconsistent evidence to challenge the credibility of a witness.

implied contract—contract expressed by conduct or implied or deduced from the facts.

implied warranty—warranty that was not made but is implied by law.

implied warranty of the merchantability—group of promises made by the seller, the most important of which is that the goods are fit for the ordinary purposes for which they are sold.

impostor rule—an exception to the rules on liability for forgery that covers situations such as the embezzling payroll clerk.

in pari delicto—equally guilty; used in reference to a transaction as to which relief will not be granted to either party because both are equally guilty of wrongdoing.

incidental authority—authority of an agent that is reasonably necessary to execute express authority.

incidental damages—incurred by the nonbreaching party as part of the process of trying to cover (buy substitute goods) or sell (selling subject matter of contract to another); includes storage fees, commissions, and the like.

income—money earned by the principal, or property in trust, and distributed by the trustee.

incontestability clause—provision that after the lapse of a specified time the insurer cannot dispute the policy on the ground of misrepresentation or fraud of the insured or similar wrongful conduct.

incorporation by reference—contract consisting of both the original or skeleton document and the detailed statement that is incorporated in it.

incorporator—one or more natural persons or corporations who sign and file appropriate incorporation forms with a designated government official.

indemnity—right of a person secondarily liable to require that a person primarily liable pay for loss sustained when the secondary party discharges the obligation that the primary party should have discharged; an undertaking to pay another a sum of money to indemnify when loss is incurred.

indemnity contract—agreement by one person, for consideration, to pay another person a sum of money in the event that the other person sustains a specified loss.

indenture trustee—usually a commercial banking institution, to represent the interests of the bondholders and ensure that the terms and covenants of the bond issue are met by the corporation.

independent contractor—contractor who undertakes to perform a specified task according to the terms of a contract but over whom the other contracting party has no control except as provided for by the contract.

indorsee—party to whom special indorsement is made.

indorsement—signature of the payee on an instrument.

indorser—secondary party (or obligor) on a note.

informal contract—simple oral or written contract.

informal settlements—negotiated disposition of a matter before an administrative agency, generally without public sanctions.

injunction—order of a court of equity to refrain from doing (negative injunction) or to do (affirmative or mandatory injunction) a specified act.

inland marine—insurance that covers domestic shipments of goods over land and inland waterways.

insider—full-time corporate employee or a director or their relatives.

insider information—privileged information on company business known only to employees.

insolvency—excess of debts and liabilities over assets, or inability to pay debts as they mature.

instruction—summary of the law given to jurors by the judge before deliberation begins.

insurable interest—the right to hold a valid insurance policy on a person or property.

insurance—a plan of security against risks by charging the loss against a fund created by the payments made by policyholders.

insurance agent—agent of an insurance company.

insurance broker—independent contractor who is not employed by any one insurance company.

insured—person to whom the promise in an insurance contract is made.

insurer—promisor in an insurance contract.

integrity—the adherence to one's values and principles despite the costs and consequences.

intentional infliction of emotional distress—tort that produces mental anguish caused by conduct that exceeds all bounds of decency.

intentional tort—civil wrong that results from intentional conduct.

inter vivos gift—any transaction that takes place between living persons and creates rights prior to the death of any of them.

interest in the authority—form of agency in which an agent has been given or paid for the right to exercise authority.

interest in the subject matter—form of agency in which an agent is given an interest in the property with which that agent is dealing.

interlineation—writing between the lines or adding to the provisions of a document, the effect thereof depending upon the nature of the document.

intermediary bank—bank between the originator and the beneficiary bank in the transfer of funds.

interrogatories—written questions used as a discovery tool that must be answered under oath.

intervenors—in administrative actions, third parties who have an interest in the issues being determined by an ALJ.

intestate—condition of dying without a will as to any property.

intestate succession—distribution, made as directed by statute, of a decedent's property not effectively disposed of by will.

invasion of privacy—tort of intentional intrusion into the private affairs of another.

invitee—person who enters another's land by invitation.

involuntary bankruptcy—proceeding in which a creditor or creditors file the petition for relief with the bankruptcy court.

issuer—party who issues a document such as a letter of credit or a document of title such as a warehouse receipt or bill of lading.

J

joint and several liability—disproportionate satisfaction of partnership debt rendering each partner liable for the entire debt with the right to contribution from other partners.

joint liability—apportions partners' responsibility for partnership debt equally.

joint tenancy—estate held jointly by two or more with the right of survivorship as between them unless modified by statute.

joint venture—relationship in which two or more persons or firms combine their labor or property for a single undertaking and share profits and losses equally unless otherwise agreed.

judge—primary officer of the court.

judgment lien—lien obtained through the courts.

judgment n.o.v. (or *non obstante veredicto*, "notwithstanding the verdict")—a judgment entered after verdict upon the motion of the losing party on the ground that the verdict is so wrong that a judgment should be entered the opposite of the verdict.

judicial branch—the branch of government (e.g., the courts) formed to interpret the laws.

jurisdiction—the power of a court to hear and determine a given class of cases; the power to act over a particular defendant.

jurisdictional rule of reason—rule that balances the vital interests, including laws and policies, of the United States with those of a foreign country.

jury—a body of citizens sworn by a court to determine by verdict the issues of fact submitted to them.

K

Kant's categorical imperative—a standard of ethics that requires that we avoid one-sided benefit for us as a result of the conduct or decision.

L

land—earth, including all things embedded in or attached thereto, whether naturally or by the act of humans.

landlord—one who leases real property to another.

law—the order or pattern of rules that society establishes to govern the conduct of individuals and the relationships among them.

lease—agreement between the owner of property and a tenant by which the former agrees to give possession of the property to the latter for payment of rent. (Parties—landlord or lessor, tenant or lessee)

leasehold estate—interest of a tenant in rented land.

legacy—gift of money made by will.

legal title—title held by the trustee in a trust situation.

legatee—beneficiary who receives a gift of personal property by will.

legislative branch—the branch of government (e.g., Congress) formed to make the laws.

lessee—one who has a possessory interest in real or personal property under a lease; a tenant.

lessor—one who conveys real or personal property by a lease; a landlord.

letter of credit—commercial device used to guarantee payment to a seller, primarily in an international business transaction.

letters of administration—written authorization given to an administrator of an estate as evidence of appointment and authority.

letters testamentary—written authorization given to an executor of an estate as evidence of appointment and authority.

liability insurance—covers the shipowner's liability if the ship causes damage to another ship or its cargo.

libel—written or visual defamation without legal justification.

license—personal privilege to do some act or series of acts upon the land of another, as the placing of a sign thereon, not amounting to an easement or a right of possession.

licensee—someone on another's premises with the permission of the occupier, whose duty is to warn the licensee of nonobvious dangers.

licensing—transfer of technology rights to a product so that it may be produced by a different business organization in a foreign country in exchange for royalties and other payments as agreed.

lien—claim or right, against through judgment or levy.

life estate—an estate for the duration of a life.

limitation-of-liability clause—provision in a contract stating that one of the parties is not liable for damages in case of breach; also called *exculpatory clause*.

limited covenant—any covenant that does not provide the complete protection of a full covenant.

limited defenses—defenses available to secondary parties if the presenting party is a holder in due course.

limited liability company (LLC)—a partnership for federal tax treatment and the limited liability feature of the corporate form of business organization.

limited liability partnership (LLP)—partnership in which at least one partner has a liability limited to the loss of the capital contribution made to the partnership.

limited partner—partner who neither takes part in the management of the partnership nor appears to the public to be a general partner.

limited partnership—partnership that can be formed by "one or more general partners and one or more limited partners."

limited (special) jurisdiction—the authority to hear only particular kinds of cases.

limited warranty—any warranty that does not provide the complete protection of a full warranty.

lineals—relationship that exists when one person is a direct descendant of the other; also called *lineal descendants*.

liquidated damages—provision stipulating the amount of damages to be paid in the event of default or breach of contract.

liquidated damages clause—specification of exact compensation in case of a breach of contract.

liquidation—process of converting property into money whether of particular items of property or of all the assets of a business or an estate.

living trust—trust created to take effect within the lifetime of the settlor; also called *inter vivos* trust.

living will—document by which individuals may indicate that if they become unable to express their wishes and are in an irreversible, incurable condition, they do not want life-sustaining medical treatments.

living-document view—the term used when a constitution is interpreted according to changes in conditions.

lottery—any plan by which a consideration is given for a chance to win a prize; it consists of three elements: (1) there must be a payment of money or something of value for an opportunity to win, (2) a prize must be available, and (3) the prize must be offered by lot or chance.

M

mailbox rule—timing for acceptance tied to proper acceptance.

maker—party who writes or creates a promissory note.

malpractice—when services are not properly rendered in accordance with commonly accepted standards; negligence by a professional in performing his or her skill.

marine insurance—policies that cover perils relating to the transportation of goods.

market power—the ability to control price and exclude competitors.

market value—price at which a share of stock can be voluntarily bought or sold in the open market.

mask work—specific form of expression embodied in a chip design, including the stencils used in manufacturing semiconductor chip products.

mass picketing—illegal tactic of employees massing together in great numbers to effectively shut down entrances of the employer's facility.

maturity date—date that a corporation is required to repay a loan to a bondholder.

means test—new standard under the Reform Act that requires the court to find that the debtor does not have the means to repay creditors; goes beyond the past requirement of petitions being granted on the simple assertion of the debtor saying, "I have debts."

mechanic's lien—claim by laborers or materials suppliers for property improvements.

mediation—the settlement of a dispute through the use of a messenger who carries to each side of the dispute the issues and offers in the case.

merchant—seller who deals in specific goods classified by the UCC.

merger (of corporations)—combining of corporations by which one absorbs the other and continues to exist, preserving its original charter and identity while the other corporation ceases to exist.

minitrial—a trial held on portions of the case or certain issues in the case.

Miranda warnings—warnings required to prevent self-incrimination in a criminal matter.

mirror image rule—common law contract rule on acceptance that requires language to be absolutely the same as the offer, unequivocal and unconditional.

misdemeanor—criminal offense with a sentence of less than one year that is neither treason nor a felony.

misrepresentation—false statement of fact made innocently without any intent to deceive.

mistrial—a court's declaration that terminates a trial and postpones it to a later date; commonly entered when evidence has been of a highly prejudicial character or when a juror has been guilty of misconduct.

money—medium of exchange.

money order—draft issued by a bank or a nonbank.

moral relativists—those who make decisions based on circumstances and not on the basis of any predefined standards.

mortgage—interest in land given by the owner to a creditor as security for the payment of the creditor for a debt, the nature of the interest depending upon the law of the state where the land is located. (Parties— mortgagor, mortgagee)

most-favored-nation—clause in treaties between countries whereby any privilege granted to one member is extended to all members of the treaty.

motion for summary judgment—request that the court decide a case on basis of law only because there are no material issues disputed by the parties.

motion to dismiss—a pleading that may be filed to attack the adverse party's pleading as not stating a cause of action or a defense.

N

National Environmental Policy Act (NEPA)—federal law that mandates study of a project's impact on the environment before it can be undertaken by any federal agency.

National Pollutant Discharge Elimination System (NPDES)—EPA system for regulating point source emissions into water.

national treatment—a WTO requirement in which a country may not discriminate between its own products and foreign products or services.

natural law—a system of principles to guide human conduct independent of, and sometimes contrary to, enacted law and discovered by man's rational intelligence.

necessaries—things indispensable or absolutely necessary for the sustenance of human life.

negligence—failure to exercise due care under the circumstances that results in harm proximately caused to one owed a duty to exercise due care.

negotiability—quality of an instrument that affords special rights and standing.

negotiable bill of lading—document of title that by its terms calls for goods to be delivered "to the bearer" or "to the order of" a named person.

negotiable instrument—drafts, promissory notes, checks, and certificates of deposit that, in proper form, give special rights as "negotiable commercial paper."

negotiable warehouse receipt—receipt that states the covered goods will be delivered "to the bearer" or "to the order of."

negotiation—the transfer of commercial paper by indorsement and delivery by the person to whom it is then payable in the case of order paper and by physical transfer in the case of bearer paper.

Noise Control Act—federal law that controls noise emissions from low-flying aircraft.

nominal damages—nominal sum awarded the plaintiff in order to establish that legal rights have been violated although the plaintiff in fact has not sustained any actual loss or damages.

nonattainment areas—"dirty" areas that do not meet federal standards under the Clean Air Act.

nonconforming use—use of land that conflicts with a zoning ordinance at the time the ordinance goes into effect.

nonconsumer lease—lease that does not satisfy the definition of a consumer lease; also known as a *commercial lease.*

nonnegotiable bill of lading—See *straight bill of lading.*

nonnegotiable instrument—contract, note, or draft that does not meet negotiability requirements of Article 3.

nonnegotiable warehouse receipt—receipt that states the covered goods received will be delivered to a specific person.

notice of dishonor—notice that an instrument has been dishonored; such notice can be oral, written, or electronic but is subject to time limitations.

notice statute—statute under which the last good-faith or bona fide purchaser holds the title.

notice-race statute—statute under which the first bona fide purchaser to record the deed holds the title.

novation—substitution for an old contract with a new one that either replaces an existing obligation with a new obligation or replaces an original party with a new party.

nuisance—conduct that harms or prejudices another in the use of land or that harms or prejudices the public.

O

obligee—promisee who can claim the benefit of the obligation.

obligor—promisor.

ocean marine—policies that cover transportation of goods in vessels in international and coastal trade.

offer—expression of an offeror's willingness to enter into a contractual agreement.

offeree—person to whom an offer is made.

offeror—person who makes an offer.

Oil Pollution Act—federal law that assigns cleanup liability for oil spills in U.S. waters.

open meeting law—law that requires advance notice of agency meeting and public access.

opening statements—statements by opposing attorneys that tell the jury what their cases will prove.

operation of law—attaching of certain consequences to certain facts because of legal principles that operate automatically as contrasted with consequences that arise because of the voluntary action of a party designed to create those consequences.

option contract—contract to hold an offer to make a contract open for a fixed period of time.

order of relief—the order from the bankruptcy judge that starts the protection for the debtor; when the order of relief is entered by the court, the debtor's creditors must stop all proceedings and work through the bankruptcy court to recover debts (if possible). Court finding that creditors have met the standards for bankruptcy petitions.

order paper—instrument payable to the order of a party.

original jurisdiction—the authority to hear a controversy when it is first brought to court.

originator—party who originates the funds transfer.

output contract—contract of a producer to sell its entire production or output to a given buyer.

outstanding—name for shares of a company that have been issued to stockholders.

overdraft—negative balance in a drawer's account.

P

par value—specified monetary amount assigned by an issuing corporation for each share of its stock.

parol evidence rule—rule that prohibits the introduction in evidence of oral or written statements made prior to or contemporaneously with the execution of a complete written contract, deed, or instrument, in the absence of fraud, accident, or mistake.

partially disclosed principal—principal whose existence is made known but whose identity is not.

partner—one of two or more persons who jointly own and carry on a business for profit.

partnership—pooling of capital resources and the business or professional talents of two or more individuals (partners) with the goal of making a profit.

partnership agreement—document prepared to evidence the contract of the parties. (Parties—partners or general partners)

party—person involved in a legal transaction; may be a natural person, an artificial person (e.g., a corporation), or an unincorporated enterprise (e.g., a governmental agency).

past consideration—something that has been performed in the past and which, therefore, cannot be consideration for a promise made in the present.

payable to order—term stating that a negotiable instrument is payable to the order of any person described in it or to a person or order.

payee—party to whom payment is to be made.

payment order—direction given by an originator to his or her bank or by any bank to a subsequent bank to make a specified funds transfer.

Pension Benefit Guaranty Corporation (PBGC)—an insurance plan to protect employees covered by defined benefit plans in case an employer is unable to meet its payment obligations from the employer's pension fund.

per capita—method of distributing estate assets on an equal-per-person basis.

perfected security interest—security interest with priority because of filing, possession, automatic, or temporary priority status.

periodic tenancy—tenancy that continues indefinitely for a specified rental period until terminated; often called a month-to-month tenancy.

personal property—property that is movable or intangible, or rights in such things.

personal representative—administrator or executor who represents decedents under UPC.

per stirpes—method for distribution of an estate that divides property equally down family lines.

physical duress—threat of physical harm to person or property.

plaintiff—party who initiates a lawsuit.

pleadings—the papers filed by the parties in an action in order to set forth the facts and frame the issues to be tried, although, under some systems, the pleadings merely give notice or a general indication of the nature of the issues.

pledge—bailment given as security for the payment of a debt or the performance of an obligation owed to the pledgee. (Parties–pledgor, pledgee)

point sources—direct discharges into bodies of water.

police power—the power to govern; the power to adopt laws for the protection of the public health, welfare, safety, and morals.

policy—paper evidencing the contract of insurance.

positive law—law enacted and codified by governmental authority.

possession—exclusive dominion and control of property.

possibility of reverter—nature of the interest held by the grantor after conveying land outright but subject to a condition or provision that may cause the grantee's interest to become forfeited and the interest to revert to the grantor or heirs.

postdate—to insert or place on an instrument a later date than the actual date on which it was executed.

postdating—inserting or placing on an instrument a later date than the actual date on which it was executed.

potentially responsible parties (PRPs)—those beyond actual polluters who could be responsible for cleanup costs.

power of attorney—written authorization to an agent by the principal.

precedent—a decision of a court that stands as the law for a particular problem in the future.

predatory lending—a practice on the part of the subprime lending market whereby lenders take advantage of less sophisticated consumers or those who are desperate for funds by using the lenders' superior bargaining positions to obtain credit terms that go well beyond compensating them for their risk.

predicate act—qualifying underlying offense for RICO liability.

preemption—the federal government's superior regulatory position over state laws on the same subject area.

preemptive right—shareholder's right upon the increase of a corporation's capital stock to be allowed to subscribe to such a percentage of the new shares as the shareholder's old shares bore to the former total capital stock.

preferences—transfers of property by a debtor to one or more specific creditors to enable these creditors to obtain payment for debts owed.

preferential transfers—certain transfers of money or security interests in the time frame just prior to bankruptcy that can be set aside if voidable.

preferred stock—stock that has a priority or preference as to payment of dividends or upon liquidation, or both.

prescription—acquisition of a right to use the land of another, as an easement, by making hostile, visible, and notorious use of the land, continuing for the period specified by the local law.

presentment—formal request for payment on an instrument.

price discrimination—the charging practice by a seller of different prices to different buyers for commodities of similar grade and quality, resulting in reduced competition or a tendency to create a monopoly.

prima facie—evidence that, if believed, is sufficient by itself to lead to a particular conclusion.

primary offerings—the original distribution of securities by the issuing corporations.

primary party—party to whom the holder or holder in due course must turn first to obtain payment.

primary picketing—legal presentations in front of a business notifying the public of a labor dispute.

primum non nocere—above all, do no harm.

principal—person or firm who employs an agent; the person who, with respect to a surety, is primarily liable to the third person or creditor; property held in trust.

principal debtor—original borrower or debtor.

prior art—a showing that an invention as a whole would have been obvious to a person of ordinary skill in the art when the invention was patented.

private carrier—carrier owned by the shipper, such as a company's own fleet of trucks.

private corporation—corporation organized for charitable and benevolent purposes or for purposes of finance, industry, and commerce.

private law—the rules and regulations parties agree to as part of their contractual relationships.

private nuisance—nuisance that affects only one or a few individuals.

privileges and immunities clause—a clause that entitles a person going into another state to make contracts, own property, and engage in business to the same extent as citizens of that state.

privity—succession or chain of relationship to the same thing or right, such as privity of contract, privity of estate, privity of possession.

privity of contract—relationship between a promisor and the promisee.

privity rule—succession or chain of relationship to the same thing or right, such as privity of contract, privity of estate, privity of possession.

pro rata—proportionately, or divided according to a rate or standard.

probate—procedure for formally establishing or proving that a given writing is the last will and testament of the person who purportedly signed it.

procedural law—the law that must be followed in enforcing rights and liabilities.

process—paperwork served personally on a defendant in a civil case.

product disparagement—false statements made about a product or business.

profit—right to take a part of the soil or produce of another's land, such as timber or water.

promisee—person to whom a promise is made.

promisor—person who makes a promise.

promissory estoppels—doctrine that a promise will be enforced although it is not supported by consideration when the promisor should have reasonably expected that the promise would induce action or forbearance of a definite and substantial character on the part of the promised and injustice can be avoided only by enforcement of the promise.

promissory note—unconditional promise in writing made by one person to another, signed by the maker engaging to pay on demand, or at a definite time, a sum certain in money to order or to bearer. (Parties—maker, payee)

promoters—persons who plan the formation of the corporation and sell or promote the idea to others.

proof of claim—written statement, signed by the creditor or an authorized representative, setting forth any claim made against the debtor and the basis for it.

property report—condensed version of a property development statement filed with the secretary of HUD and given to a prospective customer at least 48 hours before signing a contract to buy or lease property.

prosecutor—party who originates a criminal proceeding.

prospectus—information provided to each potential purchaser of securities setting forth the key information contained in the registration statement.

proxy—written authorization by a shareholder to another person to vote the stock owned by the shareholder; the person who is the holder of such a written authorization.

public corporation—corporation that has been established for governmental purposes and for the administration of public affairs.

public nuisance—nuisance that affects the community or public at large.

public policy—certain objectives relating to health, morals, and integrity of government that the law seeks to advance by declaring invalid any contract that conflicts with those objectives even though there is no statute expressly declaring such a contract illegal.

public warehouses—entities that serve the public generally without discrimination.

punitive damages—damages, in excess of those required to compensate the plaintiff for the wrong done, that are imposed in order to punish the defendant because of the particularly wanton or willful character of wrongdoing; also called *exemplary damages.*

purchase money security interest (PMSI)—the security interest in the goods a seller sells on credit that become the collateral for the creditor/seller.

Q

qualified indorsement—an indorsement that includes words such as "without recourse" that disclaims certain liability of the indorser to a maker or a drawee.

qualified privilege—media privilege to print inaccurate information without liability for defamation, so long as a retraction is printed and there was no malice.

quantum meruit—as much as deserved; an action brought for the value of the services rendered the defendant when there was no express contract as to the purchase price.

quasi contract—court-imposed obligation to prevent unjust enrichment in the absence of a contract.

quasi-judicial proceedings—forms of hearings in which the rules of evidence and procedure are more relaxed but each side still has a chance to be heard.

quasi-public corporation—private corporation furnishing services on which the public is particularly dependent, for example, a gas and electric company.

quitclaim deed—deed by which the grantor purports to give up only whatever right or title the grantor may have in the property without specifying or warranting transfer of any particular interest.

quorum—minimum number of persons, shares represented, or directors who must be present at a meeting in order to lawfully transact business.

R

race statute—statute under which the first party to record the deed holds the title.

race-notice statute—see *notice-race statute.*

Racketeer Influenced and Corrupt Organizations (RICO) Act—federal law, initially targeting organized crime that has expanded in scope and provides penalties and civil recovery for multiple criminal offenses, or a pattern of racketeering.

real property—land and all rights in land.

recognizance—obligation entered into before a court to do some act, such as to appear at a later date for a hearing. Also called a *contract of record.*

recorder—public official in charge of deeds.

recross-examination—an examination by the other side's attorney that follows the redirect examination.

redemption—buying back of one's property, which has been sold because of a default, upon paying the amount that had been originally due together with interest and costs.

redirect examination—questioning after cross-examination, in which the attorney for the witness testifying may ask the same witness other questions to overcome effects of the cross-examination.

reference to a third person—settlement that allows a nonparty to resolve the dispute.

reformation—remedy by which a written instrument is corrected when it fails to express the actual intent of both parties because of fraud, accident, or mistake.

registered bonds—bonds held by owners whose names and addresses are registered on the books of the corporation to ensure proper payment.

registration requirements—provisions of the Securities Act of 1933 requiring advance disclosure to the public of a new securities issue through filing a statement with the SEC and sending a prospectus to each potential purchaser.

registration statement—document disclosing specific financial information regarding the security, the issuer, and the underwriter.

release—an instrument by which the signing party (releasor) relinquishes claims or potential claims against one or more persons (releasees) who might otherwise be subject to liability to the releasor.

remainder interest—land interest that follows a life estate.

remand—term used when an appellate court sends a case back to trial court for additional hearings or a new trial.

remedy—action or procedure that is followed in order to enforce a right or to obtain damages for injury to a right.

rent-a-judge plan—dispute resolution through private courts with judges paid to be referees for the cases.

representative capacity—action taken by one on behalf of another, as the act of a personal representative on behalf of a decedent's estate, or action taken both on one's behalf and on behalf of others, as a shareholder bringing a representative action.

repudiation—result of a buyer or seller refusing to perform the contract as stated.

request for production of documents—discovery tool for uncovering paper evidence in a case.

requirements contract—contract to buy all requirements of the buyer from the seller.

rescission—action of one party to a contract to set the contract aside when the other party is guilty of a breach of the contract.

reservation of rights—assertion by a party to a contract that even though a tendered performance (e.g., a defective product) is accepted, the right to damages for nonconformity to the contract is reserved.

Resource Conservation and Recovery Act (RCRA)—federal law that regulates the disposal of potentially harmful substances and encourages resource conservation and recovery.

Resource Recovery Act—early federal solid waste disposal legislation that provided funding for states and local governments with recycling programs.

respondeat superior—doctrine that the principal or employer is vicariously liable for the unauthorized torts committed by an agent or employee while acting within the scope of the agency or the course of the employment, respectively.

restrictive covenants—covenants in a deed by which the grantee agrees to refrain from doing specified acts.

restrictive indorsement—an indorsement that restricts further transfer, such as in trust for or to the use of some other person, is conditional, or for collection or deposit.

reverse—the term used when the appellate court sets aside the verdict or judgment of a lower court.

reverse mortgage—mortgage in which the owners get their equity out of their home over a period of time and return the house to the lender upon their deaths.

reversible error—an error or defect in court proceedings of so serious a nature that on appeal the appellate court will set aside the proceedings of the lower court.

revoke—testator's act of taking back his or her will and its provisions.

right—legal capacity to require another person to perform or refrain from an action.

right of escheat—right of the state to take the property of a decedent that has not been distributed.

right of first refusal—right of a party to meet the terms of a proposed contract before it is executed, such as a real estate purchase agreement.

right of privacy—the right to be free from unreasonable intrusion by others.

right to cure—second chance for a seller to make a proper tender of conforming goods.

right-to-work laws—laws restricting unions and employees from negotiating clauses in their collective bargaining agreements that make union membership compulsory.

rights theory—Nozick's theory of ethics that we all have a set of rights that must be honored and protected by government.

risk—peril or contingency against which the insured is protected by the contract of insurance.

risk of loss—in contract performance, the cost of damage or injury to the goods contracted for.

Robinson-Patman Act—a federal statute designed to eliminate price discrimination in interstate commerce.

S

Safe Drinking Water Act—a federal law that establishes national standards for contaminants in drinking water.

sale on approval—term indicating that no sale takes place until the buyer approves or accepts the goods.

sale or return—sale in which the title to the property passes to the buyer at the time of the transaction but the buyer is given the option of returning the property and restoring the title to the seller.

search warrant—judicial authorization for a search of property where there is the expectation of privacy.

seasonable—timely.

secondary meaning—a legal term signifying the words in question have taken on a new meaning with the public, capable of serving a source-identifying function of a mark.

secondary parties—called secondary obligors under Revised Article 3; parties to an instrument to whom holders turn when the primary party, for whatever reason, fails to pay the instrument.

secondary picketing—picketing an employer with which a union has no dispute to persuade the employer to stop doing business with a party to the dispute; generally illegal under the NLRA.

secrecy laws—confidentiality laws applied to home-country banks.

secured party—person owed the money, whether as a seller or a lender, in a secured transaction in personal property.

secured transaction—credit sale of goods or a secured loan that provides special protection for the creditor.

securities—stocks and bonds issued by a corporation. Under some investor protection laws, the term includes any interest in an enterprise that provides unearned income to its owner.

security agreement—agreement of the creditor and the debtor that the creditor will have a security interest.

security interest—property right that enables the creditor to take possession of the property if the debtor does not pay the amount owed.

self-help repossession—creditor's right to repossess the collateral without judicial proceedings.

self-proved wills—wills that eliminate some formalities of proof by being executed according to statutory requirements.

selling on consignment—entrusting a person with possession of property for the purpose of sale.

semiconductor chip product—product placed on a piece of semiconductor material in accordance with a predetermined pattern that is intended to perform electronic circuitry functions.

service mark—mark that identifies a service.

servient tenement—land that is subject to an easement.

settlor—one who settles property in trust or creates a trust.

severalty—ownership of property by one person.

shared powers—powers that are held by both state and national governments.

Sherman Antitrust Act—a federal statute prohibiting combinations and contracts in restraint of interstate trade, now generally inapplicable to labor union activity.

shop right—right of an employer to use in business without charge an invention discovered by an employee during working hours and with the employer's material and equipment.

shopkeeper's privilege—right of a store owner to detain a suspected shoplifter based on reasonable cause and for a reasonable time without resulting liability for false imprisonment.

short-swing profit—profit realized by a corporate insider from selling securities less than six months after purchase.

sinking fund—fixed amount of money set aside each year by the borrowing corporation toward the ultimate payment of bonds.

Sixth Amendment—the U.S. constitutional amendment that guarantees a speedy trial.

slander—defamation of character by spoken words or gestures.

slander of title—malicious making of false statements as to a seller's title.

small claims courts—courts that resolve disputes between parties when those disputes do not exceed a minimal level; no lawyers are permitted; the parties represent themselves.

social contract—the agreement under Locke and Rawls as to what our ethical standards will be.

sole or individual proprietorship—form of business ownership in which one individual owns the business.

soliciting agent—salesperson.

sovereign compliance doctrine—doctrine that allows a defendant to raise as an affirmative defense to an antitrust action the fact that the defendant's actions were compelled by a foreign state.

sovereign immunity doctrine—a doctrine that states that a foreign sovereign generally cannot be sued without its consent.

special agent—agent authorized to transact a specific transaction or to do a specific act.

special indorsement—an indorsement that specifies the person to whom the instrument is indorsed.

specific legacies—identified property bequeathed by a testator; also called *specific devises*.

specific lien—right of a creditor to hold a particular property or assert a lien on the particular property of the debtor because of the creditor's having done work on or having some other association with the property, as distinguished from having a lien generally against the assets of the debtor merely because the debtor is indebted to the lien holder.

specific performance—action brought to compel the adverse party to perform a contract on the theory that merely suing for damages for its breach will not be an adequate remedy.

spendthrift trust—a trust that, prevents creditors of the beneficiary from reaching the principal or income held by the trustee and precludes beneficiary assignments.

spot zoning—allowing individual variation in zoning.

stakeholder analysis—the term used when a decision maker views a problem from different perspectives and measures the impact of a decision on various groups.

stakeholders—those who have a stake, or interest, in the activities of a corporation; stakeholders include employees, members of the community in which the corporation operates, vendors, customers, and any others who are affected by the actions and decisions of the corporation.

stale check—a check whose date is longer than six months ago.

standby letter—letter of credit for a contractor ensuring he will complete the project as contracted.

stare decisis—"let the decision stand"; the principle that the decision of a court should serve as a guide or precedent and control the decision of a similar case in the future.

status quo ante—original positions of the parties.

statute of frauds—statute that, in order to prevent fraud through the use of perjured testimony, requires that certain kinds of transactions be evidenced in writing in order to be binding or enforceable.

statute of limitations—statute that restricts the period of time within which an action may be brought.

statutory law—legislative acts declaring, commanding, or prohibiting something.

stay (or delay) of foreclosure—delay of foreclosure obtained by the mortgagor to prevent undue hardship.

stock subscription—contract or agreement to buy a specific number and kind of shares when they are issued by the corporation.

stop payment order—order by a depositor to the bank to refuse to make payment of a check when presented for payment.

straight (or nonnegotiable) bill of lading—document of title that consigns transported goods to a named person.

strict liability—civil wrong for which there is absolute liability because of the inherent danger in the underlying activity, for example, the use of explosives.

strict tort liability—product liability theory that imposes absolute liability upon the manufacturer, seller, or distributor of goods for harm caused by defective goods.

subject matter jurisdiction—judicial authority to hear a particular type of case.

sublease—a transfer of the premises by the lessee to a third person, the sublessee or subtenant, for a period of less than the term of the original lease.

sublessee—person with lease rights for a period of less than the term of the original lease (also *subtenant*).

subprime lending market—a credit market that makes loans to high-risk consumers (those who have bankruptcies, no credit history, or a poor credit history), often loaning money to pay off other debts the consumer has due.

subrogation—right of a party secondarily liable to stand in the place of the creditor after making payment to the creditor and to enforce the creditor's right against the party primarily liable in order to obtain indemnity from such primary party.

substantial impairment—material defect in a good.

substantial performance—equitable rule that if a good-faith attempt to perform does not precisely meet the terms of the agreement, the agreement will still be considered complete if the essential purpose of the contract is accomplished.

substantive law—the law that defines rights and liabilities.

substitute check—electronic image of a paper check that a bank can create and that has the same legal effect as the original instrument.

substitution—substitution of a new contract between the same parties.

sum certain—amount due under an instrument that can be computed from its face with only reference to interest rates.

summary jury trial—a mock or dry-run trial for parties to get a feel for how their cases will play to a jury.

summation—the attorney address that follows all the evidence presented in court and sums up a case and recommends a particular verdict be returned by the jury.

Superfund Amendment and Reauthorization Act—federal law that expands scope and operation of CERCLA.

Superfund sites—areas designated by the EPA for cleanup.

surety—obligor of a suretyship; primarily liable for the debt or obligation of the principal debtor.

suretyship—undertaking to pay the debt or be liable for the default of another.

symbolic delivery—delivery of goods by delivery of the means of control, such as a key or a relevant document of title, such as a negotiable bill of lading; also called constructive delivery.

T

tariff—(1) domestically—government-approved schedule of charges that may be made by a regulated business, such as a common carrier or warehouser; (2) internationally—tax imposed by a country on goods crossing its borders, without regard to whether the purpose is to raise revenue or to discourage the traffic in the taxed goods.

tax lien—lien on property for nonpayment of taxes.

teller's check—draft drawn by a bank on another bank in which it has an account.

temporary insider—someone retained by a corporation for professional services on an as-needed basis, such as an attorney, accountant, or investment banker.

temporary perfection—perfection given for a limited period of time to creditors.

tenancy at sufferance—lease arrangement in which the tenant occupies the property at the discretion of the landlord.

tenancy at will—holding of land for an indefinite period that may be terminated at any time by the landlord or by the landlord and tenant acting together.

tenancy by entirety or tenancy by the entireties—transfer of property to both husband and wife.

tenancy for years—tenancy for a fixed period of time, even though the time is less than a year.

tenancy in common—relationship that exists when two or more persons own undivided interests in property.

tenancy in partnership—ownership relationship that exists between partners under the Uniform Partnership Act.

tenant—one who holds or possesses real property by any kind of right or title; one who pays rent for the temporary use and occupation of another's real property under a lease.

tender—goods have arrived, are available for pickup, and the buyer is notified.

term insurance—policy written for a specified number of years that terminates at the end of that period.

termination statement—document (record), which may be requested by a paid-up debtor, stating that a security interest is no longer claimed under the specified financing statement.

testamentary capacity—sufficient mental capacity to understand that a writing being executed is a will and what that entails.

testamentary intent—designed to take effect at death, as by disposing of property or appointing a personal representative.

testamentary trust—trust that takes effect upon the settlor's death.

testate—condition of leaving a will upon death.

testate distribution—distribution of an estate in accordance with the will of the decedent.

testator, testatrix—man, woman who makes a will.

theory of justice—the Locke and Rawlsian standard for ethics that requires that we all agree on certain universal principles in advance.

third-party beneficiary—third person whom the parties to a contract intend to benefit by the making of the contract and to confer upon such person the right to sue for breach of contract.

time draft—bill of exchange payable at a stated time after sight or at a definite time.

tippee—individual who receives information about a corporation from an insider or temporary insider.

tort—civil wrong that interferes with one's property or person.

Toxic Substances Control Act (TOSCA)—first federal law to control the manufacture, use, and disposal of toxic substances.

trade dress—product's total image including its overall packaging look.

trade libel—written defamation about a product or service.

trade name—name under which a business is carried on and, if fictitious, must be registered.

trade secret—formula, device, or compilation of information that is used in one's business and is of such a nature that it provides an advantage over competitors who do not have the information.

trademark—mark that identifies a product.

transferee—buyer or vendee.

Transport Rule—the rule promulgated to address downwind pollution from coal and gas-fired power plants.

traveler's check—check that is payable on demand provided it is countersigned by the person whose specimen signature appears on the check.

treasury stock—corporate stock that the corporation has reacquired.

treble damages—three times the damages actually sustained.

trespass—unauthorized action with respect to person or property.

trespasser—person who is on the land of another without permission or authorization.

tripartite—three-part division (of government).

trust—transfer of property by one person to another with the understanding or declaration that such property be held for the benefit of another; the holding of property by the owner in trust for another, upon a declaration of trust, without a transfer to another person. (Parties—settlor, trustee, beneficiary)

trust agreement—instrument creating a trust; also called *deed of trust.*

trust corpus—fund or property that is transferred to the trustee also called *trust fund, trust estate,* and *trust res.*

trustee—party who has legal title to estate and manages it.

trustee in bankruptcy—impartial person elected to administer the debtor's estate.

trustor—donor or settlor who is the owner of property.

tying—the anticompetitive practice of requiring buyers to purchase one product in order to get another.

U

ultra vires—act or contract that the corporation does not have authority to do or make.

unconscionable—unreasonable, not guided or restrained by conscience and often referring to a contract grossly unfair to one party because of the superior bargaining powers of the other party.

underwriter—insurer.

undisclosed principal—principal on whose behalf an agent acts without disclosing to the third person the fact of agency or the identity of the principal.

undue influence—influence that is asserted upon another person by one who dominates that person.

Uniform Probate Code (UPC)—uniform statute on wills and administration of estates.

Uniform Simultaneous Death Act—law providing that when survivorship cannot be established, the property of each person shall be disposed of as though he or she had survived the other.

unilateral contract—contract under which only one party makes a promise.

unincorporated association—combination of two or more persons for the furtherance of a common nonprofit purpose.

universal agent—agent authorized by the principal to do all acts that can lawfully be delegated to a representative.

universal defenses—defenses that are regarded as so basic that the social interest in preserving them outweighs the social interest of giving negotiable instruments the freely transferable qualities of money; accordingly, such defenses are given universal effect and may be raised against all holders.

USA Patriot Act—federal law that, among other things, imposes reporting requirements on banks.

usage of trade—language and customs of an industry.

usury—lending money at an interest rate that is higher than the maximum rate allowed by law.

utilitarians—theory of ethics based on doing the most good for the most people in making decisions.

uttering—crime of issuing or delivering a forged instrument to another person.

V

valid contract—agreement that is binding and enforceable.

value—consideration or antecedent debt or security given in exchange for the transfer of a negotiable instrument or creation of a security interest.

variance—permission of a landowner to use the land in a specified manner that is inconsistent with the zoning ordinance.

vicarious liability—imposing liability for the fault of another.

void agreement—agreement that cannot be enforced.

voidable contract—agreement that is otherwise binding and enforceable but may be rejected at the option of one of the parties as the result of specific circumstances.

voidable title—title of goods that carries with it the contingency of an underlying problem.

voir dire **examination**—the preliminary examination of a juror or a witness to ascertain fitness to act as such.

voluntary bankruptcy—proceeding in which the debtor files the petition for relief.

voting by proxy—authorizing someone else to vote the shares owned by the shareholder.

voting trust—transfer by two or more persons of their shares of stock of a corporation to a trustee who is to vote the shares and act for such shareholders.

W

waiver—release or relinquishment of a known right or objection.

warehouse—entity engaged in the business of storing the goods of others for compensation.

warehouse receipt—receipt issued by the warehouser for stored goods; regulated by the UCC, which clothes the receipt with some degree of negotiability.

warranty—promise, either express or implied, about the nature, quality, or performance of the goods.

warranty against encumbrances—warranty that there are no liens or other encumbrances to goods except those noted by the seller.

warranty deed—deed by which the grantor conveys a specific estate or interest to the grantee and makes one or more of the covenants of title.

warranty of habitability—implied warranty that the leased property is fit for dwelling by tenants.

warranty of title—implied warranty that title to the goods is good and transfer is proper.

wasting assets corporation—corporation designed to exhaust or use up the assets of the corporation, such as by extracting oil, coal, iron, and other ores.

way of necessity—grantee's right to use land retained by the grantor for going to and from the conveyed land.

well-known mark—in international law a mark that both the Paris Convention and TRIPS recognize as deserving protection even if it is not registered in the foreign country; national law determines what "well-known" means but the WIPO offers a list suggesting that the value of the mark, the extent of its use and promotion, and its recognition in the relevant sector of the public are key factors.

White-Collar Crime Penalty Enhancement Act of 2002—federal reforms passed as a result of the collapses of companies such as Enron; provides for longer sentences and higher fines for both executives and companies.

white-collar crimes—crimes that do not use nor threaten to use force or violence or do not cause injury to persons or property.

whole life insurance—ordinary life insurance providing lifetime insurance protection.

will—instrument executed with the formality required by law by which a person makes a disposition of his or her property to take effect upon death.

writ of *certiorari*—the U.S. Supreme Court granting a right of review by the court of a lower court decision.

wrongfully dishonored—error by a bank in refusing to pay a check.

Z

zoning—restrictions imposed by government on the use of designated land to ensure an orderly physical development of the regulated area.